# the deadhead's taping compendium volume I

# the deadhead's taping compendium volume I

An In-depth Guide to the Music of
the Grateful Dead on Tape, 1959–1974

## Michael M. Getz and John R. Dwork

With: Nick Meriwether, Dougal Donaldson, Brian Dyke, Jeff Tiedrich, Eric Doherty, Michael Parrish, Paul Bodenham, Rob Goetz, Hugh Barroll, Darren Mason, Dick Latvala, Owsley "Bear" Stanley, David Gans, Steve Silberman, Blair Jackson, Les Kippel, and Barry Glassberg

And: Peter Abram, Chris Allen, Ken Babbs, Adam Bauer, Rob Bertrando, Marc Blaker, Eliza Bundledee, Kidd Candelario, A. T. Carlyle, David Cecchi, Eddie Claridge, Bob Cohen, Christian Crumlish, Dennis Donley, Rob Eaton, Todd Ellenberg, Harry Ely, Gene Estribou, Louis Falanga, Tom Ferraro, Evelynn Getz, Harry Hahn, Dan Healy, Dwight Holmes, Cherie Clark-King, Bill Kristi, Andrew Lemieux, Harvey Lubar, Adam MacConnell, Alan Mande, Jeff Mattson, Susanna Millman, Jerry Moore, Don Oldenberg, John Oleynick, Fred Ordower, Paul Pearah, John Platt, William Polits, Steve Rolphe, Amalie Rothschild, Corey Sanderson, Jean Sienkewicz, Ihor Slabicky, Larry Stein, Don Snyder, Jay Strauss, Eric Taylor, Stephen Wade, Bart Wise, and John Wood

AN OWL BOOK
HENRY HOLT AND COMPANY • NEW YORK

Henry Holt and Company, Inc.
*Publishers since 1866*
115 West 18th Street
New York, New York 10011

Henry Holt® is a registered
trademark of Henry Holt and Company, Inc.

Copyright © 1998 by John R. Dwork and Michael M. Getz
All rights reserved.
Published in Canada by Fitzhenry & Whiteside Ltd.,
195 Allstate Parkway, Markham, Ontario L3R 4T8.

Lyrics to Grateful Dead songs used by permission
of Ice Nine Publishing Company

"Deadhead" is a registered trademark of
Grateful Dead Productions and is used with permission

Library of Congress Cataloging-in-Publication Data
Getz, Michael M.
The Deadhead's taping compendium / Michael M. Getz and
John R. Dwork : with Nick Meriwether . . . [et al.].—1st ed.
  p.   cm.
"An Owl book."
Contents: v. 1. An in-depth guide to the music
of the Grateful Dead on tape, 1959–1974.
ISBN 0-8050-5398-0 (pbk: acid-free paper)
1. Grateful Dead (Musical group)—Audiotape catalogs.   2. Grateful
Dead (Musical group)—Performances.   3. Audiotapes—Reviews.
I. Dwork, John R.   II. Title.
ML156.7.G74G48   1998                                97-34141
782.42166′092′2—DC21                                     MN

Henry Holt books are available for special
promotions and premiums. For details contact:
Director, Special Markets.

First Owl Books Edition 1998

*Designed by Paula R. Szafranski*

Printed in the United States of America
All first editions are printed on acid-free paper. ∞

1  3  5  7  9  10  8  6  4  2

# Contents

| | |
|---|---:|
| List of Color Photos | vii |
| Preface | ix |
| Introduction by John R. Dwork | xi |
| Introduction by Michael M. Getz | xvii |

*Part One: Recording and Trading the Grateful Dead's Music: A Historical Overview*

| | |
|---|---:|
| **1.** "Inside" the System: The Soundmen Cometh | 5 |
| **2.** "Outside" the System: Deadheads Hear the Call | 19 |
| **3.** The Interviews: Owsley Stanley (Bear), Dick Latvala | 38 |

*Part Two: The Reviews*

| | |
|---|---:|
| **4.** How to Read the Reviews | 55 |
| **5.** Grateful Jams | 59 |
| **6.** Commonly Mislabeled Tapes | 62 |
| **7.** The Reviews: | 64 |
| **1959–1965** | 64 |
| **1966** | 83 |
| **1967** | 126 |
| **1968** | 148 |
| **1969** | 165 |
| **1970** | 214 |
| **1971** | 299 |
| **1972** | 362 |
| **1973** | 442 |
| **1974** | 514 |

*Part Three: Resources*

| | |
|---|---:|
| **8.** Recommended Listening | 559 |
| **9.** Video and Film Guide 1959–1974 | 566 |
| **10.** The Compleat Guide to Collecting and Trading Tapes | 579 |
| **11.** Resource Guide | 586 |
| Contributors | 591 |
| Acknowledgments | 595 |

# List of Color Photos

1. Trippin' in the Marin Headlands, 1967 (photo credit: Don Snyder)
2. O'Keefe Center, Toronto, Canada, 8/4/67 (photo by Herb Dreiwitz; courtesy of Joshua White)
3. O'Keefe Center, Toronto, Canada, 8/4/67 (photo by Herb Dreiwitz; courtesy of Joshua White)
4. Paloma, California, circa 1967 (photo credit: Don Synder)
5. O'Keefe Center, Toronto, Canada, 8/4/67 (photo by Herb Dreiwitz; courtesy of Joshua White)
6. York Farm, Poynette, Wisconsin, 4/26/70 (photo credit: Fred Ordower)
7. Winterland Arena, San Francisco, California, 3/24/71
8. Fillmore West, San Francisco, California, 1970
9. Fillmore West, San Francisco, California, 1970
10. Winterland Arena, San Francisco, California, 3/24/71
11. Winterland Arena, San Francisco, California, 3/24/71
12. Berkeley Community Theatre, Berkeley, California, 8/15/71
13. Berkeley Community Theatre, Berkeley, California, 8/15/71
14. Berkeley Community Theatre, Berkeley, California, 8/15/71
15. Berkeley Community Theatre, Berkeley, California, 8/15/71
16. Berkeley Community Theatre, Berkeley, California, 8/15/71
17. Winterland Arena, San Francisco, California, 12/72
18. Winterland Arena, San Francisco, California, 11/73
19. Winterland Arena, San Francisco, California, 12/11/72
20. Cow Palace, San Francisco, California, 3/23/74
21. Iowa State Fairgrounds, Des Moines, Iowa, 6/16/74 (photo credit: Ray Ellingsen)
22. Iowa State Fairgrounds, Des Moines, Iowa, 6/16/74 (photo credit: Ray Ellingsen)
23. University of Nevada, Reno, Nevada, 5/12/74
24. Campus Stadium, UCSB, Santa Barbara, California, 5/25/74
25. Bill Graham, Winterland Arena, San Francisco, California, 10/74
26. Winterland Arena, San Francisco, California, 10/74

# Preface

Welcome to *The Deadhead's Taping Compendium*. This series of books addresses the music of the Grateful Dead on tape that circulates freely in and around the Deadhead community. This first volume of the *Compendium* covers this topic from 1959 (the year from which we have our first pre–Grateful Dead recordings of individual band members) through 1974 (the year in which the Dead started a year-and-a-half-long retirement from concert touring).

More than any musical group in history, the Grateful Dead owes a large part of its success to those of us fans who call ourselves Deadheads. For most, an integral part of what it means to be a Deadhead is to passionately and relentlessly record and trade the Dead's music on tape. This facet of the Grateful Dead Experience grew in popularity without the help of record sales and with virtually no support from any of the traditional publicity vehicles that most other bands rely on. And let's not forget that almost every Deadhead trades this music for free. There is something quite marvelous about this not-for-profit aspect of the Experience in a culture in which so much emphasis is placed on making a profit.

These two activities, the recording and trading of the tapes, which to date share a fascinating almost-forty-year history, have their own distinct technical, archival, social, spiritual, and sacramental considerations. Our goal with this project is to document the history of this phenomenon, to convey the love and enthusiasm that Deadheads have for the music and the taping culture that surrounds it, and to preserve the Grateful Dead Experience so others may enjoy it in the future.

In this book we have begun to document the equipment and processes with which the tapes were recorded. We also provide a basic guide to the proper uses of current recording technology so that the music may be accurately preserved and disseminated in the future. One must remember that the evolution of home and field recording technology was in its early adolescence when the Grateful Dead began to play, and concert sound technology was only in its infancy. The result is that some of the taped music suffers from a wide variety of technical limitations and handicaps. However, with the advent of digital technology, tapers are finally able to limit the degradation of quality that occurs with multigenerational analog tape copying. Even better, as tapers are tracking down the original master recordings and transferring them to the digital realm, the inferior multigenerational quality recordings are becoming more and more a thing of the past. Every week more excellent quality recordings of this music appear in wide circulation.

Collecting Grateful Dead music provides the opportunity for all tapers to play the role of archivist. Through the process we become historians—researching, problem solving, documenting, and preserving a deep, sometimes mysterious history. The *Compendium* provides a database of the Grateful Dead's music on tape now in circulation. This body of knowledge will continue to grow and require revision as new information appears. As is the case with many "unorganized" phenomena, what eventually comes to be seen as crucial historical information is not documented until long after the fact. Case in point: For years the Grateful Dead didn't accurately mark tape boxes with dates and locations of shows. While this makes for a great deal of ambiguity, it also provides us with great opportunities for exploration and mystery solving.

The Grateful Dead taping world is its own not-so-little society with numerous subniches. There are the recordists, both ancient and modern. And then there are the tape traders who, thanks to the Internet, now span the globe and transcend the limits of the Grateful Dead's music. Recording, taping, and listening are what Deadheads do when we get together. It's an important social bond during those times when we're not attending concerts. After a day of hanging out with a friend, you usually go home with a tape or two. To this day, so much taping goes on one can almost hear the eternal whir of tape decks spinning across the globe as tapes of Grateful Dead music continue to multiply. There is always a Grateful Dead concert playing somewhere! It is our hope that this project will not only serve to document a representative part of this community but will also serve to inspire and widen it.

We have written this book for several reasons. First, much of the Dead's music is imbued with tremendous transformative power—the power to inspire, transport, amaze, mystify, enlighten, and even heal. The world *needs* music like this. We hope that this book will help guide others toward the joy and wisdom that can be gained by participating in the Experience. Also, the Deadhead community needs a written guide to serve as a focal point, something around which to gather and continue discussing that which has brought us together. And for the individual Deadhead, we hope this book will serve as a sounding board, a tool with which to objectify and confirm the feelings and opinions that arise when each of us listens to the music. Obviously, this book is not an end, but a beginning. We've only cracked the door open and taken a first serious look. Keep in mind that this is an almost-forty-year history that is still in process. Many mysteries still exist, but we hope that this book will serve as a catalyst for bringing forward many of the unsung heroes, unknown facts, and missing tapes.

We're going to begin the history of the Grateful Dead taping phenomenon by sharing with you a bit of our own stories. Every taper and every tape collection has its own history. These stories are still unfolding, too. Hop on board the bus. The long strange trip continues.

# Introduction

*by John R. Dwork*

## Searching for the Sound

If you're like me, the Grateful Dead *Experience* entered your life at a time when you needed it the most. Although it happened twenty-two years ago, I remember it as though it were yesterday. I was fifteen at the time, unable to ignore my profound suspicions that life was supposed to offer more excitement, adventure, and wonder than my daily humdrum suburban reality. Like most other fifteen-year-olds I often lay awake at night, wondering when and if *something* magical and meaningful was going to happen.

And then something *did* happen. It was the spring of 1975. I was in my room late one night, deep in thought, listening to the local classic rock radio station, when the DJ launched into a special tribute to the Grateful Dead. Until that moment I had heard only the relatively tame album versions of "Truckin'" and "Casey Jones." The DJ played an incendiary performance of "Not Fade Away" > "Goin' Down the Road" > "Not Fade Away" from the Europe '72 tour. To my utter amazement this music *leaped* out from the speakers and tickled my insides so hard I almost screamed out loud. Never before in my life had I heard anything so powerful. Nothing had ever *moved* me like this. Halfway through the jam I was off the bed, dancing wildly, playing air guitar, totally and joyously entranced by the astounding energy of this band. Fifteen minutes later, soaked with sweat, I fell to the bed exhausted, knowing that I had finally experienced something *outside* myself that mirrored the intense feelings inside my heart and mind. Though I didn't quite realize it at the time, I was in need of rituals, adventures, and sources of inspiration of mythic proportions with which to validate and inspire my own emerging worldview. By the time that "Not Fade Away" ended I had found a door to these Experiences (or did they find me?).

Now, as every Deadhead knows, the Dead's studio records barely scratch the surface of the *real* Grateful Dead Experience. The true magic is found in and around the band's live concert performances. And as we all learned quickly, concert tapes were and are the next best thing to being there. It wasn't long before I managed to snare my first live concert Dead tape: the legendary, immortal, *quintessential* second set from 2/13/70 at the Fillmore East.

If there was even the slightest doubt in my mind after hearing that radio broadcast that the Grateful Dead was the most amazing rock 'n' roll band on the face of the planet, it was completely and forever vanquished after my first listen to this tape. Only this time I wasn't just excited. I was *dumbfounded*. Could these musicians really be *improvising* so astonishingly well? Could all their shows be so ferociously hot? The fires of curiosity within me were fanned even more furiously.

As I became familiar with the music, I learned that the Dead pursued mastery of their chosen skill with intense dedication. In retrospect, I think, this has had a lasting effect on many Deadheads. We too can often be found pursuing our passions with great discipline. Also, I learned early on that the Grateful Dead's music—and in turn the Experience as a whole—was also about *taking risks*. From their coming of age at the infamous Acid Tests, these musicians' finest moments were always to be found when they were mindfully exploring terra incognita. The Acid Tests taught the Dead that sensitive, artistic exploration of chaos sooner or later gives birth to new forms of creative order—forms that often appear more vibrant, exciting, and illuminating than the old structures they follow. The Dead took this newfound wisdom—an awareness of the "tao of chaos," to borrow a phrase—and incorporated it as a central tenet in their approach to their craft. Of course, this reverence for the tao of chaos became a central part of the extended Grateful Dead mythos and, in turn, part of the Deadhead worldview. That they took such creative risks so often, and in their travels discovered breathtaking beauty, profound darkness, and enormous creative power so often, is simply incredible. And this is why we Deadheads are so enamored with the Dead's music. Time and time again they set out in search of magic and, more often than not, found it. In its own way, each such discovery is, for us Deadheads, a small, tangible miracle.

Taping not only expanded the scope of the Grateful Dead Experience, both in size, impact, and intensity; it changed our fundamental relationship with music. In Beethoven's time you only got to hear each live concert performance once. And you were lucky, and usually rich, if you got to hear more than a few concerts in your life. Even in the early years of the Dead's career the live concerts were usually experienced only once. Today, we can listen to our favorite Dead shows over and over and over again, in the comfort of our own chosen surroundings, with the audience of our choosing. No lines to go to the bathroom, no security goons shining flashlights in our faces when we get up to boogie. It's true, I miss that special sense of expectation when the hall lights first went down and the Dead took the stage—that indescribable feeling of knowing something wondrous was about to occur, of knowing I was exactly where I was supposed to be. But I'm also very happy hanging with my friends in the comfort of my own home, the lights turned down low, a stick of incense burning, a nice cold microbrew in hand, and a killer tape cranked up loud. Grateful Dead tapes allow us to enjoy life more fully. "Life may be sweeter, for this I don't know."

## The Evolution of Deadhead Taping Culture

There were several major epochs in the evolution of the Deadhead tape recording and trading scene. Before 1969 there was hardly any taping (outside the band) or tape trading going on. Things really began to heat up with the birth of several "underground" tape trading clubs in the early 1970s. This scene was fueled by four main synergists; the circulation of several particularly hot soundboard recordings (2/14/68, 10/13/68, 2/11/70, 2/13/70, 2/14/70, 5/2/70, and 5/15/70, to name a few), the rapidly rising appearance of audience recordings, an article on the underground Dead tape trading scene that appeared in the October 11, 1973, *Rolling Stone,* and several FM live concert simulcasts in the fall of 1971. In these early days coming across a decent Deadhead tape collection was a rare and very special occurrence.

The second epoch began during the Dead's 1975 hiatus from touring. Les Kippel launched *Dead Relix* (originally *Dead Relics*) magazine in September 1974 and, in turn, Deadheads dramatically increased their trading practices. When the band returned to touring in 1976, they found a whole new generation of fans waiting for them. Still, by comparison with today, tapes were still pretty hard to come by, and not many circulated widely. The late seventies saw a steady surge in the growth of the Deadhead community, and taping grew in parallel. Improvements in affordable tape recording technology helped fuel the scene.

The next and perhaps most significant transformation in the Grateful Dead taping scene took place in 1984 when Grateful Dead soundman Dan Healy decided to officially allow taping by creating a special tapers section at shows. Instantly, the scene grew dramatically larger. More tapers meant more tapes and more tapes meant more folks getting turned on to the Dead. The introduction of digital taping technology around this time also figured prominently in the next era of Grateful Dead taping. With this technology one can make tapes without losing quality in the process. Slowly, the many inferior recordings in circulation were replaced with a new wealth of pitch-corrected, low-generation, accurately databased digital clones, many of which were made from the original masters. In 1985 David Gans began his first weekly broadcast of the nationally syndicated hour-long *Grateful Dead Hour* radio show. Featuring cuts from live Dead concerts, as well as band interviews, this show also played an integral role in helping Deadheads to amass substantive collections of soundboard recordings.

The next epoch came with the appearance and dissemination of the infamous "Betty Board" tapes—a large stash of forgotten, decaying tapes belonging to former Grateful Dead sound engineer Betty Cantor-Jackson that ended up being sold at a repossession auction. All of a sudden the average Deadhead with some cash for decent tape decks and blank tapes could amass a sizable collection of pristine, killer soundboard tapes. This opened the floodgates to soundboard tapes from all sorts of other previously withheld tape stashes. With the dissemination of the Betty Boards, we entered the golden era of Grateful Dead tape trading.

The next and current major epoch came with widespread participation in the Internet. Tapers used to meet primarily at shows. Now, tapers anywhere can easily participate in in-depth, on-line discussion groups. Many have posted detailed tape collection lists on their homepages. Massive worldwide trading projects ("vines") are a daily affair. And now tapers are dramatically expanding the scope of their pursuits as awareness of other musical groups and other genres increases to include classic rock, jazz, groove rock (especially Phish), blues, and bluegrass, to name just a few. In-concert recording and tape trading are here to stay. This *Compendium* was assembled on-line. Michael lives on the west coast, while I live on the east coast, and the dozens of other participants are spread out far and wide. The taping experience has become a global phenomenon.

## Taping Philosophy and Practice

In the old days finding Dead tapes was like hunting for dinosaur bones. They were few and far between, and they were often in lousy condition when you finally unearthed them. I mean *really* lousy condition! Horribly speeded up, mislabeled, recorded with the Dolby switch in the wrong position, the volume levels set too high or low, and all this on crappy tape stock. But hey, we were happy to get what we could. Because back then, before the band allowed taping, one was lucky to have any tape of any show. These days—in the golden age of Grateful Dead music collecting—just about anyone with two decks, some blanks, and a mail address can build a mighty collection of low-generation, perfect quality soundboard tapes of the band's best live performances.

Grateful Dead scholar Steve Silberman once joked that the Grateful Dead Experience was the national pastime of the counterculture. Just like baseball: you went to the show, got a beer, went to your seat, and documented the statistics (in this case, set lists) as the "game" was played. And why not? Everybody needs a hobby, even Deadheads. Besides, the Dead were almost always more exciting than baseball. And what a hobby! Taping provides Deadheads with seemingly endless opportunities to engage in research, archiving, documentation, and communication with others who share this infatuation.

Concert recording and tape collecting give us the opportunity to pursue and acquire what we do not have. These activities challenge us, provide a quest of sorts. Part of how we judge our self-worth, our sense of accomplishment, is by setting goals and then pursuing them. For some, the adventure of learning how to make a crisp concert recording provides an exhilarating sense of accomplishment. The social status attached to a large collection is also often deeply satisfying. It can be a real joy to have someone walk into your library and gasp in amazement at how vast your collection is, and then to blow them away by playing something especially amazing. For others, it's not the size of the collection but the quality that counts. And for others, having that one great version of a favorite song is all that matters. I must have listened to "Dark Star" from 2/13/70 three hundred times the first year I had it.

## The Tapes Have Power

The development of recording technology has had a fascinating effect on the value of collectibles. With tapes—unlike stamps, coins, cards, or plates—you actually get to use what you collect. And you can make copies for your friends that have at least as much intrinsic value as your original copy.

Interesting, however, is that the value of the *tape* often decreases over time as the music on it is disseminated. But, as the tape is copied, more people who hear it may fall in love with it, and in turn the *music* becomes more valuable. As our personal taping experience evolves, our tape collections may become more like our childhood stamp collections in that what was once of high value to us becomes less important. As I became intimately familiar with the music and as my taste and awareness of music in general evolved, I began to focus on specific periods of the music, which I now prefer and listen to more often. Ultimately, the tapes are only the medium, and the real value lies with my attachment to the music they contain.

Two conflicting philosophies of tape trading have determined the growth of the tape trading scene since day one. There are those who believe that withholding information (in this case, music on tape) bestows power, and there are those who believe that sharing information bestows power.

The withholders have always found that people pay attention to them specifically because they have something desirable. Withhold information and you command attention. (So much for the Robert Hunter lyric:

"Reach out your hand if your cup be empty, if your cup is full, may it be again.")

The sharers, on the other hand, have always found that prosperity comes not from denying others what they want, but from spreading the wealth. Sharing the music allows for the good times to continue. Let's not forget this. There is a great joy also to be gained in the act of sharing. Passing the music on makes the circle complete—we give others the opportunity to find joy which was given to us when we recieved the tapes. Ultimately, the music is meant to be shared. Our scene is healthiest when the music is flowing. As Grateful Dead lyricist John Barlow says, "Information wants to be free."

## The Gray Zone

Power trips are played out all the time with the trading of "secret" tapes. These are tapes that are supposedly not meant to be shared with others. The nature of most Deadheads, though, is to share the music. As a result, most secret tapes eventually get around. With each trade the recipient is told not to pass it on. Inevitably they make that promise in order to get the tape. The old line used to go something like "If I roll you a copy of this tape you gotta promise it ain't gettin' out. It came right from the wife of the brother of the guy who drives the Dead's equipment truck on tour and if it gets out he's gonna know where it came from." "I swear on my entire tape collection, it ain't goin' nowhere" is always the automatic response. Of course, six months later everyone and their brother in Philadelphia has a copy of the tape. This cycle of false promises, betrayal, and conditional trades continues on and on. Eventually, the tape gets published in someone's list or is discussed on the Internet. As it becomes "outed," friends confront each other about the break in trust.

Secrecy and stealth have always been part of the live concert tape recording and trading scene—it's part of what makes it an adventure. Until Dan Healy created a legitimate tapers section in 1984, recordists had to tape shows stealthily. In the early days it was fairly easy to get the equipment inside the venue, but one would then have to record without the roadies spotting the setup. Sometimes they'd cut the microphone cables right on the spot.

Eventually, after taping had been allowed for a while, so many mike stands sprang up at shows that Healy could no longer see the stage properly. So he instituted a policy prohibiting taping in front of the soundboard. This created a long-lived practice of secretly recording in front of the soundboard with hand-held or head-mounted mikes. Small groups of stealth tapers would work together. It felt like a spy mission behind enemy lines.

In the mid-1980s, with the dramatic improvement in small, affordable, high quality video recording equipment, it became possible to make excellent videotapes of the concerts. This posed an overwhelming threat to the Dead's adamant policy forbidding videotaping or filming of any kind. This was a inviting challenge to more than a few recordists. At one point, things got so serious that several videographers actually experimented with broadcasting their own sound signal from a stereo recording rig in the tapers section to their video camera via wireless transmitters! The sound wasn't very good, so I'm told, but the effort seems truly remarkable.

In the end this whole subject provides an unsolvable ethical predicament. The secrecy, stealth, and unkept promises all land us squarely in a moral gray zone. But if not for the subterfuge and the leaks, how much music would we have? On one level, these actions have captured and spread the music; on another, they break rules and promises.

## Obsession

It gets much weirder, though. The Grateful Dead Experience and the taping scene have always been colored by an anarchic spirit. Though a few guides to taping etiquette have been published and posted here and there, there has always been a general lack of dogma—no *Robert's Rules of Order*. Our intense belief that the music holds power has helped both the light and the dark energies to swirl around us. Over the years many tapes have been innocently, or at least mindlessly, warped and/or morphed from their original form and/or condition. Combining songs from different shows onto one tape and then not labeling it properly, failing to label tapes at all, improperly using noise reduction circuitry, recording on fast or slow decks: these are just a few of the ways in which recorded music becomes something other than what it was. Untangling this confusion and finding one's way back to accurately labeled, low-generation copies of the music is one of the great challenges faced by serious tapers. But more than a few Deadheads along the way have *deliberately* mislabeled tapes, created deliberate cuts in jams (one did it so he could track how far his altered versions went), and refused to hold up their end in tape trades. Again, the power trip has had a far-reaching influence.

# Introduction

Somewhere along the way, many tapers, not just Deadheads, become so obsessed with recording and trading that it turns into a virtual addiction. I remember recordists at Dead shows getting into fistfights over who would get to set up in the first row of the tapers section; the actual distance being fought over was negligible, about three feet. For obsessive traders, the sole focus often becomes *getting the next tape*. Taking the time to appreciate what they have becomes rarer and rarer. Of course it's just tape collecting—no great evil here. Still, as the old Indian saying goes, what purpose is it to walk the land if all we see before us is the path?

Of course such dedication, such serious pursuit of one's passions demands that we try to see the lighter side of it all. Our scene has always been imbued with a clear sense of "crazy wisdom." We've gotten so into it that we can identify the date of show after hearing only three seconds of the middle of a space jam just from the "sound" of the recording. We have mastered the martial art of equipment sneaking, tape flipping at the speed of light, superior ticket ordering, insane tour scheduling, even sending our recording decks on tour while we stay home! We've developed our own language, our own culture, and, for some, even our own spiritual dimension. It's actually quite endearing how delightfully we've surrendered to the pursuit of oneness with the music, the art and science of the form.

Most Deadheads would probably agree that the negative aspects of this pursuit are seriously outweighed by all the good intentions and actions demonstrated by the great majority of tapers. Among most tapers, a collective sense of etiquette and respect for others, and for the music, has clearly evolved in the face of the anarchy that swirls through the scene. And most of us have learned to enjoy giving tapes as much as receiving them.

## One Long Party from Front to End

Long before the Dead stopped touring, we Deadheads were using tapes as the soundtrack to our daily lives. It's the more novel uses that stand out in my life. I'll take to my grave the sweet, sweet memory of flying a kite while dancing on top of a mountain in the Himalayas at sunset with the "China Cat Sunflower" > "I Know You Rider" Rider from 3/23/74 cranking on my Walkman as the clouds in the valley *below* me turned orange. Or floating in the warm Caribbean ocean, lover in my arms, "Bird Song" cranking on the beachfront stereo in Negril, Jamaica. Or competing in the finals of the World Flying Disc Freestyle Championships as "Not Fade Away" whips the crowd into a frenzy. Or dancing with my sixty closest friends to the "Hard to Handle" from 4/29/71 under a strobe light in a theater rented for our own little private party. With a little ingenuity and a sense of adventure the music of the Grateful Dead can help turn life into a continuous peak experience.

Still, with all these romantic memories of the Dead's music helping my life's great adventures achieve maximum profundity, I'm just as fond of the more mundane act of driving with a great Dead tape playing on the car stereo. Something quite remarkable happens when I get on the highway and put on a jazzy "Dark Star" or "Playing in the Band" from '72, '73, or '74. After a few minutes I get in this deep groove—the Zone, if you will. It's amazing how fast the miles fly by, but it's even more remarkable how this synergy between music and motion makes the creative juices in my mind flow freely. So many thoughts come flying out of my brain that I have to keep a minirecorder on hand to capture them. I'm not the only one who's found that the Dead's live jams inspire creativity in this setting. Try it some time.

For many years Deadheads have been using the music as a trigger, a catalyst, for even deeper, more profound psychic explorations. With or without drugs, listening to Grateful Dead music alters consciousness. Close your eyes and lie back in a dark room, or dance to the music with your eyes closed, and you will find that it takes you places. At its most visionary, you will find the Dead's music, more than any other music, becomes a catalyst that can spark in the mind's eye of the properly attuned listener an infinite variety of eternally unfolding, metamorphosizing, multicolored architectures of shapes, contexts, and messages. Journeying through these infinitely intertwined and interrelated architectures, one can access the full spectrum of pure emotions, being states, and sensory experiences. Such journeys often leave the Experiencer with a wealth of ineffable, mystical realizations. This music is a door to another plane, or, in my experience, to a series of constantly changing planes on which the great cosmic dance reveals itself in all its Technicolor splendor. More than a few Deadheads have found that the Dead's music can be a catalyst for genuine epiphanies.

For those of you who miss or never experienced the live concerts themselves, let me remind you that one of the great values of having this music on tape and CD is that you can select a healthier and more controlled environment and time to take this deeper journey than was provided at the concert itself.

## The Golden Age of Grateful Dead Tape Trading Is Right Now

After more than thirty years the Grateful Dead Experience, which started as a countercultural movement, has become a cultural institution. Rarely does a musical phenomenon remain relevant for so long and change so radically the worldviews and lifestyles of so many people. The Dead's music is a signpost, a beacon pointing the way toward a life filled with adventure, spirit, mystery, excitement, and communion. It is a powerful social unifier and a catalyst for deep inner travel. Even in recorded form, many of the Dead's live concert performances serve as profound examples of what is possible in the realm of human expression. Any such vehicle that opens new paths to self-expression, that allows the heart to soar, the mind to travel and expand, is a valuable tool worthy of much study. With an unprecedented number of high quality tapes in widespread circulation, the Grateful Dead musical adventure is more accessible now than ever before. You don't need a "miracle ticket." The Grateful Dead as we once knew them are gone, but the adventure lives on. "Shall we go . . . you and I while we can?"

# Introduction

*By Michael M. Getz*

The first time I had a taste of what the Grateful Dead Experience would be like for me was in 1971 at Madison Square Garden in New York City. Entering the building was like sliding down the throat of a dragon. Saying that people were excited is as much of an understatement as saying that going to church was merely dull; the place was *juiced*. The anticipation was as tangible as the wooden paddle of Sister Mary Scarme, my deranged teacher at St. Bernard's in White Plains, who had provided me with a second reason to sit on the edge of my seat. I inhaled the odors of beer, smoke, cheap cologne, sweat—and I liked them.

When the lights finally went down, the sea of seemingly random minds, over ten thousand strong, suddenly came together like scattered cards swooshed together by a magical wand into a crisp, gyrating deck. I rode this wave of collective focus in a state of enchantment. People were yelling, calling out names, cussing, cheering fine playing, or groaning in agony over a miscue. As the five players hit their stride, I could feel them moving the energy in an unselfish way, feeding off the crowd and dazzling us with their skill and timing. For within these movements was an opening, a special place for us, the sixth member, as we relied on each other to build the momentum into a mutually satisfying experience. It felt exhilarating and oddly calming despite the mayhem spontaneously erupting around me.

When it was over, I left the Garden, skipping joyfully under the blazing marquee that read:

Tonight: Knicks vs. Celtics

I was eleven years old as I walked back to the car, pumping Dad's hand while babbling nonstop about my impressions. My dad smiled politely but was clearly angry the Knicks had lost; such is the golden difference between children and adults. To enjoy the ride home I casually became sullen with him, agreeing emphatically that the players' salaries were outrageous—a point my dad ignored when the Knicks won. But I would never forget this night. I knew somehow in my young heart that it was special and worthy of being tucked away—like my Mickey Mantle autograph.

Seven years later, as a sophomore at SMU in Dallas, I discovered the Grateful Dead through a friend named George. It went like this: To get the kindest blend meant visiting his dorm room—and staying. Home court rules applied: George served as both DJ and bong tender. And he played mostly Dead on his turntable. Soon I had some of their records myself and the game was afoot.

But the real squeeze, the genuine cranium-splitting lightning bolt, came when some friends and I were in a car en route to a cabin in the Dallas countryside to spend the weekend. This was not the poetic backdrop of Texas out of Robert Hunter's "Jack Straw": there were no clouds at any altitude nor did eagles fill the sky (though smoke filled the car)—just dust and a heat that made sitting/sticking in the backseat nearly claustrophobic. But then someone popped a tape in. It was an audience recording of the Dead at Englishtown, New Jersey, on 9/3/77.

The band's live albums that I had, *Europe '72* and *The Grateful Dead* (commonly referred to as *Skullfuck* or *Skull and Roses* due to the album's lack of formal title and the intertwining skeleton and roses of the cover art) were soundboard sources, culled from performances in 1971–72. This meant the audience noise was almost completely absent because it was recorded directly off the P.A. system. I was instantly thrown into the melee of a Grateful Dead concert—only it was five years into the future from the music I knew. My dismal discomfort vanished as I was transported into the middle of the Englishtown Raceway, a full member of the crowd. The "Not Fade Away" I knew and loved from the *Skullfuck* album was sparse and nimble. The one in the car had a Who-like wallop to it as it kept swirling deeper and deeper, drawing me and the folks on the tape into a tizzy. I was floored. To this day I can feel the full weight of my jaw as it landed in my lap.

"Another bowl, sir!" I said to my friend, who complied with a grin.

Something strange happened to me in the car that day. I felt like the traveler who stumbles off the beaten track into a special, unmapped place and suddenly knows with iron certainty that he was *meant* to be there. What grabbed my attention most was the connection between the band and the audience. It felt like a high-voltage cable was being tossed back and forth, like a beach ball. I'd been to see many big-name acts, but this band arrested my mind in a very startling yet delightfully different way from the others. There was a camaraderie between musicians and listeners that made the show feel like a private, friends-only picnic. I remembered my first Knicks game.

Strange, seemingly nonsensical lyrics—like "steal your face right off your head"—were applauded with great fervor. Musically, whenever there was a sudden tempo shift, a clever modulation, or any unusual or emphatic statement by one of the players, the crowd moved right with it, responding with audible cries of some sort. This, in turn, would change the dimensions of the cable itself, stretching it, kicking it, heating it up, cooling it down. *Anything* but boring.

You could say that each side was egging the other on.

I soon became indoctrinated in some basics of the taping scene. I was fascinated to learn that hundreds of tapes were in existence and that people traded tapes not for profit but only to share the music, taking their cue from the Dead, who generously permitted it. Soon I became versed in other Deadlore: Kesey and the Pranksters, Owsley, the death of Pigpen, the spontaneity behind the song's placements, improvisational jams and transitions between the songs, and—most important—the essential influence of LSD on the band's music and origins. I found out that the Dead learned about LSD from people like Ken Kesey and Robert Hunter, who volunteered to be used by the government as guinea pigs at Stanford.

Of course, some people warned me that LSD was illegal, dangerous, and addictive; it caused its users to go certifiably insane. The media rhetoric was very strong and persuasive on this. But my guidance no longer came from my family, the government, or the media. So when Pink Floyd, Dylan, the Beatles, the Dead, and certain friends mentioned LSD as being an important experience in their lives, I had only one question: where can I get some?

Then one day my dad called to say SMU was out; in-state tuition at the University of Wisconsin, Madison, was in. Bye-bye. I arranged for a friend to drive me early the next morning to the Greyhound station. Hmm, what should I do for my last night in Dallas? George made the call. As it turned out, the goods arrived late, as in one A.M. No matter: gobble, gobble. This turned out to be one of the most important events of my life. After four hours' worth of peaking and peeling away, an astonished grin plastered to my face—my ride showed up. So I grabbed my trunk, attempted a metaphysical goodbye, and off we went to the station. And then, quite literally, the bus came by and I got on—for the second time.

Over the next few years my experiments with psychedelics taught me many valuable things about the sadly limited use of my consciousness. I did not, however, stare at the sun until blinded or attempt to tango naked with a cop while biting down on a rose; on the contrary, my reverence and appreciation for life increased tenfold. So many important questions were burning inside me that I had to find some space and get to work on them. I realized with complete certainty that I wasn't certain about anything anymore, except for what I was feeling inside: an amalgam of fear and exhilaration. How could I make a life decision such as what to do when I got out of school when I knew next to nothing yet about life itself? I also realized that nobody at school knew anything either—nothing that really *mattered,* that is. So I left Madison in 1980 (I was studying economics, for chrissakes) and went out to see a friend in Oregon who seemed to being going through the same things as I (she also had lots of tapes). Despite the guilt-laden warnings from family and friends that I'd end up sorry for throwing my life away (zzzzzzzzzzz), I left anyhow.

The sensation of being able to do what I felt like was empowering. I decided to travel a bit. I ended up hitchhiking across most of the country, rode freight trains, and had splendid adventures with people from all walks of life. I stayed in missions and Salvation Army shelters with people I had looked down upon. I slept in every conceivable place I never thought I could. At one point I lived under the steps of the San Jose public library for three months, just reading and writing whatever I pleased most of the day. I took odd jobs here and there to help cover my meager expenses.

The most significant event stemming from all of this was meeting a woman who would become my wife. We met on the road in Seattle. We both had backpacks, guitars, and worn copies of Ram Dass' *Be Here Now*. We traveled together all over the wild west, even hitching a ride on an airplane once from a private strip off the highway—in exchange for entertaining the pilot with some music.

These days we've traded the road for a family—though the adventures are no less interesting.


For me, as for many people, the experience of taking psychedelics led to a hunt to understand more about myself and how I ticked. Many of my feelings and perceptions—which I dutifully recorded in journals during the days after—seemed to be amazingly similar to passages I was coming across in the sacred texts of the great eastern religions: the Bhagavad Gita, the I Ching, the Upanishads, and the Tao Te Ching. At their core they write about the unity of opposites and a desired state of oneness that transcends polarity of these opposites. I was also finding this thread running through the work of many poets, writers, mystics, saints, scholars, musicians, cab drivers, and artists from all walks of life.

I then found a copy of physicist Fritjof Capra's book *The Tao of Physics*. In it Capra argues that science and religion meet through the discoveries of modern physics. He lines up definitions and quotations from leading physicists and their theories against passages from the above religious texts. It was remarkable to see how nearly indistinguishable they were from each other.

And then there are the lyrics of the Grateful Dead, which often touch on these very same ideas—namely, that there *is* a source to be tapped and a flowing state of consciousness that exists and can be verified through direct experience. I'm not referring here to some "higher consciousness"—a phrase that reeks of grandiosity—but to one that is already accessible within everybody. It's not about getting "higher" but about getting more real. For it is our conditioning, our pessimistic attitudes and lack of self-knowledge, that keeps the well dry. This includes embracing difficult emotions along the way—pain, grief, anger, rage, shame—instead of ignoring them in the pursuit of some pseudo high. For we all have a shadow side that needs to be acknowledged and integrated into our lives. Otherwise it's like living in a house without ever exploring the basement. Working on all sides of ourselves allows us to evolve and grow, which I believe is what we're all here for in the first place. Through their intuitive, open-ended approach, the Grateful Dead set out at each concert to connect with this source and consequently transform both themselves and their audience.

Not your ordinary rock band.

At some shows the source appeared to be just waiting; the music soars effortlessly. On these nights, it is often said, the "X Factor" is present. Other nights, though, could be sloppy and frustrating, without a puff of wind to fill the sails. Some shows fell in the middle. But because of their sophisticated improvisational approach, each Grateful Dead concert tended to stand alone, which answers the question asked by shocked people upon entering our tape lairs: *Why* do you have so many tapes of the same band?

The seemingly never-ending flow of Grateful Dead concerts has finally ceased, at least with Jerry Garcia at the helm. But their music lives on with the tapes, and continues to intrigue both the old farts and those who never saw them live. It doesn't matter. After all, I "got it" in a car before I'd seen them in person. Only the music and how it affects you counts. This book is a guide to what you can get your hands on out there in the trading world. Each show has the potential to be a unique adventure—as does the process of tracking them down. I've been trading tapes for twenty years and I still feel a pleasant rush when the doorbell rings around mail time, meaning something too big for the mail slot has arrived—like a package of new tapes?


This book itself began in such a spirit. I was browsing through the magazines at Tower Records about three years ago and came across Dick Latvala's name on the front of one called *Dupree's Diamond News*. Knowing

## Introduction

very well that Dick is the Dead's tape archivist, I flipped through the interview with him conducted by Johnny Dwork. One question raised my eyebrows. Johnny asked Dick about an uncirculated show at Long Beach on 12/15/72 because he'd heard it contained a "Dark Star" for the ages. Well, not only is December 15 my birthday, I just happened to have that tape. So I went home, spun a copy, and whipped it off in the mail to this Dwork fellow care of the magazine. He called three days later, ecstatic, and we became friends. One rap led to another and soon we decided to take on the enormous task of writing this book.

It's only fitting that a live Dead tape brought us—and this book—together.

Enjoy.

*Michael M. Getz*

# the deadhead's taping compendium volume I

# PART ONE

## Recording and Trading the Grateful Dead's Music: A Historical Overview

(photo credit: Susanna Millman)

# "Inside" the System: The Soundmen Cometh

*By John Dwork and Alexis Muellner*

*The Grateful Dead were recorded inside the system—by soundmen—and outside the system—by Deadheads—more than any other musical group in history. In the early days, before 1975, both these pioneering groups of recordists were faced with the challenge of capturing, preserving, and archiving this music with limited technological means. Superior tape stock and good noise-reduction technology were not commonly available, and desktop archiving database systems and the myriad benefits of the digital realm weren't available yet. For the soundman, the audience recordist, and the tape trader, learning how to accurately record and preserve the Dead's music on tape was a continuous process. Here is a brief overview of that process.*

If you were to walk into the Grateful Dead Vault today, you would see long, well-organized rows, from floor to ceiling, of tape reels. Thousands upon thousands of hours of inspirational music history Deadheads would give their teeth to acquire.

Thirteen years after he started working for the Grateful Dead as their official archivist, Dick Latvala continues to sort, label, and listen. Deadheads had cried out for years for the Dead to officially release live concerts on CD more than once in a blue moon. In 1993 "Dick's Picks," the now steady series of CD releases from the Vault, finally broke the Grateful Dead organization's internal aesthetic/political logjam, which had kept the official releases coming at a snail's pace.

We're lucky. What once was an unmanaged, unprotected, enormous, disordered pile of tapes destined for theft and erosion is now a well-ordered music library. Today, the Dead's vast archive can be cross-referenced and sorted by date, venue, and song. (The tape boxes are coded.) Finally, this priceless archive sleeps safely in a fireproof room protected by a special fire extinguisher system, waiting for Dick to release its shining moments on CD and/or for David Gans to play it on his nationally syndicated radio show, *The Grateful Dead Hour*.

But a look back shows that the collective Grateful Dead mind didn't get serious about archiving until the end of the sixties. For Deadheads trying to amass a strong body of good recordings made before 1968 it's been a spotty endeavor. In the early years, with band members living communally, the few dollars made at gigs went more often to food and gas than to reel-to-reel tape. And in the beginning what was recorded was often mislabeled or insufficiently labeled. Some tapes were even recorded over.

But, fortunately, some tapes of that era do exist because young engineers and sound technicians heard the call and realized that something special was happening on stage. The earliest circulated recording of Jerry, Pigpen, and Bobby playing together is of Mother McCree's Jug Band, recorded in 1964 at KZSU-FM in Palo Alto.

Michael Wanger, who went to high school with Bob Weir and was in a band with him called the Uncalled Four, recalls that his brother Peter, a Stanford University student at the time, was host of KZSU's "Live at the Top of the Tangent." Peter would go down to the Tangent at various times, record whoever was playing there on seven-inch reels, and then edit the tape for airing on his show. Says Michael, "He would pick and choose who to record and he was familiar with Jerry and Bob because of my high school connection with Bob Weir."

## Recording the Acid Tests

Merry Prankster, author, and artist Ken Babbs recalls that by the time of the Acid Tests in late '65 and '66, he and Ken Kesey were already making many recordings of their happenings.

> **Ken Babbs:** Our main thrust was that we would do things spontaneously that had a literary value in the sense that there would be a plot line to it. So we would just tape everything with that in mind.

Soon thereafter the Pranksters got to know the Grateful Dead, who quickly became the band that played at the Acid Tests.

> **Ken Babbs:** Suddenly we had a whole new dimension. We had music of a great professional nature to go along with our stuff. We never thought of the Grateful Dead as the main focus, we always thought of the band as the engine that was driving the spaceship. The music would be the engine noise. It would take you higher.

Set up on one end of the hall at the Acid Tests were several Ampex 601 two-track stereo reel-to-reel tape decks along with movie projectors, cameras, amplifiers, guitars, basses, speakers, and microphones. At the other end of the hall the Grateful Dead would set up their equipment.

Babbs used the 601 to record a master tape of the event. But often he would create live sound effects by running the tape through more than one machine at a time. The first machine recorded the signal, then the tape was led through another machine. As the signal recorded on the first machine passed over the playback head of the second machine (as much as several seconds later depending upon how far away the machines were placed from each other), it would be fed into the PA. The result: a spacey echo effect.

> **Ken Babbs:** Sometimes we'd run it through three or four machines. We'd have one long tape going through three or four machines and picking it up from each of those machines. For a while the Dead didn't have much of a PA. But then they started to get this stuff so I would go up there and tape one of my microphones on Pigpen's microphone, another on Jerry's, and so on. Then I'd have a couple on the stage and I'd run those into my tape recorder. Then all their other microphones would go into their PA. I was trying to get a good recording of them playing.

## Enter Owsley

Legendary LSD alchemist Owsley Stanley, aka Bear, first heard the Dead at the Muir Beach Acid Tests, December 5, 1965, while high on LSD. He quickly became the band's primary soundman, and began spending some of his LSD manufacturing profits on building them the best sound system money could buy. He felt the main priority of his job was simply to get good sound out to the audience—something that didn't happen at the time in rock 'n' roll music. In the mid-sixties, professional audio technology wasn't very sophisticated so at first recording the Dead was a low priority.

> **Bear:** Well, I decided since there were already microphones on stage, and all the electrical

*Ken Babbs*

signals were in the wires, that it was worth hooking up a deck and recording what was there. It just seemed to be a natural.

Dick Latvala credits Bear as the one who started taping regularly. The two have corresponded frequently in recent years, collaborating on the Dick's Picks project. Recently, when the vault was moved to a new location, Latvala combed through parts of Bear's sizable collection of master concert recordings.

**Dick Latvala:** It's in Bear's unmarked early tapes where all this unknown shit happens. There's room for discovery yet. But I've pretty much gone through it all. When I see something not labeled I have a feeling that he might have slipped some stuff in there so that people would never play it. He's crafty, he'll do that. Eventually, if I ever have time, I might do a test case of some of those scenarios. What he's shown me, like the '66 stuff, has been pretty entertaining.

**Bear:** When I met the Dead I had a 602-2 Ampex and it was a one-speed recorder, 7½ ips. I also had a 354 Ampex which used the big 10½ inch reels. It had two speeds, 7½ and 15 ips. It had both record channels on one circuit board, which was a big mistake and made it a very unreliable machine. . . .

I only had a mono Nagra in those early days. So I didn't use it with the Dead. Up until '69 I used mostly the Ampex 602. The 602 became obsolete, it was too big and too heavy; it sounded good, but it was too much to deal with. It was a tube type and (as they say in England and Australia) it had valves, or vacuum tubes in it and they, being like all vacuum tubes, stuffed up regularly (as they are wont to do). I heard about a Sony model 770-2, and I was actually able to find one that didn't have a lot of hiss in it. Most of the Sony stuff in the early days was very hissy, both cassette machines and tape decks. This one was nice and quiet.

That 770-2 was the one I did the *Bear's Choice/Dick's Picks IV* tapes (and of course the Allman Brothers at Fillmore East February 1970). I left this 770-2 at the Alembic studio when they were on Judah Street, and a few days after I went away someone walked out with it. No one knows for sure who, where or what. But I'll tell you the truth: I'd love to get it back. It had the RCA aux. input and output jacks replaced with ¼-inch phone jacks. In 1973 Nagra released a stereo version, the IV-S, and I immediately bought one, serial number 8782. This machine was "borrowed" from Weir by someone named Sam Coty, and never returned.

Most of the shows were recorded at 7½ unless we were short of tape, then maybe the rehearsal or sound check at the slower speed of 3¾, but 7½ mostly. The Sony was a two-speed machine.

Bear remembers that in the early days of recording the Dead, the tape recorder was set up at the soundboard.

**Bear:** In those days it was the way it was done, none of us questioned it, we just tried to deal with it. With the instruments, I separated them as they were onstage, either on one side or the other. I'd separate the two mikes on the drummers, so Bill's overhead was on the opposite side and Mickey's overhead was on the other, with the kick put into the same side as the drummer was on, so each drummer was captured as a stereo pair, although they were interlocked. All the kind of stuff that I did captured images that weren't real, they were real stereo, but they were artifacts rather than exact depictions of what the sound was like on the stage.

Sometimes they shifted their positions from one side to the other side of the stage from time to time in a seemingly endless search for the "perfect setup." In those days I didn't put the guitar in the PA. There was a little rhythm guitar in there but no lead, no Jerry's guitar in the PA. I didn't put Phil's bass in the PA either, because we had developed their onstage equipment to the point where they were plenty loud and didn't need reenforcement. The primitive PA systems of the time were having a hell of a time just coping with leakage and handling the voices and drums. I also never miked cymbals. The cymbal is a bigger destroyer of PA sound than anything else because it is such a broad-spectrum noise and very loud. It swamps everything and intermodulates everything. The cymbals themselves have more direct power output than any but the most modern PA systems. So there was really no need to do it. There wasn't in those days and there certainly isn't today either.

## Bear Goes on Hiatus

In mid-1966 Bear parted ways with the Grateful Dead. Bob Matthews would become the band's primary recordist for many years under the next Grateful Dead soundman, Dan Healy.

> **Bob Matthews:** Bear's version of time and having things "on time" was not one that the band could deal with. Despite the perfection of his equipment—it was the decision to leave him behind at the price of giving up the marvelous technical advantages.

## Enter Healy

Longtime Dead soundman Dan Healy first arrived on the scene in 1966 after working for McCune Sound in San Francisco. At the time Healy was living in a houseboat in Corte Madera, California. John Cippolina, the guitarist for Quicksilver Messenger Service, was living on the next houseboat over. Cippolina would bug Healy to come check out one of his shows. When Healy finally consented, the show he caught featured the Grateful Dead as the opening band. Phil Lesh's bass amp died and Healy, knowing a thing or two about electronics, was able to fix it. Later that night, while hanging out backstage with Garcia and Lesh, Healy criticized the inferior speakers in the PA being used that night. Garcia replied by daring Healy to put his sound system where his mouth was. Healy took him up on the dare and created a better-than-average public address for their next gig. Because he was familiar with studio recording techniques as well, the Dead hired Healy on the spot.

In a lecture at the New York Audio Training Institute on February 26, 1985, Dan recalled the early days.

> **Dan Healy:** In 1964, the days before there were such things as good recording studios, a four-track tape machine was brand new news. Real big new event. By ... 1966 the entire San Francisco music scene began to really start to bloom. There was a lot of call for recordings of the Jefferson Airplane, the Quicksilver Messenger Service, the Grateful Dead, the Charlatans, and all that whole sort of original generation. And so when they, the radio industry and the record-buying public, began to demand records and music from all of these groups, we hadn't yet been recorded, and we had really no experience at all. And studio recording was considerably different in those days. For one thing, multitrack recording and overdubbing as we know it today didn't exist at all. What existed in place of that was kind of a more of an older school approach which is where you played and sang everything all live at one time in the studio, which is now only done on rare occasions: mostly big bands and things like that do that, organizations that were oriented from that kind of recording realm of the thirties and the forties and fifties.
>
> So we began to be hit on by record companies, so finally, in the case of the Grateful Dead, Warner Brothers Records finally made us an offer and we accepted. We signed a contract to make albums. And so, the people that ran the studios, the engineers and the record company producers and stuff like that, were really not used to our approach, which was kind of a new sort of an approach to recording. So what happened is that I began to be asked for because I also knew all the members of all the different bands ... by then, and so they would ask for me because I understood somewhat about sound and recording and that they felt more comfortable working with someone they knew in the studio, which ... stands to reason.

## Enter Bob Matthews

When Dan Healy started working for the Grateful Dead in early 1966, Bob Matthews, an old friend of Jerry Garcia's from the early 1960s, started tagging along. Later that year, Matthews became part of the Grateful Dead organization, primarily as a recording technician.

**Bob Matthews:** I guess you could call Healy my first mentor. He was involved in recording and I hung with him. Back in those days, I'd help him set up and I would always harp on him to make sure that he brought a tape deck [a Sony 777] from McCune's whenever we did the PA 'cuz that's what I really wanted to do. So I'd basically just run the tape machine, change the reels, and label them.

Matthews says he believes the Dead's motivation to record everything they did wasn't just for posterity's sake.

**Bob Matthews:** Very early in the game the first order was to be able to review, listen, enjoy, or dissect or whatever. But the feeling that it was also for history, for the Vault, long before the Vault itself actually physically manifested, was always part of the idea. I mean, very early, we started taping every show; you can tell by how far back the tapes go.

## The Acid Test Album

Jerry and Pigpen joined the Merry Pranksters in the Sound City Recording Studios in San Francisco on January 29, 1966, for the recording of the "Acid Test LP."

**Ken Babbs:** This was not an Acid Test. Those were much bigger gatherings. This was done as a record to be played at your house. With earphones on. It was done with that in mind. It was not an Acid Test. It was just us in the studio, doing our thing.

Kesey and I and [fellow Merry Prankster] George [Foster] went in there and started laying this stuff down. The Grateful Dead had been playing the Haight down at the Straight Theater. They came down and showed up. Owlsley was there and this guy Jim the Host, who ran the recording studio, gradually started to go crazy as this thing was going on. We were hooking up all our stuff and we had the delays going. At this time we had our best delay going which we called the Figure Eight. We ran this Figure Eight thing through the delay recorder and out into the speakers and then picked it up with microphones and ran it back again. It was in stereo so you could have the microphone in one speaker that was on the opposite side of the stereo without getting any feedback. Man, did we get some great recording there.

They'd made so many recordings of themselves on the bus and at the Acid Tests that it seemed the time was right to get into the studio and make a decent recording. Babbs remembers that everyone was aching to get in there.

**Ken Babbs:** The real tragedy of all this is we must have been in there all night long, like six or eight hours. Jim the Host was responsible for editing down and mixing the session. But he took all the master tape and he made the tape that went into the record. Then those tapes got lost, destroyed, they're gone. And that guy's dead.

Soon after that, Babbs recalls, the Pranksters had a custom soundboard made.

**Ken Babbs:** We had this guy build us a soundboard: Buchla. He lived in San Francisco and he built us this thing called the Buchla Box. I think he worked on the Moog synthesizer. This guy was unbelievable. At the Trips Festival at Longshoreman's Hall [a venue with seats on all four sides of the floor], the weekend of January 22, 1966, he had ten speakers set up around there in the balcony. He had this board in which he could run the sound around in circles. He would isolate one, and have sound wheeling around the room. He had this thing like a piano that was just flat and you ran your fingers across it and it would play the notes. Made it himself, absolutely fantastic. He made up this box for us that was essentially a mixer and a mike amp and a speaker box and an earphone box.

## The Scorpio Sessions

Gene Estribou had the first four-track studio in the San Francisco area, Buena Vista Studio, and here the Dead cut their first demo in June 1966. He was introduced to the Dead by photographer Herb Greene, when the band was playing in Palo Alto and Garcia still played bluegrass.

**Gene Estribou:** First we had an Ampex three-channel instrumentation deck that Henry Jacobs brought into the studio. I had built a big horn and a studio and we had good condenser mikes and spent a lot of time optimizing the board. We went down to Western Recording and used their studio for doing some tapes that ended up being on the first 45 from Scorpio, "Don't Ease Me In" and "Stealin.' " About the same time some of the people from the big labels were searching around wondering what this San Francisco thing was. They romanced the Dead and a bunch of other groups, and I had recorded demos of Janis Joplin, Big Brother, and a bunch of others that had been in the studio. These were the first demos and recordings that happened in San Francisco.

They authorized the release but at the same time, almost simultaneously these majors were starting to court them and Warner Brothers ended up doing something with them. It was also the first time the band was under any management and half of the Dead weren't talking to them or they didn't care.

Four songs were recorded in the Buena Vista Studios, some of which had added overdubbing and vocals.

**Gene Estribou:** This was an effort going down there recording, to get a mix down that we could have as product. It was an effort to get out of the zone of indecision that you can imagine. The early Dead was trying to find themselves in a sense and get a product out when Phil wanted to do one thing and Jerry wanted to do another and Bobby was combing his hair. So it was frustrating for everybody, but we had to get something finished rather than 9,000 hours of shit that was unusable. That's basically what that was all about.

According to Garcia, fewer than 150 of the demos were pressed. Estribou, however, says it was more like 250. Some counterfeits have popped up.

## The Avalon Ballroom

Bob Cohen also worked with the Dead. He came to San Francisco from New York City in the summer of 1960. A silversmith, he had an interest in folk music and used to hang in North Beach at coffee galleries, listening to the bands. In January 1966 Bob attended the Trips Festival where he heard performances by the Grateful Dead and Big Brother and the Holding Company. Then, while working as recording engineer at the famed Avalon Ballroom, he got to hear and record many in the scene.

At the Avalon, where the Dead played many times between May 19, 1966, and April 6, 1969, Cohen said there were no signs of bootleggers.

**Bob Cohen:** They weren't doing it at the Avalon. The Avalon was too small, and if anybody did do it then they were real good. They must've done it on a little cassette or I would've caught them. I wouldn't give out any of my copies of the tapes.

The first Dead shows at the Avalon Ballroom were recorded on a Concertone ¼ track tape recorder. A little later on that was replaced by a Revox A77, it was a two-track recording most everything at fifteen inches. Then later on it was an Ampex HE440, I believe, four-track machine.

Cohen said the mikes he used were Shure SM57s and SM58s:

**Bob Cohen:** I miked the drums with one on the bass and then two other microphones, one over on the snare and the other on the other side by the tom-toms. So I would pick up the tom-toms and the cymbals. The only thing that I usually did not mike was the bass because there was usually enough bass already. The house mix was pretty close to a recording mix. I only added a few more mikes when I recorded.

Tapes were recorded off Cohen's own home-built soundboard, affectionately called the "Blue Naugie."

**Bob Cohen:** It had a blue Naugahyde front armrest. It's here. It's gigantic and it took four people to lift it. It was a 20 in, 2 out board. The average recording level you get is a +4, mine would be +30. So it had incredible dynamic range without having to use limiters. It kept the signals from distorting when recording very loud performances.

Even inside the system, way back then, it was unclear where the lines should be drawn about who had the right to record. One night, that became obvious.

**Bob Cohen:** The Dead's soundman, Dan Healy, asked, "Are you set up to record the band?" I said, "Yup." He said, "Don't record them." I said, "Fine with me." Two minutes before they're about to go on, he comes running up again and says, "OK, record them." So I got it recorded. It was a great night with a great set, recorded the whole thing, and then after the show he comes up and says, "OK. Gimme my tape." I said, "What? This is my tape recorded on my equipment. The tape belongs to both of us. I own the recording rights and the band owns the performing rights. And until we negotiate something you're not getting this tape." So we get in this big argument, and I'm playing part of this tape back, and half was on one reel and half on another. So he picked up the tape, cut it in half, and walked off with half. I've got the front half and he's got the back half. But when you play it, it really starts cooking. I'd love to find out if the other half still exists.

## Recording *Anthem of the Sun*

Bob Matthews' recording partner in the Dead organization for years was Betty Cantor-Jackson, the woman responsible for the Betty Boards. Betty came on board during the Carousel Ballroom recordings in late '67 to early '68. Matthews says he enticed her into hanging out with him by telling her she could learn how to record with him: "I just included her in everything I did, 'cuz it was my way of getting her to be my old lady."

In June of 1968 a rift developed between record company engineers and the Dead's internal sound guys. It became clear to Matthews that the band needed a liaison between it and the recording media. The band had had a brief experience with a "straight" record producer Dave Hassinger, and it hadn't worked out well.

Healy was in Dave Hassinger's face about recording techniques—specifically about pre-amp clipping. Back then, according to Bob Matthews, the recording industry accepted mike pre-amp clipping as a predistortion for disc cutting later.

**Bob Matthews:** It was point of argument in quality that Healy managed to rally the band behind, and Hassinger finally just quit and said, "Here, you do it." And that was how *Anthem of the Sun* got started, which was a lot of live recording.

With *Anthem of the Sun*, the Dead managed to do what Warner Brothers didn't want. It produced an eclectic, esoteric, jam-based sound that in a way mirrored the gestalt of the live shows of the time. *Anthem of the Sun* was pieced together using several underlying tracks recorded at live concerts on a tour of the Northwest and at the Carousel Ballroom in San Francisco in 1968. It was groundbreaking at the time, in part because it broke from the formula of producing records filled with in-studio songs, all two minutes or so in length, and meant for hit-radio airplay.

On March 25, 1985, Dan Healy delivered a lecture to the Hampshire College Grateful Dead Historical Society in Amherst, Massachusetts. He reminisced fondly about the recording of *Anthem of the Sun*.

**Dan Healy:** The first album we made was absolutely strict record company rule. It was done on a four-track, which, in those days, was like a raving new piece of equipment.

The second record, *Anthem of the Sun*, was the example of when we busted out. Our record company had assigned a producer, a poor guy named Dave Hassinger, who halfway through it had a complete total nervous breakdown and wound up in the hospital and so we wound up finishing it ourselves.

That was before the days of cassettes, they did not have cassettes... till the late sixties. And nobody really had any tape machine, that's why there's very few tapes kicking around in '65, '66, '67. So we finally built this machine that was a reel-to-reel—Viking is the name of it; I don't think they're still made anymore. But in a hi-fi era, in the sixties, that was formidable, that was the Ampex of home recorders. It was the home version, but it was the high-roller version. What we did was, we got a stereo, a two-track stereo machine. And we went to this company, Nortronics, that makes tape heads and we conned them into making a four-channel record head that applied to quarter-inch tape.

There was a [Dead] tour called "the Great Northwest Tour" that we played; in Ashland, Oregon; Portland, Oregon; Seattle; and let me see, Eugene, Oregon. And we also played in Lake Tahoe, California, at an old abandoned bowling alley that got converted into a gig hall. We had this four-channel tape machine, and in those days you had vocals mikes and maybe a couple of drum mikes and that was really stretching out there. We did all of these tapes, we derived them all. We were halfway through the *Anthem of the Sun* record which we had done, the first half, in the studio, and this guy Dave Hassinger bellied up on us, so we took it upon ourselves to finish it all. And about halfway through it, also, the one-inch eight-track format, came in.

The Kingston Trio had a recording studio called Trident Recording that was in the basement of an old building in downtown San Francisco. And by that time, the folk music era and the Kingston Trio and that kind of stuff had sort of already run its trip.... The studio was built just for the Kingston Trio, and it existed there. While we got the first eight-track on the West Coast and we took it into the studio, which was designed with a three-channel console. It had twelve inputs but it only mixed down to three: left, center, and right, they called it in those days. And so we modified it to have fader-outs, so that we had the twelve mike, front-end mike pre-amps and then the twelve input faders. Then we stayed up several nights in a row and rewired the patch bay so you could get individual access to the output of each one of these mike channels. And through that, you could record on the eight-track.

So we had all these live tapes and we had fragments of the studio stuff that we had done. If you listen to that record, you'll notice there are some parts of it that sound real studioized and there are other parts that sort of unfold into a live kind of a groove. So, we put that all together and we had some of the tapes recorded at 7½ inch and some of the tapes recorded at 15 inch. There was a whole lot of incongruities going on, but after having gone through everything that it took to lead up to that, we finally decided what the hell, go for it.

So we took this little machine that we had gone out and done several gigs with, brought it into the studio, and we transferred it onto this eight-track. In that record, if you're familiar with it, there's a lot of metamorphosis that goes on. There are a lot of things that grow out of other things in it. In many ways it's my favorite Grateful Dead album, from the point of view of really being out there, researching and trying new ideas. And you have to understand that in those days, that was considered really on the outer fringe—I mean, it was totally nonconventional. And because of that it was almost a struggle. But what happened is that we had already been committed by our record company to see us through this record, so we had some fixed budget which probably by today's standards wasn't very much, but in those days, it seemed to cover the studio time. We went ahead and pursued this. And during that time was when we really really flashed on the concept of writing, creating, generating, playing our own music in our own fashion and in our own form. And it was a very magic time in the history of the Grateful Dead.

For Matthews, the recording of this album led to an opportunity to work with a major record company, Mercury Records, as a demo recording engineer at a studio in San Mateo. There he did demos for other Bay Area bands like Santana. This new job would put Matthews in a better position to work more extensively with the Dead in the studio later on.

## The Matrix

Peter Abram owned the Matrix Coffeehouse in San Francisco when Jerry Garcia, Phil Lesh, Mickey Hart, and friends played several well-known gigs in late 1968 under the name Mickey Hart and the Hartbeats. The tapes of these shows, which enjoy wide circulation, display some of the most free-form jamming of these musicians' entire careers. The club held only 105 people. According to Abram, only around eighty people were there for those shows, which were pulled together on very short notice.

> **Peter Abram:** It would have been called Grateful Dead Jam or something like that, but Chet Helms got freaked out because he was having them at the Family Dog event the following weekend and he insisted that they not play.

A compromise was made, Abram remembers. The gig would go on, as long as the name Grateful Dead was omitted from promotions, and so Mickey Hart and the Hartbeats was born.

The experience of these shows, the loose, hangout feeling of a tiny coffeehouse venue, was reflected in the sound. Several guests sat in, including Elvin Bishop and Jack Casady. The result was a continuous stream of jams.

> **Peter Abram:** Toward the end of the night things usually loosened up and if guys like [Jack Casady] were around, they'd hop on stage and join the band. They came back with Jerry Garcia and Friends a few years later, when he was putting together the Jerry Garcia Band. And he played there every Monday and Tuesday night for two years. I recorded all that stuff on half-inch four-track tape. But when the club closed I just left them there. It was too much bulk and I didn't have a way to play them back anyway.

To record the Hartbeats' shows, Abram used a Sony 777. Though these tapes are noticeably hissy, the jamming on them is immense.

> **Peter Abram:** The heads were worn out on my machine. The tapes sounded great over the headphones, but when I played them back between sets I knew something was wrong. Owsley lent me his mikes, which helped some. At the time I was using two thirteen-dollar Calrad microphones, so whatever he had was an improvement. But since that wasn't the key problem, it didn't help.
>
> I'm not sure about the mixer; it could possibly have been a Sony of some sort. The mikes were probably Shure 57s, Electrovoice 676s.

## Recording *Aoxomoxoa,* *Workingman's Dead,* and *American Beauty*

In 1969 the Dead were looking for yet another direction in the studio.

> **Bob Matthews:** Again, Garcia and I were great, close friends. And hanging out with him at one point, I was telling him, "Hey, I got a studio down here, you can come down here and play for fun!" So they ended up down there and that's how we did *Aoxomoxoa*.

In fact, *Aoxomoxoa* was made twice.

> **Bob Matthews:** The studio Pacific Recording that was in San Mateo. Had an Ampex 440 eight-track which was a terrible transporter, it couldn't really pull the tape, resulting in different speeds at the head and the tail of the tape. As the band finished it, Ampex came out with MM1000, a 16-track, so they made the whole album over again.

Matthews said he conned Ampex into letting him use it for some remotes. That deck, serial number 33, would serve the band well for the next half a decade.

> **Bob Matthews:** The one thing we learned during *Aoxomoxoa* was that fooling around in the studio is detrimental to the feeling of the art. So, with *Workingman's Dead*, we took a whole different approach. We went in for a day and just recorded all the tunes that they had on a two-track. And then I sat and spliced them together in an order—this was

right after *Sgt. Pepper,* when people became aware of the concept of a whole album as a single unit, rather than this compilation of ingredients.

So I spliced together the two-track demos of all of that in the order that it's released in. I made copies for everyone and then they all went back out and practiced for about three weeks, and then we went into the studio and just recorded it. We did it in about three weeks. Most of it just fell together perfectly, it was really a joy. It was also in a studio that nobody had ever been able to make work before. So it was satisfying for me to be able to understand the basics of what acoustics and recording were all about and being able to take an environment that, on its own, had never been able to be used as a tool—and be able to come out with something as pleasing as *Workingman's Dead.*

Matthews recalls that shows during that summer at the Fillmore and the Avalon were also mixed and put on a shelf, though nothing has come of them yet.

After the release of *Workingman's Dead* and *Live Dead,* the band contracted with Warner Brothers to do a movie called *The Medicine Ball Caravan.* One of their requirements was that Matthews' sound company, Alembic, be contracted to do the PA and the recording of all these outdoor shows. "The night before the caravan left," says Bob Matthews, "I got into some contractual hassle and didn't go. The band ended up, not with Alembic, but with whoever the studio provided them with, and that was Steve Barncard."

The album *American Beauty* was engineered in 1970 by Barncard. A spectacular video documentary about the making of *Anthem of the Sun, Workingman's Dead,* and *American Beauty* was produced by the BBC and first shown in America on VH-1 in the spring of 1997. (Read the video chapter of this book for specifics.) This documentary features some great interview segments

*Jerry in the sound room during the recording of* Aoxomoxoa (photo courtesy of Ampex Studio)

# "Inside" the System: The Soundmen Cometh

*Recording* Aoxomoxoa (photo courtesy of Ampex Studio)

with Phil Lesh and Barncard reflecting on the making of these albums.

## The Secret Fillmore East Recordings

Amazingly, the soundboard tapes that circulated for so many years of the legendary February 11, 13, and 14, 1970, shows at the Fillmore East weren't recorded by Bear. They were secretly recorded by soundmen at the Fillmore who loved the Dead's music.

By February of 1970 Alan Mande had been working as a "mike man" at the Fillmore East for about five months. His job was to switch mike setups on stage between bands. He had already worked two runs with the Dead when they came around for the February run. "So when The Dead came around again, we were all determined to capture some of it so we'd be able to listen to it after they had gone," he recalls.

The hush-hush basement setup wasn't fully operational until February 13.

> **Alan Mande:** That was because we had heard that Bear was bringing a deck, he was going to be taping and he wanted a feed so we came up with the idea that if we're doing a feed for Bear, we may as well do an extra one too. So we just ran a separate feed under the apron at the Fillmore stage which was kind of off behind this wall at the sound shop. We had enough sense that they may not want us to do this, so we kept it hidden, which is why a lot of the breaks are there. But someone had gotten a Revox [open reel] deck, which was state of the art at the time, so we set up some fifteen-inch reels at the beginning of each set and let them roll.
>
> To get to the sound shop you had to go downstairs into this basement, where there were shelves that were off a work table that actually went into this space on the apron. We set it up in there so it would be accessible but not obvious.

When Dick Latvala was putting together *Dick's Picks IV* (from February 13 and 14, 1970), he used these secret recordings to get a seamless transition between tapes with cut points different than what exists in the Dead's vault. (See Latvala interview for the technical rundown of this process.)

> **Alan Mande:** Every time they came through and I heard them they just kept stretching my head more and more. It was just two more steps along the way. But people have said to me, "God, did you know you were at one of the greatest shows of all time?" It was another damn fine show, and personally, in my own picky Deadhead experience, I was much more turned on by the fourteenth.

Mande said someone else on the crew had a dub of these tapes made for himself on a Revox at 3¾ speed.

> **Alan Mande:** What's kind of stimulated this in the past few years is that those dubs are still existent back east, so we brought them back here [to California]. Also, when we were playing those, we found the first acoustic set from May 15, 1970. There are the 3¾ boxes, and the guy that did those stayed on a little longer than I did. So when those came out I discovered that there was some stuff on those from September 18, 19, and 20, 1970.

## Changes at the Board

In 1971, when Bear went to jail on LSD-related charges, Bob Matthews took over as the main PA engineer and recordist.

> **Bob Matthews:** We [Betty and Bob] did two live albums after that. One was *Skull and Roses* [*Grateful Dead* 1971], which was recorded in sixteen-track live, and then the other was *Europe '72*.

In early '71, Rex Jackson, the Dead's roadie (whom their philanthropic organization the Rex Foundation was posthumously named after), also started recording a lot of the shows. That lasted, according to Dick Latvala, until Grateful Dead pianist Keith Godchaux's first tour in the fall of 1971.

> **Dick Latvala:** He was using a Sony 770 and recording these shows on ¼ track tape, which now are the only ¼ track tapes in our vault. In fact, that's how *Dick's Picks II*, the Halloween show, came about—using his ¼ track tape. So anyway, then *Europe '72* was a multitrack. After that, Billy 'Kidd' Candelario started recording in late '72. Also, when Bear got out of jail he recorded some stuff in '72.

Kidd came on board as a roadie in the late sixties. He got to know the band when he was working at the Carousel Ballroom, around the time they recorded live cuts for *Anthem of the Sun*.

Before 1972, recalls Kidd, most board tapes were made at the soundboard. In late 1972, the band got a little more serious about recording and set up the recording equipment backstage.

> **Kidd Candelario:** Those tapes [made at the soundboard] were always sorta so-so because of you're mixing for the room, you're not mixing for an actual recording.
>
> For me, when I took over in '72, I was actually out in the audience with Healy, and I used to use his drum mix from the PA and then I would run that over to two mixers that I had that I would mix instruments and vocals to with his drum mix.
>
> When I could have it, I had my own room, and when I didn't, I generally would build a structure somewhere [rear, side, or back stage] with all the packing blankets and everything I could find.
>
> In my earlier years we listened every night, except for nights when we were traveling. You know, I had to lug my tape deck with me and the tapes from that show, and sometimes other tapes with me, come back to my hotel room, or at one point I sort of rebelled at that and they started giving me a room just to set up, because there was cigarette smoking going on in those days. You know, they would just trash your room, so it was better to have—actually we had a "Mr. Nagra room." And so, we would come in there and I would drag these JBL speakers and set it up. Actually, everybody came back to the hotel after they'd calmed down and cleaned up, or whatever they were doing, long about one o'clock in the morning; everybody would descend upon Mr. Nagra's room, or the taping room. I'd get that call and we'd sit there and listen to the show again.

Dick Latvala says the band listened almost solely for the purpose of doing a better job.

> **Dick Latvala:** It wasn't for the rush, that's not inherent in them. It was for other purposes, not for the fun of it. I don't think any one of them went home after a show and listened to the Grateful Dead. That's the problem I face, not having any of the people that created the music being able to determine what's releasable, because they don't see it the same way.

Though more serious attention was being given to the daily recording of shows, taping, because it was being done by road crew, still took second place to meeting the band's performance-day needs.

> **Kidd Candelario:** Not only was I recording during the show, but we were setting up drum sets and doing piano pickups, and doing a lot of other stuff like setting up the big PA. We

had the Wall of Sound to deal with, so we had actually other jobs that came first. To them, taping was, you should be there to facilitate the music rather than be off in a room taping.[1]

## Steal Your Face

In October of 1974 the Grateful Dead brought the first third of their career as a touring band to a close with five shows at Winterland. These shows were filmed for the Dead movie and recorded for the less-than-stellar double album *Steal Your Face*. Though some of the music played at these shows is excellent, many consider the audio quality to be poor.

**Bear:** It was made from totally screwed-up master tapes recorded on a twenty-four-track machine, except that the nitwit who was given the job to put Donna Godchaux's vocal on an ouboard Nagra along with a SMPTE sync track driven so hard [saturated] that the vocal was wiped by the leakage. At the same time, on the twenty-four track, there was one channel used for an "audience/ambience" mike!

Believe it or not, this continued for the whole run of shows. Weir's guitar mike fell over and the signal was lost during the first set of the first night, and this, too, continued—not only through the second set, but through the entire run!

I don't understand why they didn't just shit-can the whole movie/album idea at that point. It would have saved hundreds of thousands of dollars being flushed down the shitter. Instead we spent months on it, almost overdubbing the entire multitrack tape in the studio. There was never any possibility to salvage any of it, and the movie was a total disaster as well as the album. The performances sucked, and no one could change that.

The rotten truth is that Garcia was fascinated by the intellectual challenge of "The Movie," and couldn't see that the raw material was so badly flawed as to portend a disaster. I was originally allowed to work on the film sound, but due to my criticism about the unsuitability of the performances I was kicked off. I kept telling them that there were only one or two songs which justified full-length inclusions, and that I thought that the documentary and cartoon footage, along with carefully chosen concert footage, would edit into a very nice, reasonably short movie, and that only short bits of many of the songs were good enough to be used in the film. I stepped on some badly overinflated egos.

If this advice had been followed, the film might have not only done well, but could conceivably have won an award. As it was, it was too long for movie exhibitors to want to show; it included sixteen full-length drab, boring songs with awful poisonous green-blue lighting, and was panned mercilessly, with the result that the band lost hundreds of grand on it. The twenty-minute cartoon opener could have been an award winner if released by itself!

Ron Rakow [of Grateful Dead Records] wanted me to turn the master tape of *Steal Your Face* [ostensibly the "soundtrack" album] in to the record company. . . . I was in San Rafael, standing, looking into my fireplace, and contemplating the flames with the reel of tape in my hands and I had the strongest urge to chuck it in . . . when the phone rang, and it was Rakow, screaming and yelling about "where the hell was the tape," so I took it down to the post office and sent it off.

## Vault Gap—The Missing Links

As considerable as the Dead's vault holdings are, there are numerous gaps, the most conspicuous of which is undoubtedly the second half of 1970. Barely any tapes exist in the vault from June of that year through February of 1971. Interviews with many of the in-house engineers at the time leave it unclear where those recordings are, though all are certain they once existed.

---

1. The Wall of Sound was a 641-speaker, 26,400-watt sound system designed for the Dead in the early 1970s by Bear, Dan Healy, and other engineers at Alembic, the Dead's studio. (From *Skeleton Key* by Steve Silberman, New York: Doubleday, 1994, p. 306.)

**Dick Latvala:** When Bear left—he was arrested in 1970—he stopped taping. His last tape was the Pigpen/Janis "Lovelight" night from Euphoria on July 16, 1970. Before that, he was taping in the Bay Area but wasn't allowed to leave the area because of his arrest. So then Bob Matthews was taping. He and Betty were a team, although she played the subordinate role. Eventually, somewhere in the seventies, she took over the recording and did most of the late seventies stuff. Some of which, as you know, was abandoned by her in storage and then auctioned off to tapers. I've been trying to figure out why [all the] tapes don't exist in the Vault. I don't know what happened. There hasn't been any resolution in my mind about it. I'm bummed out that there are all these tapes missing. But then again, we've got so much already.

**Kidd Candelario:** Lots of people had access to the Vault. At one point, the Vault never had a lock on it. Anybody from our scene could actually go into the Vault. We were constantly in and out of there, putting tapes in, taking tapes out, getting cassettes to make, you know, masters, of our tapes from shows.

Kidd believes he's one of the few insiders who has returned all of the master tapes that were in his possession.

**Kidd Candelario:** The reason my tapes are in the vault is because I always wanted to get them out there. I knew that there were good shows in there. I had this knowledge of what was in the Vault and I sorta wanted to go ahead and put all this together. I feel that at one point all the Deadheads that were/are on the mailing list should have a chance to go ahead and buy them. I felt that there should be a year where everybody who was on the mailing list could buy what they wanted to, and then after that year, it should roll over to the industry. That's pretty much the way I actually thought of it originally, and then the powers that be decided that "Why should that happen?" I mean, they were looking at the dollars coming in, and, you gotta remember, they made a huge amount off of Dick's Picks without any advertising. But you know, they did spend an awful lot of money to get good results from this.

For a long time we had Phil in there helping us decide what went on, [but] having Phil in there was such a hindrance that it just got to a point where one day at a meeting I stood up and told Phil, [when] he was complaining about why things were taking so long to actually do this, that he was the problem. And that was when he threw his hands up and said, "Okay," and everybody agreed that Phil would stay out of it, and me, John Cutler, and Dick would go ahead and do this project. And at that point things got a lot easier, in part, because we're not as critical as they are. They never liked to hear their music played again, they never liked to listen to it.

So a dichotomy exists, between the edited material the band wants out and the rough-hewn, head-to-tails recordings the Deadheads say they want.

# "Outside" the System: Deadheads Hear the Call

Anyone who listens to music of the Dead in concert before 1975 will understand what motivated early Deadheads to start recording and trading: a profound realization that something incredible was happening that had to be documented, preserved, enjoyed over and over again, and shared with others.

David Cooks attended the San Francisco State Acid Test in October of 1966, but his desire to record the band didn't surface until he heard the Dead play "Viola Lee Blues" at his third Dead concert. Cooks, one of the earliest tapers, assembled one of the first extensive collections of Bay Area music, particularly recordings of John Cippolina of Quicksilver Messenger Service.

**David Cooks:** I had been to a couple of shows and I knew that something unbelievably special was going down. I knew that there was some music there that I wasn't going to be able to hear any other way and I had my serious doubts whether any record company would hire these guys. . . . They were just out there. I started recording it so that I could have tapes of them.

Cooks was present at the opening of the Carousel Ballroom on February 14, 1968. "I walked in with a reel-to-reel and plugged it in and nobody ever said shit to me," he remembers. "I just put my tape recorder on stage, spread my tapes out one at each side, and no one ever said boo. I recorded Quicksilver for years that way. Occasionally they'd question me, then they figured I was just recording them [for personal use] and let it go at that."

Eventually, Cooks got a lot of tapes from Peter Abram, the owner of the Matrix Coffeehouse. "He kind of got me into taping because he said that the bands didn't care," Cooks says. "I started going down, hanging out at the Matrix taping the shows and realizing that they didn't care at all."

In the 1960s, however, Deadhead recordists and traders were very few and far between. Cooks, for example, didn't meet another taper until mid-1972. Fewer than twenty audience-recorded shows dated before 1970 are in circulation today, though no doubt more than that were recorded. In 1970 audience recordings started to increase noticeably, and today, almost forty audience tapes from that year are in circulation.

Les Kippel realized immediately that there was something going on onstage that he absolutely had to capture.

**Les Kippel:** I first saw the Grateful Dead when I was in college. I had a friend, Robert Tirrela, who lived on Staten Island where a minimum of eight people were living in a three-room bungalow. There was a record on the turntable, and Robert said, "Hey man, this is the Grateful Dead and this is their first album. This stuff is phenomenal! They're playing at the Fillmore—you have to go see them!"

It was January 1970 when I first went to the Fillmore East to see the Grateful Dead. They came out and just blew everything away. And there I was, seeing all of this and realizing there was something there, something I had to be a part of.

The next time the Dead came to town, Kippel remembers that he discovered that Panasonic had introduced a miniature tape machine that used cassettes instead of open reels.

**Les Kippel:** I went out and bought one. It was maybe $19.99 and I used the mike that came with it. I probably used a Radio Shack tape, or something lower quality. My friends, the same ones who were in the eighteenth row before, were now in the front row, so I gave them the tape machine and told them, "You gotta record this music."

I gave them the tape machine, but by then they were so stoned on orange sunshine that they put the tape machine on the chair, put the microphone down, and all I heard the whole night was, "Hey man, pass the wine skin," not a lot of music.

Kippel said that from that point on, he realized he had to take responsibility for taping, not pass that task off to others.

**Les Kippel:** I started investigating better tape machines and better microphones, and from there, it started progressing. I didn't have any tapes at the time, I didn't know anyone taping shows; it was me doing it. I was lonely, very lonely.

Another friend of Kippel's was East Coast taper Jerry Moore. In mid-1971, Moore's high school buddy showed up with one of the first Grateful Dead bootleg albums, *Ain't It Crazy*, which featured eight tracks from the April '71 Fillmore East shows. The bootleg was purchased from someone walking up and down the street at Sheridan Square and Christopher Street in Manhattan's Greenwich Village. Moore wanted his own copy of it.

**Jerry Moore:** I went over looking for this guy and I couldn't find him. I got really pissed off and frustrated by this, so I got the idea of doing it [taping] myself.

Eddie Claridge, another of the early, hard-core tapers, was the manager at the Capitol Theater in Port Chester, New York, in the mid-seventies. Eddie consistently recorded the Dead, up to the band's final tour in 1995. The first show that blew him away was the legendary "Dark Star" medley show at the Capitol Theater on June 24, 1970. He was nineteen.

**Eddie Claridge:** My first impression was one of bewilderment. I knew I had stepped into something very serious, very different, and it would make—as it did—a lasting impression on my life.

I was living in St. Louis and I had some friends who were Deadheads. They had a couple of tapes that were very scratchy, as was everything in that era. Today, somebody could start from scratch and amass several hundred hours instantly, but early on, it was much more in the shadows.

Harvey Lubar knew very little about the Grateful Dead until June 1971. In 1972 he cofounded the Hell's Honkies Grateful Dead Tape Club—certainly one of the most famous of all the early tape trading clubs. Now, after fourteen years of not listening to the Dead at all, Harvey is a serious fan and collector once again.

**Harvey Lubar:** Although I owned *Live Dead*, I thought "Dark Star" was the most boring song. I used to go to the Fillmore East to hear loud English blues-rock bands, and it was there that I heard all kinds of wild stories about Dead concerts and people never being the same afterward. It was a very underground thing then, and as silly as it now sounds, I was scared to go to one.

In those days, Lubar recalls, bands like Mountain and Led Zeppelin ruled the Bronx. In the summer of '71, he spent lots of time with a neighbor who suggested they hang with a guitar-playing pal named Stewie Michael. Stewie, as it turned out, played guitar and worshiped Jerry Garcia.

**Harvey Lubar:** He played a red Gibson SG just like Jerry and studied every note of every solo. He also had Dead tapes. That summer, we visited him all the time and listened to his Dead tapes. My friend and I would sit there, absorb the music, and listen to Stewie talk about the significance of each solo and its context within the framework of each song.

By the time Lubar caught his first Dead show, on December 6, 1971, he was completely familiar with the tapes from '69 and '70.

**Harvey Lubar:** I was really shocked and disappointed that the Dead's set lists and playing style had changed so dramatically in only a few years. I thought we were going to be hearing "Viola Lee Blues," "Alligator" > "Caution" and the rest of the stuff that we had been listening to. Instead we got "Bertha," "Jack Straw," and "Sugaree." When I had told him what I had been expecting, Stewie just laughed.

## The Earliest Tapes to Circulate

Before the taping community came into real focus during the Dead's hiatus in 1975, very few tapes circulated.

**Eddie Claridge:** Being a Deadhead was underground, and being a tape collector was even more so. So finding those early tapes back then was sort of like finding the Dead Sea Scrolls.

Claridge says that when he first started trading there were only a handful of tapes out there and they got played an awful lot.

**Eddie Claridge:** You got to know them real well. Then all of a sudden, somebody comes out with something new and you'd fall on it like a pack of rabid dogs. Every little thing that came down the pike was a real treasure. And people weren't particularly picky as to what kind of quality it was, they just wanted it and wanted to hear it.

The first tape Claridge remembers making the rounds was in '71, from Harpur College, May 2, 1970. "Then," he says, "the tape from the El Monte Theater in December of 1970 came around. And then later in '71, there was the whole fall tour where every city had a simulcast radio show. A couple of friends and I went to several of these cities, and those tapes became readily available as well."

Another of the early great tapers was Barry Glassberg, who, twenty-five years later, can still be found taping concerts in the New York metro area. While there were many fellow Deadfreaks, as they were known back then, in Glassberg's college dorm at the State University of New York at Stony Brook, there were very few tapers. Few even used the term until the late seventies. Tape connections developed slowly.

**Barry Glassberg:** In my case, it was all by mail until I met people at shows when I started recording live in July 1973. A key moment came in late 1971 when WNEW-FM announced they would broadcast one night of the Dead's run at the Felt Forum in New York. Once again, I couldn't get tickets to any of the shows and most of the Deadheads on my dorm floor wound up going, so the next best thing was to record the show in my room. Those tapes were certainly my earliest FM concert recordings, but at that time I had no outside antenna for solid reception (Stony Brook is sixty miles east of New York City, on the fringe of decent FM reception without a roof antenna) and the tape had more background hiss than I would have liked. Nevertheless, I had the whole show with only one cut during the "Dark Star" medley (I always taped at 7½ ips on an open reel deck). By 1972–73 I also became friendly with some of the Stony Brook Student Activities Board people and acquired decent soundboard tapes of the 1970 Stony Brook Halloween late show. These two shows were my original trading tapes—what I could offer in trade for other shows. Soon after the Felt Forum shows I learned that the Dead had broadcast one show in nearly every city they performed during that fall 1971 tour. I wanted to acquire as many of those as I could, and preferably from people who also used open reel equipment [to ensure high quality].

The big break came when I saw an ad with a Berkeley, California, address in the personal ads in the student newspaper *The Statesman*. It simply read "Concert Tapes." So I sent off a letter indicating what Dead tapes I had as well as a few other non-Dead live FM broadcasts. This eventually connected me with my first trading partner, Bill Gadsden, who traded out of Trinity College in Hartford, Connecticut. He already had the Felt Forum broadcast, but he didn't have the Stony Brook Halloween soundboard. Although I didn't know the Stony Brook tapes were all in mono and exactly what generation I had, the copy was nice enough in quality (and rare enough) to get me a box of ten seven-inch reels of the best live Dead I ever heard! It included the April 26, 27, 28, 29, 1971, Fillmore East boards, the New Riders sets from April 28–29, and the Dead from September 20, 1970, Fillmore East. This last show was noticeably weaker in quality than the April 1971 tapes, but it was great material, and my first live acoustic Dead set. To this day, I still have all ten reels, and the copies of September 20, 1970, have never been replaced since I have yet to hear a better-sounding tape.

In the early seventies good-sized live concert tape collections were all but unheard of. Finding someone with more than just a handful of Dead tapes, and who was willing to share his/her entire collection, was like winning the lottery. It was through the generosity of such tapers, turning on "newbies," that tape trading began to grow exponentially.

**Harvey Lubar:** The major source for Stewie's tapes was Marty Weinberg, also known as the Legendary Marty, and his tapes as Marty Tapes. [Marty is best known for his recordings of the Capitol Theater shows in June and November of 1970.] By 1971, Marty was trading with people from all over the United States. To this day I have no idea who they were. Marty taped with a compact Uher reel-to-reel. To the best of my knowledge, the first show he taped with the Uher was June 24, 1970, Port Chester, and his last was July 31, 1971, at the Yale Bowl.

In May of 1972, Stewie and his family moved to Florida. At his suggestion, Mark and I both bought cassette machines and he copied his entire collection (sixty to seventy hours) for us. Needless to say, we were floored. All he asked for in exchange was for us never to sell the tapes and to start lots of new people out in the same way he had

*Early tapers Harvey Lubar and Jerry Moore with the Uher open-reel tape deck that Marty Weinberg used to record the Capitol Theater shows* (photo courtesy of Harvey Lubar)

helped us. Since then, I've made sure I kept that promise. The following autumn Mark and I got to work! Some of the tapes we got from Stu were 2/14/68 (FM), 6/22/69 (AUD), 2/14/70 (AUD), 5/2/70 (FM), 6/24/70 (AUD), 5/15/70 (AUD), 6/24/70 (AUD), 7/11/70 (AUD), 9/17/70 (AUD), 9/19/70 (AUD), 9/20/70 (AUD), 10/11/70 (AUD), 11/8/70 (AUD), 11/10/70 (the mislabeled Action House Tape), 4/29/71 (AUD), 7/2/71 (FM), and terrible, terrible audience tapes of the Academy of Music shows in 1972.

I started out by tearing pages from my loose-leaf notebook and writing out in longhand that I had Dead tapes and was looking to trade with others. They read, 'Trade tapes with the Hell's Honkies Tape Club.' At the bottom, I added my name and phone number. I was the one who came up with the Hell's Honkies name, and it was quite catchy. Mark and I considered taping and trading to be sort of an outlaw thing, so the name fit perfectly. I put the signs up on college campus bulletin boards all over New York City and was doing some trading in the Bronx and Manhattan. Then I got a call from Jerry Moore, someone who in the years to come would play a major role in the Hell's Honkies and in my life.

Jerry and I became close friends quickly. We were the same age, went to the same school, lived in the same area, loved the Dead, and were into tapes. Jerry was already keeping his tapes on reels but at the time didn't have very many tapes. And although I was still using a cassette machine, I had all of Stewie's collection. Around the time of October 1972, Jerry told me that he was planning on hooking up with a guy in Brooklyn named Les Kippel and that Les was the king of Dead taping. Jerry was very aggressive in tape trading and made lots of contacts. He started getting some interesting tapes so I asked my buddy and fellow Honkie Mark [Barkan] if it was okay with him to let Jerry join in our little group. The rules for being a Honkie were pretty easy: everyone had full access to each other's tapes and shared whatever was brought in. Jerry agreed, and it was a great move for us because over the next several years he became one of the main players for both taping and trading tapes.

In November of the same year, Jerry told me that he had again spoken with Les Kippel and that Les had finally invited him over. Jerry trucked off to Brooklyn, and when he returned he couldn't stop raving about Les' collection. Around that same time, lots of tapes started suddenly appearing. Among them was a terrible audience tape of 2/14/70 with the "Caution" spliced out, the San Diego acoustic sets (SBD 8/70), 10/25/69 (later revised to 5/3/69), 7/10/70 (later revised to 4/12/70), 4/6/69, parts of the Stonybrook shows from '70, and a partial audience tape of 6/5/69. The April '71 Fillmore East soundboard tapes started appearing an hour at a time, and by May 1973, 4/3/70, 11/7/71, and the "Lovelight" from 8/6/71 (first called Hollywood Bowl—no date attached) were circulating.

None of these shows were available in complete form yet, but the tape trading

JERRY                    HARVEY

**HELL'S HONKIES**
GRATEFUL DEAD
**TAPE CLUB**

MARK                     HAROLD

*Hell's Honkies trading card*

scene was growing quickly.

In late 1972 one of Stewie's old friends offered us audience tapes from the July 11 and 12, 1969, shows in Flushing Meadow Park. Commonly referred to as the Pavilion Tapes (the shows were at the 1964 World Fair's New York State Pavilion Building), these shows were considered at the time a sort of Holy Grail among tape collectors. When Jerry told Les Kippel about the Pavilion tapes, Mark and I were invited out to Brooklyn. One bright Saturday morning, Jerry, Mark, and I took the D train and headed out for parts unknown.

There were three things I remember about meeting Les for the first time. The first was a crystal clear copy of the June 21, 1969, Fillmore East (early show) audience tape. I remember trying to hide my excitement upon hearing the Dead play "The Green, Green Grass of Home" without any tape distortion.

*Jerry Moore, Harvey Lubar, Mark Barkan, and Harold Ancelowitz* (photo courtesy of Harvey Lubar)

The second thing that impressed me was the audience tapes he made from Waterbury, Connecticut, recorded back the September before. Les was telling us all kinds of stories about problems with Owsley in a motel, but all I could think of was that damn "Green, Green Grass of Home." The third, and perhaps most important thing, that impressed me was Les' business card. To me, this was both revolutionary and brilliant. My first thought was that the Honkies needed business cards, and needed them fast!

About a month later (December '72), Mark had spoken to Marty and gotten an invitation for us to visit. Marty had seen every show that the Dead ever performed in NYC and told Mark flat out that the two Pavilion shows were, without a doubt, the best shows he'd ever seen. Getting to see Marty was no small feat, and for the week preceding our visit, it was all we could talk about!

Marty lived in a huge apartment house known in the neighborhood as the Castle. It covered a full city block and had hundreds of apartments, turrets and a huge medieval courtyard. What a fitting setting to meet the legend himself! When Marty answered the door, he greeted us, shook our hands, escorted us into his room, and closed the door.

Several things stand out from that one-time meeting with Marty: first was the fact that the man played his music LOUD. Mark and I were approximately twelve feet from his speakers and although we were sitting on the floor next to each other we couldn't communicate. Of course, when you were listening to some of the greatest Grateful Dead tapes ever, there wasn't much to say.

He started by playing an absolutely perfect quality tape of the San Diego acoustic sets. Unlike everybody's else's copy, muddy in one channel, Marty's copy was simply perfect. He played for us a perfect soundboard tape of a show listed as Hollywood Bowl 1969 with "Saint Stephen" > "Drums" > "Other One" > "Cosmic Charlie," and also a Carousel Ballroom tape from '68 with a twenty-five-minute "Dancin' in the Street." His audience tape of 7/11/70 sounded like a "front of soundboard" DAT tape made today. The reels went on and on; Marty had an unbelievable tape collection, although most of his tapes have since vanished. Soon after the meeting, Marty moved. We never did get any tapes from him.

In the spring of 1973, *Rolling Stone* did an article on Les Kippel and Grateful Dead tape trading. At the end of the article, Les paid tribute to Marty by pouring an extra glass of wine, ready, just in case Marty showed up during the interview. Because of the publicity many people wrote to Les, so suddenly he was dealing with more people than he had time for. As a result, many of the letters were given to Jerry to handle. Les and Jerry had become very close and it was paying off handsomely for the Honkies. Around the same time, Mark brought in a fourth person to join the Honkies, Harold Anczelowitz. Harold never contributed much in terms of tapes, but he had a great apartment to hang out at and a good stereo system. The four of us quickly made up some business cards and gave out as many as we could. For Jerry and me, our lives revolved around tapes. We were at each other's houses almost every day listening to a new tape or discussing future trades.

### The Birth of Taper's Technique

The essential elements for getting a good audience recording have always been the same. First, of course, one must get the equipment into the venue and get a good seat. Then, several factors come into play, each of which plays a critical role in the process. Ultimately, the recording will only be as good as the microphones used to capture the sound. Mike stands, batteries, and tape stock also each play their part. Today, one is likely to find recordists fretting over this process to the point where they will spend hundreds of dollars just for mike cables and connecting adapters.

And then comes methodology. How one chooses to set recording levels, incorporate noise reduction, and flip tapes is and will always be a matter of personal taste. But in the dawn of Grateful Dead concert recording, such nuances were rarely, if ever, considered.

The first recording experiences of many early tapers often yielded little more than noise. The challenges to making live recordings were enormous. To begin with, the professional high-quality, battery-operated portable recording decks available in the mid-sixties to early seventies were very expensive, and they were few. It was hard to find microphones capable of accurately recording the high decibel music emanating out of giant PA systems. Add to that the fact that most early tapers had little or no field recording experience. Getting decks into venues was easy early on, but as taping started to get more common, smuggling equipment became an art in itself.

In the early days many tapers didn't realize that by paying the most basic attention to technique and technology, they could dramatically improve the quality of the tapes.

R. T. Carlyle, today a professional gunslinger at rodeos, first saw the Dead playing for free at the Bandshell in Central Park in New York in 1968. He was casually strolling by. He soon became one of the original members of the Free Underground Grateful Dead Tape Exchange, one of the other early, prominent tape trading clubs. He first recorded the Dead in the summer of 1970 at the Capitol Theater in Port Chester. He used a tiny, battery-operated, poor-quality Norelco cassette player and Mallory cassettes. It came with a small handheld mike and pause button with a thin cord.

> **R. T. Carlyle:** My brother-in-law used to sell tapes so he gave me a whole bunch of them. We didn't know anything about tapes, but it didn't really matter how bad it was just so long as you could make the song out; it just brought you back to the show.

Harry Ely met Jerry Garcia when his youngest son, Edward, started taking guitar lessons from Jerry at Dana Morgan's Music in Palo Alto.

> **Harry Ely:** The Dead in particular appealed to me partly because I knew that Edward, my son, knew Jerry and also because they indulged in that same kind of collective improvisation that I was used to from the small jazz bands in New York in the thirties.

But it wasn't until 1969, after recording some gospel shows at the Kaiser Auditorium in Oakland, that Ely first recorded the Dead.

> **Harry Ely:** I got a Sony tape recorder; it was a TC124. It had a little one-piece stereo microphone that came with it, which was a 46-99S. It was sort of big and awkward, but they weren't searching people very much, so I was able to put it under my belt and walk in. The microphone had an on and off switch on it, which I used as a pause button, in other words, it would stop the tape. So it turned out to make a hell of a noise every time I turned it on and off. I taped a couple that December, then March, April, and May of '70. Then, a couple of soundboards, one at Euphoria in San Rafael, and once at Winterland.

While the barriers to getting good tapes were daunting, the early frustration became a driving inspirational force, providing an incentive for early tapers to dedicate themselves to improving their art.

Ed Perlstein, who spent some of the best years of his life in front of two tape decks, is currently president of the Center to Preserve Music Culture in San Francisco, a nonprofit music archive dedicated to preserving music for future generations. Perlstein had a small portable deck he bought for listening as he traveled around Europe in the summer of 1970. When he went to see the Grateful Dead on September 18, 1970, at the Fillmore East, he took that deck. The only problem: the deck recorded as much of his friends in the audience as it did the band.

> **Ed Perlstein:** I brought it in to tape, and basically I remember I sat in the orchestra but on the left side all the way to the back. My friends and I would either be singing to the song or talking. After the show we were walking over from the Fillmore East to go to the subway and we see a limo pull up in front of a hotel and out pops Lesh and Marmaduke and a bunch of other guys. And we stood around the street corner for about an hour with Lesh. I'm not sure who stayed around but Phil was there talking and passing a J around, and I pulled out this tape deck and said, "Hey Phil, listen to this," and I put on the tape and I played it and it was some weird sound in the background with me and my friends talking or singing in the foreground. And he said, "What is that?" And I said, "Oh, it's 'A Man's World.'"

Such experiences eventually motivated Perlstein to attend sound-engineering school. A short while later, he was making pristine recordings of the Dead on an open reel deck at Winterland.

For Jerry Moore, the development of a taping methodology involved a lot of trial and error.

**Jerry Moore:** For the July RFK shows in '73 I borrowed a friend's Sony 126 portable stereo with a cassette recorder. This unit, which had no noise reduction circuitry, suffered from having an automatic recording volume level control. As a result, the dynamic range would get lost because it would record all the sound spectrum at the same volume level. The tapes probably would have turned out okay except that I was unfamiliar with the deck and I used the throwaway microphone that came with it. It looked like it should have been pointing at the stage, but it was actually made to be held vertically. It was a stereo pinpoint mike, but you were supposed to hold it up. And the pointy end wasn't apparently supposed to be facing the stage.

## Getting It Right

Only a few tapers were lucky enough to have had prior recording experience and/or good luck from the start when they first started taping the Dead. Steve Brown, an experienced early taper, is responsible for recording one of the earliest audience tapes, the Haight Street free concert on March 3, 1968.

Brown, who grew up in San Francisco, was on active duty in the U.S. Navy at the public information office in San Diego at the time. He ran a recording studio there and had access to high-quality portable tape recorders.

Brown had just recorded Cream at Winterland. The next morning, he heard that the Dead were to be the only band at the Haight Street free concert.

**Steve Brown:** So I took my Uher 440 and an extra reel or half the other side of a reel I guess is what I had, the other side of a reel that was still empty that I hadn't used yet, as well as what battery power was left, and my camera, my little Canon camera, and went down to Haight Street, and set up right underneath the marquee of the old Straight Theater. We were facing west, and a big flatbed truck had been stretched across the street at the intersection, I guess that's around Cole and Haight, over here.

The truck was, of course, being used for the stage. At around midday or so, they began playing to a complete canyon of people. I mean there were people just hanging over all of the roofs and the awnings and the balconies of all the buildings, looking out the windows. Of course the street was totally packed with folks. They just took over that whole Haight Street for about four blocks there, it was just solid bodies. I'm not sure what they opened up with because I was really kind of holding on to saving the tape for some specific stuff. The first song that I recorded that day was a twenty-two-minute jam of "Viola Lee Blues."

They went from that into "Smokestack Lightning," from that into "Lovelight." There was a brief break, I remember, when some of burglar alarms on the street went off. There was the police responding to that. And from the stage, and all, you could hear Phil and others taunting the police and you know, inciting the crowd, "Fuck the pigs"–type mentality. I don't think those were his exact words, but it was basically one of those kinds of us-against-the-man type of moments, and the whole crowd was kind of on their side. From there, I think that after the announcements and some of the things about the lost children or whatever went on, they went into a song "It Hurts Me Too," the old blues tune. I was recording this thing just holding the mike up over my head, in the air.

Brown wore several hats in those days. He had a radio show on the Navy's local San Diego radio station, and was also responsible for supplying shipboard music to the ships in the Gulf of Tonkin. After the Haight show, Brown flew back to Southern California with the freshly made Dead tape.

**Steve Brown:** I flew home that afternoon after the show on Haight Street, and went on my midnight radio show in San Diego and played the tape of the Dead on Haight Street, so it was almost a delayed broadcast, or almost, if you will, in 1968, a simulcast.

Brown, a bit more "enlightened" than other Navy music programmers, managed to slip the Dead's Haight broadcast in amid other more mainstream selections. So over the next few days, across the Vietnam Navy fleet, a twenty-two-minute "Viola Lee Blues" could be heard.

## Location, Location, Location

In 1970 and '71, certain venues were more conducive to recording than others. The Capitol Theater, for example, was a good venue because the people who produced the shows were friendly to the scene.

> **Les Kippel:** Getting tape machines into the shows then was extremely easy, since they weren't searching. The biggest concern was when you left the Fillmore in New York, the police were always there. If you were walking out of the Fillmore at four or five or six in the morning and you were stumbling all over the place, they were going to pull you over and empty your pockets out. There was no concern about tape machines; their concern was rolling paper, pipes, and drugs. So I just brought in a tape machine. No one cared until much later, when the road crew realized that this trip was happening.
>
> We were together enough so that when tickets went on sale we never went for the orchestra, we'd go for the first row of the loge. And we'd get one person at one end of the loge and another person maybe twenty or thirty feet away from the other person. Then we'd take our microphones, spread them out and put coats over each of them, remove the coats when the lights went down, and put them back when they turned the lights back on. It was perfectly planned and we got away with it!

Some early tapes suffered from being made too close to the stage. This was clearly the case at the Hollywood Palladium show on 8/6/71 in which Bob Weir can be heard suggesting that a taper who was set up very close to the stage move back several rows for a better recording.

Rob Bertrando and some of his college associates recorded that show. They called themselves the Night Crew and taped that show with a Sony 770 portable seven-inch reel deck and two battery-powered Sony ECM-22 condenser mikes. As he describes, early tapers struggled to find the best locations to record within the venues.

> **Rob Bertrando:** Obviously, the second of those two Palladium shows is widely known and loved, as much for the sound quality as for the performance. What many people don't know is that the tapers Bobby is referring to are somebody else. On the reel masters, one can hear those tapers arriving at the location of the Night Crew about a minute or so later.

By the New York Academy of Music shows in March of '72 Ed Perlstein had borrowed a better quality cassette deck and smuggled it in under his winter coat. Still, even with better equipment, the lack of an established method caused problems.

> **Ed Perlstein:** I was sitting in the orchestra about twenty rows back, and before the show this guy taps me on the shoulder and he says, "My friend and I would like to sit together, would you be interested in changing seats?" He sat third row on the side, right in front of the speakers and I was, like, no problem. So we switched. And at the time I didn't really think ahead so I didn't bring a little flashlight or a lighter or whatever. And I couldn't see what I was doing and it wasn't my deck so I wasn't familiar with it. So basically I recorded all of Bo Diddley backed by the Dead and then I recorded the Dead. Anyway, I recorded a bunch of this stuff, and they started to play "Lovelight," and I had just turned the tape over or put in another tape. Since I couldn't see what I was doing, I pushed fast-forward and play at the same time, or fast-forward and record, or something like that, so it recorded it all at the fast speed.

## Taper's Time

R. T. Carlyle remembers that in the early taping days, he rarely wore a watch and never really thought about time that much. But if you were taping a show, he said, you had to wear one. It became sort of a spiritual conflict of interest.

**R. T. Carlyle:** You constantly had to be checking your watch for when it was time to flip the tape. It was dark and it wasn't a very sophisticated situation; if you lit a cigarette lighter to look at your watch, there'd be some guy with a flashlight telling you to put your cigarette out. Anyway, I think I got dosed one night—I was definitely off in another world—and I kept looking at my watch. At a certain point, when I looked, it went "BOING!" The glass flew off, the face flew off, and springs were bouncing everywhere. It really happened, and what it was basically telling me is that you can't deal with time.

Often, early tapers dealt with the constraints posed by the time limitations of analog recording tape by pausing the deck between songs.

**Barry Glassberg:** People taped that way because they knew the first set may have been musically an hour and a half to an hour and forty-five minutes long. But if you just let the tape run from the time they walked out on stage to the time they took the break, it was probably closer to two hours. So people just said, "We're crazy recording five minutes of dead air while they tune up." I guess the saying I always had was "waste tape, not music." That carried through into the mid to late seventies when I would do your average three-hour Dead show on three ninety-minute tapes, and you would have half a side empty, and you may or may not bring it back in and reuse it.

The "legendary" Marty Weinberg was infamous for figuring out when it was getting time to change his reels by rubbing his fingers up against the tape—the result of which was a very noticeable warble in the music. Of course, timekeeping while recording eventually became a science, and the perfect tape flip was a skill soon to be perfected by many.

## The Scene Gets Focus: Tape Trading Clubs Emerge

In 1971 the Dead printed an announcement on the inside of the double album *Skull and Roses* that proclaimed, "Dead Freaks Unite," and invited all who answered the call to send in their names and addresses to receive a newsletter. For the first time Deadheads around the country began to get a sense that they were part of a widespread phenomenon. The band used the resulting mailing list to promote their records by sending out samplers. It worked—very well.

**Les Kippel:** They had innovative concepts for reproducing music and getting it out: holographic pyramids and very interesting things, which was before its time because now you have DAT machines, lasers reading CDs and CD-ROMs. They were definitely ahead of their time then.

After taping primarily East Coast shows in 1971, by 1972 Kippel felt it was time to try to find other people doing the same thing.

**Les Kippel:** I already had about thirteen tapes I had recorded myself. At that time, I was introduced to a guy named Jim who had some tapes, and we decided to trade. I came up with this idea of a tape exchange. Then there was a whole discussion about what we should call it—I'm saying 'we' because it was still the community—and we came up with the concept of a Grateful Dead tape exchange. At that point I said, "Listen, we're the first, so it should be the First Free Underground Grateful Dead Tape Exchange." It was free because we weren't in it for money; there was no fee—it was just free! It was Les, Arty, Harris, and Jim: the first four original members of the First Free Underground Grateful Dead Tape Exchange.

Kippel soon went on a "creative binge" to try to create more tape exchanges. Between 1971 and 1973 about twenty or thirty Grateful Dead tape exchanges were formed throughout the United States, Kippel recalls, as a result of his prodding people to go out and record shows.

**Les Kippel:** We would send out seed tapes, saying, "Here's a few tapes, go record a show, send the tapes to us, and we'll start exchanging." We created a flow, an exchange pattern of tapes among all these people. To us, a tape exchange was formal when you got business cards. One group would send us a card, I would send them a bunch of business cards from other tape exchanges, and we would start that way.

In 1973, Kippel met a *Rolling Stone* freelancer named Charles Rosen, who then wrote one of the first mainstream press articles on the taping scene.

**Les Kippel:** I was working with the New York City Housing Authority at the time and he did a story: "Mr. Tapes of Brooklyn Rules the Grateful Dead Tape Empire." I felt he was taking certain liberties in his exaggeration, but that was where the name Mr. Tapes came from; he penned the term.

Kippel said he got more than fifty letters in 1973 addressed to *Rolling Stone,* or to the New York City Housing Authority, from people trying to find him.

**Les Kippel:** Because of the tremendous response, that flood of sincere, curious

Grateful Dead
UNDERGROUND TAPE EXCHANGE
DeKalb, Illinois

FREE UNDERGROUND
Grateful Dead
TAPE EXCHANGE

GRATEFUL DEAD TAPE EXCHANGE
LIVE CONCERTS
HAVE TAPES, WILL TRADE

FREE
GRATEFUL DEAD
TAPE EXCHANGE
SEATTLE, WASHINGTON 98112

BROOKLYN, N.Y. 11229

KOONA-KRUMHOLTZ
Grateful Dead
Tape Club
NEW YORK

Dead Relics
Grateful Dead Tape Exchange

*Tape traders' business cards*

energy, I began thinking that I had to do something, I somehow had to put this whole trip into perspective.

We would have taping sessions where people would come to my house, we'd run tape machine to tape machine to tape machine to tape machine, etc. And I would have a clock AM/FM cassette deck that we'd use, just to check the tapes. The peak of absurdity was when I had thirteen tape machines running at once! Thirteen people there, "Okay . . . Ready, set, put your fingers on the pause button and—go!"

Kippel said it was then that he realized there had to be a better way. From out of that came the magazine *Dead Relics* (later to be renamed *Relix*), but also a proposal to the Grateful Dead.

**Les Kippel:** We had a correspondence going with the Grateful Dead on multiple levels. Our written correspondence told me they were interested in somehow creating an official tape exchange. They expressed that they were having problems with the record company at the time; Warner Brothers controlled a lot of the material that they produced, and the Dead couldn't release the material without permission from the record company. They said the record company owned the rights to everything they created. Warner Brothers, at the time, turned around and saw this entire advent of tape machines, taping, and the reproducing of music as being against their interest and possibly cutting into record sales.

The Dead always expressed concern about the quality of what was going out; they wanted to make sure that whatever went out would be of the finest quality. The idea behind *Dead Relics* was to obtain and distribute soundboard copies of shows through what was to be called the Connoisseurs Club.

**Les Kippel:** The Grateful Dead were concerned about how many people were going to get it, and they wanted to control that. But we tried to create something, of course, that would be very much in the Grateful Dead's control. It included a monthly newsletter to tape collectors.

I have a multitude of letters which say they were going to come and meet with me in New York, but they never did. And of course every time I received a letter like this, it gave me hope that maybe this free underground tape exchange could be made into something legitimate, and accepted by the organization for the benefit of all the tapers. If the proposal had been accepted, there wouldn't have been a taping section. There wouldn't have been a need for it, because the Grateful Dead would have opened up their vaults: "Well, what tape should we send out today?" And the concept was to send the tape out within two weeks after the show happened. This way, you didn't have to bring your tape machine, your poles, etc., and knock yourself out. For ten dollars you were going to get the two cassettes of the entire concert.

### The Early Equipment Choices

Those who taped shows in the 1971–73 period had few options when it came to choosing equipment that could do a decent job for the effort. There were few models of open reel machines that were portable and affordable to the average fan.

**Barry Glassberg:** The Uher only took five-inch reels; the Nagra series of seven-inch portables cost several thousand dollars; the Sony 770 was simply too large to be practical in a covert taping situation. In those early days, sound quality was the driving force behind what shows I acquired. I've often said to friends who are surprised over some of my omissions, "It's a collection, not a damned library!"

It was hard for Barry Glassberg to get used to the limitations of cassette quality. The cassette machines, which were originally designed by Norelco/Phillips as dictation devices, were available for home use in 1971, but their portable counterparts were simply not designed for live recording until 1972–73. Even then, the low- and high-end frequency response and signal-to-noise (S/N) ratio were barely acceptable.

**Barry Glassberg:** To those of us using open reel equipment at home, taping in the field with portable cassette recorders like the Sony 110A or the Sony 126 (my first purchase), would be a step down in sound quality.

Still, he ventured into the uncharted waters. Glassberg's first "mike stand" was a CB radio whip antenna, which he unfolded and then let the weight of the mike angle it toward the stage, like a fishing pole. After two months of recording in 1973, he developed something better, a ten-foot curtain rod that he hacksawed into pieces about two feet in length so that it could be telescoped and taped together once inside the arena. A single curtain rod piece or two didn't look like much of anything to security at the door. They were looking for cans, bottles, and booze as a first priority, and cameras and recorders only as a secondary consideration.

**Barry Glassberg:** The pieces usually didn't attract attention going in, and if spotted, I managed some story that usually worked. The T-bar was well concealed going into shows. Once inside a place like Roosevelt Stadium, with a soft dirt field, you jammed the reconstructed rod into the ground and held it for the duration of the show. At other arenas, I used fewer pieces, and I usually rested on my belt for support.

As tape decks and taping techniques improved, tapers realized that the recorder was no longer the limiting factor. The introduction of the Sony 152SD in June of 1973 brought cassette decks closer to the quality that could be expected with an open reel deck. If the mikes were up to it, Deadheads could now record excellent bass and high-end frequencies on cassette. The attention then shifted to using better quality directional microphones. This was very important for indoor arenas.

**Jerry Moore:** I used a couple of different pairs of AKG's D-1000, which were a handheld vocal mike, with a dynamic, cardioid pattern that cost $50–80 each. I also used D-200Es, which were dynamic microphones with a cardioid pattern. The D-200Es were better than the D-1000s due to their wider frequency response, particularly a better bass response. I also used the Sony with the ECM-99 stereo mike once or twice, which wasn't very good, though I did make a couple of decent tapes with it. I also used some Sony ECM-33P mikes, which were quite good. The 33Ps were condensers that used a nine-volt mercury battery, and were especially good in the high end. They cost about $150 each, which was a lot of money back then.

**Barry Glassberg:** In the early seventies you had the introduction of what were called "electret" condenser mikes. This was different than the traditional magnetic coil microphones which go back even to the fifties. Electret mikes have a thin diaphragm, usually made out of Mylar, almost like you have in electrostatic speakers now, the same concept. And that thin piece is between two charged plates, and a battery usually provides the power to that. And there were more and more of those kind of microphones; they were lightweight, they were cylindrical, they tended to be smaller, they didn't have the old-style conventional ball-type design and the look of microphones; they had the look of the long cigar tubes in the cases. Sony came out with a series of these. And these mikes were very directional, so-called cardioid pattern where they are more responsive to sound coming at them than from the sides, and would heavily attenuate from the rear. Those mikes, back in those days, probably sold for something like two or three hundred a pair. And a machine like the Sony 152 and the 153 when they came out also sold for maybe up to two hundred fifty or three hundred dollars, which in terms of 1990s money sounds almost like pocket change. To us poor college kids back then, people my age or a few years younger or a few years older, who were pretty much just out of college or beginning to work, it was a lot of money relative for those times.

## Challenges and Successes

The summer shows at Watkins Glen in '73 proved to be an enormous challenge to record. Barry Glassberg recalls that he didn't plan for all of the hassles getting there, such as the traffic on the single road leading to the site, the 600,000 people, or the food, water, imbibeables, and proper clothing that were needed.

**Barry Glassberg:** The closest I got to the concert stage was to the first set of speakers/scaffolds. That was certainly closer than over half the people there! I taped the mike on the scaffold as high as I could, pointed straight up! The Sony 126 was a stereo portable, but I could afford only one mike at the time, so I split the single mike for two-channel mono input.

**Les Kippel:** We were looking around for pieces of wood, anything to burn for heat, and to me, the people around me, this entire experience was negative. The only thing we could find to burn for heat were our GD tape exchange cards: they were the only thing that kept us warm.

For Kippel, the experience was so bad, he almost called it quits.

**Les Kippel:** But then came 1974, which provided a rebirth. The quality of 1974 Wall of Sound was stupendous, and they had it over a lot of soundboard tapes, because the ambiance of the room, the equipment, and the ECM-99s were exquisite in terms of catching three-dimensional warm sound, which you don't have when it comes to soundboards.

In Miami, it was exquisite. You could have dropped a pin and heard it in the audience. They didn't seem to be Deadheads, nothing else was happening, and those shows were the concert event—the Grateful Dead at the Miami front-on. And you walked in there and there was this wall of speakers. It was like, "My God . . ." We set up our tape machine and no one said anything, everyone was quiet. It used to be, in the old days, if you had your tape machine set up, and there was some idiot carrying on in front of you and interfering with the taping, you'd lean over and whisper in the person's ear, "We're taping the show, could you please do us a favor and keep it down? By the way, here's a joint, help us." And he'd be so grateful for the fat joint that he'd be very quiet. We didn't have to do that in Miami; the shows were great. And Seastones, which was Lesh and Lagin at intermission, Jerry kept the tapes running when that happened.

**Barry Glassberg:** Later, I used Nakamichis once or twice, but most of the better ones I made with the Sony ECM-33s. The Miami '74 shows were the first Dead shows I used the 152 on. Those came out fairly well, I think.

Sony introduced its first Dolby B portable, the Sony 152SD, in 1974. That gave a big boost to the taping phenomenon. Although the portable was larger than its predecessors, it was the first cassette portable to offer the chance of making high-quality audience recordings. The 152 featured manual volume control, easy-to-read averaging meters—one for each channel—with a peak light, Dolby B, a choice of tape setting (though metal tapes didn't exist yet), and mike and line mix; it had a large built-in speaker, but it didn't cut out in record mode so you had to be careful to keep the record level down to avoid getting feedback. Jerry Moore recalls that the 152 occasionally displayed a static discharge when in playback. It was replaced shortly thereafter, in 1975, with the Sony 153, on which the speaker automatically cut out in record mode. Another classic deck that represented a leap in field recording technology was the Nakamichi 550, which came out around the same time but was more expensive and larger than the 152 or the 153.

## Tape Stock and Batteries

Decent quality open reel tape stock was certainly available by the mid-sixties. According to Dick Latvala, tape stock played a crucial role, though more so over the course of time, as some tapes aged much better than others. For open reel trading, Eddie Claridge said he mostly used old BASF tape (in the gray box with the white flap and hard plastic boxes). Shortly after, Scotch 206 and 207 was available.

**Barry Glassberg:** When Maxell released the UD120 cassette tapes, they were tempting to use, especially in 1974. I never trusted the survivability of the thinner tape formulations, and in retrospect that was a very good move. I recall that some of Jerry Moore's Maxell UD120 master tapes are not playable now, twenty-five years later.

According to Eddie Claridge, up until about 1976 or so, there weren't any really good cassette tapes.

> **Eddie Claridge:** There were some of the early Ferrachrome tapes, but there were no chromium dioxide tapes. I believe the first XLII (CrO$_2$) tapes came out in late '76, which again was one of the inherent problems. There wasn't Dolby in cassette decks till '74, when the first Dolby decks came out.

Battery power was an enormously important issue in the early days before alkaline batteries had true lasting power. Many old tapes exhibit the undesirable effect of fading battery power; as the batteries died, the tape deck slowed down. Upon playback the inverse malady is displayed; the tape speeds up.

> **Barry Glassberg:** Of the many problems and glitches that occurred in my early years, I'm glad to say that I was careful enough about managing battery usage that none of my audience masters have such speed variations.

### The Tape Wars

In 1974, using the newly released Sony 152 portable stereo cassette deck and the same mikes, Rob Bertrando said he recorded two shows on his own: UCSB (University of California, Santa Barbara) in May, and the Hollywood Bowl in July.

> **Rob Bertrando:** The Bowl was recorded from the last row of the box seats, at least 200 feet from the stage, but the tapes sounded amazingly good. Unfortunately, the machine and tapes were confiscated at Santa Barbara (the equipment fortunately returned later), so no good tapes remain of that show. The method of confiscation was typical of the time: Ramrod [one of the Dead's roadies] coming off the stage, running to the mikes, and holding a knife to the cables saying, "Turn over the equipment or I cut your cords."

Bertrando's experience was common by 1974. The animosity between the band's roadies and the tapers started festering early on, as tapers started appearing in greater numbers. That's when the Dead's soundmen and roadies started clamping down on taping.

In fact, this issue goes back even further. During the two-night run in Waterbury, Connecticut, in '72, the hostility was present.

> **Les Kippel:** We were in the hotel room after the first night, or maybe the afternoon after the first night, and we were listening to our results: phenomenal. And there was a knock at the door. We went to answer it, and this guy barged in; it was Owsley, in all his splendid glory. He ran over to the tape machine: "You cannot do that, you cannot record the shows!" And he took the tape out of the machine and barged out of the room. I turned to Artie [R. T. Carlyle] and said, "Well, I guess that's it." But Artie was smiling from ear to ear and said, "I hope he enjoys the tape, because he's got a tape of me and my music." Artie had the brains to switch the tapes as soon as he saw Owsley coming into the room.

The crackdown began slowly in 1972 and progressed throughout the year.

> **Les Kippel:** Of course unauthorized taping is illegal; you're breaking the law. That's what we had to do in those days, and because we were an organization, we weren't going to let some person dictate to us that we weren't going to tape the show. We'd go in there and one person would bring in the tape machine and two people would bring in the microphones, a few people would bring the batteries and a few people bring in tapes. We'd sit in a cluster, and friends would always protect the person who was taping. If someone was coming, or we saw an usher or a crew member looking and pointing, then we'd watch. And if that person began approaching us, we'd immediately yank the tape out and put in a phony tape. Usually the only thing they'd do was take the tape, cut the microphone cable, or take the batteries.

One of the worst incidents was at the Boston Garden, on June 28, 1974.

**Jerry Moore:** It was ugly and I was toward the back. What it amounted to was a pogrom on tapers with all sorts of people running around grabbing recordists. Anyway, I was in the back of the arena with a twelve-foot pole and I got nabbed. Quite frankly, from my point of view, it was a rather elaborate and fancy operation. I was arguing with the guy who caught me. I took the tape I had in the deck out, and it was two-thirds of the way through the second set. I had already given the tape of the first set to the person I was with, so I took the tape that was in the deck and threw it under her seat. I put another tape in the deck, fast-forwarding it so it looked like I used it. It turned out the guy wanted it right then; I was arguing with him, saying, "Just a minute, just a minute!" So I gave the tape to him, but he wanted the first set too, so I went into my bag, fetched a blank, and gave that to this mastermind among Nazis. Then he wanted me to go back with him to check that there was something on the tapes, and I was thinking, "This is going to be ugly." So I told the person I was with that there's a tape under the seat, take it and scram. I got hauled backstage and somebody said, "Forget it, let him go." I was like, "Cool." I was out of there and all they got was my blank tapes.

I was back at my seat with my pole and I was wondering whether I should put it all back together again. The show was almost over and it was too much work, so I was just standing there holding the pole, thinking it over. It wasn't connected to anything at this point, but then a real lunatic came along, and grabbed me. I tried to explain to him that he got the wrong guy because I'd already been nabbed, but he started shaking the deck and threatened to break it and whatnot. I started screaming at him, he started screaming at me, and finally he came to the conclusion that I was too much work, so he went to bother someone else. I got mad about this and started thinking that this was unacceptable. So what did I do, being in a somewhat altered state, I went to the stage entrance and demanded Ron Rakow. And they told me, "Go away, kid. Don't bother us." I started screaming at them, "I want fucking Rakow and I want him NOW!!" They went and got him for me; I was yelling at him and I said, "You said this was cool! You said there was no problem! The first time was fair, they got my tapes, no problem, but this second time, this is outrageous!" He said, "Calm down, I'll get the tapes for you. Just calm down."

I was standing at the stage door; the show ended and I was still standing there. So now I was feeling rather sheepish about the whole thing. I left and went back to the hotel. Coincidentally, I was staying at the same hotel they were. I told my friends the story and they were like, "Why don't you call him?" I didn't want to bother the guy, but to make a long story short I ended up calling him. And he was like, "What'd you leave for, man? I went all around looking for the tapes until I got them back. And I came back and you were gone." So he came up to my room and I got this long holier-than-thou lecture about what a saint he is and whatnot. I'll give the guy due credit, he was trying to do a nice thing, he really was. He had three tapes in his hand, he was shaking them, and I, still in an altered state, decided to do the right thing. I said, "Thanks very much, but the tapes that the guy got were blanks."

He didn't care for that; he blew his stack, and he screamed, "I went through all this for nothing?!!" He stomped out of the room and threw the tapes over his shoulder at me. At that point I wanted to get out of there and go home. There was a show in Springfield the next day, but I wanted to go home because I was so embarrassed by the whole thing. I was talked out of it. The next day we were leaving, and we drove past a shopping mall where there were a couple of Grateful Dead equipment trucks parked.

One of the people I was with, a glutton for punishment, wanted me to go ask them what happened. I went over and I asked Rex Jackson what was going on, what the problem was. He got out of the truck and tried to strangle me. Basically, I did some of the fastest talking I've ever done in my life. I didn't know what the problem was, but I was innocent. He calmed down and he told me that he tried to take a Uher deck away the night before and the guy had hit him over the head with it. I explained to him that I wasn't that guy and I was just asking an innocent question. I had to assume that the whole scenario could explain why they didn't bother anybody for a long time after that. I figured they must have had a meeting and said, "This is too much work. We should leave these guys alone." I feel some personal responsibility for that.

Louis Falanga, now a book publisher based in the Bay Area, was so dedicated to recording the Dead that he moved out from the East Coast to the Bay Area in order to tape more shows.

**Louis Falanga:** During the Friday night show [at the closing of Winterland in October 1974] I was sitting about twenty feet away from the stage, with the Wall of Sound. After the first set, when they came back in and opened the second set with the "Dark Star" and "Morning Dew," I was sitting there with the CT-110. All my buddies were protecting the tape deck and me. I always had an extra blank tape in my pocket, just in case I got busted, so I could try to switch it real quick. So I was sitting there with my head down on the ground, trying to listen to the first set to see if it came out okay, when this guy comes up and says, "Let me listen to that!" I looked up and was about to let him listen when I saw a laminate on him. So I said, "No way!" I jumped up and said that he was trying to steal my coat. And all these people came up and pulled a bad trip on him, causing him to immediately cut my wires. By that time, I had switched the cassette and he walked off with the blank one; we resplied the wires and taped the "Dark Star" > "Morning Dew." It was a pretty intense thing when we looked up and the guy was there.

Usually Steve Parish, a road crew member, would stand on the stage checking everything out.

**Louis Falanga:** If everything were going well during the first song, he'd walk off the stage. But one time [at a Garcia Band show], he came off the stage; Jerry had just cranked into "It Takes a Lot to Laugh," which he'd never done before at the Keystone, and it was one of those "Oh wow!" kind of things. But Parish walked up to us and cut the wires on all the decks.

Ed Perlstein recorded Jerry Garcia and Merle Saunders at the Rheem Theater.

**Ed Perlstein:** I told my friends about it they said, "Oh, we'll bring our decks too." We have a hot reel-to-reel. So we had two decks going from the board. For some reason during the break we moved them up to onstage. And we were more the show than Jerry's band. We were plainly visible; we were actually onstage, we weren't behind the curtain. And I think it was Richard Lorraine or one of the other of Jerry's managers and was like screw this and pulled the plug on us in the middle of, I think, "Mystery Train."

## Creative Ways to Avoid Detection

Early on, there was always the issue of security: first, to get the equipment in and second to not get caught once inside.

**Barry Glassberg:** I was aided by my appearance relative to the average fan. I was older, had shorter hair (now gray) and was not dressed like a hippie (then) or homeless person (now). Security staff have prejudices and see stereotypes. By having the bag open and ready, I was a cooperative, forthcoming, and clean-cut person, out of place with nothing to hide! I just made sure that the tape deck was "packaged" in some way and mixed with boring medical journals and newspapers or computer printouts. It always worked.

**R. T. Carlyle:** We used to have one guy would bring in a tape machine and a microphone. They'd confiscate the microphone, figuring if you didn't have a mike, you couldn't record the show, or if they tried to take the machine, you'd make a fuss. Meanwhile, someone else would come in later, smuggling in a microphone, and they'd hook up and tape the show.

At one show Carlyle limped in on a cane as if recovering from a broken leg.

**R. T. Carlyle:** I met up with Les later on and we tied the microphone to the cane and lifted it up. It was one of our first mike stands, used to reduce audience noise. Later, I was dancing somewhere in the hall, and the usher who made a comment when I walked in with the cane came up to me and asked, "How are you dancing?" I thought quick and said, "It's a miracle! The music, the music!"

As time pressed on, innovations like setting up in the bathroom stalls became more common.

**Louis Falanga:** The stage [at the Keystone] was maybe three feet high, and you could pull your chair right up to the stage, just sit right there and put your pitcher of beer right under Jerry's feet. Since Jerry's monitor was right there, we put one microphone into the monitor and one microphone on a pitcher of beer, center stage. This was when the 152 had just come out in '74. We taped like that for the Nicky Hopkins shows, the Keith and Donna Godchaux show, the Garcia/Saunders shows, Legion of Mary, all the different variations from '74–'76. Jerry used to give us little looks when we put the mike in the monitor, but he never said anything. Those were pretty good stereo tapes, with the vocals coming from one side and the music from the other. But basically Jerry was using a little boogie amp at the time, which his microphone was turned right into. And the guitar on it was outrageous. We trailed a mike to our 152, then to these guys Lou and Mark from San Francisco who had a Nakamichi stereo deck, which then trailed to Mickey, and he plugged in at that end. We had three running decks each time at the Keystone.

Before long, band personnel and the club management knew the tapers—knew that whenever they came to the Keystone, they had a deck.

**Louis Falanga:** I noticed the fans in the Keystone bathroom that blow out air. The fan was gone from one of the panels, so there was a hole there without a window or anything. So we stuck the mikes in that hole and then picked them up from the bathroom. We used to bring two or three decks; since we knew we'd get caught, we let them check one deck and sneak the other deck in right away. They had no clue we had it. Once, we put the mikes in the hole and some guy came walking out of the bathroom with the microphones, and we had to convince him to give them back to us.

## The Vibe Gets Better

After constantly being hard on tapers, the owner of the Keystone finally gave Louis Falanga permission to record one set of a Keith and Donna Godchaux show.

**Louis Falanga:** He said we could actually set the mikes up any way we wanted. So, we ran one microphone to the middle of the stage and took the other about twenty feet back to get the PA. It's a really cool-sounding tape. He only gave us permission to tape one set, but we actually taped two.

Ed Perlstein's experience was similar. In 1973 he went to record Garcia's bluegrass group Old and In the Way in Northern California.

**Ed Perlstein:** I brought my deck in and I would go ask Jerry, "Do you mind if I plug in?" and he would say, "As long as you give me a copy." And so I did Old and In the Way at Sonoma State, and then I went to Garcia and Saunders at the UC Berkeley in January 1974, and at the Great American Music Hall. I brought my deck down to the Chateau de Liberté in Santa Cruz, which was a small house to record Bobby's group Kingfish. It was as though Kingfish was playing in your living room. It was packed and I was sweaty and I remember I immediately fell over because the guy running the board was a guy I knew from recording engineering classes. And I said that I had my deck in the car and was wondering if I could plug in, and he didn't make me ask and he was like, "Sure, go ahead. In fact we got this Ford Econoline van outside. We're doing a feed out to there and just plug in there."

Ultimately, the Deadheads won out.

**Barry Glassberg:** I've seen 352 Dead shows, taped at least 310, and got caught and shut down less than 20 times.

What kept tapers going through all the hassles and mistakes was the music, of course. But aside from that, there were moments along the way that served to inspire. Les Kippel remembers one from 1974.

**Les Kippel:** We were at the hotel, and it was, I think, Barry Brass, at that time, who got a copy of the Grateful Dead's Woodstock performance. We were so thrilled with it we were listening to it like crazy and somehow, we got a message to Phil Lesh: "We got the Woodstock tape." So, we were in the hotel room and invited him down to our room. He came down with his Heineken and said, "Let me listen to the tape."

This was like a Connoisseurs Club. Everyone was sitting around and then El Excelente came, you know, to taste a cup of coffee and give his approval, whatever, and we put the tape on for him, "Ahhh this is great, this is phenomenal, this is the best thing, I love it, this is great, I want a copy of this tape. But you gotta do me a favor." And of course we were all ears: "Yeah, what?" "I don't want to hear any of the music; I just want to hear the raps, what we said; please make me a tape." And of course we made him the tape. And we assumed he loved the tape. Those were the things that, in the early days, made the taping trip so worthwhile: when you got one over on the road crew, when you came into contact with one of the band members, when they showed appreciation for something you were doing or you were capable of providing; you enjoyed it and you felt you were doing something good for the community. That's why we kept going.

## Epilogue

The period of "retirement" in 1975 caused tape trading to accelerate. There were no new shows to see, so people could concentrate on acquiring tapes already out there.

When *Dead Relics* magazine debuted in 1974, it gave the tape trading scene further legitimacy because the magazine openly promoted trading, dealt with the bootlegging controversy, and had early articles about how to record "in the field." It was information you couldn't get anywhere else. In the first issue Mike Tannehill and Jerry Moore wrote the articles about in-concert taping. They discussed recording levels, mike orientation, what VU meters were all about, and setting levels at a live concert. Jerry wrote about getting equipment into the venue, seating location, and how to stay unobserved.

By the time the band came out of retirement in June 1976, people were much more prepared to make decent tapes.

**Barry Glassberg:** I think it's likely that there is an audience tape of every show from June 1976 onward.

## In the Next Volume of *The Deadhead's Taping Compendium*

This is by no means the end of the story of the Grateful Dead taping. We will look at the birth of the official taping section, the introduction of the digital recording format, and the story of the infamous Betty Boards. Obviously, this entire history continues to unfold. We are very interested in hearing all of your stories, both new and old.

# 3

# The Interviews

## Owsley Stanley (Bear)

Owsley Stanley, otherwise known as Bear, is the stuff legends are made of. Alchemist, artist, soundman, philosopher, Bear is the sort of person who gets to be very good at whatever he chooses to do. Bear made a place for himself in the pantheon of rock 'n' roll legends by manufacturing LSD back when it was legal. It was Owsley acid that fueled the Acid Tests. And it was at the Acid Tests that an eternal bond was formed between Bear and the Dead. Bear was blown away by the immense musical/spiritual potential exhibited by the Dead at these mythic events. He quickly noted that what the Dead needed in order to reach their potential was a decent sound system. And so he offered to be the Dead's patron. A bond was formed, and Bear started using his LSD profits to support the band and build the world's first truly acceptable rock music PA. With Bear on board as an essential catalyst, the Grateful Dead quickly took flight.

Over the years Bear also provided technical sound support for the Carousel Ballroom, Quicksilver Messenger Service, and the Jefferson Airplane and Starship, to name a few. The Dead albums *Bear's Choice* and *Dick's Picks IV* and the two Old and In the Way releases are testaments to his superlative sound engineering. These days he spends most of his time homesteading in Australia, where he creates spectacular precious metal jewelry.

*John R. Dwork: How old were you when you first saw the Grateful Dead?*

**Bear:** I was just shy of my thirty-first birthday when I first saw them at the Muir Beach Acid Test on December 6th, 1965.

*In the beginning you were able to give attention to how microphone placement on stage and how positioning of instruments and voices in the mix changed the quality of the recording. Or were you simply focused on making the PA sound satisfactory?*

It's hard to separate all those things, but I didn't start out to be a recordist. I was a soundman. My job was to get the sound out to the audience, and in 1965 and in early 1966 there wasn't any PA system in existence designed to powerfully amplify electric music. You could find PA systems in churches and baseball fields and movie theaters. But you couldn't find anything of musical quality.

By "high frequency drivers" for horns they meant 8 kHz. That was considered high frequency because it went above the sibilants in the voice, so the "high quality" music systems used a high frequency horn that had a cutoff frequency of around 8000 Hertz (cycles per second). It could only take about 2 watts or so of input power. They made another driver that was intended for the loud voice systems they used in stadiums. Those were rated between 25 and 50 watts, but only had a response out to around 2500 Hz. We went down to the JBL and Altec Lansing factories in Los Angeles, the two major manufacturers that made drivers, and said, "We'd like one that's a hybrid between these two which you could put maybe 100 watts into and have a frequency spectrum at least as far as 12,000 Hz, or further if possible." They said, "We are selling everything we make. We don't need any new products. We don't think you (and by inference, rock and roll) are important. Get lost." That was where it was left. Later Dan Healy took to renting a larger number of horns than were needed for a PA setup, replacing the blown ones on the stacks between sets. The company was forced into rebuilding the drivers or sending them down to JBL to have it done. But through it all they never refused to rent to the band. They couldn't refuse to rent to them because they wanted the money (from the rentals), which was worth a lot more than the destroyed drivers. They kept on renting them out, and the Dead kept on blowing them up, and eventually JBL got the message and designed higher powered, more durable drivers. We had to force them into it. Just like IBM, I guess, or Microsoft or Apple—once any manufacturer has gotten comfortable doing what it's doing and feels that it's making whatever you need, it resists doing anything new or even listening to people.

Dan Healy had become the Dead's soundman in '67 and was soundman for about a year, during the period they made *Anthem of the Sun*. It was recorded mostly on four-track ¼-inch machines (might have been half-inch tape, I wasn't there), but they used four-track tapes from live concerts processed with a little studio work. This was going on in the early Carousel days. He was still with the Dead when the Carousel started, and somewhere near the end of the Carousel period he got an offer from Quicksilver (he had been with Quicksilver in '65 or '66), and he went back with them and dropped the Dead. The Dead then came to me and asked me if I would like to do sound gain with them. I started at the end of June, after the Carousel closed and I worked through to the middle of 1970.

***You had been working during the hiatus from them with a bunch of different bands.***

I parted from the Grateful Dead in the fall of '66. They had decided that the system that Tim Scully and I built was too clumsy and wasn't doing what they wanted. So they wanted to go back to using standard amplifiers. I said: "Go pick out any amps you want from Leo's Music and I'll trade you for the stuff you're using." They did, and I ended up giving most of the old stuff away to places like the Straight Theater. At any rate, by then I was out of money, and the scene was in need of other things, so I went off. I've always had a wide and eclectic taste in music. Even when I was working for the Dead, I went to see other bands and recorded their music.

***Listening to the Dead's mix at concerts in the later years, I found that the musicians were so widely separated in the PA, I'd be sitting on one side of the venue and wouldn't hear some of the instrumentation from the other side of the stage.***

The split (two-stack) PA setup is the cause of those problems. The direction the speakers point and the fact the sound from the other side arrived 50, 60, 70, even as much sometimes as 120 milliseconds later, forced your mind to blank it out. Even though it was there, you wouldn't hear it. If you had taken all those speakers and put them just on one side, even on the opposite side of the stage from where you were, you'd have heard everything much better. As long as all the channels start out from a single point or line source, they all integrate in the hall. Even though some of the speakers and some of the channels point directly away from you, you'll still hear them. They'll couple into the air of the hall and may be transmitted to you by reflection, but all of the components are coherent. The sounds all have a meaningful time relationship to themselves and to each other, and your ears easily construct an image.

If you go to a concert hall to hear an orchestra, the woodwinds are all on one side and the strings all on another side and the timpani in the back and the flutes over there, and everybody's sound is going in different directions. One of the horns may be pointed at the ceiling, another one is pointed at the right wall, the next at the left wall, and yet you hear everything. If you walk around the hall you will find the mix is somewhat different everywhere. But there's no place that you can't hear everything, and it is all valid, just as there are many valid mixes for any performance of a musical piece (ask any studio engineer!). So you don't have to have a speaker pointed directly at you for each and every component of the sound that's being radiated. In fact, as Bose discovered, you can send most of the sound directly away from you and it still sounds great (some might say superior).

***In the beginning, when you were recording in smaller venues, did you have a problem getting a good tape because the room was so small that you didn't have to put certain instruments in the PA?***

I don't remember playing in any rooms that small.

***Still, you were saying that the amplification for the instrumentation was loud enough for the guitars.***

It was always loud enough for the lead guitar and loud enough for the rhythm as well. Well, no . . . I can't say that. . . . Bobby had a tendency to play too softly sometimes. He would just disappear. I had to bring him up or no one could hear him. Bob Weir has, to this very day, a tendency to listen in a somewhat overcritical fashion to what his instrument sounds like. Periodically he becomes dissatisfied with it and changes everything. He'll change his guitar, he'll change his brand of strings or their weight, or his amp, his speakers, the way that they're placed on the stage, change the brand of the wireless that he's using or the brand of the foot pedal. When he was upset with his sound, he'd play quieter and quieter. So I had to have him in the PA so that I could take care of that.

***At what point did the band start listening to tapes as a source of creative or technical reflection?***

I think we listened from the beginning. "What was it like?" We thought it might be good to hear what it really was like. Or someone might say: "Gee, I think that was terrible, let's listen and find out whether it really was." Back in those days after the show we were usually wired up and weren't ready to sleep anyway. As time went on, their vocals got better and they were singing in pitch with each other more and more. Everyone was working to try to get better. How can you get better if you don't ever listen to yourself? We were all interested in what was going on. The only way you could find out what you had done was to listen to it later. In the heat of the show, no one can tell. Whose idea was it to listen to the tapes? I think it was everyone's. They said, "You've got the tape, let's listen to it."

***What period was that?***

It was '68 through early '70.

***Was there a point at which someone said, "Hey, we should really keep these things in one place and archive them"?***

Nope. Nobody thought much about it. I learned to date them more carefully after having to deal with tapes that said simply "Saturday night" or "second set." I needed to make certain notations as to what night they were, what reel they were, what set they were, and I soon realized it was like a journal. In fact, for several years, when I went off to do my time, no one continued the practice, and for most of that time (mid-1970 to mid-1972) there were no tapes made from the board. That shows you how much interest everyone else had in taping: zilch.

***Where did you store them back then? In your house, at the office?***

In the basement of the house I was renting for a while. They were moved to Alembic's studios when I went off to jail. I came back and found them on a huge pallet in the middle of a storage room with other stuff. Tapes were missing. I've never recovered some of them. I'm now missing other tapes that were around for a while. I'm missing Fleetwood Mac and Thelonius Monk (which disappeared later), both from the Carousel. I'm also missing the original tape of Johnny Cash from when he appeared there. If any of these turn up, they will be easy to identify, as I recorded the vocals in the left channel and the instruments in the right, Beatles style.

***Did you usually record all the bands on the bill when the Grateful Dead played?***

Always. Unless they had an objection. Even when they had an objection, I still wanted to tape them (the journal, you know), but I sometimes had to give them the tapes afterward.

***Didn't you do some recordings on cassette at one point?***

I always tried to do simultaneous recordings on cassette. In the early days there were only home-type machines available. At first these were only mono. I had a little early stereo Concord that turned out later to have begun gradually running more and more slowly. I didn't know that then, because I always played the tapes back on the same machine, and rarely had the time to go back and play older ones. Later I had an Advent; but that proved to be mechanically rather unreliable. Next I had a Nakamichi but it was just too delicate for the road. When the good rugged pro Sonys came out, we went with those. I may have been one of the first to use the then new stereo cassette. There were a lot of shows that I couldn't afford tape for and neither could the band, so all we've got is cassettes. Some of them, from the Concord, were running up to 10, 15 percent slow. (I still use a Sony TC-D5 and a WM-D6C).

***Well, that can be fixed.***

Well, anything can be fixed, if you want the music badly enough. There are people cleaning up the old 78 RPM platters because it's all that's left of some of the old-time musicians' early recordings. You have to want the music real bad if you are trying to clean up an old cassette.

***What about recording tape?***

Well, I originally used some form of Scotch tape, either 201, 203, or later 207, but later on in '68 I was talked into using Ampex tape by Ron Wickersham and John Curl, who thought that it was better because it was "limper" and gave a "better head wrap." But as it turned out, the "new" Ampex tape was made in the old Shamrock factory and the adhesive that was used to glue the oxide particles onto the backing turned to snot over the years and would rub off on your hands. Subsequently, there were many tapes that you couldn't play. Somewhere along the line, someone discovered that if you heated them up to about 130°F., it would reset this adhesive for a while, but not permanently. Of course, high temperature randomizes the particles so you're basically erasing the highs off the tape while you're cooking them, reducing the highest frequency sounds, while recovering the rest. Rule Numero Uno: You don't get something for nothing. Or mistakes made now may not be apparent until much too late. I later decided I didn't really like the Ampex product and returned (thank God) to Scotch. So almost all of my later tapes are OK, like Old and In the Way, and the '70 Fillmore East shows.

One of the problems I have looking at the boxes of the first few Dick's Picks releases is that the Ampex box means "poison" to me. I thought: "Can't you use a better cover than that?" Use the Scotch box, not the Ampex box. It's poison, it's like the skull and crossbones. That is what was done for the Allman release, a modified Scotch box was made into the cover, rather successfully, too. I hope all the GDM releases get "regular" cover art when they are eventually released to the regular retail market.

*Was the soundboard always out in the audience?*

The soundboard was always out in the audience, but it was never very far out in the old days. When I did try to move it out very far, I found that I couldn't control the sound. So I moved it inward again. But it depended on the hall. Some places would only let us put it up in the front of the balcony or under the lip of the balcony overhang, which isn't a good place acoustically. They didn't want us blocking the good seats. I do prefer to be in what is called the "near field" where there's no degradation in sound quality due to the propagation through the air. Sound frequencies are absorbed nonlinearly by air, and the further away you get, the more upset the balance becomes. When you sit 150 or 200 feet away from the stage, the mix you produce isn't real, it doesn't sound right up front. So the high-priced seats have the worst sound, and that's not what you're after. It's better to have everything sound right from the speaker boxes on out. Then the sound is best. The frequency loss from distance is a natural effect that your ear will compensate for. People tend to think about things more in visual terms than in the way things actually work in the real world. The result is that a lot of the decisions that sound mixers make are based on nonacoustic, visual (how-it-looks), models. A factor in my booth setup was that it was quite small: a table and one or two chairs, unlike the monstrous mini-stage with guard rails used recently.

*You have slightly different hearing from most people, don't you?*

Yes, I suffered a traumatic injury to my right ear when I was nineteen. I was learning "clown" dives from some Hawaiians who were in the army and stationed in D.C., who were frequenting a swimming pool where I was working as a lifeguard for one summer. I made a mistake while learning one. I landed on my ear and the water column entered the ear and caused a hemorrhage in the inner ear. That was the summer of 1954. To say the least, antibiotics were pretty primitive in those days. The mass of blood in the inner ear became infected with a bacteria and fungus combination. The aftereffect was to thicken the eardrum and it also seemed to cause a kind of arthritis in the little bones that conduct the sound from the eardrum to the nerve center in the cochlea. So the quality of sound perceived in one ear is quite different from the other. I hear most of the highs with my left ear. But I use the phase information from both ears to pinpoint direction, and since the sound in each ear is quite different, I have a very sharp directional sense. As a result, a panpot that works on amplitude doesn't create a stereo effect for me. I don't hear any motion. It seems louder on one side, but I can't sense any direction to the sound, it always seems to come from the center. So I would say that I need a time arrival difference as the sound reaches my ears for me to detect it as having direction. Because of this, a mix which is stereo to my ears sounds like "super stereo" to people with normal hearing, and the usual "stereo" mix sounds like a kind of flat unbalanced mono to me.

*How many mikes were there in total onstage?*

I think most of the mixers we used had twelve inputs and I put two more directly into the tape recorder.

*How many mikes would you have on Billy [Kreutzmann] and his drum set?*

I used two mikes on each drummer's kit. One was an overhead mike, it was set above the drummer's head and would cover the entire spectrum of the top of the kit. And the other was on the bass drum on the inside towards the snare, down low. I wanted the drums to have a real 3d drum sound. Since there were two drummers, I had the overhead of one kit in the PA side opposite where that drummer was, and the bass mike in the drummer's side, the second kit had it the other way round. This gave each kit a stereo image, as I mentioned earlier. Plus, the "time" (kick) was coming from the correct side of the stage for each drummer.

There were some minor problems with the two-mike setup. It had a tendency to give a weak balance to the toms and it required careful readjustment on the tom solos. If you missed it, the sound of the toms wouldn't come quite as far in front as it should. If I were doing it today, I might use three or four mikes, and turn them on and off as needed. But you have to be very careful about that because the leakage of the desired source into more than one mike causes cancellation and buggers up the sound. If you move the mikes close to the drumheads, then you only get a portion of the sound. That's why you'll see drummers with tape all over the drumheads. It is an attempt to make the drum sound like a drum with a close mike, which is pretty much impossible due to the nature of a drum's sound.

The drumhead vibrates in a very complex fashion, and the energy radiated from the various parts of the head don't become integrated until they have traveled some distance away from the head. The tape is an attempt to modify the sound at the head to something more drumlike. Then they try to fix it up through all kinds of compensation, compression and equalization. A highly tuned drum has a really wonderful sound, but it doesn't integrate until you get twice the drumhead's diameter away from it. At that distance you can get into problems with what various kinds of microphones sound like. High-gain directional microphones can be used, but then you have the disadvantage that a directional microphone sounds a little like having a toilet paper tube up against your ear. Phasing, which gives it a directional response pattern, alters the spatiality of the sound. I always liked omnidirectional mikes, I still do.

*You'd have omnis for the drums?*

No, I used a directional Sennheiser overhead. Omnis weren't all that common in use in those days. Later on, when they became more available with sound companies, I used them more. I was very discriminating. I always found that the omnis produced a better sound. And I was always trying to get a better sound. The same high-definition sounds that I heard live on stage I wanted to hear through my headphones at home.

*How would you mike the Dead's acoustic setup in '69 and '70? Were they standing?*

No, they were usually sitting. We would put a mike on the face of the guitar, not over the sound hole, but close to the top edge of the sound hole up near the neck, rather than over the bottom part. There was usually a certain sweet spot just off the sound hole. And if you got it right, it sounded good; if the musician moved around too much though, it would change. But the boys were really good at this point and had been in the business for a number of years.

*How did you mike Pigpen's piano?*

Pig had an electric piano on stage, which went through an amp. The acoustic pianos came later, with Keith. I didn't follow any set theory when placing mikes. I would stick a mike on something and if it didn't sound right I'd move it until it did. I'd do that every time. If the musician changed something, the sound would change anyway. I hate formulas. I like it to sound good. When it came to setting up the pickup on the various amplifiers, microphones wouldn't be directly in front of the speaker. I would place them off slightly to one side and maybe even pointing in another direction. Whatever was required to adjust the way different signals would combine with each other to create a fat, thick, real stereophonic sound.

*As the musicians changed places on stage over the years, would you also change the channel they were in?*

Usually. I liked it to represent what the stage looked like to me, because, like I said, I was miking a matrix of sound. When they move themselves and their amplifiers around, they change the matrix of sound on the stage. And I was miking that matrix. I wasn't putting a specific person into a specific (artificial) position. It always represented the reality.

*The shows that you recorded in February of 1970 at the Fillmore East are, of course, much prized by Deadheads. There's a clarity to those recordings that some Deadheads think is as pristine as they've ever heard. The balance of all the instruments is just right. They're incredibly quiet, clean tapes.*

Actually, all the tapes from that period are like that. All the performances might not have been that good. There were only twelve microphones; what do you expect?

*So bass, rhythm, lead guitars. Four on the drums. Four vocal mikes and then keyboard.*

Well, fourteen mikes into the tape recorder and only twelve on stage.

*Where were the other two?*

Bass and guitar. We only had twelve-channel mixers. Too many mikes make things muddy. They get muddy because there's leakage. Leakage makes a signal appear at two different points in time due to the distance between the mikes and the source. If you then combine the channels, you create a summation or cancellation. So you keep moving things around until the phase clears between the various signal sources to produce the least interference. The fewer the microphones, the more effectively you can do that. The best possible situation is only one microphone in each channel. This is termed "binaural." It always creates this absolutely powerful sense of spatiality. But as you get more and more sources, and they get louder, you have to get creative with where the mikes are, how much level they're given, how they're put together. I liked to set it up so that the musicians' own dynamics came through.

I did the recording, mixed the PA, and mixed the monitors all at the same time. I tried to make sure the monitor was in balance with the other sound sources [amps], so that they're able to hear both. As long as they were able to hear the relationship between their instruments and the monitors, then they created the balance. And it was obvious early on that dynamics were an extremely important musical aspect that was getting lost in electrically amplified music. I've got [Jefferson] Airplane tapes, lots of nice Airplane tapes, good and even great shows, but they always turned all the amps up to ten. As a result, there was very little dynamic action in their performances, and a lot of the mikes were overloaded. These tapes are basically fuzzy and unusable for making records. Of course I wasn't making tapes to make records, just as a kind of "sonic journal" or diary of my work. The Airplane always had problems hearing their monitors.

**You were creating something that was completely different from what you would hear if you were standing in the middle of the stage.**

That's true, but it had a space. It was stereoscopic and had a dimension to it. Of course the space wasn't a real reproduction of the onstage sound sensed by the musicians and was also limited by the fact that the vocal mikes weren't stereo pairs.

**What's your opinion of Dolby sound processing?**

I like the Dolby B on cassettes. I can't tell much difference with the C. The Dolby A that was used in professional setups, I found caused a lot of artifacts that I didn't like. The Dolby B doesn't create as many artifacts at the single crossover point. People who don't use Dolby on cassettes I think are very foolish. Maybe they like to hear tape hiss and generational noise. I don't. I always Dolby things.

**What's your opinion of digital versus analog tapes?**

With digitized music you always have the horrible possibility that the standard will change to a higher sampling rate and all your precious archived music will be unusable and grainy-sounding by comparison. I would always recommend that the original tape be done in analog, even if only as a parallel recording, because you can always digitize a good analog at any time to whatever sampling rate the equipment can manage. Nagra recorders can record some components of music all the way out to 100 kHz. If you must digitize, DAT tapes are worse than useless to archive with. The magnetic medium is not appropriate for such short-wavelength recordings. It starts to decay [lose the bits of data] almost immediately. You begin to lose information *about* the sound rather than a portion of the sound, such as the higher frequencies. There are circuits which can gloss over these errors up to a point. Anyone who has any large archive in digital on tapes will probably have to spend several hours every single day copying. Once they get to be, let's say, more than eight to ten months old they begin to lose enough data that they're basically worth much less and aren't hi-fi any more. It's very difficult to deal with this because the information is lost across the spectrum. As digital dropout it's not confined to the high frequency like on analog tape. This problem is much lower on the A-DAT tapes used professionally, which are essentially VHS videocassettes and have wider tracks and run much faster past the head. Still, digital magnetic tape is not good archival, CD-R is.

**Like, for example, where you recorded something on a ferric tape you'd lose the high end.**

The ferric tapes self-erase more easily than the metal oxide ones, which include the real chrome dioxide formulations like BASF. The ferric formulations (they're all oxides, of course) are very sensitive to magnetic domain self-erasure and the highs are what go. After a while they sound dull. There's a slight advantage to Dolbying a tape, because except during the very highest passages you boost the highs during recording. So when you turn the Dolby off, your quiet highs come back, but the noise does too. But digital stuff, if you want to archive it, you're going to have to put it on an optical medium, burn a CD-R. One disk holds seventy-four minutes. If you leave it on DAT, forget it. You're going to spend your whole life recopying them. Or else you're going to have a lot of shitty-sounding music later on.

**When did you stop working with the Dead in the late sixties? And when did you return?**

I worked with the Grateful Dead from February of '66 to October, and I then rejoined them when the Carousel closed in July of '68. The courts restricted my travel in February '70 after the bust in New Orleans. They canceled my appeal bond in July of '70 and sent me to do my time. It crippled my appeal because I could not supervise the lawyers while I was locked up. I didn't get out until July of '72.

**And that's when you came back?**

Then I came back to a crew that was totally different when I left and whereas the job that I had been doing was split up amongst three other people, none of whom were willing to yield the territory. I met a lot of resistance in the scene, and after you spend a couple of years locked up your social adaptability is not very good.

**Did you do the sound for any Garcia Band shows?**

Nope. Only Old and In the Way.

**Did you record the Old and In the Way shows using the same principles that you applied with the Grateful Dead?**

Not really. Grateful Dead was recorded with the PA mikes. Old and In the Way was done with extra clip-on mikes on the mike stands which did not go into the PA. I didn't use any of the PA mikes. That's how I got stereo vocals, I used two mikes. It was not very visually attractive using those large, primitive microphones. Most were omnis. I wished they'd all been omnis. I got a very nice sense of space because of that. There's very little phasing. The guitar and bass mikes were directional (I used what I had). The sense is you get a very nice feeling of space. It feels like you're in the hall. You can hear the hall, you can hear the people when they move. It is a very realistic environment. I personally do not like directional microphones. I don't like the way they sound, and I try to avoid their use wherever I can. In most cases there's no valid criteria for using them. Sometimes they're useful for miking a drum kit on a very loud stage from overhead to have the coverage confined to the top of a drum kit and exclude some of the other stuff. You have a sound that is buried amongst other microphones in the mix so you're not aware of the phased sound. But in every other case I prefer omnis; they're best for the voice, best for any other instrument. If the sound source is loud, it's going to override anything from the free field anyway. A lot of people think like they did in the old days where mikes and PAs were primitive. A guy got up on the stage in front of an audience and the audience is loud and they didn't want it in the system. They didn't care what it sounded like, it wasn't hi-fi, it was speech.

**Did you realize there were people out in the audience making Grateful Dead tapes?**

I never saw but one guy doing that in the old days. I think it was in '69, we caught a guy in the Palladium in Hollywood with a reel-to-reel tape recorder, and we said, "Hey, that's not cool, you don't have permission to do that." We confiscated the tapes, and the guy went to the manager, who called in the cops and the cops made us give them back to the guy. We didn't have any way to erase it. Well, maybe I should've tried to substitute some other tape for it. But I wasn't in favor of tapers, not in those days. In fact, today the Grateful Dead is embarrassed by the huge number of high quality bootlegs that are flooding the market. They're having a hard time with it. One of the problems is the practice of a lot of people being allowed to plug into the soundboard. So it's a double-edged sword. Audience tapes are one thing; patching into the board by fifty or sixty people is wrong. And later when you're surprised when you find people selling hundreds of bootleg records, you can't really complain about that. I always thought it was a double-edged sword. I didn't tolerate it.

**At the same time, a lot of people would attribute the Grateful Dead's success to the decision to allow tapers to record the show.**

There would've always been those guys out there with the cassette machine up their sleeve and a mike pinned on their hat. You find those anyway. They tried to keep everyone behind the soundboard, but at any given show there could've been fifty machines in front of the board. You could never stop it completely, but it's a double-edged sword. It's good and it's bad. If the Grateful Dead want to be retirees and live off the income of records from the archives, it may be a disadvantage. On the other hand, it makes the band's music live for sure. It's very difficult to analyze it as to benefits and liabilities because it depends on the criteria by which you're judging, and what value you place on the various outcomes. I know the Grateful Dead, the Allman Brothers, David Grisman, and others do allow their fans to tape. I don't think it's a great disadvantage. But the bottom line is, as long as the band is prompt about producing good records and selling them to the public and is interested in releasing the old stuff and also is vigorous in their pursuit of people that are making money off their music, i.e., bootleggers, it may be OK. I don't have any sympathy for anyone who's bootlegging. That's artistic theft, and as an artist I resent it highly.

**Do you have a favorite period of Grateful Dead music?**

No. I thought that they were happier and the music was livelier when I was doing the sound, but how much of that is personal/subjective and how much of it is actual/objective, I don't know. I always liked the Grateful Dead, ever since I first heard them. I'd get a little upset when they didn't play well. Garcia's habits made his playing many times unacceptable to me, but I still liked them through all of their incarnations. A lot.

## Dick Latvala

Dick Latvala may be the world's luckiest Deadhead. Besides having had the good fortune to first see the Dead at the Longshoreman's Hall Trips Festival in 1966 (and plenty of times since then), Dick has the ultimate Deadhead fantasy job: he's the official tape archivist for the Grateful Dead. While Dick will quickly tell you he has many responsibilities, he does actually get paid to listen to Grateful Dead music. Dick uses this experience to choose the concerts that get released on compact disc as part of the continuing Dick's Picks project.

*John R. Dwork: What are your official responsibilities as the archivist of the Grateful Dead's tape vault?*

**Dick Latvala:** I'm supposed to know where the tapes are. In my terms, archiving means copying the stuff that's deteriorating actually. I mean, the Vault's already organized because we moved a year ago. And I had it laid out according to my specifications. That's how it was done. I organized it, then moved it, and now it's all organized.

*Is part of your job also listening?*

Absolutely. Since Dick's Picks took off the ground and looks like it's going to keep flying, maybe that's the essence of my job now. But there's only a few of us around and everyone shares in the responsibilities. I'll take the garbage out if no one's around. Doing whatever's needed seems to be the attitude, and there's a lot of things that need to be done. So I'm not sitting at home listening all the time as I would like.

*How do you store information about what's on each tape?*

I should be more professional about this in terms of centralizing all my notes and all my books, but I sort of resist that because I think it should be something you rediscover when you find something for release. I have notes over every *DeadBase* I own. I've got notes in books, binders, everywhere.

*I'm not talking about your own personal critiques. I'm talking about the actual Vault stuff.*

Oh, that's in a computer hard disk.

*Do you store it all by show, name, and reel number?*

No. I broke the Vault down into four major categories. The first is live shows. Another is record projects and other related tapes that go along with record making. Video, that's a category unto itself. Then there's masters: individual bandmember's side projects, film, you get the idea. But from my point of view the live shows are the essence of it all. It's all numbered bar codes; it just gives you necessary information, like the section number, shelf number, and tape number on the shelf.

*So for example on the computer it would say . . .*

If you wanted to find something and you had access to the databases, you'd put a find on a date and it would come up with all the ways it's stored and where it is. Any klutz could find the tape.

*Does each tape have the set list or just the tape number and date of show?*

Tape number and date of show. Wait, that's not altogether true. A lot of the dates have the set lists in them. I was doing it for Healy. We were working backward in time and got up to '74, but we got bogged down, something changed, and I never got back to doing a real comprehensive song list for each date. It didn't seem important anymore.

*Certainly one of your most important Vault releases to date is the three CD set of February 13 and 14, 1970, from the Fillmore East. How'd this come about?*

Well, I'd been trying to get this released since I first got into the position of influence at all, which was when Dan Healy started the Vault release program in 1990. I'd been trying the whole time to focus in on those two shows: February 13 and 14, 1970, or some part of that, and also Harpur College 1970. I've run those up the flagpole many times and gotten beat up over it.

*Who does the beating up?*

Depends. But it's not really important on that level. I figured out that it's more than slapping on what you think is the best thing; there's politics, there's something behind the scenes that influences the release. It's important to mention that although it's called Dick's Picks, I

*Dick Latvala: The best job in the world* (photo credit: Susanna Millman)

really don't have any final say. I'm a gathering point of information that I try to pass on to others.

*So tell us, how did* Dick's Picks IV *(February 13 and 14, 1970) come to be?*

*Dick's Picks III* was the Hollywood Sportatorium in '77. That came out in November 1995, shortly after Jerry died. And that wasn't forced; it was in the normal cycle. But we haven't released as much as I think we should. There's a lot of thought given to not appearing to be capitalizing on Jerry's death, so our pace is *not* commensurate with the demand. I was reinvestigating the February 1970 Fillmore East run when my bell was rung again. We had begun to fall into a pattern of putting one out every time the Grateful Dead Almanac (mail order catalog) came out, but that wasn't really set up until just now. It wasn't quite time for Dick's Picks to come out again, but I was thinking maybe it was a good time to bring the issue up again, see if I could get away with it. Maybe I could now. For me it was easy to put it on discs; I knew I wasn't going to use any of Bear's Choice or anything. So all these various factors came into play, that led everyone to let it go. I didn't have any resistance. It was actually sort of a miraculous occasion that everything worked right, like three CDs in a single release package; that was the first time we did that. That was a big jump. It was my endless desire to see this out. It wasn't hard to come up with the idea. What *would* be is coming up with a rare show again in this era, one that no one knows. The more I find out, the more I notice that everyone knows everything. [Laughter]

*So, really, what you said was that when the time came, everything just fit into place and the timing was right.*

Yeah, because it's not just one person determining it; a lot of things come into play. It was perfect timing, a perfect idea, and it was time. It was inevitable, right? We would have had to be stupid not to use it some year. It wasn't like it's never going to come out, it was more just a question of when. I thought, "Maybe it will work now." In terms of what years we've already released, too, it fit all the criteria.

*Was there any impetus about the fact that February 13 is widely considered one of the favorite shows of Deadheads?*

You mean in terms of me deciding to use that? Absolutely. The research, asking Deadheads the ten best shows they would like to see released, went out with *Dick's Picks III,* was on the card that we sent out, and the Internet survey. I also got information from a lot of other sources. It's not a problem for me to sit down and listen to other people's ideas. I'm into the learning phase again; I've gotten way past thinking I know everything.

*Were you able to use this information as ammunition for the release?*

That was a factor. The surveys were coming in, and people on our insight team were paying attention. But I was asking somewhat apprehensively: "What the hell am I around for if we have these surveys?" The surveys say it all.

*Have the members of the Grateful Dead actually sat down in the last decade and listened to February 13, 1970, knowing that Deadheads love it so much?*

I seriously doubt that any of the living band members have listened to that show. I don't think they like to hear themselves.

*That's understandable.*

There should be a book, or at least a chapter, written about that, how the people creating the music have a different mind-set from those receiving it. Together, the two cause the explosion that we call the Grateful Dead Experience. The audience perceives things differently from the creators. And that's the difficulty in dealing with this release thing: as an artist, even thirty years down the road, sometimes you're still too close to the art to have any objectivity to it. Often, to the extent you try, you get frustrated with it; you're the creator and you can't tell the Deadheads what they want to hear. Because your conception of it is too esoteric or sublime. The people involved with putting this on don't have the same awareness; they don't keep records of information of what happened the night before, they're on to the next thing.

*The best artists are never, or rarely, happy with their work.*

That's right. That's what causes the difficulty of getting out there some of what Deadheads say they want. Like whole shows, the tuning between songs, Jerry farting in the dressing room . . . Take for example, the whole show concept. I myself came into this whole thing with that idea and then realized it's impossible: That's the rule. With the censors I had at the time, I thought we'd never be able to release anything. Now, we're at least moving closer. And it's actually because of the surveys—thank you, Deadheads! People who have been resisting a lot of the releases which Deadheads want are becoming more amicable to ideas like whole show releases. That's pretty difficult for the people who are more directly involved with creating the music, like the band members and so forth. A lot of people have input on anything that's released because it's for money, you know, they're putting their names on it. It's authentic; they don't want to be embarrassed. I understand what Garcia meant now when he told me once that he'd never want to go through those tapes; they embarrassed him. Every time he heard one, it reminded him of what he was *trying* to do. That's the thing, see? We'll never know what he was trying to do, but what came out was pretty cool for *us* to hear.

***There's a bit of an interesting story on how you were able to get rid of reel change glitches for February 13 and 14, 1970, by using other tapes. Can you tell us about that?***

Yes. That's another example of the inside world of the Grateful Dead using and relating to the outside world of Deadheads, and them helping to make a good product. That's the purpose of the surveys. It's not like I don't know which shows are good, but there's a lot of stuff out there, so the more information the better. As people know in 2/13 and 2/14/70 there are tape flips. One of them is during "That's It for the Other One" and "China Cat" on 2/13/70 and between "Mason's Children" and "Not Fade Away" on 2/14/70. Anyway, I didn't know this until recently, but there was a whole other system of tape recording going on at the Fillmore East by John Chester [the house sound engineer]. David Gans had a DAT of the show that he got directly from a guy named Mark Morris who worked at the Fillmore East. He was a lighting guy at the shows, and he knew there was a separate system being used in the basement to tape the show. They split the signal running out to Bear at the board. Anyway, I brought David's DAT to work, and I found out that the flips weren't in the same places as the ones Bear did. Not only did we have a potentially easy patch here, but the two sources matched sonically. We didn't have to go into some esoteric means to make that flip tolerable or seamless. It was a miracle; I couldn't believe it. Over the years I listened to my old copy of 2/13 and the one we had in the Vault and I kept thinking, "This flip isn't in the same place as on my old tape," but I didn't feel like putting up the old tape, relistening to it, and really looking into it too deeply. I was just into listening for pleasure. When I found out, it all made sense.

So anyway, through David Gans, we got ahold of Mark Morris. He came over with his copy of a copy of Chester's master tape. Evidently the master went to Bill Graham and was never seen again. But the master was at 7½ ips. And the master Morris had was mostly 3¾ ips with some 7½ ips. But it definitely was a copy of Chester's tape and the only copy that the outside world would have as a master. Anyway, we used that analog tape because Gans' digital clone of that on DAT was insufficient for my expert friends John Cutler and Jeffrey Norman, my teammates in the studio making these things. They were thinking that the analog source would be much warmer and aesthetically pleasing to use as the source for the transition parts. I didn't understand this. To me, what we had sounded pretty cool. So Mark came over, brought his tapes, and we spent a day copying. And Jeffrey worked miracles at the Sonic Solution System; it was just amazing. He made it, covered the edits by using this Sonic Solution System, which can take an analog two-track *finished* tape and adjust it. It's just amazing! You can do miracles with a digital editing system like that. Does anyone know where the flips were? Have you noticed anyone who can tell where they are?

***No, you just can't tell.***

That's great. And he deserves all the credit, because he worked so fucking hard in the studio, under great stress potential. And he's so level-headed! He's not bent in any severe way, like most of us. He's not even a Deadhead, but he's turning on to the music through the live stuff over time.

***Most Deadheads don't know that there were early shows on February 13 and 14, 1970.***

Yeah, on February 11 too. There was an earlier show, and I don't know if they kicked everyone out and then started the next show or if it was two separate sets.

***The set list from the supposed early show or set goes "Cold Rain and Snow" > "Dark Star" > "Saint Stephen" > "The Eleven" > "Lovelight." Then Zacherle comes out and reintroduces the Dead all over again. It seems highly probable there was an earlier show. To what degree might you put out shows in the future that are Deadheads' choices?***

From the inside, there's a good, healthy satisfaction from sating the whims of Deadheads. I mean we're trying to do whole shows. And it's hard for those who create, produce, or have anything to do with it to eliminate the real bad parts, but they exist—bad tape flips, bad music... But by putting these shows out, we, Deadheads across the universe, have made a huge jump. People are acquainted with three CDs and how to efficiently deal with them packaging-wise. That means that the next time a Dick's Picks is ready, I can do a whole show.

Three CDs is enough room on which to fit a whole show. New doors have been opened. It's taken some time, but I think we're making some definite progress.

*Absolutely. But it's such a daunting but exciting task to take on.*

It was somewhat of a surprising thought to confront, but it makes a lot of sense. I got way more than I bargained for. That's why I need so much help; no person can keep track of even one year, let alone all of it.

*Well, Dick, if you raised your hand, I'm sure there would be no shortage of interns.*

I talk to everyone about what they think; those competent people aren't just there for the party, people with some knowledge and credibility, so to speak. 'Cause I've missed a lot. I've been going through what people say is good from the eighties. There's some great shit in there that I missed out on. Fortunately, people have been directing me toward it. Everyone's right. That's one of my assumptions: Nobody's wrong. There are so many viewpoints on this slippery subject called the "good show" it's very difficult.

*What are your favorite Dead tapes?*

I can't say. The magnitude of all of it is so staggering, my mind has been blasted apart over the years.

*Quick, the alien spacecraft is taking off to take you on a tour of the universe. You have five minutes to pack: what five tapes do you take?*

Five shows. And I'm limited just to the Grateful Dead? I've always resisted thinking like this. It's a valid question, but I've got so many dates in my head and I'm learning so much that I can't be sure that this is the essence of it all. 10/12/68, 2/14/68, 2/28/69, 11/7 and 11/8/69. Should I get into the seventies? The "Dark Star" from 9/19/70, no question about it. 2/13 and 2/14/70. Certainly 5/2/70—Harpur College. There's millions more. I haven't even gotten to my favorite years yet. Seventy-three, I could name a dozen shows worthy of taking. But I come from the sixties so I'm naming shows that I saw. That's why I got into taping. Because of my compulsion to collect and to see if I could find any of these shows from the past that moved me in real time. I wanted to see if it was the drugs talking or if it was real. And I found out it was really great.

*What are the largest holes in the Grateful Dead's Vault collection?*

Well, a large part of 1970 is basically not there, except for West Coast shows.

*The second half of the year's completely missing?*

Most of the second half of the year, including West Coast shows, is missing. That's terrible. Next problem areas are '79, '80, '81, and '82. They're basically not there. And then there are a bunch of shows missing within any of the years that are Betty Boards or surfacing Betty Boards. Things surface all the time—it's amazing. Someone told me a story about how they went to a show at Merramec College in Kirkwood, Missouri, and they found tapes for Alfred College, the night before Harpur College, under the stage setup. That's how loose things were in the past. I'm sure there were plenty of times when someone says, "Hey, put these in the truck," and the guy puts them on the back of the truck but not in the truck, and they pulled the door down, the truck takes off, and the tapes flew off onto the highway. Someone picks them up, puts them in storage, dies, and the tapes resurface. There we go and 9/19/70 comes around.

*Is it the goal of the Vault, your goal, to amass a complete collection of Grateful Dead shows? Are you interested in bringing in AUDs for shows that have no SBDs?*

No. Not me personally. Nobody's told me that they are inclined in that direction. I think that would only apply to consumers that love to hear this music at home as much as possible.

*At what rate are you able to transfer analog masters into the digital domain?*

None. We haven't done any, in a sense, deliberate archiving, because archiving means finding a medium that everyone deems acceptable and no one's agreed on one yet. That includes DATs, CDs, maybe optical discs. Everything is changing so fast in the digital realm. And there are so many thousands of tapes to transfer, and some of them aren't worth shit. I mean, no one from the inside will use them for a marketable product. So if you're going into archiving, you have to know what's good because time is of the essence. You start with what's important, but who knows what's important? Me, supposedly. But we haven't done that yet. But whenever I bake tapes, which is for anything after '74, I always double-DAT them and put them through good digital to analog converters. But I don't do that very often.

*Could you tell me year by year what tape stock the Dead have used to record shows?*

Basically it was Scotch 207 and Ampex tape.

*Open reel?*

Yeah.

*How long did they do open reel?*

You mean seven- and ten-inch style or multitrack or analog itself?

*I mean the basic idea: from 1965 to 1967 was it all two-track reels? When did they go to one-inch tape, in 1968? And when to multitrack? And then when from cassette to videotape? Then from videotape to DAT?*

In the beginning it was the analog era. There were no analog tapes in the last ten years. The last analog tapes of a live show I saw were seven-inch tapes from '81 and ten-inch tapes up to '91 with multitracks. Then there are ADATs; that's digital, you know.

*Go back to the beginning. As far back as you can go.*

Well, in the beginning, I don't know. When I first came into this gig, there were seven-inch reels and ten-inch open reels. And ten-inch reels could be two-track, four-track, eight-track, sixteen, twenty-four, and so forth. The ten-inch reels started with the Shrine, in '67 basically. They started on the seven-inch reels on 2/14/69, at the Electric Factory in Philadelphia. This gets really complex because there's so much craziness... When they were recording the stuff that went into *Anthem of the Sun*, they were using quarter-inch tape, making a four-track or a three-track. There was actually a three-track machine at one time. And there are cassettes of the older days, going back to '59, of Phil playing trumpet or something.

*Those weren't recorded on cassette back then?*

I don't know how they came to be. They were here when I got here. They were from '61, '62, '63, '64. I know what they're like 'cause I know what they sounded like in different places; it was the Wildwood Boys or something. As far as live Grateful Dead, I didn't know anything existed in the Vault from pre-'67. It wasn't until I started finding stuff in Bear's tapes or when we started collaborating, separating his Dead stuff from his non-Dead stuff, before we moved the Vault, that I found any more. I mean, he gave me some stuff from the Acid Test era, but it wasn't marked. The labeling was terrible. They taped a lot of stuff and labeled it very poorly. I've gone through that, and most of it is really terrible nonsense. Some of it could be used someday, but I don't think it's that compelling. Some of it's unique and interesting and we will use it. There aren't whole shows really, except for a few examples. The Deadheads have more stuff as tape collectors than we have... Anyway, there's hardly any two-track stuff of '68. It's mostly multitrack, four-track, or eight-track stuff in '68. Then '69 is the two-track seven-inch stuff. And Bear got pretty thorough; he taped almost every show, although there's a little missing in '69. But I found these cassettes of Bear's one day. I went, "Oh my God! I've never even heard of these shows." Some of them weren't labeled quite right, but I figured it out after a while. One would say "Louisville" and that's all, just "Louisville." When I heard them, I knew where to look, at dates I'd never seen. I went nuts on that box of tapes. I stayed up for days copying. I mean they're not usable, but they're sort of interesting as a listener. I don't think I could ever release any of it. I don't even think [David] Gans would be willing to use it on the *Dead Hour* because they're not good enough quality. But I think if you were sitting here listening, you would have no problems with it. April 26, 1969, is one of those shows.

*"Dupree's" > "Mountains of the Moon" > "China Cat" > "Doin' That Rag," "Hurts Me Too > "Hard to Handle," "Cryptical" > "Drums" > "The Other One" > "The Eleven" > "The Other One" > "Cryptical" > "It's a Sin," "Morning Dew," "Sittin' on Top of the World," "Minglewood," "Silver Threads," "Baby Blue," "Saint Stephen" > "Lovelight," and then that amazing encore of "Viola Lee Blues" > "Feedback" > "What's Become of the Baby" > "We Bid You Goodnight"! Please, pinch me. This tape is amazing!*

We don't have the encore on our reel-to-reels; they stop at "Lovelight." But I found these mislabeled cassettes and as I was going through I said to myself, "4/26? Oh yeah, that's one of the ones I need to relisten and bake, because there's squealing on the master. There were a bunch from '69 that had this. I knew I was going to get to them and bake 'em then properly one day, digitize them somehow. April 26 was on my list, but I had the cassettes and I decided to check them out. I figured if they were tolerable I could live with them for a while, just to listen to them until I baked them. So I was listening, and listening, and listening. I thought, "This is pretty listenable, pretty good." Then I got to what was labeled Reel 4, and it was actually a different show from San Mateo's Reel 1. I was listening, and after "Lovelight" they came back for an encore. They started "Viola Lee Blues" and it went on. I was thinking, "This will be a superficial." A superficial treatment of "Viola Lee," no more than ten minutes, I'm sure. But it went on for at least twenty minutes. It was intense! Then it went into "Feedback" and then "What's Become of the Baby" and then "We Bid You Goodnight"! And it lasts a total of forty-one minutes.

*A live "What's Become of the Baby"?*

Well, it was actually a tape of a studio recording from *Aoxomoxoa* that Bear was playing over which the band played live "Feedback."

*Continuing with the tape stock, didn't they switch in '71 for a brief time to cassette?*

Never. Cassettes were just an additional format. No one ever switched to cassettes. That would have been stupid. I don't think that was ever a policy. At this point, it's a useful tool because for certain shows there are only cassettes. Like I said, '79, '80, '81, '82 are basically not there in larger format. Some of the tapes aren't bad; they could possibly be used.

**Tell me when the recording medium switched from open reel.**

Well, as far as live shows go, they were recording open reel until the end of '81. They should have been recording in '82, but I don't know what happened there. I haven't gotten an answer from anyone who might have been fooling around then. But there were no tapes. The digital era started in '82. At the end of '82 is when, I believe, the first PCM tapes were made on Beta. Thereafter, it was all digital. PCM digital-videotape. Beta first, then eventually VHS. The ADAT era started—ADAT is a digital format but it started off in eight-track, but Healy got more machines as the tour went on, and eventually, by the beginning of '93, he went up to a twenty-four-track system. And for the entirety of Healy's era, there were twenty-four track-ADATs, from the beginning of the Oakland shows on. Before that, some of the Oakland shows of January or December, and some other shows in Phoenix and somewhere else, all of those were sixteen-track. The last four shows of the summer, those he did on eight-track ADAT. 7/1, that was the last show. There was Chicago, two Deer Creeks and then Buckeye in '92. 6/26 Soldier Field, 6/28 Deer Creek, 6/29 Deer Creek, 7/1 Buckeye. That was all eight-track. Then 12/2, 12/3 McNichols; 12/5, 12/6 Compton Terrace; and 12/11, 12, 13, 12/16, and 12/17 Oakland. And 1/24, 1/25, and 1/26 Oakland were sixteen-track. Then twenty-four-track starts at 2/21/93 Oakland, and it goes on that way forever until Phoenix in '94. Then it went back to DATs. Of course there are DATs through this ADAT era, but there are no reel-to-reels. Cassettes ran through '88 or '89. There are some cassettes in there and elsewhere I'm sure, but those are the last place to look for something. Sometime they might be used for a master of something, if it sounds good enough. Then there's no problem with anyone on our team using it. Anything after '74 needs to be baked, 'cause if you don't, the open reel might shed a lot or squeal; it might not rewind like any other tape you've rewound. Then you know you've got a baking problem. Ampex, much to their joy, discovered the solution to these problems. They fucked with everyone's tape library. But now, after you bake the reels, they play perfectly. You bake it for twelve hours at 130 degrees Fahrenheit. I tell you it's a miracle. It takes formerly unplayable tapes and makes them suddenly perfect, sort of like the digital editing system.

**Can you give us an idea of what kind of noise reduction the Dead used in recording shows?**

No. I'm not good at that. I know Dolby A was used in the sixties or seventies when they were professionally recording. I know what we use now is Dolby SR.

**Lets talk about the show on May 19, 1970, in St. Louis. An emcee from back then told someone in my crew that this show was never played and that the music is actually from May 1, 1970, at Alfred College in New York. Any clues on that?**

I don't know who I got this letter from but someone was communicating with me about a show in dispute. Washington University, St. Louis, was probably a show that never happened. It might really be Alfred College. Based on the Kirkwood, Missouri, Merramec College, May 14, 1970, that makes sense. The reels were probably mislabeled and were thrown in there as 5/19/70 over the years. We don't have the tape.

**What about the June 20, 1974, Atlanta and July 25, 1975, Chicago tapes?**

Yeah, they exist.

**How often did Phil do the Philo jam in fall of '72? Are there more than just those two versions? There's one from Milwaukee and another one from St. Louis.**

They did it several times. One is from the Fox Theater, October 18. October 24 is the Milwaukee show you're referring to. They did it on October 26, Cincinnati, and October 28, Cleveland. They also did it on November 26 in San Antonio.

**Have you ever done any research to try to find any tapes that are missing from the Vault by asking other Vault tape archivists—for say, the Allman Brothers, Big Brother, or Jefferson Airplane—whether there are any Dead tapes in their vaults as you have theirs in your Vault?**

Nope. Good point, though; it might be a resource. I'm somewhat doubtful of that, though, because we're more likely to have other groups' tapes than they are to have ours. I have a connection with the Allman Brothers, and he would have told me if he had any Grateful Dead. It's more likely that I have some tapes that he would like of the Allmans.

**Do you have any desire to find a way of releasing music that the Dead would never be interested in as an official CD, to be circulated amongst Deadheads and benefiting the Dead somehow?**

Yes. I'm interested and I've thought of it, but I haven't found any vehicle yet. There's Gans' *Grateful Dead Hour*, but that's still high-tech, high-quality style, and he's not likely to play anything on there that isn't imbued with some degree of competency; it has to be good quality. Things of lesser quality are what you're talking about, where could they be used. I've been thinking about that a lot, and I haven't figured what to do besides making you a tape and telling you not to tell anyone where you got it from. And you have a girlfriend who wants a copy, and before you know it ten thousand Deadheads have it. That's the way that happens; I've been through it enough times to be familiar with the cycle.

*What effect does bootlegging have on the Vault release projects?*

The very fact that bootlegs were around and so popular in late '94 allowed for the Dick's Picks series to come about. That was a joyful moment for me because I didn't have much to submit to Phil for him to listen to. And when the bootlegs were thrown out on the table, that was a sign that it was time to let go of this and let me do my thing. Now, as far as how many things get released, I don't know who decides that. I just know when my bell is rung that I'm ready. I'm told it's time and asked if I have anything. Of course I have something, day or night, any year. I'm also in a process of discovery too, so it's not like I know the best show of every year.

*It was rumored that someone in the Dead organization put cuts in leaked soundboard tapes so that they could track bootlegging. Do you know if this really happened?*

I've never heard of it; it's an interesting idea, though. The concept sounds like it's not impossible.

*Is there any preference, whether among the band or you, to release the earlier or later music?*

I would say the perspective is the more skipping around, the better, and all years are relevant. Personally, I was more inspired by the music of '68 and '69 than that of '95. But it doesn't matter; whatever you get turned on by, you like. All years have good shows, and up until the very end, there were some very good shows in there. But the more critical and brain-damaged I get seeing this over and over again, the harder it became to satisfy me.

*Do you keep the Jerry Band tapes in the Vault?*

Yes.

*Is there a move on anyone's part to release more Jerry Band stuff?*

There is a move to get the Jerry Band stuff released. I certainly would like to see the Jerry Band stuff released. I get feedback that the people want it, but it isn't my provenance to speculate on that. Dick's Picks wouldn't be involved in releasing Jerry Band stuff. Other people, like Cutler and Parish, are involved in that.

*Would you like to see the Dead's Vault made accessible via a cable subscription, or through a listening library at the Grateful Dead Museum idea that Phil is researching, or through any other format, venue, or vehicle?*

Absolutely. I don't know how it will happen or how quickly, but I certainly think that Phil is interested in having every tape accessible to anyone, so it's not formalized and limited to Dick's Picks and multitrack releases. It would be more like something stored on a big mainframe and you can download music at your house. But it's a fantasy concept because it will take forever to transfer everything. I don't foresee that happening for a while. It's the same question about how to get what we won't use made accessible to the public. There's a substantial market in passing along the music, not for money but for passing along good vibes.

# PART TWO

# The Reviews

**1. Date, Venue, Event Title**
This denotes the date, concert hall, city, and state of the show. If there is an additional title to the concert (Sufi benefit, or New Year's Eve, for example) this would be listed directly underneath this first line.

**2. Set Lists**
Here is the list of songs played, often sets and encore if known.

## 6/26/74

### Civic Center, Providence, Rhode Island

**Set 1:** Big River, Brown-Eyed Women, Beat It on Down the Line, Scarlet Begonias, Black-Throated Wind, Row Jimmy, Mexicali Blues, Deal, The Race Is On, Mississippi Half-Step, El Paso, Ship of Fools, Weather Report Suite > It Must Have Been the Roses
**Interlude:** Seastones*
**Set 2:** U.S. Blues, Me and My Uncle, Space > China Cat Sunflower > I Know You Rider, Truckin' > The Other One Jam > Spanish Jam > Wharf Rat > Sugar Magnolia
**Encore:** Eyes of the World

**4. Sources**
Herein lies the basic info for each of the different sources of the music. In this case there are 2 differencent sources for the music from this show which is in circulation.

**Personnel:** *with Ned Lagin

    **1. Source:** AUD, **Quality:** A–/B+, **Length:** 3:20, **Genealogy:** MC > RR, **Taper:** Jerry Moore
    **2. Source:** SBD, **Quality:** A+, **Length:** 2:50 (missing "Seastones," "U.S. Blues," and "Me and My Uncle"), **Genealogy:** MC > DAT > C
    **3. Source:** FM-SBD (GDH 203), **Quality:** A–/B+, **Length:** 0:20 (only "Space" through "I Know You Rider"), **Genealogy:** MC > DR

**3. Personnel**
This is where musicians other than regular members of the Grateful Dead who appear on this tape are listed.

**5. Highlights**
This is a purely subjective list of recommended highlights for those in search of "best versions" of specific songs.

**Highlights:** Space > China Cat Sunflower > I Know You Rider, Truckin' > The Other One Jam > Spanish Jam, Eyes of the World

**6. Comments**
Here is where the writer may add some specific information as to the sound quality. For instance, he or she may say that there's a buzz in the first set of songs but it disappears by the second set.

**Comments:** 7½ ips 2 track tape played on Teac Reel to Reel tape deck into PCM501ES digital processor w/Sony SL550 Beta video recorder on Maxell HGX750 tape. Dolby A decoding on transfer to DAT.

**7. Review**
Here is where the writer describes the show. The writer's name appears on the last line of the review

This night rages throughout. The energy starts high and never lets up. In addition, we are offered some unique and awe-inspiring jams. . . . The first set is very uptempo with good jams in "Scarlet Begonias" and "Weather Report Suite." Bobby also regales us with the story of the Tomb of the Unknown Speaker. The Wall of Sound suffered many casualties. "Seastones" wails with air raid and drone themes.     JOHN DOE

# How to Read the Reviews

*Despite all the seemingly complicated symbols and data, reading the reviews in this book is actually quite simple. Below is a step-by-step explanation of an actual review. First, let's look at the data itself; then we'll explain what it means:*

1. **6/26/74, Civic Center, Providence, Rhode Island**
2. **Set 1:** Big River, Brown-Eyed Women, Beat It on Down the Line, Scarlet Begonias, Black-Throated Wind, Row Jimmy, Mexicali Blues, Deal, The Race Is On, Mississippi Half-Step, El Paso, Ship of Fools, Weather Report Suite > It Must Have Been the Roses
   **Interlude:** Seastones*
   **Set 2:** U.S. Blues, Me and My Uncle, Space > China Cat Sunflower > I Know You Rider, Truckin' > The Other One Jam > Spanish Jam > Wharf Rat > Sugar Magnolia
   **Encore:** Eyes of the World
3. **Personnel:** *with Ned Lagin
4. **1. Source:** AUD, **Quality:** A–/B+, **Length:** 3:20, **Genealogy:** MC > Reel, **Taper:** Jerry Moore
   **2. Source:** SBD, **Quality:** A+, **Length:** 2:50 (missing "Seastones," "U.S. Blues," and "Me and My Uncle"), **Genealogy:** MC > DAT > C.
   **3. Source:** FM-SBD (GDH 203), **Quality:** A+, **Length:** 0:20 (only "Space" through "I Know You Rider"), **Genealogy:** MC > DR.
5. **Highlights:** Space > China Cat Sunflower > I Know You Rider, Truckin' > The Other One Jam > Spanish Jam, Eyes of the World
6. **Comments:** (This is where technical notes regarding the tape quality appear.)
7. (This is where the review of the show appears.)

Here's how to understand what it all means:

1. **Date, Venue**
   **6/26/74, Civic Center, Providence, Rhode Island**

This denotes the date, concert hall, city, and state of the show. If there is an additional title to the concert ("Sufi benefit," or New Year's Eve, for example) this would be listed directly underneath this first line.

2. **Set 1:** Big River, Brown-Eyed Women, Beat It on Down the Line, Scarlet Begonias, Black-Throated Wind, Row Jimmy, Mexicali Blues, Deal, The Race Is On, Mississippi Half-Step, El Paso, Ship of Fools, Weather Report Suite > It Must Have Been the Roses
   **Interlude:** Seastones*
   **Set 2:** U.S. Blues, Me and My Uncle, Space > China Cat Sunflower > I Know You Rider, Truckin' > The Other One Jam > Spanish Jam > Wharf Rat > Sugar Magnolia
   **Encore:** Eyes of the World

Here is the list of songs played, often by sets and encore if known. The above-mentioned "Seastones" music was an electronic music presentation performed by Phil Lesh and Ned Lagin during Grateful Dead concert intermissions only between June 23, 1974, and October 20, 1974. On those occasions at which "Seastones" segued into the Dead's second set an arrow (">") follows the word "Seastones."

Symbols and Terms

- A guest star is denoted by the asterisk symbol (*).
- Cuts in the songs are denoted as follows:
  "//Big River" = part of the beginning of the song is missing

- "Big//River" = part of the middle of the song is missing
- "Big River//" = part of the ending of the song is missing
- An ">" indicates one song segues into the next song listed (or there's only a momentary pause between the two).
- A "jam" is a structured, melodic piece of instrumental music other than a formal song. Some jams are thoroughly improvised while some routinely played thematic jams *are* given titles, e.g., the "Mind Left Body Jam" (see the review of 6/28/74, Boston Garden, Boston). The jam itself will be described, often with glowing enthusiasm, by the writer in the text.
- A "space" is a piece of freeform or improvisational instrumental conversation other than a formal song or jam. "Space" usually implies a more rhythmless and/or nonmelodic segment, often sounding creepy, dark, mysterious, even scary at times.
- A "tease", e.g., "Saint Stephen Tease," means the band strongly and clearly begins the song or states the theme without singing the words.

**3. Personnel:** *with Ned Lagin.
This is where musicians other than the regular members of the Grateful Dead who appear on this tape are listed.

**4. 1. Source:** AUD, **Quality:** A–/B+, **Length:** 3:20, **Genealogy:** MC > Reel, **Taper:** Jerry Moore
**2. Source:** SBD, **Quality:** A+, **Length:** 2:50 (missing "Seastones," "U.S. Blues," and "Me and My Uncle"), **Genealogy:** MC > DAT > C.
**3. Source:** FM-SBD (GDH 203), **Quality:** A+, **Length:** 0:20 (only "Space" through "I Know You Rider"), **Genealogy:** MC > DR.

Herein lies the basic info for each of the different sources of the music. In this case there are three different sources for the music from this show which is in circulation.

## Source

- AUD = A microphone recording originating outside the Grateful Dead's sound system, usually by members of the audience. Should the person(s) who actually taped the show be known, they will be mentioned following the "Genealogy" by the term "Taper." Sometimes information regarding the equipment used by the taper will be supplied here as well.
- SBD = a soundboard recording originating from within the Grateful Dead's sound system.
- FM-SBD (GDH #_) = a recording that in most cases originated from the band's Vault and then was broadcast by David Gans on one of his radio shows, either the nationally syndicated *Grateful Dead Hour*, or *Dead to the World*, his local KPFA (Berkeley) broadcast, or various fund-raising marathons also on KPFA. While many tapers have recorded these shows off their FM receivers during broadcast it is preferable to get a tape made off the prebroadcast cassettes, compact discs, or DATs on which David sends his show to the radio stations. This is because the pre-FM signal leaves his studio with the full bandwidth, ideally up to 20 kHz, while FM radio has a frequency limit of 15 kHz. Additionally, the *Dead Hour* can be recorded from the NPR satellite feed by someone with access to a public radio station. If possible, tapers should note on their tapes which source their copies of this music came from.
- FM-SBD = a recording or live simulcast broadcast by a radio station—in many cases by a radio station in the city in which the Dead were currently playing. FM-SBDs are distinctly different from #2 and #3 sources above; they often contain static, a very rich bass sound, and an occasional (often poorly timed) blurb by the disk jockey.

## Length

This appears in hours and minutes, telling the length of each source. Songs in parentheses denote those that are either missing or solely available from the particular source in question. In the second example, the tape contains two hours and fifty minutes (2:50) of the music from this show, and all songs except for the three mentioned in parentheses ("Seastones," "U.S. Blues," and "Me and My Uncle").

If a song is mentioned with a cut symbol attached, i.e., "Row Jimmy//", then the song *is* included but it has a cut at the end.

## Quality

Here is a grading, from A+ to F, of the sound itself on the tape (A+ is a superlative recording, F is literally unlistenable). We tried hard to give a general grade, admittedly subjective, of a tape that one can get one's hands on without too much trouble. Should one find a "C+" SBD of the above show, for example, then one knows one would be wise to continue looking for a better copy.

Somewhat different rating criteria are used for soundboard and audience recordings. An A+ quality audience recording may not be as sonically pristine as an A+ quality soundboard recording in certain areas (such as separation of instruments, audibility of vocals, and lack of ambient noise) since it exists "outside" the Dead's sound system. However, some tapers find that high-quality audience tapes are more rewarding to listen to than soundboard recordings from the same show if they have more "warmth" or convey a degree of energy or excitement that cannot be found "inside" the system (the Watkins Glen soundcheck is an excellent example of this, for while the soundboard source is thoroughly delightful, it fails to convey the energy of the audience members as they react to the band's musical prowess at that show).

Most *Dead Hour* and Betty Board (more on Betty Boards later) source tapes are "A/A+" since they come directly from the master source with no generational loss. Usually soundboard source tapes which are given a low rating (below B) have suffered from poor analog recording technique (either improper recording levels or noise reduction settings, off-speed recording equipment, or multiple generations). But even a master AUD tape may receive a low rating because of factors such as poor recording equipment, technique, or location. Generally, for SBDs, tapes within a few analog generations of the master should sound quite good, A/A–, assuming the dubbers recorded properly with good, clean equipment and conscious meter settings and that there were no glitches on the master itself (i.e., buzzes from faulty patch-cords or distortion from too-high meter levels).

Multigenerational cassettes do not get an A+ rating (especially ones with no noise reduction). These are reserved for pure digital soundboards, digitals copied off of two-track master reels or quarter track masters at 7½ ips (inches per second—the speed at which the tape moves across the head) or faster, or the best front of the board (FOB) digital audience tape (like those made with properly spaced omni-directional mikes on six-foot stands).

The number of cuts or splices does *not* effect our grading system—only the sonic quality of the music itself. In this book any tape rated C+ on up can be enjoyed without too much difficulty. The advent of DATs, which copy with zero generational loss, means that the versions of any given tape in most tapers' collections are now of uniform quality—in other words, if digital taper X has a C+ quality version of a particular tape then more than likely the version of that same tape in digital taper Y's collection will also be a C+ quality.

### Genealogy

This denotes the origin of the tape as traced from its original master source all the way to . . . our tape decks! We have tried to indicate the lowest number of analog generations through which each recording has passed. We stop counting once that tape has made it on to a widely distributed digital format.

Symbols:

MC = Master cassette recording
MR = Master reel-to-reel recording
C = Cassette recording
RR = Reel-to-reel recording
DAT = Digital Audio Tape recording
DR = Unspecified digital realm recording (usually applies to the *Grateful Dead Hour*, for which David Gans records from the master recording to either DAT or a sonic solutions digital editing system)
PCM = Recording made on the initial version of consumer digital audio. It was accomplished using a digital processor that converted the signal from analog to digital and interfaced with a videocassette recorder storing the digital data on the video portion of videotape. Either VHS or Beta videotape recorders could be used; however, Beta was preferred by most due to its standard three-hour format, which allows most Dead concerts to fit on one tape.
LP = Long-play vinyl record

Now, back to our sample review, Source #2:
MC > DAT > C . . . this means that the master cassette was copied onto a DAT first, and then onto a cassette again, before finding its way into circulation.

Another example:
MR > DAT > C > C > C . . . this means the master reel was copied onto a DAT, and then copied three times onto different cassettes before being released into general circulation.

### 5. Highlights:

This is a purely subjective list of recommended highlights for those in search of "best versions" of specific songs.

### 6. Comments:

Here is where the writer may add some specific information as to the sound quality. For instance, he or she may say that there's a buzz in the first set songs but it disappears by the second set.

Readers will occasionally see the term "Betty Board" in the comments, genealogy, and/or review sections. This term refers to a cache of master or first-generation soundboard reel-to-reel recordings formerly in the possession of Betty Cantor-Jackson, a former recordist for the Grateful Dead. In 1986 this cache of tapes, numbering in the hundreds, was sold at a repossession auction. Many of these recordings were transfered to the digital realm and were widely distributed in trading circles. They remain among the most pristine and highly treasured Grateful Dead recordings in circulation.

### 7. Review:

Here is where the writer describes the show. The writer's name appears on the last line of the review.

## A Closing Thought

This book is an ongoing project. We make no claims to have all the data or the final word on anything here. In fact, we heartily welcome and encourage readers to notify us of any information they feel is missing or needs revision. Your feedback will help make this project more complete and accurate. Should you have any info on new tapes, access to previously uncirculated tapes, upgrades to existing ones, genealogical data, who taped a specific show, etc., then *please* contact us in care of our publishers and we'll be all ears.

*The Deadhead's Taping Compendium*
Henry Holt and Company, Inc.
115 West 18th Street
New York, New York 10011

# 5

# Grateful Jams

*by William Polits*

Throughout history musical creators have taken parts of compositions by others and woven them into their works. As far back as the fifteenth century, Palestrina was famous for his masses, which parodied works by other composers. Since then Brahms gave us the great "Variations on a Theme of Haydn," and ballets by Stravinsky refer to popular song and sacred chant again and again. And in his Ninth Symphony, Beethoven even finds space in the final movement to refer to all the preceding movements. But with the advent of the Grateful Dead into the annals of music history, the practice of copping the musical material of others—and one's own—was brought to new turf: improvised music in the rock 'n' roll idiom.

Without a doubt, this ability to find fresh contexts for disparate musical strands made Grateful Dead concerts rich experiences for the band and the audience alike. The knowledge that at any moment a tiny hint could turn the whole show in a different direction had the effect of keeping listeners aware and alert to musical subtleties. The following is my humble attempt to trace some of the musical references found within the Dead's jams, in an attempt to shed some light on how these jams came to be. Any technical jargon I've used is intended not to make any of this cryptic, but rather to help pave the way for deeper levels of comprehension.

## "Uncle John's Jam"

"Uncle John's Jam" as performed on November 8, 1969, at the Fillmore is a wacky gem. It consists of a dang near note-for-note instrumental version of the song "Uncle John's Band." That's right, no vocals! This jam preceded the first live version of the song by four whole weeks and the release of the recorded version by six months.

In contrast to the tame gait of the song that all know and love so dearly, the jam is like a blistering Irish reel. If you're a listener familiar with the solid, even pace of this tune, the frenetic tempo of the jam will likely make you shake your head in disbelief. Not that it sounded the least surprising to anyone in 1969, but it might be compared to hearing a live orchestra play Beethoven's "Ode to Joy" in a fancy concert hall, with the musicians sounding like a 33 rpm LP on the 45 rpm setting.

Rewinding the tape and playing it again, you might notice there's something else that seems different. On closer listening, the jam turns up in the key of D. The song we know as "Uncle John's Band" is in the key of G. Though these two keys are closely linked harmonically, the change of key puts the melody in a contrasting register, which I have to say is very strange.

Which came first, the Dhicken or the Gegg? In this case it is arguable that, from a guitarist's point of view, the key of D is better than G for whipping out that particular melody. Then, perhaps when the tune was adapted for the group, the key change was necessary to make it singable. But I could be wrong about this.

It was played at the previous evening's performance too. The band fumbled their way through it (remember, no vocals!) on November 7, 1969, but given that they played it twice in a row, and that they got better the second time, it is likely that they practiced it a good bit.

### "Feelin' Groovy Jam"

The D–C-sharp minor—B minor–A jam that often grew out of "Dark Star" and later came between "China Cat Sunflower" and "I Know You Rider" has come to be known as the "Feelin' Groovy Jam" for good reason: it is wholly congruent with the chord pattern of the hit by Simon and Garfunkel, "The 59th St. Bridge Song," aka "Feelin' Groovy"—although Paul Simon played it with open chords in the key of G with a capo on the third fret. According to our best sources, the first "Feelin' Groovy Jam" occurred on September 26, 1969, at the Fillmore East. The first time it appeared as the filling in a "China" > "Rider" sandwich appears to have been March 19, 1973, at the Nassau Coliseum.

The way that this jam is played really varies very little from the "Dark Star" to the "China" > "Rider" contexts, apart from the consistently peppy tempos in the latter. The main difference lies in the tonal center of the music preceding and following the "Feelin' Groovy" music. In the "Dark Star" context, the last chord of the "Feelin' Groovy" progression, the A major chord, is the home key. In this respect, the "Dark Star" context is more closely related to the Simon and Garfunkel original. In the "China" > "Rider" version, the first chord of the "Feelin' Groovy Jam," D major, is the home key. To counter the ambiguity in this tonal reference, the band would do an eight-bar stint on a G-major chord to decisively close out the "Feelin' Groovy Jam" and signal the beginning of "Rider."

An interesting aspect of the "Feelin' Groovy Jam" is its similarity to the intro music of "Uncle John's Band." Specifically, the bass line from "Feelin' Groovy" is harmonically interchangeable with that from "Uncle John's Band," and the cadence is identical. This suggests that the intro of "Uncle John's Band" may be derived from New York City's 59th Street Bridge. That this jam served as a link between "China" and "Rider" illumines the hidden meaning of the word "bridge" all the more.

### "Mind Left Body Jam"

The "Mind Left Body Jam" is unmistakably lifted from the Paul Kantner song "Your Mind Has Left Your Body," from the album by Grace Slick and Paul Kantner, *Baron Von Tollbooth and the Chrome Nun*. The Grateful Dead jam is the same as the main meat of the song. The song has a few chordal quirks that the jam lacks. The song is in the key of D, as are the later versions of the jam, although earlier Dead versions of the jam are in A major. The chords go like this: A, A7, D, Dm. In the early A-major version, the Dead inserted a rocked-up interlude on the dominant chord (E major) every once in a while. This dominant chord break is absent from the later versions.

### "Spanish Jam"

"Spanish Jam" is an E-major–F-major (or E-major–D-minor/F bass) chord pattern over a Spanish dance rhythm known as a bolero; it is nearly identical to the main riff from "White Rabbit" by the Airplane or the intro to Deep Purple's version of "Hey Joe." But the true Grateful Dead antecedent for this jam may very well be that particular six-bar passage from "Born Cross-eyed" on *Anthem of the Sun*, immediately after the lyric, "Think I'll come back here again, every now and then, from time to time." This passage from *Anthem* features Phil on trumpet in a vein aptly reminiscent of Miles Davis' "Sketches of Spain."

### "Main Ten Jam"

The jam known as "The Main Ten," originally from a Mickey Hart solo album, eventually took final form as an important interlude section in the Weir-Hunter tune, "Playing in the Band." "The Main Ten," however, is decidedly in the key of E minor, whereas the interlude in "Playing" is in D major. Yet another instance of the jam growing up and then conforming to the needs of the singer. "The Main Ten Jam" finds Lesh playing the important melodic figure that eventually shows up in an ornamented pattern on Weir's fingerboard, harmonized by Garcia a major sixth above. In the song, Lesh is forced to give up this tasty melodic pattern for a more traditional bass line. This passage, originally rooted in a minor mode, formed an integral part of "Playing" jams as performed by the Dead in later years. Typically, after a late first-set foray into jamming on "Playing," Garcia would often invoke this riff in the minor mode to signal an end to the jam and a return to the interlude-bridge-chorus reprise that would bring the song to full close.

### "Philo Stomp" Jam

"Philo Stomp," named by David Gans and Dick Latvala, is a catchy tune composed of riffs that highlight

Lesh's facility playing chords on the bass. I mean, his playing goes to the point of suggesting "who the hell needs guitarists, anyway?!" The chord areas are D, A, G, B, E, A, and back to D. Bass players should have fun discovering how Lesh "voices" this one.

### "Darkness Jam"

"Darkness Jam" gets its title from the song "Darkness, Darkness" by the Youngbloods. Signaled by Garcia on lead guitar, the bold and unmistakable melody emanates, and on some versions, like the 9/19/70 Fillmore East version, Bob and Phil take the cue and supply the chordal background, gently rocking back and forth between chords with E and D roots.

### "Mountain Jam"

"Mountain Jam" consists of the main melody from Donovan's 1967 hit "First There Is a Mountain" slipped into a free jam centered on an E-major chord. For a period there, Garcia would slip it in during the "Not Fade Away" jams for melodic interest.

### Editor's Note: "Tiger" Jam

By the summer of '72 Garcia had developed a specific technique for playing a repetitive "meltdown" riff known to many as the "Tiger" jam. After many years of wondering how Garcia was able to accomplish this stunning technique, we finally obtained an uncut copy of the unreleased film known as *Sunshine Daydream* that included the "Dark Star" from August 27, 1972, in Veneta, Oregon, and, much to our delight, found that it features closeup shots of Garcia's hands while he plays this riff. One can clearly see that during this segment he rapidly repeats four consecutive descending notes while strumming very fast and brushing other deadened strings all while pumping the wah-wah pedal with his foot. This technique results in the quintessential "meltdown" sound.

# Commonly Mislabeled Tapes

*Compiled by Darren E. Mason*

## Intent

This listing is an attempt to identify commonly mislabeled tapes that are known to exist in trading circles (as of 3/18/97). Although *DeadBase IX* has an "up-to-date" listing of mislabeled tapes, it is far from exhaustive. In recent years, especially with the use of the Internet to distribute tapes worldwide, many errors, caused either through ignorance, mischief, or poor handwriting, have been observed reproducing like so many lab rabbits. In an effort to identify these mistakes and prevent their further proliferation, this list has been compiled.

## Format

The tapes are listed in chronological order, according to the mislabeled date. Additional information follows that specifically outlines the labeling error. Occasional errors in *DeadBase* are identified when appropriate. To see timings for tapes from pre-1965 through 1974, please see the detailed lists of Eric Doherty and Jeff Tiedrich at their Web sites (see Resources).

**1/17/68:** This "Golden Road" > "New Potato Caboose" is the same performance from 5/5/57 that was released by the Bay Area Tapers Group.

**2/24/68:** This tape is actually from 2/14/68, but is missing the opening song. Supposedly David Gans aired this tape on his local broadcast program, and the tape has been subsequently relabeled as 2/24/68.

**3/22/68:** Actually 8/22/68; on some tapes it is a hybrid of 8/21/68 and 8/22/68. Specifically, the "Alligator" > "Feedback" sequence is from 8/21/68 with the drums edited down to about 30 seconds.

**3/30/68:** Almost always 11/11/67; true copies definitely exist but are rather hard to find. The set list for the legit copy is "//Morning Dew," "Cryptical Envelopment" > "The Other One" > "Cryptical Envelopment" > "Dark Star" > "China Cat" > "The Eleven//."

**6/15/68:** This is a mislabeled and rearranged copy of the previous night of 6/14/68.

**9/22/68:** Actually the first set and encore from 8/21/68.

**10/13/68:** The "Morning Dew" is really from 1/14/67.

**5/3/69b:** Although this is often mislabeled as 8/29/69, true copies do exist. However, they generally possess an error in history. In particular, the tape of 5/3/69b is an audience tape recorded with a 7½ ips reel from the stage (miked monitors).

**6/6/69:** This tape commonly circulates as "Green, Green Grass of Home," "Dire Wolf," "Dupree's Diamond Blues," and "Mountains of the Moon." However, only "The Green, Green Grass of Home" is from this date. The remaining songs are from an unknown date and venue.

**7/12/69:** Audience recording. From "Alligator" to about half of the "Other One" is from 7/11/69. Following a very clean, hard-to-discern splice, the "Other One" continues to "Lovelight" except that now the recording is from 7/12/69.

**8/29/69:** This tape is a mislabeled copy of 8/30/69.

**9/6/69:** "Dancin'" > "Casey Jones" from the beginning is really a SBD copy of the same sequence from

6/22/69. Indeed, the ">" is not a segue at all but an obvious splice that has been placed at the beginning of the tape.

**11/7/69:** The portion "Dark Star" > end is often 2/13/70 without the "We Bid You Goodnight." Additionally, *DeadBase* is incorrect in its listing for 11/7/69. The true set list for 11/7/69 from the "Dark Star" on is "Dark Star" > "Uncle John's Band Jam" > "Dark Star" > "Cryptical Envelopment" > "Drums" > "Other One" > "Lovelight." 11/7/69 does not have a "Cryptical" on the down side of the "Other One," and "We Bid You Goodnight" was not played that evening.

**2/12/70:** "Clapton with Dead" is really from 2/12/70, containing Fleetwood Mac with Peter Green, Eric Clapton, and Junior Wells at the Tea Party in Boston. The encore jam complete is available in AUD source timed at 16:09; the complete tape includes introductions.

**3/21/70a:** This tape is actually the early "a" performance from 6/24/70a. For further information, see the 6/24/70a.

**4/9/70:** This tape is usually 4/12/70 rearranged. However, it is rumored that there is a correct first-set SBD in circulation.

**5/19/70:** This tape is actually from May 1, 1970, Alfred College; Alfred, New York. No show was played on May 19, 1970. It is rumored that the master Grateful Dead reels for this show (7½" size) were found under the stage at the May 14, 1970, show at Merremac Community College.

**6/24/70a:** This tape is actually from a currently unknown date and venue. It turns out that what had been circulating as 3/21/70a is the true 6/24/70a performance. What was circulating as 6/24/70a is currently unknown.

**7/10/70:** This soundboard is really 4/12/70; no soundboard copy of 7/10/70 exists to my knowledge.

**8/28/70:** This tape actually includes songs from 12/10/69 that *DeadBase* no longer lists under 12/10/69. Though the exact date for these songs is still in question, they do come from the 12/69 Thelma Theatre run.

**3/18/71:** The SBD fragment that is circulating under this date is actually from 2/18/71.

**11/14/71:** This tape is often a mislabeled copy of 11/12/71 AUD; there do exist legitimate audience copies of 11/14/71, albeit skeevy ones.

**6/17/72:** Set 2, the only set purported to circulate, is a mislabeled copy of 11/20/71 set two. The way to tell that this is really 11/20/71 is that before "Truckin'," Keith is introduced and Bobby mentions Turlock, and Jerry calls Bobby "Mr. Show Biz."

**10/21/72:** This tape is a mislabeled copy of 12/31/72. One main identifying characteristic of 12/31/72 is the presence of an "internal 'Other One'" "Drums" sequence *and* Mr. Crosby's guitar. The second set of this show, in particular the "Truckin'" > "Other One" > "Morning Dew" sequence *may* be available in AUD only, while the first set *may* be available in SBD. However, I have never heard legitimate copies of either.

**10/23/72:** The SBD version "Dark Star" > "Half Step" really has a "Weather Report Suite" prelude in the middle of the recording and actually is 11/19/72. 10/23/72 is only available in AUD format.

**2/22/73:** The SBD "Dark Star" > "Eyes" is actually from 2/26/73. In fact, the "Dark Star" from 2/22 is available only as an AUD source and is considerably shorter than the "Dark Star" from 2/26. To differentiate between the two, notice that the "Dark Star" on 2/22 is 13:38 minutes long and the "Dark Star" on 2/26 is 26:16 minutes long (these timings are approximate). To further confuse things, someone, at some point in time, spliced together songs from various '72–'74 SBD sources—their identity is as yet unknown—to create a tape that matches the set list in *DeadBase* from "Dark Star" to the end, thereby producing a legitimate sounding SBD copy of set two. However, the splices on these copies are obvious and the song versions are definitely *not* all from spring '73. Upon comparison to the true audience recording for this date, these tapes are found to be imposters.

**12/12/73:** "Pride of Cucamonga" and "Unbroken Chain" from "this soundcheck" are really 1974 studio rehearsals. This tape was furnished by Dario Wolfish with the correct information. Somehow mislabeling has occurred.

# 7

## The Reviews

## 1959–1965

By the time the Grateful Dead played their first gig under their new name in December 1965, at least two of their members were already well established in the Bay Area music scene. Jerry Garcia had been active in the folk scene on the San Mateo peninsula since the early sixties, while Pigpen had been playing blues clubs for a couple of years. Phil Lesh had also been a presence in some of the more avant-garde circles centered around the College of San Mateo. Most of the Dead's members had been playing together as a group for about a year, first in 1964 as Mother McCree's Uptown Jug Champions (without Lesh or Kreutzmann) and then, beginning around May 1965, as the Warlocks.

There are several tapes in circulation featuring members of the Grateful Dead in their previous incarnations. Most of these are tapes of Garcia's pre-Dead bands, including the Sleepy Hollow Hog Stompers (1962), the Wildwood Boys, who included future Grateful Dead lyricist Robert Hunter along with David Nelson of the New Riders (1963), Jerry and Sara, Garcia's then wife (also from 1963), and the Black Mountain Boys, also with David Nelson (1963 and 1964). A few songs are available of Mother McCree's band from 1964. As for the other band members, the pickings are slim indeed. There are a few tapes of Pigpen performing solo and with Janis Joplin, Peter Albin from Big Brother, or Jorma Kaukonen of the Jefferson Airplane, each containing only a few songs. There are two tapes relating to Phil from this period. One is a jazz recital from his student days at the college of San Mateo, the other an avant-garde performance piece composed by Phil and played by an ensemble that included Tom Constanten, later to be a short-time member of the Dead.

As you will gather from the wonderful reviews written for this chapter by Nick Meriwether, Garcia was the most prominent musician in the days before the Dead. He was a major presence in the peninsular folk and bluegrass world, playing in a myriad of bands, often simultaneously. Through these circles, Garcia crossed paths with Hunter, Pigpen, and Lesh. He also spent his time teaching guitar at Dana Morgan's music store. Among his students was a young kid named Bob Weir. Eventually Garcia and Pigpen got together with Weir to form Mother McCree's Uptown Jug Champions, later adding Bill Kreutzmann and Dana Morgan Jr., son of the music store's owner, to form the Warlocks. They started by playing covers of current pop and R&B hits, combined with old blues and jug-band standards, at a series of gigs at Magoo's Pizza Parlor in Menlo Park. Within a month, Dana Morgan had been replaced by Phil. Garcia had persuaded him to pick up the bass and learn the instrument, and within a few weeks, Lesh was playing it with the band.

Later, after occasional gigs around the San Francisco suburbs, the new band got a standing gig at the In Room in Belmont, California, on the San Mateo peninsula. The gig lasted for thirty shows in six weeks. This became their de facto rehearsal hall until they went to Mother's in San Francisco to record a demo tape. This demo has been in wide circulation for years and is one *of only two tapes available of the entire band from 1965.*

*Soon after the studio session, the band was informed that the name "Warlocks" was in use elsewhere. Needing to change their name, they gathered at Phil's house one afternoon and, while flipping through a Webster's New World Dictionary, Garcia came upon the words "Grateful Dead," which referred to a series of Scottish ballads. The Grateful Dead was born.*

*At about this same time, Ken Kesey and his group, the Merry Pranksters, began putting on the Acid Tests; they invited the Dead to perform. Eventually, they became the house band at these events. It was here that their popularity in the newly formed psychedelic scene began.*

---

### ❊ 4/59 ❊
**Unknown location, probably the College of San Mateo auditorium. The College of San Mateo Jazz Band**

I'll Remember April, Wail, Frail, Finnegan's Awake, Unknown

---

**Source:** SBD, **Quality:** B, **Length:** 0:26, **Genealogy:** MR > RR > C > DAT > [?]

**Highlights:** Finnegan's Awake

**Personnel:** Phil Lesh, trumpet, in a nineteen-piece band First trumpet (1, 3, 4), and Lesh's chart (2, 3)

**Comments:** As the earliest Dead-related tape in circulation, this is an education in Lesh's musical development. Variously dated April 5 and April 9, 1959, there is so far no way of determining precisely when the concert happened.

For an amateur tape of this age, it has remarkably good sound. Some audience noise is audible during quiet passages, especially on "I'll Remember April." Obviously assembled from longer tapes, the sound is noticeably better on the cuts at the end. Brief introductions precede each song.

In general, the music is an Ellington-style big band sound, especially apparent on "I'll Remember April," and performed by a nineteen-piece band: five trumpets, five saxophones, five trombones, and four rhythm instruments.

In a later interview, Phil remembered that "playing in a unit like that knocks your socks off.... When they're swinging together, it's really an experience. Not even a symphony orchestra is quite like it."[1] Jerry remembered Phil's work here as Stan Kenton–styled arrangements, with Phil playing "screechy Maynard Ferguson parts, pass out on the stage!"[2]

In a patronizing introduction to Lesh's first arrangement, the announcer makes it sound like a beatnik-style "hepcat" composition: "... and it's called, get this, 'Wail, Frail.'" Everyone snicker together now—those kids! It falters a little at first, but soon settles into a solid rendition of a demanding and intricate piece. These were Lesh's first two efforts at composition, which he later called "more or less mainstream stuff; I just wanted to see what would happen if I wrote it down and they played it."[3] "Ellingtonized bop" would be a good way of characterizing them: demanding and still melodic—and very tightly controlled. Lots of dynamics, strong contrasts, quick, difficult changes, and selective dissonance: rarely are both lead and backing instruments playing melodically. One may be sweet, the other discordant, always playing with harmonics, pushing the blend to the edge of cacophony. When Phil leads, as is especially apparent on "Finnegan's Awake," the band really swings. He clearly has a bandleader's confidence, and he sounds marvelous. It's so sad to think of only having one little fragment of his trumpet playing in the Dead's repertoire (on *Anthem of the Sun*). But this is so clear an indication of what would become his hallmarks as a member of the Dead: angular melodicism, complex arrangements, and powerful, dense musical textures. For someone who had turned nineteen only a month before, it is impressive.

NICK MERIWETHER

---

1. David Gans, *Conversations with the Dead* (New York: Citadel Underground, 1991), p. 93.
2. Ralph Gleason, *The Jefferson Airplane and the San Francisco Sound* (New York: Ballantine, 1969), p. 310.
3. David Gans and Peter Simon, *Playing in the Band: An Oral and Visual Portrait of the Grateful Dead* (New York: St. Martin's, 1985), p. 27.

## 🌀 1961 [?] 🌀

**Jerry Garcia and Friends
Boarshead Coffee House,
San Carlos, California [?]**

Bolshevik in Hell, Rose Connely, Long Lonesome Road, Railroad Bill, Wagoneers West, Fortune, Hand Me My Money Down, Greenback Dollar (instrumental), I'm a Good Ol' Rebel, Wealthy Old Maid

**Source:** AUD, **Quality:** B, **Length:** 0:26, **Genealogy:** MR > RR > C > DAT > [?]

**Highlights:** Long Lonesome Road, Railroad Bill

**Personnel:** [?] Jerry Garcia: guitar, 12-string guitar, banjo, vocals; Marshall Leicester: banjo, guitar, vocals; Robert Hunter: bass[?], vocals

**Comments:** This tape frequently appears appended to the Garcia and Leicester 1961 performance, usually labeled as part of that material. No mention of it appears in the current standard Garcia tapeographies, such as the one in Sandy Troy's biography of Garcia, *Captain Trips*. Most lists also have at least one phantom title, usually "Women's C/B Doin' Day," which theoretically appears between "Fortune" and "Hand Me My Money Down," though no tape so far seems to bear that out.

This is only the start of the confusion over this performance. On a good copy, it's apparent that at least three players are present, not two; most tapes in circulation only list Garcia and Hunter. No date or place is certain either, but one of Garcia's between-song quips mentions that this is the "sixth or seventh" time they've played there, so it's likely that it is the Boarshead.

Hunter starts things off with "Bolshevik in Hell," already in progress as the tape fades in. The voice sounds like Robert Hunter's distinctive baritone, and the tune is a peppy, lighthearted topical folk song. Hunter—if that's who it is—sounds good, a typical coffeehouse folkie of his day. In the patter afterward, he introduces the next song by saying that "it was written for the express purpose of being sung after the bomb was dropped." The cut in the tape that follows means we're not sure how the audience greeted this pronouncement.

But the next song, "Rose Connely," comes off well. A song that Garcia apparently never tired of, it reappeared a decade later in Old and In the Way's repertoire, in an arrangement very similar to the one here. It fades in after it has already started, and after one drop-out at the beginning, the tape sounds fine. Garcia sings lead and is in good voice, a nice folk tenor, but what will please aficionados is the fingerpicking guitar duet, the heart of this rendition. It also shows that they are fully warmed up, ready for the demands of "Long Lonesome Road." A furious, fast-paced duet, this does sound like the Garcia and Hunter familiar to us from later decades. Upbeat and good-natured, what shines here is the sweet tone and infectious rhythm. Strong interplay makes this an altogether credible folk sound, and the healthy applause at the end—only a moment before it fades out—shows that they're clicking, clearly.

Garcia provides the patter before the next song, calling it "an old chestnut" and adding that "here's this twelve-string. And I don't know if I can do it on a twelve-string, but it'll be fun to find out." He can, and "Railroad Bill" comes off well, Garcia needling the audience to join in the chorus: "It's only one word three times, think you can do it?" They do, and the full flavor and charm of a coffeehouse folk sing comes through plainly. Garcia sounds very, very good: sweet-voiced, though singing lower than he does on any other circulating tape from this period, a definite baritone part, not tenor. The audience chorusing along here actually sounds good as well: There are some good voices in the murk, one pretty soprano in particular who sings counterpoint to the chorus of "Ride, ride, ride."

Another fade-out between songs, and then we have a treat: Garcia unaccompanied on "Wagoneers West," one of the two solo a cappella Garcia songs we have. His voice sounds good, distinctive but sweet-timbred, and well suited to what he's singing: strong, colorful and unpolished, a reminder of the influence he acknowledged then of fellow Palo Altoan Joan Baez and her controlled, unaffected delivery. Garcia does not sing like a city boy, though: he interjects definite folkie-isms, and affects a passable Appalachian inflection in several places. As you listen, it's apparent that a hush has fallen over the room, and it makes you wonder, is he really going over that well? The applause at end confirms that he really did have them eating out of his hand. All in all, a wonderful folk anthem.

"Fortune" is a powerful banjo and guitar workout. Beginning strongly, it's a sweet, mournful tune, the plaintive cast giving it the lilt of a folk ballad from the British Isles. It's also a nice platform for some good picking and singing. "Hand Me My Money Down" is a rousing audience sing-along, with Garcia laughingly goading them,

"Catch on quick, don't ya?" It's clearly a favorite; the chemistry is palpable here. And it's fun, a good instrumental romp, although you get the feeling this is probably exactly what Garcia was thinking of when he later referred to this era as "my dippy folk period." Still, it shows talent, charisma, dedication, and most of all, ample evidence of his enjoyment—and pursuit—of that elusive communion of audience and performer.

"Green Back Dollar" fades in already in progress, a pleasant, fast-paced bluegrass workout, in the same mood as "Hand Me My Money Down." With the audience roaring along, it sounds like kind of a mess, sonically, and there is a definite end-of-the-evening sloppiness to it, when everything is going along so swimmingly that the band isn't particularly worried about anything, is taking lots of risks and generally having a good time. Next is an unlabeled instrumental, not marked on any tape I've encountered. As with "Green Back Dollar," it showcases some superb mandolin and banjo work, in this case more a rag than a ballad.

"I'm a Good Ol' Rebel" has Hunter singing the cowboy song with Innes Randolph's Reconstruction-era poem, "The Good Old Rebel," put to a peppy, uptempo bluegrass tune.[1] The cheerful mood sounds a bit incongruous on lines like "I hate the glorious Union,/'Tis dripping with our blood" and "three hundred thousand Yankees is stiff in Southern dust," but it gets lots of appreciative hoots and applause; the audience obviously enjoys the persona that Hunter adopts for his presentation. "Wealthy Old Maid" is also Hunter's, with the audience joining in on the chorus. A whimsical folk song, it's clearly an audience favorite, or perhaps Hunter simply does very well with the audience-singer interaction. With clever call-and-response lines, Hunter shows an excellent sense of pacing and delivery, especially on the funnier verses, which get increasingly good as the song continues. By the end, the audience is belting out the chorus, "It's a very unfortunate, very unfortunate, a very unfortunate man." Perhaps a dippy folk song, but pretty funny nonetheless. And a charming slice of what Garcia called "the Great Folk Scare," when so many talented musicians discovered the Folkways anthology and Carl Sandburg's *The American Songbag*.

NICK MERIWETHER

---

### 1962[?]
**Jerry Garcia and Friends**
**Boarshead Coffee House,**
**above the San Carlos Bookstall,**
**San Carlos, California**

Banjo Soup, Ellen Smith, Brown's Ferry Blues, Jesse James, D-tuning Session Rap, What Will Become of Me, All the Good Times Are Past, Darling Cory

---

**Source:** AUD, **Quality:** B, **Length:** 0:29, **Genealogy:** MR > RR > C > DAT > [?]

**Highlights:** Jesse James, Darling Cory

**Personnel:** Instrument voices: guitar, banjo, autoharp [some songs only], bass, fiddle [some songs only]; Jerry Garcia: vocals, Unknown: vocals

**Comments:** Like so many of the early tapes, this set has been edited and mislabeled almost beyond recognition. One of the more common mistakes calls it "Garcia and Hunter, Boarshead Folk Festival, 1962." It is usually appended with material from other early Garcia shows, and many tapeographies do not list the first song. One possibility is that it is the Wildwood Boys, circa 1962 or perhaps even early 1963; this more or less jibes with the sound of other tapes with David Nelson, Jerry Garcia, and Robert Hunter, the basic group that Hunter later recalled "had at least a dozen different names."[1] One fragment in circulation corroborates this, listing it as "1962 Boar's Head, Garcia, Hunter, Nelson." Another famous mislabel is "Garcia, Leicester, July, 1961," but even a cursory listen reveals a bass player, and there's a fiddle and possibly an autoharp on a couple of tracks, which may mean Dick Arnold as well. The most likely bassist is Hunter, of course. The July 1961 date is the most interesting mislabel—it seems to be an example of one of those tapes that hungry fans willed into existence ("Garcia's first folk gigs!"), and latched on to this conveniently vague set as a possible graft for the wish.

---

1. Garcia would have learned it as a song, not as a poem. Reported as anonymous in most anthologies, the poem was first reported as a song, stripped down to four stanzas, in John A. Lomax's historic 1906 anthology *Cowboy Songs*. Its authorship and status as a poem were not generally known until the 1954 publication of Jay Hubbell's landmark *The South in American Literature*, which devotes a chapter to Randolph. See Jay B. Hubbell, *The South in American Literature, 1607–1900* (Durham, N.C.: Duke University Press, 1954), pp. 479–81.

1. *Relix*, vol. 5, no. 2 (May–June, 1978), p. 22.

Until better information surfaces, what we have is an interesting indication of Jerry's development as a folk picker and singer. The tape is clearly an amateur audience tape: lots of crowd noise and chatter at first, along with the sounds of banjo tuning in the background, appropriate for a musician who would shortly become known for his extended tuning breaks on stage. A leisurely tune-up, with the bass an obvious presence, it moves easily from tuning with lots of chatter from the audience to a warm-up jam, which quiets the place nicely; one can't help but notice that it's just the sort of low-key start that the Dead favored. "Banjo Soup" is a pleasant, slow, steady strum-and-pick, accelerating a little as they play but basically staying grounded until part way through, where there is some stepping out, a few spins and reels to make it interesting, and it gets a good solid round of applause by the end, despite the background hum of talk.

All of the tapes I've heard have fade-outs between songs, probably to eliminate tuning and patter. It's too bad, because the between-song talk we do have can be interesting and funny, as well as informative, as the bit before "Ellen Smith" shows. "We always had a sort of basic abuse-the-audience attitude," Garcia recalled in a late interview. "Once they were in there, they were yours and you could do whatever you wanted to them. That was part of the fun of playing those little clubs."[2] With the audience attuned and attentive, Jerry's patter is relaxed and good-natured, and provides a tantalizing bit of information about the set when he notes, to great laughter, that "last night, just about this time, we were gonna do a song. We finally did do it, called 'Ellen Smith.' And ah—but the trouble was last night, a banjo string broke. A very key one: the fifth one, the one that distinguishes it from a cigar box." "Ellen Smith" is a classic coffeehouse sing-along that has a great deal of charm. Buoyed by an infectious enthusiasm, it provides a genuine insight into what kind of magic must have enticed a young, ambitious artist wavering between painting and music into the latter: just listen to what impact you could have singing and playing and sweeping an audience along with you. This is an easygoing demonstration of Jerry's mastery of the banjo, and the vocals sound quite good, admirably suited to the simplicity of the tune. Light applause afterward drifts off quickly into the chatter of an inattentive audience until Jerry finally grows impatient, saying, "Hey, you guys wanna talk?" An interesting situation to hear him in, and the only such example we have on these tapes.

None of that shows in "Brown's Ferry Blues" (listed on some tapes as "Wildwood Flower"), which features some great instrumental work. They roll into the song, and the band just belts it out, providing a showcase for Garcia's distinctive musical feel, already fully evident. Most fans unfamiliar with Garcia's early material will concur with a Deadhead friend who, on hearing this, commented, "That's our Jerry, all right." Already. A gem, "Jesse James" shows great enthusiasm, with a strong, powerful chorus, and most of all, a sense of how much chaotic fun a coffeehouse performance could be. This is the sort of feel you hear in tapes of Mother McCree's Jug Band a couple of years later, after Garcia tired of the bluegrass purist kick he went on shortly after his folkie period. Listeners will probably be mystified about why there is so much audience noise at first. Before launching into "Jesse James," Jerry gives a little warm-up patter, which sounds like it falls flat, and starts the tune with a ferocious attack. Striking hard, he accelerates the pace faster and faster, turning it into a romp, almost manic, pulling the audience along finally—and receiving lots of applause at the end.

Garcia is still interested in needling the crowd about their rudeness, noting, "Now we're gonna have a lot of fun. Which will be something different for you all, I guess"—the cynical beatnik coming out. But this goes both ways, with various audience members retorting and heckling; you can hear a faint "I want my opinion back," before Jerry launches into The Rap: "What we're gonna do now is tune. See, 'cause we're gonna play this next thing with a guitar in D-tuning, which is notoriously difficult to tune into. So, if any of you have any long-distance phone calls to make, parking tickets to pay, or anything like that, you can do it now." The end of Jerry's rap is drowned out in audience indifference and chatter, which is pretty funny, as Jerry goes valiantly on, sensing he's lost them again: "The song we're gonna do now is one that's sung by the New Lost City Ramblers. If you've ever heard the New Lost City Ramblers, you know that they play mostly old-time music, and this is an approximation of the same sort of thing. Except that we're not the New Lost City Ramblers, contrary to popular opinion. They don't look like us." Another band member pipes up: "We have to settle for the Kingston Trio," which gets another round of laughs. Jerry adds, woefully, "You know how it is," eliciting more laughter; clearly, this is the folk-purist audience. The banter and put-downs continue for a while, and the

---

2. Blair Jackson, "Hunter / Garcia: words / music," *The Golden Road*, no. 25 (Spring 1991), p. 29.

tuning really does seem to go on too long, but finally we get "What Will Become of Me," a peppy, fast-paced good-natured bluegrass rag. Then they announce the last song, which is "All Good Times Are Past and Gone," a rousing sing-along to close the set. And musically it sounds kind of horrific, actually, but in more an amusing than offensive way, partly because the humor and the enthusiasm come through clearly. "We're not getting full cooperation," says Jerry at one point, exhorting greater feats of off-key chorusing from the audience, which gives us the rowdiest slice of coffeehouse folk that we have on these tapes.

Jerry announces the encore by saying, "For those of you that are interested, we're gonna do one more. Not because any of you asked or anything, but just because we felt like it." And the communal feeling continues without a lapse, band and audience launching into "Darling Cory" as if on cue. And here, everyone sounds almost in tune with each other, with the applause at the end as much a celebration of the audience as the musicians. What it lacks in polish, it more than makes up for in spirit. This is what a hootenanny must have sounded like at its peak.

NICK MERIWETHER

---

### ❄ 6/62[?] ❄
**The Sleepy Hollow Hog Stompers**
**The Boarshead, San Carlos Jewish Community Center, San Carlos, California[?]**

Top of the Hill, Billy Grimes, Taking That Old Cannonball, Okim Dinkem Dairy, Buck Dancer's Choice, Little Birdie*, Sally Goodun, Hold the Woodpile Down, I Love Chicken Pie, Hop Up Pretty Girls, Don't Be Afraid, Shady Grove, Uncle Joe, Sweet Sunny South, Boarding House Blues, Man of Constant Sorrow†, Yonder He Goes, Three Men Went a-Hunting

* Jerry Garcia, solo banjo and vocal
† Jerry Garcia, a cappella vocal

---

**Source:** AUD, **Quality:** B, **Length:** 1:03, **Genealogy:** MR > C > DAT > [?]

**Highlights:** Buck Dancer's Choice, Little Birdie, Shady Grove

**Personnel:** Jerry Garcia: guitar, banjo, vocals; Marshall Leicester: banjo, guitar, vocals; Dick Arnold: fiddle

**Comments:** With much the same ambience as the preceding tape, this begins a few moments before the start of the set, snatches of stage banter ("Are we in tune?"), shushing going through the audience, and a fiddle starts into "Top of the Hill," which on some tapes is called "Chuck a Little Hill." A pleasant country reel, it grows quickly into a fiddle-driven bluegrass tune that highlights the tape fairly well: a clean recording, a mediocre mix, and all the boominess that seems to characterize so many tapes from this era. That notwithstanding, it is a remarkable tape—not just in terms of length (it's the longest of the extant pre-Dead tapes), but also for its exceptional sonic clarity for an amateur, early recording. The only certainty is a confirmed lineup, given in the patter between songs later in the tape. Although no one seems to know how specific dates have been attached to this set, at least two have floated around over the years: June 5 and June 11, 1962. "Top of the Hill" is a solid effort, showing good group dynamics, passable fiddle work, and some fine picking.

One of the greatest features of this tape is the between-songs patter, which is genuinely funny. The patter begins after the first song:

> **Jerry:** Thank you so much. If you're wonderin' why in an old-timey band you can't understand the words very well, it's because that we don't know 'em. And we can't figure 'em out off the record so we make up our own as we go along, see.
> **Marshall:** They're all scratchy.
> **Jerry:** That's the whole trouble, they're all scratchy. That's our voices, not the record. The fact is, we don't have any records.
> **Marshall:** Nor voices. Our mysterious gypsy violinist will now give us an obbligato here.

The camaraderie and good humor among the players comes through clearly—the tape does a good job of conveying the mood. "Billy Grimes," a classic story of an improper groom and star-crossed lovers, doesn't come across as well on tape as it did at the time, judging from the applause; this makes it a nice balance to some of the other tapes, where the playing merits more attention than it receives. Marshall sings lead on this slow-picked banjo tune, fiddle whining softly in the background.

Marshall asks for a capo afterward, "There must be somebody in this vast assemblage who has a capo," an insight into the venue and the crowd: definitely all folkies. "Taking That Old Cannonball" has a slow, sad feel, with a rolling banjo line and thoughtful vocal, a nice change from the strain that "Billy Grimes" put on Marshall's voice. Some classic patter follows:

> **Garcia:** If you're wondering about our fiddle player and why he doesn't say much, it's because he doesn't speak a word of English. You see, we found him accidentally in a little Hungarian restaurant, playing sweet tunes to the elderly matrons that would come in and sit down and . . .
> **Marshall:** That explains his dramatic, violent hair and burning eyes. Actually, we found him in—yeah, he's a passionate gypsy violinist. Really. We found him actually in a pizzeria in San Pablo. He played gypsy music.
> **Garcia:** He played in the background to curdle the mozzarella cheese. Makes for better pizza, you know.

"Okim Dinkem Dairy," on some tapes mislabeled as "Devilish Mary," has Jerry singing lead on the verses, with good bluegrass harmonies on the choruses. Another pleasant little bluegrass reel, it gets a good hand of applause. Jerry introduces the band afterward, jokey-boy style: "My name's Jerry Garcia, but I'm the only one who counts. . . . And this is Marshall Leicester, who picks the banjo, and if you'll watch closely, you'll see that never at any time do any of his fingers leave his hands," prompting Marshall: "And if you watch even more closely, you'll see that this is a guitar, not a banjo," and he introduces "Buck Dancer's Choice." A sweet, country-picked guitar introduction, the hiss is especially apparent here, unfortunately, but it is a highlight on the tape, and greeted with real enthusiasm at the end.

Jerry introduces the next song as having been "originally recorded by the Coon Creek Girls, whoever they were," and he launches into "Little Birdie," picking hard and fast until he settles into a rhythm; even then he varies a bit at first. But he sings strongly, powerfully—better than he did on many tapes from a few years later. And it is perhaps the best example in the material reviewed here of Garcia alone on banjo, a formative instrument at a formative time in his development as a player. Deadheads will immediately pick out these lines:

> *I'd rather be in some dark holler*
> *Where the sun don't ever shine*
> *Than to see you with another*
> *And to know you'll never be mine.*

Despite the very different musical setting, it shares with its offspring the tone of sweet mournfulness, though that doesn't prevent it from turning into a banjo-driven powerhouse by the end, Garcia's picking flying along until the final bar. That doesn't happen until a fretful, restive beginning has been completed, and then Jerry just leaps hard on the end of those opening measures, accelerating his picking by the second, racheting it up between verses until he's just flying along, and it's almost athletic by the end; one wonders how his voice can do it without a quaver. But he does, and he gets a solid round of applause.

Marshall announces the band's return with "tough luck, we're back," Jerry adding, "Thought you'd get away with a mere four hundred songs, did ya?" A good moment comes when Marshall aggrievedly asks Jerry, "Would you mind making up some folklore while we tune?" This gets a good laugh. A good country reel, "Sally Goodun" showcases the best tone the fiddle has had so far, but fans will probably pay even more attention to the patter afterward:

> **Garcia:** Oh, incidentally, for those who are interested, after this is over we're holding a seminar on creative folklore.
> **Leicester:** It's not really a seminar in creative folklore, it's a seminar to brainstorm a new name for our band. We were going to call ourselves the "Elves', Gnomes', Little Men's, and Leprechauns' Chowder and Marching Society and Volunteer Fire Brigade" but it won't fit on the poster.
> **Garcia:** So we settled on the Slugs.
> **Leicester:** But that can be improved.

A bit more tuning, a complaint by Jerry—"Our fiddler keeps insisting that every song we play is a fiddler's tune"—and they finish the set with "Hold the Woodpile Down," which focuses on their vocals more than their picking. After perhaps the best singing of the performance, they get a gratifyingly long round of applause at the end, even a few cries of "Bravo, bravo, just go on!" As it dies down, Jerry deadpans, "We'll be back if any of you have the stamina."

The second set opens with "I Love Chicken Pie," sometimes called "Crow Black Chicken" or "Grow Black Chicken," though there are other derivations. A rollicking folk song, it is replete with chicken squawks and other enthusiastic vocal gymnastics, but it is well played and the sound mix is particularly good.

Jerry's patter afterward shows both the folkie purist as well as the sardonic beatnik: "Thank you, thank you. We're back again to do a little of the old-time hill music that we stole from the Ramblers, and they stole from old records, and the musicians that were on the old records stole 'em from their fathers and things like that. So it's all part of the oral tradition, and that's your lesson in folklore for tonight. Now I'd like to do a song that has a rather interesting background: none!" and he continues for a while, finally turning to Marshall: "Are you finished tuning yet? I can't think of anything else to say." Still more tuning though, Marshall thoughtfully adding, "The reason we do old-time hill music is because we're not good enough to do the modern stuff," and they start out finally only to stop, Marshall incensed: "Garcia, you're in the wrong key!" Oh, oops, and the Garcia charisma is in full force as he handles it perfectly, goofing on himself and telling the crowd, "Well, folks, I'm entitled to one mistake in my life, I think, and that was it," and then they start for real. Not surprisingly, Jerry more than makes up for the gaffe, playing his fingers off in some especially flashy banjo runs.

But technical wizardry aside, it also shows how much fun they had as a group—when they are tight and flying, they sound very good indeed. But they could be relaxed and good-timey, too, and here the humor and fun show plainly in the pyrotechnics, a harbinger of the feel of the jug band to come.

The next tune is frequently not listed on tapes in circulation. Those that try usually focus on "Hop Up Pretty Girls, Don't Be Afraid," or "Johnson Boys." An unfortunate omission, since it's noteworthy for good sound quality and a nice blend of fine singing and particularly good fiddling, ending with Garcia's comment, "The big question of course is, afraid of what?"

The mood continues with "Shady Grove," one of the highlights of this tape, and it's clear the reverence Garcia has for it. Doc Watson, who learned the song from his father, once described it in terms that will strike many Heads as sounding awfully similar to Garcia's:

> "That's what 'Shady Grove' means to me—happiness. It also expresses memories of my dad and things that I can't remember, but can almost remember, as when something is mentioned and you can look back farther than your own lifetime and your own memory."[1]

Fans familiar with the 1997 Garcia-Grisman album of the same name will be delighted with this rendition.[2] Not amateurish, not Hollywood, this is simply good—very good. Here the sense of history and time is paramount, and the song as a whole is transformed from Watson's paean to happiness into a moody lyrical meditation with a plaintive instrumental accompaniment. As the lead vocal, Jerry's voice doesn't perform flawlessly, but it does well enough, and the edge of strain fits with the feeling they seem to be deliberately cultivating, an edginess, almost an angst:

> *Every night when I go home*
> *My wife, I try to please her,*
> *The more I try the worse she gets*
> *Damned if I don't leave her.*

Marshall tells the "Rufus Crisp" story next, the punch line of which is the "motto of our band," which is "The most important thing about playing yer instrument, is playing in tune." To which Garcia adds: "Now comes the second part of Rufus Crisp's little speech, and this is the part when you tune it. And this is the fun part, folks. Because there ain't nobody who can tune a banjo as bad as I can." A perfect bit of Garcia self-deprecation, but it recognized a common enough stage affliction: chasing the tuning. For a perfectionist, the nerves and strangeness of the stage could make hearing and tuning do strange things.

Thirty years later, the memory of those awful moments of chasing a tuning in public made David Nelson reminisce:

> "Jerry had a stress thing about tuning and ended up tuning too much.... He'd get stressed and nervous about playing. The stress would work itself out in tuning. Then he wouldn't be able to hear. His ears would get locked into the nervousness and he wouldn't be able to tune."[3]

---

1. Doc Watson, *The Songs of Doc Watson*, Oak, 1971.
2. David Grisman and Jerry Garcia, *Shady Grove* (San Rafael, Calif.: Acoustic Disc ACD 21, 1997).
3. David Nelson, interviewed by Sandy Troy, December 1993, quoted in Sandy Troy, *Captain Trips* (New York: Thunder's Mouth, 1994), p. 45.

In all fairness, though, difficulty with tuning seems to afflict most of the musicians Garcia is paired with at some point in these early tapes. A minute more and Garcia finishes up valiantly: "Now it's traditional at this point to break a string." And after a last spasm of tuning, almost theatrical now, they call it close enough to launch "Uncle Joe," which sounds quite good, the fiddle and banjos in great stride together for a bouncy, quick Appalachian reel, feet-pounding clear on the tape adding to the sense of a square-dance rhythm.

Slower and sweeter, "Sweet Sunny South" follows, a bittersweet banjo ballad with a leisurely loping strum that highlights the player's tone, an area in which Jerry already shows clear expertise. He follows much the same arrangement as he did thirty years later on "Shady Grove," with David Grisman. Well sung, too—for a moment it is eerily easy to forget how young he is.

> **Garcia:** This is a band tune, originally by Charlie Poole and the North Carolina Ramblers. And it's a song primarily about the woes of living in a boardinghouse.
> **Leicester:** We think it's about the woes of living in a boardinghouse. Actually we can't understand this record at all. So the words are a little Raggedy Andy once in a while.

"Boarding House Blues" is a funny, exaggerated hard-luck ballad, not a country blues at all. But it's fun and gets lots of applause, "yee haw!"s, and cheers afterward.

Jerry introduces the next tune with all of the folkie seriousness and none of the banter:

> **Garcia:** Thank you. On a sort of serious note, for a change, before there were instruments, or a lot of instruments around in the mountains, and well, way back in England and Scotland, and so forth, songs were mostly sung unaccompanied. So I'd like to sing a song that probably almost everyone is familiar with around here, you've probably heard it quite a bit. I'd like to do it unaccompanied, the way I heard a man named Roscoe Holcombe do it. It's called "Man of Constant Sorrow."

And he starts, easily, voice steady and strong and clear. A voice that's coming into its own: it does not come across as quirky, not even especially worried. And it gives an excellent insight into his determination to work around his limitations. Here it comes across as expressive and ambitious. A close listen reveals him to be in probably as good a voice as he is anywhere during these pre-Dead years, and on a good tape, it sounds fine. A simple, direct, sweet delivery, earnest and plaintive. One glitch happens in the tape toward the end, but otherwise, it's a little gem. And there's a fair amount of applause: he knew his audience.

Then it's Marshall's turn, on "Yonder He Goes," a showcase for his storytelling and picking. A talking blues on verses with nicely sung choruses, "Yonder he goes, yonder he goes, yonder he goes, can't you see." Then the full band for the closer, "Three Men Went A-Huntin'." Smooth harmonies, classic fast-paced bluegrass: it's easy to imagine this arrangement done by either the New Riders or Kingfish and having it come off well, with its guitar-driven verses and fiddle-led chorus. A pleasant portent to end the tape.

NICK MERIWETHER

---

**11/10/62**

**Jerry Garcia**
**College of San Mateo Folk Festival,**
**San Mateo, California**

Introduction, Man of Constant Sorrow

---

**Source:** SBD, **Quality:** B–, **Length:** 0:5, **Genealogy:** MR > RR > DR
**Highlights:** all

Thanks to David Gans' dissemination, we have an interesting and important slice of early Garcia: not just a rare solo a cappella song, but also a serious, substantial introduction to it. In a later interview, Hunter recalled this sort of song as one of the reasons he and Garcia worked so well together:

> "Jerry favors a certain type of folk song. He loves the mournful death-connected ballad, the [Francis James] Child ballad stuff. This is a venerable source which has always spoken to him, and to me as well, which is one reason we got together writing songs...."[1]

---

1. Blair Jackson, "Robert Hunter: The Song Goes On," *The Golden Road,* no. 16 (Spring 1988), p. 35.

Garcia begins with a disquisition on folk songs and authenticity that is the only serious side of his musicology that we have on tape from these years (although a tape of his Midnight Special show on KPFA, "The Long Black Veil," should also show this side of him, should it ever surface):

> **Garcia:** Before we break for coffee and things like that, I'd like to do a song that's maybe a little older than the things that we've been doing. What we've been doing, as it'll tell you in your program, very comprehensively, are songs "in the tradition." That means next to nothing, as far as I can tell. The songs that we've been doing have been mountain songs, roughly recorded maybe between the twenties and thirties, on commercial recording labels such as Columbia and Vocallion, Bluebird and such. One of the songs that's been a consistent favorite with country groups, dating from the old string bands up to modern bluegrass, and with ballad singers to a great degree—and lately, I've discovered, with more commercial folksong groups—in my opinion, one of the loveliest songs—mountain ballads—there is. It's a song called "Man of Constant Sorrow." I'd like to do it for you.

Not only serious but somewhat polemical as well, and an early indication of why Bruce Hornsby would later call him "the walking encyclopedia of folk music, otherwise known as Jerry Garcia." On the tape he has a scholarly tone, and his dead-center earnestness has a charm to it that mollifies his easy confidence, verging on arrogance when he delivers lines like "in my opinion." His is an opinion that matters, though, after you hear what he does with the song. It's not a polished voice, but it's definitely trained, and one that shows the same degree of intensity and earnestness that characterized his introduction. Garcia sings well, with confidence, too, which may surprise fans familiar with stories of him eschewing solo performances later in his career. Here he seems to hold the stage with ease and aplomb, with enough practice and presence of mind to give the lyric all of the benefit of the past two years' work on his voice, coaxing and shaping the little folk and country inflections he picked up from the vocal mannerisms of the performers from whom he learned the tune. He imbues the sad, plaintive ballad with sincerity, even reverence, but without transforming it into a dirge. All in all, a short tape, but a remarkable insight into what he called one of his strongest, archetypal moods, the heart of what he called his "fuzzy Christianity," and a key leitmotif in his music.

NICK MERIWETHER

---

## 1963 [?]
**Jerry Garcia and Friends**
**Top of the Tangent, Palo Alto, California**

Happy Birthday Bluegrass Rag, Nine-Pound Hammer, Darling Aller Lee, Ocean of Diamonds, Two Little Boys, Salty Dog, Rosalie McFall

---

**Source:** AUD, **Quality:** B+, **Length:** 0:19, **Genealogy:** MR > R > DAT > C

**Highlights:** Darling Aller Lee, Ocean of Diamonds, Rosalie McFall

This list generally circulates under the date March 7, 1964, as a performance by the Black Mountain Boys. If so, there are several problems, since the tape usually dated the day before this has an announced personnel quite different from the one usually stated on this tape. Compounding the mystery is that a much longer list exists, including these songs but not in this order. Since there are no tape breaks between the first four songs here, this may be an entirely different tape, but given the relatively rare overlap of songs on these early tapes, it is possible that the longer list has been rearranged by some home producer. The personnel for the longer list are reported as Garcia, Hunter, Sandy Rothman, and David Nelson; that, actually, sounds much closer to what appears here.

There are some sound problems in the beginning that stabilize fairly quickly. Good quality tapes of this are increasingly being circulated, thanks to DAT trading. It begins with Jerry speaking, interrupts him with a bad tape break, and then catches a banjo already in full stride. The first tune is just a pleasant bit of atmospherics and fun, the band singing "Happy Birthday" in a bluegrass arrangement; tapers have dubbed this the "Happy Birthday Bluegrass Rag." After another tape cut, they play "Nine-Pound Hammer," the song that won the Wildwood Boys the amateur bluegrass open in the College of San Mateo folk festival. A fun bluegrass tune, it has an ease, a looseness in feel that reminds you of Peter Rowan's attitude toward the genre: "I look at bluegrass music like this sort of glowing ball. The point is to relax the technique around the glowing ball of feeling."[1] But it still has the tightness of good players picking well.

In the patter between songs, Jerry comes across as relaxed, telling an audience member who calls out a request, "Why sure, we'll do that one, that's a *good* one, too." Which it is: "Darling Aller Lee" features good harmonies on the choruses, good mandolin picking, and a nice, comfortable arrangement that has the players trading verses and harmonizing on the choruses. Jerry asks for more requests, which produce the next song, "Ocean of Diamonds," after an obligatory bout of tuning, another indication of the quiet, loose feel to the evening. This is the other atmosphere one can imagine during this period, a late night at a coffeehouse, patrons truly rapt and attentive, possibly stoned; and a band relaxed, tight, and soaring—a necessary counterpoint to the rowdier, earlier tapes from this period. A sweetly sung, slow ballad, "Ocean of Diamonds" features subtle vocal nuances, strong harmonies, and fine understated playing in a plain, melancholy setting.

Lots of bantering back and forth with the audience over what to play next follows, with Jerry disagreeing with one suggestion—"That's kind of a *lot* like the last one"—as they tune. Garcia calls a heckler "a real smart aleck," after which they seem to be drifting into something until interrupted by a tape break. When the sound resumes, the mix has changed, and one assumes they changed things around on stage, but careful listening indicates that it's still the same show. "Two Little Boys" is a fast-picked banjo song, similar in feel to "Salty Dog," which follows; the patter before "Salty Dog" introduces it as a drink, "in case you were wondering." Here it is a fast bluegrass reel, featuring nice banjo work and strong harmonies. It sounds as if two voices and one banjo and only one guitar are present for this.

The best patter on the tape is next, probably by David Nelson: "Now this has turned out to be our most requested, least requested songs. We have three or four lists of songs that people request, and this is one of the ones that we find that, the more we do this, by George, the less people request it," which gets a good laugh. "If you have any requests," he finishes, "just write 'em on a ten-dollar bill." The last song in the set is "Rosalie McFall," which would make its triumphant reappearance on the Dead's 1980 acoustic album, *Reckoning*. A beautiful rendition, it features two guitars with Jerry singing lead in a very similar arrangement to that on *Reckoning*, but here the mandolin floats beautifully over the tune, giving it a melodic, flowing, fairly quick bluegrass feel that still retains the mournfulness of the song. Jerry's singing is positively soulful here, and the band sounds great. It is an easy leap from this to the 1980 acoustic shows, and even on into the 1990s; this is an obvious antecedent of one of Garcia's finest late compositions, "Lazy River Road." Listening to this provides a clear view into Garcia's appreciation of American folk music.

NICK MERIWETHER

---

**1963**

**Top of the Tangent, Palo Alto, California
Ron "Pigpen" McKernan,
of the Second-Story Men**

McKernan's Blues, Rocky Mountain Blues

**Source:** AUD, **Quality:** B, **Length:** 0:9, **Genealogy:** MR > R > FM > C
**Highlights:** All
**Personnel:** Ron "Pigpen" McKernan: vocals, harp, guitar

This is a fragment from an important source for pre-Dead tapes, a KFOG *Deadhead Hour* broadcast documenting the early Palo Alto folk scene, assembled from tapes provided by Richard Raffel. The Second-Story Men was Pigpen's country blues group, which featured fellow folkies Ellen Cavanaugh and future Big Brother bassist Peter Albin and his brother Rodney, who played a central role in the Bay Area folk scene and later ran the Victorian hippie palace and Haight-Ashbury institution, 1090 Page Street, where Big Brother came together. This fragment features Pigpen solo. The tape begins with Pig saying, "It's gonna be kinda difficult," which he disproves quickly, starting a nice, slow blues guitar strum. "McKernan's Blues" is a relaxed, slow blues shuffle, very similar to the arrangement and feel of "Katie Mae" on *Bear's Choice*, which is attributed to Lightnin' Hop-

---

[1]. Peter Rowan, quoted in Robert Greenfield, *Dark Star: An Oral Biography of Jerry Garcia* (New York: William Morrow, 1996), p. 152.

kins on the liner notes to that album, but credited to Pigpen by Raffel. Deadheads will recognize the tune as well as a number of the lines, such as "Folks say she must be a Cadillac, but I say she must be a T-model Ford." Pigpen sounds more than plausible: this is authentic acoustic blues, with no apologies. You can not only hear "Katie Mae" in this rendition, but you can also hear the misty origins of so much of the Dead's blues repertoire.

It's odd to hear Pigpen introduce the next number, another stately blues, but it does show his easygoing but commanding stage presence, which the Dead would prize so highly. He has an unlikely accent, but it sounds realistic: "Well, can't be much said about these blues, 'cept that, talking about a guy from Texas. Heard about the Rocky Mountains, he been out there, and he's come back to Texas again, and it's—you know, like he's telling his friends what went on in the Rocky Mountains." And Pig sounds marvelous. An altogether virtuoso performance, especially for a seventeen-year-old white kid from Palo Alto. It's easy to see why Garcia was delighted with this prodigy.

Recorded at the Top of the Tangent, this tape is one of several from that venerable folk institution. One of the two major Palo Alto folk clubs, the Tangent was an important part of the Northern California folk club circuit, which included venues in Berkeley and North Beach, and stretched as far south as San Jose, where the Off Stage held classes taught by Jorma Kaukonen (then known as Jerry) and was run by enterprising folkie David Frieberg, later of Quicksilver Messenger Service and the Airplane. Paul Kantner, Janis Joplin, Country Joe MacDonald, and a host of later rock musicians also played this circuit, making it a major tributary of the Bay Area rock scene that would emerge in a couple of years. Most of the tapes in circulation from the summer of 1964 at the Tangent were recorded by Stanford undergraduate Peter Wanger, who hosted a weekly radio show *Live from Top of the Tangent*, which he recorded himself and edited into half-hour programs.[1] Two later retrospectives drew on this material as well.

NICK MERIWETHER

---

1. Michael Wanger, interviewed by author, May 1, 1997.

---

### 2/23/63
**The Wildwood Boys**
**The Top of the Tangent,**
**Palo Alto, California**

Rolling in My Sweet Baby's Arms, Jerry's Breakdown, Standing in the Need of Prayer, Muleskinner Blues, Pike County Breakdown, Come All Ye Fair and Tender Maidens, We Shall Not Be Moved

**Source:** AUD, **Quality:** B, **Length:** 0:26, **Genealogy:** MR > R > FM > C

**Highlights:** Jerry's Breakdown, Pike County Breakdown, Come All Ye Fair and Tender Maidens

**Personnel:** Jerry Garcia: banjo, guitar, vocals; David Nelson: guitar; Robert Hunter: bass, guitar; Norm Van Mastricht: bass, guitar, dobro

This is one of the few early tapes where we have a full set, accurately dated, from the *Deadhead Hour* radio broadcast that also provided the Pigpen solo material. This set will interest fans curious about Garcia's roots but not especially enamored of folk. It has some fine playing, a wonderful atmosphere and feel, and in the course of the half-hour preserved here, it will take you through a representative slice of the Palo Alto folk scene. Recorded in 1963, it will immediately impress listeners familiar with Garcia's earliest tapes with how much he had improved.

Unlike the tape from the Tangent a year later, this starts off hot: the band sounds warmed-up and ready, especially Jerry, whose picking sounds almost amphetamine-driven. The interplay among the band members is first-rate: this is a tight band, from the first note. As is the banter, though it was essentially practical, as Jerry freely explains: "I'll just say whatever comes to mind while they finish tuning." "Jerry's Breakdown" is a showcase for his technique, quick and good. "Standing in the Need of Prayer" is pleasant and competent, but will probably strike fans more for its stage patter and the banter back and forth among band members. The best sequence comes before "Muleskinner Blues," when Jerry gives a witty, beatnik-styled putdown of Palo Alto:

**Garcia:** Well, you know, there are railroad songs, friends, and there are carpenter songs, and there are—by God, there are muleskinner songs. This here is a muleskinner song. We introduce a note of nostalgia here, realizing that Palo Alto was once a muleskinning community. [Loud, furious tuning for a moment as the audience laughs.] And many of your mothers and fathers were undoubtedly muleskinners [Tune-tune-tune.]—or better [more laughter].

And Jerry has a showman's sense of pacing; the perfect pause before he says, "—or better" still sounds funny.

Hunter also plays a major role in the set's between-song patter, something he remembered twenty years later in an interview:

> "When Garcia and Nelson and I were playing in the Wildwood Boys, I did the stagemanship. But back in those days, that's what was done. You had to have a line of patter when you were onstage. Nobody was *allowed* to just stand up there and be silent, so I used to drink a lot of beer and rave away."[1]

"Pike County Breakdown" is slower and sweeter than the first breakdown, followed by a pretty and nicely arranged "Come All Ye Fair and Tender Maidens," featuring a funny false start, Jerry saying reproachfully, "You gotta be in tune, you really do." This precedes a pretty, slow ballad, mandolin-led, with sweet harmonies—something that Jerry sought out again and again over the years, with his work with Old and In the Way and later with David Grisman. It is one of the nicer moments in the pre-Dead oeuvre. An equally intricate but much sprightlier "We Shall Not Be Moved" ends the set, with solid bluegrass harmonies in a fast-paced peppy finale. A great banjo song, it shows a tight band having a good evening.

NICK MERIWETHER

---

1. Mary Eisenhart, "Robert Hunter: Songs of Innocence, Songs of Experience," *The Golden Road*, no. 4 (Fall 1984), p. 17.

---

## 5/4/63
### Jerry and Sara Garcia
### Top of the Tangent, Palo Alto, California

Deep Elem Blues, The Weaver, I Truly Understand, All Good Times Are Past, Long Black Veil, The Man Who Wrote Home Sweet Home, Keno, Foggy Mountain Top

**Source:** AUD, **Quality:** B, **Length:** 25:40, **Origin:** common, **Genealogy:** MR > R > FM > C [?]
**Highlights:** I Truly Understand, Long Black Veil, Man Who Wrote Home Sweet Home, Foggy Mountain Top
**Personnel:** Jerry Garcia: guitar, banjo, mandolin, fiddle, vocals; Sara Ruppenthal Garcia: guitar, vocals

Another segment from the KFOG *Deadhead Hour* show on the Palo Alto folk scene, this half-hour set has some fine picking by Garcia, and shows him in an interesting stage of his musical development. This is the full set, but two songs frequently appear as filler in other tapes: "The Weaver" and "I Truly Understand." Variously dated February, May 1, and May 3, 1963, this set is actually from May 4, 1963, courtesy of Jerry's announcement of a contemporary newspaper article. Still in transition from his folk period to his bluegrass purist stage, the material here is a mix of folk, old-time, modern country, and bluegrass, a good sample of Jerry's tastes and education.

"Deep Elem Blues" Deadheads will immediately recognize as the root of the Dead's version, with largely identical lyrics and melody. Jerry plays mandolin, and quite passably, though it's not a virtuoso demonstration. The harmonies are sweet here, if less effective than on the next tune, "The Weaver"—although it's easy to see why the latter would appeal to Garcia's old-timey aesthetic. His sardonic stage persona is apparent here as well, when he exhorts the audience to "help out this next song—for a change."

Sara's soaring soprano begins "I Truly Understand," joined by Jerry's tenor, and has some nice banjo runs in the middle, emphasizing how fully developed his distinctive, appealing style on the instrument has already become, the strongest of all the various instruments he plays here. "All the Good Times Are Past" is another pleasant folk ballad. Jerry's singing here is interesting; his affected accent will grate on many, but it shows his commitment to authentic voicing. And it goes over well with the crowd, which is quiet and attentive at this point.

"Long Black Veil" features Jerry solo, just voice and guitar, preceded by a classic bit of what Garcia called "audience abuse"—truly funny, if slightly defensive patter: "With electric guitar and everything, this is called tuning." But he sings it very sweetly, with only a simple pick-strum guitar accompaniment. He introduces it as "a modern country song," perhaps a little embarrassed about its lack of pedigree, and later said it was one of the songs that he had played too much and simply worn out. Here it shows all of the polish and passion that must have made him overplay it, though.

This mood carries into the next song, which features more strong banjo—it sounds as if he really enjoys this. In the patter that follows, he comments that he and Sara just got married "last week," an ironic and appropriate introduction to "The Man Who Wrote 'Home Sweet Home' (Never Was a Married Man)," a virtuoso banjo showcase. Fans who have imagined his reference being to a long article on how two prominent local folkies wed will be disappointed: it's a bland, generic wedding write-up, and the only mention of music its description of Jerry teaching at Dana Morgan's store.[1]

"Keno the Rent Man" is a funny folk tune, with the only currently circulating fiddle playing we have from Garcia. While clearly struggling, he still shows a natural musician's feel, and his showmanship enlists the audience's sympathy. The lightest moment in the tape, it shows Jerry's sense of humor, which is a perfect complement to the song's funny lyrics, unintentionally underscored by Jerry's occasionally off-key fiddling. For the last song, "Foggy Mountain Top," he switches to mandolin, and (especially in contrast to his fiddling), he sounds quite good. With nice harmonies from Sara, this is fast-paced, high-energy, good bluegrass. A strong close to the set, it rounds out one of the better and more interesting tapes from this era.

NICK MERIWETHER

---

[1]. "Sara Lee Ruppenthal Weds," *The Palo Alto Times*, n. 107, Sat., May 4, 1963, p. 6.

---

### 1964

**Pigpen McKernan and Peter Albin**
**Top of the Tangent,**
**Palo Alto, California [?]**

John Henry, Hoochie-Coochie Man

**Source:** AUD, **Quality:** B, **Length:** 0:05, **Genealogy:** MR > RR > FM > RR > C [?]
**Highlight:** "Hoochie-Coochie Man"
**Personnel:** Ron "Pigpen" McKernan: harp, vocals, Peter Albin: guitar, vocals

A fragment from the same radio broadcast that features the Mother McCree's material discussed on the next page, this is another slice of the San Francisco Sound in the making. This tape shows the reverence for the blues of both Pigpen and Peter Albin, the future bassist for Big Brother and the Holding Company. "John Henry" is a fast-moving blues rendition of the old folk tale, with a rough, appealing character. It exudes the same ethos as Jerry's bluegrass purism; it aspires to being authentic acoustic blues. Good harp work by Pig, and though the vocals and harmonies are rough, they're appropriate for the feel they seem to be pursuing. Peter is a thoroughly competent blues guitarist.

"Hoochie-Coochie Man" is the keeper here, though: Pig just belts it out, really wrapping himself around the lyric. He sounds young, but good. This should be an instructive and informative few minutes for Deadheads who wonder about the band's roots.

NICK MERIWETHER

---

### 1964

**Pigpen and Jerry [Jorma] Kaukonen**
**Top of the Tangent,**
**Palo Alto, California [?]**

Diamond Rag Blues

**Source:** AUD, **Quality:** B, **Length:** 0:03, **Genealogy:** MR > R > C > DAT
**Personnel:** Pigpen McKernan: harp, Jorma "Jerry" Kaukonen: guitar, vocals

A tantalizing fragment of Pigpen backed by another Bay Area folk scene stalwart, Jorma Kaukonen, the only clear challenge to Garcia's preeminence as the scene's picker after Marshall Leicester went to graduate school. Jorma, then known as Jerry, specialized in acoustic blues, though, which was the appeal of pairing him with Pigpen. This tape also frequently appears with a quick two minutes of Jorma alone, on "Sweet Georgia Brown." A slow acoustic blues, "Diamond Rag Blues" will remind every Deadhead of its offspring in the Dead's repertoire, "Dupree's Diamond Blues," essentially the same narrative but reworked into the Dead's unique framework. This rendition showcases fine harp playing by Pig, and good vocals by Jorma, who also provides a comforting, lush guitar underpinning for Pig to work against. The fact that the guitar is by Jorma, a player whom Bob Weir was following around at the time with a tape recorder and studying, and who would later go on to be such an important figure in the San Francisco scene with the Airplane, makes the tape all the more historic.

NICK MERIWETHER

---

### 1964

**Mother McCree's Uptown Jug Champions
Top of the Tangent,
Palo Alto, California [?]**

I'm Satisfied with My Gal, The Rub

---

**Source:** AUD, **Quality:** B, **Length:** 0:05, **Genealogy:** MR > RR > FM, **Taper:** Peter Wanger
**Highlights:** Both, for historical reasons primarily
**Personnel:** [?] Jerry Garcia: banjo, kazoo; Bob Weir: washtub bass; Pigpen: harmonica; David Nelson: guitar; David Parker: washboard

This tape is an interesting and intriguing slice of the band that most directly preceded the Warlocks. Since it was a segment of the 1969 radio show on the roots of the Grateful Dead, *Grateful Dead, A Documentary*, produced by Michael Wanger and Vance Frost, fairly high-quality copies are in circulation.[1] Musically, it is two jug-band standards, with some vintage Garcia patter. He begins by announcing, "I got an idea. I know everybody comes to these places, and I don't know what everybody expects, or—they come, and then they listen, everybody listens and says, 'My my,' and scratch their head and kind of wonder, and half the time a lot of people don't enjoy it. You come here over a certain amount of years and you build up a lot of sort of unenjoyment," which prompts appreciative laughter, along with Bob's thumping tub bass. "And you wind up unenjoying a lot of things. So as long as you're here, and as long as some of you may be unenjoying this all, and have unenjoyed things in the past, you can all have a little boo break. And if you want, you can all just boo us," which precipitates some enthusiastic booing, though most of it sounds like it's coming from the band, not the audience, which sounds as if it's still consumed with laughter. Garcia has the jokey-boy stage presence honed by now.

"I'm Satisfied with My Gal" is a light-hearted, sprightly romp that is exactly what you'd expect from a fun, old-timey jug band. What may come as a surprise—especially if you are not familiar with Garcia's earlier bluegrass efforts—is how tight the band sounds, and how carefully worked out the arrangement is. A fast bluegrass-flavored tune, it has the distinctive jug-band chunka-chunk style, and a great kazoo solo by Garcia to distinguish it. Garcia sings lead, and it sounds like Weir is singing backup vocals, gainsaying Garcia's importuning "Yes she will!" with an equally emphatic "No she won't!"

Garcia provides another round of patter to introduce the next tune, without much success at first, as he tries to fit a word into the good-natured pandemonium swirling around him, lots of ancillary chatter and mild razzing of Garcia by other band members: "Mister Pigpen McKernan would like to play an old Lightnin' Hopkins song—he's gonna sing a song called 'The Rub.' And we're not gonna be responsible for its contents. Or his." And "The Rub," also called "Ain't It Crazy," starts in on that same chug-chug tempo. It's easy to see why Garcia would like it, too: it comes across as being fun, and fun to play, with its fast shuffle rhythm. There's a nice Pigpen harp run in the middle, but basically it's a restrained, funny, raunchy blues, made into jug-band fun. There's good banjo strumming as well.

But basically, it's a very short piece of history, though an interesting one. Weir does make the washtub bass sound good, something that had impressed Garcia at the outset. And Jerry once again shows a love for anarchy, for looseness, and for ensemble playing. It's a shame that this is the only circulating Mother McCree's tape; there is supposed to be a much longer repertoire, which

---

1. "Grateful Dead, A Documentary." Radio program. 108 minutes. Produced by Michael Wanger and Vance Frost; aired June 8, 1969, on KSAN.

David Nelson, later of the New Riders, recalled as including "Deep Elem Blues," "Washington at Valley Forge," "Beetle Um Bum," and "K. C. Moan," which Weir continues to play to this day. Nelson is credited with having added "Uptown Jug Champions" to Hunter's suggestion, which was "Mother McCree's."

What can you say about such slender evidence? Not much—or rather, you shouldn't, really. But it's tempting. Tempting to note that Weir fits in well with what's going on around him, a useful characteristic and portent of future success—and Pigpen sounds good and confident in this musical setting, as different as it must have been from his beloved acoustic blues—and Jerry sounds as good as he ever does in this period, even though nothing here is as strong as, say, "Jerry's Breakdown" as an indication of sheer prowess. This simply indicates the early chemistry in the players, and the commitment to playing and enjoying oneself in the group and in the performance.... Yeah, it's tempting to say that all of that seems evident here. Already.

NICK MERIWETHER

---

## ❦ 3/6/64[?] ❦

**Black Mountain Boys
Top of the Tangent,
Palo Alto, California [?]**

Monroe's Hornpipe, Katy Fine, Homestead on the Farm, Barefoot Nellie, She's More to Be Piticd Than Scolded, Noah's Blues, Somebody Touched Me, Who'll Sing for Me, Darling Aller Lee

---

**Source:** SBD, **Quality:** A–, **Time:** 0:28, **Origin:** fairly rare, **Genealogy:** MR > RR > DAT > C [?]
**Highlights:** Noah's Blues
**Personnel:** Jerry Garcia: banjo, vocals; David Nelson: mandolin, vocals; Eric Thompson: guitar, vocals

Though not included in most published tapeographies, this list is becoming more common in trading circles. Although this tape benefits from an announced lineup, it raises a host of questions about the tape commonly listed as occurring the next day, which is reported with a different lineup. The tape itself sounds good, though a bit more hissy than others from this era. There is one bad tape break in "Darling Aller Lee."

It fades in with a banjo already going full-tilt, guitar and mandolin playing along behind. The clarity of the mix is noticeable: this sounds cleaner than most tapes from this era, being a soundboard rather than an audience tape (though technically not a soundboard, but a PA feed). Some audience noise comes in at the end, but it sounds ambient, not miked. The first tune, "Monroe's Hornpipe," is an instrumental, which Jerry—obviously in good spirits—announces as being "about nine hundred years older than all of us put together." A solid workout, it shows the band in fine form and already warmed up. Thompson sings lead on "Katy Fine," and fans will probably find his tenor a bit grating at first, but good, tight harmonies make the choruses work well. If you like bluegrass, you'll probably find that Thompson's voice adds character to the blend, a touch of folk authenticity.

Nelson announces the band and introduces its members—including "Honest" Jerry Garcia—"we're the Black Mountain Boys, otherwise known as the Black Mountain String Band, the greatest bluegrass band since King Solomon's Mines." Jerry introduces the next song as a Carter Family song, "Homestead on the Farm," which comes off well: good harmonies and solid playing, though nothing like what they do on "Barefoot Nellie." After Jerry spends an inordinate amount of time tuning and getting flak for it, they launch into a picker's showcase, which reveals each of them to be a fine instrumentalist. It starts fast and furious, distinguished by such a first-rate breakdown a few bars after the first chorus that the audience applauds afterward. The lyrics are clear and humorous, which is what gives this music its charm—serious without taking itself too seriously. Jerry and the mandolinist are an amazing pair, and juxtaposed against the funny lyrics and funny singing, it makes for an interesting contrast.

"She's More to Be Pitied Than Scolded" is announced as a Stanley Brothers song, a pretty tune followed by some classic banter. Nelson introduces the next song as "Go Down to the Roundhouse, Mother, They Can't Corner You There." Jerry delivers the best line, though, disagreeing: "No, you've it all wrong, buddy. This is a teenaged love song that we've turned into an instrumental. And it's entitled, 'They Can Lock Me Up in Jail for Loving You, but They Can't Keep My Face From Breaking Out.'" Nelson finishes the musicology by noting that it was written by "one of the greatest bluegrass musicians, Elmer 'Liver-Lunged' Pablumpud, the granddaddy of bluegrass," and after still more tuning, Jerry finally says, "This is a hard one, here. All my students can't listen to this," as they launch into "Noah's Blues," a very fast guitar-and-banjo duel, which sounds wonderful. Both are superb pickers, and at times it seems as if Jerry really wants to accelerate things to an even greater pace, just a hint of "I want to take this up to another level, hey guys, can you—," but they're already going as fast as they can.

"Somebody Touched Me" is preceded by a good-natured argument among the band as to how to start it, which Jerry decides by saying, "See I go into it—." It's a gospel-styled bluegrass song with its call-and-response chorus of "Glory glory glory / Somebody touched me / Must the hand of the Lord." Wonderful picking workouts meet the end of each chorus: a classic bluegrass anthem.

"Who'll Sing for Me" slows the pace. Another call-and-response, each musician leads a verse, with medium-tempo harmony choruses led by Nelson. It's very well done, though the poor mix here detracts. Nelson introduces the next one as "a Civil War song, called 'Darling Aller Lee.'" A classic, fast banjo run starts it, with Thompson's reedy tenor singing lead, once again sweetened by some superb harmonies on the choruses and solid playing throughout. A bad cut mars the end of it, but it seems to be only a few seconds, almost a drop-out rather than a break. End of the set, Nelson announces, while Jerry and Eric are still picking away furiously, and they all pound out a superb closer.

The repertoire in this set is diverse, spanning bluegrass to gospel to old-timey, nineteenth-century to modern. It is worth noting that a similar eclecticism would characterize Garcia's song choices with the Dead, a commitment shared by the band's other members. This tape also suggests a few more points of comparison with Jerry's later band, in that the songs clearly have to be fun to play, and that sense of having fun, goofing around even, is apparent here, even as it also shows a real commitment to the music, to playing well, as an ensemble. At the heart of this ensemble—as with the others Garcia assembled—was individual musicianship, though. Chops were such a part of that competitive little scene, and the result shines here.

NICK MERIWETHER

---

## 5/64

**Music Now Koncerts Series**
**The San Francisco Mime Troupe Studio,**
**3450 Capp St., San Francisco, California**

6⅞ for Bernardo Moreno

**Source:** AUD, **Quality:** B, **Length:** 0:33, **Genealogy:** MR > RR > C > DAT [?]

**Personnel:** Steve Reich: piano, Tom "T. C." Constanten: prepared piano, Jon Gibson: clarinet, Gwen Watson: cello, Georges Rey: violin, Paul Breslin: bass

Five years after the San Mateo Jazz Band material, Lesh surfaces again in a very different musical context. For fans who appreciate avant-garde classical music, this will be an interesting and pleasant half hour. Most tapes date this as the May 21, 1964, performance, which is possible, although there are three other dates that are candidates; many tapes avoid the problem by citing only the month and year. Part of a series sponsored by the Mime Troupe called the "Music Now Koncerts," there were four shows—May 21, 23, 29, and 30, 1964—held at the troupe's studios, an old church in San Francisco.[1] Though Phil didn't perform, his score was one of the featured pieces, and future Dead keyboardist Tom "T. C." Constanten was a member of the orchestra. T.C.'s "Piano Piece Number Three" also frequently appears with Lesh's piece, which some Deadheads may recognize from *Anthem of the Sun,* where a part of it appears. Some tapes also feature a series of demos done by T.C. for Tarot, the band he played in after the Dead. In poorer quality tapes, it's difficult to pinpoint the cuts, especially if the applause at the end has been edited; many Deadheads believe Phil's piece was originally much longer than it actually is.

Very much the ancestor of "Seastones," this could also be described as "music as metaphor for thought," as "Seastones" was first described to fans.[2] "6⅞ for Bernardo Moreno" projects that same sense of thoughtful, intellectual structure: it's easy to see how the composer of this would get along so well with Garcia, if you consider "Late for Supper" and "Eep Hour" from Gar-

---

1. Tom Constanten, *Between Rock and Hard Places* (Eugene, Ore.: Hulugosi, 1992), p. 193.
2. *Grateful Dead Newsletter,* Spring 1974, p. 7.

cia's first solo album.[3] Essentially, "Bernardo" is a series of movements, building from sparse, almost eerie melody lines, stark and unadorned, gradually accreted by other semi-independent instrument voices, building together sometimes, stopping altogether for a few beats or measures, then abruptly starting again. The effect isn't so much unsettling as it is thought-provoking; it makes you wonder, "What is that getting at?" You don't listen to it the way you do to a song, but is a lineal and direct ancestor of "Space" in the Dead's later live shows, especially the more ethereal renditions we heard in the eighties and nineties.

It opens with a keening violin, eerie and discordant, reluctantly joined by the other members of the string section, and it develops into a tapestry of dissonance in fairly short order, all careening strings and percussion. Very reminiscent of Berio, or Cage, and maybe some Stravinsky somewhere in there as well—Stravinsky minus the melody, almost, with all the strangely orchestrated dissonance. Not at all unlistenable, though—it's interesting. At twenty-four minutes in, it sounds like nothing so much as the *musique concrète* parts of *Anthem of the Sun*, especially right before the buzz-saw sound, purportedly a gyroscope being dropped on the sounding board of the piano. (It was, coincidentally, the last straw for the tattered sensibilities of the band's label-approved producer, who, according to witnesses, apparently cleared his chair by a foot and a half.) Deadheads used to the noisy ambience of the other tapes from these years will be surprised at the volume and amount of the applause at the end, since this is the only crowd noise that appears. For Phil, it must have been especially gratifying. And for Deadheads who wondered how the band got so weird, and where some of the intellectual underpinnings to the Dionysianism came from, this tape will answer many questions.

It should also raise several others, specifically about Phil and T.C. and the connections between the San Francisco Mime Troupe and the emerging musical counterculture in the Bay Area. Phil's association with the Mime Troupe went back a while; his first credit with them is for the music he did with his friend Steve Reich for a Mime Troupe happening on February 27, 1964, called *Event III (Coffee Break)*, with projections by Elias Romero and "movement" by R. G. Davis and Fumi Spencer.[4] Part of Mime Troupe's director Ronny Davis's attitude of casting a wide net across the Bay Area artistic scene, the Music Now concerts were designed to showcase some of the new music that had been making inroads on the classical music establishment, and that San Francisco had been seeing more of in recent months, beginning with the San Francisco Symphony's performance of Webern's *Passacaglia* and culminating with the Tape Music Center's series of performances by John Cage and David Tudor the month before. At Reich's invitation, Phil prepared a piece specifically for this group of musicians, which specialized in ensemble improvisation, including what T.C. called a "jubilantly prepared piano solo" for him. What most impressed T.C., however, was Phil's handling of the arrangement of the four parts: "In the true, adventurous aleatoric spirit of the times Phil shuffled the segments anew before each performance. One of the many things I've admired him for."[5]

Mime was not the silent pantomime of Marcel Marceau. In the words of one of the troupe's most famous alumni, Emmett Grogan: "Although it incorporates the same physical movements as pantomime, it is neither silent nor restricted from using props to dramatize a dialogue. On the contrary, it uses everything from loud buffoonery to slap-stick travesty to perform dramas in which scenes imitated from life are exaggerated and broadened to make obvious what is usually subtle."[6] Which could also describe director Davis's attitude toward politics—in fact, the political aspect of the troupe's art was always a central concern for the participants, eventually alienating their business manager, Bill Graham, and culminating in the formation of the Haight's most colorful and visible activist group, the Diggers, which was spearheaded by a group of Mime Troupe alumni, including Grogan. But before the Diggers split off from the troupe, there were several years of heady experimentation with many of the same strands of the counterculture that informed the Dead, from light shows to music to dance to poetry, ranging over the most esoteric and fundamental theories of dramatic improvisation and audience-performer interaction. Even the troupe's discovery that they had attracted a core following for their weekly performances presaged the Dead's ever-expanding repertoire: "We developed a return audience and couldn't use our gimmick twice."[7]

---

3. Jerry Garcia, *Garcia* (U.S.: Grateful Dead Merchandising, GDCD 4003, 1988), 40:01 min.
4. R. G. Davis, *The San Francisco Mime Troupe* (Palo Alto, Calif.: Ramparts, 1980), p. 198.
5. Constanten, *Between Rock and Hard Places*, p. 54.
6. Emmett Grogan, *Ringolevio: A Life Played for Keeps* (Boston: Little, Brown, 1972), p. 234.
7. Davis, *The San Francisco Mime Troupe*, p. 20.

This fueled the search for a wider and wider array of "gimmicks," as they worked with painters from the San Francisco Art Institute (where Garcia was taking lessons), choreographers from San Francisco State, musicians such as Reich and Lesh and others from the Tape Music Center. It made for an interesting stew. As one participant wrote, "You would want to go to a Mime Troupe party. They were just a lot more fun to be with than most other groups, given to impromptu bands, general spontaneity, and a more diverse bunch of characters than one expected around the left."[8] Davis' mix-it-up attitude would bear particular fruit eighteen months later, at a party the Mime Troupe hosted to raise money for their legal defense (they were charged with performing without a permit). It drew all of the disparate strands of the Bay Area artistic underground together, including the composer of this piece—but this time as a performer, playing bass for a band called the Grateful Dead.

This tape is tantalizing evidence of some of the unsung artistic contributions the Mime Troupe made to the city's blossoming counterculture, as it drank from the same stew of influences roiling there. Folkies were part of that scene as well, and it is worth noting that Ronny Davis' philosophy fit in well with the folkie attitude toward purity, art, and aesthetics, though he added an edge as well—one that would fit extremely well with what one disillusioned author was dreaming up with his group of like-minded crazies and dropouts, just down the peninsula in the hills of La Honda. The author was Ken Kesey, the group the Merry Pranksters, and their new art form was an amalgam of happening theory and pop psychology, with a melange of avant-garde aesthetics, and the magic ingredient: lysergic acid diethylamide, LSD for short, or irreverently just "acid," as the Pranksters had taken to calling it. . . .

NICK MERIWETHER

---

8. Ibid., p. 11.

---

### 11/3/65
**Golden State Studios, San Francisco, California**
**The Warlocks—Autumn Records Demo—The Emergency Crew**

**Studio Session:** Can't Come Down, Mindbender, The Only Time Is Now, Caution, I Know You Rider, Early Morning Rain

**Source:** SBD, **Quality:** B, **Length:** 0:20

The earliest known recordings of the Grateful Dead, then known as the Warlocks, this tape gives a fair presentation of the band in their most naive stage of infancy. As notable for the song selection as for the actual performance, this brief session tape illustrates several key strengths of the band and just as many weaknesses.

The session begins on a comical note with "Can't Come Down." Highlighted by a classic rock 'n' roll harp accompaniment, this track, based around a simple two-chord progression, contains what are among the most hilarious lyrics ever emitted by the Grateful Dead. While the background vocals are noticeably inaccurate, the enthusiasm of the band is evident. Furthermore, the synchronicity between both Kreutzmann and Lesh is surprisingly tight, and the solos by Garcia and McKernan on the outro are also well blended. Weir's contribution is noticeably inaudible throughout the track.

The following "Mindbender" is vastly unremarkable in musical content, but it gives a prominent illustration of the mercurial Mr. Lesh's vocal abilities. Indeed, had he not abused his vocal chords, he may well have developed into the strongest singer in the band. The song's main riff is haunting, and though the interverse breaks are embarrassingly sloppy, the band makes an admirable attempt at navigating the dynamic range, most successfully on the down swoosh prior to the final verse.

"The Only Time Is Now," which had the potential to become *the* hippie anthem had it been given some room for development, further complements the vocal capabilities of Lesh. As well as being both melodically and aesthetically pleasing, Lesh's voice blends surprisingly well with the baritone of McKernan, who, though still buried, is the only other vocalist audible. The song's construction is simple, combining upper-register chord sweeps against a common time rhythm that is accentuated by Lesh's sly single-note octave shifts. Unfortunately the tape contains a disappointing muffling during the instrumental break.

Switching gears, the session continues with a rough take of what would later emerge as one of the Grateful Dead's most beloved jams, "Caution." Originating from a simple chromatic blues riff underneath a Dick Dale style surf guitar pattern, this track is highlighted by McKernan's harp licks, which far surpass most of what he performed onstage throughout his career. After a confident solo that nods to both Little Walter Jacobs and Sonny Boy Williamson II, McKernan growls through a belligerent and ever-authentic verse reading, which inexplicably fades almost immediately in an inexcusable display of incompetent engineering.

The only selection from this session to survive the test of time is "I Know You Rider," which, thirty years after its inception, showed no signs of sterility. Ironically this selection is the weakest exhibition of the day, containing little more than chords and vocals. Though the take is crisp, the execution is lifeless, with less-than-enthusiastic rhythm grooves and a barely noticeable Garcia solo.

The Beatles influence, certainly not a unique approach but an effective one nonetheless, is particularly evident in the wonderfully delightful "Early Morning Rain." Lyrically this is the most mature selection of the session, and vocally the most melodic. As they do in "Can't Come Down," the band attempts to span a wide range of dynamics, from thrust to delicate, although much more effectively in this exhibition. As well, the accompaniment combination of Garcia's Gibson with McKernan's Hammond B-3 is warm and bright, giving the selection a savory springtime attractiveness.

BRIAN DYKE

# 1966

*The beginning of 1966 found the Acid Tests, begun the fall before (see page 86), continuing in full swing nearly every weekend. In between the Dead played shows at the Matrix, a small nightclub in the Marina district of San Francisco owned by Marty Balin of the Jefferson Airplane. In February, the Dead moved down to Los Angeles for a couple of months, where they practiced for hours every day at their house on the edge of the Watts district during the week and played around town on weekends. Upon their return to San Francisco, they began playing and rehearsing in earnest. They were still a local Bay Area band at the time. More than half of their shows in 1966 were either at the Matrix, Bill Graham's Fillmore Auditorium, or Chet Helms' Avalon Ballroom. Aside from the time in Los Angeles and a week in Vancouver, all the shows took place in the San Francisco area. The band played two or three shows nearly every weekend during the summer and fall while constantly rehearsing during the week. By the end of the year, the results were really beginning to show. Their sets became tighter and more polished and their popularity grew.*

*The Dead's music at this time was made up of a combination of traditional blues including "It's a Sin," "Death Don't Have No Mercy," and "Big Boss Man"; rhythm and blues hits such as "Dancin' in the Streets," "In the Midnight Hour," and "Pain in My Heart," jug-band songs such as "Beat It on Down the Line," "Minglewood Blues," and "Viola Lee Blues," and pop covers such as "It's All Over Now, Baby Blue," "Early Morning Rain," and "She Belongs to Me." They also threw in traditional roots-based songs such as "In the Pines," "Stealin'," and "Nobody's Fault but Mine." Their only known originals at the time were the little-known "Mindbender" and "Alice D. Millionaire," and the more widely know "Cream Puff War." The music was generally played fast and loose, with Garcia's lightning-fast picking and Pigpen's authentic blues voice and Hammond B-3 dominating the sound. Kreutzmann provided a solid, if unremarkable, beat; Weir remained mostly in the background; and Lesh, while occasionally displaying moments of brilliance, had not yet mastered his instrument. The pace was often frenetic, featuring short, fast songs interspersed with the slower blues numbers. Almost all the numbers were played at a quicker tempo than they would be in later years. In many ways, the band's sound, on tapes at least, was nearly indistinguishable from other bands playing in California at the time, with its heavy use of reverb on the vocals and lack of depth in the guitar sound. What set them apart from other bands, though, were Pigpen's richly genuine blues voice and Garcia's bluegrass-influenced picking, nearly unheard of in pop music at the time. Also, in songs like "Viola Lee Blues," they began to develop the improvisational style that would be their trademark.*

*Tapes from this early period are scarce but most are of surprisingly good quality. They are concentrated in July and November (except for the Acid Tests) but dis-*

play a repertoire vastly different from what contemporary Deadheads would associate with the band. However, they are all fun to listen to and contain few dull moments. Pigpen's bouncy organ and Garcia's ringing guitar flurries often serve to astound listeners unfamiliar with this period. Every tape from this year in circulation so far is worth seeking out and adding to one's collection.

Tapes to get: 7/16, 7/17, 11/19, 12/1.

## The Acid Tests

Though known as a novelist, Ken Kesey has written occasional poems, and one of his few published ones, untitled, sounds like nothing so much as a description of his experiences with LSD:

> *Born full tilt into a river flowing—*
> *choking, blinded by sight—into a torrent's roar,*
> *no chart to tell me of the torrent's going*
> *no record of a passing here before.*[1]

It could also describe his experiences as media target in the sixties, and the powerful lessons that crucible imparted. Media glare is what led an aspiring New York author named Tom Wolfe to chronicle the entire Kesey saga in the sixties, and the book that emerged from it, *The Electric Kool-Aid Acid Test,* became a textbook in the history of the counterculture. Wolfe's account, which Kesey later said was 96 percent accurate,[2] should be supplemented by Kesey's own *The Further Inquiry* and Ken Babbs' effort, with Paul Perry, *On the Bus*. From those sources, a relatively thorough account of the era can be gleaned.

One thing that will most strike readers today is the way the Acid Tests simply evolved. Their most direct antecedent may have been the Pranksters' grand cinematic epic, colloquially titled "The Bus Trip," but their roots lay much deeper. For Kesey, the Tests were the logical extension of theories he had been developing since his first published novel, *One Flew Over the Cuckoo's Nest*. For many readers, the power of the novel lay in the degree to which its style departed from literary convention: the way Bromden's schizophrenic vision seemed to wedge its way into a reader's imagination and make him think like Bromden, see like him, feel like him. It was also strikingly original; in the words of Kesey's teacher, critic Malcolm Cowley, "That hallucinated but everyday style, smelling of motor oil, was something new in fiction."[3] It made the imagery and thought of even so damaged a narrator as Bromden seem autobiographical—and the sense of touching the author through his words was an inescapable side effect. Interestingly enough, in his 1972 work *Kesey's Garage Sale*, Kesey makes the identification between himself and Bromden explicit, moving seamlessly from a passage describing hunting with his father into that powerful, beautiful close to the first chapter of *Cuckoo's Nest*, when Bromden says:

> "It's gonna burn me that way, finally telling about all this, about the hospital, and her, and the guys—and about McMurphy. I been silent so long now it's gonna roar out of me like the floodwaters and you think the guy telling this is ranting and raving my *God*; you think this is too horrible to have really happened, this is too awful to be the truth! But, please. It's still hard for me to have a clear mind thinking on it. But it's the truth even if it didn't happen."[4]

That last sentence is a precise and perfect expression of the psychological reality of LSD, and why it was originally dubbed a psychotomimetic—psychosis-inducing—drug, as opposed to a psychedelic, mind-manifesting, one. On acid, all of those fears, hopes, revelations, and insights *are* real.

And, as most early LSD researchers discovered, that seemed to be one of the central lessons of psychedelics: their ability to permit and enhance individual insight. With another person on psychedelics, someone equally sensitized and self-aware, the possibilities for communication were profound. In a group context, the results could be fascinating indeed—as the Bus Trip demonstrated. And for a novelist who had explored in his writing themes of individuality, heroism, group dynamics, and responsibility, the implications were wonderful: group spurs to individual creativity. The artistic poten-

---

1. Michael Strelow, ed., *Kesey* (Eugene, Ore.: Northwest Review Books, 1977), p. 191.
2. Michael Strelow, "Editor's Note," in *Kesey*, p. v.
3. Malcolm Cowley, "Ken Kesey at Stanford," in Strelow, ed., *Kesey*, p. 3.
4. Ken Kesey, *Kesey's Garage Sale* (New York: Viking, 1973), p. 16. Cf. Ken Kesey, *One Flew over the Cuckoo's Nest* (New York: Viking, 1962), pp. 7–8.

tial seemed as vast as the vistas opened by the drug—in short, mind-boggling.

Before the Tests there was the bus. Originally the idea was for Kesey and a couple of friends to drive across the country to New York to launch his new book, *Sometimes a Great Notion,* and take in the World's Fair as well. As this idea took shape, the group of fellow bohemians coalesced around Kesey's place in La Honda until only a bus would hold them. And with Ken Babbs as a coconspirator, their grand artistic theories developed just as rapidly:

> "Before the bus trip we were talking about 'rapping' novels out instead of typing—because typing is so slow. We were going to take acid and stay up all night and rap out novels and tape record them. Then, to add things, we were going to act out parts, and then do the music that went with it, and then, finally, we started talking about getting the movie cameras and filming it. So we were moving very swiftly from a novel on a page to novels on audio-tape to novels on film."[5]

The first major film, of course, was the bus movie: forty hours of unedited cinema verité called *The Merry Pranksters Search for the Cool Place,* documenting their cross-country venture. Back at La Honda, the Pranksters watched and edited and reviewed and rehashed it endlessly, it seemed. One of the forums for viewing the various pieces were the Saturday night parties, which could be considered the genesis of the Acid Tests. Originally an extension of the games and audio and film experiments from the days of the bus trip, these parties added a free-form element that the bus trip always had lacked, or rather, it dropped an element the bus always had: a plot—the journey. With the parties, the potential was limitless.

One of most infamous was when famed satanist—or self-styled Diabolist—Kenneth Anger and his followers were invited; as part of the activities, a chicken was sacrificed, a gesture that the Pranksters felt was only appropriate given their guests' proclivities. Under a substantial dose of acid, however, the intensity of the ritual—the seriousness with which these Day-Glo loonies took their games—was frightening. The Diabolists left.

Live animal sacrifice did not become an established part of the Saturday night parties, but many of the elements later used in the Tests were developed in that context. With outrageousness the order of the day, and with as stellar a celebrity as Kesey nominally in charge, it was inevitable that the Saturday night parties should become the talk of the Bay Area artistic and literary scene. And just as inevitably, it percolated into the underground. One of the Pranksters was Page Browning, who mentioned to Kesey that he knew this band that would fit in very well with these grand artistic and hedonistic theories.

Right about the same time, the parties were outgrowing La Honda. The Hell's Angels made their triumphant entrance, adding a real element of volatility to the proceedings, and some of the Pranksters had moved further south, to Soquel, outside of Santa Cruz. As it turned out, that was where the first Acid Test was held, in November 1965. Besides, after a few months of evolution and development, it was time to see if this could go somewhere. From talking novels to acting them, from a small group to a larger group, from parties to more programmed—or at least more complicated—events, all of the signs seemed to point to even grander notions: why not have them in public? Why not share the vision, communicate it directly? It would be a group vision, a group creation. To some extent, that had been the bus, but it had turned the bus into a stage, and that still left the problem of audience. "You are either on the bus or off the bus" was one of the essential Prankster laws. Now it was time to see if everyone could board the bus, whether the movie could include the audience.

Critic Tony Tanner has called the bus Kesey's third novel.[6] If so, it seems reasonable to view the Tests as an outgrowth and extension of that, and of the themes Tanner explores using that analysis. The Acid Tests would keep searching for the cool place—only with all of the extras from the Bus Movie included. Now the rest of the world could participate, too. One Prankster even phrased it in those terms, calling the Acid Tests

> "really an extension of some of the things we were doing in La Honda. There was a little amphitheater up behind the house. Kesey had the whole place wired with loudspeakers and earphones and lights and things. Artsy people called them 'Happenings,' but they

---

5. Ken Babbs, quoted in Paul Perry and Ken Babbs, *On the Bus* (New York: Thunder's Mouth, 1990), pp. 89–90.

6. Tony Tanner, *City of Words* (New York: Harper and Row, 1971), p. 390.

were just a way of extending to other people what we had done in the privacy of our own bus."[7]

Literarily, if the bus can be called Kesey's third novel, then the Tests are the precursor of the form he would adopt for *Demon Box*, a series of interlinked short stories set in a loosely autobiographical milieu.

Only one ingredient was missing, one that the Pranksters didn't recognize until Page brought it along. Garcia remembered it a few years later as a casual, why-not proposition:

> "One day the idea was there: 'Why don't we have a big party, and you guys bring your instruments and play, and us Pranksters will set up all our tape recorders and bullshit, and we'll all get stoned.' That was the first acid test. The idea was of its essence formless."[8]

It also came at the perfect time in the band's career. They had been turning on while pursuing an apprenticeship at various peninsula bars, and taken their first acid trip together shortly before Page made his history-making introduction. In one account, there is the definite suggestion that they had been finally fired from their regular bar gig the day of their first appearance at one of Ken's parties. Regardless of when it exactly happened, clearly it clicked. Just as Lesh said to Luria Castell at the first Family Dog dance, at around the same time: "Lady, what this little seance needs is us."

The first Acid Test that made much of a splash was in December, right after the Rolling Stones concert in San Jose. The band had just changed its name to the Grateful Dead, and played to several hundred tripped-out young people who followed the instructions on the mysterious flyer handed out at the concert, challenging "can you pass the acid test?" One of the intrigued Stones fans was aspiring journalist Jann Wenner, future founder of *Rolling Stone*, who remembered the event variously over the years: "Here they were in the living room at someone's house playing, and it sounded great. I was staggered, and I was taking drugs at the time, too. I remember going, 'What do you guys call yourself?' And they said, 'The Grateful Dead.' And I went, 'Wow!'"[9] It was a pronouncement whose impression he phrased more succinctly in an earlier interview: "The impact, in my state of mind at that point, was severe."[10]

It also blew the Pranksters' minds—clearly, the Dead were the final element. The Tests were now a bit of everything. New rituals, strange environments, light shows; room games, word games, psychological games: it all added up to acid games. Happening theory, with an edge: this was art that would leave you changed forever, and not from without—from within. The psychological games meant there was the explicit potential for revelation, for genuine insight. It was something inherent with LSD, Kesey felt, as did the other famous group experimenting with psychedelics, the Millbrook group founded by Timothy Leary and Richard Alpert after they left Harvard. But the Millbrook group pursued the psychedelic quest with all of the high seriousness of academics, and gave their research an overtly religious connotation. Kesey and the Pranksters added the element of fun. Even so, there was always going to be the edge. That edge was not just due to the undeniable—and unpredictable—power of the drug; it was also the sensorium that the Pranksters assembled to channel the experience.

In one of his collections, Kesey describes exactly the kind of revelation he sought in the Tests, at the time when he was working at the mental hospital that shaped *One Flew over the Cuckoo's Nest*. One of the patients threatened to become unruly, even dangerous, and Kesey punctured the crisis by describing to the patient an aspect of his behavior that he had been sure was opaque to everyone else. As Kesey describes it, he blew the patient's mind. That incident is the best description of what Kesey felt LSD had the potential to do for everyone:

> "The expression 'blew his mind' was years away still, and is at present a phrase almost milked of meaning, used generally to describe everyday titillations such as the hearing of a new rock lick or the encountering of some slightly bizarre ramification of our daily deal, but imagine for a moment what is really implied: not just a shock, nor invention, but something that arrives on your own familiar wavelength and overloads all your skinny little lines of reason and forces admis-

---

7. Lee Quarnstrom, quoted in Perry and Babbs, *On the Bus*, p. 122.
8. Michael Lydon, "The Dead Zone," *Rolling Stone*, Aug. 23, 1969, reprinted in *Garcia* (New York: Rolling Stone, 1995), p. 61.
9. Joe Smith, *Off the Record* (New York: Warner, 1988), p. 237.

10. Jann Wenner, "Foreword," to Garcia, Reich, and Wenner, *Garcia: Signpost to a New Space* (Straight Arrow Books, 1972), p. 12.

sion of vistas beyond all those horizons you were certain were absolutely permanent. A delusion burst by its own rules. A fantasy split out by the butterfly fantastic."[11]

In the Sound City Acid Test, when Kesey explains to the reporter how others can reflect your blind spots to you in a sympathetic, loving manner, it also blows one's mind—which is why he ends by saying, "It's completely therapeutic."

This notion of a transformative personal insight is an extension of what Kesey had been thinking about, spurred by psychologist Fritz Perls, whose particular focus was on getting people to become fully aware of the present, to be fully focused in the Now. For Kesey, it represented nearly limitless creative potential: one could create and communicate that creation, fully and completely, with no inhibitions or blocks to filter that truth. In a 1972 interview, Kesey reminisced:

> "When we took acid ten years ago, we cut off our periphery time sense. All the stuff that had come before us, and all the stuff that was to come—we said, 'Forget that, let's deal from here on with the present. Just forget what we're going to do and what we've done. It's all contained right in this instant.' At this time I was seeing a lot of Fritz Perls who was into this thing of having to get into the present to realize our senses. He used to say he wanted to bring us to our senses of knowing what's going on right now. We really got into it. We got so we could do it and be right there, in the present, for long periods of time. When you're in the present like that, you're like Muhammad Ali when he beat Liston. You move into a state of magic. Powers are available to you that you couldn't find in the past or in the future."[12]

To an artist, it was tapping into a wellspring of creativity: pure insight, pure inspiration, as the source fuel for creation, no thought of editing; no fear. Kerouac would have approved. (Not surprisingly, though Kesey was younger than the Beats, he did write a short story while at Stanford, "The Beat Element," that made plain his admiration for them.[13]) Acid did not represent just another inebriated lark, in other words. In fact, it was an undeniable indication of how to avoid becoming trapped in the constructs and fears that were the inevitable result of learning from one's history; it was an indication of the only way to continue to discover the world anew. In a later interview Kesey elaborated, likening LSD's effects on one's thinking to being jump-started from linear thinking to lateral, which Kesey calls a wellspring of creativity: "There is lateral thinking as well as linear thinking, and in lateral thinking is where discovery lies. Linear thinking will only lead you on paths you've already traveled."[14] For a novelist, used to living in the world of frozen time that even the greatest literature is at some level, the implications for creativity were heady indeed:

> "With the taking of that acid, suddenly I was shifted over to where I was able to see where I had been looking full front at a world; and by shifting over, I was seeing it from another position. It became dimensional. . . . Everything that's going on has an allegorical level. . . . Enough stuff happened out of it that it was undeniable."[15]

This was where the threat came from, the whiff of danger, as Kesey explained:

> "We were raised over here to believe in a certain hierarchy that was up here. That all collapses when you do dope. You can't maintain it. When a person takes acid, a lot of acid, it's not going to hurt his chromosomes. It's going to hurt something that's a whole lot more dear to him—which is his image of himself."[16]

That damage could be liberating, though, which is why cultivation of games that provoked introspection were such a big part of the Tests. The essence of the Acid Tests was more than just confrontation: it was celebration. The entire encounter, and the existence of "the

---

11. Kesey, *Kesey's Garage Sale,* pp. 13–14.
12. Linda Gaboriau, "Ken Kesey: Summing Up the '60s, Sizing Up the '70s," *Crawdaddy,* Dec. 1972, p. 39.
13. "The Beat Element" [short story], 8 pp., typewritten. Kesey Manuscript Collection, privately owned. Courtesy Red House Books.
14. Peter Joseph, *Good Times: An Oral History of America in the 1960s* (New York: William Morrow, 1974), p. 382.
15. Ibid, p. 382.
16. Ibid., pp. 385–86.

Enemy," was a part of it all; the game always has an opponent, an adversary. Kesey and Company believed that the goal was to contend with that adversary—and win. People can confront their deepest, darkest fears—and emerge victorious, or better, stronger, more honest souls. Their insights into themselves, their world, their senses—their toys!—was something they could and would take home from the Acid Tests. It provided the psychological edge to the games at a Test—and made the power of games, of playing, of interpreting the world and oneself anew strong magic indeed. Richard Alpert, who later became Ram Dass, made the point explicitly:

> "The Acid Tests were extraordinary. I felt that they were sheer magic. And they were scary magic. In many ways I saw it as religious ritual. I call them scary because there were clearly bad trips going on within the framework of the Tests. They seemed to be not bad trips in the sense that they were lethal, but bad in the sense that people were getting more than they bargained for."[17]

Into this heady mixture came the Grateful Dead, the rocket fuel in what was already a jet-propelled undertaking. In a way, the band was the living embodiment of these theories already, in microcosm: their group improvisation represented exactly that sense of living fully in the Now, where insight and inspiration became communication, instantaneously. Needless to say, they fit perfectly, almost too well—and they skewed the format of the Tests. The prototype of a modern Dead show had begun. After only a few Tests, the band had become an indispensable part of the proceedings, as Mountain Girl recounted: "Those guys were really game. The more they did it, the more they got into it, and the more they would play. We tried to do an Acid Test without them and it didn't work. It wasn't the same without the band."[18]

But after only a couple of months, in which the Acid Tests went as far north as Portland and as far south as L.A., things began to fall apart. By the end, it had become an unstable mix anyway. With Kesey gone and Babbs worried, the Pranksters had become, in Garcia's words, "a semi-fascist" organization—at least in comparison to the Dead's scene, which was looser and more anarchic than ever before. As Mountain Girl recalled a few years later in an interview with Jerry, "You guys were doing up a lot of DMT and we were going on a number of not smoking any grass and not taking anything but acid and only on acid test night. We were really trying to clean up and you guys were really . . . ohhh, God . . . really weird."[19]

What the Tests provided the band, though, was exactly the sort of creative fuel that Kesey described as the central result of living in the Now, something that Bob Weir corroborated:

> "When the Dead became involved with Kesey's Acid Tests—the original ones—that was the most amazing single thing that has ever happened to me. It was one big party, one adventure incarnate. We were living on the edge all the time for a good, sustained period of time. It built to a fever pitch that was incredible. It had an amazing amount of energy."[20]

Maintaining that energy was simply too demanding, though. Before the end, the Test had turned into a more conventional presentation, a show and not a communal happening. Part of that was because the Pranksters had become so adept at the whole process. As Tom Wolfe describes their L.A. sojourn,

> "They performed with an efficiency they never knew they had before. It was if they were all picking up on Babbs' exhortation of months ago: 'We've got to learn how to function on acid.' They were soaring out of their gourds themselves, but they were pulling off acid tests that seemed like they were orchestrated."[21]

But that orchestration robbed things of the spontaneity that was supposed to be the core of it all until by the end, they were just performing for the audience, as

---

17. Ram Dass, quoted in Perry and Babbs, *On the Bus*, p. 148–49.
18. Mountain Girl interview, in Sandy Troy, *One More Saturday Night* (New York: St. Martin's Press, 1991), pp. 72–74.
19. Garcia, Reich, and Wenner, *Garcia: Signpost to a New Space*, p. 53. Ellipses in original.
20. Quoted in Jay Saporita, *Pourin' It All Out: An Insider's View of the Rock Scene* (Secaucus, N.J.: Citadel, 1980), p. 184.
21. Tom Wolfe, *The Electric Kool-Aid Acid Test* (New York: Farrar, Straus and Giroux, 1968), p. 270.

one contemporary commentator claimed.[22] Gone was the magic, that communion of minds that had drawn them all to the Tests to begin with, which even the first L.A. area Acid Test, at Paul Sawyer's Unitarian Church, had in abundance:

> "People dancing in the most ecstatic way and getting so far into the thing, the straight multitudes even, that even they took microphones, and suddenly there was no longer any separation between the entertainers and the entertained at all, none of that well-look-at-you-startled-squares condescension of the ordinary happening. Hundreds were swept up in an experience, which built up like a dream typhoon, peace on the smooth liquid centrifugal whirling edge. In short, everybody in The Movie, on the bus, and it was beautiful. . . ."[23]

And almost over. Shortly afterward, the band left the Pranksters and holed up with Owsley, sharing a house at the edge of Watts and rehearsing, gigging occasionally, and living off of the Bear while he tabbed acid and developed a sound system for them. The Pranksters themselves split apart; some fled to Mexico to join Kesey, others dispersed. There would be a few more Acid Tests, but the heyday was over by the spring of 1966. The model it left behind would be something that lodged most heavily, perhaps, in the minds of the band that had provided the soundtrack for them.

At first, though, that model represented the unattainable. In one of the interviews that is spliced into Kesey's Acid Test video, Garcia talks about the central distinction between the Tests and their later shows:

> "The nice thing about the Acid Tests was that we could play or not. And a lot of times we'd get just too high, really, to play. And we'd play for maybe a minute, and then we'd lose it. And sometimes we would play. And since there was no pressure on us—I mean, people didn't come in to see the Grateful Dead, they came to the Acid Test; it was the whole event that counted. So we weren't in the spotlight, and therefore the pressure wasn't on us. So when we did play, we played with a certain kind of freedom that you rarely get as a musician. I mean, not only did we not have to fulfill expectations about us, but we didn't have to fulfill expectations about *music,* either."[24]

And for musicians already entranced at the potential for improvisation, the implications were extreme indeed. Only a year after the Tests ended, Garcia spoke with a former student of his about the experience:

> "We've played on acid and that does things to your time sense, and it does other things. It produces an unimaginably wider scope of ideas. More consciousness means you have more of an understanding of what you're doing, and that means you can do it better because you're doing it with that much more of your mind."[25]

Years later, Garcia put it simply: "The Acid Test was the prototype for our whole basic trip. But nothing has ever come up to the level of the way the Acid Test was. It's just never been equalled, really, or the basic gist of it never developed out."[26]

The reduction of the Acid Test formula to lights and a band irked Garcia greatly, as he later complained to author Charles Reich:

> "The problem there is the form that we've been stuck with. It's unfortunate. The most historical point, I suppose, would be the Trips Festival, when another form was starting to evolve. It was turned into the most obvious kind—you take a light show, you take a rock and roll band and that's your psychedelic experience. And that's not it. That wasn't it at the Trips Festival and that's not what we were doing, either. But in order to keep on playing, we had to go with what-

---

22. mr. jones, "The Prankster's Last Prank," *Daily Californian,* Mar. 31, 1966, p. 8. Prankster Denise Kaufman, aka Mary Microgram, was supposedly the source of these reports.
23. Wolfe, *The Electric Kool-Aid Acid Test,* p. 271.
24. Jerry Garcia and Ken Kesey, interviewed by Tom Snyder, *The Tomorrow Show,* May 7, 1981.
25. Randy Groenke and Mike Cramer, "One Afternoon Long Ago," in *The Golden Road,* no. 7 (Summer 1985), p. 28.
26. Garcia, Reich, and Wenner, *Garcia: Signpost to a New Space,* p. 47.

ever form was there. Because for one thing, the form that we liked always scared everybody. It scared the people that owned the building that we'd rent, so they'd never rent twice to us. It scared the people who came, a lot of times. It scared the cops. It scared everybody. Because it represented total and utter anarchy. Indoor anarchy. That's something that people haven't learned to get off with. But our experience with these scenes is that's where you get the highest...."[27]

This state he handily defined for Reich: "To get high is to forget yourself. And to forget yourself is to see everything else. And to see everything else is to become an understanding molecule in evolution, a conscious tool of the universe."[28]

And that could well serve as an apt metaphor for the channeled inspiration that a state of peak improvisation conveys. In a 1969 interview, Garcia described his attitude toward improvisation in Acid Test–like terms:

"An ideal thing would be to go onstage with absolutely nothing in your head, and everybody get together and pick up his instrument and play and improvise the whole thing—lyrics and vocals and everything, whatever's gonna happen—and have it come out just as boss as you could want. And perhaps that's a place where we can all get. But it's in the experimental stage. It's kind of like an alchemical experiment that you have to repeat. Again and again and again, the same experiment, exactly, the same or as close to the same as you can get it, really. But naturally our music isn't like that. We don't repeat the music—the details of the music—over and over again. There's a framework for that, too. But it's like the same effort. The effort is to get higher."[29]

Early San Francisco scene chronicler James Doukas described their success in those terms when he claimed that by 1968, the Dead had "evolved into a group of musicians communicating at the highest level possible:

between themselves they could control sound with almost the same accuracy as that of speech."[30]

And a potential for communication that the band learned from the Tests. At their improvisatory peak, the Dead's jams over the years could be called the musical equivalent of the Acid Tests, with the same beguiling, exhilarating sense of potential, for anything, from a platform that suggested it all. And like the Tests, it would be an excursion filled with sweet epiphanies and powerful revelations. The Dead's drive for improvisation is quintessentially American, with elements derived from bluegrass, blues, jazz, and avant-garde classical, but their practice of it is the most audible legacy of their experience of the Acid Tests, and the most obvious artistic link. From the first definite if inchoate stirrings in 1966, through their last show, there was usually an element in the Dead's jams that approached what they began to do more formally beginning in 1967 and regularly from the mid-seventies on: a free-form group improvisation without much of anything at all in the way of arrangement, melody, or key; just communication, with each other, from within themselves, and to the audience—with them, ideally. Known as "Space" or "Drumz" (which includes the drummers' duet that precedes it), these aleatory, completely unique group compositions embodied that ethereal, intoxicating sense of not just extemporaneous instrument voices but floating arrangements as well—which was, if anything, the heart of Prankster music, too, and an insight into why Garcia was so enamored of the notion of formlessness. When Heads hear a fragment that seems to be a portent—a chord sequence, a few notes suggesting melody, a fragment of a riff—emerging in the murk, it can be a sublime epiphany for everyone, band and audience; a moment of collective unfolding revelation, Kesey's open circle, Garcia's formlessness birthing new forms. A form in which audience and band are fused into one clairvoyant whole, a vehicle for the music being played through the entire orgiastic mass. The regenerative soul of the Deadhead community can probably best be found in those moments, in which not only is everyone in the band, but more important, as lyricist John Barlow put it, "the music plays the band."

Even if Garcia describes how far short of the ideal a Dead show falls, it doesn't mean that they didn't come close—closer to that than anything else, for that matter. A *San Francisco Chronicle* reporter's description of the

---

27. Ibid., p. 65.
28. Ibid., p. 127.
29. Douglas Kent Hall and Sue C. Clark, *Rock: A World Bold as Love* (New York: Cowles, 1970), p. 164.

30. James N. Doukas, *Electric Tibet* (North Hollywood, Calif.: Dominion, 1969), p. 189.

Dead's shows as early as the fall of 1967 sounds as if it were lifted from a description of the Tests: "These aren't ordinary concerts. They're psychedelic and are extreme examples of total environmental theater, which engages all the senses: thunderous rock music, light shows that burst and flow in choruses of color, hundreds of dancing young people, incense floating through your mind."[31] And even Bill Graham tried to tap into—detractors would say cash in on—the Acid Test ethos when he took his San Francisco Scene on the road to Toronto at the end of the Summer of Love: "A total San Francisco Production with three groups, environmental lighting, sound and feeling. A total production of the feeling of the new wave from the West."[32]

Nor did the similarity end with the sixties. Long-time family member, former manager, and Rex Foundation president Danny Rifkin believes that the band's shows have long used an LSD trip as an organizing metaphor, establishing the eventual pattern of a first set comprising shorter songs, and a much longer second set, characterized by the middle segment of drums and space, with all of its dark and strange possibilities, finally ending in light, though sometimes just power.[33] And the aura of initiation, of high communication and interaction with band and fellow audience members gave shows the blend of ritual and invocation and initiation and transcendence that all good subcultural rites need. It was why Timothy Leary said that the Dead were "a twenty-year extension of the Acid Tests." And even though Garcia felt like they fell far short of the original, there was still more that linked the two forms of public outrage than not. Even the whiff of danger that Stewart Brand talked about as such a part of the Acid Test ethos: Dead shows had it, too, all the way through the end. Channeling for something that powerful was all they promised to do, and just as a four-hour dancing marathon would demonstrate exactly how well one had been caring for one's body, so too would a psychedelic romp through the synapses reveal the state of one's soul, with the soundtrack of a Dead show for a guide. Magic, but strong magic indeed.

NICK MERIWETHER

---

31. "The New Generation: Grateful Dead Are Much Alive," *San Francisco Chronicle*, Sept. 2, 1967.
32. Program, "Bill Graham Presents the San Francisco Scene," at the O'Keefe Centre for the Performing Arts, Toronto, July 31–Aug. 5, 1967, [p. 6].
33. Danny Rifkin, interviewed by Joel Selvin, Jan. 29, 1992.

---

### 1/8/66
**The Fillmore Acid Test**
**Fillmore Auditorium,**
**San Francisco, California**

Stage Banter, More Power Rap, King Bee, I'm a Hog for You, Baby, Caution, Death Don't Have No Mercy, Final remarks / Star-Spangled Banner / More final remarks

**Source:** SBD, **Quality:** B+, **Length:** 0:35, **Origin:** Part of the video *The Acid Test* (Eugene, Ore.: Key-Z Productions, 1990; 52 min.), **Genealogy:** professionally remastered VHS stereo audio

**Highlights:** King Bee, Caution

Bits and pieces of this tape have circulated since the 1990 release of the video *The Acid Test,* by Ken Kesey's Key-Z Productions. Assembled by Zane Kesey, the video is a hybrid of several sources, and the result is a classic piece of Prankster psychedelia—in part because of the difficulty in differentiating which elements came from where. This is not due to the celebrated Prankster spirit of tweaking the straights, however. The boxes housing the reels were cryptically labeled "Fillmore Acid Test"— the source of all of the audio—and "L.A. Acid Test."[1] Most if not all of the Fillmore Acid Test was recorded, apparently on four twelve-inch reels. Of the video footage marked "L.A.," however, nothing more was written on those reels or boxes, and nothing else in the archives has shed any light thus far. Nor is this especially surprising: both Bear and Dick Latvala encountered the same problem with Prankster tapes, as Latvala recalled in a recent interview: "The labeling was terrible. They taped a lot of stuff and labeled it very poorly."[2] In fact, even what we have is a lot, as Zane noted: "For the Pranksters, that much of a label was doing well—generally you'd be lucky if they wrote anything at all on it, and if they did, it might be something like 'Animal Banana Cream-puff Pimple,' which made sense to whoever wrote it—just not much to the rest of us."[3] And since many tapes, especially those of Neal Cassady, have disappeared over the years from the Prankster archives,

---

1. Zane Kesey, interviewed by author, July 30, 1996; cf. Zane Kesey, interviewed by author, May 15, 1997.
2. Dick Latvala, interviewed by John R. Dwork, April 1, 1996.
3. Zane Kesey, interviewed by author, July 30, 1996.

it may well be that we will get no more from the Keseys.[4] The video has several segments of audio that are not a part of the Fillmore Acid Test, including some obvious interview segments—some from 1966, others from 1981—as well as some pleasant little instrumental pieces, recorded much later, when the Dead and the New Riders were visiting the Keseys in Oregon.[5]

After the San Jose Acid Test, the papers were filled with stories of the "drug orgy" that had transpired—perfect advance publicity for the next few local Tests, at Muir Beach, a club in Palo Alto, and finally, a month after San Jose, San Francisco. "Dose early" was the word in the hip community, about five or six o'clock, so that one's mind would be well and truly lit by the time things got rolling at nine at the Fillmore. *Chronicle* music critic Ralph Gleason couldn't cover that show and sent a stand-in, who filed a glowing report. Watching this conventicle of the ultra-hip, which was "like the backstage crowd at the California Hall dance,"[6] he was especially impressed by the degree to which everyone was a part of it—whatever "it" was. "A strobe light was flickering at a very high frequency in one corner of the hall and a group of people were bouncing a golden balloon up and down on it. It was a most disturbing frequency. It hurt to look at them." He mentioned the Thunder Machine, streamers all over, "giant frisbees, balloons like basketballs, acrobats, girls in felt eyelashes four inches long, fluorescent painting on jeans, glasses low on the nose with eyes painted on them, people with eyes painted on their foreheads, men with foxes on their shoulders!" And the best Prankster electronics to date, replete with TV cameras and screens that showed the audience itself in various stages of communal meltdown, and, of course, "a lot of electronic equipment which sent out a low reverberation that resonated throughout the hall." Costumes, weirdness; all of the earmarks of the best Acid Test to date, and a new plateau of professionalism. For once, Gleason's standard column close of "Quite a night!" seemed understated.[7]

Gleason's enthusiastic stand-in had the irritating habit of peppering his piece with exclamation points and "Oh wow!" But he was making a point: it was a night of stark incongruities, when a scene like the Fillmore Acid Test could occur in the great wide open, in public, pay a dollar and come on in, and, once inside, find the barrel, the mysterious one that appeared and reappeared at odd intervals all over the hall, provoking a minor stampede to get at its magical contents. And all of this while the Airplane and the Charlatans provided the more responsible side of the emerging rock underground across town at California Hall, at the same time as teen-scene band the Vejtables were playing in the Marina district, a Longshoreman's Hall dance sponsored by KYA. Ironically, the most mainstream of the acts was playing the most psychedelic venue, since the Longshoreman's Hall had been the site of the first psychedelic dances in the city the previous fall, and in two more weeks would host the mammoth Trips Festival, the largest and in some ways grandest of the Acid Tests.

One side effect of all of these options was that the Dead gained a manager that night. Rock Scully was the promoter of the California Hall show, and rather than compete with Kesey's show, he arranged for buses to cart scenesters and trippers back and forth between the venues. At one point in the evening, he took one of them himself: "I split my own show, hopped on the bus and went to see the Dead. As a matter of fact, once I left California Hall, I didn't go back because when I got to the Fillmore the Dead were raising the roof. I fell in love with that band."[8]

There's enough weirdness and good music captured here to make his response understandable. The tape opens, appropriately, with what may as well be called "The More Power Rap," an interesting little document that can be considered a microcosm of the problems with taking the Acid Tests public. It starts with some vintage Kesey, though:

> **Kesey:** Hello, hello, am I coming through? Oh yes—we've been waiting for you. It's me, friends, the old pointed head. I'm nestled somewhere deep inside the bowels of the Fillmore Auditorium. And for any of you who have harbored doubts as to the seriousness of tonight's mission, the captain has assured me, that it's prearranged with the owners of the auditorium, tonight's Acid Test will remain embarked on its perilous voyage the remainder of the night. That's right: just as you feared. What's that? Turn the knob? Which one's that—ah yes, this one here?

And sounds of the audience rise, as well as the first signs of the band tuning up, prompting Kesey to warble,

---

4. Ken Kesey, *Kesey's Garage Sale*, p. 195
5. Zane Kesey, interviewed by author, May 15, 1997.
6. Michael Rossman, quoted in Ralph J. Gleason, "On the Town: It Was Quite a Weekend!," *San Francisco Chronicle*, Jan. 10, 1966.
7. Ibid.

8. Quoted in Gans and Simon, *Playing in the Band*, p. 46.

"Everybody tune up, tu-u-u-une u-u-up. The Acid Test is everywhere in this spaceship, everywhere you are, you're all acid-testing and acid-tasting." Several minutes of chaos ensue, Bobby Weir ordering someone off the stage, much debating over the sound system, microphones not working, and some great commentary from the band on all this. Bobby blithely announces, "Nothing up here is working. Ah yes, gaze upon it, friends, the electronic wasteland." Pigpen is more blunt: "No electricity on the stage. Fix it."

What is most interesting is the dynamic between the two: Kesey makes the complaints part of the proceedings, even urging them to just start playing and they'll get everything straightened out as things progress, but the Dead are having none of it; already they are a professional band, and this is a paid gig. Pig eventually falls into the spirit, singing, "Honey, you got the power," until it straightens out. "King Bee" starts slow, a New Orleans voodoo swamp mystic protopsychedelic weirdness that builds into a steadily more hypnotic trance blues state, the perfect platform for some great Garcia work in the middle—and his guitar is definitely not low in the mix. There's excellent sound here, the best of anything available this early. Pig's voice is very low in the mix, almost inaudible at times, but we get a great jangly, brittle guitar sound and a flat thumpy bass: that classic, mid-sixties PA sound. Nor is it typical of what the song became, with a very unusual Jerry solo in the middle: low, slow fretted notes, very Jorma-esque, before it flows into his signature style of cascading, concentrated runs over the fingerboard.

If you have the video soundtrack, at this point there is a segment from an interview with Kesey and Garcia in 1981, talking about the Acid Tests; otherwise, next is "I'm a Hog for You, Baby," which is interspersed with another interview segment (this time from the fall of 1966), and then has Kesey talking over the band, announcing "Operation Crystalization," in which he and a couple of the other Pranksters sound as if they are partaking of some of the evening's chemical sacraments: "Some of that high-powered rocket fuel? Well, lemme take a sip." Then we get a few moments of classic Kesey Acid Test weirdness: "Glittering, glowing, ever flowing neon, all the money that we're throwin' to the electrical company. You people out there, listen to me. This is Lothar speaking. This is a trap, a trap, you are all busted. Busted! You fools. Aaaaah! You fools! You fools!" Never trust a Prankster.

The video has several other segments interspersed here, including interviews and a brief bit of the later instrumental music, before it returns to the Fillmore for "Caution." Already in mid-jam, it opens with Pigpen singing, "I went down to gypsy woman / Find out what's wrong with me / She say, all you need . . ." He roars into "all you need, all you need," Garcia getting more and more manic behind him, running all over and around the lines, then backing off, perfect control, only to pick it up again, higher and higher, a Pigpen- and Jerry-led tour de force, leading and carrying the band forward. Psychedelicized or not, this is still very much Pig's band, a reminder of how much they relied on him in the early days to anchor the band musically just as he did socially, when they were tripping and he would settle them down from the jangles. A long, solid jam here showcases his contribution, vintage Pigpen in the days when he exhibited the most musical confidence, in many ways, weaving back and forth with Jerry, and it is easy to imagine the interplay with the audience.

A nice segue follows, though not a jam, into "Death Don't Have No Mercy." Pig's organ work is perfect here. It shone so rarely later, but here it sounds wonderful: spooky, gentle and occasionally trilling, and always eerie. A highlight of the tape, this is a very good performance; the bass sounds good, a deep, tight thump, and so strong. And faintly, in the background, you can hear someone—a woman?—wailing, either in unison with Pig or despair at the vision he's painting: "Death don't—death don't—death don't have no mercy, in this land," a sentiment that could be terrifying on acid.

Or a magnificent catharsis, the effect of which was bound to be adulterated by the premature cutoff of the power by the police: "Everybody out, the dance is over, have to clear the hall." Not missing a beat, Kesey, theatrical to the end, replies, "This is incredible! The chief security agent has taken over and informed—he has made his extraordinary announcement. And has pulled the plug on the band. Completely nullifying the engines!" Some great moments follow, as we hear the scene recounted by Wolfe and Babbs, as Pranksters wander about with microphones as the cops try to find them, even a fascinating piece of responsible discussion as one Prankster—Babbs, perhaps?—says, "We're planning on having other gigs in other cities. And if we have a hassle here, there's not gonna be another hall that'll have us. So we'd appreciate it if we'll just go a little bit more, then we'll turn on the lights and—everybody use their head."

Some nice bits of biting Bobby sarcasm, as he summarizes at the end, "Sad, isn't it? When you come to one of these things, you want to have a lot of clean fun, you know, good clean fun? So you can enjoy yourself and not hurt anybody, you know? And uh, well, that's what people come here to do, you know? And then they get kicked out, you know. It's really a pity. It's a cryin' shame." And finally, as the cops converge on him, "Arrest everybody, but don't hurt any of the equipment, you know? That's our livelihoods." A final baiting of the cops follows with a truly hideous, painful, and off-key rendition of "The Star-Spangled Banner," followed by some last-minute swearing and grumbles. The tape ends with Bobby's epitaph for the evening: "Yes, and in the end it's nothing but mindless chaos. Even as it started, he was that same old dude. Good old Mindless Chaos, hassling, ever hassling." A quintessential piece of Prankster wisdom, from the heart of the Acid Test era.

NICK MERIWETHER

---

## 1/29/66

**The Acid Test: A Sound City Production (LP)**
**Sound City Studios, 363 Sixth Street, San Francisco, California**

Ken Kesey, interviewed by Frank Frey, Ken Babbs and harmonica, Take Two: Ken Kesey, Bull, Peggy the Pistol, One-Way Ticket (A Classic) [Ken Babbs and Ken Kesey], Bells and Fairies, Levitation, Trip X, The End

**Source:** SBD, **Quality:** A, **Length:** 0:27, **Genealogy:** MR > LP > C

**Highlights:** Ken Kesey, interviewed by Frank Frey; Peggy the Pistol

**Personnel:** Ken Kesey, Ken Babbs, George Walker, Jerry Garcia, Pigpen, and other Merry Pranksters

---

One of the oddest artifacts from the Acid Test era, the Sound City Acid Test is known to most Deadheads only as a tape of a limited-release LP that came out in the spring of 1966. According to Ken Babbs, one of the prime movers behind the project, plans are afoot to re-release it officially. The LP was apparently the brainchild of the owner of the studio, known to the Pranksters only as "Jim the Host," credited on the label as Frank Frey, possibly a pseudonym to disguise the identity of someone who clearly is under the influence of LSD during the session. One issue that can be clarified is the mysterious claim made on the LP's center labels, "As photographed in *Look* magazine!" It appears that comment, at least, was premature, since no mention of the Acid Test appeared in *Look* editor George Leonard's long, thoughtful article on *California,* and the few remarks on LSD were in the context of a brief description of the Trips Festival.[1]

The center label also claims that fourteen hours were recorded, from which the LP was culled. Unfortunately, the master reels have disappeared, so this excerpt is all that remains. What remains, however, is an interesting—albeit very weird—document. Held a few days after the Trips Festival at Longshoreman's Hall, itself just after Kesey's second bust for marijuana, the Sound City Acid Test comes at an interesting juncture in the Pranksters' history. Part of the incentive was to simply experiment with a studio, as Ken Babbs recalled in a recent interview: "We'd always wanted to go into the studio. We'd done so many recordings by then: by ourselves, on the bus, at the Acid Tests. So when this opportunity to go into the studio came up we were really ready for it, because we could use all those studio facilities and get a real good recording."[2] Without an audience, however, it was clear that something was missing, and for that reason, Babbs doesn't consider it an actual Acid Test. And it's interesting to note that the Pranksters' difficulties in translating their live act to the studio would be repeated with the Acid Test house band, the Dead.

"Jim the Host" is how Ken Babbs and the other Pranksters referred to the owner of the studio, and it is his interview with Kesey that starts the album. "Jim" begins, "If you could just fill me in, and tell me a few of the details of what we're going to be doing," which prompts Kesey to say, "Well, you've already answered a lot of your question by the tone in your voice, which says it's obviously ridiculous to ask such a question," and he laughs; the Pranksters have begun pranking, as Babbs begins softly blowing on a harmonica and gradually the other Pranksters join in, weird sound effects in the background adding to the feeling that yeah, it may not be an Acid Test, but the feeling of a trip is certainly there.

Of all of the segments that Jim the Host chose to include, this is the one that will most interest fans of

---

1. George B. Leonard, "Where the California Game Is Taking Us," *Look,* vol. 30, no. 14 (June 28, 1966), pp. 108–116[?].
2. Ken Babbs, interviewed by John R. Dwork, March 22, 1997.

Kesey and historians of the era, since it provides an excellent encapsulation of the theories behind the Acid Tests. And it is perfect Prankster, seesawing from silly to serious and back again in the course of the seven minutes that make up the cut. Kesey is gentle with his interlocutor's first question, amplifying his remarks with one of the most succinct statements on record about the philosophy of the Acid Tests: "I figure that our function on this earth is to reflect the other fellow, whatever instrument that we can use, be it tape recorder or camera or pencil. Or a mirror. If I can reflect you, and the places where I see the barbs and the hang-ups, and do it with some amount of love and not with hostility, so there's as little pain as possible, it means that you can move on.... [The Acid Test is] completely therapeutic."

But maintaining seriousness is definitely not the function of the Test, so the interview veers into the silly and the weird immediately, Ken pointing out the Pranksters as examples of his "therapy": "some of the lamest and loopiest and looniest people in the Bay Area." And how does he achieve this therapy? "Well, as navigator of this venture, I try as much as possible to set out in a direction that, in the first place, is practically impossible to achieve, and then along the way, mess up the minds of the crew with as many chemicals as we can lay our hands on, so it's almost certain that we can't get there." Still groping, still the straight man, Jim the Host (or Frank Frey) gamely asks, "Well, would you say that it was deliberately self-defeating, then?," as the Pranksters giggle in the background. And this prompts another veer into the serious, Kesey expanding on a theme he addressed in one of his seminal lectures, delivered the summer before to a group of English teachers:

> **Kesey:** This is about as deliberately self-defeating as anything has ever been in history. Most of the people, I think, involved with this realize that there's nothing to be gained. That every time you try to lay your hands on something and get hold of it, that you've sold yourself down the river—that it's a lie. The first Prankster rule is that nothing lasts. And if you start there, and really believe that nothing lasts, you try to achieve nothing at all times.

To which the great straight line is, "Well, if you're trying to achieve nothing, then why do you put so much effort into achieving nothing?," provoking gales of Prankster laughter, and Ken's tentative response, "We, uh, we have nothing else to do?"

After the laughter dies down, Kesey delivers the last serious statement of the album and the interview.

> **Kesey:** Organized disorganization is like nothing. That's a self-cancelling fact, like nonmusic. See, none of us are musicians, or navigators. Or technicians. We're all completely bumbling amateurs. First, because like Galileo or Columbus or anybody who makes any sort of discovery at all in this world, they have to do it by accident. We have to do something that will almost ensure accident. And since a human being is so damn proficient at grooving himself a rut and staying in it at all costs, so that he doesn't get hurt, we have to do something to break us out of that rut. The outlet of our minds, which has been going along this same kind of thinking for so many thousands of years that we don't even realize it, that our thoughts are going nowhere new. You don't—you can't have a new idea. You can't just sit down there on the toilet and begin to strain and go forward and find a new idea. You can be enlightened, which is like 'ah!' And to do that, though, you have to wander into a new area.

This, in turn, explains why the Pranksters valued their amateur musical—and nonmusical—efforts so highly:

> **Kesey:** Imagine how it used to be like when people started talking. The first guy that ever realized he could use this mechanism in his throat to make a sound that would communicate a feeling, emotion, or effect in the brain of another being over there. At that time, we probably were humming all the time. We probably were just making continual noises. It's done, like I was saying before, to emphasize something that's going on with us. There is, right now, between you and I, a weirder thing happening than usually happens, just because we're getting close enough to begin to examine it. You get a lot of people examining it for a long time, it gets very weird. It gets extremely weird.

But the weirdness has a distinct intellectual purpose, and this is the basis of the artistic appeal of the venture for an award-winning novelist:

**Kesey:** The trip is an open circle, I think. Everything else is closed circle. The trip means there is still a place in what is happening for me to fit into. Or for you to fit into. If you're listening to the radio, it's a closed circle. It's already happened, you know. This all has to do with time. You see, when I say something now, it's taken how long for the voice to get to you, to your ears and to your head. So that whatever I do happens at a point in time, and finally reaches you . . . by then it's a closed circle. There's no place for you to interrupt. Everything is closed circles between people. When you get an open circle, it's dangerous—it's like children, or animals. It means they demand you doing weird things, like playing a harmonica that is going nowhere, that any moment you can add to it your own kind of noise and it's part of it. This is different from Beethoven's Fifth, which is finished, and there's no place for me in it, except as an audience.

Theory expounded, interview segment ended, and now we're into the trip. A classically strange moment comes when Jim the Host asks, "What are you doing, Ken?" Kesey replies, in a voice that is instantly identifiable as that of someone tripping fairly hard, "Just goofing," to which another Prankster says, "Let him do it, whatever he's doing." A tenet of those who trip together: when someone needs support, you provide it, responding quickly to that tone of need so clearly sounded in a tripper's voice—a voice bereft of pretension, tripping heavily, speaking pure thought, no filter to block the instinct to communicate. It's probably the most arresting moment on the album, and an interesting moment in recorded psychedelia.

Struggling gamely on, Jim the Host pursues Kesey through a series of cat-and-mouse questions, such as "What about death," as Kesey banters easily with him, the stoned and the straight, harmonica blowing in the background along with various weird Prankster musical effects.

"Take Two" is a Kesey song-poem, a ditty, as it's labeled on the LP, probably spun on the spot: "Take two, take two. Take two, ladies and gentlemen. Here we are indisposed, as it were, at this end of the Sound City situation, and we're entitled to Take Two. Of what, may I ask? [Lots of strange Prankster effects cut in here.] God knows, I am answered," to more sound effects, as he intones:

*Take two—they're small.*
*Take two—that's all.*
*Take two—then quit.*
*Take two, man, and then—I said split.*

A quick cut and Jim the Host is once again attempting to communicate with Kesey, in the aptly titled cut "Bull." By now almost frantic, he sounds like a confused and frightened student at an irritated guru's feet:

**Jim the Host:** No, I am interested in you, because you and I—put the microphone away—[loud Prankster discordance going on throughout Jim's speech]—you're two different people, you can communicate with me so beautifully in one language, the other language that you can communicate in so beautifully, I'm trying to understand because I'm a learner. I learned some basics today and I'm trying—and I'm quite with the basics. I'm as smart as you in one way, you know that.

This prompts some of the best banter, as Kesey replies, quickly, "We're all as smart as each other." "Nah, no."

Kesey won't give up, though: "Everyone I know is a lot smarter than I am."

This doesn't slow Jim down in the slightest: "I can talk as fast, and as quickly, and I can write as well. The other thing that you have—the other philosophy, the basic thing that you have—the beautiful thing that you have—," which we don't hear as it fades out.

"Peggy the Pistol" is the only part of the proceedings that Babbs remembers as having been practiced before, and the polish is evident. Sung by Kesey, it is a slow, weird blues:

*Have you ever heard the story 'bout Peggy the pistol*
*She didn't shoot a gun, but she shot a lot of crystal*
*She had the meth habit, she had it bad*
*Now lemme tell you 'bout the trip she had*

In the next few verses, Peggy thinks that she overdoses, wakes up in a strange dream world—"She had landed in the crack, between tick and tock / In a land as still as a frozen clock"—and sees various people—Jesus, Anne Frank, Buddha, Lee Harvey Oswald—in a style reminiscent of Dylan's parade through literary history in "Desolation Row."

"One-Way Ticket (A Classic)" is an extended riff on a theme Kesey has invoked in several places, from journals to published writings, starting with the line "There's always somebody there, right in the alley, waitin' for you to go slippin' past and say, 'hey buddy, you wanna buy a hot trip to Heaven?' "[3] Following the ramble through the various twists of Kesey's rap, as distorted by Prankster electric mayhem, is difficult, but the effort will at least provide an indication of what they wanted the studio to do for their efforts. And as the rap develops, the subject seems to become the Acid Tests themselves: the "hot ticket" to insight and ecstasy itself. Lots of clues suggest this in the course of the ramble: "Best thing since education. It's nonreachable communication. It's nonreachable communication! It's somebody else—it's somebody over the plane, astral, astral, astral." But the best part is Kesey's use of the metaphor of a country jubilee for what the experience could be:

> **Kesey:** I mean it was jubilation, and it is rejoicin', everywhere. And everybody's joinin' in and they's clappin' hands, and they's shriekin' at the top of their voice, and it sounds to the unbeholden ear that these people have completely and totally wigged out and to some sort of absolute divinity. But it's not that, it's just good, honest-to-God ticket—it's just good, honest-to-God ticket to that one-way road of the only Heaven Gates we all know. And I say, it's all beautiful, and golden, and harmonious. And there's nothing but sweet mellow hands layin' on you, and I mean to tell you if this sounds like something you've heard when you was a little kid it's because it's *still* true, brothers, oh brothers.

"Bells and Fairies" is another slice of Kesey's narratives, country storytelling with personified animals like Tommy Robin, which rapidly devolves into banter with other Pranksters, riffing and rhyming: "Straight? Without deviation?"

"Oh, worse than that—I think inebriation."
"Ooh, it's an abomination. . . ."

More jokes, more banter, always laced with the occasional comment that reminds you of how easily the tripping brain passes from silliness to inspired lunacy to high seriousness. When Kesey says, "Hm. We still got it going. The crossover once means that we can slip back and forth, because we are, once again, teleported above the past into the present, and sometimes tickling the toes of the future," it is as accurate a summation and as serious an assessment of the Acid Tests as we have.

For Deadheads, the only mention that the band gets—and the only comment from Garcia on the LP—is at the very end of the album when Kesey asks, "I would let the Dead sing some," which prompts some off-key warbling as Jerry tries a warm-up note, finally saying, "My voice is completely shot, Ken. I can't even hold—can't keep a pitched note. *Aaaah*—see? *Eeeeenh*—ehh," which elicits a massive Prankster response, "*Eeeeeh*," as they mock him. And on that appropriately Pranksterish note, the album ends.

As the last Acid Test that Kesey did before fleeing to Mexico, the Sound City LP documents a culmination of the Pranksters' Acid Test expertise, as well as the peak of their recording techniques at the time. It also seems like vintage Prankster, especially in the baiting of Jim the Host, with the added bonus, as Ken Babbs put it, of hearing him as he "gradually started to go crazy."[4] But the cloud of Kesey's bust hung over the proceedings, making this feel as if it were also an attempt to record the venture before it came to a halt.

On January 17, a judge had found Kesey guilty of the pot charge from the raid on La Honda and sentenced him to six months on a work farm and a three-year probation. Two days later he was arrested along with Mountain Girl on the roof of a North Beach apartment, after throwing pebbles at Margo St. James' apartment; 3.54 grams of marijuana was retrieved from the alley where Kesey had thrown it after a struggle with one of the officers. A journal entry of his, undated but from this period, could well describe how he was proceeding: "You are on the spring lamb," he begins. In a series of cautionary, and fairly funny, remarks, describing martyrdom by modern media but invoking Christological terms, he ends by writing:[5]

---

3. Kesey liked this phrase, using it again in his "Be-Foreward," to Wavy Gravy, *The Hog Farm and Friends* (New York: Links, 1974), p. 13: "I swallowed it [the capsule] like Moses getting a good deal on a hot ticket from heaven."

4. Ken Babbs, interviewed by John R. Dwork, March 22, 1997.
5. Kesey, undated journal page, Kesey Manuscript Collection, privately owned. Courtesy Red House Books.

*Well, you must never take nor give children nor candy without a permit.*
*Second, you must bite the fiend that hands you.*
*Lastly, do not movie unless you are an actor trussed up for marketing.*
*And be sure you keep the shadow's left when you come down the aisle on the way to the border.*
*Or you're—I seem to hear someone calling—a dead man!*[6]

Or a jailed one. The border—Edge City, literally—is where Kesey headed next, after a Pranked-up suicide that he acknowledged in his note would probably fool no one. He was right, and it set the stage for his triumphant and celebrated fugitive appearance in the last Acid Test he and the Pranksters gave, at San Francisco State, the following fall.

In "In One-Way Ticket" (A Classic) one of Kesey's best lines is "But there was no way of answering that question because he had passed outside the sphere of verbal communication." Which could serve as a fairly good summation of the entire LP. For students of the Acid Tests, and Keseyphiles especially, this is an interesting if demanding half hour. For Deadheads expecting a polished audio invocation of the spirit of the Acid Test, it may be a thought-provoking disappointment.

NICK MERIWETHER

---

### 2/12/66
**Watts Acid Test**
**Youth Opportunities Center, Compton, California**

Who Cares Rap, Good Mornin', Li'l Schoolgirl

---

**Source:** FM-SBD, **Quality:** B, **Length:** 0:06, **Genealogy:** MR > Gans FM
**Highlights:** Historical curiosity only

This tape is a strange little curio that will provide an interesting bit of historical depth to Deadheads who know the story of the infamous Watts Acid Test. According to Vault archivist Dick Latvala, the material here comes from two different seven-inch reel boxes, the Pigpen rap in an unlabeled one, the other marked "Longshoreman's Hall #1," with no other information. The intriguing thing is that both tapes have identical ambiences, and Bobby's comment at the end of the Pigpen rap—"someday Ron'll take acid"—is on the tape labeled Longshoreman's Hall, right before the band goes into "Schoolgirl," and Weir's comment has the same ambience and feel as the segment with Pigpen's rap.

Deadheads familiar with Tom Wolfe's *The Electric Kool-Aid Acid Test* or Ken Babbs and Paul Perry's *On the Bus* will be familiar with the story of the Watts Test. It was held in a community center in Watts just a few days after the riots, when the signs could not have been less auspicious for a Test. Hugh Romney (not yet Wavy Gravy), the stand-up comic who became affiliated with the Pranksters and hosted them for a couple of weeks in L.A., remembered the challenge posed by the situation: "It is the eve of Lincoln's birthday, and the city of Watts is still smoldering from recent race riots. Somehow it is cosmically appropriate for the Merry Pranksters to rent this giant warehouse amid those smoldering embers. Word is out, and most every hip person in southern California shows up."[1] But with Kesey gone, there was already a fair amount of stress on the Pranksters as they adapted to Babbs' more heavy-handed style and contended with a scene that had grown to an unwieldy extent. This combination of factors that would culminate shortly after the Watts Test in a series of schisms, as the Dead cleaved off and stayed with Owsley and half of the Pranksters absconded with the bus and went to join Kesey, leaving a number of Pranksters—even Cassady—behind.

What is most famous about the Watts Test has always been the story of the "Who Cares woman," the subject of this snippet of tape. The most common story in circulation is the one that Romney tells, which he describes as the moment at which he "passed the Acid Test."[2] As the master of the punch, Romney spent the first part of the evening guarding the dosed Kool-Aid, warding off the unsuspecting from what several Pranksters had thoughtfully spiked, each unbeknownst to the others. When preliminary calculations proved to be grievously incorrect, the realization dawned, in the immortal words of one Prankster:

---

6. Kesey, undated journal page, [p. 1]. Kesey Manuscript Collection, privately owned. Courtesy Red House Books.

1. Wavy Gravy, *Something Good for a Change: Random Notes on Peace Thru Living* (New York: St. Martin's, 1992), p. 96.
2. Ibid., p. 96.

"After a couple of cups, when I was as high as I had ever been, somebody recomputed and realized that each cup held three hundred micrograms [a strong to somewhat heavy dose]. I remember hearing that and realizing that I had just gulped down two thousand micrograms. The rest of the evening was as weird as you might expect."[3]

The tape begins with strange electronic audio effects reverberating, a very trippy, psychedelic-sounding Prankster-style audio environment, with voices in the foreground. In general, there is a boominess to the sound, as if it were a big hall. Then the first loud voice comes through, a woman's voice saying loudly, "Who cares?" Slightly edgy sounding, she doesn't sound happy, although it may just be exasperation. "Nobody cares!" is the response, perhaps by Babbs; it sounds perfectly appropriate, a theatrical, stentorian pronouncement, no weirdness yet, really, a feeling bolstered by the comments of Bobby, who has been talking in the background, sounding as if he's trying to navigate a complex of microphones: "I hear you can talk to anybody.... It's just a little bit less louder—." He is cut off by Babbs again, intoning the Prankster mantra "Freak freely," which is exactly what proceeds to happen as the Who Cares woman comes unglued. Bobby continues to test microphones as this drama unfolds, making for a strange technical background to the ordeal, little fragments like "this was quite a bit louder, then if you back off," as his voice trails off, giving way to Pigpen, who seems to be the only one in a position of power who actually wants to ameliorate the situation. In classic singsong fashion, a cappella, he croons, "I want to tell ya little story now," just as if it were "Lovelight" and he had brought the band down to nothing and now was stepping out. Not a moment too soon, since the woman is screaming now, her voice sounding far away, in the back of the hall, a sustained disturbance that doesn't abate as Pigpen winds into it, "Ever'thin's gonna be all right now. I wanna know, do you feel good?," chuckling, trying to calm the waters. You can imagine his motive, onstage, band hopeless and helpless behind him, circle of heavily tripping people in front, Prankster mayhem all around, and the edgy sense that no one knows how much they've taken or whether this first headlong rush into the high is going to stop, and how much higher things will be getting, and Pigpen is going to smooth the trajectory.

"I wanna know, can you find yo' mind?," and now the audience is relaxing a little—this is weird but he's clearly in control, this is fine, we know how to respond—and they chorus, "Oh, yes!" Now he can tease, gently, "If you can, you better get on out of this place." But he has to back away from the teasing as the competition for the group's mood begins again, and he falls silent in the face of the Who Cares woman's howls. Pig gets one line off—"An' I wanna tell everybody a little story right now"—before she cuts him off, wailing strongly, clearly very unhappy, screaming again and again, "Who cares?! Who cares!"

This is the point where most written accounts begin, corroborated by the other voices that lend a hand—or an irritant. As Romney recalled, following Babbs' Law (the Pranksters were fond of codifying their insights into laws, e.g., "Never trust a Prankster"), which states that "if you take a bad situation and irritate it, it will get worse," some Pranksters had found the woman and stuck even more microphones around her, with the result found throughout this tape. Romney, deep in the midst of the heaviest trip he had ever embarked upon—which was heavy indeed, since he had worked up to more than five hundred micrograms by then—went in search of her, if only to, as he put it, "get her to shut the fuck up."[4] His emphatic response is explained not only by the degree of his own chemical siege, but also by the attempt to handle someone else's heavily amplified bummer on an already overloaded psyche. It is probably his voice that we hear saying, "It's okay, it's okay," soothingly, precipitating the group rescue that dominates the remainder of the tape. It takes a while, though: the screams continue, "Who cares! Who cares! Please stop! Please stop!," as someone else—Babbs?—first tries to drown out her pleas "Ba-lupda-lop-lop," chant-singing ineffectively until we hear another Prankster uttering the immortal line, "It's easier to do it over a microphone than anywhere else." Babbs' Law writ large on the group mind, recorded for posterity.

And clearly, extreme measures were called for: re-enter Pigpen, who shines for the rest of the tape. "Now do you understand about it now?" Bobby coaches the audience in the response lines—"*Yeah!*"—and feeding back to Pigpen: "Well, if you don't understand then you better listen to what I got to say right now." And the only sober voice takes over, calm and focused and acting the perfect emcee. "I wanna tell everybody in da house

---

3. Lee Quarnstrom, quoted in Perry and Babbs, *On the Bus*, p. 161.

4. Wavy Gravy, quoted in Perry and Babbs, *On the Bus*, p. 161.

right now—*yeah*—there's many many things you got to do one more time—*yeah*—you gotta think about yo' neighbors—*yeah*," and now we hear a drum flourish for accent, the first musical accompaniment to Pig's rap so far. "You got to think about yo' friends—*yeah*—you got to think about yo' brothers!" He is in superb form, voice rising into a high sing-along, impassioned now, drum roll behind him solid, the audience responding "*yeah!*" as he gets to the main point: "You got to think about yo' sister—*yeah*—You got to think about everybody that means something to you." And even a rebuke for the Pranksters, or so it sounds: "Now do you think you know somethin'?—*yeah*—If you think that you know something—*ow* goddamn it! What's *wrong* wit' you?!"

A ride that he maintains beautifully, with only a minor lapse when a Prankster or perhaps a band member starts monkeying with the microphones, and Pig snarls sotto voce, "Get that microphone away from me goddamn it, before I fix you right," before recovering quickly: "You know before I got interrupted by that man, aw, I was trying to say—I was trying to say something to all you peoples standin' around here. An' my main point of business tonight is—" and he launches into his blues-scat-sing, "that you got to love ever'body!" He moves and weaves through the audience like a benevolent dictator of consciousness, soaring above Bobby, who spends the rest of the tape talking about the microphones as the audience is pulled along by Uncle Piggers, who plays a first-rate country preacher, exhorting and eliciting "*yeahs!*" and whipping the crowd into security again before he delivers the salvation they all need to hear: "I wanna know, do you wonda what I'm talkin' 'bout now?—*yeah*—I'm talkin' 'bout somebody who lost a little bit of love—*yeah*—Somebody lost a little bit of friendship!—*yeah*—I wanna know, do you know what I'm talkin' about now!—*yeah*—You know what I'm talkin' about now!" And they've gotten it, things have calmed, and he finishes: "I think maybe you hearin' what I'm sayin'."

Indeed. For Deadheads who wondered how this nonpsychedelic bluesman fit in so well with his crazed acid-munching contemporaries, this tape explains it better than any interview or account. When Bobby ends the tape by saying, "Someday Ron'll take acid" and laughs, it neatly underscores the point that he doesn't have to. He understands perfectly.

After Bobby's comment, the guitar and bass begin noodling as the band launches into "Good Mornin', Li'l Schoolgirl," a workmanlike and in places inspired rendition, which also makes one wonder whether it is from the same performance; by some accounts, the band was simply too high to really function well that night, though the condition of those commentators makes their accounts suspect. As one Prankster recalled, the Watts Acid Test was the last trip for a number of the Pranksters for a long, long time—the overdosing had been simply too extreme. But the tape provides a confirmation of Pigpen's centrality to the Acid Test scene, something that has never been well documented, as well as illustrating why the event was such a watershed for Wavy. As he put it, "That was when I passed my Acid Test. I realized that when you get to the very bottom of the human soul and you're sinking, but you'll still reach for someone who is sinking worse than you are, everybody's going to get high. You don't need acid to get there." An elegant summation of so many of the lessons psychedelics can remind one of, as well as impart.

NICK MERIWETHER

---

### 3/12/66
**Danish Hall, Los Angeles, California
Pico Acid Test**

Viola Lee Blues, You See a Broken Heart, Midnight Hour

---

**Source:** FM-SBD, **Quality:** B+, varies in quality and mix, **Length:** 0:29, **Genealogy:** MR > RR > DR

This tape is unique in that it represents the most music we have in circulation from any of the Acid Tests—almost a half hour, recorded toward the end of the period of time when the Dead were woodshedding in L.A. The Pico Acid Test happened after Kesey had fled to Mexico and the band had parted ways with the Pranksters, opting to stay in L.A. with Owsley and work on new material. "You See a Broken Heart" is probably one of the originals that emerged from this time.

After a smattering of applause, as if it were just after the band had been introduced, "Viola Lee" opens the tape and the set. During these first couple of years, the Dead used this song to set a mood, regardless of where it appears: tapes from 1966 and '67 show it all over the set, but most frequently as an opener or closer. Already they're playing with how best to arrange the material, even as they're pursuing all the various ways of opening each one up. Sound quality is poor, especially at first; there is a boomy, muffled feeling, and several distinct shifts in the mix happen early in the tape. But a few minutes in, the mix has settled, your ears have adjusted—and this is an actual Acid Test, so they're probably high, but damn they sound good. One advantage of a soundboard tape seems to be that no matter how old, the event it documents is almost always "recapturable." The drums are lost in a wash, but the vocals are pretty clear, and Garcia's leads come through crisply enough; Pig's organ is clear, too. And it's a nice version: slow groove, heavy and relaxed—maybe a little sloppy at first, but they settle in and it rapidly takes on a weird cast. An excellent, fully developed and thoroughly freaky breakdown jam opens up in the middle, though it takes them a good ten minutes to get there; nice and leisurely at first, it soon builds into that trademark density, manic, intense, complex, and ferocious.

"You See a Broken Heart" is Pig's tune, although here it comes across as pop-flavored R&B: "You see a broken heart / My baby's tryin' to set me free / Well I got tears (tears!) tears (tears!) tears in my eyes," and so on, with the band chorusing behind him. A painful lyric pattern, but a good groove for Jerry to work out against, and a nice solo at the end, a classic nightclub-style guitar statement, with Pig exhorting, "Just a little bit softer, just a little bit softer now, just a little bit louder," working the band. A crowd pleaser at the time, judging from the reaction, though probably not to most contemporary Deadheads' liking.

"Midnight Hour" is the capper. A good, solid rendition, it showcases perfectly credible harmonies—a rejoinder to those who claim that the band didn't learn how to sing until the *Workingman's Dead* era. Peppy and up-tempo, it shows none of the sloppiness that mars some of the 1966–67 recordings of this, but what is most unusual is Garcia's leads, played unusually low on the neck at first, then dropping back to playing complementary rhythm guitar with Weir. Only after Pig has finished rapping does he really step out. It ends in a mammoth, manic organ and guitar breakdown that roars and rages for several minutes. *Vintage Dead* wanted to capture this on vinyl, and fell so far short. Some strange sonic effects pop up at the end, as it settles into a nice if somewhat amphetamine-amplified groove, as if spinning into the ground in fine style, but then building slowly back into a monster cacophonous chorus, wailing and shrieking into the second verse, now almost so slow as to be off-key—worth having on its own merits. And as an Acid Test, it's the best music we have available.

NICK MERIWETHER

---

### 🌀 10/2/66 🌀

**"Whatever It Is" Festival
(the San Francisco State Acid Test)
San Francisco State University,
San Francisco, California**

The Head Has Become Fat Rap, A Mexican Story: 25 Bennies, A Tarnished Galahad, Get It Off the Ground Rap, Acid Test Graduation Announcement, Prankster Music, Prankster Raga, Final Kesey Rap and Repeat, Closing Jam

---

**Source:** SBD, **Quality:** B+, **Length:** 0:45 (LP), 1:40 [tape], **Genealogy:** 1. MR > LP (bootleg) > C; 2. MR > RR > C; 3. MR > DAT > C

**Highlights:** A Mexican Story: 25 Bennies, Closing Jam

The portion of this Test that usually circulates is from a much-bootlegged LP, which has excerpts from this material spliced in with footage from a 1981 television interview with Jerry and Kesey, reminiscing about the glory days.[1] (Interestingly enough, this was the same approach used on the video *The Acid Test*, available from Key-Z Productions.) Recordings from the vinyl are usually of good quality, albeit with the standard surface noise. In the spring of 1997, a master reel was located in a San Francisco archive and disseminated. It is characterized by superb quality and a very weird mix, replete with shifts from speaker to speaker, strange stereo/mono changes, and a host of Prankster manipulations, with the result being almost a cross between a source tape for the happening and a recording of the actual event. Perhaps the best-labeled Acid Test recording in existence,

---

1. *The Electric Kool-Aid Acid Test. San Francisco State College, October 1st–2nd, 1966.* [USA]: United Fan Club Society, SMS 001-1, 1986. NB: Several pressings of this bootleg LP exist. The most recent pressing has slick white inner labels captioned "Stellar Music Special Series 1 Show 1. The San Francisco Acid Test (A Musical Study)."

the San Francisco State master reel gave us what look like fairly complete credits, noting that the tape was recorded between 4 A.M. and 6 A.M. (corroborated by several commentaries), and providing what appears to be complete attributions: "Voices, Ken Kesey, Hugh Romney. Guitar: Kesey. Violin: Dale. Organ: Jerry Garcia. Engineering: Steve Newman, Kesey, Mountain Girl." It is worth noting that the bootleg LP also credited these participants and their roles, as well as claiming—or making the reasonable supposition—that the electric guitar that makes a fragmentary appearance occasionally was played by Garcia as well.

About halfway through the tape, in one of the room games that the Pranksters played at the Acid Tests, Kesey makes a particularly allegorical comment—one of many that infuse the recording—about future archaeologists examining this: "They can understand what's happened, they can at least see the bones there." Which could serve as a reasonable summation of this tape: it does provide a good indication of what went on during those couple of hours, as the San Francisco State Acid Test was winding to a close. As a tape, the S.F. State Test is something of an extension of what the Sound City LP is getting at: acid wisdom from Ken, some of the universal lessons of the intensely personal visions he believed an acid-magnified consciousness could convey. Here the raps and riffs sound much more like fables; the morals and the storytelling aspects are made much more plain and less pranked, although the electronics and tape effects work very well here, perhaps the best we have on tape.

By the fall of 1966, the Acid Test era seemed over. A few days after the San Francisco State Test, LSD would become illegal, which in many commentators' minds—including participants like Garcia—effectively ended them. Kesey had been gone for eight months, hiding out in Mexico, leaving the Pranksters to fragment and the Dead to emerge as a professional, regularly gigging band. This last Test captures them—or at least Garcia—as they were moving into 710 Ashbury, for the year-long stint that would earn them their greatest fame as the Haight-Ashbury's best-known musical residents. (The band played at the San Francisco State Test, but no known tape exists of the performance, although one participant wrote that they played "Midnight Hour," apparently the source for that commonly cited fact.)[2] Everything felt as if it were in transition. Just as the counterculture caught on and moved into the mainstream, the backlash began brewing as well, and the outlawing of LSD was only the cusp of the wave of repression to come. So why not? A last Test, before it all becomes illegal—and a Grand Prank, to celebrate the fugitive Kesey's return.

San Francisco State seemed like a convivial home for it. An incubator for the artistic underground in the city, State could claim a number of famous Haight-Ashbury habitués, and it would go on to play a major role in the nationwide campus protests that defined such a visible part of the sixties. How the Acid Test came to its sedate campus out at the southern edge of the city was a matter that seems to have largely escaped everyone involved. For Kesey, it was merely the most visible manifestation to date of his announced intention to be "salt in J. Edgar Hoover's wounds." But that shrouded the preparations in even more of a smokescreen than typical Prankster last-minute, chaotic planning. Even as late as the Monday before the festival was to begin, the student newspaper *The Daily Gater* was reporting that the event was "apparently taking shape, with its organizers—whoever they are—hard at work to ensure its successful production, wherever it is."[3] By the day of the event, the *Gater* was sounding gloomy warnings, complaining about the secrecy, the planning, even the intentions, and wishing the event "a hell of a lot of success. Anything less could spell catastrophe for the College's future activities."[4]

Finally, the day of the event, beneath banner headlines proclaiming "Whatever It Is, It's Here," Associated Students president Jim Nixon announced that the purpose of the three-day event was "to expose the students at SF State to the variety of experiences available to them on campus."[5] In a cryptic close to the piece, which discussed the budget—a whopping $7,800, more than the income generated by five "traditional" campus activities, the campus newspaper sniffed—Nixon noted that "it would be a mistake to assume that an event like this will be of interest to a majority of the student body. But you must always remember that interesting things are always put on by an interested minority."[6] But Stew-

---

2. Reynolds, Frank, as told to Michael McClure. *Freewheelin' Frank, Secretary of the Angels.* New York: Grove, 1967, p. 138.

3. Larry Maatz, "'Whatever It Is' Might Even Happen," *The Daily* (San Francisco State University) *Gater*, Sept. 26, 1966, p. 5.
4. Ben Fong-Torres, "Editor's Desk: 'Whatever It Is' Will Be, Will Be . . . ," *The Daily* (San Francisco State University) *Gater*, Sept. 30, 1966, p. 2.
5. "Whatever It Is, It's Happening," *The Daily* (San Francisco State University) *Gater*, Sept. 30, 1966, p. 1.
6. Ibid., p. 1.

art Brand, credited as the "prime organizer" for the festival—posed in full psychedelic American Indian regalia, underneath the caption " 'Tour guide' for the campus mind excursion"—said that he believed it would turn a profit, grandly announcing, "We are providing a collection of creative materials that are very rare in an atmosphere very unlike most atmospheres."[7]

With LSD not yet illegal, the word was out in the underground that this would be the last great acid bash in San Francisco—certainly the last by the fabled Day-Glo pied pipers, the Merry Pranksters. As the event approached, the psychedelic overtones became increasingly overt. By Friday, the calendar editor was saying that this would be more than "rock 'n roll excitement," it would be "total excitement for that matter."[8] More blunt was the front-page article the day of the festival's opening, which closed by noting that "for those participants suffering an overdose of WII, a non habit forming reality producing drug will be dispensed at various points on the campus."[9] Nor was the drug angle downplayed in the reports afterward, the lead account in the student newspaper mentioning "a gaggle of reclining students whose bloodstream were charged with all sorts of spectacular chemicals."[10] And editor Ben Fong-Torres' lead column afterward prominently discussed one student dancing to the Dead whose whacked-out gyrations showed that she "was either crazy or on a too-good trip."[11]

Sprawled over the campus, in more than a half-dozen locations, the festival began at three P.M. on Friday and ran through Sunday morning, when a core crew cleaned it all up. Over the course of the weekend, students who paid their dollar—outsiders paid two—would walk through a symbolic archway in the Commons, have "Enter" stamped on their foreheads, "and Happen," as the *Gater* put it. During the next two days, what they could see included Mimi Fariña with the Only Alternative and His Other Possibilities, the Final Solution, the San Andreas Fault Finders, a rock workshop, a light show by Bill Ham, Ron Boise's Thunder Machine music sculpture, and performances by the Mime Troupe, the Congress of Wonders, the Committee, and Ann Halprin's Dancer's Workshop Annex. Even some faculty got involved: an art instructor's sculpture, "Tensed Membrane," provided a backdrop for the light show, and another assistant professor led a series of games in the Sculpture Garden.

The dances were held in the gym, a scene described by one poetic participant: "Scaffolds are built throughout the gymnasium, where people stand working projectors that play technicolor films against the ceiling in all beauty of violets and purples and reddest of ruby reds."[12] Steve Newman, program director for campus radio station KRTG (and credited on the tape as one of the engineers), helped coordinate the seemingly endless miles of cables snaking back and forth. Partly due to his efforts, State students who were still awake at four A.M. could tune in and hear America's Favorite Fugitive broadcasting live, along with Neal Cassady and Hugh Romney.

The secretary of the San Francisco chapter of the Hell's Angels provided an appropriately acid-drenched assessment:

> "The sandman draws circles, as singers and poets gather tonight under a searchlight for guidance. The trees which surround this garden-like college spring their flavors and smells of green leaves. As my poet Michael [McClure] says—'All of the birds and beasts were there.' The date is 10/1/66. We have before us all the eyes of those who have come to enjoy and give joyously to one another the mindwaves of their recent escapades into the hollowness of the night. THIS IS AT SAN FRANCISCO STATE COLLEGE—THE SCENE IS KNOWN AS AN ACID TEST."[13]

And the featured attraction would not be going on until well after the Dead's set had ended.

At that point, however, it was the worst-kept secret in the underground. Before Friday, the student newspaper was coy about specifying who would appear, always careful to say "among the scheduled performers," hinting at more, and afterward the lead editorial cited

---

7. *The Daily* (San Francisco State University) *Gater,* Sept. 30, 1966, p. 1.
8. Skip Wag, "What's in the Bag: Enticement and Excitement," *The Daily* (San Francisco State University) *Gater,* Sept. 30, 1966, p. 5.
9. Larry Maatz, "Whatever It Is, It's Happening: Non-Program for 48 Hours," *The Daily* (San Francisco State University) *Gater,* Sept. 30, 1966, p. 1.
10. Phil Garlington, "Whatever It Was . . . It Was," *The Daily* (San Francisco State University) *Gater,* Oct. 5, 1966, p. 4.
11. Ben Fong-Torres, "Whatever's Right: Upon Re-Entry from Whatever . . . ," *The Daily* (San Francisco State University) *Gater,* Oct. 5, 1966, p. 7.

12. Reynolds, *Freewheelin' Frank: Secretary of the Angels,* p. 137.
13. Ibid., p. 137.

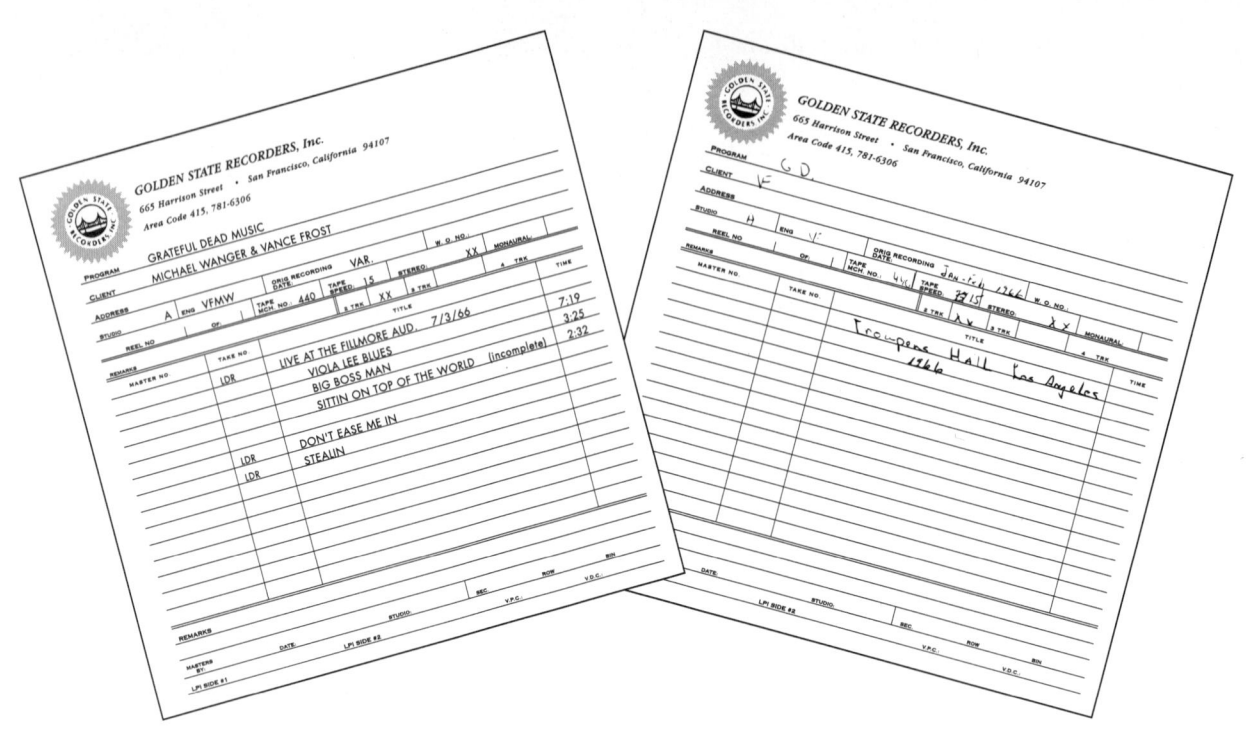

*Golden State recording studio tape box notes (7/3/66)*

"rumors" that Kesey had been around.[14] The paper's city editor went further: Kesey had been there all right, "incognito as hell," stated his October 5 lead article.[15] Finally, a couple of days later, the *Gater* gleefully reported that Kesey had "performed his Acid Test" hidden in Studio B of the campus radio station, in the California Building. It also breathlessly announced his plans for the Acid Test Graduation, "providing the police don't surprise him first."[16] A few days later they would do just that, but for the evening, the Greatest Prank was about to take place: Kesey would host another Acid Test, an outlaw celebrating the outlawing of the drug he had helped make notorious. How perfect.

And a classic, curious blend of the paranoid and the Prankster, Kesey walking around in the afternoon like a fearless man, but insisting that the setup for the broadcast be very, very secure, as Wolfe reported:

> "a very tight ship, this fantasy, even up to the Hell's Angels standing guard outside the stu-

dio. Except that by the time they get all the wiring hooked up, and start rapping, Neal Cassady with a microphone inside the hall—introducing KEN KEEEEE-ZEEEEEE it is about 4 A.M. and now October 2nd. Kesey is hidden [in] the studio, talking over the hugest Prankster hookup of wires, running long over the college campus to the gymnasium."[17]

Angel Freewheelin' Frank, though, offers the best description:

> "This night brought many smiles. It also brought me to the college radio station. As I approached the doorway my acid mind was running wild. A page in a black cap was leading me.... We walked through the swinging doors, and there in front of me, sitting on a stool with an electric guitar plugged into a large amplifier with wires running all over the floor and around his head and

---

14. Ben Fong-Torres, "Whatever's Right: Upon Re-Entry from Whatever...", *The Daily* (San Francisco State University) *Gater*, Oct. 5, 1966, p. 7.
15. Phil Garlington, "Whatever It Was... It Was," *The Daily* (San Francisco State University) *Gater*, Oct. 5, 1966, p. 4.
16. "Hunted 'Psychedelic' Novelist Performs 'Acid Test' Here," *The Daily* (San Francisco State University) *Gater*, Oct. 7, 1966, p. 1.
17. Wolfe, *The Electric Kool-Aid Acid Test*, p. 352. Cf. anon., liner notes to *The Electric Kool-Aid Acid Test*. San Francisco State College, October 1st–2nd, 1966. [USA]: United Fan Club Society, SMS 001-1, 1986.

across the floor and around other people, sat none other than the god of LSD on the West Coast—Ken Kesey... This god of LSD was now sitting on this stool, with a pair of earphones across his neck, twanging away at a guitar and quoting weird poetry into the night, all lit up by the electricity of this neon room, surrounded by so many windows and blinking things that said ON THE AIR, ON THE AIR... The men on the other side looked as though they were going crazy trying to transmit. I ran up and hugged him, feeling an immediate charge of electricity surge through me. This god reminds me of a satellite that flies around in the skies. He's so wired up it scares one.... I placed the set of earphones on my ears and through them came the echoing of wired up instruments and the voice of Ken Kesey speaking to faraway worlds in the universe. 'Am I getting through down there? Up there? In miles there aren't numbers enough to measure... You out there... Among the faraway galaxies running wild... Can you see these people in here? Let them see it's their brains projecting onto the ceiling...' I closed my eyes and let my visions blacken and then they swirled in the clouds and I saw visions of my God."[18]

The tape begins with music in the background, the organ prominent; only the left channel at first, then the right cuts in as Kesey says "Giddyap! Whoa! Whoa, here boy!" as competent raga-sounding rock plays in the background, underpinning Kesey's triumphant announcement: "Anybody there? Okay good, good, good. We've finally done it. Oh, my God, we have done it. We have not only done it, but we've done it and got away with it." Hugh Romney and Neal Cassady were supposedly in the gymnasium, speaking back to him, but their voices are almost inaudible.

After some banter, Ken exhorting the audience in the gym to move around—"I like to see a lot of movement"—he begins his first soliloquy, addressed to Romney: "Hey, Hugh? You know what I realized watching a lot of this stuff go on here for the last day or so? The head—man, listen to this, this is a real exclusive—the *head* has become *fat*. That's terrible news, the head is the only hope of this nation and most of the world." It is a classic Kesey riff: an acid rap with Ken commenting on the scene, himself, and making a connection between both, the allegory of his own life and the recent history of the counterculture made plain. As avatar, he seems to be thinking in similar terms to the Acid Test graduation: "The stomach has been overworked for so many years. The head—is—tired!," and he plunks on the guitar for emphasis. "The spine is getting hard! And deep inside the cellular dance, a new direction is being fired at will, or won't!! The head has become fat!" Jerry is joining in on the organ now, as Ken drops into rhyme, singing, "Now what do you think—of that!" Always the entertainer, always aware of the position the Test—and the chemicals—have put him in, Jerry playing along, providing a wheezing, sinister-sounding chord progression in the background, perfectly synched with Kesey as the "that" gets twisted and reverbed and sent out to mingle with Jerry's strange organ warble and crescendo. This is the essence of the Acid Tests, in a sense: improvised synergy, communication between them exactly as it could be with the audience, with everyone; not knowing where Kesey was going with the story but somehow anticipating, well, if simply.

As the rap progresses, it is impossible to dismiss the idea that this is all thinly veiled metaphor for Kesey's own experiences: "No fear, the die is near, last year—but this year, we drink out of a different cup-cup-cup. Last year it was just go ahead on, but that's gone. It's now go ahead on up, up up up. Naked naked naked. Listen-listen. The stars tell a story, they listen. Listen," and strange Prankster music begins as he sings softly, "Listen. And that's the way it's going to be, be, be. Listen listen listen. Listen to the territory between you and me," as the music is taking off, just plain weird and getting more so.

Part of the territory he wants to explore is outlined in his Mexico Story, which he debuts here. Interestingly, it is in the form that Kesey returns to in his collection of interlinked stories *Demon Box* (1986), that of the short story rooted in autobiography. For Keseyphiles, this recording provides some useful pieces of the puzzle, such as when he says, "You see, you're in the bottom of a shack," heavy reverb underscoring that this is the start of a heavy story. It offers insight also into what made the Acid Tests so appealing for an author, used to giving readings and lectures and talks where the performance and its techniques hadn't changed in a couple of thousand years; here was rock music, showing the possibili-

---

18. Reynolds, *Freewheelin' Frank: Secretary of the Angels*, pp. 139–41.

ties. But he couldn't do that in a staid reading. With the Acid Tests, however, he could do anything he wanted.

> **Kesey:** -shack-shack-shack. And a telegram and says, "The jig is up. Come back. They're on to you-you-you." And so you go out to the edge of the shack 'cause the jungle's right there, and you move off into the jungle, and you decide it's gonna be paranoid anyway, folks, so you might as well take twenty-five bennies and really get out there and do it all, because you know how it is when you're coming down off bennies and you're out there in the woods, and they've already put *Federales* in the streets. And they've arrested two heads who they thought was you.

The rest of the story focuses on Ken's encounters with "a little woodcutter about four feet tall." Three times Kesey encounters him, and each time he wants to make contact, say something, "you want to sit for a minute and sing to him with the guitar"—Kesey pronounces it "GI-tar," with a country twang to it—"because you've come a long way and carried it long and far, and it'd be nice, but there's this human ice that's gone between, and you can't do it." On through a wonderful allegorical fall: "And you run into the jungle, twenty-five bennies, scared and high, and you fall off a cliff and you realize you can't exactly do that, you can only fall down, and if you grab a-hold, you can keep from hittin' hard enough at the bottom. And finally when you get down at the bottom of the dip you find there's exactly what you were lookin' for, a little pool where you could take a bath, and there's this same little Mexican woodcutter, right down there at the bottom, and he's shy." One more missed opportunity for contact until the final encounter, a little way farther in Kesey's jungle run: "And you still want to play the guitar with him but you can't make it. And you go on, and you realize: that you're given three chances to have your wishes come true: but you gotta take 'em."

Listening to a fugitive with a long jail sentence hanging over his head make this sort of responsible pronouncement must have made an impression on the trippers awake to hear it. But Kesey is an entertainer, so he moves quickly into a song that he announces as being one that he wrote in Mexico, "A Tarnished Galahad." Printed later as the epigram to *Demon Box,* he introduces it as "Written later, on the run, in Mexico" and, after the last line, writes, "pretty much what happened."

Here he says, "This came after I just got a thing from Mountain Girl, after her trial up here when the judge, speaking, the judge he says, he says, 'You're just a tarnished Galahad.' . . . I get that in a clipping, from the States." And he strums the guitar loudly, a bit awkwardly, commenting a little self-consciously, "That's mighty loud, isn't it?" But he launches into it, and sings well, if amateurishly:

> *Down to five pesos from five thousand dollars*
> *Down to the dregs from the lip-smacking foam*
> *Down to a dopefiend from a prize-winning scholar*
> *Down to a hut from a five-acre home.*

A catalogue of woes and decisions made and consequences reaped, the chorus is especially telling:

> *Tarnished Galahad—did your sword get busted?*
> *Tarnished Galahad—there's no better name!*
> *Keep running and hiding 'til the next time you're busted*
> *And locked away to suffer your guilt, and shame.*

For those who see Kesey only as the carefree psychedelic Chief Prankster, this will be a rebuttal. And when he finishes, after the emotional final chorus, his self-consciousness comes through once again, a touch of embarrassment at the honesty and passion of his confession: "That gives you some idea of what was goin' on this summer. Now tell me what's been happenin' with you, Hugh."

Which doesn't happen. Instead, a brief reprise of some of the lines from "A Mexico Story"—"the jungle bennies is wild, twenty-five of 'em running through there without a smile"—gives way to a long, free-form rap that is basically the group gestalt of the Acid Test. As someone—definitely Garcia-sounding—begins to play an electric guitar, Kesey starts an Acid Test game, urging Romney to get a group of people to participate, and he harangues and implores them to go along with it, riffing over the exhortations, "We'll pioneer our ass off for you, just give us something soft to land on, to lay on, till we can just rest on." Part of the way through, Kesey comments, "I hope we can get it off the ground. We haven't been able to do so well so far. It's like an enormous industrial display, of all the chemicals and materials that we could possibly array. And we can't—even with all this stuff—get away, get away, get away. We've got to get off, we've got to get off, we need some kind of launching pad, we've got to get off. . . ." This is the essence of Kesey's rap: the prosaic, in terms of high symbolism; room games elevated to happenings, courtesy of the Pranksters and perhaps a tab of Owsley's finest.

And perhaps the most pithy remark of the Test shines here, when Kesey says, "Let's work at it! Let's get it. It spent fifty thousand years sittin' here, eatin' meat, suckin' on its thumb. We can get it up, we can do it. We won't do it now, but we can at least threaten to do it," as cousin Dale saws away on the violin, torturing it for emphasis, Kesey expanding the rap to include the Fillmore riots going on that night, Goldwater's campaign, and it all comes to rest and center on what's happening here, now, in this Test. Perls would have been proud of his student. Grail located, Kesey urges them on, providing as neat a summary of the Tests and the power of belief they so unequivocally express: "We've finally found the cup. We won't throw it down—go ahead up, c'mon, please. C'mon! Do it! Just a little bit. Lift it! Lift it! You don't believe it! You people are sittin' there listenin' to this shit, you paid your dollar, for Christ's sakes! You got your ticket, you might as well, you might as well believe it! You can lift it, you've had it long enough and you can lift it, lift it, lift it, you can get it off the *ground*!" He's singing by the end, as the music swells and builds from minor key suspense to major-key crescendo—a nice flourish with Dale caterwauling and Jerry plinking and wheezing.

In the heart of this rap, Kesey makes a number of the connections between his own writing and the themes and theories he's been batting around for the past couple of years. More than just the power of belief, and the specific power of group improvisation—group belief as opposed to the role of the individual—Kesey makes the point specifically: "It can't be done alone. We can't make it by ourselves. As soon as you do it alone, you get like Nijinsky and you sit for thirty-five years on the shelves of insanity, saying, 'I'm God, if I'm by myself.' We've *got* to do it together," the music swelling now, "Up! I think we've got Jerry Garcia coming that way, he'll try to move it up. Think it off, think it off, think it off the ground.... There, that's the way. There's a figure eight in eternity, and we can plug it into something. There's a last chance that we can put it in," as the music swells one final time, very abstractly now, true Prankster music with a competent electric guitar filigree overlaid as Ken finishes up with a particularly good image: "Let's hear those cells bump together. Let's hear the marmalade of us going down in here with 'em."

A few minutes later and the Prankster has returned, as Kesey begins to bait the audience a bit:

**Kesey:** Do you know that the railroad track that we've been riding on is owned, completely, completely owned, absolutely bought and paid for by the Devil! Do you know the sky that we've been breathing, did you know that the sun we've been underneath and the shadow that we been tryin' hard for so long underneath this leavin'—belongs to the Devil. Do you now that these books that we've been readin' and these looks that we've been givin' each other, belongs to the Horned Brother under the ground. Do you know that we've only one chance to reach out and touch that last living rod. It's good to be God, it's good to be God, God, God.

This must have been strange indeed to hear echoing around your brain at five A.M. and zonked to the gills on 250 micrograms of the Bear's best. As Stewart Brand was fond of saying, "There was always a whiff of danger" to the Acid Tests.

Kesey seesaws back into seriousness for a moment, though, telling Hugh, "The only way isn't the lonely way, although it may be lonely finding it sometimes." Then he makes another oracular pronouncement: "I think it's more complicated than that. I really do feel that we're faced with a serious problem. Why? Because you know what we have here. We have an army, a nirvana army. An army, all around, but they don't hup to the old new tunes." What does the leader of a movement do? Especially when the Establishment isn't pleased at all. "And they know they're an army and we know it. But we don't know exactly what direction we're marching, and we can't say because we don't know it all! But some of you out there sittin' do. And the ones that do, move!" A classic Kesey exhortation, and a large part of what gives this Acid Test its particular focus and intensity: Kesey is behaving as a leader. And his concern tonight is how to challenge, how to harness this energy, these insights, these initiates.

As always, though, Kesey seems to know when to shift from serious to silly, and as the electric guitar chords strum, he sings a strange ditty that rolls from comic to macabre to serious, from immediate to abstract: "The butcher is back, the butcher is back, with the cat in the hat, the butcher is back. He's cuttin' up pieces and feedin' them—to me 'n' you. The butcher is back, the butcher is back, the butcher is back. It's full of worms and blood, it's meat, and it's all we're going to have to eat until we read nothing, but nothing. The butcher is back. And now it's cut up nicely and packaged. Let's sell it to each other, marinate [sic] it for about twenty-four straight hours, get it out there on that barbecue pit, that'll make it a real social hit. I know some fun people from Atherton," which goes through a nicely reverbed delay and repeat, capped with another single line of insight: "The only way out of this armor is to love it."

Then comes an interesting moment, when Kesey announces that he's going to smoke a joint; why not? "That's one of the nice things about being exiled." And he rambles a bit before getting to his point, which is to announce the Acid Test Graduation. "It's no longer 'Can you pass the Acid Test?' but 'Did you pass the Acid Test?' " To be held a couple of weeks later, location still undetermined, but he declares, it will be a particularly mammoth final prank:

> Kesey: It may be down in Union Square, in your own living room, but just be there, we're going to get some makeup and a lot of costumes, and we're going to, as Stewart Brand says, 'up level everything.' One last time before we split. Because if I'm laid finger on before this happens, ah, you know what it is. They tell me it's five years for runnin'. The cops are everywhere, there's no gettin' around it. There's cops inside and outside. Lookin' for power. Every place but home. And then look down. And then look out, because power don't work, man, that's plugged and doubt, then look out! For one long, emancipated twisted hour. We sit there looking for power. We look up and down, in and out, all around until the doubt was gone. What's happening?

Indeed.

A last song ends his broadcast, Kesey singing a ditty that has a definite theme of escape, "Let's send at to the moon, me to the moon, we don't do it soon, the moon is gonna starve," until his final, unceremonious sign-off: "I'm ready to rest. My ass hurts. Get somebody else to do something, we're tired."

This ends the main part of the show, although there is still a fair amount of tape left. The remainder consists of selected excerpts and repeats from the earlier portions, put to Prankster music and audio weirdness. As strange as any experiment in *musique concrète*, this is a foreshadowing of what Garcia would do in a more melodic and structured fashion on his solo debut album. A thumping heartbeat is going on underneath it all as the piano takes off, spinning out in a well-improvised jam, eerie singing still going on, faintly, in the background, shifting gradually to chanting, as the piano accompaniment blends to match it. Animal noises, flying saucer sound effects, waves crashing; then a flute screech, seabirds calling . . . ocean surf, again, until it strips down to just the heartbeat, interrupted by a muezzin-style yell, followed by a weird chorus of horns, and we are taken back into Kesey's head, and bits and pieces of the first forty-five minutes get recycled in interesting ways for most of the rest of the tape.

The last segment is a jam session, faded into while already going. Flute, guitar, and percussion are obvious, and somewhat competent, though amateurish. Some crowd noise in the background, even a baby crying—until there is a tape cut, followed by silence and then very strange noises: screeches, whines, just noise, but gradually built into soundscapes. If you listen to the Residents, you'll enjoy these final few moments a great deal; or if you like *musique concrète* then you'll appreciate the fragment we get before plunging back into weirdness, reminiscent of some of the stranger parts of Pink Floyd's *Ummagumma* and its weird, keening tweets and whistles, like electronic bird calls—until the tape suddenly stops. Six A.M., and time to clean up the last Acid Test.

Afterward it drew mixed reviews among the Pranksters. Without Babbs, something was definitely missing, and the general air of paranoia hadn't helped. But some of the complaints may have to do with why it made such a good tape. Even Hank Harrison got it partly right when he said that it was "perhaps the least popular and most analyzable Trips Festival."[19] Despite the factual error (Harrison also claims Kesey wasn't even present), he does have a point about the relative accessibility of this tape, something that Kesey archivist Zane Kesey commented on recently, noting that the State Test had "the most definite beginning and end, really."[20] For that reason, if no other, it may be a good tape for those who only want to sample the weirdness.

At State, however, the event was immediately labeled a success. Spokesmen were quick to point out that not only had they broken even—or come close, or

---

19. Harrison, *The Dead Book*, p. 140.
20. Zane Kesey, interviewed by author, May 15, 1997.

made a slight profit, depending on which source and how they did the accounting—it was, at the least, the most profitable undertaking in the history of the Associated Students.[21] And the lead article on the event came to the altogether reasonable conclusion that "the startling thing about Whatever It Was is that over 5,000 volatile students plunged into a weekend of somewhat nightmarish activity without serious damage to themselves or the campus," mentioning that dances had been banned the previous semester because of fighting and vandalism.[22] In an editorial the following week, Ben Fong-Torres tallied the negatives—one stolen microphone, too many "straights," and the fact that many people involved were "overreaching, searching for an emotion or atmosphere they will never be comfortable with"—and pronounced the event an unqualified success. Commenting on how pleased he was at the organizers' response to his critical editorial the Friday before, he concluded, "We only wish that more than 6,000 showed up and that publicity, before and after, could have been fuller. The world at large deserves—and some of it needs—to realize what's going on here."[23]

Preferably long after Kesey had left the scene, however. With the Graduation, he would bow out of the public eye once again, after just one more hit of that media glare, a small pinch more for J. Edgar's abraded sensibilities. It was also appropriate, given his stature as counterculture icon, though it obviously risked a great deal. And Kesey felt, quite reasonably, that he had already sacrificed a great deal because of that role, which was the source of his irritation with a young reporter who questioned his motives for calling for a "graduation" from LSD: "If you don't realize that I've been helping you with every fiber in my body . . ."[24] He could well have been thinking of a few lines he dashed off in his journal, back in Palo Alto before all of this went down: "The find of how it hurts when you take the blame / you can be the patient to a mr. hyde as well as crutch to the lame."[25] Kesey's days of being a crutch to the scene would end in a final, fittingly public bummer, at the Acid Test Graduation, held a few weeks after the San Francisco State Test.

It was the end of the Acid Tests and the end of the era. For the Dead, it signified their emergence as royalty in the Haight, and the symbolism of the torch being passed from the Pranksters to them was accompanied by Mountain Girl's departure to the Dead camp shortly afterward. State was the first real contact she had had with Jerry since the Watts Acid Test the previous February; for her, and to a number of observers, this final Test was where she was, as she put it, "establishing a relationship with Jerry," and she moved into 710 Ashbury a little later.[26] A friend watching their interaction saw it more as Garcia wooing her: "I watched MG and Jerry connect. As far as I know, it went boom! He played to her all night. You could feel it."[27] In a few days, Kesey would be arrested, throwing plans for the Acid Test Graduation into turmoil as the word on the streets was that he had cut a deal with the authorities, even as Bill Graham was hearing the opposite. Out of fear that Kesey's grand parting prank would be a massive psychedelic free-for-all, Graham withdrew, leaving the Pranksters with only a loft in San Francisco's South of Market district, and not even the Dead as a draw. The Anonymous Artists of America, a band featuring Jerry's first wife and fellow folkie, Sara, supplied the soundtrack instead. Appropriately enough, that night—which Kesey called "an awful high voltage humiliating public freakout!"—is the only bad trip at an Acid Test that he has ever written about.[28]

A reporter interviewed Kesey in July 1967, at the San Mateo Honor Camp where he was completing his sentence, and asked him, "What did you want to create through the Acid Tests?" And Kesey replied,

> "Ah, here's where you've got to stop writing, because you can't get this down on paper. Well, okay, I got aboard a spacecraft one time, and I saw I was to be taken to outer

---

21. " 'Whatever It Is' Triumphs," *The Daily* (San Francisco State University) *Gater,* Oct. 4, 1966, p. 1.
22. Phil Garlington, "Whatever It Was . . . It Was," *The Daily* (San Francisco State University) *Gater,* Oct. 5, 1966, p. 4.
23. Ben Fong-Torres, "Editor's Desk: What Mattered About 'Whatever,' " *The Daily* (San Francisco State University) *Gater,* Oct. 5, 1966, p. 2.
24. Wolfe, *The Electric Kool-Aid Acid Test,* p. 31.
25. Kesey, undated journal page, Blue Notebook [p. 11]. Kesey Manuscript Collection, privately owned. Courtesy Red House Books.

26. Sandy Troy, "An Interview with Mountain Girl," *One More Saturday Night,* p. 80. Cf. Greenfield, *Dark Star,* pp. 84–85.
27. Valerie [Tangerine] Ann Steinbrecher, quoted in Cynthia Robins, "She Never Got Off the Bus: The Hard Life and High Times of Carolyn Garcia," *San Francisco Examiner Magazine,* May 25, 1997, p. 21.
28. Ken Kesey, "Foreword," to Wavy Gravy, *The Hog Farm and Friends* (New York: Links, 1974), p. 14. The other bad trip appears in "Over the Border," in *Garage Sale.*

space on a trip by myself, and I would have to spend the rest of my life in what society would consider an insane asylum, and I would be sad and lonely. So, I saw I would have to take everybody with me, I would have to turn on the whole world."[29]

The Tests were proof of what the phrase "turn on" meant: to open oneself up to new experiences, and more than that, to incorporate them into one's perspective; to use Norman O. Brown's terms, it meant that one was a system, not a satellite. The legacy of the Acid Tests is more than just the artifacts they left, it is also the example of its creation: everything new is done by amateurs, as Kesey says in the Sound City Test, so get out there and do it; create; be. The apotheosis of turning on.

In a poem he wrote around this time, called "Advise," Kesey could well be offering his final thoughts on the whole experience—Tests, Pranksters, media, and the sixties:

> *This I say to every mind*
> *who also is a head;*
> *"Spend not so much time justifying . . .*
> *and justify instead."*[30]

It recalls the old Prankster saying from the days of the bus trip: "Always stay in your own movie." If nothing else, the San Francisco State Test was a graceful abdication, and a sign of the succession. The next movie would last thirty years, a rolling Acid Test called Grateful Dead.

NICK MERIWETHER

## The First Grateful Dead Record: The Scorpio Single

### 1966

**San Francisco: Scorpio 201, 1966**

Stealin' b/w Don't Ease Me In

For years record collectors have known about this odd single, technically considered the first Grateful Dead record, but Deadheads have generally only encountered it as filler on early tapes. Culled from sessions held in San Francisco in 1966 (see "The Scorpio Sessions" review) the single has peppy, well-performed arrangements of two songs popular in the Palo Alto folk scene,[1] one of which, "Don't Ease Me In," stayed in the band's repertoire for the rest of its career. "Stealin'," interestingly enough, appeared again thirty years later on the Jerry Garcia–David Grisman release *Shady Grove*, where Jerry plays the old standard in an arrangement not far removed at all from this early release.

"Release," however, is a loaded word to use here: by all accounts, the record received limited distribution at best. Twenty years later, Garcia recalled that fewer than 150 copies were pressed, and "the Psychedelic Shop probably had 20 or 30 of them."[2] Record historians estimate that even fewer survived: one contemporary reviewer thought that fewer than twenty remained as soon as a year later.[3] Even the producer, Gene Estribou, thirty years later, remembered at most 250 copies. Part of this had to do with the band's irritation—by all accounts, their reaction ranged from embarrassment to antipathy, and some sources have claimed that the single was "withdrawn," or never even released, for this reason. But perhaps the greatest factor was that with Warner and other major labels sniffing around, this little project became a dead letter before it even got off the ground.

The product of Gene Estribou, a local music enthusiast who wanted to form his own record company, the single came from sessions that are common trading fodder today. Many tapes, especially from the early years, have the two sides as filler, which has caused considerable confusion over the years. Were it not for the strange circumstances surrounding it, and the fact that it is the first record by the band recording as the Grateful Dead, it wouldn't merit a footnote. (The Autumn Records demo predates this, but it appears under the name-in-transition the Emergency Crew, and was never released.) Nonetheless, it is an interesting document musically, and historically, it points out several important aspects of the band at the time. Musically it documents how they are progressing from a folk-blues band to full-fledged rock. The arrangements here show Garcia's

---

29. Burton H. Wolfe, *The Hippies* (New York: Signet, 1968), p. 202.
30. Strelow, ed., *Kesey*, p. 191.

1. John Cohen, "The Tradition Lives," liner notes to David Grisman and Jerry Garcia, *Shady Grove* (San Rafael, Calif.: Acoustic Disc ACD 21, 1997) [p. 17].
2. Blair Jackson, "Singles! A Look at the Dead's 'Forgotten' Records," *The Golden Road*, no 4 (Fall 1984), pp. 30–31.
3. Greg Shaw, reported in *Electric Frog* (Richland, Wash.), no. 3 (June 1967), p. 4.

skill, and Pigpen's dominance. This is usually the greatest surprise for fans: neither rendition is built around Jerry; he's just a player, and less of a presence than Pig. Moreover, it shows the band moving away from the teen-pop sound that Tom Donahue pulled out of them a few months before in their Autumn Records demo, and which at least part of their audience still demanded. Clearly, this is a band that is learning to do things its own way. It also shows a band that wants to adapt itself to the technology of the time—it wants to make a record, have a hit single, and learn how to use the studio to capture "their sound." That they failed to do so also makes it something of a harbinger of all of the problems that they feared they would encounter in making the transition from a performing band to a recording group. This is largely why they would choose a local producer, someone whom they thought they could control more easily than an L.A. industry insider, but even then it resulted in a product they all considered inferior.

Quality and representativeness notwithstanding, it has been more widely disseminated in the decades since then than it ever was at the time, boosted by more than one counterfeit pressing. In a way, this little single is probably more historic because of its status as the first Dead collectible to be widely counterfeited. (The only way to tell, according to knowledgeable collectors, is by an actual analysis of the grooves themselves; the labels are virtually perfect.) Critics of mid-sixties rock hold it in fairly high regard. Deadheads will probably agree with Blair Jackson's assessment of the renditions as "good and punchy,"[4] an estimation echoed by other rock historians of the era. Brian Hogg probably comes closer by calling them "pleasant workouts, interesting rather than startling."[5]

More interesting is the story of its creation. Both cuts come from sessions held in Estribou's home-built studio in San Francisco, dubbed Buena Vista Studios, sometime in the spring of 1966. The two tracks released on the single were finished at Western Recorders, a peninsula studio, as Estribou and his partner put the finishing touches on Buena Vista, which had rapidly grown into the first four-track studio in the area. The incentive for recording was there, but the direction it took was far from decided, as Estribou recalled: "It was an effort to get out of the zone of indecision, as you can imagine. The early Dead was trying to find themselves in a sense and get a product out when Phil wanted to do one thing and Jerry wanted to do another."[6] The single emerged in part so that the band would have a demo available for any major label expressing interest, which accounted for the dissension among the band about the single's quality. "So it was frustrating for everybody," Estribou summarized, "but we had to get something finished rather than nine thousand hours of shit that was unusable."[7]

In a contemporary interview, Garcia explained: "Well that [single] was with the same producer [as we're now working with], but we did it before we rushed off to L.A. and we never got in on the mixing of it and we didn't really like the cuts and the performances were bad and the recordings were bad and everything else was bad so we didn't want it out." Nonetheless, he ends up being even-handed in his assessment of the record, saying it may not be worse than much of what's being played on the radio (no great generalization in August 1966), but it simply isn't representative: "the big thing about it is that it doesn't sound like us." His band members were less charitable. When Garcia hedged, "It's not that bad, but . . . ," Pigpen's response was "Bullshit." Weir's advice for the interviewer, who said he owned a copy, was "Go burn it."[8]

Part of the reason for its disappearance had nothing to do with the band's objections. One aspect of the story that has confused collectors for years is the existence of another label in San Francisco named Scorpio. Founded by the Weiss brothers, owners of Fantasy Records, Scorpio recorded a number of local bands, several of whom went on to play with the Dead at various gigs at the Fillmore and the Avalon. The most famous of these were the Golliwogs, who later renamed themselves Creedence Clearwater Revival; as the Golliwogs, they recorded a number of singles that still arouse considerable interest today. Oddly enough, the only Scorpio single to do well—the Golliwogs' "Brown-Eyed Girl"—charted at about the same time this single hit the stores.[9] Scorpio's obscurity explains why Estribou had never heard of them. Garcia explained at the time: "What happened with the Scorpio label was that the guy went ahead and applied for it, had the labels printed up and everything like that, but after the record came out and after he had the labels out they discovered that there was some other label named Scor-

---

4. Blair Jackson, "Singles! A Look at the Dead's 'Forgotten' Records," *The Golden Road,* no. 4 (Fall 1984), p. 30.
5. Brian Hogg, "Grateful Dead: The Longest-Lasting Acid-Rock Band of the Sixties," *Record Collector* (London), no. 64 (December 1984), pp. 32–38.

6. Gene Estribou, interviewed by John R. Dwork, Feb. 12, 1997.
7. Gene Estribou, interviewed by John R. Dwork, Feb. 12, 1997.
8. *Mojo Navigator,* vol. 1, no. 4 (Aug. 30, 1966), pp. 1–6.
9. Alec Palao, liner notes to "Nuggets from the Golden State: The Scorpio Records Story," U.K.: Ace / Big Beat, CDWIKD 129, 1994.

pio, so the big clearing house, wherever it is, said 'No, you can't use that name.' "[10] Estribou essentially confirmed this. With the confusion over the labels, the brevity of the pressing, and the Warner contract in hand, the stage was set for the single to sink, leaving only a few traces of the first record in the band's history.[11]

NICK MERIWETHER

## Other Reviews from 1966

### 3/25/66
### Trouper's Hall, Los Angeles, California

Stealin', Jam, Hey Little One, Hog for You Baby, You Don't Have to Ask, Cold Rain and Snow, Next Time You See Me

**Source:** SBD, **Quality:** B+ (clean, with poor bass and poor mix in places; good for the era), **Length:** 0:35, **Genealogy:** MR > RR > DAT

**Highlights:** Stealin', You Don't Have to Ask, Jam

**Comments:** Very good quality copies of this tape are now common in tapers' circles, slowly edging out the abysmal ones that have been around for years. This material was also part of one of earliest bootleg CDs of the band, *Greetings from the Living Dead*.[1] Good copies made from DAT will sound crisp with no muddiness in the bass; clean copies that sound compressed are probably from this bootleg or its descendants, which show a substantial degree of generational loss, as well as suffering from "dolbilation," critic Thomas Storch's inimitable term for improper Dolby encoding.[2]

This performance is required listening for Deadheads who wish to learn how the band evolved, a gem from a very significant period in the band's development, their days of woodshedding with Owsley and playing the Acid Tests and a few small venues like this. While they were there, the Bear acted as their patron, boarding them in a drafty house at the edge of Watts, the band practicing downstairs as the pill press thumped away upstairs, producing Owsley's little colored tablets—still legal at the time—which were the fuel for the Acid Tests. This is the only tape of a Trouper's Hall gig available to date, although the band performed there several times that spring according to various sources, and even this tape is incomplete, according to *DeadBase*. It is a great snapshot of the band at the time, though, right in the middle of their L.A. sojourn, and really at the ebb of the Acid Test era. From then on, even at the Trips Festivals that spring, they would be a professional, gigging band, playing for money, and performing without Kesey—with one appropriately weird exception seven months after this gig (see 10/2/66).

A retired actors club in Hollywood, Trouper's Hall was called a box by local performers, famed for poor acoustics and a vicious echo. For the band, the Trouper's Hall gig was their earliest exercise in producing their own shows on foreign turf. "We did everything ourselves, all in two days," one family member recalled. "We plastered handbills all over Hollywood. Stage decor was a few lengths of paisley cloth purchased that afternoon at a fabric store. For a box office, we had a card table and a cigar box. Our not-quite-full house must have had over a hundred people; and when the night was over, our net take was $75. At 2 o'clock in the morning, we went over to Cantor's Deli on Fairfax and spent it all on dinner for everybody—with dessert."[3]

The highlights require a bit of explanation: "Stealin'," because of the feel of the performance; "You Don't Have to Ask," because of its range, from teen pop to psychedelia; and the Jam, because it's state-of-the-art Dead, circa early 1966, and because it shows a band on the way to full-bore psychedelia.

---

10. *Mojo Navigator*, vol. 1, no. 5 (Sept. 7, 1966), pp. 1–5.
11. The "Scorpio" single was to be included on a CD that was almost released in 1986. It was scraped when Garcia went into his coma. It included "You Don't Have to Ask," "Stealin'," "I Know You Rider," "Don't Ease Me In," "Cardboard Cowboy," "Can't Come Down," "Caution," and "Early Morning Rain" from this session; "Fire in the City" with Jon Hendricks, "Tastebud," "Lindy," and "Alice D. Millionaire," from some unknown studio session; "The Barbed Wire Whipping Party" from the *Aoxomoxoa* sessions; Mickey's "Fire on the Mountain"; the studio version of "Mason's Children"; "Lovelight" from 7/16/70 with Janis; and "Cream Puff War," "There's Something on Your Mind," and "I Just Want to Make Love to You" from 11/29/66 at the Matrix. The name of the album was to be *The Birth of the Dead*.

---

1. *Greetings from the Living Dead* (Italy: Living Legend, LLR CD 008, 1988). One compact disc, 0:60. The liner notes state: "San Francisco, March, 1966—Viola Lee Blues, Big Boss Man, Sittin' on Top of the World, Dancin' in the Street, I Know You Rider, He Was a Friend of Mine, Los Angeles, January, 1966—Hey Little One, I'm a Hog for You Baby, You Don't Have to Ask, Cold Rain and Snow (pt. 1), You Lied and Cheated, Me and My Uncle, Cold Rain and Snow (pt. 2), Jam." The song titles and track listing are correct; the dates and locations are not.

2. Thomas Storch, "Dead in Their Boots," *Gray Areas*, vol. 2, no. 3 (Spring 1993), pp. 88–96.
3. Brandelius, *Grateful Dead Family Album*, p. 43.

Every tape I have heard of this begins with "Stealin'" already in progress, usually at Garcia's line "In this whole wide world." The mix varies and wobbles a bit at first, but youthful energy comes through from the start—the Dead charisma is definitely there. Peppy, good-natured, with fine vocals, it is too brief, and would probably feel that way even without the cut beginning.

The Jam makes up for the brevity of "Stealin'." It's a long organ and guitar workout, with Garcia giving a one-man demonstration of the connection between rock, jazz, and bluegrass. Though not like the immense tapestries they weave later, it is quite good—especially since it's *so* early. All those hours of practice are apparent here, but not in that expansive, gentle way that they would become known for in just a few years, as exemplified by the sweet-voiced meanderings that coalesce into "Dark Star" on *Live Dead*. Here the confidence shows in their willingness to launch themselves into the vortex. The tempo is quick, but the desire to reach the groove is already apparent. And successful. Eight minutes in, and "wow" is the only appropriate response.

"Hey Little One" shows their affinity for a good, well-crafted pop ballad, with some good signature guitar licks by Jerry and good singing, for the era, by him, too; the end is especially strong, with Jerry just belting it out. "Hog for You Baby" is where Pig really wants the Dead to sound like an R&B band, and they provide a fair impersonation of one when Jerry is soloing, but not so great when they're singing and the tinny organ—a Farfisa?—is wheezing. Just not heavy enough to be credible. From a shaky start, which makes them sound like a cheesy nightclub band, they recover for a fine first jam and solo and settle into a solid Motown rhythm. Already, this is a band that demonstrates its diversity, and even more, its desire to be diverse, and at times the strain shows. But at times it doesn't, and most Heads will concur with one of my friend's assessments: "Already, they have the touch."

Bobby sings lead on "You Don't Have to Ask," and Jerry sounds warmed up and ready—this is his tempo, his forte, a quick steady pound, and he just soars over it, fast-picking as if he were back in a Palo Alto coffeehouse doing "Jerry's Breakdown." Pretty good harmonies, too: this is altogether credible. The band sounds as if they all like this song, and it careens and tilts and flies, with much of the same feel that they captured in "The Golden Road" on their debut LP, but with a much longer, fuller workout here. Most interesting is how it shows a distinct spaciness in the improvisations at the end, the sort of jam that toys with ensemble arrangements and dynamics, not just solo-based ones. And it goes places—not just exploring, but traveling too. It has progressed a great deal from the more formal treatment they gave it in the Autumn Records studio sessions four months earlier.

On most tapes there is an end-of-set announcement, and then "Cold Rain and Snow," still an organ showcase for Pig, who is the dominant presence in the song, both vocally and instrumentally. His singing really shines here: strong, confident, in control. "Next Time You See Me," pleasant though short, ends in a spectacular tape foul-up, if you have it: the unique sound of a reel-to-reel dying, or running out of tape, or perhaps simply committing hara-kiri over the dynamic range the band has forced it to endure.

Trouper's Hall was basically the other half of the band's L.A. performing experience outside of the Acid Tests. A wonderful shot of them on stage there appears in Gans and Simon's *Playing in the Band*, possibly from the same show (it's dated March 1966).[4] A perfect stage photo, it is especially useful for tapers interested in the band's setup at the time. Most of all, though, it shows how young they were—a useful reminder for fans first listening to the era, who may be disappointed in how different they sound from their late-sixties glory. This tape, however, shows them well on the way there.

NICK MERIWETHER

## 7/3/66
### The Fillmore Auditorium, San Francisco, California

Viola Lee Blues, Big Boss Man, Sittin' on Top of the World, Dancin' in the Streets, I Know You Rider, He Was a Friend of Mine, Next Time You See Me

**Source:** SBD, **Quality:** A (for the era), **Length:** 0:33, **Genealogy:** MR > RR > [multiple reel generations?] > DAT > C

**Highlights:** The entire set is recommended.

This is one of the oldest circulating 1966 sets, common in trading circles when I first began trading in the mid-eighties. Provenance is especially difficult for this tape,

---
4. Gans and Simon, *Playing in the Band*, p. 44.

since multiple reel generations were common in the early days of tapers. The best copy I have heard comes from a DAT made from an early ten-inch reel, with the Scorpio single sandwiched between "Sittin' on Top of the World" and "Dancin'."

Musically, it is a set that requires restraint in description, else you run out of adjectives on "Viola Lee Blues" alone. And "Viola" . . . sounds just great. When I first heard this set, it had been lovingly rearranged by some avid amateur producer, whose concept of catharsis placed this at the end of the show. It's an instinct most Heads will sympathize with; my first reaction was "Here is *the jam*." A long but brisk descent into classic Dead heavy improvisation: confident, strong, and enthusiastic: this is why listening to early era Dead can be fun. And instructive.

The chugging rhythm also informs "Big Boss Man," the whole band solidly in the groove already, relaxed, easy-going, all confidence and grace. "Dancin'" is where critics will be tempted to say that the band's woodshedding earlier that spring has paid off. It shines, and already it shows what the band would use it for over the next couple of decades: as an unlikely and therefore inspired platform for improvisation. It gets "out there": both melody and rhythm are abstracted so well—and so far from the song—that it has you worried about the return. And a classic Dead decision: to take a contemporary teen pop anthem and transmogrify it into their own weird, decidedly noncommercial vehicle.

In those days, commerciality was closely tied to eating, though, so in a perfect little note of irony, most tapes then have Jerry making an embarrassed little plug for a clothing store on Haight Street, for which the band had recently done an advertisement, a photo of the band that is one of the classic early shots. "Rider" is still in that fast, happy arrangement immortalized on the Sunflower LP *Vintage Dead*. It features some fine guitar moves by Jerry, as if this is the tempo he is most comfortable working in; you can almost hear the banjo theory behind what he's working out on these classic chord changes. Unfortunately, a bad cut ends this and launches us into "He Was a Friend of Mine," and the cut is so brutal that it takes many moments before you realize that *they* aren't suffering; they still sound good—quite good, though not as good, mostly because Garcia's voice shows that weird vibrato effect he was playing with then. But it's a nice version, sweet and mournful, especially the guitar tone. The last verse is exquisite: no vibrato in Garcia's voice, and Lesh's bass lopes and runs all over the place, in that same slow but inexorable beat that "The Wheel" cap-

tured so elegantly years later. It makes for a hypnotic, groove-oriented tune that masks how quick it really is: it simply floats through and over and around, sinuously. One of those "instant classic" folk songs, it shows here that under the Dead's hands it can also be a great vehicle for a jam, or for the free dancing that was coming into play with the Dead already. It offers so many instrumental flourishes and nuances to bend and shake around, so many good solos, especially Garcia's.

In 1966 tapes, Pig always comes across as a confident band leader, and he sounds good and strong on "Next Time You See Me." Here it is quicker than a few months earlier at Trouper's Hall, but no real jam—strictly a blues for Pigpen to take and make soar. Picky Deadheads who can miss the early jams—which are a feature of this set—would still do well to listen to this. In 1966, it is still Pigpen's band.

NICK MERIWETHER

---

### ❊ 9/66 ❊

**The Avalon Ballroom and the Matrix Club, San Francisco, California**

*Vintage Dead* (LP). MGM / Sunflower, SNF 5001, 1973, 39:50 min. I Know Your Rider, It Hurts Me Too, Baby Blue, Dancin' in the Streets, Midnight Hour

*Historic Dead* (LP). MGM / Sunflower, SNF 5004, 1973, 28:51 min. Good Mornin', Li'l Schoolgirl, Lindy, Stealin' [Matrix], The Same Thing [Matrix]

---

**Source:** SBD, **Quality:** A, **Length:** total Avalon material: 0:55, total Matrix material: 0:15, **Genealogy:** LP > C

**Highlights:** I Know You Rider, Dancin', Midnight Hour, The Same Thing

**Comments:** The material from these two albums has floated through the taping world for years, in an impressive number of guises. The front cover of one of the albums reproduces the Avalon poster for the shows on September 16 and 17, 1966, which has probably been the best source for dating some of the material; Robert Cohen's liner notes state the year of the Avalon tracks, and Peter Abram has confirmed the year of the Matrix material. Numerous other creative interpretations have circulated, though, ranging from Acid Tests to Warlocks gigs.

Both albums have their gems, and the audio quality is unimpeachable. To an album buyer at the time, however, *Historic Dead* must have appeared anemic: at just under thirty minutes, it feels like a rip-off. With only four songs, two very short indeed (three minutes and under), we do get an eleven-minute "Schoolgirl," and—most important—a remarkable "The Same Thing," at just over twelve, so it can definitely be considered a useful document of the predebut album period of their development. It is, however, fairly easy to see why the band hated both of these efforts: by 1973, they were phenomenally unrepresentative of their sound, in addition to the whole sleaziness of the way they came out. But a tape of both albums is an important addition to a collection of the era, especially one from a clean set of albums, recorded with a good turntable and cartridge.

**VINTAGE DEAD**

The early arrangement of "I Know You Rider" is always something of a critical—or taste, or aesthetic—benchmark for Deadheads: either it is pop-poisoned juvenilia or else raw, essential garage-band Dead, rough energy with only a thin veneer of polish and a great deal of depth. Here some listeners will find good if somewhat rough harmonies and amphetamine-fueled guitar leads over a roaring, raging locomotive of rhythm, drums exploding behind and a bass charging over a melody line with more rhythm licks than most funk, charging alongside and under Garcia's glissandos, mutating into two-stringed counterpoint to the harmonies, organ trilling out and away from it all: a snapshot of them at their peak for the time.

A fast introduction, almost rushed, to "Hurts Me Too" makes it feel off-kilter at first, as if it had lost a first verse somewhere. But from the outset it moves, and Pig sounds great; the band sounds tight if not inspired—solid. And a good "first" jam, which furthers the impression that it has been edited. Despite some nice final flourishes, it's a low-energy rendition, all told. A medium-slow groove characterizes "Baby Blue," Pigpen playing a prominent organ role and sounding good. Garcia plays his chunky, percussive rhythm style to great effect. When he plays rhythm during these years, the band always seems to achieve a certain propulsive precision that is simply inexorable: a superb groove, and an early indication of its prowess as a dance band. This is not Garcia's finest vocal showing, but even that seems somehow fitting, making it a good solid groove from their garage-band years, betrayed only by the craft evident in their arrangement of the ending.

A hard start begins "Dancin' in the Streets," an aggressive pound with good vocal harmonies overlaid; it feels like a harbinger of good things. Pigpen's organ finally plays the lead position in the mix—a nice contribution by the album. Despite the very good voices for the era—perhaps the best vocals on these two LPs—the highlight is Pig's organ, which plays in this arrangement the most sophisticated part that it does anywhere on any tape in circulation, all sweeping atmospheres above and trills behind Garcia's restless leads, darting and running and lashing the band on, worrying the melody, shaking and shepherding it with complete dominance and aplomb. By the end, even Pig gets aggressive and abstracted, Garcia soloing high and weird over the increasing diffusion and polyphonous mélange below, each instrument so entwined that there doesn't seem to be any room for Garcia's leads down there, but he drops into the soup and calms it for the return to the vocals, "All we need is music, sweet music. . . ." Good harmonies, once again. At the end, it feels as if they've said a lot in eight minutes.

In a nice bit of sixties history, Chet Helms announces the band next: "Ladies and gentlemen: the Grateful Dead!" Out of place in the middle of a tape, but it's appropriate if one recalls this would have been the start of the second side of the album. And the distinctive thump of "Midnight Hour" begins, a groove they command from the outset. Pig is in fine form, rapping and bantering, nothing too substantive, but the seeds of the grand group narratives that he would weave with the band and audience later are already clear in his rapping here. And it is his tune; he calls the band members back and sets them loose, whips them up and slows them down. It is as superb a demonstration of his musicianship and stagemanship as any tape from this era. In a review of what could well be the night of this performance, Ralph Gleason lavished particular praise on this song: "The band went into 'Midnight Hour' and Pig Pen made it into a one-man blues project. He sang for almost twenty minutes, stabbing the phrases out into the crowd like a preacher, using the words to riff like a big band, building to a climax after climax, coming down in a release and soaring up again. He is one of the best blues singers of his generation. . . ."[1] It's an apt description.

---

1. Ralph J. Gleason, "On the Town: All That Jazz and Rock Paid Off," *San Francisco Chronicle*, Sept. 13, 1966.

## HISTORIC DEAD

"Good Mornin', Li'l Schoolgirl" sounds odd in the beginning—the band sounds self-conscious, or perhaps it is simply one of their more understated openings. They're not in a real hurry, and the cleaned-up recording is something of a shock if you're used to hearing amateur, multiple-generation tapes over three decades old. The sound is punchy, almost artificially clean in places, but the result is an imminently listenable tape. Heads with refined sonic sensibilities and without access to DAT trading might want to seek this out as the best sound quality of anything from 1966.

By the end of the first verse, things have picked up. With excellent and unusual guitar and harmonica interplay in the jam following the first verse, the whole band swings into it hard. Pig shines in the end of this first crescendo, then everything pares down to sparse and percussive, slowly fleshing out, building as Garcia calls for stranger and stranger rhythm patterns from Lesh and Kreutzmann, thinning out finally into Pig, soulful and sweet, importuning and sighing: a confident and worthwhile rendition.

Slowed to a raggedy blues, "Lindy" comes across as a perfectly respectable jug-band holdover, and a first-rate, heavily reverbed Garcia solo goes a long way toward making it serious fun. That seems a description tailor-made for "Stealin'," which captures the Dead's energy here in the way that only a few of the songs did in 1966. One of the two songs provided by Peter Abram to the project, it is another live cut from the Matrix, though many Heads have tapes listing them as studio, for some reason. Though clean, a good recording reveals the live ambience.

"The Same Thing" starts very slow, especially for 1966, which will immediately strike fans as interesting. Already in fine form and voice, this gives every indication of turning into a Pigpen showcase. From his opening line, "What makes a man go crazy, / When a woman wears her dress so tight," this is highly competent blues—superior to any of their blues on the debut album, and a slice largely missing from the recordings in circulation. And of the Matrix tracks we have, this is the finest, though the caliber of the audio can be partially attributed to the professional production. From the stately opening, it builds nicely, if quickly, with Garcia in charge, pulling at the leash, slowed beautifully by Lesh and Kreutzmann. Critics of Lesh who dismiss his blues chops will be interested to see how conservatively—and how well—he plays here, on a slow blues at

that. Garcia plays especially fluid leads over Pig's last lines, floating out farther and farther as it gets heavier and heavier, dynamics working up to a fever pitch and intensity, Lesh driving the bottom end toward what seems as if it will become one of their trademark, awesome crescendoes—an expectation neatly foiled as Garcia strips the lead down to a few repeated chords and interconnecting riffs, rhythm reduced to a solid groove now, and a graceful feint back at melody before the groove returns full force for a romp to the close, but with a high-velocity, single-minded meander on the way there. A short twelve minutes. Best at high volume.

Exactly how these albums came to see the light of day is murky, a classic tale of music industry chicanery. Originally part of a project that was to release live albums from a host of the San Francisco bands, the Dead's albums were all that was salvaged. Robert Cohen, Chet Helms' partner in the Avalon Ballroom, was hired to engineer and master the tapes, and completed work on not only the Dead's tracks but a number of others as well, including some from the Charlatans and the Airplane.[2] The original project fell through, however, and when the studio where Cohen had done the mastering was not paid, they held the masters as collateral against their fees. MGM, one of several labels with allegedly shady distribution connections at the time, bought the tapes and contacted Cohen, blithely announcing their impending release, over Cohen's protests. With releases from the band—a point disputed by them, though under Lenny Hart's management they certainly signed other poor contracts—the two albums were completed, with Cohen's production. When Cohen found out that MGM planned to release other tapes from the original project without the bands' permissions, he took matters into his own hands and erased the tapes. When *Vintage Dead* came out, it included his elegiac liner notes: "That is the Grateful Dead. This closeness, this ability to become one being is perhaps the greatest asset that any group can have. They perform best on stage with an audience in front of them. They have fun on stage and this is obviously where they want to be. This is why I recorded them."

Pilloried for erasing the tapes, Cohen left the music business entirely and now refers to the entire debacle as "that ill-fated nightmare." Nonetheless, the two documents made a definite contribution to Deadhead knowl-

---

2. Bob Cohen, interviewed by Joel Selvin, Jan. 6, 1993.

Reviews: November 1966

edge of this early period in the band's development, especially during the 1970s and 1980s, when so few good quality recordings from this era circulated.

NICK MERIWETHER

---

### ❦ 11/29/66 ❦
### The Matrix Club, San Francisco, California

**Set 1:** Sick and Tired, Standing on the Corner, Mindbender, Hurts Me Too, Viola Lee Blues, I Know You Rider, It's a Sin, Sick and Tired, Cream Puff War
**Set 2:** Me and My Uncle, The Same Thing, Stealin', Big Boy Pete, One Kind Favor, Viola Lee Blues
**Set 3:** Down So Long, Something on Your Mind, Lindy, Good Mornin', Li'l Schoolgirl, I Just Want to Make Love to You

---

**Source:** SBD, **Quality:** A–, **Length:** 1:40:42, **Genealogy:** MR > RR > C > DAT
**Highlights:** The Same Thing, Viola Lee Blues

This evening's performance, at least the first set, has vexed Deadheads for years because of the vagaries in dating all but the last song. Wonderful sound quality is available—almost as good as the Sunflower records, and the sets here cover a much wider range of material. Originally considered to be from the Matrix show on November 29, 1966, the first set has most recently been identified as February 23, 1966, and even that is uncertain, according to *DeadBase*. An additional complicating factor is that it sounds like a Peter Abram tape, but he is certain that he didn't tape them that night. A surprising number of tapes circulate with virtually identical set lists on adjacent tape sides, one attributed to 2/23/66 and the other to 11/29/66. Perhaps the most complete tape shows no break between "Sick and Tired" and "Standing on the Corner"; it also lacks breaks between the last three songs of the first set, throwing some question on the set now commonly credited as 2/23/66, which follows a slightly different order than the set above. And some tapes also list two more songs, "Early Morning Rain" and "Cold Rain and Snow," which are missing here. What we have, however, is interesting if only tentatively dated.

As Marty Balin's showcase club for his new band, the Jefferson Airplane, the Matrix opened in August of 1965, on Friday the 13th, beginning a checkered seven-year history that was marked by a host of problems with the city and the neighborhood over noise. Along the way it was bought by one of its patrons, Peter Abram, a Berkeley grad student who dropped out to pursue his long-time hobby, making tapes of this new music that was sweeping San Francisco. He bought the club so he could make tapes of what he thought was the most innovative and important new music to be heard in decades—which no one else was recording. In time, tapes that he recorded would be bought and released by several major labels, providing collectors with a taste of early Steppenwolf, the Doors, the Great Society, the Velvet Underground, and a couple of Grateful Dead cuts on the controversial MGM/Sunflower release, *Historic Dead*. Over the years, despite the hassles, the Matrix was a perfect small venue for intimate jam sessions that drew Jerry Garcia, Merl Saunders, Elvin Bishop, and a host of other Bay Area and national talents who relished performing in front of club audiences.

In 1966, the Matrix was a featured venue for the nascent Dead. In this set, perhaps the most salient characteristic is the brevity of the songs, and the short breaks the band takes between them; this is a band that still shows all the signs of its apprenticeship in the bars of the peninsula. Another facet that will interest fans unfamiliar with this era is how willing they are to sound like a typical teen rock outfit; although they already clearly show their other influences, contemporary pop was also a major referent in 1966, though one that quickly diminished as they solidified their feel. It is yet another reminder that the dividing line between pop and rock wasn't very clear in 1966—especially for a group of musicians who counted the Beatles as a major reason for getting involved with electric music. For Garcia in particular, who had run out of places to play as a bluegrass musician, a big part of the appeal of being a rock band was gigging—which meant getting audiences to like you. Therefore, you played some contemporary hits. And as their Autumn Records sessions showed, they could certainly ape the teen rock sound that Autumn's owner, Big Daddy Tom Donahue, believed would sell.

These sets show all of that, and more. A soundboard, the tape listens like an Abram tape: excellent sound for the time though the tape malfunction on "Cream Puff

War" is a demonstration of what Abram later called his jinx of recording the band: "I don't know why this is true but it seems as though every time I get near the Grateful Dead something goes wrong with the recording."[1] Regardless, his tapes are prized by collectors for their warmth and sonic quality in an era when even studio recordings showed all their limitations clearly.

True to form, they open with "Sick and Tired," Pig's song in every way, with a good harp solo and a solid groove. It is interesting primarily in that it showcases Garcia as a rhythm guitarist, playing no real solos, just little fills and riffs, and also shows Lesh playing a conventional bass line—and, critics of his "soulfulness" will be interested to note, he knows how to play that traditional chunky, heavy bass line that he abandoned later. "Standing on the Corner," a fifties tune first recorded by Dean Martin and then the Four Lads, sounds like Garcia's protopunk anthem, all angry teen angst and cynicism: "Think I'll fling myself into space / I'm not doin' it 'cause I'm desperate / I'm just doin' it to save some face." The solos are weak—they come across as stilted, all relegated to a conventional "and now we solo" section—but lyrically it is fascinating to hear the Dead throw themselves into this kind of material: angry young post-Beat bohemians, on the cusp of hippiedom, summarized by the line: "There's a lot of new things / Runnin' 'round my mind." It establishes a mood and theme—the realm of the mind—that is also the focus of the next tune, "Mindbender," one of their earliest originals, which Deadheads may recognize as "Confusion's Prince." Perhaps the outstanding teen-style tune they did before the first album, "Mindbender" is lyrically and instrumentally a delight. Oblique but obvious in its drug imagery, you can see how it would go over well with their audiences: "If only I could be less blind / If only I knew what to find / Everywhere and all the time / It's bending my mind."

Only with "Hurts Me Too," the next song, do they sound like what they would become. You could be forgiven for thinking, at first, that it was a late-sixties version, which indicates how good they already were with Pigpen's beloved blues. Pig is especially good, his singing exceptional, and the band finds a nice groove, not too slow, a little faster than on *Europe '72*, for example. Midtempo blues is what the Dead really showed total mastery of in this early period, and it shows to beautiful effect here. No wonder Peter Abram pulled tape; this really was a treasure of the moment, and the idea of being able to capture it must have been intoxicating. The recording has problems here: the mix is poor, and Garcia's guitar is difficult to pick out, as are the keyboards in places. As on many tapes from this era, the drums sound hollow and boomy, but the vocals are clear, Pigpen's harp is wonderful, and the bass and drums work together with a punch and metrical precision that more than compensates for the deficiencies in tonal quality. In a column that appeared in the Berkeley student newspaper the day after the phantom February 23 show, Rolling Stone founder Jann Wenner, writing under the pseudonym Mr. Jones, concluded: "The group which, if it ever makes it, will make it the biggest, is the Grateful Dead."[2] This tape shows why he was so impressed.

"Viola Lee Blues" is an eight-minute workout, played here a little slower than seems to have been normal for them, but at my favorite tempo for this tune: powerful, languorous, and still intense. It shows, even in 1966 (whether February or November), they could already "do it." This is also where Lesh really shines, loping and leading and thumping, playing at least three different parts of the arrangement in the course of the song, refusing to be pinned down. Five minutes in and they've reached that first emotional and melodic plateau—already eminently capable of carving out that signature Dead mood, the balletic sense of a jam, building and ebbing and rising and moving and effusing that elusive sense of progress. All of their ideas and eclecticism shines in this, with even a ragalike riff and solo from Jerry about seven minutes in. It's a reminder that even as they demonstrate how distinctive they had already become, they are still very much a product of their time.

"I Know You Rider" is manic, fun, and magic. A showcase song for them in '66, it shows them bridging many of their major influences, from folk to teen rock to serious, amphetamine-driven weirdness. This is still solidly anchored in the fun side of that axis, but the jamming shows how seriously they took their fun. Both "It's a Sin" and "Sick and Tired" are Pigpen powerhouses, supple and tight, and like the song that follows to close the set, they show the degree to which they've been practicing. Fans familiar with the difficult structure and phrasing—both musical and lyrical—of "Cream Puff War" will easily see the fruits of the band's hours in the heliport in Sausalito, their first serious practice space; no

---

1. Peter Abram, interviewed by John R. Dwork, Jan. 23, 1997.

2. mr. jones [Jann Wenner], "Bob Dylan's T.B. and Acid-Rock," *Daily Californian*, Feb. 24, 1966, p. 12.

hitches or breaks mar its bumpy demanding steamroll. A medium tempo version, this is not as fast as the one on their debut album, and a sense of measured restraint, of almost wondering, comes through strongly here. Garcia is in good voice, belting it out over not the greatest mix—certainly not headphone quality. The band, however, sounds absolutely fine; though not stepping out at all, it is a letter-perfect rendition, though a little tentative until the final jam, which sounds as if it may be going places until a horrible cut at the end, a leading candidate for unkindest of 1966.

"Me and My Uncle" opens the second set, introduced by Garcia in a Hollywood Southern accent as "a cowboy song." Weir sings lead over a good, quick groove, which sounds as if it owes its feel to bluegrass licks flying over a swampy organ stew. Wonderful tension shows through the juxtaposition of styles and influences, with a pronounced New Orleans flavor emerging during the jams. Weir doesn't come across as well as he does elsewhere in this tape—not very clear in the mix, and his voice quavers a bit, but it sets the stage for "The Same Thing," which seizes the New Orleans touch and pounces on it. It starts wonderfully slow, everybody gradually joining in, and a few moments in, you will be amazed that for a song that apparently had such a small position in the repertoire, it certainly packs one of their best blues punches: one of their best slow blues from this era. On a good tape at high volume, it is difficult to tell that this is 1966. Garcia has something to say in his solos; the band shows a perfect sense of ebb and sway; and Pig is in fine and subtle voice, coaxing and wheedling the melody over and around the other instruments, ambling purposefully along in a sure-footed shuffle, wheeling and flexing into a first-rate example of why the Dead so impressed Jann Wenner when he saw them during these months. They already show a keen sense of exploration, with jams that seem to turn inside out and in on themselves, warping rhythm and melody and beat in a wonderful, cathartic workout.

Garcia introduces the next tune with a bit of musicology, saying, "This is an old jug-band song, called 'Stealin'." A nice, easy loping version, this is well played and low-key, pleasant if undistinguished—until the next tune, that is, which makes "Stealin'" look masterful. "We're gonna do a rock 'n' roll song," Garcia says next, "a famous old rock 'n' roll song." Which they do, and "Big Boy Pete" is a reminder that they really could sound like a teen rock outfit back then; this really isn't that far away from the strangely named outfit that auditioned for Tom Donahue only a year earlier. And this rendition makes you wonder why Donahue passed on them, since this sound seems not far removed at all from what Autumn Records did pursue. But the Dead also did these other, weird things; they were just a little too early, both for the scene and for Big Daddy Donahue himself, who hadn't completed his psychedelic metamorphosis yet.

"Pete" includes an excellent bit of guitar work from Garcia, though, and Pig sounds good. By the end, the entire band is nothing if not tight. The audience applause is very sparse, though; Peter Abram remembers around eighty people at these shows, but even so, there's not much noise. "Pete" was not a favored song among the cognoscenti. Some nice long tuning follows, and Jerry picks into the melody of "See That My Grave Is Kept Clean" (or "One Kind Favor") with everybody swinging in behind him for a long leisurely spin into that smoky New Orleans sound again, a slow steady groove, powerful and sparse, with a touch of syncopation to keep it heavy and somber without letting it become ponderous—barely controlled power, in fact, with Garcia hitting strong high notes, Phil playing loud and hard, Pig being sparse and atmospheric on the organ: wow. It's easy to forget the date here, too. This cut is perfect headphone listening. A superb and unusual Garcia solo in the middle of the song is all high notes and rippling duel-stringed runs that don't sound much like his signature sound at all, which was already well defined by 1966. Jerry takes a verse and does a perfectly serviceable job, even kicking the band into final high pitch for the last chorus, but Pig is clearly the vocal dynamo on that stage.

As Jerry is bantering with the crowd—"we're changing our name to comic relief"—you can hear faint requests offstage for "Early Morning Rain," and Garcia keeps talking to a Marty in the audience whose voice isn't audible on the tape, but it certainly could be Marty Balin. "Early Morning Rain" is peppy and energetic, well done but not inspired; it's tempting to say that this is not what they most enjoy. A quick and competent job and on into "Viola Lee Blues," which they start with a vengeance, fast but not manic, pounding rapidly into a hard-driving rhythm, generating waves of sound so that when they slide into drums only for a few seconds as they wind into the jams, it really does approximate the ebb and flow of surf, giant breakers gathering into swells that come crashing down seconds later.

And they sound great. From a strong, confident, medium-fast-tempo opening, they give all the signs of a canter on the verge of breaking into a gallop. Good voices, good guitar tone, and a very good opening jam by a tight, nimble band. They navigate this clip—this complexity—quite well, especially Pigpen, who is not a small presence here, either, and is fairly weird. It's difficult to imagine him being increasingly left behind in the explorations of the later sixties, given what we see here, the subtlety and range of his contribution to the sound textures being woven. By the end it cranks into a marvelous, frenetic, discordant though still melodic maelstrom, the antecedent for their reputation of rolling thunder if ever there was one. What is most striking is the degree to which Garcia's ringing guitar maintains a chiming tonality, a sweetness in the howling cacophony raging around him—until they abruptly topple back into the verse, for a last reprise and the close. Eleven minutes and forty-four seconds of the Dead in full regalia.

The third set begins with "Down So Long," a phrase made most famous by fellow Bay Area folkie Richard Fariña with his novel *Been Down So Long It Looks Like Up to Me*. Fariña's wife Mimi shared the stage with the Dead on a few occasions, and his sister-in-law, Joan Baez, inspired Jerry when he was first starting out as a folkie. All Dead songs have their fans, and even near universally deplored songs in the later repertoire like "Day Job" had adherents, but this definitely seems to be one of the duds in the early repertoire. If you can listen for the interplay, though, it shows why it gets such a good treatment: a few nice opportunities for instrumental flourishes, some good group counterpoint, and an odd platform for Garcia to solo against, including a campy, slowed ending.

"Something on Your Mind" is a Pigpen-led ballad, bluesy and sad and violent and lovelorn and stricken and fundamentally Pig—another of his moods. "Lindy" is its typical, semi-silly self, a calliope-wheezy electric jug-band rag, and pretty charming at that. "Good Mornin', Li'l Schoolgirl" returns things to serious, predictably long but featuring several unpredictable quirks. A midtempo groove and a vocal marathon for Pig, in good form, voice bending and roaring and wheezing convincingly, smoothly. All of Lesh's trumpet-solo-style bass lines are evident here, bucking beneath Garcia and soaring over Kreutzmann's floating, rock-steady beat, even a few moments of near-solo at one point, before they all swing hard into the final jam, Pig anxious and and exhortative, preaching with the band, and at last his organ plays a prominent part, needling and then settling down and weirding out until he finally calls everyone back into line for a final verse, though it seemed as if only dissolution were possible from there.

It was a good night for the band, and especially for Garcia. All the years spent in so many bands show strongly here in his sense of when to play behind and with others, and when to step out. The last song shows this as well: "I Just Want to Make Love to You" begins like one of those initially unpromising-sounding "teen-beat" songs, but one already evident characteristic of the Dead is their ability to use the most unlikely vehicles as launching platforms. And the tune has a distinct bridge and middle section that would appeal to their love of challenge, which is perhaps why we get into a good jam at the end and an easy jump into the weird, as if the pace gave them the velocity for the leap. It feels cut off too soon, interestingly enough, but not by Weir—by Pigpen.

A tiny touch of vestigial Dead showmanship and whimsy, the Merrie Melodies tune ends the set, preceded by Jerry saying, "Well, it's about that time again." Bobby helps date the show afterward by saying, "We all will be back tomorrow night," to which Jerry, the deadpan beatnik, adds—establishing the proper note—"In spite of it all."

NICK MERIWETHER

---

### 12/1/66
**The Matrix Club,
San Francisco, California**

**Set 1:** New Minglewood Blues, Betty and Dupree, Next Time You See Me, I Know You Rider, Big Boss Man, One Kind Favor (See That My Grave Is Kept Clean), Alice D. Millionaire, Me and My Uncle, Cream Puff War

**Set 2:** You Don't Love Me, Beat It on Down the Line, Hurts Me Too, On the Road Again, Yonder's Wall\*, My Own Fault\*, Down So Long, Cold Rain and Snow, Viola Lee Blues

**Set 3:** Deep Elem, Something on Your Mind, Big Boy Pete, Death Don't Have No Mercy, Lindy, Dancin', Me and My Uncle

\* With guest vocalist.

# Reviews: December 1966

**Source:** SBD, **Quality:** A–: some rough spots, but basically very good for the time, **Length:** 2:40, **Genealogy:** MR > RR > C > DAT

**Highlights:** Betty and Dupree, I Know You Rider, My Own Fault, Viola Lee Blues

As the last of the Dead's three-day stint at the Matrix, it's somewhat appropriate that this also be the most complete set of tapes we have from the run. Unfortunately, the sound is poor at first. Part of that may have to do with the club's acoustics; more likely is that the engineer, Peter Abram, was having problems with his tape deck, which he remembered years later: "The heads were worn out on my machine. The tapes sounded great over the headphones, but when I played them back between sets I knew something was wrong."[1] With the loan of Owsley's microphones and judicious manipulation of the tape during playback, Abram produced thoroughly passable results, especially by the standards of the time, when four-track was not yet state-of-the-art. (It apparently allowed Columbia to claim that tapes made by him six months earlier were "professionally recorded," even though they were made on a portable Akai reel-to-reel.)[2] By the end of the first song, the sound has stabilized as Abram and Owsley get the mix balanced, without requiring that phenomenon of Deadhead adaptation that, in the opinion of non-Deadheads, seems to grant aficionados the ability to listen despite the crippling deficiencies of beloved tapes.

"New Minglewood Blues" opens with Weir singing lead, screaming fairly convincingly at the right moments, along with some good Garcia. This is definitely their teen-angst-ridden arrangement of it, and it comes across as a garage-band rocker that careens and tilts and whines through an organ-dominated landscape where Garcia alternates between rhythm and lead, bass line careening; it rocks and roars. Some great stage banter follows, a perfect stage-setting bit of atmosphere by Garcia: "Welcome to another evening of confusion and high-frequency stimulation, and Sucrets, cold beer on tap, lurid night club atmosphere, and—and beatniks. More beatniks than you can count on the fingers of two hands," as the band tunes and noodles in the background, so reminiscent of the Black Mountain Boys or the Wildwood Boys bantering in a Palo Alto coffeehouse. This mood is furthered by the next song, "Betty and Dupree," which dates back to those days. A sweet folk tune, it has some good organ work and boasts a tight arrangement; the Mother McCree's influence seems especially pronounced here. On "Next Time You See Me" Pig holds forth with such an easy confidence: a relaxed but commanding vocal presence, along with nice understated organ fill work. Throughout there is good Garcia-Pigpen interplay, between harp and guitar especially, but basically this is Pig's song and showcase.

Lots of tuning follows this, another hallmark of the Dead already in place, cut off by another bit of coffeehouse musicology: "This is a famous old folk song," and one that they would continue to play for the entirety of their career. "I Know You Rider" starts by trilling into the riff from this first, early arrangement, which made it into such a speed workout, and then Kreutzmann just launches, a hard drum roll that Phil leaps on, pounding into a propulsive groove. One of their signature songs from this era, it is all manic energy and melody driven to the brink of cacophony, interplay as ferocious and serious and playful and competitive as siblings wrestling. The swing and sweep of organ, guitar, and bass against that roaring drum barrage is a harbinger of the sound to come.

More signs of their folkie roots show in "One Kind Favor," which folkies call "See That My Grave Is Kept Clean." With that sinister New Orleans sound again, courtesy of Pig's organ and Jerry's reedy tenor vocal, it goes exploring, pushed by a very good Jerry solo that weaves and floats, covering a large amount of ground before Pig begins and the groove descends another level, and the band really is in that New Orleans flailing funk, pounding down at the end, back to a swing and closure. Now there is a gratifying amount of applause from the audience; it wasn't just the tape that made it sound sparse the last time. A reminder that the Dead didn't necessarily mean that much then, although they already carried the promise of a great show.

Many tapes list the next song as "No Time to Cry," the band's ode to Augustus Owsley Stanley. Its proper title is "Alice D. Millionaire," the homonymic title taken from the headlines when Owsley was arrested. Weir recently called this one of their earliest—if not their first—"group compositions,"[3] which makes it especially appropriate given that its subject is their benefactor, part of whose value to the band was his sponsorship while they were practicing and working up material. Pig sounds good here, though everybody else sounds off. Slower than the studio version, perhaps the

---

1. Peter Abram, interviewed by John R. Dwork, Jan. 23, 1997.
2. Alec Palao, *Cream Puff War*, no. 1 (Jan. 1991), p. 11.
3. Bob Weir, interviewed by Michael Wanger, Apr. 22, 1997.

laid-back tempo was a good idea, but the harmonies don't come off well at all. Pig sails out clear and strong, though—he handles this style well.

In stark contrast, they launch into a tight, fast, well-jammed introduction to "Me and My Uncle," Bobby singing lead—not terrifically well—against Pig's careening organ, prominent and powerful. Faster tempos work better for them on many songs during this era. Not even that saves this false start, though, and the band grinds to a halt, Jerry saying, "We can't agree on the words so we won't do that one," to audience laughter and applause. A creditable run-through follows, finally, before "Cream Puff War," a highlight. Clearly, this tempo is their forte: careening, on the verge of out-of-control, with no one sure who is holding the reins. All good old-fashioned teenage exhilaration and exuberance, with one long, proto–Dead jam. There's some very good and interesting guitar work in Garcia's solo, all over the neck as he coaxes out low, sweet runs and manic, high-fretted glissandos so filled with notes they seem about to abstract from the melody, as if he were mimicking a hard-bop Charlie Parker solo, but more melodically . . . And then that incredible, amphetamine-driven introductory riff: wow. And that's the end of the first set. They've hooked the audience.

An interesting set to contemplate, too: a classic, nightclub-styled set, forty minutes on, fifteen-minute break, and then back for another. It makes this set a particularly good representative to have from this era, as the nightclub-era Dead was changing to reflect all of the lessons learned over the last year, and not just lyrically—as "Mindbender," "Cream Puff War," and "The Golden Road" all showed already—but musically as well. The latter evolution would take several more years.

With the first song out of the second set, they've picked up precisely where they left off; "Beat It on Down the Line" is filled with great manic energy from the first note. A wonderful organ workout here, Pig just raging over the keys, rolls and sweeps propelling this frenzy, then finally Garcia's statement, right after the phrase "coal mine"; he spins the pace to a dizzying level but only briefly, as if to say it's Pig's tune, and be respectful. All of the years spent listening to other musicians, to creating a group feeling and not just using others as one's backdrop, shines here, with the perfectly appropriate level of solo and group work. "It Hurts Me Too" is a typically competent 1966 version. There's eagerness apparent beneath the slow, powerful start—suggesting that it chafed a bit to drop to this stately pace—but it settles quickly into a sweet and nicely balanced blues, with a satisfying and discursive Garcia solo before the last verse. "On the Road Again" is a good, fast rendition and a tight arrangement, peppier than the version that appears on *Reckoning,* the band's 1980 live acoustic album.

Announcing a mystery guest, Garcia says, "We'd like to have a friend come up and sing a song or two," and a white blues singer, perhaps Jerry Pond (he's listed on the bill with the Dead) sings the next two tunes, "Yonder's Wall" and "My Own Fault." The band hits a good, powerful sinuous groove, in full stride now, slowing to a nice section in "My Own Fault," stripped down and beautifully executed—impressive. A first-rate blues solo by Garcia, playing counterpoint to the harp, is one of the best moments on the tape, re-creating a time and place and feel that most tapes lack. Thank you, Peter Abram. A classic Matrix homey moment comes at the end when Garcia thanks him, saying, "You done good," to warm applause.

"Down So Long," an upbeat folk tune, comes across here as fluff and fun, distinguished by a little flourish at the end that shows how strongly they are still in the milieu of professional bar bands, replete with a stock of performer's clichés. Perhaps it is simply a lackluster performance; the follow-up, "Cold Rain," certainly is. Workmanlike, but there are better renditions in this era. Maybe they're just tired of it tonight?

"Viola Lee Blues" makes up for the ebb, though, a grand and thorough catharsis, and ample proof of their already well-developed powers of recovery. Extended jams built on a groove that stays entrenched and mesmerizing, it is classic early Dead. Fans expecting the next tune to take the form that they gave "Deep Elem Blues" in later years will be surprised here. An extremely unorthodox arrangement, it sounds weird and angular, with chord changes that only approximate the version more familiar to Deadheads from *Reckoning.* But it rewards listeners with an extremely good jam, a reminder of the effort they were making at jamming off with strange structures, already growing into a hallmark feature of their sound.

Pigpen fans will find "Something on Your Mind" a treat, a slow beaten blues featuring a couple of early raps, advice to the lovelorn by Uncle Piggers. It's something of a textbook blues rap, in fact, as he floats off the storyline suggested by the lyrics, telling a story, illustrating the moral, and segueing elegantly back into the melody for another spin, capping it at the close with another, sillier rap; this is the point of departure for measuring how much he grows in this position over the years. This mood crashes hard with "Big Boy Pete," a pop ditty that despite its classic status simply hurts. A sop to the teen scene, it is competently executed, just tough to swallow.

"Death Don't Have No Mercy" atones for it with a display of dynamics and control that is one of the highlights of the evening. Slow, stately, and mysterious at first, it shifts from anguish to dirge beautifully, with one of the longer, better-articulated Garcia solos on tape in this era. Exquisite and fully developed, it is a showcase for him, roaring into a complexity and speed that is the antithesis of the say-nothing guitar histrionics of later rock genres. Far from having nothing to say and an abundance of technique to show it, here he has so much to say that it all piles up together, leaping from idea to notion because Garcia is already two thoughts beyond that already, and his fingers have to work even faster to catch up. This great finale doesn't end the set, despite the feeling that it should. After "Lindy," more an interlude than anything else, we get "Dancin' in the Streets," where the Dead take teen pop and make serious music out of it—indeed, there are moments when it doesn't sound like 1966 Dead at all. Part way in and the jam has lifted off, so deep and free of the melody you can't even remember how you got there, carried along by Garcia's thin, Strat-like filigreed runs, perilously close to what some critics called the San Francisco Sound, a vibrato-laden fast guitar lick being one of the defining motifs.[4] And it takes us farther and farther away from the melody, overtly psychedelic, fast gentle guitar notes liquid over that rumbling, powerful groove, still propelling, always threatening: quintessential Dead.

Hard on the heels of that workout, Garcia opens "Me and My Uncle" with a lick that sounds as if it could have come straight from the sessions that produced their backing tracks for Jon Hendricks' "Fire in the City," a chunky, staccato opening that takes the edge of the repetitiousness. Though not significantly different from the rendition they opened with, it comes off quite well and leaves the crowd clearly pleased.

Showmen to the last, they end with a complete merry-go-round tuning, and now it doesn't sound campy, but simply kind of fun: 'Hey, we know how to play that role.' After three sets, there may not have seemed much else to say. A nice closer to round off an evening more characterized by what *Newsweek*, in a story that came out a couple of weeks after this gig, called "their hard, hoarse, screeching sound," which in their view, was "pure San Francisco." Fortunately, these tapes disprove the other central comment they chose to quote from a member of the band: " 'I don't believe the live sound, the live excitement, can be recorded,' says 24-year-old lead guitarist Jerry Garcia."[5] But what we get here is a fine approximation.

As the last of the Matrix sets by the band, this tape also represents the end of the teen-beat era for the Dead: from now on, the tapes show an increasing departure from the bar-derived format of short set, short songs with one long one to close. Though the Matrix would go on to host the legendary Mickey and the Hartbeats shows almost two years later, as well as the Garcia-Saunders gigs after that, this largely marked the end of the easy days of playing locally in one-hundred-seat clubs. A noteworthy run, as club manager and engineer Peter Abram noted: "That was actually the only time in my time at the club that the Grateful Dead played. Other times it was bits and pieces of the band, basically because we were a little small for their following."[6]

Loss of that intimacy drove a number of the San Francisco musicians to play after-hours clubs after their regular gigs, which is part of what gave the club its celebrated attractions. Looking back thirty years later, one musician explained the appeal: "There was really only one hippie nightclub in San Francisco, the Matrix."[7] Like its larger cousins the Fillmore and the Avalon, the Matrix was a focal point of the conflict between the city and the hippies over public space. The first of the successful hippie rock venues (only Mother's, in North Beach, preceded it, and it survived only briefly), the Matrix opened in August of 1965 with the Jefferson Airplane, and hosted a glittering array of bands in its tiny, 105-person confines until it closed for the last time in 1972. It changed owners, appearance, and clientele in the interim, but it is justly revered as the recording venue that produced a treasure trove of live tapes, from the Dead to the Great Society to a young Steppenwolf to the Doors.

Those tapes are an integral part of the Matrix's history. After its first year, the club was bought by recording engineer and taping enthusiast Peter Abram, in large part so he could continue his efforts unimpeded: "The

---

4. See, for example, Bruce Harrah-Conforth, "The Rise and Fall of a Modern Folk Community: Haight-Ashbury, 1965–1967" (Ph.D. dissertation, folklore, Indiana University, 1990), p. 208.

5. "The Nitty Gritty Sound," *Newsweek*, Dec. 19, 1966, p. 102.
6. Peter Abram, interviewed by John R. Dwork, Jan. 23, 1997.
7. Darby Slick, *Don't You Want Somebody to Love: Reflections on the San Francisco Sound* (Berkeley, Calif.: SLG Press, 1991), p. 82.

only reason I bought it was because I enjoyed making the recordings—if I didn't buy the place, I couldn't make the recordings. The club was a necessary evil so I could continue with my hobby."[8] The commercial implications were clear enough, too, as a newsletter pointed out: "We believe in the live sound and hope to produce that sound, exactly as it is performed, on our own record label."[9] At the time, the idea of a label seemed like a viable option, as Abram explained to a San Francisco State student reporter: "Since there are only two recording companies in San Francisco, we feel that there should be another one and the Matrix can certainly provide that."[10]

Considered by many hippies to be the best and least pretentious of the San Francisco clubs, the Matrix was host to legendary musicians' jam sessions and was the place chosen by Chet Helms, later the colorful impresario of the Avalon, to debut the new group Big Brother and the Holding Company. In the San Francisco scene, the Matrix served as a public woodshed for fledgling groups to hone their chops. As Peter Abram said, "Basically, it was a stepping stone to the Fillmore."[11] The crowds were not entirely hippies, though. It had a musicians' feel, but whether it was size or location—in the well-to-do Marina district—the Matrix wasn't intimidating to the occasional straight. Darby Slick, lead guitarist for the Great Society, summed it up: "All of the musicians used to come by and listen to each other, and enough of the hip people were there, along with plenty of straight people, to make a good mix."[12]

For musicians and audience, it was an intimate and informal space; the storeroom, for example, was the dressing room, and the recording booth was originally built over a toilet that they hadn't bothered to remove. But it made for an easy intimacy that comes through on the tapes and in the memoirs of the musicians who played there. One of them recalled: "It feels as if I have spent a thousand nights in the Matrix listening to the most beautiful music on the planet."[13]

NICK MERIWETHER

---

8. Peter Abram, interviewed by John R. Dwork, Jan. 23, 1997.
9. Gary L. Jackson, *The Matrix Newsletter*, vol. 1, no. 2 (Feb. 15, 1968), p. 1.
10. *The Daily* (San Francisco State University) *Gater*, Mar. 7, 1968, p. 5.
11. Peter Abram, interviewed by John R. Dwork, Jan. 23, 1997.
12. Slick, *Don't You Want Somebody to Love*, p. 82.
13. Ibid., p. 93.

---

## 12/31/66

**New Year's Eve
Fillmore Auditorium,
San Francisco, California**

Baby What You // Want Me to Do, Jam > Janis // Tune (unknown title)

**Source:** AUD, **Quality:** F, **Length:** 0:45
**Personnel:** Includes members of Quicksilver Messenger Service, Big Brother and the Holding Company, Jefferson Airplane, and the Grateful Dead. Exact personnel unknown.
**Comments:** The presence of any members of the Grateful Dead on this tape has been debated.

This all-star jam, presumably the evening's finale, is exactly what one would expect from New Year's Eve 1966. Drunken, ragged, and undeniably festive, this virtually unlistenable audience tape depicts a group of obviously exhausted musicians backing a no-worse-for-the-wear Janis Joplin, who seemingly could go on for hours. In fact, she almost does. Barely able to stand up straight and finger the correct chords, the tape begins with a sluggish rendition of "Baby What You Want Me to Do." What better way to start off the New Year? Although the tempo is painfully stagnant, the guitar solo, presumably from Jorma Kaukonen, hits a few fine chops. Though Janis' vocals are ragged, she does manage to remember most of the lyrics, and when all else fails, resorts to either repeating the first verse, or ad-libbing some of her own. The majority of the jam is sloppy and embarrassing. While the rhythm section manages to keep reasonably accurate time, the guitarists spread themselves far too thin, shifting between out of tune and out of time. After a lame attempt to muster some audience enthusiasm, a guitar solo (possibly John Cippolina) emerges, consisting of pathetic, poorly constructed licks that thankfully last only a moment. Attempting to reground the shuffle with straight rhythm chords, the resulting gibberish nearly causes the jam to collapse. What follows is ten minutes of pointless drivel, eventually disintegrating into a feedback passage hinting at the finale. Unfortunately, it's only a tease. Upshifting, the tempo is increased and the players try to lock into the same groove, again attempting to ground themselves. After five or so minutes of repetitive riffing,

Grace and Janis come to the rescue, trading a few verses worth of sisterly sneers before settling into a Janis vocal, with Grace contributing her trademark screeches in the background. While this passage is obviously a grand step up from the preceding instrumental exhibition, it seems to go on forever until, almost in relief, the jam abruptly collapses.

BRIAN DYKE

**Source:** SBD, **Quality:** A–, **Length:** 1:30

**Comments:** Aside from the instrumental takes of "Cardboard Cowboy," the first take of "Stealin'," and the final two takes of "Don't Ease Me In," this tape is an exact duplicate of the tape circulating as "2/5/66 Questing Beast Rehearsals."

BRIAN DYKE

## ?? 1966
### Unknown Location

**Studio Rehearsal:** Early in the Morning (02/??/66), Cardboard Cowboy (instrumental), Cardboard Cowboy// (instrumental), Cardboard Cowboy (instrumental), Cardboard Cowboy (instrumental), Cardboard Cowboy, Stealin' (instrumental), I Know You Rider// (instrumental), I Know You Rider, Cold Rain and Snow// (instrumental), Cold Rain and Snow// (instrumental), Cold Rain and Snow// (instrumental), Cold Rain and Snow// (instrumental), Cold Rain and Snow (instrumental), Cold Rain and Snow (instrumental), Stealin'// (instrumental), Stealin'// (instrumental), Stealin' (instrumental), Stealin', I Know You Rider, Don't Ease Me In// (instrumental), Don't Ease Me In// (instrumental), Don't Ease Me In (instrumental), Don't Ease Me In// (instrumental), Don't Ease Me In// (instrumental), Don't Ease Me In// (instrumental), Don't Ease Me In// (instrumental), Don't Ease Me In (instrumental), Don't Ease Me In// (instrumental), Don't Ease Me In// (instrumental), Don't Ease Me In (instrumental), Don't Ease Me In (instrumental), Don't Ease Me In// (instrumental), Don't Ease Me In// (instrumental), You Don't Have to Ask// (instrumental), You Don't Have to Ask// (instrumental), You Don't Have to Ask, Early in the Morning (instrumental).

## ?? 1966
### Unknown Location

**Apartment Demos:** Two Women, Michael, Katie Mae, New Orleans > That Train, Instrumental, Shotgun, C. C. Rider, Katie Mae, Hitchhiking Woman, Two Women, When I Was a Boy, Shotgun

**Source:** SBD, **Quality:** Varies from A to C, **Length:** 0:50

**Comments:** These tracks appear on the tape often circulating with the label "Bring Me My Shotgun" and "Pigpen Studio Demos," although aside from "New Orleans" > "That Train," this entire tape is in actuality an inferior duplicate of the tape circulating as "??/??/70 Pigpen in the Studio." The track listed as "New Orleans" is actually a variation of "Baby Please Don't Go." Tape is annotated as "Apartment Demos," but overdubs suggest that at least some tracks are actually studio demos.

Armed only with a harp, this pair of tunes is foot-stompin' parlor blues at its finest. "New Orleans," a loose variation on the more common "Baby Please Don't Go," is highlighted by an extremely thick Delta-style harp accompaniment. The reed choking is Sonny Boy slick, and Pigpen's bending has the blaze of a locomotive smokestack. Understandably, Pigpen is a tad winded on the lyrics, barely able to catch his breath from the intra-verse chops. "That Train" is smoother and more restrained, giving Pigpen the opportunity to thrust more emotion into the vocals, and a more measured attack on the harp licks.

BRIAN DYKE

# 1967

By their second year, the Grateful Dead had established themselves as one of the premier bands of the San Francisco Sound, headlining their own shows on equal billing with the Jefferson Airplane, Big Brother, and Quicksilver Messenger Service. They had signed on with Warner Brothers and quickly recorded their first album. They followed up the album with their first shows in New York and a series of shows in Los Angeles. Ironically, they played only a handful of paid shows in San Francisco during the famed Summer of Love, mostly performing out of the Bay Area. There are not many tapes in circulation from the beginning of the year, nor do many set lists exist. However, from what does exist, the substance of shows up until about August appears to be much the same as 1966 shows. The tapes that do exist from the early part of the year bear this out. Listening to these tapes it becomes apparent that, perhaps more than any other album, the Dead's first accurately captures their live concert sound during the time of recording.

A few new originals were added to the repertoire in 1967. "The Golden Road (to Unlimited Devotion)" was written as a tribute to the Dead's fan club of the same name and is typical of the bubbly, fast-paced music they were playing in the 1966 and early 1967. "Alligator" and "New Potato Caboose," however, were somewhat of a departure from that style. "Alligator," the first with lyrics by Hunter, had an open end that invited improvisation, and "New Potato Caboose" bore a more complex song structure than the band had previously attempted.

Most tapes in circulation from 1967 are concentrated in the latter part of the year, from August to November. They include the very first known audience tape from the Hollywood Bowl in Los Angeles on September 15; however, most are very good quality soundboards. On September 29, Mickey Hart joined the band on drums for "Alligator," and it was instantly apparent that everything was going to become infinitely more interesting from then on. It is interesting to hear how quickly the band developed after Mickey's arrival. His addition provided them with a fuller, more sophisticated sound with a greater number of musical possibilities on most of their songs. The difference is audible when comparing tapes like the Toronto shows in August with ones like the L.A. Shrine shows from November.

Within a month of Mickey's arrival, work began on the live tracks to Anthem of the Sun. This landmark album captured the beginnings of the more experimental phase of the Dead's music. With the addition of more psychedelic songs such as the "Cryptical/Other One" suite, "New Potato Caboose," and "Caution," the music began to stretch out and segues between songs became more developed. Pigpen was still very much the front man on the big show-stopping songs, and he was adding to his repertoire with songs like "Turn On Your Lovelight." However, what made the band really stand out, were the unusual song structures they wrote and the lyrics of Robert Hunter.

Tapes to get: 3/18, 10/22, 11/11.

---

## 1/14/67

**The Great Human Be-In,
Polo Fields, Golden Gate Park,
San Francisco, California**

Morning Dew, Good Morning, Li'l Schoolgirl*, Viola Lee Blues

* With Charles Lloyd.

---

**Source:** SBD, **Quality:** B (clean, but low fidelity and technical problems), **Length:** 0:30, **Genealogy:** MR > RR > DAT > C

**Highlights:** An unusual set and a historic occasion

The Dead played a half-hour set during this four-hour festival, and bits and pieces of it have floated through taper circles for years. Frequently one or two songs will appear with a couple of the poets' and activists' speeches, sometimes with a fragment of Quicksilver Messenger Service's set. Occasionally the songs are identified as Acid Test material, with wildly inaccurate dates. Compounding these difficulties is the fact that this tape, more than most, seems to have called forth the amateur producer instinct, so most tapes have cuts and a rearranged song sequence. Among the speeches frequently included are those by Allen Ginsberg, Michael McClure, Timothy Leary, Lenore Kandel, and a six-minute "Peace Dance" that directly precedes the Dead's set. Missing in action are Gary Snyder, Lawrence Ferlinghetti, Maretta, and the other bands, except for about two minutes of Quicksilver.

Later in their career, especially after Woodstock, the band was fond of claiming that they religiously failed to live up to their potential when public pressure was high. If this is any indication, that gremlin hasn't reared its head yet. "Morning Dew" leads things off, and it is the curio and treat in this set, currently their earliest known performance of it and the earliest recording in circulation. A strong, confident opener, its greatest surprise is the falsetto Jerry gives on one of the "I guess it doesn't matter" lines at the end.

After a break in the tape, Bobby's voice says, "Let's get it," and they begin that distinctive groove that marks "Schoolgirl." Good, steady, strong—this is perfect afternoon dance music. Many tapes begin with this tune, and the PA system sounds fairly rocky at first, but it improves. Heads will be interested to hear a jazz flutist with the Dead, especially one as distinctive as Lloyd; the spellbinder here, though, is his long intense rap-roar-chant-scat-sing, alternating back and forth with his flute solo. The Dead just cook along behind him, complementing him remarkably well despite the fact that he is not their style of soloist at all, more Parker or Ornette in a raw mood than the ensemble cloak the Dead sought to create. But the blend was good enough, for Lloyd would go on to appeal to that same audience by recording a live album at the Fillmore, and a few months later, Paul Williams, editor of the respected rock magazine *Crawdaddy*, wrote that Lloyd was one of a number of "head-brothers," jazz musicians "whose attitude and structural approach bring them close to the same artistic goals that rock aspires to."[1] This was the band's first interaction with Lloyd, whom Garcia spoke highly of several times over the years, and clearly it clicked. Lloyd's band would open for the Dead for a six-night engagement at a new Bay Area rock club in a couple of months, a run distinguished by the attendance one night of Garcia's mother. Their paths crossed after that as well.

"Viola Lee Blues" features some good solo work by Jerry, but basically he keeps it reined in; this is not an example of the supreme brinkmanship that it gets elsewhere during this period. The band hits a good groove immediately, though, with no loss of energy or concentration. Some microphone problems plague the proceedings, and part way in you can hear someone—Bobby?—calling to Phil, then saying "testing" into the microphone, but it opens out into a satisfying, well-explored jam. Kreutzmann sounds especially good at the end, just a fury of percussion. Finally, almost at the close of the song, the vocals come through, faint harmonies giving way to Phil belting out "you've got a friend somewhere," though the others are still very, very muted, as if only one microphone were working, picking up their voices ambiently. Still, a good, tight instrumental version, vocal screw-ups notwithstanding. Overall, the good mood shines here, despite the equipment problems.

And what a day—one of the events where history was made, and the Dead, once again, were there. The Human Be-In was a pivotal event in the history of Haight-Ashbury, and one of the burgeoning counterculture's brightest moments. Shortly afterward, one of the organizers wrote an elegiac description:

> "Human beings, human beings, human beings being in at the Human Be-In, San Francisco, January 14th, 1967. Polo Grounds, trees, park all around, twenty thousand people, children, feathered multitudes, a thousand visions and a thousand Christs.... A holy dance a hot day in January.... Marijuana flags tied into capes hanging from the shoulders of beautiful little children, dancing for the people and themselves to the music of the Grateful Dead. All listen to the chanting of the poets singing 'Peace in America, Peace in Vietnam, Peace in Mississippi, Peace in Saigon.' And for once all is sanity."[2]

---

1. Williams, Paul, "What Went On," in *Outlaw Blues* (New York: Dutton, 1969), p. 83.

2. Michael Bowen, "The Haight-Ashbury Human Be-In," *Inner Space*, no. 4 (March 1967), [unnumbered page].

That was painter Michael Bowen, who captures the sense of optimism and hope that most of the Haight-Ashbury community felt in the aftermath of this unexpected triumph.

The Be-In had its genesis several months earlier, when Bowen and a friend saw an angry crowd forming in response to the bust of 1090 Page Street, the sprawling Victorian run by Rodney Albin that had housed the jam sessions that gave birth to Big Brother and the Holding Company. Bowen's friend Allen Cohen remembers:

> "The idea for the Be-In came from Michael and me. I remember we were sitting in a Haight Street café when 1090 got busted, sometime in August or September, 1966. I saw this group of angry people streaming past my window, and I thought, 'Here it goes again, the same old confrontation-conflict-violence cycle.' It seemed so pointless. We knew that LSD was going to become illegal on October 6, and Michael and I had this idea: instead of a protest, let's have a celebration."[3]

As a celebration, it would have some teeth: not just hippies being irrelevant again, but hippies making a pointed statement that their philosophy had a political edge to it as well. By the end of 1966, many hippies felt that some sort of political statement was necessary. Moreover, allowing for the differences of expression, there seemed to be a great deal that the various factions within the youth underground could agree on. When Bowen and Cohen saw angry, catalyzed hippies in the streets, the potential for unity seemed undeniable. "We saw an entire youth movement," Cohen remembered many years later, "with a certain conflict between the politically active part and the spaced-out part. There were extremes on both sides, but in the middle were people exploring, within and without; most people, after all, were against the war and wanted a more peaceful and tolerant society. And antimaterialism was a unifying thread amongst the camps."[4]

As was the threat of being drafted and the immense potential for being harassed by the police. All in all, the time seemed right for a conventicle—a gathering of the tribes. The grand ambition was for it to demonstrate, unequivocally, the solidarity of youth; as Cohen put it, "The Be-In was going to sponsor unity, bring the hippies and the politicos together."[5]

The name came from a comment made by Richard Alpert at one of the free concerts in the Panhandle: "It's a human be-in." The most prominent of these free shows was called the Love Pageant Rally, held on October 6, 1966, the day that LSD became illegal. With the success of that, the planning for the grand event went ahead in earnest; to the Be-In's organizers, "The event had the feel of a new community ritual, and the idea for the Human Be-In, a larger more inclusive event that would rock the world, was born."[6]

Other names that were suggested were Pow-Wow and Gathering of the Tribes, which also went on the posters advertising the event. The poster artists, including Michael Bowen, Rick Griffin, and Stanley Mouse, designed a series of stunning images to advertise it. The *Oracle*, the Haight's famed multicolored newspaper, and the *Berkeley Barb* covered the planning and announcement of the event; Allen Cohen secured the necessary permits from a sympathetic Parks and Rec official. The final date was chosen after consulting two famed local astrologists.

With unity as its driving theme, the event expanded to include more than simply a celebration of the Haight-Ashbury and youth in general. It also would acknowledge their forebears, the bohemian elders of the Bay Area, symbolized by Michael Bowen's participation as one of the organizers. An important bridge figure between the Beats and the hippies, Bowen was a North Beach habitué and an accomplished painter who started in the Beat era of the fifties, and who went on to become one of the Haight's more colorful and influential characters, a Psychedelic Ranger who trumpeted the hippie philosophy, the community's yang to the Diggers' confrontational politics. In a series of meetings that fall and winter, the program took shape. The stage would be shared by all of the representatives of the Bay Area youth movement, as well as their elders: the Beats and Timothy Leary, Allen Ginsberg, Gary Snyder, Michael McClure, Lenore Kandell, and Lawrence Ferlinghetti all consented quickly to the idea.

Advertising was done through the various underground newspapers, the *Oracle* and the *Barb,* and

---

3. Allen Cohen, interviewed by author, Oct. 23, 1991.
4. Allen Cohen, interviewed by author, Oct. 23, 1991.

5. Allen Cohen, interviewed by author, Oct. 23, 1991.
6. Allen Cohen, "The San Francisco Oracle, A Brief History," in *The San Francisco Oracle Facsimile Edition* (Berkeley: Regents Press, 1991), p. xxviii.

through the posters that papered the Bay Area. The posters probably would have sufficed, but the use of print media was a calculated—and prophetic—move. Organizers thought it couldn't backfire, as Allen Cohen noted:

> "Michael and I were practical. We wanted to change the world. The means to do this were LSD and the media, which was being used against us, to reach the public. We weren't concerned with distortion; they couldn't distort what they couldn't understand, or so the thinking went. In fact, we figured that the more it got maligned, the more interest it would receive."[7]

Which it did. On January 13, the "inspirers" of the festival published a proclamation in the venerable underground newspaper *The Berkeley Barb*:

> "Materialism and empire have thwarted and veiled the spiritual foundations of man and woman and their relations in America. Profit and Desire are one-tenth of the divinity of man. We declare the necessity of spiritual exercise, experience and celebration for the proper education of man. We declare and prophesy the end of wars, police states, economic oppression and racism. When the Berkeley political activists and the love generation of the Haight Ashbury and thousands of young men and women from every state in the nation embrace at the Gathering of the Tribes for a Human Be-In at the Polo Field in Golden Gate Park the spiritual revolution will be manifest and proven. In unity we shall shower the country with waves of ecstasy and purification. Fear will be washed away; ignorance will be exposed to sunlight; profits and empire will lie drying on deserted beaches; violence will be submerged and transmuted in rhythm and dancing; racism will be purified by the salt of forgiveness. Spiritual revolution to transform the materialistic bruted body and mind of America is NOW here with the young budding."[8]

It was a clarion call to the classic hippie philosophy, expressed in the ringing political tone of the Berkeley radicals. It seemed as if the tribes had indeed united. Later commentary placed the success at the feet of the community; as one Barb commentator said, "It took nothing to assemble the people. A few posters and some talk. Everyone wanted to be assembled. Everyone wanted something to take place . . ."[9]

The planning had not been not an entirely smooth process, however. The Diggers threatened a boycott, which was only averted after an initially tense and confrontational meeting between emissaries Snyder and Ginsberg and two Digger representatives, Emmett Grogan and Peter Berg. After Snyder declared his political bent as an old Wobbly, in an attempt to establish a common ground with the Diggers, Berg lit into him:

> "I responded with probably more heat and volume than was necessary that the current Diggers should be seen as successors to the moribund Wobblies and bearers of the grand anarchist tradition begun with the Paris Commune. Forcing the issue that prompted our meeting, I added that the Love Generation otherworldliness would undo whatever hope for actively transforming society might exist among the mob who would come to the Be-In."[10]

After a series of rapid-fire Zen-like questions from Snyder, the two emerged with a sense of respect that enlisted the Diggers as allies rather than antagonists, and Berg and Grogan pledged that the Diggers would serve free food as their contribution.

Finally, the night before the Be-In, the last planning session took place in the Haight with a meeting of nine luminaries—from Ginsberg to Freewheelin' Frank of the Angels—debating the batting order, and finally locking horns over whether Leary would be allotted the seven minutes accorded a poet, or whether as prophet he should have half an hour.[11] Democracy eventually won out, and Tim received the standard seven minutes. Now the only issue was whether the weather would

---

7. Allen Cohen, interviewed by author, Oct. 23, 1991.
8. *The Berkeley Barb,* vol. 4, no. 2 (Jan. 13, 1967), p. 1.
9. Ed Denson, "What Happened at the Hippening," *The Berkeley Barb,* vol. 4, no. 3 (Jan. 20, 1967), p. 4.
10. Peter Berg, "Beating the Drum with Gary," *Gary Snyder: Dimensions of a Life* (San Francisco: Sierra Club, 1991), p. 379.
11. Jane Kramer, *Allen Ginsberg in America* (New York: Random House, 1969), pp. 3–4.

cooperate—and how many people would actually care to show up.

The weather cooperated. January 14 dawned bright and clear, the sort of near–Indian summer day that San Francisco sometimes rewards its citizens with after drowning them in clammy fog for long gray weeks at a time. That morning people began walking down Haight Street toward the park at 9 A.M. And so many of the accounts make a point of emphasizing the sense of disbelief among the gathering throng—hey, there's so many of us!—slowly building as they wandered through the two miles of park before topping the crest of the dirt running track circling the field. The sight that greeted them was astounding, by all accounts: "It was the Polo Field itself that presented a new world. It was a medieval scene, with banners flying, bright and uncommitted; the day was miraculous, as days can be in San Francisco at their best, and the world was new and clean and pastoral."[12] Tom Wolfe described it in even more baroque terms:

> thousands of them piled in, in high costume, ringing bells, chanting, dancing ecstatically, blowing their minds one way and another and making their favorite satiric gesture to the cops, handing them flowers, burying the bastids in fruity petals of love. Oh Christ, Tom, the thing was fantastic, a freaking mindblower, thousands of high-loving heads out there messing up the minds of the cops and everybody else in a fiesta of love and euphoria.[13]

The fiesta didn't formally begin until 1 P.M., but the thousands who had arrived that morning got to watch Ginsberg and a small clutch of participants start things a couple of hours earlier, circumnavigating the field in an ancient Hindu blessing ritual to purify a place before a *mela*, or holy gathering, happens, while chanting *dharanis*, Buddhist short-form prayers. It set a tone that was to carry through to the end of the proceedings. Promptly at one the program began, with Gary Snyder blowing on a conch shell. For the next four hours, there was a stream of speakers and bands, as well as a few unplanned moments of silence when the PA failed. Lenore Kandell delivered the ringing lines, "Let it go,

whatever you do is beautiful." Ginsberg gave a gentle benediction, "Peace in your heart dear / Peace in the Park here." McClure gave one of his trademark poetic invocations, a one-line poem repeated nine times, once for each word, with the emphasis shifting from first to last: "This is really it, and it is all perfect." And among the politicos, the speech that aroused the greatest reaction—and was shortly to become a catch-phrase of the counterculture—was not by Jerry Rubin, but Dr. Timothy Leary, intoning his mantra, "Turn on, tune in, drop out."

Years later, what Leary remembered was not his own speech but the music—and specifically the Dead:

> "It's a powerful memory. It was miraculous. That was the first time there was that kind of a show in numbers. There was no advertising, only underground radio and word of mouth, and wow! They jammed, and suddenly forty or fifty thousand people showed up. It was awesome. It was a small little stage, and Hell's Angels around there wasn't room for anybody else! We thought, 'Shit! Good Lord! Look at all these people!' We got a sense of the demographic power the music had. Of course Owsley was there, but the Dead! They were the only band I remember from that day."[14]

In addition to the Dead, the other seminal Haight-Ashbury bands played: Big Brother and the Holding Company, Quicksilver Messenger Service, and the Jefferson Airplane. For all of them, it was the largest crowd they had performed before. Garcia was awestruck: "When there was the Be-In up here I'd never seen so many people in my life. It was really fantastic. I almost didn't believe it. It was a totally underground movement. It was all the people into dope of any sort, and like 20,000 people came out in the Park and everyone had a good time. There was no violence, no hassling."[15]

Or rather, only one hassle: at some point, the power was cut from the generators to the stage, prompting an announcement that the Hell's Angels would guard the cables from then on. Even that interruption fulfilled one planner's hope: the night before, the hippie one reporter

---

12. Helen Swick Perry, *The Human Be-In* (New York: Basic, 1970), p. 86.
13. Wolfe, *The Electric Kool-Aid Acid Test*, p. 13.
14. Linda Kelly, *Deadheads* (New York: Citadel Underground, 1995), pp. 91–92.
15. Randy Groenke and Mike Cramer, "One Afternoon Long Ago," in *The Golden Road*, no. 7 (Summer 1985), p. 28.

identified only as Buddha said to Ginsberg, "Man, I'd just as soon no one says a word tomorrow. Just beautiful silence. Just everybody sitting around smiling and digging everybody else."[16] In the diary of one participant, the silence afforded exactly that:

> The best part of the January 14, 1967 first Human Be-in was that there was absolute quiet for hours. The cables were cut; the important people, the Leary's, the Kendalls [sic], Ginsburgs [sic], even the Grateful Dead were hushed, and the rest of us, 25,000 strong, looked around, grooved and recognized each other for the first time. Something new was born that day. 25,000 people, most of them on acid, dreamed a vision of love. . . . What really mattered that day was not words or even music but an orange with the word LOVE carved in it. It was an icon for the grateful hope of 25,000 people who lived each other, felt each other, recognized for the first time the potential of the entire human race.[17]

So many little touches made impressions on the throng. Hell's Angels baby-sitting lost children. Owsley's lieutenants distributing free samples of the latest batch of acid, widely rumored to be the strongest yet, nicknamed White Lightning.[18] Diggers handing out free turkey sandwiches, which one claimed had been "salted down" with crushed White Lightnings; recipients were chosen carefully as a result, sandwiches finding "those who looked like they needed something to eat, physically or spiritually."[19] But perhaps the most singular event of the day was the descent of a parachutist, which prompted some of the most wildly varying accounts of the whole event. People variously reported seeing a paisley parachute, an alien, an anonymous hippie who walked off "never to be seen again," and more prosaically, the director of a local sky-diving school. With streamers flying, he landed—but not exactly where he had intended. In the only painful collision of cultures in the event, he missed the Polo Field and landed next to it, where one of San Francisco's prestigious high society clubs, the Olympic Club, was having a rugby game, enjoying the same weather though not the same consciousness. One of those participants, describing their own scene replete with chitchatting society matrons and the city's power brokers grunting on the field, explained their view of the adjoining festivities:

> The only problem in this very perfect scene is that five hundred yards away there was a Be-In—thousands of wild-looking, laughing, dancing, cavorting maniacs listening to the crazy strains of Janis Joplin, Grateful Dead, Jefferson Airplane, Quicksilver Messenger Service, Big Brother and the Holding Company, Timothy Leary, Allen Ginsberg, blowing their brains out. Meanwhile the kids and the people were sheepishly passing joints, some ripped on acid, some just popping whatever they could get, some just looking on. Everyone dressing funny, acting funny, dancing funny.[20]

And obliviously barrelling over the rugby teams to see this offering from the sky.

But basically the day was something of an unanticipated miracle, to most observers and participants. Paul Kantner would plagiarize veteran *San Francisco Chronicle* music critic Ralph J. Gleason's paean to the event in his song "Won't You Try / Saturday Afternoon," which seems to embody a feeling in most of the positive reports.[21] At the end of the day, Ginsberg led a group of stalwarts around the field practicing "kitchen yoga," and cleaning up. Parks and Rec officials later said they had never seen so little damage and trash from such a large gathering, in all the park's history. The final event was a walk to the ocean, only a few blocks away, for a closing ceremony on the beach. The Great Human Be-In was over—except for the aftershocks, and the reams of paper that would be devoted to its assessment.

No one was sure what it meant, but anything that big had to mean something. One older hippie sympathizer commented on the expressions on the faces of the people leaving: "It would seem almost as if they had been to early morning mass, which had turned out to be a huge picnic."[22] To understand the sense of optimism

---

16. Kramer, *Allen Ginsberg in America*, p. 5.
17. Elizabeth Gips, *Diary of a Haight-Ashbury Pilgrim* (Santa Cruz, Calif.: Changes, 1993), p. 28.
18. Charles Perry, *The Haight-Ashbury, A History* (New York: Random House, 1984), p. 125.
19. Grogan, *Ringolevio*, p. 274.

---

20. Michael Stepanian, *Pot Shots* (New York: Delta, 1972), p. 19.
21. Appears on the album Jefferson Airplane, *After Bathing at Baxter's* (U.S.: RCA, 4545 2 R, 1967).
22. Perry, *The Human Be-In*, p. 86.

that flooded most of the participants, read a few of the more breathless reports. Michael Bowen wrote a letter to a small periodical a few weeks later that put it in classic psychedelic terms:

> Hara Kiri of the Ego is required, egodectomy must be performed even at the risk of the patient's human body. Air full of incense, orange smoke, rainbow colored flags, a dreamscape, a cosmic relief for the agonies of countless ghosts of ancient, naked Indians and they came back and we are they and they are us and all are ONE and harmony must return to this planet Earth, the illuminated hallucination, deep drums, steady blood veined beat, hearts deep underneath the grass and ground of the polo field, rumbling drums heard through my feet melting with the sound of the Grateful Dead.[23]

One member of the Dead's family portrayed it as the organic, natural process of the neighborhood becoming conscious: "Our awareness of a larger community grew until it peaked that fine day in January of 1967, the day of the Tribal Stomp at the Polo Fields to be known as the 'Human Be-in.'"[24] Michael McClure explained the feeling in perhaps the most poetic terms:

> Exuberance and intellectual and spiritual excitement cause love structures to come into being. More and more complicated associations of events and persons and organizations of matter join together. There were bigger dances, greater and greater joinings of hands reaching farther and farther until at last a Human Be-in was necessary to express the complication of feelings.[25]

The only negative reports, aside from the Olympic Club (who handily defeated their opponents anyway), were from some of the politicos. The *Barb*, for example, was dismissive: "The hippies presented an in-group scene for believers with a mostly local cast doing things that hadn't been thought out in a way that showed they weren't ready for that step...." Their overall assessment: "Nothing happened at the Be-In, and the opportunity to gather all of those people was wasted."[26] Emmett Grogan agreed, and perhaps that disappointment is the reason for the Dead's fundamentally positive impression of the Be-In; as the politics of playing free impinged on their stage that spring and summer, they were moved to complain to Joan Didion: "In the Park there are always twenty or thirty people below the stand, ready to take the crowd on some militant trip."[27]

Not all the Diggers concurred with Grogan. Berg, for example, later wrote that the Be-In "proved to be an astounding panoramic display of the influences bursting into popular consciousness at that time (including declarations against war and racism) wrapped in the glow of pot and Owsley's donated acid."[28] Even the police, whose tactics had provoked the first protests that led to the gathering, seemed to feel the spirit. Or perhaps they realized the futility of arrests in a crowd of those dimensions. If so, their frustration would tend to explain why their moratorium was so short-lived. That night they swept Haight Street and made more than four dozen arrests. (In a wonderful ironic touch, the hip lawyer who represented the detainees was one of the Olympic Club's rugby players from earlier that day.)

If the overwhelming reaction was that the event had been a success, less clear was what it all meant. One audience member recalled: "It was difficult to sort out what happened. It was a religious rite in which nothing in particular happened. And yet it was a day that marked for me at least the end of something and the beginning of something else. There was clearly a renewal of the spirit of man, unplanned, non-political."[29] The consensus was that the gathering had fulfilled its aims: to assemble the various factions of the youth movement and show them what they could achieve—and a peaceful crowd of that size, with no violence or mayhem to mar it, was an achievement in itself. It was an echo of the feeling that had swept many heads when they saw the crowds at the first Family Dog dance in the fall of 1965: "Wow—there're so many of us." One of the Haight's spokesmen put it best when he said that the

---

23. Michael Bowen, "The Haight-Ashbury Human Be-In," *Inner Space*, no. 4 (March 1967), [unnumbered page].
24. Rosie McGee, quoted in Brandelius, *The Grateful Dead Family Album*, p. 40
25. Michael McClure, "Spiritual Occasions," foreword to Gene Anthony, *Summer of Love: Haight-Ashbury at Its Highest* (Berkeley: Celestial Arts, 1980), p. 6.
26. Ed Denson, "What Happened at the Hippening," *The Berkeley Barb*, vol. 4, no. 3 (Jan. 20, 1967), p. 4.
27. Joan Didion, *Slouching Towards Bethlehem* (New York: Simon and Schuster, 1979), p. 121.
28. Berg, "Beating the Drum with Gary," in *Gary Snyder: Dimensions of a Life*, p. 380.
29. Perry, *The Human Be-In*, p. 88.

Be-In was "the first time the San Francisco hippies walked out of their apartments, walked out into the middle of that big green grassy polo field, and saw each other all together at once in one place."[30] As Garcia reminisced a few years later to Charles Reich, "The first really pure event was the Be-In, which was the first time that the whole head scene was actually out in force."[31] And it was the start of the Dead's season of playing in the park, a point that Bill Graham was eager to impress upon fans when the Dead traveled north six months later: "They were the first to play in the Park for free, now it is happening every week-end, and sometimes during the week...."[32] The Be-In would always represent the peak of those concerts.

It's difficult to say what the impact of gathering all of the poets together had on the multitudes. The reactions we have focus mostly on the size and composition of the crowd, some of the more colorful events, and the bands—especially the Dead. But the impact on the speakers was quite profound. Leary would reprint Allen Cohen's "Prophecy of a Declaration of Independence" in its entirety in the last paragraph of his *Politics of Ecstasy,* published a year after the Be-In.[33] And for the Beats, it was a startling affirmation that their struggle continued, albeit in a different guise, both politically and artistically. Looking back later, Ferlinghetti told biographer Barry Silesky that "to the participants [of the Be-In] it truly seemed a new age had arrived, with a new vision of life and love on earth."[34] One of the most powerful connections between the groups brought together that day was, on the surface, an unlikely alliance: between the Diggers and the Beats. More understandable—at least to most observers—was the clear kinship felt by the musicians on the stage and the older poets. For the latter, the event was something of a watershed in their perceptions of this new group of bohemians, and of themselves as well. Part of this was simply due to the respect they had been shown, as another of Ferlinghetti's biographers noted: "They were recognized as older voices who had sought all along a culture of freedom and peace."[35] But, in classic Beat fashion, the Be-In provided the poets on stage with their own poetic epiphanies, an individual reaction that also neatly expressed the Haight-Ashbury belief that genuine political change came only through individual changes in consciousness. For Ferlinghetti, for example, it was especially significant because he had taken LSD for the first time on New Year's Day, two weeks earlier. A few weeks after the Be-In, at a reading in Berlin, he would read his poem "After the Cries of Birds," which one of his biographers has described as "an attempt to bring his personal and public sense together in an apocalyptic vision of mankind."[36] It was rooted in this new counterculture, as Ferlinghetti explained: "Beginning in Rock and Roll folk dances at Fillmore Auditorium Fall 1965 ... mixed with trips to my cabin Bixby Canyon Big Sur"—where Kerouac had written his novel *Big Sur*—"After a definite break, a breakthrough, my first trip on LSD ... In the end there is no way to go but In. Into ourselves ... Pause & begin again."[37]

For Allen Ginsberg, the Be-In launched him into the public eye. In the words of one of his biographers, "Allen really became the Allen that we know in 1967. He got out into the public and could never really withdraw completely again. The Be-In skyrocketed the whole Ginsberg cottage industry into outer space. It was the greatest visibility that he had up to that point."[38] And McClure's commentary makes plain the impact it had on him. When Gene Anthony wrote his account of the Summer of Love, McClure was the person he asked to introduce the volume.

Even the politicos felt some degree of transformation. A few years later, in his memoir *Growing Up at Thirty-Seven,*[39] Jerry Rubin couched his own maturation and aging in terms that sounded as if they could have been quotes taken from one of the more literate Haight Street conversations.

---

30. Stephen Gaskin, *Haight-Ashbury Flashbacks* (Berkeley: Ronin, 1990), p. 46.
31. Garcia, Reich, and Wenner, *Garcia: Signpost to a New Space,* p. 60.
32. Program, "Bill Graham Presents the San Francisco Scene," at the O'Keefe Centre for the Performing Arts, Toronto, July 31–Aug. 5, 1967, [p. 6]. Garcia recalled the Be-In as the start of their season of playing for free in the park as well; see Garcia, Reich, and Wenner, *Garcia: Signpost to a New Space,* p. 61.
33. Timothy Leary, *The Politics of Ecstasy* (New York: Putnam, 1968; reprint, Berkeley: Ronin, 1990), p. 371.
34. Barry Silesky, *Ferlinghetti: The Artist in His Time* (New York: Warner, 1990), p. 149.
35. Larry Smith, *Lawrence Ferlinghetti, Poet-at-Large* (Carbondale: Southern Illinois University Press, 1983), p. 43.
36. Ibid., p. 41.
37. Lawrence Ferlinghetti, "Genesis of *After the Cries of the Birds,*" in *Poetics of the New American Poets,* ed. Donald Allen and Warren Tallman (New York: Grove, 1973), p. 449.
38. Barry Miles, *Ginsberg: A Biography* (New York: Simon and Schuster, 1989), p. 395.
39. See especially Chapter 16, "Uniting the Personal and the Political," in Jerry Rubin, *Growing Up at Thirty-Seven* (New York: M. Evans, 1976), pp. 197–208.

One point made by many spectators and commentators was the symbolism of the torch being passed on the stage at the Be-In, the acknowledgment of the bohemian elders of the counterculture and their unruly, fractious, and talented apprentices. What that torch meant to the various participants—other than a certain respect for altered states of consciousness for creative purposes—no one especially wanted to elaborate. Though most critics of either the Beats or the hippies mention how much the former influenced the latter, no one has systematically explored these links. Nor is this the place for such a discussion, but there are a few major points of comparison that Deadheads will probably find helpful in their understanding of the band and the cultural milieu from which they sprang. Some of the acknowledgments are explicit, such as Garcia's comments about Kerouac or Lesh on Ginsberg, and some are shared affinities, such as both groups' admiration for Joyce, Blake, and Whitman.[40] And almost every articulate musician in the Haight has gone on record discussing the influence of *On the Road* or *Howl* or *Naked Lunch* on their intellectual development—or alienation. In addition, the record is filled with casual and serious interaction, such as Garcia visiting Kenneth Patchen and studying under Wally Hedrick, and as the sixties wore on there were parties and concerts. As Leary reminisced, "There was a small culture, and we all knew each other, and we'd all meet and hang out."[41] But what has never been much discussed are the striking similarities the two groups of bohemians had toward art and aesthetics—which formed the core of their mutual admiration.

Generalizing across such a large group is difficult, but there are a number of broad points of comparison that are helpful. In addition to obviously shared sources of inspiration—everything from Blake to mysticism to visionary poetics, especially a fascination with symbolism and archetype—what truly bound the two groups after the Be-In was their realization that they had a similar sense of audience engagement, of the need for and the power of a direct emotional connection with their audience. Making the audience a part of the performance was a hallmark of Beat readings, just as the bands differentiated between good and bad nights by the degree to which they felt that connection had happened or not. Looking back several years later, Michael McClure remembered the sense of unity with an audience as a central part of the Beat ethos, and something that continued into the sixties. Describing how rock star Peter Gabriel would fall off the stage into fans' hands, McClure said: "That was wonderful because it gave some idea of what it was like in the sixties, or some idea of what the expression of our poetry was like in the mid-fifties, when the audience was as much a part of it as we were. The audience was yelling, 'Go, go go! . . .'"[42]

Inspiration was the oil of divinity that made the bond between performer and audience concrete, so it is not surprising to discover a similar attitude toward courting it, and letting it be as much of a guide as possible. McClure describes a feature of his poetics as letting the energy of a system shape the system, a concept he phrases in terms of biophysiologist Harold Morowitz: "the flow of energy through a system acts to organize that system." In McClure's paraphrase,

> The systemless system must be loosely, yet complexly, looped, and allow for invention and stochastic structuring (and possibly chance) so that it may accommodate both Negative Capability and agnosia—knowing through not knowing. Such a system is a kind of deep spirit-thought and is capable of creating stepping stones through the torrent, and through the torrent, of the search for vocal rage—for inspired and heightened expression. It is the surge of our physical energy that carries us through—and we need no vanity about having it—it is an inheritance. It is also the surge that organizes the system into tribes. It spurts and it radiates. It is the energy that defines poetry. *The Kingfishers* is an ode to energy and of energy. Like us, the exterior is an extension of the interior. It is myriad, it is one.[43]

This is what McClure began to imagine as pre-anagogic, borrowing from Charles Olson's theory of projective verse—*anagogic* means "leading out," and projective verse was poetry that transmitted the form of

---

40. Michael McClure, *Lighting the Corners: On Art, Nature, and the Visionary* (Albuquerque: University of New Mexico Press, 1993), p. 170. Cf. Slick, "Rejoyce," etc., etc.

41. Linda Kelly, *Deadheads* (New York: Citadel Underground, 1995), p. 31.

42. McClure, *Lighting the Corners*, p. 172.

43. Michael McClure, *Scratching the Beat Surface* (San Francisco: Northpoint, 1982), p. 57.

what the poet perceived, clearly, onto the paper; in essence, it made the poet a part of the medium. And he could just as easily have been one of several San Francisco rock musicians describing the way a song develops in a group setting, or how a jam unfolds at a peak moment of group improvisation—the energy shaping the performance, structuring the arrangement and building the mood, just as McClure recounts. Critic Allen Williamson has discussed the same thing in Snyder's work:

> An "I" whose energies are completely absorbed by an object or an action does not remember that he/she is an "I." In Suzuki's words again, "When you do something, you should burn yourself completely, like a good bonfire, leaving no trace of yourself." How can poetry convey this lapsing into perfect attentiveness?[44]

The notion that transcendence lies at the heart of a successful performance—be it poetic or musical—was an attitude that had perfect resonance with the Haight. Ferlinghetti's words—"In the end there is no way to go but In. Into ourselves . . . Pause & begin again."—have the same ring of the Haight-Ashbury's own poet laureate, Ashleigh Brilliant, who wrote, "If you love this old world and wish truly / To improve it before you are dead, / You don't have to press others unduly / Better start with the world inside *your* head."[45] It was an attitude that terrified middle America, as *Time* magazine reported: "The middle-class ego, to the hippie, is the jacket that makes society straight, and must be destroyed before freedom can be achieved. One East Coast hippie held a 'funeral' for his former self. 'You must follow the river inside you to its source,' he said, 'and then out again.'"[46] Naturally, the scare tactics failed completely, and the article came to epitomize the mass-media exploitation of the Haight; in the eyes of many commentators, it turned the trickle of immigration into the Haight into a flood. Some of the most positive accounts of the Be-In make that point explicitly. One member of the Dead family called it "a day of innocence and hope; and in many ways the last moments of naivete for a neighborhood that had just gone public."[47] A Ginsberg biographer was more blunt: "It was the last innocent, idealistic hippie event."[48]

Even if it is difficult to describe the Be-In without making reference to the gathering gloom, what is abundantly clear is that it represented a high point in the nascent underground's history. In retrospect, the Be-In really was the start of the Summer of Love—both flowers and warts. But if it also signifies the beginning of the end, in January the end was still a long way off, and for that day, it looked like it might end in victory. Monterey Pop hadn't happened yet, and the sight of such an immense aggregation of talent in San Francisco, from defiant and uncompromised elders to so many unsigned and un-sold-out musicians, could not help but create the giddy hope that this hippie revolution going on in the Haight might actually work. As one participant put it, "The Human Be-In had somehow appealed to everybody, square and hip, young and old, who had been in any proximity to it. In a divided and sick world, this was a new and exciting idea—that all people should just *be*."[49]

Michael McClure may well have provided us with the best summation:

> The Be-In was a spiritual occasion culminating from the countless preceding events, dances, thoughts, breaths, lovemakings, illuminations. The Be-In was a blossom. It was a flower. It was out in the weather. It didn't have all its petals. There were worms in the rose. It was perfect in its imperfections. It was what it was—and there had never been anything like it before.[50]

Perhaps the only sentiment that everyone there could have agreed with.

NICK MERIWETHER

---

44. Alan Williamson, "Some Tenses of Snyder," *Gary Snyder: Dimensions of a Life* (San Francisco: Sierra Club, 1991), p. 218.
45. Gene Anthony, *Summer of Love: Haight-Ashbury at Its Highest* (Berkeley: Celestial Arts, 1980), p. 173.
46. Joe David Brown, ed., *The Hippies* (New York: Time, 1967), p. 6.
47. Rosie McGee, quoted in Brandelius, *The Grateful Dead Family Album*, p. 40.
48. Miles, *Ginsberg: A Biography*, p. 395.
49. Perry, *The Human Be-In*, p. 89.
50. Michael McClure, "Spiritual Occasions," foreword to Anthony, *Summer of Love*, p. 7.

## 1/[?]/67

**RCA Studio A, Los Angeles, California**

**Studio Session:** King Bee, Lucky Man Jam, New Minglewood Blues, I Know You Rider, Cold Rain and Snow, Cream Puff War

**Source:** SBD, **Quality:** B+, **Length:** 0:45
**Highlights:** King Bee, Lucky Man Jam
**Comments:** This tape also circulates labeled "Grateful Dead Outtakes." The King Bee and Lucky Man Jam circulate labeled "?/?/66 Sessions" as well.

Although this tape is obviously from a session for the Grateful Dead's debut LP, the real meat is in the first two tracks, the unreleased "King Bee" and "Lucky Man Jam." These tracks, both done instrumentally, provide a great illustration of the Grateful Dead's blues roots. "King Bee" is classic Louisiana slow blues with a twist of Chicago thrown in, and the "Lucky Man Jam" is about as shufflin' swing as the boys can pull off. The rest of the material, all instrumental except for "Cream Puff War," is not unlike what did appear on the band's debut LP.

BRIAN DYKE

## 1/27/67

**Avalon Ballroom, San Francisco, California**

Morning Dew, Cold Rain and Snow, Viola Lee Blues, Alligator > Caution, New Potato Caboose//.

**Source:** SBD, **Quality:** C–, **Length:** 1:20
**Highlights:** Viola Lee Blues, Alligator > Caution
**Comments:** There's a good amount of hiss, a couple of dropouts, and a fairly narrow mix to this tape. The drums, not having much definition on this tape, come across as just cymbals and snare. It's also difficult to hear Bobby, but overall the tape is "listenable" due to Jerry and Pigpen not being trapped by the muddiness.

This interesting little musical snippet is worth seeking out, especially for those of us who love the formative years. It contains some of the earliest performances of "New Potato Caboose," "Alligator," "Caution," and "Morning Dew." It's great to hear these songs in development, even though the tape sounds a bit like it went through the wash. The tape starts out with a solid "Morning Dew" in which Phil melodically pulls the band forward and holds down the groove. The contrast of Jerry's matter-of-fact vocals with the band's serious intention is beautiful. "Cold Rain and Snow" is a quick hundred-yard dash, but it's a real solid upbeat version. "Viola Lee Blues" is the song that makes this tape shine for me: 19 minutes and 15 seconds of absolute magic! It opens with that familiar groove-infected rhythmic bounce that instinctively makes your leg start bouncing and shaking. This roller coaster of a song presents us with so many tension-resolution executions that you get butterflies in your stomach. Jerry's first two leads, which really breathe, are completely enchanting. After everyone takes their turn soloing, they venture out into an intense jam that culminates in a frenzied chaotic whirlwind that pushes right up against the boundaries of delirium. This jam, an amazing musical journey in itself, ends with some scary, spacy feedback. When they finally return to the opening theme, you realize the ride is over. For my money, "Viola Lee Blues" was one of the best springboards for their brand of improvisational explorations.

"Alligator" starts out with plenty of raw energy, then veers into a truly hypnotic grooving drum duel. The end of the jam comes smashing back in with the ferocious battle cry of "ALLIGATOR!" The drummers steer the band into "Caution" and the stage is set for Pig do his stuff. After blowing a sweet harp solo and laying his vocals down on the band's groove, Pig coaxes the band into some well-jammed passages before the song closes. This tape finishes with a smooth and melodic "New Potato Caboose," which unfortunately fades out before the end of the song.

This tape is testimony to the Dead's ability to push the boundaries of improvisation to the extreme edge, remaining musical without overplaying. This tape is worth searching for, and should be in your collection, as long as you can deal with the less-than-desirable sound quality.

COREY SANDERSON

## 3/18/67
### Winterland Arena, San Francisco, California

**First Set:** //Me and My Uncle, Next Time You See Me, He Was a Friend of Mine, Smokestack Lightning, Morning Dew, It Hurts Me Too, //Beat It on Down the Line, Dancin' in the Streets
**Second Set:** //The Golden Road (to Unlimited Devotion), Cream Puff War, The Same Thing, Cold Rain and Snow, Viola Lee Blues, Death Don't Have No Mercy//

**Source:** SBD, **Quality:** B+, **Length:** 1:30
**Highlights:** Dancin' in the Streets, The Same Thing, Viola Lee Blues
**Comments:** This soundboard tape first appeared in circulation during the summer of 1989, along with the tape from 11/19/66. It was the Dead's third performance at Winterland, and their first album had been released the day before. This tape is quite hissy, but is still very good quality for one from '67: Jerry and Billy are the most prominent in the mix, with the others a bit lower and a rather muddy bottom end.

During this show Jerry's and Bobby's vocals range from crooning to outright screaming, and one can feel the band's youthful energy from the very first tune. Jerry's fingers seem to fly over the strings during his solos—he plays soooo many notes in such a short time! "Smokestack Lightning," the first number with Pigpen on harmonica, has a more laid-back feeling and a slower tempo than the three previous tunes. "Dancin' in the Streets" is the best tune of the first set, with Bobby singing, "Spring of the year / the time is here / for dancin' in the streets!" Although their vocals are a tad off-key, the boys' playing is spacy and goes further out there than any tune so far. This innovative jam is a gem!

Following second set opener "The Golden Road (to Unlimited Devotion)," Jerry says, "Thank you, thank you; thank you, thank you, thank you. Welcome to set two of ours, the post–Chuck Berry set. We'd like to continue the proceedings with a song we affectionately call 'Cream Puff War.' " This tune is another screamer, with the vocals mixed high. It is well played, with lots of jamming squeezed into six minutes. The incredibly hot "Same Thing" ties with "Viola Lee Blues" as best tune of the second set. The band expertly, yet gradually, builds up the intensity. Almost imperceptibly, they switch from a minor to a major key during the jam, and the only flaw is the abrupt ending, during which Jerry hits a bad note!

At 14:18, "Viola Lee Blues" is one of the longest tunes of the show. It starts out fairly structured and straightforward, until a lovely, long jam begins toward the end. It builds in both intensity and speed to a screeching crescendo, then launches back into the melody riff. What a way to end the show!

JOLIE GOODMAN

## 4/[?]/67
### The Tom Donahue Show, KMPX-FM

**Interview:** Jerry Garcia, Phil Lesh

**Source:** FM, **Quality:** A, **Length:** 2:00
**Highlights:** All. The material selected is such an eclectic mixture of musical tastes that the entire show is worth seeking out.
**Comments:** This show was rebroadcast on KPFA-FM on February 18, 1995. The show circulates both complete and with the musical selections edited out.

Garcia and Lesh act as guest DJs for this program, giving brief synopses for each selection.

BRIAN DYKE

## 5/5/67
### Fillmore Auditorium, San Francisco, California

[Stage banter], The Golden Road > New Potato Caboose, Alligator, He Was a Friend of Mine//

**Source:** SBD, **Quality:** B, **Length:** 0:37
**Highlights:** "The Golden Road," Bobby's inarticulate lysergic insight that we're all primates

Before the explosion of tape availability starting in the late eighties, there were certain gems from the early days that had really made the rounds. This is one such tape. It's probably the "Golden Road" from this performance that gave this fragment legs. In recent years a handful from '67 and '66 have surfaced, but back in '85 (when I first got this tape) this was the only "Golden Road" I could find.

The tape itself came to mislabeled as a Fillmore West Acid Test 2/6/67. Not only was there no Acid Test on that date, but there was no Fillmore West in 1967 either. It probably got called an Acid Test along the way because of the trippy stage banter, labeled on my original as "The Effects of Vitamin A." My first copy of this was an audience tape, but a soundboard is now available. Some tapes have "He Was a Friend of Mine" first (before the chatter), but the soundboard shows that it clearly comes after "Alligator."

"The Golden Road" is energetic and over quickly, segueing neatly into "New Potato." (Bobby says "This one is for Laughlin," who, if memory serves correctly, was a well-known Bay Area entertainment agent/manager back then) before launching into the first verse. The jam is nice and rubbery, if not quite as mind-blowing as some of the 1968 versions (such as the incredible one captured on *Two from the Vault*). The "Alligator" is worthy of the period, but nothing special. It sounds a little desultory. While tuning up for the next song, Phil says, "Hey I just saw a narc down in the audience... He was right around in there. If you see one step on him." "He Was a Friend of Mine" is warbled sweetly, if a tad off-key.

The date is speculation. Here's the illustrious Jeff Tiedrich's opinion on the date.

> In *DeadBase 9* this set list was moved to 9/29/67 (Straight Theatre), because the *DeadBase* authors have a notion that this is the famous "Alligator" where Mickey Hart sat in on a two-hour-long "Alligator" > "Caution" and henceforth became a member of the band.
>
> This premise seems to be based on the circumstance that *DeadBase*'s copy of this tape cuts halfway through "Alligator." You can read more about their reasoning in their review of 5/5/67 on page 378 of *DeadBase 7*. Unfortunately, this premise falls apart when you hear the more complete fragment. "Alligator" does NOT segue into a two-hour "Caution." It merely ends quite normally

after 15 or so minutes, followed by (there are no splices on the tape) some off-mike banter:

> **Phil:** Why don't we turn down for this next one?
> **Garcia:** What?
> **Phil:** Why don't we TURN DOOOOWNNNN for this next one?

and then "He Was a Friend" begins. Sorry Charlie, it ain't 9/29/67, much as we all want it to be.

Bottom line: Let's keep searching for a true date.

CHRISTIAN CRUMLISH

---

**6/18/67**

**Monterey County Fairgrounds, Monterey, California**

**Monterey International Pop Festival**

Viola Lee Blues, Cold Rain and Snow.

---

**Source:** FM-SBD, **Quality:** A, **Length:** 0:20

The Monterey Pop Festival, which made instant stars of many groups, was far from one of the Dead's musical high points. All that circulates of their mainstage performance is two songs. (They gave a free unofficial concert on another stage, of which no tape circulates.) The opener, "Viola Lee Blues," is aggressive, with Phil's bass lines cascading over Garcia's lead riffs. Unfortunately, this cuts before the end and, on the soundboard, is spliced right into the other surviving tune, a standard-issue-of-the-era, speed-freak run-through of "Cold Rain and Snow." Unfortunately, not known to exist on tape are the legendary jams at Monterey Peninsula College that weekend, where the Dead, Hendrix, the Airplane, and many of the other festival performers held long, open-ended jam sessions.

MICHAEL PARRISH

## 7/23/67
**Neal Cassady at the Grand Reopening of the Straight Theater**

**Straight Theater, Haight Street, San Francisco, California**

Neal Cassady raps, backed by the Dead

**Source:** SBD, **Quality:** B+, **Length:** 0:07, **Origin:** fairly common, **Genealogy:** MR > RR > acetate > DAT
**Highlights:** All

For literary Deadheads, this will be something of a treat. As one of the few recordings circulating of Cowboy Neal, aka Dean Moriarty, aka Speed Limit ("the Fastestmanalive"), it is an interesting glimpse of the man lionized by Kerouac, Kesey, Tom Wolfe, Ginsberg, John Clellon Holmes, and in the Dead songs "The Other One" and "Cassidy." For fans who have encountered Neal only as a subject, this brief monologue is especially interesting because it is a taste of what his artistry was all about: the free-form rap, a performance designed to inveigle an audience and draw them into his multifaceted perspective.

Oddly enough, it is the only piece of the Dead backing Neal in circulation: none of the extant Acid Test material we have shows this kind of interplay between Neal and the audience, and Neal and the backing musicians—though several critics agree that this is a poor example of that. Nonetheless, what we hear is a loud echo of what those dozen Acid Tests must have done for both Neal and the band, for there is a definite synergy between the performers, even if the audience doesn't entirely understand the badinage. For fans of the era, then, it is more than just a Neal rap: it is the ethos of the Acid Test, in a way that we don't really have otherwise. Most interesting of all, however, is that it makes the case for the connection between the Acid Tests and the band's signature sonic philosophy. When the Dead start playing behind Neal, Heads will immediately recognize the link.

The tape also comes from an interesting moment in the history of the San Francisco counterculture. Recorded at the grand opening of the Straight Theater, the event has caused some confusion among tapers over the years because of the number of openings the Straight had. This was a function of its ongoing battles with City Hall over permits, itself a part of the long-running fight over public space that was such a defining part of the hippies' struggle with San Francisco. It was also something of a reunion of the Acid Test participants, for the first time since the San Francisco State Acid Test the previous fall. Sadly, it is the last "hipalogue"—as one of Neal's biographers called these raps—that we have of Neal. In a little over seven months, he would be dead by the side of the railroad tracks outside San Miguel de Allende.

All recordings of this in circulation come from one source, the acetate included in Hank Harrison's *The Dead Book,* the earliest monograph on the band. Whatever source tape it was drawn from has since disappeared from view, though the generational loss has been offset by the digital cleanup provided by more than one assiduous DAT collector. Most interesting, however, is the fact that the entire rap has been transcribed and published with annotations by Ken Babbs, Kesey's lieutenant and the other guiding hand shaping the Acid Tests.[1] It is a bit odd to see Neal reduced to print, but Babbs' annotations

*An Electric Circus newspaper ad in 1967*

---
1. Ken Babbs, with Kim Spurlock, "Neal Cassady at the Grand Opening of the Straight Theatre," *Chemical Imbalance: The Magazine of Convulsive Beauty*, vol. 2, no. 3 (1991), pp. 86–92.

do a marvelous job of decoding Neal's dizzying stream of references. Even if the performance is a less-than-representative slice of Neal, it is still, in the words of his first biographer, "as veined with subtle treasure as any previous effort."[2]

It is also a slice of Neal when he is not at his best, as Robert Hunter said in an interview a decade later: "That little record that Hank Harrison put into his *Dead Book,* though, gives you a good idea of his rap. He was like that, except he was not in top form on the record except for a few moments."[3] Harrison even warned readers of that in his book: "It is significant that the audience, consisting mostly of young people from Haight Street, did not know who he was and were jeering him from the floor."[4] Part of this is because it is an unusual moment for Neal—unusual in terms of monologue, more so in terms of audience and scene. As his biographer notes, on the tape he sounds "oddly self-conscious. Neal appears to be sampling himself as a figure in history, to be at once burdened and consoled by his enshrinement in the pantheon of American heroes. He is also, and above all, giving the public what he thinks it wants—and demands—of him."[5]

For readers who know his persona, it is strange to hear him in this context, as a formal performer, on stage in front of an audience, and not as a performer-participant, a shaping force for a communal gathering in which everyone, Neal included, was melted into a puddle together. This may have been what Garcia meant when he said that Neal, at his purest, "was a tool of the cosmos." He performed, but you were invited to participate; there was interaction with Neal, through this ongoing, developing creation, his art form. Monologue isn't a truly accurate term since it was always more than a single narrative: Neal had several storylines going at once, moving among them and between them in bits and spurts, gracefully blending them with the perfect connection here, a catch-phrase there; it made for the most marvelous of platforms for his rap, which was nothing less than the ongoing explication of the themes that Neal saw running in his life, in life in general, and in American culture overall. It was a trait that made him immediately appealing to the writers drawn to him, who dealt with those same issues and in similar ways—but never so immediately. Neal did it all in real time. And that made it a performance, the source of his appeal for musicians—and a large part of why the Dead found him so compelling an avatar. Garcia wrote: "Neal represented a model to me of how far you could take it in the individual way, in the sense that you weren't going to *have* a work, you were going to *be* the work. Work in real time, which is a lot like musician's work."[6] And Neal provided confirmation that Garcia's commitment to performance and to a collective effort were as valid as any traditional, individual form of artistic expression.

The tape begins with Garcia introducing him, saying "hand that man a microphone." And Neal steps up, beginning the rap fitfully, like a musician noodling as he decides what to play; a few catch-phrases from the backstock of themes that he played with, and the band begins their equivalent of the same, a few riffs tootled out, as if to save Neal from the silence and confusion that greeted him. Some heckling prompts a classic Nealism: "I knew I should have worn more paisley," and that seems to launch him, finally; now there is enough to work against, between the audience and the band behind him, starting up strongly now, providing a context to rap over and in. And Neal, relieved, kicks into it, bouncing into the rhythm; a good pun—"menopausal"—riffed off a blank spot in the sonic backdrop, and then comes the line that really leaps out, the one that was a harbinger of the end: "You can work yourself into anything, but how do you get out of it?" That was Neal's abiding dilemma at that point, according to his friends, and the one for which he never found an answer, except to burn out.

Another pause swallows things before he lurches on, spinning more riffs, puns, but mostly in-jokes and Beat references that largely escape the majority of the audience, one imagines; this is where Babbs' annotations shine. There is a certain genius at work here, but a more specialized—and probably intimate—audience is required, or perhaps it is simply the failure of the Acid Test format to work outside that guaranteed chemical stage. Just as that thought may strike some listeners, where Neal makes the "lost my extension" remark, the band begins a lyrical, melodic weirdness, not a full-on space jam but the start of one, it sounds; a space noodle, one that grows and mushrooms for several seconds, now minutes—and shades of 1969, this is as weird as they get, ever, in the height of the *Live Dead* years. A little longer and it's undeniable: this is the link between the Acid Tests

---

2. William Plummer, *The Holy Goof* (New York: Paragon House, 1990), pp. 154–55.
3. *Dead Relix,* vol. 5, no. 2 (May–June 1978), p. 24.
4. Hank Harrison, *The Dead Book* (New York: Links, 1973), [p. 180].
5. Plummer, *The Holy Goof,* pp. 154–55.

---

6. Jerry Garcia, "Behind the Wheel with Neal," preface to Perry and Babbs, *On the Bus,* p. xviii.

and the heart of the Dead's improvisational genius, which is, for so many fans, epitomized by that wonderful, amorphous, yet focused prelude to "Dark Star" on *Live Dead* or any one of a dozen shows from that era. And this is the tape that shows that connection, that debt, so unequivocally—corroboration of the lofty claim Harrison makes in the book for it, which is that "the totality [of the tape] is reminiscent of the acid tests." Most interesting of all, Harrison calls the Dead's backing jam "Prankster music."[7] For Deadheads, this alone makes it a tape of history, as close to the heart of the alchemical soup of the Acid Tests as we have in circulation.

Unfortunately, that seems to be at the expense of capturing the best of Neal. Compressing Cassady into a recording was always a goal of the Pranksters, just as pinning him with written words was for his literary friends. That both tasks still meet with failure, now almost thirty years after his death, is something he would find vastly amusing, partly because of its futility, but mostly because of the irony. The essence of Neal was spontaneity, the present, and actually, a shade into the future, a few steps ahead of Now—the perfect opposite of measured retrospect. But the Beats are museum exhibits now, as are the Hippies, and Neal's place in history is anchored in both of those countercultures; in fact, he is the most visible, colorful, and important link between those two great bohemian movements, and in exactly the ways that he would have appreciated: symbolic and actual. For Neal was really about that marginal, wonderful space between reality and myth: he lived as if life were mythopoetic, on a personal and still grand scale. It was a lifestyle before that term had come to mean consumerism, when it meant the art of living, and it impressed almost all who encountered him, from the major figures such as Kerouac and Kesey to a host of minor ones, some of whom provide the clearest indication of his power. Poet and biographer Aram Saroyan called him "that flashing, dashing enterprise of absolute glad creases and speeches, mixes and dishes, food and thought complexes: Neal."[8]

Darby Slick, an early leader in the San Francisco music scene and author of the San Francisco anthem "Somebody to Love," said of Neal: "To listen to him was to be roller-coastered through a fun house, every room of which was built by a different demon. There was no time to adjust to one jarring juxtaposition before the next was presented.... It was like listening to someone talk improvised poetry, so fast and strong that it almost literally hurt my brain."[9] Pigpen said it perhaps the most succinctly: "That cat Moriarty from the Doldrums is just about so crazy as a man can be."[10]

After the heyday of the Pranksters, when Neal was on the West Coast he stayed with Robert Hunter, who made a number of tapes of his raps and explained their power to an interviewer a decade after Neal's death: "He did one tape that I would play, and I'd swear that every time I played that tape that there would be a different conversation with me on it. He was flying circles above me ... I hear myself kind of bumbling around with what appeared to be a seventy-eyed creature. I was Flakey Foont to his Mr. Natural there."[11]

Not surprisingly, this sentiment is echoed by Kesey. "He was far out, folks. I realize more and more just how far out he was as the years pass since his death and each time I penetrate what I thought was virgin territory I find Neal's familiar restless footprints messing through the choicest glens. I mean, friends and neighbors, I mean he was far out, just one hell of a hero and the tales of his exploits will always be blowing around us...."[12]

Those exploits are the crux of the difficulty with understanding Neal, for he was, of course, more than just a monologuist. Indeed, his raps are indistinguishable from the kind of life he lived, and the way he lived it. A perfect illustration comes in Ken Kesey's *Garage Sale*, where he tells the story of Neal before an incredulous judge: "Mr. Cassady, how is it possible for one man to incur twenty-seven moving violations in the course of one month!" And Neal duly launches into a response, marshalling the techniques cultivated in years of speed-rapping before God and his awed fellows, all sweetness and oozing sincerity from every phrase, excuses piled upon explanation and it was all a mistake, you understand, and on and on, through debacle after debacle, easily recalling all the proper dates, times, street numbers, each officer's name, all as casually as if he were legitimately the victim of all these darned misunderstandings, you see—not difficult for a man who had read all of Proust's *Remembrance of Things Past* and could quote, as Kesey points out, "long machine-

---

7. Harrison, *The Dead Book*, p. 180.
8. Aram Saroyan, *Genesis Angels: The Saga of Lou Welch and the Beat Generation* (New York: William Morrow, 1979), p. 125.
9. Darby Slick, *Don't You Want Somebody to Love: Reflections on the San Francisco Sound* (Berkeley, Calif.: SLG Press, 1991), p. 108.
10. Jerrilyn Brandelius, *The Grateful Dead Family Album* (New York: Warner, 1989), p. 51.
11. *Dead Relix*, vol. 5, no. 2 (May–June 1978), p. 24.
12. Kesey, "Lord Buckley, Roland Kirk, and Neal Cassady," in *Kesey's Garage Sale*, p. 195.

gunning bursts when tempted." All the charges were dropped, of course. "T'weren't nuthin, Chief," Neal commented to a dumbfounded Kesey afterward. "Even a bad dog won't bite if you talk to him right."[13]

If Neal himself is impossible to pin down, his impact on the artists around him may be the closest we come to sketching a picture of him. And perhaps that story is as good a way as any of summarizing that impact: Neal was a life-as-art model, a modern-day minstrel for whom the live performance was everything, and that performance was his life, his mind, his art. His rap was his own inspired, dedicated connection with the world around him, honed into such a personal medium that it largely vanished with him, except for the tributes and a few pieces like this tape. It was all his movie, and he was happy for you to be a part of it. Kesey warns against mythologizing Neal beyond his art: the stories of Neal's exploits, as he put it, "really veer one from the mark Neal had in mind. Only through the actual speedshifting grind and gasp and zoom of his high compression voice do you get the sense of the urgent sermon that Neal was driving madcap into every road-blocked head he came across."[14] This recording does not do justice to the impact that Neal had, but it is an indication, albeit imperfect, of the magnitude of that impression.

NICK MERIWETHER

---

### 8/4/67
#### O'Keefe Center, Toronto, Canada
Alligator, New Potato Caboose, Viola Lee Blues

---

**Source:** SBD, **Quality:** B+, **Length:** 0:40
**Highlights:** All

I cannot speak too highly of this one cassette-tape side of psychedelic madness. It is positively ferocious with music that just drips. "Alligator" features a jam every bit as intense as the "Caution" from 2/14/70. The scene at this concert was very hip with light show projections illuminating a triptych of enormous screens above and behind the band. Very far out, man!

JOHN R. DWORK

---

13. Ibid., p. 195.
14. Ibid., p. 195.

---

### 9/3/67
#### Rio Nido
Midnight Hour

---

**1. Source:** SBD, **Quality:** A, **Length:** 0:32
**2. Source:** SBD-CD, **Quality:** A, **Length:** 0:32, **Genealogy:** MR > DR > C; Officially released on *Fallout from the Phil Zone* (U.S.: Grateful Dead Records, GDCD 4052, 1997), 2:03:52

One of those "historic song" tapes, Rio Nido is famed for one song and one song only. Usually this kind of tape gets attention because the rendition stands out from a mediocre set, or because of a guest, or simply because it represents an apogee in the band's performance of the tune. In this case, it's because one song is all we have, but it is "primal Dead"—what Vault keeper Dick Latvala calls truly transcendent shows, where the band has the famed X factor and the performance is not only greater than the sum of the parts on stage, but in the whole hall.[1] Long after this compendium was in the works, it was officially released on *Fallout from the Phil Zone*, a compilation of superb odds and ends assembled by Lesh, who wrote in the liner notes that the band "played our little hearts out," despite an audience of only about twenty-five people.[2]

"Midnight Hour" is one of band's signature pieces in this era, and here it is a tour de force led by Pigpen, only a few days shy of his twenty-second birthday. It also shows what the band had become, what they could do as a five-piece, only a couple of weeks before Mickey Hart joined. In addition to superb musicianship, the real appeal of this tape is the ample good humor that comes across: Pig and the boys sound friendly and relaxed, warm and appealing—and good. At thirty-two minutes, it feels like a band with time on its hands.

A year earlier, the tune had already become known as one of the Dead's hallmark jams. Jann Wenner, in his pre–*Rolling Stone* days, described it in the spring of '66 as the highlight of a gig at Berkeley, calling it "one of their best numbers, and the best version of that song I've heard any group do."[3] Here, over a year later, it has

---

1. Steve Silberman and David Shenk, *Skeleton Key* (New York: Doubleday, 1994), p. 230.
2. Phil Lesh, Liner Notes to Grateful Dead, *Fallout from the Phil Zone* (U.S.: Grateful Dead Records GDCD 4052, 1997), [p. 3].

incorporated even more of the Dead ethos. One of the central improvements fans will notice is how carefully they are listening to each other: the dynamics, the ebb and flow of complexity, the smoothness of the transitions in the arrangement from sparse to dense, all are noticeably better than in any version from the previous year. Of course, this is a dangerous generalization: who knows what we're missing, in the dozens and dozens of performances that were not taped, or haven't been circulated yet. But based on what we have available now, it shows how much they've improved, how much closer they can come to that alchemical summoning of the group mind's muse.

Pig's cajoling and rapping will delight most fans, especially Deadheads who don't know the range he had as a frontman. He whips the band in and out of intensity, melody, and rhythm; since it's a soundboard tape, it's impossible to tell how well his exhortations and cajolery are being received. And the band sounds great in this capacity, replete with backing chorus of "get on up," in a classic R&B style revue, cooking along behind this charismatic dynamo. Some of Pig's banter is hysterical—such as when, after repeated injunctions to "get on up and dance," he finally begins auctioning off Bobby as a dance partner: "Hey Bobby, c'mon man, you can put down your guitar and go dance with her"—perhaps not an implication Bobby appreciated. At one point, Pig says he's "disappointed" with the crowd: "I thought you were going to get up and dance." But the band sounds so good one wonders whether this is just part of the act, whether Pig just wants a greater frenzy. So is it a bad—a "dead"—audience, as Pig implies, or is this merely a great emcee rapping and interacting and working the crowd? More probably the latter, given the caliber of the performance and firsthand recollections.

The band played a two-day run at Rio Nido, and only two songs are known to be in tapers' hands; only this is in circulation now. Historically, the tape falls at an interesting juncture in the band's career. The day before, in a *San Francisco Chronicle* column praising their debut album, manager Rock Scully said that the band had decided to leave the Haight, saying, "We've been squeezed out by tourists and Tenderloin types."[4] Despite the loss of their spiritual home, what is most significant about the Rio Nido gigs is that during these shows the band gained a full-time lyricist: Robert Hunter, just back from a long recuperative stay in New Mexico. After making a circuitous *On the Road*–style odyssey to get back to San Francisco, Hunter went up to Rio Nido and saw the band performing "Alligator," one of his first songs, and it floored him. "It was the biggest thrill for me. It was gestalt—I knew I was the missing link, I knew it. It was my lifework—I knew it."[5] If what he heard was anything like this, we know why.

NICK MERIWETHER

---

## 9/15/67

**Bill Graham Presents the San Francisco Scene in Los Angeles**

**Hollywood Bowl, Hollywood, California**

Viola Lee Blues, Cold Rain and Snow, Beat It on Down the Line > Good Mornin', Li'l Schoolgirl, Morning Dew, Alligator > Caution > Feedback

---

**Source:** AUD, **Quality:** C+, **Length:** 1:10
**Highlights:** Beat It on Down the Line > Good Mornin', Li'l Schoolgirl

In what amounted to their major concert debut in the Los Angeles area, the Dead came on before the (at the time) vastly more popular Jefferson Airplane and gave a schizophrenic look at their present and future, a performance that was midway between jamming out extended versions of album songs and the luminous group improvisations that would begin to emerge a few months hence. The first half of their set, captured on one relatively distant audience recording, consists of fairly straight renditions of stuff from their first album, mostly delivered at the same delirious tempos at which the songs were recorded. A great deal of goofy rapping goes on between songs, including Garcia's threat to raffle off Pigpen before "Beat It on Down the Line." The second half of the set was given over to a long, driving, but ultimately somewhat meandering "Alligator" > "Caution" > "Feedback" that ended with a goofy bit of vaudeville chorus and probably left many in the audience scratching their heads.

MICHAEL PARRISH

---

3. mr. jones [Jann Wenner], "The Return of Nowhere Man," *Daily Californian,* May 12, 1966, p. 12.
4. "The New Generation," *San Francisco Chronicle,* Sept. 2, 1967.

5. Robert Hunter, interviewed by Joel Selvin, Jan. 7, 1992.

## Reviews: October 1967

### ✺ 10/22/67 ✺
**Marijuana Defense Benefit, Winterland, San Francisco, California**

Morning Dew, New Potato Caboose, Cryptical Envelopment > The Other One > Cryptical Reprise

**1. Source:** SBD, **Quality:** A+, **Length:** 0:40, **Genealogy:** MR > DAT > C > DAT
**2. Source:** FM-SBD (GDH 300), **Quality:** A+, **Length:** 0:30 (Cryptical Envelopment through Cryptical Reprise), **Genealogy:** MR > RR > DR
**Highlights:** Different lyrics in The Other One

Looking for a perfect example of *proto*–primal Dead? This is it. Garcia's vibratto singing makes his voice quiver like a windsock in a hard-drivin' nor'easter. Pigpen's organ is more prominent in the mix than Keith Godchaux's piano ever was. Bobby's guitar? Virtually nonexistent in the mix. The vocals waver steadily in and out of key. But who cares? The quality is superb and the band is going for it. You can enjoy this show just for the sheer effort exerted.

This "Other One" is unique in that it sports different lyrics! I asked Dick Latvala to make an attempt at deciphering them and this is what he came up with:

> (second verse)
> When I woke up this morning
> My head was not intact
> Asked my friends about it
> Gonna find out where it's at
> Came up inside me
> Blew the dust clouds all away
> The heat came by and busted me
> For smilin' on a cloudy day . . .
>
> (third verse)
> Well the heat down in jail
> They weren't very smart
> They taught me how to read and write
> They taught me my precious heart
> Well breakin' out of jail
> I learned that right away
> They didn't need to tell me
> 'Bout smilin' first then running away . . .

JOHN R. DWORK

### ✺ 10/31/67 ✺
**Billed as "Trip or Freak" for Halloween, Winterland Arena, San Francisco, California**

Alligator > Drums > Caution//, Cryptical Envelopment > The Other One > Cryptical Reprise

**Source:** SBD, **Quality:** C/C+, **Length:** 0:45
**Highlights:** Alligator, Cryptical Reprise

Halloween + Winterland + 1967 = Tribal Stomp! First prize goes to the drummers, who weave thunderous rhythms akin to the spirit of Olatunji and King Sunny Ade. "Alligator!" becomes the battle cry, chanted fervently, until Garcia shreds it all with some Townshend-like power strums. Lesh responds with the rolling and tumbling bass lines to "Caution" and off they march. Pigpen tosses up some street-corner-sounding harmonica only to be immediately smothered by Garcia. Undaunted, Pig hits the mike for his "gypsy woman" rap. Weir follows with his "all you need" rap. Behind the vocals the band provides spooky, eerie Halloween treats of their own. Coming together, they reach a fine peak—but then the music cuts. Damn.

"The Other One" has that early horseback riding feel to it as well as different lyrics (see the review of 10/22/67 for Dick Latvala's interpretation). No jam has evolved yet so they head quickly back into the "Cryptical" reprise. Ah, but what a version it is. Garcia wisely hangs back and allows the band—especially those percolating drummers—to get alongside him, rather than trailing him (which, in my opinion, is too often the case). The result is simply a ten-minute gush of glorious musical energy. What's unique here is how Garcia takes the helm at the final peak, finds the melody that usually follows verse 2 of "The Other One"'s "in a circle," and firmly closes the song with it. Very slick.

MICHAEL M. GETZ

## 11/10/67
### Shrine Auditorium, Los Angeles, California

Viola Lee Blues, It Hurts Me Too, Morning Dew, Good Mornin', Li'l Schoolgirl, Alligator > Drums > Alligator Reprise > Caution

**Source:** SBD, **Quality:** A–, **Length:** 1:00
**Highlights:** Good Mornin', Li'l Schoolgirl

My original review statement for this tape was "very electric," that is, until my uncle's seventeen-year-old blind dog started to bark when given a chance to state his opinion. That was when it became all too apparent that this show is more than just electric, it's unique as well! Putting sound quality aside (which, for the age of the show, is an excellent mix), the music flows evenly, and when it comes to doing his part, each band member is right on. "Viola Lee Blues" is boilerplate primal Dead. It's what I'd call "boogie-delic," since Garcia frequently lets loose with some serious short cuts and fast rips from his guitar. The jam during that song alone makes the entire tape worth listening to repeatedly. For "It Hurts Me Too," Pigpen wails true to form, and Garcia produces a B. B. King–like sound; it is one of the better versions I've come upon. "Morning Dew" is powerful as well, albeit short and somewhat subdued; nonetheless, Garcia's vocals will break any true Deadhead's heart.

Going into "Schoolgirl," the electric blues feel returns and Pigpen's harmonica has never been more precise. There's another clean jam before they break from "Schoolgirl" and move into one of the most interesting versions of "Alligator" I've ever heard! Pigpen's organ is wild, the guitars are crisp and sharp. If you want to call the jam and drums in the middle a "DRUMZ" entity all its own, it may very well be! There's some spaciness to it all, although it does seem rather tight and planned out. Exiting that and entering back into "Alligator" leaves you begging for more. (More of that trippy "Alligator" chant is thrown in during the performance.) The tape wraps itself up with one of the more careful versions of "Caution," but in itself, it's quite a good version. The only thought in my head as I finished listening was, it needs a warning label, "Caution: This Tape Kicks Ass!"

— SCOTT HAYMAKER

## 11/11/67
### Shrine Auditorium, Los Angeles, California

Turn On Your Lovelight, Death Don't Have No Mercy, Good Mornin' Li'l Schoolgirl, Cryptical Envelopment > The Other One > Cryptical Reprise > New Potato Caboose, Alligator > Caution//

**Source:** SBD, **Quality:** A–, **Length:** 1:20
**Highlights:** Turn On Your Lovelight, The Other One

It takes only a few words to describe this tape: electric and eclectic, this is one wild show! Following on the heels of the previous night at the same venue, the group seems to take 11/10's energy and momentum and continue rolling it right along. The tape begins with an extremely tight version of "Lovelight." However, for the first few lines, Pig has some microphone troubles before somebody decides to turn him up. Once they do, it's evident why this is one of his signature tunes. Pigpen's razor sharp vocal raps interspersed with Garcia's intense guitar work hint of things to come. During the next song, "Death Don't Have No Mercy," Garcia nails it. Pigpen accompanies on this one as well, and once again, the audience is treated to some very intense jamming. "Schoolgirl" brings them around to exploring a blues groove with excellent harmonica work providing the highlights. Next, a high-energy "Cryptical Envelopment" is finished with quickly by the band in order to explore a strong version of "The Other One" (hampered only slightly by Weir).

If I had to peg where the "eclectic" aspect came into play, it would be during "New Potato Caboose." This is an extremely spacy version, which isn't new, but it contains some incredibly strong bass work, some even stronger guitar work, and intense organ playing by Pigpen. By the time "Alligator" hits, Pigpen is rolling and really into it, and Garcia's guitar work is impressive. The drums are short, but very tasteful. Garcia even contributes an "Alligator" chant before an incredible crescendo finish, which could only be followed by one thing: "Caution." Talk about a group effort! The band's work together is very tight here, and their ferocious jamming leaves the listener longing for more. In truth, I was quite disappointed when the tape finally rolled an end.

— SCOTT HAYMAKER

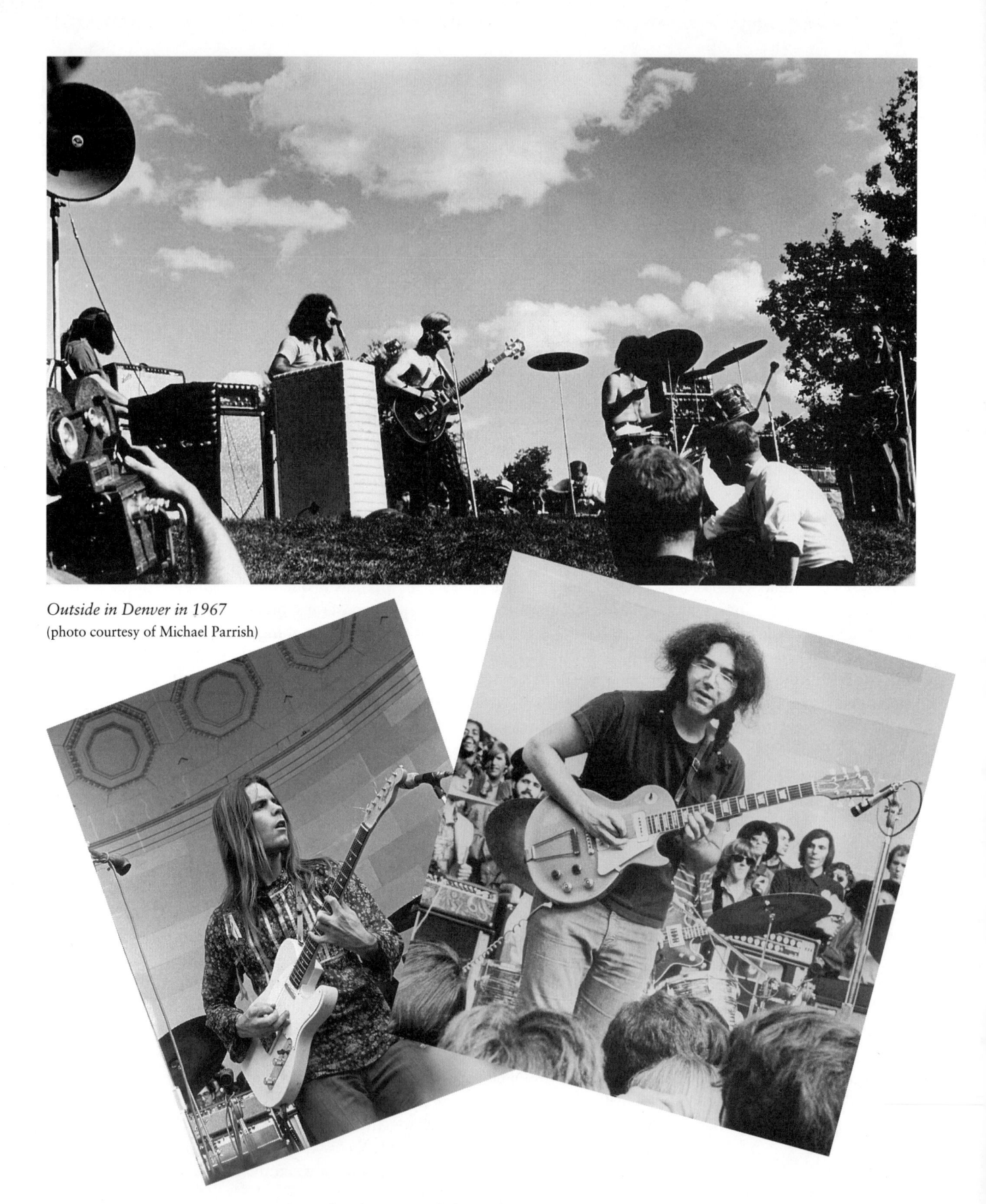

*Outside in Denver in 1967*
(photo courtesy of Michael Parrish)

*Central Park, New York City, 1968* (photo courtesy of Cotter Michaels)

## 11/14/67
### American Studios, North Hollywood, California

Born Cross-Eyed, Dark Star

**Source:** SBD, **Quality:** A, **Length:** 0:10
**Highlights:** All
**Comments:** Some tapes of this session are accompanied by an instrumental "Alice D. Millionaire" and "I Know You Rider" from an unknown 1966 session, as well as "The Other One" > "Death Don't Have No Mercy" that circulates as 11/1[?]/67.

While "Born Cross-Eyed" is nearly identical to its officially released counterpart on *Anthem of the Sun,* "Dark Star" is similar in style but instrumentally interpreted with a trifle more transparency. Notable is the absence of the keyboard, replaced by delightfully delicate hand percussion. Both of these tracks are very possibly the shortest renditions in circulation.

BRIAN DYKE

## 11/19/67
### Unknown Location Studio Rehearsal

//Cryptical Envelopment > The Other One > Cryptical Reprise, //Alligator > Caution, Turn On Your Lovelight, Alligator Reprise > Caution Reprise, Cryptical Envelopment > The Other One > Cryptical Reprise, Viola Lee Blues

**Source:** SBD, **Quality:** B, **Length:** 0:45
**Highlights:** The entire rehearsal
**Comments:** Some tapes of this studio session contain a second loop of "Alligator" > "Caution" and "That's It for the Other One." As well, some tapes in circulation have an unidentified "Viola Lee Blues" that is definitely not from these sessions. Finally, "Lovelight" circulates individually labeled 11/19/67, which very well may be the correct date.

Beginning with an extremely ragged rendition of "That's It for the Other One," this rehearsal shifts gears quickly during the "Cryptical Envelopment outro, erupting in a blazing series of spiraling licks from Garcia. The instrumental "Alligator," completely standard fare, is focused mainly on perfecting the verse pattern. After a weak ad-lib attempt behind the Drums segment, however, Garcia explodes with a simply delightful solo consisting of some of the finest blues licks and bends ever exhibited. This leads into an all-out eruption, the band furiously jamming in an absolute maniacal passage that even a modern-day headbanger would appreciate. The segue into "Caution" occurs at mach ten with traces of R&B thrown in by Lesh. The verse portion of "Caution" is an unfortunate return to sloppiness.

Well performed all around, the "Lovelight" is perhaps the closest vocal interpretation by Pig that we have of Bobby Bland's definitive rendition. Though unfortunately minimal, this jam, rich in reverb, offers Garcia showcasing licks sweet as honey. Surprisingly, the band calls it quits following the return to the verse.

BRIAN DYKE

## Undated/67
### 710 Ashbury Street, San Francisco, California

**Interview:** Jerry Garcia

**Source:** AUD, **Quality:** C, **Length:** 1:20
**Highlights:** Moments after commenting on the recent theft of the band's equipment, the interview is interrupted by an ecstatic Bob Weir, who promptly announces that the gear has been recovered, to which Garcia nonchalantly responds, "Far out, man."
**Lowlights:** "It's gettin' hard to buy things like cymbals and, uh, guitar strings now, 'cause they're making bullets out of them."

Following a scattered discussion covering musical gear, musical tastes, perceptions, and climate, Garcia embarks on a lengthy and uncharacteristically candid discussion about political ideologies, at times speaking so vehemently and convincingly that he remotely resembles a grassroots politician.

BRIAN DYKE

## Undated/67
### Unknown Location
**Interview:** Jerry Garcia, Bill Kreutzmann, Phil Lesh

**Source:** FM, **Quality:** B, **Length:** 0:06
**Host:** "One thing I know about the Dead, it seems like the instruments, everything is right together, there's never any sloppiness."

This interview, conducted by a truly obnoxious and borderline moronic host, contains Garcia's description of the origin of the band's name, followed by a few ridiculous and irrelevant questions before it breaks off.

BRIAN DYKE

## 1968

For stage improvisation and playing in the moment, what would become the overriding characteristic of the Dead's music, 1968 was probably the pivotal year. They had made the commitment to following a musical thread wherever it led, not to be satisfied with performing from a prescribed set list. They were in full experimental mode, attempting to take many of their showcase songs to their furthest extent. Adding to the mix of these shows, the band introduced three new original songs early in the year: "China Cat Sunflower," "The Eleven," and the ultimate free-form song, "Dark Star." Each of these had an open ending that encouraged musical exploration. Many times the transition to another song would occur by dissolving one song into a long, exploratory jam of feedback mixed with subtly defined instrumental progressions and then rematerializing into the next song. At other times, the band would mark the transition by building to an apocalyptic meltdown that would descend into a meditation of light feedback before changing over. The tapes that have appeared from the early part of the year are excellent examples of these jams. Within these improvisations would appear the "Spanish Jam," the first of several instrumental themes that became commonplace in the Dead's space jams. A haunting progression with a definite slow flamenco flavor, containing themes reminiscent of Miles Davis' sketches of Spain, this jam would start out softly, played as almost a suggestion, and build to a full-fledged musical expression, sometimes lasting several minutes.

In mid-July, Anthem of the Sun was released, a landmark album of visionary music that mixed live and studio tracks, often within the same song. Much of the live material was taken from late 1967 and early 1968. The album featured show staples such as the "Other One" suite often segueing into "New Potato Caboose," as well as "Alligator" > "Caution." Missing, however, was the other concert staple of the time, "Dark Star" > "China Cat" > "The Eleven," which, although interesting in form, was not as mature in development. Almost as soon as the album was released, "China Cat" was replaced in that combo with the brand new "Saint Stephen." The resulting combo of "Dark Star" > "Saint Stephen" > "The Eleven" would become the centerpiece of shows for the next year. It is interesting to note that the Dead's first two live albums, Anthem of the Sun and Live Dead, were released just as a key song on the album was being phased out. On Anthem, it was "New Potato Caboose," certainly definitive of the Dead's sound at the time, but rare by the end of the year. On Live Dead, the song was "The Eleven," played less than a dozen times after the album's release.

The band had begun taping its shows on a regular basis by this time, even when it wasn't planning a live album. The taping bug had even begun to creep into the audience. On March 3, the first good-quality audience tape was made by Steve Brown at a free show on Haight Street. However, in most cases, the portable equipment and the techniques used were not sufficient to make good recordings yet. Consequently, there are only a few reasonably listenable audience tapes made in the entire year, most notably May 18 at San Jose, June 14 at the Fillmore East, and August 28 at the Avalon.

Most shows were still in the Bay Area, but there were brief forays into other parts of the country, though not in so organized a fashion that would have allowed fans to follow on tour. Also, the band's repertoire focusing on their new songs had not expanded to the point of allowing much variation between shows.

Tapes to get: 1/20, 1/22, 2/2–2/3, 2/14, 3/3, 8/21–8/23.

## 1/20/68
### Eureka Municipal Auditorium, Eureka, California

//Clementine > New Potato Caboose > Born Cross-Eyed > Feedback > Spanish Jam > Caution Jam > Dark Star//

**Source:** FM-SBD (GDH 342), **Quality:** A–, **Length:** 0:40, **Genealogy:** MR > DR
**Highlights:** Every note of this extended jam

Here is a classic example of the young Grateful Dead's go-for-anything attitude and adventurous set list building. In particular, Pigpen's keyboard playing is quite impressive. Each tune flows into another and the whole is intensely asymmetrical. Pig's playing on a faded-into "Clementine" is simply beautiful, the result of a pleasant jam that drips effortlessly into a serene "New Potato Caboose." A raucous "Born Cross-Eyed" moves on to space jamming which segues into a "Spanish Jam." Nonetheless, Garcia and Weir provide a blistering theme alongside Pigpen's keyboard. At the conclusion, Billy changes the pace. Lesh begins the grumbling notes to "Caution," which quickly drops into the opening of "Dark Star," where, unfortunately, the tape fades out. This was the first show of their infamous Great Northwest Tour, during which the Dead's live performances were used in conjunction with studio work to produce *Anthem of the Sun*.

ROBERT A. GOETZ

## 1/22/68
### Eagle's Auditorium, Seattle, Washington

Alligator//, Feedback > Spanish Jam > Dark Star > China Cat Sunflower > The Eleven Jam > Caution//

**Source:** FM-SBD (GDH 337), **Quality:** A–, **Length:** 0:15 (Alligator)
**Highlights:** Alligator, Spanish Jam > Dark Star

Continuing the Great Northwest Tour, this tape begins with a tight and inspired version of "Alligator." A young Pigpen energizes slowly and clearly sings the lyrics with Garcia, Weir, and Lesh screaming behind in a frolicsome manner. With Garcia providing the lead, a major jam is invoked before the band returns to the conclusion of the tune. Next is a faded-in Feedback space, allowing for the entrance of a Bobby-led "Spanish Jam." This flows into the relatively new song, "Dark Star." Garcia sings the first verse quickly, and before launching into the second verse, the band plays a few meandering jams. It is a treat to acquire such an early performance; one can hear through the jams exactly how "Dark Star" was meant to develop into one of the Dead's most significant improvisatory launch pads. This moves into "China Cat," another early performance of a signature tune, which transforms itself perfectly into an impressive "Eleven Jam." The "Eleven Jam" then moves into a "Caution Jam," which is cut after about two minutes.

ROBERT A. GOETZ

## 2/2/68
### Crystal Ballroom, Portland, Oregon

Viola Lee Blues, Cryptical Envelopment > The Other One > Clementine > Good Mornin', Li'l Schoolgirl

**Source:** FM-SBD (GDH 310), **Quality:** A, **Length:** 0:40, **Genealogy:** MR > DR
**Highlights:** All, essential early Grateful Dead

During both "Viola Lee" and "The Other One," Garcia and Lesh play some truly puncturing notes, revealing the rudiments of a rather twisted, aesthetic partnership that never fails to entertain. T.C. sounds wonderfully medieval throughout this tape—especially on the Hunter-Lesh composition, "Clementine" (of which no versions circulated until the mid-1990s). This song has a lilting shuffle with bardlike lyrics of lost love and, of course, roses. The segue into "Schoolgirl" is superb. This version has two well-played harmonica solos by Pigpen and some very strange guitar sounds by Garcia near the end that are worth hearing at least twice.

MICHAEL M. GETZ

# REVIEWS: February 1968

### ❀ 2/3/68 ❀
#### Crystal Ballroom, Portland, Oregon

Dark Star > China Cat Sunflower > The Eleven > Space//, Cryptical Envelopment > The Other One > Cryptical Reprise > New Potato Caboose > Born Cross-Eyed

**Source:** FM-SBD (GDH 304 and 310), **Quality:** A, **Length:** 0:45, **Genealogy:** MR > DR

**Highlights:** The Eleven > Space, New Potato Caboose

A very short, eventless, but cute "Dark Star" explodes into a funky, raplike version of "China Cat" to get things started here. Steamrolling into a strong, precise take on "The Eleven," Phil grabs the helm at the end and steers the band into what begins to be an interesting Space. However, the tape cuts and that's that.

"The Other One," like "Dark Star," is still played from the cradle. But they give the cradle a good rock, and this is essential listening for anyone interested in how this song evolves into one of the Dead's trademark pieces of improvisation. In fact, this song was to never leave their repertoire.

The "New Potato" is stunningly beautiful, easily one of the finest versions in circulation. "Born Cross-Eyed," despite some solid musicianship, falls beneath the weight of the strained, overambitious vocals that eventually led to its being dropped from future performances.

MICHAEL M. GETZ

### ❀ 2/14/68 ❀
#### Carousel Ballroom, San Francisco, California

**Set 1:** Dark Star > China Cat Sunflower > The Eleven > Turn On Your Lovelight
**Set 2:** Cryptical Envelopment > The Other One > Cryptical Reprise > New Potato Caboose > Born Cross-Eyed > Spanish Jam, Alligator > Drums > Jam > Caution > Feedback
**Encore:** Midnight Hour

**1. Source:** SBD, **Quality:** A–, **Length:** 2:00, **Genealogy:** MR > PCM > DAT

**2. Source:** FM-SBD (KMPX), **Quality:** B–, **Length:** 2:00, **Genealogy:** Master FM

**3. Source:** FM-SBD (GDH 365), **Quality:** A–, **Length:** 0:30 (Cryptical Envelopment through Spanish Jam), **Genealogy:** MC > DAT

**Highlights:** Spanish Jam, Alligator > Jam > Caution > Feedback

The Carousel Ballroom, situated in the heart of downtown San Francisco at Van Ness and Market Street, was cooperatively run by the Dead, Quicksilver Messenger Service, and the Jefferson Airplane as an alternative to the more commercial events put on by Bill Graham. Not surprisingly, this very loose business venture only produced shows for six months in 1968 before folding in the red. Also not surprisingly, Bill Graham immediately stepped in and picked up the lease, moving his operations away from the increasingly dangerous neighborhood where the original Fillmore Auditorium was located. Renamed the Fillmore West, Graham hosted shows there until the final one on July 2, 1971. While it was the Carousel, it was legendary for shows that pushed the limits of what was permitted and acceptable in a public dance hall, the Acid Test ethos living on in notorious gigs put on not only by the bands themselves, but also by the Diggers, the Hell's Angels, and a host of others. The Dead played a total of sixteen shows in 1968 from January 17 through their final performance on June 19, though there were probably numerous uncredited or lost shows. Today the Carousel is a car dealership, with cars stored on the fabled dance floor itself.

For years this show was available only as a so-so FM recording from KMPX in San Francisco. But in 1996 a beautiful soundboard surfaced from its long, er, honeymoon. Much of this music was used, along with the 11/67 Shrine shows in L.A., as the foundation for *Anthem of the Sun*.

Set 1 starts out with a dose of Psychedelic Castle Music (PCM)—"Dark Star," "China Cat," and "The Eleven," pungently performed—that succeeds in transporting the listener back to the Middle Ages and evoking a magnanimous feeling to combat the decay of the corrupt King's court. Some things never change. While Weir winks at the ladies-in-waiting, the band weaves a Tolkienesque spell fueled largely by Hunter's bardlike lyrical landscapes and T.C.'s swirling, medieval keyboards. Had they played "Saint Stephen" and "Clementine" (two other PCM standards) while handing out jugs of wine and slabs of sizzling beef, the Carousel may well never have come back. However, Pigpen and Weir (looking slightly flushed) bring us back to the present with a short but rousing version of "Turn On Your Lovelight" to close both the set and the doorway to the past.

Set 2 opens with a dedication to Neal Cassady by Garcia, who has often cited Neal as his number one hero/influence. The lyrics to "Cryptical" take on a new meaning as Garcia emphatically sings, "You know he had to die," as if Cassady's death was inevitable. One can only wonder about Garcia's ensuing similar attitudes and the lifestyle that led to his own early death.

Weir pays his own homage by singing "tripping through the lily fields," as opposed to "skipping." "The Other One" is confident, slashing, and fully juiced. The "Cryptical" reprise features some hyper needlepointing by the whole gang before segueing crisply into an intricately juggled "New Potato." The closing jam is monstrous. Although the vocals of "Born Cross-Eyed" are strained and overwrought, the piece is still musically compelling. Everything up to this point makes for a fine evening, but it's the next hour of music that reveals the transformative power of this band, made even more remarkable by the fact that they had only been playing together for three years.

As "Born Cross-Eyed" fades out, lurid, sinister notes spring up like zombies from the grave: marching music for the rotting, decomposing Vietnam era. Garcia bends and bends, crying out like a banshee under the sword. The music barely contains a pulse as it shudders along, stranger than a mist, toppling over gravestones and yet leaving not so much as a footprint. A gong roll from Mickey, a bit of feedback, and then it's gone.

Officially this was called the "Spanish Jam," but the Dead used the chords merely as a framework to express something else, something even more primal that simply needed to come out. And due to the Dead's open-ended approach, this "thing" was able to.

Enter the "Alligator." The relief and jubilation can immediately be felt as Pigpen wags his tail through the opening verses, pulling the Carousel back to its feet. During the short drum solo, Weir steps up to the mike and says, "Burn down the Fillmore, gas the Avalon!" and then, "Come on everyone—get up and dance! It won't ruin ya!" Sliding gracefully out of the drums, Garcia and Lesh lead the band into a long, southern-flavored jam. This one doesn't rise or fall much, just zooms effortlessly on the wings of pure improvisation. Simply a beautiful jam until . . . Uh-oh, cries of "Alligator!" reemerge. Lesh rolls out the "Caution" carpet with a swagger to his notes. Garcia double-pumps his guitar and fires off round after round of ferocious, eye-blurring buckshot. These guys are *hot*. Steals your face, bone, and brain. Lots of variations on the "Caution" theme follow, all of them burning embers of coal.

As "Caution" limps away, dazed and riddled, the Dead take us to yet one more realm. The following "Feedback" is such a force of nature that I can only urge everyone to sit down and let this thing grab you by your collars. It feels like the universe has been turned inside out, revealing the band as mere mortal puppets all along. That Other presence—call it the X Factor, Fitness, or what you will—makes itself known in a *huge* way. You can feel it as tangibly as you can a tap on the shoulder. It's rare for this Thing to take such a near-visual form; just a sense of it is usually enough to make a special show. But on February 14, 1968, the damn thing broke out of its cage and pranced around the Carousel. The guy with the key to the cage was, of course, Lesh: he creates an eerie, childlike emotional vortex through which the other members easily lock on to.

Serious listening to this show reveals such a sheer depth of soul-waking power that it astonishes me to remember just how young a band they were at the time. Free advice: if you have the tapes, go back for another listen; if you don't, get moving.

MICHAEL M. GETZ

## 3/3/68

**Haight Street at Cole,
San Francisco, California**

Viola Lee Blues, Smokestack Lightning, Turn On Your Lovelight, Hurts Me Too//

**Source:** AUD, **Quality:** B, **Length:** 0:45, **Genealogy:** MR > DAT > Gans FM, > **Taper:** Steve Brown, Uher open reel deck

**Highlights:** A historic occasion and a rare tape; worth having for those reasons.

The first thing that hits you about this tape is its quality: this is a really, really bad sounding tape. And then you read the history of it: made by a fan on a big old Uher, with a cheap mike that he stuck up over the crowd, and recorded three and a half songs—less than an hour of the show—before the batteries ran out.[1] And then it sounds—well, kind of marvelous. An illegal document, a slice of history—and in this case, what a history. Bear out on bail, headed back fairly soon; the Carousel Ballroom up and running, a major risk and investment by the Dead and their partners, including the Airplane; and a band in transition. This could be considered one of the Dead's first conscious acts of history: a gig they put together themselves, performing for free, on an illegally blocked-off Haight Street, as a thank-you and farewell to the scene that they had become so inextricably associated with, and this was a perfect way to acknowledge that debt.

So on March 3, 1968, Haight Street was filled with hippies and the Dead set up on a flatbed truck, running their power from the old Straight Theater, another casualty of the city's increasingly intolerant attitude toward the long-haired throngs of young people making their way to the Haight throughout the previous year. Even though the band had already moved out, and the Diggers had held their famous Death of Hippie ceremony a few months earlier, publicly laying to rest their vision of the Haight-Ashbury, all that was forgotten for one bright afternoon. A free concert by the Dead, on Haight Street—it really was the Summer of Love, one last time.

"Viola Lee Blues" starts things off, and ninety seconds in, it's clear that the band means to groove. Mid-tempo, that marvelous range where the Dead lock into a trance and usually sail out into hypnosis pretty quickly. Three minutes in, and if you're listening to the version cleaned up by David Gans and broadcast on the *Grateful Dead Hour,* then you're no longer even aware of the tape; the universe it defines is whole and complete and mesmerizing all in itself, and then you're into a marvelous first breakdown, with that quintessential Dead hypno-groove-jamming stretching out and rolling over and around you, sinuous and powerful. This is a band that has improved a great deal since its performance of the same tune nine months earlier, at another big outdoor performance, the Monterey Pop Festival. But that was an L.A. exercise they mistrusted from the outset, and this was for the home crowd, on their old familiar turf. Many superb photographs of this gig have been published, but perhaps the most evocative are those of Jerry walking up to the stage through admiring well-wishers, looking relaxed in a crowd treating him with respect and affection but not putting him above them, really; he was still searching in 1968, and the band was still a few months away from their turn into the serious psychedelia that would culminate in the shows that produced *Live Dead.* Those long, delicate, intense exploratory jams that for most Heads define the *Live Dead* era really begin unfolding in earnest in 1968, and a taste of them shows up in places here.

A marvelous crescendo shows the band's classic beboplike controlled cacophony in the verse "Some got six months, some got one solid . . ." Pig's organ is pretty low in the mix, but what will strike Heads most is that it's also no longer his song. This is, in fact, the proto-Dead—drum-driven guitar mania, with Pig and his organ as only part of the stew. Very good, rhythmic, powerful Phil on this—Reddy Kilowatt, indeed, and worth any Deadhead's time. By now, the tape flaws have all but evaporated and you're immersed—not oblivious, but this is amply listenable. Thank you, Steve—and thank you, David Gans, for the digital cleanup and dissemination.

Lots of crowd interplay is evident on the tape. This sounds like a fun show, even down to that damn whistle that some fan is helpfully tootling at various points.

"Smokestack" returns the band to Pig, and he gives it a first-rate harp intro. And vocally Piggers sounds great. After one verse, though, the band wrests it away from him, jamming it as far from the melody as they can, as the crowd roars in appreciation—a reminder that audience tapes have their advantages. Smoky, hypnotic, and weird, this is a superb rendition. Then a bad

---

1. Steve Brown, Letter to the Editor, in *The Golden Road,* no. 8 (Fall 1985).

cut into "Lovelight," already going; maybe a tape flip here? But "Lovelight" is on and roaring, despite loud audience noise at first. "A show of sonic cascades" is how I first described the tape to a friend, and there is so much of that here, waves of jams, Pig's organ perfect, Garcia's tripled leads running beautifully against the barrage, simplifying into dueling lead lines with Phil, manic and growing more so, and the band just roars into overdrive—play this part loud. You will marvel at the morons who talked their way through this, their ignorance faithfully recorded along with the bliss.

Some great stage banter and classic period announcements in the middle: a sixties-style harangue—"stop hassling the cops, man"—and set of announcements—Weir: "Rodrigo is lookin' for Perez—"; audience member: "LBJ is looking for peace!," which gets a laugh.

A nice "Hurts Me Too" begins, which is unfortunately all that we get, a tantalizing little bit of Pigpen singing and blowing harp, then a fade-out, if you have the Gans version, or a lingering death by battery failure if you have one of the many other multiple-gen copies, drawing you into torture, moment by moment, as you try to kid yourself, "No, really, I can still get it, I can listen through the hideous, warping distortion—" until you scream. Better to go with the Gans on this one, completion be damned.

If you're a Deadhead, you—by definition—love history; you love, to be specific, something like three decades' worth of the stuff. Thus it stands to reason that you should be aware of those moments of—we'll call them "High History," when the Recording Angel or muse of whatever is standing there incarnate, taking notes, and for various reasons, history is made. Garcia discussed that sense of history in the making in a brief interview in the early seventies, describing Woodstock: "It was like I knew I was at a place where history was being made. You could tell.... When you were there there was a sense of timelessness about it. You knew that nothing so big and so strong could be anything but important, and important enough to mark somewhere."[2] The Haight Street show is one of those moments. If you've never heard of it, check out the photos of the event, which are ubiquitous in the Dead scene, or look up a friend who has the Jerry memorial issue of the *Grateful Dead Almanac,* the band's newsletter, the cover of which reproduces one of those shots.[3] Even Thomas Albright's mammoth academic study *Art in the Bay Area, 1945–1980* features a picture from that day as its representative shot of a San Francisco rock band.[4]

If you're a fiend for sound quality, you'll turn up your nose at this tape. As well you should, if sonic quality is your sole criterion for judging a tape. But if so, then you exclude yourself from a notion of what it sounded like—how it felt—to be in the Haight, "Ground Zero of the counterculture," as Wavy Gravy says, on a street filled with fellow Deadheads and hippies (and narks and cops and dogs and tourists and the occasional mystified straight person trying to get to a shop and wondering what the hell was going on) . . . and it's San Francisco in the sixties, or at least fifty minutes of one of the nicer moments in that complicated, bittersweet story. A marvelous piece of history, one sunny afternoon in 1968, as the era drew to a close.

NICK MERIWETHER

---

### 3/16/68
**Carousel Ballroom, San Francisco, California**

**Set 1:** Dark Star > China Cat Sunflower > The Eleven > Jam > Good Mornin', Li'l Schoolgirl
**Set 2:** It Hurts Me Too, Cryptical Envelopment > The Other One > Cryptical Reprise//, //Alligator > Caution//, //Feedback > We Bid You Goodnight
**Encore:** Morning Dew

**Source:** SBD, **Quality:** A–, **Length:** 1:30, **Genealogy:** MC > DAT

**Highlights:** The Eleven > Jam, Schoolgirl, Alligator > Caution

---

The ten-minute "Dark Star" opener is soft, callow, and barely arousing. It's fun listening, though, knowing that in only a few months it will begin to develop calluses from repeated usage and will gradually become the band's most beloved transportational tune, peaking

---

2. Peter Joseph, *Good Times: An Oral History of America in the 1960s* (New York: William Morrow, 1974).

3. *Grateful Dead Almanac,* Fall 1995, ed. Gary Lambert (Novato, Calif.).
4. Thomas Albright, *Art in the Bay Area, 1945–1980* (Berkeley: University of California Press, 1985).

timewise with a forty-eight-minute performance on May 11, 1972. "China Cat" is up next. The band regains its swing as all the players vigorously pounce upon it. "The Eleven" is fully explored before yielding to a jazzy jam at the end that contains a strong "Caution" feel. "Schoolgirl" follows this and showcases the Dead's superb blues improvisations.

The second set opens with stage banter, a silly ditty, and then another blues number; "It Hurts Me Too" is efficient but not much else. A rowdy, resolute "The Other One" follows that, bordering on belligerence. The "Cryptical" reprise is quickly cut. "Alligator" is missing the first verse but contains a keenly focused jam that rises ever so carefully before exploding into "Caution"—another must-hear. Pigpen delivers a nice harmonica solo while the band backs him, oh-so-raucously, before the tape cuts. A dark, dreadful "Feedback" cuts in for a few minutes before melting into a somber "Bid You Goodnight" show closer.

Despite the cuts, this is a wonderful-sounding soundboard from an important era in the Dead's history. Get it.

MICHAEL M. GETZ

### 3/29/68
**Carousel Ballroom, San Francisco, California**

//Morning Dew, //Turn On Your Lovelight > Cryptical Envelopment > The Other One > Cryptical Reprise > New Potato Caboose > Born Cross-Eyed//

**Source:** SBD, **Quality:** B+, **Length:** 0:35
**Highlights:** Cryptical Reprise, New Potato Caboose

Though "Morning Dew" cuts in at the first verse, it is inspired and worth some ear. "Turn On Your Lovelight" picks up near the end and features some smokin' vocals by Pigpen and Weir (who sings lead on the last verse). "The Other One" is short but energetic and worth a listen, if only for evolutionary perspective. The "Cryptical" reprise spins round and round, carefully woven by Garcia until he gently lays it down into a meticulously played "New Potato." "Born Cross-Eyed" cuts out right as it begins.

MICHAEL M. GETZ

### 3/26/68
**Carousel Ballroom, San Francisco, California**

//Good Mornin', Li'l Schoolgirl, Death Don't Have No Mercy, Sittin' on Top of the World, Dark Star

**Source:** SBD, **Quality:** B+, **Length:** 0:30
**Highlights:** Death Don't Have No Mercy

"Schoolgirl" cuts in after the first jam but the band is clearly revved up, as the second jam confirms. Garcia does very well with the vocals on "Death Don't" (not a given for this song) to complement the strong ensemble work by his fellow musicians. "Sittin' on Top of the World" rocks. The embryonic "Dark Star" is just beginning to open its eyes as it stretches out carefully for ten minutes or so before uniquely ending without any segue into another song.

MICHAEL M. GETZ

*Jerry on Haight Street, 1968* (photo credit: Steve Brown)

## 3/30/68
### Carousel Ballroom, San Francisco, California

**Set 1:** //Morning Dew, Cryptical Envelopment > The Other One > Cryptical Reprise > Dark Star > China Cat Sunflower > The//Eleven > Turn On Your Lovelight
**Set 2:** //Born Cross-Eyed > Feedback > Spanish Jam > Death Don't Have No Mercy//, Turn On Your // Lovelight Reprise, Beat It on Down the Line, Dancin' in the Streets

**Source:** SBD, **Quality:** B+/C–, **Length:** 1:40
**Highlights:** The Eleven > Turn On Your Lovelight, Spanish Jam

Although "Dew" cuts in on the fourth verse, Garcia smokes his solo down to the butt. Between songs, Weir and Pig briefly toy with the Rascals' version of "Good Lovin'." "The Other One" has a very confident gait, due mainly to Lesh's unwavering, take-no-prisoners groove. The "Cryptical" reprise features an onslaught of ensemble punches before Garcia and Lesh steer the band into a ten-minute "Dark Star." This one stretches out lightly, purring a bit, before erupting into a hissing version of "China Cat." The following "Eleven" struggles initially to maintain this high energy level but soon finds itself rumbling downhill like a jazzed-up boulder in a matter of minutes. The Dead then take this energy to a solid peak, hold it squarely, and—ta da!—do a slight of hand to reveal the first of two "Lovelight's." Very slick. Pigpen takes charge right off the bat with some creamy vocals. The only jam comes after the first verse and is another controlled exercise in pinpointing the energy as one mind. "Turn On Your Lovelight" finishes up with some bizarre, gospel-like vocals by Pigpen, Weir, Lesh, and Garcia that may be described as sucking, grunting, chanting, and squealing. No kiddin'. Picture a Baptist church in the Deep South where the holy water got replaced with Kool-Aid one fine Sunday morning....

A very hot "Born Cross-Eyed" rocks open the second set. This dissolves like Tang into a, rather lurid "Feedback" that lasts for almost five minutes. A spidery "Spanish Jam" crawls forth that's very similar to 2/14/68. Only this one's got more meat on the bones. Garcia wails and moans, as if playing in a cemetery. "Death Don't" begins as usual—but cuts after the first verse. The second "Turn On Your Lovelight" has a big cut in the middle and starts with even more goofy grunting by all the vocalists. Weir then takes the final verse with Pigpen backing him up. At this point the sound quality changes—for the worse. The mikes have somehow moved closer to the audience and talking can clearly be heard for the first time. "Beat It on Down the Line" is typically tight and eventless. Garcia then asks the crowd, "What do you want to hear, man?" Someone yells out, " 'Morning Dew'!" Garcia unsarcastically responds, " 'Morning Dew,' huh?" as if they hadn't played it. Hmmm. Of course, they played "Turn On Your Lovelight" twice; perhaps the songs are out of order. Garcia then tells the crowd, "At the count of three, everybody yell out your choice and we'll pick out the one we hear best in all the confusion—maybe." The Dead settle on "Dancin'" despite the insistent yelling by someone for—Mother McCree's!? Uh-huh. "Dancin'" has some early level drops but produces a short and feisty jam.

MICHAEL M. GETZ

## 3/31/68
### Carousel Ballroom, San Francisco, California

//Caution > Feedback > We Bid You Goodnight

**Source:** SBD, **Quality:** B+, **Length:** 0:20
**Highlights:** Caution > Feedback

A swingin' "All you need" rap begins this slice of "Caution." After a short jam, a full-fledged, thundering "Caution" theme erupts. Phil's notes are so thick and pervasive that they resonate up and down the spine like he's a musical chiropractor. The segue into "Feedback" comes seemingly out of nowhere and feels like someone throwing a heavy purple velvet rug over your head—it's insidious. And then—dum-de-dum—the Dead are telling us that "Jesus loves you the best" in "We Bid You Goodnight." Strange band, eh?

MICHAEL M. GETZ

## 5/18/68
### Santa Clara County Fairgrounds, San Jose, California

Alligator > Caution > Feedback

**Source:** AUD, **Quality:** C–, **Length:** 0:40, **Genealogy:** MR (3¾ ips) > DR **Taper:** Jorma Kaukonen?
**Highlights:** All.

This audience tape, reportedly recorded by Jorma Kaukonen using on-stage mikes, has a vacant sound, swims a bit, and has a few drops. In essence, it stinks. Plus, it's a short set to boot. So why bother even hearing it? Well, because it has a rip-snortin' "Alligator," that's why! Billy provides the fierce, staccato rhythm, sounding like he's kicking boxes around in a damp basement à la Elvin Jones. After Pigpen serves up the first verses, Garcia comes out of nowhere to *screech* some notes; Lesh responds by blanketing everyone and then starting up "Caution." But wait! Instead, the band spontaneously turns it all up a notch and goes off into hyperjam. Garcia nails every note and chord that comes to mind, playing them as fast as possible. Someone yells: "Alligator!" and the band goes back into "Caution." Pigpen tries to slow it down and do his "All you need" rap, but Garcia and Lesh just blow right by him. Pigpen tries it again later—again he's ignored. But the swelling groove that's been released has a mind of its own. And what it wants is to be left alone to "Feedback." And it has its way. Monstrous. Brutal. Right up to the end.

Pigpen doesn't even get to say goodnight.

MICHAEL M. GETZ

## 6/14/68
### Fillmore East, New York, New York

Feedback > The Eleven > Saint Stephen, Alligator > Drums > Turn On Your Lovelight > Caution > Feedback//

**Source:** AUD, **Quality:** C+, **Length:** 1:00
**Highlights:** Every intense minute!
**Comments:** The quality of this tape varies throughout; when the band is playing softly, it's actually one of the best pre-1970 audience recordings we've heard. When they crank it up, the bass obviously distorts, though not nearly to a point of unlistenability. Over the years I've had several copies of this tape, and some have more hiss from multiple generations than others. If the copy you get sounds godawful, keep trying; low-generation copies are worth getting. Dick Latvala has said that no soundboard of this show exists in the Vault.

Imagine this: It's the Dead's first performance at the Fillmore East. The lights go down and the stage is bathed in deep blue light. Dry ice fog begins to roll out over the stage floor. One by one, the Dead walk out to their instruments. Then, from out of electric silence, they begin to play eerie, bone-chilling "Feedback!" Jerry's guitar howls madly as he shoves it against his amp, the volume cranked up ALL THE WAY. After a few minutes of this deliciously mad aural hell, Phil begins, slowly at first, to lay down the bottom line of "The Eleven" with fat, juicy chords. As he picks the tempo up, Jerry comes in to fully shape the song. WOW! This is truly heavy! After a fully developed "Eleven" jam (you can tell the band is *waaay* stoked!), they descend flawlessly into a textbook example of "Saint Stephen." When this is over, they abruptly stop—an interesting phenomenon for the Deadheads used to hearing "Saint Stephen" almost always segue into another song.

"Alligator" is fairly short, as the band jumps quickly into a bluesy, snaky "Turn On Your Lovelight." Jerry plays call and response on his guitar to Pig's scat vocals. This is the "vintage" Dead at its majestic peak: pure psychedelic heaven. And as if this weren't already enough to convert even the biggest skeptic, the band then segues seamlessly from "Turn On Your Lovelight" into "Caution," a version that has to be heard to be believed. "Caution" is astounding! Pigpen plays a surprisingly long harmonica solo while the drummers whisper the tempo in the background. The rest of the band comes back, and, after fully exploring the more intense side of "Caution," they dissolve back into "Feedback." While all the tapes I've ever heard of this show cut during the "Feedback," I know from someone who was at this show that the Dead ended it exactly opposite from the way it began: "Feedback" fading out under blue lights and fog, musicians leaving one by one. Now, how's *that* for a debut performance?!

JOHN R. DWORK

## 8/21/68
### Fillmore West, San Francisco, California

Cryptical Envelopment > The Other One > Cryptical Envelopment Reprise > Good Mornin', Li'l Schoolgirl, Alligator > Feedback, Dark Star > Saint Stephen > The Eleven > Death Don't Have No Mercy > Turn On Your Lovelight// Midnight Hour

**Source:** SBD, **Quality:** A/A+, **Length:** 1:50
**Highlights:** The Other One Suite > Schoolgirl, Death Don't Have No Mercy, Midnight Hour

The *very* electric "Other One" suite > "Schoolgirl," which usually comes separate from the rest of this show's music on its own tape, circulates in much better sound quality than the rest of the show. The "Schoolgirl" is one of the best we've ever heard (Jerry goes absolutely nuts). Before time and generational travel gave the second tape of this performance a moderate amount of hiss, it must have been a gem. The vocals are panned either hard left or right, giving a nice effect to the tape. "Alligator" features a brief instrumental exploration of Donovan's "First There Is a Mountain" theme, which eventually turns into the "We Bid You Goodnight" riff that now finishes "Goin' Down the Road." "Dark Star," fading in on the tape shortly after it starts, closely resembles the version found on *Two from the Vault*. The "Turn On Your Lovelight" cuts. "Death Don't Have No Mercy" and "Midnight Hour" both shine. For those who have the option to get this show from a DAT or Beta source, you may want to rearrange the order so "The Eleven" doesn't suffer through a cassette flip.

JOHN R. DWORK

## 8/22/68
### Fillmore West, San Francisco, California

Dark Star, Cryptical Envelopment > The Other One > New Potato Caboose, Saint Stephen > The Eleven > Death Don't Have No Mercy, Alligator > Caution > Feedback

**Source:** SBD, **Quality:** A/A+, **Length:** 1:30
**Highlights:** A perfect early Dark Star and Death Don't Have No Mercy. One of the better versions of the Alligator > Caution > Feedback medley
**Comments:** This clean tape features lots of low end.

Simply amazing! This is absolutely one of the best finds from 1968. Bill Graham introduces the band as "Clean-cut but morally corrupt: the Grateful Dead." And the boys launch into "Dark Star." Whoa, very heavy! Yes, this early version features the same excessively repetitive organ riff found in most other very early "Dark Stars," but this version doesn't drag; instead the organ provides a soft and dark, almost spooky, Gothic feel. Jerry lets his guitar sing in perfect eerie accompaniment. His voice is a bit too far back in the mix when he sings the verse, but everything else in the mix is extremely sweet. It ends as softly as it begins—just perfect.

"The Other One" suite is also very tight, but suffers ever so briefly from a minuscule cut right before the "Cryptical" reprise. Unfortunately, Phil's bass is out of tune during his solo in the middle of "New Potato Caboose." Garcia comes to the rescue with a long climax that builds for many minutes. The "Saint Stephen" > "The Eleven" is excellent standard fare for the time, but the "Death Don't Have No Mercy" is especially sublime. The real gem of this whole performance, though, is the final medley. When the guitarists return after the "Alligator" drum solo, the music *seethes and boils* with psychedelic energy. The "Feedback" is just divine. This is a great jam to listen to on headphones with a single candle burning, or in the car at top volume.

JOHN R. DWORK

## 8/23/68
### Shrine Auditorium, Los Angeles, California

Alligator > Caution > Feedback

1. **Source:** SBD, **Quality:** A+, **Length:** 0:34, **Genealogy:** The same 8-track recordings used in making *Two from the Vault*
2. **Source:** FM-SBD (GDH 364), **Quality:** A+, **Length:** 0:34, **Genealogy:** MR > DR
**Highlights:** Every incredible moment!

This is about as good as improvised, psychedelic, lights-out-with-the-headphones-on music gets. It's especially sweet due to the fact that it's widely available in CD-quality sound. Recorded on multitrack at the same show *Two from the Vault* was culled from, this is every bit as hot as the phenomenal "New Potato Caboose" featured on that recording. The jamming is screamingly intense and filled with all sorts of witty, improvisational themes discovered by a perfectly synergized band. Once discovered, these themes are eloquently explored and then left in the ensembles creative warp engine's wake. The "Feedback" finale is one of the longest we've ever heard. This addendum to *Two from the Vault* is one of the best finds of the first half of the 1990s—it is a must-have tape.

JOHN R. DWORK

---

### 8/24/68

**Shrine Auditorium, Los Angeles, California**

Good Mornin', Li'l Schoolgirl, Dark Star > Saint Stephen > The Eleven > Death Don't Have No Mercy, Cryptical Envelopment > The Other One > Cryptical Reprise > New Potato Caboose > Turn On Your Lovelight, Morning Dew

---

**Source:** SBD, **Quality:** A+, **Length:** 3:00, **Genealogy:** *Two from the Vault* CD

**Highlights:** The quintessential "New Potato Caboose"

This is what Dick Latvala calls "primal Dead," and rightly so. For it is this period of the Dead's music that seethes, boils, and overflows with primordial, cosmic, psychedelic energy. At the same time, it is both intensely raw and breathtakingly developed. While listening to primal Dead, my mind's eye paints pictures of exploding galaxies: both scary and beautiful at once. This concert, which the Dead released as *Two from the Vault*, contains such music.

The first CD in this two-disc package starts with a tight "Good Mornin', Li'l Schoolgirl," typical of the time. Next up is "Dark Star" > "Saint Stephen" > "The Eleven" > "Death Don't Have No Mercy." The "Dark Star" is young and undeveloped, a far cry from the more mature versions from 1969 and beyond. On one hand it is handicapped by Pigpen's monotonous eight-note organ riff, played over and over and over again—although it was that very riff that kept the Dead playing in time with one another when all of them (besides Pig) were tripping! However, "Saint Stephen" > "The Eleven" is, in a word, ferocious (although definitely not as amazing as the version on *Live Dead*). "Death Don't Have No Mercy," however, is arguably as polished and passionate as the version that appears on that seminal album.

The true magic of this recording starts on the second CD with a mind-melting suite of "That's It for the Other One" > "New Potato Caboose." "The Other One," nearly sixteen minutes long, is blisteringly hot, but the "New Potato Caboose" that follows defies accurate description. This fourteen-minute masterpiece is nothing less than a musical holy grail: a definitive version of the Grateful Dead at their transportational best. Starting as a beautifully poetic meditation set to melody, it rises to an indescribably joyous jam. Just when one thinks the band can't be any more inspired, Phil launches into an outrageous interpretation of "The Minute Waltz"—*simply unbelievable!* Unlike the previously better-known version of this jam (10/13/68, KMPX-FM broadcast), this one doesn't fall apart; it just keeps going and going and going. Then, as if this isn't already enough to blow the mind of even the most jaded Deadhead, Jerry launches into yet another jam that builds and builds and builds until he ends the whole magnificent performance with a perfect climax of cascading notes. One is left breathless, grinning ear to ear. It's even more impressive when compared with the "New Potato" played just two nights earlier at the Fillmore West, which was nowhere near as well developed. *Two from the Vault* is a must-have CD, simply because of this jam.

Next up is "Turn On Your Lovelight," as finger-snappin' funky and as well improvised as any other from 1968. Finally, the CD comes to a close with a rather weird version of "Morning Dew," during which the band's stage power is cut and the song ends abruptly, never to be finished.

JOHN R. DWORK

## 8/28/68
**Avalon Ballroom, San Francisco, California**

Good Morning, Li'l//Schoolgirl, Dark Star > Saint Stephen > Death Don't Have No Mercy, Turn On Your Lovelight

**Source:** AUD, **Quality:** B, **Length:** 1:00
**Highlights:** Good Mornin', Li'l Schoolgirl

Though all the instruments on this tape can be heard and identified, there's an FM-like static that hangs over the sound. The recording sounds very similar to the March 1968 Carousel Ballroom shows—only this tape has taken more hits (generations). If it's the same taper, then *please*—whoever you are (or were)—get in touch with us and tell us your story.

Bill Graham begins things in his own inimitable way: "Named after a code name that's like nine hundred years old by now—the grateful, Grateful Dead!" Of course. "Schoolgirl" is a psychedelic blues delight: Lesh and Garcia toss ideas back and forth like Day-Glo jellybeans. An exceptional version (despite a brief cut). "Dark Star" continues this trend: it's basically a trippy duet with minimal accompaniment. "Saint Stephen" is played very fast. "The Eleven" sounds overrehearsed, void of the risk taking that highlights the interesting versions. The Lesh-led segue into "Death Don't Have No Mercy," though, is downright sinister. But the song itself plods. "Turn On Your Lovelight" is barely average as the band sounds tired and ready to go home.

MICHAEL M. GETZ

## 9/2/68
**Betty Nelson's Organic Raspberry Farm, Sultan, Washington**

Dark Star > Saint Stephen > The Eleven//, Cryptical Envelopment > The Other One > Cryptical Reprise, Alligator > Caution Jam > Feedback

**Source:** SBD, **Quality:** B+, **Length:** 1:15
**Highlights:** The Eleven Jam, Cryptical, Alligator, Caution, Feedback

This tape serves as an early example of the Dead evolving into the *Live Dead*–styled form. Several of the jams obtain the magical essence so typical of that period. After an introduction, the band opens with a traditionally formed "Dark Star." Although somewhat short, only about ten minutes, the between-verse jams are quite intricate. Several meandering themes arise with Garcia leading like a leaf flowing down a stream. The following "Saint Stephen," uptempo and rousing, rips through the air like a thunderbolt. The "Eleven" jam is long and impressive. Kreutzmann and Hart, in particular, provide for a manic rhythm session with Weir and Lesh. Garcia somehow keeps the pace, and the result is several blistering jams. It eventually winds down and probably moves into "Death Don't Have No Mercy," but the tape fades out just before it begins.

August 20, 1968, is the first documented time the band played the omnipotent nexus of "Dark Star" > "Saint Stephen > "The Eleven" > "Death Don't Have No Mercy." This connection must have developed through some type of natural selection, very similar to how the human body naturally evolved an intricate biochemical cellular respiratory system—perfection through selection. "That's It for the Other One" fades into the opening lyrics of the "He Had to Die" section: it is a short version, but the jams just soar. And once again the rhythm is impressive. The "Alligator" > "Caution" > "Feedback" is probably the zenith of this tape, with deeply spaced and maniacal jams throughout. The "Caution" finale sounds like a volcano erupting. During the final "All you need!" chorus, Pigpen and Weir scream in unison while Lesh sings in a haunting bass voice—deranged!

ROBERT A. GOETZ

## 10/8/68
### Mickey Hart and the Hartbeats
### Matrix, San Francisco, California

**Set 1:** Clementine, The Eleven > Jam, Death Don't Have No Mercy[‡], The Seven, Dark Star > Cosmic Charlie[‡] > Jam
**Set 2:** Jam > The Other One Jam[*§], Jam[*§], Jam[*§], Baby Please Come Back[†], Jam[§]

[*] with Elvin Bishop, [†] Bishop vocal, [‡] Garcia vocal, [§] without Garcia

**Source:** SBD, **Quality:** A, **Length:** 3:00, **Genealogy:** MR > RR > C > PCM > DAT
**Highlights:** Dark Star > Cosmic Charlie, second set opening jam
**Comments:** All cuts are instrumental unless otherwise noted.

In late 1968, Jerry and Phil grew frustrated with what they saw as the technical limitations of Pigpen's and Weir's instrumental abilities. In interviews, both Garcia and Weir himself suggest that Weir and Pigpen were actually let go for a couple of months, although no Dead shows from this period seem to lack either member. However, Garcia, Mickey Hart, and (sometimes) Lesh took up residence at the tiny Matrix coffeehouse for a half dozen or so nights from October to December 1968 as Mickey Hart and the Hartbeats. In the process, they managed to create some of the most remarkable instrumental music played by these musicians. Much of the material consists of long instrumental versions (peppered with a few Garcia vocals) of familiar Dead material intermixed with free-form jams and guest appearances by other San Francisco musicians. Although these tapes are in wide circulation, many have appeared with one or more alternate (or completely erroneous) dates, or as tapes that combine material from two or more nights. Listed here are all of the nonoverlapping pieces of Hartbeats music in circulation that I am aware of: 10/8, 10/10, 10/30, 12/16, 12/24, and another jam segment labeled as ??/??/68. Dates used here are based on low-generation tapes received from careful and reliable sources, and correspond with two different sources of soundboard masters in the Dead's Vault.

This, the earliest identified Hartbeats performance, opens with an instrumental based on the rarely performed "Clementine," a Hunter-Garcia song with a long, complex melody that was recorded for, but left off of, *Aoxomoxoa*. The tune dissipates momentarily when Garcia stops, thinking his amp has gone out, but continues soon thereafter, moving into a high-speed version of "The Eleven"—with Garcia playing the vocal melody lines during the "numerology" part of the song—and eventually into "Death Don't Have No Mercy." A single-chord jam then opens up into a busy version of "The Seven," which never quite jells and eventually sputters to a stop. A relatively brief but tasty "Dark Star" jam abruptly jumps into a fast, raucous version of "Cosmic Charlie," another tune that was coming together in the studio at about the same time. The next piece is a speedy, Freddy King–style guitar blues jam that references the descending guitar figure that normally appeared in the middle of live versions of "Good Mornin', Li'l Schoolgirl."

The second set begins with a long, languid jam featuring Garcia and Jack Casady. A high point occurs late in the jam, when Casady starts playing a slow, stately Bolero-like melody over which Garcia starts with little stinging leads, moves into some furious single-note soloing, and winds down up with a coda of funky rhythmic chops. After this lengthy jam, Garcia leaves to make way for five blues jams featuring Elvin Bishop (whose band was originally scheduled to play at the Matrix that night) and the Hartbeats. The third jam is wild, with Bishop's crazed string-bending inspiring Casady to some equally uninhibited pyrotechnics. Bishop sings the slow blues, "Baby Please Come Back to Me," before the evening ends, somewhat anticlimactically, with another twelve-bar blues workout.

MICHAEL PARRISH

## 10/10/68

**Mickey Hart and the Hartbeats (Garcia, Hart, Kreutzmann, and Jack Casady)**

**Matrix, San Francisco, California**

**Set 1:** Jam, It's a Sin‡, Jam*, Look Over Yonder's Wall*†, New Potato Caboose
**Set 2:** Turn On Your Lovelight > Drums > Caution > The Other One > Jam with bells > Death Don't Have No Mercy‡, Dark Star > The Eleven > The Seven

* "Marvin" on harmonica, † "Marvin" vocal, ‡ Garcia vocal

**Source:** SBD, **Quality:** A, **Length:** 3:00, **Genealogy:** MR > RR > C > PCM > DAT
**Highlight:** The Seven
**Comments:** All cuts are instrumental unless otherwise indicated.

The evening opens with a lengthy, moody jam that commences with Garcia playing a distinctive, repeating guitar figure. Casady eventually takes over on bass, and the jam comes to an end with waves of soft guitar feedback over bass chording. Next is a rare Garcia vocal version of Marty Robbins' slow blues number, "It's a Sin." Then Garcia calls a harmonica player, "Marvin" (who is not Paul Butterfield, although he is, on some tapes, identified as such), up from the audience to sit in on a few tunes. The first of the three is based on the descending riff that usually appears between verses of "Good Mornin', Li'l Schoolgirl," and the third is a vocal version of "Look over Yonder's Wall." A wide-ranging improvisation follows, starting with the middle portion of "Clementine" and moving on to quote extensively from various parts of "New Potato Caboose."

A long continuous piece then begins with an ominously slow "Turn On Your Lovelight," which leads into the only drum duel among known Hartbeats tapes. This concludes with the rapid-fire "taketa-taketa" drum and vocal chant bit common to that era. A "Caution" jam leads into a long, somewhat aimless "Other One" flowing into a quiet space jam featuring bell-like percussion. This then flows into an apocalyptic "Death Don't Have No Mercy." The night concludes in fine fashion with a subdued "Dark Star" jam, leading into the Dead's two early tributes to strange time signatures: "The Eleven" followed by "The Seven." It is a testament to Casady's musicianship that he navigated through the heady changes of these pieces—notably the tricky, abrupt transition from "Eleven" to "Seven"—without mishap. He even managed to push Garcia, particularly during the middle of "The Eleven." The speedy rendition of "The Seven" is one of the most exciting versions in circulation of this rarely performed piece.

MICHAEL PARRISH

## 10/12/68

**Avalon Ballroom, San Francisco, California**

**Set 1:** Dark Star > Saint Stephen > The Eleven > Death Don't Have No Mercy
**Set 2:** Cryptical Envelopment > Drums > The Other One > Cryptical Reprise > New Potato Caboose > Jam One > Drums > Jam Two > Feedback//

**1. Source:** SBD, **Quality:** A, **Length:** 1:19, **Genealogy:** MR > DAT
**2. Source:** FM-SBD (KPFA), **Quality:** A, **Length:** 1:00 (thru Jam 1), **Genealogy:** MR > DAT
**3. Source:** FM-SBD (GDH 052), **Quality:** A, **Length:** 0:35 ("The Other One" > Jam 1), **Genealogy:** MR > DR
**Highlights:** Jam between post-Caboose drums and feedback

An indubitable authority has determined that this is 10/12/68, not 10/13/68—the night Jimi Hendrix showed up to sit in but was not asked onstage because he had stood up the Dead and Quicksilver at the Sausalito heliport the night before. Although it's a bummer that no known tape exists of the October 13 show, it would have been even more of a shame had it been the one time Hendrix jammed with the Dead.

Regardless, this hot show, 10/12/68, opens with a still somewhat young "Dark Star," glorious and full of energy. It features impressive jamming, mostly due to Garcia's peeling off the notes at a dizzying rate. With headphones, this "Star" is quite a trip. "Saint Stephen" begins with a somber air, then careens forward into

"The Eleven," which has unbelievable, rapidly intensifying energy, and an electric transition into an alternately soulful, haunting, and soaring "Death Don't Have No Mercy." Garcia then tells the crowd the band is going to "stop for about five minutes to get our hands dry. In the meantime, you can do whatever you like while we're waiting around." High on the possibilities, the crowd responds with high-pitched "Really, really?"s and an intrepid "Anything?" along with a sincere "Thank you, Mr. Garcia."

Maintaining their gripping intensity throughout "That's It for the Other One," the Dead then find their way into a sublime, psychedelic "New Potato Caboose." This is followed by the best part of the show: fifteen minutes "found" only in the mid-nineties. A sweet, wild, and beautiful jam struts into seven minutes of feedback ended by a cut, perhaps close to the end of the show. Prior to this addition, "New Potato Caboose" ended prematurely; this was, for many years, misattributed to the midnight curfew imposed upon the Avalon by the authorities.

BILL KRISTI

however, is strong, if relatively low-key, and Garcia's rapid-fire soloing is clearly its highlight.

The ten-minute "Dark Star" is simple and sweet, with muted gongs and rudimentary keyboards setting an almost devotional mood. The band then rocks strongly into a muscular "Saint Stephen," during which the three singers put in particularly energetic unison vocals that continue into the introduction to "The Eleven." This without a doubt rocks just as hard as its predecessor. A fast, amorphous jam eventually leads into an energized "Caution," the beginning of which finds Pigpen laying down some tasty organ licks before he starts to spit the vocals out. The "All you need!" section features more rocking, albeit ragged, vocal choruses before segueing into another rapid-fire Garcia solo, which eventually dissolves into a slow jam melting into a show-ending wash of "Feedback." Although this show may not be one of the Dead's most consistent performances of the time, this flawed tape is worth seeking out because of the raw, visceral nature of the performance.

MICHAEL PARRISH

---

### 10/20/68
#### Greek Theater, Berkeley, California

//Good Mornin', Li'l Schoolgirl, Turn On Your Lovelight, Dark Star > Saint Stephen > The Eleven > Caution > Feedback

**Source:** SBD, **Quality:** B, **Length:** 1:15
**Highlights:** Turn On Your Lovelight, the jam

In their second performance at what would become perhaps their most popular venue fifteen years later, the Dead performed an erratic set preserved on an equally problematic soundboard tape (which didn't surface until 1996). Although the tape's audio is excellent in spots, it suffers from speed fluctuations, reel squeaks, radical volume shifts in the mix, and dropouts. Things get underway with a ragged "Schoolgirl" that eventually establishes a strong, sloppy groove. A lone "Turn On Your Lovelight" jumps out in an unusual spot between "Schoolgirl" and the jam. Lesh introduces the tune by saying, "Now this one's for dancing." Tempo fluctuations in the recording of "Turn On Your Lovelight" render it all but unlistenable. The performance itself,

---

### 10/30/68
#### Mickey Hart and the Hartbeats (Garcia, Lesh, Kreutzmann, and Hart)
#### Matrix, San Francisco, California

**Set 1:** Dark Star > Death Letter Blues‡, The Other One > Saint Stephen Jam > Turn On Your Lovelight, Clementine > The Eleven > Death Don't Have No Mercy‡
**Set 2:** Jam*, Baby Please Come Back†, Clementine, Dark Star//

* with Elvin Bishop, † Bishop vocal, ‡ Garcia vocal

**Source:** SBD, **Quality:** A, **Length:** 3:00, **Genealogy:** MR > RR > DAT
**Highlights:** Jam > Death Letter Blues, Clementine
**Comments:** All selections are instrumental unless otherwise noted.

This seems to be the only full Hartbeats show in circulation with Phil Lesh playing bass, and it is probably the best example of the group jamming on the standard Dead repertoire of the time. As incredible a job as

Casady does on the other Hartbeats shows, it is still a revelation to hear Garcia build on Lesh's seemingly endless store of melodic ideas. The opener is a mellow, stratospheric "Dark Star" jam that meanders into an amorphous portion that is mostly extended Lesh improvisation. Ultimately, Garcia cranks up a nasty, fuzzy tone on his guitar, building a blues jam that flows into a short, speedy vocal version of Son House's "Death Letter Blues." After a bit of tuning, Lesh cranks out his patented "Other One" introductory riff to herald a long, intricate "Other One" jam. This abruptly changes into a loud, syncopated improvisation on the instrumental break in "Saint Stephen," and wraps up with a frenetic instrumental "Turn On Your Lovelight." After another lengthy pause, the Hartbeats groove into a slow, sensuous instrumental rendition of "Clementine" that shows how marvelous the melodic skeleton of this song really is, particularly the middle passage's insistent, repetitive bass figure. A sweet, low-key version of "The Eleven" gives way to an impassioned, set-closing "Death Don't Have No Mercy."

The second half of the show begins with Elvin Bishop, on second guitar, sitting in on a bittersweet, late-night improvisational jam that moves into conventional twelve-bar blues, during which Bishop and Garcia trade some remarkable leads. The dueling guitars continue into the next number, an energized version of "Baby Please Come Back to Me," which Bishop played on October 8. After Bishop's exit, the Hartbeats play around with another improvisation based on the middle of "Clementine." At the end of this, Garcia dismisses the audience's applause, saying, "That isn't necessary. We're here primarily to screw around, so don't expect anything that isn't screwing around. We will be screwing around, unless otherwise stated in advance." The last piece of music on this tape is another "Dark Star" jam, which cuts abruptly after about thirty minutes.

MICHAEL PARRISH

## 11/1/68
### The Silver Dollar Fair, Chico, California

Dark Star > Cryptical Envelopment > The Other One > Cryptical Reprise > New Potato Caboose//, //Caution > Feedback > We Bid You Goodnight

**Source:** SBD, **Quality:** A−, **Length:** 0:45
**Highlights:** Cryptical Reprise, Feedback

"Dark Star" is sung/told with a theatrical spin à la Rod Serling. Though some punctilious leads by Garcia drive the jam between verses, it never really gets out there; rather, it's an exercise in precision. "The Other One" continues this trend until Weir ignites the band with some ferocious, throat-scrapin' singing. Also, before doing the first verse, he goes "Yoo hoo" into the mike as if he's looking for a lost pet of some kind. The band hits a full stride during the "Cryptical" reprise. Toward the end Garcia does that fast, bluegrass-styled fingerpickin' that will become a staple in future "Dark Stars."

The segue into "New Potato" sounds like a door opening into another world—but it fades out before we can experience what lies behind it. A few bars of "Caution" cut in before dropping violently into a long, tumultuous "Feedback." A short but sincere "Bid You Goodnight" emerges as the kids from Chico take their hands from over their eyes and gratefully clap along.

MICHAEL M. GETZ

## 12/16/68
### Mickey Hart and the Hartbeats (Garcia, Hart, and Jack Casady)
### Matrix, San Francisco, California

**Set 1:** Jam
**Set 2:** Jam

**Source:** SBD, **Quality:** A, **Length:** 1:22
**Highlights:** The second set
**Comments:** Spencer Dryden sits in on the first set, David Getz on the second.

Possibly because of the absence of both Kreutzmann and Lesh, no familiar Dead material is played this evening. The first two sets are each extended jams containing some of the most inventive free-form improvisation from the Hartbeats shows. Spencer Dryden sits in for the first set, a slow jam that begins with conventional blues changes before delving into deep space and building up to a high-energy finish.

For the second jam, Big Brother's David Getz takes the second drum position for a slow, sensuous groove session with the same feel as contemporary "Dark Star" renditions, replete with a very *out there* jam during which Casady wildly flails away on his bass as Garcia solos with controlled feedback. They eventually move into a passage with the rhythmic pattern and chord progression that later becomes "Fire on the Mountain," before wrapping up with a happy little Caribbean melody.

MICHAEL PARRISH

---

### 12/24/68
#### Matrix, San Francisco, California

Jam, Feel It, Three O'Clock in the Morning, Mojo Worker, Jam

---

**Source:** SBD, **Quality:** A, **Length:** 1:30
**Highlights:** Three O'Clock in the Morning
**Personnel:** Jerry Garcia, Elvin Bishop, and Steve Miller with the Harvey Mandel Band

This tape, sometimes identified as a Hartbeats show and even as the third set of 12/16/68, consists (based on a label on the master reel) of an "open stage" jam featuring guitarists Garcia, Elvin Bishop, and Steve Miller, the keyboard player from Bishop's band, sitting in with the Harvey Mandel Band. The first piece on the tape is a tedious, thirty-five-minute jam in D minor that, nonetheless, is notable for some blistering feedback-drenched guitar work by Mandel, one of the best, and most underrated, guitarists in San Francisco at the time. Miller then sings a soulful "Feel It" from the Bishop band's repertoire, which is followed by Bishop's singing of a fast, funky blues, "Three O'Clock in the Morning," on which Garcia and Mandel trade rapid-fire leads. Miller sings another number, "Mojo Worker," before the evening concludes with another twelve-bar guitar jam.

MICHAEL PARRISH

---

### Fall/68 (?)
#### Unknown Location

//Jam > Cryptical Envelopment > The Other One > Cryptical Reprise > New Potato Caboose, Alligator > Caution//

---

**Source:** SBD, **Quality:** A−, **Length:** 0:45, **Genealogy:** MC > C
**Highlights:** New Potato Caboose

This tape, probably from the fall of '68, starts out with a short, pleasant jam out of (probably) "He Was a Friend of Mine." During a very laid-back "Other One," Garcia uncharacteristically allows Tom Constanten to strut a bit, even playing off him at times. This makes for an interesting, well-dispersed version. The "Cryptical" reprise perks the band up before descending perfectly into an inspired and even well-sung "New Potato." The portion of "Alligator" that follows is sleek. Garcia's leads are way, way out there though he seems a bit isolated from the rest of the band. The cut occurs during the middle of the second jam, so who knows how it turns out.

MICHAEL M. GETZ

---

### Undated/68
#### Mickey Hart and the Hartbeats (Garcia, Lesh, Hart, and Kreutzmann)
#### Matrix, San Francisco, California

Jam//

---

**Source:** SBD, **Quality:** B, **Length:** 0:20
**Highlights:** All

This mysterious fragment consists of another version of the jam that opens 10/30/68. It is notable for Garcia's inspired and frenetic soloing, which has a rather unusual Latin feel.

MICHAEL PARRISH

## 12/??/68
### Alembic Studios, San Francisco, California

//Turn On Your Lovelight, Dark Star > Saint Stephen (x) > The Eleven (x)

**Source:** SBD, **Quality:** B, **Length:** 1:00
**Highlights:** Dark Star
**Comments:** This studio rehearsal tape also circulates labeled "11/6/68 Studio Sessions."

This rehearsal breaks in on a brief "Lovelight" with vocals by Garcia, and an extremely rough yet funky organ track in the background. The "Dark Star," although rudimentary, is not at all unimpressive, featuring sparkling leads from Garcia and thick, lush bass support from Lesh. Focusing primarily on perfecting the song's structure and correct chord changes, this "Star" slowly unravels itself note by note, before peaking prior to the final verse, when Garcia and Lesh hit an eruptive passage that is absolutely delightful, lasting around three minutes before the final verse and clumsy wrap-up.

And then the tide changes. . . .

After stumbling several times on both the final verse and the bridge of "Saint Stephen," the band falls flat on its face during "The Eleven," going through several takes, weak on vocal harmonies, weaker on chord changes, and absolutely pathetic on the jam. Young and persistent, the band painstakingly goes through try after try of the various sections, part by part, section by section, working diligently to achieve that sound that would eventually be perfected only a few months later. At various points, Lesh can faintly be heard barking and scolding at his bandmates, perhaps an arrogant illustration but, as your ears will hear, completely justified. It's an understandably complicated piece of material, which we must begrudgingly admit becomes a trifle more bearable with each take.

BRIAN DYKE

## 1968 or 1969
### Golden State Recorders, San Francisco, California

Documentary

**Source:** FM, **Quality:** B, **Length:** 1:30
**Highlights:** Lesh saying, "I feel that we did a horrible job of raiding the Quicksilver because if we had been really Indians and we had really been raiding them, they would have killed us all. They had guns, man!"
**Comments:** Produced by Michael Wanger and Vance Frost.

This radio documentary contains a wide assortment of interviews, not only from members of the Grateful Dead, but from other prominent Bay Area figures as well. Although there are a few minor factual inaccuracies, this provides a solid background in early Grateful Dead history.

Aside from the pair of 1964 Mother McCree's Uptown Jug Champions tracks, the bulk of the background music is unremarkable.

BRIAN DYKE

# 1969

*By the beginning of 1969, "Dark Star," "Saint Stephen," and "The Eleven" had become fully developed as quintessential Grateful Dead concert material. The combination was played almost nightly, and for the first several months of the year reached incredible peaks nearly every time. However, the repetition of this material, nearly to the exclusion of the band's other material, probably served to drain the interest of the musicians over time. This result was likely no matter how improvised the songs were and what peaks were reached. In the preceding year, the band had all but discarded much of its material from the first two years. By April, however, the band began to reintroduce some of this older material into its repertoire. Also getting mixed into a regular rotation was material from* Aoxomoxoa, *the very odd album released in June 1969. By this time, the band had the ability to careen instantly from one song* into another and, with the expanded collection of songs, created some amazing musical moments. Shows like April 5 at the Avalon Ballroom and May 24 in West Hollywood, Florida, exemplify these attempts to break out of the mold they had created. Adding to the richness of the Dead's sound at this time was the fanciful keyboard playing of Tom (T. C.) Constanten. From his first appearance with the band on November 23, 1968, in Athens, Ohio, T. C. brought with him a wealth of knowledge of classical and avante-garde styles, as well as those from old ragtime and minstrel shows. As a result, he was able to mesh perfectly with the music whether it meant soaring the psychedelic stratosphere of "Dark Star" or bouncing in the calliope rhythms of "Dupree's Diamond Blues."

With seven people now in the band, each bringing their own depth of knowledge and experience in some form of particularly American music, the Dead were able to call on increasingly greater combinations of musical influences in their performances. Yet it all remained undeniably American. On June 11, the Dead, minus Pigpen, T.C., and Kreutzmann, played an extraordinary show at the California Hall in San Francisco. Together with David Nelson and John Dawson, old friends from pre-Warlocks days, they played a long acoustic set of old and new covers ranging from country classics, to Everly Brothers pop hits, to old railroad songs. Garcia had already introduced a couple of acoustic numbers into the band's set, "Dupree's Diamond Blues" and "Mountains of the Moon." By mid-year, Garcia and Weir were exerting a country roots-based influence into the music. Weir developed his cowboy persona, and Garcia explored the musical style that had been his forte in the early sixties. New covers like "Silver Threads and Golden Needles," "Ol' Slewfoot," and "Green, Green Grass of Home," were being introduced as well, together with new originals with similar themes such as "Dire Wolf" and "Casey Jones."

This trend continued throughout the summer and into the fall. The lyrics to most of Hunter's new songs contained themes of folklore or a harkening to a simpler time, in keeping in sync with the movement out of the cities of many of the Dead's contemporaries from the early psychedelic scene. Beginning in September and continuing into November and December, a great change occurred in the band's concerts. The evolution away from the nightly psychedelic crescendos began and "Uncle John's Band" was born. "Dark Star" and "Saint Stephen" were now played only every third or fourth show at best, and "The Eleven" was very nearly played out; it would only be performed a handful times after the end of the year. In their place came songs of the new style, like "High Time," "Easy Wind," and "Black Peter," which would appear on Workingman's Dead. Some songs not seen since 1967 also reappeared, like "Dancin' in the Street," as well as new covers like "Hard to Handle" and "Good Lovin'." The pace of shows had slowed down significantly. Many shows were now a collection of individually crafted songs with few of the wild segues seen earlier in the year. One pleasant result of the Dead's new style was that Pigpen continued and even expanded his role as the show stopper, developing "Good Lovin'" and "Lovelight" into huge events and introducing his own brand of improvised rapping. Much of the emphasis had shifted to deliver well-crafted songs and vocal harmonies, and this culminated on December 19 at the Fillmore with the first entirely acoustic set performed by the Dead.

Throughout the year, the crew was consistently taping nearly every show. The fan base had grown to nationwide proportions, and the band was a favorite on college campuses. Most shows in the major cities were taped by the audience; however, the equipment and techniques were still insufficient to get consistently good quality tapes made. The exceptions include May 3 at Winterland, December 10 at the Thelma Theater in Los Angeles, and June 22 in Central Park in New York. For years, soundboard tapes were few and far between and weren't especially representative of the normal show fare. Starting in the late eighties, however, a veritable flood of tapes from 1969, of varying quality, appeared in circulation, some from pristine reels, others from noisy, multigeneration cassettes with merely average, but not crisp, dynamics. Most were far more listenable than the ragtag collection that had preceded them. The music they contained, though, was astounding and far more revealing from a historical viewpoint. From the magnificent Fillmore West shows in February and the wild shows in April, May, and June, and March to the Thelma Theater shows in December, tapes from this year will remain among the most sought after of any in the Dead's career.

Tapes to get: 2/22, 2/28, 3/1, 4/5–4/6, 4/21–4/22, 5/24, 7/11, 9/6, 11/8, 11/15, 12/12, 12/30.

## 1/26/69
### Avalon Ballroom, San Francisco, California

**Set 1:** Cryptical Envelopment > Drums > The Other One > Cryptical Envelopment > Clementine > Death Don't Have No Mercy
**Set 2:** //The Eleven > Turn On Your Lovelight

1. **Source:** SBD, **Quality:** A/A–, **Length:** 1:15, **Genealogy:** MR > C > C > DAT
2. **Source:** FM-SBD (GDH 300), **Quality:** A+, **Length:** 0:15 (Clementine)

**Highlights:** All, especially The Eleven > Turn On Your Lovelight (the same ones that appear on *Live Dead*)

By and large, Deadheads are notorious for holding strong opinions on the merits of this show or that, whether date A is superior to date B, etc. When talk turns to official albums, this can get even more pointed. People often hold opinions entrenched in years of glorious association or dismissal. There is an exception to this: I have never met a Deadhead who does not like *Live Dead*. For just about everyone, this album contains the essence of the Dead in incandescent improvisatory mode, served up with an overwhelming feeling of immediacy, of being in the midst of some absolutely vital creation with no obvious signs of manipulation after the fact. Of course, the fact that it's actually constructed from several different shows somehow doesn't detract from its documentary qualities. The Avalon, 1/26/69, gave us some of the major reasons for that album's success: "The Eleven" and "Turn On Your Lovelight." By checking out this superb show, you can discover just what preceded those sublime performances.

The opening "Cryptical Envelopment" > "The Other One" is played with a sense of control, flowing along an eccentric circular rhythmic path in a measured way, without losing any dynamic power in the process. The final "Cryptical" jam stretches out nicely with Garcia's guitar and Constanten's organ trading phrases over waves of bass and drums, alternately winding up the inner tensions of the song and releasing them in flurries of notes and concise phrases.

"Clementine" is a rarely performed number, yet delightful as it is, it's not difficult to see why it was dropped. Structurally complex, it has much in common with *Aoxomoxoa*-era material, but its skipping jazz rhythm sets it apart from anything else in the Dead's repertoire of the time. Paradoxically, at this, the height of their full-on, pure psychedelic improvisation phase, the Dead were about to make a great stylistic change: a move toward song-oriented material where the likes of "Clementine," with its serpentine twists and turns and a space-jazz ambience, wouldn't fit. This is a shame, as the song is really rather special, even if half the time you get the feeling that Garcia hasn't a clue as to how the melody should go or just which words make up the lyrics. A jam at the song's end drifts into a measured "Death Don't Have No Mercy" that, though less tortured than other versions, still burns with emotion and builds gracefully toward its powerfully sung conclusion.

From the second set comes some of the most affecting music we've ever heard: "The Eleven" > "Turn On Your Lovelight" as used on *Live Dead*. Sure, for picky Deadheads, it's easy to point to other versions of these numbers that are longer, or spacier, or meet some such other categoric imperative, but it's necessary to recognize that these versions have an intensity equaled by few others and are graced with an elegance matched by none. Certainly, the overwhelming mythic status afforded the material on *Live Dead* makes it next to impossible for long-time devotees to view it objectively, but rest assured, the playing here represents an unassailable peak of achievement in the history of the Grateful Dead. Although there are other shows that reach, even surpass, its level of musicianship, but none will affect you as profoundly as these tracks as included on *Live Dead*.

— PAUL BODENHAM

## 2/2/69
### Guthrie Theater, Minneapolis, Minnesota

//Good Mornin', Li'l Schoolgirl, Dark Star > Saint Stephen > The Eleven//, //Death Don't Have No Mercy, Cryptical Envelopment > The Other One > Cryptical Reprise > Turn On Your Lovelight

**Source:** SBD, **Quality:** B+, **Length:** 1:25, **Genealogy:** MR > C > C > C > DAT

**Highlights:** The Eleven, The Other One > Lovelight

It seems strange to refer to a Dead show, especially a 1969 one, as "concise," but that's the word that springs to mind when listening to this tape. Here we have a good portion of the Dead's 1969 live repertoire performed in less than ninety minutes, and there is hardly a note wasted during the set. Much of the show is a dramatic flow of dynamic ideas between Garcia and the drummers, who constantly pass rhythms and phrases across the stage. The mix is slightly muddy, and for most of the time the contributions of Phil and Bobby are rather difficult to isolate. Curiously enough, T.C.'s organ frequently cuts through, sending clusters of keyboard notes spinning out of the thunder. There is nothing out of the ordinary as far as arrangements go; there are no new twists to the standard architecture of an early 1969 set. However, it's very much a high-energy '69 show with Garcia, Hart, and Kreutzmann especially displaying a keen ear for each other's ideas. The interplay and speedy changes of direction here are quite extraordinary, being closer to the inspired group creations of later years—say '73–'74.

Halfway through "Turn On Your Lovelight" Pigpen shouts, "Talk to me!" and the band does just that. In tongues. Listen up.

PAUL BODENHAM

*Pigpen, 1969* (photo credit: Fred Ordower)

---

### ☸ 2/14/69 ☸
### Electric Factory, Philadelphia, Pennsylvania

**Set 1:** //Good Mornin', Li'l Schoolgirl, //Dark Star > Saint Stephen > The Eleven > Turn On//Your Lovelight
**Set 2:** Morning Dew, Cryptical Envelopment > Drums > The Other One > Cryptical Reprise > Death Don't Have No Mercy, Alligator > Caution > We Bid You Goodnight.

**Source:** SBD, **Quality:** B+/A–, **Length:** 3:10, **Genealogy:** MR > C > C > DAT
**Highlights:** Saint Stephen, That's It for the Other One

---

A very washed-out version of this soundboard emerged in the early nineties batch of 1968 and 1969 soundboards. In 1994, a significant upgrade began circulating. This is not one of the greats from 1969. Still, it's an interesting show. The band is clearly warming up for the recording of *Live Dead*. Many of the arrangements we've come to know and love are being hammered into place. The show also gives us a glimpse at the remarkable transformations the band was working on "Dark Star." We still hear many traces from 1968. T.C. echoes Pigpen's organ part at the start. Jerry's opening leads could have come straight from the Hartbeats. Although "Space" doesn't find a place in this jam, the band does introduce the "revolving jam" to "Dark Star" just before the second verse. It sounds as if they are still feeling their way around this jam. T.C. nicely frames the second verse, which moves smoothly into a terrific "Saint Stephen." This one is hot, every bit the wild romp of *Live Dead*. "The Eleven" and "Turn On Your Lovelight" are fine, very close to their *Live Dead* arrangements. "Turn On Your Lovelight" suffers from an internal chop. The band loosens up considerably in the second set. An elegant "Morning Dew" gives birth to a powerful jam. Then comes a potent and freewheeling "That's It for the Other One." This is what I listen to this show for. After Bob muffs the "Spanish Lady" entrance, the band builds a wide-ranging jam between the verses. The "Cryptical" reprise jam opens with Jerry's guitar sweetly singing, then roars after the vocals end. Jerry, Phil, and T.C. build to a climax, then they quiet and slow to "Death Don't Have No Mercy." This is fairly sleepy until Jerry's fiery solo. The show closes with another wonderful romp through "Alligator" and "Caution." "Alligator" features some improvised lyrics after "stumbles and hops." The transition jam features a strong three-way conversation between Jerry, Phil, and T.C. After "Caution" is wailing and moaning, feedback almost returns to the "Caution" theme but instead quiets and leaves us with a short "We Bid You Goodnight."

HUGH BARROLL

## 2/21/69
### The Dream Bowl, Vallejo, California

Good Mornin', Li'l Schoolgirl, Doin' That Rag, Dark Star > Saint Stephen > The Eleven > Turn On Your Lovelight, Morning Dew

**Source:** SBD, **Quality:** B+, **Length:** 1:40, **Genealogy:** MR > C > C > DAT
**Highlights:** The whole tape

A monster, monster, monster of a performance! Fierce jamming throughout. The sound quality is pretty good as well. "Doin' That Rag" ends oddly with Phil screaming, "Hey You MOTHERFUCKERS!" The "Dark Star," during which Garcia's guitar *howls,* is one of the few pre-1970 versions in which Bobby's guitar playing is extremely noticeable in the mix. The height of passion on this tape, however, flowers during "The Eleven," which seems to go on forever. "Turn On Your Lovelight" rises and falls again and again as the Dead intentionally bake a tasty musical soufflé brimming with delicious Garcia licks and Pigpen raps. This is one juicy tape—don't pass it up!

JOHN R. DWORK

## 2/22/69
### Dream Bowl, Vallejo, California

**Set 1:** Dupree's Diamond Blues > Mountains of the Moon > Dark Star > Cryptical Envelopment > Drums > The Other One > Cryptical Reprise > Death Don't Have No Mercy
**Set 2:** Doin' That Rag > Saint Stephen > The Eleven > Turn On Your Lovelight

**1. Source:** SBD, **Quality:** B+, **Length:** 2:00, **Genealogy:** MR > C > C > DAT

**2. Source:** FM-SBD (GDH190 & 191), **Quality:** A, **Length:** "Mountains of the Moon" through "The Other One," "Doin' That Rag" through "Turn On Your Lovelight," **Genealogy:** MR > DAT
**Highlights:** Cryptical Reprise, Death Don't Have No Mercy

While not quite on the ferocious level of the previous night's performance this show is still a hot one. The jamming really heats up as they go back into the "Cryptical" reprise—the climax is immense. The "Death Don't Have No Mercy" that follows may be the best version I've ever heard. Be careful if you're transferring this from DAT to cassette as the jam is too long to fit on even a hundred-minute tape. (I suggest putting the "Doin' That Rag" > "Eleven" > "Turn On Your Lovelight" on a second tape.)

JOHN R. DWORK

## 2/27–3/2/69
### Fillmore West, San Francisco, California

These four nights at Market and Van Ness stand as a landmark of sorts in the canon of live Dead performances. In the nineties, it is hard to imagine a four-night run during which both "Dark Star" > "Saint Stephen" > "The Eleven" and the "That's It for the Other One" suite would be played every night, but that's exactly what happened during this run. One or both of the middle nights of the stand, 2/28/69 and 3/1/69, are on many tapers' top-ten lists, and the Thursday show gave us the archetypal "Dark Star" > "Saint Stephen" that made it onto *Live Dead*. Whether it was the phase of the moon, the outstanding billing in which they were paired—with British folk gods Pentangle and the Sir Douglas Quintet—or the knowledge that the shows were being recorded for a live album, the band performed at the top of their game for four nights running.

## 2/27/69
### Fillmore West, San Francisco, California

**Set 1:** Good Mornin', Li'l Schoolgirl, Doin' That Rag, Cryptical Envelopment > Drums > The Other One > Cryptical Reprise
**Set 2:** Dark Star > Saint Stephen

1. **Source:** SBD, **Quality:** B **Length:** 0:40 ("Schoolgirl" through "Cryptical Reprise").
2. **Source:** CD (*Live Dead*), **Quality:** A, **Length:** 0:30 ("Dark Star" > "Saint Stephen"), **Genealogy:** CD
**Highlights:** Dark Star > Saint Stephen

Only a relatively muddy fragment of the Thursday show's first set is in circulation. After the first of a weekend of bizarre Bill Graham introductions ("The only group in the business who can drive you insane and still make it all worthwhile"), the band tore into a convincing version of "Schoolgirl," a fairly routine opener for the time, with Pigpen going wild on harmonica. An energetic, good-humored "Doin' That Rag" follows. The board concludes with the least focused of the three versions we have of the run's takes of "That's It for the Other One." This one kicks into high gear following the vocal introduction with a long, linear Garcia solo. It ends rather abruptly, without returning to the "Cryptical" vocal conclusion, as some high-energy, spiraling guitar figures melt away into a soft wash of feedback and Weir produces ringing sounds reminiscent of Big Ben's chimes.

All we have of set 2 is what most tapers consider the archetypal versions of "Dark Star" > "Saint Stephen." On the album, the airy "Dark Star" fades in from the bittersweet melody of the open-ended conclusion of "Mountains of the Moon," moving into the bewitching extraterrestrial landscape of one of the most elegant "Dark Star"s ever performed. Certainly longer, more intense, and stranger versions exist, but this quietly surreal, relatively slow version, with Garcia's buttery guitar lines, Phil's loping bass, and T.C.'s understated keyboards, was an entirely justifiable choice for the band's first live album. The middle part has a chamber music feel rare in this song, thanks in large part to Constanten's baroque improvisations. A particularly sweet vocal on the second verse led into the familiar ascending bass segment that, in a short burst of "Feedback," led into the muscular, extremely well-sung (and occasionally screamed) version of "Saint Stephen," which again is distinguished by T.C.'s swirling organ. At this point, we can only imagine what the rest of this jam might have sounded like.

MICHAEL PARRISH

## 2/28/69
### Fillmore West, San Francisco, California

**Set 1:** //Morning Dew, Good Mornin', Li'l Schoolgirl, Doin' That Rag, King Bee > Turn On Your Lovelight
**Set 2:** Cryptical Envelopment > The Other One > Cryptical Reprise > Dark Star > Saint Stephen// > //The Eleven > Death Don't Have No Mercy, Alligator > Drums > Alligator > Caution > Feedback > We Bid You Goodnight

**Source:** SBD, **Quality:** A, **Length:** 2:50, **Genealogy:** MR > C > C > DAT. **Second Set:** MR > RR (3¾ ips) > RR (7½ ips) > PCM > DAT. **Last Set:** Unknown
**Highlights:** King Bee, and the entire second set

The Friday night show, at nearly three hours, was an extremely long show for 1969. The soundboard tape starts a bit after the start of the weekend's sole "Morning Dew," a soulful, energized version that set a ferocious groove that was maintained, and built upon, for

*At the Fillmore West 3/1/69* (photo credit: Michael Parrish)

# Reviews: February 1969

the rest of the night. The rest of the first set was mostly Pigpen's show. Another ripping "Schoolgirl" was again followed by "Doin' That Rag." "King Bee" is dark and lumbering, with swooping bass lines, and leads right into the set closer, a relatively mellow "Turn On Your Lovelight."

Bill Graham introduced the band for the second set as "The last of the Gay Desperadoes." Weir screams as Garcia counts down to a long, cascading version of "That's It for the Other One," which again is terminated by an instrumental passage that decreases in volume to a whisper, and then gives way to the familiar opening figure of "Dark Star." Friday's "Star" is, like the performances of the two subsequent nights, very much cut from the same cloth as Thursday's. Friday's is markedly more subdued; it features Mickey's hand percussion more prominently, and the bass and keyboards are much less evident. "Saint Stephen" is energized, if not quite as manic as the previous night's version. A tape cut excises the end of "Saint Stephen" and the very beginning of "The Eleven," which is executed flawlessly, with Garcia and Lesh thrusting and parrying at a breathtaking pace. A meandering transitional passage gives way to an emotional "Death Don't Have No Mercy." Although the audience had more than gotten their three bucks' worth by this point, the highlight of Friday's show came in the forty-minute jam that wrapped up the show. "Alligator" starts relatively sedately but, after being bisected by a short but furious drum duet, evolves into an incredibly speedy instrumental passage as the rest of the band tries their best to keep pace with the pumped-up percussionists. The jam builds until both Garcia and Weir are ripping out chords as fast

*At the Fillmore West 3/1/69* (photo credit: Michael Parrish)

as they can, dropping into an absolutely amazing "Caution," with Pigpen's urgent vocal matching the intensity of the instrumentalists. Near the end of the instrumental passage, the band—incredibly—speeds up until guitars, bass, and the ricocheting drums create an apocalyptic din that dissolves into a long, but considerably more sedate, passage of "Feedback." A brief, sloppy snippet of "We Bid You Goodnight" is marred by some grating static from one of the musician's reverb units, which prompted Garcia to sign off by saying, "Goodnight from all the electronic mice."

MICHAEL PARRISH

---

### 3/1/69
**Fillmore West, San Francisco, California**

**Set 1:** Cryptical Envelopment > The Other One > Cryptical Reprise > New Potato Caboose > Doin' That Rag > Cosmic Charlie
**Set 2:** Dupree's Diamond Blues > Mountains of the Moon, Dark Star > Saint Stephen > The Eleven//> Turn on Your Lovelight//
**Encore:** Hey Jude

---

**1. Source:** SBD, **Quality:** A, **Length:** 2:30, **Genealogy:** (Set 1) MR > C > DAT. (Set 2) MR > C > C > DAT
**2. Source:** FM-SBD (DHH 47), **Quality:** A, **Length:** Dark Star through The Eleven.
**Highlights:** Set 1, Saint Stephen > The Eleven

Little did I know that, when I conned my parents into driving me up to San Francisco to finally see the Grateful Dead for the first time, that I would be witness to one of the band's peak performances. Even though I only heard the first set (the folks picked me up at the witching hour), I witnessed an intensity of purpose that night that was rarely, if ever, equaled in the ensuing quarter-century of shows. Following a rocking set by Frumious Bandersnatch (subbing that night for the Sir Douglas Quintet) and a luminous, sit-down acoustic set by Pentangle, Bill Graham introduced the band as "The American version of the Japanese film, *Magnificent Seven*," and the band tore into one of the most amazing versions of "That's It for the Other One" ever, a textbook example of X-chemistry from which my poor brain has never recovered. Particularly notable during the entire night was Phil's supple improvisation; as was so often the case, the rest of the band followed his lead. A jagged guitar figure at the end drops down into the quiet beginning of a real rarity, one of the last live performances of "New Potato Caboose." This piece was difficult to execute live, but the Saturday version fulfilled, and exceeded, the potential of the *Anthem* version, which I consider one of the Dead's finest hours on record. In the middle of "New Potato," Phil embarks on a frenetic (but frustratingly out of tune) bass excursion that leads back into the driving instrumental coda. This in turn builds to a peak, giving way to another vigorous "Doin' That Rag," which leads, without a missed beat, into a supercharged version of "Cosmic Charlie," which emerges through a blast of Chuck Berry–derived riffing. Whew! In one of its earliest concert appearances, "Charlie" charged along at its original speedy tempo and cadence, more of a punk song than the mellow rumination it became on *Aoxomoxoa* and beyond.

For years I was haunted by Weir's parting words after the opening set—"We'll be back to do a second set later—a long one"—wondering what I had missed. When the soundboards of this show finally circulated in the mid-eighties, it showed he had been true to his word. In what was a rather common conceit for the time, the band opened (after yet another perfectly goofy Graham intro: "The Great High Hope"), with a spry, acoustic "Dupree's," replete with Constanten's amusement park keyboards. This leads into a long, spacy "Mountains of the Moon," on which T.C.'s keyboard sound mutates into that of a harpsichord. "Dark Star" has a denser texture than those of previous nights, thanks to the prominence of Weir's structural chording and T.C.'s organ. Weir was full of beans on the exuberant "Stephen," screaming and quipping, "Except in California!" after "One man gathers what another man spills." What I consider the run's best version of "The Eleven" starts with an introduction featuring fine vocals and some nice rudimentary drumming, leading into a short bass-heavy jam out of which emerges, at a relatively speedy tempo, the body of the song, with Garcia, Lesh, and Constanten jockeying for melody lines. A dramatic moment, sadly cut on the soundboard, occurs when the rest of the band drops out and Garcia solos briefly, then introduces the melody of "Turn On Your Lovelight," with everyone else dropping in hot on his heels. "Turn On Your Lovelight" is adrenaline-laced, full of dramatic cordial stabs and more screaming from Weir. An intense middle passage features a short Pigpen rap and an extended section where Garcia and Weir traded ringing E chords that fade down before building back into the song's typically big finish. At a loss for an encore selection, the band opted for a sloppy, ad-hoc version of "Hey Jude," with Pigpen taking the lead and the guitarists falling in on some painfully off-key background harmonies. Undoubtedly fun to hear at the show, "Jude" makes for somewhat painful listening after the fact, an anticlimactic conclusion to an otherwise extraordinary performance.

MICHAEL PARRISH

---

### 3/2/69
**Fillmore West, San Francisco, California**

**Set 2:** Dark Star > Saint Stephen > The Eleven > Turn On Your Lovelight//

---

1. **Source:** SBD, **Quality:** A, **Length:** 0:45
2. **Source:** FM-SBD (GDH 387), **Quality:** A, **Length:** "Dark Star" through "Saint Stephen"

**Highlights:** Dark Star, The Eleven

Only a fragment of the second-set jam of this show circulates, albeit in a very fine quality soundboard. What would be, in a different context, a stellar set pales somewhat in comparison to those of the previous three nights, but only slightly. Somehow avoiding another Graham intro (Garcia gleefully remarks, "Free turf"), the band dives headlong into another "Dark Star" that is very much the sibling of those played on the other three nights, but dominated by Garcia's fat guitar sound. A relatively subdued "Saint Stephen" follows. "The Eleven" is smooth and melodic, lacking some of the intensity of the preceding nights, but featuring an extended jam with some particularly tasty Garcia-Lesh interplay that leads right into "Turn On Your Lovelight," which cuts early, at the drum break.

MICHAEL PARRISH

---

### 3/15/69
**Hilton Hotel, San Francisco, California**

Hard to Handle, Good Mornin', Li'l Schoolgirl, Dark Star > Saint Stephen > The//Eleven > Turn On Your Lovelight

---

**Source:** SBD, **Quality:** B+, **Length:** 1:15
**Comments:** Fair-to-middling sound quality with a bias toward one channel.
**Highlights:** Saint Stephen, The Eleven > Turn On Your Lovelight

Being charitable I'd have to say that the opener, "Hard to Handle," verges on a complete mess. It's sloppy in the extreme and has contains fluffs and fumbles galore, which a valiant effort by Pigpen cannot hope to overcome. "Schoolgirl" is an attempt at redemption, but Garcia's guitar, all angles and abrasive surfaces, gives a sense of trying too hard, and the result isn't really up to much. However, the classic song sequence that follows is another thing entirely. It's as if the band tries to relax during the beginning of "Dark Star" and await a favorable visitation from their collective muse. This unspoken desire to let the inspiration arise without being forced works a treat and eventually pays off with some fine playing.

The "Dark Star" is a relatively concise reading of the modes and themes of the arrangement we know so well from *Live Dead,* but it would be fair to say that it doesn't catch fire like some versions of this era. "Saint Stephen" is tight, in complete contrast to the R&B covers earlier in the set. The band has by now definitely found its feet, and as it moves smoothly into "The Eleven," you just *know* that something magical is going

*Fillmore West, 3/1/69* (photo credit: Michael Parrish)

to happen. Well, it does, but you have to wait for it as the beginning of this version is more competent than inspired. However, toward the middle of the jam someone up in Heaven pushes all the right buttons and . . . BOOOOM! we're off! A surge in the cosmic power supply just about doubles the energy and the level of creativity; a tidal wave of pure, unadulterated joy propels us into a short but perfect "Turn On Your Lovelight," where at last everything is as it should be.

This transformation from floundering bar band to Allah's cosmic messengers in just over an hour is an extraordinary spectacle, and it's worth wading through the stodge at the beginning in order to fully appreciate the end result.

PAUL BODENHAM

## 3/27/69
### Merced, California

**Set 1:** Good Mornin', Li'l Schoolgirl, Dark Star > Saint Stephen > The Eleven//, //Death Don't Have No Mercy > Turn On Your Lovelight
**Set 2:** Cryptical Envelopment > Drums > The Other One > Cryptical Reprise

**Source:** SBD, **Quality:** A–, **Length:** 1:15, **Genealogy:** MC > PCM > RR > PCM
**Highlights:** Dark Star > Turn On Your Lovelight

This is a slightly hissy soundboard that surfaced around 1991 as part of an unusually large batch of 1968 and 1969 soundboards. On the road to Las Vegas, the band makes a side trip to the verdant Central Valley and treats the good people of Merced to an excellent show. We have almost all of this show, although "The Eleven" is cut and T.C. is practically inaudible. Pigpen storms out with a raw and bluesy "Schoolgirl." His harp is in fine form. A snaky Pigpen rap leads into the jam. Next up is a warning about the electronic gnats (relatives of the electronic mice, no doubt). Then a wonderful twenty-three-minute "Dark Star" greets us. The initial jamming stays close to the "Dark Star" theme, while voyaging through elegant variations. A piercing Jerry lead brings us to the first verse. After the verse, gongs set the tone for a brief "Space"/"Feedback" section. Jerry, Phil, and T.C. reestablish the "Dark Star" thread, then, with Bobby, set up a circular jam. A quiet section ends when Jerry awakes and escalates the energy. The jam peaks, then quietly spaces out. A spacy lead guitar wanders well out, then returns for the second verse. The delicate transition leads to a stomping "Saint Stephen," with a powerful jam careening nearly out of control. "High Green Chilly" suffers from T.C.'s inaudibility. The fifteen minutes we get of "The Eleven" are a delight. Before the verse, Phil and Jerry favor us with an extended dialogue, repeatedly building toward the verse and each time finding a new way to escape. After the verse, Jerry is on top of a high-energy jam that builds up to "The Eleven" theme, then quiets and slows. After the quiet jam, a high-energy jam starts to form just as the tape chops. After a chopped beginning, "Death Don't Have No Mercy" generates two powerful and jagged Jerry solos. The band then bounces into a classic '69 "Turn On Your Lovelight"—twenty-two uncut minutes of sheer delight. After breaking for some Cokes, the band opens and closes the second set with "That's It for the Other One." It's a powerhouse version that doesn't break new ground. It features a high-energy revolving jam that is nicely moving into "Feedback" when the band abruptly stops. With the house lights rudely turned on, the show ends.

HUGH BARROLL

## 3/29/69
### Ice Palace, Las Vegas, Nevada

Morning Dew, Good Mornin', Li'l Schoolgirl, Doin' That Rag, Dark Star > Saint Stephen > The Eleven > Turn On Your Lovelight

**Source:** SBD, **Quality:** A–, **Length:** 1:20, **Genealogy:** MR > C > C > DAT
**Highlights:** Dark Star, The Eleven

Only a few weeks after their great four-night stand at the Fillmore West, which produced the majority of the *Live Dead* album, the Dead play their only ever gig at this big Las Vegas casino. In 1969 this could not have been the most sympathetic of venues. Although Pigpen is rock-steady on "Schoolgirl" and Garcia is playing well throughout, ably assisted by Phil, the band as a whole is somewhat scrappy on its "Star" > "Stephen" > "Eleven" > "Turn On Your Lovelight" sequence when compared with the myriad of excellent versions that litter this period.

Nevertheless there are moments of real excitement, as when Garcia takes off after the first verse of "Dark Star" and in his intense and very fast dueting with Phil on "The Eleven." Pigpen, however, never really gets a handle on what is a relatively short "Turn On Your Lovelight," and the show ends rather abruptly—possibly, one feels, so the management could bring the dancing girls back on. The sly comment from Bob that "Dark Star" was a song written "just this morning, especially for the Ice Palace" sounds like a dig at their surroundings, and it's probably significant that the band never came back.

JAMES SWIFT

---

### 4/4/69

**Avalon Ballroom,
San Francisco, California**

**Set 1:** Cryptical Envelopment > Drums > The Other One > Cryptical Reprise > Death Don't//Have No Mercy
**Set 2:** Dark Star > Saint Stephen > The Eleven > Feedback

**Source:** SBD, **Quality:** B+, **Length:** 1:15, **Genealogy:** MR > C > C
**Highlights:** The Other One, Dark Star, The Eleven > Feedback

Garcia gears up "The Other One" by sporting a slide on his guitar up through verse one. The effect is tremendously energizing, and it's strange he never used it again on this tune (to my knowledge). But the energy dwindles during a sluggish middle jam so the drummers simply cease playing in protest. The band regroups for a few minutes, but despite a strong effort the music is too restless and out of synch. During the "Cryptical" reprise, though, the pushing pays off with some nice, hard-rocking jams—not pretty but worth a grin. "Death Don't" contains a sharp jam and some fine singing by Garcia, but a cut swipes three of the last four minutes.

"Dark Star" opens the second set but initially suffers from the same stubborn tension that hampered the first set. But after the first verse Garcia reaches into his bag of tricks to pinpoint the knot and kneads it with some searing, well-aimed licks. The toxins disperse and the music takes a tangible sigh of relief. An odd but interesting jam opens up and the band—now more relaxed—goes with it and rides it out. It grows slowly, building in intensity. Garcia takes it to a peak and then switches his guitar to that "choking sitar" sound. But instead of returning to the "Dark Star" melody, he opens up a new space with it. The drummers evidently approve because they go absolutely ballistic. This wave eventually recedes, the band quiets down, and then "Dark Star" reappears. They slowly elevate it with great care, gently but firmly lifting it upward until they arch beautifully into the final verses. Complete rejuvenation right before our ears.

All cylinders clicking, the Dead prance joyfully through "Saint Stephen." The vocals are very confident and jovial. "The Eleven," too, has all those extra touches of the band-in-flow. After some swingin' jams, it drives straight off the road and over a cliff into "Feedback." T.C. provides a parachute of Gothic sounds while Weir and Garcia can be heard slowly scraping against the side, like fingernails upon a blackboard. Oddly, this ends the show after just a few minutes' of tonal weirdness.

MICHAEL M. GETZ

---

### 4/5/69

**Avalon Ballroom,
San Francisco, California**

**Set 1:** Dupree's Diamond Blues, Mountains of the Moon > Dark Star > Saint Stephen > (William Tell bridge) > Turn On Your Lovelight
**Set 2:** Hard to Handle, Cosmic Charlie, China Cat Sunflower > Doin' That Rag, Cryptical Envelopment > The Other One > Cryptical Reprise > The Eleven > It's a Sin, Alligator > Feedback > We Bid You Goodnight

**Source:** SBD, **Quality:** B+, **Length:** 3:00, **Genealogy:** MR > C > C > DAT
**Highlights:** Alligator, Feedback

"Dupree's" through "Turn On Your Lovelight" is perhaps the shortest pre-80s first set I have ever heard. The "Dark Star" however, is yet another classic, not to be missed. The second set starts out real slowly with Jerry on pedal steel for "Hard to Handle" and "Cosmic Charlie," both of which are just AWFUL! Things don't begin to percolate again until well into "The Other One" and then the energy dissipates quickly as they leave a rather short "Eleven" and settle into the rare and bluesy "It's a Sin," complete with vocals and harmonica. Amazingly, Jerry calls out to the audience asking, "Whadya wanna hear that'll last ten minutes, we got ten minutes left?" After tuning up (during which one can hear the unmistakable beginning of "Weather Report Suite" emanating from Bobby's guitar!) they deliver a hard, raw "Alligator" featuring an East Indian–style percussive vocal jam (da da da diga da diga da) that segues into serious "Feedback"—the best part of the second set by a serious margin. Musically speaking, this second set may be the weakest I've yet heard from 1969, which is very odd considering the juicy set list as it appears on paper.

JOHN R. DWORK

### 4/6/69
**Avalon Ballroom, San Francisco, California**

**Set 1:** Radio announcer > //Good Mornin', Little Schoolgirl, Beat It on Down the Line, It's All Over Now, Baby Blue
**Set 2:** Cryptical > Drums > The Other One > Cryptical Reprise, Death Don't Have No Mercy, Turn On Your Lovelight, Viola Lee Blues, King Bee

**Source:** FM-SBD, **Quality:** A–, **Length:** 1:40, **Genealogy:** MR > RR > PCM
**Highlights:** The Other One suite, Baby Blue, Viola Lee Blues
**Comments:** "King Bee" appears at the end of the tape and may be an encore or, possibly, an excerpt from the first set since the second set is ended abruptly.

For years, this was one of the only high-quality 1969 tapes in circulation. Ironically, it was marked by a unique set list featuring a rare "It's All Over Now, Baby Blue" (actually a breakout after a two-year hiatus).

Most cassettes of this show had the set list rearranged to allow the songs to fit on a ninety-minute tape. The beginning of "Good Mornin', Li'l Schoolgirl" is missing as the show was joined in progress. Although "Schoolgirl" was a common show opener at the time, the timing of the show compared with the other nights of the run indicates that more songs may be missing. Nevertheless, the tape remains a classic with an explosive "Cryptical" suite that settles into a chilling "Death Don't Have No Mercy." Right at the transition, an audience member is heard to shout out, "I don't want to die," probably anticipating the next song. Phil responds by menacing the poor fellow with a flurry of bass notes. A crushing "Viola Lee Blues" ends the set. It is one of the finest versions on tape but was ended abuptly as the plug was pulled right at the end of the song's crescendo. The band quickly recovered and performed an a cappella version of the final chorus. Not a bad demonstration of ad-libbing considering it was one of only a few versions played in the two-year period between 1968 and 1970.

DOUGAL DONALDSON

### 4/13/69
**Ballroom, University of Colorado, Boulder, Colorado**

//Dark Star > Saint Stephen > The Eleven Jam > Death Don't Have No Mercy

**Source:** AUD, **Quality:** B, **Length:** 0:45, **Genealogy:** MC > C > DAT, **Taper:** Owsley
**Highlights:** Dark Star, The Eleven > Death Don't Have No Mercy

A classic *Live Dead* set. The "Dark Star" fades in highly energized during the pre-verse jam. Several themes are touched on and Garcia puts forth 110 percent effort. At times it is slow and drippy, at others furtively weird, and others like a beast on top a tower screaming for a love of life. The "Saint Stephen" is average, but "The Eleven" is highly exceptional. Garcia rips through the themes with a frenzied rage—listening to it makes you stop and open your mouth in awe. Ultimately it drops into a morbid "Death Don't Have No Mercy." This tape leads you in and out of several different emotional realms: tranquility, psychosis, passion, mania, and melancholia.

ROBERT A. GOETZ

## 4/15/69
### The Music Box, Omaha, Nebraska

Morning Dew, It Hurts Me Too, China Cat Sunflower > Doin' That Rag

**Source:** SBD, **Quality:** B, **Length:** 0:35, **Genealogy:** MC > C > DAT, **Taper:** Owsley
**Highlights:** Doin' That Rag

"Morning Dew": holy shades of 1978. Garcia's over-enunciation makes his vocals sound hysterically unconvincing. Musically, though, the song is explosive. Lesh drops depth charges. Weir, on the other hand, plays little and when he does, his playing is distracted and aimless. The vocals on "Hurts Me Too" are a painful contrast to Garcia's; Pigpen sings effortlessly and from the heart. Solid version. "China Cat" opens with some deliriously carnivalesque keyboards by T.C. Garcia sounds much more comfortable here vocally, away from the ballad and into the psychedelic. The transitional jam is pure raunch and roll. The "Rag" they settle into is surprisingly sparse and nimble. Garcia almost cracks up at one point, urged on by his mates. The climax is perfectly played with the band stopping the speeding, runaway train precisely a quarter of an inch from the mother and her baby carriage. The Dead have always had good brakes.

MICHAEL M. GETZ

## 4/21/69
### The Ark, Boston, Massachusetts

**Set 1:** Hard to Handle, Morning Dew, Cryptical Envelopment > Drums > The Other One > Cryptical Envelopment > Sittin' on Top of the World, Alligator > Drums > Jam > Doin' That Rag
**Set 2:** Foxy Lady Jam, Dark Star > Saint Stephen > The Eleven > Turn On Your Lovelight
**Encore:** Viola Lee Blues > Feedback

1. **Source:** SBD, **Quality:** B, **Length:** 3:00, **Genealogy:** MC > C > DAT
2. **Source:** SBD, **Quality:** B, **Length:** 3:00, **Genealogy:** MC > PCM > RR (7½ ips, dolby B corrected) > PCM > DAT
**Highlights:** The whole show!

WOW! From the moment it walks out on stage, this band breathes fire like a two-tailed dragon. The pinnacle of the show is witnessed during the great exploratory jams throughout the "Dark Star" and "The Eleven," which just keep on building. Note the long "Turn On Your Lovelight," during which Jerry plays bluesy slide guitar—very hip. An obstinate East Coast crowd refuses to let the Dead leave the stage without an encore. The band members, obviously tired, drag their dragon tails back out on stage to deliver a "Viola Lee" that, despite a slow start, builds to a ferocious climax.

JOHN R. DWORK

## 4/22/69
### The Ark, Boston, Massachusetts

**Set 1:** Sittin' on Top of the World, Morning Dew, Beat It on Down the Line, Good Mornin', Li'l Schoolgirl, Doin' That Rag, Cryptical Envelopment > The Other One > Drums > Cryptical Reprise > Death Don't Have No Mercy
**Set 2:** Dupree's Diamond Blues, Mountains of the Moon > Dark Star > Saint Stephen > The Eleven > Turn On Your Lovelight > Caution Jam > Turn On Your Lovelight

1. **Source:** SBD, **Quality:** B-, **Length:** 3:10, **Genealogy:** MC > C > DAT
2. **Source:** SBD, **Quality:** B-, **Length:** 310, **Genealogy:** MC > PCM > RR (7½ ips, dolby B corrected) > PCM > DAT
**Highlights:** The Other One, the entire second set

Early in this recording Garcia says, "We're going to do some short old stuff, or some old stuff anyway, something, you know, since we're the only ones here, we can do anything we want, anything, absolutely anything, so if you think of anything weird enough for us to do, we'd be more than delighted to do it, perhaps, perhaps." OK. Howzabout a fearsome "Other One"? Perhaps a haunting rendition of "Mountains of the Moon," played first on acoustic guitar complete with jam, which segues directly into a fully electric "Dark Star" > "Saint Stephen" > "The Eleven" > "Turn On Your Lovelight," just like on *Live Dead*? Well, that's indeed what Garcia felt like playing. The quality of this soundboard source tape is good, the playing just a tad rough, like most shows in this era. This is a pretty good example of the Dead just on the verge of adolescence, about to ascend to a greater maturity. It's refreshing to go back and check this out once in a while. The energy is high, and you can tell that the band is on to something and knows it. No MIDI effects here folks, just Good Ol' Grateful Dead; check it out.

JOHN R. DWORK

## 4/23/69
### The Ark, Boston, Massachusetts

**Set 1:** Introduction, He Was a Friend of Mine, Dark Star > Saint Stephen//, //It's a Sin > Saint Stephen Reprise > Cryptical Envelopment > Drums > The Other One > Cryptical Reprise > Sittin' on Top of the World, Turn On Your Lovelight
**Set 2:** Morning Dew, Hard to Handle, Doin' That Rag, Alligator > Drums > Caution Jam > The Eleven > Jam > Caution//, //Feedback > We Bid You Goodnight
**Encore:** Not Fade Away (aborted), It's All Over Now, Baby Blue

**Source:** SBD, **Quality:** A, **Length:** 2:35
**Highlights:** The entire show

On the heels of two sensational shows, the Dead wrap up their three-night stint at the Ark with an epic blowout performance.

Cries of "Speech!" and "Hear, hear!" from the stage begin the tape. An unknown man, sounding like he's making the big confession at an AA meeting, says to the crowd: "Listen, I said this last night and I'm gonna say it again. Monday night [April 21] I didn't know how to introduce the people up here 'cause I'd never heard them live. Well, last night [April 22] I did and tonight I know even better that this is the best fucking rock and roll band in the *world*." Applause. Then Weir: "At your service."

During most of the show, Garcia pulls out strange-sounding, highly creative leads like rabbits from a hat; some are cute and cuddly, but others are voodoolike, sinister, and seemingly interbred with alien blood. The rest of the band is also in peak form as they manage to stay rooted in the Great Now and give us some powerful music.

"He Was a Friend" opens the show with a downhome flavor. Yet it's a tad deranged and—wanting more of this—the boys sense they need to spread out: thus, "Dark Star." This one is hard to describe: the darn thing moves sideways and is unpredictable. The band is so linked up that even a slight hint by someone immediately gets a response and leads to a new direction. Right after the first verses are sung, the earth feels like it's cracking open, torn fiercely apart by a huge gust of energy from the band. It's a mighty blow that comes out of nowhere and epitomizes the *Steal Your Face* logo. I felt stunned before I started laughing out loud by myself.

Things calm down suddenly and a new space emerges. Lesh takes the helm and wraps himself around the music like a boa constrictor working its prey: squeeze and release, squeeze harder and release . . . over and over with precise increments in the pressure. Assorted crevices are dutifully explored with great zeal. Finally, after twenty-five minutes, the band goes into "Saint Stephen." But a reel flip cuts it after only two minutes and the music returns for the end of "It's a Sin." This zooms straight into a rockin' "Saint Stephen" reprise.

"The Other One" is elevated by some superb tandem drumming that pounds relentlessly throughout this scorching version. During the "Cryptical" reprise, following the last wail of "he had to die-uh-uh," the drummers *nail* their skins 1 . . . 2 with all their strength—and on the third beat the rest of the band explodes. Then they repeat this three more times: one, two, ka-boom. It's savage. The Dead have fiddled with this sequence before but never to such a tremendous and exhilarating effect.

"Lovelight," though briefer than the previous two nights (only fifteen minutes here!), is flawless and full of juicy, well-roasted Pig. The band backs him up snugly and even manages more odd and creative jamming behind him. It's hard to believe the show's only half over.

The heat continues as the Dead deliver outstanding versions of "Dew," "Hard to Handle," and "Rag" to start the second set. "Alligator" brings wild applause. Following the drums, the boys do their "na na na na na"

Burn-down-the-Fillmore thing to delight the crowd further. Then it's off to jam heaven. First, a "Caution" jam spiced with an "Other One" flavor shoots out of the gate. Then T.C. squeezes out a familiar signal during a pause. The drummers catch it right away and begin the offbeat pattern to "The Eleven." Everyone joins in, although it starts out hesitantly. Soon, though, it builds into a swift, solid version. After singing the first verses, Garcia starts playing strange, out-there notes. The band follows suit and they all abandon "The Eleven" for a free jam. Garcia slips in a "Goin' Down the Road Feelin' Bad" coda, denying Phil's "Caution" teases. But then Garcia seems to say, "Well, all right," and almost storms into "Caution," reaches a peak... and then plays the coda again. Then he simply wails, building to another pre-"Caution" flurry, but drops back down again, leading the band into more free jamming. Some noodling follows this. Then—utter chaos. Monster belches. While everyone's distracted, Garcia slips into a genuine "Caution" right under their noses. Phil rolls into it big time.

Pig struts to the mike with his obligatory "gypsy woman" rap. Weir joins in for some yelping on the "All you need" rap. Then Garcia and Lesh chime in for some wild yelling of ooohs and ahhhhs. Fun, fun, fun. As Pig yells, "Just a touch—" the band melts the stage with a feedback-driven electrical storm. "Caution" climbs back up yet again. This time it goes faster, faster, faster—doo doo doo doo doo doo—boom!

Pig returns, mojo rappin'. More "All you need" and then—the tape cuts. The middle of "Feedback" emerges. The mood here is intense but calming, slowly bringing it all to a close, rung by rung into a pure stillness. The boys sing a quaint, heartfelt "Bid You Goodnight" to close an amazing evening of music. You can hear this fact in their singing.

They come back to encore "Not Fade Away" but find themselves out of tune so they bail. An inspired but oddly enunciated "Baby Blue" is played instead, and when it ends Weir slyly remarks to the crowd, "Always leave 'em guessing." Lesh sincerely adds, "We'll see y'all when we're back in town. You've been good people." On both sides, Phil.

MICHAEL M. GETZ

## 4/26/69
### Electric Theater, Chicago, Illinois

**Set 1:** Dupree's Diamond Blues > Mountains of the Moon > Dark Star Prelude > China Cat Sunflower > Doin' That Rag, It Hurts Me Too > Hard to Handle, Cryptical Envelopment > Drums > The Other One > The Eleven Jam > The Other One Reprise > It's a Sin, Morning Dew, Sittin' on Top of the World, New Minglewood Blues, Silver Threads and Golden Needles
**Set 2:** It's All Over Now, Baby Blue, Saint Stephen > Lovelight
**Encore:** Viola Lee Blues > Feedback > What's Become of the Baby? > We Bid You Goodnight

**1. Source:** SBD **Quality:** A: a very good soundboard tape, with a near-perfect mix of instruments and voices; some hiss **Length:** 2:55 **Genealogy:** MC > C > DAT

**2. Source:** SBD-CD (Fallout from the Phil Zone), **Length:** 0:20 (just "Viola Lee Blues")

**Highlights:** If you are a Grateful Dead tape collector, this show is a must-have: Dupree's Diamond Blues, Mountains of the Moon, Doin That Rag, The Other One > The Eleven Jam > The Other One, Viola Lee Blues > Feedback > What's Become of the Baby? > We Bid You Goodnight.

**Comment:** A complete show of two sets, and the mother-of-all-encores. Chicago's early shows are woefully underrepresented among tapes in circulation. In fact, prior to the recent release of this show, the earliest available Chicago concert was from August 1971. The '68 and '69 shows all took place at the same venue; my friend Stephen Wade remembers his forays there that began with the Grateful Dead's first Chicago appearance on November 27, 1968:

Chicago's Electric Theater eventually became known as Aaron Russo's Kinetic Playground. Located on the north side between an ice skating rink and a shop filled with granite burial monuments, an evening's entertainment typically included three acts for a $5.00 admission. Near the entrance stood a maze of enclosed seating areas, light sculptures, and mirrored surfaces. Passing through these shifting ambiguous spaces, illuminated by dim purplish light, patrons entered the hall. Musicians played in intimate proximity to the audience, the stage raised only three or four feet above the floor. The room was devoid of fixed seating, leaving the audience free to lie still, wander, or dance. Slides filled with heated colored oils, followed by dense psychedelic images, and rapturous strobe displays enveloped listeners in a sensorium of that era. The Electric Theater was Chicago's Fillmore.

Now, take yourself there, to the Electric Theater. It's April 26, 1969. With this introduction from the emcee—"Something serious for Jerry here: Everybody settle back and relax, because these people are gonna be here awhile and see what they can do for you. Ladies and gentlemen: The Grateful Dead"—the Dead embark on one of the most mind-blowing trips of their career, soaring nimbly and absorbedly across musical genres from blues to bluegrass, folk to jug band, rock 'n' roll to pure psychedelic fury.

The show opens with a sweet medley that includes their very finest renditions of "Dupree's," "Mountains of the Moon," and "Doin' That Rag," three tunes that best exemplify the Dead's derivative music, drawing on earlier ragtime and Elizabethan song modes. Woven in is a celestial "Dark Star" prelude. (Call it a tease if you like, but they never actually begin "Dark Star," taking us instead to the very precipice before dropping us into a "China Cat" so spirited that we soon stop wondering what happened to "Dark Star.")

Pigpen joins the show for a solid "It Hurts Me Too" and a bumpy "Hard to Handle," with Jerry playing slide guitar on both. While "It Hurts Me Too" showcased some of Jerry's best slide playing over the years, "Hard to Handle" began to jell only after he put down the slide and began fingering those raucous riffs that later characterized the tune.

While we ponder, "How did they *do* that?" the Dead sneak us from a dazzling "Other One" into a raucous "Eleven" jam—and back—with Phil powerfully leading the way through these segues. Apparently, the boys get so excited by the chase that they forget all about the final verses of "Cryptical Envelopment," jumping instead from the end of "The Other One" directly into a fine version of "It's a Sin." So be it—is your brain still intact?

"Morning Dew" is a delicate song that the Dead didn't always perform consistently. To really pull it off right, things need to be just right. On this night, they are. Winding down the first set, the boys rock through two traditional numbers just fine, "Sittin' on Top of the World" and "New Minglewood Blues," except that nobody cues in the drummers as to when "Minglewood" is supposed to end. The first set closes with the debut performance of the country number "Silver Threads and Golden Needles." Its warm round of applause from the audience is probably an indicator of what and how much the crowd has been ingesting, for the performance is hideous. This is the coming-out party for Jerry's pedal steel guitar; what is phenomenal is how well he was playing it when recording *Workingman's Dead*. On this particular night, however, it sounds like he was plucking it for the first time.

Weir's enigmatic "This is the home stretch for us—on account of we're going home" announces the second set, which opens with "It's All Over Now, Baby Blue." The performance is as good as, but no better than, other ones of the era. The band turns it on with an inspired "Saint Stephen," after which Pigpen returns to center stage. I like the '69 versions of "Turn On Your Lovelight" when the band really gave it their all behind Pigpen. Jerry's melodic, driving riffs are reminiscent of the *Live Dead* version. The crowd cheers for more after the raucous, thirty-five-minute "Lovelight." They get it. As Bob Weir calls out "Hey, Bear!" the Dead launch into the Mother of all Encores.

Years ago, a San Francisco writer observed that the Dead's "Viola Lee Blues" was the first truly psychedelic song. (Quite a transformation from the Cannon's Jug Stompers' version, recorded in 1928!) They didn't play "Viola Lee" that often after 1967; it seems they treated it with a certain reverence, saving it for those times when the stars were aligned just so. "Viola Lee" is no ordinary song—and this is no ordinary "Viola Lee." What follows is a forty-minute psychedelic tour de force.

Once again, Phil is concert maestro as well as bassmeister; the ensemble follows his every lead. The baby steps of "Caution" and the melody lines of "The Seven" are interwoven with the more usual "Viola Lee" motifs, all overlaying the requisite *accelerando* tempo that characterizes the "Viola Lee" jam. (Note that this is undoubtedly the only "The Seven" performed in 8/4 time!) As is their wont, the Dead extend the "Viola" finale into a twenty-minute "Feedback," every bit as forceful, subtle, and expressive as the *Live Dead* version. What distinguishes this rendition is the apparent segue into the otherwise never performed "What's Become of the Baby?" It is said that this was not an actual performance of that tune, but rather the playing of a studio recording through the sound system during "Feedback." That may well be the case—though the "What's Become of the Baby?" heard here is clearly different from the *Aoxomoxoa* album version. Regardless... Encore! Encore!

DWIGHT HOLMES

## 4/27/69
### Labor Temple, Minneapolis, Minnesota

Turn On Your Lovelight > Me and My Uncle > Sittin' on Top of the World, Dark Star > Saint Stephen > The Eleven > Turn On Your Lovelight Reprise

**1. Source:** FM-SBD (GDH 309, 435, and 436), **Quality:** A, **Length:** 1:40, **Genealogy:** MC > DAT
**2. Source:** SBD, **Quality:** A, **Length:** 1:40, **Genealogy:** MC > DAT
**Highlights:** Turn On Your Lovelight, Dark Star, The Eleven, Turn On Your Lovelight Reprise

One of the best shows from 1969, this one caps off one of the finest weeks in the band's career. The Dead waste little time here as they charge out of the gate into a long, sizzling "Turn On Your Lovelight." Instead of ending it, Garcia and Lesh create a beautiful door through which "Me And My Uncle" struts in. They nearly return to "Turn On Your Lovelight" but suddenly careen into a lively, rockin' "Sittin' on Top of the World." The following "Dark Star" is an intense and eerie rendition from a year that had plenty to behold. This one is long and lean, slithering across the desert like a snake in search of prey. This develops into a strong "Saint Stephen" but the "Eleven" that follows is simply orgasmic. Speaking of (hopefully) love, the Dead end this show with a second "Turn On Your Lovelight" that's equally delicious.

MICHAEL M. GETZ

## 5/3/69
### Evening Show, Winterland Arena, San Francisco, California

Bill Graham Introduction: "Samurai Seven," He Was a Friend of Mine, Cryptical Envelopment > Drums > The Other One > Cryptical Reprise, Doin' That Rag, Me and My Uncle

**1. Source:** AUD, **Quality:** A, **Length:** 0:45, **Genealogy:** MR > PCM > DAT, **Taper:** George Jackson with a Sony 770, 7½ ips quarter track and two Sony condenser mikes at the front of the stage near the keyboard position.
**2. Source:** FM-SBD (GDH 213), **Quality:** A, **Length:** The Other One Suite
**Highlights:** All but Me and My Uncle
**Comments:** The audience tape is so excellent that many people think it is a soundboard.

The opening "He Was a Friend of Mine" is very sweet, if somewhat uneven. It's one of the better versions. "The Other One" smokes from "Cryptical" onward a twenty-minute jammed-out rendition that makes you wanna drop in your tracks. Phil plays with a subtly demonic style that foreshadows the wickedness that was to possess his bass playing in the early seventies. There is also a quiet, groovy part before the second "Cryptical" that reveals the band evolving toward a more wide-ranging improvisational style. "Doin' That Rag" is a typical '69 rendition, which is to say it's great! All in all, despite its brevity, this tape is a gem that everyone should have, both because of the performance and the sound quality.

PAUL PEARAH

## 5/23/69
### Big Rock Pow Wow, Seminole Indian Village, West Hollywood, Florida

Hard to Handle, Morning Dew, Me and My Uncle, Dark Star > Saint Stephen > The Eleven > Turn On Your Lovelight

**1. Source:** SBD, **Quality:** A-, **Length:** 1:40, **Genealogy:** MR > C > C > DAT

**2. Source:** FM-SBD (GDH 098), **Quality:** B, **Length:** Morning Dew through The Eleven

**Highlights:** Dark Star > Saint Stephen > The Eleven > Turn On Your Lovelight

Although tapes of both "Big Rock Pow Wows" had existed for a few years prior, soundboards only became widely circulated in the summer of '93. For two nights, the Dead were only a few of many fine artists to play this Indian festival; the most notable were Johnny Winter, NRBQ, and the late, great Muddy Waters. The mix is typical 1969 Dead, with an earthy rumbling provided by Phil's bass that occasionally reaches bottom-end distortion. Weir's guitar spurts through grungily, and Jerry's rings with a fat, heavily fuzzed tone. All vocals have plenty of room in the mix to propel their musical counterparts. At first, Pigpen and his blues band—uh, the Dead—take a while to find their groove, as a rough "Hard to Handle" stumbles and lurches for stable ground. The *Live Dead* suite delivers the goods, as the "Dark Star" rides bubbling territory reminiscent of several of the Mickey and the Hartbeats gigs of the previous year: interstellar space at its raw essence. "Saint Stephen" climbs steadily before roaring into a muscular "Eleven" groove, which in turn explodes into a pile-driving "Turn On Your Lovelight" that commands your pelvis to shake. There's nothing really extraordinary here for 1969, but the last sixty-two minutes of this tape showcase a wide variety of moods and ambitious tempo changes, the music playing the band by the time Pigpen dominates "Turn On Your Lovelight."

JOHN WOOD

*Jerry Garcia*

## 5/24/69

**Big Rock Pow Wow, Seminole Indian Village, West Hollywood, Florida**

Turn On Your Lovelight, Doin' That Rag > He Was a Friend of Mine > China Cat Sunflower > The Eleven > Death Don't Have No Mercy//, Alligator > Drums > Saint Stephen > Feedback > We Bid You Goodnight

**Source:** SBD, **Quality:** B+, **Length:** 1:30, **Genealogy:** MR > C > C > DAT

**Highlights:** Doin That Rag > He Was a Friend of Mine > China Cat > The Eleven > Death Don't Have No Mercy

**Comments:** The mix is quite similar to 5/23, with its principal difference its overall clarity, although areas of muddy distortion and cluttered chaos still reign.

For fans of onstage band dialogue, this incredible tape begins with a cluelessly naive emcee vainly attempting to seat the audience. Alas, Pigpen has other ideas, "Don't sit. Stand up!" he challenges the crowd. Yet the anal-retentive emcee persists, only to be upped again by Pigpen's command, "Don't be programmin' it, baby. Let's just get it on!" Well, this is the perfect excuse the Dead need to rip through a version of "Turn On Your Lovelight" that no one in their right mind could ever sit through. As good as this somewhat sloppy, but very high-energy "Lovelight" is, what really turns this into a must-have tape is the stretch from "Doin' That Rag" through "Death Don't Have No Mercy" where the core of IT exists. Although this amazing progression of songs is a little rough around the edges, the beauty of every segue from "He Was a Friend of Mine" on is just perfect. "Doin' That Rag" moves slow and slinkily, accented by a passionate, creepy Garcia vocal. Note by note, the subtle buildup from the soft and eerie "He Was a Friend of Mine" transforms seamlessly into "China Cat," its bridge glued by Weir's churning guitar when it joyfully finds the traditional opening lines of the latter. This is four months before "China Cat" discovered "I Know You Rider" as its significant other, yet one minute of its jam reeks "Rider" before gliding into the chaotic euphoria of "The Eleven." Eventually, joyous emotions turn to the deep despair of a brooding, soul-ravaged "Death Don't Have No Mercy." A shriveled "Alligator" quickly surrenders to a brief drum solo accented by an Indian chant, then drives into a straightforward "Saint Stephen" sans its infamous intro. The Dead likely played under a time limit at that point, as the sequence from "Alligator" to the closing strains of "We Bid You Goodnight" elapses a compact twenty-two minutes. Believe it or not, this set was followed by the Youngbloods, known for their infamous cover of "Get Together." File under "what's wrong with this picture?!"

JOHN WOOD

## 5/29/69

### Robertson Gym, Santa Barbara, California

Morning Dew, Cryptical Envelopment > Drums > The Other One > Cryptical Envelopment > Good Mornin', Li'l Schoolgirl, Me and My Uncle, Alligator > Drums > Turn On Your Lovelight

**Source:** SBD, **Quality:** B, **Length:** 1:20
**Highlights:** Alligator > Drums > Turn On Your Lovelight

Words like "subtle" and "understatement" aren't needed in this review so that's the last time you're going to read them. This show has the lads insisting on nothing less than a full-on torrent of rhythms and an abiding belief in the transcendent qualities of exhaustive high-energy improvisation. The recording is mostly trebly lo-fi with a side order of hiss and a smidgen of phased distortion, although I'm sure better-quality versions must be around someplace. It's probably only one for hard-core fans of '69 shows and those of us not bothered by a lack of high-quality sound reproduction.

"Cryptical Envelopment" > "The Other One" develops into a flailing example of psychedelic thrash, and although I'm sure there are musical subtleties to be discovered here, they are comprehensively masked by the quality of the recording. Things cool down slightly for a "Good Mornin', Li'l Schoolgirl," but it's still infused with a restless energy and it doesn't take long before the band slips back into top gear for an edgy "Me and My Uncle." "Alligator" > "Turn On Your Lovelight" is, as you might expect in these circumstances, a riot of flying cross-rhythms culminating in an extended, overheated R&B workout. A mystery guest sits in on congas (and the odd vocal interjection during "Turn On Your Lovelight"), bringing some hot African-Latin patterns to the lengthy "Drums" section. For whatever technical reason, this orgy of percussion is probably the best-sounding segment of the tape, and it's so fine that it's a good reason to search out a copy of this show. Add to that an extended passage that features Garcia's alternately chattering and swooping guitar lines playing over the tapestry of drums and you get another reason for tracking this one down. Pigpen roars out "Turn On Your Lovelight" in a typically lusty voice but without developing any raps. His first attempt at the second verse is all but drowned out in monumental howling guitars and an explosion of drums. It's quite a show-stopper and successfully brings to a close eighty minutes of full-on cosmic fun. I'm sure that better-quality copies will reveal many layers of tonal delights and sonic interplay that are for the most part swallowed whole in this version, but until such a time we'll have to put up with this and as long as you're into hot '69 shows you'll enjoy this no matter what its shortcomings are.

PAUL BODENHAM

## 5/31/69
### McArthur Court, Eugene, Oregon

**Set 1:** Hard to Handle, Cold Rain and Snow, Ken Babbs Rap > Bob's Yellow Dog Story, Green, Green Grass of Home, Me and My Uncle, Cryptical Envelopment > Drums > The Other One > Cryptical Reprise > Sittin' on Top of the World, It Hurts Me Too, Turn On Your Lovelight
**Set 2:** He Was a Friend of Mine, Dark Star > Doin' That Rag//, //Cosmic Charlie
**Encore:** It's All Over Now, Baby Blue*, We Bid You Goodnight*

* mono

**Source:** SBD, **Quality:** A, **Length:** 2:20
**Highlights:** All

A very clean '69 tape this, with an "in yer face" drums 'n' Jerry mix that unfortunately leaves Phil and, to a lesser extent, Bob struggling to be heard. They're still there, but you'll have to concentrate to pick up on them. Naw, don't put yourself out: just turn the volume up, your neighbors need to hear another hot '69 show.

A hyperactive "Hard to Handle" kicks off the proceedings in an enjoyable if slightly confused and unfocused rush. No raps, no stretching out, just a relatively brief opening statement. "Cold Rain and Snow" is just plain unhinged, belting along at an impossible velocity, the absolute opposite of the arrangements of later years. And then? Well, equipment malfunctions give us a good ten minutes of thoroughly demented mile-a-minute jabber from Ken Babbs "Therearemoreofusthananyoneelseinthisroom . . . ," the collective Grateful Dead Slide Whistle Impressionists, and, if that wasn't enough, Weir wants to tell us a "stow-ray": three cheers for the Yellow Dog Joke. Again.

Easing into a tasty "Green, Green Grass of Home" and shifting up a gear or two for a "Me and My Uncle" the band at last find themselves able to stretch out a touch and dive into a truly tumultuous "The Other One." Throughout this first set, Garcia comes perilously close to playing too much, if you can imagine such a thing. Notes spill out in a continuous flow that, exhilarating as it is, occasionally lacks pace or dynamics.

However, "The Other One" suite finds everyone listening to one another, seemingly for the first time in this show; their collective playing improves and everything begins to flow. The segue into a rocket-riding "Sittin' on Top of the World" is handled beautifully.

Pigpen takes control for the rest of the first set, taking things way, way down for an emotional "It Hurts Me Too" before unleashing an outrageous "Lovelight," which might not be quite the longest, most high-energy version you've ever heard but has to be one of the most outrageous to end a *first* set: hell, these guys are just warming up.

Despite, or maybe because of, its length—around fifteen minutes long, "He Was a Friend of Mine" doesn't do anything for me, I'm afraid. Yeah, there are admittedly a few tasty moments but not enough to stop you casting glances at your watch/clock/sundial. Garcia's vocal embellishments overload a melody that is frankly a bit feeble to start with, but you may wish to disagree. However, I just know we'll *all* love the "Dark Star," which is a truly fabulous creation: lines snake out, washed in dazzling feedback, interlocking rhythms emerge and fade away, tensions arise and are dissipated in a performance that seems so effortlessly organic and natural it's hard to imagine that it's being performed by the same outfit that threw itself at "Hard to Handle" two hours ago. The basis of this version is still the arrangement that graces *Live Dead,* but by now it's become more flexible as the band senses its potency and the true nature of this structure as a means to reach the stars. "Doin' That Rag" is fine but, following such an epic stretch of improvisation, it doesn't really emerge from the shadow of the "Star."

You like "Cosmic Charlie"? Yeah, me too. Which means that there are at least two of us totally pissed off that all that exists of that tune on this tape is the last ten seconds. I really wish someone had edited that tiny fragment out. Oh, well, always leave 'em wanting more . . .

The encore, "It's All Over Now, Baby Blue," doesn't so much begin as drift into your consciousness, featuring an obtuse and low-key spoken word fragment courtesy of Ken Babbs. It's not as dramatic as some, and in the context of this show that's just as well. Coupled with a brief, tired, but heartfelt "We Bid You Goodnight," it's a fine end to a show stuffed positively full of surprises.

PAUL BODENHAM

## 6/5/69
**Fillmore West, San Francisco, California**

Morning Dew, Doin' That Rag, He Was a Friend of Mine, Hard to Handle, Cosmic Charlie, //Cryptical Envelopment > The Other One > Cryptical Reprise, China Cat Sunflower > Sittin' on Top of the World > Dark Star > Saint Stephen//

1. **Source:** SBD, **Quality:** A, **Length:** 1:50, **Genealogy:** MR > RR > DAT
2. **Source:** FM-SBD (GDH 055 and 089), **Quality:** A, **Length:** "Doin' That Rag" through "Hard to Handle," "Cryptical Envelopment" through "Dark Star"
3. **Source:** SBD, **Quality:** A, **Length:** 1:30

**Highlights:** He Was a Friend of Mine, Cosmic Charlie, China Cat Sunflower > Sittin' on Top of the World

This tape has appeared piecemeal since a chunk first surfaced on the Grateful Dead Hour radio show a couple of years ago; nearly the entire show now exists from at least two different soundboard sources. Not quite as amazing as the Saturday show with Janis, it nonetheless has an interesting song selection, and in particular a tasty, unusual juxtaposition of tunes that closes things out. Opening with a powerful, well-sung "Morning Dew," the early parts of the set also include a slow, pretty (and relatively rare) "He Was a Friend of Mine" as well as a trippy "Cosmic Charlie," uncharacteristically set off by itself. The jam starts with a sizzling "China Cat" that leads into a rapid-fire "Sittin' on Top of the World" before settling down into a long, dense "Dark Star" that in turn leads into a particularly volatile "Saint Stephen" that features some nice bells from Mickey during the bridge and cuts near the end.

MICHAEL PARRISH

## 6/6/69
**Fillmore West, San Francisco, California**

Green, Green Grass of Home

**Source:** FM-SBD (GDH 089), **Quality:** B, **Length:** 0:05

**Highlights:** All

**Comments:** The "Dire Wolf," "Dupree's Diamond Blues," and "Mountains of the Moon" that often accompany this selection are not from this performance.

In a time most noted for marvelously exquisite "Dark Stars," ferocious "Eleven"s and rambunctiously bawdy "Turn On Your Lovelight"s, this rendition of "Green, Green Grass of Home" provides a contrasting illustration of the Dead's country roots. Assuming the balladeer role nonchalantly, Weir displays absolutely heavenly vocal eloquence, and Garcia's solo is as sweet and soothing as a Kentucky sunset.

BRIAN DYKE

## 6/7/69
**Fillmore West, San Francisco, California**

Dire Wolf, Dupree's Diamond Blues, Mountains of the Moon > Dark Star > Saint Stephen > The Eleven// > Sittin' on Top of the World > Cold Rain and Snow > Doin' That Rag, Me and My Uncle, Turn On Your Lovelight (with Janis Joplin)

1. **Source:** SBD, **Quality:** B/B-, **Length:** 1:40, **Genealogy:** MR > C > C > DAT
2. **Source:** FM-SBD (GDH 089), **Quality:** A, **Length:** "Dire Wolf" through "Mountains of the Moon"

**Highlights:** Virtually every moment

**Comment:** The raspy distortion on this tape is known as stiction which is what happens on old tapes when the oxides begin to stick to the back of the tape on the reel. It makes the reels work harder. It can sometimes be alleviated by reducing the tension on the capstan.

One of great shows of 1969! The second half of this tape has been around in worse quality for years, but the first forty-five minutes turn out to be even hotter. After an all-acoustic "Dire Wolf" and a partially acoustic "Mountains of the Moon," the Dead pull off a brilliant "Dark Star" that just keeps getting hotter and hotter till the end. The "Saint Stephen" is perfect, with a breathtaking a cappella lyric sung by Garcia with only a xylo-

*Bobby* (photo credit: Fred Ordower)

phone accompaniment in the background. This tape is a bit mysterious in that the first forty-five minutes are superb quality. But just as "The Eleven" ends, and it appears that Phil is about to lead the rest of the band into "Death Don't Have No Mercy," there is a very noticeable splice and a completely different-sounding soundboard quality cuts in with the start of "Sittin' on Top." Hmmm? Well, regardless of whether this is all from the same show, the music is amazing to the very end. Unfortunately the same high-end "raspy" distortion that's been on the older circulated versions of this second half begins to kick in during "Doin' That Rag." This version of "Turn On Your Lovelight" becomes a classic as Janis Joplin sits in to trade vocal scat improvisations with her sometime sweetie Pigpen McKernan, yet this song sounds again as though it's from a different source. All told, it seems to us like this is tape is a composite from *three* different sources. But it doesn't matter because the magical music is all here and good enough, even at its worst quality, to enjoy thoroughly. Absolutely don't pass this one by!

JOHN R. DWORK

### 6/13/69
**Convention Center, Fresno, California**

Hard to Handle, Me and My Uncle, Sittin' on Top of the World, Beat It on Down the Line, Good Mornin', Li'l Schoolgirl*, China Cat Sunflower > Morning Dew, Saint Stephen > The Eleven > Turn On Your Lovelight*

* with Ronnie Hawkins

**Source:** SBD, **Quality:** B-, **Length:** 1:40, **Genealogy:** MR > C > C > DAT

**Highlights:** Sittin' on Top of the World, Good Morning, Li'l Schoolgirl, China Cat Sunflower > Morning Dew, Saint Stephen > The Eleven > Turn On Your Lovelight

This set gets better with each and every song, steadily rising in intensity until the vibe on stage explodes with unbounded energy. "Li'l Schoolgirl" features Ronnie Hawkins on guest vocals. The segue between "China Cat" and "Morning Dew" is as smooth as could be. "Turn On Your Lovelight" features some very tasteful flute playing (but by whom? We don't know—perhaps Charles Lloyd?), and again Hawkins appears at the end to scream his lungs out in unison with Pigpen.

JOHN R. DWORK

## 6/14/69
### Monterey Performing Arts Center, Monterey, California

Turn On Your Lovelight 1 > Me and My Uncle > Doin' That Rag > He Was a Friend of Mine, Dire Wolf, Dark Star > Saint Stephen > The Eleven > Turn On Your Lovelight 2 > Drums > Turn On Your Lovelight 3

**Source:** SBD, **Quality:** B, **Length:** 1:50
**Highlights:** All three Turn On Your Lovelights, Dark Star, The Eleven

A well-stacked "Turn On Your Lovelight" sandwich forms the basis for this scrumptious show. The top slice takes a little while to come together as the band does some light stretching to get loose. When Pigpen returns to the mike, he gets right into it: "You can make it if you try!" he croons with a chef's authority.

Garcia and Lesh are in their most playful modes, tossing vaguely familiar melodies back and forth, teasing each other to supply the next notes. Pigpen is into singing lots of falsetto at this show. At one point, Garcia mimics him on the guitar and they go back and forth, just two kids in a sandbox. Even T.C. is given lots of room to play; Garcia actually holds back at moments. As "Turn On Your Lovelight" gets fully stretched out, Lesh seizes the moment with some notes made of C-4 plastic explosives. The weirdness has begun. Strains of "Feedback" emerge. "Turn On Your Lovelight" dissolves; chaos reigns. After a few minutes, a strange Spanish-flavored theme pops to the surface. When Pigpen returns, he sounds different, darker and very much like Jagger doing "Midnight Rambler."

As this mood passes, the band suddenly gallops happily into a rowdy, hootin' and hollerin' "Me and My Uncle." "Doin' that Rag" immediately follows but the band struggles with it all the way through—an odd rhythmic choice. "He Was a Friend" is sung endearingly and has a sweet solo by Garcia. "China Cat" begins but the band finds itself out of tune. After tuning up they opt for a different song: "Dire Wolf." But the cute, twinklish vocals can't make up for the song's clear lack of rehearsal. Another strong "China Cat" tease begins before yielding to . . . "Dark Star." OK.

It begins innocently enough as the band gets dug in, feeling each other out. But after just a few minutes, it becomes clear that they're in synch and *ready*. The pace picks up furiously before dropping down into the first verse. A mere formality. Amidst T.C.'s frantic keyboard runs and Garcia and Weir's screeching guitar feedback, Lesh gets himself behind the wheel of a bulldozer, bringing a storm of woe to all in his path. Garcia tries, too late, to create some order of notes before having to quickly duck and narrowly avoid leaving his face upon Lesh's grinning treads. Suddenly you are *there,* inside the music, inside the current of "Dark Star."

Had Lesh not broken the rules and followed his gut, this might have been just a decent "Dark Star," instead of the transcendental one that it is. Garcia does manage to squeeze in his obligatory "choking sitar" pattern of notes, but Lesh quickly overrides this with an impatient flurry of notes, implying, "Man, we've *done* that before." The Dead ride out the storm in style, neither pushing too hard nor being intimidated by it, until they land gently into the last verse.

"Saint Stephen" is unflawed but sounds *so* structured and constricted compared to its predecessor. "The Eleven," again Lesh-driven, feeds mightily off the storm once again, producing some intense, angular jamming. The return to "Turn On Your Lovelight" feels triumphant. After slowing it down following some minimal but effective feedback, the band do their "shine on me" vocal jam. But a sudden burst of energy by the drummers gives way to an unusually placed but inspired drum solo. The drums wind down and an "Alligator"-like chorus of "ya ya ya ya ya ya ya ya!" cries out ceremoniously and then they go back to "Turn On Your Lovelight" for the third time. An unknown vocalist takes the first line before Pigpen and Weir complete the sandwich with another burning "shine on me" vocal jam.

A must-have tape for any collection.

MICHAEL M. GETZ

## 6/21/69
### Early Show, Fillmore East, New York, New York

Green, Green Grass of Home, Me and My Uncle > High Time > China Cat Sunflower > Morning Dew, Alligator > Drums > The//Other One > Cryptical Envelopment > Slewfoot, //Cosmic Charlie

**Source:** AUD, **Quality:** C/C+, **Length:** 0:55

**Highlights:** Morning Dew, The Other One, the rare Slewfoot, Cosmic Charlie, and the stage patter and interaction with the audience!

**Comments:** All instruments, including pedal steel, T.C.'s organ, guitars, bass, and drum, are audible, although the bass range (bass and drums) is muddy; vocals are clear and not too low in the mix. The hiss on my copy is relatively unobtrusive. Taper talk is minimal, and entertaining when audible.

This show and the one from the following day were among the tapes I first acquired back in 1971 and '72; when I traded for a better-quality copy a couple of years back, it was like finding an old friend again. Even before the music began, I could tell—from the ambience and the tape talk—that this was the same show (and source) that I'd had twenty-some years ago. This tape is not for the collector who abhors all but the crispiest soundboards. The best preparation for enjoying "skeevy aud" tapes like this is to have grown up, as I did, in a small town in an era when FM stations were rare (and played nothing but classical music), and even AM stations were few in number and mostly concentrated in large cities. I spent my childhood and adolescent evenings with my ear pressed to the radio, listening to my favorite baseball team (the Cubs—when they were on the road, of course, since they had no night games at home) and to my favorite Top 40 deejays on Chicago AM stations WGN and WLS. From two hundred miles away, the sound quality was quite akin to that of some of these "skeevy aud" tapes we have from the late sixties shows. I credit this early training for my ability to fully enjoy these tapes, despite their being sound-quality challenged. This is a very tight, compact show, offering a peephole into the full range of what the Dead was doing musically in mid-1969. Though none of the jams are of epic duration, they are characteristic of the very best telepathic jamming that the Dead could produce on a good night; at the same time you hear the group obviously enjoying themselves with some of their early, exploratory forays into "country music," both of a traditional sort ("Green, Green Grass of Home"; "Slewfoot"), highlighted by some of Jerry's earliest-known pedal steel playing, as well as of their own creation ("High Time"). The tape begins with the emcee announcing simply "From San Francisco, the Grateful Dead," followed immediately by the first notes of "Green, Green Grass of Home," with Jerry playing a very soulful, mournful pedal steel. The audience shows their appreciation for this perhaps surprising opener with warm applause, followed by some inaudible patter, and audience laughter. You are drawn into the show with the strong sense that there's a real rapport between the crowd and the band—and that everybody's having a real good time. Jerry says, "There'll be a brief pause while we allow you to consider these new developments," followed again by laughter, a drum roll or two, and someone on stage saying, "Thank you." "Me and My Uncle" follows and is notable for that characteristic calliopelike T.C. organ sound, and the variant lyrics "left him lyin' there by the side of the road." It segues into a sweet if unpolished "High Time," which leads directly into a hot and raucous "China Cat," still arranged very much as on *Aoxomoxoa* (which had just been released the previous day); a nice though not extended jam leads into a very hot version of "Morning Dew," showcasing Jerry's guitar and vocals at their best.

At this point the crowd's energy has been raised to a fever pitch, and people begin calling out requests: "Saint Stephen," "Saint Stephen!!" . . . (pandemonium) . . . "Alligator!" One of the tapers comments: "Phil Lesh always changes his hairstyle. . . . He looks like he oughta have an old mule and be hunting for gold or something. . . ." The audience request for "Alligator" seems to have fallen on receptive ears, as Phil quips: "Alligator who?" To which Jerry fires back, "Alligator yourself, looks like you got the wrong end . . . ," just as the drummers lead them into "Alligator"—Pigpen's only appearance of the show. Jerry's guitar leads the band, uptempo, out of the drum duet, and into one of the finest renditions of "That's It for the Other One" of 1969. "Cryptical Envelopment" provides a poignant conclusion to the suite, bringing us down from the psychedelic heights and abruptly into backwoods Tennessee: "One, two, three, four, high on a mountain, what do you see? Bear tracks, bear tracks lookin' back at me . . ." A rare, rowdy, and fun rendition of "Slewfoot," with Jerry again sitting at the pedal steel. After this, just fifty minutes into the show, who would be ready to leave the Fillmore? Appropriately, the boys bring out "Cosmic Charlie," imploring everyone to "go on home, your momma's callin' you."

DWIGHT R. HOLMES

## ❊ 6/22/69 ❊
### Central Park, New York, New York

Dancin' in the Street, Jam > Casey Jones, Hard to Handle, Me and My Uncle, Sittin' on Top of the World, Silver Threads and Golden Needles, //Dark Star > The Other One > Saint Stephen > It's a Sin, //Turn On Your Lovelight

**Source:** AUD, **Quality:** B+, **Length:** 1:25

**Highlights:** Sittin' on Top of the World, Dark Star, Turn On Your Lovelight

**Comments:** The song order on my tape is different from what usually circulates; however, it conforms more closely with the copy of this show I had on one of my old reels from the time. Furthermore, I concur with Bart Wise (who pointed this out to me) that the tape flip in "Dark Star" at the end of side A here is heard in the middle of side B in the more common arrangement, which would seem to support the idea that this song order is the original one, and that the more common song order results from someone rearranging things in order to have the entire "Dark Star" > "Other One" > "Saint Stephen" > "It's a Sin" sequence on one side of the tape. Also, ending the show with "Turn On Your Lovelight" seems more plausible than closing with "It's a Sin," doesn't it? In any case, there is no hard proof since, on all versions that circulate, there are "hard" cuts between each of the songs, most of them displaying that distinctive *whirrrr* sound of the microphone's on/off switch.

The Dead are in good spirits throughout the show, from the opening "Dancin' in the Street" right on through to the end of a rousing "Turn On Your Lovelight." Fans of "Dancin'" will want this tape, as it's the only rendition of this tune in circulation between 3/18/67 and 12/5/69. It doesn't yet feature the more extended jam of the later '70 versions, but the arrangement is similar. You won't hear any stage patter in this show—perhaps because the boys were talked out from the night before, more likely because the open-air free concert did not offer the kind of intimate environment that lends itself to that kind of rapport with the audience. What you will hear are the loud and frequently obnoxious protestations from the audience, such as "Hey sit down, ya fuckin' speed freaks, sit down!" This is particularly pronounced during the jam that leads into "Casey Jones," but continues pretty much throughout the show. Don't let that distract you from some fine music, however.

This inaugural (at least, among circulating shows) "Casey Jones" is a very countrified rendition, with Jerry fingerpicking the leads; it is rather quaint, compared to the hard-driving versions of a year later, but a fun rendition nonetheless. "Hard to Handle" gets off to a clumsy start, but, with Jerry playing straight guitar (rather than slide) this song is much improved over what it was just a couple of months earlier. After a solid "Me and My Uncle," the boys ratchet things up a notch with a rockin' version of "Sittin' on Top of the World" that really gets the crowd going. Jerry then sits down at the pedal steel for "Silver Threads," while the boys do try their very best on the vocals.

"Dark Star" is powerful, if short (10:40 before it flips on my cassette tape of this show, and 2:00 after). The X factor is evident in the jam before the only verse, which successfully quiets the raucous audience. This is a good tape for T.C. fans, as his organ is right up front in the mix, and he is right in there with all that is going on musically, throughout the show—especially in "Dark Star" and "The Other One." "Saint Stephen" melts prematurely (after "and lower down, and lower down again . . .") into the last ever "It's a Sin" (that we know of), which spotlights Jerry and Pigpen at their blues best. The rest of the show is Pigpen's: a classic Dead dance-till-you-drop "Turn On Your Lovelight"—and the crowd loves it.

DWIGHT R. HOLMES

## 6/28/69
### Veterans Auditorium, Santa Rosa, California

Slewfoot*, Silver Threads and Golden Needles(*?), Mama Tried‡, Me and My Uncle*†, Doin' That Rag, High Time, King Bee, Sitting on Top of the World, Turn On Your Lovelight

\* with Peter Grant, banjo; † with John Dawson (vocals); ‡ with Peter Grant on dobro

**Source:** SBD, **Quality:** A, **Length:** 1:15, **Genealogy:** MR > DAT > C > DAT
**Highlights:** Mama Tried, High Time, Lovelight

The second of two consecutive dates at the Santa Rosa Veterans Auditorium starts off in the same manner as the first: with Weir singing a spirited "Slewfoot" (introduced by Phil as "a ladies' choice"). As in the previous night's show, Weir plays acoustic guitar, Garcia plays pedal steel, and Peter Grant sits in on five-string banjo. "Silver Threads" follows, with Garcia still playing pedal steel. For "Mama Tried," played at the same slow tempo as the previous night's version, Garcia switches to electric guitar. Grant, still sitting in on banjo, contributes an interesting un-banjolike string-bending solo. Between songs, Weir introduces John Dawson and also identifies "the guy playing banjo back there" as Peter Grant. "They're good boys," assures Weir. Dawson and Weir then sing a duet on "Me and My Uncle," something they would later do during 1970 New Riders sets.

As with the previous evening's show, this unfamiliar material is met with polite applause. A more enthusiastic welcome is given to the opening chords of "Doin' That Rag" (*Aoxomoxoa* had been released eight days before this show), with the band in a more familiar, all-electric-and-no-guests configuration. A nice, long ending to "Doin' That Rag" provides us with the first real jamming of the night. At the conclusion of the a cappella ending to "Rag," Garcia begins strumming the opening chords of a picture-perfect "High Time," nicely done with very tight harmonies.

Now for some macho strutting—it's Pigpen time! Garcia lays down a slow, grinding pattern and Pig wails his groaning harmonica over it while the drummers kick in with a determined groove. "I'm a King Bee," Pigpen tells us, "buzzing all around your hive." Yes, ladies and gentlemen, he makes us believe it, taking us through a welcome change of pace from the country-gentleman songs that opened the show. Garcia does a little strutting, too, contributing a very bluesy solo.

A straightforward "Sittin' on Top of the World" follows, and then the spotlight returns to Pigpen as the band kicks into high gear with "Turn On Your Lovelight." This longish "Lovelight" serves as the high point of the show, with lengthy stretches of jamming (often boiled down to just Garcia and the drummers) punctuated by Pigpen, his "rider" always within arm's reach, over his left shoulder, taking great pains to explain to us exactly where our hands should *not* be. A nice rave-up at the end, with Pigpen and Weir exhorting us to come on please, keep on rolling home and let it shine, brings a short but enjoyable show to a close. (The emcee explains afterward that the Dead would love to play all night but they're up against Santa Rosa's midnight curfew.)

JEFF TIEDRICH

## 7/10/69
### Playboy Studios, New York, New York

Mountains of the Moon, Saint Stephen, Turn On Your Lovelight

**Source:** TV, **Quality:** A, **Length:** 0:30 (only part with the Dead)
**Highlights:** Mountains of the Moon

This video, from the *Playboy After Dark* series, documents the hilarious meeting between the hip straight world of Hugh Hefner and the hip freak world of the Grateful Dead. The setting of these shows is supposed to be a hip party at Hugh's penthouse with the guest stars just happening to drop by while the party is in progress. It is obvious from looking at the tape that the party at Hugh's turned into something far more genuine than what the producers ever bargained for. Hugh manages to pose a couple of bland questions to Garcia, who fields them in his typical glib way and makes it somewhat entertaining. His colorful Mexican poncho is nearly too much for the TV cameras; with a radiant smile he positively vibrates on screen. The performance of "Mountains of the Moon" is a joy to watch. Garcia plays it beautifully and is backed up by T.C. on harpsichord. It is very sweet. The "Saint Stephen," on the other hand, is performed all-out as the band attempts to get the stiff crowd loosened up and dancing. You can see some of them getting into the spirit, but most assume the standard *Playboy After Dark* position of sitting before the performers and nodding their heads. Weir is practically drooling over the abundance of beautiful women and can be seen making eye contact with more than one. At the very end of the show, the band is shown playing "Lovelight." Videotapes of this show are in wide circulation as the entire series was rebroadcast on the Playboy channel several years ago.

DOUGAL DONALDSON

## 7/11/69

### State Pavilion, Flushing, New York

Bob Weir's Joke Time, Dupree's Diamond Blues, Dire Wolf, Hard to Handle*, Silver Threads and Golden Needles*, Casey Jones, Sittin' on Top of the World, Big Boss Man, Mama Tried, High Time//, //Drums > Alligator Jam > The Other One > Death Don't Have No Mercy > Turn On Your Lovelight//

* Garcia on pedal steel guitar

**1. Source:** SBD, **Quality:** B, **Length:** 1:20
**2. Source:** AUD, **Quality:** B, **Length:** 0:45 ("Alligator Jam" through "The Other One")
**Highlights:** Alligator Jam > The Other One
**Comments:** This tape is afflicted by a mix featuring lots of bass and treble but very little in between. This gives an initial impression that it runs fast. There's also a fair amount of hiss, so this is another test of exactly who can handle a less-than-perfect recording.

Although there are lots of shows out there that will test your levels of tolerance more than this one, the rather thin, hollow sound is strangely wearing. However, this is still a must-have tape because of its illustration of the Dead in transition, and a peculiarly schizophrenic snapshot it is too, with one side a series of rather rough 'n' ready versions of songs old and new, and the other an extensive slab of spirited stretching out.

With technical problems affecting his amplifiers, Bob Weir tells us a joke or two to keep us entertained ("the Five Hundred Million Bricks" and "The Man with the Cigar" for those Weir-the-Comedian fans among us). Then it's on with the show, beginning with "Dupree's Diamond Blues" and "Dire Wolf," both spewed out at quite an accelerated rate. The real oddity of this set is the brief "Hard to Handle" featuring Garcia on pedal steel. In most other respects, this version is their standard take on this number for the time, but it's a miserable failure mostly because the airy tone of the pedal steel just isn't gutsy enough to cut it in the usual arrangement. After the first listen, you'll be fast-forwarding past this "Hard to Handle" every time. Much better, however, is the use of this instrument on "Silver Threads and Golden Needles," albeit in a traditional fashion.

The real core of this performance is in the "Alligator" jam. Now, this could possibly be a proper, full-length "Alligator," but my tape cuts directly into "Drums" and doesn't indicate whether this is actually the beginning of a jam or whether the song that would usually precede it is, for some reason, absent. But then, who cares when they unleash such a serpentine slice of hardcore '69 improv? The drummers set up a boiling caldera of volcanic drums, charging through the "Indian" rhythmic phrase used around this time to end drum duets, this time without the usual percussive vocal from the drummers. The jam is given shape by Lesh's bass and Weir's slashes of rhythm as Garcia rolls out those endless phrases that snake all over the place, eventually drawing the band into a speedy version of the "We Bid You Goodnight" theme as used at the end of "Goin' Down the Road" before heading out into "The Other One" territory. These jams are quite exhausting, and "Death Don't Have No Mercy" almost comes as a blessed relief, although that is short-lived as this version stokes itself up into an emotional overload that demonstrates these guys ain't going softly into anyone's dark night. The climax is a jagged, chaotic, howl that only just remains coherent. Not everyone's cup of Earl Grey, but I reckon it's superb.

Less-than-perfect recordings don't necessarily detract from the musicality of a performance; often they work like an alternate mix. I would imagine better versions of this tape are in circulation. If you feel uncomfortable with less-than-perfect sound quality, taste and try before you trade, but my guess is that you'll still want this date.

PAUL BODENHAM

## 7/12/69
### New York State Pavilion, Flushing Meadow, Queens, New York

//Dark Star > The Other One > Saint Stephen > The Eleven > Turn On Your Lovelight

**Source:** SBD, **Quality:** B, **Length:** 1:04
**Highlights:** The Eleven, Turn On Your Lovelight

The band is in high goofiness at this show. The tape begins in the middle of "Dark Star," which dissolves smoothly into "The Other One." Bobby launches immediately into the first verse and, after only a short jam (five minutes), sings the second verse. The rest of the band must have had their heads spinning because they fumble the ending and then can't seem to decide what to do next. Someone verbally suggests going back into "Dark Star," but Jerry takes over with "Saint Stephen." Following that is an epic twenty-minute version of "The Eleven" and a hilarious "Turn On Your Lovelight." It's hard to tell what is happening during "Turn On Your Lovelight," but from what I can tell, Bobby pulls some woman out of the audience and does a man-on-the-street interview with her in mid-song, and the woman starts singing a song of her own in a husky, bluesy voice. Meanwhile, Pigpen has jumped behind the drum set and drags Mickey out to the microphone to do some singing and shouting. Sheer lunacy.

DOUGAL DONALDSON

## 8/16/69
### Woodstock Music and Art Fair, Max Yasgur's Farm, Bethel, New York

Saint//Stephen . . . > Mama Tried (equipment break, stage raps), Dark Star > High Time, Turn On Your Lovelight

1. **Source:** SBD, **Quality:** B+, **Length:** 1:13
2. **Source:** SBD Vinyl (Bootleg Record), **Quality:** C-, **Length:** 1:13, **Genealogy:** MR > C > LP
3. **Source:** AUD, **Quality:** C-, **Length:** 1:13
**Highlights:** Lovelight, the bizarre tripping rap

If any show in the Grateful Dead's history has the greatest reverse mystique, it's their appearance at Woodstock. Over the years, the Dead made much of their reputation for "blowing it" whenever they appeared at a big event (even if this was not strictly true—as when they blew everybody's mind at Monterey, according to Eric Burdon, or at the Human Be-In, according to Tim Leary and Allen Ginsberg), and Woodstock was the granddaddy of disappointments. The story of rain and wind; giant tie-dyed backdrops acting as sails, pushing the stage off its moorings; speaker tower stacks threatening to tip over; and painful blue electric shocks for the musicians have been told and retold many times.

So it is that whenever a Dead tape collector remembers that the Dead played Woodstock and starts asking around for that show, she or he will be told that the show is hard to find, and not worth listening to. In a sense, the community has internalized the conventional wisdom that the Dead were awful at Woodstock. In a sense, this is true: the "Saint Stephen" is incomplete, there's a long stretch of tripped-out jabber on the tape (during equipment problems—which were mainly, it seems from the off-mike talk, *monitor* problems), the "Dark Star" is loose to the point of meandering, and there's someone talking shit during the beginning of "Lovelight." These are all strikes against this show as a candidate for easy listening.

However, as a collector's item, the Woodstock show should not be missed, especially now that a soundboard copy (of admittedly dubious pedigree) seems to have circulated well enough to have generated at least one bootleg CD (which, warbly as it is, compares favorably to my older audience tape of the same material). The "Saint Stephen" may be incomplete, but it's still curious the way it segues into "Mama Tried" without ever finishing. Imagine the people tripping in the audience and what it must have seemed like to them?! And though the "Dark Star" is not the best one from 1969 you'll ever hear, it's part of the ongoing dialogue and evolution of that song from '68 to '72. The "High Time" is "early" (it wouldn't come out on an album for another five months or so) and tentative, but points in the direction of the Dead's next step, and the "Lovelight" is full-on and raging, giving the Woodstock audience a clear idea of what the Dead were famed for. Compared to the pedestrian "greatest hits" style set list the Dead played at the U.S. Festival in 1982, the Woodstock mini-set is a winner.

One mystery remains: who exactly is doing most or all of the talking during the equipment break? There's clear evidence that the man is under lysergic influence, from the nervous heh-heh-hehs to the bizarro logic and his semifluid ability to pick up words or phrases thrown at him by the alternately joking and annoyed band members and weave them into his monologue.

An announcer starts the Dead set by saying, "Will everybody *please* sit down. Let the people behind you have a chance to see the show. Just relax those muscles in your legs. Sit down for a few minutes please." My recordings all have a lot of distortion on the man's voice, and there are warbly distortions throughout the tape. He then introduces the band, "One of the best fuckin' rock groups in the world, the Grateful Dead!"

"Saint Stephen" is cut between "in and out of the garden he goes" and "wishing well with a golden bell." Instead of the "lady finger" bridge, there's a weird transition into "Mama Tried" (I wonder if they meant to go back to "Saint Stephen" at all, before the equipment problems). There's a clear hint of "High Time" before the long stage raps. Here's a short excerpt of what is said between this noodling and the beginning of "Dark Star":

> **Man on Stage:** Well are we we we . . . Once again we're too slow, our timing is off just a hair right here, and I'll tell you why—it's because, uh, the only place we really feel comfortable is in home, you know, when we got our family around us, and our family's a big one, and we're feeling pretty comfortable up here, but but heh*
>
> We want to get the family so big that even in this scene—and it's happening—we're, uh, we'll feel comfortable even when we're like this, and the rain comes down, and everyone's in terrible shape. Yeah! So that's what we're working at. If he's gonna do it, we'll do it. Yeah it is, I know it—it's all happening right.

There's a peaceful, mellow "Dark Star" intro, typical of '69. The first verse comes around 7:40. There's a more tense jam around 11:14 with Phil all over the place. The jam meanders and at 24:12, when it seems to be going back into second verse, it wanders into "High Time." You can hear radio chatter coming over the mikes while Jerry is singing, ". . . nothing's for certain." (Phil once commented on how similar this was to Spinal Tap's experience at the Air Force base.) "High Time" ends sort of weakly and dribbles into "Lovelight." During the opening chords of "Lovelight," someone starts rapping (loudly):

> *Whoa yeah ah I've*
> *I've seen the sun rise!*
> *I've seen the sun rise over the lake the great the great*
> *the great*
> *lake the lake the lake*
> *and set over over over the the Pacific Ocean*
> *and rise over the Atlantic*
> *and just ah thing I'd like to say here tonight*
> *for everyone here*
> *and that's*
> *there's another coast*
> *yeah*
> *it's just another coast*
> *it's a third coast*
> *uh uh uh*
> *oh the greatest fresh water reservoir in the world*
> *oh the greatest fresh water reservoir in the world*
> *and more miles of coastline just measurin' just measurin'*
>
> [Pig starts: "without a warning . . ."]
>
> [over Pig's vocals]
> *oh right in the middle*
> *right in the middle*
> *right in the middle*
>
> *ah the third coast*
> *yeah the third coast*
>
> *and I'm not talking about Chicago blues either!*

---

* Tripping logic backtrack.

"Lovelight" has a real nice jam at 21:50, and Pig stops the band several times with his trademarked "Now wait a minute!" The song fades out at 28:04 with Pig chanting, "All I need that's all I need."

CHRISTIAN CRUMLISH

band seems pretty laid-back, even during the "Cryptical" suite, but that's usually the case in the mellow Northwest.

DOUGAL DONALDSON

## 8/20/69
### Aqua Theater, Seattle, Washington

Big Boss Man, Sittin' on Top of the World, Cryptical Envelopment > Drums > The Other One > Dark Star > Cosmic Charlie

**Source:** SBD, **Quality:** A-, **Length:** 0:37, **Genealogy:** MR > C > C > DAT
**Highlights:** Cosmic Charlie

A sweet little snippet of the next show after Woodstock, this tape features the shortest "Dark Star" of the year, clocking in at less than seven minutes from the first faint notes of the song to the "Cosmic Charlie" segue. The

## 8/30/69
### Family Dog at the Great Highway, San Francisco, California

Dark // Star > Saint Stephen > The Eleven Jam > Drums > High Time//

**Source:** SBD, **Quality:** C+, **Length:** 0:40
**Highlights:** First ten minutes of the "Dark Star" are superb.
**Comments:** My copy of this show is a decent soundboard with a mix only slightly biased toward Phil, who becomes saturated several times during the show. The drums and vocals are also a little low, but dynamically all but the very high end is solid. Hiss is present but tolerable. Very listenable.

. . .

The show opens with a nice "Dark Star." Although some "Dark Star"s from '69 seem to rip you out of your seat, this one has a more laid-back feel to it. It starts in a spacy fashion and meanders to a Bobby-led jam that is delightfully melodic. Phil and the drums are strong and in control, fitting in with the direction of the song. The jamming is strong and very tight, leading up to about the ten-minute mark, where Jerry breaks out the first verse. After the first verse, the show slides into a "Saint Stephen," while remaining in the same low, lovely gear. Unfortunately, all good things must come to an end, and eventually all sense of order is lost. The jamming becomes futile, and the band just seems to lose its way. The bridge to the "Eleven Jam," or more precisely, everything after the "William Tell" verse, has notable flashes of attention-grabbing greatness, but even several listenings couldn't convince me this was a special show. Out of the brief "Eleven" comes a respectable drum solo that crashes into a "High Time" that on my tape cuts early.

DAVID R. CECCHI

### 9/1/69
**Baton Rouge International Speedway, Prairieville, Louisiana**

Casey Jones, Morning Dew > Mama Tried > High Time, Easy Wind, Yellow Dog Story, //Dark Star > Saint Stephen > The Eleven > Turn On Your Lovelight//

**Source:** SBD, **Quality:** B/B+, **Length:** 1:25
**Highlights:** //Easy Wind, Dark Star > Saint Stephen > The Eleven > Turn On Your Lovelight//
**Comments:** This is basically a decent, well-balanced mix (with T.C. right up front for a pleasant change), but most versions in circulation I've heard are just about drowned in hiss. A certain amount of distortion creeps in during "Turn On Your Lovelight," but if you've listened that far you're not going to complain. Still worth checking out, mind you, for the versions of the newer songs at a formative stage, not to mention an always welcome version of "The Eleven."

"Casey Jones" kicks off in a frenzied blur, but "High Time" is performed so tentatively that it's hardly there at all. "Easy Wind," on the other hand, is suited to this predominantly loose feel; Pigpen fans will find it quite tasty. "Morning Dew" is, as always, entertaining but as with most sixties versions it's played way too fast to contain much of the drama and heart-stopping dynamics of later versions. And just when you thought it was safe to listen to the band in between songs . . . you get another Bobby joke. Me, I like 'em, but I suspect that the hearty laughter from the rest of band means they've heard this old chestnut once too often.

Side two of my cassette is another story entirely. Here the band is functioning well in music they know backwards, and it shows in the effortless way they navigate through the extended improvisations of "Dark Star" and thunder into a raging "Saint Stephen" with absolutely no hesitation, no need to think rationally about what they're doing (well, that's how it sounds anyway!). "The Eleven" is full of tortuous twists and turns and gets cranked up to such a level that you know that it can only be resolved in a hot "Turn On Your Lovelight," which of course is exactly what we get. Well, only about half of it, unfortunately. Oh well, look on the bright side, we do get to hear another "Yellow Dog" story.

PAUL BODENHAM

### 9/6/69
**Family Dog at the Great Highway, San Francisco, California**

Good Mornin', Li'l Schoolgirl, Doin' That Rag, He Was a Friend of Mine, Big Boy Pete > Good Lovin', It's All Over Now

**Source:** SBD, **Quality:** A-, **Length:** 0:45, **Genealogy:** MR > C > C > DAT
**Highlights:** Big Boy Pete, Good Lovin' (with Jerry on vocals), It's All Over Now
**Comments:** Many tapes list the songs "Dancin' in the Street" and Jam > "Casey Jones" to open the show; however, these are actually from 6/22/69, Central Park, New York City. All in all, this tape is excellent in quality, fidelity, and dynamics. It is a very good mix—all the instruments and vocals can be heard clearly. The cymbals are very clear, even with Dolby B. It seems to be just a bit inconsistent in pitch, however, which is the reason for the A- rating.

The influence of Tom Constanten can be heard from the first strains of "Good Mornin', Li'l Schoolgirl." The band is much looser than during the previous two years, in no small part due to T.C.'s freer and more creative keyboard playing, with Pigpen's blues roots shining through. Toward the end, the band plays in a triplet beat reminiscent of "Truckin'." The tune culminates with Pigpen declaring, "I don't care if you're only sweet fifteen years of age!" During "Doin' That Rag" I thought about what a strange tune this is, clearly showing the influence of psychedelics in the Dead's songwriting. But it wouldn't be nearly as weird without T.C. and his strange keyboards in the background! T.C. and Phil are very prominent under the vocals, with Jerry singing, "And the faces are crawlin' up and down your sleeve" (instead of the usual "aces," referring to playing cards). At thirteen minutes "He Was a Friend of Mine" is the longest tune on this tape. It is much improved over the few earlier versions, although this version is rather slow. Although the vocals are a bit off-key at times, the three- and four-part harmonies that appear on *Workingman's Dead* can be heard here.

"Big Boy Pete" is my favorite tune on this tape—the first upbeat tune they play here, and it rocks! Phil is incredible on the bass, especially on the fills between the vocals. Not only is this tune flawless, but the band sounds like they're really having fun. This tape is also worth collecting for Jerry's lead vocals on this fast, four-minute "Good Lovin'." In only the second performance of this tune, Pigpen merely sings the fills during the chorus, such as "All I need is love" and "Some of your lovin', baby." This tape also contains the first performance of "It's All Over Now," which is fairly boring with its straight 4/4 beat. Pigpen plays some nice harmonica, but the band makes several mistakes. It's interesting that they didn't play this tune again until November 20, 1970, and then not again until September 25, 1976. All in all, this is a fairly unremarkable show, definitely not in the top ten of 1969.

JOLIE GOODMAN

**Source:** FM-SBD (GDH 393), **Quality:** A, **Length:** 0:30, **Genealogy:** MR > DR
**Highlights:** All (but only for the novelty factor)
**Personnel:** Jerry Garcia, Jorma Kaukonen, Joey Covington, plus other unknown musicians

One of the lewdest and most rambunctious sets we've yet to encounter, this tape was discovered by Dick Latvala and David Gars in the Vault labeled "Jam with the Airplane 9/7/69." While the complete personnel lineup is unknown, we can clearly ascertain the presence of Jerry Garcia and Jorma Kaukonen. Immediately delving into absurdity, the tape begins with a godawful rendition of "Peggy Sue," sung by Jorma, and executed at the level that you would expect from your average high school garage band. Somehow, the band(s) pull together for a surprisingly solid version of "That'll Be the Day," sung by Garcia, and pretty damn well at that. "Johnny B. Goode," sung by Garcia, is ridiculously sloppy; Jorma's rebound of "Baby What You Want Me to Do" is pretty standard, not unlike the thousands of renditions we've heard him crank out since: musically enthusiastic, yet vocally preposterous to the point of being painful. The following jam, appearing out of nowhere, starts simply from a surf riff by Garcia, ad-libbed and extenuated all the way into a unique arrangement of "Big Railroad Blues." The concluding "Louie Louie" > "Twist and Shout" > "Blue Moon," sung by Joey Covington, the drummer at that time for the Jefferson Airplane, is arguably the poorest yet most hilarious five minutes in Dead/Airplane tape history. By now, it is clear that the effects of inebriation have taken their toll, and for a moment you feel as though you're in the midst of a sixties college fraternity party. This is true party music at its best *and* worst!

BRIAN DYKE

---

### ❊ 9/7/69 ❊
**The Family Dog at the Great Highway, San Francisco, California**

Peggy Sue, That'll Be the Day, Johnny B. Goode, Baby What You Want Me to Do, Big Railroad Blues, Louie Louie > Twist and Shout > Blue Moon

---

### ❊ 9/26/69 ❊
**Early Show, Fillmore East, New York, New York**

//Dark Star > Saint Stephen// > The//Eleven > King Bee > Death Don't Have No Mercy//

**Source:** AUD, **Quality:** C+, **Length:** 0:45
**Highlights:** Dark Star, Saint Stephen, The Eleven, King Bee

**Comments:** This is a partial concert tape, of a single sequence of songs, cut in the beginning, cut in the end, and with three very brief breaks or splices in the middle. My tape of this show is of poorer sound quality than my tapes of the 27th (at the same venue) and the 28th and 29th (at the Café au Go-Go). It is also a bit slow—the times given below reflect speed correction. All instruments appear to be audible, though the bass and percussion instruments come through quite muddy. The vocals are well balanced in the mix. There is a problem with some distortion that is evident during peak levels (e.g., "Saint Stephen," "King Bee"), especially affecting Phil's bass guitar. There are a couple of breaks in the tape. Most distracting of all, my tape suffers from bleed-through of some other, indeterminate music. Fortunately, this bleed-through is hardly noticeable in the beginning, and really only becomes a nuisance during the last two songs.

The forty-five minutes we are privileged to hear are spirited, high-energy, and uptempo throughout. The boys are in fine form, as they were for all of these late September New York shows. Nevertheless, due mainly to its poor sound quality, this tape will likely be of most interest to "completists" who are collecting everything (or, perhaps, everything in this four-show/five-night run in New York). It should also be of genuine interest to "Dark Star" connoisseurs, as this "Dark Star" is the closest of any to the one from 6/24/70 in both tempo and mood. (This is a bit of an enigma, of course, given that at least twenty "Dark Star" performances intervened between these two.) Not that it is an equal, but the character is strikingly similar, with that same upbeat, bouncy pace. The tape begins some moments into the piece, with a nice jam leading into the first verse (3:42 from the beginning). After an intriguing "Space" segment, there is an enthusiastic "Feelin' Groovy Jam," 11:00 from the start, which then, after some meanderings, leads back to the "Dark Star" theme and closing verse. "Dark Star" passes the baton to "Saint Stephen" at the 16:59 mark.

While shows are seldom remembered for their "Saint Stephen"s or their "Eleven"s, rarely do these songs ever disappoint. These two tunes, particularly when in tandem, are generally performed with genuine and infectious enthusiasm, and this concert was no exception. In short, they rock. (There is what sounds like a splice at the end of the jam, just before the last verse of "Saint Stephen," with a change of sound quality—but no music is lost. It's as if a different microphone were connected or something. During "The Eleven" there are two momentary breaks, where it sounds as if the switch on the microphone was turned off and then immediately back on again, or as if the reel was taking up slack.) Then there is one of those special Grateful Dead moments: a segue into "King Bee" that is so smooth, so polished, you would think they'd played it exactly this way every day for the last month or so. Pigpen is in fine form on vocals and harmonica. "King Bee" is somewhat truncated, however, as they pull off another smooth transition into "Death Don't Have No Mercy." This last tune is cut within seconds of the end, just shy of the forty-five-minute mark.

DWIGHT HOLMES

---

### 9/27/69
**Early Show, Fillmore East, New York, New York**

Morning Dew, Mama Tried, Next Time You See Me, Casey Jones, China Cat Sunflower > High Time, //Dire Wolf, Me and My Uncle

**Source:** AUD, **Quality:** C+, **Length:** 0:45
**Highlights:** China Cat > High Time

"The magnificent seven from San Francisco—the Grateful Dead" was Bill Graham's introduction for this evening's performance. This forty-five-minute audience recording is fairly easy to listen to, due primarily to a good overall mix with decent levels. Despite the usual amount of glitches and slightly nasty dropouts common to so many early audience recordings, it manages to capture the ambience of the evening, offsetting any technical imperfections for the most part. It's lucky this audience tape has survived because there is no soundboard circulating from this show.

"Morning Dew" starts out effortlessly. Jerry sings as though the song were a lullaby. His voice has a gentle soothing, comforting quality to it. The final jam closes the song with a feeling of contentment and conviction. Bobby dishes up a quick and warmed-over version of "Mama Tried," but Jerry's playing through the second verse is so aggressive that it is on the edge of being distracting. "Next Time You See Me" is a straight-ahead version that highlights Pigpen and Jerry as they share solo duties. "Casey Jones," the tightest and most playful song from this show, is actually a pretty hot version. It's sassy! The pairing of "China Cat Sunflower" and "High Time" is the real treasure of this tape. From the onset "China Cat" has a frolicsome, cowbell-punctuated rhythm that floods your ears with merriment. The song descends and dissipates, and then, like the phoenix rising from the ashes, a very unexpected "High Time" is born. These early live versions of "High Time" have methodical fluid drum accents that add to the overall solemn feeling that the song offers. This pairing really works, and I wish that they had explored this combination (and others) much more. "High Time" has such a deeply somber tone that it contrasts perfectly with the fun and energetic "China Cat Sunflower" that precedes it. The beginning of "Dire Wolf" is missing, but it's a fairly spiritless version, so it's not too profound a loss. "Me and My Uncle" is a mediocre version with nothing worth mentioning. The end of the tape contains the "Take Me Out to the Ball Game" tuning and some noodling for posterity's sake.

COREY SANDERSON

### 9/30/69
**Café au Go-Go, New York, New York**

//China Cat Sunflower > I Know You Rider, Merry-Go-Round Theme > Take Me Out to the Ballgame > Alligator > Drums > The Other One

**Source:** AUD, **Quality:** A-, **Length:** 0:30
**Highlights:** China Cat Sunflower > I Know You Rider, Drums > The Other One
**Comments:** A partial tape with unknown missing songs. My tape is sixth generation. This would be a solid A- quality tape except that the vocals are too low in the mix throughout—especially during "Alligator," when Pigpen is barely audible. Weir's vocals are also too low during "The Other One," as are Garcia's in "China Cat." Other than that, this is a crisp recording. The microphone placement is quite good for the drums—almost as if the mike is onstage somewhere where the voice monitors are not picked up.

Yet another partial tape of a New York early show—shorter than its three predecessors, all of which are forty-five minutes in length—this one opens about forty seconds into the opening song. And, as with the three previous tapes of this run, this one leaves you thirsting for more: the Dead are clearly enjoying themselves again. This show is perhaps most notable for the debut (at least on tape) of the "China Cat Sunflower" > "I Know You Rider" pairing. Don't expect any stunning jams as they segue from one tune into the other—they would have twenty-five years to fine-tune this transition—but this is apparently the night it all began. The arrangement of "I Know You Rider" is, not surprisingly, similar to that of the '66 versions (as heard on *Historic Dead*). September 30 was right at the end of the '69 baseball season—the year the amazing Mets, perpetual cellar dwellers of the National League, scorched my Cubs, coming from eleven games back to win the pennant by a mile, and eventually the World Series too. New York is absolutely baseball crazy about this time, and the Dead are playing "Take Me Out to the Ballgame"! But why, exactly—was it a request? Actually, it turns out they are stalling for time, to let the new pitcher get warmed up. In a few minutes they signal his arrival with the announcement, "And here he is!" followed by the opening notes of "Alligator." Pigpen is center stage. The fact that the vocals are so low in the mix definitely detracts from this version. As if to make up for that flaw, the Dead really shift into high gear: the result is worthy. Aside from the low mix on the microphones, this is a fine audience recording for '69. The drum duet after "Alligator" sustains the high energy of the drums duo from the previous night's show, building toward the end, when they really get the crowd fired up just as they go into "The Other One." Things just get better from there; this is a stellar version. The only disappointment is that the tape is over.

DWIGHT HOLMES

### 10/24/69
**Winterland Arena, San Francisco, California**

//Casey Jones, Dire Wolf > High Time, Hard to Handle, China Cat Sunflower > I Know You Rider, Easy Wind, //The Other One > Cryptical Reprise > Cosmic Charlie//

**Source:** AUD, **Quality:** B+, **Length:** 0:45
**Highlights:** Casey Jones, Easy Wind

*Winterland Arena, 10/24/69* (photo credit: Michael Parrish)

For this show, one of their many co-bills with the Airplane, the Dead played one longish set, a fragment of which exists in this reasonably good audience tape. My second show, this was my first foray into Winterland, which seemed vast compared to the Fillmore West, and horribly oversold at that. I remember being pleased but bewildered by the material, most of which was totally unfamiliar to me. Still-evolving versions of "Casey Jones," "Dire Wolf" (with some tasty organ from T.C.), and "High Time" get things rolling. The most striking thing on the tape is the wonderful, gutsy version of "Easy Wind," which has an entirely different, jazz-blues feel than later versions, thanks in part to Constanten's trebly organ. One of the earliest versions of the "China Cat Sunflower" > "I Know You Rider" pairing finds the band still working its way through the coupling, although "Rider" is about as spirited as this song gets. Unfortunately, the energized "Other One" > "Cosmic Charlie" jam is cut at both the start and finish on the audience tape.

MICHAEL PARRISH

## 10/25/69
### Winterland Arena, San Francisco, California

Dark Star > Saint Stephen > The Eleven//, Good Lovin' > Drums > Jam//

**1. Source:** SBD, **Quality:** A, **Length:** 0:30 (Star through Eleven), **Genealogy:** MR > C > PCM > DAT
**2. Source:** SBD, **Quality:** B+, **Length:** 0:10 (Good Lovin')

"Dark Star" comes out swiftly, very bassy, and with both drummers playing hand instruments. Garcia and Lesh are so far out in front of the mix that they nearly come off as a duet. After a short, meandering space, the drummers curl up with their kits. A light, double-time frolic steers into a jazz-influenced jam reminiscent of 1973. Lesh attempts a "Feelin' Groovy Jam" that only half sticks with the rest of the band. Another theme develops that sounds strongly like "Hypnotized," the tune Weir wrote for his 1970s band, Kingfish. But the Dead stubbornly mix these two themes to the point of suffocation. "Saint Stephen" unites the band with some crisp, flawless playing. "The Eleven" cuts after only three minutes. Someone announces, "Once again, and with no interruptions—the Grateful Dead!" The beginning of a second set? Or making note of the fact that they played the night before, too? Regardless, "Good Lovin'" comes out. Unfortunately, it cuts shortly after the drums.

MICHAEL M. GETZ

## 10/31/69
### Halloween, San Jose State University, San Jose, California

Casey Jones, Yellow Dog Story, Dire Wolf, It Hurts Me Too, Cryptical Envelopment > Drums > The Other One > Cryptical Envelopment > //China Cat Sunflower > I Know You Rider, High Time, Sittin' on Top of the World, Next Time You See Me > Easy Wind//, Turn On Your Lovelight

**Source:** SBD, **Quality:** B, **Length:** 1:51, **Genealogy:** MR > RR > C > Beta HF > PCM
**Highlights:** Turn On Your Lovelight

Another in the line of mediocre cassette boards that appeared in the early 1990s from this very transitional period in the Dead's career. This Halloween night at San Jose State features a fun-filled if routinely played show that included a handful of *Workingman's Dead* songs, a long drum segment in the "Cryptical" suite, and a nice segue out of "Cryptical" into "China Cat." By midway through the show, Pigpen takes over the stage with three songs in a row, including his new "Easy Wind" (only the third performance), and a rousing half-hour-long "Turn On Your Lovelight."

DOUGAL DONALDSON

## 11/7/69
### Fillmore Auditorium, San Francisco, California

Morning Dew, Mama Tried, Next Time You See Me, Good Lovin', China Cat Sunflower > I Know You Rider, Dark Star > Feelin' Groovy Jam > Uncle John's Jam > Dark Star Reprise > Cryptical > Drums > The Other One > Turn On Your Lovelight//

**Source:** SBD, **Quality:** A-, **Length:** 1:40, **Genealogy:** MR > C > DAT
**Highlights:** Dark Star, The Other One, Turn On Your Lovelight
**Comments:** Though this tape has a light but audible flutter, the sound is quite bright, rich, and strong.

Overshadowed, perhaps justifiably, by the following night, this show should nevertheless not be overlooked. The band is on a performing roll and every song here is worth a listen. Highlights? How about Garcia's chilling final vocal on "Morning Dew"? And who but the good ol' Grateful Dead would follow this apocalyptic dirge with the chirpy Merle Haggard tune, "Mama Tried"? After this, someone from the audience plays "The Star-Spangled Banner" on a pump flute, much to the merriment of all. The Dead respond with a slew of ditties themselves. The "Good Lovin'" is short but pumped up enough to get the crowd sweating.

"Dark Star" begins with a very quiet, inward-facing stroll. Garcia delicately needlepoints his way on the guitar, slowly and assuredly, suddenly intensifying his notes—just to get a rise out of Lesh—before dropping back down again, rung by rung, into his darkened corner. He sneaks out to sing the first verse, sounding like he's looking out of the "Blues for Allah" cover into the Great Void. Afterward, the band seems tense, poised and cobralike. The mood is thick with possibilities. Ceremonial gong rolls fade away, leaving a staring silence onstage, save for the pulse of a high hat. Some feedback takes form, growing like those magic rocks you'd beg your parents for at gas stations in the South. The sounds are strange, eerie, yet somehow comforting. Lesh rumbles chillingly. T.C. sounds like he's scoring a Bela Lugosi flick.

Suddenly the band takes off from this place. Lesh steers the band into a brief "Feelin' Groovy Jam." This dissolves into an "Uncle John's Jam" complete with Garcia playing the spirited melody. However, the playing has become messy and continues this way through the "Dark Star" reprise. At this point, someone needs to step up.

Someone does. Phil Lesh strikes hard and early in "The Other One," never letting up, manhandling every nuance, intimidating all comers and having himself one whopper of a monkey spank. Garcia foolishly tries to claw his way in, but Lesh merely swats him away. The following "Turn On Your Lovelight" features Pigpen at the top of his game, rapping easily to the crowd and having a ball. Behind him the band juggles one musical idea after another, in a constant flux, restlessly creative, in peak form. The cut is harsh but comes after a full fifteen minutes worth of great music.

MICHAEL M. GETZ

## 11/8/69
### Fillmore Auditorium, San Francisco, California

Good Mornin', Li'l Schoolgirl, Casey Jones, Dire Wolf, Easy Wind, China Cat//, I Know You Rider > High Times, Mama Tried, Good Lovin', Cumberland Blues, Dark Star > The Other One > Dark Star > Uncle John's Band > Dark Star > Saint Stephen > The Eleven Jam > Caution > Feedback > We Bid You Goodnight

**1. Source:** SBD, **Quality:** A-, **Length:** 1:20, **Genealogy:** MR > C > DAT
**2. Source:** SBD, **Quality:** B
**Highlights:** Every note of this phenomenal, extended jam

This tape is an odyssey. Many consider it to be one of the Grateful Dead's finest early performances. Lesh and Garcia, in particular, stand out with stellar statements. The true voyage of this show begins with a delicate "Dark Star." With the exception of Pigpen providing the rhythm, this "Star" is a Lesh-Garcia duet. While slow and carefully constructed, the improvisational jams between the two are deeply ruminative. After the lyrics, the band spaces out for a while before Garcia wanders into a fantastic "Star" jam. Lesh, the ultimate opportunist, intricately molds the jam from "Star" into a "Feelin' Groovy" strut. Near its conclusion Lesh begins dropping "Other One" teases, and like a dehydrated man sighting a desert mirage, Garcia follows into a blistering "Other One." Several jams occur before the first verse, all of which feature a maniacal Lesh and a sinister Garcia. Just before the lyrics, Lesh begins hinting at a "Caution" jam, but instead Garcia soars back into the "Dark Star." The transition from "The Other One" back to the "Dark Star" is so subtle that one is stuck wondering if they ever left it. Once again Lesh imitates Joe Montana by calling an audible and leads the band from the "Dark Star" into, of all things, a breathtaking instrumental "Uncle John's Band" *jam*. This indescribably joyous, uptempo interpretation must be heard to be believed. The transition back to "Dark Star" quickly leads into the second verse. "Saint Stephen" arises and jolts the entire band into cognizance. It is alive and full of electricity; the final jam is particularly hot. An exceptionally solid "Eleven Jam" provides the typical lightning leads, but what is really impressive is the transition. Garcia and the band really reach some deep improvisational territories. Ultimately Lesh gets his way and "Caution" is entered. Several long, bending and psychedelically sinister jams result before Pig brings the band back to more earthly realms with a long and detailed choral discourse. A cut occurs—Pig was singing about his mojo working, and after the cut, someone *other* than Pigpen (perhaps Mickey Hart?) is singing a sly slur about giving someone a sad smile while trucking down the line because "you too have been there before." The band enters a "Main Ten Jam" before returning for a scorching "Caution" finale. An extended "Feedback" ends with Garcia opening a bittersweet and slightly out of tune "Bid You Goodnight."

ROBERT A. GOETZ

## 11/15/69
### Lanai Theater, Crockett, California

Casey Jones, Me and My Uncle, Easy Wind, Cumberland Blues > China Cat Sunflower > I Know You Rider, High Time, Next Time You See Me, Mama Tried, Big Boss Man, Cosmic Charlie, Dire Wolf, Cold Rain and Snow, Good Lovin', Turn On Your Lovelight

**Source:** SBD, **Quality:** B+, **Length:** 2:15.

**Highlights:** Easy Wind, China Cat Sunflower > I Know You Rider, Cosmic Charlie, Good Lovin', Turn On Your Lovelight

This show is often underrated because of the great show a week earlier and the standard-looking set list that lacks the long string of songs found in many of the jams from 1969. After the band works its way into form with the first couple of songs, Pigpen leads it through a very bold and bluesy "Easy Wind." Pig, as he so often did, sparks the band and lifts them to a higher level. This is evident in the fast-paced "Cumberland Blues," which flows into an ebullient "China Cat Sunflower," which in turn pours into a right as rain "I Know You Rider." A pretty but rough-edged "High Time" is followed by Pig upping the ante with both "Next Time You See Me" and "Big Boss Man." A sweet and colorful "Cosmic Charlie" has the charged ending that they would sometimes forgo. After a plaintive backwoods "Dire Wolf" and the doleful matter-of-factness of "Cold Rain and Snow," Pigpen caps the show with a pair of songs. As was often the case when the Dead hit one of "those" moments, it is almost impossible to discern if it is the band or Pigpen who is leading the way. The energy and spirit of both unpredictability and joy are evident as the Dead alternately charge, brake, and charge again while Pigpen serves up his best blues improvisation as well as acting as social director.

— ANDREW J. LEMIEUX

## 11/21/69
### Building A, Cal Expo, Sacramento, California

**Set 1:** Cold Rain and Snow, Cumberland Blues, Easy Wind
**Set 2:** Tuning Up > Introduction, Good Lovin' > Drums > Good Lovin', China Cat Sunflower > I Know You Rider, High Time, Me and My Uncle, Turn On Your Lovelight//

**Source:** SBD, **Quality:** A, **Length:** 1:20, **Genealogy:** MR > RR > RR > PCM > DAT

**Highlights:** Cold Rain and Snow, Easy Wind, Good Lovin'

**Comments:** *DeadBase* lists this as a two-set show. The tapes that I've heard from this show have only the last half of the first set, and in the second set, the end of "Turn On Your Lovelight" is cut. It's only recently that the portion of the first set has become available. Although the songs on the tape that I have are out of order for a better fit, I will review the show in order. The tapes that I have heard of this show are all in stereo. In first set's mix the guitars and vocals are equally in both channels with the drums split to the left and right channels. Set 2 is also stereo, but it is a very strange, three-channel mix. Again, most of the band is centered—that's three guitars, two drummers, and all the vocals. Lesh's bass is hard to pick out. The right channel occasionally has either the bass or tom drum from one of the drummers. The organ is way over on the left side, and it is clearly audible.

The first set portion starts off with a very nice version of "Cold Rain and Snow." Throughout the whole song, Tom Constanten is there, and the mix has plenty of organ. Next, Garcia asks that the monitors be made "a taste louder." The band then jumps into a very short "Cumberland Blues," played by the book. "Easy Wind" follows, and for some reason it sounds particularly dark and evil! The jam after the verses starts off with a short harp solo by Pigpen, and then it's T.C. and Garcia, trading licks and solos. Here is T.C. at work demonstrating that he's got his licks down! Pigpen comes back for the closing verses, and that's almost it for the set. Apparently, the first set was plagued with sound and equipment problems. Bob Weir steps up to the mike: "Well, needless to say, here we are hung up again, caught in the shards of an electronic wasteland." Someone from the band says, "Tell them a joke, Bobby." Weir, in his inimitable style, proceeds to tell the "stow-ree" of the "short fat ugly squat little yellow dog."

The second set starts off with the band launching into a very nice version of "Good Lovin'." Next up, a version of "China" > "Rider" in which the "China Cat" remains true to the album version. Hearing it played this way, you realize how much it changed over the years. Garcia starts the transition into "I Know You Rider," but everyone is too into the "China Cat" jam to notice, so he goes exploring another theme for a few bars. "Me and My Uncle" starts out with T.C. playing lead on the first verse, and Garcia taking over after that. The song ends with a little "Dark Star" tuning tease, which is not to be. After the first set of lyrics in "Turn On Your Lovelight," the band goes off into a long jam. Pigpen comes back with "Now wait a minute..." and starts off a short rap that leads into "Well she's got...." He starts another rap, getting to "...my, my, my rider...," Mickey Hart starts on the guiro, and bummer of bummers, the tape fades out!

The songs played at this show are all "standards," but they give T.C. who is very prominent in the mix, a great opportunity to show his stuff. If you like Tom Constanten, this tape is for you.

IHOR SLABICKY

## 12/4/69
### Fillmore West, San Francisco, California

Casey Jones, Black Peter, Big Boss Man, Me and My Uncle, Cumberland Blues, Dire Wolf, Dark Star > High Time, Good Mornin'// Li'l Schoolgirl, Good Lovin', China Cat Sunflower > I Know You Rider, Uncle John's Band

**Source:** SBD, **Quality:** B-, **Length:** 2:15
**Highlights:** Not one minute
**Comments:** This show begins and ends with a dull, muddy, and poorly mixed sound with the central and potentially more interesting segment being even worse. There are lower-quality tapes around, some of which are infinitely more listenable than this show due to their musicality—an attribute sorely lacking here.

. . .

After a spoken introduction inviting people to Altamont (a bad omen if ever there was one), the set begins with a lumbering "Casey Jones" and progresses through some of the least inspired Dead music I've ever heard. Lots of T.C. in the mix is always welcome, but that's little compensation for virtually no Phil and the fact that the drummers sound like they're playing a wet cardboard box and a tin tray while Bob Weir seems to be totally absent for much of the time. "Black Peter" is an early performance and sounds it: a long intro, played very slowly and a sense that no one knows what's going on. Weir shows up for a dismal "Me and My Uncle" and sounds like he's been dosed, which I suppose is a possible explanation of the relatively poor musicianship on display here. Things wake up slightly for the Pigpen numbers but inspiration is thin on the ground and there's precious little here to excite even the most rabid Deadhead.

"Dark Star" > "High Time" sounds like a wonderful pairing, but seeing as the recording quality takes another dive shortly after the beginning, any moments of delight that may exist are successfully masked by a sound that is even muddier than before. In all honesty, you're extremely unlikely to want to listen to this all the way through in order to check whether there are any bright moments: it's not *fun*. Your trusted reviewer *did* sit through it all, and, believe me, I can think of at least a thousand things I'd rather do than repeat the exercise.

"China Cat Sunflower" > "I Know You Rider" is more like it, the band desperately trying to crank it up and salvage something from this lackluster performance, but it all slips away with an early "Uncle John's Band," which once again is decidedly hesitant and not a little formless. "Well, seeing as we blew most of the set just trying to remember how to play, so we're gonna blow this part of the set trying to sing a song we barely know," says Garcia by way of a warning just before it begins. Following a certain amount of floundering, it becomes obvious that they've forgotten how to end the song, and they decide to repeat the first verse instead.

Although it's perfectly true that every Dead show, no matter how dire, has at least a moment or two of sheer magic hidden away in it, considering just how many great shows there are out in the big wide world, you really don't want to worry about this one.

PAUL BODENHAM

## 12/5/69

**Fillmore West, San Francisco, California**

Me and My Uncle, Casey Jones, Black Peter, Mama Tried, Hurts Me Too, Cumberland Blues, Cryptical Envelopment > Drums > The Other One > The Eleven Jam > Cryptical Reprise > Cosmic Charlie, Dancin' in the Streets, Dire Wolf, China Cat Sunflower > I Know You Rider > High Time, Uncle John's Band > //The Main Ten > It's All Over Now, Baby Blue

**Source:** AUD, **Quality:** B-, **Length:** 2:15, **Genealogy:** MC > DAT, **Taper:** Harry Ely, with a Sony TC124 deck and a F995 mike

**Highlights:** Hurts Me Too, Dancin' in the Streets

This show is divided up nicely on two cassette tapes so the connected "Cryptical" suite is not disturbed by the tape flip. This audience recording has a pleasing mix and doesn't sound far away, as so many of the early audience tapes do. It is also surprisingly free from the large numbers of glitches and the wind tunnel hiss that handicap so many early audience recordings. This performance exudes an heavily countrified feel, reminding the listener of the band's roots.

"Me and My Uncle" and "Casey Jones" are both decent versions. "Black Peter," almost reaching the ten-minute mark, is a splendid long version that has a sweet and sorrowful tone. Bobby skips through a standard "Mama Tried," before Pigpen testifies in a tormented "Hurts Me Too" that would make Elmore James proud. Pig adds his usual great harp work between these emotionally troubled verses.

"Cumberland Blues" is warm, but "Dancin' in the Streets" is hot—a real scorcher from the get-go. Even though this version won't topple those of Harpur College '70 or Cornell University '77, it is extremely worthy in its own right. This mix favors the bass, drums, and keyboards, thereby accentuating the truly outstanding jam. "Dire Wolf" reminds the listener of how easily the Dead could jump from one style to another.

The second side of the tape starts with a pleasant "China Cat Sunflower" that segues into a softer "I Know You Rider," which in turn mellows further by descending into a thoughtful "High Time." The jam out of "Uncle John's Band" provides a rhythmic, almost jazzy platform for them to step off nicely into the "Main Ten." This grooves nicely for a few minutes before setting up a beautiful, heartfelt, eleven-minute-long "It's All Over Now, Baby Blue."

The second cassette tape from this show contains the "Other One" suite. We can all appreciate how great it is when the combined songs aren't interrupted and the flow isn't broken by a tape flip or switch. This is, however, one of the least exciting "Other One" suites in circulation; the band struggles all the way through. "Cryptical" drags. The drum solo is directionless. The audience, apparently unimpressed, starts talking. The entrance into "The Other One" is plopped down like an afterthought. The high point of the whole cluster is reached when Bobby comes in with his potently sung lyrics, obviously sounding frustrated that things aren't working. His tone of voice is aggravated, and it sounds as though he's trying to help everyone find their place. The "Eleven Jam" is a little less than average as there isn't much jamming. The "Cryptical" reprise, this time sweet and pretty, transitions smoothly into an average, almost goofy "Cosmic Charlie," which helps bring things to a close on a lighter note.

COREY SANDERSON

## 12/7/69

**Fillmore West, San Francisco, California**

Black Peter, Hard to Handle, Cumberland Blues, Mama Tried > Easy Wind, Dancin' in the Streets//, //Good Lovin', China Cat Sunflower > I Know You Rider, Saint Stephen > The Eleven > Turn On Your Lovelight

**Source:** SBD, **Quality:** C-, **Length:** 1:47, **Genealogy:** MR > C > Beta HF > PCM

**Highlights:** Black Peter (for Altamont, I am sure), Turn On Your Lovelight

**Comments:** One of the series of late 1969 soundboards that came into circulation in the early nineties, this show is one of the worst-sounding of the batch, although none of the batch was of pristine quality. There is an abnormal amount of hiss and almost no high end of music. Once you can mentally adjust to the sound, however, the music is there.

...

These tapes are quite interesting to anyone wanting to dig into a transitional time with the band. This is the beginning of "Uncle John's Band," the kind of band that one would see playing "down by the riverside." The heavy country roots-based music that had been introduced into shows during the fall was pervasive in shows now. In addition to the return of old covers like "Dancin' in the Streets" and "Big Boss Man," and the debuts of new covers like "Hard to Handle" and "Good Lovin'," new originals were brought out for this run of shows. This was ironic because these shows were grouped around the infamous concert at Altamont. This show was the day after and the tape begins appropriately with "Black Peter." With the exception of "Mama Tried" and "China Cat Sunflower," all of the first nine songs here had been either revived in the previous three months or were brand-new altogether. Songwise, this was almost a new band people were seeing. Coupled with the events at Altamont the previous day, this shook up the audience quite a bit. Happily, the band came through at the end with the old standard of 1969, "Saint Stephen" > "The Eleven" and a good, long "Turn On Your Lovelight." At least there was some reminder of the intensity of shows past.

DOUGAL DONALDSON

---

### 12/10/69
**Thelma Theater, Los Angeles, California**

Me and My Uncle, Cold Rain and Snow, Casey Jones, Good Mornin', Li'l Schoolgirl*, Morning Dew*, Black Queen*

* with Stephen Stills

---

**Source:** SBD, **Quality:** A, **Length:** 0:44, **Genealogy:** MR > RR > C

**Highlights:** Black Queen

**Comments:** Well, finally we have a tape we can count on as actually being from this night. As you will read in the reviews of the following night, a tape has been circulating for years labeled as this night. Listening to this tape, however, it is clear that the versions of "Me and My Uncle," "Cold Rain and Snow," and "Casey Jones" are not the same as those on the previously circulated version. We still are not absolutely sure where *that* tape is from, but we can feel fairly secure that *this* tape is labeled correctly.

This tape appears to begin somewhere in mid-set. "Me and My Uncle" kicks it off in the chunky, loping pace typical of late 1969, with Weir affecting his classic cowboy voice. An upbeat "Cold Rain" comes next, slowed down considerably from the high-speed versions of the early days, but still played as rock 'n' roll. Garcia applys a forceful attack on his guitar and is more considerate of the lyrics than the earlier style. Phil joyously chimes in on the chorus, completely off-key. "Casey Jones" is a typically unimpressive version. That song would not reach maturity for several years. At this point, Stephen Stills joins the stage for the remainder of the show. As the band launches into "Schoolgirl," his presence is apparent from the beginning. His guitar pierces the mix with classic sixties blues riffs. Pigpen, however, plays it straight, forcing Stills to keep up and find his own places to interject riffs and solos. Unfortunately, he never gets a chance as Garcia immediately grabs the first solo and Pigpen follows him up with a harmonica solo. Vocally, this is one of the more unique and interesting versions of this song. Next up is "Morning Dew." Stills appears to be more comfortable, but this is a hard song for a stranger to find his place. He makes a good effort, though. You can hear Garcia giving him a verbal warning of the coming bridge, and they manage to turn it into a decent duet. Stills takes the solo for the first part of an extended final jam, and then turns it over to Garcia to finish off. Now, Stills having found his feet with the band, it becomes his turn to do a number. He picks "Black Queen," a song that would also be played at the other guest appearance by Stills years later. He leads the band through a long intro and then launches into the lyrics, with its card-playing references foreshadowing themes that were just beginning to become common in Dead songs. The first jam does not really go anywhere as the band is waiting for Stills to lead the way. The second jam finally develops into a nice, rocked-out jam, with shades of "Mason's Children," before seamlessly transforming into "Turn On Your Lovelight." Unfortunately, here the tape fades. One suspects that with Stills' blues background and proper warmup, it must have been good. Maybe, someday, the rest of the tape, and the mystery of these shows, will all be revealed.

DOUGAL DONALDSON

## Reviews: December 1969

### 12/11/69
#### Early Show, Thelma Theater, Los Angeles, California

Casey Jones, Cold Rain and Snow, Mama Tried, Dire Wolf, Hurts Me Too, China Cat Sunflower > I Know You Rider, Black Peter > Me and My Uncle, Hard to Handle, Dark Star//, //Cryptical Envelopment > Drums > The Other One > Cryptical Envelopment > Cosmic Charlie//

**Source:** AUD, **Quality:** B+, **Length:** 1:52, **Genealogy:** MR > RR > Beta HF > PCM

**Highlights:** Casey Jones, Dire Wolf, It Hurts Me Too, Dark Star

**Comments:** The debate over the origin of this tape has raged for decades. It was originally circulated as the Kaleidoscope in Los Angeles from 12/10/69. I have also seen it labeled as being from the Straight Theater in San Francisco. Both places had closed by this date. While the material does fit the time frame, another tape from 12/10/69 has surfaced from a more reliable source that has a different ending. The other tape ends with "Good Mornin', Li'l Schoolgirl," "Morning Dew," and "Black Queen," all with Stephen Stills performing with the band. The real truth about this tape came out when, in the early 1990s, among a batch of mediocre-quality soundboard tapes, the soundboard of 12/11/69 appeared. This tape had many of the same songs in the same order, and, after very close listening, it is clear that these songs are the same versions. Several hours of close listening to key parts of the two tapes confirms that they are without question from the same night (12/11/69). The evidence is as follows: (1) On the soundboard of 12/10/69, "Casey Jones" is different from these two. (2) In the transition from "Black Peter" to "Me and My Uncle," Garcia's guitar lead into the first verse of "Uncle" is identical. (3) The false start to "Dark Star" is identical. (4) During and just after the first verse of "Dark Star," the gongs, Garcia's lead, and Lesh's bass notes are identical. (5) There is a great jam just before the second verse of "Dark Star" that builds nicely until the moment that Garcia pulls the ripcord and brings the band softly back into the main theme and the verse. This is identical on the two tapes. (6) The very end of "Dark Star" is cut and then you hear Garcia count off the lead into "Cryptical." Definitely not part of the same jam. However, the "Cryptical"/"Other One"/"Cosmic Charlie" segment does not match the one from 12/11/69. It is not clear where that version originated. It, too, is an audience tape and has nearly the same ambient sound as this tape. Although the "Other One" is very similar to the one on the 12/11 soundboard, it is not identical. It does not match any other version I have heard on tape and may indeed be from 12/10/69, the only surviving portion of that audience tape.

The show itself is the second of a four-show run in Southern California, three shows at the Thelma Theater and one out toward the desert in San Bernardino. The band, having recovered from the previous week's debacle at Altamont, set about making up for the dismal set of shows from the Fillmore West where they debuted their new material that would appear on *Workingman's Dead*. Having not played in the Southland since March in Pasadena, and not in L.A. proper in nearly a year, the band decided to give the locals a mix of both the new and old material. Opening with a laid-back "Casey Jones" and the new, slower version of "Cold Rain and Snow," it was clear that this was going to be a mellow, sit-down show. The "Mama Tried" and "Dire Wolf" were also of the campfire sing-along variety. Next came Pigpen's slow, bluesy "Hurts Me Too." Things finally begin to

*Jerry on the pedal steel guitar, 1969*
(photo credit: Fred Ordower)

pick up with "China Cat" > "I Know You Rider." A nice long "Black Peter" is followed immediately by "Me and My Uncle" and a very short "Hard to Handle." Pigpen had still not quite developed this song to the heights it would achieve by 1971.

The "Dark Star" is the gem of this tape. After quickly taking the main theme into the first verse, T.C. meanders through the sparse feedback-laden jam, drifting among the plunking notes of Weir and Garcia. Finally, Weir comes up with the "Feelin' Groovy Jam," which is joined by the rest of the band. This leads directly into a wonderful nameless jam before Garcia's ripcord lead-in to the main theme again and then the second verse. Wherever the "Cryptical"/"Other One"/"Cosmic Charlie" combo came from, it, too, is stellar. "The Other One" rocks with primitive intensity, and the "Cryptical" reprise floats softly up to the ether, where it is transformed into "Cosmic Charlie." Unfortunately, it is here that the tape is cut.

DOUGAL DONALDSON

---

## 🌀 12/11/69 🌀

### Thelma Theater, Los Angeles, California

**Set 1 (or Early Show):** //Black Peter > Me and My Uncle, Hard to Handle, Dark Star > Saint Stephen > The Eleven > Cumberland Blues
**Set 2 (or Late Show):** Morning Dew, Next Time You See Me, Sittin' on Top of the World, Beat It on Down the Line, Big Boss Man, Good Lovin', High Time, Dancin' in the Streets, Easy Wind, Cryptical Envelopment > Drums > The Other One > Cryptical Reprise > Cosmic Charlie

---

**Source:** SBD, **Quality:** B, **Length:** 2:33, **Genealogy:** MR > C? > Beta HF > PCM
**Highlights:** Dark Star, The Eleven, Dancin' in the Streets, The Other One

Yet another of the dull, hissy soundboards that came from late 1969, this show was an excellent example of the peaks that the band was able to obtain while in the midst of transition. The focus of shows in this month was clearly on the *Workingman's Dead* material. You can also tell that the band was fairly subdued by the debacle of Altamont. This show was able to mix the new material in with the classic, but now rare, material from the beginning of the year. It is not clear whether this night actually had two shows. At the end of "Cumberland Blues," the emcee comes on and says, "A very beautiful group, the Grateful Dead." This usually would only happen at the end of a show. It would, however, explain the length of both this show and the following night's. Both are far longer than nearly every other show from 1969. However, there is also the question of why the Thursday and Friday night shows (12/11 and 12/12) would get two sets, but the Saturday night show, at San Bernadino, would get only one. Possibly the band was worn out after four shows on consecutive nights. Regardless, the music from this night was excellent. The "Dark Star" > "Saint Stephen" > "The Eleven" is every bit as mature and interesting as any from the year. The "Dark Star" is missing some of the familiar themes from versions in the early part of the year, but does have some interesting segments. Although possibly lacking some of the fury of earlier in the year, "The Eleven" is strong throughout and the band is never at a loss for where to take the jam. As "The Eleven" is winding down, you can hear a hint of "Cumberland," which then appears suddenly a few seconds later.

The second show is equally interesting with a large sampling of songs from all four years of the band's existence. The "Morning Dew" is a welcome surprise, and together with "Sittin' on Top of the World," "Beat It on Down the Line," and "Dancin' in the Streets," makes this show a throwback to 1967. However, interspersed with newer songs like "Next Time You See Me," "High Time," and "Easy Wind," it keeps the audience firmly grounded in the present as well. Although his songs were generously sprinkled throughout the set, Pigpen was not a dominating force this night. The highlights all belonged to the ensemble playing of the whole band. The set ends with a blistering "Cryptical" > "Other One" suite that sweetly melts into a short but pleasant "Cosmic Charlie." The band seems to want to continue on at this point but can't think of what to do. Garcia says, "Fuck it," Weir says, "Later," and off they go back to the hotel to get ready for the third and final night.

DOUGAL DONALDSON

## 12/12/69

**Thelma Theater, Los Angeles, California**

**Set 1 (or Early Show):** Cold Rain and Snow, Me and My Uncle, Easy Wind, Cumberland Blues, Black Peter, Next Time You See Me, China Cat Sunflower > I Know You Rider, Turn On Your Lovelight
**Set 2 (or Late Show):** Hard to Handle, Casey Jones, Mama Tried > High Time, Dire Wolf, Good Lovin'//, King Bee, Uncle John's Band > He Was a Friend of Mine, Alligator > Drums > Alligator > Caution > Feedback > We Bid You Goodnight

**1. Source:** SBD, **Quality:** A, **Length:** 3:15, **Genealogy:** MR > C? > Beta HF > PCM
**2. Source:** FM (DHD 378), **Quality:** A, **Length:** 0:55 ("China Cat Sunflower" > "I Know You Rider," "Turn On Your Lovelight," "Hard to Handle," "Casey Jones")
**3. Source:** FM (DHD 120), **Quality:** A, **Length:** 0:55 ("Uncle John's Band" > "He Was a Friend of Mine," "Alligator" > "Drums" > "Alligator" > "Caution"//) "Caution" cuts at about twelve minutes before the end of the show.

**Highlights:** Turn On Your Lovelight, Uncle John's Band, He Was a Friend of Mine, Alligator, Caution

**Comments:** It is uncertain whether this was two sets or two shows. The show is extraordinarily long for it to be one show. Also, on the previous night, an emcee came onstage and asked the crowd to give the band a hand after first set ended, indicating that that evening offered two shows, not two sets. There were shows in this period that were sold as early or late shows; however, no advertising or witness has been found to corroborate either theory.

If the previous night featured the ensemble playing of the band, this night belonged all to Pigpen. His songs take up over half the entire evening. Both shows end with unbelievable versions of his biggest show stoppers. "Turn On Your Lovelight" is over thirty minutes long and swings back and forth between Pigpen's long wailing raps and mind-blowing jamming from the rest of the band. Even Pigpen seems to acknowledge the ridiculous length of this version. Toward the end of the song, he says, "When you think it's all over, it isn't. Got to get it on one more time, the love shines on me, right through the trees." Ultimately, this whole run of shows was but a warm-up to the final hour of this night. Fortunately, this is where the A-quality soundboard cuts in. It begins with a lovely, but stumbling, version of "Uncle John's Band" that seamlessly transforms into a hauntingly beautiful version of a surprising "He Was a Friend of Mine" (the next to last version ever). Next comes one of the most tremendous versions of "Alligator" > "Caution" on tape, rivaling even the versions from late 1967 and early 1968 that were used for *Anthem of the Sun*. The "Alligator" jam after the drums is monstrous and storms into the opening riffs of "Caution." The band jams out on "Caution" long enough that you think they are going to skip the vocal part altogether, but Pigpen finally comes through. After a couple of verses and a whole lot of "All you needs," the band launches into a brilliantly fierce jam and winds down to a brief pause. This is where the excellent-sounding tape fades out. What is missed on that tape, but is in the lesser-quality tape, is a frightfully intense session of the classic "Caution" melody, groups of eight notes rising and falling like a roller coaster followed by three huge bombs. All the time, Garcia is scrubbing furiously in and out of this rhythm. Eventually, it all descends into Pigpen's "mojo hand" wail and a massive feedback storm that eventually blows itself out into a calm, floating cloud before evaporating into "We Bid You Goodnight."

DOUGAL DONALDSON

## 12/13/69

**Swing Auditorium, San Bernardino, California**

Casey Jones, Hard to Handle, Black Peter, Mama Tried > China Cat //Sunflower > I Know You Rider, High Time, Good Lovin' > Drums > Good Lovin' > Cumberland, Saint Stephen > Turn On Your Lovelight

**Source:** SBD, **Quality:** B, **Length:** 1:25, **Genealogy:** MR > C? > Beta HF > PCM

After three amazing shows in downtown L.A., the band just is not able to get any energy happening for a fourth night. This show ranks with some of the most lackluster performances in the band's history. The tenor of shows at this time was already fairly laid-back, but this night's was nearly unconscious. The playing seems tired and the set selection is certainly uninspired. The only brief flash of inspiration comes during the "Cumberland Blues," which is one of the better, if not the longest, versions of the month. Getting to that moment, however, the band had to slog through an hour's worth of songs where both they and the audience seem half-asleep. The "Good Lovin'" features an interminably long drum set that seems to enable the band to go splash some water on their faces and perk up some. It doesn't last long, however, as after a respectable "Good Lovin'" and the "Cumberland Blues" comes an embarrassing version of "Turn On Your Lovelight." This version is so pathetic that the band gives up halfway through it, and the song dwindles to an end without the usual crescendo. So much for Saturday night.

DOUGAL DONALDSON

---

### 12/19/69
**Fillmore Auditorium, San Francisco, California**

**Acoustic Set:** Monkey and the Engineer, Little Sadie, Long Black Limousine, I've Been All Around This World
**Electric Set:** Mason's Children, China Cat Sunflower > I Know You Rider, Black Peter, Hard to Handle, Cumberland Blues//, Good Lovin', Cryptical Envelopment > Drums > The Other One > Cryptical Reprise, Uncle John's Band > Turn On Your Lovelight

---

**1. Source:** SBD, **Quality:** B-, **Length:** 2:00, **Genealogy:** RR > C? > Beta HF > PCM
**2. Source:** AUD, **Quality:** C-, **Length:** 2:00, **Taper:** Harry Ely
**3. Source:** FM-SBD (GDH 158 and 159), **Quality:** A, **Length:** 0:40 (Acoustic Set and "Cryptical" through "Uncle John's"), **Genealogy:** MR > DAT
**Highlights:** Little Sadie, Uncle John's Band, Turn On Your Lovelight

This show is highly significant in that it appears to be the first to feature an acoustic set (Jerry says that while Phil is missing, he and Bobby will regale the crowd with a few numbers). Granted, it was brought about fully by accident because there were significant technical problems. It was successful enough, however, that they tried it again the next week in Dallas and then numerous times in 1970. The first five songs of this show (four acoustic and one electric) had never before been played by the Dead. This came right after a whole raft of new songs had been introduced in the previous few months. Once out of the way, though, the band settles into the usual song selection, performing a solid "China Cat" > "Rider," the typical lengthy "Black Peter," and a rocking "Cumberland Blues." "Black Peter," in December 1969, generally averaged between twelve and fifteen minutes, which always surprises people nowadays who are used to hearing versions from 1970 and 1971, when it had been considerably shortened to its length on *Workingman's Dead*. Fully half the show is the final jam of the "Other One" suite that segues nicely into a sweet "Uncle John's Band" and winds up to a long (nearly twenty-five minutes) "Turn On Your Lovelight." Even though Pigpen had not yet fully developed his storytelling style in that song, the versions in late 1969 were all clocking in at a minimum of twenty minutes, with some stretching over thirty minutes. This version had the usual peaks and valleys of intensity with Pigpen and the rest of the band trading off the lead until the song spiraled up to a huge climax that left the audience exhausted.

DOUGAL DONALDSON

---

### 12/26/69
**McFarlin Auditorium, Southern Methodist University, Dallas, Texas**

**Acoustic Set:** Monkey and the Engineer, Little Sadie, Long Black Limousine, I've Been All Around This World, The Master's Bouquet, Black Peter, Uncle John's Band
**Electric Set:** //Casey Jones, Me and My Uncle, Cold Rain and Snow, China Cat Sunflower > I Know You Rider > High Time, Dark Star//, //Turn On Your Lovelight

---

**Source:** SBD, **Quality:** B-/C+, **Length:** 1:40, **Genealogy:** MC > C > C
**Highlights:** Little Sadie, Long Black Limousine, I've Been All Around This World, The Master's Bouquet

The acoustic set is very down-home and features splendid versions of "Little Sadie," "Black Limo," and "All Around This World." The old spiritual "Master's Bouquet" makes a rare appearance with Christmas just around the corner. There is plenty of stage banter in the form of consternation for the missing Phil (who shows up) and Billy (who does not).

With Billy back, the electric set nonetheless starts out rather low-key. In all fairness, too much music is missing to give this show a fair shake. "Dark Star," which cuts after only two minutes, actually goes into a big jam > "Dark Star" > "New Speedway Boogie." One can only imagine. "Turn On Your Lovelight" begins in the middle to give us only the last ten minutes' worth. But hey—it's a raucous, inspired ending at that. Weir and Pigpen do one of their infamous screaming duets that brings the house down. After the final yelps, some guy takes the mike and zings the crowd with "You've just had it done to you by the Grateful Dead, folks!" Nice line.

MICHAEL M. GETZ

and finally Jerry telling the kids to "Remember the other guy—don't create fear in anyone."

"Hard to Handle," featuring a strong, extended jam that brings the vibe of anarchy onstage up to the level out in the rowdy audience. The band moves into "Mason's Children" but stops so Pigpen can warn the crowd again about the towers, ending when someone chimes in, "You've been warned, now do what you want." But the band seems a little distracted, which makes for tough sledding during the harmonies on "Mason's Children." They begin to cook again in the middle of the tune, with a psychedelic solo from Jerry and Phil right there.

Given the supercharged atmosphere the Dead wisely chooses to play "Turn On Your Lovelight." They are more confident now, pulling off a gorgeous a cappella "shine on me" near the middle. Pig sings while Jerry talks back with his guitar. Classic stuff. Unfortunately, the tape cuts out before the set ends.

With all the audience interaction and Pig's strength as the front man this tape emits the raw but high-energy feelings of a primal '69 show.

ERIC TAYLOR

## 12/28/69
### Miami Pop Festival, International Speedway, Hollywood, Florida

//Good Lovin', Cold Rain and Snow, Hard to Handle, Mason's Children, Turn On Your Lovelight//

**Source:** SBD, **Quality:** B-, **Length:** 2:15, **Genealogy:** MR > R > R > PCM > DAT

**Highlights:** Hard to Handle, Mason's Children, Turn On Your Lovelight, and "the vibe"

This is definitely a festival gig. This tape begins near the end of "Good Lovin'." The band's obviously playing intensely, with Pigpen at the helm. Phil sounds particularly clear during "Cold Rain." Pigpen's organ reminds me of Country Joe and the Fish during that period. On my tape vocals are a bit distorted.

Then it's major tune-up time—always a real big part of those early shows. Just before "Hard to Handle," Pigpen creates apparent anarchy when he invites the audience to "come closer." What ensues is Phil and Bobby asking, pleading, "Watch the wires and towers,"

## 12/29/69
### Boston Tea Party, Boston, Massachusetts

**Set 1:** //Mama Tried, Black Peter, Easy Wind, Me and My Uncle, China Cat Sunflower > I Know You Rider, High Time, Hard to Handle, Mason's Children
**Set 2:** Cumberland Blues, Casey Jones, Good Lovin' > Drums//

**Source:** SBD, **Quality:** B-/C+, **Length:** 1:40, **Genealogy:** MC > C > C > C

**Highlights:** Mason's Children

This seems like a mere warm-up for the following night (which cooks!). Despite a soulful rendering of "Black Peter" and solid takes on "Hard to Handle" and "China Cat" > "I Know You Rider," it's hard to fairly assess this show because—like 12/26/69—so much of the second set is missing. However, the "Mason's Children" is worth special mention as it's played in that straight-ahead, in-yo'-face jamming style a la "Viola Lee Blues."

MICHAEL M. GETZ

## 12/30/69

**Boston Tea Party, Boston, Massachusetts**

**Set 1:** Good Lovin', Mama Tried, New Speedway Boogie, Casey Jones, Black Peter, Me and My Uncle, Midnight Hour, Cumberland Blues, Cryptical Envelopment > Drums > The Other One// > Cosmic Charlie
**Set 2:** Uncle John's Band > Mason's Children, China Cat Sunflower > I Know You Rider, Dark Star//, //Alligator > Drums > The Eleven > Alligator Reprise > We Bid You Goodnight

**Source:** SBD, **Quality:** A-, **Length:** 2:30, **Genealogy:** MC > C > C > C > DAT

**Highlights:** The Other One, Black Peter, Dark Star//Alligator > The Eleven > Alligator > We Bid You Goodnight

**Comments:** This is a great soundboard tape (for the time), with a near-perfect mix of instruments and voices. My tape, of unknown generation, has a fair amount of hiss. (Usually on a ninety-minute tape and a hundred-minute tape, with the side A of tape 2 having about twenty minutes blank; this is in order to get the "Dark Star" > "Alligator" > "Drums" > "The Eleven" > "Alligator" > "We Bid You Goodnight" sequence on a single fifty-minute side.) The two sets are complete except for two gaps: one of unknown duration between the middle of "Dark Star," which cuts to the end of the verses in "Alligator"; the other, presumably shorter, from the second verse of "The Other One" to the beginning of the segued "Cosmic Charlie."

The Dead are generally thought of as a sixties band. However, as we know, the sixties were just the beginning of their long, strange trip. This concert, on the cusp of a new decade, was also on the cusp of major changes in the structure and style of the band: These were the final days of the seven-man ensemble, Tom Constanten being heard here for one of the last times. Meanwhile, the sound and songs that would emerge in 1970 as *Workingman's Dead* had begun to come into their own. Don't get me wrong, though: This is not one of those shows you'll want to collect for historical value. Au contraire: this is a show that will blow you away, time and time again. Typically, perhaps, the Dead treat us to the full range of their repertoire on this night. There are the extended and exploratory ragas "Dark Star" and "The Other One," juxtaposed with the short and sweet country tunes "Mama Tried" and "Me and My Uncle"; there are songs on the wax, such as "Uncle John's Band" and "Cumberland Blues," together with "Alligator" and "The Eleven," songs we would soon know were on the wane. And then there is the tune pulled out of a hat, the all-but-forgotten "Midnight Hour."

"Good Lovin'" is a solid opener, the band is tight, as are the vocals. In fact, one of the things that stands out about this show is the quality vocal work (we are talking within the context of the Grateful Dead, of course). Following a tight and spirited "Mama Tried" we hear the first "New Speedway Boogie" available on tape, appearing just a very few weeks after the tragic episode at the Altamont Speedway free concert, which moved Robert Hunter to write it. The vocals may seem a bit overproduced, but Jerry's slide guitar solo is superb. Another song introduced within the previous month is "Black Peter," which comes off very nicely indeed. The highlight of the first set, however, is unquestionably "The Other One." From the thunderous, opening Phil bomb coming out of "Drums," to the end of the song, Lesh takes his unique lead bass to new heights (and depths). It is Phil who clearly sets the pace here but by steering, not pulling; it is the coordinated performance of the ensemble that makes this an awesome peformance you are likely never to forget. "Cosmic Charlie" is a delightful way to wind down the set, though this rendition is not quite up to the standards set five months later on that legendary night in Binghamton, New York.

The second set opens with two more tunes that were less than a month old: "Uncle John's Band" and "Mason's Children." It is interesting to note that they both feel a bit rough around the edges, and that "Mason" would soon fade from the rotation. "Uncle John's Band," on the other hand, would undergo a rearrangement, quickly becoming a linchpin of the Dead's repertoire. (In fact, this was perhaps the last rendition of "Uncle John's Band" without the G-B-C-D chords in the introduction and between verses.) Following a solid performance of the familiar "China Cat Sunflower" > "I Know You Rider" sequence, the Dead open the doors and lead us into the Magic Kingdom. No one knows just how long the gap is that wrenches you out of "Dark Star" just when things are starting to build into a very sweet jam and drops you unceremoniously amid the last verse of "Alligator"; for all we know, there might even have been a "Saint Stephen" in there as well! But no one belittles the Sphinx just because its face has been disfigured; similarly, no connoisseur of "Dark Star" will disparage this performance, incomplete though the record of it may be. This "Dark Star" is typical of the late '69 renditions: very mellow and sweet, not the haunting D sharp space, while retaining all of the essential ingredients of "Dark Star" à la *Live Dead*. T.C.'s organ is right up front in the mix, which really helps to make this "Dark Star" special. The polite but sincere applause from the audience, as Jerry begins the words to the first verse, reveals the intimate feel that pervades this whole show, and particularly during this visceral, fifty-minute sequence. Throughout, there is no hurry. Things develop with patience, deliberation, equanimity. Coming out of the verse, Mickey's toys (the gongs, bells, etc.) and T.C.'s organ paint fairy landscapes for us, somewhat as in "Leave the Castle" on *Anthem of the Sun*. For long stretches we hear feedback, then space, then a familiar "Dark Star riff, and then a tease of a jam, but it's enveloped and quietly shrouded in T.C.'s waterfall. Finally, Phil and Bobby pull things out of the abyss and into, finally, what we later came to call the "Feelin' Groovy Jam." After a couple minutes of tight, spirited jamming, just as we sense an imminent transition into another motif 19:20 after it all began—WHACK! (The tape is cut.) And suddenly it's "'or! Alligator running round my door...." With the "Alligator" and "The Eleven" that follow, we are held in the same intense but mellow iron-velvet grip of a Grateful Dead Experience. Neither of these songs would be played more a few times again, ever. But there is no hint of boredom or inattentiveness in this performance. The boys are gettin' down. Enjoy it, folks; it doesn't get any better than this.

DWIGHT HOLMES

### ??/69
#### Unknown Location
I'm a Lovin' Man, Buckey's Theme

**Source:** SBD, **Quality:** A, **Length:** 0:10
**Highlights:** All
**Personnel:** Jerry Garcia, Ron McKernan, John Tenney, and Bob Weir. The bass player is unidentified.

**Comments:** Supposedly, these are outtakes from a Pigpen solo LP that was never completed. An absolutely delightful pair of tracks, this brief excerpt shows Weir and Pigpen truly in their element. Heartfelt and soulful, "I'm a Lovin' Man" is a unique country/bluegrass selection, with just a touch of rockabilly thrown in for good measure. The combination of smooth-as-silk Weir verse with Hank Williams–gruff Pigpen vocals oozes elegance against Garcia and Tenney's illustrious pedal steel/fiddle blends. It's a shame that this was not released. Little is known about the instrumental "Buckey's Theme." This selection is picture-perfect for square dancing with its knee-slappin' swing rhythm. Garcia's pedal steel solos are simply enormous, while Tenney's fiddling is subtly sensuous. It's unfortunate that it's less than five minutes long.

BRIAN DYKE

### ??/69
#### Action House, Island Park, New York
Doin' That Rag > The Seven > Good Lovin' > Drums > Good Lovin' > Saint Stephen > The Eleven//

**Source:** AUD, **Quality:** C (many versions that circulate are pitched way too fast), **Length:** 0:45
**Highlights:** The entire medley—especially "The Seven"
**Comments:** This show has circulated for at least two decades under several guises. Most Deadheads know this as the mysterious Action House tape variously dated as: ?/?/69, 7/11/69, 11/11/69, and 11/9/70. It was generally attached to what appears to be an actual fragment of 11/9/70 Action House, Island Park, New York. It has also circulated for years as 9/29/69 Café au Go-Go, New York, New York. Chances are, this will always be a mystery.

Regardless, this wild medley represents one of the highwater marks from a very good jamming year for the Dead. Opening with a long, loose version of "Doin' That Rag," the band goes from an instrumental restatement of the last line of the chorus straight into one of only a handful of known full-band performances of "The Seven." This version is marked by some stunning harmonic interplay between Weir and Garcia on the fast parts. This jam—which in spirit and energy is a kissing cousin of

"The Eleven"—sounds like classical music on acid: it is joyously melodic, breathtakingly fast, stop-on-a-dime tight—in a word, mind-blowing! After restating each facet of the piece several times, the band explodes instantly into a version of "Good Lovin'" that is unbelievably frenetic even when this tape is pitched correctly. This turn leads into a crisp "Saint Stephen" on which both guitars and keyboards favor a percussive attack. A slow, slightly ponderous (and truncated) version of "The Eleven" follows "Stephen" and the "William Tell" bridge. Despite the quality, this is must-have music for collectors of primal Dead.

JOHN R. DWORK AND MICHAEL PARRISH

*Phil*

conversation equivalent to a roundtable chat where everyone is talking at the same time. Somehow, the ensemble manages to synchronize for the first climax, which is hampered by a completely inappropriate harp contribution. On the first dissolution, MacDonald gives a truly lame rap attempt, with remote nods to "Turn On Your Lovelight" and "Mellow Down Easy," before leading into the next theme, a swinging blues shuffle. The synchronicity improves to a listenable level, as the guitarists seemingly attempt to take turns showcasing their licks, but quickly the harmony disintegrates when the unidentified harp player again butts in with a painstakingly awful solo that is neither in time nor in tune. As the jam accelerates, Hart makes a valiant effort to steady the groove, but the density of such a large assembly of egos onstage simply overwhelms his attempt, resulting in a long and irrational passage of unfocused drivel. Dissolving once again, nearly to silence, the jam then turns to a brief feedback jam, again teasing the finish, but slowly rising into a surprisingly schmaltzy fifties-style ballad theme. Switching between breezy spring keyboard drifts and fiery lead guitar descensions, this passage is simple and virtuous. As the theme winds down, the ensemble gradually erupts, bringing the pulse to a respectable, albeit long-winded, climax and conclusion.

BRIAN DYKE

---

### ??/69
**Fillmore West, San Francisco, California**

**Jam:** Donovan's Reef

**Source:** SBD (CD), **Quality:** A-, **Length:** 0:40
**Highlights:** The last ten minutes
**Personnel:** Jack Casady, Jerry Garcia, Mickey Hart, Jorma Kaukonen, Country Joe MacDonald, Steve Miller, and others

This track, which appears on Country Joe and the Fish's *Live! Fillmore West '69* CD, features an all-star lineup reminiscent of the 1968 Mickey Hart and the Hartbeats performances. While the selection certainly sounds promising throughout the intro and verse, which is raspy in execution and ridiculous in content, the jam that emerges is unfocused and random. Each guitarist quickly slips out of time, and the rhythm supply of Casady and Hart is painstakingly irregular. The musicians leave little space between phrases, making for a terminally dense

---

### ??/69[?]
**Location Unknown**

**Radio Commercials:** *Aoxomoxoa* (x3), *Live Dead*, *Workingman's Dead* (x3), *American Beauty*, *Europe '72* (x2), *Bear's Choice*, Cheetah Club, Port Chester Apology, Anti-Heroin PSA, Planned Parenthood

**Source:** FM, **Quality:** Varies from A to B, **Length:** 0:15

**Highlights:** All

In the grand Grateful Dead tradition of not approaching anything related to marketing in a serious manner, these radio commercials are ingeniously constructed not only to grab one's attention, but to provide enough entertainment to arouse interest in the product as well.

Among the most comical spots are for *Aoxomoxoa,* which the narrator alludes to by confessing that he's not able to pronounce the title. The first, with "Dupree's Diamond Blues" as backdrop, is fairly straightforward in effect. The second contains a hilarious mock interview where a female fan is asked to rate "What's Become of the Baby" in *American Bandstand* fashion, of course scoring it in the high nineties for rhythm, danceability, and lyrical content (yeah, right!). The final spot, against a backdrop of "Doin' That Rag," is narrated in a hyperbolous fashion so rapidly that its content is completely diminished, although its comic value is certainly undeniable.

The *Live Dead* commercial is narrated in Howard Cosell style, with the "Saint Stephen" climax as background music.

The commercials for *Workingman's Dead,* which the narrator describes as country flavored, are all identical in script, varying only in background, with one containing excerpts from "Dire Wolf" and "New Speedway Boogie"; one containing excerpts from "Easy Wind," "Cumberland Blues," and "Uncle John's Band"; and yet another containing excerpts from "Uncle John's Band," "Black Peter," and "Casey Jones." Each ends with the slogan "Steal it!"

Another comical spot is the *American Beauty* commercial, with a "Truckin'" backdrop, in which the narrator describes a young and very pristine fan named Trisha. After describing a series of satirical and borderline risqué transformations that she undergoes after hearing the Grateful Dead, the narrator then retracts each description by listing its possible consequences. This leads into the pitch to purchase the record, stating that its contents are a near substitute for the aforementioned descriptions. This commercial is far too hilarious to be adequately described.

The spots for *Europe '72* are both narrated in sports announcer style; the first resembles an athletic team lineup announcement, and the second, an ad for Tower Records, is a mock horse race. Both ads are backdropped by "Sugar Magnolia," with the ads emphasizing the ridiculously low price of $4.99.

The spot for *Bear's Choice* quotes briefly from a March 11, 1973, *New York Times* piece before leading into an excerpt from "Wake Up, Little Susie" and subsequent promo and slogan: "You can't eat caviar every day, and a good hamburger is a good hamburger," ending with a bit from "Hard to Handle."

The Cheetah Club commercial, with a "Viola Lee Blues" background, is speculated to be bogus, alluding to an event on Friday, August 11. Directed specifically to hippies, the narration runs through the band's personnel lineup before giving the promo for the event.

The Port Chester apology, issued because of the cancellation of a series of shows in late 1970 that were rescheduled for February 1971, is as much of a clowning session as an actual statement. Following a delicious banjo intro, Garcia and Hart give a lighthearted and heavily overdubbed apology.

In his public-service announcement, Weir introduces himself and gives a seemingly sincere warning about the negative repercussions of heroin use, based of course on observations of others rather than personal experience. It's real brief.

Perhaps the most perplexing commercial of the lot is Garcia's spot for Planned Parenthood. The interview begins somewhat seriously with Garcia expressing regrets of his shortcomings as a parent, but he quickly reduces his credibility by remarking, "You know, really I don't have anything to say about it; if I understood that stuff, I wouldn't be in trouble all the time," followed by his trademark giggling.

BRIAN DYKE

# 1970

*The year 1970 was one of great transition. Acoustic music was fully integrated into most major-venue shows by this time, often combined with two electric sets and a set by the New Riders of the Purple Sage featuring Garcia on pedal steel. Billed as "An Evening with the Grateful Dead," it contained four whopping sets of music that would carry late into the evening, sometimes until daybreak. The sound of* Workingman's Dead, *having been integrated into shows in the last months of 1969, was* now dominant. "The Eleven," "Alligator," and "Caution," once staples of a Dead show, barely made it past the first two months. "The Eleven" was replaced in the "Dark Star" > "Saint Stephen" sequence by the old rock 'n' roll standard "Not Fade Away," a much simpler song to perform, but one that still provided a solid base for musical exploration.

"Dark Star" and the "Cryptical" > "Other One" suite had become the only frameworks of the long, psychedelic jams, and they remained so until "Playing in the Band" blossomed in 1972 By 1970, the "Cryptical"/"Other One" suite had become a fierce, driving behemoth of a song that often attained a primal energy that recalled the rawness of early days. In many of the more popular versions, the music reached ecstatic peaks not only in the central "Other One" portion, but also in the final "Cryptical" reprise, where the intensity would rise and fall before finally washing into the lilting opening bars of a "Cosmic Charlie" or, in some cases, "Attics of My Life." "Dark Star," on the other hand, would often dissolve from the main theme to a meditation of textural, non-rhythmic sounds including "Feedback," then build up to an intense free-form jam before transitioning back into the familiar, comfortable main theme again. The free-form jam sometimes developed into another of their quintessential musical progressions, this one an instrumental melody, would commonly become known as the "Feelin' Groovy Jam," similar to Paul Simon's "59th Street Bridge Song."

These two songs, "Dark Star" and "The Other One," no longer were the centerpiece of every show, however. As in the latter part of 1969, many shows would consist of a series of individual songs and end with a raging version of "Turn On Your Lovelight" or "Viola Lee Blues," which enjoyed a brief comeback in 1970. "Dancin' in the Streets" and "Good Lovin'" also had brief stints as songs that contained free-form jams in the more extended versions from 1970.

More new songs began to creep into the repertoire from the American Beauty album that was put out at the end of 1970. The songs from the two albums Workingman's Dead and American Beauty acted as bookends to the year that marked a dramatic new direction, both in the studio and in concert. Many of the songs from American Beauty, one of their most successful records, debuted in August at a run of shows at the Fillmore West. Like the Workingman's Dead songs the year before, these songs dominated shows for the remainder of the year. As these songs had a slightly harder edge than the folksy flavor of Workingman's Dead, the shows, too, began to develop a more modern, urban sound. Even "The Other One" began to sound more tamed and structured, often being stripped of the "Cryptical" segments and paired with "Truckin'."

During this time, Weir finally began to gain more confidence in his playing and consequently became more pronounced in the mix. There was a paradigm shift in his singing and playing in which the cowboy persona began to drop away and the rock 'n' roller started to emerge. With the addition to the repertoire of songs like "Not Fade Away," "Sugar Magnolia" and "Truckin'," Weir found a milieu in which to be the front man for the band. He developed a wonderful, intuitive

*Fillmore East program, 1/2–3/70*

(at first, although gangly and tinny) style of rhythm guitar and even began to play some great leads on the songs like "Easy Wind" (see September 20, 1970 at the Fillmore East) and "China Cat Sunflower."

This year has always been very popular among tapers. A major reason for this was the wide availability, until recent years, of a larger body of circulated tapes than for prior years. These include a good number of Fillmore East tapes, mostly made by venue soundmen patching a soundboard feed to a tape deck in the basement. There are also a couple of FM broadcast recordings, various other soundboards, and a set of very good—for the time—audience recordings made at the Capitol Theater in Port Chester, New York.

Unfortunately no one knows whether any more soundboard tapes will appear from 1970. During the last half of the year, Bear, who was responsible for recording many of the tapes from that era, was in jail, and as of this writing, there are very few soundboards from those months in the Vault. Hopefully, they have only been misplaced and will eventually turn up.

Tapes to get: 2/11, 2/13, 2/14, 4/12, 5/2, 5/6, 6/24, 9/18–20, 11/5–8.

## 1/2/70
### Late Show, Fillmore East, New York, New York

2001 Theme, /Mason's Children, Casey// Jones, Black Peter, Mama Tried, Hard to Handle, Cumberland Blues, Cryptical Envelopment > Drums > The Other One > Cryptical Envelopment > Cosmic Charlie

**1. Source:** SBD, **Quality:** B+, **Length:** 0:47, **Genealogy:** SBD > RR? > C? > Beta HF1 > PCM
**2. Source:** SBD-CD (Fallout from the Phil Zone), **Quality:** A, **Length:** 0:06 (Mason's Children)
**3. Source:** AUD, **Quality:** C, **Length:** 1:00
**Highlights:** Cumberland

The band returns to New York City, where they first tested the waters of their new roots-based style. After announcing their arrival on stage with the theme for *2001: A Space Odyssey*, they jump right in. More songs have been added to their repertoire from the soon-to-be-recorded *Workingman's Dead* album. This is one of the series of relatively low quality soundboards from this period that are, as a whole, historically interesting but contain few real musical highlights. This show sounds particularly homey and laid-back. The organ in "Casey Jones" and "Black Peter" is played casually, like a low whistle. "Cumberland" contains a unique jam in the middle that resembles the verse but ultimately falls apart. Possibly it was intended to be a verse, but the vocalists were asleep at the wheel and the band lost its place. Finally, the drums in the "Cryptical" begin to pick up the tempo of the show, ending with a crescendo of cymbals before roaring into "The Other One." Unfortunately, it is here that the soundboard cuts. The audience tape contains the remainder of the show which includes a mellow, floating "Cosmic Charlie."

DOUGAL DONALDSON

# Reviews: January 1970

*At the Fillmore East, 1/3/70* (photo credit: Amalie Rothschild)

### ✺ 1/3/70 ✺
**Early Show, Fillmore East,
New York City, New York**

//Morning Dew, Me and My Uncle, Hard to Handle, Cumberland Blues, Cold Rain and Snow, Alligator > Drums > China Cat Jam > Goin' Down the Road Jam > Alligator > Feedback
**Encore:** Uncle John's Band

**Source:** SBD, **Quality:** A−, **Length:** 1:05, **Genealogy:** MR > C > C

**Highlights:** Morning Dew, Alligator > Drums > China Cat Jam > Goin' Down the Road Jam > Alligator > Feedback

**Comments:** "Dew" is missing only the first ten seconds.

This is an interesting period for the Grateful Dead in that it features both the 1969 sound with Tom Constanten on organ and that unique 1970-style intensity. T.C. left the Dead only a few weeks later. The "Morning Dew" is made all the more wonderful by T.C.'s playing during the climax jam. "Me and My Uncle" is the usual boring cheese cowboy song. The "Hard to Handle" was a bit raw but nice—this song got better in 1971. The T.C. introduction in "Cumberland" is spectacular, and Bobby plays great rhythm throughout. "Cold Rain and Snow" is super sloppy. The "Alligator," however, is the best song of the night. The drum solo is crappy, as are many of the old ones, but hey, we didn't have "Corinna," "I Need a Miracle," or "Easy Answers" back then, so drum solos were great times during which to make a bathroom run. Jerry does a mellow post-drum solo jam with the drums still playing along, and then Phil joins in. This jam sounds remarkably like the "Caution" jam played on 2/14/70. This leads first into a "China Cat" jam, then immediately into a "Goin' Down the Road" jam, then just as quickly into another "Caution" tease and then into a *great* exploration of "Feedback." One imagines that they were either confused about what to play next or they were incredibly stoned. Either way, this is one *incredible* version of "Alligator." Right as they are tuning up for the encore, you hear band members complain about hearing "feedback" (as in the crowd yelling what they should play). This cracks me up since they just ended the first show with intense "Feedback." Make up your minds, fellas. The encore, "Uncle John's Band," played in classic *Workingman's Dead* style, is very sweet.

DARIO WOLFISH

### 1/3/70
**Late Show, Fillmore East,
New York City, New York**

Casey Jones, Mama Tried, Big Boss Man, China Cat Sunflower > I Know You Rider > (a High Time tease?), Mason's Children, Cryptical Envelopment > The Other One > Cryptical// Reprise > Cosmic Charlie, Uncle John's Band > Black Peter, Dire Wolf, Good Lovin', Dancin' in the Streets
**Encore:** Saint Stephen > Midnight Hour

**Source:** SBD, **Quality:** A−, **Length:** 2:15, **Genealogy:** MR > C > C
**Highlights:** The Other One > Cryptical Reprise, Dancin', Saint Stephen > Midnight Hour

The "Casey Jones" and "Mama Tried" are uneventful, as they usually are. There are sound problems during "Big Boss Man." ("Come on, Bear, give me some fuckin' monitors.") The "China Cat" starts with those T.C. *Aoxomoxoa* riffs, which are really cool. It's hard to tell whether there's a "High Time" tease or whether the tape cuts right as they go into "High Time." "Mason's Children" is very much like the version played on 2/14/70 with a T.C. twist. Jerry and Phil come out swinging on "The Other One." YEOW! This jam is a lot like the one they did at Harpur College on 5/2/70. Jerry plays this really neat repetitive rhythm jam while Phil plays a lead bass solo. It's kind of a role reversal. Only Phil and Jerry could pull that off. There is a wicked cut in the "Cryptical" reprise. I had to splice it together since my source's tape had a big pause before the music resumes. T.C. shines again during "Cosmic Charlie." The "Uncle John's Band" > "Black Peter" is a *Workingman's Dead* feast. "Black Peter" is sung with tremendous emotion. "Dire Wolf" is average. There's an extremely short drum solo in "Good Lovin'," which is unusual for a 1970 version. Phil plays a short duet with the drums, and Jerry comes in and they proceed to kick some butt! Although this is pretty short, the classic 1970-style high-octane jam knocks me out. The "Dancin'," very much like the version on 2/14/70, especially the Jerry solos, is superlative. The transition in the "Saint Stephen" > "Midnight Hour" encore is incredible. Both of the songs are slower than most 1970 versions. Very much like during the slow but boiling "Lovelight" from 2/13/70, Pig and Jerry are unusually mellow on this fine, fine "Midnight Hour."

This is a great show. I wish I had been there.

DARIO WOLFISH

### 1/10/70
**Community Concourse,
San Diego, California**

China Cat Sunflower > I Know You Rider, Me and My Uncle, Dire Wolf, Hard to Handle, Casey Jones, Mason's Children > Black Peter, Good Lovin' > Drums > Good Lovin', Cold Rain and Snow, Turn On Your Lovelight

**1. Source:** SBD, **Quality:** B+, **Length:** 1:25, **Genealogy:** MR > C > C > PCM > DAT
**2. Source:** FM-SBD (GDH 003 and 007) **Quality:** A, **Length:** 0:45 (Mason's Children, Black Peter, Cold Rain and Snow, Turn On Your Lovelight), **Genealogy:** MR > RR > LP
**Highlights:** Hard to Handle, Mason's Children, Black Peter, Good Lovin', Lovelight
**Comments:** A well-balanced FM mix with a better-than-average sound quality because it dates from a 1980 broadcast.

Hot poop and no mistake, this is a tremendously enjoyable hour and a half, packed with soulful and energetic playing. If you wanted to be *really* picky, I suppose you could point out that "Casey Jones" is a bit rushed, or that the performance of "Dire Wolf" is a little on the weedy side, but the rest of this tape is most definitely ON and is guaranteed to bring a broad grin to your face. "Hard to Handle" is an exceptionally tight version and shorter than most with no Bobby solo or jam before Jerry steps out. An other surefire favorite is the confident reading of "Mason's Children," which glides into a delicate "Black Peter" that features sweet Garcia vocals (dig the brief falsetto accent—wonderful!). The solo is brief, but it rages with a suppressed emotion that is finally revealed. "Good Lovin'" signals imminent damage to the fixtures and fittings of your living room as it *demands* that you dance with total abandon RIGHT NOW. The dialogue of the drums at its heart is a pure percussive joy with cross-rhythms skittering out over that powerful energy pulse. Oops, there goes your TV. Oh well, now you'll just have to listen to more tapes like this one. "Lovelight" stretches out without overreaching itself, maintaining its momentum nicely. No Pigpen rap, unfortunately, but there's a helluva lot of rhythmic interplay going on here that remains well focused, so you're kept on your toes throughout.

PAUL BODENHAM

---

### 1/16/70

**Springer's Inn, Portland, Oregon**

**Set 1:** Monitor Madness Rap, Casey Jones, Mama Tried, Black Peter, Hard to Handle, China Cat Sunflower// > I Know You Rider, High Time, Good Lovin', Dancin' in the Streets, Alligator > Drums > The Eleven Jam > Death Don't Have No Mercy
**Set 2:** Cumberland Blues//

**Source:** SBD, **Quality:** B, **Length:** 1:30, **Genealogy:** MR > RR > DAT
**Highlights:** Solos on High Time, shreddingly thick mix

Tonight the band sounds thick, big, and wet. This is a great and very fat-sounding soundboard, although there is a bit of distortion, probably from some too-hot levels somewhere along the taping chain. The mix is great. In general, the rhythms are tight, the tempos solid and hot. The opening three numbers are all straight and strong, if slightly unfocused. "Black Peter" stands out, with a clear and mournful reading of the lyric by Jerry and magnificent dynamic range of the band. "Hard to Handle" brings Pig on, and the jam stretches up and out.

"China Cat Sunflower" is ultrapeppy with a great ensemble performance in the solo section. "High Time," however, is so slow it falls off the map. "Good Lovin'" is awesome, with the three string-pickers joining forces to make an awesome choir of musical demons. The jam here features augmented-ninth chords from Garcia's axe for a tangy Hendrix-esque flavor. "Dancin' in the Streets" features shriek-o-rama vocals by all, which blow Weir away, but send channels of energy into the jam that cooks with a ripping double-time "Dark Star" hint. Energy continues hot through the late-set jam. Not to be missed is the section from "Drums" leading up the "Eleven Jam." This prelude material to "The Eleven" is familiar. But here, the dynamic level falls while the rhythmic tension is honed razor-sharp so that when Billy hits the snare twice, to signal "The Eleven" rhythm proper, the feeling of relaxation is complete.

WILLIAM POLITS

---

### 1/17/70

**Oregon State University Gym, Corvallis, Oregon**

//Dire Wolf, China Cat Sunflower > I Know You Rider, Hard to Handle, Cumberland Blues, Me and My Uncle, Black Peter, Good Lovin', Mason's Children > High //Time, Dark Star > Saint Stephen > The Eleven > Turn On Your Lovelight//

**Source:** SBD, **Quality:** B/B– (slight oversaturation on the vocals), **Length:** 2:00, **Genealogy:** MR > RR > Beta HF > PCM > DAT
**Highlights:** Cumberland Blues, Mason's Children, Dark Star

These tapes enjoyed heavy circulation at the beginning of 1990 and with very good cause. Less than four weeks from when this band would deliver three quintessential performances at the Fillmore East, this tape shows us a creative relationship in a state of accelerated evolution. While their country tunes are just beginning to jell, their psychedelic journeys are really beginning to mature. The first highlight is "Cumberland Blues," which is literally driven by Lesh's thumping bass. "Me and My Uncle" and "Black Peter" are played with feeling and nerve. "Mason's Children," one of only fifteen that we know of, stands apart from the others by virtue of an unusual and particularly inspired jam at its climax. A heartfelt reading of "High Time" is tarnished by a brief glitch in its epicenter. "Dark Star," a classic of the time, features numerous thematic forays, some familiar and others unique to this date. The "Feelin' Groovy Jam," well on its way to being perfected just a few weeks later, is delicately explored here.

JOHN R. DWORK

---

### 2/1/70
**The Warehouse, New Orleans, Louisiana**

//The Other One > Turn On Your Lovelight

---

**Source:** SBD, **Quality:** B+, **Length:** 0:45, **Genealogy:** MR > RR > RR > PCM > DAT
**Highlights:** Turn On Your Lovelight
**Personnel:** With Peter Green on guitar

The music fades during the last few minutes of "The Other One" before bolting splendidly into a nearly forty-minute "Lovelight." Peter Green takes the stage and starts bending and blending in right away. Instead of having an adverse effect, his presence fires up the others into playing more carefully so as not to sound like some guitar army. The three guitars weave in and out of each other beautifully and with careful concern for the overall sound. Green shows a deft touch for the tricky tempo changes that make "Lovelight" such a delight. He also stands tough in the batter's box, getting at least a piece of the sharp curves the Dead pitch forth from their improvisational mound of ideas. Thus we have a "Lovelight" with an extra kick that comes across with an almost Who-like delivery.

Pigpen's voice, too, is in top form: charmingly bluesy one moment, raunchy and suggestive the next. Green tries to get into it vocally with Pigpen at one point, but Pig shrugs him off like an obese panhandler. To his credit, Green doesn't try again.

There are several annoying channel drops, though they last only a minute together until the end; the last one zaps the final two minutes and does take a bit away from the hot ending.

MICHAEL M. GETZ

---

### 2/2/70
**Fox Theater, St. Louis, Missouri**

Dark Star > Saint Stephen > Mason's Children//

---

**1. Source:** SBD, **Quality:** A, **Length:** 0:33, **Genealogy:** MR > RR > RR > PCM > DAT
**2. Source:** FM-SBD (GDH 047 and 242), **Quality:** A, **Length:** 0:33, **Genealogy:** MR > DR
**Highlights:** All of what little we have

This show, performed a mere two days after the boys' infamous bust in New Orleans, and less than two weeks before the epic February 11, 13, and 14, 1970, shows at the Fillmore East, sees the Dead sparkling throughout the brief portion that's in circulation. A crisp and confident "Dark Star" immediately triggers synaptic resonance with *Live Dead*, lingers briefly in a number of beautiful spots before drifting into a still embryonic version of the soon to be perfected "Feelin' Groovy Jam," and then comes back perfectly into the last verse of "Dark Star." "Saint Stephen" rocks on all cylinders before evolving into a fully matured rendition of "Mason's Children," which is unfortunately and brutally cut just as they begin to open up the jam. Sounds like the reel-to-reel tape simply ran out. Great while it lasts, though!

ADAM HUNTER BAUER

---

### 2/4/70
**Family Dog at the Great Highway, San Francisco, California**

Hard to Handle, China Cat Sunflower > I Know You Rider

---

**Source:** SBD, **Quality:** B, **Length:** 0:20

**Comments:** These three songs were filmed and aired for a PBS special that was shown on December 13, 1970.

"Hard to Handle" is muscular but flexes aimlessly, without any poise, ultimately lying flat in the sand. "China Cat," featuring many fine improvisational strokes by the whole band, restores some grace. "Rider," though, gets bogged down in the band's futile attempt to sing three-part harmony while holding down the rhythm. It trudges along, leaving the inventive "China Cat"—and this tape—a distant memory.

MICHAEL M. GETZ

## 2/5/70
### Fillmore West, San Francisco, California

Big Boss Man, Black Peter, Mason's Children, The Race Is On

**Source:** AUD, **Quality:** C+, **Length:** 0:30
**Highlights:** Big Boss Man, Black Peter

Pigpen delivers a kick to the pants of the "Boss Man" with some deliciously surly vocals. "Black Peter" is handled with grace and delicacy; a superb job of concentration makes this one of the best early versions available, a real fireside rendering. A botched jam in the middle of "Mason's" is quickly forgotten and yields to a slick space that reminded me of the Stones' "Can't You Hear Me Knockin'." It ends too soon, though, as does the last jam, despite being turned up a few notches. Yup, yet another one of those frustrating moments when we wonder why on earth they didn't shoot for the moon. The final song here, "Race Is On," is highlighted by Garcia's exuberant pedal steel playing.

MICHAEL M. GETZ

## 2/7/70
### Fillmore West, San Francisco, California

Green, Green Grass of Home, Sawmill, Seasons, China Cat Sunflower > I Know You Rider > High Time, Big Boss Man, Me and My Uncle, Hard to Handle, Cold Rain and Snow

**Source:** AUD, **Quality:** B, **Length:** 1:10
**Highlights:** All

The Dead's run at the Fillmores during the first half of February 1970 was notable both for the level of playing (February 5, 13, and 14 in particular) and the diversity of shows presented. I attended the early parts of both the Friday and Sunday shows of the Fillmore West run, and was puzzled and frustrated by the pedal steel guitar that sat forlorn and unused at center stage while I was there. As this tape shows, I should have gone on Saturday, February 7, instead, as the abbreviated performance that night began with one of the last of Garcia's pedal steel performances onstage with the Dead, as opposed to the New Riders. "Green, Green Grass of Home" had become a standby of these pedal steel interludes, and the version here is appropriately mournful, with lots of weepy steel and an emotive Weir vocal. "Sawmill" was a tune that Weir performed many times in guest slots with the New Riders, but this seems to be the only Dead version that survives on tape. The tune's catchy melody and rapid tempo is greatly enhanced by a wonderfully convoluted Lesh bass line and restrained percussion from what sounds like both drummers. The "unplugged" set concluded with one of the few Dead performances of "Seasons," another slow-tempo Weir-sung weeper.

The electric set is notable chiefly for its conventionality, and in the complete absence of an extended jam. "China Cat" starts out assertively enough, leading into a passionate "I Know You Rider" that flows, as it did so often back then, into an elegant "High Time." A long interval follows during which Weir bitches about Bear's notoriously finicky monitor system, followed by instrumental snatches of the "Looney Tunes" theme and a country hoedown. When the monitor issue is resolved, Weir lets on that he likes his monitors loud "because it makes me feel like a rooster crowing!" Pigpen snapped

*Bob at the Fillmore West, 2/8/70 (photo credit: Michael Parrish)*

### 2/8/70
### Fillmore West, San Francisco, California

**Set 1:** Smokestack Lightning, Morning Dew, Dire Wolf, Me and My Uncle, Sittin' on Top of the World, China Cat Sunflower > I Know You Rider, Hurts Me Too
**Set 2:** Dark Star > Saint Stephen > Not Fade Away > Saint Stephen > // Turn On Your Lovelight//

**1. Source:** SBD, **Quality:** B, **Length:** 0:40 (//"Dark Star" through "Lovelight"//)
**2. Source:** AUD, **Quality:** C+, **Length:** 2:50
**Highlights:** Smokestack Lightning!!
**Comments:** Early 1970: what a time for the Grateful Dead! Some of the greatest shows the Dead ever played came out of this period, and this show, though not the best ever, is worthy of its company. The tape I have is from a very listenable audience source with a soundboard portion patched in on the backside. During the audience segments, every member of the band is clearly heard, vocals are clear, and drums are loud and strong. The soundboard portion is a little thin, but has nice extension on the high end. Again, vocals and guitars are clear.

The first set opens with an amazing "Smokestack Lightning." Over seventeen minutes long and bluesy as all heck, it deserves to be listed as one of the most notable in the band's history. Initially, Pig stays low in the groove, singing just enough to keep the mood as the group begins to find the jam. Building slowly but steeply, the song winds through a few choruses with some exceptional work by all included. Near the thirteen-minute mark, the band explodes into an unforgettable climax that gives new meaning to the word "energy." Guitars screaming, drums pounding, bass driving the whole thing, the moment takes the song to a new level. Whew!

After Bobby alludes to things to come with a "We're waiting for Bear to turn on his lovelight," the band launches into a "Morning Dew." Jerry's voice is strong and clear, and the song, while short, manages to capture a hint of what had come before. The jam has an obvious bluesy feel and is a little slower than normal, both of which add to the overall uniqueness of this version. The next three songs, "Dire Wolf," "Me and My Uncle,"

back with "More like a bantam hen!" as the band charged into an authoritative, rocking "Big Boss Man." "Me and My Uncle" was notable for its unusually rapid tempo and for Pigpen's tasty organ fills. "Hard to Handle" and a typically fine "Cold Rain and Snow" close out the audience tape of this show. Although it doesn't scale the improvisational peaks of some of the other shows that week, the Saturday Fillmore West set showcases the stone country and short-song facets of the mercurial early '70 Grateful Dead.

MICHAEL PARRISH

and "Sittin' on Top of the World," allow the band to relax and settle down. "Dire Wolf" and "Sittin' on Top of the World" are done acoustically, with the latter having a noticeable playful feel to it. The tempo is up, the vocals are strong, and the guitar work is sharp. That attitude is carried into a "China Cat Sunflower" > "I Know You Rider" pair, which opens at a quick pace and maintains it for the duration. While everyone works well with one another, the drums manage to steal the spotlight. Maniacal throughout, the drumming really defines where the songs are going to go.

The second set starts the soundboard portion, and with it comes a "Dark Star." This "Star" starts out with great focus but quickly becomes quite spacy. After some extensive noodling, the song gets back into a focused groove. After a splice, a "Feelin' Groovy" jam clearly materializes out of the fog. A brief and routinely powerful "Saint Stephen" comes next, more as a conclusion to the "Dark Star" than a separate song. Out of the "Stephen," after an uncomfortable pause, comes a "Not Fade Away." On only the fourth time the song's been played, the pace is cautious and has clearly not developed. Vocals are weak, and the players obviously haven't found their role in the new material. When the song does shift back into "Saint Stephen," the band is eager to prove it can still rock and turns out a ferocious conclusion. The first few notes of the "Lovelight" survive before the soundboard tape comes to an end far too soon (although most of the "Lovelight" is available from an audience recording).

DAVID R. CECCHI

---

BILL GRAHAM PRESENTS IN NEW YORK

# GRATEFUL DEAD

# LOVE

## ALLMAN BROTHERS

## JOSHUA LIGHT SHOW

FILLMORE EAST
February 11, 13 & 14, 1970

*Fillmore East program, 2/11, 2/13 & 2/14, 1970*

---

## The Legendary February 1970 Three-Night Stand at the Fillmore East

### 2/11/70
**Fillmore East, New York, New York**

**Set 2:** Not Fade Away, Cumberland Blues, Cold Rain and Snow, High Time, Me and My Uncle, Dark Star > Spanish Jam* > Turn on Your Lovelight†
**Encore:** Uncle John's Band

\* with Duane Allman, Gregg Allman, Mick Fleetwood, Butch Trucks, Danny Kirwin, and Peter Green
† also with Berry Oakley

**1. Source:** SBD, **Quality:** A+, **Length:** 0:45 (//"Dark Star" > "Spanish Jam" > "Turn on Your Lovelight"//), **Genealogy:** MR > RR > RR, **Tapers:** John Chester and Alan Mande recorded this show in the basement of the Fillmore using a Revox reel-to-reel tape deck with 15-inch reels.

**2. Source:** AUD, **Quality:** C+, **Length:** 1:30 (the entire electric set)

**Highlights:** Not Fade Away, High Time, Spanish Jam

*Back row, left to right: Jerry Garcia, Bill Kreutzmann, Barry Oakley, unknown, Butch Trucks, Duane Allman, Mickey Hart. Front row, left to right: Mick Fleetwood, Peter Green, Pigpen, Bob Weir, Danny Kirwin, Gregg Allman* (photo credit: Amalie Rothschild)

*Good times at the Fillmore East, 2/13/70* (photo credit: Amalie Rothschild)

## 🌀 2/13/70 🌀
### Late Show, Fillmore East, New York, New York

**Electric Set 1:** China Cat Sunflower > I Know You Rider, Me and My Uncle, Dire Wolf, Smokestack Lightning
**Acoustic Set:** Monkey and the Engineer, Little Sadie, Wake Up, Little Susie > Black Peter, Uncle John's Band, Katie Mae
**Electric Set 2:** Dark Star > Cryptical Envelopment > Drums > The Other One > Cryptical Reprise > Turn On Your Lovelight > We Bid You Goodnight

**1. Source:** SBD, **Quality:** A+, **Length:** 3:00, **Genealogy:** MR > RR > RR, **Tapers:** John Chester and Alan Mande recorded this show in the basement of the Fillmore using a Revox reel-to-reel tape deck with 15-inch reels.

**2. Source:** CD, *Dick's Picks IV,* **Quality:** A+, **Length:** ("Dark Star" > "Cryptical Envelopment" > "The Other One" > "Cryptical Envelopment" > "Lovelight" only), **Genealogy:** MR > DR > CD, **Taper:** Bear

**3. Source:** CD, *Bear's Choice,* **Quality:** A+, **Length:** "Smokestack Lightning" only, **Taper:** Bear

**4. Source:** AUD, **Quality:** C+, **Length:** 3:00

**Highlights:** Smokestack Lightning, Dark Star > Cryptical > The Other One > Cryptical Reprise > Turn On Your Lovelight > We Bid You Goodnight

## 🌀 2/14/70 🌀
### Late Show, Fillmore East, New York, New York

**Electric Set 1:** Casey Jones, Mama Tried, Hard to Handle
**Acoustic Set:** Monkey and the Engineer, Dark Hollow, All Around This World, Wake Up, Little Susie > Black Peter, Uncle John's Band, Katie Mae
**Electric Set 2:** Dancin' in the Streets, China Cat Sunflower > I Know You Rider > High Time, Dire Wolf, Alligator > Drums > Me and My Uncle > Not Fade Away > Mason's Children > Caution > Feedback > We Bid You Goodnight

**1. Source:** SBD, **Quality:** A+, **Length:** 2:30 (entire show), **Genealogy:** MR > RR > RR, **Tapers:** John Chester and Alan Mande recorded this show in the basement of the Fillmore using a Revox reel-to-reel tape deck with 15-inch reels.

**2. Source:** CD, *Dick's Picks IV,* **Quality:** A+, **Length:** "Casey Jones," "Dancin' in the Streets," "China Cat Sunflower" > "I Know You Rider" > "High Time," "Dire Wolf," "Alligator" > "Drums" > "Me and My Uncle" > "Not Fade Away" > "Mason's Children" > "Caution" > "Feedback" > "We Bid You Goodnight" only, **Genealogy:** MR > DR > CD

**3. Source:** FM-SBD (GDH 073 and 240), **Quality:** A+, **Length:** "Casey Jones," "Mama Tried," "Not Fade Away" > "We Bid You Goodnight," **Genealogy:** MR > DR

**4. Source:** CD, *Bear's Choice,* **Quality:** A+, **Length:** "Hard to Handle," "Dark Hollow," "All Around This World" only

**5. Source:** AUD, **Quality:** C+, **Length:** 2:30

**Highlights:** Dancing in the Streets, High Time, Alligator > Drums > Me and My Uncle > Not Fade Away > Mason's Children > Caution > Feedback > We Bid You Goodnight

What makes this the best-loved run in the history of the Grateful Dead?

Consider the fact that in early '70, the Dead were at one of the turning points in their evolution, moving from the dense, acid-fueled sonic experimentation of the

*The Dead, 2/13/70* (photo credit: Amalie Rothschild)

*Aoxomoxoa* era into a role as country-inflected bards of a gone world: a river of American mythos, of miners and last-ditch gamblers, inspired by Dylan and by Robbie Robertson's songs for the Band.

Each show of the run featured an acoustic segment, with Garcia strumming new originals like "Uncle John's Band" alongside Pigpen's gritty, unadorned renditions of Lightnin' Hopkins' "Katie Mae," and the bluegrass and old-time chestnuts Garcia grew up playing in coffeehouses south of San Francisco, in groups like Mother McCree's Uptown Jug Champions. With songs like "Dire Wolf," "High Time," and "Black Peter" (all of which would appear on *Workingman's Dead,* the album the Dead began recording the month they played them at the Fillmore), Garcia and Hunter made that turf their own, penning Old West miniatures that will be the folksongs of the twenty-first century.

Factor in the monster jam at the late show on the 11th, when the Dead were joined from "Dark Star" onward by members of the Allman Brothers Band (who were still virtually unknown in New York), along with "rattlesnake" blues guitarist Peter Green, whose journeyman gig was replacing Eric Clapton in John Mayall's Bluesbreakers, before he joined Fleetwood Mac.

For the Deadheads who were lucky enough to be there, consider the fact that the Dead were just beginning to build a fire on the East Coast, especially in the Big Apple, which was proving to be acutely receptive to their kind of alchemy. In 1970, the Dead played at the Fillmore East nearly every other month. Says former *Goldmine* editor Jeff Tamarkin, "There was a missionary sense among the early New York Deadheads that this couldn't be kept a secret, the word had to be spread. You wanted all of your friends to be there with you, to experience what you'd experienced."

Though canonizing any single incarnation of the Dead as "the best" would be as misguided as trying to choose "the best" Miles Davis session, the Fillmore run of February 1970 gives us the Dead in the full flourishing of their powers, with both psychedelic past and bardic future at their command, playing shows that lasted until the rising sun sparkled in the snow-dusted sidewalks of Second Avenue.

Part of the magic of this run had to do with the vibes of the Fillmore itself, and the state of Freakdom—"hippie" was a loathed term—in New York City at that moment.

The Fillmore had formerly been the Loew's Commodore theater, where, in its heyday, you could trade a nickel for a whole day of features, newsreels, and short subjects. By the late sixties, a new influx was transforming the neighborhood—which was just then

# Reviews: February 1970

becoming known as the East Village—into a bustling center of psychedelic bohemia. Right around the corner was St. Mark's Place, which was to Manhattan what the Haight-Ashbury was to San Francisco, but edgier. ("Flower power" had a harder time cutting it on the Lower East Side than in Golden Gate Park.)

When Bill Graham bought out Loew's in 1968, he brought in the bands, like Janis Joplin; Jimi Hendrix; Miles Davis; the Doors; Crosby, Stills, Nash & Young; and the Who, and the blockbuster double and triple bills (Neil Young, Miles Davis, and Steve Miller on one night; the Who, Chuck Berry, and Albert King on another), that had made his Fillmore West a cultural landmark.

*Washington Post* reporter Don Oldenburg went to his first Dead show on the 13th. He remembers that the street outside the Fillmore was "crawling with molecular energy. An unreal streetlight-illuminated scene surrounded by the darkness of that end of town late at night made it feel like we all were on stage. A guy who looked like Jimi Hendrix but wasn't walked by murmuring, 'Acid, acid,' in a fog that seemed to emanate from him." (The Hendrix lookalike was undoubtedly the legendary dealer SuperSpade.)

As Blair Jackson describes it in *Skeleton Key*, "The scene outside was completely crazed. Everyone was decked out in their countercultural finery, and either rapping with each other, or wandering up and down the line."[1]

"When I walked up to the box office," recalls Gary Lambert, the editor of the *Grateful Dead Almanac*, "I was chagrined to find that the Dead seemed to be catching on—I could no longer count on effortlessly copping seats in the first 10 rows. Still, I was somewhere in the orchestra for all three nights. I remember that this was the first run at the Fillmore for which I purchased tickets at the newly inflated price of—$5.50! Believe it or not, this was considered obscenely exorbitant at the time, and brought yet another wave of vituperation from 'the community' toward the resident capitalist, Bill Graham."

Once inside the venue, says Blair Jackson, "You were transported to a magical world that was completely under Graham's control," with the amenities of a golden-age moviehouse, if funkier than it had once been.

"On the ground floor," Lambert remembers, "there was a conventional refreshment stand, serving up the hot dogs, popcorn, sodas and such, that had doubtless been sold at the venue since its days as the Loew's Commodore. But up on the balcony level was the perfect stoned-hippie-food concession, offering up fresh fruit and juices, bagels with cream cheese and, best of all, Dannon Yogurt, in a wide selection of flavors. Yogurt never tasted so good! Even now, a quarter-century later, a mere spoonful of Dannon sets loose a Proustian torrent of Fillmore memories."

Unlike the Fillmore West, there were seats at the Fillmore East, rather than an open floor. Cartoons were shown during the breaks between sets to keep people in their seats, because the lobby was small. Dead shows at the Fillmore even gave off their own distinctive aroma, a heady mixture of patchouli oil, incense, and pungent Moroccan hash, all blending with the building's own antique mustiness.

Fillmore crew member Alan Mande, who helped tape these shows, recollects that, while the other members of the Dead clustered around an octopus of hoses leading to a nitrous oxide tank in the upstairs dressing rooms, Pigpen held court in the sound shop in the basement "with a bottle of Jack Daniel's, and at least six gorgeous women."

*Ad for shows at the Fillmore East, 2/11, 13, 14—Note: "2 shows nightly"*

---

[1] Steven Silberman and David Shenk, *Skeleton Key: A Dictionary for Deadheads* (New York: Doubleday, 1994), 91.

*The coffin is brought on stage with Zacherle, Fillmore East 2/14/70*
(photo credit: Amalie Rothschild)

As Richard Kostelanetz, in his memoir *The Fillmore East,* described the regulars, "The audience seemed a microcosm of a new society that was free of both race prejudice and class prejudice, free of middle-class inhibitions about pleasure, free of censorship, acutely sensitive to political and social evil."[2]

A significant boost to the lysergic vibe was provided by the Joshua Light Show, throbbing across a translucent screen twenty feet tall by thirty feet wide behind the performers. The Joshua Light Show was the crème de la crème of light shows, with eight carousel slide projectors wired for 1,200-watt bulbs, three overhead projectors fitted with dishes of swirling fluids, and two film projectors running simultaneously, beaming floods of color and hypnogogic imagery onto the screen in time to the music. The light show staff was paid $1,000 a week for their art, which drew crowds of students from the New York University film school next door.

Augmenting the light show was the Dead's "pyrotechnician," Boots, appearing at peak moments in the music to catapult fire signs toward the ceiling, throwing neon afterimages behind every dilated pupil in the room.

At this point in their career, the band members were still willing to engage the rowdy New York audience in banter from the stage, and one of the delights of the run was the nonstop stream of hilarious tune-up shtick—in the spirit of Garcia's clowning in the Jug Champions—often at the expense of Bear and the stage crew. During the tuning for "I've Been All Around This World" on the 14th, Weir warned the audience that you could lose a finger using a "Bill Russell double-action capo," and glanced over at Garcia, who, of course, was minus a finger.

The early show on the 14th featured this episode of the Blackjack Garcia/Bobby Ace comedy hour:

> **Weir:** We're going to investigate this here crackling sound.
> **Garcia:** Everybody hold your breath.
> **Weir:** Ahh! It just went away. Hey, could we have more monitors? I want to shout and scream.
> **Garcia:** Yeah, we need more monitors here. [Feedback]
> **Weir:** Not much of an improvement. It ain't like it was last night. *I want it like it was last night!* [More feedback] The swamp's fightin' off the alligators.
> [Garcia plays the opening notes of "Dark Star."]
> **Weir:** I hope none of you heard that.
> **Garcia:** Seen any good movies lately?
> [More feedback]

---

[2] Richard Kostalanetz and Raeanne Robinson, *The Fillmore East: Recollections of a Rock Theater* (New York: Schirmer Books, 1996).

**Pigpen:** I got mice in my guitar.
**Garcia:** Let's wait until this passing squeech goes by.
[Blast of piercing feedback]
**Weir:** We're gonna hang out up here and bleed up your ears.
**Garcia:** That's nice, very nice, euphonious, you might even say.
**Weir:** Put a spotlight on the PA man.
**Lesh:** He deserves a spotlight. The narrow-beamed spotlight focuses.
**Weir:** He's responsible for our loss of high-frequency hearing, did you know that?
**Lesh:** Yes, it's hard for us to discern spoken words in quiet rooms.
**Weir:** Sibilances and such.
**Lesh:** Consonant [inaudible]. Are we through now?
**Garcia:** Jeez, we just started, man.
**Woman in the audience:** Yeah, man!
**Weir:** Usher, eject that chick!
**Garcia:** "Yeah, man." This is outta sight, really, man. Nothing's weirder than coming to New York.
**Lesh:** [Counting off "Dark Star"] 1, 2, 3, 4 . . .

Also on the 14th, the festivities began with a memorable introduction by the legendary WNEW-FM deejay Zacherle, known by many as the ominous voice of "Chill-l-l-l-e-r-r-r Theater." After being delivered onto the stage in a wooden casket, Zacherle introduced himself as Jonathan Schwartz (WNEW's morning deejay) before giving the Dead the punchiest intro of their career: "The Grateful Goddamned Dead!"

And the band's presence was having its usual effect on the local crew. Right after one of the acoustic interludes on the 14th, Garcia can be heard looking for "the microphone guy." The crew member in question had other things on his mind at that moment. "Everything went fine on the 13th, but on the 14th, I got totally Owsleyized," he recalls. "When I heard them calling for me to come back onstage to set stuff up, I was tripping out of my mind, laying on my back in one of the aisles."

For Deadheads, part of the golden aura of this run can be attributed to the fact that high-quality recordings of the late shows have been available in trading circles for years. For many Deadheads who came of age in the seventies and eighties, low-gen dubs of 2/13 and 2/14/70 were a Holy Grail that could be acquired with a reasonable effort. The odyssey of these tapes offers a fascinating perspective on how tape trading can influence the perceived history of a band.

As the sound crew set up for the first show on the 11th, Bear patched in his Sony 770-2 to record the performance on 7-inch reels. There was another patch into the soundboard those nights, but only the Fillmore crew knew it. John Chester, who ran the house PA, was feeding a second deck, a Revox with 15-inch reels, through the "snake" running under the apron of the stage.

One of the men on Chester's crew was Alan Mande, a twenty-four-year-old stage technician with a background in the traditional theater. "I got hired because I knew how to move things around in the dark quick," said Mande. Mande would play a significant role in Deadhead history by dubbing Chester's reels after the run, and giving copies to one of the key figures in the nascent Dead tape trading scene, Bob Menke, a couple of years later.

The copy of the 13th was on a half-track reel, and the 14th was on low-grade cassette. Dubs of those tapes trickled out for years afterward, with copies of copies crisscrossing the globe by mail and backpack, converting casual fans into full-fledged Heads wherever they went.

"The run in February of 1970 provided the quintessential snapshot of the Grateful Dead at their finest," says John Scott, the editor of *DeadBase*. "There are several defining stands in Grateful Dead history, but none is as notorious as this, and none is more deserving of the attention, providing showcase versions of almost all the Dead's important songs. Even after 27 years, these shows have not lost their power to surprise and amaze."

One of the people surprised and amazed by the tapes was Dick Latvala, who was one of the first generation of Dead tape traders, years before he was hired as the band's official archivist. Latvala was so impressed by the Dead's performance on the 13th (which Latvala hails, with characteristic hyperbole, as "one of the most intense nights in the history of the planet almost!") that he sent an ad in to *Relix*, one of the first of the tape traders' journals, offering anyone who had been to the February run free rent at his house in Hawaii for a month.

Twenty years later, by the time Latvala had gotten the job of selecting historical performances for official release, the Fillmore run had become so highly regarded by Heads who had heard hissy copies of the Chester reels that Latvala was deluged with postcards requesting the release of the master tapes on CD. "2/13/70—IT'S TIME!" read one, and Latvala didn't argue.

There were, however, gaps on the master reels Bear had made, where the tapes had to be flipped during extended jams. It turned out to be a good thing that the hidden deck had been running 15-inch reels. To create a complete master for *Dick's Picks IV*, Jeffrey Norman of the Dead's studio was able to mend the gaps by digitally patching in music recorded on Chester's deck.

The existence of two different source tapes also explains why some Deadheads have believed for years that there was only one show each night (*DeadBase* lists only one). The Fillmore crew hadn't taped the early shows, which had to end at 11 P.M. each night. There was too much stage work to do in a limited time to worry about tapes. The copies in circulation were dubs of Chester's reels. "One day at the studio about eight years ago," says Latvala, "Bear found a box of stuff, and he came up to the Vault and said, 'These should probably be upstairs with the Dead's stuff.' He opens this box, and there's 2/11, 2/13, and 2/14/70! I just about had a heart attack." There were also master reels of the 5/2/70 performance at Harpur College in the box.

The rediscovery of the early shows is welcome news, but the truth is that the tapes of the late shows that were already in circulation capture the best of the run, with tighter, more focused playing, smoother transitions, and subtler dynamics.

There was so much great music played at the Fillmore that week, it's not surprising that the Dead were able to mine these tapes for two of their most inspiring official live releases: *Bear's Choice* and *Dick's Picks IV*. (The Allman Brothers have also released their own sets from this run.) But the rest of the performances are worth seeking out on tape as well—especially those of the 11th, which certainly deserve the *Dick's Picks* treatment someday.

Highlights of the best unreleased moments of the run would have to include the late show on the 11th, which begins with an introduction by Keeva Krystal, an old waiter friend of Bill Graham's from his days as a busboy in the Borscht Belt: "Ladies and gentlemen, San Francisco men and their music, the Grateful Dead." The Dead launch into "Not Fade Away," and it's a walloping version—more like a pull-out-the-stops set closer than an opener. Jerry is full of fire, the rhythm section pounding out the primal rock 'n' roll beat with roof-shaking confidence. The band pushes the tune in several interesting directions, including an outstanding lead spot by Bob, reminiscent of the diamond-edged leads he would take coming out of "China Cat" in '72. It's one of the very best two or three performances of the tune, out of hundreds.

The "High Time" on the 11th is also fine, played with conviction and passionately sung. Even "Me and My Uncle" has volcanic energy boiling just under the surface. The first "Dark Star" of the run is a strong version, if not as seamless and lovely as the definitive version two nights later. During this era of the Dead, Phil Lesh's bass was fully a co-lead voice with Garcia's guitar, weaving melodic counterpoint around Garcia's probing lines, rather than metronomically keeping the beat. Two weeks before these shows, Tom Constanten had left the band, which left new space in the music for the sinewy, stripped-down power of the guitars.

The three-headed guitar beast rears its head right away in the run's first version of "Dark Star," with Garcia, especially, playing aggressively from the start. More and more instrumental voices are added into the mix, until "Dark Star" evolves into a rolling ocean of electrified strings and percussion, punctuated by Duane Allman's down-home slide voicings and Peter Green's barbed-wire twang, surging into a more bluesy mode than one usually associates with "Dark Star."

Then magic happens. For the first time in two years, Weir begins strumming the theme he lifted from a horn line on Gil Evans' "Solea," from Miles Davis' haunting 1960 masterwork, *Sketches of Spain*. (According to Lesh, Weir first introduced what became known as the "Spanish Jam" to the band at rehearsals at San Francisco's Potrero Theater in late 1967.) The changes are a perfect setting for the multiple guitarists, who add their own stinging accents to Weir's moody theme.

The jam shifts abruptly into a marathon workout on Bobby "Blue" Bland's "Turn On Your Lovelight," with Gregg Allman interjecting somewhat superfluous "Can you feel it, baby!" amens to Pigpen's roadhouse praises of his superhuman lover, who's "nine foot tall, six foot wide, and wriggles like pigs fightin' in a sack." (It may have been Allman's tepid vocal interjections that turned Dick Latvala off to this show, until he listened to it again—after *Dick's Picks IV* had already been selected—and decided that it might be worth releasing someday.)

By the time the steam-raising "Lovelight" winds up, bass duty has shifted from Lesh to the Allmans' Berry Oakley, and there are over thirteen people onstage for the raucous conclusion. Many collectors' copies of the show cut before the final few minutes of "Lovelight," and it's worth noting, if only as consolation, that Berry Oakley's speakers were so shredded by the end of the set that his bass sounds like a very large kazoo. (Tragically, both Duane Allman and Berry Oakley would die in separate road accidents, in 1971 and '72, respectively.)

There are unmined jewels from the other nights, too, like a ragged but haunted "Little Sadie"—which Garcia learned from an early-sixties Clarence Ashley–Doc Watson session—from the late show on the 13th, with a verse dropped from versions of the tune played at the Warfield ten years later, and a fine "Black Peter" from the 13th.

The unreleased music that has naturally aroused the most curiosity among collectors is the early show from the 14th, boasting one of the last performances of the classic "primal Dead" suite of "Dark Star" > "Saint Stephen" > "The Eleven" > "Lovelight." (It may in fact be the last, if they finished the second set on April 24, 1970, with something other than "Lovelight.") News of this discovery sent frissons of anticipation through the online taping world—as if a second disc of *Sergeant Pepper's Lonely Hearts Club Band* had turned up in the basement of Abbey Road studios.

The "Dark Star" has a distinctly harder edged sound than the previous night's, and is much more fragmented. The flowing, effortless qualities of the version of the 13th are subverted by more dissonant leads, bristling percussion, and an unwillingness—especially on Garcia's part—to cruise along in the melodic pathways cleared the night before. Lesh and Weir try their damnedest to lead the band into the "Feelin' Groovy Jam" that had worked so well on the 13th, but Garcia vetoes it twice. The set is most valuable as a glimpse into the ways the band was determined to reinvent itself night after night, set after set, even if that meant abandoning a proven approach. The Grateful Dead was a beast that thrived on metamorphosis.

The "Saint Stephen" > "The Eleven" sequence (with a couple of ill-timed cuts, unfortunately) still makes for thrilling listening. "The Eleven" sounds a bit forced, though; perhaps they were already losing their taste for playing it.

The highlight of the run, of course—if not the highlight of their thirty years on the road—was the late show on the 13th, when the Dead played a seamless hour of music that launched a million trips: one of the most coherent, fluid, subtle, and adventurous passages of twentieth-century music in any idiom.

This night's "Dark Star" unfolds with a glorious, stately majesty. Theme after improvised theme circulates among the players like shapes in water. Listening intently to one another, responding to the minutest gestures, the band reaches a level of empathy equaled only by, say, the Bill Evans Trio with Scott LaFaro and Paul Motian. When the "Dark Star" theme yields to the bright, cascading "Feelin' Groovy Jam," it's one of the most purely life-affirming moments in the band's career.

As the band moves through "Dark Star," "That's It for the Other One," and into "Lovelight," the dynamic range modulates from the barest rustling ("Dark Star") to liquid thunder ("The Other One"), touching on every emotion from buoyant joy to volcanic dissonance that roars like a force of nature. Time seems infinitely elastic, the band accelerating and decelerating together, breathing music, as if the sounds being generated were the thoughts of a single flowing harmonious consciousness.

It was in one of those moments of uncanny clarity that Alan Mande paused behind an amp to look out into the Fillmore, at all the faces illuminated by the lightshow phantoms playing on the screen behind the stage.

"I'd spent these years in the theater helping to maintain a fragile suspension of disbelief," Mande recalls, "knowing that if I just stepped out onstage, it would totally break the illusion. I looked out at that moment and saw all these people in ecstasy, and I knew that if I walked onstage, it wouldn't matter at all. I said, 'This is where it's at. This is real power.' My life turned around one hundred eighty degrees that night."

"I'll always be thankful," he continues, "because Jerry came and got me, and took me there. And I stayed there, on the bus, until August 9th, the day he died."

STEVE SILBERMAN

# Flashback:
## The Fillmore East, February 13, 1970

Six of us took the train down to NYC from New Haven and bought tickets at the box office window, which next to walking in free wasn't even much of a miracle in those days. Tickets sold for $3.50, $4.50, and $5.50. Outside, the old opera house was crawling with molecular energy. An unreal streetlight-illuminated scene surrounded by the greater darkness of that end of town late at night made it feel like we all were on stage. A guy who looked like Jimi Hendrix but wasn't walked by us murmuring, "Acid, acid," in a fog that seemed to emanate from him. We stepped into the tripping crowd that gathered in front of the closed doors, waiting, milling. Noises and voices barked from no distinct direction. Inside, the Dead were playing out the end of the early show that decades later folks would debate whether it even occurred. My first GD show. Nothing to do but smile, smile, smile.

When the doors opened, we plowed six abreast into the doors. A few Heads lay unconscious on the stairs as we stepped by them. A band called Love opened the show, followed by a relatively little-known group from the South called the Allman Brothers. Love was eminently forgettable; the Allman Brothers turned heads that night with a strong muscle-flexing set, closing after forty-five minutes (or so) with a holyshit "Whipping Post," then bidding adieu—Duane, I think it was, saying, "We know who y'all came here to see . . ."

Stage dark. 'Round 1 or 2 A.M. or a little after, Bill Graham (at least we swore it was his voice) announces something like "The Fillmore East welcomes the Grateful Dead." Onstage spotlight moves to a black casket that's propped up back where Pigpen used to hold out with the percussions. The casket opens and out comes what some of us there remember to be Jerry. Others say it was Zacherle, the New York radio guy known to do strange and macabre stunts. Stage lights shine and the boys start in with "China Cat" (though I swore for years it was "Cosmic Charlie").

Great scene at the Fillmore East. Immediate big dose of energy moves like wind blowing off the stage at the audience till you think your hair's pulled straight back. Dead played all night long, virtually nonstop, spelling each other at times, doing a little acoustic here, mostly brazen psychedelic though. The "Dark Star"'ll stay with me forever. "The Other One" and "Cryptical" too.

They closed the show with Pig doing an incredible "Lovelight" (I wasn't in any state of mind to time anything, but I'd swear it was thirty, forty minutes). Left everyone standing on the armrests of their chairs screaming and clapping so loud that when the band stopped playing, said goodnight, and walked off the stage, the sound didn't drop a decibel.

That went on for fifteen minutes till the boys came back out (Jerry, Bobby, and Phil, at least) and calmed the crowd with a long "We Bid You Goodnight" that starts loud and gets quieter and quieter with each refrain. When they finished and walked offstage, the crowd turned and walked out in total silence. Pin drop. Totally spent. It's hazy morning sunshine on the streets of New York City and in the brains of a good many Heads pouring out of the Fillmore. It had to be close to 7 A.M. To this day, I've never seen a show to match it—and I've seen plenty of shows.

DON OLDENBURG

---

### 2/27/70

**The Family Dog, San Francisco, California**

Cold Rain and Snow, Me and My Uncle, Dancin' in the Streets, Easy Wind, Good Lovin' > Dru//ms > //Jam//, Good Lovin', China Cat Sunflower > I Know You Rider > High Time, Hard to Handle, Not Fade Away > Turn On Your Lovelight

**1. Source:** SBD, **Quality:** A–, **Length:** 1:50, **Genealogy:** MR > PCM > DAT

**2. Source:** FM-SBD (GDH 094-144-210), **Quality:** A, **Length:** 0:40, ("Dancin' " > "Good Lovin'," "Not Fade Away" > "Turn On Your Lovelight"), **Genealogy:** MC > DAT

**Highlights:** High Time, Hard to Handle, Not Fade Away

Inventive but not startlingly so, this fine tape rides on a fairly mellow vibe regardless of the song being performed. Things tend not to reach real escape velocity, but it's nonetheless enjoyable and does include some moments of pure pleasure. "Dancin' in the Streets" certainly swings with some tasty interplay, all well presented in a mix that fairly sparkles with clarity. A plea to open the doors to let some fresh air into the venue naturally enough leads into a strong, bluesy "Easy Wind," Pigpen at one point losing his grip on the rhythm but transforming the slip into a neat vocal improvisation on the general theme. "Good Lovin'" rolls along with a tasty duet from the drummers but no Pigpen rap and a sadly chopped jam, though I suspect that little is missing here. A solid "China Cat Sunflower" > "I Know You Rider" with Phil's vocals distinctively high in the mix during the a cappella section leads into a sublime "High Time," a definite reason for searching out this show: perfectly paced, full of delicate playing and a great vocal from Jerry. "Hard to Handle" is all spiky guitars and a howl of testosterone-fueled Pig out on the prowl. You keep expecting it to really fly off into the ozone but it resolutely stays (relatively) earthbound. However, it's a wonderfully smoky, brooding performance full of pent-up sexual energy with a gorgeous moment of quiet reflection just before the vocal reprise that is almost at odds with the rest of the song but fits perfectly.

"Not Fade Away," at around seven minutes, is a trifle short considering the number of ideas being tossed around in it, but it segues into an overlong (thirty-minute) "Lovelight" that in comparison doesn't really contain enough substance to merit its length. Pigpen is, for Pigpen, rather restrained, but the fragments of blues songs in lieu of a rap are a nice touch.

PAUL BODENHAM

## 3/1/70
### Family Dog at the Great Highway, San Francisco, California

New Speedway Boogie Jam, Casey Jones, Big Boy Pete, Morning Dew, Hard to Handle, Me and My Uncle//, Cryptical Envelopment > Drums > The Other One > Cryptical Reprise > Black Peter, Beat it on Down the Line, Dire Wolf, Good Lovin', Cumberland Blues, China Cat// Sunflower > I Know You Rider, Uncle John's Band, Dancin' in the Streets, It's All Over Now, Baby Blue

**Source:** AUD, **Quality:** C, **Length:** 2:15, **Taper:** Harry Ely
**Highlights:** Big Boy Pete, Morning Dew, Hard to Handle, Cryptical > Drums > The Other One > Cryptical > Black Peter//

This tape is a fair but listenable audience recording. It seems at times a little compressed and muffled, but overall it has a decent mix. Most of these early audience tapes haven't enjoyed the circulation the soundboards have, for obvious reasons. They do, however, occasionally provide a little ambience to help reminisce, reminding us of the times when stadium gigs weren't the norm. There isn't much hiss on this tape, but there is some kind of static, slightly akin to the pops and cracks of vinyl, that can be slightly annoying especially during the soft passages. The first number, a soft and smooth vamp on the "New Speedway Boogie" theme, is completely enjoyable even without the solos or lyrics. There seems to be plenty of mischievous action onstage during this jam, as there are frequent outbursts of laughter and chuckling by the audience. Bobby is "greeted by a big blue spark" when he steps up to the microphone, and proceeds to describe to the audience the hazardous lifestyle of a musician. After finally solving the feedback problem, they break into "Casey Jones." This version has an upbeat marching feel thanks to the drummers, who are tenaciously locked into the groove. The seldom-played "Big Boy Pete" is next, re-creating that early rhythm and blues sound of the early 1960s. "Morning Dew," one of the highlights of this show, is a truly splendid version. The jam smokes and Jerry's vocal passages are smooth and silky—his voice is on tonight. "Hard to Handle," another noteworthy performance of the evening, briskly rocks the whole way through. There's only a little bit of "Me and My Uncle," as it cuts in shortly before the ending is reached.

This "Cryptical" suite is remarkable. From the first few pretty notes you know that what lies ahead will be delightful. "Drums," tumbling in slow and slightly heavy with lots of vigor, is filled with grooving melodic passages. When the drummers have finished, they roll (with Phil's help!) headfirst into a killer rendition of "The Other One." This is the musical peak of the show. Bobby sings with powerful conviction as the jam sways back and forth, weaving in and out of the theme, eventually returning back safely to the lyrics. Things then descend back into a sweet and now slightly bouncy (thanks again to Phil) "Cryptical" reprise that soars and concludes with a lofty jam at the end. The ending motion delicately slips into a potentially great "Black Peter," which is ruined by a glitch that chops right as the band reaches the most intense level. Except for this technical flaw, this suite is delicious.

The next part of the tape deteriorates in both technical and musical quality. An average "Good Lovin'" is followed by an ordinary "China Cat Sunflower" with a glitch so bad it makes you dive for the stop button. Once the music returns, the transition into "I Know You Rider" is exceptionally smooth, but it unfortunately leads into an uneventful version. "Uncle John's Band" is seven minutes of pure torture. This is one of the most lethargic and insipid performances of this song I have ever heard. As if this lame performance weren't enough, it is coupled with some meatball who is apparently clapping to some other beat, to some other song, somewhere else. To top it all off, the tape slows over time, which makes this truly aggravating to listen to. "Dancin'" is a good solid straight-ahead performance. "Baby Blue," the soft and slow ballad for the evening, features Jerry doing his best interpretation of Dylan.

COREY SANDERSON

## 3/8/70
### Civic Auditorium, Santa Monica, California

Black Peter, China Cat Sunflower > I Know You Rider, High// Time, Dire Wolf//, //Not Fade Away > Good Lovin' > Drums > The Other One > Not Fade Away > Turn on Your Lovelight//

**Source:** AUD, **Quality:** C+, **Length:** 1:15

**Highlights:** China Cat Sunflower > I Know You Rider, //Not Fade Away > Good Lovin' > Drums > The Other One > Not Fade Away > Lovelight

This show sticks out in my mind as one of the better early shows that has survived as an audience recording. This fairly difficult to find tape is well worth your time if you happen to come across it because this was one of those magic nights when the boys were on. The energy of the fired-up crowd intermingling with the super-charged music makes this an extremely enjoyable show to listen to. This audience recording, which is less-than-perfect, comes complete with hiss, talking, clapping, screaming, and cut songs. Unfortunately, there is no soundboard from this show circulating, so we'll just have to be grateful for what we have.

"Black Peter" is a sincere and beautiful version, soaring and flowing as Jerry's lead surges and swells with the band's serious intent and gentleness. The band works the dynamics of this song as they ascend dramatically, then ease gently back down to earth. The only word to describe this "China Cat Sunflower" > "I Know You Rider" combo is thunderous. "China Cat" is frisky and vivacious, bouncing and rocking in delight. The jam, leaving the stratosphere via Jerry's searing lead, stays out there the whole time. The intensity doesn't let up for a minute, finally coming back in like a tidal wave, cascading into "I Know You Rider." This monstrous pairing is hot. You really have to hear this one! I'm always left with a big smile on my face, and I can honestly say this is one of those "China" > "Rider" combos that visits my tape deck frequently.

"High Time" is a passionate version that unfortunately has a unpleasant glitch. We get only a couple of seconds of "Dire Wolf." The tape immediately jumps into "Not Fade Away" in the middle of a heated jam. Unfortunately, I can't tell how much is missing. This great jam flies into a maniacal "Drums" complete with frenzied multilayered grooves providing enough rhythms to keep the entire universe vibrating for another few billion years. "Drums" then dives into an uptempo pedal-to-the-metal "Good Lovin'." They break into a fantastic "Other One" right before the end of the first side of my cassette, which continues after the tape flip has been negotiated. The second side is where the really hot jamming resides! This "Other One" is fast-paced, sounding like everyone is possessed as they furiously race along. They tease the audience by slowing and quieting down for a few moments, sounding like they're all out of energy and ready to call it quits, then they suddenly jump down into a fiery "Not Fade Away"! They hit the ground full force with Bobby doing a fantastic job with the vocal duties on this early version. Then, after a few short minutes, unbelievably they break into an outrageous uptempo "Lovelight" that is one of the craziest versions ever performed. Pig is the master of ceremonies for this one, providing the crowd with everything they could ever want. This monumental rendition goes on seemingly forever, spanning a full twenty-three minutes before unfortunately cutting. If you're a "Lovelight" fan, you need to get a copy of this one. This is a definite must-have show. If you let this one pass you by solely because it's not a crispy soundboard, you'll miss out on a very hot night in Grateful Dead history.

COREY SANDERSON

## 3/20/70
### Early Show, Capitol Theater, Port Chester, New York

Casey Jones > Black Peter, Good Lovin', Mama Tried, High Time, Cryptical Envelopment > Drums > The Other One > Cryptical Reprise, Cosmic Charlie
**Encore:** New Minglewood Blues

**Source:** AUD, **Quality:** B−, **Length:** 1:20

**Highlights:** Casey Jones > Black Peter, New Minglewood Blues

**Comments:** This is a moderately acceptable audience tape. There is a strong overlay of hiss on the tape, and a somewhat muddy quality to the recording. Most instruments and vocals are audible, but often the drums are hard to pick out. Audience noise is not bothersome during the music sections. The sound becomes very muffled for about five minutes at the beginning of the second side of the tape (during "The Other One"), and there are some speed problems with the last fifteen minutes of the show. There are no cuts between songs, so this is most likely the complete show, except for some of the drum sequence lost at the tape flip.

The show begins with some preparatory noodling that explodes into a cheerful "Casey Jones" as soon as the announcer is done introducing the band. This sunny song melts into the rather dire "Black Peter" at the end. The transition is smooth enough that it seems clear that it was planned beforehand, which betrays either some sense of humor or perhaps perversity on the part of the band in juxtaposing two such diametrically opposed sensibilities. The strange duo works in stirring up the listener's thoughts and feelings.

"Good Lovin'" is a solid piece of work, with speedy, energetic jamming in a straightforward structure. One of the fun things about this show is the audience participation between songs: people seem to be taking joy in yelling out the most odd song suggestions they can think of, good examples being "White Rabbit" and "Twenty-two." (Huh?) After "Mama Tried," Garcia announces that the band is listening for "just the right voice," and lets people yell frantically for another couple of minutes before launching into the slowest song the Dead play, "High Time." Although there are a few missed chords during this version, there is a very pleasant "chilling out" feeling after the maelstrom of hysterical screaming just before the song.

"The Other One" is played as the full extended suite, with a long drum solo in the middle. The "Cryptical Envelopment" portion at the beginning is particularly well played and satisfying, while the "Cryptical" portion at the end is short and not as fully explored as was normal for the period. "Cosmic Charlie" is sloppy and seems like an afterthought rather than a necessary close to the show. The encore, "New Minglewood Blues," on the other hand, is electrifying. The band is playing with bone-crunching power as Bobby sounds like he's shredding his vocal cords, shrieking and howling over and over, even in the middle of verses. This version of "Minglewood" acts as an outrageous ending to a short but worthwhile show.

BART WISE

---

### 3/20/70
**Late Show, Capitol Theater, Port Chester, New York**

**(Electric) Set 1:** //I Know You Rider, Hard to Handle
**Acoustic Set:** //Deep Elem Blues, Friend of the Devil, Don't Ease Me In > Black Peter//, //Uncle John's Band, Katie Mae
**(Electric) Set 2:** Good Lovin' > Drums > Not Fade Away > Drums > Good Lovin', Viola Lee Blues, High Time, Turn //On Your Lovelight
**Encore:** We Bid You Goodnight

**1.** .**Source:** SBD, **Quality:** B+, **Length:** 2:00, **Genealogy:** MR > PCM > DAT
**2. Source:** SBD, **Quality:** B+, **Length:** 1:00, **Genealogy:** MR > RR > DAT
**Highlights:** Hard to Handle, Black Peter, Turn On Your Lovelight
**Comments:** This tape is a pretty nice soundboard recording. All the instruments and vocals are easily discernible, and the dynamics of the performance are well preserved. There is some hiss throughout the tape, as well as a low-level hum that sounds like a grounding problem with the soundboard; neither of these faults is too obtrusive. The entire electric content of the show also circulates condensed onto one ninety-minute tape without the acoustic set.

The performance is worth checking out, although it is not nearly as good as the unbelievable Port Chester shows from June 24, 1970, or the first week of November 1970, and really is not even as good as the early show from 3/21/70. The tape limps in halfway through "I Know You Rider" with many a cough and sputter from an aging reel. The final few minutes of "Rider" are unremarkable, but the version of "Hard to Handle" that follows is quite interesting. It is full of energy from the get-go, and Pigpen's vocal jam after the initial verses has markedly different words from his usual rap. Phil steps in with an excellent solo, wringing prolonged, powerful, emphatic notes out of his bass. In another break from form, Pigpen chimes in with a second rap after Phil steps back. Pigpen hesitates a moment at the end of his rap to let the others jam, and when no one picks up the cue, he launches into the final reprise. Altogether a pretty unusual version of the song.

The tape of this acoustic set comes in a few seconds into "Deep Elem Blues," a fine version with great singing and snaky, fluid guitar playing. "Friend of the Devil" follows, where we find Garcia playing free with both the melody and the lyrics; the listener gets the sense that the singer has abandoned himself entirely to forces beyond his control, a desperate sort of feeling that fits well with the meaning of the lyrics. An uptempo "Don't Ease Me In" ends in sloppiness from which "Black Peter" emerges, a surprise juxtaposition that somehow works well. "Black Peter" as delivered is gripping, a dissociative fever vision neither fully in this world nor in the next. Sadly, the very end of "Black Peter" is missing. A significant portion of the beginning of "Uncle John's Band" is missing, and Pigpen sings his signature acoustic tune in predictable yet involving fashion.

The second electric set begins with a jam that should be great but turns out to be disappointing. The "Not Fade Away" following the first "Drums" segment in "Good Lovin'" is basically a sucker punch, short and unfulfilling, and the jam before the final "Good Lovin'" reprise is also given short shrift. The "Viola Lee Blues" that follows, however, has a great beginning groove, with sweeping, crystalline notes from Garcia and a punchy Phil backbone. The central buildup in the song is short and less satisfying than the next night's version, but there is enough energy for a fun listen here. "High Time" is fine, but the last song of the set is where the action really is.

"Turn On Your Lovelight" begins energetically, as usual. There is a very brief barely noticeable cut near the end of the first sung verse. At first Pigpen seems to be leading the band down the usual pathways, but it's not long before he reveals a really inventive mood. Among other fun shenanigans, Pigpen makes the rest of the band turn their backs so he can share a "secret" with the audience, and drives the audience several times into a wild frenzy of clapping and shouting. You'd have to work hard to sit still through this version of the song. The sense of catharsis and epiphany is so strong that guitars ringing at the end summon visions of bells ringing in some high church of rock 'n' roll. The crowd claps long and hard, and, humorously, even as the announcer is trying to explain that the Dead are too tired to play an encore, he is interrupted by the triumphant voices belting out the Dead's gospel good-bye. Let it shine!

BART WISE

---

### 3/21/70
**Early Show, Capitol Theater, Port Chester, New York**

Walkin' the Dog, Me and My Uncle, Death Don't Have No Mercy, Good Lovin', Dire Wolf, Big Boss Man, He Was a Friend of Mine > Viola Lee Blues > The Seven > Cumberland Blues

**Source:** AUD, **Quality:** B+, **Length:** 1:30, **Genealogy:** MC > C > DAT

**Highlights:** Walkin' the Dog, Death Don't Have No Mercy, He Was a Friend of Mine > Viola Lee Blues > The Seven > Cumberland Blues

Although this show is not as explosive as the late show, it is nevertheless a fine example of the magic of the Grateful Dead, circa 1970. It opens with the rarely played shenanigan-ish "Walkin' the Dog," and shortly thereafter Jerry plays a heartfelt "Death Don't Have No Mercy." Pigpen keeps things rolling with an improvisational and solid "Good Lovin'" that ends rather abruptly. "Big Boss Man" is another rarely played treat, but the Dead saved the best for last, as was often the case in 1970. The jam begins with a liltingly poignant "He Was a Friend of Mine" before giving way to the roller-coaster-like, electrically charged cacophony that is "Viola Lee Blues." The band doesn't stop short there, but they shift into "The Seven" before ending with "Cumberland Blues," a song that benefits here from the momentum of the jam.

ANDREW J. LEMIEUX

## 3/21/70
### Late Show, Capitol Theater, Port Chester, New York

**Electric Set 1:** Casey Jones, Dancin' in the Streets, Easy Wind
**Acoustic Set:** Friend of the Devil, Deep Elem Blues, Don't Ease Me In, Black Peter, Wake Up, Little Susie, Uncle John's Band, Katie Mae
**Electric Set 2:** Cosmic Charlie, Saint Stephen > Not Fade Away > Saint Stephen > China Cat Sunflower Jam > Not Fade Away, Midnight Hour > Turn On Your Lovelight
**Encore:** We Bid You Goodnight

**1. Source:** AUD, **Quality:** A–, **Length:** 1:30, **Genealogy:** MC > C > DAT
**2. Source:** SBD, **Quality:** B+, **Length:** 1:20, (Electric Set 2)
**Highlights:** Dancin' in the Streets, Katie Mae, the whole second electric set

This show opens with a short electric set, which is often missing from tapes that circulate of the show. After "Casey Jones" comes a very solid and well-jammed "Dancin' in the Streets." Although it is not as dynamic as the version from May 2, 1970, it is classic 1970 Grateful Dead and a hint of what is yet to come. Pigpen ends this short set with "Easy Wind," which is only fitting since he ends all three sets of this show and pushes this show over the top at its conclusion. The acoustic set is a nice contrast, a quieter, but by no means less poignant, Grateful Dead. "Friend of the Devil" is quicker and played in more of a bluegrass style than the latter-era ballad versions. A plaintive "Black Peter" and pretty "Uncle John's Band" are also very well played. Pigpen closes this set with the too rarely played "Katie Mae."

The second electric set is what makes this show my favorite from among many outstanding shows in 1970, my favorite year of Grateful Dead music. It begins with a well-played "Cosmic Charlie," and then the jam begins. The incendiary playing that rounds out this set would be hard to appreciate fully without the crowd reaction that the audience tape provides. A powerful and tightly played "Saint Stephen" weaves into the tribal stomp of "Not Fade Away." The Dead then return to finish "Saint Stephen," and Jerry rips off a lightning-quick "China Cat Sunflower" jam that catches the crowd by surprise before they make their way back to wind-up "Not Fade Away." Pigpen is able to take the band and crowd to yet another, even higher frenzy with his urging and vocal improvisation during the concluding combination of "Midnight Hour" > "Turn On Your Lovelight." The Dead range from exploratory to explosive and leave the crowd stomping and clapping out the beat long after the band has stopped. Pigpen comes out to tell the crowd, "All right, baby, it's your show!" before the rest of the band makes their way to the stage to cool things out with a gentle "We Bid You Goodnight."

— ANDREW J. LEMIEUX

## 3/24/70
### Pirate's World, Dania, Florida

//Morning Dew, Mama Tried, Good Lovin' > Drums > Good Lovin' Reprise, Don't Ease Me In, Cold Rain and Snow, High Time, Dark// Star > The Other One > Saint Stephen > Drums > Not Fade Away > Turn On Your Lovelight > Me and My Uncle

**Source:** SBD, **Quality:** A, **Length:** 1:30, **Genealogy:** MR > RR > DAT > C > DAT
**Highlights:** Good Lovin', High Time, Dark Star, Saint Stephen

Now here's an interesting tape. The Dead are facing a tough challenge: time. Nothing is known yet about what other bands are on the bill, but the Dead are given only a ninety-minute set to work their magic. They come out high-spirited and really go for it, though. Unfortunately, there's a feeling of haste, especially after the "Dark Star," as they quickly cram their "hits" in to beat the clock. They do a fine job considering the task—and considering how this is *not* the way they prefer to unfold their unique brand of music.

"Don't Ease" has a terrific groove. "Good Lovin'" is very solid and slickly delivered (though still too short). "High Time" is very sweetly done. "Dark Star" starts out perky and promising, but a sudden cut forces us to wonder how much we missed. "Dark Star" continues on in a new space that has a healthy dose of strange, eerie, rhythmless sounds. This cascades into a thundering jam that peaks when Lesh grabs the wheel and takes the band into one round of the "Feelin' Groovy Jam." Garcia then grabs the wheel from Lesh and steers the band into an intense and rousing "Dark Star" jam. Hints of "Darkness, Darkness" flutter by before Lesh pulls both the rug and the plug by slamming into the "Other One." A short but robust version slips into "Saint Stephen." There are several focal flubs but the last jam is an all-out, in-your-face assault on the gates of heaven. Ah but they *just* miss. Nonetheless, it's exciting as hell. A brief "Drums" brings on the shortest and least interesting "Not Fade Away" I've heard yet. The segue into "Lovelight," though, is spotless. And the playing is excellent, featuring some killer crescendos. But the time limit puts a squeeze on it—despite Pigpen's typically entertaining rap on the sexual merits of his old lady. And then Weir said, "Say, we've still got a few minutes left, guys. How 'bout 'Me and My Uncle,' man?"

So they did.

MICHAEL M. GETZ

---

### 4/3/70
### Field House, University of Cincinnati, Cincinnati, Ohio

**Electric Set 1:** //Casey Jones, China Cat Sunflower > I Know You Rider, Hard to Handle, Dancin' in the Streets, Me and My Uncle
**Acoustic Set:** Friend of the Devil, Deep Elem Blues, Candyman, Wake Up, Little Susie > Black Peter, Uncle John's Band, Katie Mae
**Second Set:** //Good Lovin', Cryptical Envelopment > Drums > The Other One > Cryptical Envelopment > Cosmic Charlie, Not Fade Away > Turn On Your Lovelight

**Source:** SBD, **Quality:** B+, **Length:** 2:15, **Genealogy:** MR > RR > RR > RR > PCM > DAT

**Highlights:** Wake Up, Little Susie, Katie Mae, Cryptical Envelopment > Cosmic Charlie

**Comments:** My analog cassette of this show is a soundboard of unknown generation. The sound fades in and out a bit for the first half of the first side. The bass is boomy and distorted for most of the show, but the sound is clear enough so you can hear the snares vibrating. However, the drums are too low in the mix in some places. There's also an intermittent buzz throughout the entire tape, which can be very annoying. My B+ rating is due to the distortion and the buzz. The flip right before the very end of "Lovelight" could have been avoided by either flipping before "Not Fade Away" or putting the last side on half of a one hundred-minute tape.

Given that Ken Kesey and the Merry Pranksters were also on the bill, one might think this show would be a guaranteed wild night. For 1970, though, this ended up being a relatively low-key performance. This was, however, new ground for the University of Cincinnati, so reported the student newspaper from that week, as they experimented with general admission seating ($3 per ticket!) for the first time. The opening act was the Lemon Pipers of "Green Tambourine" fame.

At the end of "Casey Jones," Phil says, "We're having a little trouble with the monitors because they're *not* on!" This is quite typical of technical problems that plagued the band during this period, and continues at least through the acoustic set. The segue between "China Cat Sunflower" and "I Know You Rider" is flawless, with beautiful harmonies on "I Know You Rider." Their vocals are more expressive than in the earlier years. Bobby explains that "Dancin' in the Streets" is a "drummer's choice," but I'll never get used to this version because the backing vocals are always off-key. The jam is strong, however—one of those that if you turned the tape on in the middle, you'd have no idea what song it was, yet they somehow manage to bring it back to the original riff without missing a beat. It gets very jazzy in the middle, with a rhythm that foreshadows "Eyes of the World." The acoustic set is great! Jerry sings an extra verse in "Friend of the Devil": "I went down to the levee but the devil caught my scent, so I coughed up two hundred bills to pay back what was lent." This is the first performance of "Candyman," which doesn't yet have its syncopated beat in this fast version. "Wake Up, Little Susie" is incredible—it's my favorite acoustic tune from this show. Pigpen grumbles over the placement of his guitar mike before "Katie Mae," explaining that "I got weak fingers, so it's got to be close!" His guitar work is the best I've heard on this tune. "The Other One" seems a bit lackluster in places, but the instrumental at the end of "Cryptical Envelopment" is awesome, beginning with the gorgeous quiet guitar work by Jerry and Bob (my favorite part), then

*Jerry and Bob, 4/10/70* (photo credit: Michael Parrish)

building back up until Phil goes nuts and they tear it up at the end. The segue into "Cosmic Charlie" comes out of some brief space. This version is incredible! Wish I had been there. Jerry and Bob's vocals are surprisingly together, and the falsetto part sounds silly (an early taste of the Bee Gees influence?!). The instrumental at the end is quite powerful, with a some fuzz effects on the guitars. This would have been a great show-ender: "Go on home, your momma's callin' you!" The "Not Fade Away" is relatively low energy and Pigpen's rap during "Lovelight" is quite short. However, they build up to a frenetic tizzy at the end, with Bobby screaming and Pigpen howling, going on and on so it seems as if the show will never end.

JOLIE GOODMAN

## 4/9/70
### Fillmore West, San Francisco, California

**Electric Set 1:** Good Mornin', Li'l Schoolgirl, Mama Tried, China Cat Sunflower > I Know You Rider, Viola Lee Blues
**Acoustic Set:** Candyman, Friend of the Devil, Deep Elem Blues, Black Peter//, Uncle John's Band, Katie Mae
**Electric Set 2:** Good Lovin' > Drums > Good Lovin' Reprise, Cowboy Song, It's a Man's World, Cryptical Envelopment > Drums > The Other One > Cryptical Reprise//, //Me and My Uncle, Casey Jones, Not Fade Away > Turn On Your Lovelight//

1. **Source:** AUD, **Quality:** B (second electric set) B– (acoustic set), **Length:** 1:30, **Taper:** Harry Ely
2. **Source:** SBD, **Quality:** A–, **Length:** 0:45 (first electric set)

**Highlights:** Good Mornin', Li'l Schoolgirl, Viola Lee Blues, I Know You Rider, It's a Man's World, Not Fade Away

**Comments:** "Cowboy Song" is a guess at the title.

This was the first show of a four-night run in which the Miles Davis Quintet opened for the Dead. Quite a contrast, to say the least. Like Charles Ives, Peter and Caspar Brotzman, Evan Parker, Elliott Carter, John Coltrane and others, Miles created a dense force of

*Phil and Bob, 4/10/70* (photo credit: Michael Parrish)

nature and hurled it at his audience. In referring to Ives on his radio show, "Eyes of Chaos," Lesh once remarked that one must adjust the way one listens to this kind of music by letting it pass through and simply feeling its power. Should one instead go into it, locking in on particular sounds, a brain-knot will ensue, causing discomfort. Consequently, music of this kind invites comments such as "I can only listen to twenty minutes of that stuff—then it's *too* much." Indeed, this is true, unless one steps back a pace or two, as Lesh advises. It's worth a try for any adventurous lover of music. Lesh is also on record as saying that while he sat on the side of the stage during Miles' set, he felt mesmerized and a little intimidated about going on next.

Nonetheless, the Dead opened the first electric set with one of the finest versions of "Schoolgirl" ever. All three jams sparkle with ingenuity and contain lots of open space to let the audience in. Surely this was comforting to many in the crowd who were no doubt blown away by Miles.

There's a wonderful moment during "China Cat" when Garcia gets lost two-thirds of the way through and—knowing so—spits forth a flurry of "ahhh, what the hell, folks!" notes and *burns* a path toward *Rider*. On the way he also jokingly teases "Goin' Down the Road." "Rider" itself finds the whole band clicking, but Garcia stands out as a man possessed: he snaps, crackles, and pops his notes till they sound like rim shots. The set ends with a "Viola Lee" that is played savagely, with neither remorse nor mercy. Not a dry eye in the house, indeed.

The acoustic set is distinctly fresh and relaxed. The harmonies are achingly youthful, gleeful, overwrought, and sometimes off-key—but they're sung with complete sincerity. For a bunch of radical, consciousness-exploring drug users, they sure sound like a bunch of nice fellers here. Strange, too, for the crowd to be presented with an immense "Viola Lee" one minute—and then, almost apologetically, lulled back to the suburbs by this gentle, innocent acoustic set. Who *are* these guys?

Back in the electric saddle again, an average "Good Lovin'," despite Lesh's attempts to get it going with a power stunt on the G-C-D theme. "Cowboy Song" sounds like a mixture of "Casey Jones" and the "Goin' Down the Road" coda. The swingin' beat delights the crowd and is sung very loosely by an unknown vocalist (definitely not David Bromberg, so he says). The first known version of "Man's World" is played superbly. Pig tears through it vocally while the boys provide some inspired backing vocals themselves. Lesh is so into Pigpen here that he shadows his singing, countering it with his own sly interpretations. Great fun.

Pigpen gets the honor of nailing the "Other One" introduction with a fierce organ blast. Garcia slows it down to a whisper after the first verse before slowly and carefully rebuilding it with sharper, more piercing notes till the jam has more purpose and less recklessness than before. However, it's too controlled, too safe, and covers little creative ground.

During the "Cryptical" reprise, though, after Garcia's ". . . he had to die-eye-eye-eye-yuhhhhhhhh" yelp, Lesh seals it all with an ear-splittin' note that brings audible cries of ecstasy from the crowd. Garcia grows wings for "Not Fade Away," soaring higher and higher with each measure, until he seemingly elevates the band with him. Ah, but wait. A second listen reveals a less obvious (and certainly more sinister) force in and around Garcia that perhaps is even responsible for the sudden shifts in the wind's velocity that Garcia so effortlessly rides upon. I refer, of course, to Mr. Lesh. I guess it's one of those chicken or the egg jams.

"Lovelight" smoothly emerges after "Not Fade Away," and the crowd loves it. There are some explosive moments, but it cuts after ten minutes, right as the band settles down to back up Pigpen's obligatory sermon on the importance of family values, predating Dan Quayle by twenty years.

MICHAEL M. GETZ

---

### ✺ 4/12/70 ✺

**Fillmore West, San Francisco, California**

**Electric Set 1:** Good Mornin', Li'l Schoolgirl, Casey Jones, Mama Tried, China Cat Sunflower > I Know You Rider, Good Lovin'
**Acoustic Set:** Candyman, Deep Elem Blues, Dire Wolf, Black Peter
**Electric Set 2:** Dancin' in the Streets, Uncle John's Band, It's a Man's World, Viola Lee Blues > Feedback

**1. Source:** SBD, **Quality:** B+, **Length:** 1:40 (all)

**2. Source:** FM-SBD (GDH), **Quality:** A, **Length:** 0:55 ("Dire Wolf," "Black Peter," and "Dancin' in the Streets" through "Viola Lee Blues")

**3. Source:** SBD-CD (Fallout from the Phil Zone), **Quality:** A, **Length:** 11:40 ("Dancin' in the Streets")

**Highlights:** Deep Elem Blues, Dancin' in the Streets, Viola Lee Blues

For the last night of their four-night stand with Miles Davis, the Dead played competently, although they were hardly a match for the visionary music that Davis and his Bitch's Brew collaborators had just laid down. A relatively linear collection of single songs, the Sunday night show definitely didn't, as a whole, showcase the band doing what they do best, although some spectacular highs were achieved during the extended pieces. Bill Graham's introduction was "If the Dead End Kids were alive today, they would be called the Grateful Dead," which led into a sure, slow "Schoolgirl." "Casey Jones" is bright and punchy. A mid-set treat is a rare, funky version of "Deep Elem Blues."

The show's centerpiece is a long, jazzy "Dancin' in the Streets"—easily one of hottest versions performed by the Dead and one of the more notable jams from 1970. Immediately following the introductory lyrics, a polished, high-energy improvisation begins to evolve. At first, the band keeps this statement very tight, much like the eloquent yet controlled version played on February 14, 1970. But the jam keeps elongating into even more ecstatic realms. As Phil begins to drop *massive* chordal bombs, Jerry fingerpicks with remarkable speed and precision. Obviously feeding off each other, Phil and Jerry then begin *hacking* away at their strings, very much like the "Dancin'" from September 18, 1970. This is the legendary Grateful Dead that makes the blind see and the lame walk! Eventually, after pulling off several magnificent crescendos, Jerry starts to hint at a return to the closing lyrics. But Phil will have no part of this; he launches into a fully articulated "Feelin' Groovy Jam." Moments later, as the band settles back into the closing lyrics, the listener may get the urge to compare this version to that played on May 2, 1970. Amazingly, the "Dancin'" from April 12 is so inspired one would be hard pressed to say that the version from Harpur College is truly better. You'll just have to own both.

The rest of the evening is just as tasty. The long version of "It's a Man's World" features some slippery Garcia leads and an impassioned Pigpen vocal. "Viola Lee Blues" was a relative rarity by this time, but it also features some incredible rapid-fire soloing by Jerry and Phil before easing back into the final chorus, which is followed by a brief, apocalyptic feedback segment. This tape was first circulated when it was broadcast, without a date identification, on KMPX in the late '71. It was frequently labeled as 7/12/70 Fillmore East in later years before it showed up as a clean, low-generation soundboard a couple of years ago, and then the "Dancin'" was released on the Phil Zone CD.

MICHAEL PARRISH

---

### 4/24/70
**Mammoth Gardens, Denver, Colorado**

**Acoustic Set:** I Know You Rider, The Monkey and the Engineer, Friend of the Devil, Me and My Uncle, Candyman, Uncle John's Band

**Electric Set:** Easy Wind, Cumberland Blues, Dire Wolf, Dark Star > Saint Stephen > The Eleven > Drums

**Source:** AUD, **Quality:** C, **Length:** 1:40
**Highlights:** Dark Star

---

The quality and the brevity of this tape make it impossible to accurately judge this show. It's a shame no better tape exists because I remember the show as incredibly psychedelic—and I wasn't tripping. In my case the acoustic set and good pot were mind-expanders for me; we never expected an acoustic set from the Dead, but we got one. Since I'd grown up on folk music, what I heard bonded me to the band. This was the period after the old dancing ballroom shows where most rock audiences sat on the floor (in this case an old roller-skating rink) and danced only if the music virtually forced them to. Acoustic music kept everyone on the floor.

It took the second set on this warm, electric spring night—and it *was* electric indeed—to get people moving. I remember the "Dark Star" being punctuated with the percussionists playing wind chimes. It got quiet and sorta scary, as "Dark Star" could. And then it climbed to a fierce, extended ending.

But what stands out strongest in my mind was Pigpen shooting a pistol off toward the ceiling during "Saint Stephen" just before the *oh-so-sweet* "one man gathers what another one spills" lyric. The tape does have that moment. After that, I just can't recall much,

# Reviews: May 1970

except I do remember after the show walking out of the Gardens into the warm night air and feeling my whole body full of smiles. I had become a Deadhead. The next week the Dead headed East to do their now famous Spring of '70 East Coast college run. A whole lot more kids like me were about to get on the bus.

ERIC TAYLOR

---

## 5/1/70
### Alfred College, Alfred, New York

//The Other One > Cryptical Reprise, High Time, Turn On Your Lovelight//

---

**Source:** SBD, **Quality:** A–, **Length:** 0:52, **Genealogy:** MR > RR > PCM > DAT

**Comments:** It has long been thought that these songs were played on May 19, 1970, on the campus of Washington University in St. Louis, Missouri, but a little research determined that the Washington University show never happened. I was first told by a long time taper from New York City that what was listed under 5/19/70 was actually from 5/1/70 Alfred College. He said that some of band's reels for 5/1/70 were found under the stage on May 14, 1970, at Merramec Community College, Kirkwood, Missouri. Soon after the show one of the parties with the reels disappeared, and some of the reels were never recovered.

So did the May 19, 1970, show ever happen? If the rest of our tapes are correct, the band went from Missouri to New York to Pennsylvania to Connecticut back to Missouri and then off to England. Not too likely. I then found someone in St. Louis who used to work for Velvet Plastic Productions, the company that brought the Dead into town. This guy emceed the April 17, 1969, show at Washington University, and he did not remember the Dead returning in 1970. He then sent me this:

> I've made some inquiries at W.U. about the supposed "phantom show" there in 1970, and it seems, at this point, that it never happened! I reviewed the documents of the era in the school library with appropriate staff, and even talked by phone with the lady (now retired) who would have known if the Dead had played in Graham Chapel. The consensus seems to be that it never happened! Not only was the school shut down early for spring break as a result of the tumult that followed Kent State, but it doesn't make sense that the band would return to town so soon after playing at Merramec C.C. only a few days before. The bottom line: it appears that *DeadBase* is wrong.

I confirmed this with another source who went to all the St. Louis shows from 1969 onward. The Grateful Dead did not play on May 19, 1970, in St. Louis.

The music we do have on tape, //"Other One" > "Lovelight//," was originally called "Larry's Tape," after the guy who found it. Larry dubbed over the tuning because he did not want to listen to it, which explains why most tapes have cuts after each song. A new, much cleaner and slightly longer tape is starting to circulate from first-generation reels dubbed by Larry's friend. I wrote Dick Latvala, Grateful Dead tape archivist, to see if he could shed any light on the situation. He replied, "We have reel #2 from Alfred College (5/1/70), that says on the tape box that the New Riders were on part of the

*Mickey, 5/70* (photo credit: Michael Parrish)

reel. This implies that we must have the very start of 5/1/70 and reels #3, 4, 5 (or however many there were) were the ones that were found under the stage. Also, our reel is 7" at 2 × 7½ ips." So while we may not be able to say with complete certainty that these songs were played on May 1 at Alfred College, it is the best lead we have.

The tape cuts in during "The Other One" about two minutes before Bobby starts singing, "Spanish lady . . ." The pace is fast and furious. The drummers are falling all over themselves propelling the band forward. As they slow it down and glide into "Cryptical," the beauty of their ensemble playing shines through. Jerry is the first to hint at "Cryptical," as if to say, "Hey, follow me, this is going to be fun!" "High Time" gets a decent playing but nothing special. The tuning is cut out between all the songs on my tape. Pigpen sends the crowd home with a little encouragement to "turn on your lovelight."

ERIC DOHERTY

## 5/2/70
### Harpur College, Binghamton, New York

**Acoustic Set:** Don't Ease Me In, I Know You Rider, Friend of the Devil, Dire Wolf, Beat It on Down the Line > Black Peter, Candyman, Cumberland, Deep Elem Blues, Cold Jordan*, Uncle John's Band
**New Riders Set:** Lovin' Games (?), Henry, Saw Mill†, Race Is On†, Mama Tried†, Me and My Uncle†, The Weight†
**Electric Set 1:** //Saint Stephen > Cryptical Envelopment > The Other One > Cryptical Reprise > Cosmic Charlie, Casey Jones, Good Lovin', Cold Rain and Snow, It's a Man's World, Dancin' in the Streets
**Electric Set 2:** Morning Dew, Viola Lee Blues > Feedback > We Bid You Goodnight

* with the New Riders
† with Weir and Garcia

**1. Source:** SBD-CD (*Dick's Picks VIII*), **Quality:** A, **Length:** 2:57 (missing "Cold Rain and Snow" and NRPS set)

**2. Source:** SBD, **Quality:** A, **Length:** 3:40 (all), **Genealogy:** MR > RR > RR > DAT
**3. Source:** FM-SBD, **Quality:** B (although very hissy, this part is in stereo), **Length:** 1:20 (just the the acoustic and New Riders sets)
**4. Source:** SBD, **Quality:** A, **Length:** 3:00 (no NRPS set), **Genealogy:** MR > DAT
**Highlights:** Cold Jordan, Uncle John's Band, Cryptical > The Other One > Cryptical > Cosmic Charlie, Good Lovin', It's a Man's World, Dancin' in the Streets, Viola Lee Blues > Feedback > We Bid You Goodnight
**Comments:** All known copies of the electric sets both in circulation and in the Vault are only available as mono recordings.

One of the most valuable lessons the Grateful Dead taught me was how to be ready for and appreciate

*Jerry on pedal steel guitar, 5/70* (photo credit: Michael Parrish)

serendipity when it graciously appears. So, it seemed par for the course when, on the first day I sat down to write this review, I picked up a copy of Camille Paglia's *Sex, Art, and American Culture* for the first time and opened immediately to the page in the middle of the book on which she describes her experiences attending Harpur College in the late sixties!

"Harpur," she wrote, "with its strong presence of avant-garde, intellectual Jewish students from New York City, was seething with raw creative energy. People called it Berkeley East."[1]

Knowing this now, is it any wonder the Dead played so powerfully when they breezed through this state college campus in the spring of 1970?

For all the media coverage we've seen in the past few years documenting who and what Deadheads are, nothing is said anymore about what we Deadheads were like when the Dead first rose to legendary status. The truth of it is, that when the Dead started attracting *serious* attention on the East Coast in 1970, a large part of this fanatical following comprised upper-middle-class white college kids. Never mind that this was the height of the turbulent sixties, the college experience, with its wealth of novel social and cultural experiences, tends to provide an environment extremely conducive to profound shifts in worldview and consciousness expansion. It would be hard to imagine going to college in 1970, attending a Dead show like the one at Harpur, and *not* being transformed into a raving Deadhead.

Additionally, 1969–70 was a very intense year in America, both politically and socially. Between the first-ever lunar landing, Woodstock, Altamont, the Vietnam War, the antiwar moratoriums and demonstrations (particularly the one at Kent State in Ohio—just two days away—at which the National Guard killed four innocent student bystanders), young adults had plenty going on around them to fire them up and blow their minds. The Grateful Dead, along with the Jefferson Airplane and Jimi Hendrix, provided the perfect soundtrack for those times.

Jerry Garcia and his troupe of traveling troubadours brought their "Evening with the Grateful Dead Family" show to at least eleven colleges back East that spring (some are perhaps still unidentified): Alfred, Harpur, Wesleyan, M.I.T. (two shows), Delhi, Worcester, Merramec, Temple, Fairfield, and Washington University. This was a very smart move. *Live Dead* had hit the record stores just a few months before, and the band

*Bobby*

was perfectly positioned to attract huge crowds of new, soon-to-be-faithful fans. It was a beautiful accident waiting to happen.

The Harpur show is widely considered to be one of the Dead's best-ever performances. It's not that the music on 5/2/70 is played with amazing technical perfection. Quite the contrary: it's raw and ragged. It is, however, played with an unparalleled degree of intensity: so intense at times that it's scary. This is a very, very important point. The Dead were probably better than any other band on the planet at playing music that expresses darkness and ugliness as well as beauty and joy. It's not that they championed darkness or worshiped evil, but that they allowed themselves to freely explore the entire range of emotions and colors of life and art—both the sunshine and the shadow worlds. In a post–World War culture obsessed with achieving psychological security, the safe pop love song of the 1950s and early 1960s was the accepted and desirable norm. The Grateful Dead playing screaming "Feedback" was not. Listen to the "Other One" from this show. This *isn't* pretty music. It is the sound of flesh ripping apart, of suns exploding. Of lightning screamin', "I AM!"

But the beautiful horror of the shadow world is still a ways away when the Dead first take the stage on May 2—armed with nothing more ominous and foreboding than acoustic guitars. Still the expectant crowd goes nuts from the start. Jerry says, "Relax, we've got you all night." After Weir tells the audience to behave, Pigpen, in true Prankster fashion, tells them to ignore Bobby. By "Black Peter" they manage to at least contain themselves until the more upbeat tunes. Instrumentally, Jerry goes nuts from the start, but he's probably quite stoned because he's obviously a bit out of synch with Weir and Pig.

---

1. Camille Paglia, *Sex, Art, and American Culture* (New York: Vintage, 1992), p. 125.

Unlike the unexplainable mono recording of the electric sets, this acoustic set is a stereo soundboard source recording. Why the difference, and where, if anywhere, the stereo recording of the electric set might be is anybody's guess. Additionally, a story has spread over the years that the "Candyman" > "Cumberland Blues" medley that most everyone has is actually a composite made by a radio deejay who needed to cut some time from the music in order to fit it all in during his show. Listen carefully and you'll hear it for certain. Regardless, "Cumberland," which is complete, rocks out! The two other highlights from this set are the "Cold Jordan," which features members of the New Riders, and the all-around strong, set-closing "Uncle John's Band" complete with tasteful percussion highlights.

Only a few songs from the New Riders set circulate, but they're worth getting since they usually appear on the same tape as the acoustic set and they feature Jerry on pedal steel. Marmaduke introduces "Bobby 'Ace' Weir," who sits in for four songs.

The acoustic set was the sweet, folksy, bring-the-boys-home-to-yer-mama Grateful Dead, but the impending electric set is the raw, rude, sexy GD we all really secretly pine for. This is the *meat*, so to speak. It's a real bummer that a tape of the electric set doesn't start until smack dab in the middle of "Saint Stephen." Regardless, it's immediately obvious that a wild ride is already in progress. "Cryptical" brings the energy down briefly but sets the tone for what quickly becomes one of the heaviest "Other Ones" you'll ever hear. Phil's instrument unleashes a monster opening statement. Jerry's Gibson guitar tone is fat, electric, and VERY LOUD!

When listening to the music of the Grateful Dead I have always experienced synesthesia; I don't just hear the music, I *see* it too. When I listen to this "Other One," a clear vision of Yamantaka, the Tibetan Buddhist deity who scares away evil by assuming a wrathful guise, appears clearly in my mind's eye. Yamantaka appears as a ferocious, multiheaded beast engulfed in flames, grasping a skull cup overflowing with brain meat. This bodhisattva doesn't fuck around, and neither do the Dead during this "Other One." Three days later, in Harpur College's student paper, the concert's reviewer describes Garcia's guitar work during "The Other One" as "cosmic."

Back into the reprise of "Cryptical" Jerry and Bobby give birth to a brief yet stunning contrapuntal conversation in which Bobby strums out a luscious melody while Jerry counters with a brilliant, minimalist statement of singular harmonic notes. Once they reach the far side of the reprise's lyrics, Jerry returns to shred mode, commanding his guitar to scream as though the beautifully horrific moment of death has truly arrived. Phil equals Jerry's enormous statement on the low end of the register. Absolutely incredible! From the ashes of "Cryptical" rises what may be the most triumphant version of "Cosmic Charlie" in circulation. It's not the wildest—that honor is still claimed by the version played on 3/1/69. There is an unusual sense of joy exuding from this "Cosmic Charlie." One gets the feeling the Dead know they've hit a home run with this medley of songs and are excited to be rounding third base. Save for one brief off-note sung by Bobby, this song is delivered with absolute perfection.

"Casey Jones" is fairly nondescript, which is odd, considering how fired up they all are. "Good Lovin'," on the other hand, is so hyperkinetic it's almost impossible to dance to! The drummers are the demonic driving force behind this mad version—they start the song at breakneck speed. Once into the lyrics Phil's backup vocals are off-key. But who cares?! Something intense is obviously about to happen. During the drum solo Billy and Mickey continue to go nuts. Jerry's the first one to come back in with a relatively quiet but very fast, tiny lead-in. Phil steps quickly into the spotlight and seriously ups the ante by playing with frightening intensity. "Oh yeah?" Jerry seems to reply with even greater ferocity. The jam builds instantly to an all-hands-on-deck, red-alert, Latin-flavored war dance. If I had been at this show, I would've stopped dancing and simply stared in utter disbelief with my jaw agape. This is the male beast aspect of the Grateful Dead cocking its hairy head upward and bellowing flames high in the air. Very heavy indeed!

"Cold Rain and Snow" follows. Despite several retuning attempts in midsong and a passionate effort throughout, the band can't bring their instruments in tune together.

Then it's Pigpen's turn at the helm again, and he leads the sextet through yet another classic Grateful Dead moment: a shining rendition of the James Brown tune "It's a Man's World." I can't think of a more perfect *blue* moment in Grateful Dead history. Garcia plays this one just right: no screaming leads here, just a perfect amalgam of soul and blues riffs as a emotionally evocative instrumental support structure for Pigpen's mournful lyrical refrain.

And then comes "Dancin' in the Streets." The Dead's treatment of this tune—which shortly after this performance all but disappeared for several years from the band's standard repertoire—was more about building a psychedelic groove than about giving the audience an opportunity to do the traditional Motown frug. No doubt there are many versions we still have yet to hear (for lack of circulating tapes from this time period), but this version discovers creative spaces more eloquent and blissful than most versions in circulation, save 4/12/70, perhaps. Once the opening verses are sung and the improvisation begins, the modality is the same as "Dark Star," but it's much more of a guitar solo than a jam, with the band laying down an enormously muscular groove. The jam starts out with Garcia playing sharp chords and Weir playing a lead figure that becomes his mantra throughout the rest of the instrumental voyage. Off of this mantra, which Bobby does different permutations of but never really strays far from, Jerry plays melodic lines simple enough to sing; one of the reasons we love this version so much is that we can sing Garcia's guitar lead. Jerry does pluck a few "wrong" notes but manages to make them sound beautiful, proving that for a master musician there really are no wrong notes. Once again his playing is highlighted by the tonality of his Gibson guitar—the notes sound fatter, rounder, more electric than his Fender Strat sound. At several points he takes advantage of these tonal characteristics and repeatedly plucks specific notes that resonate fully with the guitar-amp-room combination present that evening. Phil builds his playing around the root, but makes beautiful forays outward, delivering brilliant exclamation points throughout. The jam changes direction with the introduction of a pattern of two parallel major 7th chords. Mickey picks up on this and starts playing his cowbell. All of a sudden there is again a joyous Latin feel in the air—one of the most notable aspects of this particular version.

After fully exploring this samba for a while, Jerry starts playing chords up high on the neck, giving the drummers the chance to extrapolate on the groove with Mickey playing the cowbell again. Jerry then returns with a strong lead against which Phil plays a choppy, walking line until the band pulls the entire groove back to a brief, quiet interlude. Once again they return to the same "Dark Star"–like modality this amazing improvisational voyage started with. Jerry plays thirds over an open A string reminiscent of his playing in "Cosmic Charlie." Again, the band becomes quiet and Jerry does this stunning little fingerpicking riff much like that on the *Live Dead* version of "Dark Star."

This leads into a triumphant return to the bridge of the song, "And all we need is music." Gorgeous! The band sets this monumental version to rest with a strong sustained moment of feedback, which cuts on many circulating tapes.

The tape then comes back in to capture Phil saying, "OK now, you folks should all follow the fine example of this fellow over here who got it on with his girlfriend. We're gonna take a short break and I want you to all feel each other for a few minutes while we ... But we'll come back and play some more, honest we will."

The student newspaper's reviewer reported that during this break people were walking around looking dazed! You would have been too!

Back on stage—who knows how much later—the Dead march through an intense reading of "Morning Dew." Garcia's guitar screams again. The hole that the Dead ripped in the fabric of normal reality on this evening is now torn open even further. This is not happy music. *Intense* is the operative word here. The stage was now set for one more apocalyptic climax: "Viola Lee Blues."

Perhaps the most amazing thing about the finale to this show is how LOUD Garcia's guitar is during "Viola Lee Blues." You can tell he's got the amp turned *all the way up*. And I've never heard a "Viola Lee" that comes close to this one in intensity. It is as though Garcia is possessed—or maybe just a wee bit *dosed* perhaps?

"Viola Lee" is, of course, an exercise in stretching volume and time. The faster they go, the louder they get. This works in three sections. First, they jam on the groove of the tune, building that in intensity. Then, this gradually doubles up in feel. And then, they play faster and faster until the ear-shattering climax. This, of course, resolves back into the tune as if it had been there all along.

By 1970, by which point the Dead were pretty much through with "Viola Lee Blues," they had really mastered the art of the gradual buildup. They were now playing the song in a much more relaxed, less frantic style, more attentive to building tension in the groove— as opposed to the classic sixties style in which the tune bounces along at a frenetic pace from the get-go. During the climax of this particular version Garcia is playing dissonant, clashing clusters of notes against Phil's flurry of incredibly brief notes. Bobby clangs away with all-out abandon. The result is some of my favorite NOISE!

When the band returns from the clanging climax, they fall back into the basic groove of the song really slowly, and not exactly at the place you were expecting. But they're totally in sync, as though lovers were smoking a cigarette after a mind-bending orgasm. As the final verse disperses, the Dead melt into one of the most delicious short "Feedback" jams you'll ever hear. From out of the ghostlands of electric noise, Jerry begins to cry a mournful, lonely reading of "We Bid You Goodnight."

I can only imagine that this must have been one of those magical Grateful Dead Experiences after which, sober or not, one walks around in a daze for hours, still too brimming with energy to go to sleep. Listen to 5/2/70 from beginning to end and then try to appreciate just how far the Dead journeyed in this one performance. From the gentle American folk roots groove of "Don't Ease Me In" and "I Know You Rider" to the howling 13th dimension terror of "The Other One" and "Viola Lee Blues." Amazing. This was indeed *a trip* for the ages. Could those in attendance have learned anything anywhere near as enlightening in class at 9 A.M. the next morning? I doubt it. Twenty years after I first heard it, I'm still learning things from this concert. I hope you can too.

JOHN R. DWORK WITH JEFF MATTSON

## 5/3/70
### Wesleyan University, Middletown, Connecticut

Me and My Uncle, New Speedway Boogie, Good// Lovin' > Drums > Good Lovin' Reprise, Dire Wolf, Don't Ease Me In, Turn On Your Lovelight > The Main Ten > Uncle John's Band > Turn On Your Lovelight

**Source:** AUD, **Quality:** D, **Length:** 1:30
**Highlights:** Turn On Your Lovelight > The Main Ten Jam > Uncle John's Band > Lovelight

What could have possibly been more fun than a Grateful Dead show on your campus lawn in 1970? This outdoor show took place at the foot of Foss Hill on the campus at Wesleyan University on the afternoon of May 3, 1970. All we have is one audience tape made by a couple of students. According to some inside research, a group of sociology students were doing their senior project on group dynamics and used the Dead show as their centerpiece. The tape that exists was made by two of the students as part of their sociology study—not to document the music. Supposedly there is also a film of the audience made for the same purpose. At times the audience talking is as loud as the music, and the sound quality changes throughout the show as the taper moves the microphone around.

Because they were not making the tape to document the music, there is some interesting commentary during and between songs. The tape starts with a lolloping version of "Me and My Uncle." "New Speedway Boogie" gets drowned out by the crowd noise and chatter, but when you cannot hear the music, listen to the people talking. Just as "Good Lovin'" starts the taper says, "This is song number seven," which means that four songs are missing before "Me and My Uncle." There are some tape cuts between songs, but the taper calls out the time before each song so we know the order is correct.

The drugs must have kicked in before "Good Lovin'" because he gets the time wrong, and before "Dire Wolf" he starts mumbling into the recorder and laughing uncontrollably. Don't you wish all homework was this much fun? Before "Dire Wolf" you can hear someone comment about the sociology department and people going up the hill, further documentation of the purpose of the tape and the location. As "Lovelight" starts, the taper pretends he is on the radio and introduces the song to "radio land." So what drug makes people lose track of time, laugh uncontrollably, and play at being a deejay?

The highlight of the tape begins with "Lovelight." Jerry's guitar is gently soaring over the crowd while Pigpen raps. Pig's songs are among my favorites because he created wonderful tension. The band would absolutely let loose and dive deep into the fiery pit of the song between his vocal raps. It is as if Pigpen slowed the band down, held them back, and then let them loose. Bob picks up the "Main Ten" theme and begins to punctuate it behind Pigpen's singing. Mickey adds in with some percussion and Phil joins in with his bass line. After about one minute, the jam quickly dissolves into a tight but short "Uncle John's Band." Back into "Lovelight" they go with Bob and Pigpen embroiled in a screaming match at the end of the song. The taper comments, "The guys are going into a frenzy." After the show there is an interesting PA announcement about bringing down the establishment and peaceful demonstration. Hey, it's 1970 and only the day before Kent State.

I received a letter from a Wesleyan alumn a year ago. It read, "I got the Wesleyan alumni magazine a couple of years back—it had a big color photo from the show. At the center was the spitting image of Jerry Garcia, but the caption informed that this was really a professor (the one who sanctioned said sociology project) who had just passed on. He's smiling from ear to ear in the midst of the crowd, who look exactly like the kids I went to school with 20 years later...."

ERIC DOHERTY

### 5/6/70
**Kresge Plaza, Massachusetts Institute of Technology, Cambridge, Massachusetts**

Dancin' in the Streets, China Cat Sunflower > I Know You Rider, Next Time, Morning Dew, Good Lovin' > Drums > Good Lovin', Casey Jones, Saint Stephen > Jam > Not Fade Away

**Source:** SBD, **Quality:** B+, **Length:** 1:30, **Genealogy:** MR > RR > PCM > DAT

**Highlights:** Dancin' in the Streets, China Cat Sunflower > I Know You Rider, Morning Dew, Good Lovin'

This was a legendary free concert given on campus during the countrywide protests following the shooting of students at Kent State. This free show, played outside on a cold afternoon in May, preceded the Dead's indoor concert there the following night. The tape quality is generally very good but with a few drops in volume, mostly during "Casey Jones."

Maybe it was the event or maybe it was just due to the cold weather, but the band does crank out a fair bit of energy here, with "Dancin' in the Streets" working up a good head of (paisley) steam, flowing into a tasty jam before a return to the verse structure. "China Cat Sunflower" > "I Know You Rider" also features some energetic jamming during the midsection, but the "Morning Dew" is the highlight of the first side of this tape, its chilling subject a timely comment on the reason why everyone was gathered there that afternoon. Colossal bass notes and yet another sensitive Garcia vocal on this classic.

"Good Lovin'" suffers a false start, with the band falling apart as Pigpen berates the sound crew for a malfunctioning microphone. Once the problem is solved, they roll into an exceptional version of the song with Pigpen bellowing out the vocals in between explosions of drums, the guitars circling around Lesh's taut bass lines.

"Casey Jones" is marred by a peculiar dropout on the tape, but things recover for an extended "Saint Stephen" > "Not Fade Away." You can *hear* fingers getting cold and stiff during this performance; the will is there, but Garcia's lines get progressively more ragged and—unintentionally—slightly dissonant. This isn't exactly torture for us, but then we're probably listening to it somewhere nice and warm. "It's too fuckin' cold to play," says Bobby at the end of the show. Considering the invention and creativity on display during this mini-

*"Freek" weekend at MIT, 5/5/70*

"Dancin' in the Streets" outside at MIT, 5/6/70 (photo courtesy of MIT Yearbook)

show, it's a real shame that the weather wasn't more clement. Ah well . . .

PAUL BODENHAM

## Flashback:
### May 6, 1970

In the spring of 1970 I was the sole Deadhead at MIT's radio station WTBS (call letters since changed). Of course it was thrilling to watch the Dead set up to play. I asked their sound guy if I could get a feed off his board. When he agreed, I bent the arms of the technical staff (at the station) to help me run it down one of our existing telco lines on the campus to the station where our head engineer at the time (I believe named Larry Killgallen) recorded the show onto an Ampex 350.

Over the next few years, as the number of Deadheads grew, these tapes took on more importance. Somewhere in the winter of '70–'71, a bus full of freaks (ostensibly some lagaers from the Hog Farm) broke down in Boston. I befriended the like-minded souls. At one point I "lent" them the master tapes; they in turn were to give me a set they had from a Cincinnati gig. It was not clear what I ended up with after all was said and done; I was prone to being under a bit of a haze in those days!

By the summer of 1971 my interest in the Dead had waned, though I kept a fond place for them in my heart. Someone once told me that concert had ended up on a bootleg.

PETER KAYE

## 5/7/70

**DuPont Gymnasium, Massachusetts Institute of Technology, Cambridge, Massachusetts**

**Acoustic Set:** Don't Ease Me In, I Know You Rider, Friend of the Devil, Me and My Uncle, Deep Elem Blues, Candyman, Cumberland Blues, New Speedway Boogie, Black Peter, Uncle John's Band
**Electric Set:** Good Lovin', Cold Rain and Snow, Dire Wolf, Easy Wind, Beat It on Down the Line, High Time//, //Cryptical Envelopment > Drums > The Other One > Cryptical Reprise > Cosmic Charlie, Casey Jones, King Bee, Not Fade// Away > Turn On Your Lovelight > Saint Stephen Jam > Darkness, Darkness Jam > China Cat Sunflower Jam > Turn On Your Lovelight

**Source:** AUD, **Quality:** B, **Length:** 3:00, **Genealogy:** MC > RR > PCM > DAT

**Highlights:** Cryptical Envelopment > Drums > The Other One > Cryptical Envelopment Reprise > Cosmic Charlie, King Bee, Not Fade// Away > Turn On Your Lovelight > Saint Stephen Jam > Darkness, Darkness Jam > China Cat Sunflower Jam > Turn On Your Lovelight

**Comments:** The acoustic set sounds remarkably different than the electric set. Because it's much more quiet during the acoustic set, the echoey ambience of the gymnasium really comes through strong. This would've been a much better tape if the concert hadn't happened in a gymnasium. It seems as though the recordist did the best job possible under these circumstances.

This is a great companion tape to 5/2/70 in that it is so completely different in almost every way. Because it's an audience recording one gets to hear a decent recording of what the band sounded like during this legendary week from "outside" the sound system. Unlike the show at Harpur, this audience is virtually *silent* during the acoustic set. Surely this had to have made at least a subtle difference in the Dead's energy level. While this is a very fine show indeed, it just doesn't get to that mind-blowing level that the attendees at Harpur certainly witnessed. Still, the band is charged and obviously itching to play. With the full-length New Riders set (not reviewed here), this show ends up be very long: three full tapes.

The acoustic set is good, but not amazing. The same rings true for the beginning of the electric set. The "Other One" suite, though extremely intense, just doesn't have the same monstrous energy as the version from 5/2/70. The band is attentive, even inspired, but it just doesn't tear at the fabric of reality in the same way as at Harpur just five nights earlier.

This show's final medley, however, is the stuff we Deadheads love the most about the spring '70 tour. "Lovelight" starts off with great vim and vigor. The magic really begins, though, when Jerry explodes into a double-time "Saint Stephen" jam. This leads almost directly into the first "Darkness, Darkness" jam. In fact, this may be the best version of that jam that you'll find. Once they've played this through to its appropriate conclusion, there's a moment during which it's obvious that no one on stage has any idea what should happen next. But this is the magical Grateful Dead warmed up, relaxed, in the groove, and flowing. One gets the feeling that during this moment of uncertainty the band is so connected that no one is worried that they have no clue what's coming next. Bobby finally suggests "China Cat," and as he states the theme several times, Jerry dances over his lines with joyous excitement. Then the band falls back into "Lovelight" like Pigpen falling into bed after a four-day creep. Ah, delicious!

JOHN R. DWORK

## 5/9/70

**Worcester Polytechnic Institute, Worcester, Massachusetts**

Deep Elem Blues, Friend of the Devil, Silver Threads and Golden Needles, Black Peter

**Source:** SBD, **Quality:** D–, **Length:** 0:25
**Highlights:** Pigpen's harmonica solos and some stage banter:

> Garcia: Phil, Mickey, and a few others are still en route . . . missing.

Well, the sound sucks. But Pigpen's harmonica shines through, showing off his strong feel for acoustic music and giving these songs a nice, down-home flavor. Other than that . . .

MICHAEL M. GETZ

## 5/14/70
### Merramec Community College, Kirkwood, Missouri

**Acoustic Set:** Don't Ease Me In, Friend of the Devil, Deep Elem Blues, Silver Threads and Golden Needles, Candyman
**Electric Set:** Casey Jones, China Cat Sunflower > I Know You Rider, Mama Tried, High Time, Good Lovin' > Drums > Good Lovin', Attics of My Life, Good Mornin', Li'l Schoolgirl, New Speedway Boogie > Saint Stephen > Nobody's Fault but Mine Jam > New Speedway Boogie Reprise, Not Fade Away > Turn On Your Lovelight

**1. Source:** FM-SBD (KPFA, GDH 352 and 353), **Quality:** A, **Length:** 1:40 (entire electric set), **Genealogy:** MR > DAT > radio broadcast
**2. Source:** SBD, **Quality:** C, **Length:** 0:25 (acoustic set only), **Genealogy:** MR > RR > PCM > DAT
**Highlights:** Deep Elem Blues, New Speedway Boogie > Nobody's Fault Jam > New Speedway Boogie, Not Fade Away, Turn On Your Lovelight

> Someone: Hi, folks! This is Willie Mays!
> Someone else: This is a commercial: Acid Rescue is here! They're wearing red coats and handing out cards.

Although the acoustic set is muffled a bit, the instruments can be made out with effort. This relaxed and confident set, typical for 1970, is highlighted by a "Deep Elem" that has a punchy Garcia lead and is driven by a seductively thick groove.

This show was played while the Dead were recording their *Workingman's Dead* album; thus, singing and harmonies are the main focus, even in this electric set. Also, Mickey is absent for unknown reasons, reducing their firepower. "I Know You Rider" and "High Time" stand out. "Attics," though, is almost comical. There's oddly no jam at all between "China" and "Rider," and "Good Lovin'" features only a short, aimless one. Things finally heat up with a very intense "New Speedway" made possible by Garcia's blazing slide guitar solo on the sandwiched-in "Nobody's" jam. Garcia's vocals, too, are so emphatic that he sounds like some hillbilly preacher mixing business with a twang. "Saint Stephen" rocks, continuing the momentum, and "Not Fade Away" contains the first long and inspired ensemble jam of the show. After one verse, Lesh bolts the band into a swift, richly textured "Lovelight." Inventiveness glows in every nook as the boys end this show with a bang.

MICHAEL M. GETZ

## 5/15/70
### Early Show, Fillmore East, New York, New York

**Acoustic Set 1:** Don't Ease Me In, I Know You Rider, The Rub, Friend of the Devil, Long Black Limousine, Candyman, Cumberland Blues*, New Speedway Boogie*, Cold Jordan*
**Electric Set:** Casey Jones, Easy Wind, Attics of My Life, Saint Stephen > Cryptical Envelopment > Drums > The Other One > Cryptical Reprise > Cosmic Charlie
**Encore:** New Minglewood Blues

* with Marmaduke Dawson and David Nelson

**1. Source:** SBD, **Quality:** A, **Length:** 1:52, **Genealogy:** MR > RR > RR > PCM > DAT
**2. Source:** SBD, **Quality:** A, **Length:** 1:52, **Genealogy:** MR > DAT
**3. Source:** SBD-CD (Fallout from the Phil Zone), **Quality:** A, **Length:** 8:04 ("Easy Wind")
**Highlights:** Cumberland Blues, New Speedway Boogie, Easy Wind, The Other One suite

This very fine tape, whose amazing moments redeem ordinary ones, is full of banter, beginning with Bill Graham introducing the band "during the calisthenics."

> Graham: From Marin Junior College, Mr. Philip Lesh.
> Weir: That's a lie.
> Garcia: That ain't Philip Lesh.

A sweet acoustic set opened with nice Garcia vocals on "Don't Ease," and crooning on "Rider," followed by a hot "Rub," their third ever, on which Pig and his harmonica just drip the blues. Their fourth "Limousine" (of five ever) is chillingly beautiful, with Weir in very fine voice. As the band is joined by Marmaduke and David Nelson, the show really picks up steam, with "Cumberland" absolutely barreling along, and it remains hot while Garcia belts out fine vocals on "Speedway." But the audience ain't heard nothin' yet. During "Easy Wind" Pigpen leads on harmonica into a jam (featuring a remarkable Weir lead) that must have set the Fillmore on fire, followed by their first Attics ever. After intense "Saint Stephen" jamming, an incredibly electric Other One redefines "incendiary." Weir's overly aggressive screaming makes the "Minglewood" closer a truly humorous oddity.

BILL KRISTY

---

### 5/15/70
**Late Show, Fillmore East, New York, New York**

**Acoustic Set:** Ballad of Casey Jones, Silver Threads and Golden Needles, Black Peter, Friend of the Devil, Uncle John's Band, Candyman, She's Mine, Katie Mae, I Hear a Voice Callin'*
**Electric Set:** China Cat Sunflower > I Know You Rider, Cumberland Blues, Hard to Handle, Beat it on Down the Line, Morning Dew, Good Lovin', Dire Wolf, Next Time You See Me, Dark Star > Saint //Stephen > Not Fade Away// > Turn On Your Lovelight
**Encore:** Cold Jordan

* with David Nelson

---

1. **Source:** SBD, **Quality:** A, **Length:** 2:52, **Genealogy:** MR > RR > RR > PCM > DAT
2. **Source:** SBD, **Quality:** A, **Length:** 1:52, **Genealogy:** MR > DAT

**Highlights:** China Cat Sunflower > I Know You Rider, Cumberland Blues, Hard to Handle, Good Lovin'

A great quality tape begins with the day's second sweet acoustic set, opening with a beautiful version of the

---

> BILL GRAHAM PRESENTS IN NEW YORK
> AN EVENING WITH THE
> **GRATEFUL DEAD**
> FEATURING
> THE NEW RIDERS OF THE PURPLE SAGE
> JOE'S LIGHTS
> May 15, 1970
>
> **GUESS WHO**
> **COLD BLOOD**
> **BUDDY MILES**
> JOE'S LIGHTS
> May 15, 1970
>
> FILLMORE EAST

*Fillmore East program, 5/15/70*

first "Ballad of Casey Jones" the band ever played (they played only one more). While tuning before "Friend of the Devil," Garcia says they "got a request to do this here, we did this in the first show and we're gonna do it again now." Weir adds "thus breaking a long-standing tradition, and we love to break traditions." Actually, on March 20, 1970, they had played four songs twice. None were sung by Weir, but both shows on September 27, 1969, featured "Mama Tried," prior to which a flip through set lists indicates it had been a long-standing tradition to not repeat songs on the same day (5/3/69 requires that this be qualified) at the same venue. Garcia's guitar playing is just beautiful on "Uncle John's." After the day's second "Candyman," when David Nelson is announced, Pig's "wait a minute, don't I get to play one?" gets strong audience support, so he plays "She's Mine" (the second of four times played) and Katie Mae. David Nelson then does join them on their first-ever performance of

"I Hear a Voice Callin'," for some extremely sweet harmony.

So incredible it simply defies belief, this amazing second set made it a very special day to be a Deadhead. They again redefine incendiary with searingly hot jamming on "China Cat." "Rider" and "Cumberland" (each the day's second) and "Hard to Handle" had so much energy they must have caused an East Coast blackout. "Beat It on Down" and "Dew" alternate hot and beautiful, with Garcia really nailing the vocals. Then a hot "Good Lovin'," with Lesh, Garcia, and Weir building to an awesome jam, and a "Dark Star" of particularly wide-ranging, spacey improvisation. It is a shame most of the "Saint Stephen" is missing, because what remains is magnificent, as are the "Not Fade Away" and "Lovelight" that follow. Garcia just peels off the notes during "Lovelight," and Lesh builds a solid sonic wall of bass. After three minutes of clapping, they encore acoustic with the day's second (and third ever) "Cold Jordan."

BILL KRISTY

## 5/24/70

**Hollywood Festival, Lower Finney Green Farm, Newcastle-Under-Lyme, England**

Casey Jones, China Cat Sunflower > I Know You Rider, Hard to Handle, Me and My Uncle, Cryptical Envelopment > Drums > The Other One > Cryptical Reprise > Attics of My Life, Good Lovin', Cold Rain and Snow, Dark Star > Saint Stephen > Not Fade Away > Turn On Your Lovelight

**1. Source:** SBD, **Quality:** B+, **Length:** 1:30 ("Cryptical Envelopment" through "Turn On Your Lovelight" only)
**2. Source:** AUD, **Quality:** C, **Length:** 0:30 ("Casey" through "Me and My Uncle" only)
**3. Source:** AUD, **Quality:** B–, **Length:** 2:00, **Genealogy:** MC > C > C > DAT (master recording is on a C-120 cassette)
**Highlights:** The Other One, Dark Star

The Dead on the same bill as Black Sabbath? Hmm... Sounds a trifle unusual. This overequalized soundboard fits on a ninety-minute tape, but is missing the first five songs of this one-set performance. This "Cryptical" starts off sluggishly; the band seems a bit out of it for the opening verses. However, turning the stage over to the drummers, the momentum slowly begins to build and the energy clearly begins to rise, leading into a powerful, attacking "Other One." As the band noodles on the main theme, Garcia races his leads a step or two ahead of the rest of the band, rushing off in the opposite direction of the verse. At times, he strays far out enough to throw the timing of the rest of the band off, but upon each instrumental climax the band recenters itself. Though well delivered, Weir's vocals are way back in the mix, which hampers the otherwise strong delivery of the first verse. During the jam between verses one and two, it becomes clear that the drummers are playing on a level way above the rest of the band, as they pound away on their crash cymbals like breaking glass. The energy sustains throughout the jam, lasting several minutes before the second verse. Love that triplet run that Garcia throws in after "It trembled and exploded..."! The band lands a tad clumsily on the outro, but is rescued by Weir, whose outro rhythms are extra chunky. Unfortunately, Garcia's leads are a tad below par. The boys really blow it on the following "Attics," which is so far out of tune vocally that it's almost ridiculous. Ah, well, a bit of comic relief never hurts. "Quick, better go into 'Good Lovin' ' as a rescue measure." Another fantastic "Drums" segment between the second and third verse: Mickey really cooks on this while Billy holds the back rhythms steady. The jam builds slowly, teasing "Caution" before returning to the refrain. "Cold Rain and Snow" is executed with every bit as much energy as the preceding tunes before the boys launch into "Dark Star." Wasting no time, this "Star" takes off immediately, with Garcia leading the way. No new ground is broken on the first jam; the band merely weaves in and out of the main theme before returning for the first verse. From the verse the boys go into an instant meltdown, all band members silent except for Lesh, who uses heavy bass bombs to establish footing. Slowly, the guitarists return with cautious blasts of feedback before trickling on some well-placed spaghetti licks. Taking the cue, Lesh and Weir lead the way out on the jam, which eventually falls into a beautiful Weir-led jazz jam. Weir goes nuts here, coaxing lush rhythm textures out of his ES-335. Garcia's solo begins brilliantly as he plays around the rhythm jam, but alas, a few minutes into it he runs out of gas. Flustered, the boys return to the second verse, which leads into

"Saint Stephen." This is badly hampered by a seemingly asleep Garcia—unfortunate, because the rest of the band is really cooking at this point. Midway into "Not Fade Away," Captain Trips gets a second wind, perfectly timed, leading the band through a sweet "Goin Down' the Road" tease. The set-ending "Lovelight" is anticlimactic, but nonetheless well executed, wrapping up the Dead's European debut.

Wonder whose Harley that really is in the background between "Good Lovin'" and "Cold Rain and Snow"?

BRIAN DYKE

## 5/??/70
### Newcastle-Under-Lyme, England

**Interview:** Jerry Garcia, Jon McIntyre, Bob Weir

**Source:** AUD, **Quality:** D, **Length:** 0:06

**Highlights:** Garcia: "It's not, it's not specific questions, it's the idea of, it's just that the assumption that any of us would have any real answers to real questions, and the whole idea of what questions are anyway, and also, and above and beyond that, the whole idea of interviews, and above and beyond that, the whole idea of the kind of attention that it all implies. I mean, I object to the whole thing."

**Comments:** The Dead performed on May 24 at the Hollywood Festival. Based on the background tuning and feedback, it is possible that the interview took place on the day of the performance.

The quality of this tape renders much of the interview nearly inaudible.

BRIAN DYKE

## 6/4/70
### Fillmore West, San Francisco, California

Not Fade Away > Midnight Hour > Jams > Midnight Hour Reprise
**Encore:** It's All Over Now, Baby Blue

**Source:** SBD, **Quality:** A–, **Length:** 0:30, **Genealogy:** MR > DAT

**Highlights:** Jams, Baby Blue, Weir's guitar playing

A strongly percussive "Not Fade Away" evolves into a jam featuring a "Saint Stephen" melody played in a different key. Of note is Weir's absolutely sensational guitar work. "Midnight Hour" finds Pigpen sounding very lethargic. He wisely aborts his rap segment and Garcia takes the band into uncharted waters; all, that is, except for Pigpen who stubbornly continues to play the "Midnight Hour" chords over and over, well into the jam. But the music picks up, invigorated, and suddenly the band sounds like the Allman Brothers as they play a few minutes of "Mountain Jam." Weir plays some lead here and truly sounds like a different guitarist. This jam veers into a "China Cat" tease before the band deftly reprises "Midnight Hour."

"Baby Blue" is long, slow, and, of course, very bluesy. Weir strikes again with more sparkling playing, even throwing in some lead work to nicely complement Garcia. Jerry sings it with great feeling, carefully evoking Dylan's words of shattered innocence, lost love, and, perhaps, the end of naïveté and Beaver Cleaver.

MICHAEL M. GETZ

## 6/5/70
### Fillmore West, San Francisco, California

**Acoustic Set:** Dire Wolf, I Know You Rider, Silver Threads and Golden Needles, Friend of the Devil, Me and My Uncle, Black Peter, New Speedway Boogie
**Electric Set:** Cold Rain and Snow, Easy Wind, Mama Tried, It's a Man's World, Uncle John's Band, Cryptical Envelopment > Drums > The Other One > Cryptical Reprise > Attics of My Life, Hard to Handle, Saint Stephen > Casey Jones

1. **Source:** AUD, **Quality:** A–, **Length:** 2:15 (all)
2. **Source:** FM-SBD (GDH 051), **Quality:** A–, **Length:** 0:25 ("I Know You Rider" through "Black Peter")

**Highlights:** Me and My Uncle, Attics of My Life

*Scenes from Fillmore West, 1970*

# Reviews: June 1970

*Fillmore West, 1970*

This show is available in a nice, albeit hissy, audience recording and features an acoustic and electric set. To facilitate an uncut "That's It for the Other One," the order of songs is a bit scrambled. The 1970 acoustic sets served as both a warm-up for the electric sets that followed, and a display of the vast and overlooked country/folk influences of the band's origins. This particular acoustic set is an excellent example of the Grateful Dead's roots, and provides a valuable retrospective look at how these influences have been transcended over time. Compare the acoustic sets from 1970 to the ones in 1980 sometime as a reference. Despite very ragged playing, this acoustic set contains several highlights. Of particular note is the song selection. "Dire Wolf" opens the show in standard fashion, sticking closely to the electric arrangement. Garcia appears to be handling all vocal chores solo on this rendition. Continuing the warm-up, the boys pull out an acoustic

*Fillmore West, 1970*

Reviews: June 1970

*Fillmore West, 1970*

"I Know You Rider," similar to the version performed by Hot Tuna. Pretty standard fare here, highlighted by Garcia pulling out the uncommon "I'd rather drink muddy water" line. All right, now it's Bob's turn to sing, and Mr. Weir rises to the occasion with a wonderful "Silver Threads and Golden Needles." Although hampered by sound problems, this version shows Weir in excellent form, well above that of his bandmates. Following "Friend of the Devil," which is again hampered by feedback, is the set's highlight, "Me and My Uncle." So confidently does Weir sing this one, I consider it the definitive version of this overcriticized selection. Indeed, Weir authoritatively assumes the storyteller's role in this tale of tragedy. Garcia continues the motif with a soulful "Black Peter" before closing the set with a raw "New Speedway Boogie."

Returning for the electric set, the boys spend a few numbers preparing their chops, highlighted by "Easy Wind," before attempting to get serious with a full "That's It for the Other One." Showing great promise at the start, this one fails to make it out of the starting gate. After a brief and floundering "Drums" segment the band kicks in. Unfortunately, Garcia appears stuck and is unable to assert himself. Despite furious crunches from Weir, the rhythm section is very disoriented, with the drummers in particular lagging badly. Surrendering, Weir leads the boys into the verse, which he executes with the same confidence as was previously displayed that evening. Too bad the rest of the band isn't as hot. Feedback rears its ugly head during the jam between the first and second verse, and it is evident that the boys are becoming frustrated. Garcia, in particular, appears to have given up completely and is merely going through the motions, and poorly at that. Of course, as the communication among band members disintegrates, the jam becomes painfully disjointed. Weir again attempts to come to the rescue in the second verse, but receives little help from his fellow band members, and even less from Bear, the scapegoat of sound on this evening. Following the second verse, Garcia immediately launches into the outro, but the attempt to bring it down only yields more feedback, and the boys finally, in ungraceful fashion, throw in the towel, leading into "Attics of My Life." Nice rebound! The vocals are nearly in tune, and Garcia's solos on this version are as bright as a morning sunrise in December. Giving their vocal chords a rest, the boys turn things over to Pigpen, who goes back to basics with "Hard to Handle" and "It's a Man's, Man's, Man's World." These are tame versions, but well played nonetheless. The set closing "Uncle John's Band" and double encore of "Saint Stephen" > "Casey Jones" make for a dose of classic 1970 Dead at its finest, sending this uneven performance off on a high note.

BRIAN DYKE

## 6/13/70
### Civic Auditorium, Honolulu, Hawaii

Cold Rain and Snow, Easy Wind, Uncle John's Band, Candyman, Me and My Uncle, Good Lovin', China Cat Sunflower > I Know You Rider, New Speedway Boogie, Casey Jones, Turn On Your Lovelight//

**1. Source:** AUD, **Quality:** B–, **Length:** 1:30
**2. Source:** FM-SBD (KPFA *Dead Hour*), **Quality:** A, **Length:** 0:30 ("Good Lovin'" and "China Cat Sunflower" > "I Know You Rider"), **Genealogy:** MR > DAT

**Highlights:** Good Lovin', New Speedway Boogie, Turn On Your Lovelight

**Comments:** Many of the tunes on the audience recording come in already in progress as the recordist turned on the tape deck once the song had started. For years *DeadBase* has listed two guests, Dino Valenti and Gary Duncan, on "Good Lovin'" and "Lovelight," but I cannot hear any additional musicians on these tunes despite careful, repeated listening.

No big jams here, but a hot tape nonetheless. The emphasis is on raw, explosive energy—you can clearly hear a bloodcurdling yelp of preorgasmic anticipation from someone in the audience at the start of the "Good Lovin'." The drum solo inside "Good Lovin'" features a short but hip Asian Indian–style vocal percussive rap (*da da digida da*) by Mickey. The "China Cat" > "Rider" is only average. "New Speedway" is another highlight. Garcia screams through this reading with fire and brimstone. He even throws in an instrumental measure or two of "Nobody's Fault but Mine." An unknown piano player can clearly be heard here (perhaps one of the supposed guest artists?). The "Lovelight" is very fast and contains several very inspired, fairly developed psychedelic blues instrumental passages.

JOHN R. DWORK

## 6/21/70

**American Indian Benefit,
Pauley Ballroom, University of California,
Berkeley, California**

Frozen Logger, Casey Jones, Cumberland Blues, Easy Wind, Mama Tried, Candyman, //Not Fade Away > Saint Stephen > Drums > Good Lovin'//

**Source:** AUD, **Quality:** C, **Length:** 1:10, **Taper:** Harry Ely

**Highlights:** Easy Wind, Not Fade Away > Saint Stephen

This show, a benefit for one of the Dead's favorite charities, marked one of the few times that they played at UC Berkeley's intimate Pauley Ballroom. The show opened with a rare full band version of one of Weir's periodic goofs, the novelty tune "Frozen Logger," complete with circus rhythms and a wobbly lead vocal. A stretch of relatively stock (for mid-1970), well-played, shorter tunes is notably interrupted by an extended, intense, and jagged version of "Easy Wind." Another highlight is a slow, emotion-packed version of "Candyman." The jam that ends the tape reverses a familiar pattern; the tape starts abruptly in the middle of a long, simmering "Not Fade Away" and then eases slyly into a fine, driving "Saint Stephen." After a quick drum break, the band moves into a kicking "Good Lovin'," leading into still more drums and then back again into "Good Lovin'," during which the master tape apparently ran out. This tape has also been listed sometimes as "Spring '70."

MICHAEL PARRISH

## 6/24/70

**Early Show, Capitol Theater,
Port Chester, New York**

Cold Rain and Snow, Me and My Uncle, Easy Wind, New Minglewood Blues, Alligator > Drums > The Other One > Attics > The Other One > Cosmic Charlie > Good Lovin' > Drums > China Cat Sunflower > I Know You Rider > Good Lovin'

**1. Source:** AUD, **Quality:** B–/B (Some copies, but not the original, cut in on Cold Rain and Snow. Also, there is a brief muffling during Minglewood Blues. Every copy we researched has the same tape cuts and audience comments—for example, during the Drums > Good Lovin' someone close to the mike sings, "da da dadadada da da da da," just before Phil plays that line on his bass.), **Length:** 1:30, **Taper:** Marty Weinberg, Uher 7-inch open reel deck, **Genealogy:** MR > DAT

**2. Source:** AUD, **Quality:** B/B–, **Length:** 1:15, **Taper:** Marty Weinberg, Uher 7-inch open reel deck, **Genealogy:** MR > PCM > DAT

**Highlights:** The whole show

**Comments:** There is even more mystery surrounding the origin and exact historical details regarding these tapes than existed before this project began. These tapes have circulated since shortly after they were originally recorded, and numerous tapers claim to have gotten them from at least two distinct sources. It's been known since the early 1970s that the legendary Marty Weinberg recorded these shows. There's also been an unconfirmed rumor that the brother of one of the security guards at the venue also recorded some of these shows as well as the November run at this venue. A close listen, however, to numerous tapes from different sources that contain the electric music played at this show reveal they are in fact from a single source. A distinct exclamation from an audience member close to the microphone, "Yeah, yeah . . . oh no," can be heard during the transition between "Dark Star" and "Saint Stephen" on every copy we listened to.

There is some question as to whether the acoustic music that circulates from this show is even from this date at all. *DeadBase* lists "Friend of the Devil," "Candyman" > "Cumberland," and "Cold Jordan" as the music that follows "Monkey and the Engineer." Obviously, this doesn't mesh with the music we have.

An even more hotly contested question is whether or not this set is actually the early show. In fact, the music listed in the review below as coming from the early show has usually circulated with the date 6/25/70. We've seen the newspaper ads, and the Dead only played on June 24. It would be technically accurate, though, if the late show started after midnight (which was a common occurrence in those days), to label it as being from the 25th.

To make matters more complicated, it appears that the Dead always kept the acoustic music for the beginning of the *late* show whenever they played the Capitol Theater in 1970. Therefore it would seem to make the most sense that the acoustic show was the late show and somewhere down the line (early on) someone mislabeled the tape. We may never know the absolute truth.

For now, it seems the commonsense thing to do is to simply label both tapes 6/24/70.

From the very start of this early show, both the inspirational temperature and volume on stage and in the audience are turned *waaay* up. The jam in "Easy Wind" is quite impressive, and "Minglewood" is a perfect showcase for Bobby's screaming—this song used to be a raw and rowdy barn burner.

"Alligator" starts off as usual with its sing-songy lyrics leading into "Drums." Amusingly, during the long, winding drum solo, on Marty Weinberg's recording one can clearly hear a woman say, "Pray for 'Not Fade Away.'" The jam on "Alligator" never really materializes. Jerry comes in just as he normally does at the beginning of the post-drum "Alligator" jam, with a guitar/drum duet. But he quickly suggests "The Other One." The drummers get the hint and change the tempo to match. Jerry then fades out so the drummers can fully diverge into the pre–"Other One" shuffle. This accomplished, the whole band comes in with the formal opening to "The Other One." Bobby sings the words immediately, and before you know it they're playing "Attics of My Life"—certainly one of the shortest post-1969 "Other Ones" ever!

"Attics of My Life" is arguably the Dead's most sacred lyrics, and perhaps even the most spiritual words ever sung by any rock 'n' roll group. But there's something particularly special about all the versions of this lyrical meditation played at the Capitol Theater shows, both on this night and on November 7, 1970. Perhaps it's the total hush that falls over the audience. This is one of those examples of where a soundboard tape may be less preferable.

With this beautiful action meditation completed, Jerry leads the band immediately back into the second half of "The Other One." The jam here is longer, but not by much. This in turn leads into the reprise of "Cryptical Envelopment." But before Jerry even gets to the "well you know he had to die" screamin' vocal finale, he steers the band into "Cosmic Charlie." Again, the same woman in the audience who prayed for "Not Fade Away" during the drum solo can be heard pegging "Cosmic Charlie" before they fully commit to it—good call, madam!

There are only a few examples I can think of besides this performance where the band plays "Good Lovin'" into another song and then back into "Good Lovin'": 1/2/72: "Good Lovin'" > "China Cat" > "Good Lovin'"; 11/6/70: "Good Lovin'" > "Main Ten Jam" > "Good Lovin'"; and my favorite of all, 4/14/72: "Good Lovin'" > "Caution" > "Who Do You Love" > "Caution" > "Good Lovin'". All treats not to be missed.

This "Good Lovin'" leads directly into yet another drum solo. One of the best "China Cats" from 1970 rises up out of this drum solo, although it contains several of Marty's trademark warbles, created when he touched the reel several times as it was recording in order to determine how much tape was left; the result is that the music distorts for between a half and two seconds or so. Also, for a brief moment, most of the high end, particularly the cymbals, is muffled. "I Know You Rider" leads quickly back into a rousing but short "Good Lovin'" reprise.

From a look at the set lists from both the early and late shows on this evening, it's obvious that the Dead were going nuts with the medley idea. They're so into switching songs they don't even bother to fully play one before moving onto the next. Quite an unusual night.

JOHN R. DWORK WITH KIPP ARMSTRONG

---

**6/24/70**

**Late Show, Capitol Theater, Port Chester, New York**

**Acoustic Set:** Big Railroad Blues, Deep Elem, Monkey and the Engineer, The Rub, Silver Threads and Golden Needles//
**Electric Set:** Not Fade Away > Easy Wind, Dark Star > Attics of My Life > Dark Star > Sugar Magnolia > Dark Star > Saint Stephen > China Cat Sunflower > I Know You Rider, Uncle John's Band

---

**Source:** AUD, **Quality:** B/B–, **Length:** 0:30 (just the acoustic music)

**Highlights:** The whole show

Ah, the infamous Capitol Theater shows of 1970. What treats! Both the early and late show from this June night as well as the six shows from the four nights in November have long been famous among Deadheads because of the fine audience recordings available from at least two different sources. The legendary Marty Weinberg recorded many of these shows on a compact Uher reel-to-reel deck. Also, another set of fine recordings may have been in the balcony by the brother of one of the security guards. A tip of the hat to these gents, because without their efforts we wouldn't have this superlative music.

As for this set of shows: what a night indeed! Almost every song in both the early and late shows is played fantastically. And look at the set lists; what a fantasy for Deadheads!

This electric set starts very much the same way as the electric set on 2/11/70 starts, with an enormously high-energy "Not Fade Away." Only this version is even longer. The band is off and running out of the gate at a full, breathtaking gallop. Right out of the starting gate you know this is going to be a very special set. After a long jam Bobby returns to the words and then Phil leads the band through an absolutely seamless transition into an equally hot "Easy Wind." Zowie!

Now, imagine being at a Grateful Dead show in 1970 and having Jerry step to the microphone and say, "We have a little bit of technical preparation, Mickey has to get his gongs together . . . we're gonna do 'Dark Star.' " You'd have puppies, right? Well, the audience screams in delight. Jerry then quips, "There'll be a respectable minute or two of silence onstage while Mickey fiddles aimlessly around the stage." A long, delicious minute of horny anticipation ensues. Pigpen steps to a mike and snorts, "This is gonna suck somethin' good!" Another luscious minute goes by, and then the band launches into "Dark Star" with a feeling of confidence that's so intense you could cut the good vibes in the air with a knife. It is one of my all-time favorite beginnings to my favorite song.

Remarkably, it takes the musicians all of about two minutes before they hit a delicious groove that leads directly into the first verse. Mickey plays the gongs behind Jerry's pleading voice. The crowd cannot contain itself, emiting yelps of orgasmic delight. Words sung, the band quickly descends to a heavenly gong/feedback passage. Not a peep from the audience now. From out of this wonderful noise Phil hints at "Attics." Jerry follows gently, softly suggesting the tune. Billy confirms the tempo and they lock into the song. Immediately, the audience recognizes what the band is up to, and they cheer briefly. It's at this point you realize most of those concert-goers at this late show were probably also at the early show—how else could they know so quickly, so instantaneously that it would be "Attics"? As far as I'm concerned, this is the greatest argument supporting the notion that the "Alligator" > "Other One" > "Attics" > "Other One" > "Cryptical" > "Cosmic Charlie" set we have listed for the early show really is from 6/24/70.

Anyway, "Attics" is *perfect*! This may be the best early version we have. Just as Jerry segued instantly from "Attics" back into the "Other One" during the early show, here he ascends back into the gorgeous "Dark Star" modality without a moment's hesitation. Once Jerry brings the pre–second verse 1970-style "Dark Star" theme to a blistering crescendo, Bobby starts to play the same blissful chords as in a 1970 "Dancin' in the Streets" jam. Phil builds the tension by playing high up on the neck. The band has reached that sacred space in which everyone in attendance is grinning ear to ear. After exploring this slowed-down instrumental "Dancin'" type theme, Jerry returns to a the "Dark Star" theme. This in turn falls toward a "Feelin' Groovy Jam." But wait, could it be? Whoa! The band steers rapidly into "Sugar Magnolia." Incredible! Bobby sings the opening verse, but then skips the second and instead sings the "She's got everything delightful" refrain. Then Jerry steers the band back into "Dark Star" faster than can you say "dream telepathy experiment." Quickly, he sings the second verse.

As "Dark Star" ends in classic *Live Dead* fashion, the audience energy builds in anticipation. Everyone in the house is praying for "Saint Stephen." And of course they get it. The instrumental crescendo is enormous, and the return to the final verse is hit as well as you'll ever hear it. Continuing in the same medley-esque fashion, Jerry instantaneously states the opening theme to "China Cat." The instrumental break is executed with textbook perfection. This is the immortal Grateful Dead! Both the following jam and the "I Know You Rider" are, as you'd expect by this point, absolutely perfect. A standardly perfect "Uncle John's" ends the set on a spiritual note. It's rumored that the band returned to play "Swing Low, Sweet Chariot" as an encore, but I have never seen this cut in circulation. A pity indeed!

This is one of those astounding nights that makes one wonder why the Grateful Dead weren't more popular than the pope.

JOHN R. DWORK WITH KIPP ARMSTRONG

## 7/11/70

**Fillmore East, New York, New York**

**Acoustic Set:** Friend of the Devil, New Speedway Boogie, So Sad (to Watch Good Love Go Bad), Rosalie McFall, I Hear a Voice Callin'*, Cold Jordan*, Swing Low, Sweet Chariot*

**Electric Set:** Not Fade Away, Casey Jones, Mama Tried, Good Lovin'†, Sittin' on Top of the World, Minglewood Blues//, High Time//, Cumberland Blues, China Cat Sunflower > I Know //You Rider, Me and My Uncle, Morning //Dew

* with members of NRPS on mandolin and vocals
† Weir on vocals

**Source:** AUD, **Quality:** C+, **Length:** 1:55, **Taper:** R.T. Carlyle

**Highlights:** So Sad (to Watch Good Love Go Bad), Good Lovin'

This tape began life as a pretty poor quality recording, and even relatively low-generation copies are tough to listen to. The band sounds echoey and distant, and there is audience chatter throughout, as well as sporadic crackling in the left channel. Hiss is present but not overwhelming on low-gen copies. On the positive side, all the instruments are discernible in both the acoustic and electric sets, The original taper apparently started the tape only after it became clear that an actual song had started, so the first few seconds of every song on the tape are cut. Since it sounds as if no significant amount of any song has been lost, I have chosen to simply note the songs as complete in the above set list.

The music in the acoustic set is more satisfying taken as a whole than the music in the electric set. An easygoing "Friend of the Devil" precedes a long version of "New Speedway Boogie." This version begins with a two-minute instrumental section that combines with audience clapping to create a positively hypnotic vibe. Garcia's singing is strong, and he sounds invested in the meaning of the words. The version is marred, however, by an extended and directionless jam at the end.

The true gem of the entire show is the unique rendition of the Everly Brothers tune "So Sad (to Watch Good Love Go Bad)." Weir's singing is tender and bittersweet, and when Garcia chimes in on the choruses, it literally brings tears to one's eyes. "So Sad" reveals the Dead in a more human mood than we usually experience, and it seems too bad they didn't choose to play this song a little more often.

The acoustic set is rounded out with a bevy of traditional songs. The final three songs are all religious in nature and all feature mandolin playing and extra voices, with members of NRPS who have joined in. The effect is to create a country church type of atmosphere which fits well with Garcia singing in his "old and wise like the hills" voice.

The electric set is rather different from the usual. First of all, there are no Pigpen vocals at all, even though you can hear him playing organ in several songs ("Not Fade Away," "Me and My Uncle," "Morning Dew"). Was he too drunk to sing? Sore throat that night? Probably no one remembers anymore, but the set is pretty uninspired in general. The big jam in "Not Fade Away" doesn't seem to have much story or direction to it, and never seems to jell into anything really compelling, even though the band seems to be trying new things. It is easy to blow by the versions of "Casey Jones" and "Mama Tried" that follow without missing anything of importance.

The version of "Good Lovin'" contains both the worst and the best pieces of the whole electric set, and is worth listening to. Weir sings the vocal parts that Pigpen usually handled, evoking visions of many a Bob-version of the song to come. It's actually pretty amazing how similar his phrasing and melodic choices are to those he would make in singing the song in the late seventies and up to the present; you can even hear that "got to have love" line that would later become standard. Following the drum solo, however, is an amazingly energetic jam. Garcia plays lots of notes very quickly; it sounds as if he is surging forward in a wild, hyperactive flight of fancy that the others can't catch up with at all. His playing displays very specific and well-formed ideas in kaleidoscopic succession; it's a joy to hear. Garcia eventually steps back to allow Lesh an extended solo over the La Bamba beat, which resolves back into the vocal reprise.

It sounds as if the band was largely on cruise control for the rest of the set. "Sittin' on Top of the World" is a nice choice to follow "Good Lovin'," and "High Time" seems well done, with confident, on-key harmonies. "Me and My Uncle" is slower than normal, and it suffers for this. There are numerous successive dropouts in the middle of both "I Know You Rider" and "Morning

Dew." There is a lot of crowd excitement at the beginning of "Morning Dew," which suggests it might be an encore.

BART WISE

## 7/12/70
### Fillmore East, New York, New York

**Acoustic Set:** Dire Wolf, The Rub, How Long Blues, Dark Hollow, Friend of the Devil, Candyman, Katie Mae, She's Mine, Rosalie McFall, Cocaine Blues, Wake Up, Little Susie
**Electric Set:** Easy Wind, Mama Tried, Attics of My Life, China Cat Sunflower > I Know You Rider, It's a Man's World, Cryptical Envelopment > Drums > The Other One > Me and My Uncle > The Other One > Dancin' in the Streets, Cold Rain and Snow, High Time, Turn On Your Lovelight > Saint Stephen Jam > Turn On Your Lovelight//

**Source:** AUD, **Quality:** C+, **Length:** 3:20
**Highlights:** The whole show

This is a heavy show in which the Dead play songs that deal with serious themes—accordingly, the band gives them serious attention. I think this show would be much more widely traded if a soundboard version were in circulation.

Any acoustic music from this time period is incredible, and performance-wise, this set ranks right up there with 8/18/70 and 9/20/70. During this portion of the set, the Dead offer up fine versions of rare songs such as "The Rub," "How Long Blues," "Cocaine Blues," "She's Mine," and a beautiful "Katie Mae." The electric portion of the evening opens with a typically great "Easy Wind." Pigpen offers a solid foundation on which the band can expand this into a show-stopping blues exploration. Other highlights include a tender "Attics," a twangy "China Cat" > "Rider," and a serious "Man's World" that contains some interesting blues improvisation on Garcia's part.

The next big highlight of this show is the obviously lethal combination of "Cryptical" > "Drums" > "Other One" > "Me and My Uncle" > "Other One" > "Dancing in the Streets." The jam starts off as usual; however, during the "Drums" sequence Pigpen entices the crowd to stand up, and they go crazy in anticipation of the jams to come. This leads into "The Other One," which showcases nice rhythm work by Weir that blends perfectly with the leads that Jerry offers up. Slowly and subtly, the band winds its way down that country road via "Me and My Uncle." Although not as intense as 11/7/71 or 12/1/71, this combination is both imaginative and effective. As the band winds down, the ensuing "Other One" > "Dancin' in the Streets" appears in its wake. They take this version *waay* out there. This monster of a show ends with a rippin' "Lovelight," containing a "Saint Stephen" jam that brings the crowd to its knees. This tape should be sought out by every true fan of 1970-style Dead music.

JAMIE JOHANSEN

## 7/14/70
### Euphoria Ballroom, San Rafael, California

Don't Ease Me In, Friend of the Devil, Dire Wolf, Dark Hollow, //Candyman, Black Peter, How Long Blues, Deep Elem Blues, New Speedway Boogie, Cumberland Blues

**1. Source:** SBD, **Quality:** A+, **Length:** 0:55
**2. Source:** AUD, **Quality:** B–, **Length:** 0:05 ("Don't Ease Me In")
**Highlights:** How Long Blues, Deep Elem Blues, New Speedway Boogie

The audience recording of "Don't Ease Me In," which begins this show, ignores that plea and does just that: it virtually gives you an ambient fade into the proceedings as you're led through the screaming crowd toward the band. Wzzrp! and there you are, onstage with Bobby and Jerry in time for the second song. Gradually the number of performers increases, and the atmosphere shifts from a cozy strum-along toward an acoustic set with rather more bite to it. PA problems (which, incidentally, do not affect the sound of the tape) are one of the reasons for a fair amount of lighthearted banter with Bear and members of the audience, but this chat is actually quite at odds with the material performed. Just look at that song list and reflect on the subject matter: a pretty comprehensive selection of types of emotional turmoil and pain, loss, unavoidable fate, and imminent death—what a catalogue of miseries to cram into an hour!

Although this tape is widely known for David Crosby supposedly adding high vocal harmonies on the final two songs, I can't say that I'm *totally* convinced that it's him, but maybe that's just me being an old curmudgeon. Many people's favorite track is going to be the lengthy "New Speedway Boogie," which has a great blend of acoustic instrumentation plus Garcia's spellbinding vocal, not to mention his wiry electric guitar improvisations. Whoever does join the harmonies toward the end does a great job; the effect of those ghostly voices is unforgettable. This is one of the best versions of the song available.

PAUL BODENHAM

### 7/16/70
#### Euphoria Ballroom, San Rafael, California

Turn On Your Lovelight

**Source:** SBD, **Quality:** B–, **Length:** 0:25
**Personnel:** Janis Joplin on vocals

"It ain't music but it's a lot of fun," Janis screeches out at one point. Which is true in that they never actually sing this "Lovelight" but merely rap and jam it. The fun is a subjective experience for Pig and the Rock Goddess.

With this awesome, gutsy, soulful spread of talent on stage, I personally found this rendition a disappointment. It starts out bouncin' into a likable call-and-response moment with Janis and Jerry's guitar. Then . . . trying to get a rise out of the crowd? Or maybe at a loss for words? Possibly takin' too many pauses to jack off Mr. Daniel's? But this whole "gettin' it on," "gettin' it down" thang starts happening. "Daddy [Ron] likes to butt-fuck. . . . Janis don't like that. . . . Maybe they could get it together. . . ." and on and on into much senseless babble. Truly lacking the rich high that "Lovelight" can carry.

*Ticket from 7/11/70, Fillmore East*

The whole piece is set in the early muddy psychedelic sound. A groovin' wa-wa solo from Jerry leads right back into more talky talk. Rappin' their way to a party that never quite happens. Oh well.

ELIZA BUNDLEDEE

### 7/30/70
#### The Matrix, San Francisco, California

To Lay Me Down, Dire Wolf, Candyman, Rosalie McFall, I Hear a Voice Callin', Swing Low, Sweet Chariot

**Source:** SBD, **Quality:** C+, **Length:** 0:30
**Highlights:** To Lay Me Down
**Comments:** There is a slight hiss in the sound quality but not so much that it disturbs the music.

"To Lay Me Down" is a pretty song that evokes feelings of sadness. It features lovely harmonies with the instruments and vocals all strung together with a gentle drum beat. This is a melodic song remembering nice times.

"Dire Wolf" is cute even though it seems to be about how the singer might be murdered. That would be too bad.

Next comes "Candyman," a slow riding beat that makes you feel like swaying. The interesting lyrics inspire one to question their meaning. I thought the song was over when—to my surprise—it opened up into a beautiful interlude laced with slow and easy vocal harmonies.

Ahhh—with this "Rosalie McFall" my feelings are lightened with just the right upbeat rhythms that can change one's mood. This elevating beat comes to a close as the band enters into "Swing Low, Sweet Chariot." With nice echoing vocal harmonies, this song is quite sweet.

This selection of songs concludes with "I Hear a Voice Calling." Like its predecessors, this song highlights the band's roots in country/mountain vocal harmonies.

EVELYNN GETZ

## 8/5/70
**Community Concourse, San Diego, California**

**Set 1:** Candyman, El Paso, Rosalie McFall, Cocaine Blues, Drink Up and Go Home, I Hear a Voice Callin', Cold Jordan, Swing Low, Sweet Chariot
**Set 2:** Deep Elem Blues, Dark Hollow, Friend of the Devil, Mama Tried, To Lay Me Down, Dire Wolf, The Ballad of Casey Jones

**Source:** SBD, **Quality:** B+, **Length:** 1:10
**Highlights:** El Paso, Cocaine Blues, Cold Jordan, oh hell, all of it!

A rather weird mix rather lets down what otherwise is an enjoyable two-set acoustic show to what sounds like a very small but appreciative audience. With the guitars way up front the vocals languish somewhere behind, it's not the best mix you could wish for but the generally spirited playing makes up for any shortcomings. It's rather on the hissy side too, which doesn't help matters, but the overall quality of the performances and the relative rarity of the material will make it a desirable item for many. A few members of the New Riders join the guys on vocals and some strong mandolin playing on several selections, as they do at various contemporary shows, providing more reasons why you should check this tape out.

The two very brief sets are a great mixture of standards from most 1970 acoustic shows plus some real rarities, especially in acoustic versions. This whole show has a good-time vibe running through it, and any shortcomings are rendered unimportant by the verve with which the material is performed. In fact, this whole show has the endearing quality of a low-key get-together with a bunch of friends, and although this means that the songs are delivered largely without any intense emotions, the show still includes some moments of magic.

Highlights? Well, there's "El Paso," played in a stately waltz time that suits it perfectly even though this engenders a feeling pretty much at odds with the story being told. The moralizing of "Cocaine Blues" has an effervescent tongue-in-cheek quality you'd expect, while "Drink Up and Go Home" is played so straight it's quite worrying. All the gospel tunes are played well, with "Cold Jordan" once again winning a leading position in the "most infectious tune" stakes; one listen guarantees you'll wander around whistling it for a week. In the second set the sparky "Mama Tried" and a surprisingly tight and engaging "To Lay Me Down" win the honors.

The only real disappointment with this show is its brevity. As long as the mix doesn't irritate, you'll find it a warm and thoroughly enjoyable listen.

PAUL BODENHAM

## 8/18/70
**Fillmore West, San Francisco, California**

**Acoustic Set:** Truckin', Dire Wolf, Friend of the Devil, Dark Hollow, Ripple > Brokedown Palace, Operator, Rosalie McFall, New Speedway Boogie, Cold Jordan*, Swing Low, Sweet Chariot*
**Electric Set:** Dancin' in the Streets, Next Time You See Me, Mama Tried, Cryptical Envelopment > Drums > The Other One > Cryptical Reprise, Sugar Magnolia, Attics of My Life, It's a Man's World, Not Fade Away, Casey Jones > Uncle John's Band

* with guest on mandolin—most likely David Nelson

**Source:** AUD, **Quality:** C, **Length:** 2:40, **Genealogy:** MC > RR > DAT
**Highlights:** It's a Man's World, New Speedway Boogie, Dancin' in the Streets, Not Fade Away
**Comments:** This show, as well as that on the night following, first appeared in tape circulation in 1974, when the original recordist contacted my partner for a trade. These shows catch the Dead as they were introducing the music that would later appear on *American Beauty*. We took the original cassette masters from both shows and transferred them to reels. Then, in 1990, I transferred my reels to PCM/Beta. The taper noted that it was Pigpen who played a stand-up piano throughout the acoustic set.

Overall, the show is pretty mellow, but there are several points where the Dead are in classic 1970 form. The

"New Speedway Boogie" is excellent, as is the "Dancin' in the Streets" and the "Not Fade Away." But the highlight of the show is unquestionably "It's a Man's World"—Pigpen and Jerry shine throughout, and even the harmonies are in tune. However, I have one question: What happened to Pigpen at the end of the show? He normally came out at the end of "Not Fade Away" to sing with Bobby, but instead we get Jerry. The song ends, and unfortunately, there's no Pigpen show-stopper to end the concert.

HARVEY LUBAR

## 8/19/70

### Fillmore West, San Francisco, California

**Acoustic Set:** Monkey and the Engineer//, How Long Blues, Friend of the Devil, Dark Hollow, Candyman, Ripple > Brokedown Palace, Truckin'//, Cocaine Blues//, Rosalie McFall//, Cumberland Blues, Wake Up, Little Susie, New Speedway Boogie, Cold Jordan*, Swing Low, Sweet Chariot*
**Electric Set:** Cold Rain and Snow, Me and My Uncle, Easy Wind, China Cat Sunflower > I Know You Rider, Saint Stephen > Sugar Magnolia, New Minglewood Blues, Casey Jones, Not Fade Away† > Turn On Your Lovelight†

* with guest on mandolin—most probably David Nelson
† with David Crosby on guitar

*At the Fillmore West, 8/19/70* (photo credit: Michael Parrish)

**Source:** AUD, **Quality:** D+, **Length:** 1:30, **Genealogy:** MC > RR > DAT
**Highlights:** Easy Wind, Not Fade Away > Turn On Your Lovelight

The Dead were really comfortable playing the music from *Workingman's Dead,* and at the same time beginning to introduce the music from *American Beauty.* The sound quality of this tape is even poorer than the previous night's and, as a result, is rarely played in my house. The letter that accompanied the cassette masters flatly stated that David Crosby played on the "Not Fade Away" > "Lovelight," and as the taper put it, "Although you can't hear him on the tape, he was definitely influencing Garcia's guitar playing." The band does an excellent version of "Easy Wind," but again, due to the poor sound quality, the power of the song is completely lost.

HARVEY LUBAR

## 8/30/70

### KQED Studios, San Francisco, California

**Broadcast for the TV show "Calibration"**

Easy Wind, Candyman, Casey Jones, Brokedown Palace, Uncle John's Band

**Source:** FM-SBD (KQED), **Quality:** B+, **Length:** 0:35, **Genealogy:** MR > RR > FM
**Highlights:** Easy Wind, Candyman, Brokedown Palace
**Comments:** The sound is a bit muffled with a few accidental feedbacks and all-around sound tweaks.

This live set of five tunes was introduced, on air, as an introduction to the four-track recorder. I found this quite evident in the listening. Each instrument could be easily distinguished. For a beginner in the realm of listening to a band sound, one who struggles to decipher who's who, this is a great place to start.

All the songs are basically played straight with no frills. Pigpen sings it clean on "Easy Wind" with a zippy

# Reviews: August 1970

*Fillmore West, 1970*

harmonica solo. Jerry flies with a comfy psychedelic blues lead while Bobby colors the rhythm with chunky chords topped with snappy up-clucks.

Next in this lineup is "Candyman." It is a real treat to hear young Jerry's voice, precigarette, etc., destruction, complete with a taste of vibrato à la country slang. A bit dry though. A few moments of gentle, imperfect, but tender harmony vocals.

Cruisin' right along like the little engine that could with "Casey Jones." Jerry's vocals are clear and driven yet jump tracks in the mix, which unfortunately continues for the duration of this selection of songs. The drummers stir the soup in this forward-headed tune.

After happy applause from the friendly studio audience, the band rocks gently with determination into "Brokedown Palace." Pretty. Pretty. Pretty. Nice harmony vocals, Phil! Maybe it's pushed an ounce over speed but it's a lovely yummy nonetheless.

The band continues to ride a brisk wind with "Uncle John's Band," yet somehow remains grounded. Soft and sweet cradled in the bosom of a roasting machine. Beautiful a cappella vocals toward the end, followed by a rippling roll of the drumsticks, bring this quintuplet of melodies to a close.

ELIZA BUNDLEDEE

*Fillmore West, 1970*

## 9/17/70
### Fillmore East, New York, New York

**Acoustic Set:** Truckin', Monkey and the Engineer, Dark Hollow, Friend of the Devil, Ripple, Brokedown Palace, Box of Rain, Rosalie McFall, Cold Jordan > Swing Low, Sweet Chariot//

**Electric Set:** Dark Star > Feelin' Groovy Jam > Saint Stephen > Good Lovin'

**1. Source:** AUD, **Quality:** C+, **Length:** 0:45 (Just the acoustic set), **Taper:** Jack Toner

**2. Source:** AUD, **Quality:** C+ (This very old audience recording is usually too fast and needs pitch correction), **Length:** 0:45 (Just the electric set segment), **Genealogy:** MR > C > C > DAT, **Taper:** Marty Weinberg

**Comments:** The acoustic set, which only appeared on the scene in widespread circulation in 1997, seems from the ambient quality of the recording to be from a different source than the electric segment, which has circulated far and wide for many years.

**Highlights:** Good Lovin'

Although the original recording of this acoustic set could be brighter, have less audience chatter and have better "presence," the music itself is simply gorgeous. In fact, this may be one of the nicest acoustic sets from 1970. This concert happened right around the time the band was recording *American Beauty* and as a result this set has the feel of that sacred album. "Brokedown Palace" features a rare, tasteful piano accompaniment. The shiniest gem here is obviously the only known acoustic live performance of "Box of Rain." What can be said except Wow! Though the quality of the recording makes it challenging to fully appreciate, or even hear clearly for that matter, it appears that Jerry plays pedal steel on this tune. A mandolin is added into the equation for "Rosalie McFall" and stays through the next two tunes. Unfortunately, "Sweet Chariot" cuts moments after it begins. If the soundboard of this set ever reappears, it would make a very tasty candidate for a Vault release.

After the traditional beginning and first vocal break, "Dark Star" drops into a disjointed experimentation with minimalist "Space" "Feedback." This section is so quiet that the audience begins applause, obviously thinking that the song has ended. After a few minutes the band gets back into a regular "Dark Star" groove that evolves into a very percussive "Feelin' Groovy Jam." A ship-shape Saint Stephen follows and leads to a short drum solo from out of which a high-spirited "Good Lovin'" bounds, with Jerry and the drummers trading licks during the intro. Phil comes in during the drum solo and the three of them really start to cook.

— HARRY HAHN

## 9/18/70
### Fillmore East, New York, New York

**Acoustic Set:** Truckin', Black Peter
**Electric Set:** Sugar Magnolia, Candyman, Cryptical Envelopment > The Other One > Cryptical Reprise > Brokedown Palace, It's a Man's World, Till the Morning Comes, Me and My Uncle, Operator, Dancin' in the Streets, Saint Stephen > Not Fade Away > Good Lovin'
**Encore:** We Bid You Goodnight

**1. Source:** AUD, **Quality:** C, **Length:** 0:10 (acoustic tunes only), **Taper:** Jack Toner

**2. Source:** SBD, **Quality:** A+, **Length:** 0:50 (electric tunes only), **Genealogy:** MR > DAT

**3. Source:** FM-SBD (GDH 241), **Quality:** A, **Length:** "Operator," "Dancin' in the Streets"

**4. Source:** AUD, **Quality:** D, **Length:** 1:50, **Taper:** Marty Weinberg

**Highlights:** The jams in and around Saint Stephen > Not Fade Away

On this night and the two that follow, we hear some of the finest guitar work that Bobby had thus far contributed to the Dead. Much of late 1970 displays this intensified effort by Bobby; it's his "diamond in the rough" period in which he's finally starting to shine as a guitarist. The two acoustic tunes, which only came into widespread circulation in 1997, are fairly poor by comparison to other acoustic audience recordings of the time. "Truckin'" is standard fare. The "Black Peter" is unusual in that Garcia stops playing all of a sudden in midtune either due to some technical dilemma or because the band is having trouble keeping it together—it's hard to tell which due to the poor quality. Garcia quips that it's insane up on stage and the audience goes nuts accordingly.

My excellent soundboard tape begins (out of order) with a respectable if uninspired "Operator." The energy level exuded during the jam in "Dancin'" is enormous, but it fails to develop with the same sort of poetic beauty found in many others of this year. Unfortunately, it also suffers from a small glitch during the early part of the jam. During the "ladyfinger" section of "Saint Stephen," Jerry breaks out in laughter. We are also treated to some delicate, beautiful percussive work with the glockenspiel here. As "Saint Stephen" progresses, Bobby really starts to rock. By the time we hit "Not Fade Away," he's picking right at Jerry's pace, leading the band through a very "China Cat"-like instrumental jam and then into the "We Bid You Goodnight"-like jam we normally hear at the end of "Goin' Down the Road." "Not Fade Away"'s final vocals feature a Bobby and Pigpen call-and-response in which we hear Bob seeming to destroy his voice. The drum solo in "Good Lovin'," which was usually too long in 1970 doesn't get too far here before Phil joins in to add some very funky bass lines. Then Bobby joins in again with blistering picking. At this point we find Jerry playing some very juxtaposing syncopations. It all evolves into a traditional but hot "Good Lovin'." The transition to the second set of vocals features the terrific trading of licks between each band member common to "Good Lovin'" in this period. "We Bid You Goodnight" is the short version: beautiful, but without the biblical verses.

HARRY HAHN

*Ticket stub for September 18, 1970, at Fillmore East*

## 9/19/70
### Fillmore East, New York, New York

Morning Dew, Me and My Uncle, Good Mornin', Li'l Schoolgirl, Cold Rain and Snow, Easy Wind, Dark Star > Saint Stephen > Not Fade Away > Darkness, Darkness Jam > Turn On Your Lovelight

**1. Source:** SBD, **Quality:** A+, **Length:** 1:05 ("Dark Star" through "Lovelight"), **Genealogy:** MR > DAT
**2. Source:** FM-SBD (GDH 311 and 312), **Quality:** A, **Length:** 1:05 ("Dark Star" through "Lovelight")
**3. Source:** AUD, **Quality:** F/D+, **Length:** 1:50, **Taper:** Marty Weinberg?
**Highlights:** Morning Dew, Easy Wind, Dark Star > Saint Stephen > Not Fade Away > Darkness, Darkness Jam > Turn On Your Lovelight

A bread-and-butter classic show from this era. Due to the supremely inferior quality of the audience recording, the first forty-five minutes—"Morning Dew" through "Easy Wind"—takes real patience to listen to. The music warbles a bit and echoes. If the legendary Marty was indeed the recordist of this segment then it wasn't his usual superb job. Each song fades in as it starts and out as it ends. The music, however, smokes. The band plays every song with the focus and intense energy we've come to expect from shows at the Fillmore East. The audience is, of course, the synergistic antagonist here, screaming at every peak onstage—egging the Dead on to higher and higher swells. Jerry's vocals are passionate throughout and Bobby rips through a great solo in "Easy Wind"—a telling prelude to the quintessential version played on September 20.

The exquisitely beautiful "Dark Star" starts the soundboard tape off with delicate, hypnotic rhythmic percussion and superb rhythm guitar licks. As on 9/17, after the first vocals we get a very quiet minimalist "Space" section, but since this tape is a soundboard, we can actually hear what the band is doing. The jamming becomes more and more intense and melodic, eventually evolving into a joyous "Feelin' Groovy Jam." Bobby is right on the mark during this section, and Jerry gives him plenty of room until stepping in to bring the band around to the second vocals. Following a flawless "Saint Stephen," a raucous "Not Fade Away" ensues. After the first vocal break we find Bobby front and center again, as he and Jerry quickly find their way into a short but strong "Darkness, Darkness" jam. "Lovelight" cooks along in its usual way, with both guitars equally audible in the mix. Pigpen eventually gets the audience involved by way of playing matchmaker and romantic adviser for the men in the audience. As usual he advises a very, shall we say, *direct* approach. Suffice it to say that even Bobby is taken aback by Pig's language. Pigpen even passes his microphone into the crowd and encourages audience members to declare their interest in one another through the PA. Eventually the band takes over again and builds the jam into something sounding very much like "Let It Rock." This ends abruptly when Pig takes control back, eventually leading to the usual, triumphant ending, which is punctuated by yet another Pigpen expletive. Let it shine, shine, shine.

HARRY HAHN

---

## 9/20/70
### Fillmore East, New York, New York

**Acoustic Set:** Uncle John's Band, Deep Elem Blues, Friend of the Devil, Big Railroad Blues, Dark Hollow, Ripple, To Lay Me Down, Truckin', Rosalie McFall, Cumberland Blues, New Speedway Boogie, Brokedown Palace
**Electric Set:** Casey Jones, China Cat Sunflower > I Know You Rider, Candyman, Sittin' on Top of the World, Big Boy Pete, Me and My Uncle, Easy Wind, Mama Tried, Sugar Magnolia, Attics of My Life, //Good Lovin', Not Fade Away > Caution > Feedback > We Bid You Goodnight

---

**1. Source:** SBD, **Quality:** B/A+, **Length:** 2:55, **Genealogy:** MR > RR > RR > DAT
**2. Source:** FM-SBD (GDH 148 and 311), **Quality:** A+, **Length:** 0:30 ("Big Railroad Blues," "Ripple," "Casey Jones" through "I Know You Rider")
**3. Source:** AUD, **Quality:** D+, **Length:** 1:50, **Taper:** Marty Weinberg
**Highlights:** One of the better acoustic sets from 1970, Easy Wind
**Personnel:** David Grisman (?) on mandolin, David Nelson on mandolin

Featuring one of the best acoustic sets from 1970, this tape is also one of the most glitch-free, with a very tasty song selection and guest musicians to boot. Throughout the first few songs on an uncredited mandolinist, who we believe is David Grisman, adds a beautiful touch. An unusually slow "Big Railroad Blues" has Bobby announce David Nelson with "another mandolin." "To Lay Me Down" has outstanding piano, organ, and mandolin work along with Jerry's beautiful vocals. A very early "Truckin'" appears in a rare acoustic version. Other favorites include "Rosalie McFall" and "New Speedway Boogie."

This second set is a great follow-up to the acoustic first set, with some great song selections and fine Bobby work. The song list speaks for itself; for starters you've gotta love any set with "Sittin' on Top of the World" and "Big Boy Pete," especially when both versions are this good. "Easy Wind" is arguably one of the best-ever versions. This is due largely to the outstanding lead guitar work of Mr. Weir. Yes, that's right, lead guitar. This is Bob's finest hour as he takes a remarkable, piercing lead. As usual his guitar tone is shrill, but his relentless picking entices Jerry into a no-holds-barred duel. Despite his worthy opponent, Weir holds his own, in effect announcing, "I have arrived." It's really a remarkable moment. Again we get a ripping early version of "Sugar Magnolia" that features some really cool distortion tones from Garcia and kooky vocal "do-do-do's" that were soon abandoned. Only the final portion of what was most likely a great "Good Lovin'" shows up on this tape, and it's probably not in its original position here.

"Not Fade Away" appears for the third night in a row yet is very different from its predecessors. This one progresses like the one on 9/18, through an end of "Goin' Down the Road"–style jam, but then Phil begins suggesting "Caution." The band, however, first needs to end "Not Fade Away," so they go back to finish up business and then immediately jump into "Caution." As expected, we get a healthy portion of Pig's vocal ramblings with the band's increasingly weird backup. The jam works back up into a strong "down the tracks" theme and crescendo followed up by semiaudible Pigpen vocals and then a nice bit of harmonica work. Unfortunately, there is a major handicap in this tape due to the fact that everyone's copy switches abruptly at this point, in mid-jam, from excellent (if usually somewhat hissy) quality to worse quality. (It is rumored that this turn for the worse is on the master tape though no one knows why.) At this point we find ourselves back on track with Garcia seriously stoking the fire before descending into "Feedback." After about seven minutes of inspired aural weirdness, a fully extended version of "We Bid You Goodnight" closes the book. Audience members on this night were treated to the full spectrum of positive Grateful Dead musical styles and energy.

HARRY HAHN

## 10/4/70
### Winterland Arena, San Francisco, California

KSAN crew talk, Truckin'//, Till the Morning Comes, Brokedown Palace, Next Time You See Me, Cold Rain and Snow, China Cat Sunflower > I Know You Rider, Good Lovin' > Drums > Good Lovin', Sugar Magnolia, Casey Jones, Uncle John's Band.

**Source:** FM-SBD (KSAN and KQED), **Quality:** B–, **Length:** 1:30, **Genealogy:** MR > RR > PCM > DAT

**Highlights:** Till the Morning Comes, China Cat Sunflower > I Know You Rider, Good Lovin', Uncle John's Band

**Comments:** On October 4, 1970, the Grateful Dead, along with other groups playing at Winterland, took part in one of the first live television simulcasts with quad sound. The concert was broadcast on KQED television, and the quadraphonic sound was broadcast on two San Francisco FM stations: KSAN and KQED. I assume that my tape of this show is from the KSAN broadcast, as it includes two of their *verrrry* spacey promos. The last half of this show ("China Cat Sunflower" > "I Know You Rider," "Good Lovin'," "Casey Jones," "Sugar Magnolia," and "Uncle John's Band") appears on the infamous "Mammary Productions" bootleg album that first appeared at the head shops of the East Village in late spring of 1971. To this Deadfreak, that bootleg album was the nicest treat since seeing the Dead at the Fillmore East earlier that year, in April.

On my tape, "Truckin'" is missing; the tape starts off with an announcer stating that "they are setting levels." It then goes right into a rhythmically infectious "Till The Morning Comes" that invokes an image of a puppy dog's tail, wagging as happily as it can—one of the best renditions ever of this seldom played song. This upbeat spirit doesn't last long, because the band then wanders through a "Brokedown Palace," Pigpen does a very short "Next Time You See Me," and they run through some "Cold Rain and Snow."

Philheads take note: By this time with the band, Lesh has developed his phat bass sound—that thunking sound of a thick rubber band, amplified and equalized so that you can just lean on the notes. He is ON this night.

After "Cold Rain and Snow," there are a lot of requests shouted out from the audience. Weir proceeds to tell them, in his uniquely twisted way, that they're shouting out a bunch of meaningless words to them, because the band doesn't know the names of the songs. What follows are two more highlights of the show.

Within fifteen seconds of the start of "China Cat Sunflower," you know that this version is going to be good—very, very good. Lesh and Weir trade licks between lyrics, and with Lesh's phat sound so prominent in the mix, I wonder who really is playing lead. The transitional jam seems short, but it is complete, with Weir playing plenty of sproingy chords as only he could do back then. "I Know You Rider" is great, and when Garcia sings "I wish I was a headlight," you can almost feel that cool Colorado rain hitting you in the face, as you look out the engine cabin, heading on the gleaming tracks, in a river canyon, surrounded by mountains and trees. This is a real mind melter: a "China" > "Rider" you can use to set a standard by which all others can be judged.

The groove continues, with the drummers beginning "Good Lovin'." After Pigpen finishes the verses, Kreutzmann and Hart start a spirited game of tag on the drums, which dissolves into a lively Follow the Leader. When the band joins in, Lesh's bass raises the hairs on the back of my neck. Garcia leads the jam back to "Good Lovin'," with everyone getting to solo a couple of bars before Pigpen wraps up the song with "and I was feelin' . . ."

"Sugar Magnolia" follows, with plenty of wah-wah from Garcia. A nice start, and the band jams out to the "Sunshine Daydream" verses. Unfortunately, Weir misses the first intro, doesn't get the words timed to the music for the second attempt, and the song quickly dies.

"Casey Jones" starts off a little rough; Garcia flubs a verse, but it recovers nicely. "Uncle John's Band" is another gem. Again, Lesh's bass playing is just as interesting to follow as Garcia's lead. Weir and Lesh sing some very nice backups to Garcia's lead vocals. The post–"take his children home" jam doesn't develop much past the album version, but it is intense.

In retrospect, even the screwups are great, because they're so fall-off-the-edge obvious. Despite some severe lyric flubs and a lackluster first half (except for "Till the Morning Comes"), this show has a number of great, standard-setting versions of classic Grateful Dead songs.

IHOR SLABICKY

## 10/4/70
### Winterland Arena, San Francisco, California
**Interview:** Ron "Pigpen" McKernan

**Source:** AUD, **Quality:** B, **Length:** 0:03
**Highlights:** "If I can't put it in my pocket, it ain't worth taking."

BRIAN DYKE

## 10/10/70
### Colden Auditorium, Queen's College, Queens, New York

**Set 1:** Truckin', Deep Elem Blues, Hard to Handle, Sugar Magnolia, Candyman, Cryptical Envelopment > Drums > The Other One > Not Fade Away > Goin' Down the Road Feelin' Bad > Not Fade Away
**Set 2:** Casey Jones, Cold Rain and Snow, Me and My Uncle

**Source:** AUD, **Quality:** C+, **Length:** 1:30
**Highlights:** Hard to Handle, Not Fade Away

This show is not the hottest from this momentous year, but it certainly has its moments, especially the first set. The opening "Truckin'" sets the tone for the rest of the tape, a solid version with flashes of brilliance. Next up is a rare, electric "Deep Elem" that showcases the band's love for traditional numbers. This is followed by a routinely hot "Hard to Handle" that features some nice bombs by Phil, excellent rhythm by Weir, and tasty leads from Garcia. A supercharged "Sugar Magnolia" keeps the show moving right along. Workhorse versions of "Cryptical" and "The Other One" lead into a hot "Not Fade Away." What comes next is Grateful Dead archival history. Now, in *DeadBase* and on my tape the label says that "Goin' Down the Road" comes next. This would be the first known instance of this magical pairing. However, on the tape that I have there is only a "Goin' Down the Road" jam, and I can't hear the cut for the life of me. In either case, the music is hot as the band ends this set with the conclusion of "Not Fade Away." The second set starts with a rockin', crowd-drivin' "Casey Jones" that only hints at what the second set has to offer.

DWIGHT HOLMES

## 10/11/70
### Marion Shea Auditorium, Patterson State College, Wayne, New Jersey

Casey Jones, Hurts Me Too, Mama Tried, Till the Morning Comes, Dancin' in the Streets, Candyman, //Sittin' on Top of the World, Morning Dew//, //Dark Star > Saint Stephen > Not Fade Away > Goin' Down the Road Feelin' Bad > Not Fade Away Reprise

**Source:** AUD, **Quality:** D+, **Length:** 1:30
**Highlights:** Morning Dew, Candyman, Dark Star > Saint Stephen > Not Fade Away > Goin' Down The Road Feelin' Band > Not Fade Away Reprise
**Comments:** This tape has an aggravating swishing hiss that terribly distorts the sound during certain songs. The closest way to describe it is like hearing the ocean in a seashell. The music on this tape, however, is quite good for the most part, making it frustrating that there isn't a better tape available.

This show starts out with a fairly standard version of "Casey Jones," followed by a favorable "Hurts Me Too." Phil, playing with his usual full warm sound, holds things together as the rest of the band settles into the feel. Once this is accomplished, Pigpen takes full advantage of his harp solo, laying it out smooth and sad. Pig seemingly isn't his usual self, as the lyrics are sung with a halfhearted enthusiasm that unfortunately keeps this song from really shining. "Mama Tried" is an average attempt, but next we hear the seldom played (only during the latter part of this year) "Till the Morning Comes." This is a solid version with a good sense of momentum, except for the end where things become slightly inconsistent transitioning from the solos back to the main theme.

"Dancin' in the Streets" starts off with a good deal of energy but soon becomes unrecognizable because the sound quality diminishes to unlistenable standards. "Candyman," a completely delightful treat (pun intended), showcases Jerry's melodic singing at its most sincere. The entire band plays well enough to make this one of the longest and most beautiful versions ever played. "Sittin' on Top of the World" is almost completely missing. What follows, however, is a slow and deliberate "Morning Dew" that not only is relaxed and sincere, but also maintains an high level of intensity. The jam has a serious feel as it gathers energy and momentum. The transition back into the lyrics is noticeably delicate and smooth. Unfortunately, seemingly as with all good versions, it cuts.

The second side of the tape ventures out with "Dark Star" spanning a wonderfully weird and wild twenty minutes. On the tape, "Dark Star" starts out already in progress, but probably only thirty seconds from the beginning. I doubt too much is missing. This smooth and energetic jam flows into the main theme and then casually slips into the first lyrics about four minutes later. After the drummers slowly fade the groove out, taking on their spacey percussive role, everyone slips into new territory into a seemingly alternate plane of reality as they break new ground. Screeching and shrieking, they journey into space with an almost industrial-sounding edge complete with sinister overtones, as if they are trying to warn us of some kind of impending doom. With a massive amount of tension built up, there is an air of anticipation as the drums slowly creep back in to fill out the jam. Returning to the main theme right before the nineteen-minute mark, they ease into the second lyrics. This version, although it doesn't have extremely large peaks and valleys, stays pretty even and maintains a consistent level of intensity. Overall, this is quite a good performance, and the crowd gives a raucous amount of applause at the finale. If you like "Dark Star" scary and weird (who doesn't?), then this one will be of special interest to you.

"Saint Stephen," at its usual energetic high level of intensity, is well jammed throughout. It then jumps down into a revved-up "Not Fade Away." The transition into the very new "Goin' Down the Road" is completely seamless, melting so extremely well it sounds as if they've been doing it for years. After a little time spent settling into the feel, things really get going as the crowd does their part by hollering and clapping. Finishing up, the song leaps back into "Not Fade Away" for a good bit, then finally lands on the last chord, much to everyone's delight.

COREY SANDERSON

## 10/21/70
**Unknown Location**

Jam 1, Jam 2, Jam 3 (Hopkins), Jam 4 (Blues)

**Source:** SBD, **Quality:** B+, **Length:** 0:40
**Highlights:** Every note
**Personnel:** Jack Casady, Papa John Creach, Jerry Garcia, Nicky Hopkins, Jorma Kaukonen, Merl Saunders, Will Scarlet [?]

**Comments:** Reviewer's tape has no listing for a drummer. Some tapes in circulation list Spencer Dryden as an additional participant, while others list Joey Covington. Also, this reviewer's tape label credits Will Scarlet, although the tape contains no evidence of a harp player at all.

This tape, a forty-minute all-star session, consists of four instrumental jams, each containing a specific theme. Unlike most jams which consist of a backing section beneath a testosterone-rich set of stringmen, this session displays each of the participants in a solo context. Wisely, the jammers refrain from the temptation of terminal density; in fact, rarely do more than four ever play at the same time.

The first jam, lasting around twelve minutes, is based around a pair of similar descending riffs. Beginning with the keyboard players, each instrumentalist uses his allotment to loosen up, exhibiting mainly standby licks and phrases without too much risk taking. Somewhat notable is that each guitarist employs a tone cleaner than is characteristic, leaving the distortion responsibilities to Hopkins and Saunders.

Jam 2 begins with a keyboard-fiddle triad, ever a dynamic contrast in range, with Hopkins and Saunders supplying plenty of low end percussion against Creach's upper-register vibrato. Boldly and assertively, the instrumentalists drive the jam with focused intensity, responding to each other's chops in true improvisational fashion. As Creach gives a courteous bow to allow Saunders to step forward, Hopkins calls out a few chords before leading the way into a brief but stunningly bold dueling keyboard jam. Returning to the fold, Creach adds some directive chopping of his own with a series of phrases that shift between curt and conversational. Just as the jam begins to melt, Casady steps forward with a few riffs before being shoved aside by the drummer, who, along with Creach, marches the boys militantly into Jam 3, a gruff and belligerent jam sans guitar. The musicianship displayed here is confident and rhythmic, as if each instrumentalist is strutting arrogantly while the guitarists sit on the sidelines. While Casady and the drummer hold the pulse of the jam, Creach and Saunders trade licks in a unique blend of meticulously accurate lead phrases with abrupt off-beat responses. As the jam nears its conclusion, seemingly at least, the tempo increases and a brief drums-keyboard shuffle emerges, lasting only a few minutes before, strangely, the tape fades.

And, of course, what jam session would be complete without a headcuttin' blues finale? Obviously, this is the most traditional of the jams in that it is dominated by the dueling guitarists, with a solid but standard bass and percussion accompaniment. As notable as the musicianship itself is the diverse tonal range, as both guitarists shift between crystal clean and reverberated raunch. Taking turns, both in twenty-four- and twelve-bar increments, the guitarists alternate between rhythm and counter-rhythm and lead in a textbook display of blues diversity. While Kaukonen is consistent in exhibiting his traditional style of blazing hammers and pulls amidst a throttling vibrato, Garcia employs a schizophrenic approach that blends screaming and straight in-your-face leads with restrained and rationally timed rhythmic phrases. Though jams such as these often go on endlessly at the expense of the audience, the musicians here wisely recognize the appropriate conclusion, giving a graceful and climactic finish to an afternoon of ballistic musical exhibitionism.

BRIAN DYKE

---

### 10/23/70
**McDonough Arena, Georgetown University, Washington, D.C.**

Casey Jones, Mama Tried, Hard to Handle, China Cat Sunflower > I Know You Rider, Sugar Magnolia, Candyman//, Drums// > Good Lovin' > Drums > Good Lovin', Me and My Uncle, Truckin' > The Other One// > Not Fade Away > Goin' Down the Road Feelin' Bad > Not Fade Away Reprise
**Encore:** Uncle John's Band

---

**1. Source:** AUD, **Quality:** C, **Length:** 1:30, **Genealogy:** MC > C > DAT, **Taper:** Cary Wolfson, Sony TC124 recorder with a 1 point stereo mike 15 feet back from stage

**2. Source:** AUD, **Quality:** C, **Length:** 1:30, **Genealogy:** Unknown

**Highlights:** Hard to Handle, Candyman, Good Lovin', The Other One

**Comments:** I suspect that the tape that circulates is not complete, even though the information in *DeadBase IX* indicates that it is. I state this based upon the annotated stage banter opposite. Specifically, the announcer's opening statement, "Once again . . . ," seems to indicate that the band was either onstage earlier in the evening (more likely), perhaps performing acoustic numbers, or that it had been there on a previous date (less likely). However, since "Casey Jones" is supposed to be the opening song of the night, and the band has never played this venue before, this comment seems *very* out of place. Moreover, the announcers first reference to "changing things around" also suggests that some music preceded the songs on this tape. Unfortunately, there is no circulating soundboard to either support or refute these irregularities.

This ninety-minute tape and the show it archives is scattered with the focused energy and raw power that made 1970 such a unique and well-loved year for the Dead. Indeed, although numerous technical flaws and occasional musical missteps occur during this show, when viewed in the aggregate this tape is a must for any serious collector of 1970 shows. For the interested listener, particular attention should be paid to a stellar version of "Hard to Handle," a unique rendition of "Good Lovin'," and one of the sweetest presentations of "Candyman" I have ever heard.

The cassette I have is a surprisingly clean audience recording that suffers only from some slight hiss and an occasional oversaturation of treble. Unfortunately for the listener, however, the tape of this show is marred by unusually loud audience chatter. Various interjections and comments made by folks near the taper not only dominate most of the mid-song breaks on this tape, but they are also audible during many of the quieter parts such as during "Candyman" and "Uncle John's Band." Nevertheless, the music from this night shines through the clutter and is well worth the price of admission. This portentous mood is immediately suggested by the opening sequence of stage banter:

> **Announcer:** We're going to give you a hell of a long show so it will be just a very short break while they change around a second.
> **Pigpen:** (screams)
> **Taper:** (screams) (he does this *a lot*)
> **Phil:** Inflammatory.
> **Bobby:** It's kind of hot and sticky.
> **Announcer:** I think they are about ready. Once again, the Grateful Dead.

After the show opener, a rousing and energetic offering of "Casey Jones," some amusing stage chatter by Jerry, the kind that makes me laugh out loud, can be heard:

> **Garcia:** Hey, could you turn on the monitors? The monitors here. Yeah. Now they are starting to come in. Monitors, monitors, a-hah. Monitors, monitors, monitor . . .

After this humorous interlude, and contrary to the audible requests by the audience for "Candyman" or "Dark Star," Pigpen follows up a standard version of "Mama Tried" by lashing out with an exceptional version of "Hard to Handle." This rendition has the kind of mojo comparable to the epochal versions of April and August 1971. Indeed, with this effort, it is clear that the band is beginning to push the envelope of where this song can go. The raw mid-verse jam is, long, well-structured, and incorporates many tempos. By the time Pigpen is ready to return to the mike, Jerry is pushing his axe hard and free, creating a very clear picture of what this song could become, given the right moment.

*Ticket stub for October 23, 1970, McDonough Arena*

After a nicely performed "China Cat Sunflower" suite, the only flaw being a somewhat awkward bridge, an intricate, yet raw "Sugar Magnolia" presents itself. This version is unusual, if only for the oddly performed "Sunshine Daydream" sequence that ends it. The transition sounds ill-timed and the ending comes off sounding rushed. Not withstanding, the solo before this oddity is fun and well worth a listen. With the exception of the "Uncle John's Band" encore, the only ballad of the night, "Candyman," follows. Even though this song is technically marred by a slight song-ending cut, it is a truly wonderful version. This ode is complemented by passionate vocals and subtle playing that allow this song to become a perfect ending to the first side of my tape.

The second side of this tape starts off with an unusual sequence of percussion preceding the beginning of "Good Lovin'." This skin-rattling lasts for some forty seconds (it could be longer since there is a splice in the tape during this portion), and while at all times vaguely related to the usual "Good Lovin'" intro, it is nevertheless unique enough to merit a mention. Following the standard first verse, Mickey and Billy return to what they started, this time giving the endeavor seriously creative attention. The playing is interesting and, after a time, explodes to provide Jerry the perfect environment to offer up his contribution to this song. His powerful playing rises to the call and proves to reflect the kind of roaring jam that made 1970 so famous. Recall that these are the days when the song stood alone and Pigpen's famous rap of 1971–72 has not really made it into the rotation. What the listener instead receives is pure, raw guitar work colored with a blues edge. The exploration here is not a long spacey improvisation, but rather a compact, energy-driven treat. The final chorus, pumped by Bobby's rhythm, caps the song perfectly.

Following a standard "Me and My Uncle," the final suite of the tape gets underway. The initiating "Truckin'," however, starts out in rather humdrum fashion. The vocals lack punch, the words stumble, and the playing is more embellishment than magic. Bobby tries to inject some fire with the "If you got a warrant, I guess you're gonna come in" verse, but to only marginal effect. In fact, with the exception of Jerry playing a bit with the post-vocals jam, the remainder of the song is uninteresting. Perhaps, since things don't seem to be working, a quick switch occurs and the band fires off into "The Other One." This version, although also a tad slow, has an energy level that seems to be up a notch or two from "Truckin'." Thanks to some dexterous work by Jerry, the listener's ear is treated to an interesting exploration by the band following the first verse of the song. A variety of tempos are traversed and peaks realized before the band returns to the final verse. Although not as epochal as in the glory years of 1972, this version of "The Other One" is a keeper and saves a lackluster "Truckin'" from sure disaster. The final musical ensemble, ending with "Not Fade Away," is quite competently played and provides a respectable cap to the evening's fun.

DARREN E. MASON

## 10/24/70

### Kiel Opera House, St. Louis, Missouri

Dancin' in the Streets, Hurts Me Too, Me and My Uncle, Friend of the Devil, Cold Rain and Snow, Attics of My Life, Good Lovin', Casey Jones, Saint Stephen > Not Fade Away > Goin' Down the Road Feelin' Bad > Not Fade Away Reprise > Turn On Your Lovelight

**Source:** SBD, **Quality:** A–, **Length:** 1:50, **Genealogy:** MR > RR > RR > PCM > DAT

**Highlights:** The mellow tunes, Good Lovin'

This show is available in very good quality and is well worth seeking out. The only problem is that the volume on my tape fluctuates, and there are a few minor cuts. About two minutes into the only circulating set, the jamming starts on "Dancin'," and the show boogies throughout, with some mellow numbers thrown in for balance. It's actually the soulful tunes like "Friend of the Devil," "Hurts Me Too," and "Cold Rain and Snow" that I enjoy the most on this tape; there are so many hot versions of "Good Lovin'," "Not Fade Away" > "Goin' Down the Road" > "Not Fade Away," and "Lovelight" from back then that it's hard to compare, but I would have to say that the "Good Lovin'" is a standout! Get it.

PAUL J. PEARAH

## 10/30/70

### Early Show, Gymnasium, SUNY–Stony Brook, New York

Cold Rain and Snow, Truckin', Sugar Magnolia, Next Time You See Me, Me and// My Uncle, Good Lovin' > Drums > Cumberland// Blues > Good Lovin', Casey Jones

**1. Source:** SBD, **Quality:** A–, **Length:** 1:30, **Genealogy:** MR > RR > RR > PCM > DAT
**2. Source:** SBD, **Quality:** A, **Length:** 1:30, **Genealogy:** MR > DAT

**Highlights:** Next Time You See Me

Veteran taper Barry Glassberg recalls that both shows on this date featured the Dead and the New Riders, who played one set each per show. The sound system was being run by students, not the Dead's crew, which resulted in the band getting really pissed off (and, so it seems, drunk). These circumstances conspired to foster some of the weakest shows of one of the strongest years in the Dead's touring history.

Jerry's guitar lacks energy, and Phil's bass is too low in the mix (the fatal flaw). "Truckin'" features howlingly awful harmonies, but a nice outro. Or maybe you're just glad it's over. All in all, this is a clean recording of a lackluster show. Unfortunately, the late show wasn't much better.

PAUL J. PEARAH

## 10/30/70
### Late Show, Gymnasium, SUNY–Stony Brook, New York

**Set List:** Smokestack Lightning, Beat It on Down the Line, China Cat Sunflower > I Know You Rider, Friend of the Devil, Truckin', Candyman, Hurts Me Too, Dancin' in the Streets, Big Railroad Blues, Saint Stephen > Not Fade Away > Goin' Down the Road Feelin' Bad > Not Fade Away, Turn On Your Lovelight

1. **Source:** SBD, **Quality:** A, **Length:** 1:50, **Genealogy:** MR > RR > RR > PCM > DAT
2. **Source:** SBD, **Quality:** A, **Length:** 1:50, **Genealogy:** MR > DAT

**Highlights:** Dancin' in the Streets, Smokestack Lightning, Turn On Your Lovelight

Excerpts from an actual e-mail exchange regarding the early and late shows:

> All in all, a pretty loose night, never really found the groove.
>
> Unremarkable. Lazy. Indifferent. In general, =yawn=.
>
> <whew!> was holding back...i've always found all 4 of those shows (10-30a&b, 10-31 a&b) to be yawners.
>
> Dancin', Smokestack, and Lovelight have their moments, but this show just isn't up to the 1970 standard. Consider these shows as a soundcheck/rehearsal for the Port Chester run.
>
> I think it is a mellow show...well-played and executed, just without the highlights one expects from a 1970 show. The Saint Stephen > Not Fade Away > Going Down the Road Feeling Bad > Not Fade Away is basically uneventful.
>
> If I had to take 500 Dead tapes to the proverbial sound-system-equipped desert island, this wouldn't be one of 'em.

PAUL J. PEARAH

## 10/31/70
### Early Show, SUNY–Stony Brook, New York

Till the Morning Comes, Hard to Handle, Mama Tried, China Cat Sunflower > I Know You Rider//, Dire Wolf, Me and My Uncle, Dark Hollow, Brokedown// Palace, Viola Lee Blues > Cumberland Blues, Uncle John's Band

1. **Source:** SBD, **Quality:** A, **Length:** 1:25, **Genealogy:** MR > DAT
2. **Source:** SBD, **Quality:** B–, **Length:** 1:25, **Genealogy:** MR > RR > RR > PCM > DAT
3. **Source:** FM-SBD (DHH 07), **Quality:** A, **Length:** Till the Morning Comes

**Highlights:** Till the Morning Comes, Dark Hollow (electric), Viola Lee Blues > Cumberland Blues, Uncle John's Band

Kicking off a show with a fine "Till the Morning Comes" is enough to get any Deadhead salivating like one of Pavlov's canine pals. Well, mop up that drool and enjoy the rest of the set; it may not all fall into the same category as far as rarity value is concerned, but it does include some totally unique moments. "Hard to Handle" stretches out nicely with great interlocking rhythmic interplay building up to the release of Jerry's solo. The "China" > "Rider" combo fires on all cylinders, opening up nicely during Rider before... *fading out!!* Oh pooh, and I was so enjoying that...

The tracks on side 2 of my cassette are all eminently enjoyable; check the rarely performed electric version of "Dark Hollow" and the delicate reading of "Brokedown Palace." However, the centerpiece of this show for me is the very last performance of "Viola Lee Blues." This may not be the most intense version around, but its basic structure ensures that dramatic tension is continually increased to a point of cathartic release. In most versions this is achieved through the whole song imploding in a supernova of glorious, full-on noise but what makes this one unique is the increasing tensions of "Viola Lee Blues" into its musical polar opposite, an airy, sprightly "Cumberland Blues." "Viola Lee Blues" isn't a musically open structure; it creates an overwhelming feeling of claustrophobia that complements the lyrics beautifully. "Cumberland Blues" is a piece that can be radically interpreted, which presumably is precisely why it remained on the playlist for the next twenty-five years and "Viola Lee" didn't. Emotionally, "Viola Lee Blues" may well be one-dimensional, but that one does happen to be the fifth dimension—which makes it a shame that such High Magick should be abandoned. Anyway, this pairing is real hot and the transition is absolutely sublime, so go check it out, folks.

"Uncle John's Band" is a stunner as well: great vocals and a well-developed jam before the final verse that comes closer to the performance styles of later years rather than the norm for a show of this date.

PAUL BODENHAM

---

### 🌀 10/31/70 🌀

**Late Show, SUNY–Stony Brook, New York**

Casey// Jones, Sugar// Magnolia, Next Time You See Me, The Other One > Cosmic// Charlie, Big Boss Man, Mama// Tried, Drums > Good Lovin' > Drums > Good Lovin', Saint Stephen > Not Fade Away > Goin' Down the Road Feelin' Bad > Not Fade Away Reprise

---

**1. Source:** SBD, **Quality:** A–, **Length:** 1:25, **Genealogy:** MR > DAT

**2. Source:** SBD, **Quality:** B–, **Length:** 1:25, **Genealogy:** MR > RR > RR > PCM > DAT

**Highlights:** Good Lovin', Not Fade Away, Goin' Down the Road Feelin' Bad

A series of cuts in the first two songs makes for unsettled listening; although they're none too serious, they do spoil the momentum that is building nicely after the early show. Thankfully, no tape glitches mar "The Other One," but even though the band is up for it, the performance is stymied by monitor problems (apparent through missed vocal cues). "The Other One" still contains some electrifying moments, especially from the drummers, who pack in some fine percussive interplay and not just in their featured duet. In fact, the drummers are superb throughout this show, laying down a flare path of churning beats on all the numbers that stretch out and even managing to squeeze *two* drum duets into "Good Lovin'."

Putting it charitably, "Cosmic Charlie" is a mess although it's obviously due to monitor problems, which provoke Bobby into a tirade against some nameless soundman. After Pigpen threatens to rip off the head of the aforementioned sound engineer and defecate in it, the problems seem to get resolved, thereby saving the show from a decline into fecal ultraviolence.

If a certain amount of frustration with the sound system adversely affects the music for a few numbers, the rest of the show has everyone in tune and spiraling outward in an orgasmic surge of energy. The drum sound at the beginning of "Not Fade Away" is absolutely *immense;* rolling breaks and the crash and shimmer of cymbals drive the band onward. If not exactly full of radical and unique ideas, on the whole the band's playing here has a willful sense of purpose and determination, not to mention a certain degree of wild abandon that cuts through any shortcomings in the tape recording and delivers enough pure fun to satisfy most folks.

PAUL BODENHAM

---

### 🌀 11/5/70 🌀

**Capitol Theater, Port Chester, New York**

Hard to Handle, Sittin' on Top of the World, Mama Tried, Truckin' > Drums > The Other One, Dark Star > Saint Stephen > Not Fade Away// > Goin' Down the Road > Not Fade Away Reprise//, China Cat Sunflower > I Know You Rider//

---

**Source:** AUD, **Quality:** B– (occasional bass oversaturation), **Length:** 1:05

**Highlights:** The whole show

**Comments:** As with the tapes from 6/24/70, there is even more mystery surrounding the origin and exact historical details of these tapes than existed before this project began.

These tapes have circulated since shortly after they were recorded, and numerous tapers claim to have gotten them from at least two distinct sources. It's been known since the early 1970s that the legendary Marty Weinberg recorded these shows. There's also been an unconfirmed rumor that the brother of one of the security guards at the Capitol Theater also recorded some of the shows as well as the June 24th shows. A close listen, however, to numerous tapes from different sources that contain the electric music played at these shows at the

Capitol Theater reveal that they are in fact largely from a single source. We could only find differences in the acoustic sets of two: 11/7 and 11/8. We went back as close to each of the two supposedly different master sources as we could get. Some of the tapes we listened to were twenty years old. We got copies of each source from four unconnected tapers, three on the East Coast, one on the West Coast. We logged all glitches, cuts, and near-field audience chatter. Ultimately, we relied only upon audience chatter as this seemed to be the truly definitive difference between tapes. In some situations, we found shows edited together from many different sources/generations—the late show from 11/7, for example. Will we ever get to the bottom of this? Perhaps some things are meant to remain a mystery. Hopefully, one of you who reads this will come forward with two or more completely distinct tapes from these shows to settle the mystery once and for all.

*Ticket stub for November 5, 1970, at Capitol Theater*

Ladies and gentlemen, fasten your seat belts for a run of shows that rides like a fantastic theme park attraction. The first highlight on opening night is a breathtaking "Hard to Handle"—one of the best versions from all of 1970. Phil plays the very same climactic jam found in "Hard to Handle"s from the April 1971 run!

"Truckin'" is, in a word, *ferocious*. The whole band is intensely animated, especially Bobby, who sings like there's no tomorrow. The segue into "The Other One" is the most seamless transition you'll ever hear. Most unexpectedly, the band quickly abandons "The Other One" for an extremely short drum solo. Moments later, they jump back into "The Other One" head-on, with as much gusto as they displayed during "Truckin'". It's a fairly short version, though. Marty's recording has a small glitch and several moments of high-end muffle within "The Other One" but nothing too horrendous.

Many tapes of this show are labeled "Other One" > "Dark Star" > . This is inaccurate, as the band comes to a full stop after "The Other One"'s second verse before heading off into a typical 1970-style "Dark Star" from silence. After a short intro, Jerry belts out the lyrics, and the band then quickly descends into a fully elaborated, luscious, minimalist "Feedback" space. You may find yourself holding your breath; for several minutes not a single peep can be heard from the audience. The band builds ever so slowly into—you guessed it—the "Feelin' Groovy Jam." Not the best reading of this jam, but heavenly nonetheless. Once stated, this gives way rapidly to the second verse of "Dark Star." With the opening notes to "Saint Stephen" the audience takes its cue and releases shrieks of expectant joy. Instantly, every pair of hands (except those of the recordists, appparently) in the theater are clapping as though it were Sunday morning in church. As usual, Mickey plays the glockenspiel during the "ladyfinger" verse. Oddly enough, the undesirable effect of bass oversaturation on the tape helps to positively accentuate Phil's spectacular lead during the jam.

"Not Fade Away" is every bit as wild a ride as "Truckin'" was. The band hurtles down the track like a runaway train. As the jam progresses, Pigpen steps to the mike and starts to play harmonica. Suddenly, the tape cuts. Bummer. *DeadBase* claims that the rest of the set went "Goin' Down the Road" > "Not Fade Away" > "Lovelight." We may never know for sure. Both my sources (perhaps from the same source long ago) have a "China Cat" > "I Know You Rider" (which cuts) tagged on to the end. Though I haven't been able to match it up with another "China" > "Rider" from the run, this version feels too laid-back to have been from this point in this show.

JOHN R. DWORK WITH KIPP ARMSTRONG

---

### 🌀 11/6/70 🌀
**Early Show, Capitol Theater, Port Chester, New York**

Casey Jones, Me and My Uncle, King Bee, China Cat > I Know You Rider, Easy Wind, Truckin', Candy//man, Sugar Magnolia, Good Lovin' > Drums > Main Ten Jam > Good Lovin'

---

**Source:** AUD, **Quality:** B+/A–, **Length:** 1:20, **Taper:** Marty Weinberg, Uher 7-inch open reel deck, **Genealogy:** MR > DAT

**Highlights:** Good Lovin' > Drums > Main Ten Jam > Good Lovin'

This might be the least interesting show of the run. Still, it's delightful. After a tight but uneventful opening, Jerry really begins to shine on "King Bee" by crying the blues on slide guitar. When Phil keeps his volume down, Marty's tape is amazingly crisp; once Phil cranks, the tape becomes a touch oversaturated.

Though this "Sugar Magnolia" is very young—too young, in fact—the transition between "Sugar Magnolia" and "sunshine daydream" is the same very memorable twangy solo guitar bridge Garcia plays on the famous 10/4/71 Winterland radio broadcast.

The obvious pinnacle of this set is the "Good Lovin'" > "Drums" > "Main Ten Jam" > "Good Lovin'." The band finally lets it all hang out here. The "Main Ten Jam" is stunning. Unlike the tail end of the equally hot "Good Lovin'" sandwich played on this same stage several months earlier, on June 24, the return to this "Good Lovin'" features a full jam. Before the guitarists let Pigpen bring this journey to a final rest, they bring it down low, to a very brief silence, and then each states the familiar "Good Lovin'" theme one at a time until they all join in unison to break back into the melody. Wow!

JOHN R. DWORK WITH KIPP ARMSTRONG

---

### 11/6/70
**Late Show, Capitol Theater, Port Chester, New York**

**Soundcheck:** Candyman, Uncle John's Band, Attics of My Life, Drum Solo, Bass Solo
**Acoustic Set:** Don't Ease Me In, Deep Elem, Dark Hollow, Friend of the Devil, The Rub, Black Peter, El Paso//, //Uncle John's Band
**Electric Set:** Casey Jones, Alligator > Drums > Jam > Not Fade Away > Goin' Down the Road Feelin' Bad > Mountain Jam > Not Fade Away Reprise > Caution > Turn On Your Lovelight

---

**Source:** AUD, **Quality:** B+ (several extremely quick but definitely distracting glitches, not cuts, appear in the first three songs of the acoustic set), **Length:** 1:20, **Taper:** Marty Weinberg, Uher 7-inch open reel deck, **Genealogy:** MR > DAT
**Highlights:** The entire show is spectacular!
**Comments:** The presence of a soundcheck on tape provides us with a mystery. On one hand this would seem to confirm that there was indeed a recordist present who had insider access (the fabled brother of a security guard, perhaps). How would a regular audience member be allowed to hang out, much less record, such a practice session? At the same time all four of our tapes of this show, which came from very different sources, contain the same markings—for example, the glitch right before the lyrics in the "Not Fade Away" reprise. This same glitch occurs on the tape we are sure came from Marty.

This soundcheck is significant only in that it was one of the first, if not the only, recordings of a soundcheck in circulation back in the early seventies. Hearing them work on "Attics of My Life" confirms that the entrancing effect it had when performed for an audience later at these shows was a direct result of focused practice. The Phil bass solo is just puttering around, nothing well formed at all.

Shortly thereafter, with an audience in attendance, the acoustic set turns out fairly standard for the time—in other words: *très* sweet. Upon recognizing the beginning of each tune, the audience claps, screams, and squeals, but once they settle down they're very quiet. At one point between songs, two audience members yell out, "Louder," to which Garcia, without missing a beat replies, "Listen more carefully." The audience cracks up and Bobby replies, "Next," as a compliment to Jerry's quick wit.

My DAT tape, purported to be only one generation removed from Marty's master, has an "Uncle John's Band" to end the acoustic set, whereas *DeadBase* suggests "Brokedown Palace" ended this set (alas, the mystery continues). My tape continues with what many believe to be the early show (*DeadBase* suggests that there were early shows on 11/6 and 11/7 but not on 11/5 and 11/8). I tend to believe in the two-show theory myself as the 6th was a Friday, the 7th a Saturday. If you can manage to find one of the low-gen digital copies made from Marty's tapes, you'll be surprised how good they sound in comparison to the multi-gen copies that have circulated widely for years.

The electric set of this show is not only my favorite set of the run, it's one of my favorite sets of the entire year! As it progresses, one gets the distinct feeling that the band is having so much fun it doesn't want to stop. It's one of those perfect examples of when the music plays the band.

Just after Pigpen sings the opening to "Alligator," Billy goes into his obligatory drum solo. Now, I'm of the belief that most GD drum solos, back before the Billy and Mickey began to get really adventurous in the late seventies, were pretty boring. But the drum jams at these shows are much more high-energy than most others I've heard from this early period. (It helps to hear on these audience tapes how vociferously the audience claps along.) Well, for this drum jam Jerry decides to stay onstage with Billy for a guitar-drum duet, and boy, what a difference. This one is as good as it gets. You must listen to this very carefully; it's simply incredible. Jerry goes as *nuts* here as on the better "Alligator"s from the summer of 1968. When the rest of the band joins in, they too are very inspired. The first thought that comes to mind at this juncture in the jam is how hot the Dead were when they broke from "Me and My Uncle" into "Not Fade Away" on 2/14/70. That's what this set is about. You dig?

After a blisteringly hot "Not Fade Away" > "Goin' Down the Road" > "Not Fade Away, during which Jerry floats effortlessly in and out of an instrumental recitation of the "Mountain Jam" theme, the guitarists strum as if to end the set. But no, they're *waay* too revved up, so into "Caution" they fly. Pigpen's harmonic playing is superlative. Phil is ferocious. The band is on fire. In fact, they're still too hot to stop playing, so, as "Caution" melts into a fiery climax, Phil explodes into one of the hottest "Lovelight"s I've ever heard. At one point, only Billy is playing while the audience claps along. The guitarists are just sitting back, waiting to hear where Pigpen's rap is going to lead them. Again, the audience squeals in delight. The air is crackling with electric energy! Bobby steps to the mike and demands, "Hey Pigpen, tell 'em about the bear." To which Pigpen replies:

*The bear, whew,*
*Well you all know about the bear you know, ha,*
*he's kind of hairy [pronounced "haayreee"].*
*When he begin to move, his chops kinda open up just a*
*touch you know,*
*he comes sneakin' around them young ladies' windows*
*late in the evenin' time,*
*he's got something on his mind you know,*
*so he may just come up kinda scrabblin' and a*
*screetchin' up around yer window you know,*
*scratchin' on yer wall a little bit or somethin',*
*and he might go kinda, 'growl, snort, snort,' you know,*
*so if any of you young ladies feel any kinda noses this*
*evenin',*
*there's some guy in the audience standing close around*
*you who's got some*
*ideas on his mind that makes you hungry*
*[at which point ladies in the audience scream in*
*delight],*
*but you know that old bear, man he come out of the*
*hills,*
*just kinda steppin' quiet in the evenin' time,*
*he just a-snifflin' and a-snufflin' all around yer*
*windows and your backdoors,*
*so you girls better watch out,*
*cause that ol' bear is always hungry,*
*and he's big and hairy,*
*he just can't do without,*
*he be comin' up on your windowsill,*
*he figure like you got a pie sittin' out there on your*
*windowsill coolin' off or somethin',*
*at night time when it gets cooled down a little bit, ha,*
*that ain't the kind of pie he's lookin for,*
*scuffling around your windows*
*[and the band starts to play behind him].*
*I told you he was hairy,*
*well I ain't got to worry about no bear, ha!*
*You oughta see my old lady,*
*she can whip a dozen of 'em . . .*

At which point Pig goes back into the traditional "Lovelight" rap. Everyone, the band and audience alike, are just goin' nuts . . . Now *this* is a textbook example of primal Dead! Ten minutes later, when Pig finishes singing and the song is over, the band strums on and on, stretching the closing crescendo to a full seventy seconds. Phew! For the love of Dead, get this tape.

JOHN R. DWORK WITH KIPP ARMSTRONG

## 11/7/70
### Late Show, Capitol Theater, Port Chester, New York

**Acoustic Set:** Deep Elem, Monkey and the Engineer, Big Railroad Blues, Operator, El Paso, How Long Blues, Ripple, Brokedown Palace, Uncle John's Band
**Electric Set:** Cumberland Blues, Cold Rain and Snow, Hurts Me Too, Beat It on Down the Line, Truckin' > Drums > The Other One > Casey Jones, Attics of My Life, Sugar Magnolia, Big Boss Man, Mama Tried, China Cat > I Know You Rider, King Bee, Good Lovin'

**1. Source:** AUD, **Quality:** B–, **Length:** 0:35 (acoustic set only), **Taper:** Jack Toner
**2. Source:** AUD, **Quality:** B–/B, **Length:** 2:20 (missing "How Long Blues," "Brokedown Palace," "Uncle John's Band")
**Highlights:** Cold Rain and Snow, Attics of My Life
**Comments:** The correct order of this show is uncertain. There are many high-generation tapes of this set circulating so it's not uncommon to find a wide disparity in quality—even sometimes on the same tape. The first source listed here for the acoustic set only showed up in wide circulation in 1997, and it appears to be a more likely order than the tapes from Marty's recordings of this set, which appear in many different orders throughout the tape trading scene. As for the electric music, it seems highly unlikely, given how hot all the shows from this run were, that "King Bee," a real sleeper here, was the second-to-last song of this late show. Also, it seems more likely from the energy that "Cold Rain" opened the electric set, not "Cumberland Blues."

The acoustic set from this performance is excellent standard fare for the time. The song selection, however, is particularly hip. "Deep Elem" suffers mildly for a moment or two from what sounds like a ruffling or adjusting of the rig.

*DeadBase* lists "Cumberland" as the final song of the acoustic set; however, listening to the tape reveals that it is actually played with electric guitars. "Cold Rain and Snow" is one of the better versions I've ever heard. Jerry refuses to end it and goes the extra measure. To no avail, the crowd yells for "Dark Star" between songs. While hot enough to please, the "Truckin'" from this show isn't as hot as the version from 11/5/70. And on this evening the band goes straight into "Drums" rather than creating the seamless transition into the "Other One" theme as was the case on 11/5. The drum solo on this evening, however, is far better developed. The crowd listens attentively as Billy brings the energy way down, playing many different rhythms for quite some time and then raising the energy way up again.

Though not as "heavy" as the rendition on 6/24/70 this "Attics" is, again, one of the soulful highlights of the entire Capitol Theater series in 1970. "King Bee" is forgettable. "Good Lovin'" is highly energized but doesn't go to the same magical places as some of the other versions from this run.

JOHN R. DWORK WITH KIPP ARMSTRONG

## 11/8/70
### Capitol Theater, Port Chester, New York

**Acoustic Set:** Dire Wolf, I Know You Rider, Dark Hollow, Rosalie McFall, El Paso, Operator, Ripple, Friend of the Devil, Wake Up, Little Susie, Uncle John's Band
**Electric Set:** Morning Dew, Me and My Uncle, Mystery Train > My Babe, //Around and Around, New Orleans > Searchin', It's All Over Now, Baby Blue, Casey Jones, //Truckin' > Dark Star > Main Ten Jam > Dancin' in the //Streets, Not Fade Away > Goin' Down the Road Feelin' Bad// > Not Fade Away Reprise > Good Lovin'

**1. Source:** AUD, **Quality:** B/B– (Marty tended to stop the deck between songs. As a result, the beginnings of "El Paso," "Operator," "Morning Dew," "Around and Around," and "Truckin'" are missing. There is a brief but serious warble in "Baby Blue," and some, but not all, copies of "Morning Dew" come in once the song is in progress), **Length:** 3:10, **Taper:** Marty Weinberg, Uher 7-inch open reel deck, **Genealogy:** MR > DAT
**2. Source:** AUD, **Quality:** B, **Length:** 0:45 (unknown how much of this source exists as it has been combined with Marty's tapes. We only know that the acoustic set

is from a different recording because there is none of the same audience commentary that exists on Marty's tape.)

**Highlights:** The whole show

**Comments:** The tapes recorded by the legendary Marty contain small cuts at the onset of numerous songs, as though he were trying to conserve tape. None, however, miss more than a few notes. Some copies have a small glitch in "Dire Wolf."

While the energy level on 11/6 easily equals and maybe even surpasses that of this evening's performance, 11/8 has long been thought of by many Deadheads as being the more noteworthy show because of its unusual set list and superlative second-set jam.

Things get going with yet another fine acoustic set, which is notable for the last-ever performance of "Operator." There's an amusing moment in the interlude between "Dark Hollow" and "Rosalie McFall" during which Bobby tells the audience about Godzilla's ability to breathe radioactive fire, to which one can hear a member of the audience reply, "Have him join the band!"

This show really begins to get interesting when Jerry leads his fellow cohorts through the only versions of "Mystery Train" and "My Babe" they ever played. While very gentle, "Mystery Train" is also very together for a first-time performance, as though they practiced this a good deal before breaking it out. (Or this may simply be a testament to how tight the band was in those days.) "Mystery Train" leads into "My Babe" so smoothly you'd think they'd have been doing this segue for years.

This first-ever performance of "Around and Around" more closely resembles the classic sixties delivery by the Rolling Stones than any other version I've heard the Dead deliver. When the tape comes in, several seconds into the song, we find the whole band going nuts behind Bobby, who is screaming his lungs out as though the song were ending! The band doesn't stretch out with a jam, but the energy is so explosive it doesn't much matter.

Obviously in a party mood, Bobby leads the band through yet another barn burner—the only performance ever by the Dead of the old classic rocker "New Orleans." Why Bobby dropped this from his repertoire I'll never know; it's one of the best high-energy tunes I've ever heard him do. This segues effortlessly into Pigpen singing "Searchin'," the Leiber and Stoller tune first made popular by the Coasters. The band continues to deliver a spirited and exciting sermon with strong readings of "Baby Blue," "Casey Jones," and "Truckin'."

As if this wasn't already a sweet enough show, we are treated to yet another thoroughly magnificent "Dark Star." This reading was one of the early one-verse-only "Dark Star"s, a sign of things to come. After a very confident exploratory opening passage, Mickey plays the theme to "Dark Star" on the glockenspiel as an intro to the verse. This leads immediately into feedback. Suddenly, a toy duck quacks—the audience laughs. A human voice cries out, *something* hisses, a gong trembles. Someone lets rip a bloodcurdling scream, cymbals crash, more feedback moans and cries. Mickey plays in the theme to "Saint Stephen" on the glockenspiel. And then the band returns from atonal madness to the final recitation of the "Main Ten Jam." Stunning!

This evolves into a breathtaking melodic theme jam very much in the "Dark Star" vein. Bobby, Phil, and Jerry take turns presenting riffs that subtly change the direction of the whole. Phil makes a major suggestion, Billy hears it and shifts tempo, and the whole band gets the hint. They quiet down for just a second, and then burst into "Dancin' in the Streets." *Very* sweet!

Most unfortunately Marty's tape cuts during "Dancin'," and the balcony tape of the rest of the show, which many folks have tagged on after this cut, features as much audience clapping in the mix as anything else. This makes it a bit of a challenge to fully enjoy the obviously marvelous instrumental interplay. Years later, when Harvey Lubar tracked down Marty's original tapes from these shows, the final reel was missing, so while low-gen DATS of this show do circulate, the final segment from mid-"Dancin'" on is only available from copies made before digital technology. Therefore, when the "Dancin'" resumes it's usually not of the same quality of what precedes it.

The Dead drive this monster show home with a powerful rock 'n' roll medley. "Not Fade Away" starts as usual, red hot. Surprisingly, this performance of "Goin' Down the Road" is mellow, so much so that it almost serves as Jerry's prefinale slow song: another sign of things to come, as this song lost most of its energy for the first half of 1971 until Jerry revitalized it in the fall when Keith came on board. Jerry also sings a different verse: "My momma told me, son don't go down there."

With this sleepy digression disposed of, the band revs it up again with a two-song home run to triumphantly end one of the Dead's all-time highest-energy runs of their entire career. I would highly advise all collectors who have become used to the pristine quality of soundboard recordings—of which there are now so many—to make the investment and obtain these audience recordings. While I, like many of you, vastly prefer being "inside" the Dead's sound system, these tapes convey a sense of excitement that soundboard tapes cannot match. I will fondly revisit these tapes, warts and all, for the rest of my life. I hope you will too.

JOHN R. DWORK WITH KIPP ARMSTRONG

---

### ❦ 11/9/70 ❦
### Action House, Island Park, New York

Attics of My Life, Mama Tried, Walking the Dog, Minglewood Blues, Morning Dew, Deep Elem Blues

---

**Source:** AUD, **Quality:** D+/C+, **Length:** 0:40

**Highlights:** Attics of My Life, Morning Dew, Deep Elem Blues

**Comments:** The sound fluctuates; "Attics," "Dew," and "Deep Elem" are a cut above the other songs, which sound pretty poor.

"Attics" is surprisingly well sung, slow, deliberate, and full of endearing harmonies. The crowd is respectfully quiet, too. Weir screams his bloody head off on every line of "Minglewood." "Morning Dew" is exceptional in every sense: the mid-jam is unexplosive but instead tender and very carefully rendered; Lesh plays his trademark wiggling bass runs to perfection; and the climax rides gracefully to a precise peak behind the intertwining strumming of Weir and Garcia.

"Deep Elem" is also a gem. Garcia's bluegrass roots sprout from his mouth with some goofy, hillbilly singing. The instrumental break is unusually long as everyone chips in some hot licks.

MICHAEL M. GETZ

---

### ❦ 11/11/70 ❦
### 46th St. Rock Palace, Brooklyn, New York

**First Set:** Casey Jones, Me and My Uncle, Cold Rain and Snow, China Cat Sunflower > I Know You Rider, Big Railroad Blues, Mama Tried, It Hurts Me Too, Cryptical Envelopment > Drums > The Other One > Cryptical Envelopment > Sugar Magnolia, Hard to Handle, Truckin'

**Second Set:** Good Lovin' > Drums > Jam > La Bamba, Jam > Good Lovin', Cumberland Blues, Goin' Down the Road Feelin' Bad*, John's Other†, ///(unknown)†, //Around and Around†, (unknown blues song)†, Not Fade Away† > Hey Bo Diddley† > Jam† > Ja//m† > (unknown)†

* with Jack Casady
† with Casady, Jorma Kaukonen, and Papa John Creach

---

**Source:** AUD, **Quality:** B–, **Length:** 2:50, **Taper:** Mike Tannenbaum

**Highlights:** Not Fade Away and the jams!

This show was originally booked for November 26th according to the ticket stub. Mike Tannenbaum was the taper, and he probably taped from his 5th row center seats. This fine show never saw the light of day until December 1996 when an old friend of his, Kevin Ryan, wrote me a letter.

The tapes cut out after each song with the familiar "zipping" sound made by a reel to reel machine. The "Drum" jam coming out of "Cryptical" is surprisingly good as is Jerry's lead from "Drums" back into "The Other One." "Hard to Handle" is great and includes a "Saint Stephen Jam." Before "Truckin'" someone in the crowd yells out, "Play 'Lovelight'." Our intrepid taper replies, "Play whatever the hell you want."

A logical set break would come after "Truckin'," but the tapes reveal little with all the presong banter cut out. "Good Lovin'" starts off with a drum duet of unknown length since the tape cuts in and out until the guitars kick in. What is this, "La Bamba"? Out of "Good Lovin'" comes a short "La Bamba" jam with a few muttered

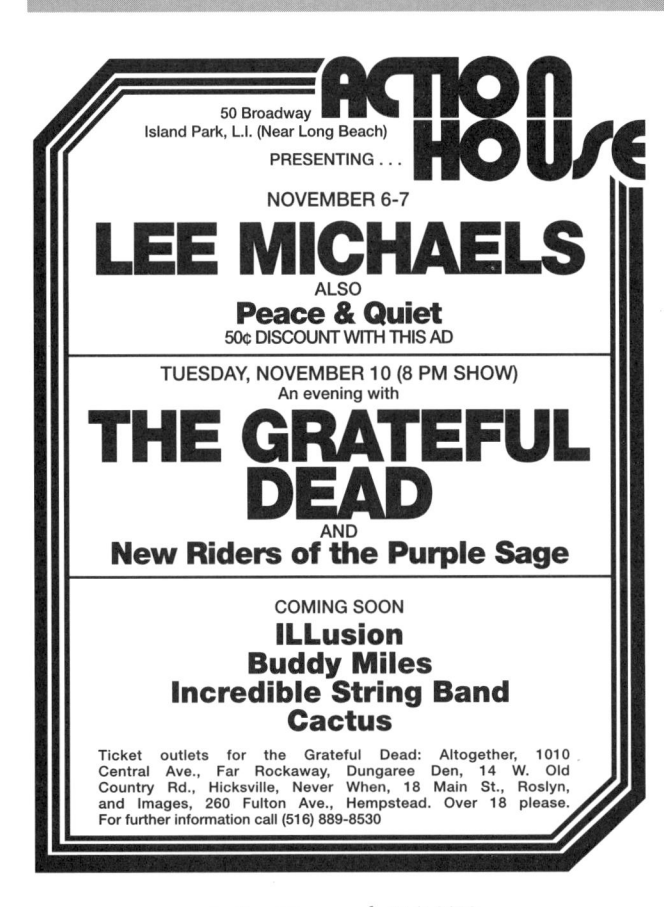

*Action House ad, 11/10/70*

lyrics. It lasts about thirty seconds but still sparks the crowd. This is the earliest known attempt at "La Bamba" and predates what we thought was the first version in 1987. What other treasures are yet undiscovered?

"Goin' Down the Road Feelin' Bad" starts off quiet and slow. All previous versions of "Goin' Down the Road" came out of "Not Fade Away" in the fury of the jam, but this version is allowed to build from the ground up. A few minutes into "Goin' Down the Road" the crowd lets out a yell as Jack Casady of the Jefferson Airplane joins the band. You can hear the crowd calling out "Jefferson Airplane" and "Casady." Jorma Kaukonen may be in the mix too but it is very hard to tell from this audience tape. Jerry later introduces Jack Casady and Jorma Kaukonen and clearly Papa John Creach is on stage as the band launches into "John's Other."

The highlight of the whole night is the "Not Fade Away" and ensuing jams. Blazing new trails of electric wonder, San Francisco's finest show a rowdy New York crowd what it means to rock!

ERIC DOHERTY

## 11/16/70
### Fillmore East, New York, New York

//Good Lovin'*

* with Jorma Kaukonen on guitar

**Source:** SBD, **Quality:** C–, **Length:** 0:10

Let me say first here that I normally find Jorma Kaukonen's playing most interesting and creative. However, this tape cuts in to find Jorma screeching inside a net the Dead have provided for him. Then he stops. A Lesh-led point develops to Garcia's counterpoint. Jorma steps back in with more abrasive, dentist-chair leads. Well, not "leads": stings. It's as if he's expressing himself while an angry hornet's nest is trapped inside his underpants. Lesh and Garcia back off, hold the rhythm, and wait for it all to end. When Jorma lets up, they quickly close the net, reprise "Good Lovin'," and rush for their aspirin bottles.

MICHAEL M. GETZ

## 11/20/70
### The Palestra, Rochester, New York

**Set 2:** Truckin' > Drums// > //The Other One > Saint// Stephen > Not Fade Away > Goin' Down the Road Feelin' Bad > Not Fade Away Reprise > King Bee, Casey Jones
**Set 3:** Around and Around*, Jam* > It's All Over Now*, Jam* > Darlin' Corey* > Jam*

* with Jorma Kaukonen on guitar

**Source:** AUD, **Quality:** D+, **Length:** 1:30, **Genealogy:** MR > RR > DAT
**Highlights:** King Bee, third set with Jorma Kaukonen

This is a fun performance that suffers greatly both from the mediocre quality in which it circulates as well from the nasty cuts on the first side of the tape. This tape starts in the second set with a real bluesy "Truckin'" that leads into "Drums." Next, the tape cuts and we wind up inside "The Other One" not knowing how much time has elapsed. The following songs on this side are well played and are full of that 1970 energy. The highlight of this set is the "King Bee" that builds out of a hot, hot, hot "Not Fade Away." This version features a prowling Pigpen putting his own salty spin on this blues classic, with nice backup, particularly from Garcia. After "Casey Jones," Jerry tells the crowd that the band will return shortly. For the abbreviated third set, the band is joined by the Jefferson Airplane's Jorma Kaukonen. The songs that he plays on are more fun than anything, especially the rockin' "Around," giving the band a chance to relive the carefree atmosphere of Northern California before the hippie tour buses. What is interesting about Jorma's performance are the jams that lead in and out of their songs. In each jam the players formulate a theme, even hints of "Darkness Jam," and weave in and out of it at will, usually a blues-centered jam. It is obvious that the Dead appreciate the new blood, and the interplay among the musicians is interesting. Overall, I recommend this tape because of the set list and the guest appearance; it's a must-have for every serious collector.

MICHAEL PARRISH

### 11/21/70
#### Sargent Gym, Boston University, Boston, Massachusetts

**Set List:** Cryptical Envelopment* > Drums > The Other One* > Cryptical Envelopment* > Cosmic Charlie*

* supposedly with Ned Lagin

**Source:** SBD?, **Quality:** B+, **Length:** 0:25
**Highlights:** The entire show
**Comments:** *DeadBase* lists a "Drums" before "The Other One," but there isn't one.

This was the only show at which Ned Lagin played with the Dead before his regular Seastones performances (also known as "Phil and Ned," or "Warp Ten") and occasional onstage collaborations in 1974 and his final appearance with them at Kezar Stadium in 1975. It is sad to report, therefore, that he is at no point audible on the tape (we assume he was playing keyboards, as usual). However, maybe it was his presence that inspired the Dead to play with a particular diligence and attention to detail on this night. Garcia is in great voice as he takes his time on the introductory "Cryptical." "The Other One" erupts straight out of this with a long and very unusual flowing jam from Jerry over Phil's strong bass underpinning. Even more unusually, the same jam continues, as energetic and mellifluous as ever, after the first verse. There is none of the typical frenzied abandon about the playing here, although the energy levels are never in doubt. After "Cryptical" reappears, there is a long and gentle descent to take us into a "Cosmic Charlie" whose introduction sounds more than ever like that of the Beatles' "Revolution," before its trademark rolling beat and hypnotic vocals take over. A very fine show, curious for its sense of restraint in a suite of songs notable for their impetuous fury elsewhere in this year, as well as for its inaudible guest.

JAMES SWIFT

### 11/21/70
#### WBCN Studios, Boston, Massachusetts

Jam*, El Paso, Big River, I Know You Rider, Instrumental, Dark Hollow, Angie, Let Me In 83968

* Acoustic

**Source:** FM-SBD, **Quality:** B, **Length:** 0:35, **Genealogy:** FM > C
**Personnel:** Duane Allman, Gregg Allman, Jerry Garcia, Ron McKernan, and Bob Weir
**Highlights:** The complete performance

This late-night acoustic studio jam, although playful and full of amusing banter, is fairly uneventful and poorly mixed. Disappointingly absent are any of Duane's trademark slide licks. Fatigue from the Grateful Dead performance earlier in the evening is painfully apparent, especially from a vocal standpoint. Although the narration lists Garcia, McKernan, and Weir as being present, Pigpen is apparently only present as a spectator. As well, the Allmans seemingly only perform on the final two selections, having arrived at the studio sans instruments. Perhaps this was initially a social visit that transpired into a brief impromptu jam.

Although obviously tired, the boys boldly stomp

through a traditional acoustic set, none of which is poorly performed, but it's slightly lacking in the energy department. Notable is Garcia's use of the "Loser" opening lick on the intro to "Big River," which he good-naturedly stumbles on while singing. The instrumental is filled with impressive country licks from Garcia, but is hampered by a continuous fade-in/fade-out in the mix. Of course, Weir's readings on "Dark Hollow" and the rare "Let Me In 83968" ring with authenticity. While on paper it would certainly be considered a highlight, Duane's instrumental, "Angie," is a trifle rushed. Nonetheless, despite the disappointments of this performance, the intersong banter and rarity make this tape worth seeking out.

BRIAN DYKE

---

### 11/23/70

**Anderson Theater, New York, New York**

Casey Jones, //Friend of the Devil, Cold Rain and Snow, King Bee, //I Know You Rider, //Hard to Handle*, Big Railroad Blues, Mama Tried, Not Fade Away* > Goin' Down the Road Feelin' Bad[†] > Not Fade Away Reprise[†], Truckin' > Jam > The Other One[‡], Uncle John's Band[‡]

* with Steve Winwood
[†] with Winwood and Chris Wood
[‡] with Ramblin' Jack Elliot on harp

---

**1. Source:** SBD, **Quality:** B+, **Length:** 1:30, **Genealogy:** MR > RR > PCM > DAT

**2. Source:** SBD-FM (GDH), **Quality:** A, **Length:** 1:30

**Highlights:** Big Railroad Blues, Truckin', The Other One, Uncle John's Band.

Versions of this legendary Hell's Angels benefit gig have been circulating on tape, vinyl, and CD for years, but now a crystal-clear mix has surfaced, albeit one that has more than a few potentially irritating edits. Overall, it's the Dead plus a few pals having a good time, playing music that doesn't quite scale the heights but nevertheless reaches enough of the right places to guarantee a whale/wail of a time. The mix subtly shifts around in a rather organic fashion and changes the instrumental focus, something that is rather enjoyable. The contributions of the others (definitely Steve Winwood, probably Chris Wood, and Ramblin' Jack Elliot), with the exception of Winwood's organ, hardly push the Dead into new possibilities, let alone steal the limelight, but as party music goes, this set is rather fine and in this nice 'n' clean edition is worth checking.

The first forty-five minutes are a mixture of raucous good-time music making and tantalizing fragments. After a sparky "Casey Jones," "Friend of the Devil" fades in just in time for Jerry to sing a chorus before his solo, after a strong "Cold Rain and Snow" and a "King Bee" made almost scary by Pigpen's lascivious vocal delivery. The following pair of songs are presented in severely truncated form, but at least you get the whole of "I Know You Rider" because the music fades in right at the climax of a jam presumably following "China Cat Sunflower." Hearing this taken out of its normal context does make you listen afresh as it erupts from the speakers fully formed. The fact that "Hard to Handle" is cut down to around four minutes is extremely frustrating, especially as it features some cool jazz Hammond organ playing by Steve Winwood. In fact, everyone seems up for this one, which makes its fragmentation even more galling. "Big Railroad Blues" is taken at quite a lick and who cares that it lacks a little light 'n' shade; it's a glorious thrash-along, with Mickey's drumming verging on the unhinged, a blues harp that will not stop wailing, and Garcia dragging up an extra verse from somewhere to hammer home the despairing vibe of the lyrics.

Once again "Not Fade Away" is used as a vehicle for group improvisation with guests, not that any of 'em get to say much. Winwood shines on an all-too-brief solo spot that has him dissecting arrhythmic jazz/blues lines before Garcia elbows him back into the shadows. If that really is Chris Wood singing on this, er—why? Maybe he left his sax and flute on the bus, but his singing here is perfunctory and mercifully brief, kept to the main theme with a minute or so of scat singing in the middle. Overall, you've heard better versions, but the transition into "Goin' Down the Road Feelin' Bad" is a joy to hear and throughout the drummers sneak forward in the mix, maybe thinking that we won't notice until their pounding sends stuff cascading from our shelves.

"Truckin'" develops into a tasty jam with Billy, Mickey, and Phil playing a round of "Blow the Speakers"; it's this interplay that has largely been indistinct on previous editions of this show, and when he rises up in the mix occasionally Phil really does have a wonderful sound here. "The Other One" features more crunchy drum 'n' bass team work and a great, if rather brief, central jam that, rather than space out, tends to drift in a most appealing fashion. Then a hidden surprise: listen carefully and you'll catch Ramblin' Jack Elliot riffing along on harp at the end. A few moments' respite and the guys wrap it all up with undoubtedly the most sublime moments of the whole show, a truly gorgeous "Uncle John's Band" that draws you in with an atypical intro, again featuring Ramblin' Jack blowing wistful, lyrical harp, rather in the style of Will Scarlet. The performance of this number is as good as any I've heard, especially from 1970, and following the outstanding jam at the end comes some deliciously fragile vocal harmonies that must have moved all the bikers in the house to tears. Well, maybe not.

PAUL BODENHAM

## 11/28/70
### Unknown Location, Chicago, Illinois
**Interview:** Jerry Garcia, Phil Lesh, Bob Weir

**Source:** FM, **Quality:** C, **Length:** 0:20

**Comments:** Interview conducted by John Ryan for "The Underground News."

Following a general discussion of the New Riders of the Purple Sage and a short tale of Garcia and Weir's first encounter, the interviewer boldly inquires about the political climate regarding the Black Panthers and the Hell's Angel's, to which the interviewees are understandably evasive. After more pressing about political topics with nil results, the interviewer then returns to general questions regarding the New Riders.

BRIAN DYKE

## 11/29/70
### The Club Agora, Columbus, Ohio

**Set 1:** Don't Ease Me In, Cumberland Blues, Beat It on Down the Line, Next Time You See Me, Morning// Dew, Brokedown Palace, Me and Bobby McGee, Truckin' > Drums > The Other One > Me and My Uncle, Casey Jones
**Set 2:** Dire Wolf, Good Lovin' > Sugar Magnolia, Not Fade Away > Goin' Down the Road Feelin' Bad// > //Not Fade Away Reprise//

**Source:** AUD, **Quality:** C, **Length:** 2:15
**Highlights:** Brokedown Palace, Drums > The Other One > Me and My Uncle, Good Lovin'

This audience recording, which has been available for years, is a fairly decent show to have. The quality is fair, the levels are where they should be, and the performance is good for the most part. "Don't Ease Me In," "Cumberland Blues," "Beat It on Down the Line," "Next Time You See Me," and "Morning Dew" are all standard fare—nothing amazing here.

Continuing the tranquil feeling with one of my favorite Jerry ballads, they play the still-young "Brokedown Palace." The supporting harmonies, combined with Jerry's lyrical solo, remind me of how great "Brokedown Palace" was as an encore. This debut performance of "Bobby McGee" finds Bobby Weir's voice sounding surprisingly full and seemingly well practiced. This version unfortunately lacks the emotional power that some of the later versions provide.

Side 2 starts with a young and energized "Truckin'." With plenty of Pigpen and Phil in the mix, the full audio range is covered. Jerry's confident playing has an aggressive presence, darting between Bobby's enthusiastic lyrics and Phil's punctuated bass lines. After "Truckin'," Bill and Mickey venture out on safari for a wild and dangerous tour of "Drums." With blistering polyrhythms and bombastic hits exploding from their kits, they shower the audience with musical shrapnel. Completely locked in and playing off each other, they bring the audience to a heightened rhythmic climax confirmed by yelps and squeals of delight. They wind down, transforming and rolling into an intensely abstract "The Other One." Jerry's sharp playing is interspersed with

Bobby's aggressive lyrics. Pigpen wails away in the background, filling out the musical backdrop. They jam for a while, leading into a slower section and then twist into a spacey midsection jam. The main groove, which is invisible, gets passed around with everyone getting a chance to hint at it. Everyone meets back at the main theme to conclude the song. Transitioning into "Me and My Uncle," usually which might on first thought be considered a poor song to segue into from such an intense jam, is actually a superb choice here. This version has almost the same level of intensity as "The Other One"; it's just wrapped up in a different package. The playing is hot all the way through, leaving the crowd satisfied. A simple and spirited "Casey Jones" nicely closes out the first set.

"Good Lovin'" starts out with Pig already way into full effect. He furnishes a long and well-developed rap, which is temporarily interrupted by the tape switch. Pig brings his usual no-holds-barred, spontaneously inventive, comical storytelling prowess to this particular version. Pig raps away, with Jerry replying back through his musical commentary. "Good Lovin'," apparently starting to meander, is almost immediately yanked back on course as Phil delivers a quick but great bass solo. The ending finds the crowd absolutely delighted.

"Not Fade Away" starts without its usual punch. The drums have seemingly lost a little of their presence in the mix. The tape sounds muffled, as if someone is standing in front of the microphone or it's being hidden (to avoid detection?). The transition into "Goin' Down the Road" starts smoothly, but the tape cuts, providing an uneasy silence for almost three seconds. The levels reappear, with apparently the majority of the song missing. The tape picks up toward the end of "Not Fade Away," which unfortunately cuts.

COREY SANDERSON

## 11/70
### Wally Heider's Studio C, San Francisco, California

**Studio Sessions:** Song With No Words[7], Laughing[4]//, Laughing[4], Song With No Words[7], Song With No Words[7], Tamalpais High[3], Tamalpais High[3], Orleans[8]//, Orleans[8], Orleans[8], Cowboy Movie[2], Cowboy Movie[2]//, Cowboy Movie[2], Cowboy Movie[2]//, Tamalpais High[3], What Are Their Names[5], Song With No Words[7], Orleans[8], I'd Swear There Was Somebody Here[8], Music Is Love[1]//, Laughing[4], Laughing[4], Traction in the Rain[6]//, Traction in the Rain[6], Traction in the Rain[6], I'd Swear There Was Somebody Here[8], I'd Swear There Was Somebody Here[8], Music Is Love[1], Music Is Love[1], The Wall Song[9], Kids and Dogs[10], Cowboy Movie Jam[11], Coast Road[12]

[1] David Crosby, Graham Nash, Neil Young
[2] David Crosby, Jerry Garcia, Mickey Hart, Bill Kreutzmann, Phil Lesh
[3] David Crosby, Jerry Garcia, Jorma Kaukonen, Bill Kreutzmann, Phil Lesh
[4] David Crosby, Jerry Garcia, Bill Kreutzmann, Phil Lesh, Joni Mitchell
[5] David Crosby, David Freiberg, Jerry Garcia, Paul Kantner, Bill Kreutzmann, Phil Lesh, Graham Nash, Joni Mitchell, Grace Slick, Neil Young
[6] Laura Allan, David Crosby, Graham Nash
[7] David Crosby, Jerry Garcia, Jorma Kaukonen, Graham Nash, Greg Rollie, Michael Shrieve
[8] David Crosby
[9] David Crosby, Jerry Garcia, Bill Kreutzmann, Phil Lesh, Graham Nash
[10] David Crosby, Jerry Garcia
[11] David Crosby, Jerry Garcia, Jorma Kaukonen, Bill Kreutzmann, Phil Lesh, Neil Young
[12] Laura Allan, David Crosby

**Source:** SBD, **Quality:** A, **Length:** 2:30
**Highlights:** The Wall Song, Kids and Dogs, Cowboy Movie Jam, Coast Road
**Comments:** Commonly traded soundboards are in wide circulation. "Kids and Dogs" appeared on *Grate-*

*ful Dead Hour* 319. "Cowboy Movie Jam" appeared on the *Deadhead Hour* on August 25, 1996, on KFOG. These tapes often circulate accompanying the January 1971 "Planet Earth Rock 'n' Roll Orchestra" tape. "The Wall Song" is actually an outtake from the LP *Graham Nash/David Crosby*, believed to have been recorded on November 11, 1971. Personnel listings derived from Stephen Barncard's notes, and refer to LP renditions. Personnel listings have not been deduced for the missing instrumental or vocal tracks that appear on the tape. Special thanks to Steve Silberman for providing assistance with tape data.

Although this tape often appears labeled as "If I Could Only Remember My Name Outtakes," the bulk of the material is actually derived from the identical tracks as the LP in rough and vastly inferior mix. Virtually every imaginable approach is documented here, with some sections completely absent, and several ranges of prominence in between. One has to wonder if this tape is actually just a joke conjured up by a bored engineer.

The tape begins with a bare version of "Song With No Words," containing only the vocals accompanied by acoustic guitar. Following are two horrifically inappropriate takes of "Laughing," one of which breaks off prematurely, the other lacking both the lead vocal track and the bulk of Garcia's illustrious pedal steel. An additional two takes of "Song With No Words" follow, the first containing a buried Kaukonen and accentuated Rollie, the second containing prominent Kaukonen and diminished Rollie. Similarly, the subsequent two takes of "Tamalpais High" are missing key instrumental passages, one of Kaukonen and one of Garcia. The three takes of "Orleans" are, in order, the intro only, the complete take minus one guitar track, and a take virtually identical to the version that appeared on the LP.

The following four takes of "Cowboy Movie" are very possibly two loops of the same pair of takes, the first missing Garcia's right channel lead, the second missing Garcia's left channel lead.

Following the first tape flip, the mix approach improves slightly on a few tracks, with a "Tamalpais High" that, though instrumental, is well blended from each instrumental perspective. "What Are Their Names," also instrumental, is mixed more effectively than the LP version, with bolder guitar passages and hollower vocals, giving the song a whispery, eerier feel. "Orleans" also contains a more hollow vocal approach, but the absence of the upper register fingerpicking accompaniment hampers the otherwise suitable mix. Nearly as horrific as the preceding takes that lack Garcia's pedal steel are the next two takes of "Laughing," the first missing Garcia's pedal steel until the outro, the second missing Crosby's electric tracks completely, with Lesh barely audible. The concluding takes of "Traction in the Rain" and "Music Is Love" are all disappointingly lacking of vocal, string, and percussion passages. And finally, who really knows what the difference is on *any* of the takes of "*I'd Swear There Was Somebody Here*"? There may be a longer echo, there may be a shorter delay, but by now, who's paying attention?

Appearing near the end of the tape is "The Wall Song," which appeared on the 1972 LP *Graham Nash/David Crosby*. Backed by Garcia, Kreutzmann, and Lesh, the lads give a solid and uncharacteristically focused approach on this outtake, which Crosby sings solo. Although the verse interpretation is not as polished as the album version, the outro contains a magnificent Garcia solo that weaves masterfully between the rhythm of Kreutzmann and Lesh, unlike the LP version which fades immediately upon the completion of the final verse.

Widely regarded as the one that got away, "Kids and Dogs" is perhaps the finest moment between Crosby and Garcia. Affectionately referred to as the result of Bong Telepathy, the piece begins with two distinctly different passages from each instrumentalist, with Crosby strumming obscure modal phrases against Garcia's sweetly divine lead lines. After a delightful meandering, the guitarists settle into the melody, hummed beautifully and illustriously by Crosby. The conversation that emerges is intuitive and exploratory, with Crosby retaining the chord melodies as Garcia launches from the structure into a whirling dance of notes. The overdub is utter perfection, as the solo switches seamlessly from acoustic Garcia to electric Garcia and back to acoustic Garcia, dripping honey from each note. Easing back into the melody, the guitarists pluck gently bright and summery colors into the conclusion.

The tape continues with "Cowboy Movie Jam." Although there are faint traces of vocals in the background, they're overshadowed by the whopping four guitars that appear. With rock-solid support from Kreutzmann and Lesh on rhythm, the guitarists patiently, and at some points hesitantly, take turns contributing licks. At the onset, each statement is curt and to the point, gradually building into a four-way conversation of long inquisitions and simplistic responses. Unfortunately, just as the passage appears to take off with a comical series of delayed rhythm riffs from Neil Young, the tape fades.

The concluding "Coast Road," an Allan-Crosby duet, begins with a beautifully mystical acoustic passage, divine in content and deeply rich in ambiance. The vocals contain only a trace of awkwardness, overshadowed by the delicately gentle accompaniment. Slowly fading to near silence, Crosby picks in lush colors, while Allan's accompaniment sweeps through the background with transparent tranquillity.

MICHAEL PARRISH

---

### 12/12/70
#### Sonoma State College, Sonoma, California

**Set List:** Me and My Uncle, Truckin', Brokedown Palace, Hard to Handle, Mama Tried, China Cat Sunflower > I Know You Rider, Not Fade Away > Goin' Down the Road Feelin' Bad > Darkness, Darkness Jam > Saint Stephen Jam > Not Fade Away Reprise, Good Lovin' > Uncle John's Band

**Source:** SBD, **Quality:** A–, **Length:** 1:30
**Highlights:** Brokedown Palace, Darkness, Darkness Jam > Saint Stephen Jam > Not Fade Away

---

This show begins in a relatively routine manner but closes with a couple of extended, surprising improvisations on relatively familiar material. The early part of the set features a nice "Brokedown Palace," but the first corker is what starts out as a standard "Not Fade Away" > "Goin' Down the Road." The jam at the end of the second tune winds slowly and unquestionably into an instrumental version of "Darkness, Darkness," which was an FM hit at the time for the Dead's Marin County neighbors, the Youngbloods. Garcia's emotive playing of the vocal melody is exquisite, and leads into a volatile, unmistakable version of the introductory instrumental riffs from "Saint Stephen" before punting on the intro to the song and instead heading back into a full-bore reprise of "Not Fade Away," with Weir screaming his lungs out. A longish "Good Lovin'" with a relatively insubstantial Pigpen rap rolls smoothly into a strong "Uncle John's Band" closer.

MICHAEL PARRISH

## The Crosby-Garcia Collaborations

Late 1970 and early 1971 were the heyday of the Planet Rock and Roll Orchestra, a loose aggregation of members of the Dead; The Airplane; Quicksilver; and Crosby, Stills, Nash, and Young that logged an amazing amount of studio time jamming together and produced a few classic recordings like the first Crosby solo album, *If Only I Could Remember My Name,* and Paul Kantner's *Blows Against the Empire*. For a week or two at the end of 1970, one subset of this group formed a loose performing entity consisting of Garcia, Crosby, Lesh, and Hart. This aggregation—which had several names, including Jerry and the Jets and David and the Dorks—played out a few times, including the Matrix show discussed here and the one show I was lucky enough to catch, on December 21, at San Rafael's Pepperland. That show, billed as an Acoustic Dead show, was a complete surprise to most of the audience, particularly since Crosby, Stills, Nash, and Young, then at the zenith of their popularity, were much bigger stars than Garcia and the hometown team. Unlike many impromptu jamming aggregations of the era, this was a serious, although regrettably short-lived group that managed some memorable music during their week or so together, fortunately captured on these two tapes.

*Jerry Garcia and David Crosby, 12/21/70* (photo credit: Michael Parrish)

## 12/??/70 (Probably 12/15, afternoon)

**The Matrix, San Francisco, California**
**David Crosby, Jerry Garcia, Phil Lesh, Mickey Hart**

**Rehearsal:** Alabama Bound, Eight Miles High (2×), Cowboy Movie (4×), Wall Song, Bertha (3×), Bird Song

**Source:** SBD, **Quality:** A–, **Length:** 0:45
**Highlights:** Bertha, Bird Song

This rehearsal tape reveals the musicians taking first crack at some later classic material, and road-testing and jettisoning the Byrds' hit "Eight Miles High," which the Dead musicians never seemed to get a handle on. Notable are what seem to be the first attempts at "Bird Song" and (in a very different meter) "Bertha." It is fun to hear Crosby sing harmony on "Bertha" and to have Garcia chime in behind David on "Cowboy Movie," which they run through repeatedly.

BRIAN DYKE

## 12/15/70

**The Matrix, San Francisco, California**
**David Crosby, Jerry Garcia, Phil Lesh, Mickey Hart**

Drop Down Mama, Cowboy Movie, Triad, Wall Song, Bertha, Deep Elem Blues, Motherless Children, Laughing

**Source:** SBD, **Quality:** B+, **Length:** 1:00
**Highlights:** Bertha, Cowboy Movie, Wall Song

The Matrix show is a joy, with the musicians running through energized versions of newly rehearsed material like "Cowboy Movie," "Bertha," and "Laughing." Garcia and Crosby also took turns on old blues material: Jerry brought out "Deep Elem Blues" and Crosby sang "Alabama Bound," "Drop Down Mama," and "Motherless Children." Another rarity for the time was Crosby's "Triad," which was best known at the time from the Airplane's version on *Crown of Creation*—he had yet to record it, or perform it live with Stills, Nash, and Young. This group could also jam ferociously; check out the interplay among Garcia, Lesh, and Crosby's electric 12-string on "Cowboy Movie" and "Wall Song."

BRIAN DYKE

## 12/23/70

**Winterland Arena, San Francisco, California**
**Benefit for the Montessori School and Bear**

Hard to Handle, Candyman, Me and My Uncle, Cold Rain and Snow

**Source:** SBD, **Quality:** A, **Length:** 0:25, **Genealogy:** MR > C > DAT
**Highlights:** Candyman, Cold Rain and Snow

This superb-sounding, and consistently well-performed, chunk of one of the Dead's many benefits emerged a couple of years ago. On "Hard to Handle," Phil and the drummers lock midsong into a meaty, extended groove. A sweet "Candyman" follows, with delicately elegant Garcia-Lesh interplay, followed in turn by a rote "Me and My Uncle." "Cold Rain and Snow" is appropriately chunky and lumbering. The tape, which ends with Lesh cranking out the bass line from the chorus of "Saint Stephen," is a superb example of how well the Dead executed even the most basic material on a good night during late 1970.

MICHAEL PARRISH

## 12/26/70
### Legion Stadium, El Monte, California

**Set 1:** Cold Rain and Snow, Mama Tried, Frozen Logger, Easy Wind, Till the Morning Comes, Truckin', Friend of the Devil, Me and My Uncle, Candyman, Big Railroad Blues, New Minglewood Blues, Black Peter, Beat It on Down the Line, Morning Dew, Casey Jones
**Set 2:** Dire Wolf, China Cat Sunflower > I Know You Rider

**Source:** SBD, **Quality:** A, **Length:** 1:50, **Genealogy:** MR > RR > RR > Beta HF > PCM > DAT
**Highlights:** Easy Wind, Minglewood, Black Peter, Dew
**Comments:** Obviously the second set of this show is incomplete.

It's the day after Christmas and the band is definitely *not* hung over. This is an important period of transition: a month after the release of *American Beauty*. It sees the snappier country-rock-flavored songs of their repertoire that Bob Weir loved highlighted and Weir taking (or being pushed into?) his future place as a major frontman for the band rather than just the amiable space cadet he had been before. The format is getting much closer to the alternating lead vocalist roles that Garcia and Weir took in the future. However, one consequence of this is the unfortunate relegation of Pigpen to singing on only one track, the lengthy and excellent "Easy Wind." Garcia has a fat and raunchy guitar sound and style throughout the show, and he and Weir are structuring their playing together in a focused manner that is a definite departure, particularly evident on the carefully crafted "Morning Dew." There are a few rarities in the show too. The short "Frozen Logger" acts mainly as a vocal tuning for Weir, who is having mike problems. The band play their fifth and last version of "Till The Morning Comes." Also "Easy Wind" (although not exactly uncommon itself at the time, this song was soon inexplicably to be dropped from the repertoire) contains a rare Bob Weir guitar solo. In a perfect juxtaposition of the two guitarists' starkly different styles, Weir kicks things off with his jagged and angular playing, throwing out staccato threads of notes until Garcia plunges in with his fluent and easy soloing. All who advocated Weir taking over as lead guitarist after Garcia died should listen to this one. His future consummate excellence as a rhythm guitarist is starting to show, but if he had ever played lead for three hours straight, I think a high proportion of fans would have been leaving shows with bad headaches! Finally, however, what we have of this show is less truly remarkable in itself than tantalizing as to what they might have done while in such good form in the missing set 2. Despite some excellent soloing and singing, there are no true extended band workouts in what we have—maybe Dick Latvala will oblige us with the rest one day and we'll see what the jams have to offer!

JAMES SWIFT

## 12/27/70
### KPPC Studios, Pasadena, California

**Studio Session:** Silver Threads and Golden Needles, Cold Jordan, I Hear a Voice Callin', Swing Low, Sweet Chariot

**Source:** SBD, **Quality:** B, **Length:** 0:20
**Highlights:** All except Silver Threads and Golden Needles
**Personnel:** John Dawson, Jerry Garcia, David Nelson, and Bob Weir

Although this studio jam may lack the charm characteristic of many other late-1970 performances of these selections, it certainly displays the playful lightheartedness that that these boys are known to exhibit to a tee. Serving mainly as a promotionary vehicle for the Grateful Dead's remaining performances at nearby Legion Stadium, this studio performance was broadcast live on KPPC-FM. Perhaps cognizant of the restrictions of FM radio as well as the conservative climate of the community, the boys wisely choose to begin with a "Silver Threads and Golden Needles" (which comes off rather ragged) before embarking on a triad of delightful gospel selections. Brilliant marketing indeed; after all, what better way to woo new listeners than with a heartfelt "Jordan," a harmonious "I Hear a Voice Callin'," or a heavenly "Swing Low, Sweet Chariot"? While each selection is kept uncharacteristically concise, the interplay is nonetheless impeccable. As well, the intrasong banter is, as usual, hilarious, as the boys playfully mimic and tease each other as well as the host. Before the conclusion, the boys deliver a brief but delicious instrumental coda, blending bluegrass and country turnarounds so masterfully that the host quips, "That was a great wrestling match!"

BRIAN DYKE

### 12/27/70
#### KPPC Studios, Pasadena, California
**Interview:** John "Marmaduke" Dawson, David Nelson, Jerry Garcia, Bob Weir

**Source:** FM, **Quality:** B, **Length:** 1:00

**Highlights:** "'Cause a pedal steel guitar, you know, in 1970, in Palo Alto, is like a Volkswagen in Chicago in 1953 kinda thing. It's very obscure, nobody's heard of one before. You might have seen such a thing wandering around on the streets, but you didn't know quite what it was." (Dawson)

This radio appearance serves mainly to promote the upcoming performances at Legion Stadium, as well as the latest LP material from both the Grateful Dead and the New Riders of the Purple Sage, from which a few tracks are aired. Aside from some hilarious commentary by Dawson on his early encounters with his cohorts, this interview consists of evasive clowning around and playful drivel.

BRIAN DYKE

### 12/28/70
#### Legion Stadium, El Monte, California

**Set 1:** Cold Rain and Snow, Truckin', Hurts Me Too, Me and My Uncle, Beat It on Down the Line, China Cat Sunflower > I Know You Rider, Cryptical Envelopment > Drums > The Other One > Cryptical Reprise > Sugar Magnolia, Casey Jones
**Set 2:** Smokestack Lightning, Big Railroad Blues, Me and Bobby McGee, Deep Elem Blues, Cumberland Blues, Morning Dew > Good Lovin' > Drums > Good Lovin' > Uncle John's Band

**Source:** AUD, **Quality:** B–, **Length:** 2:45, **Genealogy:** MR > PCM > DAT

**Highlights:** The entire second set except Morning Dew

This performance signifies the end of one of the Grateful Dead's strongest years, as well as illustrating several of the stumbling blocks that perhaps were persuasive in their shift to the tighter sound that would emerge just a month later. Beginning with a sluggish rendition of "Cold Rain and Snow," it is immediately evident that the band is suffering from exhaustion. Attempting to kick-start the performance with a premature "Truckin'," the boys barely are able to achieve average status, with an outro that could best be described as sleepy. Of course, the opening is rescued by Pigpen, who soulfully digs into "It Hurts Me Too." The emotional content of this reading overshadows the mediocre musicianship displayed by both Garcia and Pigpen. Once they turn things over to Weir, the momentum gradually increases, ironically, with the following "Me and My Uncle" and "Beat It on Down the Line." Ordinarily considered a highlight, the "China Cat Sunflower" > "I Know You Rider" followed by "Cryptical Envelopment" is extremely uneven. Although the intro of "China" > "Rider" shows great promise, the band gives a lazy execution all the way through without putting much effort into the jam or the verses.

Continuing with "Cryptical," the band struggles through the intro before turning the stage over to the drummers. What begins as a humiliating and sloppy segment of "Drums" suddenly turns the corner at the three-quarter mark when Kreutzmann and Hart miraculously fall into The Groove, settling comfortably in the familiar tribal rhythm that lays the setting for the "Other One" that follows. Through the first verse, this version is solidly performed, albeit lacking in the intense climaxes that are characteristic. A calculating Garcia chooses to wisely insert the appropriate quarter notes to the corresponding intervals, a nice contrast to the blazing sixteenth and thirty-second note runs we're accustomed to. Following a powerful verse from Weir, the jam downshifts and, unfortunately, begins to fall apart almost immediately. Unfocused, the frontmen take turns laying back as the jam disintegrates, and a series of brief on/off passages result. Just as frustration begins to rear its head, the band quickly returns to the main groove, marching promptly back into the verse and the return to "Cryptical," whose finish is executed much more gracefully than its intro. Fading into silence, the band hints momentarily at "Black Peter," only to blast off into an extremely ragged yet hellaciously fun "Sugar Mag." The combination of Garcia's Clapton/Cream wah-wah tone and Weir's obnoxiously hilarious yawping during "Sunshine Daydream" make this one a difficult piece to stay seated during. The set closer of "Casey Jones" is downright explosive, and allotted the most energy of the set.

Returning for the second set, and obviously refreshed, the Dead ignore the audience request for "Morning Dew" and choose instead to deal out a perfect five-card poker hand of selections, beginning with "Smokestack Lightning." Even though none of the tracks could be described as mind-blowing or out of this world in delivery, the selection itself makes up for the execution. "Deep Elem Blues" followed by "Cumberland"? Who could not love this band?

The concluding forty-five minutes of the performance is a mixed bag. After rushing through a "Morning Dew" that is much too fast and nowhere near its usual level, the band turns the stage over to Pigpen, who climaxes the evening with his trademark "Good Lovin'." Heavily laced with testosterone, the rhythm section is given their chance to showcase for a while before the frontmen break in for the jam. Notwithstanding a few shaky spots, this is an extremely focused passage. The thundering drive from Hart, Kreutzmann, and Lesh nicely complements Garcia's blues licks and Weir's double stop-off beats. And Pigpen's ad-libs, as usual, are excellent all around. After several climactic teases, the eruption and finish is executed with an uncharacteristic flamboyance that hints subtly at "La Bamba," a great example of how the transition from masculine to matrimonious can be made over the course of just a few notes. The show-closing "Uncle John's Band" is not unlike any other version from 1970: in other words, perfect. Packed with emotion, harmony, and energy, what a wonderful sendoff to what would be the end of an era.

BRIAN DYKE

---

**12/31/70**

**Winterland Arena,
San Francisco, California**

Dire Wolf, Big Railroad Blues, Cumberland Blues, Cryptical Envelopment > Drums > The Other One > Cryptical Reprise > Black Peter, Sugar Magnolia, China Cat Sunflower > I Know You Rider, Good Lovin' > Uncle John's Band

---

**1. Source:** FM-SBD (GDH), **Quality:** A, **Length:** 0:30 ("Dire Wolf," "Cryptical" > "Drums" > "Other One" > "Black Peter," "Sugar Magnolia")
**2. Source:** FM-SBD (KSAN), **Quality:** C–, **Length:** 1:35
**Comments:** Ninety minutes of highly degraded, almost unlistenable FM soundboard. The mix varies throughout the entire performance.

This tape begins midset, and the boys are seemingly blowing off steam from an otherwise outstanding year. Obviously suffering from overindulgence, the Dead manage to acceptably drag their way through "Big Railroad Blues," followed by standard readings of "Cumberland Blues" and "Dire Wolf." What follows is one of the most embarrassing passages of Grateful Dead music that I've yet to hear. Ordinarily a highlight, "Cryptical Envelopment" fails to get out of the starting gate, with weak vocals by Garcia and sloppy musicianship by his companions. The "Drums" segment is too long and too sloppy at the onset, perhaps indicating that someone had a few too many before going onstage. The transition into "The Other One" is even sloppier, with Weir trying to hold things steady while the rest of the band falls apart. Somehow, they manage to pull together for the verse, which is badly hampered by a warbling mix on the tape. The delivery is strong, but the band lazily fades on the jam between verses one and two. Lesh aimlessly meanders and Garcia's leads are badly uninspired. This results in a sequentially amusing alteration between unguided meltdowns and overextenuated theme statements. The ensuing musical jibberish becomes horrifically embarrassing, making the listener scream out in agony, "Hey guys, make up your minds!" Returning to the final verse at last, the boys give a solid reading of the final verse and call it quits instantaneously, fading into "Black Peter." Isn't it amazing how quickly the tide can turn? This is 1970 Dead at its finest. Soulful but methodical. Accurate. Confident. Too bad they're unable to maintain those attributes during the rest of the set. Hampered by sound fluctuations, "Sugar Magnolia" is average at best, though certainly a crowd pleaser, and the set-closing "China Cat Sunflower" > "I Know You Rider" is textbook standard.

Returning for what appears to be an encore, the Dead wisely hand the ball to Pigpen, whose reading of "Good Lovin'" pulls out all the stops. Talk about rebounds! Perhaps trying to overcome embarrassment, the Dead pour their hearts into this fabulous New Year's Eve closer. Although it takes a while to get going, the jam is deeper than the traditional "Good Lovin'" jam, with Garcia and Lesh tag-teaming on short, melodic phrases. Also unique to this is the subdued percussion section, though probably a blessing given their preceding performance. As Lesh erupts into a thundering bass solo, Garcia adds texture to the jam with straight rock 'n' roll riffing. Of course, Pigpen picks the perfect moment to jump back in, soulfully ad-libbing behind the Dead's thundering drive. Just as the momentum is about to peak, swoosh, the band sinks back to ground level as if to say, "Let's try that again!" Pigpen's gut-wrenching ad-libs continue as the momentum of the band behind him ascends once more, with Lesh acting as a bassist and percussionist simultaneously as he drives the rest of the band. Eventually peaking in a kinetic frenzy of furious twanging from the frontman, the band returns to the coda before an immediate segue into a ragged "Uncle John's Band." Although far from perfect, this is a tremendous sendoff to a fabulous year of performances.

BRIAN DYKE

## 12/70–1/71
### Wally Heider's Studio, San Francisco, California

**Studio Sessions:** 01/02/71: (Mountain Song Intro) Walkin' in the Mountains[1], Is It Really Monday[2], Under Anesthesia (You Sit There)[1], Loser[3], Over Jordan (Wayfaring Stranger)[4]
1/3/71: The Mountain Song[5] (4×)
1/14/71: Wild Turkey (Leather Winged Bat)[6], Jorma and Jerry's Jam—1 (Electric Bat)[7]
12/13/70: The Wall Song[8]
??/??/??: The Wall Song[1]
1/11/71: Eep Hour[9]

[1] David Crosby
[2] David Crosby, Jerry Garcia, Phil Lesh
[3] Papa John Creach, David Crosby, Jerry Garcia, Phil Lesh
[4] David Crosby, Jerry Garcia
[5] Jack Casady, David Crosby, Jerry Garcia, Mickey Hart, Paul Kantner, Grace Slick
[6] Jack Casady, Jorma Kaukonen, Mickey Hart
[7] Jack Casady, Jerry Garcia, Mickey Hart, Jorma Kaukonen
[8] David Crosby, Jerry Garcia, Bill Kreutzmann, Phil Lesh, Graham Nash
[9] Unknown Personnel

**Source:** SBD ("Loser" appeared on *Grateful Dead Hour* 318), **Quality:** A, **Length:** 1:30
**Highlights:** All
**Comments:** Parentheses refer to alternate song titles for tracks. Special thanks to Steve Silberman for providing assistance with tape data.

The personnel for these studio sessions, referred to as the Planet Earth Rock 'n' Roll Orchestra, or PERRO for short, comprise a virtual who's who of Bay Area musicians, assembled during a time when, as Paul Kantner has stated, "None of our schedules conflicted." From these sessions arose numerous recordings, among them, David Crosby's *If I Could Only Remember My Name*, Jefferson Airplane/Starship's *Blows Against the Empire*, the David Freiberg/Paul Kantner/Grace Slick collaboration of *The Ballad of Baron Von Tollbooth and the*

*Chrome Nun,* and the Paul Kantner/Grace Slick *Sunfighter*. The tape begins with "Walkin' in the Mountains," an absolutely exquisite Crosby passage that, while brief, immediately breathes gusts of warm spring ambience into the mood. Lyrically incomplete, the tune quickly builds to a thunderous chord progression before abruptly breaking off. The following "Is It Really Monday," another Crosby composition supported by subtle Garcia and Lesh, is somber, based around a restrained acoustic fingerpicking accompaniment remotely nodding to Depression-era country blues. Upon dissolution, the track segues into "You Sit There." Lyrically, this selection is somewhat satirical, yet the haunting acoustic accompaniment and deep Crosby vocal give the tune a deeply morose feel. Not to be taken too seriously, Crosby immediately launches into a loose variation of "Hey Joe" on the conclusion before belching into the mike and quipping, "If I write another tune in E minor, I'm gonna get fired."

The leadership then switches to Garcia, who patiently walks his colleagues through a very infantile rendition of "Loser." With only the first verse nailed, Garcia hums through the remaining verses and refrain. Although Crosby and Lesh lend minor support, it is overshadowed by the colossal contribution of Papa John Creach, whose fiddle is simply divine. At various points, the song breaks down, with Garcia talking through chord changes and demonstrating strumming techniques.

A disappointingly incomplete fragment, "Over Jordan" begins with a Crosby fingerpick, quickly aided by Garcia. Crosby whispers a few verses before building to the bridge climax and immediately dissolving. After restarting, the song again dissolves quickly.

The tape then continues with "The Mountain Song," containing an all-star ensemble of Crosby, Garcia, Kantner, Slick, and presumably Casady and Hart. Although this exhibition is only a faint glimpse of the actual song, it is considerably more aesthetically pleasing than the electrosynthesized version that appeared on Paul Kantner's 1983 LP, *Planet Earth Rock and Roll Orchestra*. While the musicians utilize a prominent acoustic guitar approach, this tune is highlighted by Kantner's simply luscious banjo accompaniment and Slick's boldly assertive piano. And, demonstrating true creativity, each take is itself a unique entity. The first two takes are actually the same, differentiated only by minor mix variations. The chorus slowly builds to a thundering pulse before, with Garcia surprisingly handling the bulk of the vocals and Crosby and Slick weaving in between the refrain with scat improvs. After teasing a fade, Garcia immediately launches into a graceful meandering that meshes effortlessly against Kantner's banjo. The third take is approached from a more soothing perspective, slower, with whispering vocals that are highlighted by Crosby and Slick's wondrous harmonies. The final and longest take begins with Crosby's intro from "Walkin' in the Mountains," executed a hair sloppier than the version that appears at the beginning of the tape, but segueing perfectly into the chord progression and refrain. Unlike the preceding passages, the momentum on the chorus remains constant, and leads directly into the jam. The blend of Kantner's banjo and Garcia's acoustic fingerpicking is exquisite, and further complemented by Slick's pulsating piano. As the jam descends to a whisper, the jammers return to the refrain, with Crosby and Slick again weaving between Garcia's vocals until the conclusion, which features a delightfully tasty turnaround lick from Garcia.

The tape then takes a much-needed switch in mood with Leather Winged Bat, an instrumental jam by Casady, Hart, and Kaukonen. After delivering a raunchy intro, Kaukonen quickly shifts to a smoother and nasal chord progression that contrasts nicely with his overdubbed wah-wah punches. Kaukonen's solo is fiery yet restrained, based primarily on a few standby licks. The following "Electric Bat," a duet between Garcia and Kaukonen, is structured around a simple pair of riffs, as the guitarists take turns soloing. Kaukonen takes the first lead, with a blaze of squealing bends and rich sustains. The chops are methodical and venomous, each note directly aimed and precisely fired. Conversely, Garcia's solo, considerably briefer, is unfocused and abstractly random. The lines are long and exploratory, hitting the G string on occasion but quickly wandering afar, not at all unlike what would later become defined in the great jams of the Grateful Dead's "Playin' in the Band" and "Dark Star." As the groove set by Casady and Hart becomes subdued, Garcia accelerates his spiral until, brilliantly, the groove transforms into a combination of funk rumbles from Garcia and Hart that contrast wonderfully with Casady's rock solid pulse. After tagging back to Kaukonen, the jam immediately circles for the landing, perhaps only a tad premature.

The following "Wall Song," the earliest recording of the tape, is slightly lacking in assertion with Nash's piano a noticeable absence. However, this take contains a complete outro jam that is disappointingly absent from the definitive David Crosby/Graham Nash LP rendition, with illustrious Crosby strumming in the right channel that responds delicately to Garcia's poignant solo in the left channel. Like the preceding passage, this track dissolves without notice and perhaps just a tad prematurely. The next version of "The Wall Song" is a solo Crosby acoustic demo, and illustrates only the basic framework of the tune.

Concluding the tape, mysteriously, is "Eep Hour." The personnel on this are unknown. Some speculate that Casady supplies the bass although it is well known that Garcia played every instrument except drums on his first solo album on which "Eep Hour" appeared. The identity of the guitarist(s) is unknown. It is possible that Garcia plays several parts and that they're overdubbed individually; it is also possible that several guitarists play simultaneously. Nonetheless, what appears here is a beautiful acoustic excursion, mildly Spanish flavored, and heartily chaotic.

BRIAN DYKE

---

## ??/70
### Unknown Location

**Studio Demo:** C. C. Rider, Instrumental (×4), Bring Me My Shotgun, Katie Mae, //Bring Me My Shotgun, Hitchhiking Woman, Piano Riff, I Got Two Women, Santa Fe Queen, Gas Station Rap, Hobo Jungle Rap//, Passing// Through, Easy Rider, In the Still of the Night, Big Boy Pete

**Source:** SBD, **Quality:** Varies from A to B, **Length:** 1:00
**Highlights:** All

---

**Comments:** This material circulates in just about every form and fragment imaginable, often labeled differently and often as filler at the end of tapes. With the exception of the last four tracks and three of the four takes of "Instrumental," all of these selections appear in inferior quality on a tape that circulates as either "Bring Me My Shotgun" (annotated as "Apartment Demos 1966") or "Pigpen Studio Demos 1964–73." Furthermore, "I Got Two Women" is sometimes listed as "Two Women," "Bring Me My Shotgun" is frequently listed as "Shotgun," "Santa Fe Queen" is often listed as "When I Was a Boy," and "Gas Station Rap" is often listed as "Michael" and "Poor Michael Went Down."

While some say that Ron "Pigpen" McKernan's definitive moments came during the peak of his most soulful "Hard to Handle"s or most rambunctious "Turn On Your Lovelights"s, many feel that his finest performances were elicited solo with just his guitar and harmonica, when he would ooze soul and emotion from both heart and string. This demo tape presents Pigpen in several lights: a bluesman, a folk singer, a balladeer, and a jester. Although this tape contains more than several musical shortcomings, they are far overshadowed by the sincerity of delivery. The tape begins with a traditional folk-style "C. C. Rider." Presumably, this was done first as a solo acoustic guitar passage, with the harp fills overdubbed later. The string accompaniment is fingerpicked in fine fashion, and the intraverse harp fills are bold and brisk.

"Instrumental," done in four takes at varying tempos, is based around a catchy riff combination of fingerpicked melodies and half-chord shuffles. On the first two takes, the pattern and range is notably undynamic, although the execution itself is surprisingly clean and mistake-free. The third take illustrates maturation, with a less static and more responsive conversation emerging in the phrases. The final take is slightly ragged, hampered by subtle but sloppy variations in tempo.

The first signs of brilliance come during the following Lightnin' Hopkins trifecta, "Katie Mae" sandwiched between two takes of "Shotgun." The first take of "Shotgun" is executed as a solo guitar piece with later harp overdubbing, the second sans harmonica. Take 1 is ornery in execution, with gruff vocals and a salty harp accompaniment. The solo begins with some boldly plucked Hopkins licks, but quickly shifts to a standard rhythm shuffle. The second take is less belligerent and contains a few minor miscues, both rhythmically and instrumentally, which overshadow the otherwise fine delivery. "Katie Mae," delivered in a considerably more subdued fashion than Hopkins' original, is noticeably deeper than the preceding passages. The vocals are dripping in authenticity, and Pigpen's licks are downright venomous, aside from a few less-than-masculine string bends.

"Hitchhiking Woman" begins as a common-time country blues before breaking down and reemerging as a slow blues in 12/8. Very possibly the only exhibition on record of Pigpen playing slide, the style is directly derived from the bag of Robert Johnson. The rhythm is strikingly accurate, and while the slide chops are in actuality somewhat sloppy, they're far from embarrassing and kept mercifully brief.

"Piano Riff," an extremely brief instrumental selection, is a boogie-woogie blues from the text of Memphis Slim. Unfortunately, it lasts less than a minute. Sigh. "I Got Two Women," which collapses and restarts, is perhaps the lowest highlight of the tape. After delivering an absolutely delicious intro lick, Pigpen scratches his way through the track halfheartedly with lackluster vocals and embarrassingly sloppy shuffling.

The tape then shifts from blues to folk with "Santa Fe Queen," an incomplete tale about a youngster who runs away from home. This is perhaps the most eloquent exhibition of the tape. The vocal is melodic and heartfelt, and though the song construction is utterly simplistic, it's effective for accompanying the narrative. Like "Piano Riff," however, the tune is disappointingly brief, lasting only two verses. "Gas Station Rap," a somewhat similar tune but one that contains a definitive ending and moral, is a sad tale that is delivered with such commitment that one wonders if it is autobiographical. A classic tragedy, the song tells of a young lad who arrives penniless in an unfamiliar town. A local merchant takes pity on the lad and gives him a job. With the selfishness of youth, the lad decides that the pay is insufficient and, with the aid of a few friends, commits a foolish robbery. Of course, the youngsters are caught, and while the narrator and anonymous accomplice manage to narrowly avert death, their coconspirator is caught in the chase and shot down. Again, the musical accompaniment is kept simple, serving only to lay the setting for the narrative. The folk motif continues with "Hobo Jungle Rap," a simple one-chord monologue in which Pigpen describes his first encounters with the local hobos. After quickly dissolving as a song, the monologue continues as a spoken word narration. In it, Pigpen talks briefly about his first experiences hopping freight trains, adding a sweet lick from his guitar here and there. Much to our dismay, however, the tape breaks off prematurely.

Following the tape flip, the subsequent two tracks are disturbingly haunting. All of the preceding selections are based around traditional blues and folk approaches, but these songs are derived from a deeper spiritual influence, remotely similar to that of Charlie Patton or Son House. Vocally, these are emotionally harrowing, and the musical approach is dark, almost occultish. "Passing Through," while admittedly not a very dynamic selection and further hampered by feedback blasts, is a chilling tale of weary travel, with loneliness and despondency prevailing. "Easy Rider," which at the outset sounds distinctly similar to the Rolling Stones' "Sister Morphine," is only slightly less morbid lyrically, but far eerier in execution. Unlike "Passing Through," which is delivered from an emotional and perhaps autobiographical approach, this tune is presented in the form of a narrative, focused intently on setting as well as character.

Following a brief rap, the tape concludes with a fragmentary and comic attempt at the fifties sock hop classic, "In the Still of the Night," complete with teen idol falsetto, before the finale of "Big Boy Pete," which is playful and immature.

BRIAN DYKE

# 1971

*After a few warm-up shows on the West Coast, 1971 began in earnest with a run of six shows at the Capitol Theater in Port Chester, New York. These shows marked the end of the transitional period that began in late 1969. The music had become slicker and less jangly, with some of the rough edges smoothed out, and the sound production was significantly improved. Continuing the trend of the past year, many of the long jams had completely disappeared, and nearly every show was now two sets, mostly consisting of single songs and with one or sometimes both sets ending with two to four songs strung together. For many years, the Port Chester shows were partially available only on barely listenable audience tapes. The whole run is now documented in its entirety as part of the original stash of Betty Boards. (For an explanation of "Betty Boards" see "How to Read the Reviews", p. 58.)*

*In a couple of ways, these shows also marked the beginning of another, more subtle, period of change. Firstly, following the opening show of the run, Mickey Hart left the band for an indefinite period due to the improprieties of his father who had been managing the band. This loss, although significant to the band, was not overtly noticeable in the music, as Kreutzmann had developed his drumming skills to the point that he could more than make up for the sudden loss. In fact, some of the drum solos he performed at the Port Chester shows were excellent. While the loss of Mickey took away some of the richness of the band's sound, it allowed them to move more into the jazz idiom. The music opened up and began an entirely new transitional period that would produce some of the most profound music in the band's history. Secondly, five new Hunter-Garcia songs were debuted at these shows, beginning a three-year period of incredibly prolific songwriting by this team. By 1974, Hunter and Garcia added twenty-five new songs to the repertoire, in addition to several new songs written by the new team of Weir and John Barlow. In all, between 1971 and 1974, thirty-eight new original songs were introduced as well as a score of new covers. This huge increase in repertoire enabled the set lists to become far more varied and interesting, making up for the lack of the traditional extended jams and the loss of old favorites.*

*Many of the Pigpen songs performed around this time fit right in with the Dead's new sound. They were simple, faithful renderings of old roots songs like "Big Boss Man," "It Hurts Me Too," or "Next Time You See Me," much tighter and more professionally done than in the early years. In fact, many of the most stunning versions of Pigpen's show-stopper songs, come from 1971. (Examples include the "Good Lovin'" from 4/17 at Princeton and 4/26 at the Fillmore East, or the "Lovelight" from 4/27 at the Fillmore East.) With all the focus on the new songs and style, however, Pigpen was not really able to shine in all his glory until one of the final songs of a show. Unfortunately, even as his style and playing was becoming more profound, by midyear it appeared that his health was already suffering. He took a break from touring in August to try to recover from his long history of alcohol abuse. He returned in December, but he never regained the energy and power he once held onstage.*

*Another subtle change for the band this year happened when the Fillmores East and West closed down for good. Although the closing runs for the band at these venues are counted among the greatest, or at least most important, shows of all time, it meant losing their home bases on either coast. In the taping world, these shows were particularly significant in that they were among some of the first truly high quality, both in terms of performance and sound, tapes to be circulated to the general Deadhead community both in terms of performance and sound. Throughout the seventies and eighties, they were among the most cherished tapes in any Deadhead's collection. Their distribution around the country clued people in to the fact that the content and quality of performances varied from show to show, and that tapes were a way of getting to hear the finest performances without having to travel to New York or San Francisco. In the late seventies, another batch of tapes appeared from the shows leading up to the closing of the Fillmore East in April. These tapes were of slightly less than excellent quality, but of far inferior shows on the whole. They demonstrated the Dead in a more run-of-the-mill setting, playing more run-of-the-mill shows.*

*Filling in for Pigpen in the fall was a new keyboard player, Keith Godchaux. He turned out to be the godsend the band needed. Keith was already a fan of the band and knew all the songs, and he played a great piano, a combination of barrelhouse and jazz. His playing style immediately meshed with the band's latest new direction. However, this changeover resulted in more than a few uneven shows. These were the first shows to be played without one of the founding members, but where Mickey Hart was a second percussionist, Pigpen had been the front man and lead vocalist from the beginning. The period from October through December was, for many years, one of the best-documented periods in the band's history. Half the shows played in that time were broadcast on local radio stations, providing early tapers with a rich supply of very high quality tapes featuring Keith and the band's rollicking new sound and occasional deep space explorations. What these tapes also show, however, is a monotony that was beginning to creep into the show as the band was learning a new batch of songs, a new sound, and bringing a new instrumentalist up to speed. Many of the songs in the first set sounded identical to every other version in those first two months. The saving grace of this time was provided by Bob Weir. He stepped up his role as the band's front man in contrast to Pigpen's psychedelic blues man, growling out songs with his own psychedelic rock 'n' roll showmanship, screaming out the lyrics in a forceful, explicit manner. Pigpen's return in December helped to focus the music a little more, even though his contribution to the band, for a time, was negligible. With Pig on* stage, the band seemed to regain its confidence and played some outstanding free-form jams. Listen to the "Other One"s from December 1 at the Boston Music Hall and December 14 in Ann Arbor, Michigan, and the "Dark Star"s from December 5 at the Felt Forum in New York City and December 15 in Ann Arbor to hear how the band was beginning to stretch out more and investigate unknown corners of these songs. These jams were the beginnings of a new form of Grateful Dead space jams that would dominate shows for the next three years. The Dead were adapting their music to Keith's rollicking jazz style and Weir's emergence as a rock 'n' roll star, and they seemed to like it.

Tapes to get: 2/18, 2/23, 4/5–4/6, 4/26–4/29, 8/6, 10/21, 10/29, 11/7, 12/2, 12/5, 12/15.

---

### ??/71
### Unknown Location

**Live Outtakes:** Cold Rain and Snow, Cold Rain and Snow//, Cold Rain and Snow//, Cold Rain and Snow//, Cold Rain and Snow, Me and My Uncle, Cold Rain and Snow, Me and My Uncle

**Source:** SBD, **Quality:** A, **Length:** 0:35

These tracks, labeled simply, "Outtakes," are perhaps selections considered but not used for the Grateful Dead's 1971 LP, *Skull and Roses*. Although six takes of "Cold Rain and Snow" and two takes of "Me and My Uncle" appear on the tape, they are actually derived from the same rendition of each selection, differentiated only by mix variations. Like the material that did appear on *Skull and Roses*, the execution is solid but not spectacular.

BRIAN DYKE

---

### 2/??/71
### Unknown Location

**Studio Rehearsals:** Playing in the Band, Greatest Story Ever Told, Bird Song, Wharf Rat

**Source:** SBD, **Quality:** A–, **Length:** 0:35

The material at this rehearsal, all of which would be debuted just a few weeks later at the storied Capitol Theater run, is extremely rough. It is distinctly possible that this is the band's first rundown of these tracks. One might have never guessed that they would eventually find place among the Grateful Dead's most revered classics.

The rehearsal begins with "Playing in the Band," the boys cautiously wading through the changes in structure from verse to bridge. On the first take, the intro is executed before each verse, and Weir's vocals, while confident, are mistimed, as is most of the musical interplay between. Unable to synchronize, the boys go down for the count at the bridge and, after deciding to go straight into the second verse from the change, rise again for the second take. Weir mutters the vocals on this one, and in the refrain the drummers abandon ship, followed quickly by the rest of the band. Take three, completely instrumental, staggers unremarkably all the way through.

The following "Bird Song" begins with a lengthy repetition of the intro, followed by the lyrics. On the first refrain Lesh and Weir join in for a rough harmony, on the second verse Weir increases his presence on rhythm. Steadily, the boys make it all the way through the take, with Garcia eliciting a few delicious country licks on the outro. A second take ends abruptly when Garcia realizes that he's out of tune, likewise for the third and fourth, when he decides to give Weir a bit of coaching on the rhythm. Finally, at the end of the fifth take, Garcia remarks, "That's the right groove," prompting the band to move on to its next task, "Greatest Story Ever Told." While the preceding selections are rough and infantile, this track is downright disinteresting, with Weir struggling with the lyrical timing as the rest of the band half-heartedly stumbles through the arrangement.

Although the concluding "Wharf Rat" is the smoothest execution of the day, it consists of little more than chords and lyrics.

BRIAN DYKE

## 1/22/71
### Lane Community College, Eugene, Oregon

Ken Babbs Introduction, Casey Jones, Beat it on Down the Line, Hurts Me Too, Me and My Uncle, Cold Rain and Snow, Hard to Handle, Brokedown Palace, Johnny B. Goode, China Cat Sunflower > I Know You Rider

**Source:** SBD, **Quality:** B–, **Length:** 1:10

This tape has no extraordinary moments or jams. After an introduction by Ken Babbs, the band enters a very sloppy first set. Each song is either a barely average or a horrible version. Maybe they were simply inebriated? Early 1971 is considered by many to be one of the poorer Dead runs. This performance is evidence for that argument.

ROBERT A. GOETZ

## 2/18/71
### ESP Experiment Show
### Capitol Theater, Port Chester, New York

**Set 1:** Bertha*, Truckin', Hurts Me Too, Loser*, Greatest Story Ever Told* > Johnny B. Goode*, Mama Tried, Hard to Handle, Dark Star > Wharf Rat* > Dark Star Reprise > Me and My Uncle
**Set 2:** Casey Jones//, Playing in the Band*, Me and Bobby McGee, Candyman, Big Boss Man, Sugar Magnolia, Saint Stephen > Not Fade Away > Goin' Down the Road Feelin' Bad > Not Fade Away Reprise > Uncle John's Band//

* First time played

**1. Source:** SBD, **Quality:** A (//"Bertha," //"Playing in the Band"), **Length:** 3:00, **Genealogy:** Betty Board, MR > RR > PCM > DAT

**2. Source:** FM-SBD (GDH 002, 072, 161 and 256), **Quality:** A+, **Length:** ("Bertha," "Loser" > "Johnny B. Goode," "Dark Star" through "Me and My Uncle," "Playing in the Band")

**Highlights:** Bertha, Hard to Handle, Dark Star, Not Fade Away

**Comments:** Betty Board—7½ ips, ¼ track, 7-inch reel, recorded on Sony 770. Played on Teac reel-to-reel into PCM 501 ES series digital processor at 14 bit, using Sony SL550 Beta video recorder and Maxell H GX 750 tape.

This night marked the beginning of a new era in Grateful Dead performances, as well as in tapes. The sound quality and mix of the music on this tape is far superior to any soundboard tape coming out of 1970 other than those released on CD. There is an improved separation of the instruments and a warmer, softer sound to the music. With this show came the debut of several new songs, most of which would be eventually featured on the *Skull and Roses* album. In fact, this run of shows was originally recorded on multitrack tape for that album, and although none of the material was used, it may account for why such a good quality tape was made. Chronologically, this is the first of the Betty Boards, and with this whole run now available as Betty Boards, we are able to get an extraordinary insight into what it was like to attend a run of shows back in the old days.

The show starts out with a brand-new song that would become a favorite of Deadheads, "Bertha." It is a remarkably tight version for a debuted song, showing that the band must have been rehearsing the new songs since the beginning of the year. They still had not settled on any one way to end it, because each of the versions in this run of shows was done slightly differently. The next song is "Truckin'," during which there is a slight increase in the level on the tape and a sudden rise in Phil's levels in the mix during the second chorus. The jam after the final verse lasts a short two minutes before it fades into the final verse reprise. Pigpen follows this up with a soulful rendition of "It Hurts Me Too" that contains nice slide work by Jerry and some phat Phil notes sprinkled throughout. "Loser," another song making its debut here, came off rather tentatively as did the first-ever "Greatest Story Ever Told." Some of the tentativeness may have been due to their anticipation of "Johnny B. Goode," a song that harkened back to the ultra-high energy style of the pre–*Anthem of the Sun* days. The band just explodes into it at a breakneck pace that never quits. It is the first of the new songs with a true rock 'n' roll quality. The old standard "Mama Tried" is next followed by a blistering version of "Hard to Handle." The set ends with what would become a true rarity, a first-set "Dark Star." This version is relatively short and simple, creating a loose framework that flows into the first performance of one of Garcia's favorite Hunter ballads, "Wharf Rat." Pigpen opens the song with a pretty harpsichord effect. The drummers maintain the song's signature march beat throughout the song, except during the bridge, and the song is given a solid, but quick, run-through. With the new song out of the way, the band stretches out and is more inventive for the second half of "Dark Star." There is a beautiful, unique jam that flows effortlessly with a high clear sound, similar to the "Feelin' Groovy Jam," but this has an older, timeless feel. The jam's theme is gorgeous and is never repeated on any other tape available. It must have been one of those moments of inspiration where the band just played for the moment and the moment never came again. There is a slow transition to "Me and My Uncle," with Mickey on wood blocks.

The second set opens with the ever popular "Casey Jones." There is much ado about the house lights before the beginning of the song. This could be related to the ESP experiments being conducted during this run. Apparently, during the show, pictures would be shown up on a screen behind the band. The audience was to focus on these pictures and try and "transmit" them psychically to subjects in a nearby lab. The brightness of the house lights may have affected the visibility of the pictures. Also, people who were there indicated that not a lot of attention was paid to the conduct of the experiment.

Next was the first performance of "Playing in the Band," the only one with Mickey Hart for three and a half years. Mickey's presence is very noticeable, especially if compared with other early versions of this song after he leaves. "Bobby McGee" is also typical of the more laid-back feel. "Candyman" is much like the acoustic versions played in 1970, with long-drawn-out vocals ending each chorus, followed by a brief rest, and continuing with the next verse or solo. The band must not have liked the electric versions much as it was nearly two years before it appeared again, and then with a slightly altered arrangement. A rather perfunctory "Big Boss Man" came next. "Sugar Magnolia" followed, showing off Jerry's wah-wah effect, which gave it a bouncy sound like giant cartoon springs spiraling around in all directions. As usual, there was some scratching of asses while deciding on an appropriate way to end this show.

They open the final jam with a very tight "Saint Stephen," with an extended jam at the end (some of which is missing during the tape switch, unfortunately). From there they go right into "Not Fade Away," which starts out fairly standard with a short jam going into an exceptionally sweet "Goin' Down the Road" intro. "Goin' Down the Road" gets a incredibly rocked-out ending before going back into a "Not Fade Away" reprise that showcases the full frontal assault of these "six proud walkers" for the last time ever. Because of the financial improprieties of his father, this would be Mickey's last show with the band, and he would not return until long after Pigpen had died. However, they do go out with a flourish on this song. While "Not Fade Away" is still rattling its ending, Garcia plucks the beautiful opening chords to "Uncle John's Band" seemingly out of nowhere. The rest of the band seems a little surprised and pauses a moment to catch the timing before jumping right in.

The tape ends with the crowd clapping for more, but you can hear Dylan's "Lay Lady Lay" come over the PA as the deck is shut off. Overall, this was a show that demonstrated a band very psyched to show off a bunch of new songs. They succeeded and then some. This is certainly one of the best shows of the year, if not one of the all-time classics.

DOUGAL DONALDSON

---

### 2/19/71
**ESP Experiment Show**
**Capitol Theater, Port Chester, New York**

**Set 1:** Truckin', Loser, Cumberland Blues, It Hurts Me Too, Bertha, Playing in the Band, Dark Hollow, Smokestack Lightning, China Cat Sunflower > I Know You Rider
**Set 2:** Greatest Story Ever Told > Johnny B. Goode, Bird Song// Easy Wind, Deal, Cryptical Envelopment > Drums > The Other// One > Wharf Rat, Good Lovin', Casey Jones

**1. Source:** SBD, **Quality:** A+, **Length:** 2:35, **Genealogy:** Betty Board, MR > RR > PCM > DAT

**2. Source:** FM-SBD (DHH 04, 05, 24; GDH 180, 209), **Quality:** A, **Length:** ("Hurts Me Too," "Dark Hollow," "Smokestack," "Easy Wind"), **Genealogy:** MR > DAT

**Highlights:** Smokestack Lightning, Easy Wind, Deal, The Other One

**Comments:** A multitrack version of this show was very nearly to be *Three from the Vault*, but was ultimately rejected. Betty Board—7½ ips, ¼ track, 7-inch reel, recorded on Sony 770. Played on Teac reel-to-reel into PCM 501 ES series digital processor at 14 bit, using Sony SL550 Beta video recorder and Maxell H GX 750 tape.

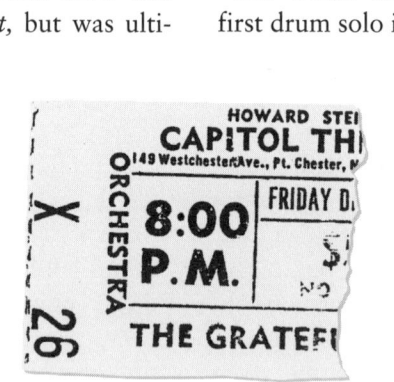

This is the first show after Mickey Hart's departure from the band. It starts off tentatively with a standard "Truckin'." "Loser" and "Cumberland" follow with Garcia stumbling through the lyrics. The band is audibly distracted by either Mickey's absence or the pictures being flashed up on the screen behind them for the ESP experiment. Pigpen is able to whip the band into shape as he delivers a flawless version of "It Hurts Me Too." This picks the band up for "Bertha," featuring some nice organ work between verses. "Playing in the Band" gives one the sense that the band knew from the beginning that there would be a long spacey part in the middle. There's a brief hesitation before the final chorus that would become in later years the launching pad for the space jam. Now the set gets interesting when Weir breaks out a rare version of the folksy "Dark Hollow" and Pigpen leads the band through an excellent "Smokestack Lightning." There is a great blues jam in the middle of "Smokestack" that sounds both unique and familiar at the same time. A short, fast, but tight version of "China Cat" > "Rider" closes up the set.

The second set kicks off with chunky versions of "Greatest Story" and "Johnny B. Goode." Next comes the first-ever "Bird Song," played as if they had been doing it for years, effortlessly putting together a light, floating jam that would become the song's signature. Unfortunately, the tape runs out just before reentry into the final verse. "Easy Wind" provides an excellent example of just how good a drummer Kreutzmann is. This show was his first one as the lone drummer in three

*Ticket stub for 1971 run at the Capitol Theater, Port Chester*

and a half years, and he comes through like a pro. He delivers crisp rolls, a solid beat, and lots of cymbal fills. This is most evident in "Easy Wind," which has a complex drum pattern. "Deal" is one of those instances where a new song is broken out and it never quite sounds the same again. Garcia gives it a little extra soul that seemed to be missing from subsequent versions. Finally, we get to the show's big question: can they play "The Other One" with one drummer? Kreutzmann's first drum solo is more than adequate, and the jamming is nearly indistinguishable from the previous night's in the fullness of sound. This "Other One" is like when you shoot one of those old toy rockets. It starts off at a furious pace, then the momentum slows as the rocket climbs and climbs. Eventually it runs out of fuel and seems to hang in the air for a moment before it begins to fall, gathering speed until it crashes to earth once again—this time into their second effort with "Wharf Rat." Having just made it through one drum solo, Kreutzmann skips it in "Good Lovin'," thus keeping the band's momentum going and ending the show on a solid note.

DOUGAL DONALDSON

---

### 2/20/71

**ESP Experiment Show**
**Capitol Theater, Port Chester, New York**

**Set 1:** Casey Jones, Me and My Uncle, Hard to Handle, Bertha, Playing in the Band, Bird Song, Big Boss Man, Cryptical Envelopment > Drums > The Other One > Wharf Rat, Sugar Magnolia

**Set 2:** Truckin', Loser, Next Time You See Me, Greatest Story Ever Told > Johnny B. Goode, Ripple, Not Fade Away > Goin' Down the Road Feelin' Bad > Not Fade Away Reprise > Turn On Your Lovelight

**1. Source:** SBD, **Quality:** A, **Length:** 2:25, **Genealogy:** Betty Board, MR > RR > PCM > DAT

**2. Source:** FM-SBD (DHH 04), **Quality:** A–, **Length:** The Other One through Sugar Magnolia

**Highlights:** The Other One, Ripple, Turn On Your Lovelight

**Comments:** Betty Board—7½ ips, ¼ track, 7-inch reel, recorded on Sony 770. Played on Teac reel-to-reel into PCM 501 ES series digital processor at 14 bit, using Sony SL550 Beta video recorder and Maxell H GX 750 tape.

This show features every new song from this run except "Deal" and includes a rare electric "Ripple." You almost can't tell the difference in sound between this show without Mickey and the first of the run with Mickey. Part of this may be due to the simpler songs being played and the extraordinary ability of Billy to add the fills while never missing a beat. Some of the percussive effects like the wood blocks and the rhythm fish are missing, but the overall effect of the drum unit remained the same. There were some variations with this night's versions over previous ones. "Bertha" was missing the jam after the final chorus. The "Cryptical Envelopment" suite was missing the final "He Had to Die" part, although this would become normal during the year. Garcia misses some lyrics in "Wharf Rat." The solo in "Loser" begins with Garcia doing some minor tuning before really getting into the jam. The band as a whole did not seem to have quite the level of energy it possessed on the first night of this run—that is, until the final jam. They decided to combine the straight-ahead rock 'n' roll medley of "Not Fade Away" > "Goin' Down the Road" with the more improvisational "Turn On Your Lovelight." The combination is excellent. The band is peaking at the end of "Goin' Down the Road" and appears to be going into the "Not Fade Away" reprise when they suddenly break into the "Lovelight." Pigpen tries to get the guys in the audience to "get going" with the women, but they seem to be too stoned or polite to follow his advice, so he gives up and starts telling a story about how he's "walking down the street, looking for what's going on." This story will be developed with several variations in the next two months until it becomes the classic and well-known "Good Lovin'" rap from Princeton, New Jersey, on April 17. He meets the guy with "the business" but he's only got a buck and a quarter. So the guy sends him on down to the fat girl down at the end of the block. Finally the story dissolves into a plea for everyone to raise their hands. At this point the band takes over and brings the song to an amazing climax.

DOUGAL DONALDSON

---

### ❋ 2/21/71 ❋
**ESP Experiment Show**
**Capitol Theater, Port Chester, New York**

**Set 1:** Cold Rain and Snow, Me and Bobby McGee, Loser, Easy Wind, Playing in the Band, Bertha, Me and My Uncle, Ripple, Next Time You See Me, Sugar Magnolia, Greatest Story Ever Told > Johnny B. Goode

**Second 2:** China Cat Sunflower > I Know You Rider, Bird Song, Cumberland Blues, King Bee, Beat It on Down the Line, Wharf Rat > Truckin', Casey Jones, Good Lovin' > Uncle John's Band

**Source:** SBD, **Quality:** A+, **Length:** 2:35, **Genealogy:** Betty Board, MR > RR > PCM > DAT

**Highlights:** China Cat Sunflower > I Know You Rider, Good Lovin', Uncle John's Band

**Comments:** Betty Board—7½ ips, ¼ track, 7-inch reel, recorded on Sony 770. Played on Teac reel-to-reel into PCM 501 ES series digital processor at 14 bit, using Sony SL550 Beta video recorder and Maxell H GX 750 tape.

This show also features all of the new songs of the week except "Deal." It also shows the Dead playing more unevenly than on any of the other nights on this run. Pigpen has trouble with the lyrics in "Easy Wind" and the band has to stop playing "Ripple" and restart it as they are so out of sync. By the second set, though, the band is able to find a small groove. "China Cat" > "Rider" had been much better developed by this time, and this night's version of it is exemplary. It is also one of the few uncut versions of this combo from 1971, one of the great mysteries in taping lore. "King Bee" had been making a short-lived comeback at this time, with this night's version being typical. The band could not come up with a cohesive jam, however, as they strung together several songs that were normally part of connected jams but this night were kept separate, although they were well played. "Wharf Rat" is beautiful, with Jerry's soulful crooning lending it a sweetness that countered the march beat effectively. "Truckin'" is well jammed and could easily have gone into some other song but the boys cannot figure out how or what and, instead, decide to end it.

Finally, at the end, it is Pigpen to the rescue with a wonderful "Good Lovin'" that featured not so much the storytelling aspect of Pigpen's rap, but the beautiful wailing blues voice that could be an improvisational instrument in itself. In 1971, this song ranked up there with "Lovelight" as the Pigpen jam song of choice. After Kreutzmann's drum solo, the band returns with a fresh jazzy lead-in to Pigpen's vocals. Pigpen implores the crowd to raise their hands (the theme for the week) and asks, "Do you believe in the people?" Amazingly, there is none of the sexist storytelling or matchmaking efforts in the entire song, making it a thoroughly enjoyable version for all. Finally, after a lengthy vocal rap, he leads the band back into the chorus and a crashing ending where Garcia floats the opening chords to "Uncle John's Band" out of the ashes once again. This time the band is ready, and what follows is one of the finest versions of the song played for several years.

DOUGAL DONALDSON

---

### 2/23/71

**ESP Experiment Show**
**Capitol Theater, Port Chester, New York**

**Set 1:** Uncle John's Band, Loser, Playing in the Band, Big Boss Man, China Cat Sunflower > I Know You Rider, Me and Bobby //McGee, Bertha, Next Time You See Me, Morning Dew, Sugar Magnolia, Casey Jones

**Set 2:** Me and My Uncle, Bird Song, Truckin' > Drums > The Other One > Wharf //Rat, Greatest Story Ever Told > Good Lovin', Not Fade Away > Goin' Down the Road > Not Fade Away > Johnny B. Goode

1. **Source:** SBD, **Quality:** A+, **Length:** 2:40, **Genealogy:** Betty Board > MR > RR > PCM > DAT
2. **Source:** FM-SBD (DHH 04 and 05, GDH 010 and 027), **Quality:** A, **Length:** 0:30 ("Uncle John's," "Big Boss Man," "Bertha" through "Casey Jones," "Bird Song")

**Highlights:** Uncle John's Band, Morning Dew, Bird Song, The Other One, Goin' Down the Road

**Comments:** Betty Board—7½ ips, ¼ track, 7-inch reel, recorded on Sony 770. Played on Teac reel-to-reel into PCM 501 ES series digital processor at 14 bit, using Sony SL550 Beta video recorder and Maxell H GX 750 tape.

This show is my personal favorite of the Port Chester run. It is undeniably the most solid set list and has just about everything one could ask for in a Grateful Dead show. For starters, the show opens with a solid "Uncle John's Band," has a rocking "China Cat" > "Rider" early on, and ends with "Morning Dew," "Sugar Magnolia," and "Casey Jones." In a couple of years, that would be a definitive show-ender. Here, it is just a prelude to a wonderful second set.

The second set of this show has two distinct characters. The first half is spacey and ethereal, combining "Bird Song" with a powerful "Truckin'" that starts off with a slow growl and continues on with Phil's pumping bass leading the way. A solid drum solo follows, building to a ferocious bass intro to "The Other One." This "Other One" is typical of many in 1971, with a monster jam leading to the first verse followed by a more sparse jam where the band is searching for ideas on which to act. Here the jam features Phil dropping huge bombs while Garcia and Weir interlace their dripping feedback. This begins to disintegrate until Garcia and Kreutzmann pick up the pieces and form a musical pattern that the rest of the band latches on to, and eventually turns into another crescendo that seamlessly returns to the main theme. A soulful, soaring "Wharf Rat" concludes the jam. That song seemed to evolve quickly in its first week as the band tried to find where and how it would fit best.

The second half of the set is stand-on-your-seat rockin' with the added twist of having the "Greatest Story" > "Johnny B. Goode" combo split up by the typical 1971 show-closers, "Good Lovin'" and "Not Fade" > "Goin' Down the Road." The "Good Lovin'" is notable in that there was no drum solo nor does Pigpen do any kind of rap as was the norm in 1971. The band keeps the rock 'n' roll energy up throughout this and the remaining songs of the set. The "Not Fade" > "Goin' Down the Road" is scorching and is climaxed with an equally hot "Johnny B. Goode." The crowd is audibly more vocal at the end of this show than at any of the others this week, and they have every reason to be.

DOUGAL DONALDSON

# Reviews: February 1971

## 2/24/71
### ESP Experiment Show
### Capitol Theater, Port Chester, New York

**Set 1:** Casey Jones, Me and My Uncle, Cumberland Blues, Next Time You See Me, Bird Song, Me and Bobby McGee, Bertha, Hard to Handle, Loser, Playing in the Band, Good Lovin'
**Set 2:** Sugar Magnolia, King Bee, Greatest Story Ever Told > Johnny B. Goode, Deal, New Minglewood Blues, Truckin' > Not Fade Away > Goin' Down the Road > Not Fade Away Reprise > Turn On Your Lovelight

**Source:** SBD, **Quality:** A+, **Length:** 2:42, **Genealogy:** Betty Board MR > RR > PCM > DAT
**Highlights:** King Bee, Minglewood
**Comments:** Betty Board—7½ ips, ¼ track, 7-inch reel, recorded on Sony 770. Played on Teac reel-to-reel into PCM 501 ES series digital processor at 14 bit, using Sony SL550 Beta video recorder and Maxell H GX 750 tape.

The last night of a long run. In fact, this was the longest run at one venue they had ever done outside of the Bay Area. As would often be the case at the end of a run like this, the band settles back with even less agenda than usual and lets their evening run its own course, and it becomes a review of the past week's shows with a couple of extras thrown in. They play every one of the new songs except "Wharf Rat," which was played at each of the other shows. The band takes some time to get into a groove, especially in the first set where none of the songs are notable.

The second set is much better played, however, and far more interesting, with rare versions of "King Bee" and "Minglewood," both given tight performances here. The show's finale makes this tape worth getting. "Truckin'" kicks it off it high gear, followed closely by a bouncy "Not Fade Away." "Goin' Down the Road" smokes much as it has all week. At the end the band seems to be debating whether to return to "Not Fade Away" or launch into "Lovelight." As it is the final night, they do both, building up steam with the "Not Fade Away" reprise and shooting right into a blazing "Lovelight." This is a classic 1971 version with an extended rap that features a successful matchmaking effort by Pigpen. He brings a woman up onstage and then requests volunteers to get together with her. Sending them on their way, he closes the song, and the run, in a shattering climax.

DOUGAL DONALDSON

## 3/3/71
### Airwaves Benefit
### Fillmore West, San Francisco, California

**Set 1:** Casey Jones, Hard to Handle, Playing in the Band, Loser, Me and Bobby McGee, Next Time You See Me, King Bee, Beat It on Down the Line, Bertha
**Set 2:** Me and My Uncle, Truckin' > Drums > The Other One > Wharf Rat, King Bee, Greatest Story Ever Told > Johnny B. Goode.
**Encore:** Good Lovin'

**Source:** SBD, **Quality:** A–, **Length:** 2:15
**Highlights:** Good Lovin'

Early 1971 was a strong period for song development; many new songs were introduced into the rotation, and their structures defined. However, this was also arguably their weakest period in terms of improvisational jamming. Indeed, this performance illustrates the shoot-'em-up bar band approach that the band had adopted at the time. Opening with a standard rendition of "Casey Jones," the band then attempts to loosen their collar with a respectable version of "Hard to Handle." The "Playing in the Band" that follows is picture-perfect for 1971; it successfully presents the structure of the tune in its earliest pre-embellished form. The rest of the set is similar, with the Dead cranking out tight renditions of each song, but without any noteworthy exploration. The second set starts off with an album-worthy reading of "Me and My Uncle" that, again, is tight and succinct with no real improvisation. The following "Truckin'" is made interesting by mix variations, with Pig's organ way out front until the second verse. Tame and structured, this version is probably most notable for the superb vocals from the frontmen—when they're audible, that is. On the outro, Jerry briefly teases the "Dust

My Broom" riff before returning to the much safer E blues scale, where he continues with his standby licks. Eventually, the jam fades into "Drums," which sounds very rehearsed and fails to elicit a noteworthy response. Continuing in the same vein, the following "Other One" is very polished, but conversely refrains from irrational musical regurgitation. Indeed, each note makes sense, each lick, each chop having a definite place within the song's parameter. The vocal delivery from Weir is confidently executed, as are the backups from Lesh and Garcia. On the jam between verses 1 and 2, the boys loosen up by a hair, displaying the first remote sign of emotion for the evening. Garcia even goes so far as to bend a string, between split-second outbursts of feedback that were probably unintentional. On the second verse, Weir overarticulates the lyrics, and the backups are a hair out of tune. Good sign. Opting for the sudden ending without an outro jam, the boys begin a very young "Wharf Rat" that appears without any real segue or resolution. Garcia's vocals on this are scratchy; at times he talks his way through the verses. Things begin to look better on the outro jam as the musicians show signs of restlessness, and the ending is much more graceful than that of the preceding "Other One."

The show concludes with a sluggish rendition of "King Bee." Pigpen scratches his strongest Slim Harpo imitations through this one, but is hampered by amateur harp licks and a weak solo from Garcia. Could've benefited from a slide on this one. The finale of "Greatest Story" > "Johnny B. Goode" is sleepily executed and lacks the energy of the many other interpretations from this era. The "Good Lovin'" encore highlights this performance: strong rhythms from Lesh and inspired jamming from Garcia. Cautious to stay within the framework, Lesh, Weir, and Kreutzmann pound the foundation like a hammer around Garcia's pentatonic phrases. Just as it looks as if Lesh and Kreutzmann are to take over, Pigpen begins the rap. This is perfectly complemented by Kreutzmann's shuffling off-beats. The boys tease further unraveling following the rap, if only briefly, before Garcia leads the band back into the chorus, wrapping up an uneven evening at the Fillmore.

BRIAN DYKE

---

### 3/14/71
**University of Wisconsin Field House, Madison, Wisconsin**

Truckin', Bertha, Hard to Handle, Good Lovin', Wharf //Rat, Uncle John's Band, Casey Jones

**Source:** AUD, **Quality:** C/B–, **Length:** 1:00, **Tapers:** Stephen Wade and Fred Ordower
**Highlights:** Hard to Handle, Good Lovin'

The quintet's performance at Madison anticipates the spare style recorded a few weeks later on the *Skull and Roses* album. This concert, like that compilation, marks a retreat from the psychedelic septet of 1969 and 1970. Madison recalled the band's earlier involvement with vernacular song forms such as the Chicago blues. Not surprisingly, the evening's highlights, "Hard to Handle" and "Good Lovin'," reasserted Pigpen's role. In Madison, the Dead had returned to the discipline of the discrete song. Accordingly, the tape reveals no segues or medleys. "It's the prototype Grateful Dead. Basic unit," said Jerry Garcia of *Skull and Roses*. "We're a regular shoot-'em-up saloon band."[1] That night the band encored with the prototypical song of the shoot-'em-up saloon band: "Johnny B. Goode." The concert took place at a small college field house at the University of Wisconsin. Stage lighting was minimal, leaving the hall, and sometimes the band members, in darkness. Our tape, too, is marred by poor audio fidelity, and its muffled sound is further aggravated by the occasional intrusion of my own voice. Matched parabolic mikes on telescoping stands and high-quality cassette technology remained yet in the future. The only surviving documents from the Madison concert are this fragment of tape and some color photographs. Our pictures show Jerry Garcia's guitar was neither of his red Gibson SGs, but a black Les Paul. Perhaps this choice of an instrument long associated with a harsher blues sound aided his impulse to return to the earthiness of saloon band rock 'n' roll. Certainly Pigpen's role in the band served that purpose. That wintery night in Madison the band accompanied him with impassioned maturity. They were drawing from the great models of the

---

[1] Blair Jackson, *The Music Never Stopped* (Delilah Books, 1982), 125.

past, using the lessons of pith, economy, and coherence in the service of their own originality.

STEPHEN WADE

---

### ❋ 3/21/71 ❋
### Exposition Center, Milwaukee, Wisconsin

**Set 2:** Me and My Uncle, Hard to Handle, Loser, Beat It on Down the Line, Me and Bobby McGee, Not Fade Away > Goin' Down the Road Feelin' Bad

---

**Source:** AUD, **Quality:** B+, **Length:** 0:40, **Genealogy:** unknown generation reel, apparently from a bootleg vinyl album (pops and clicks are present). All between-song matter has been edited out.

**Highlights:** Hard to Handle, Beat It on Down the Line

As one listens to this decent-sounding and competently played audience tape, one question comes to the forefront: "Where are the jams?" This very short set is largely typical for the time in that it lacks any long improvisations or multiple-song segues. But not even a "Dark Star" or "Other One"? Odd indeed.

*Phil, 1969* (photo credit: Fred Ordower)

The playing however, is superb. "Me and My Uncle" is picture-perfect, differing only slightly from the cut on the Dead's second live album. "Hard to Handle" is played in typical 1971 style, with first Weir and then Garcia taking energetic solos. "Loser" is well played, and "Beat It on Down the Line" is remarkably tight. The energy level dips slightly with "Me and Bobby McGee" but bounces right back on a bubbly "Not Fade Away"—but even here, the Dead refuse to stretch it out. The transitional jam between "Not Fade Away" and "Goin' Down the Road Feelin' Bad" is short and lacking in any peaks and valleys. Just some familiar riffing, inoffensive but unspectacular, to fill the spaces. "Goin' Down the Road Feelin' Bad" is very short and comes to an abrupt close without its usual journey back into "Not Fade Away"—an odd end to a baffling set. Did the Dead suddenly remember that they'd left a pie in the oven?

JEFF TIEDRICH

*Pigpen at the piano, 3/21/71* (photo credit: Fred Ordower)

*Jerry and Bob get down to business* (photo credit: Fred Ordower)

*The band, 8/23/71* (photo credit: Fred Ordower)

*On stage at Winterland, 3/24/71* (photo credit: Michael Parrish)

## ☀ 03/24/71 ☀

### Sufi Benefit
### Winterland Arena,
### San Francisco, California

**Set 1:** Bertha, Sugar Magnolia, King Bee, Beat It on Down the Line, Casey Jones, Hard to Handle, Greatest Story Ever Told > Johnny B. Goode
**Set 2:** Next Time You See Me > Loser, Truckin' > Drums > The Other One, Playing in the Band, Not Fade Away > Goin' Down the Road Feelin' Bad > Not Fade Away Reprise
**Encore:** Uncle John's Band

**1. Source:** AUD, **Quality:** A–, **Length:** 2:15
**2. Source:** FM-SBD (GDH 125), **Quality:** A–, **Length:** 1:00 (Bertha, Casey Jones, Hard to Handle, Truckin' > The Other One), **Genealogy:** MR > DAT > broadcast
**Highlights:** King Bee, Hard to Handle

This performance does little to dispute the argument that early 1971 was one of the weakest periods in Grateful Dead history. Sandwiched between an overrated run at the Port Chester Capitol Theater in February and an even more overrated run at the Fillmore East in April, this show depicts the Grateful Dead at the peak of its "bar band" era. The play is average, the emotional factors absent, and the summation is a very rehearsed and unimprovised performance. Not that the tunes are played poorly. Quite the contrary: the first set consists of tight, album-worthy readings of each track, containing little improvisational risk-taking. This is clearly a band that's been rehearsing, and the robotic outcome is evidence of that point. Most noteworthy is the strong vocal delivery. Coming on the heels of their two strongest vocal albums, the boys are undoubtedly polishing their voices, letting the music take second priority. Weir, in particular, roars on "Sugar Magnolia," and even gives "Beat It on Down the Line" a slight blast. As well, Pigpen's gruff delivery on "King Bee" and "Hard to Handle" are classic '71 Dead defined. It's unfortunate that musically the band is unable to match the level of soul that is put into these tracks vocally.

Set 2 kicks off with a solid pairing of "Next Time You See Me" > "Loser" before what might have become the set's highlight. However, this version of "Truckin'" > "Drums" > "The Other One" is rather tame, each band member asserting his standby licks without stretching too far into space. Again, this is highlighted by strong vocal deliveries from the frontmen. Concluding this lackluster performance is an average, if uneventful, interpretation of "Not Fade Away" > "Goin' Down the Road" > "Not Fade Away." The band shows signs of energy on the jam-out "Not Fade," but instead quickly rushes through an uninspired "Goin' Down the Road" before returning to "Not Fade." The "Uncle John's Band" encore, although strong vocally, is hampered by a clumsy and obviously tired Garcia.

BRIAN DYKE

*The Dead with the Sufi Choir on stage at Winterland, 3/24/71* (photo credit: Michael Parrish)

## 4/4/71
### Manhattan Center, New York, New York

**Set 2:** Hard to Handle, Deal//, Sugar Magnolia, Casey Jones, Good// Lovin', Goin' Down the Road Feelin' Bad > Saint Stephen > Not Fade Away > Uncle John's Band

**Source:** AUD, **Quality:** D+, **Length:** 1:30
**Highlight:** Casey Jones

Rarely can a complete performance by the Grateful Dead be characterized as a failure. Throughout the thousands of hours we have endured both in live and reproduced settings, our obsession as tapers is defined by the premise that each passage of music has something to offer. Of course, there are rare exceptions, and not coincidentally, many of them lurk within the first six months of 1971. More important than hoarse vocals, miscued solos, or sluggish rhythms, this April performance lacks one of the most prominent elements of the quintessential Grateful Dead concert: emotion. Missing the entire first set, the tape begins with a lackluster rendition of "Hard to Handle." Although full of tasty licks from each member, the bar band sound is exacerbated by Garcia's borderline offensive use of the wah-wah, and the rhythm section's admirable but complacent effort is poor compensation. A standard reading of "Deal" and a few rambunctious moments of clowning around from Weir give way to "Sugar Magnolia." The band races through this enthusiastically, keeping the soloing to a minimum and skimping heavily on the "Sunshine Daydream" conclusion. In desperation, and to the delight of the crowd, the Dead roar through what was destined to become a perennial barroom favorite, "Casey Jones." Truly characteristic for 1971, this elicits the most energy of the evening, both from the band and the audience. Unfortunately, the energy level is unsustainable and the band barely survives an uncharacteristically sterile "Good Lovin'." Although Pigpen's improv is in fine form, the band lags desperately behind him, waiting until the final few moments to kick into overdrive.

What would ordinarily provide the evening's climactic interlude is a rendition of "Goin' Down the Road" > "Saint Stephen" > "Not Fade Away" that is rushed and nowhere near the level we've come to expect from that period. Although the introductory solo begins rather confidently, Garcia suddenly runs out of gas midway and leads hastily into the verse. While the vocals are quite acceptable, musically this is an extremely disappointing passage, completely lacking in aggression, assertion, and emotion. As boredom begins to sink in, the band quickly segues into an embarrassingly sterile "Saint Stephen." Serving as little more than a lead in to "Not Fade Away," as well as a cowardly means to kill a few more minutes of stage time, the boys manage to catch their breath during this passage and conclude the performance with an enthusiastic "Not Fade Away." Although this is given a standard reading through the verses, the boys manage to blast some energy into the wrap-up, highlighted by coda shrieks from Weir that are second to none. The brief but piercing feedback jam, perhaps accidental, makes for a perfect transition into the finale of "Uncle John's Band," whose delivery is neither passionate nor pathetic.

BRIAN DYKE

## 4/5/71
### Manhattan Center, New York, New York

**Set 1:** Cold Rain and Snow, Me and Bobby McGee, The Rub, Loser, Playing in the Band, Big Railroad Blues, Me and My Uncle, Big Boss Man, China Cat Sunflower > I Know You Rider, Casey Jones
**Set 2:** King Bee, Bertha, Truckin' > The Other// One > Wharf Rat > Sugar Magnolia, Not Fade Away > Goin' Down the Road Feelin' Bad > Not Fade Away Reprise, Turn On// Your Lovelight

**1. Source:** SBD, **Quality:** A+, **Length:** 2:50, **Genealogy:** Betty Board, MR > RR > PCM > DAT
**2. Source:** FM-SBD (DHH 53), **Quality:** A+, **Length:** "Not Fade Away" through "Lovelight"
**Highlights:** Big Railroad Blues, The Other One, Goin' Down the Road Feelin' Bad, Lovelight
**Comments:** Betty Board—7½ ips, ¼ track, 7-inch reel, recorded on Sony 770. Played on Teac reel-to-reel into PCM 501 ES series digital processor at 14 bit, using Sony SL550 Beta video recorder and Maxell H GX 750 tape.

One hundred seventy minutes of pure, unadulterated mad-eyed brilliance, this show is an absolute cracker

*April 1971, Fillmore East* (photo credit: Amalie Rothschild)

from start to finish. When at the very end, Pigpen asks the audience, "Do you feel all right?" no one doubts the answer. As with most shows of the period, long space-outs or rambling jams are largely absent; for most of this date, the musical creativeness is distilled into more concise forms. If you're looking for paradise in a '71 show, this is it.

The recording quality of this show is superb. Certain selections of the show were chosen for inclusion on the *Skull and Roses* album ("Big Railroad Blues" and "Not Fade Away" > "Goin' Down the Road"), and the mix and general ambient sound is close to that. My copy has what sounds like FM interference on it in places, but it's no big deal and, a few (admittedly horrendous) cuts aside, this is a primo quality recording that should be widely available in a good condition.

Picking highlights out of this is a hard one as there really isn't any thing under par; it's just one of those shows that shines from the first note onward. Highlights of the first set include the yodeling in "Me and Bobby McGee" (a hit in the Tyrol, I'm sure), the blazing "Big Railroad Blues" we're all familiar with, and a glorious "China Cat Sunflower" > "I Know You Rider." The second set hasn't got a moment of the merely average in it. Sure, you've heard other '71 shows with the same or very similar track listings, but this really does transcend most of them. From the headlong rush out into deep space of "The Other One" through the fluid and quite frankly astonishing interplay of "Goin' Down the Road" (I've been listening to this track for the best part of twenty-four years and it *still* raises goose bumps), we finally move into a long and incident-packed "Lovelight" where Pigpen takes total control and unbelievably raises the temperature even higher. After Pig's lead, the band winds the show up to a textbook definition of "fever pitch." The result: The Manhattan Center filled with a *totally* demented audience. Yeah Pig, we feel all right. This must be Heaven indeed.

PAUL BODENHAM

## 4/6/71
### Dance Marathon
### Manhattan Center, New York, New York

**Set 1:** Bertha, Beat It on Down the Line, It Hurts Me Too, Me and Bobby McGee, Dire Wolf, Oh Boy, I'm a Hog for You, Baby, Playing in the //Band, Midnight Hour, Mama Tried, Cumberland Blues, Casey Jones

**Set 2:** Greatest Story Ever Told > Johnny B. Goode, //Loser, Good Lovin', Sugar Magnolia, Not Fade //Away > Goin' Down the Road Feelin' Bad > Not Fade Away Reprise > Truckin'

**Source:** SBD, **Quality:** A+, **Length:** 2:37, **Genealogy:** Betty Board, MR > RR > PCM > DAT

**Comments:** Betty Board—7½ ips, ¼ track, 7-inch reel, recorded on Sony 770. Played on Teac reel-to-reel into PCM 501 ES series digital processor at 14 bit, using Sony SL550 Beta video recorder and Maxell H GX 750 tape.

**Highlights:** It Hurts Me Too, Midnight Hour, Greatest Story, Truckin'

There's something about New York City that brought out the best in the Dead. This show is no exception. From the extremely rare songs in the first set to the hellacious "Truckin'" that ends the show, the boys were cooking from beginning to end here. This show was the end of a three-show run billed as a dance marathon; however, judging from the pleas from the band for the crowd to step back, and from eyewitness reports, there was simply no room for anyone to do anything but cram up against their neighbor. By the middle of the first set, the band was having a great time one-upping each other on song selection. Garcia dusted off "Dire Wolf" for one of only three versions that year, Weir answered with the only electric "Oh Boy," and Pigpen finished them off with the only post-1966 version of "I'm a Hog for You, Baby," which had both Weir and Garcia cheerfully chipping in on vocals. Just to prove his mastery at dusting off old classics, Pigpen added a rare mid-first-set "Midnight Hour."

The second set contained mostly standards from the period, starting off with a chunky "Greatest Story"/ "Johnny B. Goode." Pig's only entry was a raucous "Good Lovin'" where he exorted the crowd to turn to the person next to them and say, "HOWDY" (as if they weren't already close enough), and then to take off their clothes and have a good ol' time. The show closes with an amazingly rocking "Not Fade Away" > "Goin' Down the Road" sandwich and then pulls out all the stops on a "Truckin'" that is more reminiscent of 1977 than 1971. Alone this show would have been typically legendary of New York shows; however, within a few weeks, it would be eclipsed by several of the five shows at the Fillmore East. Fortunately, there are tapes of nearly all of them available.

DOUGAL DONALDSON

*Ticket stub for 4/6/71 at Manhattan Center, New York*

## 4/7/71
### Boston Music Hall,
### Boston, Massachusetts

**Set 1:** Me and My Uncle, Next Time You See Me, Casey Jones, Playing in the Band, Loser, Me and Bobby McGee, Hard to Handle, Sugar Magnolia

**Set 2:** China Cat Sunflower > I Know You Rider, Saint Stephen > Drums > Jam // Not Fade Away > Goin' Down the Road Feelin' Bad > Not Fade Away Reprise > Johnny B. Goode

**Source:** SBD, **Quality:** A–, **Length:** 1:40, **Genealogy:** Betty Board, MR > RR > PCM > DAT

**Highlights:** Next Time You See Me, Hard to Handle, China Cat Sunflower > I Know You Rider

**Comments:** Betty Board—7½ ips, ¼ track, 7-inch reel, recorded on Sony 770. Played on Teac reel-to-reel into PCM 501 ES series digital processor at 14 bit, using Sony SL550 Beta video recorder and Maxell H GX 750 tape. For the entire first set, Phil is a bit low in the mix, as compared with the mix of other 4/71 soundboards in which Phil vibrates furniture (the reels had a comment on them, "First night for new mixer").

1

2

3

4

5

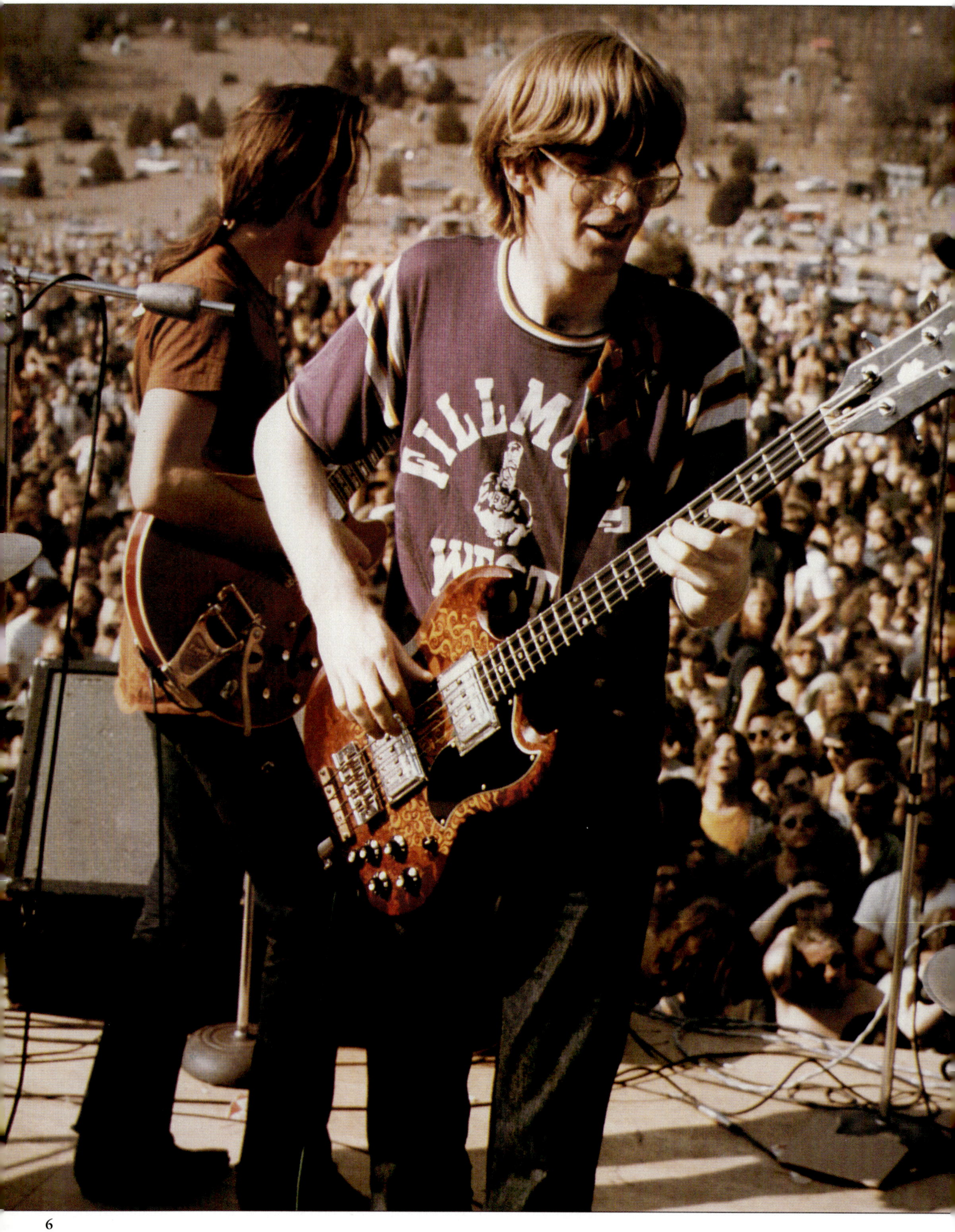

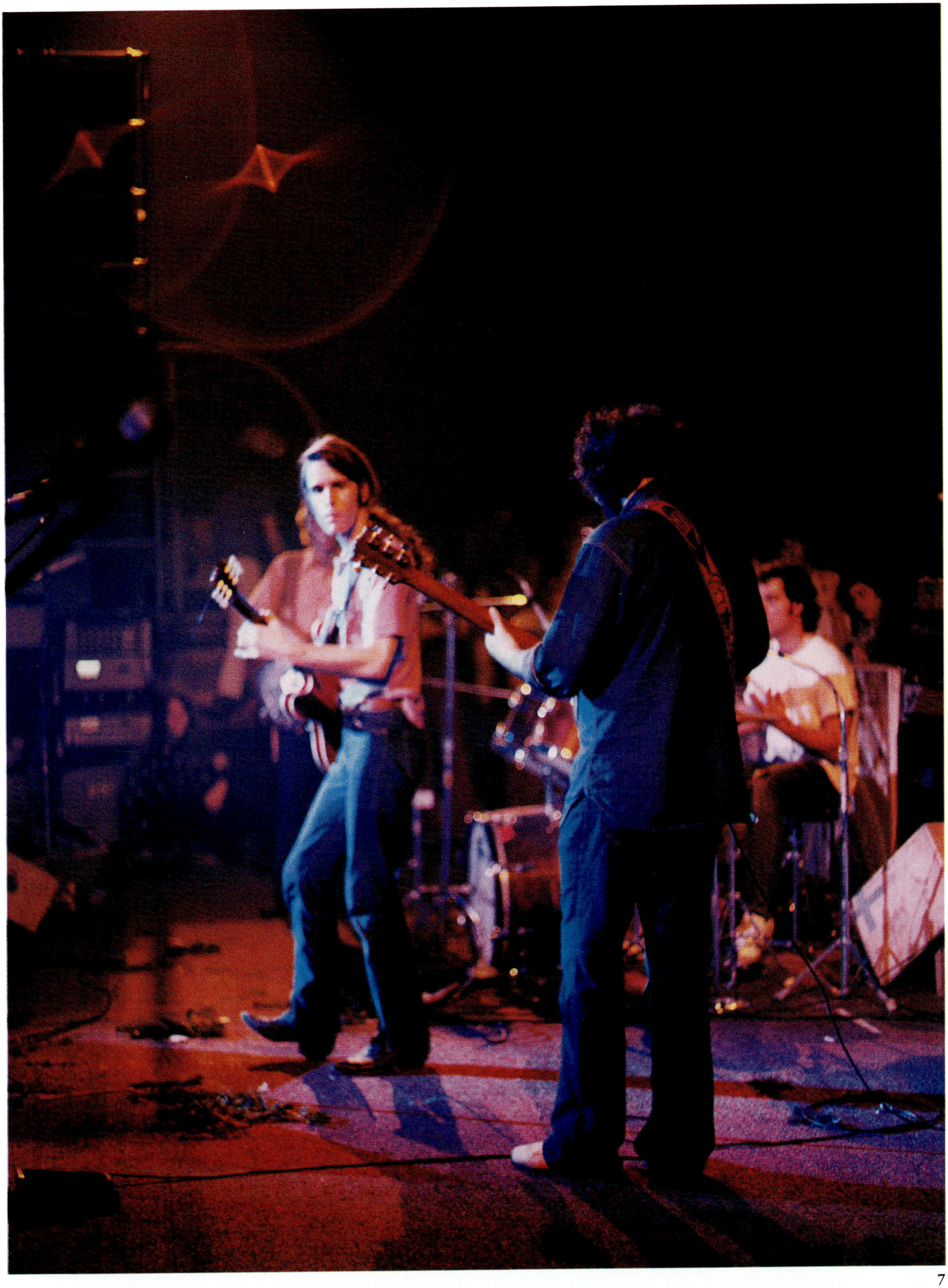

8

9

10

11

12

13

14

15

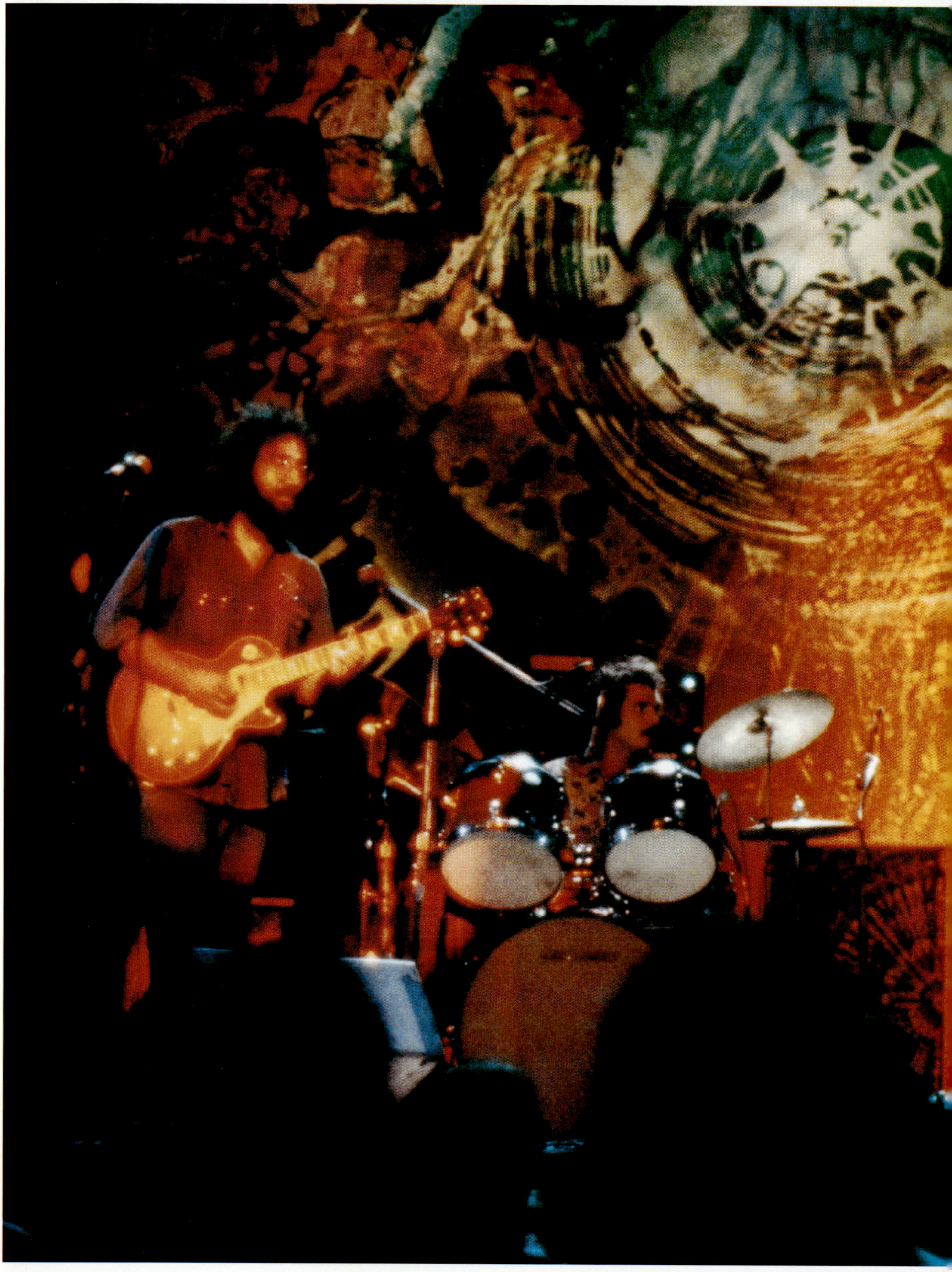

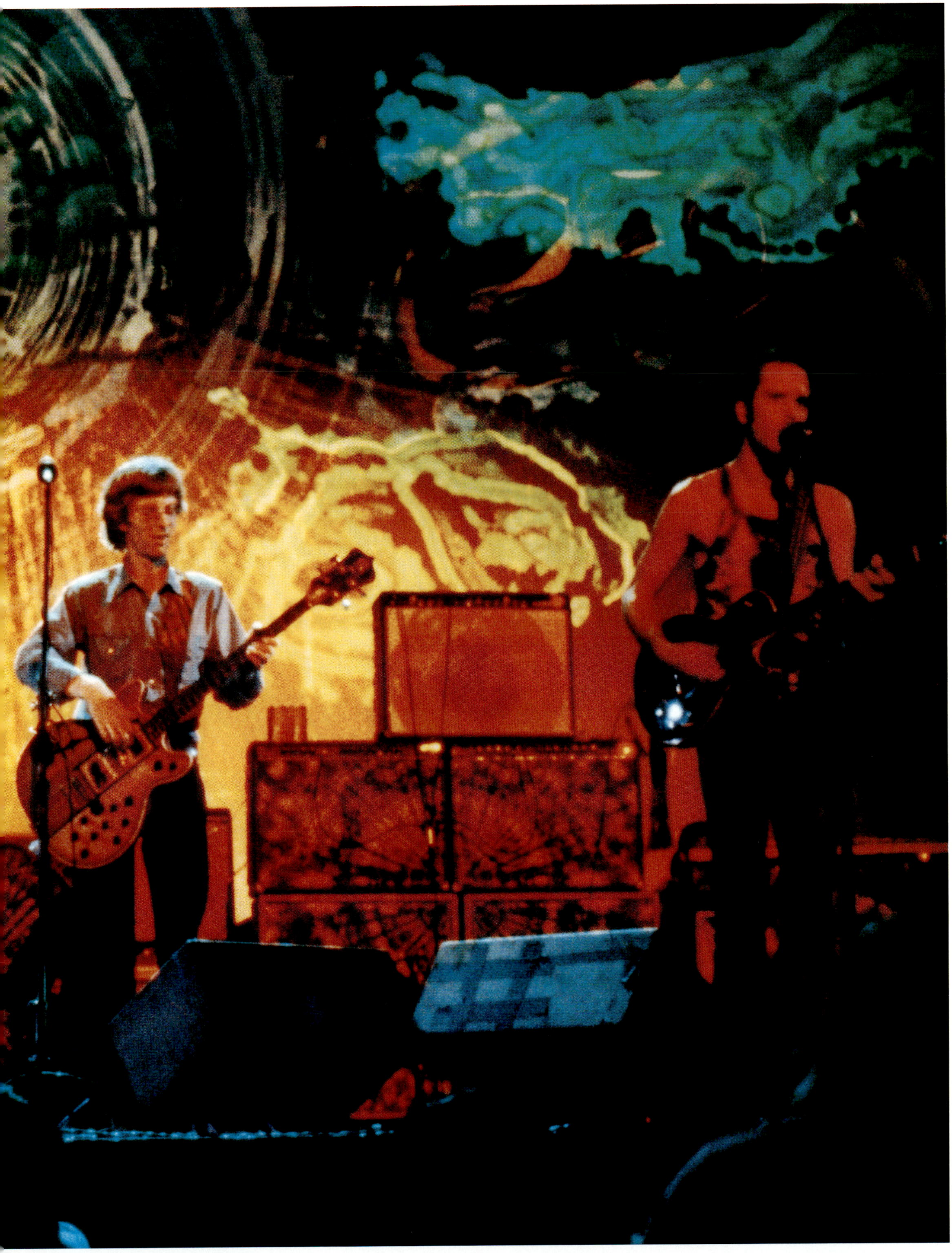

17

18

19

20

21

22

23

24

26

25

Highlights of the first set for me include a real nice version of "Next Time You See Me." Garcia's chops are outstanding and laced with a solid dose of attitude. Weir's got a real sweet groove going. When listening to "Hard to Handle," be prepared to steady up for a major testosterone rush, very possibly causing the unprepared listener to emit savage primal screams, tearing at one's hair and finally—potentially embarrassing—rending garments. "Hard to Handle" is, in this reporter's opinion, one of the most stompin' Dead tunes ever to hit the rotation. This was one of fourteen "Hard to Handle"s played in April '71, and every one of them that I've heard is a ripsnorter. This one finds Pigpen in a fine groove and features exceptional cut-it-up guitar work by Jerry and Bob. If you're breathing, you're moving.

In the second set, Phil seems to be up a bit more in the mix. During "China Cat" everyone is strong out of the chute. Guitars are high in the mix. Bobby slips off-key for a short chord to start the second jam, which throws it off for a brief moment. Phil comes in from out of nowhere and *blasts* back into the mix with a vengeance, peppering the jam with lead bass runs and then letting loose with a power chord and holding it for five full seconds while waiting for Garcia to reach his next peak. Bobby delivers the archetypal "China Cat" lead licks, which then dissolves into "comic book colors on a violin river . . ." After "in the eagle winged palace of the Queen Chinee," Garcia barely finished singing "Chinee" when, all lyrics now behind him, he leads the freakfest into a short body-twitching, hair-whipping scorcher and then drops it right into the interjam, which has Jerry bendin', Bobby strokin', and Phil dancin'.

Weir's axe work is great throughout, and the return of Phil to the mix wakes you up and gets you going like a blast of cool clean October air coming off the Washington coast. And as in most "China Cat" > "I Know You Rider"s played anywhere anytime, the tasty synthesis of guitar and bass work has me shaking my head in bemused giddiness. As "I Know You Rider" begins to materialize, Phil's bass is cranked way up before dropping off, and then it's set about right. The levels are a bit unsteady throughout the song. Extra-special treats for me are the goose-bump high harmonies by Phil and strong lead lines by Jerry. Bob's vocals are also right perfect.

Saint Stephen is crisp yet contained. Phil comes in vocally about halfway 'twixt now and then . . . Jerry singing the bridge with typically restrained approach, gently so as not to outpace the notes or Bob's massaging the strings to give that familiar second voice in the distance, like the indistinguishable unseen voice over the telephone in the old cartoons . . . building to the blistering rationalization that "one man gathers what another man spills." But first Bill and then Phil blast the whole blessed affair off into the zone of contention, and then, as they near the crescendo and as Jerry attempts to slam the brakes into "Did he doubt or did he try?," someone's apparently not ready—and the control tower signals the pilot as he pulls full back on the throttle and takes it around for another pass before attempting a safe landing. It's at this moment that Phil takes charge and tosses out a few massive cluster bombs, signaling to all that it's time to land this baby, which they do.

Phil alone sings "Fortune comes a-crawlin'" before Jerry joins him in "calliope woman/ Spinnin' that curious sense of your own . . . ," and after "answer man," it collides into "Drums," which rolls along for a couple of minutes, Phil joining in for a brief moment, and then we get a noodle out of Jerry, and Bill, and just as they really start to roll—my tape splices right into . . . "Not Fade Away."

"Not Fade Away" is kind of laid-back, as is "Goin' Down the Road" (like a good number of versions of this medley on this tour—a condition that would disappear by the fall of the year). Garcia picks it up some after the first verse, stretching notes to reach the high spots, using more finesse than fire, keeping it contained, kicks it back into "Not Fade Away," with Pig joining into the chorus, and then, in a moment that sent shivers up my spine the first time I heard it, during the final "Not fade away"s, as Pigpen and Bobby are going round, Pig makes a prophetic declaration, singing, "I won't fade away!"

"Johnny B. Goode" starts with a big Pig scream. It's a nice big fat version, with Pig sharing the vocals on the "Go, Johnny, Go"s. A couple of weeks later, on April 27, along with the Beach Boys, Pig joined in and sang the whole dang thang. "Because of the curfew stuff," Garcia apologizes, "we've got to knock off, I'm sorry, see ya later."

JAY STRAUSS

## 4/8/71
### Boston Music Hall, Boston, Massachusetts

**Set 1:** Truckin', Bertha, Next Time You See Me, Playing in the Band, //Loser, Beat It on Down the Line, Second// That Emotion, Sugar Magnolia, China Cat Sunflower > I Know You Rider, Casey Jones

**Set 2:** Dark// Star > Saint Stephen > Not Fade Away > Goin' Down the Road Feelin' Bad > Not Fade Away Reprise, Sing Me Back Home, Cumberland Blues, Greatest Story Ever Told > Johnny B. Goode, Good Lovin'

**Source:** SBD, **Quality:** A, **Length:** 2:30, **Genealogy:** Betty Board, MR > RR > PCM > DAT

**Highlights:** Second That Emotion, China Cat > I Know You Rider, Dark Star, Not Fade Away, Sing Me Back Home, Cumberland Blues, Good Lovin'

**Comments:** Betty Board—7½ ips, ¼ track, 7-inch reel, recorded on Sony 770. Played on Teac reel-to-reel into PCM 501 ES series digital processor at 14 bit, using Sony SL550 Beta video recorder and Maxell H GX 750 tape.

April 8, 1971, is outstanding on many levels, but one component of the X Factor here will shine brightest: PHIL! He's way up in the mix, and it was a damn fine use of the board. If you like Phil, you'll want this show. If you love Phil, you'll need CPR. Nine times out of ten, what makes a killer "Truckin'" for me is the instrumental blowout after the last words are sung. But this version smokes from the get go. After "Bertha," during tune-up, there's all sorts of strange noise in the right channel, including conversation and something sounding like a kazoo. As "Next Time You See Me" starts, the noise continues. This chatter disappears when the music picks up. During "Playing," there is more humming in the right channel. "Next Time You See Me," however, is perfect. Weir's chord shuffle is real cool. Phil starts "Beat It on Down the Line" alone, bangs out eighteen beats, then Billy kicks in for a beat, stops, and then Weir says, "Hey wait a minute... you said seventeen" "It's up to you." Phil decides on lucky seven, and it's off to the races with Bill and Phil leading the way through a scorcher. Weir's got a fun, unusual lead-in to the "China" intro. "Crazy cat peekin'" and Jerry tears into the sweet melodic climb up, while Bob's taking those short shots/jabs. Garcia's lead dances, wild yet fluid *kata* around the outside. Bob, with short strokes of color, performs Tai Chi in the center. Phil and Bill are tempting the cobra on the outer perimeter. "In the eagle wing palace of the ... Queen Chinee," and it slows almost to a stop as they decide who will lead them through the small door to the interjam. Bob and Phil poke their heads through. Jerry lags on the perimeter until he finds the groove, all the while measuring up the various possibilities, and again it sputters momentarily until Garcia whispers, in beckoning notes, *Yo, fellers, over here*— and slowly, gently, they venture into the first verse of "I Know You Rider." "Wish I was a headlight" is not angrily trumpeted, but rather quietly spoken, as if not to wake the children, or perhaps to get their attention.

"Dark Star" is pure exhilaration as Garcia, reaching from the soul, implores the cosmos to reveal its secrets in a beautifully melodic, soaring climb through the unexplored, yet not unfamiliar, "attics of my mind." Phil, resonant and booming, follows the contours of the mountainous landscape while Bob adds the context from which the beast takes life. In the first verse, there is a short fade-out. As I listen closely, through headphones, I feel as though I am peering directly into the soul of the Grateful Dead. "Mirror shatters"... There is a cut at "recedes in the night//" and then it comes back in at "the transitive nightfall of diamonds." Then it fades quickly into "Saint Stephen." Which is nicely sculpted and blasts off into the jam, which (it's still basketball season) has me relating to a three-on-one fast break with Phil leading the way and passing to Jerry and Bob, who pass back and forth; this court's a hundred yards long, with great jamming, everything's clicking on the fast break, and they're running and passing fast and hard through the flow, and then, as Phil flies up and is about to slam it home, they're forced to pull up because, of course, "Saint Stephen" has remained, and all he lost he shall regain....

Phil drives the low register forcefully into "Not Fade Away." Weir leads them into "Goin' Down the Road" with majestically rhythmic chords and riffs. It sounds like someone is tapping the tambourine. Great first jam—Garcia's lines are crisp yet circuitous, like casual conversation. They find their way back to "Not Fade Away," where Pigpen joins them to bring it home. We get a real nice "Sing Me Back Home" before the tape flip. Great stuff, with Jerry singing it home, almost whispering at times, and Phil accompanying with vibrant melodies. A great "Cumberland Blues" ensues with PHIL!! leading the way. It's Phil and Jerry dueling it out and Weir pulling wild chords out of his bag of tricks. It's more fun than a barrel of dosed monkeys. Raucous, rowdy, drunken "Greatest Story"—guaranteed to prime the pump. After a real nice "Johnny B. Goode" that just keeps building, the reel pauses. Billy cues up the "Good Lovin'"; Phil beats it into a pulp with an upper-range assault that one of my friends likened to having Mr. Lesh reach into his chest and pounding his heart like a speed bag. Billy's all over it. This "Good Lovin'" is outstanding—Pig and Phil are the soul of it. There must have been something going down in the 'hood, because here's some of the Pig's rap (somewhat indistinguishable, to me): "Just a-look after your neighbor, say how ya doin . . . Ain't no use in fussin' and fightin', ain't no use in carryin' on, no there ain't. . . . Everybody put up their guns and put 'em home/ . . . Walk the streets all alone and we'll be all right if everybody else is a-doin' the same. . . ." Weir is all over it during Pig's rap—really fantastic stuff. The guitars are so strong that I get the sense that Pig is distracted and having some trouble focusing on his rap. Me too. Weir: "Hey that's all the time there is so we'll see y'all later." Wow.

JAY STRAUSS

### 4/10/71

**East Hall, Franklin and Marshall College, Lancaster, Pennsylvania**

**Set 1:** Casey Jones, Me and Bobby McGee, Next Time You See Me, Loser, Beat It on Down the Line, Hard to Handle, Bertha, Playing in the Band, Deal, Good Lovin', Truckin'

**Source:** AUD, **Quality:** D–, **Length:** 1:15
**Highlights:** When it ends

Ouch! This was by far the most painful tape I had to review. A poorly made audience tape, the music is so garbled and unintelligible that you cannot tell whether the songs are any good or not. The only exceptional feature about this tape is its rarity. However, that circumstance probably came about because nobody wanted the tape! The bass is completely distorted, the vocals sound like they are coming through a vacuum cleaner tube, and the rest is simply white noise. It takes almost a minute to discern that it is the Grateful Dead, much less what song is being played. Please, make it stop!

DOUGAL DONALDSON

### 4/17/71

**Dillon Gym, Princeton University, Princeton, New Jersey**

**Set 1:** Truckin', Big Railroad Blues, Big Boss Man, Bird Song, Playin' in the Band, Hard to Handle, Loser, Mama Tried, Casey Jones, Sugar Magnolia
**Set 2:** Good Lovin', Me and Bobby McGee, Deal, Beat It on Down the Line, King Bee, Bertha, Sing Me Back Home, Goin' Down the Road Feelin' Bad, Lovelight

**Source:** SBD, **Quality:** A– (slight hiss; a few rough spots), **Length:** 2:43, **Genealogy:** MR > RR > DAT
**Highlights:** Good Lovin', Bird Song, Sugar Magnolia

Good-quality soundboards of this show, with clean sound and even a good headphone mix, are now common in tape-trading circles after years of poor ones, although most tapes still suffer from butchered sequencing, especially in the second set. Immortalizing the nadir in this history, an eight-song Italian bootleg CD came out in 1990; beware of anyone offering a one-hour tape with a suspicious-looking song sequence of "Truckin'," "Big Boss Man," "Bird Song," "Hard to Handle," "Good Lovin'," "Bertha," "Goin' Down the Road," "Lovelight."[1]

The show itself is famous to Heads for the Pigpen rap on "Good Lovin'," but legendary to Princeton Deadheads for the apocryphal story of Jerry being told by a campus cop before the show to extinguish his joint—prompting the retort "I'll never play here again"—and for the student who fully groked the Dead's message of freedom and jumped up on the stage to express his acid-fueled revelation, leaving a tremendous impression on witnesses though nary a trace on the tapes.

For the band, it was a gig on a different sort of tour: lots of short trips, centered around buses and not airplanes. Garcia recalled a few months afterward, "That was really fun, we were just able to hang together all the time, we didn't have to go through a lot of airports and all that. And we got to see some of the countryside. It was a little more like travelling and less like matter transmis-

---
1. Grateful Dead, *My Head Is Dead* (Italy: The Genuine Pig, TGP CD 124, 1990), 59:26 min.

sion."[2] The Princeton show, the eighth stop of the tour, seems to exude that mellow, friendly vibe. Despite the fame of the band, there was still a casualness and an intimacy between band and fans; one long-time Deadfreak (as Heads were then called) wandered backstage before the show and chatted with Phil, posing a question very much on most fans' minds: "I asked him what it was like with just one drummer again, and he said it was like riding one surefooted horse that you know inside out."[3] Down to a five-piece configuration for the first time since 1967, they were back to what Garcia called "prototype Grateful Dead." As difficult a blow as Mickey's departure was, it came at a creative peak for the band, hard on the heels of what Hunter considered the best period of collaboration with Garcia,[4] and the time when he felt most attuned as lyricist for the fans: "I was them and they were me, and I felt very much that I was speaking for us. They knew what I meant, and I knew what they would like it to mean, and it seemed to work."[5] In 1971, it was still a very intimate relationship between fans and band, a small circle of initiates who "got it." As Hunter recalled, "The Deadheads and the Dead were a rather close symbiotic unit at that point."[6] It gave concerts the group gestalt that impressed and mystified outsiders, and gave the band new converts at every outing. It was part of why many students called this show the most significant event of their tenure on campus.

Set 1 opens with "Truckin'," announced by its signature rhythm, that heavy steady beat, very slow here, clearly working the vocals for everything they can; the lyrics don't sound rushed at all, which makes one wonder if this is what Hunter had in mind when he wrote it, or whether this was the band's compromise with their density. Regardless, it comes off well, Garcia's guitar doing interesting and weird little flourishes over and around Weir's vocals, but the highlight is, as always, the final jam, relentless and thorough and sinuous and strong, winding down to smooth melody before the final chorus, marked by solid singing, even a good set of screams by Bobby: a solid opener. The sparseness of the ending and its singular beauty will remind you of what stripping down to one drummer could do for that kind of implied beat; the rhythm can get so much more spacious with only Kreutzmann.

Kreutzmann also plays a prominent role in the next song, "Big Railroad Blues," giving Garcia a rock-steady platform. And he shines—a nicely executed lead vocal, with perfectly elegant guitar sweetening—and the whole band responds. Weir's comping is exquisite, Lesh runs rings around and through things, and Kreutzmann gives it a metronomic precision without being either heavy-handed or predictable: remarkable. The audience is psyched, though not as much as they should be, it sounds like. This is the first time you get the sense that it is an Ivy League crowd, and a seated one at that.

Pig sounds great on "Big Boss Man," continuing the laid-back feeling, chugging and affectionate in a good harp solo; it's a rough transition to Garcia's companion solo, but once he starts moving, he finds something to say, and builds to a strong close. "Bird Song" is a treat and a highlight of the show. With the mellow mood of the evening so far, the start promises one of those mournful, sweet elegies that the Dead already had the conviction, power, and sheer authority to make sound sincere but not pompous. The jam, just moments into the song, right after the first verse, is one of those that incline one to think that anybody hearing it would become a Deadhead. Restrained and confident, they come across as saying something definite, concrete; but the sense of symbolism, of intending emotional and not literal truths, is the central theme. A few minutes in there is an archetypal Dead moment, sounding loose and sloppy coming out of a jam as the guitarists force a line prematurely, or perhaps it's Kreutzmann lagging, but it's so off-kilter it almost hurts. Being the Dead, they right themselves within a couple of measures—which is not so unusual. What is unusual is that it precipitates some of the sweetest moments in the show, a few hauntingly lovely bars of improvisation around one of "Bird Song"'s signature riffs; not just a recovery, but a graceful compensation—not overdone, simply elegant. Those sublime moments are a big part of the affection Deadheads feel for the band: seeing—hearing—their human pitfalls and their inspired, near-superhuman recoveries.

And in classic Dead self-deprecation, after the enthusiasm dies down, Weir deadpans, "We're gonna tune up": the casualness on the stage is a sign of their swagger. They're doing well, if not transcendently, and the sense they give is that by now there's no real news in that. A new song, though, is certainly news and most fans there hadn't heard one of the dozen or so performances of "Playing in the Band," only a couple of

---

2. Garcia, Reich, and Wenner, *Garcia: Signpost to a New Space*, p. 112.
3. John Zias, e-mail to author, Feb. 1, 1997.
4. Jeff Tamarkin, "Robert Hunter: Keeping It Alive in '85," *Relix*, June–Aug. 1985.
5. Mary Eisenhart, "Robert Hunter: Lifetime Member of the Dead Poets Society," *Bay Area Music Magazine*, Aug. 9, 1991, p. 44.
6. Blair Jackson, "Robert Hunter: The Song Goes On," *The Golden Road*, no. 16 (Spring 1988), p. 32.

months after its debut in February. For a young song, though, it comes off well: no faltering, no missteps, just solidly pounding into one of Bobby's first masterpieces. Solid if all too brief, it always has something to share, and here it has a great deal. Weir's tunes seem to work especially well when given lots of variations in dynamics and sonic density, which "Playing" receives here. "Hard to Handle" has a solid Pigpen funk groove, expressive and controlled. Good groove in the middle, Phil playing a solid funk bass for a few measures before breaking into a classic, soaring, syncopated baroque line dancing heavily through and over and around Garcia, Weir comping beautifully through the tangle, and Kreutzmann reveling in the freedom to float. The result is one of their finest moments in the show, that long extended jam a couple of minutes in; you'll know when you hit it. A reminder of why Ralph J. Gleason, the pioneering jazz critic for the *San Francisco Chronicle*, called what the Dead were doing in the sixties "really jazz even though the sound of the electric guitars at first inhibits you from saying that."[7] Led by a relentless bass line, climbing over the melody, a swirling Garcia lead over it all, they finally resolve into the melody; this is a song that works particularly well with the one-drummer arrangement.

"Loser" begins softly, slowly; even sweetly. This is the mood they sculpt in this set, and tonight overall. Jerry is in good voice, the band does well with the song's laid-back anguish, especially good harmonies, one of those times when a clean soundboard is almost a distraction—a little audience reaction wouldn't hurt here, a confirmation from the crowd that they too were spellbound. But a clean board tape shows highlights lost in hissy, high-gen tapes, and it is a treat to hear all of the nuances of Garcia's flicks of filigree over Pigpen's sepulchral, understated organ, moaning softly in the background. A superb performance.

Even "Mama Tried" gets the slow treatment, and it too, benefits. Bobby sings in a relaxed and expressive way, but the crowd doesn't seem especially interested in this cowboy Dead, saving its enthusiasm for "Casey Jones," which gets an appreciative cheer as it starts. The band sounds loose and strong, good harmonies still the order of the day; almost a polished pop band, in fact. Still the good ol' Grateful Dead, but it makes you wonder why this didn't do at least as well as their big hit, "Touch of Grey." (Well, the lyrics, for one thing . . .) But it's tight, powerful, and polished, until the first jam—which is also tight but pretty raw, and quite determined. Everything smooths out into precision for the final verses, swelling and bucking as they wind up the vocals, faint screams from the audience getting louder, clearly working things up to fever pitch, and they swing faster and faster, pounding and roaring, racheting it up more, as fast as things have gotten tonight, and even more, just building and toying with the audience, and it sounds as if Weir says *no, one more time*, still faster, finally ended by Garcia's last line: "And you know that notion / Just crossed my mind." Younger Heads used to eighties and nineties shows will be interested to hear a strong final jam cut off by Garcia, but they emerge from the pandemonium on a still-melodic note, which may have been the reason for the call. And it leaves the crowd hungry, in good shape for "Sugar Magnolia" to close the set. With a nice flanging effect on Garcia's guitar to open, it moves determinedly from a sweet, steady introduction, with Lesh clearly psyched, bouncing and running over everyone. The vocals sound good, though the mix isn't optimal. Instruments are clear, however, and Weir's voice carrries well, though it isn't until the final jam that it becomes a highlight of the show and a reminder of how much the band already really liked this song. As a tunesmith, Weir truly tapped the vital part of what made the Dead such a performing powerhouse.

Set 2 opens with the hallmark of the show, and the highlight of the tape, "Good Lovin'." A superb rendition, it clocks in at thirty minutes long, with a six-minute drum solo in the middle, and shows the Dead at their most expansive, layering level after level of improvisation over the melody, abstracting and exploring every nuance it suggests to them, from sparse to orchestral, sweet and lyrical to hard-driving and dense, funk to near-folk simplicity and sparseness. The long, powerful drum solo by Kreutzmann segues seamlessly into a high-energy Garcia run, pushing the whole band into a steamroll back into the song. Some more nice Jerry work over the jam at the "a dollar and a quarter" line, the band cooking along perfectly behind Pig until he's ready to fall into the groove, switching smoothly from rap to scat to full-fledged singing, riffing and using the whole blues vocalist palette as if the entire routine were rehearsed and cued with the band. As Pig winds up they abstract and simplify to nothing in just a few moments, now down to just a cymbal, a drum tap, and then the build-up begins, all of them now, faster and subtler than you can write, can only feel, and GODDAMN what you would give to be in Dillon Gym then, an undergraduate at Princeton, having your mind well and truly blown by

---

7. Ralph J. Gleason, "The Sound of a New Generation," *San Francisco Chronicle*, April 7, 1967.

an alternative standard of excellence every bit as powerful—and a hell of a lot more visceral than the one ensrhined in the ivy-coated halls outside.

Pigpen fans can find the rap transcribed in a couple of places, including an earlier edition of *DeadBase* as well as David Gans' *Playing in the Band*, but transcriptions don't capture the range and emotion of Pigpen's delivery. From an easy start, he begins casually, "I was goin' down the street one day, right after me and my old lady got in a fight. I see this dude on the corner, he say, 'Hey man, you look like you kinda lonesome.' " Thus begins one of Pigpen's most famous raps, one which Lesh remembered years later as definitive: "Rather than try and describe what Pigpen did, I'd say you should listen to him. The best thing I could recommend is a tape from Princeton University in 1971. That 'Good Lovin' is the quintessential Pigpen: the tape will explain it all."[8]

And it does, over the course of an extended narrative, with Pigpen acting as showman, preacher, barker, and matchmaker, bantering with a pimp and making it all come across with a kind of innocence and honesty that would be hard to imagine anyone taking real offense at. Pigpen rolls through the set-up: "He said, 'Well, hey, listen—I just got into bidness' "—the band still going, definitely still wedded to the melody, Pig lifting above it phrase by phrase—"He say, 'Watchoo want?' Well, I said, 'You got any dope?' "—and on through a laundry list before reaching what's really on Pig's mind, what's on every hormone-crazed acid-soaked brain in the place, the band toying with melody still, but thinning it, more and more sparsely now as Pig-the-narrator says, "Oh yeah?" knowingly, after this semi-confession before the clincher: "He said, 'No, man. I got myself a Cadillac!' " Two men who understand each other now, and an audience on the edge of their seats, the dicker-and-barter around Pig's poverty—"And I got to tell him, 'Well, I got about a dollar and a quarter' "—and Jerry is dancing and weaving around the story now, Pig singing again, "I just want a little bit," band cooked up to hot now as Pig delivers the clincher: "This fella slow down and a-turn around, scratch his head just a little bit an' he say, 'I got an I-DEEEEEEEA!' " Pig singing a high, full-throated blues wail now, band up and suddenly out, down to drumbeats only for the denouement, narrator aching for his feminine solace for the evening: "He say, 'Look down on the corner. See that girl?' I said, 'What girl?"—drums only now, beat-beat-beat—"He said, 'The big one!' 'That's a GIRL? I thought that was the Brooklyn Bridge!' He say, 'How much you got?' I say, 'A dollar and a quarter.' 'SOLD! The Brooklyn Bridge!' "

And the audience roars, Pigpen taking them through the end, "She said, 'It's all right now, Daddy, show me what you can do,' and don't you know, now, people, she treated me nice and fine," band fully engaged for another segment, Pig explaining, "That's all I need, a little bit of love, a little bit of love in my soul," band back into a nice long spacey guitar solo over no drums for a minute, the perfect musical inverse of what we began with, sweet and slow now, just the prettified melody, Garcia leading things into heaviness again, insistent calls traded with Lesh, weaving back into sparseness, then back into power as Pig returns for a vocal coda, finishing up the story of his date, a recap of the trouble that led to it, and finally back to the theme of what the doctor ordered for his lovesick heart; "He said, 'Now, son, I know exactly what's wrong with you: you need a little bit of lovin', good ol' love, nothin' on the side, need a love, a good ol' love, don't blow your pride," ending with a "Yes I do" which positions them perfectly for the first verse's reprise, as letter-perfect a wind-up as could have been choreographed.

A gentle, smooth, country-style introduction opens "Me and Bobby McGee," everything in balance: Weir singing softly and understatedly, Garcia sounding like he's delivering a eulogy, Pigpen mashing sweet organ fills, and Lesh hitting a bass line alternatingly sparse and melodic in his trademark style. After the first verse and chorus, it builds up into some power, then grows more emotional, still swinging alternately between sorrow and anguish and touching on resolution, strength, resilience. Weir is an excellent narrator here, Garcia an excellent accompanist to his vocal, playing never intrusive, always pertinent, two-stringed harmony as Lesh performs the equivalent in elegant counterpoint, an octave down. A solid closer, lots of audience interaction, "Yeahs!" yelled from the floor. A bit surprising to hear things slow down again, then, for a languorous crawl into "Deal," chugging into life so slowly that you wonder what they can do with it, how long it will take to gracefully bring this up to room temperature without damage. But a few bars into Garcia's solo, the chug shows signs of filling in easily, becoming the showcase for him that it did in the nineties with his own band, when he seemingly made a speciality of inserting some of his most expressive, dynamic, and versatile solos into otherwise almost soporifically slowed renditions.

A great moment follows as the band argues over the start of the next tune, Garcia finally saying, "Just tell us

---

8. Quoted in Gans and Simon, *Playing in the Band*, p. 129.

how many beats," provoking a somewhat exasperated "Seven!" from Weir, and they swing into "Beat It on Down the Line," a peppy version overall, if relatively subdued until Garcia's first solo, which cranks things up a few notches. Preceded by a nice little strange tuning fragment, "King Bee" uncoils with a slow, smoky introduction, and after things settle, Pigpen leads the band into the song, an easy lope into a fairly rare song in the repertoire: here it was close to the end of its tenure, the second to last time it would make an appearance. And in the course of its leisurely exposition, it does a good job of encapsulating the set as a whole: lots of nuances, some power beneath the laid-back aura, and an ease that borders on overconfidence in places.

After an appropriate pause, we get a leisurely stroll into "Bertha," Pig's organ very faint in the mix, but Jerry in fine voice. He muffs a lyric in the beginning, atoning with some first-rate jamming before the second chorus; not the best singing, but a clear tape will still yield some treasures. "Sing Me Back Home" has Jerry singing lead again, in good voice: slow, simple and sweet. There are some missed harmonies in the beginning, but the final verse and chorus are letter-perfect. Another pause and "Goin' Down the Road Feelin' Bad" starts, easing into that rolling inexorability, sweet and swift, Garcia's guitar ringing happily from the first note, and the band seems serious, picking up and hitting on the groove with total concentration; this bodes well. Good singing, much better than a moment ago, and a wonderful jam—a show where they were especially good at finding the slow, sweet spaces in the jams. And a gorgeous rendition overall, with a semi-sparse tapering off, Garcia calling them back for a last little flourish and coda, building back up to *something*, but unclear as to what or where, just nice little fragments and spins. Something definite is in the groupmind, but the jam just explores for a few minutes, the arrangement unfolding as spontaneously as the individual musicians' parts, the spirit of improvisation taken to its furthest melodic limits . . . maybe "Not Fade Away"? A perfect little tease, but almost sharply they launch into "Lovelight." Audience singing along with "let it shine on me," which is nice to hear, Pig's clearly pleased, the band's cooking solidly—in that classic "Lovelight" groove, worked into a complex, tangled whirlwind of a jam within a couple of minutes, playing with a stretched-out, opened-up arrangement where the drums and bass leave wide open spaces in the rhythm, jazzy, moving swiftly—and then Piggers begins introducing people to each other, breaking through that legendary Ivy League reserve with ease, matchmaking couples with a humor and kindness that has none of the lascivious undercurrent of the rap on "Good Lovin'," before the band falls back into a good, solid chunk of melody to close the song and the set. It still ends too quickly, especially without an encore, but a nice ovation follows anyway, a solid indication of the impact the Dead had made on this secluded outpost of academe.

Experienced tourheads found the show somewhat wanting, according to some reports. Spoiled by powerhouse performances at the Fillmore East, Princeton's laid-back vibe simply didn't measure up. Even so, it ranked; as one veteran wrote, "a solid performance nonetheless."[9] Acoustics seem to be a central memory for many fans. One writer remembered that "the show had more distractions than most, because it was a gym as opposed to the Fillmore ambience, and the sound wasn't the best."[10] But everyone remembers Pigpen: "Musically of course, the highlight was that epic Pig rap (the famous Brooklyn Bridge one) on 'Good Lovin'.' He was the definitive emcee that night."[11]

For Princeton, it was a huge event, especially at this point in the campus's history. Joining most other campuses, Princeton had already begun a seismic swing to the left, accelerated by the previous spring when they joined the nationwide protests and strikes over the invasion of Cambodia and the Kent State killings. When exams were canceled—an unthinkable event there—the somewhat sardonic and half-disbelieving term was coined on campus, "Even Princeton."[12]

And the counterculture was in full bloom, too. When asked what the reaction was to the announcement of the show, one alum's immediate response was: "The campus was *psyched*. At least half the student body had tried pot, and I'd guess a quarter smoked regularly."[13] Whole blocks of tickets were bought by hip eating clubs, Princeton's social and eating facilities for upperclassmen that had replaced fraternities in the late nineteenth century. Freaks or not, one Deadhead who traveled to Dillon remembered differently: "What I remember about that show is, since it was at an Ivy League school, there was a bit of preppie atmosphere (much different from today's definition of preppie)—meaning, there were lots of campus police and they were very nervous because they didn't see the likes of that kind of crowd very often."[14]

---

9. Jerry Gill, e-mail to author, Jan. 30, 1997.
10. John Zias, e-mail to author, Feb. 1, 1997.
11. John Zias, e-mail to author, Feb. 1, 1997.
12. Confidential source.
13. Confidential source.
14. Jerry Gill, e-mail to author, Jan. 30, 1997.

Despite campus police, and the seated arrangement, joints passed freely along the rows of the turned-on segment of the student body, feasting on preinflation pot prices of fifteen dollars an ounce—less, if you had a good connection. For a small group of alums who kindly shared their recollections, their connection was a mild-mannered Southerner, a former football player who routinely turned on his friends with a trunkful of good smokin' weed when he returned from the Deep South after breaks. A good proper Princetonian, one of his friends remembered him as "a little uptight, didn't show his emotions much, and that night, tripping heavily, he decided to let those emotions show a little more, I guess—let people see the real him."[15]

No one, apparently, can remember exactly when this transpired, though—and the band never missed a beat.[16] As one alum recalled, "out of nowhere, this *body* appears on stage. No shirt, gyrating wildly—not dangerous, but dancing. Energetically."[17] Experienced Heads took it in stride, in classic empathic fashion; one tourhead remembered that "it was hilarious because the band had a distinctly 'no big deal' reaction to it, in fact they were rather amused, but the school cops overreacted of course."[18] He was hustled offstage by the proctors (campus police), and then it was off to the infirmary for a shot of Thorazine. Unfortunately, that was the end of the concert for this batch of partiers: once they determined their friend would be fine, they wandered off to repair their shattered psyches. Another alum recounted dealing with the aftermath: "The rest of them spent the remainder of the night in my room talking about it, and how freaked out they were—tripping, as they were, too. I played head doctor to the rest of them until almost dawn."[19]

For the campus, it was a success. The reviews were good, the proctors didn't seem too upset, and the students were pacified—certainly diverted. And it left in its wake a number of war stories that would grow into myths still circulating on campus decades later, providing a sense of local history to the seed groups of Deadheads that sprang up there over the ensuing years. Even twenty-five years on, the participants I spoke with were emphatic: "It was one of the more memorable occasions of my Princeton career," as one of them put it.[20] And the guy who jumped onstage? No ill effects, according to his clubmates: "He showed up fine the next day for dinner, looking kinda sheepish."[21]

NICK MERIWETHER

---

### 4/18/71
**Lusk Field House, SUNY, Cortland, New York**

**Set 1:** Cold Rain and Snow, Me and My Uncle, Bertha, Me and Bobby McGee, Next Time You See Me, China Cat Sunflower > I Know You Rider > Casey Jones
**Set 2:** Second That Emotion, Truckin', Around and Around, Good Lovin' > Drums > Pigpen Rap > Good Lovin'

---

**Source:** SBD, **Quality:** B, **Length:** 1:30
**Highlights:** Cold Rain and Snow, China Cat > Rider > Casey Jones, and Pigpen's rap are well worth the price of admission.

This is the typical April 1971 one-night-stand show. The mix on this tape has lots of emphasis on the lead vocals, which almost overpower the playing. My tape of this show has a complete first set, and only excerpts of the second set. The first set starts off with a slow and languid "Cold Rain and Snow," played at a walking pace. The notes wash over you, each one clear and distinct. A beautiful start, and the crowd loves it! Jerry Garcia makes an announcement for Fred Burns to come up to the stage. "Me and My Uncle" follows, and the pace keeps building. With "Bertha," the band is in stride—not too fast and not too slow. Lesh's bass is going "thonk, thu-thonk, thonk thoink" in all the right places. "Me and Bobby McGee" is next, with a rock-steady rhythm. Garcia plays a very nice bridge solo, and during the "hey-ley-ley-la" chorus, Weir throws in a "Where are those miracles?" By this point, the band is feeling loose. Garcia gets on the lighting techs' case to turn down the lighting in the hall. The rest of the band joins in, commenting that the hall is not the spacecraft assembly building, although it is remarkably similar. Pigpen finally gets a chance to sing, doing a very short but bouncy "Next Time You See Me," finishing off by trading solos with Garcia. Once

---

15. Confidential source.
16. John Zias, e-mail to author, Feb. 1, 1997.
17. Confidential source.
18. Jerry Gill, e-mail to author, Jan. 30, 1997.
19. Confidential source.
20. Confidential source.

21. Confidential source.

again, Bob Weir comments about "the lights creeping back up," and that turning them down would be "most equitable." The band asks the audience how they like the lights, and Pigpen gets in with a kind word for Mr. Electrician Man. The second-set excerpt starts off with "Second That Emotion," the fourth of six times the band ever played it. Garcia mumbles through the start of the second verse, and rips open a stupendous solo for the third. "Truckin'" closes with a wide-open jam, with Garcia exploring a number of short themes, before Lesh "thonks" that it is time for the final verses. "Around and Around" well, it's around, mostly as filler. "Good Lovin'" is the final song on the tape. Pigpen finishes off the verses with an "... is all I need!" and on the next beat, Kreutzmann launches into a drum solo. The drum kit is miked in stereo, so it's very easy to follow along with Kreutzmann as he builds a progression. The entry back into the jam is very rough. Lesh breaks in when it seems that Kreutzmann still has a few ideas left to play out. However, watching the great jam that develops out of this is just so much fun! Pigpen comes back with "Good old lovin', makes you feel so good..." He continues on with a rap coming somewhere out of the recesses of his mind, urging you to put down your things, and get some of that good old love. He then goes downtown, meets up with a "bidness man," and starts up one of his "dollar and a quarter for some nookie" deals. Weir plays around with a short jam that he fully develops several nights later at the Fillmore East during "The Other One." Unfortunately for what promises to be a great rap, we never do find out if Pigpen made his deal or not, as the jam leads into the closing lyrics of the song.

IHOR SLABICKY

## 4/21/71

**Rhode Island Auditorium, Providence, Rhode Island**

**Set 1:** Casey Jones, Mama Tried, Big Boss Man, Loser, Truckin' > Drums > The Other One > Wharf Rat, Hard to Handle, Cumberland Blues, Bird Song, Me and Bobby McGee
**Set 2:** Bertha, Sugar Magnolia, Good Lovin' > Not Fade Away > Goin' Down the Road Feelin' Bad > Not Fade Away Reprise
**Encore:** Uncle John's Band > Johnny B. Goode

**Source:** SBD, **Quality:** B, **Length:** 2:15
**Highlights:** The whole show

This is one of THOSE shows. The Dead manage to deliver an extremely high-caliber performance that has been unfairly overshadowed by the five-night closing of the Fillmore East. Overflowing with massive amounts of energy, it is strong the whole way through. The low-generation soundboard source of this tape has a good mix with minimal hiss and provides some real nice definition to the vocals and instruments. The vocals have just the right amount of reverb, the drums are especially well defined, the guitars sound bright, and Phil's bass sounds exceptionally warm and full.

A spirited "Casey Jones," saturated with its own rhythmic groove, kicks off this show. A rebellious "Mama Tried" really shows the defiant tones as well as an edge to everyone's playing. Pigpen lays down his sarcastic and condescending vocals in a bluesy "Big Boss Man." The high point of this song is Pig's harp solo, heavily flavored with the blues. The still young "Loser" was a perfect choice for this show, as it bubbles over with energy, especially in the chorus.

A very worthy "Truckin'" shuffles down the road with a great lively feel. "Drums" follows, moving in for the kill without the slightest hesitation. This is "Drums" at its best, starting out fast and furious, settling way down deep, and pumping out melodic, pulsating grooves like there's no tomorrow. This transition time when Mickey left the band allowed Billy to open up and play more fully. Keeping up the pace, the band drives right up into "The Other One" with continued intensity. Then they give a quick little energetic jam before descending back down, just in time for the first set of lyrics. They finish up strong, then make a solid transition into "Wharf Rat." Jerry's well-told and frustrating story is convincingly sad. This smooth ballad grows into a sincerely delightful version.

A scorching "Hard to Handle" jams the whole way through with everyone playing their absolute best as they reach the zenith in the big jam. This is a "Hard to Handle" that you definitely should have—it's a blast! The band then launches into a foot-stomping "Cumberland Blues" for an extra-special good time. "Bird Song," one of my favorite versions, clocking in at just under eight minutes, is about as passionate as you could find for a short, early version. "Me and Bobby McGee" is just as perfect, ending a HOT first set.

A fired-up "Bertha" starts off set 2. Jerry doesn't solo through the chorus as he does in many later versions, which allows the full warm notes from Phil's bass to rise up instead. "Sugar Magnolia" is a passionate and inspiring version guaranteed to make you feel warm and fuzzy all over. "Good Lovin'" is filled with great playing from everyone, with kudos especially to master storyteller Pigpen who's got his mojo workin' for this one. Afterward, the boys lead into a feverish "Not Fade Away," transitioning into a version of "Goin' Down the Road" that is so exquisite it is guaranteed to cause severe giggling and goose bumps to the listener. The driving and relentless momentum pushes the jam back into the reprise of "Not Fade Away," which even surpasses the energy level at the beginning of this musical sandwich. The high energy ending of this second set leaves the crowd satisfied.

The "Uncle John's Band" encore is wonderful, especially when it jumps into a phenomenal, lightning-quick "Johnny B. Goode." This is a fine show through and through.

COREY SANDERSON

## 4/22/71

### Municipal Auditorium, Bangor, Maine

**Set 1:** Bertha, Me and My Uncle, Next Time You See Me, Loser, Playing in the Band, Cumberland Blues, Hard to// Handle, Deal, Me and Bobby McGee, Casey Jones
**Set 2:** China Cat Sunflower > I Know You Rider, Greatest Story Ever Told > Beat It on Down the Line, Sing Me Back Home, Good Lovin', Johnny B. Goode

**Source:** SBD, **Quality:** A/B+, **Length:** 2:00, **Genealogy:** MR > RR > RR > PCM > DAT

**Highlights:** Next Time You See Me, Cumberland, Hard to Handle, China Cat, Bobby McGee, Sing Me Back Home, Good Lovin'

This was the only time the Dead ever played the 7,000-seat Municipal Auditorium. With outstanding shows in New York, Boston, and Princeton preceding this one and only three days till they were to start the beloved Fillmore East run, this show may have been a bit of a calm between the hurricane and the tidal wave. 4/22 is impressive on several levels, and has many great moments. Although it's definitely worth having, I would not suggest that this one is a barn burner.

This was the seventeenth "Bertha," and the fifth time they had opened with it. Jerry experiments with early vocal phrasings. Phil's driving bottom stands out. Bobby's chiseled counterpoint is really nice. During "Loser" Weir carves the form and fills in the spaces with the determined visualization of a master craftsman. Phil's bass dances along beside Garcia's vocal. Phil's prominent place in the mix underscores the high drama of this song and gives one the eerie feeling that the protagonist will, sadly, not pull his inside straight. After an immature "Playing in the Band," Bob offers, "That's what happens when the bearded clam gets on the loose...." (Do we really want to know what he's responding to?!) Then he launches into a hot "Cumberland Blues." Phil quickly inhabits the upper end, with upright bass style beats to set the pulse (thunk thunk thunk...). Bobby adds to the canvas with rhythmic color strokes while Jerry's darting lines are moving forward, in, through, and around, just on the edge of losing equilibrium, while simultaneously completely controlled.

After it's done, Phil announces, "OK, now we're gonna do a Microphone Monitor Level Test..." speaking with the quiet solemnity of the announcer at a pro wrestling match who's whipping up the crowd for the good guy.

After extensive banter Pigpen starts to rap:

*Well, I was walkin' down the street picking up some hubcaps...*

Garcia and Kreutzmann, however, were apparently not in the mood to hear about Pigpen's litterbug patrol efforts so they kick right into "Hard to Handle." Phil and Bill are behind the wheel driving the rhythm section with Bob providing that angular slashing discord, keeping it off-balanced and really interesting. Rap master Pigpen is in the house... and he's kicking it old school style, so you best be gettin' out the way. After a taste of rapid-fire rappin', Phil takes over with rich-textured, low-end tremors while Weir and Garcia try to rassle the beast under control. (There's a small cut, a blip really, about halfway through the jam.) Maestro Lesh alternates rhythm and melody as he rampages through the middle of a big phat all-round good ole GD jam. Everyone else settles down a touch to bring it on home, but they can't stop Garcia who's only just gettin' warmed up—until the harsh realization hits that everyone's bailed on him—and they bring it down for a soft landing. Pigpen comes in a beat or two too soon—or too late—back into "baaaby here I am . . ."—but what's a few beats between friends. Phil wraps up the tune, and side A of my cassette with a four-part concussion bombing.

After a well-sung and nicely jammed "Deal," a strong "Bobby McGee," and an only average "Casey Jones," they take a break.

Next: "China Cat." While Bob and Jerry queue up their respective opening melodies, Phil "the Underboss" Lesh puts the "b" in bottom. (Slight warble in the tape in first verse at "silver kimono.") As they turn the corner, you know, THAT corner, which signals the move toward the second verse, Phil discharges a "ba-BOOM!!," like a skier who, schussing smooth and happy down an easy run, decides at the last second to try for a gnarly jump up ahead. But now he has to make a nasty turn to get there, so he digs his skis into the mountain, shifts his weight, and barrels into the turn—ba-BOOM. After the second verse, another quick turn has them in the musical transition where trails merge, and with a quick glance uphill to check for danger, they blast off into the interjam zone. Weir's running an upper-fret, somewhat tense and frustrated solo into "I Know You Rider," which contrasts with Garcia's more lighthearted leads, assuring Bobby that all is well.

Later on, Pigpen's return for "Good Lovin'" must've kicked the whole place into high gear because the energy on the stage comes searing through the tape. All instruments seem to be crackling with high voltage. Pig digs right into the lyric. Phil clears my sinuses as Billy starts the drum solo. Billy is *dancing*—he spanks them skins. The rest of the fellas snake back in; Phil catches a neat descending riff right before Pig starts to rap. Pig's rapid-fire delivery tries to keep up with the rest of the speedsters who clearly ain't ready to *wait a minute*: ". . . gotta give it 'cause I want it 'cause I need it gotta have it . . ." Phil rips into, he's high, he's low, he's using uppercuts, jabs, body shots. When he hits the speedbag, it really gets ugly.

Johnny B. Goode starts with the urgency of a full-bladdered Deadhead who's next on line for the bathroom when he hears the first note of "Dark Star." They must've really been trying to get through this tune before the cops pulled the plug. At four minutes long, they were screaming through it.

JAY STRAUSS

## 4/24/71
### Joe College Weekend
### Duke University, Durham, North Carolina

Truckin', Deal, Hard to Handle, Me and Bobby McGee, Playing in the Band, Cumberland Blues, Next Time You See Me, Loser, Sugar Magnolia, Casey Jones, Good Lovin', Me and My Uncle, Sing Me Back Home > Greatest Story Ever Told > Johnny B. Goode, Not Fade Away > Goin' Down the Road Feelin' Bad > Not Fade Away Reprise
**Encore:** Uncle John's Band

**Source:** SBD, **Quality:** A, **Length:** 2:25, **Genealogy:** MR > PCM > DAT

**Highlights:** Good Lovin', Sing Me Back Home > Greatest Story > Johnny B. Goode

For this stop on their East Coast college tour, the Dead played a free outdoor show on a bill with several other groups, including the Beach Boys, with whom they would jam at the Fillmore East a few nights later. An energetic, if pretty routine show, the early part is distinguished by a pretty "Bobby McGee" and a relatively raunchy "Bertha." This must-have version of "Good Lovin'" is a preview of the insanely intense version the Dead would play two nights later at the Fillmore. A sensitive "Sing Me Back Home" segued into the skeletal Pump Song incarnation of "Greatest Story" that the band was playing in early '71, crashing headlong into a full-tilt "Johnny B. Goode." It was back to arena, rock 'n' roll to finish with a rockin' "Not Fade Away," "Goin' Down the Road" medley and a mellow "Uncle John's" encore.

MICHAEL PARRISH

## The Dead's Last Stand at the Fillmore East, April 1971

The April 1971 Fillmore East shows are legendary for many reasons. The Dead played what many regard as some of their best 1971 shows there; there were guest

BILL GRAHAM PRESENTS IN NEW YORK

**PROCOL HARUM**

WINTER CONSORT

TEEGARDEN & VAN WINKLE

JOE'S LIGHTS

April 23-24, 1971

---

**GRATEFUL DEAD**

featuring

THE NEW RIDERS
OF THE PURPLE SAGE

JOE'S LIGHTS

April 25-29, 1971

FILLMORE EAST

*Fillmore East program, April 25–29, 1971*

musicians three of the five nights; and it was the last time the Dead played the venerable theater on New York's seedy Lower East Side. Excellent soundboard tapes of four of the five shows have been in circulation *forever*, it seems, and this is no doubt one reason why the shows are held in such high esteem: "favorite tapes" lists have invariably been stacked in favor of "crispy" soundboards through the years. There's certainly much to enjoy in these shows, but they are not that far away from the mainstream early '71 shows, which were, generally speaking, more tentative (lots of new songs being broken in) and less adventurous than shows later in the year, particularly after Keith Godchaux joined the band. One thing that makes tapes from this era interesting is that, since Pigpen rarely contributed much instrumentally, much of the time we get to hear the Grateful Dead Quartet—Jerry, Bob, Phil, and Billy—and there's a wonderful clarity and definition to the playing that you don't hear once keyboards become prominent in the mix again.

## 4/25/71

Fillmore East, New York, New York

**Set 2:** //Good Lovin' > Drums > Good Lovin', Sing Me Back Home, Not Fade Away > Goin' Down the Road Feelin' Bad > Not Fade Away Reprise

**Source:** SBD, **Quality:** C+, **Length:** 0:45
**Highlights:** Good Lovin' > Drums > Good Lovin'

Considering how common tapes from the other shows in this run are, it's shocking that no one seems to have this one. I tried every tape source I know, up to and including Dick Latvala himself, and never came up with more than a forty-minute segment from the middle of "Good Lovin'" on. I suppose we can assume the show exists on multitrack, like the other nights, but for whatever reason, it seems to have not filtered down to the cassette level. The one side I have is a soundboard of poor quality, with lots of dropouts and mangled tape noises, but your mileage may vary, as they say.

It's a shame that there isn't more of the show around, because what's here is excellent, especially the "Good Lovin'," which features a hilarious rap by Pigpen that's somewhat similar to the famous Princeton rap eight nights earlier. If the band was tired from having played Duke University in North Carolina the previous night, you can't tell from the tape—it's high-energy and nicely focused. "Sing Me Back Home" is as lovely as always, and the "Not Fade Away" > "Goin' Down the Road" sequence is lively, if not particularly jammed out.

— BLAIR JACKSON

*Ticket stub for 4/25/71 at the Fillmore East*

## 4/26/71

**Fillmore East, New York, New York**

**Set 1:** Bertha, Me and My Uncle, Big Boss Man, Loser, Playing in the Band, Hard to Handle, Dark Star > Wharf Rat, Casey Jones
**Set 2:** Sugar Magnolia*, It Hurts Me Too*, Beat It on Down the Line*, China Cat Sunflower > I Know You Rider, Deal, Mama Tried, Good Lovin' > Drums > Good Lovin', Sing Me Back Home, Not Fade Away > Goin' Down the Road Feelin' Bad > Not Fade Away Reprise

* with Duane Allman on guitar

**Source:** SBD, **Quality:** B+, **Length:** 2:30, **Genealogy:** MR > PCM > DAT

**Comments:** "Big Boss Man" and "Wharf Rat" appear on the release *Skull and Roses*.

This was one of two shows in this run I went to (the other was the 28th), and it was just three weeks after I'd seen the Dead two nights at Manhattan Center (April 4 and 5, 1971, the most uncomfortably crowded Dead shows I ever saw). My seat was in literally the last row of the Fillmore balcony, and you know what? It didn't matter at all! I can vividly recall standing on my seat most of the night and "boogying"—that's what we did in the seventies, all you whipper-snappers!—until I was exhausted.

There are no real surprises early on in the set. "Bertha" was a common opener in this era and always got the place rockin'. "Big Boss Man" is a little zippier than most versions. "Playing in the Band" was still a new song at this point and hadn't developed into a jamming vehicle yet—think of the version on *Skull and Roses* and you get the idea. Weir is particularly strong in the middle jam on "Hard to Handle," which is just the tune the band needs to flex its muscles before "Dark Star," which was a first-set rarity even then. This version has both moments of deep space and some soft, gentle, rhythmic passages before it slides into "Wharf Rat," another one of the tunes introduced in February '71. The set-ending "Casey Jones" rocks hard, but frankly this tune did not vary much from night to night (including Garcia's brief solo) so one version is fairly similar to the next.

When the Dead came out for the second set, they brought Duane Allman with them. Alas, this was the only time I ever saw him perform; he died in November '71. One could argue that the three tunes he plays on didn't give him much of a chance to stretch out and strut his stuff, but he kills on the songs anyway. As was often the case with guests, Duane is mixed a little low, but it's still crystal clear what he's adding to each song. On "Sugar Mag" he adds a wicked slide solo that acts as a nice counterpoint to Jerry's wah-wah work. "It Hurts Me Too" also benefits from his fine slide work. "Beat It on Down" also has a nice solo, but the song is too short and limiting to give Duane the space he needs. Having Duane play obviously juiced the band somewhat, because the "China Cat" > "Rider" that follows his departure just smokes, with Phil's bass rumbling all over the jams. The first seconds of "Good Lovin'" are cut. While I prefer the previous night's performance, this version is among many Heads' all-time favorites. The big, highly rhythmic jam, which includes a fully articulated "Saint Stephen" Jam, chugs along powerfully. Again, Weir is amazingly strong and inventive here. "Not Fade Away" has almost no jam at all on it, though to be honest, I can't recall that bothering me one iota at the time. I was not a picky Deadhead in 1971, just a grateful one.

BLAIR JACKSON

## 4/27/71

**Fillmore East, New York, New York**

**Set 1:** Truckin', Mama Tried, Bertha, Next Time You See Me, Cumberland Blues, Me and Bobby McGee, Loser, Hard to Handle, China Cat Sunflower > I Know You Rider, Casey Jones
**Set 2:** Sugar Magnolia, Deal, Me and My Uncle, Bird Song, Playing in the Band, Searchin'*, Riot in Cell Block #9*, Help Me Rhonda*, Okie from Muskogee*, Johnny B. Goode*, Sing Me Back Home, Uncle John's Band > Turn On Your Lovelight

* with members of the Beach Boys

**Source:** SBD, **Quality:** A, **Length:** 3:00

No surprises in the first set here—your standard '71 set of mainly short tunes—but the execution is nearly flawless. The "Truckin'" has a nice jam, and everything else, though not extended beyond normal lengths, is played with vigor and power, particularly "Cumberland," "Loser," and "China Cat." The second set starts with a handful of short tunes, all nicely played, and then at mid-set the Dead are joined onstage by members of the Beach Boys for a wild mini-set of rock 'n' roll classics, one Beach Boys song, and Merle Haggard's right-wing screed, "Okie from Muskogee" (which includes the immortal lines "We don't smoke marijuana in Muskogee/ We don't take our trips on LSD . . ."). If you've ever seen pictures of the Beach Boys from this era, you know that in the early seventies they were not the short-haired, clean-cut crew they were in the mid-sixties (and again in the late seventies). At the Fillmore, they appeared in Caftans and sported long hair and bushy beards—yep, they were heads! The playing and singing is pretty sloppy during this segment, but it's still a fun ride, a true curiosity that probably belongs in every serious tape collection. Then, the Dead-only finale, with "Sing Me Back Home" and "Uncle John's" going into a cool "Lovelight"—the only version of the series—are a nice wrap-up to a show that is all over the map. The "Lovelight" is Pig at his best as he tries to play matchmaker for kids in the audience: How does a guy convince the young lovely next to him to go home and go to bed with him? Just ask her and "Tell 'em Pigpen says it's OK!" Wish I'd thought of that in 1971.

BLAIR JACKSON

*Ticket stubs from 4/26/71 and 4/29/71 at the Fillmore East*

## 4/28/71

**Fillmore East, New York, New York**

**Set 1:** Truckin', Beat It on Down the Line, Loser, El Paso, The Rub, Bird Song, Playing in the Band, Cumberland Blues, Ripple, Me and Bobby McGee, King Bee, //Bertha
**Set 2:** Morning Dew, Me and My Uncle, Deal, Hard to Handle, Cryptical Envelopment > Drums > The Other One > //Wharf Rat, Sugar Magnolia, Dark Star* > Saint Stephen* > Not Fade Away* > Goin' Down the Road Feelin' Bad* > Not Fade Away Reprise*

* with Tom Constanten on keyboards

1. **Source:** SBD, **Quality:** A+, **Length:** 3:00
2. **Source:** FM-SBD (GDH 030, 031, 060, 199, and 210), **Quality:** A+, **Length:** "Truckin'," "Loser" > "The Rub," "Dark Star" through "Not Fade Away" Reprise, "Cumberland Blues," "Ripple," "Morning Dew," "Me and My Uncle"

I had better seats for this show than the 26th, which was great because it was more my style of show all the way around. The first set is wonderful through and through, with "Truckin'" once again a standout, along with excellent versions of "Loser," "Cumberland," "Me and Bobby McGee" (always one of my favorites in this era), a rare electric "Ripple" (sounding like a Buck Owens tune), and the set-ending "Bertha." Even in its relative infancy it was obvious that "Bird Song" would become a great improvisational vehicle for the group, but it doesn't really blossom until '72.

The second set was, not surprisingly, more overwhelming. The second set opener, "Morning Dew," was a complete surprise to me—at that point I'd seen the band ten times, and it was only the second time I'd heard the song live. I'd also only heard "Cryptical" one other time, so that was another treat; as was frequently the case in '71, that went into the still-new "Wharf Rat." But the real fireworks in this show occur at the end of the second set, when Tom Constanten joined the group for "Dark Star" > "Saint Stephen and the familiar "Not Fade Away" > "Goin' Down the Road" medley. This was the only time I saw T.C. with the Dead, and you can tell from the tape that his being there *did* make a difference. The sound of his organ wheedling in and out of the fray was such an integral part of the first Dead album I loved—*Live Dead*—hearing him at the Fillmore almost felt like I was seeing for the first time the band I had fallen in love with. On tapes of 4/28, T.C. is mixed a little lower than I remember from the concert, but of course that could have been a function of where I was sitting at the show. There are certainly much longer and trippier versions of "Dark Star" out there, but this one has a character of its own. For the first several minutes, Billy plays only maracas and cymbals as Phil and Jerry dance around each other in an elegant pas de deux. After the first verse there's a segment dominated by feedback, and that's followed by a slowly accelerating passage that then leads back (too quickly) to the second verse. The "Saint Stephen" that follows rocks hard and is marred only by Bob muffing the final verse, which Jerry clearly thinks is pretty darn funny. T.C. adds some nice, typically ornate flourishes throughout; even on "Not Fade Away."

BLAIR JACKSON

---

### 4/29/71

**Fillmore East, New York, New York**

**Set 1:** Truckin', Bertha, It Hurts Me Too, Cumberland Blues > Me and My Uncle, Bird Song, Playing in the Band, Loser, Dark Hollow, Hard to Handle, Ripple, Me and Bobby McGee, Casey Jones
**Set 2:** Morning Dew, New Minglewood Blues, Sugar Magnolia, Black Peter, Beat It on Down the Line, Second That Emotion, Alligator > Drums > Jam > Goin' Down the Road Feelin' Bad > Cold Rain and Snow, China Cat Sunflower > I Know You Rider, Greatest Story Ever Told > Johnny B. Goode
**Encore 1:** Uncle John's Band
**Encore 2:** Bill Graham's Rap, Midnight Hour > We Bid You Goodnight

**1. Source:** SBD, **Quality:** A+, **Length:** 3:25, **Genealogy:** MR > PCM > DAT
**2. Source:** FM-SBD (DHH 13, GDH 062 and 259), **Quality:** A+, **Length:** "Truckin'," "Bird Song," "Play-ing," "Dark Hollow," "Second That Emotion" through "Cold Rain and Snow," "Sugar Magnolia"

Ah yes, the Dead's final performance at the Fillmore East. As most of you probably know, the Dead are not exactly famous for rising to or even acknowledging big occasions (Woodstock, Egypt, Harmonic Convergence '87, etc.). But this one is a keeper, to say the least, and it's obvious from listening to it that the Dead knew the night had special meaning—after all, the Fillmore East was one of the greatest venues they ever played. The first set is solid from beginning to end, with lots of their coolest uptempo material including "Truckin'," the spry combo of "Cumberland" and "Me and My Uncle," and a superlative "Hard to Handle." This version of "Hard to Handle" is regarded by many as one of the best the group ever played, and it's easy to see why. The jam percolates slowly, Weir and Lesh leading the way at the outset, with Jerry mainly playing supporting chords. Once Garcia's lead begins, though, the jam ascends to a spectacular climax where the lines of Garcia, Lesh, and Weir seem to collide in midflight and explode in a glorious fireball; the crowd's ecstatic reaction, clearly audible on even soundboard tapes, says it all. The Dead also deliver fine readings of "new" tunes like "Playing" and "Bird Song," two electrified acoustic numbers ("Ripple" and "Dark Hollow") and, of course, the de rigueur "Casey Jones" closer.

The second set is where most of the action is, however. Once again there are excellent versions of "Morning Dew" and "Sugar Magnolia," but early on there's also the lone "Black Peter" from the series, and at mid-set the final version of "Second That Emotion" (which reverted to Garcia's solo repertoire for some reason; too bad, since the Dead handled it nicely). After that, though, the band tackles "Alligator" for the first time since the fall of '70, and for what turned out to be the last time ever. The song part of the tune is a little sluggish perhaps, but the jam after Billy's drum solo is widely recognized as one of the best the Dead ever played—it journeys through hints and snatches of "The Other One," "Good Lovin'," "Goin' Down the Road," and "Saint Stephen" before landing beautifully at "Goin' Down the Road." Garcia's tone all through this jam is breathtakingly beautiful and clear; rarely has he sounded more expressive. "Goin' Down the Road" then eases into a lovely, elegiac "Cold Rain and Snow," sung with great feeling by Mr. G. From there, it's party time with "China Cat" > "Rider" and "Greatest Story" > "Johnny B. Goode." Wow!

But wait, there's more. The band comes back and plays a warm, tuneful "Uncle John's" and then, after Bill Graham harangues the crowd for calling out for even more (New Yawkers—never satisfied), the Dead return a second time for a fun, if not terribly inspired, "Midnight Hour" (Pig's final version) and "We Bid You Goodnight," which was a rarity in that period. Great show, great run.

BLAIR JACKSON

---

## ❊ 5/29/71 ❊
### Winterland Arena, San Francisco, California

Casey Jones, Me and Bobby McGee, It Hurts Me Too, Promised Land, Loser, Playing in the Band, Hard to Handle, Me and My Uncle, Truckin' > Drums > The Other One > Wharf Rat, Sing Me Back Home, Cumberland Blues, Sugar Magnolia, Deal, Not Fade Away > Goin' Down the Road Feelin' Bad > Not Fade Away Reprise

---

**Source:** AUD, **Quality:** B to C, **Length:** 2:15 (missing "Me and My Uncle")

**Highlights:** Truckin' > Drums > The Other One > Wharf Rat

The Dead played only two shows in May 1971. This is the first of them, one month to the day after their historic final show at the Fillmore East. Were they rusty after their brief vacation? Not a bit; this show gets off the ground in fine style with a chuggin' "Casey Jones," a song always well received by audiences. Weir sings an earnest "Me and Bobby McGee" and then things get down and dirty with "It Hurts Me Too" as Pigpen and Garcia trade off on appropriately bluesy solos. What follows is the Dead's first-time-ever performance of "The Promised Land," a Chuck Berry song they would play more than 420 times over the next twenty-four years. This initial offering is well rehearsed and rocks along rather well. The next two songs—"Loser" and "Playing in the Band"—are presented in a straightforward and workmanlike manner, well played but unremarkable. "Hard to Handle," however, is a gem. This song is neatly bisected by a very long jam, which, in mid-'71 style, starts out quiet and slowly builds to a fever pitch, gaining ever more intensity until exploding into the final verse—a nifty bit of tension-and-release, a game the Dead played better than anybody. Every good Dead show needs a centerpiece, and this one is no exception. This evening's extended jam begins with "Truckin'," full of energy with Lesh driving the post-song jam along with a pumping shuffle. This short jam winds quickly down and comes to an almost complete stop before turning into a brief drum solo. Eventually, Kreutzmann starts pounding out that familiar rhythm and Phil makes it official with his famous "Other One" intro. It only takes a few minutes of jamming on "The Other One"'s main theme before the Dead get down to the business of deconstructing it. But after only a brief exploration, Weir rounds up the boys and heads right into the singing of the first verse. Fans of weird-ass space music are not denied, however, for immediately following the verse Garcia start spiraling into hypnotic triplets while Lesh tries to see if he can vibrate Winterland into pieces. Through all this, Weir and Kreutzmann do their best to keep things on a rhythmic track. These diverging streams of musical consciousness play tug-of-war and for a while, but it's a losing battle for the Forces of Extreme Weirdness. But eventually Lesh convinces the beat-minded troops that the true path to enlightenment is paved with dissonance, drowning everyone out with some seriously loud and low rumblings. Has the December 8 time signature been vanquished at last? No! Here comes Billy to the rescue, revitalizing the "Other One" beat. One by one the rest of the band falls into formation and Weir crosses the t's and dots the i's by singing the final verse. After such a heated battle, it's only natural for the weary to want a little rest and relaxation, so Garcia heads right into a slow and soulful "Wharf Rat." It's played perfectly; a requisite cool-down after a glimpse into the edge of hyperspace. Our boys can't help but wring just little bit more craziness from the music, winding down the short jam after "Wharf Rat" with some right proper discordance.

The final leg of the journey begins on an even slower course with Sing Me Back Home. Garcia's solo on this song soars high above the arena, does a few tricky loops, and dives back down just in time for the final verse. "Enough of this slooooow stuff already," the band seems to be saying as they churn out high-octane versions of "Cumberland Blues" and "Sugar Magnolia." As the final notes of "Sugar Magnolia" reverberate into Winterland's rafters, Garcia winds up and offers a nice, fat "Deal" down the center of the plate. The rest of the band smacks it over the fence. Played in typical, slowed-down 1971 fashion, it's a good counterpoint to the intensity of the previous two selections.

Like the man said, all things must pass. The final piece of the evening is "Not Fade Away" > "Goin' Down the Road Feelin' Bad" > "Not Fade Away," the suite that closed about half the shows from this era. It's a fitting coda. Kreutzmann rocks, Garcia rolls, Weir chunks, and Lesh throbs through a short and compact version of this sandwich. It's satisfying and well played and a nice capper to some two-odd hours of pleasure.

JEFF TIEDRICH

## 5/30/71
### Winterland Arena, San Francisco, California

**Set 1:** Bertha, Me and Bobby McGee, The Rub, Playing in the Band, Loser, Next Time You See Me, Morning Dew, Promised Land, Good Lovin'
**Set 2:** China Cat Sunflower > I Know You Rider, Sugar Magnolia//, //Cumberland Blues, Me and My Uncle, Deal, Truckin' > Turn On Your Lovelight, Uncle John's Band, Casey Jones
**Encore:** Johnny B. Goode

**Source:** AUD, **Quality:** B to C, **Length:** 2:15
**Highlights:** The Rub, Morning Dew, Good Lovin'

The second night of a two-night stand at the Winterland Arena in San Francisco, this show starts off in familiar fashion with an uptempo "Bertha." However, an attempt to change the arrangement by placing the instrumental break in a different place backfires with Weir attempting to sing a chorus where none exists. After a quick recovery, everything comes back to normal. "Me and Bobby McGee" follows, with Garcia playing some unusual (for him) double-stop bent notes during his instrumental part. A nice, rare electric version of "The Rub" is next, bouncy and full of energy. Phil's throbbing bass lines dominate a slow "Loser." "Playing in the Band" is presented in its pre-Keith incarnation: slow and lacking the mid-song jam, without which any version pales in comparison. Bobby introduces a rockin' version of "Next Time You See Me" with "here comes the Pigpen Shuffle, right on time!" Good harmonica work shines during this song.

"Morning Dew" rarely shows up in the middle of a first set, but here it is, and it fits in splendidly. Garcia's vocals are particularly strong. "Promised Land," played here for only the second time, is an interesting curiosity as Garcia, still feeling his way around the song, plays some stereotypical Chuck Berryesque riffs. The set ends in fine form with an unusual "Good Lovin'." Things start normally but it's the mid-song jam that, bears notice. After Pigpen's standard macho posturing, Garcia and Company launch into some serious jamming. What makes this "Good Lovin'" unique is that, instead of a straight-ahead churn back into the vocals, the band starts winding down, playing slower and slower (and grittier and grittier). Eventually things melt down into a good old free-form space jam—in the middle of "Good Lovin'"! Unfortunately, just as things get interesting, a splice in the tape brings us back to the band jamming on the standard "Good Lovin'" chords. Quelle disappointment! We'll never know just how far out the boys got.

Set 2 opens with decent versions of "China Cat Sunflower" and "I Know You Rider," connected by a very well-thought-out Weir-led jam. Unlike most "China" > "Rider" jams of this era, Garcia does not contribute much lead work to the transition. "Sugar Magnolia" is next, and the crowd greets it with much enthusiasm. Unfortunately, the end of this song is cut, as is the beginning of the next song, a speedy "Cumberland Blues." Lesh and Garcia bounce off each other nicely during the instrumental parts, with one playing high up while the other plays low, and vice versa. Era-standard versions of "Me and My Uncle" and "Deal" follow.

The crowd greets "Truckin'" with so much hollering and clapping, continuing throughout the song, that at times they drown out the music. Clearly, this is the crowd-pleaser of the evening—until the band jams into the next song: "Turn On Your Lovelight." At that point the audience nearly goes into mass convulsions.

Unfortunately, it's at this point that something goes seriously wrong with the taper's deck. Perhaps the batteries started to go south. From "Lovelight" on, the music becomes muddier and muddier and it becomes impossible to pick out just what it is that Pigpen is rapping about. Every now and then, some interesting phrase rises out of the muck. One tantalizing instance follows thusly:

**Pigpen:** mumble mumble hungry. Does he want some baloney? No. mumble mumble want some mumble mumble? No! Mumble mumble. Mumble mumble mumble? No! He wants a little bit of PUSSY! Mumble mumble . . .

It is also apparent that at some point Pigpen is playing matchmaker—always a crowd-pleasing moment—trying to get various men and women in the audience to hook up with each other.

"Uncle John's Band," "Casey Jones," and "Johnny B. Goode" end the show, but sadly, by this time the tape is so degraded and inaudible that these songs are almost unrecognizable, making it pointless to evaluate them. Here is a show that cries out for the soundboard to circulate!

JEFF TIEDRICH

## 6/21/71

### Chateau d'Herouville, Herouville, France

Hard to Handle, Deal, //China Cat Sunflower > I Know You Rider, Morning Dew, Playing in the Band, Big Boss Man, Black Peter, Bertha, Casey Jones, Cryptical Envelopment > Drums > The Other One > Wharf Rat, Sugar Magnolia, Sing Me Back Home, Johnny B. Goode

**1. Source:** SBD, **Quality:** A, **Length:** 1:30 ("Playing" through "Johnny B. Goode")
**2. Source:** AUD, **Quality:** C–, **Length:** 0:30 ("Hard to Handle" through "Morning Dew")
**Highlights:** Big Boss Man, The Other One, Sugar Magnolia

The Dead's second show on European soil is an interesting one. However, for once in the annals of the Grateful Dead, this had less to do with the music played than with the particularly bizarre circumstances that surrounded its performance. They were invited to a free festival that was to take place at the country hang-out of a Paris fashion designer, Jean Bouquin; apparently it was organized just to ease his boredom and amuse his high-fashion friends. However, this ostensible purpose may have had something more behind it because the band was to be lodged at the nearby chateau at Herouville, owned by a composer friend of Bouquin's and recently refurbished with all modern comforts and luxuries. These included a health spa, a tennis court, and a swimming pool but also a new state-of-the-art recording studio that one suspects he might have liked the Dead to take a fancy to, famed as they were at the time for their endless studio noodling. But the real reason the Dead were persuaded to come over was that Bouquin paid for transport not only for the band, their own sound system, and a full sound crew, but also of about half of the huge extended family that surrounded the Dead. It was a free holiday and not to be turned down.

Fate intervened, however, in the shape of one of the biggest downpours in that area this century. The festival site was totally washed away and the Dead were marooned in the chateau. Apparently the distractions included an open cellar and a procession of leggy French girls who came and went at convenient intervals. Phil was in hog heaven in any case because Chopin had once lived in the chateau, and Pigpen never stirred due to the stash of duty-free Wild Turkey he had taken care to acquire on the journey. Despite all this and a day trip to Paris, during which a bemused Deadhead met Garcia halfway up the Eiffel Tower, the band members were restless and started to make plans to play. In the end they just set up outside the chateau and played for free for over three hours to about two hundred people, mainly just yokels from the local village, including the mayor, the fire brigade, a load of small children, and a camera crew from a Paris TV station who broadcast the show the next week (where's the video?!). The story is that everyone just got unbelievably drunk, pushed each other in the swimming pool throughout, and thoroughly enjoyed themselves. The music itself is never less than competent, but then again, it is rarely inspiring. However, to be fair, this must be placed in the context of the fact, virtually unheard of at the time, that the band had only played two shows in the past two months and had not played live at all for the previous three weeks. Apparently we don't have quite the full show, but many of the versions played are rather short and workmanlike. The notable exception to this is "The Other One," which is both long and interesting. The jam goes in a number of very unusual directions, although not in a particularly focused manner, finally sliding into a "Wharf Rat" that never quite makes it. The band headed back to San Francisco, and more normal forms of weirdness, the next day.

JAMES SWIFT

## 7/2/71
### Fillmore West, San Francisco, California

**Set 1:** Bertha, Me and Bobby McGee, Next Time You See Me, China Cat Sunflower > I Know You Rider, Playing in the Band, Loser, The Rub, Me and My Uncle, Big Railroad Blues, Hard to Handle, Deal, Promised Land, Good Lovin'
**Set 2:** Sugar Magnolia, Sing Me Back Home, Mama Tried, Cryptical Envelopment > Drums > The Other One > Cryptical Reprise, Big Boss Man, Casey Jones, Not Fade Away > Goin' Down the Road Feelin' Bad > Not Fade Away Reprise
**Encore:** Johnny B. Goode

1. **Source:** Pre-FM SBD, **Quality:** A, **Length:** 3:15
2. **Source:** FM-SBD (KSAN, San Francisco), **Quality:** B+, **Length:** 3:00, **Genealogy:** MR > DAT
3. **Source:** LP *Last Days of the Fillmore*, **Quality:** B+, **Length:** 0:10 ("Casey Jones" and "Johnny B. Goode" only), **Genealogy:** LP
4. **Source:** FM-SBD (GDH 145 and 146), **Quality:** A, **Length:** "Bertha" through "Next Time," "The Rub," "Hard to Handle" through "Good Lovin'," "Sugar Magnolia" > "Sing Me Back Home," "Cryptical Envelopment" through "Big Boss Man"

**Highlights:** Bertha, The Rub

The Dead's fine set during the Fillmore West's closing week was a fitting farewell to the site of many of their most memorable performances. It is worth noting that Garcia had already been onstage playing pedal steel for over two hours, first with the Rowan Brothers and later in the New Riders, before the Dead started their three-hour set with a memorable, churning version of "Bertha," their stock opener for that era. As the first FM broadcast of 1971, this performance marked the first time many of the *Skull and Roses* tunes, like "Playing in the Band" and "Big Boss Man," entered into wide trading circulation. The FM versions of this tape were eventually superseded by a crisp soundboard version that began circulating near the end of the eighties. The first set is an expertly played textbook example of the new short song format the Dead adopted in 1971, and features almost exclusively material introduced since the beginning of the year. Highlights include one of Weir's best versions of "Bobby McGee," a loose, good-humored version of "The Rub," a slow, funky "Deal," and a long, energetic "Good Lovin'."

In a switch from later tradition, the second set opens with a smokin' "Sugar Magnolia" and a particularly sweet "Sing Me Back Home." Lesh dedicates the majestic version of "That's It for the Other One" to Bear, who had been incarcerated for several months at Terminal Island on drug charges. One of Kreutzmann's more engaging drum solos follows Garcia's vocal introduction, and the song's long instrumental excursions meander down to a low-key conclusion. Set 2 finished in fine fashion with a rave-up "Not Fade Away" > "Goin' Down the Road" > "Not Fade Away." The audience claps for well over ten minutes before the band returns with one of the performances that made it into the Fillmore movie and CD, a ripping "Johnny B. Goode" that the usually close-mouthed Garcia prefaces by shouting, "All right folks, here's the one it's all about!" The Dead's last gig at the Fillmore West stands as an affectionate, finely executed farewell to one of their favorite early venues.

MICHAEL PARRISH

## 7/31/71
### Yale Bowl, New Haven, Connecticut

**Set 1:** Truckin', Sugaree, Mr. Charlie, Mama Tried, Big Railroad Blues, Hard to Handle, Loser, Playing in the Band > Dark Star > Bird Song, El Paso, Me and Bobby McGee
**Set 2:** Bertha, Big Boss Man, Me and My Uncle, Deal, China Cat Sunflower > I Know You Rider, Sing Me Back Home, Sugar Magnolia, Casey Jones, Not Fade Away > Goin' Down the Road Feelin' Bad > Darkness Jam > Not Fade Away Reprise
**Encore:** Uncle John's Band > Johnny B. Goode

**Source:** AUD, **Quality:** B, **Length:** 3:00
**Highlights:** The entire show

The year 1971 is widely regarded as a weaker one for the Grateful Dead during the seventies. Of course, there are exceptions to that statement, and this summer spectacular is one of the most prominent. Indeed, this Ivy League visit oozes energy from the first note to the last, combining all elements of great jamming, tight rhythms, confident vocals, and synchronized musicianship. After opening confidently with a supercharged "Truckin'," the Dead break out a pair of first-timers. The "Sugaree" is perfectly succinct, immature, but sounding oh-so-good. Garcia's tone is blisteringly bright, semidistorted with just the right amount of sustain. And I love those precision bends! This exemplifies how well the Dead can turn nervous reluctance into passionate emotion on any given night. The set continues at a high-energy pace through the standard '71 repertoire before the highlight: "Playing" > "Dark Star" > "Bird Song." While the "Playing" is certainly nothing to write home about, the "Dark Star" is manic and highly energized, one of the best of the few versions played in '71. Segueing rapidly into the outer depths, the band noodles aimlessly, rushing, before restating the theme to ground themselves at the three-minute mark. Garcia quickly loses himself and the rest of the band as he attempts to find the Zone, resulting in a premature meltdown, which flounders around for a few minutes like an infant left unnurtured. As the jam ascends rather suddenly, Phil again attempts to restate the theme and is joined by Garcia a few seconds later, bringing the band into a slightly disoriented "Dark Star" that begins to soar with energy, continuing for a few moments before arriving at the first verse. Coming out of the verse, Lesh and Garcia trade heavy riffs complemented by Weir's calculated and pointed feedback bombs. Provoked, Kreutzmann begins to spastically increase the pace, and the resulting chaos leaves the listener trembling in bewilderment. A frantic "Feelin' Groovy Jam" emerges out of this, complemented by a well-timed yawp from an anonymous member of the audience. At this point, the band is completely locked in to each other, the energy has peaked, and the groove has climaxed. For a split second, Garcia does a comical "Bertha" tease, before beginning to unravel with spiraling sixteenth-note descensions. This lands gracefully at what appears to be the second verse, but the boys take their time, dancing restlessly around the theme. Garcia's melodic phrases at this point are a heavenly delight, each note a savory taste of musical bliss. Seemingly from nowhere, "Bird Song" bursts forth dramatically, and the band's cosmic direction shifts gears in drastic fashion. Just a tad rushed, the music that follows comes through the band rather than from the band, oozing color and imagery from each note. This is an immense "Bird Song"—very rocked out!! The set-closing combo of "El Paso" and "Bobby McGee" continues the energy level set by the preceding tunes in more standardized fashion.

The Dead return to the bandstand and, still obviously pumped, blaze confidently through more of their regular set. Each tune is executed with ragged festivity, the boys and the audience in great spirits at this point. Mid-set, the band decides to get serious with a fantastically charged "China" > "Rider." This version features some of Garcia's clearest vocals, and a fantastically unique jam on the transition. Kreutzmann, in particular, is having a great time shuffling the rhythm up a bit, almost hinting at "Not Fade Away" at times. Although hardly an original finale for 1971, the concluding forty-five minutes of this performance is solid '71 Dead all the way. The execution is understandably clumsy, but this is good summer rockin' nonetheless. Halfway into the "Darkness Jam," it becomes obvious that the band is getting out of tune (must've been hot that day) and the boys wisely wrap the set up in quick, yet solid fashion. Retuned, the boys return to the stage with a heart-warming encore of "Uncle John's Band" > "Johnny B. Goode," sending this show off with a smile.

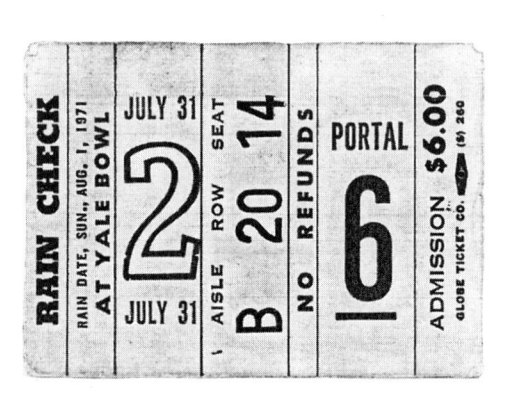

*Ticket stub for 7/31/71 at the Yale Bowl, New Haven*

BRIAN DYKE

## 8/5/71
### Hollywood Palladium, Los Angeles, California

**Set 1:** Bertha, Me and My Uncle, Mr. Charlie, Sugaree, El Paso, Cryptical Envelopment > Drums > The Other One > Wharf Rat, Me and Bobby McGee, Casey Jones
**Set 2:** Truckin', Loser, Sugar Magnolia//, //Not Fade Away > Goin' Down the Road Feelin' Bad > Not Fade Away Reprise, Johnny B. Goode

**Source:** AUD, **Quality:** A–, **Length:** 1:40, **Genealogy:** MR > RR > PCM > DAT, **Taper:** Rob Bertrando
**Highlights:** Bertha, The Other One
**Comments:** One of the finest audience tapes made prior to 1974. Sony ECM-22 condenser mikes into a Sony 770 portable 7-inch reel deck. Master tapes dubbed to PCM. This is the less known of the two audience tapes that came out of this run in Los Angeles.

The show the following night was much more solid all the way through and has always been preferred. This performance is no slouch, however, either as a tape or a show. The sound quality on the tape is very nearly as good as the second show. The added deficiencies may be as much from the difference in PA sound as in microphone placement. The show begins with a unique "Bertha" that features a long introductory jam before the first verse. Garcia's mike must have been out, but the band did not miss a beat, and we get to hear one of the best versions ever of that song. The rest of the set was spotty but featured a nice version of "Sugaree," only the second ever, and a "Cryptical" > "Other One" suite that did not reach the peak of the following night's, but was powerful in its own right. The second set never really got off the ground until the final "Not Fade Away" > "Goin' Down the Road" sandwich, although, to be fair, part of the set is missing where the batteries began to die and had to be changed. You can hear the tape start to warble during "Loser" and "Sugar Magnolia." Bird Song," which was performed between "Sugar Magnolia" and "Not Fade Away," does not appear on this tape.

DOUGAL DONALDSON

## 8/6/71
### Hollywood Palladium, Los Angeles, California

**Set 1:** Bertha, Playing in the Band, Loser, Mr. Charlie, Cumberland Blues, Brokedown Palace, Me and Bobby McGee, Hard to Handle, Casey Jones
**Set 2:** Saint Stephen, Truckin' > Drums > The Other One > Me and My Uncle > The Other One > Deal, Sugar Magnolia, Morning Dew, Turn On Your Lovelight

**Source:** AUD, **Quality:** A, **Length:** 2:15, **Genealogy:** MR > RR > PCM > DAT, **Taper:** Rob Bertrando
**Highlights:** Mr. Charlie, Cumberland, Hard to Handle, The Other One > Me and My Uncle
**Comments:** One of the best-known, best-quality audience tapes in existence. (Rob Bertrando's recollection of the recording of this show can be found on page 27.)

This show is a mindblower. Stellar versions of songs litter the first set, including a tight "Mr. Charlie," a blistering "Cumberland Blues," and what some feel is the best version of "Hard to Handle" ever recorded (rumor has it that Garcia dropped to his knees during the jam's climax). The second set opened with one of the last "Saint Stephen"s until the postvacation era. Then things got interesting. "Truckin'" and "The Other One" were de rigueur in those days, but this night's versions were out of this world. "The Other One" crackled from the beginning and, after the first verse, steamrolled into "Me and My Uncle." This combo would reoccur several times in the fall and winter tours, but this was the first time this had been done all year. The ambience of the tape really brings it alive, and you can hear the earliest suggestions of the song as it begins to form itself into the consciousness of the music. After a couple of false beginnings, the band builds up the tempo into an a full frontal assault on "The Other One" that transitions perfectly into "Me and My Uncle" with a simple chord change from Weir. The die is cast and the band charges right into the first verse. One of the all-time great segues and one that, because of the ubiquitousness of the tape, would leap into one's mind as a possibility whenever the band approached the same level of intensity in a free-form jam. After "Me and My Uncle" concludes, the band completes "The Other One" and then allows the audience to recover by flowing into a mellow "Deal." However, the fun is not over yet. A tremendous "Morning Dew" follows, and the finale of "Turn On Your Lovelight" brings the show to a trembling close. It's in the opening notes of "Lovelight" that you can really understand just how good this tape is. You are able to hear every note of each instrument, each tap of the cymbal, each inflection of Pigpen's voice. It is amazing that such a tape, one that is rarely equalled even in the high-tech digital nineties, could have been made in 1971 with equipment that was not particularly exceptional. Why doesn't every tape sound this good?

DOUGAL DONALDSON

---

### 8/14/71
**Berkeley Community Theatre, Berkeley, California**

**Set 1:** Bertha, Me and My Uncle, Mr. Charlie, Sugaree, El Paso, Big Railroad Blues, Big Boss Man, Brokedown Palace, Playing in the Band, Hard to Handle, Cumberland Blues, Loser, Promised Land
**Set 2:** Truckin' > Drums > The Other One, Me and Bobby McGee, Sugar Magnolia, Not Fade Away > Goin' Down the Road Feelin' Bad > Not Fade Away
**Encore:** Johnny B. Goode, Uncle John's Band

---

**Source:** SBD, **Quality:** A, **Length:** 3:20, **Genealogy:** See below

**Highlights:** Bertha, Me and My Uncle, El Paso, Promised Land, The Other One, Not Fade Away, Johnny B. Goode

**Comments:** The nicest gifts are those given or received unexpectedly. That was certainly the case in April 1997 with these previously uncirculating and rich-sounding soundboard tapes. Out of the blue I was approached by a trader who had had the good fortune to discover in his friend's sister's music collection (she had worked for the Grateful Dead in their business office) first-generation soundboard tapes of the two August 1971 Berkeley shows that Jerry had given her as a gift. Her brother had inherited the tapes when she passed away, and had packed them carefully away, not realizing they were shows that did not circulate and were not in the Vault either. When my friend came upon them, he recognized what he had discovered, offered them to me in a trade, and had them transferred to DAT. Hence, my unexpected good fortune and gratitude, as well as this review! The set list for the first night had previously been mixed up and incomplete, and the history for the tapes, for those keeping score at home, went: master reels > the tapes Jerry gave to Bonnie > both my friend's and my copies.

The first set opens with an introduction by Bill Graham and energetic versions of both "Bertha" and "Me and My Uncle." There is some amusing stage banter from Bobby, Jerry, and Phil throughout the set as they tune up between songs. The witticisms and the prominence of Phil's bass in the mix of these shows are two of my favorite aspects of 1971 Grateful Dead music. "El Paso" is played in the slower, more deliberate style that is better suited to this song. Some of the songs, such as "Sugaree" and "Playing in the Band," were fairly new to the repertoire and are not explored the way they soon would be, but all of the Pigpen numbers are delivered with confidence and power, and "Hard to Handle," as is often the case in 1971, shines. The version of "Promised Land," which ends the set, is also crackling with energy and well played.

A significant portion of the "Truckin'" that opens the second set is marred by a sound that resembles an air-raid drill in a blender accompanied by a kazoo. It clears up right at the "busted, down on Bourbon Street" line, and is fine after that. The drums build the rhythm and tension before giving way to a version of "The Other One" that is seized by Phil's thunderous opening and is quickly matched by Jerry's nimble run of notes. It dissolves just as fast as it began before building again and charging in to the first verse. This version of "The Other One" does not have the weaving of songs that some earlier and later versions from 1971 had, but it is just as engaging due to its powerful beginning, its melodious deep space exploration and jam, and its tight climax. A cheerful and rollicking "Sugar Magnolia" is followed by one of those tasty "Not Fade Away" > "Goin' Down the Road Feelin' Bad" > "Not Fade Away" reprise sandwiches that has the Pigpen and Bobby special sauce ending.

Bill Graham comes back out to wish David Crosby, who has just joined the band onstage, a happy birthday. Much as on 9/10/72, he cannot be heard contributing to the music, and is perhaps just a witness to the magic onstage with the best seat in the house! The first encore, "Johnny B. Goode," ends with a Bobby scream that is second only to the "Minglewood Blues" from 5/15/70a. The second encore is a happy and mellow "Uncle John's Band."

ANDY LEMIEUX

---

### 8/15/71
#### Berkeley Community Theatre, Berkeley, California

**Set 1:** Big Railroad Blues, Playing in the Band, Mr. Charlie, Cumberland Blues, Sugaree, Promised Land, Big Boss Man, China Cat Sunflower > I Know You Rider, Me and Bobby McGee, Casey Jones
**Set 2:** Truckin' > Drums > The Other One > Me and My Uncle > The Other One Reprise > Wharf Rat, //Turn On Your Lovelight
**Encore:** Johnny B. Goode > We Bid You Goodnight

---

**Source:** SBD, **Quality:** A, **Length:** 2:15
**Highlights:** Big Railroad Blues, Playing in the Band, Sugaree, Truckin', The Other One, Wharf Rat, Turn On Your Lovelight, We Bid You Goodnight

As with the previous night at the BCT, this show begins in full swing and fine form with a rockin' "Big Railroad Blues." This version is highly charged and tightly played. Equally noteworthy is the fact that Phil is again very prominent in the mix. The first set repeats many of the previous night's songs; a few of them are better played the second time around. Both "Playing in the Band" and "Cumberland Blues" are stretched out a bit more this time around, and the "Sugaree" has more bite to it than the night before, both lyrically and musically. There is some interesting noodling and more amusing talk between the band and the audience on this evening too, regarding a drunken man who repeatedly asked for "White Rabbit" at a previous show and reminds the band of someone who is yelling requests in a similar fashion at this show. The "China Cat Sunflower" > "I Know You Rider" combination is also well played in set 1 after Bobby's lament of the broken-string blues, and although it never ranges too far, it does hint at the flawless and extended versions that would come the following year.

The second set opens with a "Truckin'" that shifts from fat and bouncy to fiery with the postvocal jam and builds in intensity before giving way to Billy's drum solo prelude to "The Other One." Phil's rumbling attack is answered with the counterpoint of Garcia's fervent lead before it briefly dissolves, only to be reintroduced more deliberately before giving way to the first verse and another much deeper and pensive space that is very much in the realm of "Dark Star." This space regains momentum and drops down in to "Me and My Uncle," and then returns as Jerry introduces a jazzier feel to the jam. Phil follows this up with another resounding roll that gives way to the second verse of "The Other One," which in turn gives way to a wistful "Wharf Rat," complete with a very stately ending. The beginning of "Turn On Your Lovelight" is clipped, but it picks up before the opening verse and away the band goes charging, stopping, starting—swinging and swaying along behind Pigpen's seductive pleading and strutting before winding down with the double-team cheerleading of Pigpen and Bobby. An unbridled "Johnny B. Goode" encore leads in to the last known version of "We Bid You Goodnight" with Pigpen, and it is a beauty!

ANDY LEMIEUX

---

### 8/21/71
#### Mickey's Barn, Novato, California

**Set List:** //Ghost Riders in the Sky, Winin' Boy Blues, Pre–Fire on the Mountain Jam, Wall //Song, Rock 'n' Roll Jam, Rock, Roll, 'n' Surf Jam, Screamin' Finale Jam

---

**Source:** SBD, **Quality:** B+, **Length:** 1:30
**Highlights:** All
**Personnel:** John Cippolina, David Crosby, Jerry Garcia, Mickey Hart, Nicky Hopkins, Phil Lesh, Merl Saunders, and Bob Weir

**Comments:** This tape also circulates labeled 9/20/71, which very well may be the correct date.

This all-star jam session from mid-1971 contains several passages of musical experimentation and expertise, often within a few moments of both at the same time.

The tape breaks in on "Ghost Riders in the Sky," most notable for the excellent double-stop leads from Cippolina. Quickly, the boys launch into a ragged rendition of "Winin' Boy Blues," sung by Weir. Although he certainly ain't no Jelly Roll Morton, he does handle the vocal chores with an authority atypical of the Grateful Dead during that period. The following jam, based on just two chords, is a stylistic derivative of "Fire on the Mountain," but executed with considerably more fury and drive. The jamming here is far from spectacular; it even contains a few points that Garcia stumbles through. Rather, the approach seems to be to explore a variety of rhythmic patterns, ranging from constricted to chaotic. The Hart-Lesh presence is volatile, almost erupting in a testosterone-laced head-cuttin' segment. The jam then switches to a rhythm virtually identical to "Fire on the Mountain." Beginning smoothly, the ascension that occurs here is directly proportional to the amount of force applied to each instrument. Soon, the boys are slamming at head-banging proportions. Wisely, the guitarists abandon ship, and Lesh is left to his lonesome for the conclusion, which is monstrous. "Wall Song," which starts rather sluggishly, features some dark soloing from Garcia, but doesn't really begin to jell until the tempo is increased by Lesh, when a fine jam emerges among the fellows. Briefly, one can hear Cippolina playing slide, but mix complications prevent it from being audible. Eventually the jam settles into a sweet duet between Cippolina and Garcia that segues back into the main tempo, when Cippolina unleashes some sweet whistles before the tape fade and subsequent flip.

Picking up on side B, the jam quickly dissolves. The following jam is straight ahead rock 'n' roll, and, like the pre–"Fire on the Mountain" jam, is based simply around two chords. While certainly tight and succinct, this jam is pretty standard all around, with some fine soloing but without any real improvisation until the final minutes, when the boys begin to get rambunctious. Pausing for a few moments to tune up, the fellas continue with yet another two-chord rock 'n' roll jam, this time with a subtle fifties surf feel. Unlike the previous jam, this cooks from start to finish. Though the previous jams had a distinctive Hart-Lesh presence, this is a six-stringer's jam, with all three guitarists wailing like a pack of teenage schoolboys. The concluding jam, this time based around a three-chord structure, is slightly hampered from the tired and slightly out-of-tune instruments of all. Nonetheless, the boys continue to wail relentlessly away until the tape breaks off.

BRIAN DYKE

---

### 8/23/71
#### Auditorium Theater, Chicago, Illinois

**Set 1:** Big Railroad Blues, Playing in the Band, Mr. Charlie, //Sugaree, //El Paso, //Next Time You See Me, Bertha, Me and Bobby McGee, Cumberland Blues

**Set 2:** Big Boss Man, Loser//, Bird Song, //Cryptical //Envelopment > Drums > The Other One > Me and My Uncle > The Other// One > Cryptical Reprise > Wharf Rat, Deal, Brokedown Palace, Empty Pages

---

**Source:** AUD, **Quality:** B, **Length:** 2:15, **Tapers:** Stephen Wade and Fred Ordower

**Highlights:** Cryptical > Drums > The Other One > Me and My Uncle > The Other One, Empty Pages

**Comments:** Empty Pages is patched from a different, inferior source.

This show was recorded by Fred Ordower and Stephen Wade. As with 3/14/71, which they also taped, they have lost track of their master reels; I acquired this show via a trade and loaned it to Stephen so that he could write this review. As I was listening to the first set through headphones, I was delighted to hear proof that this tape was indeed a "child" of their own recording: Stephen's voice, unmistakably saying to the usher, "But I don't wanna sit in my seat," as the Dead start rockin' with "Cumberland Blues." Unfortunately, the tape gives us no such proof to tell us definitively which show this is, 8/23 or 8/24/71. Even Dick Latvala was unable to confirm this. Stephen taped the show, and he is fairly certain that this was the first night. That's good enough for me.

DWIGHT HOLMES

## Flashback

Copies of this performance usually identify the concert as occurring on the following night. Although years have passed since we made this tape, I believe that my friends and I attended the first evening of the engagement. We rented an open-reel Uher tape recorder, and attached the microphone to a portable flood-light stand borrowed from my father, a former professional photographer. I remember the usher's baffled look as we assembled our apparatus and stacked our reels of tape in readiness for the night ahead. The concert represents the first performance given by the Grateful Dead at the Auditorium Theater, a renowned architectural landmark. Although the band would play there on a few other occasions, the facility would eventually ban the group's appearances. It was a formal hall, splendid and grand, but the Grateful Dead's audience throbbed with youthful energy, and destroyed some of the building's decorations and stairway banisters. While no vandal, I too remember feeling confined by the fixed, albeit plush, seats. The band performed competently and presented an evening marked by diversity: contemporary country hits, Chicago-style blues, and recently recorded Grateful Dead songs. Of the three forms, I think the shorter blues numbers showed to best effect. Although various musical themes emerged during "The Other One" medley, the transitions seemed arbitrary rather than organic. The quality of discovery—surely one of the Grateful Dead's strengths—was muted despite the band's efforts. Perhaps the hall inhibited the musicians as much as it bound the peregrinations of the listeners.

STEPHEN WADE

## 8/26/71
### Gaellc Park, Bronx, New York

**Set 1:** //Bertha, Playing in the Band, Mr.// Charlie, Sugaree, El Paso, Big Boss Man, Big Railroad Blues, Hard to Handle, Beat It on Down the Line, Loser, Sugar Magnolia, Empty Pages, Good// Lovin', //Casey Jones

**Set 2:** China Cat Sunflower > I Know You Rider, Cumberland Blues, Truckin' > Drums > The Other// One//, //Saint Stephen > Not Fade Away > Goin' Down the Road Feelin' Bad > Not Fade Away Reprise

1. **Source:** AUD, **Quality:** C–, **Length:** 3:00
2. **Source:** FM-SBD (GDH), **Quality:** A, **Length:** 0:30 ("Saint Stephen" through "Not Fade Away" reprise)

**Highlights:** Mr. Charlie, Big Boss Man, Big Railroad Blues, Hard to Handle, Loser, Sugar Magnolia, Empty Pages, Good Lovin', Casey Jones, Cumberland Blues, Truckin'

**Comments:** Until the mid-1990s this show was only in circulation as a very hissy, thin-sounding audience tape on which the high end occasionally swooshes in and out. It's fascinating to observe the enormous difference between the energy one gets from the two differently sourced tapes. The audience tape *surges* as the crowd clearly reacts with glee at the high energy coming off the stage during most of this show. Although it's ultimately a pretty lousy-sounding tape, there's a great outdoorsy feel to it with just enough audience noise to make you feel like you're in the twentieth row but not enough to interfere with the music (if you can ignore the warble and trebly mix). Conversely, the soundboard segment, though very clean, is flat, dry, unemotional.

This show is notable for Pigpen's superlative first-set performance, particularly his recitation of "Empty Pages," one of only two versions in circulation. (The other was from the performance two days prior in Chicago.) This was Pig's last show until December 1, 1971, and he rocks throughout. "Big Boss Man" is rambunctious, "Mr. Charlie" impeccable. There's a great "let's do it" that can be heard on the audience tape just before "Hard to Handle" starts. This version is almost as good as 8/6 or 4/29—almost. "Good Lovin'," although missing much of the jam, positively *screams* as

Jerry lets rip an incendiary guitar lead at the onset. I should also mention that during "Loser" Jerry sings the "Sweet Suzie" line that we all love so much, but that disappeared quickly thereafter from that song.

From the first note this set burns. "Cumberland Blues" and "Truckin'" feature Jerry at his finest, and the effect is intensified by hearing the audience go nuts whenever he lets it rip or when Bobby roars through the words. "The Other One," which is moderately adventurous, suffers from a few warbles that sound as though the recordist was touching his finger to an open reel as it was recording to gauge how much tape was left. The mid-song cut comes right as the band starts to play softly and ends just as they are about to launch back into the second verse. The next cut comes just as the song (and the ninety-minute cassette side) ends. "Saint Stephen" comes in seconds after the song starts. I hope someday to get the whole show as a soundboard so I can compare the two fully—I'm curious how much good jamming we're missing and whether or not I'll still prefer the audience tape for the excitement provided by the audience reactions.

JOHN R. DWORK

*Ticket stub for 7/30/71 at Gaelic Park*

"Bertha," which they fail to make it through successfully, the band moves unremarkably through a combination of new material and old standards. While certainly they are shaking off the cobwebs, the energy level displayed is admirable nonetheless. Weir gets a tad confused on "One More Saturday Night," singing the first and second verses twice, but hey, it's still in development, right? Switching to balladry, "Brokedown Palace" is perhaps best described as ordinary, unlike the following "Tennessee Jed," which is executed as if it had been a mainstay in the repertoire for years. This version is full of delightful chicken scratches from Garcia. Specifically, the last jam before the finish features some exceptional twang, complemented deliciously by the Lesh/Weir sideways rhythm backings. After the musicians catch their breath, the momentum steadies during "Candyman" before combusting once again with a ferociously roaring "Cumberland Blues." Before the first chorus has unwound, Garcia has already sprinted up the frets with a perfectly intonated series of string bends. Inexplicably, he calls a premature halt, prompting Weir for the final verses before expressing displeasure at the feedback, which hampers the concluding, and incomplete, "El Paso."

BRIAN DYKE

---

### 9/28/71

**Veteran's Memorial Building, Santa Venetia, California**

**Rehearsal:** Bertha, One More Saturday Night, Brokedown Palace, //Tennessee Jed, //Candyman, Cumberland Blues, El Paso//

---

**Source:** SBD, **Quality:** B+, **Length:** 0:30
**Highlights:** Tennessee Jed, Cumberland Blues
**Comments:** *DeadBase IV* does not list a rehearsal on this date; however, Dick Latvala confirmed the dates and lists of these rehearsal sessions.

This tape, supposedly the first of the Godchaux rehearsals, shows the band to be in rusty form, having not performed live for over a month. Perhaps needing to regroup a bit after a month off, this is mainly, "Oh yeah, how does that go?" material. Beginning simply with

---

### 9/29/71

**Veteran's Memorial Building, Santa Venetia, California**

**Rehearsal:** China Cat Sunflower > I Know You Rider, Bertha, Mexicali Blues, Brokedown Palace, Bird Song, Tennessee Jed, Truckin', Me and Bobby McGee, Mexicali Blues

---

**Source:** SBD, **Quality:** B+, **Length:** 0:30
**Highlights:** China Cat Sunflower > I Know You Rider, Mexicali Blues, Brokedown Palace, Bird Song

The previous day's session showed only a glimpse of the brilliance that would be revealed only a few weeks later, but this following rehearsal contains several displays of it. As in its predecessor, however, there lurk traces of hesitation as well. The band begins with a "China Cat Sunflower" > "I Know You Rider" that is every bit as solid though not nearly as exploratory as those on the Great Fall Tour. While Garcia takes a few minutes to get into form, the presence of Weir is commandingly stated from the opening measures. Casually weaving through the chordal maze, Weir confidently leads his bandmates into the verses with his trademark rhythmic chunks. The following "Bertha" attains about the same level as it did the previous day: solid, but not spectacular. Again, Weir gets a bit frisky with the rhythm, prompting Garcia to unveil a few sweet interverse licks before completely blowing his solo. Swapping places, Garcia goes nuts on "Mexicali Blues," soloing furiously underneath each verse while Weir simultaneously croons the vocals and putzes on rhythm. The following "Brokedown Palace" is simply gorgeous, especially complemented by Keith Godchaux's first showcasing of his abilities, successfully overshadowing Weir's rhythm. Sweet and innocent, these licks sound much like a child playing a xylophone. Graduating to more complicated material, "Bird Song" begins as a simple guitarists' duet between Garcia and Weir. As Garcia unwinds out of the first refrain, Kreutzmann subtly joins in, adding simple tom-tom rhythms that oppose Weir's rhythm perfectly. Out of the second refrain they are joined by Lesh, making a full ensemble save for the absence of Godchaux, and ready to launch. Wasting no time, the boys immediately head for deep space, when, for no obvious reason, the band abruptly calls a halt mid-meltdown, and after some obnoxious quibbling from Garcia, shifts swiftly to "Tennessee Jed," with Godchaux seemingly on organ?? Ugh! Undoubtedly unique, this is more distracting than anything else, hampering what is otherwise a smokin' version. Following this, the rehearsal concludes without any notable occurrences.

BRIAN DYKE

---

### 9/30/71
**Veteran's Memorial Building, Santa Venetia, California**

**Rehearsal:** Brown-Eyed Women, Playing in the Band, Jack Straw, //Deep Elem Blues, //Big Railroad Blues, Attics of My Life, Tennessee Jed

**Source:** SBD, **Quality:** B+, **Length:** 0:40
**Highlights:** The whole rehearsal

Unlike the previous rehearsals, in which Godchaux seemed a bit intimidated, this tape, from day 3, unleashes the confidence and assertion that would soon be the definitive characteristics of Grateful Dead Keyboard Player #3. Beginning with a unique intro into "Brown-Eyed Women," which would have been nice to hear in a live setting, the band triumphantly and enthusiastically roars through these selections without a trace of hesitation. The interverse segment of "Playing in the Band" features some wonderful Godchaux-Weir blends, and the jam is methodically perfect, slowly unraveling note by note against the thick rhythm grooves before quickly returning to the reprise. The yet-to-be-performed "Jack Straw," sporting an earlier version of lyrics, is without any notable occurrences. Conversely, the colossal combination of "Deep Elem Blues" and "Big Railroad Blues" is a ballistic boogie jam from start to finish. Godchaux is really in fine form on this one, adding colorful fills that complement perfectly Kreutzmann and Weir's chunky rhythm. The interplay between Garcia and Godchaux begins to ascend spectacularly during "Deep Elem Blues," where they trade biting Strat solos with pristine piano boogies. Though the ballad of the day, "Attics of My Life," is beautifully sparse, the concluding "Tennessee Jed" is gung ho from start to finish, high in energy and amazing musically. Garcia's solos are very hot, and his Telecaster-like tone combined with authoritative country chops has the sting of a honeybee.

BRIAN DYKE

## 10/1/71
### Veteran's Memorial Building, Santa Venetia, California

**Rehearsal:** Deal, Tennessee Jed, Jam > Brown-Eyed Women, Casey Jones, Jack Straw, Mexicali Blues, Saturday Night, Loser//, Keith Jamming, Cold Rain and Snow, Ripple, Cumberland Blues, Uncle John's Band

**Source:** SBD, **Quality:** A/B, **Length:** 0:50
**Highlights:** Cold Rain and Snow, Ripple, Uncle John's Band

This tape, the final of the Godchaux rehearsals, is considerably more subdued than the previous day's smoker. Somewhat restless, the band appears anxious to play live. After some amusing egging on of the immaculate Bob Weir, the rehearsal begins unremarkably with "Casey Jones," followed by another attempt at the new material, "Jack Straw" and "One More Saturday Night." These are only slightly improved from the previous days' versions: still incomplete lyrically, but somewhat more comfortable musically. Particularly tasty is Garcia's fingerpicking on the verse of "Jack Straw." Following a bland "Tennessee Jed" that pales compared to that of the previous day is a jam combining funk patterns by Kreutzmann, straight-ahead rhythm pumps from Lesh, and off-beat antirhythm slashes from Weir. Eventually settling into "Brown-Eyed Women," the band at this point sounds downright sleepy. As if on cue, Godchaux takes the lead with a commanding boogie-woogie jam that appears to lead into "Greatest Story Ever Told," yet dissolves into "Cold Rain and Snow" instead, which oozes authority from start to finish. "Ripple," in which the musicians enter one by one, is simply beautiful, and one cannot help but wonder why this selection was not afforded a heavier rotation in the repertoire. Although the Garcia-Lesh blend is far from in tune, the heartfelt emotion cannot be denied. The same can be said of "Uncle John's Band," which is every bit as delightful as the picture-perfect version from Minneapolis on the opening night of the tour.

BRIAN DYKE

## 10/19/71
### Northrup Auditorium, Minneapolis, Minnesota

**Set 1:** Bertha, Me and My Uncle, Sugaree, Beat It on Down the Line, Cumberland Blues, Tennessee Jed, Black Peter, Jack Straw, Big Railroad Blues, Brown-Eyed Women//, Mexicali Blues, Comes a Time, Playing in the Band, One More Saturday Night, Casey Jones
**Set 2:** Truckin', Ramble On Rose, Me and Bobby McGee, Brokedown Palace, Cryptical Envelopment > Drums > The Other One > Cryptical Reprise// > Wharf Rat, Sugar Magnolia, Uncle John's Band > Not Fade Away > Goin' Down the Road Feelin' //Bad > Not Fade Away Reprise

**1. Source:** SBD, **Quality:** A, **Length:** 2:30
**2. Source:** FM-SBD (KQRS), **Quality:** B, **Length:** 2:30
**3. Source:** FM-SBD (GDH 047 and 066), **Quality:** A, **Length:** 1:00 ("Comes a Time," "Saturday Night," "Casey Jones," "Tennessee Jed," "Jack Straw," "Truckin'," "The Other One")
**Highlights:** Sugaree, Beat It on Down the Line, Truckin', The Other One
**Comments:** This show is now available in a superb soundboard version, although many will have the rather thin FM recording. Although the FM recording has a fair amount of hiss, it nonetheless has a pleasant live-on-stage ambience: the real feel of an *event*. And an event it certainly is, as this is the debut of not only Keith Godchaux but also of no fewer than *six* new songs.

Keith plays both organ and piano during this show, and his swirls and flourishes on both keyboards color and embellish every tune in a refreshingly audible fashion. This makes a welcome change from most of the keyboard contributions of Pigpen and Tom Constanten, which were usually buried beneath amped-up guitars. The Dead have never given new members an easy time of it: throwing them into the deep end of their performance art and expecting them to keep up. Well, Mr. Godchaux acquits himself admirably, handling every curve they throw him with aplomb. The new songs are, well, new songs, and although you might expect them to be performed in a rather tentative fashion, this isn't the case: they're all rather rushed performances, but though they obviously lack the nuances and subtleties brought to them in time, they remain enjoyable as much for their rough edges as for any innate musicality. Oh, and the first-ever "One More Saturday Night" (a great high-octane thrash) is performed on a Tuesday!

Hot tips? Well, "Sugaree" is kept on a tight rein that rather suits it, and the following "Beat It on Down the Line," with a count-in of twenty beats, is positively unhinged, rocketing along at a totally demented velocity, Keith pounding out staccato rhythms like he's always been there. This is actually the point where Inspiration takes a hold of the band, just about everything they're familiar with after this point gets a great reading. "Truckin'" is a raucous stomp, with the obligatory "forgotten lyrics" gaps we all listen out for, but it's the "Cryptical Envelopment" > "Other One" > "Cryptical" reprise segment of the show that really pulls the stops out. Keith plays excellent organ throughout, gliding from rather baroque T.C.–like passages to some bizarre tumbling runs in the space-out sections that are unique. The final "Cryptical" jam contains moments where Garcia leads the ensemble into places of sheer unadulterated beauty that once again show the adeptness of the Dead in discovering totally new angles to explore in the midst of almost overfamiliar constructions.

PAUL BODENHAM

---

### 10/19/71
**Northrup Auditorium, Minneapolis, Minnesota**
**Interview:** Jerry Garcia

**Source:** FM, **Quality:** B, **Length:** 0:10
**Highlights:** "It's kinda like, uh, uh, it's kind of another version of the sidewalk superintendent trip."

In this preconcert interview, Garcia speaks candidly about performance procedures and logistics, his current outside musical activities, and the absence of Pigpen and the addition of Keith Godchaux to the Grateful Dead.

BRIAN DYKE

---

### 10/21/71
**Auditorium Theater, Chicago, Illinois**
**Set 1:** Truckin', Loser, Beat It on Down the Line, Tennessee Jed, Playing in the Band, Big Railroad Blues, Jack Straw, Cumberland Blues//, //Comes a Time, Mexicali Blues, Cold Rain and Snow, One More Saturday Night
**Set 2:** Casey Jones, Me and My Uncle, Dark Star > Sittin' on Top of the World > Dark Star > Me and Bobby McGee, Brown-Eyed Women, Ramble On Rose, Sugar Magnolia
**Encore:** Saint Stephen > Johnny B. Goode

**Source:** FM-SBD, **Quality:** B+, **Length:** 2:45
**Highlights:** The entire second set except Casey Jones. And Keith Godchaux's piano playing.

The 1971 fall tour served as a prelude for what is arguably the Dead's finest period, 1972–74. Here the boys honed their chops, perfected their standards, broke in a new band member, and began the gravitation toward looser and more free-flowing sound. And, as a cherry on the sundae, many of these shows are readily available as fine FM broadcasts. This Chicago performance features a solid first set whose main focus is to further rehearse the material debuted two nights earlier in Minneapolis, as well as to afford Godchaux the opportunity to get comfortable with the band's style. As Phil puts it during a moment of banter, "He's doing one hell of a job." A close listen to this tape shows that to be an understatement. Remember, this was Keith's second gig with the band, making this display of energy a truly awesome spectacle indeed. Each tune in the first set is played solidly; most notable is the extended jam on "Playing in the Band." One of the earliest, this short passage hints at things to come upon maturation. The jam is kept within a very strict parameter, yet features some of the fullest playing of the evening as the boys weave around the main frame searching for potential gateways to try on the next visit. The rest of the set is executed fantastically, the bandmates obviously in good spirits, judging from the wisecracks they make from the stage.

The show's highlight comes near the beginning of the second set as the Dead break out a fantastic "Dark Star"

> "Sittin' on Top of the World" > "Dark Star" > "Me and Bobby McGee." While the rest of the band starts slowly and gently, Godchaux wastes no time with his melting piano fills that immediately stretch the jam outward. Provoked, Garcia and Godchaux lead the way on an outward spiral into meltdown paradise. A brief jam that noodles incessantly emerges before the boys launch into the main theme and verse, with each member locked into the groove perfectly. The verse is executed solidly, but is overshadowed by the following meltdown that spotlights the rookie's ability to intuitively respond to each member's musical interrogations. Godchaux then leads the band through a jam that complements the traditional confusion themes stated by Garcia with echoes of serenity and joy. As the interplay between Garcia and Godchaux builds to a climax, the band falls into the "Feelin' Groovy Jam," at which time Weir begins to assert himself by adding concise rhythms that border on comedic. In response, Garcia and Godchaux lead the jam further out into space before suddenly launching into an unexpected "Sittin' on Top of the World." The band really cooks on this one, with Godchaux hammering out his best boogie-woogie licks behind Garcia's bluesy soloing. At the song's conclusion, the band immediately segues into the second verse of "Dark Star," featuring wonderful backup vocals from Phil. In turn, this flows sweetly into "Me and Bobby McGee." Now it's Weir's turn to take over, as he trades strong vocals with thick juicy rhythms. This continues through "Sugar Magnolia," with Weir the driving force behind the band as they charge through the end of the set. The "Saint Stephen" > "Johnny B. Goode" encore is every bit as energized as the preceding set as the boys conclude one of the years finest performances.

BRIAN DYKE

---

### 10/23/71

**Easttown Theatre, Detroit, Michigan**

**Set 1:** Bertha, Playing in the Band, Loser, Mexicali Blues, Sugaree, Jack Straw, Big Railroad Blues, El Paso, Ramble On Rose, Me and Bobby McGee, Cumberland Blues, Brokedown Palace, One More Saturday Night

**Set 2:** //Casey Jones, Me and My Uncle, Tennessee Jed, Sugar Magnolia, Comes// a Time, Truckin', Brown-Eyed Women, Not Fade Away > Goin' Down the Road Feelin' Bad > Not Fade Away Reprise

**Source:** FM-SBD, **Quality:** B+, **Length:** 2:45
**Highlights:** Not Fade Away > Goin Down the Road > Not Fade Away Reprise

Coming on the heels of a fantastic pair of shows in Minneapolis and Chicago, this fall '71 performance is significantly less adventurous and considerably sloppier than either of its predecessors. Beginning clumsily, the boys warm their chops with a standard opening of "Bertha." From the opening notes, it is evident that the energy level is lower than the preceding performances. The following "Playing in the Band" follows the same pattern as the previous reading two nights earlier in Chicago. The jam is kept brief but is cautiously extended just a hair beyond the song's parameter. The set continues unremarkably through the standard '71 selections until the boys start to loosen up during "Jack Straw." Garcia in particular seems to be getting restless on the attack during the final solo. The Dead continue to build momentum bit by bit throughout the rest of the set, and by "Ramble On Rose," they have the groove locked in tightly. The final songs of the set are executed with much more confidence as Lesh and Godchaux begin to assert themselves. "Cumberland Blues" is a smoker all the way, the entire band going pedal to the metal on the jam, nicely complemented by Lesh's backup vocals. The "Saturday Night" set closer is still underdeveloped, but Weir's comical liberties with the lyrics make it a fun version regardless.

The second set is carried predominately by Weir and Garcia, with Lesh and Godchaux disappointingly quiet throughout. Much like the first set, the play is fairly standard, with sudden blasts of energy when least expected. After opening with "Casey Jones," Weir blazes authoritatively through "Me and My Uncle." Likewise, "Tennessee Jed" is Garcia hot all the way through, featuring some luscious string bending against Weir's sideways rhythm. Unfortunately, the boys run out of gas early, as the following "Sugar Mag" is a sleeper and "Comes a Time" is barely average. Ah, maybe they were just pacing themselves for the concluding thirty minutes, which starts with "Truckin'." Solidly played, the jam features some of Garcia and Weir's strongest licks of the evening, but for some reason the boys decide to call it quits just as the sparks begin to fly, and return to the coda for a very abrupt and graceless ending. Sigh. The following "Brown-Eyed Women" is completely lackluster, but the Dead manage to rebound with a hot set-closing "Not Fade Away" > "Goin' Down the Road Feelin' Bad" > "Not Fade Away." The first jam is led by Garcia but soon is turned over to Lesh, who commands angular offbeats from stage left. (Or was it stage right at the time?) A great jam emerges with Jerry singing triplets out of his Strat, Weir supplying the rhythm, and Lesh leading the march with staccato bass weaves. Eventually this is brought down to simmer, and for the first time of the evening, Keith begins to assert himself with sharp jabs in between Garcia's leads. At first, the jam seems to have flickered out, but Garcia relentlessly thrusts the band to peak once again as the segue into "Goin' Down the Road" begins. As Garcia screams sixteenth notes from his axe, the jam is slowly brought back to a full boil. Of course, in true roller-coaster fashion, the band brings the jam to ground level again on the outro theme, taking their time with a soft spacey melody before lurching back into "Not Fade Away" for the finale, which features one of Weir's strongest yawps on the final "Not Fade Away" chant.

BRIAN DYKE

## 10/26/71

**The Palestra, University of Rochester, Rochester, New York**

**Set 1:** Bertha, Playing in the Band, Sugaree, Me and My Uncle, Tennessee Jed, Big Railroad Blues, Me and Bobby McGee, Cumberland Blues, Cold Rain and Snow, Mexicali Blues, Loser, Beat It on Down the Line, El Paso, Comes a Time, One More Saturday Night
**Set 2:** Ramble On Rose, Truckin' > Drums > The Other One > Johnny B. Goode, Sugar Magnolia

**Source:** FM (WCMF), **Quality:** C+, **Length:** 0:45
**Highlights:** Truckin' > Drums > The Other One > Johnny B. Goode
**Comments:** Severe problems between the FM patch and the PA system leave much of this show inaudible. *However*, there are forty-five minutes where the sound is unscathed and it's very much worth hearing.

This book was written for moments like this: digging up an old B side of a mediocre-quality tape and finding some spectacular music on it. Nobody talks about this tape. This should change. For here is a jewel hidden within an already well-respected and well-represented era. Dig it up and be amazed!

The tape starts with the first set closer, "Saturday Night." It rocks ferociously. Set 2 starts with a strong, well-sung "Truckin'." The ensuing jam features an interesting counterpoint: Garcia does a bluesy, wildly enthusiastic lead on one side, and Lesh, on the other, brings in his jazz roots with a dapper, swing-styled bass line that has a nasty edge to it. The result is like two relentless grave diggers intently shoveling earth under the glow of a lantern. Both "The Other One" and a "Truckin'" reprise are repeatedly teased before finally giving way to a five-minute drum solo by Billy.

As expected, Lesh unleashes a hissing intro to "The Other One." Immediately weird and full of those playful pauses that characterize the jams from the fall of '71, this version is like the weeble that won't fall down. Normally, Billy drops out completely at least once to allow the others to scrape the bottom of the sea in search of odd sound growths. But not this show. The reason is Garcia. He has built up a steady momentum since the post-"Truckin'" jam and seems ready to burst. When Weir sings the "Spanish lady" line Garcia rumbles enticingly. But when Weir completes the line, ". . . it trembles and explodes . . ." Garcia incinerates his guitar in a display of raw, naked energy. It'll floor you. The rest of the band, remarkably, doesn't lose a beat, though they must have tossed Garcia looks of utter amazement.

Garcia has nothing to lose now: the cat's out. He instantly takes charge and overruns his mates at a fever pitch. The rest of the band grab their hats and do all they can to stay with him.

But he's gone, lost in the whirl of pure inspiration. He plays sounds I'd never heard before—and haven't heard since. "The Other One" careens wildly as Garcia turns it inside out. This is a dizzying, breathtaking, virtuosic performance.

When "The Other One" finally skids to a halt, rubber burnin', Garcia slams savagely into J.B. Goode and plays every R&B lick he knows within the five minutes he's given, making it one of the hottest versions ever played. Lesh steps up and propels a sinewy "Sugar Mag" with some thick, bouncing notes. The heat is starting to wear off, though. Nonetheless, I urge you to go find this tape and give it a listen.

MICHAEL M. GETZ

---

## 10/27/71

### Onondaga County War Memorial, Syracuse, New York

**Set 1:** Casey Jones, Me and My Uncle, Deal, Jack Straw, Tennessee Jed, Beat it on Down the Line, Sug//aree, Playing in the Band, Comes a Time, Mexicali Blues, Frozen Logger, Big Railroad Blues, Cumberland// Blues, One More Saturday Night
**Set 2:** Bertha, Me and Bobby McGee, Ramble On Rose, Sugar// Magnolia, //Drums > Goin' Down the Road Feelin' Bad > Not Fade Away Reprise

**Source:** FM-SBD (WAER Syracuse), **Quality:** A–, **Length:** 2:15
**Highlights:** Playing in the Band, Cumberland Blues, One More Saturday Night, Drums > Goin' Down the Road Feelin' Bad

---

Shuffled in among the year's finest performances, this fall of 1971 show depicts the Dead's enthusiasm level at a high level. Unlike so many performances from the same period, there is nothing here that would stand out as being mind-blowing. However, the intensity with which even the simplest selection is executed makes this performance worth having. Although from the opening notes each band member is clearly operating at an acceptable level, it becomes immediately obvious that the rookie, Keith Godchaux, is performing on a level well above that of his companions—a high-testosterone approach to music that would not be heard again until 1990 with the integration of Bruce Hornsby. After opening with a superslick reading of "Casey Jones," the band roars through a predictable combination of new and old material, making even the new songs sound as if they've been performing them for years. And, when least expected, outbursts of pure exhilaration pop up. The mid-set "Playing in the Band," still in its infant stage, is simply luscious, with the interplay between Garcia and Godchaux as tight as an old married couple of several score years. Although this was the honeymoon tour, Keith's ability to intuit the direction of the music is simply astounding, making the shifts from chaos to tranquillity with an unmatchable gracefulness. Following with a beautiful "Comes a Time," the band seemingly catches its breath for a few tunes before unleashing a phenomenally roaring pairing of "Cumberland Blues" and "One More Saturday Night." Although "Cumberland Blues" is fairly sleepy at the onset, following a brief splice, the song is concluded at incredible intensity, at times so exciting that the band seems in awe of the reckless abandon being displayed. Clutching the moment, the band maintains the energy with an equally enthused "One More Saturday Night" set closer.

From the opening notes of "Bertha," the boys crank out 100 percent, opting managing a tight and flawless approach that echoes their performances from earlier in the year. Unfortunately, what one would hope to be the highlight of the night, "Truckin'" > "The Other One," is missing, and the tape breaks in on a very focused and direct "Drums" segment based on the "Not Fade Away" rhythm, setting the path for a one-of-a-kind jam with heavy Allmanesque overtones. Abetted by the illustrious rhythm support of Kreutzmann and Lesh, Garcia throws a unique twist of Dickey Betts licks that furiously revolve around a single note, aided by Godchaux's bell tinkling underneath. Quick to peak, Weir assumes the lead into a brief "China Cat" jam that veers straight into "Goin' Down the Road." Like most late '71 versions, this is about as hot as Grateful Dead rock 'n' roll gets, filled to the brim with Garcia's patented mix of country-folk shuffling > rock 'n' roll soloing and Kreutzmann's and Lesh's thundering drive. Sadly, the band blows up during the final moments, and the "Not Fade Away" coda, only one verse long, fails to achieve impressive status, despite a passionate effort from Weir on vocals.

BRIAN DYKE

## 10/29/71
### Allan Theater, Cleveland, Ohio

**Set 1:** Introduction by Sam Cutler, Truckin', Sugaree, El Paso, Loser, Playing in the Band, //Brown-Eyed Women, Beat It on Down the Line, Brokedown Palace, Jack Straw, Tennessee Jed, Mexicali Blues, Big Railroad Blues, Casey Jones
**Set 2:** Cryptical Envelopment > Drums > The Other One > Me and My Uncle > Cryptical Reprise > De//al, Sugar Magnolia, Ramble On Rose, Not Fade Away > Goin' Down the Road Feelin' Bad > Not Fade Away Reprise
**Encore:** One More Saturday Night

**Source:** SBD, **Quality:** A–, **Length:** 2:53, **Genealogy:** 7-inch MR quarter track > C > DAT
**Highlights:** The high quality of this tape, but no songs in particular

Hello, Cleveland! This tape starts with road manager Sam Cutler saying, "OK Cleveland, let's welcome the Grateful Dead—the Grateful Dead." The band jumps quickly into the standard opener for this tour, i.e., "Truckin'." Typically these were all pretty good and this is no exception. The "Sugaree" that follows is again very typical for this era—nothing earth-shattering but well done all the same. The set plods along in typical late '71 fashion, with standard fare showing no brilliance but maintaining a steady and energetic pace nonetheless. For those keeping track, "Beat It" had eleven hits at the start. "Brokedown" was very nice with exceptionally in-tune vocals. "Jack Straw" is the first real low point of the set, very sloppy and tired. The remainder of the set is average with nothing notable happening except for the

few words spoken by the band between some songs. For instance, Weir's "If you've ever been down to Mexico dodging bullets, then you'll know what I mean" before "Mexicali," and Garcia's "This aha, this tune is called aha, 'Big Railroad Blues.'"

The second set opens with a nice, almost whimsical "Cryptical" that glides its way into a long Billy K. drums solo. The cascading "Other One" ebbs and flows beautifully, reminiscent of a "Dark Star" jam with long melodic dialogue that segues smoothly into "Me and My Uncle." The transition from "Me and My Uncle" is flawless as it pounds its way back into "The Other One," where Weir finally gets to the second verse, having skipped the first altogether. The last part of "Cryptical" is short and very uneventful, the surprise is the "Deal" that follows, an unusual end to an interesting jam. There is a reel flip in the middle of "Deal," however. The rest of the set is on par with the first. All in all, a solid show but nothing exceptional. The high quality of the recording itself, though, makes it a must for collectors.

ROB EATON

## 10/30/71
### Taft Auditorium, Cincinnati, Ohio

**Set 1:** //Bertha, Me and My Uncle, Sugaree, Beat it on Down the Line, Loser, Playing in the Band, Tennessee Jed, Big Railroad Blues, Me and Bobby McGee, Brown-Eyed Women, One More Saturday Night
**Set 2:** Casey Jones, Mexicali Blues, Comes a Time, El Paso, Ramble On Rose, Sugar Magnolia, Truckin', Not Fade Away > Goin' Down the Road Feelin' Bad > Not Fade Away Reprise

**Source:** FM-SBD (WEBN), **Quality:** B+, **Length:** 2:40, **Genealogy:** MR > DAT
**Highlights:** Beat It on Down the Line, Tennessee Jed, Big Railroad Blues, Me and Bobby McGee, One More Saturday Night
**Comments:** In general, the sound quality of this show is quite good. Unfortunately, due to the fact that this is an FM broadcast, they have cranked up the levels of the cheering audience whenever the band finishes a song. There is also a slight bit of source static at the end of the second set. Other than that, things are great.

This show contains plenty of comical band-audience interaction throughout the whole evening. Although the set list doesn't contain songs known for extreme and extensive jamming, the performance is filled with sharp and fairly compelling performances that still deliver that good ol' Grateful Dead feeling.

A slightly clipped "Bertha" leads off the first set with gobs of energy. A quick and energized "Me and My Uncle" makes way for a solid "Sugaree," played lightly but with enough gusto to provide the usual serious feel. This urgent and mighty "Beat It on Down the Line" is played extremely well, with Jerry's picture-perfect solo being extremely noteworthy. Smooth but slightly raspy Garcia vocals intermingled with hot solos and praise-worthy harmonies makes "Loser" a definite show highlight.

Side 2 of cassette one finds the very new and brightly played "Tennessee Jed." Keith has now been turned up in the mix, filling out the whole sound. "Jack Straw," "Big Railroad Blues," "Me and Bobby McGee," "Brown-Eyed Women" are all played eloquently. "One More Saturday Night" caps off the first set with loads of intense energy. Its noteworthy feature is Bobby driving the band forward, extending the ending for another round and finally concluding for a well-deserved set break.

A slow and deliberate "Casey Jones" starts out the second set with a laid-back comfortable feeling. "Comes a Time," another fresh and unpretentious song, features Jerry's crystal-clear voice emotionally educating us on the more sobering realities of life.

A solid "Truckin'," moves along, keeping a decent pace with a graceful jam in the middle. The authoritative opening beats of "Not Fade Away" jump out of the speakers, which causes you to stand up and take notice. Billy isn't messing around on this one, and neither is the rest of the band; everyone sounds intensely serious, making this quite an inspired version. They transition into an equally pleasing "Goin' Down the Road," with intermittent interference from Bobby's vocal mike, jamming for quite a while before reaching the lyrics. The ending becomes gentle and pretty, nicely contrasting with the leap into an even hotter reprise of "Not Fade Away."

With all that, it's easy to understand why this show would be a worthwhile addition to your collection.

COREY SANDERSON

---

### 10/31/71
#### Ohio Theatre, Columbus, Ohio

**Set 1:** Deal, Playing in the Band, One More Saturday Night
**Set 2:** Dark Star > Sugar Magnolia, Saint Stephen > Not Fade Away > Goin' Down the Road Feelin' Bad > Not Fade Away Reprise
**Encore:** Johnny B. Goode

**1. Source:** FM-SBD (*Grateful Dead Hour*), **Quality:** A+, **Length:** 0:20 (first set songs and encore only), **Genealogy:** MR > DR

**2. Source:** CD-SBD (*Dick's Picks II*), **Quality:** A+, **Length:** 1:00 ("Dark Star" > "Sugar Magnolia," "Saint Stephen" > "Not Fade Away" > "Goin' Down the Road Feelin' Bad" > "Not Fade Away" Reprise), **Genealogy:** MR > CD

**Highlights:** Jam between Goin' Down the Road Feelin' Bad and Not Fade Away

This is a strange release. Since the music was previously uncirculated and it's taken from the wonderful fall of '71 tour—it's a wise choice. So why don't I ever listen to it?

First, Keith is buried in the mix. So what we have here is basically a quartet. Second, though the band gives a strong effort, the music falls mostly flat.

"Dark Star" is played intricately and looks good on the surface, but it's too careful and pensive, void of any feeling. All the players have moments where they turn it up a notch but never as a unified thrust. An interesting jam emerges halfway through in the form of a rough draft of what will become "Hypnotized," a tune Weir will eventually pen for his future band, Kingfish. This leads into a spacey melt for a few minutes that starts to show signs of life—until Weir kills it dead by going into a decent "Sugar Mag."

"Saint Stephen" starts out stiff until the closing jam when they make a run at getting fluid. Alas, they fall short again. The "Not Fade Away" sandwich is the most inspired portion of the show. The band loosens up as Billy adds a spark with some boogie-down drumming. The transition into "Goin' Down the Road" features some scorching licks by Garcia who has found a groove at last. The whole band jells and delivers a crisp version. On the way back to "Not Fade Away," the boys take a pleasant detour by jamming on a variation of "Not Fade Away." Oddly, this can't hold a candle to 11/15/71, two weeks later, when the band takes this same spot and gets *way* out there. Definitely a strange release.

MICHAEL M. GETZ

## 11/7/71

**Harding Theater, San Francisco, California**

**Set 1:** Truckin', Brown-Eyed Women, Beat It on Down the Line, Hideaway, Sugaree, Jack Straw, Tennessee Jed, Cumberland Blues, El Paso, Big Railroad Blues, Comes a Time, Mexicali Blues, One More Saturday Night
**Set 2:** Ramble On Rose, Me and Bobby McGee, Loser, Sugar Magnolia, Dark Star > Drums > The Other One > Me and My Uncle > The Other One Reprise > Deal, Brokedown Palace, Playing in the Band, Casey Jones, Not Fade Away > Goin' Down the Road Feelin' Bad > Not Fade Away Reprise
**Encore:** Johnny B. Goode, Uncle John's Band

**1. Source:** FM-SBD, **Quality:** A/A+ (except "Saturday Night": on most, but not all, tapes this song has several glitches), **Length:** 3:20, **Genealogy:** MR > PCM > DAT, pre-FM MR > DAT
**2. Source:** FM-SBD (DHH 38), **Quality:** A, **Length:** "Hideaway," "Dark Star" through "The Other One" Reprise, "Brokedown," "Playing in the Band"
**Highlights:** While the whole show is a gem (minus the Jack Straw), the Saturday Night, Not Fade Away > Goin' Down the Road > Not Fade Away Reprise, and Johnny B. Goode are all-time best versions. Hideaway and Dark Star are also exceptionally tasty treats.

One careful listen and I'm sure many Deadheads will agree: this classic show is one of the Dead's most notable performances from 1971. The band is on FIRE! Especially Jerry—it's as though some great electrified spirit is just screaming out of his guitar. From the middle of the first set on, every song is played with textbook precision and unbridled passion. Actually, this show is more like a performance from the triumphant Europe '72 tour: the band tirelessly tears through a deliriously long set list, takes absurdly long tune-ups between songs, and delivers astounding jams one right after the other. With perhaps the one exception that "Dark Star," while exquisite, had yet to be stretched *waaay* out again.

Excluding "Jack Straw," every song from the first set is a delight! "Hideaway," a classic 1950s instrumental ditty, is played just this once as a time killer while the sound crew tries to restore power to the stage monitors. "Jack Straw," which is played way too slow, features a funny moment; after they sing the lyric, "my old buddy, you're moving way too slow," Bobby quips, "Ain't that a fact." But then the band proceeds to kick ass. Every song *screams*. Even "Comes a Time" is one of the strongest versions I've ever heard. And you can tell the band is having oodles of fun from the continuous stream of smart-alec jokes and comments traded back and forth with the audience. The "Saturday Night" closer is the most impressive version this reviewer has ever heard—Phil in particular goes completely NUTS! If you get a copy of this "Saturday Night" with distortion, keep searching; it's available undamaged elsewhere. And speaking of Phil going nuts—it's important to note that the tapes of this show feature some of the best-sounding bass guitar tones you'll ever hear. It's not just that Phil plays well; the timbre of his Alembic bass is indescribably phat.

The second set is a work of art. The "Dark Star," while not as blissful or developed as, say, the one from 10/21/71, is an eloquent exercise in subtle melodic meditation. On the other hand, "The Other One" is a short, well-formed assault on the psyche fiercely led by Commander Jerry but supported by the big low-end artillery courtesy of General Lesh.

After a superb "Other One" reprise, the band stops abruptly. Phil apologizes by informing the audience that they "probably wouldn't have stopped there but we got a broken string." Ultimately, the spacey songs are well performed but not the highlight of this show. That honor belongs to the rock 'n' roll numbers.

While researching this book, I had the privilege of hearing the (uncirculated) "Not Fade Away" > "Goin' Down the Road" > "Not Fade Away" from the previous night at the Harding Theater, and, in my humble opinion, it isn't nearly as good. The only one I think comes close is 10/31/71, on which Jerry may actually play more impressively (hard to imagine) but the whole band doesn't quite play as perfectly in sync—ultimately it's a toss-up. Over the past sixteen years however I've deejayed *dozens* of large Deadhead tape parties, and this "Not Fade Away" > "Goin' Down the Road" > "Not Fade Away" gets people dancing like very few other pieces of music. It is the Grateful Dead at their most rocked-out. Put this on with the "Hard to Handle" from 4/29/71 and you've got yourself a serious party.

JOHN R. DWORK

### 11/11/71
#### Municipal Auditorium, Atlanta, Georgia

**Set 1:** Bertha, Me and My Uncle, Suga//ree, Playing in the Band, Jack Straw, Big Railroad Blues, Mexicali Blues, One More Saturday Night
**Set 2:** Truckin', Sugar Magnolia, Not Fade Away > Goin' Down the Road Feelin' Bad > Not Fade Away Reprise, Johnny B. Goode

**Source:** SBD, **Quality:** B, **Length:** 1:30

The fall of '71 was a tremendous period for the Dead, with few exceptions. This is one of them. The playing is solid but colorless and dry. It does have a few moments of inspiration ("Bertha," "Sugar Magnolia"), and there's even some dark humor: after Weir announces that Pigpen is home sick in bed, someone in the crowd repeatedly—and seemingly without malice—keeps yelling, "Where's the Pigpen?" But unless there's a big jam missing somewhere—and this is a strong possibility because the Dead rotated "Dark Star" and "The Other One" nearly every show in this period—everything here is available in much hotter form. Save a blank.

MICHAEL M. GETZ

### 11/12/71
#### Civic Auditorium, San Antonio, Texas

**Set 1:** Truckin', Lo//ser, Beat It on //Down the Line, Sugaree, Jack Straw, Tennessee Jed, El// Paso, //Brown-Eyed Women, Mexicali Blues, Black Peter, One More Saturday Night
**Set 2:** Ramble On Rose, Me and My Uncle, Cryptical Envelopment > Drums > The Other One > Cryptical Reprise > Big Railroad Blues, Sugar Magnolia, Casey Jones
**Encore:** Johnny B. Goode

**1. Source:** FM-SBD, **Quality:** B, **Length:** 3:00
**2. Source:** FM-SBD (GDH), **Quality:** A+, **Length:** 0:40 ("Cryptical Envelopment" through "Big Railroad Blues")

**Highlights:** Black Peter, Cryptical > Drums > The Other One > Cryptical Reprise > Big Railroad Blues

These tapes have a pleasurable mix featuring a wide dynamic range with all the instruments receiving equal attention. The contribution of the piano, usually lost from the mix, fills out the sound incredibly well for these shows. If you are a Keith fan, you'll especially love this show, as he plays extremely well and is easily audible. The later part of this year, a time of great energy, change, and maturation, already shows the beginnings of the monumental Europe '72 sound in development. Aside from the fact that this is Keith's beginning with the band, we also have Billy taking on the role of being the primary timekeeper. In the absence of Mickey, Billy does a fantastic job of filling in the music and making a transition smooth for the whole band. This whole show is good, and some of it sounds as though it could be from the *Europe '72* album.

"Truckin'," laid-back and shuffling in stride, winds around and then evolves into a decent jam. "Loser," which had the potential to be a great version, is chopped up by two meddling glitches that really hurt. These defects sound as if they could've been avoided by popping out those little cassette erase tabs. Just a friendly reminder! Nine mighty beats kick off a piano-filled and very peppy "Beat It on Down the Line." This is a well-played version that leaves you quite satisfied (even with one glitch). "Sugaree" shakes it up good with Phil and Keith landing hard on their respective notes. Although this version doesn't reach extreme proportions, it jams along steady and smooth. "Jack Straw" starts out slightly unsure, but soon transforms into a solid version. "Tennessee Jed" is upbeat and slightly funky with the perfect amount of energy to make it really sparkle. "El Paso" is mediocre, with two audio defects.

"Brown-Eyed Women" is nice even with the one glitch. "Mexicali" gallops along in typical cowboy fashion. "Black Peter," which is perfectly gorgeous, is played with sincerity and passion. It's for this reason that this version has always been a favorite of mine. A rousing "Saturday Night" (the right channel drops out for a couple of seconds) closes out the set with plenty of flair.

The second set starts with a playfully hot "Ramble On Rose" as Keith aggressively takes charge with some graceful keyboard work. Everyone is all warmed up and ready to go as they sprint through "Me and My Uncle." The "Cryptical" suite is quite remarkable, featuring some truly incredible playing that makes this the highlight of the show. "Cryptical" starts off light, leading into a drum solo that is so melodic you can almost sing along. Billy builds up plenty of tension by launching oscillating rhythms from his drum kit—so much so, that your ears strain to hear the roll into "The Other One," which is hiding right around the corner. This immediately opens up into a ferociously sharp jam that speeds off like some maniac zipping past you in the passing lane. Changing directions, they head off into a spacey exploration that drifts off into nothingness. Out of this minimalist space Billy starts up the groove as he dances around the main theme. Phil follows Billy's cue, leading in at the appropriate time with the rest of the band right on his heels. They build a deliciously layered jam, reaching some serious levels of intensity *before* the first lyrics! This is a full and fierce twelve minutes of wonderful jamming. Bobby's entrance hits the song at full speed. Things then evolve into another spacey and slightly scary jam that lasts another eight minutes. As they happily wind things down, they drift into a soft and pretty "Cryptical" reprise. The surprise of the evening is that the suite is not over yet, for they break into a blistering "Big Railroad Blues." Talk about unexpected!

A spirited "Sugar Magnolia" pleases everyone. "Casey Jones," the second-set closer, is laid-back and bouncy. The encore of "Johnny B. Goode," loaded with lots of guitar and piano, makes sure the crowd leaves satisfied. Although the first set has quite a few defects the second set is extremely hot and is a highly valued musical snapshot that deserves to be in your collection.

COREY SANDERSON

---

### 11/14/71
**Texas Christian University, Fort Worth, Texas**

**Set 1:** //Tennessee Jed, Mexicali Blues, Jack Straw, Me and Bobby McGee, China Cat Sunflower > I Know You Rider, El Paso > Sugaree, Big Railroad Blues
**Set 2:** Truckin' > Drums > The Other One Jam > Me and My Uncle//, Loser, Playing in the Band, Casey Jones

**Source:** AUD, **Quality:** C+/B−, **Length:** 1:30
**Highlights:** The Other One jam

---

The sound here is muffled and hissy, and fluctuates a grade or so as the taper appears to be rather mobile. Texas, you know. Fortunately, the highlights are of the higher grade.

The songs here are all well played. The transition between "China" and "Rider," though, is exceptional due to Lesh's sinister, ear-popping bursts that are a delight to hear. "Truckin'" has a hefty jam that gets way out there until—bam—they slyly reprise it. Slick.

The best reason to hear this tape is the "Other One" jam. This version sounds much more like the fall of '79 shows than anything in 1971. It's got large teeth and the gait of a boxer. Lesh is all over this sucka with some booming notes that resound splendidly on this tape. Without singing a verse, they go eloquently from deep space straight into an "Uncle" that fades out almost immediately. The "Playing" is of interest in that it has an embryonic but feisty three-minute jam in it.

MICHAEL M. GETZ

# Reviews: November 1971

## 11/15/71
### Municipal Auditorium, Austin, Texas

**Set 1:** Truckin', Bertha, Playing in the Band, Deal, Jack Straw, Loser, Beat It on Down the Line, Dark Star > El Paso > Space > Casey Jones

**Set 2:** Me and My Uncle, Ramble On Rose, Mexicali Blues, Brokedown Palace, Me and Bobby McGee, Cumberland Blues, Sugar Magnolia, You Win Again, Not Fade Away > Jam > Goin' Down the Road Feelin' Bad > Not Fade Away Reprise

**Encore:** Johnny B. Goode

**1. Source:** FM-SBD (WREK), **Quality:** C, **Length:** 3:00, **Genealogy:** MR > RR > PCM > DAT

**2. Source:** SBD, **Quality:** B/B+, **Length:** 1:30 ("Dark Star" through "One More Saturday Night" and "Cumberland" through "Encore")

**Highlights:** Dark Star, Space Jam

The available soundboard to this show contains all the highlights (except a hot "Truckin'" to open the show); plus, it's a whole grade better in quality, too. There's some hiss but all the instruments come through crisply.

There are two wonderful pieces of improvisation, one for each set. The first, of course, is "Dark Star." This one prances forward very confidently from its unusual first-set location. Garcia, Lesh, and Keith instantly weave intricate, spiraling patterns of notes around each other, hewing any rough edges. A drumless "Space" follows. But after some hesitation, Lesh and Billy link up, give it a swift kick, and off they all zoom . . . nowhere special. So they go into verse 1. A few Phil bombs later, Keith comes up with a delightful, dizzying burst on the keys that propels the band into a fast-paced, inspired jam. The band is cookin' now. Yet, right as they start to go deep, Cowboy Bob slips "El Paso" into the foray. To his credit, Garcia shows real patience as he shifts directions subtly, concealing his disappointment at not being able to mine what appeared to be a rich vein. A space emerges on the heels of "El Paso" that steadily descends into a polite—but effective—meltdown. A straight-ahead jam follows that has lots of mustard being slapped down by the whole band. Lesh sounds like he's playing thick snakes instead of strings.

The Dead finally land, gently, whispering quietly among themselves until they slam into a chug-a-luggin' "Casey Jones" to end a hot thirty-five minutes of music.

The second-set jam comes in a strange spot. Normally, the transition between "Not Fade Away" and "Goin' Down the Road" lasts only a few minutes or so. But this one stretches out for an exciting fifteen-plus minutes' worth. The band goes in and out of several beautiful places, re-mining the aborted vein from "Dark Star," and play without any concern for *having* to rush into anything. Unique and well worth obtaining.

MICHAEL M. GETZ

## 11/17/71
### Civic Auditorium, Albuquerque, New Mexico

**Set 1:** //Truckin', Sugaree, Beat It on Down the Line, Tennessee Jed, El // Paso, Big Railroad Blues, Jack Straw, Deal, Playing in the Band, Cumberland Blues, Me and Bobby McGee, You Win Again, Mexicali Blues, Casey Jones, One More Saturday Night//

**Set 2:** Ramble On Rose, Cryptical Envelopment > Drums > The Other One > Uncle John's Band Jam > Me and My Uncle > The Other One Reprise > Wharf Rat, Not Fade Away > Goin' Down the Road Feelin' Bad > Not Fade Away Reprise

**Source:** FM-SBD, **Quality:** C+, **Length:** 3:00

**Highlights:** Sugaree, Big Railroad Blues, Playing in the Band, Cumberland Blues, Me and Bobby McGee, Casey Jones, Ramble On Rose, Wharf Rat, Not Fade Away > Goin' Down the Road > Not Fade Away Reprise

**Comments:** The tapes from this show have a less than average sound, even on the lower-generation copies, due to the fact that they are heavy on the midrange and light on the lows and highs. They are, however, completely listenable and still very enjoyable.

The first set, comprising a full fifteen songs, will make anyone long for the good old days when hour and a half first sets were the status quo. One of the highlights is the opener, colorful and energized "Truckin'" leads into a mini–symphonic jam where everybody's distinct sound meshes together wonderfully. "Sugaree" reaches some decent, almost funky proportions. Thirteen beats kick off a "Beat It on Down the Line" that speeds along like the day you overslept and had to race to work. A rollicking "Tennessee Jed" prances along and features a substantial solo section that seems to keep stretching out and bubbling over with energy. Staccato piano work and bluesy guitar phrases, make this version of "Big Railroad Blues" really shine. Jack Straw is smooth and lyrical, with Garcia gently bending the notes in the opening phrase.

By this time "Playing in the Band" had really started to mature. The frame of the song had been stretched to be less rigid as well as allowing for extended jams. This way-too-short jam touches on the boundaries of amazing! Things are going along so great that you can't figure out why on earth Bobby would lead everyone back into the lyrics. It's completely baffling. "Cumberland Blues" is played with determination and "Bobby McGee" has extra bounce and a more upbeat feel than most of the other versions from this year.

A surprisingly hot "Casey Jones" features Keith flying up and down the keyboard. The ending momentum finds half of the band wanting to continue, with the other half wanting to end, causing a humorous kind of musical car crash. Most of "One More Saturday Night" is missing, but a spunky "Ramble On Rose" from the start of set 2 finishes side B of my first set cassette tape off nicely.

A focused "Cryptical" starts tape two. "Drums," digs down deep, providing an entrancing tribal rhythmic groove. The entrance into "The Other One," however, is unfortunately not incredibly inspiring, as Phil seems to be the only one paying attention. Despite the fairly weak introduction, the jamming that follows more than makes up for any dissatisfaction. Phil's staccato lines drive the band along at a steady pace until everyone switches into a softer and gentler side of the jam. What follows is a delicate and spacey exploration with no sense of time and no markers to remember what song they are in the middle of. Jerry pulls out strange notes, seemingly leading everyone around. The jamming continues with the lyrics finally appearing through the mist. There's a surprisingly smooth transition into a heavily strummed "Me and My Uncle." Upon the final chord, Jerry jumps right back into the "Other One" theme. They finish up strongly. They slip down into a very solemn "Wharf Rat," which brings to mind the beautifully sad music of a funeral procession. This powerful version, loaded with dark overtones and seemingly apologetic vocals, gives the listener a sense of depression at the frustrations encountered in all our lives. When Jerry sings, "I know that the life I'm living's no good," time stretches and slows down as if this were the most important sentence he's ever uttered. I don't know of a sadder, more heart-wrenching version.

"Not Fade Away" is relentlessly hot and features wonderful communication between Jerry's solo and the band's accents. Phil drops a "Lovelight" fake in right before slipping into "Goin' Down the Road." This is a real sweaty and driving version that covers a lot of ground before smoothly closing out. They jump back into an even hotter "Not Fade Away" reprise, landing on the final chord like an explosion. This is a show worth having.

COREY SANDERSON

---

### 11/20/71

**Pauley Pavilion, University of California at Los Angeles, California**

**Set 1:** Bertha, Me and My Uncle, Sugaree, //Beat It on Down the Line, Tennessee Jed, //Mexicali Blues, //Brown-Eyed Women, El Paso, Big Railroad Blues, Jack Straw, //Cumberland Blues, Playing in the Band, Casey Jones, One More Saturday Night
**Set 2:** Tru//ckin' > Drums > The Other One > Ramble On Rose > Sugar Magnolia, You Win Again, Not Fade// Away > China Cat Sunflower Jam > Goin' Down the Road Feelin' Bad > Not Fade Away Reprise

---

**Source:** FM-SBD, **Quality:** A, **Length:** 2:40
**Highlights:** Truckin' > Drums > The Other One > Ramble On Rose

This performance is fairly sleepy until midway into the first set. Garcia, in particular, lags throughout the beginning, running through his usual licks, but without any substantive improvisation. In fact, the "Sugaree" is completely devoid of any Garcia soloing. As well, both Garcia and Weir seem tired, and their attempts at singing suggest as much. Later into the set, as each member begins to wake up, the band begins to loosen and assert itself more confidently, starting with "Big Railroad Blues" and continuing throughout the set. As usual, "Cumberland Blues" cooks from start to finish, and this rendition features Garcia's most furious soloing of the evening. By contrast, "Playing in the Band" is slow and methodical. Hesitant, and obviously afraid of entering uncharted territory, the boys approach this with extreme caution. The "Playing" jam is still maturing; compare this version to that of Chicago or Detroit the previous month to witness the transition. Slowly unwinding out of the verse, the band members noodle individually on the main theme for only a few moments apiece, being very careful not to step on each other. As it becomes obvious that the band is potentially veering off into different directions, the frontmen come full circle and casually return to the reprise. The Dead then finish the set predictably, but respectably, with "Casey Jones" and "One More Saturday Night," with Keith the only one sticking out here.

Returning for the second set, refreshed and confident, the boys pick "Truckin'" to be the platform to launch from. Wow, is this the same band? The first set varied from sleepy to solid, but this is balls-out Grateful Dead all the way. The outro jam is highlighted by some fabulous interplay between Garcia and Godchaux that like a roller coaster varies between simmer and boil. The "Drums" segment is minimalistically graceful, albeit brief, leading into a fantastically charged "Other One." As Garcia fumbles on the theme, Keith rages on the grand piano, falling into an unintentional meltdown that takes a few minutes to steady. The band then enters abruptly into march mode, straying periodically like soldiers falling out of line. Weir's vocal execution is subdued, setting the tone for the jam between verses 1 and 2. As the rest of the band sways between spatial brilliance and instrumental complacency, Godchaux interjects clear, jazzy fills that bring the jam into a frenzied display of chaos. Following the heavy feedback bombs from Weir and Lesh, Garcia and Kreutzmann march the band into a funky shuffle that eventually emerges into a great "Rhythm and Blues and Space Jam." As the rest of the band swings loosely, Garcia frantically scrambles like a paranoid schizophrenic in a straitjacket before dissolving into a second meltdown. Seizing the opportunity to fire more feedback bombs, the band makes a sharp turn that for a moment sounds like a sunrise. Calm and serene, this lasts only a moment before Lesh and Kreutzmann take another sharp turn into "Rhythm and Blues and Space Jam #2." More focused than its predecessor, this stays inside the parameter, but allows the band to get funky nonetheless. After it dissolves, the boys immediately return to the second verse. Even though Garcia's leads are in fine form, the rhythm section really takes charge here, with Godchaux and Kreutzmann in complete synchronicity. Once again, Weir gives a subdued reading of the verse before Jerry leads the troupe into "Ramble On Rose." Before the rest of the band has a chance to get started, though, Keith goes nuts with some maniacal ragtime trills that would make Scott Joplin blush. While the band plays solidly here, it is obvious that Godchaux has risen far above his colleagues. Perhaps inspired by Keith's enthusiasm, Weir starts prematurely on "Sugar Magnolia," which cooks from start to finish. The following "You Win Again" is light, considering the preceding selections, but is played flawlessly. (*Love* Garcia's chicken-pickin' turnarounds.) As the band clowns around, trying to decide what to close the set with (is there more than one option?), Billy fiddles on some nonsensical rhythms before leading the band into "Not Fade Away." Late 1971 was a great period for hot "Not Fade Away"s (they certainly had enough rehearsal), and this rendition is no exception. While the vocals are right on, the jam is what really sparkles. Out of the first verse Garcia takes the lead, slithering around the band like a snake until reaching the "China Cat" jam, which he masterfully uses to set up the segue into "Goin' Down the Road." The band stumbles briefly on the first verse, but rebounds quickly for an otherwise solid execution. During the jam before the final chorus, it starts to become evident that the band has peaked and that it's time to wrap it up and say goodnight. The return to "Not Fade Away" is textbook standard, with Weir's trademark shrieking sending this one off with a bang.

BRIAN DYKE

## 12/1/71
### Boston Music Hall, Boston, Massachusetts

**Set 2:** Cryptical Envelopment > Drums > The Other One > Me and My Uncle > The Other One Reprise > Not Fade Away > Goin' Down the Road Feelin' Bad > Not Fade Away Reprise

**Source:** FM-SBD (GDH 188), **Quality:** A+, **Length:** 0:45, **Genealogy:** MR > RR > DR
**Highlights:** All

Here's a snapshot from the second set of a band performing with unbridled confidence. It's often impossible to tell who is leading the jams. Often unheralded, but here precisely displayed, is the band's sharpened skill at *listening* to each other. The music rises and falls, slivered with the Taoist shreds of beauty and violence, as if prescripted. They halt, race ahead, stagger, shuffle, and spin to and fro as one six-legged creature. Nobody gets left behind on this bus.

Here we have a classic "Other One" sandwich. Ah, but how to describe this? Take the following ingredients in their jams: full band; without Billy only; Lesh and Garcia only; Billy only on cymbals; "Me and My Uncle" fakes; "Other One" fakes; "Space" with rhythm; and an atonal, rhythmless "Space." Add one egg and get baked.

The "Not Fade Away" sandwich is ferocious and closes the show with a bang. When it ends, David Gans aptly calls it "a classic marriage." Indeed. With everything said about the superb ensemble work here, the game ball must go to Phil Lesh. He is unwavering in his commitment to play the strangest, least repetitive combinations of notes he can muster. He's absolutely relentless and a joy to listen to. His performance here ranks right up there with 9/11/73.

MICHAEL M. GETZ

---

## 12/2/71
### Boston Music Hall, Boston, Massachusetts

**Set 1:** Bertha, Playing in the Band, Mr. Charlie, Sugaree, Beat It on Down the Line, Black Peter, Next Time You See Me, Jack Straw, Tennessee Jed, Mexicali Blues, Smokestack Lightning, Big Railroad Blues, Casey Jones, One More Saturday Night
**Set 2:** Sugar Magnolia, Deal, El Paso, Brokedown Palace, Uncle John's Band, Not Fade Away > Turn On Your Lovelight > Goin' Down the Road Feelin' Bad > Not Fade Away Reprise
**Encore:** Johnny B. Goode

**Source:** FM-SBD, **Quality:** A–, **Length:** 3:00, **Genealogy:** FM > RR > Beta HF > PCM
**Highlights:** Black Peter, Smokestack Lightning, Brokedown Palace

This is the third show featuring both Pigpen and Keith Godchaux (although no Pig tunes from the previous two night circulate yet). Pigpen had not played live since August, and it is apparent that he has not yet regained his stride. He contributes very little, even though he sings on the two longest songs in the show. The show begins rather clumsily with a perfunctory "Bertha." The "Playing in the Band" is one of the first versions to feature a "Space jam". At this point, the tape lacks any punch; it sounds flat and there is little Phil present. It is clear but lacks the full sound of other FM broadcasts from this period. After "Sugaree," the sound improves and becomes more what one is accustomed to. "Black Peter" is one of the highlights of the first set, with Keith playing sweet riffs during the bridge verse. Later in the set, the band sneaks into a surprise "Smokestack Lightning," one of the last versions sung by Pigpen. Although Pigpen turns introspective and begins moaning, "I been gone so long," several times this is a very mellow version that never really takes off. The rest of the band eventually pulls him out of it, and they are able to finish the song.

The second set is short and unremarkable as well. One of the highlights actually takes place between songs after "Sugar Magnolia" where there is a lightly played jam that is like a hybrid of "Sugar Magnolia" and "The Wheel," which Garcia had just finished recording on his solo album. "Brokedown" gives a perfect example of the charm of the Dead's true vocal style: no golden throats here, but rife with feeling. The show stumbles to a close with a standard "Not Fade Away," a lackluster "Lovelight," and only a slightly above average "Goin' Down the Road." This was a strange tour for the band because they were simultaneously breaking in Keith and dealing with Pigpen's waning contribution. Pig's health was in serious danger by this time, and he was not able to withstand the rigors of the road. Consequently, there were more than the usual number of below-par shows in an otherwise hot season. This show was one of them.

DOUGAL DONALDSON

## 12/4/71

### Felt Forum, New York, New York

**Set 1:** Introduction by Bill Graham, Truckin', Sugaree, Mr. Charlie, Beat It on Down the Line, Jack Straw, Run, Rudolph, Run, You Win Again, Me and Bobby McGee, Comes a Time, El Paso, Smokestack Lightning, //Cumberland Blues, One More Saturday Night
**Set 2:** Ramble On Rose, Me and My Uncle > The Other One > Mexicali Blues > The Other One Reprise > Wharf Rat, Casey Jones
**Encore:** Johnny B. Goode

**Source:** SBD, **Quality:** A, **Length:** 2:38, **Genealogy:** MR > RR > DAT
**Highlights:** Run, Rudolph, Run, Smokestack Lightning, second-set jam

Opening night of a four-show run. Pig had rejoined the band a few nights prior in Boston, but this show would prove to be the big return of what many considered to be the nucleus of the group. The tape starts with Bob and Phil goofing with the crowd, followed by Bill Graham introducing the band as "The food that feeds us all . . . the Grateful Dead." The band quickly pounds out a rousing version of "Truckin'" that's a few seconds short of twelve minutes long, quickly followed by an equally long "Sugaree." For the most part, the set is more upbeat than normal for late '71, but the real gems of the set are the Pig songs. A rare "Run, Rudolph, Run" and an inspiring "Smokestack Lightning" round out this fresh and spontaneous first set.

The second set starts with an average "Ramble On Rose" followed by "Me and My Uncle," which segues into "The Other One," a rare start to a jam for any year. The absence of a drum solo during "The Other One" keeps this version shorter then normal and more introspective than some. The playing doesn't stretch as deep as some of the better shows from the fall of '71, e.g., 10/31 and 12/15. The highlight of the second set is the unique layout of the jam that starts with "Me and My Uncle" and ends with "Wharf Rat." This appears to be the only time in the band's history that these songs were arranged in this manner, which makes it a must for serious collectors. The second set is short and overall not up to the high energy level of the first set, but it's still a great listen. Because of the ten-inch reel-to-reel format and its 7½ ips tape speed, the entire show only contains one cut (at the start of "Cumberland Blues")—not bad for an old tape!

ROB EATON

## 12/5/71

### Felt Forum, New York, New York

**Set 1:** Bertha, Beat It on Down the Line, Big Boss Man, Brown-Eyed Women, Muddy Water, Jack Straw, Mr. Charlie, Tennessee Jed, El Paso, Deal, Playing in the Band, Next Time You See Me, Comes a Time, Casey Jones, One More Saturday Night
**Set 2:** Truckin', Ramble On Rose, Hurts Me Too, Sugaree, Sugar Magnolia, Dark Star > Me and My Uncle > Dark Star Reprise > Sittin' on Top of the World, Me and Bobby McGee, Big Railroad Blues, Mexicali Blues, You Win Again, Not Fade Away > Goin' Down the Road Feelin' Bad > Not Fade Away Reprise

**Source:** FM-SBD, **Quality:** A−/B+, **Length:** 3:00

**Highlights:** Muddy Water, Comes a Time, Dark Star > Me and My Uncle > Dark Star > Sittin' on Top of the World, Not Fade Away > Goin' Down the Road Feelin' Bad > Not Fade Away Reprise

The second night of the only Felt Forum run ever was broadcast live on WNEW-FM, making this tape fairly common. The broadcast featured a "you were there" sound by mixing the board feed with microphones placed in the audience. Keith was starting to settle into his role as the new keyboardist. Pigpen, out of the hospital, had joined the tour a few nights earlier in Boston, although his contributions to the show were rather minimal. The occasion of a broadcast in the Big Apple was used to showcase the newer songs. They played a total of thirteen tunes that were less than one year old; six of them had been added to the repertoire for this current tour, which had begun almost two months earlier. I was fortunate to be in the tenth row for this highly entertaining show.

Following a classic introduction by Bill Graham the boys launch into a rocking "Bertha." Bobby registers a complaint about the monitors and then welcomes the radio audience as the band kicks off a quick and snappy "Beat It on Down the Line." More monitor complaints lead the way into the first Pigpen tune of the night, "Big Boss Man." Although his voice sounds clear and crisp, his energy seems subdued. The lack of organ playing throughout the show is not due to a poor mix; Pig was just not playing. He was standing and/or sitting behind the organ looking kinda down until it was his turn to take a lead vocal. Jerry, on the other hand, was being very playful and energetic as he tossed off a few bars of "Love in Bloom." Bobby, picking up on Jerry's playfulness and mindful of the radio audience, fills some dead air (pun intended) by exhorting the listeners to take a trip to the fridge while Phil "changes the batteries in his bass."

The first musical highlight comes with Jerry's performance of the only-time-ever "Muddy Water," which is well played but short. Short tunes rule the show as there is very little extended jamming in the first set. Jerry's guitar tone is particularly sweet, typified by his solo during "Deal." Some nice jamming begins in "Playing in the Band"; you can hear it evolve into an exploration of sorts, although it comes back to earth far too soon. Jerry's soulful singing and playing on "Comes a Time" make this my favorite musical moment in the first set. Phil's bass provides the perfect accent to Jerry's lead. Keith breaks from his percussive style to add some nice little licks between the Jerry/Phil sandwich. After Jerry gives the crowd "something to ease the pain" ("Casey Jones"), Bobby brings the set to a close with a rocking "One More Saturday Night."

The second set kicks off with "our big AM radio hit," "Truckin'," which was nice but not yet like the raging jams that emerged during the 1972 European tour. Before the next song starts, Phil can be heard playing around with what sounds to these ears like a "Mason's Children," but it dissolves into "Ramble On Rose." A nice but tame "Hurts Me Too" gets Pig up in the spotlight. After "Sugar Mag" they take an extended tuning break, during which there's a huddle to plot the course that would take us on the most adventurous musical excursion of the night.

A unique "Dark Star" starts to build to the point where one would expect to hear "Daaaaark Star crashes . . ." but there's a seamless shift into an uptempo "Me and My Uncle" instead. As the last note of "Uncle" is played, whoosh, the band dissolves back into "Dark Star." This is where it really gets interesting as the music takes you on a journey through the cosmos, finding new worlds along the way. Different themes emerge throughout until one of them turns into "Top of the World," returning us to earth, rock 'n' rolling to the beat. It's only now that we begin to realize there were no lyrics on the "Dark Star."

This upbeat show continues with decent versions of "Bobby McGee," "Big Railroad Blues," and "Mexicali Blues." Jerry goes country, covering Hank Williams' "You Win Again." "Not Fade Away" gives way to a "China Cat" riff before segueing into "Goin' Down the Road." This rocks right back into "Not Fade Away" as Pig and Bobby rave up the ending. The "Johnny B. Goode" encore is not on any of the FM tapes. I recall Bobby saying to the audience something like: "They've had to cut off the broadcast so you're gonna get to hear a song that the radio audience missed." I've not heard an audience tape of the "Johnny B. Goode," but I remember it as an anticlimax to this wonderful show.

This FM source tape with the unobtrusive audience mix is highly recommended, especially if you'd like to feel what it was like to attend a late 1971 show.

MARC BLAKER

## 12/10/71
**Fox Theater, Saint Louis, Missouri**

**Set 1:** Bertha, Me and My Uncle, Mr. Charlie, Loser, Beat It on Down the Line, Sugaree, Jack Straw, Next Time You See Me, Tennessee Jed//, El Paso, Big Railroad Blues, Casey Jones
**Set 2:** Good Lovin', Brokedown Palace, Playing in the Band, Run, Rudolph, Run, Deal, Sugar Magnolia, Comes a Time, Truckin' > Drums > The Other One > Sittin' on Top of the World > The Other One Reprise > Not Fade Away > Goin' Down the Road Feelin' Bad > Not Fade Away Reprise
**Encore:** One More Saturday Night

**Source:** FM-SBD (KADI), **Quality:** B–, **Length:** 3:00
**Highlights:** Good Lovin', Truckin' through the end

The first set is a playful, uplifting strut. The band is in fine form, making it appear effortless. Pigpen is relaxed and vibrant on his two tunes. "Casey Jones" is taken to a blistering peak to close the set.

Pigpen opens the second set with a fired-up "Good Lovin'." The band, led by Lesh's bubbling, insistent bass lines, charges into a straight-ahead jam. This turns very spacey for a few minutes before Pigpen suddenly slips in quietly to jam vocally with the existing patterns. He sings his rap, making it all up on the spot. Stuff like:

> She got overdrive
> And it keeps me alive
> 'specially in the morning
> Some folks say she must be a Cadillac
> I say she must be a T-Model Ford!

After Pigpen switches to his love of pony riding, the band steadily builds the reprising chords behind him, tighter and tighter, until they all climax explosively together.

Before "Truckin'," Weir tells the crowd and radio audience his now famous line: "This next number rose straight to the top of the charts in Turloc, California. Number one, numero uno, I'll have you know. So all I'm saying is I wish you'd all get hip and buy the new single."

"Truckin'" features Garcia playing his lead razor-sharp, like on the single. Boy, guess they really *are* trying to sell this thing. The closing jam is led by Lesh into a slick, one-minded jam that slowly ungoo's into a spacey, pre–"Other One" feel. Garcia, however, slyly slips in a few "Truckin'" notes into the equation and—without pause—they reprise the darn thing. Then, as if Xing an item off a laundry list, they pick right up where they'd been before. Soon Billy solos just long enough (fourteen seconds) to propel Lesh's rumbling intro to the genuine "Other One."

It's astonishing how quickly—in just seven weeks—Keith not only caught on as the new keyboardist, but how brazenly he goes after Garcia and Lesh to push the musical directions. Unlike T.C. or Pigpen, who mostly provided rhythm and dabs of color here and there, Keith pounces and prowls like a caged animal. On this song he kicks, spits, licks, and tricks his way to the forefront of the flow, growling alongside the two elderly statesmen.

At Lesh's signal, "The Other One" sprints forward like a spider across the kitchen floor. The E to D pole is lightly brushed against, as the jam seemingly runs by itself, the peaks and valleys abundant and pleasantly weird. Billy lets up as a short Zen-like regrouping space ensues. Then Billy returns with a nice chug-a-lug beat. The others lock in and they dash into a crisp "Sittin' on Top of the World" (which Keith had been hinting at for a full minute before the rest of the band comes on board). "The Other One" returns, stronger, bolder, and with some attitude. But then Billy drops out yet again. He returns quickly with some skip-along snare slaps, invigorating the band into a swifter space. Finally the band rises into . . . verse 2? Yes. Well, they close the song and burst into "Not Fade Away." After finishing the verses, the band simply ignites in a rush of energy as they dash off into the unknown. Along the way, they do a full-fledged "China Cat" tease and a brief "Mountain Jam" tease before Garcia picks the notes to "Goin' Down the Road." He sings, "going where the water tastes like . . . (long, long pause) . . . wiiiiiiiiiiiiiiiiiiiiii-iiiiiiiiiine-uhhhhhhhh," with tremendous feeling. His solos are so deft, so sly, so quick, and so colorfully patterned—he could have completed every needlepoint project at every nursing home in the Chicago area from this one song alone.

The transition back to "Not Fade Away" features a gorgeous exchange between Keith and Lesh that's worth listening for. Pigpen joins in on the vocal climax, pushing Weir to turn his throat into burnt toast; he does. The

# Reviews: December 1971

"Saturday Night" encore, like nearly all versions from the fall of '71, is red hot.

MICHAEL M. GETZ

---

### 12/14/71
#### Hill Auditorium, Ann Arbor, Michigan

**Set 1:** Truckin', Sugaree, Mr. Charlie, Beat It on Down the Line, Loser, Jack Straw, Next Time You See Me, Tennessee Jed, El Paso, Big Railroad Blues, Me and My Uncle, Run, Rudolph, Run, Black Peter, Playing in the Band, Casey Jones
**Set 2:** Ramble On Rose, Mexicali Blues, Big Boss Man, Cryptical Envelopment > Drums > The Other One > Wharf Rat, Sugar Magnolia, You Win Again, Not Fade Away > Goin' Down the Road Feelin' Bad > Not Fade Away Reprise

---

**Source:** SBD, **Quality:** A, **Length:** 2:45, **Genealogy:** Betty Board 10-inch reel, ½ tape 7½ ips

**Highlights:** Run, Rudolph, Run, Black Peter, Cryptical Envelopment > Drums > The Other One > Wharf Rat, Not Fade Away > Goin' Down the Road > Not Fade Away Reprise

This tape is a good way to discover the feeling of a typical show from the fall of '71. Highlights from this tour include a blizzard of rollicking keyboard work by the newly initiated Keith Godchaux, and numerous astounding performances of "The Other One" and "Not Fade Away" > "Goin' Down the Road" > "Not Fade Away." 12/14/71 is one of the infamous Betty Board tapes so good-quality copies have been circulating for a number of years in analog and DAT quality.

The first set is not spectacular, but it is pretty solid. The highlights are a rocking "Run, Rudolph, Run" and a sweet "Black Peter."

After a few songs in the second set, they hit the peak of the show: "The Other One." It's not really a peak as much as a wonderful series of rolling hills in which they build up an intense jam, and then go back down and let it space out a bit, then build it up again, then let it go back down again, etc. Earlier "Other One"s ('67–'69) were usually played at a breakneck pace without variation, and later versions ('72–'74) sometimes traversed deep space, but 12/14/71 and its close relatives (10/29/71, 11/12/71, and 11/17/71) have a lot of variation that keeps them focused and very interesting all the way through.

There is some goofing around with a "Stars and Stripes" intro before "You Win Again," and then they go into the other highlight of the night, the closing seventeen-minute "Not Fade Away" > "Goin' Down the Road" > "Not Fade Away." It seems to go on and on. When you think that they've been going on forever and will be ending the song soon, you realize that they're just starting "Goin' Down the Road." There is no encore, but after this monster medley who cares? This is definitely a keeper. Check it out.

JOHN OLEYNICK

*Ticket stub for 12/14/71 at the Hill Auditorium, Ann Arbor*

---

### 12/15/71
#### Hill Auditorium, Ann Arbor, Michigan

**Set 1:** Bertha, Me and Bobby McGee, Mr. Charlie, China Cat Sunflower > I Know You Rider, Beat It on Down the Line, Hurts Me Too, Cumberland Blues, Jack Straw, You Win Again, Run, Rudolph, Run, Playing in the Band, Brown-Eyed Women, Mexicali Blues, Big Railroad Blues, Brokedown Palace, El Paso, Casey Jones//
**Set 2:** Dark Star > Deal, Sugar Magnolia, Turn On Your Lovelight > King Bee > Mannish Boy > Turn On Your Lovelight Reprise//, One More Saturday Night

---

**Source:** FM-SBD, **Quality:** A–/A, **Length:** 2:40

**Highlights:** Dark Star, Lovelight > Mannish Boy > King Bee > Lovelight

The majority of 1971 is considered by many to be a relatively average year, with the exception of the fall. The acquisition of Keith Godchaux required the Dead to change its sound dramatically, and the result was the beginning of one of their finest eras: Fall 1971 through 1974. This tape is exquisite in performance, and the transitional sound is indeed apparent. Pigpen missed their October and November shows and returned on December 1. His absence allowed Godchaux time to melt into the band, and his playing on December 15 sounds as though he had been with the band since the early days. The first set is seemingly endless and all of the songs are performed tightly and almost in a sterile manner. Obviously the band was learning several new songs and giving Godchaux warm-up time. Interestingly, the songs "Mr. Charlie," "Jack Straw," "Playing," "Brown-Eyed Women," and "Mexicali" were in their formative stages, and the band was really polishing them. Just five months later, however, these songs would drastically change into a slower and more patient format, creating their lasting image.

The second set picks up with "Dark Star." It begins with Garcia inspecting the area with a tight rhythm. The jams meander a bit until Lesh finds a groove. The band follows it with Garcia picking outerspace notes. The rhythm ceases and Garcia dives beneath it, pulling them farther and farther down. The sound gets really mean until Garcia soars upward, leaving the band scrambling to catch him. He ultimately lands into the lyrics of the "Star" and/or the Garden of Eden. After the lyrics, Lesh attacks the auditorium with massive bombs leading into several atonal jams. Finally they give the crowd a chance to catch their breath as Garcia segues into "Deal." This "Dark Star" really provides an example of how the band was changing. The jam format is markedly different from their 1968 through summer 1971 versions. It is slower paced, drippier, and less conscious at times, and simply stellar. The "Deal" and "Sugar Magnolia" are totally flawless; the band is 100 percent on. The "Lovelight" that follows displays one of the finer Pigpen performances. On four different occasions he stops the band in the middle of their jam to sing. On the second time Weir calls out, "This story better be good!" Pig follows by going off on pocket pool. The third time he sings about meeting a woman, telling her he has no money in his pocket but that if she wants to see what he does, she better come with him. The band jams on into a bluesy strut and Pigpen begins singing "King Bee," which quickly goes into "Mannish Boy." The band provides their trademark bluesy psychotic rhythm before falling back into the "Lovelight." The finale is spectacular. Pigpen starts singing about how no "jockstrap" is gonna take his woman away from him—remember this was at the University of Michigan. He ends it with his stellar screams of "Baaaaybay." The final three seconds are cut, but nonetheless one of the best "Lovelights" has transpired. They end the show with a stomping version of "Saturday Night."

ROBERT A. GOETZ

---

## 12/31/71
### New Year's Eve
### Winterland Arena, San Francisco, California

**Set 1:** Dancin' in the Streets, Mr. Charlie, Brown-Eyed Women, Beat It on Down the Line, You Win Again, Jack Straw, Sugaree, El Paso, Chinatown Shuffle, Tennessee Jed, Mexicali Blues, China Cat Sunflower > I Know You Rider, Next Time You See Me, Playing in the Band, Loser, One More Saturday Night*
**Set 2:** Truckin' > Drums > The Other One > Me and My Uncle > The Other One Reprise, Jam > Black Peter, Big River, The Same Thing, Ramble On Rose, Sugar Magnolia, Not Fade Away > Goin' Down the Road > Not Fade Away Reprise
**Encore:** Casey Jones

* Donna Jean Godchaux's debut on vocals

---

**Source:** SBD, **Quality:** B+ (Set 1), A (Set 2), **Length:** 3:10

**Highlights:** Dancin' in the Streets, Brown-Eyed Women, Tennessee Jed, China Cat Sunflower > I Know You Rider, Truckin' > Drums > The Other One > Me and My Uncle > The Other One, Black Peter, The Same Thing, Goin' Down the Road Feelin' Bad

This show comes at the end of a critical year for the Dead. The Godchauxs had been installed—this was

Donna's first appearance—and like it or not, Pigpen's influence on the band was in terminal decline, especially after his first prolonged absence from the band that autumn. This is not to say that there was not life left in the old beast, but it is clear the new Dead were on their way.

Opening on the chimes of midnight, it's straight into a rousing "Dancin'," with some nicely understated work from Garcia that foreshadows the post-1976 arrangement of the song. This would in fact be the last version of this underplayed part of the Dead's repertoire until then. Going on what Weir says afterward about the stage being "a fuckin' mess," the radio presenter's descriptions of a nude man running about as part of the celebrations, and the shrieks from the stage of "Happy New Year," none apparently from the band, the party was already well under way. This is a great show, with the band showing off its multifaceted talents to great effect. Early on in the first set a whole batch of the new material is dropped on the audience. "Mr. Charlie," "Brown-Eyed Women," the inexplicably short-lived "You Win Again," "Jack Straw," "Sugaree," "El Paso," "Tennessee Jed," and "Mexicali Blues": all played superbly. "Chinatown Shuffle" is premiered in a snappy version, and the band sounds confident and refreshed that it isn't trotting out the standards of the last three or so years. Having said that, by the time the band hits "China Cat," it does so with great relish. Jerry unleashes one of his killer spiral solos, and this inspires the band into wonderfully sympathetic playing. The Pig has his say on "Next Time You See Me," and they finish up with a great "Loser" and a "Saturday Night" that features Donna's trademark vocals for the first time.

Set 2: After the "short break" it's back to work with a characteristic intro from Bill Graham, sincere and somewhat awkward, yet also direct, honest, and passionate. "Truckin'" sets the scene for what is to come with Garcia tearing off fiery licks while Weir shouts himself hoarse. Kreutzmann knocks himself out on his solo, making nearly as much noise as he used to with the aid of Mickey, and eventually Phil rides in, all guns blazing, to take the band into "The Other One." A huge canvas of sound unfurls with everyone chipping in, and after ten minutes or so the band somehow shoehorns the jam into "Me and My Uncle," a trick akin to forcing a quart into a pint pot. This is an exceptional version and begs the question of why this was the second-to-last time they ever tried this particular combination. The explosion back into "The Other One" is marked by a deeply dissonant and spacey jam that eventually freewheels its way back into the vocals and then into an attempt at a swift transition into "Black Peter," which is aborted as the band goes out of tune. However, after a little light doodling Garcia goes on to deliver a particularly poignant version of this song. The first attempt at "Big River" is followed by a showstopping rendition of "The Same Thing" which would be the last one for twenty years—another song criminally underplayed by the band. "Not Fade Away" leads into an effortlessly energetic and fluid "Goin' Down the Road" and then a "Not Fade Away" reprise that screams its way to a conclusion at 3:45 in the morning. It's 1972.

JAMES SWIFT

---

### ??/71
**Unknown Location**

**Rehearsal:** Playing in the Band

**Source:** SBD, **Quality:** A–, **Length:** 0:05

Obviously still mastering the basic tracks, the boys go down for the count at the bridge and, after a little how-to from Weir, fail to answer the bell. The less that's said about this one, the better.

BRIAN DYKE

## ??/71
### Unknown Location

**Studio Sessions:** Fire on the Mountain[1], Ghost Riders in the Sky[2], It Makes Me Mad #1[3], You Know I Will[4], Is Anybody There[5], Night of the Vampire[6], It Makes Me Mad #2[7]

1 Frieberg, Garcia, Hart, Melton
2 Cippolina, Frieberg, Hart, McPherson
3 McDonald, McPherson, Schuster
4 McDonald, McPherson, Schuster
5 Frieberg, Hart, McDonald, McPherson
6 Hart, Hunter, Lesh, Melton
7 Frieberg, Garcia, Hart, Melton

**Source:** SBD, **Quality:** B, **Length:** 0:25
**Personnel:** With John Cippolina, David Freiberg, Robert Hunter, Kate McDonald, Jim McPherson, Barry Melton, and Steven Schuster
**Highlights:** All

Not only is this unreleased Mickey Hart LP a brilliant mainstream effort, it's an illustration of Hart's versatility and a satirical masterpiece as well! The tape begins with "Fire on the Mountain," which, though rhythmically similar to the Grateful Dead interpretation, is delivered vocally by Hart in a primitive raplike fashion. As well, this rendition contains lyrics not found in the Dead's version. Garcia's solo is frisky and energized, but is overshadowed by Hart's authoritative vocal delivery. "Ghost Riders in the Sky," a loose satire on cowboy themes, is surprisingly legitimate. The combination of gruff baritone vocals with rough-and-tumble licks from Cippolina gives this selection a tough-as-leather authenticity. The tape contains two takes of "It Makes Me Mad," the first of which features a hilarious but incomprehensible vocal track through a layer or two of distortion. Rather than recite lyrics, the vocals here are seemingly only phonetic rumblings that are enunciated with masterful timing, with a word or two thrown in on occasion. The second take, in contrast, contains a very Slickish vocal approach, complete with verse snarling and refrain screeching. Yielding a slight nod to the mainstream, "You Know I Will" is a pleasant male-female duet that blends gracefully the lyrical and vocal characteristics of disco with the rhythm and melodic attributes of Motown. "Is Anybody There," on the other hand, is a hollow, slightly somber, ballad that is minutely reminiscent of Procul Harum's "Whiter Shade of Pale." Very uncharacteristic of Hart, these two selections might very well have become FM staples had they been given the opportunity. The final highlight of the tape, "Night of the Vampire," is an absolutely gut-busting parody of heavy metal. This tune contains all of the necessary elements: Alice Cooper vocal impersonations, falsetto screeching, Wolfman Jack–like narration, Transylvanian accent chanting, and comical spoken commentary by Hart. An absolutely hilarious exhibition, this track will induce side pain from excessive laughter!

BRIAN DYKE

## ?? 1971–?? 1973
### Unknown Location

**Demos:** C. C. Rider, Katie Mae, Hitchhiking Woman, Two Women, Queen of Santa Fe, Bring Me My Shotgun, Instrumental, Poor Michael Went Down, Queen of Santa Fe, I Believe, She's Mine, No Tomorrow//

**Source:** SBD, **Quality:** A–, **Length:** 0:45
**Comments:** It is unknown as of yet if any or all of these tracks are duplicates of those on the tapes circulating as "Bring Me My Shotgun" and "Pigpen Studio Demos 1964–73."

BRIAN DYKE

# 1972

*The year 1972 started out in much the same way as 1971 had ended. Many of the new songs introduced in that previous year began to mature and lose their monotony. Keith had found his niche within the band surprisingly quickly and Pigpen was starting to get back in the groove again. A new expansive direction had taken hold and began to dominate their "Space" jams, which were nearly a nightly exercise. The band was in its prime, had a new mind-set, and was peaking musically. All this occurred* just in time for the Dead's historic and triumphant tour across Europe. After a three-month break from touring, the Dead bade farewell to the U.S.A. with a six-show run in New York and flew to Europe. Although this tour, like most, contained its share of uneven or unspectacular shows (such as April 24 in Duesseldorf, May 10 in Amsterdam, and May 23 in London) in which the band sounded tired and distracted, the majority of the shows featured the Dead breaking entirely new ground and performing some of the most astounding and celebrated shows in their entire history. Listen to the tapes from April 8 in London, April 26 in Frankfurt (the CD Hundred Year Hall), April 29 in Hamburg, May 11 in Rotterdam, and, especially, May 26 in London, and you will hear a band that is right on top of its game. This tour, unfortunately, also became Pigpen's swan song, as he was dead within a year of the tour's end, never having toured again. Somehow, though, the combination of the old giving its final heave and the new looking ahead to fresh musical frontiers gave many of the shows on this tour that added spark. The band seemed to play endlessly; several shows contained well over three hours of music, much more than in previous years.

Upon their return from Europe, Pigpen went home to attempt again to recover from his now serious health problems. Musically, however, the band never looked back and they carried their European momentum into the summer tours. Instead of retaining the same themes, however, the band upped the ante and became even more intense. They entered what many people consider their golden age. Whereas fans of blues and R&B favor the early years, country fans the period from 1969 to 1971, and rock 'n' roll fans the late seventies and eighties, this "golden age" was the period most favored by jazz aficionados. "Dark Star" and "The Other One" became infinitely more interesting as the band moved away from roots-based, frenetic psychedelia and on to an visionary, jazz-based sound. Garcia's apocalyptic, wildly spiraling "wah-wah" notes at the peak of these jams became known to many Deadheads as the "Tiger's Roar" and emerged as almost nightly occurrences. The "Space"s preceding the "Tiger"s were often just as intense, with the band going off to investigate unseen corners of the songs while sometimes barely hanging on to a thread of the song's basic theme. "Dark Star" and "The Other One" had been greatly expanded from the usual length of any previous year and were often a straight line to outer space, reaching heights never dreamed of before. "Playing in the Band" also had been transformed into a song with the ability to enter deep space. Now the band was able to whip into an incredible frenzy at least twice a show and, many times, they did.

Other changes occurred in the band's sound. Donna Godchaux, Keith's wife, joined the band, singing on several numbers—most notably "Playing in the Band." She provided a much-needed replacement to Phil's high harmony, which frequently was inconsistent, and gave them a quality vocal sound for the first time. Donna possessed an excellent voice and had an impressive country music background; she was a backup singer for Elvis Presley during some studio sessions in Alabama in the late sixties. Throughout her career with the Dead, however, she was plagued by the occasional inability to hear herself properly in the monitor mix and, consequently, was often quite off-key.

The Dead's traditional musical influences were giving way to the band's own unique flavor. At the same time, Hunter's lyrics evoked a distinctly American folk tradition. Songs like "Ramble On Rose," "Jack Straw," "Tennessee Jed," and "Brown-Eyed Women" carried powerful images of American life, past and present, that contrasted sharply with the emerging pop culture of the seventies. He created his own set of contemporary mythological archetypes that the growing audience could latch on to. In fact, it was common throughout the Dead's history for fans to engage in "Deadspeak," using phrases lifted from the Dead's songs, to convey an idea in the course of conversation. The Weir-Barlow team also produced unique songs as Weir leaned toward increasingly complex structures in tunes like "Greatest Story Ever Told" and "Black-Throated Wind." These songs contributed to the extraordinary variety of musical styles being performed at shows in 1972.

Fall 1972, beginning in September and lasting through November, marked the band's return to daily touring and they put forth probably their most consistently fine tour of all time. Each night provided a solid arrangement of first-set songs, usually culminating with a now mature and expanded "Playing in the Band." The second sets featured songs leading up to a meltdown during "Dark Star," "The Other One," or "Truckin'," and finally ending with the scorching rock 'n' roll of "Sugar Magnolia" and the "Not Fade Away" > "Goin' Down the Road" medley. Musically, this tour marks some of the creative improvisational jamming ever.

For years, good-quality tapes from this era were nearly nonexistent with the exception of a few European soundboards. Many shows in the States were only being taped by whatever local tapehead happened to attend a show. They weren't always Deadheads and they didn't always attend each show in the run. At this time there wasn't yet a contingent of people on tour, and so it is difficult to track down those who were actually taping. The tapes that did appear, mostly from shows on either coast, are of mediocre quality compared to those of later years. In the early eighties, a handful of soundboards from September 28 in Jersey City, the Texas shows in November, and December 11 from Winterland appeared, providing a very different picture of this year than that offered by European shows and beginning the demand for tapes from this year. Since then, tapes have come into circulation ranging in quality from average to spectacular, usually in small batches. We now have a reasonable sample of shows from every part of this year, but there are still more to uncover in this, the most highly sought after year.

Tapes to get: 4/8, 4/11, 4/14, 4/26, 4/29, 5/3–5/4, 5/11, 5/26, 7/18, 8/27, 9/17, 9/23–9/24, 11/19, 12/31.

### 3/5/72
**American Indian Benefit**
**Winterland Arena,**
**San Francisco, California**

Tennessee Jed, Jack Straw, China Cat Sunflower > I Know You Rider, Mexicali Blues, You Win Again, El Paso, Casey Jones, Good Lovin', Not Fade Away > Goin' Down the Road Feelin' Bad > Not Fade Away Reprise
**Encore:** One More Saturday Night

1. **Source:** SBD, **Quality:** A–, **Length:** 1:20
2. **Source:** AUD, **Quality:** A, **Length:** 1:10, **Genealogy:** MR > C > C > C
**Highlights:** Good Lovin'

Notable as Pigpen's last San Francisco show, the Dead's performance this night followed lengthy performances by Yogi Phlegm and the New Riders that put the headliners up against what (that night at least) was a hard-and-fast 2 A.M. curfew. An earlier highlight, preserved on an audience tape, occurred when Garcia and Lesh subbed for two late-arriving members of Yogi Phlegm, performing "Big Boss Man" and "How Blue Can You Get" with Phlegmsters Bill Champlin and Bill Vitt. The soundboard tape of the Dead's show is missing the first six songs, which included the maiden voyage of "Black-Throated Wind." The rest of the tape consists principally of first-set material nicely, if unspectacularly, played. The highlight is the truncated second-set jam, featuring Pig's only vocal of the evening, on a rocked-out "Good Lovin'" that also featured the debut of the new falsetto vocal chorus that was so much a part of the European tour versions of that song. Watching the clock for once, the band wound up with a routine "Not Fade Away" > "Goin' Down the Road" > "Not Fade Away" medley and a quick "Saturday Night" encore.

MICHAEL PARRISH

### 3/23/72
**Academy of Music, New York, New York**

**Set 1:** China Cat Sunflower > I Know You Rider, //Black-Throated Wind, Chinatown Shuffle, Brown-Eyed Women, Beat It on Down the Line, Looks like Rain, Mr. Charlie, Jack Straw, Next Time You See Me
**Set 2:** Playing in the Band, Truckin', Ramble On Rose, Two Souls in Communion, Mexicali Blues, Big Boss Man, Dark Star, Not Fade Away > Goin' Down the Road Feelin' Bad > Not Fade Away Reprise

**Source:** AUD, **Quality:** C/C–, **Length:** 2:15, **Taper:** Marty Weinberg, R. T. Carlyle, and Ed Perlstein all taped this show.
**Highlights:** Two Souls in Communion, Dark Star

The sound quality, as you have probably deduced from the above rating, leaves a lot to be desired. There isn't much hiss or many technical glitches present on this recording, but all the recordings sound far away with very minimal definition to the music. This performance, though masked behind this low-quality recording, was a very solid night musically for the Dead during their seven-night stand in New York. Even though the sound quality is poor and this tape will probably not be spreading through taping circles like wildfire, I still want to provide a few general comments. To start, this show definitely sounds like a real good time with a set list that has something for everyone. The crowd is completely enthralled; they scream, yell, holler, and clap away, usually competing with the music for the peaking levels on the tape. This show featured the debut of "Two Souls in Communion," one of five Pigpen tunes from this night, all performed with their usual flair. The whole first set was played extremely well, with all songs actually becoming fine versions. For some unknown reason, the version of "Dark Star" on the second tape sounds a couple of notches better than all the other songs from this show. It might even be from another audience master or taped from a better location. There is a cleaner definition to the music that almost makes it listenable! The crowd is extremely quiet, which helps make "Dark Star" stand out in quality from the rest of the show. This "Star" is a good, weird version that contains an interesting jam that sounds like an intermingling of "Goin' Down the Road Feelin' Bad" and "I Know You Rider." There are even hints of "China Cat Sunflower" dropped in for good measure. If there were a circulating soundboard from this show, it would be a worthwhile recording to own. If you're a "Dark Star" fan, you might want to check this tape out if it comes your way. All in all, the show sounds as if it were an extremely fun night in New York City with the Dead.

COREY SANDERSON

*Ticket stub for the 1972 run at the Academy of Music, New York City*

---

### 3/25/72
**Hell's Angels Party**
**Academy of Music,**
**New York, New York**

**Set 1:** Hey Bo Diddley* > Mannish Boy* > Jam*, Take It Off*, Mona*
**Set 2:** //How Sweet It Is, Last Train to Jacksonville, Next Time You See Me, Brown-Eyed Women, Smokestack Lightning, Sittin' on Top of the World, //Sugaree, //Looks like Rain//, Bertha, Mr. Charlie, //Playing in the Band, //Turn On Your Lovelight

* with Bo Diddley

**Source:** AUD, **Quality:** C–/D, **Length:** 2:10, **Taper:** Marty Weinberg, R. T. Carlyle, and Ed Perlstein all taped this show.

**Highlights:** Mannish Boy > Jam, Take It Off Baby, Smokestack Lightning, Playing in the Band

This night at the Academy of Music proved to be a night of "firsts" and "onlys." Although the tape I have is exceptionally grungy, the music from this evening shines through to the patient ear. From the opening shouts of guest Bo Diddley, who yelled, "Are you ready up there?" numerous times to the anxious crowd, to a gorgeous "Playing in the Band" late in the second set, this show was filled with memorable moments that any loyal fan of the Grateful Dead should hear.

The first set of this show opened with a three-song medley, "Hey Bo Diddley" > "Mannish Boy" > "Jam," that was energetically led by Bo Diddley, who sat in throughout the first set. "Hey Bo Diddley" was merely a tool to warm up the band, featuring no major solo. However, the second song of the suite, "Mannish Boy," proved to be a nicely done blues number, highlighted by a midsong exploration of distortion by Diddley, which Jerry eventually joined in on. This subsequently descends into a jam that is crackling with energy, much more so than anything heard thus far; the band was heating up! Both Jerry and Bobby join Bo in a some heavy rhythmic jams that build to a crescendo, followed by a plea from Bo to the crowd to join in and clap. Of course, the crowd is overjoyed and enthusiastically joins in. The band builds the jam again, with Jerry really starting to shine; I imagine they were having oh-so-much fun with such a blues legend.

Unfortunately for the listener and contrary to *DeadBase IX*, this jam comes to a finale and ends; it does not segue into "Take It Off." "Take It Off" is another treat nevertheless. Phil takes off, forming a backbone of bass while Bo pleads with the crowd's ladies to "Take it off, baby!" and sing along. "You've got everything a man could want!" Bo cries as the jam begins to take off, finally reaching a peak and then coming to a conclusion. Again contrary to *DeadBase IX*, there is not a segue from "Take It Off" into "Mona." This time Bobby leads the way into Mona, with Phil pounding out the notes. Jerry, Bobby, and Bo fill the air with riff after riff. However, as with most songs in this set, Mona is uncharacteristically short, and ends with Bo's standard three-chord riff. No matter, this first set is a crowd pleaser!

As the second set begins, the listener finds the return of the "good old Grateful Dead," this time led by Pigpen, who was essentially silent during the first set. The set opens with a couple of never-before-heard songs: "How Sweet It Is," which is cut in the beginning of my tape, and "Last Train to Jacksonville." "How Sweet It Is" is still an early formative version of this long-played Jerry Garcia Band song; "Last Train to Jacksonville" is the first time that Donna's voice fills the air as an "official" member of the band. Both are "once only" treats. The highlights of this set, however, are the Pigpen tunes. "Next Time You See Me," though plagued by a drop in recording quality (if that is possible), is energetic throughout and features some nice solo work by Garcia. It is simply too bad that Jerry was so low in the mix, unlike the person next to the microphone who contributed incessant clapping. The "Smokestack Lightning" is excellent, one of the best I have heard: long, bluesy, with a fantastic solo by Garcia toward the end. As the jam containing Garcia's solo rises to a crescendo, it suddenly descends into a *major* "Truckin'" tease, led by who else but Phil! This turn by the band only adds to the fervor, raising the energy up a notch. Even after the subsequent jam returns to the basic "Smokestack Lightning" chords, we are again treated to another rising crescendo of jams, this time led by Garcia. Wow!

Though Pigpen's version of "Mr. Charlie" is quite good, the next highlight arrives in a fantastic "Playing in the Band." Even though this song is horribly cut, picking up in the mid-verse jam, it is extremely spacey. The noodling is solid, energetic, fearlessly explorational, and very representative of the many massive versions to come in 1972–74. Perhaps the finest component of this rendition is Lesh's dominating bass notes that really take the band wherever it needs to go. This version would most likely rank higher if it were complete and available in a higher-quality recording.

My tape is missing the "Good Lovin'" that is supposed to follow "Playing in the Band" and only picks up the "Lovelight" well into the song, just as the usual post-first-verse jam starts to rise to a climax. Huge notes by Phil coupled with great rhythm work by Bobby dominate the mix as the final vocals by Pig begin. Unfortunately, because so much of this is missing, the total time of this version is under eight minutes.

— DARREN MASON

---

## 3/26/72

**Academy of Music, New York, New York**

**Set 1:** Greatest Story Ever Told, Cold Rain and Snow, Chinatown Shuffle, Black-Throated Wind, You Win Again, Mr. Charlie, Jack Straw, //Loser, Looks like Rain, Big Railroad Blues, Big Boss Man, Playing in the Band//

**Source:** AUD, **Quality:** D, **Length:** 1:30, **Taper:** Marty Weinberg, R. T. Carlyle, and Ed Perlstein all taped this show.

**Highlights:** Big Railroad Blues

The tape from this show is a *really* lousy recording. The band sounds quite far away—no doubt this show was taped by the same person who recorded the show two nights earlier. On my tape the levels are fine but there's a *serious* amount of hiss. Even the lowest generation available would barely be listenable and not really desirable. The music from this show, however, is decent, with the version of "Big Railroad Blues" standing out. There isn't really any need to look for this one because it was just an average night musically for the Dead, captured on a lousy recording.

— COREY SANDERSON

## 3/27/72

**Academy of Music, New York, New York**

**Set 1:** Bertha, Black-Throated Wind, Chinatown Shuffle, Brown-Eyed Women, China Cat Sunflower > I Know You Rider > Me and Bobby McGee, Mr. Charlie, Looks like Rain//, Deal, It Hurts Me Too, Cumberland Blues, Playing in// the Band
**Set 2:** Greatest Story Ever Told, Ramble On Rose, Big Boss Man, El Paso, Good// Lovin'//, Me and My Uncle, Two Souls in Communion, Sugar Magnolia > Sunshine Daydream, Loser, Casey Jones, One More Saturday Night

**Source:** AUD, **Quality:** D–/F+, **Length:** 3:00, **Taper:** Marty Weinberg, R. T. Carlyle, and Ed Perlstein all taped this show.

**Highlights:** My highlights are weighted toward the songs one can actually hear well enough to appreciate: Playing in the Band, China Cat > I Know You Rider, Good Lovin', Two Souls in Communion.

March 27 was the second-to-last in the seven-day run at the Academy of Music. Several songs played at this show were in their early incarnations; this was the fourth "Looks like Rain," featuring Garcia on pedal steel; the third of "Black-Throated Wind"; the fifth of twenty-six Chinatown Shuffle"s; and the second of only nine "Two Souls in Communion"s. These last two would be around for a painfully short time, and leave us, along with their singer, much too soon. Also, this was Donna's first official run.

Less than a year after the closing of the Fillmore East, and with only three Big Apple shows in the interim, New York City Heads were fiendin' for a fix. Those who have experienced New York intensity will not be surprised to hear that this seven-day run was met with more than just a little enthusiasm. A friend of mine with twenty-seven years of GD experience insists that this was one of the best runs the Dead ever played. He went on to say that the Academy of Music had phenomenal acoustics and was the best-sounding place the Dead ever played. While that debate rages, we're left to stew in the ironic reality that these tapes are among the worst quality I've ever heard. They are so bad that upon hearing the first song, my son said, "I can tell it's 'Bertha,' but only by the vibrations." Not much hiss on my copy, but with a lot of distortion and almost no highs or lows, it sounds as if it were recorded through the speaker at a McDonald's drive-thru. That's why, if you please, I would like some fries with these. No offense to the kind soul who gave us our only taste of this show, but in my opinion, only three types of people will want these tapes: the completists, the nostalgic (you were at the show), and the mildly sadistic (you want to end a party that's gone on too long). On the other hand, though it's real tough to get accustomed to the poor quality, there is some fantastic music on this tape. Of dubious comfort is the fact that when Phil's bass is quiet (don't hold your breath), you can more easily hear what's happening elsewhere.

Thumbing his nose at such foolish notions, Phil thunders through the "Black-Throated Wind" while Garcia tears it up to shreds. Afterward, you can hear all sorts of tunes being requested between songs. Despite the quality, it's evident that the "China Cat" is s-s-smokin'. Weir, Garcia, and Lesh are all over this thing like politicians at a Fourth of July parade. You really can't hear Billy at all, and if Pigpen or Keith is doing anything, it's lost in the distortion. What you can hear is that as they move into "I Know You Rider," they are feeding the crowd and the crowd is feeding the beast. Whatever it was recorded on, it was no match for the sinister and evil Lesh monster and his repeated saturation bombardment of the innocent, unsuspecting equipment. Sadly, it didn't stand a chance. During the "Wish I was a headlight . . . ," Phil was all over the place, dancing into the upper register. By the time they end it, the crowd is going ballistic. Any confusion about the tape quality will be eradicated if you'll buy the following comment; even Donna's wail in the "Playing in the Band" that ends the first set can barely pierce through this recording. On the plus side, this song takes absolutely no time to reach the end of the runway and hurl itself into deep space. It's ENORMOUS. If a rocket could express its emotions as it explodes through the earth's atmosphere, this is the musical cacophony it would be screaming into the heavens: Mayday Mayday, Houston, some acoustical panels have shaken loose and we have complete meltdown. There's a cut just a few seconds before the song ends, at 10:02.

The second set starts with a blow-it-out assault of the "Greatest Story Ever Told," and finally you can hear

Keith, who lays into it, through the quagmire. A while later Phil serves up "Good Lovin'." You can hardly hear a word Pigpen's singing, but the background groove is quite tasty. Everyone else is going round feeding off each other; notably kick-ass are Jerry, Phil, and Bob jousting repeatedly for their pleasure and ours. This is a fantastic "Good Lovin'." With apologies to the truly suffering, if there is any mercy in this world, soundboards of this show will turn up in my lifetime. It's twenty-one minutes long; there's a small cut at sixteen minutes in, and then it cuts at twenty-one minutes, which is just a few seconds before it ends. After "Me and My Uncle," "Two Souls in Communion" is a floating, grinding, forward-thrusting body rush of a Pigpen love song. Bobby, whose heartstrings are tugging by this time, pulls out his own tender love song, a no-holds-barred "Sugar Magnolia" > "Sunshine Daydream," with Phil roughing it up in the red zone, that reduces the recording tape deck to a pile of ashes. It's a sad case of oversaturation bombing. The "Loser" finds Bobby and Keith dancin' in a ring around the sun. "Casey Jones" ends the show with Keith dancin' all over them bones, while Phil renovates the joint. The encore, on this Monday evening in late March, is the twenty-first performance of "One More Saturday Night." For some reason (Phil) the tape deck really appears to have about had it, and the sound is more muffled than it was moments ago. Who knows, maybe it was an alternate side of the street parking night in New York, and the taper decided to get closer to the door. Anyway, if you listen carefully, you'll hear Keith beating the white out of his ivories.

JAY STRAUSS

---

### 3/28/72
**Academy of Music, New York, New York**

**Set 1:** Truckin', Tennessee Jed, Chinatown Shuffle, Black-Throated Wind, You Win Again, Mr. Charlie, Mexicali Blues, Brokedown Palace, Next Time You See Me, Cumberland Blues, Looks like Rain, Big Railroad Blues, El Paso, China Cat Sunflower > I Know You Rider, Casey Jones//
**Set 2:** Playing in the Band, Sugaree, Two Souls in Communion, Sugar Magnolia > The Other One, It Hurts Me Too, Not Fade Away > Goin' Down the Road Feelin' Bad > Not Fade Away Reprise
**Encore:** Sidewalks of New York > One More Saturday Night//

**Source:** AUD, **Quality:** D, **Length:** 3:00, **Taper:** Marty Weinberg, R. T. Carlyle, and Ed Perlstein all taped this show.

**Highlights:** Truckin, Cumberland Blues, China Cat Sunflower > I Know You Rider, Sugar Magnolia > The Other One

**Comments:** This tape is of very poor quality, especially the first set, which is considerably worse than 3/25/72. The main problem with the recording is that Phil is oversaturated, causing distortion to ring through one's home speakers. Nevertheless, as is the case with many of the Academy of Music shows, there is some great music underneath the tape defects.

This show opens with a "bring the house down" version of "Truckin'." The jam after the vocals is very well played and hard driving, eventually decaying into a space that is dominated by Jerry and Phil, both tossing riffs and bombs back and forth with incredible speed. A rousing opening to the final show of the seven-day run.

After a standard run of first-set songs, highlighted by a "Mexicali Blues" that was preceded by teases of "El Paso" and a very well played "Cumberland Blues," a mistake in *DeadBase IX* is revealed. What follows "Looks like Rain" is not "Big River" but instead, with no splices present, a rollicking version of "Big Railroad Blues." The highlight of set 1 was a very nice suite of "China Cat Sunflower" > "I Know You Rider" right before the set-closing "Casey Jones." The post–"China Cat Sunflower" jam is very lively and visits many different destinations along the way to "I Know You Rider." Though not as long as many 1974 versions, the sheer frenzied energy still makes this version a treat. As usual, Phil's bass is all over the place, sending notes this way and that.

The second set begins, like the first, with a rousing number. Although not as spectacular as the version played three days earlier, this "Playing in the Band" has its moments; it's complete and well played. The highlight of this show, however, is the mid-second-set suite "Sugar Magnolia" > "The Other One," an amazing "once only" performance that is always on the top of my list. The opening chords are well received, accompanied by the annoying clapping that is omnipresent in most audience tapes of the era. A lively version of "Sugar Magnolia" commences, complemented by some nice board work by Keith and a wailing solo by Jerry. As the "Sunshine Daydream" segment draws to a close, Phil picks the "Other One" bass line out of nowhere, with the band following suit. Effortlessly, the band slips into the mid-verse "Other One" jam, leaving no hints about whence they came; you almost forget you were even listening to "Sugar Magnolia," the change is that complete. Most notable during this transition is a very brief (under four chords) hint of "Eyes of the World," which is immediately snuffed out by the dominating "Other One" theme. Following a nice exploratory jam, we are left with just Keith's keys and a slight note of bass. Then, a thundering tone from Phil reenergizes the band, causing everyone to take off with a renewed sense of purpose, jamming to a frenzy of strumming, distortion, and chaos. This eventually decays to a segment of very spacey contributions from the whole band. However, as has already happened in this fantastic portion of music, the chaos again becomes full of energy and takes form. Unfortunately, it is at this point that we are interrupted by a distracting tape flip. The second side of the cassette tape continues where the previous side left off, with the music again led by Phil until, between fifteen and twenty minutes in, the familiar "Other One" signature jam begins, culminating in the first verse of this awesome version. The mid-verse jam, though not as chaotic as the first, is more energetic. Many avenues of structured jams are explored, but just as the precursor chords to verse two appear, my tape cuts, this time for good. The listener is unsympathetically left drooling for more.

The second set closes with a standard serving of "Not Fade Away" > "Goin' Down the Road" > "Not Fade Away" and an encore of "Sidewalks of New York" > "One More Saturday Night." Unfortunately, nothing in this final segment of songs comes close to what preceded it. The "Sidewalks of New York," a once-only version, is very short with no vocals.

DARREN MASON

---

### ❊ 4/7/72 ❊
### Empire Pool, Wembley, England

**Set 1:** Greatest Story Ever Told, Sugaree, Chinatown Shuffle, China Cat Sunflower > I Know You Rider, Big Boss Man, Black-Throated Wind, Loser, Mr. Charlie, Beat It on Down the Line, Tennessee Jed, Playing in the Band, Casey Jones
**Set 2:** Truckin' > Jam > Drums > The Other One > Me and My Uncle Jam > The Other One > El Paso > The Other One > Wharf Rat, Ramble On Rose, Sugar Magnolia//, Not Fade Away > Goin' Down the Road Feelin' Bad > Not Fade Away Reprise
**Encore:** One More Saturday Night

---

**Source:** AUD, **Quality:** C–/F+, **Length:** 3:00
**Highlights:** Truckin' through Wharf Rat
**Comments:** It is very unfortunate that a majority of this show, which kicks off the notorious European tour of 1972, circulates only in terrible quality. Indeed, a substantial portion of this tape is easily one of the worst-sounding tapes I have in my collection, requiring heroic patience to listen to. Not only is the bass exceedingly oversaturated, but the hiss floor is high and the keyboards are essentially inaudible. Fortunately for the listener, however, most of the best music from this show does circulate in a somewhat listenable (lower generation?) audience tape that has been spliced into the previously described horror.

This first performance by the band at the Empire Pool, which is kicked off by a friendly introduction from Sam Cutler welcoming the band back to England, was essentially the warm-up show before they headed out to weave their magic across Europe. Although the second set is quite good, the entire show does not measure up when compared to the sheer giants they would play in the next two months. Nevertheless, the substantial "Truckin'" > "Other One" montage in the second set makes it worth the effort to acquire this somewhat rare tape.

The first set is unnotable, except for the fact that the band pulls off a well-played "China Cat Sunflower" > "I Know You Rider" suite. I have always been fond of this pairing in Europe—not because the band was pushing the envelope of improvisation, as they would in the years to come, but rather because they were just beginning to experiment with what *could* happen during the bridge. This version, and many others from the same time period, form the initial groundwork to the masterful renditions that would fill the air in 1974.

At the beginning of side B of my first cassette tape of this show, a few standard numbers follow "China Cat Sunflower," and then a spliced-in sequence from a fifth-generation tape appears. Although the sound is still quite grungy, the hiss floor is nearly gone and stage banter can be heard.

From here, "Beat It on Down the Line" begins. Oddly, you never hear Bobby mention Jesse Fuller on the tape; I imagine this was lost to a tape pause or some such gremlin. Following a mediocre "Playing in the Band," the first set closes with a standard rendition of "Casey Jones."

Fortunately, in set 2 the band removes the gloves and decides to hit hard. Indeed, before a single break is taken, it will journey through more than sixty minutes of a diverse musical landscape. This segment alone makes this skeevy audience tape worth hearing. The canonical pairing of "Truckin'" with "The Other One" was one that would truly blossom during the year 1972. There are so many great versions of this suite that would occur in the months to come (9/17/72 and 12/31/72 among them). This version is in some sense a nice view of the "genesis" rendition. "Truckin'" starts out slow but picks up steam as the final verses of "We better get back truckin' on!" are belted out by Bobby. Unfortunately, my tape returns to truly horrid quality at this point. What was a fairly clean audience recording is replaced by muddied boom.

Nevertheless, the spirit of the jam can be discerned and just as it is beginning to loosen up and achieve that "spacey" quality that we are familiar with in this suite, the tape cuts and is continued on tape two. Fortunately, whoever did the transfer up the line, restarts on tape two well ahead of where the cut occurs, so that no music is lost. The "Space" out of "Truckin'" is a very eerie jam, reminiscent of some old horror film theme. The playing drifts in and out of melodic sparse notes, to whiney feedback, to frenetic jamming. All too soon, however, before the playing really takes shape, the band descends into "Drums."

"The Other One" begins with a fury following the skin beating punctuated by the ear-rattling tones of Phil. Then, after the usual rhythmic structures that signify this song have passed, the band once again returns to the spacey and loose melodies that preceded it. This time, however, the diversion is longer and touches on the boundaries of "Dark Star." The band members complement each other in detailed scales that slowly intertwine. The "Space" decays into chaos and Phil: form without structure.

After this interlude, Bobby and Jerry tease back into "The Other One," slowly building the structure from before. Following the nearly unintelligible vocals of the first verse, the listener is granted another pardon and the nice fifth generation audio is respliced back into the tape, there to remain until the show is over. With the band clearly audible in the tape, I found the final jam is to be imaginative and energetic. Eventually, perhaps five to six minutes after the final verse of "The Other One," a very energetic "Me and My Uncle" jam builds out of some "Space" and very quickly reaches breakneck speed. However, they cut it short and return to "Space," much to the chagrin of the crowd who reply with boos. Of course, the band simply has bigger fish to fry. Indeed, the order of the day is more melodic "Space," quite beautifully played. This return to melancholy has a purpose, however: to set the mood for one of my favorite covers, "El Paso," which is seamlessly created out of the musical sea. Following "El Paso," the return to "The Other One" is a fast, furious, and hot jam that, once again, decays into the oscillatory theme that has preceded it: unstructured "Space" mixed in with intermittent revisits to rhythm. Ultimately, the band sings the second verse of this mammoth rendition, signaling that the time has come to shift gears, this time into a very pretty "Wharf Rat." Not long into the song, my tape again cuts. Fortunately, the song is started again on side B of cassette tape two.

To close "Wharf Rat," which ends with applause and foot stomping, Phil makes an announcement to the obviously excited audience: "Hey, everybody. About thirty-five to forty minutes ago the hall landlord [(?)] started putting pressure on us about you people standing in the aisles and it seems to violate fire regulations, etc. So would you all please return to your seats and listen from here?" Unexpectedly, the audience greets this announcement with very little booing and jeering, a far cry from what has happened in other places at other times.

After "Ramble On Rose" and "Sugar Magnolia," which cuts during the jam before the "Sunshine Daydream" (the sound is reminiscent of the tape running out), the final ensemble beginning with "Not Fade Away" closes this first night in Europe. While well played, it does not even begin to approach the interesting music that followed it.

DARREN E. MASON

## ❊ 4/8/72 ❊
### Empire Pool, Wembley, England

**Set 1:** Bertha, Me and My Uncle, Mr. Charlie, Deal, Black-Throated Wind, Next Time You See Me, Cumberland Blues, Brown-Eyed Women, Beat it on Down the Line, Tennessee Jed, Playing in the Band, Good Lovin', Looks like Rain, Casey Jones
**Set 2:** Truckin', Big Railroad Blues, Hurts Me Too, Dark Star > Sugar Magnolia > Caution
**Encore:** One More Saturday Night.

**1. Source:** FM-SBD (GDH 427 and 428), **Quality:** A, **Length:** 1:00 ("Dark Star" > "Sugar Magnolia" > "Caution")
**2. Source:** SBD—LP, *Glastonbury Faire*, **Quality:** A, **Length:** 0:20 (excerpt from the middle of "Dark Star"), **Genealogy:** LP > C
**3. Source:** AUD, **Quality:** F–, **Length:** 3:20 (the whole show)
**Highlights:** Playing in the Band, Good Lovin', Dark Star > Sugar Magnolia > Caution

For a short while, from April through November '72, the Dead gained access to a musical space—or, more accurately, transcended to a level of musical consciousness that was deeper, more complex, more evolved, more articulate, more powerful than any other that "spoke through them" before or afterward. This period contains more than a few passages of improvisational music that hold the power to bring the listener to and through the furthest depths of inner consciousness. It is as powerful a vehicle for inner, visionary travel as any music ever created. The "Dark Star" from 4/8/72 represents one very clear pinnacle in this short, brilliant epoch.

You don't have to go any farther than this concert to find strong arguments in defense of the claim that the Dead were true visionary artists. The mystical psychedelic experience was a central facet of their worldview and livelihood. By April of '72 their kinesthetic skills, intellectual awareness, musical prowess, and familiarity with each other allowed these musicians to let go and allow the music to play the band on a much more refined, fearless, and evocative level than ever before. Bobby's guitar skills had finally arrived. And Jerry had become a true avatar, channeling the most articulate psychedelic statements ever to fly out of an electric guitar. Fortunately, excellent quality tapes of such profound improvisational journeys preserve and offer us this music as catalysts for ongoing visionary Experiences.

"Dark Star" is, of course, a vehicle in which a very special collective artistic journey can be taken. It's the quintessential example of the musicians' decision to knowingly take a huge risk, to cast off together into the unknown, to explore new realms. Somehow, almost every single time the Dead took that risk, they charted new, breathtaking musical constellations. Another thing that makes "Dark Star" so special is that it was just as likely to find and explore the evil, dark, and scary emotions as it was to find and explore the most stunning examples of emotional beauty (the "Feelin' Groovy Jam" for example). And so, deservedly mythic in stature, "Dark Star" was the Dead's own psychedelic bus. When that bus came by, we all got on. It was an adventure with ever-changing but always exciting results.

For maximal enjoyment I would suggest that you listen to the "Dark Star"s from both 4/8 and 8/27/72 in the recommended "set and setting," then read the review of 8/27 in this compendium, and *then* read this review. Under these circumstances I think you will find that the following analysis is fair. It is my belief that these two *enormous* "Dark Star"s represent two interrelated and mutually dependent spheres of aesthetic/spiritual experience. Emotionally, the "Dark Star" from 8/27 brings the inner journeyer through a metaphorical death/rebirth experience. The frighteningly fast apocalyptic meltdown in that "Dark Star" is stunning in its sheer darkness, speed, and terror—not cheap terror like you'd see on television, but *real* terror. This is not casual listening music. It's as emotionally serious a piece of music as I've ever heard. I've had the great honor of playing that "Dark Star" on a top-notch sound system in an intimate environment for small groups of listeners (more than 1,000 people in total over the past seventeen years!), and virtually every single one of them agrees with this observation.

By contrast, the "Dark Star" from 4/8 seems to clearly represent to me the opposite energy; for the most part it feels like an exploration of beauty and nirvana. Yes, on 4/8 they do get pretty "out there," but they seem compelled to return to far more melodic, structured, bright, happy jams. And so I value these two performances as the yin and yang of visionary "Dark Star"s. When I want to psychically experience the metaphorical death/rebirth *Experience* I listen to 8/27/72. When I want to visit the heavenly realms, I put on 4/8/72. Together, the two provide me with a balanced set of catalysts for visiting the outer edges of my inner emotional/spiritual landscape.

The second set of this show is easily one of the most entrancing I've ever heard, and, dare I say, it features one of my four favorite "Dark Star"s. (The other three are 8/27/72, 2/13/70, and 9/27/72.) Until 1996 only two thoroughly frustrating tapes of this show circulated. First, a stunning twenty-minute excerpt from the middle of the "Dark Star" was released in 1973 as part of a record showcasing several bands from the long-famous Glastonbury Faire in England. Many Deadheads transferred this tease of a snippet to tape long ago so it is in fairly wide circulation. The other frustrating source of this show (which is in far narrower distribution) is the worst audience recording I've ever heard. It sounds like someone recorded the "Dark Star" > "Sugar Magnolia" > "Caution" from the bathroom on a dirty, misaligned, three-dollar, high school AV department Wollensak tape deck purchased at a crap-filled tag sale and then intentionally bumped the tape down five generations, missetting the Dolby switch every time! It's so bad it's worth getting just for the good laugh. Thankfully, the "Dark Star" > "Sugar Magnolia" > "Caution" was finally played on the radio by David Gans in 1996, and now we can all properly rejoice in the bliss of this very special music. This horrid audience tape does feature the entire show, and though it's virtually impossible to appreciate the music, it's still apparent that the highlights are a raging "Playing in the Band" in its dramatically expanded form and an equally immense "Good Lovin'."

Ah, the music here is *phenomenal*. The "Dark Star" contains numerous melodic explorations every bit as beautiful as the "Feelin' Groovy Jam" (but different). It starts like every other version from the first half of 1972; however, it quickly develops into a psychedelic jam whose tempo, rhythm, and energy are far more animated than the typical pre-lyrics jam of that time; in fact, you might mistake this particular segment as coming from the middle of a 1972 performance of "Playing in the Band." Interestingly, and unlike so many other "Dark Star"s from 1972, Jerry sings the words here rather quickly. Then the band launches into the jams that make this version so special. Much more than usual, Bobby and Keith are as responsible for this deluge of inspiration as Jerry and Phil.

Listen to the twenty minutes that follow the words and then imagine what a tease it was to have only this part of the show for eighteen years! You can begin to imagine how delightful it was to finally acquire the rest of the set.

The highlight of this "Dark Star" is a heavenly jam at its finale that rises out of controlled madness and congeals into pure bliss. It's an early permutation of the "Mind Left Body Jam," although while the chord progression is the same it's rhythmically different (they're actually in the groove for "Sugar Magnolia"). What makes this particular permutation of this four-chord progression so memorable is Garcia's sweet, sweet statement that dances over the top of the melody. It's one of my favorite Garcia instrumental passages.

Once again Bobby sees a perfect opening and starts playing the opening statement of "Sugar Magnolia." This segue from "Star" to "Sugar" is sinfully sweet—one of the most perfect transitions of the band's entire career. "Sugar Magnolia" > "Sunshine Daydream" is a standard full-tilt rock 'n' roll explosion. As Bobby screams his lungs out at the close of this rocker, Phil starts pumping out the frenetic signature underpinnings of what quickly becomes the first "Caution" played since November 6, 1970. Whoa! Upon first listen you may find yourself thinking, as I did, *The boys mean business here!*

The band tears through a blistering jam that threatens to never end. Eventually, Pigpen commits a small vocal flub, coming in with the opening line a bit early; it's so small a flub one might not notice it on casual listening. He backs off quickly and the band continues to go nuts for a few more minutes before Pig eventually gets to sing. It's obvious the guitarists are loving what they're doing and don't want to stop. What I love about this and the five other final versions of "Caution" from 1972, all performed on this European tour, is that they are reexaminations of the Dead's primal form, the type of song they first used as a vehicle for moving energy upward and outward, only by 1972 it was in the context of a more mature musical perspective. Another good example of this is the comparison between, say, the version of "Not Fade Away" from February 14, 1970, and the version from September 10, 1974 (on *Dick's Picks VII*). It's the same song, but these two readings are very different musical statements because the band's music had changed so much. As for this performance of "Caution," well, it's both a bit rough, being the first time out, and *amazing*! At one point the energy swells so intensely one is clearly reminded of the astounding jam between "Lovelight" and "Goin' Down the Road" from Frankfurt on April 26. Also, as with the jam following "Lovelight" from Bickershaw on May 7, Garcia explores in this "Caution" a deep, psychedelic blues realm by playing slide for a few minutes.

This concert shows the Dead at what was obviously an all-time energy peak and very, very psyched to be starting their historic tour of Europe. Dick Latvala has told me that this show is on his short list for eventual releases. Let's hope he has his way real soon.

JOHN R. DWORK

---

### 4/11/72

**City Hall, Newcastle upon Tyne, England**

**Set 1:** Greatest Story Ever Told, Deal, Mr. Charlie, Black-Throated Wind, Tennessee Jed, Big Boss Man, Beat It on Down the Line, Sugaree, Jack Straw, Chinatown Shuffle, China Cat Sunflower > I Know You Rider, Playing in the Band, Next Time You See Me, Brown-Eyed Women, Looks like Rain//, Big Railroad Blues, Casey Jones
**Set 2:** Good Lovin', Truckin' > Drums > The Other One > Comes a Time//
**Encore:** Brokedown Palace

---

**Source:** SBD, **Quality:** B (Most copies are very hissy; some older copies are off-speed by as much as 8 percent!), **Length:** 3:00 (missing "Sugar Mag" from between "Comes a Time" and "Brokedown")

**Highlights:** Virtually every song is a must-have version. Casey Jones, Good Lovin, Truckin', and The Other One shine very brightly.

Someday, when this show is released on CD, I think many will come to think of it as one of the Dead's very best. At the moment, however, this show isn't very well known to most traders. It's a shame, because the band plays with *immense* ferocity and focus from the very first note to the last. It doesn't help matters much that the tapes in circulation of this show, when available, are almost always very hissy and off-speed (I've gotten copies that are too fast and too slow). Oh, but the music! This show starts off with a ferocious "Greatest Story"—one of the strongest openers I've ever heard them play. Donna *wails!* Phil shakes the earth. "Tennessee Jed" also is one of the tightest versions ever. The "China" > "Rider," though not as polished as the version on *Europe '72,* is actually hotter! "Playing in the Band" is as good as almost any other version, save a precious handful. It's amazing to here the audience only claps politely at the conclusion of this psychedelic supernova. If I had been there, I would have been screaming in joyous disbelief. Shortly thereafter, Garcia sits down at the pedal steel guitar for "Looks like Rain" and turns it into a genuine tearjerker. Again, one of the best versions ever! This would be a splendidly rare addition as a Vault release some day. The shiniest gem to be gleaned from this concert is the second-set opener, "Good Lovin'." Everyone is totally in sync, particularly Billy. After Pigpen sings the song's standard verses and adds a few minutes of impassioned improvising with the band embellishing right in step behind him (just like in any good version of "Lovelight"), he steps back and lets the instrumentalists take over. All I can say is that the ensuing jam is a breathtaking example of the Grateful Dead doing what they're best at: transcending to a level at which all musicians are part of one collective brilliantly creative gestalt—in the moment, listening to each other, obviously having tons of fun.

At the risk of sounding like a broken record, "Ramble On Rose" is also one of their best-ever versions. In particular, Keith is right there alongside Garcia laying down some especially sweet licks. "Truckin'" is enormous—arguably the best version I've ever heard. This monster version quickly melts into a sea of Phil-dominated noodling. Soon Bobby casts an overlay of lush, dissonant chords. Jerry's guitar starts to wail. And then the whole band is in deep, blissful, melodic space. They descend into a short drum solo that serves as a launching pad for one very intense "Other One." After the words, the band finds itself quickly again in that same ineffable place we hear them traveling through on *Hundred Year Hall* during the "Lovelight"—where the music plays the band at breakneck speed, too fast for the artist to premeditate. They simply *are* conduits through which the music unfolds.

Amazingly, they then gallop right into a full-fledged "Feelin' Groovy Jam" (sort of like on 3/31/73 Buffalo), which in turn melts down into eerie "Space" again. Jerry's guitar starts to cry lonely, mournful notes. Shortly thereafter the whole band begins tearing into a very scary, apocalyptic meltdown. This in turn explodes into yet another galloping jam, which then tumbles back into the second verse of "The Other One." Incredible! Unfortunately, "Comes a Time" cuts. As is the case with virtually every *Europe '72* show, you should make every effort to get this tape—you won't be sorry!

JOHN R. DWORK

## 4/14/72
### Tivoli Concert Hall, Copenhagen, Denmark

**Set 1:** Bertha, Me and My Uncle, Mr. Charlie, You Win Again, Black-Throated Wind, Chinatown Shuffle, Loser, Me and Bobby McGee, Cumberland Blues, Playing in the Band, Tennessee Jed, El Paso, Big Boss Man, Beat It on Down the Line, Casey Jones
**Set 2:** Truckin', Hurts Me Too, Brown-Eyed Women, Looks Like Rain, Dark Star > Sugar Magnolia, Good Lovin' > Caution > Who Do You Love > Caution > Good Lovin', Ramble On Rose, Not Fade Away > Goin' Down the Road Feelin' Bad > Not Fade Away Reprise
**Encore:** One More Saturday Night

**1. Source:** SBD, **Quality:** B, **Length:** 3:00 (missing "Ramble On Rose")
**2. Source:** FM-SBD (Radio Copenhagen), **Quality:** B–/C+ (*very* hissy), **Length:** 3:00 (missing "Ramble On Rose")
**3. Source:** AUD, **Quality:** C, **Length:** 3:30
**Highlights:** Don't miss a minute of this show! The "Feelin' Groovy Jam" in the "Dark Star" is the most aggressive version I've heard. The Pigpen rap in the "Good Lovin'" medley is one of his wildest ever.
**Comments:** This show originally circulated in the 1970s as an *extremely* hissy FM broadcast soundboard tape that suffered from a good number of cuts. Then, in the 1980s, a better copy emerged, and then, in the mid-nineties, a much improved soundboard tape finally began to circulate. Still, as is the case with all non–Betty board tapes from this tour, it has more hiss and less depth (especially on the low end) than one would like.

Give a careful listen to this show and you might end up considering it to be one of the Dead's all-time highest energy shows, as I do. It's profoundly inspired from beginning to end with extended segments of extraordinary jamming all over the place. As with so many other shows from this tour, the band marches along, song after song, with textbook accuracy. The mix is also interesting in that Keith Godchaux is turned *waaay* up—no complaints here. Man, could he tickle those ivories. In the first set, the "Black-Throated Wind" and the "Playing in the Band," both Pigpen tunes, are of particular interest. "Playing in the Band" drips with transcendent psychedelic energy as Jerry dances all around the "Main Ten" theme repeatedly. During the breaks between songs it's also amusing to hear the band tease the audience about their inability to understand English. At first the crowd is rather placid. But as the band rips through each song with enormous energy, the crowd is quickly transformed. In no time at all, the crowd goes nuts, clapping in anticipation between many songs.

Things get immediately legendary in the second set. In fact, all the music from here on out is so hyperkinetic that one has to wonder if the band was high on some sort of "up" drug! (At one point Phil asks the audience if they mind if the band gets high!) Phil steps up to the mike, tells the rest of the band that it's time to "issue the call," and then launches into one of the most blistering versions of "Truckin'" ever. Of course Bobby forgets a few of the words as usual, but Jerry's instrumental ferocity quickly makes up for this lyrical divot. A superb "Hurts Me Too" is highlighted by Jerry's magnificently mournful slide guitar work. After a strong "Brown-Eyed Women" the band delivers one of the best-ever readings of "Looks Like Rain" with Jerry's pedal steel guitar work crying mournfully behind Bobby's haunting lyrics.

The "Dark Star," while not in the handful of best-ever versions, is certainly up near the top. This one is all Garcia; he's manic, as if possessed by some hyperactive spirit (perhaps Lady Cocaine?). His playing here reminds me very much of his playing of the same song at Roosevelt Stadium on 7/18/72. The band quickly soars off into a very upbeat "Space," one of the most fully developed pre-lyric improvisations ever! Jerry's guitar is *wail-*

*ing* while Bobby clangs away in unison, stating high, bell-like harmonics. Both Jerry's and Bobby's guitar sounds are at times so piercing, so powerfully shrill, they actually hurt the ears at points (although it's that good kind of screaming guitar hurt, like on the "Dark Star" from *Live Dead*). It's a long time till Jerry gets around to singing the lyrics, but none of them are in a rush as it's obvious they're totally lost in the moment. Then, after the vocals, the band yells for a Garcia-led melodic instrumental jam not unlike the joyous melodic jams found in the "Dark Star"s played on Empire Pool 4/8/72 and Philly 9/21/72.

Even more amazing is the breakneck "Feelin' Groovy Jam" that follows. Jerry is in the midst of playing a stunning yet dark, frenetic lead when Phil launches into the "Feelin' Groovy" theme at the high tempo the band is already playing at. Bobby joins Phil quickly, but Jerry seems reluctant to break out of his dark mode—he just keeps hammering away as though thoroughly mesmerized by the savage energy emanating from his guitar. The result is as novel as the jam at the tail end of "Lovelight" on 4/26/72 in Frankfurt (on the *Hundred Year Hall* release), during which Jerry plays "Goin' Down the Road" while Bobby and Billy play "Not Fade Away" on top of one another. Only *here* Jerry is playing hellish music while Phil and Bobby are playing music from heaven. This juxtaposition is miraculous because it somehow works. Jerry does his best to get out of the "Feelin' Groovy" mode by bringing the jam to a quick climax. Phil and Bobby are stubborn however, and keep coming back to "Feelin' Groovy." Yet Jerry is just as stubborn—he's found a groove that feels delicious and he just wants to stay there. Eventually, Jerry relents to a degree and comes around harmonically for a brief instant. This outrageous passage is by no means the sweetest "Feelin' Groovy Jam," but it's definitely the fastest and most offbeat. It's so breathlessly fast one almost laughs in disbelief. By this point the listener is absolutely convinced Jerry is high on something.

The segue between "Dark Star" and "Sugar Mags" is one of the most magnificent musical moments of the night. Garcia's guitar is howling, screaming, moaning deep sobs as Bobby plays the opening phrases to "Sugar Mags." The rest of the band all falls into place with Bobby—the rest of the band, that is, except Garcia, who continues to wail away as though in deep aural hell. As he repeats a deliciously bent note for what seems like a short infinity, one wonders if he is again going to stubbornly stick to his guns. But no: he resolves the note into consonant bliss and joins the band for "Sugar Mags."

Somehow, this incongruous mix of chaos and structured song work perfectly together. Brilliant!

As if this wasn't already astonishing enough, the band then rips into one of the great improvised medleys of their career: "Good Lovin'" > "Caution" > "Who Do You Love" > "Caution" > "Good Lovin'." In between the first part of "Caution" and "Who Do You Love," Pigpen sticks in one of his all time greatest vocal raps. Granted, as you read in the transcription below, it's rather sexist—to say the least—but it's still amazing.

*Early in, in the morning,*
*oh, oh, everybody needs a little bit of lovin',*
*late in the evenin', you know it's true,*
*late in the evenin', you know it's true,*
*you got ta have it,*
*I don't care who you are,*
*you got ta have it,*
*I don't care who you are,*
*you got ta have some love in the mornin',*
*a taste in the afternoon,*
*just a little more round the midnight hour,*
*darn it soon.*
*You know that love will drive a man to drink,*
*make a professor forget how to think,*
*do many strange, strange things to your mind,*
*try to rope a [inaudible] to find yourself on a straight*
    *line,*
*what's the matter with you,*
*I got you all turned around,*
*I just [inaudible] yes I do,*
*ain't nothin but it's somethin',*
*no no,*
*nothin but it's time baby,*
*no no no,*
*huh, so ease in slow, so ease in slow,*
*my, my, my, my,*
*oh you know I ask my rider sometime in the morning,*
*sit up please, darlin', turn on over,*
*s'all I need before I go to work,*
*s'all I need before I go to work,*
*is just a little bit o' yer sweet thing,*
*just a little bit o' your sweet thing,*
*I know you got it darlin', I been there before,*
*I just wanna come back home one mo' time again,*
*yes I wanna come on back home one more time again,*
*raise up, and ease on over,*
*raise on up, now baby and ease on over,*
*that's all I need, that's all I need,*
*what made you think that a hawg could all night long,*

*what make you think that a tomcat prowl along,*
*what made you think that a rabbit hunt a hound,*
*same old thing now darlin' please turn your damper down,*
*give it to me baby,*
*it's gettin' to me,*
*it's gettin' to me, yes it is.*
*[the band then jams]*
*Now boy I wanna tell all you fellas,*
*I wanna tell all you fellas something,*
*I dunno, if you think that you cool,*
*I dunno if you ever been anyone's fool,*
*I tell you one thing that I want you to understand,*
*just one thing now for you to understand,*
*I don't care how strong a man you are,*
*I don't care how strong you can get,*
*I tell you there's one thing you can't miss,*
*I know you need it, I know you want it,*
*I know you got to have it, I know you're gonna get it,*
*let me tell you something,*
*women who got them tricks,*
*you know it ain't, got them, got them evil chicks,*
*wind around, 'round a little finger if you let 'em,*
*wind you 'round, turn you every way but loose,*
*turn you every way but loose,*
*turn you every way but loose,*
*you know I come home one morning,*
*come home one mornin', I've been out on a four-day creep,*
*drinkin' and gamblin' hey all, all next week,*
*walkin' the dog,*
*lay up here in the bed*
*you know I'm gonna lay down and rest my weary head,*
*drinkin' and gamblin' for days and nights on end,*
*sure make a man kinda cry, yes I know little friend,*
*yes I'll tell you somethin',*
*the second that I lay down,*
*here comes my old lady, say turn on around,*
*you know I can get you to do it,*
*every ol' time no matter how tired you is,*
*I can get you to do it every time,*
*yes I can, huh,*
*'cause them women,*
*and women got to leave their lovin' ways,*
*women got to leave their lovin' ways,*
*make a man go crazy, can't control himself,*
*don't know what they doin',*
*no no can't control yourself,*
*they can do anything they want to do,*
*any damn old thing, all a man can do is but keep on*

*lovin' my my,*
*keep on lovin',*
*ah huh,*
*one thing that I ask my baby please momma, a favor to me,*
*ease ease on over, ease on over,*
*raise yourself up,*
*turn on over baby, raise yourself up, c'mon now turn on over,*
*a little lovin',*
*early in the mornin', awright*
*I asked my little girl one time,*
*she begin to run and hide,*
*asked my little girl, she begin to run and hide, run and hide girl,*
*I said baby, all I wanna do is jump in your saddle and ride,*
*jump in your saddle and ride,*
*jump in your saddle and ride,*
*you're my sweet little mare, I ride you everywhere,*
*you know you're my sweet little mare and I ride you everywhere,*
*lemme jump in your saddle, now baby, let me ride,*
*let me jump in your saddle and ride,*
*she start on easy, mama just a work on slow,*
*start out walkin', start out walkin' real slow,*
*then you ease on up just a little bit,*
*ease on up just more, ease on up a little more, my my my my,*
*jump up in your saddle and ride, my my, my my my my my my,*
*[inaudible] All I got to do now,*
*'bout time I [inaudible] out on a four-day ride,*
*turn the outlaws back, I was lookin' to help my hide,*
*little old girl seventeen years old,*
*daddy had a big old shotgun,*
*carryin a double-on load,*
*caught me on top of that horse,*
*for havin' my fun,*
*had to turn up and pack up, started him to run,*
*'cause you know he's gonna shoot me,*
*gotta keep on truckin' my my,*
*I could fly, fly, fly,*
*I could fly that night, fly that night,*
*I could fly that night, fly that night,*
*shotgun after me the sheriff behind,*
*shotgun after me the sheriff behind,*
*keep on runnin',*
*keep on rollin',*
*keep on movin',*

*keep on goin',*
*keep on a-runnin',*
*with a piece in my hand,*
*keep on runnin',*
*to save my soul.*
*[the band jams again]*
*Feel all right, yes I did,*
*and now I ain't no tail dragger,*
*no, my wife's on my tracks,*
*go down to little girl's house,*
*ain't nobody can track me back,*
*I know when there's some cookin' bacon,*
*I can smell it a mile away,*
*I know when that sweet [inaudible],*
*I can smell it a mile away,*
*I asked my baby turn around,*
*asked my baby turn around,*
*if you can't turn around, turn your damper down,*
*can't turn around, turn your damper down*
*It smell too good yes it do,*
*feel like eatin' some of that pie now, some cherry pie,*
*how your bakery starts?*
*Can't turn your damper down, mama turn your oven around,*
*if you can't turn your damper down, mama turn your oven down,*
*can't keep it under control,*
*all the boys in the neighborhood tell 'em that your bakery shop is good,*
*let 'em try some cherry pie they go droppin' by, my my,*
*yes I will,*
*yes I will*
*[The band jams again]*

Dick Latvala is quick to point out that the Dead played much better versions of "Caution" and "Good Lovin'" elsewhere on this tour. The spontaneity of this medley, however, and the breathtaking call and response between Pigpen's vocals and Garcia's guitar licks make this a very, very special jam not to be passed by.

And as if this weren't enough they then tear through one of the most high-energy "Not Fade Away" > "Goin' Down the Road" > "Not Fade Away" medleys I've ever heard. Right after the first "Not Fade Away" jam climaxes, Bobby leads Jerry into a well-formed "China Cat Sunflower" instrumental before they settle into "Goin' Down the Road." When it's all over, the formerly placid audience is screaming in delight. Who wouldn't be?! When the Dead get around to putting this show out on CD, they should consider editing out Donna's off-key screams during "Goin' Down the Road." Otherwise, this blissfully frenetic show is a genuine treasure.

JOHN R. DWORK WITH JEFF MATTSON

---

### 4/16/72
**Aarhus University, Aarhus, Denmark**

**Set 1:** //Greatest Story Ever Told, Sugaree, Chinatown Shuffle, Black-Throated Wind, Tennessee Jed, China Cat Sunflower > I Know You Rider//, Mexicali Blues, Loser, //Playing in the Band
**Set 2:** //The Other One > Not Fade Away > Goin' Down the Road Feelin' Bad//

---

**Source:** SBD, **Quality:** B–, **Length:** 1:20
**Highlights:** The Other One, Not Fade Away, Goin' Down the Road
**Comments:** A muddy, flat, and compressed sound makes this tape a bit of a disappointment; however, the mix is well-balanced most of the time, and with a little perseverance you'll find yourself listening to the music rather than the quality of the recording.

As compilation tapes go, this isn't so bad as it balances short songs with a few extended numbers from the second set. I've no idea as to how these sections of the show in question were chosen. The brutal edits here are gonna drive the completists among us to distraction.

The first edit we encounter drops us into a "Greatest Story Ever Told" already in full flight. "Sugaree" is a fine version that builds dramatically, and it's a real shame that this number usually found itself close to the beginning of a show before the band had developed a good head of steam. The rest of the first set numbers are played in a solid if not overly inventive fashion: they're certainly entertaining and hit the spot without any real fireworks. It should be noted, however, that Phil is ON for this show, and despite the poor sound quality, this is a good reason to check it out. Unfortunately for us, when the band really starts to kick, we get our second edit: the appalling cut that condemns most of "I Know You Rider" to oblivion—and after a "China Cat Sunflower" that is really rather uplifting too. A crime.

We're dropped directly into the climax of the free-playing jam toward the end of "Playing in the Band," which certainly makes you catch your breath as white-hot noise floods into your room just before the last chorus. God knows what the rest of this number sounded like, but the last five minutes are priceless. Things aren't edited in such a brutal fashion during "The Other One," giving us a chance to discover just how the jam evolves, but you still don't get enough of it before Phil and Billy lead everyone into a storming "Not Fade Away" > "Goin' Down the Road" combo that is a pure adrenaline rush that stands in stark contrast to the relatively laid-back first-set material. Being plunged into the middle of a jam is enjoyably disorienting, and being forced to listen to the end product of an exploratory performance before you hear its source does lend a different perspective to the song in question. Overall, this date is another well-played Europe '72 show, and we're not going to rest until we get to hear all of 'em in good-quality editions.

PAUL BODENHAM

---

### 4/17/72
**Tivoli Concert Hall, Copenhagen, Denmark**

**Set 1:** Cold Rain and Snow, Me and Bobby McGee, Chinatown Shuffle, China Cat Sunflower > I Know You Rider, Jack Straw, He's Gone, Next Time You See Me, Black-Throated Wind
**Set 2:** (broadcast): Casey Jones, Playing in the Band, Sugaree, One More Saturday Night (end of TV show), It Hurts Me Too, Ramble On Rose, El Paso, Big Railroad Blues, Truckin' > Jam
**Set 3:** Dark Star > Jam > Sugar Magnolia > Caution > Johnny B. Goode

---

**1. Source:** SBD, **Quality:** A, **Length:** 2:36, **Genealogy:** MR > DAT
**2. Source:** SBD-Video, **Quality:** A (mono), **Length:** "Casey Jones" through "Saturday Night"
**Highlights:** "Big Railroad Blues" and all of set 3.
**Comments:** The tape and show are crisp and worth the effort to find.

This show opens with a strong uptempo "Cold Rain and Snow" that sets the pace for the entire night. The high-energy "Bobby McGee" that follows has some beautiful interplay between Keith and Jerry. "Chinatown Shuffle" highlights an outstanding Pig vocal, especially for 1972. "China Cat" is slower than normal but maintains a steady groove that slips into the typical long jam that glides into a very good "I Know You Rider." "He's Gone" is played for the first time, and this classic tune has a slightly different arrangement to it. "Next Time You See Me" ("Lied and Cheated") and "Black-Throated Wind" finish a nice, strong set.

Then the band breaks and gets ready to do the TV shoot. "Casey Jones," which opens the second set and the TV portion, is one of the best versions of this song ever played. Weir is very strong in this classic rendition, which is quickly followed by a powerful but short "Playing in the Band." "Sugaree" is crisp and clean; "Saturday Night" is strong and rockin'. The band takes a short pause, then eases into a nice bluesy "It Hurts Me Too" followed by "Ramble On Rose," which again has some great Bobby playing. El Paso is as you'd expect from '72 and is followed by one of the best-ever versions of "Big Railroad Blues." Anyone who has the album *Europe '72* will certainly remember the photo of the band in the pullout all wearing clown masks. Well, this "Big Railroad Blues" is the song the band was playing when those photos were snapped (just a little trivia). The set ends with a short but hot "Truckin'."

After yet another short break, the band returns for what will be a classic set. In any other year this set would be one of the best but surrounded by shows like April 8, 14, 16, and 29, it falls in the cracks of obscurity. Don't be fooled: this is a great set and a great show. Set 3 starts with none other than "Dark Star" (can one ever tire of this song?) with its free-form jam that ebbs and flows into "Sugar Magnolia," which seamlessly winds its way into a "Caution" that contains some inspired Pig vocals. This builds and ends with a powerful "Johnny B. Goode." Overall, an outstanding show!

ROB EATON

---

### 4/21/72
**Beat Club, Bremen, West Germany**

**Soundcheck:** Loser, Black-Throated Wind
**Set:** Bertha, Playing in the Band, Truckin' > The Other One > Jam, One More Saturday Night*

* Different source

**1. Source:** SBD, **Quality:** B, **Length:** 1:20
**2. Source:** SBD-video, **Quality:** B– (mono), **Length:** One More Saturday Night
**Highlights:** The Other One

For a band that frequently failed to produce the goods on special occasions, this stab at fame via a German TV program in the midst of the Europe '72 tour isn't at all bad. Certainly you can track down tapes with varying set lists in a range of sound qualities, but this one is worth looking for as it's a proper stereo soundboard tape and not a mono TV version. The quality isn't great—it sounds ever so slightly overloaded and on the verge of distortion—but that shouldn't put you off.

As with most Dead studio recordings, a sense of urgency is largely absent, which rather undermines the performances that would otherwise be imbued with drama and more defined dynamics. Both "Loser" and "Black-Throated Wind" are respectable performances, but neither has much of a spark. Long pauses and a few cryptic comments from various members of the band eventually lead us to a raucous "Bertha" that is satisfyingly ragged but right. "Playing in the Band" stretches out into a respectable jam, but although it's never less than entertaining, it still lacks that extra special quality that comes with a proper live show. The first version of "Truckin'" suffers a breakdown within a couple of minutes as Mr. Weir once again forgets the words while version two begins by plodding along with an absence of grace. However, once the song itself has been negotiated and the band heads out into freer territory, the music loosens up considerably and attains a fluidity that you'd hardly think likely after such an inauspicious beginning. By the time they hit "The Other One" they are actually in cracking form: lines snake out and contract and create an impressive sound pool in the midst of a sterile TV studio. But there's more, as "The Other One" winds down into a poignant and unique meandering jam that has moments of great beauty. It's as if the Dead themselves are rather taken aback by this turn of events, because the jam melts into silence with no one having much idea how to resolve it. About four seconds of silence is followed by a simple chord progression that sets up a roaring cataclysm of unearthly noise that sounds good, but I do wish they'd have let the jam trail away instead. "One More Saturday Night" on this tape is much poorer quality than the rest of the session, it is in mono and so probably comes from a TV broadcast. It's pleasantly manic, mind you, and a fitting end to what is, on the whole, a tape worth tracking down and checking out.

PAUL BODENHAM

---

## 🌀 4/24/72 🌀
### Rheinhalle, Dusseldorf, West Germany

**Set 1:** Good Lovin', Casey Jones
**Set 2:** Dark// Star > Me and My Uncle > Dark Star > Wharf Rat > Sugar Magnolia

**Source:** SBD, **Quality:** B+, **Length:** 3:00
**Highlights:** Good Lovin', Dark Star > Me and My Uncle > Dark Star > Wharf Rat > Sugar Magnolia

Another solid show from the Europe '72 tour with yet another superlative journey through deepest space in the "Dark Star" jams. However, tapes of the whole show aren't in wide circulation, and most are a compilation of the end of the first set and the "Dark Star" segment of the second. Sound quality can be a little muddy, but there must be decent versions around someplace.

"Good Lovin'" was performed on most of the European dates, and it's interesting how the different versions compare with one another. They're nearly all fairly lengthy, and the one featured here is no exception, being even longer than usual and having a number of short spacey jams woven into the fabric of what is basically a straightforward rock song. Pigpen's "Good Lovin'" raps on this tour tend to be a little repetitive, but that's hardly a problem when his delivery is as sharp and energetic as it is here. Nearly always appearing toward the end of the first set, "Good Lovin'" is used as an opportunity to flex those improvisational muscles that haven't been utilized during a first set that concentrates on more concise song forms. The band leaps at the chance to stre-e-etch out some. Tonight the good people of Dusseldorf got a superfine rendition of this classic.

"Dark Star" > "Me and My Uncle" > "Dark Star" > "Wharf Rat" > "Sugar Magnolia" provides the heart of this show and yeah, you guessed, it's a real smoker. From the majestic way the theme unfolds (and it's one of those "Star"s where it takes a good fifteen minutes to reach the first verse), you know these guys are not going to avoid taking an interesting detour if it seems entertaining enough. From the depths of some zoned-out

# 4/26/72

## Jahrhundert Halle, Frankfurt, West Germany

**Set 1:** Bertha, Me and My Uncle, Next Time You See Me, China Cat Sunflower > I Know You Rider, Jack Straw, Big Railroad Blues, Playing in the Band
**Set 2:** Truckin' > Drums > The Other One > Comes a Time > Sugar Magnolia, Turn On Your Lovelight > Goin' Down the Road Feelin' Bad > One More Saturday Night

**Source:** SBD-CD (*Hundred Year Hall*) **Quality:** A+, **Length:** 2:20

**Highlights:** Playing in the Band, The Other One, Comes a Time, One More Saturday Night

**Comments:** The following tunes were omitted from *Hundred Year Hall* CD: Mr. Charlie, He's Gone, Black-Throated Wind, Chinatown Shuffle, Loser, Beat It on Down the Line, You Win Again, Good Lovin', Dire Wolf, El Paso, Tennessee Jed, Greatest Story Ever Told, Two Souls in Communion, Casey Jones

Thankfully this concert has now been released on CD, albeit in a heavily edited edition, as *Hundred Year Hall* in the indispensible From the Vaults series. It is a priceless document that is a long overdue reexamination of live Dead circa 1972. For many people this period represents a major change in the sound of the Dead: a time when they displayed equal amounts of youthful exuberance and a newfound sophistication. Subsequently, and quite naturally, they developed away from the rough-edged rock 'n' roll band with a head full of drugs/John Coltrane/Merle Haggard/drugs/Stockhausen/Howlin' Wolf/drugs; their abilities began to consistently match their aspirations.

The first set, represented on the CD by a selection of short 'n' sharp songs and a few of the more long-form numbers, is as good an illustration of the incremental nature of inspiration in a Dead set as you're going to find. For me at least, "Bertha," "Me and My Uncle," and "Jack Straw," although very welcome, aren't exceptional in any respect; they are played in a straight ahead, workmanlike fashion with no frills. "Next Time You See Me" is tasty, although that's partly due to not having heard it recorded this well before. However, "China Cat Sunflower" > "I Know You Rider" is the sound of a

*Jerry in Frankfurt, 4/26/72*
(photo credit: David Lemieux)

angular jam we're sucked back into the bright, garish Technicolor wide-screen action of a frantic "Me and My Uncle" that, having told the tale, drops us off the edge of the world into a poignant and rather pretty atonal space. The transition into "Wharf Rat" is far more measured, helping us acclimate to more structured music, but by the time they burst into "Sugar Magnolia" we're all flying at warp factor 9. Again.

PAUL BODENHAM

*Europe '72 Tour* (photo credit: David Lemieux)

band discovering that their feet don't quite touch the floor anymore, and "Playing in the Band" is the realization that questions like "Which way is up?" no longer have any relevance. Ladies and gentlemen, we have liftoff!

Music from the second set concentrates on the jams, and although I hesitate to employ such an overused word as awesome, I'm inclined to believe that it is the only word that can do this outrageous soundscape justice: the playing here is such an overwhelming experience, especially when presented with such clarity. "Truckin'" is strong, even though lyrics are forgotten by the cartload. This number is the basic propulsion unit that sets up the majestic "Other One" that follows. A drum solo at this juncture ought to undermine the buildup, but Billy's energetic tom-tom rolls and skittering snares keep things boiling nicely before Mr. Lesh unleashes *that* rumble and we're off into hyperspace. The conversations that run through this astonishing piece of music making are so intertwined that they must surely be the product of one mind. Its waves ebb and flow, one moment featuring tight clusters of richly detailed sounds only to dissolve into near-silence and near-empty space. Bobby throws in a guide toward a "Spanish Jam," but the idea isn't taken up. Instead we glide into a jewel-like "Comes a Time" that is a beautiful contrast to the preceding mayhem. "Lovelight" is virtually shorn of Pigpen raps (he does sound tired), but this version still struts along like the prime piece of R&B it is, with a great transition into "Goin' Down the Road Feelin' Bad" that includes a tussle between Billy and Bobby who'd dearly like to thrash into "Not Fade Away" and Jerry who plainly doesn't. Garcia is having none of it, and eventually, after a forceful battle of wills, the others concede defeat and slip into "Goin' Down the Road" like a couple of pussycats. This segment is much loved by some, although I'd have to say I find it entertaining more for its level of musical conflict than for any intrinsic musical values. Once we arrive there, "Goin' Down the Road Feelin' Bad" isn't quite the firework we'd all like it to be, but "One More Saturday Night" most definitely is—a heavenly technicolor explosion right there in your living room.

PAUL BODENHAM

## 4/29/72
### Musikhalle, Hamburg, West Germany

**Set 1:** Playing in the Band, Sugaree, Mr. Charlie, Black-Throated Wind, China Cat Sunflower > I Know You Rider, Big Boss Man, Jack Straw, Chinatown Shuffle, Me and My Uncle, Big Railroad// Blues, Good Lovin', Casey Jones
**Set 2:** Greatest Story Ever Told, He's Gone, Next Time You See Me, Dark// Star > Sugar Magnolia > Caution, One More Saturday Night, Uncle John's Band

1. **Source:** SBD, **Quality:** B/B– (some warbling distortion), **Length:** 3:30
2. **Source:** AUD, **Quality:** B+, **Length:** 3:30
**Highlights:** Dark Star > Sugar Magnolia > Caution

After a daring start, diving in at the deep end with an energetic "Playing in the Band," much of this performance is a little on the average side. Certainly there are fine moments, and if you can track down a decent-sounding tape, you're unlikely to take it off the deck. The first set especially suffers from tape warble and could put off the more fainthearted, but from "Next Time You See Me" the second set sounds fine. Decent audience tapes (for the time) exist, although these don't have such good-quality vocals. All that having been said, however, from "Dark Star" onward this is well worth checking out: the "Star" itself is a monumental version full of invention and as touched by genius as you could hope for.

With one of those long, long intros, unwinding slowly and eventually crystalizing into the song's main theme, this epic version packs an extraordinary number of different moods into its jams: from the serene to the hair-raisingly cataclysmic, from perfect peace to Phil doing his impressions of the Big Bang, this "Dark Star" is stuffed full of the kind of creativity largely absent from the rest of the show, or at least from the part that precedes it. The passage from a deep, abstract "Space" into a blazing, joyful "Sugar Magnolia" is so sudden that you're left gasping for breath at such an example of group mindreading. The closing "Caution" is also a version full of twists and turns, angular spaces and irrepressible rhythm. Pigpen adds a note of confession to his raps, referring to his recent change of lifestyle. The closing "Uncle John's Band" is a fine, well-focused version with excellent vocals.

Keith Godchaux is due special honor for his contributions throughout this show. His '72 playing is generally full of lightning-fast conversation with everyone else and a fearless attitude when plunged into the furthest-out jams. His work here is thoroughly enjoyable throughout.

PAUL BODENHAM

## 5/3/72
### L'Olympia Theatre, Paris, France

**Set 1:** Bertha, Me and My Uncle, Mr. Charlie, Sugaree, Black-Throated Wind, Chinatown Shuffle, China Cat Sunflower > I Know You Rider, Beat It on Down the Line, He's Gone, Next Time You See Me, Playing in the Band, Good Lovin', Sing Me Back Home, Casey Jones
**Set 2:** Greatest Story Ever Told, Ramble On Rose, It Hurts Me Too, Truckin' > The Other One > Drums > The Other// One > Me and Bobby McGee > The Other One Reprise > Wharf Rat, Jack Straw, Sugar Magnolia > Not Fade Away > Goin' Down the Road Feelin' Bad > Not Fade Away Reprise, One More Saturday Night

**Source:** SBD, **Quality:** A, **Length:** 3:20, **Genealogy:** MR > PCM > DAT
**Highlights:** Good Lovin', It Hurts Me Too, Truckin' > The Other One

Another bright, well-mixed show, if usually a little on the hissy side. Still, the music, as expected, is of a predictably high quality, and we mean HIGH. Most tapes in circulation tend to include a severely edited first set, starting with the hot "China" > "Rider," which is a shame, but that shouldn't put off anyone but the most ardent completists out there. Most of us would find the heady mix of self-contained songs and the extensive jamming of the second set ample reward for tracking these tapes down.

Pigpen's vocals, although a little on the thin and reedy side, are packed with emotion and delivered with a soulful intensity that, especially on "It Hurts Me Too," becomes almost too painful to listen to. Unbelievably, "Good Lovin'" is played at thirteen of the twenty-two Europe '72 tour shows so you'd expect them to get rather good at it. This one is a definite goodie: it's long but still remains focused, blending its rhythmic drive with some distinctly weird spaces without losing the plot. Pig's in control, and his rap, although not deviating from the Europe '72 norm, is less repetitive than some, and when Pig raps you listen up.

This show's jam section is quite a blowout. "Truckin'" builds up the momentum, and all of a sudden the ground has been removed from beneath our feet, leaving us suspended above a tapestry of stars. This "Space" contains moments of tranquillity but it's mostly another exercise in creating an arc of ever-increasing intensity that breaks into a classic "The Other One." Following a brief drum solo, Phil gives us an all too brief bass solo before a tortuous midsection that is about as strange as it gets: chortling Garcia guitar, poignant, dark, lonely tones and clusters of notes mutating into gossamer feedback courtesy of Phil before Bobby leads everyone into "Me and Bobby McGee," just about the last place you'd expect such a trip to deliver you to. "The Other One" reprise is kept short, basically little more than the last verse but enough to create a dynamic contrast with the smoky "Wharf Rat" that follows. "Jack Straw" is the version from *Europe '72,* so we're all familiar with that. The rest of the show is an efficient high-octane finish: exciting, energetic stuff without the finesse of the jam section, but that's just fine, thanks.

PAUL BODENHAM

## 5/4/72
### L'Olympia Theatre, Paris, France

**Set 1:** Greatest Story Ever Told, Deal, Mr. Charlie, Beat It on Down the Line, Brown-Eyed Women, Chinatown Shuffle, Playing in the Band, You Win Again, It Hurts Me Too, He's Gone, El Paso, Big Railroad Blues, Two Souls in Communion, Casey Jones
**Set 2:** Good Lovin', Next Time You See Me, Ramble On Rose, Jack Straw, Dark Star > Sugar Magnolia

**1. Source:** SBD, **Quality:** A, **Length:** 3:00, **Genealogy:** MR > PCM > PCM > DAT (Set 1), MR > C > PCM > DAT (No "Sugar Mags")
**2. Source:** FM-SBD (GDH 415), **Quality:** A, **Length:** "Two Souls in Communion," **Genealogy:** MR > DR

**Highlights:** You Win Again, It Hurts Me Too, Dark Star > Sugar Magnolia

**Comments:** Until recently this show was only available as a compilation of first- and second-set material, and the quality depended on just who your friends were. Now, there's a spiffy high-quality version doing the rounds, and it's a highly desirable addition to any collection of '72 performances. One interesting point about these Europe '72 shows is that they often sound so much better than the *Europe '72* album. Presumably because that album has a fair number of studio overdubs added to the original live tapes from so many different venues, the ambient sound qualities have been all but eliminated in order to balance and disguise the differing sources. This unfortunately leaves us with a curiously cold and rather uninvolving sound. Good soundboards like this one let you in on the real deal and restore the performances to their original state: music played to a real audience in a real room someplace, not some antiseptic void.

Finding their feet during a spirited "Mr. Charlie," the band quietly progresses through several levels of divine inspiration to deliver a satisfying three hours of wonderment. First-set gems include a great sequence of a relatively short but supercharged "Playing in the Band," a rather tasty reading of "You Win Again," and the painfully emotional "It Hurts Me Too."

No matter what kind of buzz you're looking for, the second set will have something for you. The "Good

Lovin'" is just about the longest of the tour, clocking in at over twenty minutes, but despite a spirited performance from Pigpen and a few inspired moments its power is dissipated way before the end: the detail is frequently engrossing but the big picture is lost. The forty or so minutes of "Dark Star" will attract most and, yeah, it's yet another fine example of a '72 "Star." What it lacks in out 'n' out weirdness it makes up for with a great deal of energetic, although fairly linear, jamming. A series of rhythmic waves eventually lead to the first verse before the spare, glittering notes and bass hum of free space create the chasms of sound we all long for. Billy draws on Phil's bass tones to introduce a rollin' and rumblin' tom-tom-driven drum interlude before the band comes together on another rush of joyous energy. The "Sugar Magnolia" is the version from *Europe '72*, and knowing just what it grows out of only enhances its grace and power. Well worth checking out.

PAUL BODENHAM

---

## 5/7/72

### Bickershaw Festival, North Wigan, Great Britain

**Set 1:** Truckin', China Cat Sunflower > I Know You Rider, Dire Wolf, Me and My Uncle, Casey Jones
**Set 2:** Dark Star > The Other One > Sing Me Back Home

---

**1. Source:** AUD, **Quality:** A–, **Length:** 2:15
**2. Source:** SBD, **Quality:** B+/B–, **Length:** 0:45 ("Dark Star" through "Sing Me Back Home")
**3. Source:** SBD, **Quality:** A, **Length:** 1:15 ("The Other One" through end of show), **Genealogy:** Betty Board
**Highlights:** Casey Jones, Dark Star > The Other One > Sing Me Back Home
**Comments:** Betty Board—10-inch reel; ½ track, 7½ ips.

Thankfully, some enterprising souls had the presence of mind to set up a recording rig and put this, my first show, down for posterity, as well as my enjoyment almost twenty-five years later. My tape copies are now a mix of this audience recording with a couple of different sourced boards. Listening now, I wish I'd kept the whole audience source tapes.

Anyway, after a weekend of rain the Dead closed the festival and brought some sunshine with them. With a dedication "To all our muddy friends" "Truckin'" opened and we were dancing. I remember the thrill of hearing some of these songs for the first time—some for the last too, as it turned out. And the sheer power of the live Experience, since at that point in time my frame of reference consisted of the albums released thus far. The concert consisted of a long two-hour first set of mostly the shorter tunes and a longer second set following. But it's only now, with hindsight and tape, that I can see the highs and lows; it was *all* a buzz at the time. Pig was in good voice, though maybe not good enough to give us a "Caution" as in other European shows. It was just great to get a "Star" and an "Other One." To have that dissolve into "Sing Me Back Home" was bliss.

A fair share of halts to sort out the "technical problems" and to chat to us about things like the flight over, the weather, and the Anti-Festivals Bill going through Parliament at the time. A few songs had yet to settle down—"He's Gone," for instance, or "Playing"—but "China" > "Rider" was all I could have wanted. A great transition. We all sang "Happy Birthday" to Billy too. Oh, and I nearly forgot Joe's Light Show with the film screens on either side of the stage: Iron Man during "The Other One" and bouncing ball lyrics with a train crossing from one screen to another during "Casey Jones."

JAKE FROST

# Reviews: May 1972

## 5/10/72
### Concertgebouwe, Amsterdam, The Netherlands

**Set 1:** //Bertha, Me and My Uncle, Mr. Charlie, China Cat Sunflower > I Know You Rider, Black-Throated Wind, Loser, Next Time, El Paso, He's Gone, Chinatown Shuffle, Playing in the Band, Big Railroad Blues, Jack Straw, Tennessee Jed, Big Boss Man, Greatest Story Ever Told, Casey Jones

**Set 2:** Truckin' > Drums > The Other One > Me and Bobby McGee > The Other One > Wharf Rat, Beat It on Down the Line, Two Souls in Communion, Ramble On Rose, Sing Me Back Home, Sugar Magnolia > Not Fade Away > Goin' Down the Road Feelin' Bad > Not Fade Away Reprise

**Source:** SBD, **Quality:** A, **Length:** 3:36, **Genealogy:** MR > R

**Highlights:** All except I Know You Rider

**Comments:** Sound is very good; show is even better!

The tape cuts into the intro of "Bertha," a common phenomenon in those days for whatever reason. The show starts slightly out of sync with many miscues but quickly recovers in fine form into what will turn out to be an outstanding set. "Me and My Uncle" and "Mr. Charlie" are standard versions with an outstanding Pig vocal on "Mr. Charlie." "China Cat" has one of the longest intros ever with some vintage Keith piano work—boy, I miss Keith! The "China Cat" jam, shorter than normal, weaves its way into a lethargic and mellow "I Know You Rider," the only flaw of the show. "Black-Throated Wind" is very solid; Phil leads the way with some very solid bass lines. The rest of the set is just exceptional with other highlights being the very melodic "Playing in the Band" jam and Keith's piano solo in "Chinatown Shuffle." There are also stellar versions of "Tennessee Jed," "Big Boss Man," and "Greatest Story Ever Told."

The second set starts out with one of the best "Truckin'" > "Other One"s ever done, taking the listener far and wide with jam after jam after jam. There are actually six different jams within this sequence. The highlight is an amazing "Other One" that's a journey unto itself. The entire jam is sixty-two minutes of the most amazing Dead you've ever heard. The rest of the set never lets you down with its beautiful "Sing Me Back Home" and rousing "Not Fade Away." The sheer length of this show is indication enough that the Dead were in the groove and enjoying the night. I can't overemphasize the magnitude of this show. Often overlooked on this classic tour, 5/10 stands out in my opinion as one of the best all-around shows of the year. Do yourself a favor and find this tape: you won't be disappointed!

ROB EATON

## 5/11/72
### Concertgebouwe, Rotterdam, The Netherlands

**Set 1:** Playing in the Band, Sugaree, Mr. Charlie, Black-Throated Wind, Deal, Chinatown Shuffle, Mexicali Blues, It Hurts Me Too, China Cat Sunflower > I Know You Rider//, Beat It on Down the Line, Brown-Eyed Women, Jack Straw, Big Railroad Blues, Good Lovin', Casey Jones

**Set 2:** Morning Dew, Me and My Uncle, Two Souls in Communion, El Paso, Tennessee Jed, Next Time You See Me, Dark Star > Drums > Dark Star > Sugar Magnolia > Caution > Truc//kin' > Uncle John's Band, One More Saturday Night

**Source:** SBD, **Quality:** A, **Length:** 3:40

**Highlights:** Morning Dew, Dark Star > Sugar Magnolia > Caution

Prepare thyself to deal with a miracle, as they say. This is probably the finest quality recording taken from this tour in unofficial circulation, and along with that it's also one of the best shows of 1972. Simply put, this is a lengthy sojourn in Heaven. Whatever you're looking for in a '72 show you're guaranteed to find it here: the older favorites played with style, the newer songs with assurance that belies their relative youth; emotive singing, especially from Pigpen; inspired improvisation; and a "Dark Star" that features some of the highest Dead Magick to be found anywhere. (For what it's worth, this

"Star" is just possibly my personal favorite version of all time.) Once you've heard it, you're going to break out in a sweat just thinking about it.

You can just feel it in your bones that this is going to be an archetypal hot show from the way they plunge straight into a heavyweight no-nonsense version of "Playing in the Band" for starters. Inside five minutes this show is spacing out in serious style. With total honesty (would I lie to you people?) I can say that there isn't a duff moment playing-wise during the first set. For whatever unfortunate technical reason the a cappella section at the end of "I Know You Rider" fades out, spoiling a perfect moment, but the performance is of a frighteningly high standard throughout.

The second set kicks off with some excellent songs: "Morning Dew" and "Two Souls" really shine, but it's still dominated totally by a supernova "Dark Star," stretching out beyond thirty-five minutes with an interconnecting flow of jams. It's not as hyperactive as some; the band takes its time exploring every nuance of a relatively small number of musical concepts. It drifts in a dream state for much of its duration, which makes the outbursts from Phil seem even more seismic than they would otherwise. Don't be misled by that, though: Mr. Lesh coaxes some truly devastating bass notes out of the ether here, great clusters of chords trailing bat shrieks and insect whine feedback: a whole spectrum of sound in waves that rise up through the floor and blow your windows out.

The "Sugar Magnolia" is a hot one, but coming after such an experience it sounds a trifle daunted by it all. Not for long. Pig takes control and "Caution" blends beautifully driving R&B rhythms, several spaced-out moments where everything almost, just almost, spins out of control. Pigpen raps through fragments of old blues numbers, pouring out "Who Do You Love?" at some length, which leads some people to list it as a separate song in the jam. It's still very much a part of what we'd all recognize as "Caution," though. In case all that wasn't enough, you still get a powerhouse "Truckin'," ending on a perfect note with a superb "Uncle John's Band." There you go: the show the words "too much" were created for.

PAUL BODENHAM

## 5/16/72

### Luxembourg, Radio Luxembourg

**Set 1:** Introduction by "Kid" Jensen, Bertha, Me and My Uncle, Mr. Charlie, Sugaree, Black-Throated Wind, Chinatown Shuffle, China Cat Sunflower > I Know You Rider, Beat It on Down the Line, It Hurts Me Too, Tennessee Jed, Playing in the Band, Promised Land

**Set 2:** Truckin' > Drums > The Other One, Sing Me Back Home, Sugar Magnolia, Not Fade Away > Goin' Down the Road Feelin' Bad > Not Fade Away Reprise, One More Saturday Night

**Source:** SBD, **Quality:** A+, **Length:** 2:40, **Genealogy:** MR > RR > DAT > C > DAT

**Highlights:** Playing in the Band, Sing Me Back Home, Truckin' > The Other One

Yet another revelation from the archives, especially for those of us in Britain who, regardless of the relative proximity to Luxembourg and despite the supposedly high-powered transmitters, never heard a Radio Luxembourg broadcast with anything remotely resembling the clarity of these tapes. Imagine a thin, distant radio signal that fades out to static every ten minutes before fading back in. Then imagine trying to enjoy to this show! These tapes, however, are primo quality recordings with only the occasional temporary glitch in the mix, which is usually rectified promptly.

Overall, the playing here is frequently inspired and everyone seems up for it from the word "go." The gorgeous clarity of this recording allows us to pick up on every nuance in the performance; the subtlety of some of the exchanges here could only be apparent on such a good recording. These tapes come recommended for those with a taste for '72 shows but an aversion to hissy or otherwise poor quality recordings.

Once again it's almost impossible to choose the best tracks because they're all of such consistently high quality and they all contribute to the overall development of this show. There are certainly no below-par performances here, and, although other Euro '72 shows probably contain higher peaks, this is still one to track down because of its consistency. Outstanding performances from the first set include a dazzling "China Cat Sunflower" > "I Know You Rider" with a lovely rolling solo from Bobby and a succinct transition jam, a brief but raging "Beat It on Down the Line," and a stunning "Playing in the Band"; Garcia's stratospheric harmonics ring out over the subtle, elastic, rhythmic patterns laid down by everyone else. An A+ for effort is awarded to Donna here: her wailing isn't quite the bloodcurdling howl she's capable of but it's close.

The second set is all high-octane stuff, the only respite being the tight version of "Sing Me Back Home," which features excellent vocal harmonies and Garcia once again expertly plucking harmonic tones during the superbly emotional solo. The "Truckin'" > "The Other One" adventure is as dynamic and overwhelming as you'd expect (Weir forgets some of the lyrics in "Truckin'" as well, so that's a comforting and familiar moment we can all enjoy). Phil punctuates the free space with more of those ground-shaking bass chords graced with feedback we all love—although it seems a little unfair to single out the contributions of one musician when this is really such a collective creation.

PAUL BODENHAM

---

## 🌀 5/18/72 🌀

### Kongressaal Deutsches Museum, Munich, West Germany

**Set 1:** Truckin', Sugaree, Mr. Charlie, Jack Straw, Tennessee Jed, Chinatown Shuffle, Black-Throated Wind, China Cat Sunflower > I Know You Rider, El Paso, It Hurts Me Too, You Win Again, Playing in the Band, Good Lovin', Casey Jones
**Set 2:** Sitting on Top of the World > Me and My Uncle, Ramble On Rose, Beat It on Down the Line, Dark// Star > Morning Dew > Sugar Magnolia > Sing Me Back Home

---

**Source:** SBD, **Quality:** B–, **Length:** 3:30, **Genealogy:** MR > C > DAT
**Highlights:** Beat It on Down the Line, Morning Dew, Dark Star, Sing Me Back Home

Somebody, somewhere has a pristine copy of this soundboard tape. Unfortunately most of us don't know this person and are consequently stuck with this version. It's hissy and plagued with a thin, trebly wobble of a sound that many will find irritating, verging on the unlistenable. This is a great shame because the show itself, what we have of it, is excellent and one that rewards those willing to persevere and grit their teeth.

Oh my, what have we here?! Yet another Europe '72 "Good Lovin'." What a surprise! Once again it's a good one, but you're likely to find yourself struggling to cope with the sound quality rather than appreciating its finer musical moments. The pairing of "Sitting on Top of the World" and "Me and My Uncle" is an explosive one and something to look forward to on the better quality tape that is sure to come our way sooner or later if we all behave like good boys and girls. After a sing-along with Jerry "Ramble On Rose," we get another burst of incandescent rock 'n' roll energy with a warp drive "Beat It on Down the Line," sleek and streamlined behind the distortion—which, if you've stuck with the tape this far, somehow seems a bit more tolerable.

The "Dark Star," unfortunately split over two sides of the tape, isn't a gentle, immersive meditation but a no-messin' wrestle with primal forces, building up to some dramatic peaks prior to the first verse. Over on the second side Phil dons the hat of Mr. Sonic Apocalypse with more bass than your neighbors are likely to find tolerable—if you've still got neighbors, of course. The rest of this song cycle is a masterful use of dynamics, the highs and lows of a classic "Morning Dew," a rush of pure undiluted joy in "Sugar Magnolia," and one of '72's better versions of "Sing Me Back Home" as a fitting conclusion.

With so many of the Europe '72 tour shows available, this isn't going to be on the want list of those of us who find they can only listen to high quality tapes these days. That's a shame as there's some classic brainmelt material here.

PAUL BODENHAM

## 5/23/72

**The Strand Lyceum, London, England**

**Set 1:** Promised Land, Sugaree, Mr. Charlie, Black-Throated Wind, Tennessee Jed, Next Time You See Me, Jack Straw, China Cat Sunflower > I Know You Rider, Me and My Uncle, Chinatown Shuffle, Big Railroad Blues, Two Souls in Communion, Playing in the Band//, Sittin' on Top of the World, Rockin' Pneumonia, Mexicali Blues, Good Lovin', Casey Jones
**Set 2:** Ramble On Rose, Dark Star > Morning// Dew, He's Gone, Sugar Magnolia, Comes a Time, Goin' Down the Road Feelin' Bad > Not Fade Away > Hey Bo Diddley > Not Fade Away Reprise
**Encore:** Uncle John's Band.

**Source:** SBD, **Quality:** B, **Length:** 3:35
**Highlights:** Rockin' Pneumonia, Two Souls in Communion, Good Lovin', Dark Star > Morning Dew
**Comments:** Most of the first set of this show sounds muddy and indistinct, although from "Sitting on Top of the World" onward (usually the beginning of the second tape), things improve markedly and you get rather more clarity. Since the following night at this venue is available in excellent quality, you should be able to track this one down in a better version than the one I'm reviewing. Less than perfect sound quality aside, this is a truly breathtaking show and its musicality demands that you get your hands on a copy. No excuses.

The band play to such a consistently high standard throughout this show that it's hard to single out songs as "the best." Of course, on rarity value alone you'd want to get your hands on "Rockin' Pneumonia," which follows a brief but power-packed "Sittin' on Top of the World" that is worth checking out in itself. Other essential versions contained in this majestic performance include possibly *the* best version of "Two Souls in Communion": perfectly paced, sung with great feeling by Pig, and graced with a Garcia solo pared down to a bare, emotional essence. True, the backing vocals at the climax of the song are a little on the shaky side but what the hell. "Good Lovin'" is one of the best from the Europe '72 tour. It's kept relatively short and contains no Pigpen rap, but the concentration of energy works wonders. The following "Casey Jones" is also one of the tour's best, building up its head of steam and heading for destruction with playing of great precision.

In a show of such high standards you expect the second set jams to be exemplary, and here you won't be disappointed. The "Dark Star" is as magnificent as you could wish: the initial jams build inexorably toward the first verse and the later sonic interplay is full of moments of sheer delight as the group mind takes the whole enterprise to another level, culminating in a glorious feedback frenzy: an eternity or two of beautiful chaos. The "Morning Dew" is yet another superb rendition, unfortunately marred by a brief cut. Still, it's a great way to follow such an epic "Star."

— PAUL BODENHAM

## 5/25/72

**The Strand Lyceum, London, England**

**Set 1:** Promised Land, Brown-Eyed Women, Big Boss Man, Black-Throated Wind, Tennessee Jed, Mr. Charlie, Jack Straw, China Cat Sunflower > I Know You Rider, Me and Bobby McGee, Good Lovin', Playing in the Band, Brokedown Palace, Casey Jones
**Set 2:** Me and My Uncle, Big Railroad Blues, Chinatown Shuffle, Ramble On Rose, Uncle John's Band > Wharf Rat > Dark Star > Sugar Magnolia, Comes a Time, El Paso, Sittin' on Top of the World, Goin' Down the Road Feelin' Bad > One More Saturday Night

**Source:** AUD, **Quality:** D−, **Length:** 3:40
**Highlight:** Dark Star
**Comments:** This is easily one of the worst-sounding tapes in circulation, but don't dismiss it too quickly.

Despite the poor quality of the tape, there *is* a "Dark Star"—and an excellent one at that, despite the difficult sound. Garcia and Lesh can be made out well enough;

Weir and Keith trickle in at spots. Pigpen and Billy are buried, though.

As "Dark Star" segues effortlessly out of "Wharf Rat," what can be heard immediately is that Garcia and Lesh are having a closely knit, very intimate musical conversation. They rise and fall, engage and retreat, and enter and pull out as if playing each other's instruments. There are sudden arguments, playful buttock pinches, and fake tantrums—all while exploring the guts of their relationship. After seven or eight minutes of increasingly serious play, Lesh steers the music down a damp, mist-shrouded ravine where they halt. Shyly and cautiously, they turn slowly to face one another, the longing in their eyes evident. Phil's notes stiffen; Jerry feedbacks coyly. A picture comes to mind: inside an Italian restaurant, two men sit quietly at a candlelit table in the corner; one hand reaches out over the tablecloth, past the bread, through the wineglasses, and meets another hand, fingers lightly touching, while "Seastones" plays softly on a roving violin.

Garcia is the first to snap out of this interlude, and looks over embarrassed at Lesh, who averts his eyes. Garcia mumbles something to Lesh about how good the 'Niners look this year before taking the band into verse one of "Dark Star." He sounds weary but serious; it is the second to last night of the tour. An off-beat, funky jam ensues as the drums mysteriously appear on the tape. This serves, though, simply as a windup for a stunning "Feelin' Groovy Jam" that grows in intensity with each lap around the track. So in sync is the band that the segue out is virtually invisible. Next up is a slow-down "Space" that contains that razor's edge so prominent in 1972. The tiger stirs, one eye open, lightly growling. The strumming intensifies, but instead of peaking the jam is pushed forward, moaning but alive, out of the dungeon and into the bright sunlight where Weir—donning shades—slams appropriately into a hard-rockin' Sugar Magnolia.

MICHAEL M. GETZ

## 5/26/72

### The Strand Lyceum, London, England

**Set 1:** Promised Land, Sugaree, Mr. Charlie, Black-Throated Wind, Loser, Next Time You See Me, El Paso, Dire Wolf, Two Souls in Communion, Playing in the Band, He's Gone, Cumberland Blues, Jack Straw, Chinatown Shuffle, China Cat Sunflower > I Know You Rider, Not Fade Away > Goin' Down the Road Feelin' Bad > Not Fade Away Reprise
**Set 2:** Truckin' > The Other One > Morning Dew > The Other One > Sing Me Back Home, Me and My Uncle, Ramble On Rose, Sugar Magnolia, Casey Jones
**Encore:** One More Saturday Night

**Source:** SBD, **Quality:** A, **Length:** 4:00 (complete show except for "Cumberland Blues")

**Highlights:** Truckin' > The Other One > Morning Dew > The Other One > Sing Me Back Home

This is IT, folks. This is THE ONE. This is the one night when everything converged perfectly to produce some of the finest four hours of music the Dead ever assembled on stage.

This was the final show of a four-night stand at London's Strand Lyceum, as well as the final show of the legendary Europe '72 tour. This two-month tour produced the most consistently amazing collection of shows, each one better than the last. And this one, in my opinion, was the best of all. This show is notable for being the last in circulation featuring contributions from Pigpen. He appeared briefly at the Dead's June 17, 1972, show in Hollywood, but no tape circulates and he retired from the band after that due to his failing health. But he's in good form here, singing respectable versions of "Mr. Charlie," "Next Time You See Me," "Two Souls in Communion" and "Chinatown Shuffle."

There's so much to say about the amazing second set that I will only touch briefly on two set 1 highlights. The first is "Playing in the Band." What is notable about this rendition is that it is one of the first to break through the 7/4 beat and diffuse into a free-form jam. The Dead had begun, over the previous months, to stretch this song out but had always kept things within the confines of 7/4 time.

The second highlight is the set closer: "Not Fade Away" > "Goin' Down the Road Feelin' Bad" > "Not Fade Away." Since the very first time this combination appeared (October 10, 1970), it had never before appeared in the first set of a show, and it never would again. And it's an excellent, long, and intense version. Suffice to say that the entire set is well played, two hours long, and sets a perfect table for what comes next.

Set 2 opens with a song that will be immediately recognizable to the CD-buying public: the amazing "Truckin'" that was chosen for the *Europe '72* album. (Weir's "... top of the chart in Turlock, California" intro is, sadly, absent from most circulating copies of this tape.) This is the high water mark of "Truckin'," the standard by which all others must be judged. Keith's driving chords and Phil's thumping bass anchor the song to solid ground as it chugs steadily along. Vocal harmonies are tight. The jam that immediately follows is an intricately woven fabric of sound, building upon the beat and rhythm of "Truckin'," with Phil shuffling on the high strings of his bass and Weir laying down a steady chunka-chunka. Keith, however, is the real hero of this jam: he quite effectively mimics Garcia's sparkling guitar runs, and the two of them wrap bright chromatic melodies around each other. After a few minutes of this high-powered frolic, the real magic begins. The band begins to wind down and lowers the level of intensity. It's at this point that the usual 1972 arrangement of "Truckin'" brings the band back into a reprise of the final verse. But not tonight; instead Garcia veers off onto a sharp left-hand turn and, with some deft guitar work, takes the rest of the band down the rabbit hole.

Here's where things get interesting, and where it becomes apparent that we're in for some truly spectacular improvisation. Telepathy must have been in high gear on this evening, for *every* musical idea thrown out by any band member is immediately picked up and built upon. Not a single note is wasted and not a single avenue goes unexplored. Complex polyrhythms and tonalities coalesce out of nowhere, live and breathe for half a minute, and then the band will turn, en masse, on a dime and head off in another direction. And it's all gold. Not one sour note, not one uninteresting tangent. This is pure improvisation at its finest.

About seventeen minutes into the set, the jam begins to wind down. It's at this point that, on *Europe '72*, a studio-dubbed pulsing bass note closes the selection. Back in the real world, fortunately, we're treated instead to a very short bass solo consisting primarily of low-register power chords, after which Lesh introduces "The Other One" theme. The rest of the band follows suit and produces a brief exploration of that song, after which comes a brief drum solo followed by some bass-and-drums interplay. One by one, the entire ensemble falls into place and produces more of the brilliant improvisation that marks this entire extended song selection. Eventually, Weir brings things to a head, refusing to be diverted from chording a strong return to "The Other One" theme, and, as soon as the entire band is on the same page, he sings the first verse.

Soon afterward, however, we're back in the Enchanted Forest. The area mapped out between the first and second verses of "The Other One" has, like "Dark Star," always been reserved for the band's most free-form explorations, and tonight's menu is no exception. Things get *very* strange indeed. The band is still locked in a perfect mind meld, but now their thoughts are sinister. The music turns dark and discordant. As galaxies are born, flare brilliantly, and die, the band searches for new and uncharted areas of the universe. And, as the band quiets down until only Weir and Godchaux are delicately polishing off chromatic tone clusters, you realize that you're on familiar ground: the spacey jam that appears with "Morning Dew" on the *Europe '72* CD. Once again, the level of intensity picks up until we are body-slammed by a thick slab of complex tonality. Garcia frantically ascends the fretboard while pulling off chromatic triplets while Weir, Lesh, and even Godchaux coax ear-splitting feedback from their instruments. Billy sits behind all of this, confidently grinding out his unique polyrhythms that are tied to no particular time signature—just free-form drumming.

Just as tension reaches its highest point—as you start to grind your molars into dust—the band releases the latch on the intense feedback and, once again turning on a dime, creates some breathing space, a great collective musical exhale. Garcia, mindful of the delicate moment, opens "Morning Dew" not, as usual, with a power chord, but rather with some gentle fretwork that gradually builds into the song.

Like "Truckin'" before it, this is the benchmark "Morning Dew," the version against which all others must be compared. Each band member manages to build a delicate framework around this song, with (here's the collective mind at work again) very little overlapping of musical ideas. As one instrument makes a tonal point, it recedes into the background and another steps forward. Meanwhile, Garcia's singing is sweet and soulful. But it's the rave-up at the end of the song that bears notice. It's very short when compared to most of the Dead's versions, but it builds to a perfect crescendo. And, as Garcia's final vocal line fades into the night (it's here that the CD ends), Billy drums the rest of the band back into "The Other One."

It's only a brief bit of high-energy jamming on "The Other One"'s beat before Weir sings the second verse (but be sure to check out Keith's stunning chordal run just prior to the vocals). Afterward, the band, to give us some time scrape our brains off the ceiling and pour them back between our ears, entertains us with a skillful rendition of "Sing Me Back Home." Garcia's solo during this song is particularly powerful.

And, some seventy-five minutes after this extended song segment began, it comes to a quiet close. We've been to the mountain and back, folks, and every moment is worth savoring.

But the show's not over. It's amazing that the band would have any energy left at all (we're now over three hours, excluding the set break, into the show), but we're treated to excellent versions of "Me and My Uncle," "Ramble On Rose," "Sugar Magnolia," and "Casey Jones" to end the set.

The encore is "One More Saturday Night," a blistering, speedy version that has the crowd on its feet, clapping and chanting for more. The sound of fireworks exploding can be heard on the tape and that's that. An amazing close to an amazing tour.

JEFF TIEDRICH

### 6/17/72
**Hollywood Bowl, Hollywood, California**

**Set 1:** Promised Land, Sugaree, Black-Throated Wind, Tennessee Jed, Me and My Uncle, China Cat Sunflower > I Know You Rider, Playing in the Band, Loser, Beat It on Down the Line, Stella Blue, El Paso, Casey Jones

**Source:** AUD, **Quality:** C–, **Length:** 1:30
**Highlights:** "China Cat Sunflower" > "I Know You Rider," "Playing in the Band," "Stella Blue"

In my years of tape collecting, this show has been rarer than hen's teeth. Having sat in box 73 (front row!) with a headful of substances, I have long sought verification that the playing was as memorable as originally imprinted on my psyche. Alas, this skeevy audience source recording is all that circulates, although you will find the second set from 11/20/71 occasionally masquerading as the second set from this show. It's especially unfortunate, because this is Pigpen's last performance with the band, that his sole tune of the show ("Rockin' Pneumonia") appears in the noncirculating second set. After an afternoon set by the New Riders, the Dead took the stage for a long (thirteen songs!) fast-paced first set highlighted by a fine "China Cat Sunflower" > "I Know You Rider," "Playing in the Band" sequence. Also noteworthy is the debut of "Stella Blue," making its first of fourteen first-set appearances. Although the playing is far from pedestrian, the poor quality and missing second set make this tape one for the completist only.

DENNIS DONLEY

### 7/16/72
**Dillon Stadium, Hartford, Connecticut**

**Set 1:** Promised Land, //Cold Rain and Snow, Black-Throated Wind, Sugaree, Playing in the Band//, Tennessee Jed, Jack Straw, Deal, Mexicali Blues, Cumberland Blues > Me and My Uncle, Mississippi Half-Step > Sing Me Back Home//, Casey Jones
**Set 2:** Truckin' > Drums > The Other One > He's Gone > The Other One Reprise > Looks like Rain, Ramble On Rose, Not Fade Away* > Goin' Down the Road Feelin' Bad* > Hey Bo Diddley*

* with Dickey Betts and Berry Oakley

**Source:** AUD, **Quality:** C/C+, **Length:** 3:00 (missing "Sugar Magnolia" and the "Johnny B. Goode" encore)
**Highlights:** Mississippi Half-Step, The Other One > He's Gone > The Other One Reprise, Not Fade Away > Goin' Down the Road > Hey Bo Diddley

This is the second stateside performance since their incredible European tour, and, as one would expect, there are numerous sparkling moments to be found

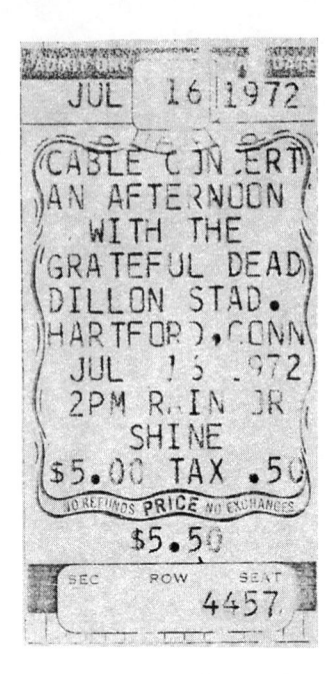

*Ticket stub for 7/16/72 at Dillon Stadium, Hartford*

throughout. Unfortunately, this mediocre audience recording is punctuated with volume fluctuations that shift from the right channels to the left and back again throughout many songs.

The first set is surprisingly sloppy, although the band, especially Garcia and Weir, are evidently having an enormous amount of fun. This is the first-ever performance of "Mississippi Half-Step," and it's delivered with tremendous focus and intent.

The highlights of the second set begin with a short drum solo that sets up a fully elaborated "Other One." Like all other versions of the time this is *serious* psychedelic music. After guitar phrases twist, violently for a while the energy finally fades to a melodic, spacey jam, and then grinds to a halt, disappearing with wraithlike swiftness into rumbles and noodles that in turn segue into a mind-bending bass solo. This evolves into another amazing jam, which then descends into "He's Gone."

A crisp soundboard recording might reveal further nuances worthy of being declared highlights, but meanwhile the obvious pinnacle of this show is the finale, which features Dickey Betts and Berry Oakley from the Allman Brothers Band. "Not Fade Away" is blistering, building higher and higher with furiously fast jamming. The party atmosphere escalates to even greater, more joyous heights when they slide into a monster version of "Goin' Down the Road." It's hard to imagine, but this energy level explodes to an even higher plateau as the troupe segues into "Hey Bo Diddley"! We really need the soundboard of this, don't you think? All in all, an amazing jam.

CHERIE CLARK-KING

---

## 7/18/72

### Roosevelt Stadium, Jersey City, New Jersey

**Set 1:** //Bertha, Me and My Uncle, Bird Song, Promised Land, Sugaree, Black-Throated Wind, China Cat > I Know You Rider, Jack Straw, Loser, Beat It on Down the Line, Stella Blue, //El Paso, Casey Jones
**Set 2:** Greatest Story, Playing in the Band, Brown-Eyed Women, Tennessee Jed, Truckin' > Dark Star > Comes a Time, Sugar Magnolia
**Set 3:** Ramble On Rose, Mississippi Half-Step > Sing Me Back Home, Not Fade Away > Goin' Down the Road Feelin' Bad > Not Fade Away Reprise

---

**1. Source:** AUD, **Quality:** B–, a bit echoey, **Length:** 3:30 (missing "Greatest Story," "Sugar Magnolia," and "Saturday Night" encore), **Taper:** Louis Falanga, Les Kippel

**2. Source:** SBD, **Quality:** B+/A–, hissy (//"Bertha," "Stella Blue"//, //"El Paso," "Comes a Time"//), **Length:** 3:00 (missing "Greatest Story," "Sugar Magnolia," entire third set and encore)

**Highlights:** The whole show—especially Bird Song, Playing in the Band, Tennessee Jed, Truckin' > Dark Star > Comes a Time

**Comments:** Technical problems with the signal from the piano mildly hamper various songs with brief outbursts of static.

Roosevelt Stadium was a very weird place to experience a concert. Buried in the back end of an industrial neighborhood in the middle of nowheresville, New Jersey, this former minor league baseball stadium had an indescribably wild ambience. Getting there was work—at best a real adventure, at worst a nightmare. Getting home was always a drag. But the hero's adventure almost always paid off in gold. This show is proof of that.

This was only the second East Coast show since their legendary spring tour of Europe, and the Grateful Dead obviously had something to prove to this, its fanatical New York area audience. Since their previous East Coast tour in March, they had obviously ascended to a new level of musical prowess, and almost every song played at this show proudly proclaims this evolution. Jerry in particular is *possessed* at this show—his playing is quite literally out of this world.

Unfortunately, this show is plagued by intermittent technical problems on stage: a buzz and a crackle in the PA, to be specific. At one point Phil apologizes for this and explains that it is emanating from the piano.

My soundboard tape starts smack dab in the middle of a "Bertha" delivered with a full head of full-steam. "Me and My Uncle" is no less animated with Keith overlaying some mighty tasty rolls at just the right moments. The band is obviously fired up! After Bobby explains that Pigpen isn't feeling well Jerry launches, and I mean *launches,* into the first "Bird Song" since August 24, 1971. It's absolutely incredible to experience how confident they all are with this, it's first performance in almost a year. Jerry's guitar *soars* to breathtaking heights immediately out of the first verse. It's as if they have been playing this tune forever. "Promised Land" is so high spirited it almost seems a shame it's so short. Again, Keith *shreds.* "Casey Jones" is highly energized, yet is oddly missing the same spirit of so many versions of that year.

One of the highlights of this concert, and of the entire summer for that matter, is "Playing in the Band." Once the first verse is disposed of, the band *explodes* out of the gate. Billy in particular is a standout force, propelling the band forward with muscular rolls. Although Jerry starts out gingerly by playing the "Main Ten" theme, he too is soon off and moving. And when he finally gets up into high gear, the result is extraordinary. Much like during the cosmic "Playing in the Band" from 8/27/72, his guitar tones here are *searing,* like a knife. Though there was always something special about outdoor Grateful Dead concerts, there was something extramagical about the tone of Garcia's guitar back then when he played outdoors on hot summer days. Surprisingly, while Jerry takes off *waay* out in front of the band, Keith, of all people, is closest in his jetstream, laying down complementary melodies and lead lines that soar. Interaction here is key. Weir has his moment in the sun, pounding out a melody in octaves. Reaching toward a ragingly psychedelic climax, Jerry sustains one note for a long time. This resolves back into the "Main Ten" theme, around which Keith wraps delicious flourishes. To say the least, this is very deep music. It sounds as though the jam might be over, but the muses of electricity have more to say, and the musicians are their willing messengers for a few more minutes.

As opposed to many "Playing in the Band"s from both '72 and '73 in which the Dead return to the final lyrics from out of deep space by first quieting down, this version finds them returning at light speed. Donna heralds the triumphant return from the cosmos with as emphatic a screaming banshee wail as any she ever let rip. If you're looking for "peak experience" visionary Grateful Dead music, this "Playing in the Band" is it.

"Brown-Eyed Women" is short and sweet. "Tennessee Jed," on the other hand, is as funky as it gets. Jerry's lead guitar solo is *soooo* twangy, that, well, this has to be one of the best-ever versions. How could you not love Jerry just for this solo? It's that good.

This rendition of "Truckin'" is easily one of my two favorites (the other is 4/11/72, Newcastle, England). The whole band is supercharged and totally synched. Bobby screams his lungs out just perfectly, and again, Jerry's lead guitar work is incendiary. The jam is long and fiery, and then, after the closing verse, the band settles quickly into what is obviously a prelude to something very special.

The air is thick, saturated as though magic is about to burst forth from the ether. Jerry begins to play a series of high-pitched "pick harmonics" that are produced by tweaking the strings with pick and right-hand finger at a set distance from the fretted note while using the brighter-sounding bridge pickup. This leads into a lush moment of silence. All the focus here is on Jerry, who shines like a true avatar fulfilling the role of tantric conduit through which some divine higher power speaks. From out of this delicious void the traditional opening riff of "Dark Star" is born. And off they go! Eventually, Jerry picks up the pace from the standard relaxed forays usually associated with the pre-verse segment. His playing becomes intense, pushing the time with relentlessly cascading riffs. At one point he finds a riff and, in classic Garcia style, repeats it, in this case centering around one note, playing up to it, and then down to it, building the intensity, and finally releasing the jam into a higher plane. This is the magic of Jerry Garcia as no others ever managed to achieve.

Meanwhile, Phil, though frustratingly low in the mix, can clearly be heard laying down some of the fastest fretwork of his career. While Billy keeps the tempo cruising, Jerry's guitar cries out the essential lead lines that come during the instrumental climax to "Dark Star."

After the verse is sung with resounding confidence, the band quickly dispenses with tonality. Jerry uses his wah-wah pedal to achieve shrill harmonics and to color his tone. He overbends his strings to play the notes in between the notes. The music becomes more and more chaotic. There is no tempo, no perceivable rhythm. Phil fills the bottom end with overamped double-stops and chords. Jerry starts playing a "Tiger" meltdown that quickly evolves into chordal shapes played in random patterns on different sets of strings and frets. The notes are no longer important; it's the sounds and how they feed off each other that matter. The Dead make beautiful noise like no others.

From out of this small apocalypse Jerry begins to play the sad chords of "Comes a Time." Unfortunately, this is where the soundboard tape in circulation cuts. I had never heard the audience tape of this show before reviewing it for this book. It was a remarkable experience because some of my first concerts were at this venue. I remember clearly the echo one would hear when sitting in the covered bleachers. Unlike the audience recording of 7/31/73 made at Roosevelt Stadium, this tape has that same echo. Putting on this "Comes a Time" sent goose bumps up and down my arms as I was instantly and profoundly transported back in time to the stadium. The audience recording of this show is quite good despite the echo and hearing Jerry sing "Comes a Time" from out in the bleachers instead of from "inside" the system was wonderful.

Before embarking on the "Not Fade Away" > "Goin' Down the Road" > "Not Fade Away" medley, Bobby steps to the microphone and says, "We're gonna light up and relax for a minute and then we're gonna rock 'n' roll." And boy, do they ever. This offering doesn't feature any particularly amazing Garcia leads like the earlier two sets did, but the whole band sings and plays its heart out as hard as ever. Donna lets forth several gutteral wails à la "Playing in the Band." This is the good ol' Grateful Dead driving the show home with every available ounce of effort. Altogether one of my favorite shows. You *must* check it out.

JOHN R. DWORK WITH JEFF MATTSON

---

### 7/21/72

**Paramount Northwest Theatre, Seattle, Washington**

**Set 1:** //Sugaree, Black-Throated Wind, Cumberland Blues, Me and Bobby McGee, Loser, Mexicali Blues, China Cat Sunflower// > I Know You Rider, Beat It on Down the Line, Stella Blue, Playing in the Band, Tennessee Jed
**Set 2:** Casey Jones, Me and My Uncle, Deal, Jack Straw, He's Gone, Truckin' > Drums > Bass/Drums > The Other One > Comes a Time, Sugar Magnolia > Ramble On Rose//

**Source:** SBD, **Quality:** A, **Length:** 3:00
**Highlights:** Playing in the Band, Bass/Drums > The Other One

Many Deadheads are of the opinion that the ten-show West Coast run that occurred between the legendary shows at Roosevelt Stadium in July and the Field Trip in Oregon in late August was lower in focus and intensity than the magnificent shows that framed them. This show, however, is certainly one of the better ones from this brief summer lull. Though not of the same intensity as 7/18 and 8/27, it rocks solidly throughout.

Most of set 1 is standard fare for the time: tight renditions with nicely articulated jams—nothing mind-blowing though. This "Playing in the Band" is another 1972 intergalactic voyage. It's very much like the version from 8/27/72—a raging psychedelic maelstrom—only this version is obviously lacking the chemical synergist necessary for the band to take the song to the truly cosmic level.

The second set starts with a promising scream of excitement from somewhere onstage—a good indicator of the high energy that was about to follow. The band launches immediately into "Casey Jones" and delivers a version worthy of the scream that introduced it. Bobby starts to lead the band into a "Weather Report Suite Prelude," but this is abandoned after only fifteen seconds or so. Bobby guffaws, then chuckles, "Well anyway, this one's about history," and they're off and galloping again, this time through a spirited "Me and My Uncle." Though delivered with the same gusto as the two tunes that precede it, "Deal" is unmemorable in that it is missing the rise and fall dynamic of the many masterful versions Jerry would unleash in the decades to follow.

"He's Gone," though one of the shortest versions of the year (maybe ever), is delivered with unusual gusto, making it one of my favorite early versions.

After a few minutes of tuning and joking around, Bobby explains, "This here's why they call it the boogie band," before embarking on the evening's jam. The Dead keep the energy high for "Truckin'," though not on the same manic level as in the previous version they performed on July 18 in New Jersey.

The drum-bass duet is notable less for Phil's playing as for the rapid panning effect that swooshes Billy's dominant cymbal work from one channel to the other at a very rapid pace. This is the only such percussion panning effect I can recall hearing on a pre-'74 tape. Once the rest of the band steps in, it's "Other One" time, and how! Jerry noodles away in top psychedelic form while Keith runs drippy tracers around him. After the lyrics Jerry delivers a strong "Tiger" meltdown, though the vibe gets nowhere near as heavy as the apocalyptic post-"Tiger" meltdowns of many "Dark Star"s and "Other One"s in August and September 1972. "Comes a Time" is simply good, nothing as heart-wrenching as this song can be. Likewise, "Sugar Magnolia" is hot but, despite Bobby's frantic yelping, fails to ascend to the searing temperature of so many other versions from this year.

*DeadBase* lists "Ramble On Rose" as the encore; however, the tape reveals Jerry leading the band directly into it from "Sugar Magnolia." Regardless, it cuts shortly after starting up—too soon to tell how far the band takes it or what may follow afterward.

JOHN R. DWORK

---

## 7/22/72
**Paramount Northwest Theatre, Seattle, Washington**

**Set 1:** Bird Song, Beat it on Down the Line, Sugaree, Black-Throated Wind, Big Railroad Blues, Cumberland Blues, Brown-Eyed Women, El Paso, Tennessee Jed, Playing in the Band//
**Set 2:** China Cat Sunflower > I Know You Rider, Mexicali Blues, Deal, Promised Land, Stella Blue, Mississippi Half-Step, Me and Bobby McGee, Ramble On Rose, Morning Dew, Uncle John's Band, One More Saturday Night

**Source:** SBD, **Quality:** A/B+ **Length:** 2:28
**Highlights:** China Cat Sunflower > I Know You Rider, Morning Dew
**Comments:** Inconsistent mix, fluctuates at times, occasional tape glitches. The mix in this recording is not quite balanced right; everything is audible but the drums come through in front and there are some fluctuations to the mix.

A competent performance, with strong vocals and good playing, but nothing to write home about. That is, not too many extended solos or segued songs, and a fairly ordinary song selection. The vocals are probably the show's strongest point, especially the force Jerry puts into "Stella Blue" and "Morning Dew," the latter featuring some strong guitar work as well. His deliberate vocals on "China Cat Sunflower" also stand out. "Me and Bobby McGee" is nice to come across, but not exceptional. One highlight that suffers from a tape cut is "Playing in the Band," which offers the first extended jam of the show. Sadly, this piece is cut midway through the jamming after the verses.

Fans of intersong banter will enjoy Bob's long story after "Stella Blue" about the man with the short, fat, squat, ugly yellow dog and the man with the big, black, slick, mean-looking dog. Jerry noodles around with "Heart and Soul" in the background.

DAN DESARO

## 7/25/72
### Paramount Theatre, Portland, Oregon

**Set 1:** Promised Land, Sugaree, Me and My Uncle, Bird Song, Black-Throated Wind, Cumberland Blues, Jack Straw, Big Railroad Blues, El Paso, Tennessee Jed, Playing in the Band, Loser, Beat It on Down the Line, Casey Jones
**Second Set:** He's Gone, Greatest Story Ever Told, China Cat Sunflower > I Know You Rider, Mexicali Blues, Truckin' > Jam > Drums > The Other One > Space > The Other One > Lesh Solo > The Other One > Wharf Rat, Sing Me Back Home, Not Fade Away > Goin' Down the Road Feelin' Bad > Not Fade Away Reprise

**Source:** SBD, **Quality:** A–, **Length:** 3:00, **Genealogy:** MC > DAT > C
**Highlights:** Space

This is an odd show. The band is clearly in sync with each other and the crowd seems into it, too. There aren't any musical flubs. But it's *so* amazingly mellow and relaxed, completely void of any of those good ol' nasty emotions I personally like, e.g., rage and tension. This isn't exactly elevator music, by any means. Each song is focused and carried out in true Grateful Dead fashion. And the music isn't exactly boring. It's just . . . odd.

"Bird Song" and "Playing" are spacey and comforting. But they're *so* gentle and soft that I felt compelled to throw my copy of Robert Bly's *Iron John* at the stereo. Billy is the only one who seems aware of this soft-male attitude on stage as he continually attempts to kick some urgency into the others. But he's mostly ignored.

"The Other One" features a long, often intriguing jam. This turns into a beautifully mellow, drumless melody that sounds very familiar (and practiced). I've never heard it before on any tapes. It fits perfectly into the band's mood with its lullaby-like charm. The rest of the show is standard fare, including (unfortunately) Lesh's solo. For those who prefer a laid-back, very West Coast show, this is definitely the one. It's hard to believe, though, that this is the same band that opened '72 with the fine Academy of Music run, the stellar Europe '72 tour, and then ripped nearly every show from Kesey Farm (8/27) on through New Year's. Go figure.

MICHAEL M. GETZ

## 7/26/72
### Paramount Theatre, Portland, Oregon

**Set 1:** Cold Rain and Snow, Mexican Hat Dance Tuning, Black-Throated Wind, Mississippi Half-Step, Mexicali Blues, Sugaree, El Paso, China Cat Sunflower > I Know You Rider, Jack Straw, Tennessee Jed, Playing in the Band, //Casey Jones
**Set 2:** Promised Land, He's Gone, Me and My Uncle, You Win Again, Greatest Story Ever Told, Ramble On Rose, Dark Star > Comes a Time, Sugar Magnolia, Brown-Eyed Women//, Beat It on Down the Line, Stella Blue, Not Fade Away > Goin' Down the Road Feelin' Bad > Not Fade Away Reprise
**Encore:** One More Saturday Night

**1. Source:** SBD, **Quality:** A, **Length:** 2:45, **Genealogy:** MR > DAT
**2. Source:** FM-SBD (GDH 131, 143, and 414), **Quality:** A+, **Length:** 2:00 ("Mexican Hat Dance" through "Black-Throated Wind," "China Cat Sunflower" > "I Know You Rider," "He's Gone," "You Win Again" through "Sugar Magnolia," "Comes a Time"), **Genealogy:** MR > RR > DR
**Highlights:** Dark Star > Comes a Time, Playing, Not Fade Away > Goin' Down the Road > Not Fade Away Reprise, Saturday Night

Tapes of this show first emerged in the early '90s, and though not a typical favorite or even a very widely circulated show, this soundboard is well worth having if you're an avid or even average collector. The Grateful Dead performed six shows at Portland's Paramount Theatre: one pair each in July 1972, June 1976, and October 1977. This show was from the band's first run at the venue, and although it was the second night of the run, technical problems still plagued both sets.

The selection and quantity of songs played, as well as the show's length, are the most satisfying aspects of the show. A twelve-song first set lasting, nearly one hour and forty-five minutes and full of many mid-'72 standards is surpassed by a sixteen-song second set lasting well over two hours plus an encore. Seven shows and two months to the day after the final Europe 72 show, this Wednesday performance is also only the sixth show following Pigpen's last appearance onstage with the band.

The vocals are crystal-clear right from the start, but unfortunately they are much too high in the mix. The instruments, and Kreutzmann's drum kit in particular, are relegated to the background. The technical difficulties are apparent early on as Weir complains of monitor problems right after the "Mexican Hat Dance" tuning. First-set favorites include a twelve-minute "China" > "Rider" firmly planted in mid-set and the fourteen-minute "Playing in the Band" that features Donna Godchaux and precedes the "Casey Jones" set closer. "Half-Step," the third song in set 1, marked only the fourth time the song had been performed live; nonetheless, it already sounded reasonably well developed. "Casey Jones" has a cut very early on and is missing part of the first verse, most likely due to a reel change.

Set 2 substantially outshines its predecessor, beginning with a three-minute high-energy "Promised Land" that had already become a common set opener even though the Dead had only played it together a little more than a dozen times. Similarly, the next up was only their fifteenth rendition of the soon to be standard second-set tune "He's Gone." Following "Me and My Uncle" was a choice "You Win Again," which would only be played twice before being retired exactly two months later. "Greatest Story" followed, with that delightfully raw, characteristically early-'70s "Pump Song" urgency. Next we're treated to a Garcia hat trick: "Ramble On" and a splendid "Dark Star" into a heartfelt "Comes a Time." "Dark Star" is the definitive highlight of the show! It includes both verses, which became quite a rarity in 1972 and the years to follow. It is soothing, graceful, soaring, and long—clocking in at over thirty minutes. "Brown-Eyed Women" is cut, also likely attributable to a master reel change. The second-set-closing medley of "Not Fade Away" > "Goin' Down the Road" > "Not Fade Away," though not unique, is overflowing with energy and excitement, and it's well over twenty minutes long. Finally, the "Saturday Night" encore is well performed, fun, and energized.

ERIC VANDERCAR

### 8/12/72
**Sacramento Memorial Auditorium, Sacramento, California**

**Set 1:** Promised Land, Sugaree, Me and My Uncle, Bird Song, Black-Throated Wind, Deal, El Paso//, //Tennessee Jed, Playing in the Band, Big Railroad Blues, Cumberland Blues, Stella Blue, Jack Straw, Casey Jones
**Set 2:** Greatest Story Ever Told, Ramble On Rose, Beat It on Down the Line, He's Gone > Drums > The Other One > Black Peter > The Other One Reprise > Truckin', Mississippi Half Step, Sugar Magnolia

**Source:** SBD, **Quality:** A–, **Length:** 3:10
**Highlights:** Bird Song, The Other One > Black Peter > The Other One

A nice soundboard of this exemplary post–Europe '72 era show circulates. The band was evolving quickly as it experimented and stretched to fill the void left by Pigpen. Who would have thought that you could fill a void with space?!

The first selection that lends intrigue is "Bird Song." It's an unhurried, jammed-out version that breathes very well, and has that jazz-space signature sound of the golden '72–'74 era. That sound is back again in the twelve-minute "Playing in the Band," during which Garcia plays with a unique wah-wah tone. This is followed by five more songs in the first set!

The second set begins innocently enough with "He's Gone," but there's a certain sorta sound about that segue into "The Other One" that lets you know that it's gonna happen tonight. Sure enough, "The Other One" melts into deep, primordial space, and culminates into a cacophony reminiscent of the jam later dubbed "The Tiger." What could emerge from that but, uh, "Black Peter"? And a sweet version it is. This is the only time that "Black Peter" was sandwiched inside "The Other One," which ends the segue with a reprise into a ferocious "Truckin'." Unfortunately, the tape ends there, but I suspect that I have heard the highlights of the show.

PAUL J. PEARAH

## 8/20/72
### Civic Auditorium, San Jose, California

**Set 1:** //Bertha//, Me and My Uncle, Sugaree, Beat It on Down the Line, Bird Song, Jack Straw, Friend of the Devil, Black-Throated Wind, //Cumberland Blues, El Paso, Loser, Playing in the Band

**Source:** SBD, **Quality:** B–, **Length:** 1:30, **Genealogy:** MC > C > C > C, **Taper:** Bear
**Highlights:** Playing in the Band

It's extremely rare to find a mediocre set of music from the Dead in 1972. Yet here it is. Even "Bird Song" lies grounded, stuffed with worms, too lazy to fly. But the Dead do snap out of it for yet another outstanding "Playing in the Band" to close the set. This one has Garcia plugging in the ol' Black and Decker to drill a hole in your brain. Great filler.

MICHAEL M. GETZ

## 8/21/72
### Berkeley Community Theatre, Berkeley, California

**Set 1:** Promised Land, He's Gone, Black-Throated Wind, Friend of the Devil, Jack Straw, China Cat Sunflower > I Know You Rider, Me and My Uncle, Sugaree, Beat It on Down the Line, Stella Blue, Playing in the Band, Brown-Eyed Women, Mexicali Blues
**Set 2:** Greatest Story Ever Told, Ramble On Rose, Dark Star > El Paso, Space > Deal, Sugar Magnolia, Mississippi Half-Step, Uncle John's Band > One More Saturday Night

**1. Source:** SBD, **Quality:** A, **Length:** 3:10
**2. Source:** SBD, **Quality:** A, **Length:** 3:10, **Genealogy:** Betty Board, 10-inch reel, ½ track, 7½ ips, MR > PCM > DAT
**3. Source:** AUD, **Quality:** C–, **Length:** 3:00 ("Greatest Story"//)
**4. Source:** FM-SBD (DHH 25), **Quality:** A, **Length:** "Half-Step," "One More Saturday Night"
**Highlights:** Dark Star

What could have been dismissed as a run of the mill, unremarkable Monday night opener in a four-show run at the Berkeley Community Theater cannot be because of the vigorous "Dark Star" contained in the second set. The first set is generously littered with long waits between songs, filled with noodling, tons of audience noise, and even Phil lending his two cents about vegetables.

The second set has a noticeably superior sound quality than the first: less noise, hiss, and distraction. Getting right to the one highlight of the evening, this "Dark Star" begins with about nine minutes of standard, delicious exploratory cruising before Jerry sings the only verse. Off into the deep unknown we go. Garcia and Lesh's dissonant waves crisscross for a while before taking the plunge into full-fledged *chaos jazz* jamming. The whole band grinds and spits, weaving back and forth between euphoria and the dark abyss. As the turbulent spirits leave the stage and the band settles down, Keith takes a piano solo. Garcia valiantly tries (just, if one listens carefully, as on the tail end of Dark Star on 8/27/72) to lead the tide toward "Morning Dew," which glistens for a moment at the surface before disappearing into jazz piano scat again. As everyone joins the jazz composition, the piece begins to resemble the prequel leading into any number of Weir cowboy numbers, finally slowing down to segue into "El Paso." Afterward Garcia and Lesh noodle "Dark Star" space quietly for several minutes before Jerry nods at "Deal," a honey-drenched mellow rendition. Jerry's vocals shine, Keith tickles the ivories, and in the wink of an eye, it's over, except for Bobby throwing his hat into the ring for nomination as mayor (with Jerry prompting, "of Fremont!").

Of course, nothing can remotely compare to what we were given at the end of this famous week, namely what arguably turned out to be what many consider one of the best Dead shows ever: August 27, 1972.

CHERIE CLARK-KING

## 8/22/72
### Berkeley Community Theatre, Berkeley, California

**Set 1:** Black-Throated Wind, Bird Song, Beat It on Down the Line, Tennessee// Jed, Me and My Uncle, Friend of the Devil, Playing in the Band, He's Gone//, The Promised Land

**Set 2:** Brown-Eyed Women, Mexicali Blues, Truckin' > Jam// > Truckin' > Drums > Bass Jam > The Other One > Bass Solo > The Other One Reprise > Stella Blue, El Paso, Ramble On Rose, Not Fade Away > Goin' Down the Road Feelin' Bad > Hey Bo Diddley > Not Fade Away Reprise

**1. Source:** SBD, **Quality:** B+, **Length:** 1:30 (set 1), **Genealogy:** MR > RR > C > C > C (?)

**2. Source:** SBD, **Quality:** A+ (left channel is missing from "Brown-Eyed Women" through middle of "Truckin'"), **Length:** 1:30 (set 2), **Genealogy:** Betty Board, 10-inch reel, ½ track, 7½ ips, MR > PCM > DAT

**3. Source:** FM-SBD (DHH 25), **Quality:** A, **Length:** "Stella Blue," "Not Fade Away" through "Hey Bo Diddley"

**Highlights:** Bird Song, The Other One (and Bass Solo), Not Fade Away > Goin' Down the Road > Hey Bo Diddley > Not Fade Away Reprise

**Comments:** I put this show together from two different sources. The sound quality of both is relatively good. My copy of the first source is a fourth-generation soundboard I obtained from Michael Getz. My second source was the first of two tapes that constitute the first release of the Bay Area Tapers Group (BATG), an Internet-based tape-distribution club. It was released by the East Bay Group and is Tape A of Release No. 1 in the BATG system.

"Friend of the Devil" is slower than on *Workingman's*, but it's not the latter-day Loggins and Messina–esque arrangement. There's a cut in the "Playing in the Band" jam of probably a minute or so (judging from the continuity). The jam itself is great overall with perhaps an anticlimactic ending. After "Playing in the Band," Jerry says to the crowd, "Yeah, we'll get into all that top 40 shit later, man. Don't you worry about it." "He's Gone," already slower by this point than on *Europe '72*, is cut after one verse!

There's a vague "White Christmas" tuning tease before "Truckin'." I look at the set list of the tape as it starts to play, end up spacing out during the "Truckin'" jam, Drums, a little bass solo go by, first hint of "The Other One." Space out some more, listen to Phil take over the "Other One" riff and then go off, keeping a rhythm going the whole time but wandering into fully fanned chords and picking a top-and-bottom jive at the same time, never losing a grip, folding it back into "The Other One" lickety-split. The recording level fades out in the solo briefly. The full-on "Other One" is wah-wah heavy, it gets spacey, with sounds of plucked strings, a Sun Ra Arkestra feel, and then resolves into a melodic country-rock jam (brief, a minute or so).

In "Stella Blue," an early rendition, Jerry sings uncertainly—"All the worlds combine"—languid, a little off. The end is heartfelt but a little stilted ("Steh!-eh-ella Blue") with just hints at the majesty of later versions. After this, Bobby announces "Listen, Pigpen isn't here tonight. He's home sick, he's gonna be sick for a while. That's what the doctor says. So I guess what we'll have to do is send all your best wishes back to him 'cause he can't be here." (Cheer goes up from from crowd.)

The closing "Not Fade Away" > "Goin' Down the Road" jam unleashes a lot of energy, typical of that combination in that period. The rare "Hey Bo Diddley" inserted before the "Not Fade Away" reprise is more fully played than might be expected from other insertions around the same time.

CHRISTIAN CRUMLISH

## 8/24/72
### Berkeley Community Theatre, Berkeley, California

**Set 1:** Promised Land, Sugaree, Jack Straw, China Cat Sunflower > I Know You Rider, Me and My Uncle, Bird Song, Beat It on Down the Line, Tennessee Jed, Playing in the Band, Casey Jones

**Set 2:** Mississippi Half-Step, Mexicali Blues, Brown-Eyed Women, Truckin', Dark// Star > Morning Dew, Sugar Magnolia, Ramble On Rose, Greatest Story Ever Told, Sing Me Back Home, One More Saturday Night, Uncle John's Band

**1. Source:** SBD, **Quality:** A, **Length:** 3:20, **Genealogy:** MR > RR > RR > DAT

**2. Source:** FM-SBD (GDH 051, 105, and 366), **Quality:** A, **Length:** 1:20 ("Promised Land," "Bird Song," "Casey Jones," "Dark Star" through "Morning Dew")

**Highlights:** Brown-Eyed Women, Mexicali Blues, Bird Song, China Cat > I Know You Rider, Truckin', Dark Star > Morning Dew

**Comments:** An archetypal hot show, this date is in circulation in various levels of quality, and as luck would have it, those with truly superb sound quality and a spot-on mix are the ones that are heavily edited: my original copy of this show has lots of sparkle but lacks the "Dark Star" > "Morning Dew" combo that is the heart of the second set. A more complete version is unfortunately a bit muddy (although it is still mixed well).

Recorded just a couple of days before the legendary Kesey's Creamery benefit show at the Old Renaissance Fairgrounds in Oregon, this gig is as strong as you might expect: the guys are most definitely on a roll, and just about all of this show *glows*. The shorter songs are sung with passion and tightly played (my favorites being "Brown-Eyed Women" and "Mexicali Blues"—both versions are near enough perfect), while all the long numbers are developed with dynamic interplay and not a few stellar moments: "Bird Song" unrolls with more than the usual loose-limbed grace, "China" > "Rider" includes a glorious jam and transition section (again), the "Playing in the Band" is energetic and subtly spacey, while "Truckin'" is explosive energy that just cannot be contained, and it's maybe surprising that they end it rather than search for a segue into something else.

The "Dark Star" > "Morning Dew" combination is quite stunning, with some of the best and unique multilayered improvisations of the period blossoming in the "Star." As Keith smears electric keyboards over the cross-rhythms set up by the others, the feel of contemporary Miles Davis music is evoked so be prepared to visit some enjoyably strange soundworlds here. Highly recommended. A big tick and a gold star to everyone concerned.

PAUL BODENHAM

## 8/25/72
### Berkeley Community Theatre, Berkeley, California

**Set 1:** Bill Graham Intro, Cold Rain and Snow, Black-Throated Wind, He's Gone, Beat It on Down the Line, Loser, Frozen Logger, El Paso

**Source:** SBD, **Quality:** A+, **Length:** 0:50, **Genealogy:** Betty Board, 10″ reel, ½ track, 7½ ips, MR > PCM > DAT

This was the last in the series of four shows at the Community Theatre in Berkeley. It was the first Bay Area appearance after the landmark Europe '72 tour and the first without Pigpen. The run was going well, and with Bill Graham finally introducing the band in its new configuration, the musicians seem ready. This show starts off well with the uncommon "Cold Rain and Snow" (at that time played only about once a month), and containing a first-set "He's Gone." There's also the appearance of the rare "Frozen Logger." All indications are that the band is playing well and is comfortable after three nights with an intimate (and identical) crowd. Unfortunately, all that is available is the first forty-five-minute reel. Not even the set list is available from the remainder of the show, making it the last Bay Area show for which there is no list in circulation.

DOUGAL DONALDSON

# Reviews: August 1972

## ❈ 8/27/72 ❈
### Field Trip
### Old Renaissance Fairgrounds, Veneta, Oregon

**Set 1:** Promised Land, Sugaree, Me and My Uncle, Deal, Black-Throated Wind, China Cat Sunflower > I Know You Rider, Mexicali Blues, Bertha
**Set 2:** Playing in the Band, He's Gone, Jack Straw, Bird Song, Greatest Story Ever Told
**Set 3:** Dark Star > El Paso > Sing Me Back Home, Sugar Magnolia
**Encore:** Casey Jones, One More Saturday Night

**1. Source:** SBD, **Quality:** A/A+, **Length:** 3:10, **Genealogy:** transferred from the Alembic Studios 15 ips, 16 track tape, **Genealogy:** MR > DR

**2. Source:** SBD (GDH 205 and 206), **Quality:** A, **Length:** 1:50 ("China Cat" > "Rider," "Playing in the Band," "Bird Song," "Greatest Story Ever Told," "Dark Star" > "El Paso" > "Sing Me Back Home"), **Genealogy:** MR > DR

**3. Source:** SBD, **Quality:** A (complete until the middle of "Dark Star," which is cut), **Length:** 1:50, **Genealogy:** Betty Board, 10-inch reel, ½ track, 7½ ips, MR > PCM > DAT

**Highlights:** Promised Land, Black-Throated Wind, China Cat Sunflower > I Know You Rider, Playing in the Band, Bird Song, Greatest Story Ever Told, Dark Star > El Paso > Sing Me Back Home, Sugar Magnolia, Casey Jones, One More Saturday Night

Because art is by nature subjective, it's impossible to critique Grateful Dead shows with any sort of *absolute* objectivity. Well, obviously this hasn't stopped us Deadheads from comparing great shows and debating about which ones are the *best*. Such debates have ensued continuously for at least a quarter of a century. Surveys taken by the Grateful Dead fanzine *Dupree's Diamond News* over the years and feedback submitted to Dick Latvala suggest that a majority of Deadheads believe February 13, 1970, and May 8, 1977, are at least the most *popular* Grateful Dead performances of all time, if not the *best*. But I will offer here the argument that the Dead's legendary "Field Trip" concert on August 27, 1972, at the Old Renaissance Fairgrounds in Veneta, Oregon, is the most *important* show of their career.

Why? First and foremost, because I believe 8/27/72 was the quintessential Grateful Dead live concert *Experience*—not just a display of technically and emotionally brilliant musicianship but also a spiritually transcendent vision quest ritual for audience and band alike. One of the greatest appeals of the live Grateful Dead concert is that it was a ritual during which the band set out to explore the uncharted realms of the creative collective unconscious. They took great risks in the hope of finding great art. Through the improvisatory segments of the show the band would search for wondrous, cosmic, beautiful, even ugly and scary universal truths. When the Dead came upon such magnificent realms of experience, those of us who were present and properly attuned were often transported into states of profound realization and intense emotional release and connection. Part of what made the Dead so special was *our* collective participation in the unfolding of those amazing moments: we took those magical trips with them. The Dead provided a setting in which we could take risks, and together with them we could find treasured, sacred moments that gave meaning and hope to our lives. When it worked, the Grateful Dead concert Experience was one of the highest, most evolved activities humans have ever collectively engaged in. The concerts were sacred, peaceful, intelligent, artistic celebrations of life. The show on August 27, 1972, was both one of the Dead's finest, most powerful musical performances and one of Grateful Dead community's all-time finest rituals. One would be hard-pressed to find a more potent combination of these two essential ingredients in any other show.

Amazingly the Dead allowed a film crew to document this concert. This yet-to-be-released film (which circulates on video), *Sunshine Daydream,* is perhaps the best audiovisual evidence ever recorded of the Dead and Deadheads peacefully and joyously celebrating life together. If you haven't seen it try to imagine a film of the Dead, high as kites, playing a fully articulated, *screamingly* psychedelic "Dark Star" in a lush, natural, outdoor environment as the setting sun bathes everything in sight with a warm orange glow. It is hard to watch this film and not be seriously moved. Part of what makes this show so important is that the film offers us the ability to see the Dead playing their hearts out at the peak of their career. We live in a world filled with a wealth of audio recordings that provide ample evidence to support the argument that the Dead were

*The original poster announcing the 8/27/72 Field Trip*

artists of immense proportions. And yet very little visual evidence exists to support that mighty claim. *Sunshine Daydream* is just such a rare, in-depth visual record of the Dead playing at the height of their creative powers in a magically surreal setting, and so it's enormously significant. I am quite certain that someday, when this film is finally released, it will be widely recognized as the most insightful visual document of the entire Grateful Dead Experience.

There is another crucial point to consider in this argument. If the Dead's music on tape can be used as a tool to access different levels of consciousness and deep-felt emotional and spiritual states, then the music from this show is as potent a vehicle for such voyages as any other that exists in circulation. I know; over the past seventeen years I have hosted intimate "listening sessions" for more than one thousand Deadheads at which the specific goal was to see exactly how far the Dead's music could take the conscious, focused mind through inner space. Many different pieces of music, both Dead and non-Dead, have been used in these sessions. None however, have displayed the power of 8/27/72 to elicit such *profound* visionary states. Psychically speaking, on that day, the Dead truly went where no musicians had ever gone before—to the farthest reaches of improvisatory psychedelic space, to the heart of darkness and back again, to heaven on Earth. The music created on that day is so powerful that even today, when encountered under the appropriate set and setting, it offers the attuned listener, time and time again, a transcendant visionary Experience. Hear me when I tell you that this miraculous Experience is repeatable.

If the Grateful Dead were, as Mickey Hart has often said, "in the transportation business," then for the many reasons offered herein, this performance is arguably the most perfect example of that power we have yet found. Please permit me to elaborate.

**A SPECIAL TIME IN THE DEAD'S CAREER**
Before 1972 the Grateful Dead's musical evolution had brought them through several clearly identifiable stages. By 1967 the Dead had just begun to effectively harness the intense power of psychedelics as catalysts for the creation of visionary music. But the resulting efforts at this time were still raw and rough-edged, overflowing with too much youthful, psychedelic vibrancy. Powerful as an atom bomb, the early Grateful Dead beast was still untamed. By 1969 we saw a band whose psychedelic sound had matured considerably; the overwhelming power was still there, but they were learning how to intelligently harness and effectively structure it. The year 1970 brought the start of an important new era. With greater emphasis given to singing well and a return in part to acoustic American folk music, the Dead were beginning to show signs not only of focus and maturity but of an awareness of *nuance*. Any great musician will tell you that, in music, the most powerful sound is silence. The emergence of this greater awareness in the Dead can be heard throughout the spring of 1970 in breathtakingly exquisite performances such as 2/13/70. Musically speaking, 1971 seemed to be contractive by comparison. I remember reading a Garcia quote about *Skull and Roses,* the live double album from 1971, in which he said that the Dead were trying to achieve a super-tight "shoot 'em up" bar band sound.

As 1972 rolled around, however, the Dead's music took a dramatic shift up in power, focus, and intensity. It can be argued that their tour of Europe in the spring of that year was their strongest to date. The Dead replaced many of the acoustic folk traditionals of the previous two years with a strong repertoire of their own electrified American classics including "Jack Straw," "Tennessee Jed," and "Ramble On Rose." At every single show on the European tour, the band would march through this well-developed repertoire with Herculean power. But the jams really shined on this tour. Not just a few here or there: at virtually every performance the band reached breathtaking new plateaus. Songs like "Dark Star," "Playing in the Band," "Bird Song," "Good Lovin'," "China Cat" > "Rider," and "The Other One" became vehicles, portals through which to access and explore deep inner spaces as far removed from everyday consciousness as any musicians—or concertgoers—had ever traveled before. By the summer of '72 Jerry Garcia had become a true musical avatar. As a whole, the band had arrived at a point at which its music displayed both immense power *and* awareness.

By August other important changes were taking place. Keith and Donna had become perfectly integrated into the group's collective creative mind. Pigpen was sick at home, and the band was quickly gravitating away from his blues-based sound and toward rock played in a jazz idiom. Except for Pigpen, the band was vibrantly healthy. They were at an age, their late twenties, when youthful stamina plays a critical role in an artist's ability to play his or her heart out at every performance.

**"We'd sure like to thank the Springfield Creamery for making it possible for us to**

*play out here in front of all you folks and God and everybody. This is where we really get off the best."*
—Phil Lesh, August 27, 1972

## RECIPE FOR A MIRACLE: COMING HOME TO THE PRANKSTER FAMILY

By August of 1972, Jerry, Phil, Bobby, Billy, Keith, and Donna had become so awesomely skilled at their chosen craft and so in sync with one another that they were on the verge of achieving a level of creative prowess above and beyond anything that had come before. All it would take was the right set and setting to create a concert of miraculous proportions.

Oregon was the original home of many members of the Dead's extended family. Some of the roadies were from Pendleton, and many of the Merry Pranksters, including Ken Kesey and Ken Babbs, had settled around Eugene. Many hippies who had come of age in the Bay Area in the sixties eventually moved up north to settle. By 1972 Eugene was, in the eyes of many, the epicenter of the West Coast Rainbow Nation. For the Dead, a visit to Oregon would be a homecoming.

In the summer of 1972 Ken Kesey's family creamery business was in need of an infusion of cash. Black Maria, a Merry Prankster family member, traveled to the Bay Area to ask the Dead if they'd do a benefit for the creamery. On the last day of July, the Dead gave the go-ahead. The Keseys had only twenty-seven days to prepare for the event. Tickets were printed on the creamery's yogurt labels, and family friends signed on to build the stage. And talk about mellow: if can you imagine, back then they didn't need to get a concert permit—they just rented an appropriate site and set to work!

In keeping with their tradition as the hosts of highly unusual events, the Kesey clan assembled all the proper catalysts to insure that this event would be special. More than just a fund-raiser and a concert for the local community, this was to be a party for the extended Grateful Dead/Prankster family. They billed it as "The Field Trip."

*Tickets for 8/27/72 were printed on the Springfield Creamery's yogurt labels (note the delightful "Acidophilus Presents" wording)*

## THE FIELD

If you've ever been to Stonehenge, Red Rocks, the Grand Canyon, or Swayambunath, Nepal, then you know what it means when people speak of power spots or "energy centers." There are certain places on this planet that, through a combination of powerful environmental surroundings and inexplicable or unseen energy forces, are conducive to deeply significant spiritual occurrences. The Oregon Country Fairgrounds and the surrounding fields are such an area. The first time I set eyes on this place I couldn't help but call it "god's country." In August it is beautiful, almost beyond description. Vast fields are covered in a sea of tiny yellow wildflowers which sway silently in a warm summer wind. These fields are bordered everywhere with blackberry bushes bearing infinite bushels of dark, sweet fruit. Gently rolling hills dressed in evergreen trees draped with chartreuse tufts of Spanish moss surround these expanses. Up above are big puffy clouds dotted by soaring hawks. The fat old sun blankets the land with a deep, penetrating heat. But none of this description does true justice to the feeling one gets when there. Where else but in such a lush setting, so intimately connected with nature, could the Dead play music of such cosmic proportions?

## THE WEATHER

Another one of the crucial synergistic factors was the record-breaking temperature recorded in Oregon that day. With the brutal August sun creating an all-time Oregon high of 108 degrees, INTENSE became the operative word on that field. Lack of proper planning put the stage, and henceforth the instruments, on the wrong side of the field. The result was that the musicians—or more important, their instruments—were directly exposed to the afternoon sun! This resulted in some very strange aural effects. But the astounding heat of that day made for a collective trial by fire for everyone present, not just the band. This was 1972, mind you, and there weren't such things as ice cream or soda stands on the site, which even today qualifies as rural. At one point the water ran out. The Keseys got hold of a water truck from the fairgrounds, but just as they were about to spray the crowd, Ken's brother Chuck realized that it was a truck used to empty portable toilets! Talk about tragedy narrowly averted! Potable water was eventually resupplied, much to everyone's relief.

**THE PSYCHEDELIC FACTOR**

Any discussion of this concert—in fact any discussion about the Dead's most important musical work—would be incomplete without a serious look at the intimate role that psychedelic sacraments played in creating that music and in listening to it.

We all know the Grateful Dead would not have become the legendary exploratory artists they are had it not been for the power of psychedelics—particularly LSD. In the early part of their career, at least through 1974, the Dead directed a good share of their focus toward making psychedelic music—music influenced by and created while under the influence of psychoactive drugs. This focus resulted in many hours of music that conveys the energies, the fundamental character of the psychedelic experience. Knowledge of this heritage is important in this context because on August 27, 1972, members of the band "checked in" with the catalysts that had helped to shape their music. As a result, with all the other synergistic factors that I have just described falling into place, the music that emanated from the Dead on that day is arguably some of the most powerful psychedelic music ever created and, in turn, is also some of the most visionary music this planet has yet witnessed.

Accordingly, it has been a long-standing tradition for Deadheads to participate in focused "listening sessions" during which the music of this show (and others, of course) is used, with or without other mind-expanding catalysts, as a tool for heightened sensory exploration and meditative spiritual introspection. Engaged in responsibly, such Experiences can result in tremendously healing soul work.

The music of 8/27/72 is particularly powerful in that it affords those who encounter it in a focused setting the opportunity to experience the full spectrum of mental/physical/emotional being states available through taking visionary journeys. In his groundbreaking books *Beyond the Brain* and *The Adventure of Self-Discovery*[1] Stanislov Grof, one of the world's leading experts in altered states of consciousness, eloquently describes the more profound levels of heightened awareness one may experience during a visionary experience. The first level is the Sensory Barrier, in which there is an increased awareness of and within the five senses. The second is the Biographical/Recollective realm, in which one relives emotionally relevant memories. The third is the Perinatal realm, in which the unlocking of sensory, emotional, and physical experiences encountered during the birth process is experienced. The fourth level is the Transpersonal realm, in which one transcends individuality and becomes one with universal awareness, or cosmic consciousness. These are the more recognizable levels of awareness that one can move through when under the influence of psychedelics. The music of 8/27/72 is unique in that it has a tendency to bring the attuned listener to and through the deeper levels discussed here.

With this in mind, I should warn that one must take great care in deciding whether or not to combine this extremely evocative music with the more powerful mind-altering drugs, as the combination tends to result in the accessing of the Biographical/Recollective and Perinatal realms. As I will explain in great detail further on, parts of this concert display almost terrifying emotional intensity. For those whose psyches surpress potentially painful and difficult memories from their early lives, hearing such music when in a highly sensitized and emotionally amplified state of consciousness can be deeply disturbing (although often cathartic). Additionally, accessing the Transpersonal realm may result in the shattering of one's fundamental worldview, although with that said it should also be noted that many Deadheads have taken this communion with cosmic consciousness, this realization of nonduality, to be one of the most enlightening and ultimately rewarding experiences of their lives. In the seventeen years during which I have introduced people to this music, I have seen both difficult and joyous journeys come from listening to it in a focused setting.

The amazing thing about this music is that it affords the listener the opportunity to have such journeys *repeatedly*. On that day, with all the essential elements aligned, the band was able to function as a receiver and transmitter for universal consciousness. When people tune in to and resonate with this level of consciousness, they can access a holographic dimension that contains all of the archetypal energies, mythological images, and evolutionary history of the universe. Some might call this "god consciousness," or communion with The One. Regardless of what one chooses to call such a sacred communion, this is the sort of spiritual Experience that has nurtured and inspired many human souls since day one.

---

1. Stanislov Grof, *Beyond the Brain* (Albany, N.Y.: SUNY Press: 1985), and *The Adventure of Self-Discovery* (Albany, N.Y.: 1988).

Once access to cosmic consciousness is gained it can be shared with others who participate in the ritual. *It is highly significant that the Dead were pioneers of amplified music, sound powered by electricity, which for the first time in the history of Western culture allowed for the externalization of cosmic consciousness in a vibratory field so large that thousands of people could collectively experience it at one time.* Given the Dead's ability to act as the world's most powerful amplifier of psychedelic/transcendental harmonics, it should come as no surpise that they enjoy such a fervent following!

There is also something very different about the tonal quality of the tapes of 8/27/72. Listening to a good soundboard tape of this show under the right circumstances isn't like listening to a tape of most other shows, for while you can lose yourself in good tapes of many other shows, there's almost always some awareness that you're listening to a tape. Remarkably, I've found that with 8/27/72 (and with 2/13/70 as well) you can get completely "inside" the music, which surrounds you, causing the boundaries between you and the music to dissolve much more easily. While listening to the jams you feel almost as though you are flying. Once you are "inside," the music allows the listener to transcend the limitations of time and space.

Another characteristic of the Dead's music that sets it apart from that of other rock bands, and in turn plays such a critical role at this show, is the deep emotion inherent within it. The Dead were one of the first contemporary bands to stray from the confines of rock's wimpy love-song mentality and play music that also dealt with birth, death, enlightenment, sadness, and the mysterious, mythical, primal underbelly of American life ("Wharf Rat," "Cumberland Blues," etc.). This concert was made all the more special because the Dead chose on that day to play their more improvisational, spiritual, and bittersweet songs.

It's also crucial to note that the emotional state of the music evolves in tandem with band's own psychedelic trip that day. As they "get off" (during "China Cat Sunflower"), the music soars to a new, profoundly joyous level—a birth of sorts. At the apex of the hot afternoon concert (during "Playing in the Band," "Bird Song" and "Greatest Story") the energy is crisp, electric, brimming with youthful vitality like a flower in peak summer bloom. As the day begins to fade, the music turns heavy and mysterious, like the approach of death ("Dark Star"). And then, mirroring the classic rebirth archetype, the music emerges from the heart of darkness and transcends to joy ("Sugar Magnolia"). At the end of the show there is great reason to celebrate: the psychic (or psychedelic) gauntlet has been run and life has been reaffirmed. At virtually every turn the Dead chose on that day the perfect song to frame the emotional states they experienced as they evolved through their own psychic voyage.

These points make up the most important qualities that set this show apart from most others. On August 27, 1972, the Dead played music that resonates and harmonizes with the essence of life's most fundamental phases: birth, youth, maturity, death, and rebirth. Anyone who has had a psychedelic experience knows that all such voyages are evolutionary and usually mirror these phases, each of which presents the voyager with a different set of physical and psychological experiences (oftentimes they run in tandem with the Sensory, Biographical/Recollective, Perinatal, and Transpersonal realms).

To this day and beyond, the listener can attune to these same deep levels of awareness and peak life phases just by listening under the proper circumstances to the tapes of that show. Seventeen years of sharing this music with many others have proven to me that perhaps more than any other show it provides serious "transportation" music for the soul. (Given the enormity of this music, it would be advisable not to put a tape of the heavier segments on the stereo as background music for, say, your average social get-together.)

**THE CONCERT BEGINS**

In true Merry Prankster fashion, the original prankster Ken Babbs serves as emcee for the gig, showing up on the side of the stage from time to time, dosed to the gills, first to introduce the bands and then occasionally to make suitably trippy announcements. After an opening set by the New Riders of the Purple Sage, the Dead take the stage. Cutting off a lengthy introduction by Babbs, Phil steps to the microphone in a silly wide-brimmed floppy hat and thanks "the Springfield Creamery for making it possible for us to play out here in front of all you folks and God and everybody. This is where we really get off the best." Whoa! Is this a good omen or what? And this is only the first of the band's several mentions of "God" on that day. I know of no other show at which the Dead acknowledge the possibility of a higher force.

The Dead start up with a crisp rendition of "Promised Land." The sun is high in the sky; it is brutally hot. Then the Dead downshift into a slower mode and move unremarkably through acceptable versions of

"Sugaree," "Me and My Uncle," "Deal," and "Black-Throated Wind." To this point it is nothing more than what one would expect of a hot, run-of-the-mill outdoor show played in 1972.

But what happens next is remarkable and can perhaps best be described as an "unfolding." Jerry launches into "China Cat." At first it is controlled, a well-structured psychedelic mantra being marched through its regular paces. But as Jerry flies out of the first verse and bounds briefly into an instrumental interlude, one begins to feel reality vibrate and shift. The second verse trembles with intense energy as though all Heaven is about to burst forth. Something is about to change.

WHOOSH! VROOM! As the Dead leap off into instrumental space, one is struck with a clear sense that the energy level is rapidly emerging into a vibrant new realm. The band is beginning to peak and the musical colors are starting to swirl. Bobby takes the first lead. He's so amazingly on, so hot, so totally committed to *goin' for it,* that the listener can't help but smile in awe. The power is mesmerizing. This is one of Bobby's finest shining moments. Jerry picks up where Bobby leaves off and brings the group to an even higher plateau. As he peaks at the traditional point in the jam, the band members take a musical breath as though to settle down for "I Know You Rider." But they've just "gotten off," and realize the music is almost effortlessly pouring itself out of them. One can just *feel* Garcia grooving immensely in this newfound state of consciousness. He takes advantage of the chemically stimulated tactile and nervous system rush by refusing to settle into "Rider," jamming on instead. Jerry fingerpicks the band through yet another climax. Not to be outdone, and as if to musically verify that he too has arrived at a similar state of heightened consciousness, Phil pounds out a devilishly smart segue between the songs. (And what's even better is that this moment is captured perfectly on film. The movie cuts from an audience shot to an extreme close-up of Phil's finger at this precise moment. It's incredibly reassuring that at least one filmmaker in the world of rock music had the sensitivity to cut to a musician's fingers when it counted the most.)

In terms of the evolutionary progression of the concert (and the visionary Experience which is beginning to unfold) the "China Cat" > "I Know You Rider" evokes feelings of birth and youth—as the Dead's own psychedelic voyage is born, so is a newborn youthful vibrancy expressed in the music.

"Mexicali Blues" and "Bertha" follow to close this first sunstroked set. Although the merciless rays of the sun bring the guitars slightly out of tune, both of these songs are among the most rocked-out versions ever. Jerry is very obviously beginning to peak, as one would expect during the first hour or so of a psychedelic voyage, and the lightning-fast cascades of notes that result are so blindingly intense it's almost funny. Too high and too hot to play in tune, the band takes a break.

### SET 2: COSMIC MUSIC IS BORN BETWEEN MOTHER EARTH AND FATHER SUN

With the sun still high in the sky, the band takes the stage once again. They open with what is arguably the most psychedelic "Playing in the Band" of their career. The song starts a bit laid-back—it's still hot as hell and they're clearly tripping. But once they finish the opening lyrics and begin to jam, another transformation occurs. With the words out of the way, the need to play according to some preordained structure disappears and deep astral space travel immediately becomes the modus operandi. The musical conversation begins to soar, metamorphosing rapidly from one surreal climax to the next. One moment the music is turbulent and chaotic; the next it is a tightly bound ascending spiral soaring upward and inward. As the ensemble's creative intuition leads it further into uncharted realms, a miraculous series of musical epiphanies begin to occur. As each peaks, it then dissolves and is replaced by newer, more complex, fractal music patterns. For the "expanded" listener this swirling, melting, boiling music appears to mimic the chaotic evolutionary character of nature. One thought is inescapable: this is unlike any other music the Dead have ever played.... This is *VERY SERIOUS!!*

It quickly becomes evident that Jerry in particular has moved into an optimal performance level. After years of serious devotion to mastering a creative discipline, a musician may arrive at a point where there is no longer separation between player and instrument: they are one. As one, they become a conduit through which a higher energy can express itself. The marriage of instrument/body/mind/spirit becomes a tuner-amplifier. One gets the feeling when listening to this particular "Playing in the Band" that Jerry, who is playing music faster than he could possibly consciously think it, as fast as he's ever played for that matter, is allowing the spirit of the music to play itself through him. One might go so far as to say that he is amplifying the normally unperceived holographic, harmonic signature of cosmic consciousness. More simply said: he's tripping! And amazingly he's completely on the mark—not one breathtakingly fast note is off! This is the Grateful Dead doing what they labored for years to accomplish, playing visionary music of the highest caliber, going where no artists had gone before.

The "Playing in the Band" continues to evolve from one crescendo to another. Surprisingly Jerry is the one who tries on several occasions to bring the intensity down. But Billy, Phil, and Bobby are hopelessly wired together in thirteenth gear. So Jerry gives in and each time delivers an ever more intense climax. For the "expanded" listener whose psyche is open to this music, this section can elicit ecstatic, kaleidoscopic visions—a dazzling cascade of spectacularly intricate, multilayered, architectural, crystalline, cellular, geometric, liquid images all morphing into and out of one another in perfect time to the rhythm, tempo, and flavor of the music. It is, in the truest sense of the word, mind-blowing. In terms of the birth-life-death-rebirth cycle, this music harmonizes with life-energy during its most vibrant, self-actualized phase. The music has become powerful enough to trigger within the listener mental/physical/spiritual connections with the Biographical/Recollective, Perinatal, and Transpersonal levels of consciousness.

After one of the most intense musical climaxes we've ever heard Garcia pull off, during which he pumps his wah-wah pedal while rapidly fanning clusters of notes to achieve a matrix of harmonically pulsing sheets of sound, the band finds its way back to more earthly realms. Following a triumphant, wailing scream by Donna, the band rips through the final verse, closing the song with a perfect signature ending to one of the Dead's most intergalactic musical space voyages.

> "That old sun is making our instruments get mighty strange."
> —Bob Weir, August 27, 1972

With that epic flood unleashed there's simply no denying the musicians are peaking, and they wisely turn the intensity dial down several giant notches, settling into a slow, soulful recitation of "He's Gone"—a good choice for regrounding. "Jack Straw" follows and the film editor's interpretation of this song in the original unreleased version of *Sunshine Daydream* is adorable, but we won't reveal its sweet surprise for those who haven't seen it.

The Dead are unusual among rock bands in that a good portion of their music captures so poignantly the immense beauty of nature ("Eyes," "Let It Grow," "Here Comes Sunshine," etc.). So it should come as no surprise that Jerry would choose, in such a stunning natural setting, to play "Bird Song." Many would argue this is the best version ever played. When performed well this song conveys a sense of femininity inherent in nature. On 8/27 Jerry's bittersweet instrumental improvisations are astoundingly evocative of these feelings. His guitar cries; the notes soar and then disappear. During the chorus you can feel the band members struggling to avoid allowing vibrato inflections in their voices. Many people who have tried to sing while under the influence of a psychedelic describe how hard it is to keep the voice from "quivering." It can take enormous effort to keep the voice steady. Somehow they pull it off. With Jerry's guitar notes eerily floating in and out from the heat, the final jam is both immense and as fragile as a spider's web.

In need of yet another respite from the still-intense sun, the band closes the second set, but not before delivering a blistering version of "Greatest Story." Once again Jerry's screaming guitar notes seem to float in and out as Donna wails with all-out abandon. This version is one of the all-time best, following closely on the heels of the 9/28/72 Stanley Theater version, famous for its ferocious "Saint Stephen" jam.

This set, with the exception of "He's Gone," epitomizes the radiant quality of life being born and then rising into its peak. For the listener attuned to the resonance of this cosmic harmonic signature, this is music full of hope and bright, positive energy.

### THIRD SET: THE APOCALYPSE AND BEYOND

What happens next can only be described as transcendent. The third and final set of this show is in my opinion one of the most profound sets of music performed by any band in the entire history of music as we know it. In spiritual terms this set metaphorically represents an apocalyptic journey through the experience of death followed by the most intensely bittersweet reflection on the transitory quality of life and a phoenix-like rebirth into a heavenly state of eternal bliss. This is *the* heavy Dead set to end all heavy Dead sets.

The band takes the stage as the sun, thank God, begins to set. A dog on stage barks, and then, the band launches into... "Dark Star." Immediately, one gets the strange sensation that this is like no other "Dark Star" ever played. The tonal qualities of the instruments make the band sound as if they're truly in another dimension. Jerry's notes melt, bend, and contort in strange, unearthly ways. Bobby's guitar is more shrill than we've ever heard. The tape displays a subtle-yet-totally-noticeable, bizarre echo—as though a perfectly placed audience microphone is ever so gently mixed in. And yet one can hear no audience at any time. This effect is not present on any other Grateful Dead tape (the audio/soundboard mix tapes from 10/16–20/74 don't even sound quite like this). Whatever the cause, the net result adds to the surreal nature of this music. From the get-go this "Dark Star" really is unique.

Perhaps the most hypnotic, most striking, most telling visual image of the Grateful Dead to be found anywhere is the footage in *Sunshine Daydream* of Jerry during the first few minutes of this set. Obviously high as a kite, eyes intensely transfixed on some point out in space, Jerry appears to be in a trance. When we show the film to people for the first time, their immediate remark is often that it appears as though he is listening with all his attention for some transmission from a faraway place. And at one point a naked, long-haired, writhing man (seen earlier in the film) is visible here, undulating in total trance directly behind Garcia's head. With the sun brushing its final golden rays on the stage, the calm presence and sensitivity displayed by Jerry and the band during this quintessential moment is enough to make you hold your breath and shake your head in awe. It's the heaviest Grateful Dead moment I've ever seen. Really.

The Dead sail forth, at first cautiously exploring a number of closely related themes, each for a few moments, before moving on in search of a slightly deeper groove. It's as though they're testing the waters (or space, as it were). Throughout these initial delicate explorations, they maintain a steady, mostly slow tempo, methodically searching for *it* . . . the X Factor. At one point Jerry starts to intersperse his run of leads with the repeated toll of an open A string, as though accentuating an OM in the recitation of a chanted mantra. The A note becomes like a chiming gong, evoking a more sacred space. This evocation succeeds and accesses a deeper space. The collective musical mind is synchronized. While this pre-verse jam by no means approaches the intensity of the "Playing in the Band" from earlier in the day, it hints at a impending meltdown of much scarier proportions. Whereas the "Playing in the Band" offered a maelstrom of psychedelia, this moment didn't need a torrent of notes to enfold the listener in a profoundly altered state.

Amidst this very "Dark Star"–sounding jam a space opens and Phil quickly interjects a lovely, almost classical melody—Bach on acid, if you will!

The band then comes briefly to a familiar way station, the lyrics. Jerry sings, "Shall we go, you and I, while we can, through the transitive nightfall of diamonds," and suddenly it becomes clear that this is the end of the universe as we know it. One by one the troupe casts off into the unknown—first Phil with a confident lead statement, then Billy, who changes tempo to support Phil, then Bobby with a lush cross-rhythm, then Keith, and then Jerry with violin-like volume swells (which he accomplishes by moving the volume control on his guitar with his right pinky finger while picking with the same hand. This is one of the beauties of a Fender Stratocaster).

The Dead quickly throw all caution (what little of it is left) to the wind and surrender to the deepest, farthest-out-there part of their collective musical subconscious.

Perhaps the best way to describe the immense, at times *frightening*, series of jams that follow is to liken them to the progression of perceptions that advanced Tibetan Buddhist lamas say one experiences at the moment of death. Whether high or not, the listener hears music that has the power to elicit some very heavy feelings. It is not uncommon to see one's life flash before one's eyes.

Just when you can't imagine the music getting any more densely jazzy and psychedelic, the Dead come to yet another significant boundary marker. Jerry, Bobby, and Keith sign off as a drum and bass solo begins. Now, while Phil did occasionally step out front and solo throughout 1972–74, he has never been particularly famous for his bass solos. Unlike his other peers of the time—Jack Casady, for example—Phil's solos were often quirky, frustratingly halted, or minimalist. On this day, however, Phil was nothing less than monstrous. His solo, accompanied by Billy, is perhaps the fastest, jazziest, most rhythmic two minutes of his career. Unlike any other of his other solos, here he shows not the slightest mental or physical hesitation. He's playing such intelligent music so fast one can only conclude the music is playing him. Unfortunately, even the very best two-track audio- and videotapes in circulation are poorly mixed during this segment. Phil is slightly behind the drums. If only for the bass solo, let's hope the Dead pull out the sixteen-track Alembic recording of this set and remix it properly.

Eventually Jerry leads the rest of the band back in to the conversation and again the whole flavor of the "Dark Star" changes. Now, Jerry seems to know, if only subconsciously or perhaps intuitively, where he's going. No longer a delicate exploration, the journey proceeds at blinding speed toward the furthest imaginable reaches of improvisational visionary jazz-rock. Notes fly off Jerry's guitar like sparks off a grindstone. Keith Godchaux brilliantly weaves piano notes around Garcia's blazing guitar work.

Shortly after this new direction, Jerry and Phil fall ever so briefly into the "Feelin' Groovy Jam." Despite this version's brevity it is nonetheless significant, for as they float in and out of it, one can clearly see Phil in the film breaking into a delicious smile, eyes *brimming*, nodding to Jerry in deep satisfaction. This cinematic moment offers indelible proof that the "Feelin' Groovy Jam" was just as special to the band as it is to the listener.

But the "Feelin' Groovy Jam" is far too happy a vibe for this journey. Jerry is intent on bringing the ship of the Dead to and through the great abyss. With no hesitation the notes get darker, louder, faster, scarier. This is now the most serious musical vibe the Dead have ever elicited.

## DEEPER INTO SPACE THEY TRAVEL

By the summer of '72 Garcia had developed a stunning technique for playing a repetitive meltdown riff (known to many as the "Tiger Jam"). After many years of wondering how Garcia was able to accomplish this, I finally obtained an uncut copy of *Sunshine Daydream* that included "Dark Star" and, much to my delight, found that it features closeup shots of Garcia's hands while he plays this riff. One can clearly see that during this segment he rapidly repeats four consecutive descending notes while strumming very fast and brushing other deadened strings and while pumping the wah-wah pedal with his foot. This technique results in the quintessential meltdown riff.

Finally the music seems as if it can go no further: the deepest depths of the soul have been plumbed . . . the cathartic voyage through metaphorical apocaplyse has been made . . . the actual moment of symbolic death is upon us. An eerie sense of calm pervades the air. Jerry's notes cry more mournfully than ever before, and I do mean cry. It is as if the soul has lifted and, after taking one last look at the body, turns and moves into the white light (insert whichever death passage metaphor works for your own worldview). As Jerry's guitar sobs, Phil leans into his amp and hits a series of majestic power chords. Together they rise into one final mind-blowing crescendo. The moment of great passage is complete. It's as heavy a musical moment as the Grateful Dead ever had.

So, having made this intense journey, where to next? Watching the film one can clearly see Jerry turn to his bandmates and begin to play "Morning Dew" (quite fitting, considering that "Morning Dew" is about the morning after a nuclear holocaust). But Bobby has other plans. Instead of letting Jerry continue the voyage through such somber places he launches the band into a far more lyrical mode—with a waltz. He leads them into "El Paso." The shift in mood and the return to recognizable melody are, in their own way, both revelatory and apropros. (One should note, however, that despite its carefree and danceable vibe this song too is about death.)

While some would shake their heads in frustration at Bobby's censuring of "Morning Dew" this act did, in fact, set up another wondrous moment. After "El Paso," Phil leads the band into "Sing Me Back Home." This tune, performed by the Dead in the gospel vein, was written by Merle Haggard after having had a deeply felt experience in jail. A man by the name of Jimmy Hendrix (no relation to the rock icon) was sentenced to death for killing a cop. As Jimmy passed by Merle's cell on the way to his execution, he asked the warden to let Merle sing him one last song. Merle obliged and the seed for "Sing Me Back Home" was planted. The Dead first broke this tune out in 1971, but it didn't really come to life until the Europe '72 tour, where they worked it up into a real tear-jerking gospel number with Donna singing soulful accompaniment to Jerry's lead vocal. By August the band had this number wired.

As it turns out, the Dead couldn't have chosen a more opportune time to let this sad number rip. "Dark Star" > "El Paso" leads the listener through a phase in the musical journey that first resonates with the emotional qualities associated with apocalyptic death and then passage into the ethereal world of the great beyond. "Sing Me Back Home" fits the journey's spiritual progression perfectly; it metaphorically elicits feelings that the soul, having left the body and ascended to the great beyond, now looks back on life one last time and recognizes the bittersweet, transitory quality of mortal life.

The heartbreaking climax peaks first with a soulful, gutsy scream delivered by Donna Jean, only to be eclipsed by the all-time most soulful cry ever to leave the vocal cords of Mr. Garcia. Embodying all the emotion of the final sad sigh of a human life, this version is arguably the most spiritual moment in the Grateful Dead's career. I've played this for hundreds of Deadheads over the past fourteen years, and it is the one version that brings tears to more eyes than any other musical offering.

With this epic spiritual swan song delivered, the Dead could only drive the concert home with one tune: "Sugar Magnolia." With the very last light of day fading quickly, Bobby leads the band through what is one of the finest versions of this song ever played. The jam and the "sunshine daydream" go on and on with Donna wailing like a banshee above Bobby's screams and Garcia's instrumental attack. And what a fitting end for such a cosmic summer day under the sun. Having experienced such a transcendental musical experience in such a breathtaking setting, one can only ask if it has indeed been anything more real (surreal?) than a daydream. For the listener who is harmonizing with the spiritual progression of this concert, "Sugar Mags" conveys a feeling of rebirth. One is reborn into joy and life once more.

A credo is a statement of belief. In the case of music it can be an affirmation that such creative expression has the power to evoke a connection with the sacred. While obviously not created intentionally, if the Grateful Dead have any such thing as a musical credo, this third set is it.

The band encores with what was certainly the strangest choice of the day, "Casey Jones." Far removed from the spiritually immense journey just completed, this song seems to suggest that the Dead has landed, its trip is over, and it's back to business as usual, just like any other encore that has ever been.

Until several years ago, "Casey Jones" was considered within the greater tape trading community to be the only encore at this show. For years, however, there was a tape on which Bobby can be heard counting off, "One, two, one, two, three, four ..." before the tape goes blank. This puzzled us because not even *DeadBase* had the second encore listed. But then, just a while back, a pristine copy of the entire show surfaced, including a smokin' "One More Saturday Night" encore (although the show was on a Sunday). As with the "Casey Jones," the band sounds as if they've "landed." Nevertheless it's a rip-roarin' rock 'n' roll stomp, a tremendous version by anyone's standards.

## IN RETROSPECT

Over the past two decades I and others have dedicated countless hours of scholarly and meditative attention to the Grateful Dead phenomenon. In that time, having enjoyed hundreds of simply stellar shows, both in the flesh and via tape, we have found this show to contain the Dead's most transcendent and soulful music. Amazingly, tapes of this show continue to provide the opportunity for intense psychic exploration. Used properly this music is nothing less than a transportation device, rendering deep corners of the subconscious, psychic, and transpersonal realms accessible. *Sunshine Daydream* is priceless. It's the most powerful visual Grateful Dead imagery we have, eloquently capturing the Dead going full-tilt boogie at a pinnacle in their career, and it shows us what a gathering of the tribe can be in all its glory. We strongly urge you to petition the Dead for its release (or better yet, for a more extensive re-edit).

Barring some unexpected emergence from within the band's Vault of an equivalent landmark performance, we feel 8/27/72 deserves to be honored as the show that serves as the most potent example of what the Grateful Dead Experience was at its best: kindred spirits gathering in harmony with Mother Earth to embark together in creating a transformational ritual that feeds the soul. This is how I would like our scene to be remembered. Find copies of the video- and audiotapes and experience them for yourself. Do so in the proper set and setting. For many of you it will be nothing less than an enlightening experience. Enjoy.

JOHN R. DWORK WITH ALEX THOMSON, JEFF MATTSON, MIKE SAMETT, AND ALEXIS MUELLNER.
MANY THANKS TO KEN, ZANE, STEPHANIE, SUE, AND CHUCK KESEY

## 9/3/72

**Folsom Field, University of Colorado, Boulder, Colorado**

**Set 1:** Promised Land, Sugaree, Me and My Uncle, Tennessee Jed, Black-Throated Wind, Bird Song, Beat It on Down the Line, Mississippi Half-Step, Playing in the Band, Casey Jones
**Set 2:** Bertha, El Paso, Brown-Eyed Women, Mexicali Blues, China Cat Sunflower > I Know You Rider, Truckin', Loser, He's Gone > The Other One Jam > Drum Solo > Bass Solo > The Other One > Wharf Rat, Johnny B. Goode
**Set 3:** Cold Rain and Snow, Sugar Magnolia, Deal, Jack Straw, Ramble On Rose, Rockin' Pneumonia, Not Fade Away > Goin' Down the Road Feelin' Bad > Not Fade Away Reprise
**Encore:** One More Saturday Night

**1. Source:** AUD, **Quality:** B to B+, **Length:** 3:45 (Complete show except for "Cold Rain and Snow." Almost all between-song tunings have been sloppily edited out; many songs have the first couple of notes clipped.)
**2. Source:** SBD, **Quality:** B+, **Length:** 1:40 ("El Paso" through "Wharf Rat")

**Highlights:** Not much to choose from. Mississippi Half-Step has the highest energy level of any song from this show. Keith lays down some nice riffs during Brown-Eyed Women.

This is a very well-played and competent show, but has very few high points and never reaches the psychedelic intensity of other 1972 shows. The show starts off with a familiar sequence: "Promised Land," "Sugaree," and "Me and My Uncle." One might call even call this an overfamiliar start; about a third of all summer and fall 1972 shows started with "Promised Land" followed by "Sugaree." Things chug along nicely through "Tennessee Jed" and "Black-Throated Wind." "Bird Song" follows next, bringing us the evening's first real song of interest. It's played in standard '72 style, with nice, mellow jams between every verse. The fast "Beat It on Down the Line" that follows is a nice contrast to the long, slow "Bird Song."

"Mississippi Half-Step," still a reasonably new song (this is its eighth performance), and "Playing in the Band" are high points of set 2. "Half-Step" features some very bouncy soloing by Garcia, and "Playing in the Band," while never leaving the contraints of the 7/4 time signature, still manages to have some high-energy jamming wrung out of it. Along with the 8/27/72 version, we have a nice indication of where this song is going; only a month later, the band would start to crank out a steady string of the nice, long, and spacey versions that we've come to know and love.

"Casey Jones" is the first-set closer. The crowd comes alive for this, greeting it with the loudest cheering of the day.

Set 2, again, starts off in familiar fashion: a speedy "Bertha" gets things rolling nicely. Before "El Paso," Bobby gets off a bit of his trademark weird humor. Parodying Tina Turner's famous introduction to her version of "Proud Mary," he says:

> "Every now and then, we get the feeling that you'd like to hear us do something nice and straight. Well, we never ever do anything nice and straight. Well, we're going to take the beginning of this song and we're going to start out nice and straight. And then we're going to take the end of the song and we're going to finish it up REAL WEIRD."

(No, they don't—it's a very straightforward reading of "El Paso.") After running through competent versions of "Brown-Eyed Women," "Mexicali Blues," and "China Cat" > "Rider," Weir once again introduces "Truckin'" as the "number one song in Turlock, California. That's north of Visalia." "Truckin'" comes to a rather abrupt stop after only a short bit of postsong jamming, resulting from, Weir explains after the song, a broken string.

After "Loser," the band launches into its extended song sequence for the set. A mellow "He's Gone" very niftily segues into "The Other One," with Keith and Bobby responsible for revving up the slow ending of "He's Gone" by laying down a cascade of triplets until the rest of the band falls in line, comfortably jamming into the rhythmic pattern of "The Other One." After a few minutes of playing with the theme, things wind down into a short drums solo, followed by a VERY short Lesh solo, ending of course with the famous "Other One" intro and, not long after that, the singing of the first verse.

It's at this point where things get ultimately disappointing (perhaps because of the torrential downpour that occurred during this set). During the '72–'74 era, "Other One"s are at their most interesting. Between the two verses, the band usually tears apart the fabric of space and time, and patches it together in new and unusual ways.

At this show, however, things don't really get off the ground. There is some nice mellow and polyrhythmic jamming, and immediately following the first verse, there's a nice bit of something that Keith should have done more often: he puts the sound of his grand piano through a wah-wah pedal and he wrings quite a bit of feedback out of this setup. But other than this, there's not a lot of the tension-and-release roller-coaster ride that makes the Dead's extended jamming a pleasure to experience. Just at the part of the jam where things start to get nice and intense, with Garcia doing his signature tiger-growl guitar while the rest of the band dissolves into feedback behind him, Weir starts chording the "Other One" rhythm and after a short bit of jamming sings the second verse. Jeez, Bobby, what's your hurry? "Wharf Rat," slow and sweet, closes out the jam. As with the first set, the "Johnny B. Goode" that closes it gets the loudest applause of the set.

Set 3 is an oddity. It made up of a bunch of "set 1" songs: "Cold Rain" (no doubt in honor of the weather that day), "Deal," "Ramble on Rose," and so on. "Rockin' Pneumonia" is the high point of the set. A thoroughly unremarkable "Not Fade Away" > "Goin' Down the Road" > "Not Fade Away" reprise sequence closes the set, followed by a "Saturday Night" encore.

JEFF TIEDRICH

---

## 9/9/72

**Hollywood Palladium, Los Angeles, California**

**Set 1:** Promised Land, Sugaree, Me and My Uncle, Bird Song, Black-Throated Wind, Tennessee Jed, Mexicali Blues, Deal, Playing in the Band, Loser, Johnny B. Goode
**Set 2:** China Cat Sunflower > I Know You Rider, Friend of the Devil, Jack Straw, He's Gone > Truckin' > The Other// One, Stella// Blue, Casey Jones
**Encore:** One More Saturday Night//

**1. Source:** AUD, **Quality:** B+, **Length:** 1:30 (first set), **Genealogy:** MC > RR > DAT
**2. Source:** SBD, **Quality:** B, **Length:** 3:00
**Highlights:** Playing in the Band, Truckin' > The Other One

This tape shows the band once again, as it did in Eugene and September 3, 1972, in Boulder, jumping smoothly from theme to theme and creating some way-out jams. These jams are lightning quick and give the band a chance to explore the many frontiers that "Playing" would later uncover. The "China Cat" > "Rider" transition isn't as intense as August 27, 1972, but it is above average. The fireworks of the night, however, involve a tight "He's Gone" > "Truckin'" that enters a stellar version of "The Other One." At the conclusion of "Truckin'" Garcia launches into a magnificent stroll through jam alley. This "Truckin'" jam scorches into a deep wandering drift that builds into a maniacal pace, finally landing into a "Truckin'" reprise (which is cut out of the tape). After the reprise and another "Truckin'" strut, the band suddenly drops off, leaving only Lesh, who immediately attacks with a blistering "Other One" jam. The band follows for a few minutes before dropping and giving the reins over to Mr. Kreutzmann. Lesh opens the gates again with a thunder bass roll and commences one of the finer Lesh versus Garcia "Other One"s. The initial jam is monstrous and features an angry-sounding Lesh. Garcia slowly blends into this jam a tense overtone that naturally drifts into a deeper platform from which to improvise. Lesh follows for a few minutes but returns to more powerful bass bombs, sending the pace back to a brisk sprint. After a monstrous peak is reached, Jerry fools the band by not surging into the first verse but dropping into another deep meander. Ultimately Jerry crafts a strong enough base and launches straight upward, leaving the band behind. As with many Garcia leads, once the band finally catches up with him, he effortlessly leads them into verse number one. A bizarre and intrusive haze is created after the verse by Lesh, Godchaux, and Garcia. Jerry's playing basically resembles a kite high in the sky catching wind occasionally and drifting downward at times. Eventually the theme gets too weird with Godchaux's eerie organ and Lesh's bombs. Jerry takes the cue and finely crafts a respectful but not evil "Tiger" jam. Afterward the band drifts and one by one exits the jam until only Jerry remains. He enters an abstract deep acid-type jam that barely makes sense. This goes on for about five minutes and is truly impressive. The band returns and after some further jamming returns to the conclusion of "The Other One." This "Other One" demonstrates how Jerry used improvisational platforms to create his own language.

ROBERT A. GOETZ

---

### 9/10/72

**Hollywood Palladium, Hollywood, California**

**Set 1:** //Bertha, Greatest Story Ever Told, Mississippi Half-Step, Black-Throated Wind, Bird Song, Promised Land//, Deal, El Paso, Sugaree, Playing in// the Band
**Set 2:** //He's Gone > Truckin', Ramble On Rose, Beat It on Down the Line//, Dark Star* > Jack Straw* > Sing Me Back Home*, Sugar Magnolia*
**Encore:** One More Saturday Night

* with David Crosby on guitar

---

**Source:** SBD, **Quality:** B, **Length:** 3:00
**Highlights:** Playing in the Band

This performance features ups and downs. The first set begins with an upbeat "Bertha and a wild "Greatest Story." The "Half-Step" has impressive jams, but the Rio Grandeo chorus lacks the right harmony. At this point in time the band jumped directly into the Rio Grandeo after the final "Half-Step" verse and again to conclude the song. The transition is poor because Garcia has no opportunity to develop the momentum of it. The band changed this format on December 10, 1972, and thereafter to the now familiar version—in fact that version is probably one of their best. The following "Black-Throated Wind" and "Bird Song" are typically impressive. The band closes the set with an incredible "Playing in the Band." The jam format is once again similar to August 27, 1972, in Eugene, in that the band flows from one jam to the next, ultimately reaching some incredible peaks.

The second set begins with an average performance of "He's Gone" > "Truckin'." The "He's Gone" lags a bit, and the "Truckin'" jams, although hot, don't reach any magical peaks. The "Dark Star" is unfortunately cut into the tail end of the jam preceding the verse. One would assume, considering the time and the little bit that exists, that it is well done. David Crosby joins the band following the post-lyric jam and, to be polite, slightly gets in the way. Garcia brings the jam to outer space and performs an average "Tiger" but the jam never really takes off. Kreutzmann does a drum solo, and the band returns for a short transition into an average "Jack Straw" that goes into "Sing Me Back Home." In comparison to 8/27/72, this version lacks divine inspiration. The "Sugar Magnolia" is tight, but on the "Sunshine Daydream" jam Crosby really inhibits the momentum. Garcia at first struggles to find the rhythm and eventually locates an average jam. Weir and Donna, however, provide an impressive number of screams for the conclusion. The "Saturday Night" encore is typically hot.

ROBERT A. GOETZ

## 9/15/72
### Boston Music Hall, Boston, Massachusetts

**Set 1:** China Cat Sunflower > I Know You Rider, Friend of the Devil, Playing in the Band
**Set 2:** Bird Song, Truckin' > The Other One > Sugar Magnolia
**Encore:** One More Saturday Night//

1. **Source:** AUD, **Quality:** B, **Length:** 1:30
2. **Source:** SBD, **Quality:** A, **Length:** 0:20 ("The Other One"), **Genealogy:** MR > DAT

**Highlights:** China Cat Sunflower > I Know You Rider, Friend of the Devil, Playing in the Band, Bird Song, Sugar Magnolia

This chopped-up tape includes highlights from the first and second sets. The band lets loose a great "China" > "Rider" near the beginning of the first set featuring a long and twisted Weir solo and prolonged Garcia segue jam into the "Rider." Weir stands way out of the "Friend of the Devil," matching Garcia's harmony like a charm. The following "Playing in the Band" is another stellar version. Weir really directs the pace, immediately setting a fast, untamed speed. The "Playing in the Band" continues with the previous four versions' impulsivity and has the Dead doing psychedelic sprinting. Garcia matches Weir's pace from the start, racing down various hallways of confusing themes. When the jam finishes its zenith and begins the descent to the reprise, Garcia twists it in such a way that a certain tension is created centering around whether or not they will indeed make it to the reprise. Of course they do make it to the reprise, and a sense of overwhelming relief is present. The second set features one of their finest versions of "Bird Song." This particular one is tropical in nature. Garcia soars from branch to branch including some blistering jams in between. Weir provides the appropriate jungle sounds to a tee. The "Truckin'" is sloppily hot with Weir trashing his vocal cords at the song's conclusion. Garcia begins with the strut and immediately switches to outer space "Truckin'." The jam meanders a bit before abruptly dropping into a short "Other One" drum solo. Lesh launches the band with a bass roll and the pre-lyric jams are standardly solid. The pace is quite rapid and they don't slow down to meander. Weir, as with the first set "Playing," is definitely setting the pace, and the result is that they cruise from jam to jam, ultimately landing in the first verse. Garcia opens things up a bit after the first verse, and the band slowly falls into a deep abyss. The band reaches some pretty intense levels with Garcia managing to squeeze in two "Tigers" before returning to a smoking "Other One" finale jam. Although this "Other One" is impressively performed, the band doesn't venture out from the typical 1972 themes the way they do on the 9/17/72 in Baltimore or 12/31/71 at Winterland versions. They follow with an astonishingly hot "Sugar Magnolia." Weir screams in between the verses. Garcia reaches a ferocious momentum during the "Sunshine Daydream" jam, and Donna and Bob close the tune perfectly. The "Saturday Night" encore features Weir screaming wildly again but unfortunately is cut halfway through.

*Ticket stub for 9/15/72 at Boston Music Hall*

ROBERT A. GOETZ

# Reviews: September 1972

## 9/16/72
### Boston Music Hall, Boston, Massachusetts

**Set 2:** Dark Star//

**Source:** SBD, **Quality:** A, **Length:** 0:30, **Genealogy:** MR > DAT
**Highlights:** Dark Star

Deep into the second set the band decided to open things up and performed "Dark Star." As they launch into it with the opening chords, it sounds like they have all jumped off a cliff into a hidden ocean. The band kept a rapid pace the previous evening through their outer space jams, but on September 16, 1972, they really slowed it down. This "Dark Star" is a prime example. The pre-verse jams are slow and completely contemplative. It is one of the Dead's great masterpieces. The entire band is completely in sync from the beginning. While Garcia initially meanders around searching the area, Weir is already hinting toward new themes, and just like that they have captured a deep peaceful aura. This "Star" is lethargic in formation and flows like a film of crashing ocean waves in slow motion. Garcia slowly goes up and down bending various themes while the band slowly and hypnotically follows. The final eight minutes before the first verse feature Garcia in improvisational heaven with the band right behind him. This version definitely rivals 9/18/72 at Roosevelt Stadium and 11/11/73 at Winterland. Truly amazing. After the verse Weir and Lesh engage in a beautiful melody, bringing the band down a path into oblivion. The band is in absolutely no hurry to end this jam, and Garcia slowly molds it into a long climb straight upward into psychosis. Incredibly, Garcia transforms the theme into a raging storm of desire culminating in a twisted "Tiger." This jam lasts about ten minutes and is honestly one of their best post—"Dark Star" jams. After the storm subsides, Kreutzmann picks up the pace and the band races slowly into an awesome funk jam that eventually flows into a "Brokedown Palace" but unfortunately is cut just before the transition.

ROBERT A. GOETZ

*Ticket stub for 9/17/72 at Baltimore Civic Center*

## 9/17/72
### Baltimore Civic Center, Baltimore, Maryland

**Set 1:** Promised Land, Sugaree, Black-Throated Wind, Friend of the Devil, El Paso, Bird Song, Big River, Tennessee Jed, Mexicali Blues, China Cat Sunflower > I Know You Rider, Playing in the Band, Casey Jones
**Set 2:** Truckin', Loser, Jack Straw, Mississippi Half-Step, Me and My Uncle, He's Gone > The Other// One > Sing Me Back Home, Sugar Magnolia
**Encore:** One More Saturday Night

**Source:** AUD, **Quality:** B+, **Length:** 3:00
**Highlights:** Promised Land, Black-Throated Wind, Bird Song, Tennessee Jed, China Cat Sunflower > I Know You Rider, Playing in the Band, Truckin', He's Gone > The Other One > Sing Me Back Home, Sugar Magnolia, One More Saturday Night

On certain evenings in the Dead's illustrious career, they were "on" and on others they were *completely* on. On September 17, 1972, the band was completely on. In particular the band shows how well it worked together in creating new, diverse, sweet, psychotic, and definitely strange improvisational themes. Each song and jam performance on this night was exceptional. The first set provides stellar versions of "Promised Land," "Black-Throated Wind," "Bird Song," "Teneessee Jed," "China Cat" > "Rider," and of course, "Playing in the Band." The "Playing" jam begins with the regular fall '72 themes. About halfway through, however, Garcia begins to space out and the band drops all rhythm around him. The sound gets quiet and almost eerie. Weir begins a new theme and Jerry follows it, leading to a unique "Playing" jam that once again results in Garcia winding up in the lost zone. The band begins hinting at the "Playing in the Band" reprise and for a few seconds they all mold together helping Jerry realize the location—it has a joyful, homecoming sound. This version of

"Playing in the Band" shows just how deep and lost their jams were beginning to get. A marked transition occurred here between the previous August and early September "Playing"s and the subsequent versions. The band started to cast themselves deep into oblivion and work their way out as a team instead of just creating massive psychedelic jams. We see that no band member is really in control and how well they communicate with each other on stage.

The second set begins with a stomping version of "Truckin'" and features exceptional versions of "Loser," "Half-Step," and "He's Gone" > "Other One." "He's Gone" is slow and hypnotic: a foreshadow of what follows. After a short choral finale, the band sneaks around a bit before Lesh drops a thunder bass roll into "The Other One." The crowd cheers but little do they suspect the intensity that will follow. Garcia immediately responds and the band jams solidly for a few minutes before melting into a drum solo. Lesh returns the band with another thunder roll and Garcia bends them into a deep and even somewhat pleasant "Other One" jam. After the first set of lyrics, the band seems to enter a faraway universe. After inspecting and locating alien lifeforms Garcia begins communication. Apparently it fails because he leads the band into a slow-building whirlpool that develops into a massive, dark jam. Near its conclusion Garcia soars out of it and carries the band into an outer atmosphere. The jam simply is too much: Garcia builds it into a high-pitched "Tiger" like few others. The band continues to press forward, and Garcia does another "Tiger" before he finally does one last psychomelt into the ground. Peace is felt by all, and one feels as though a great battle has taken place; no one ever said "The Other One" was a "nice" song. Weir begins a new theme that builds into one of their finest transitions back into "The Other One." Upon reentry to our solar system, the band begins the traditional "Other One" jam, and upon reentry to the Baltimore Civic Center Lesh lets rip a massive blast of feedback. Truly one of the most spontaneously directed, improvisational, psychotic, and well-balanced "Other One" masterpieces has transpired. The chaser to this strong beverage is a sedating and depressing "Sing Me Back Home"—an appropriate moral to the story.

ROBERT A. GOETZ

---

### 9/19/72
#### Roosevelt Stadium, Jersey City, New Jersey

**Set 1:** //Bertha, //Greatest Story Ever Told, //Bird Song, //Black-Throated Wind, //Big Railroad Blues, //Me and My Uncle, //Sugaree, //Jack Straw, //Tennessee Jed, //Promised Land
**Set 2:** //Mississippi Half-Step, //Mexicali Blues, Brokedown Palace, //Beat It on Down the Line, //Deal, //Big River, //He's Gone > The Other One > Stella Blue//, //Sugar Magnolia, //Casey Jones, //One More Saturday Night
**Encore:** //Johnny B. Goode

**Source:** AUD, **Quality:** B–, **Length:** 3:00, **Taper:** Jerry Moore, Les Kippel
**Highlights:** Greatest Story, Big Railroad Blues, Tennessee Jed, Mississippi Half-Step

The Dead entered Jersey City on a hot streak and kept the drive alive. A sloppy but well-jammed first set results in one of the year's best first sets because of ferocious Garcia leads, the tight band rhythm, and intense screaming during nearly all of the songs. Each song performance is exceptional, but the "Greatest Story," "Big Railroad Blues," and "Tennessee Jed" stand out. This is rowdy Grateful Dead at its best. Instead of delivering a clean and flawless first set like December 11, 1972, at Winterland, the band makes errors, but even the errors sound awesome and well placed. The set cannot be immortalized, however, for it lacks a "Playing in the Band." The band probably would have done it but had to cut the set short because of piano problems.

The second set retains the pace and energy from the start with a fantastic "Half-Step" complete with stadium fireworks. Ultimately the band set into a relaxed state and enter "He's Gone," which has the bottom fall out of it into "The Other One." After the standard theme Garcia drops the band through harmonics into a deeper state. Lesh immediately kicks in with a groovy rhythm identical to that performed on the 9/23 Waterbury, Connecticut, and 9/28 Jersey City "Other One"s. The band follows this for a bit before Jerry surges the jam upward into a ferocious "Other One" theme, landing on top of verse one. Afterward the band drifts aimlessly, led only by Lesh sans Garcia. The theme Lesh creates is calming but suspiciously ominous considering Garcia's absence. Upon returning Jerry immediately directs the jam toward a "Tiger." The development toward the peak is long, deranged, and impressive but much tamer and less creative than on September 17 or 23, 1972. The transition back to "The Other One" is a struggle because Garcia refuses to enter a lucid frame of mind from which to build off of. Eventually they do return, and after a fine series of "Other One" jams enter a depressing "Stella Blue" rivaling that of August 22 in Berkeley. Unfortunately a complete comparison cannot be made because the final jam here is cut. The Dead end the show with rock 'n' roll and leave on a high note. For the most part they performed very well this evening but lacked a certain creative intensity. "The Other One" is indeed impressive, but it doesn't venture outside of reality into the paranormal.

ROBERT A. GOETZ

## 9/21/72

### The Spectrum, Philadelphia, Pennsylvania

**Set 1:** //Promised Land, Bird Song, El Paso, China Cat Sunflower > I Know You Rider, Black-Throated Wind, Big Railroad Blues, Jack Straw, Loser, Big River, Ramble On Rose, Cumberland Blues, Playing in the Band
**Set 2:** He's Gone > Truckin', Black Peter, Dark Star > Morning Dew, Beat It on Down the Line, Mississippi Half-Step, Sugar Magnolia, //Friend of the Devil, Not Fade Away > Goin' Down the Road Feelin' Bad > Not Fade Away Reprise
**Encore:** One More Saturday Night

    **1. Source:** SBD, **Quality:** A–, **Length:** 3:10 (missing "Big Railroad" through "Big River"), **Taper:** Les Kippel
    **2. Source:** SBD, **Quality:** A, **Length:** 0:45 (mid–"Dark Star" through "Not Fade Away" reprise without "Beat It on Down the Line," "Mississippi Half-Step," "Friend of the Devil")
    **3. Source:** AUD, **Quality:** B, **Length:** 3:30

**Highlights:** China Cat > Rider, Cumberland, Playing, Truckin, Dark Star > Morning Dew, Not Fade Away > Goin' Down the Road > Not Fade Away Reprise, Saturday Night

This long and somewhat underrated performance features the Dead continuing the September 1972 momentum. After a solid "Promised Land" the band enters a "Bird Song," and one can see just how tight they really are. During the first jam Garcia exits (a broken string?), and Godchaux picks up the improvisational lead perfectly while the rest continue as if nothing has happened. Garcia eventually returns and leads them into a typical hot selection of jams. The "China" > "Rider" is spectacular. Weir begins the jam into "Rider" with a long and winding solo before Garcia takes his turn and puts forth an awesome series of jams that molds into the "Rider." After a stellar bluegrass rendition of "Cumberland" that has Lesh standing out, the band launches into one of their all time finest versions of "Playing in the Band." No particular band member stands out in this version: rather, the band forms into one exploring instrument of communication. Instead of a long series of jams, there is only one long slow jam spanning over fifteen minutes that reaches several highs and lows. The band is really in sync—each member is really on. The second set opens with a great "He's Gone" that leads into a rousing version of "Truckin'." The "Dark Star" is long and hypnotic. While the band struggles to create a sense of structured jam, Garcia refuses and fuses a unique sense of weirdness. This "Dark Star" is quite abstract. I think of this jam as representing Garcia's exodus from society. The pre-verse jam is Garcia's trial by jury, in which he is found guilty. During the postjam he creates an intense escape. The jam is long and twisted, ultimately culminating in a slow "Tiger." After wandering around in its aftermath, Garcia begins teasing a "Morning Dew" but first enters an utterly breathtaking, heavenly jam that eventually melts beautifully into the "Dew." This stunning jam is quite like the brilliant jam that serves as a segue between "Dark Star" and "Sugar Magnolia" on April 8, 1972, in England. The "Dew" is slow and intense. The finale builds from the ground into a gigantic climax—truly one of their best. The band ends the show with some rock 'n' roll. The "Sugar Magnolia" > "Sunshine Daydream" jam has the band reaching incredible heights. The "Not Fade Away" transition jam into "Goin' Down the Road" is superb and rivals the August 22, 1972, in Berkeley version. Weir closes the show by trashing his vocal cords while managing to stay in tune, and the encore "Saturday Night" is, as usual, stomping.

ROBERT A. GOETZ

> ## 9/23/72
> ### The Palace Theatre, Waterbury, Connecticut
>
> **Set 1:** Big River, Sugaree, Mexicali Blues, Friend of the Devil, Black-Throated Wind, China Cat Sunflower > I Know You Rider, Jack Straw, Bird Song, El Paso, Deal, Playing in the Band
> **Set 2:** Promised Land > Bertha > Greatest Story, It's All Over Now, Baby Blue, Cryptical Envelopment > Drums > The Other One > Wharf// Rat, Beat It on Down the Line, Sugar Magnolia > Goin' Down the Road Feelin' Bad > Not Fade Away > One More Saturday Night

**1. Source:** SBD, **Quality:** B+, **Length:** 1:30 ("Playing in the Band" through "Wharf Rat"), **Taper:** Les Kippel
**2. Source:** AUD, **Quality:** C–, **Length:** 3:20
**Highlights:** Playing in the Band, Cryptical Envelopment > Drums > The Other One > Wharf Rat

A relatively average first set ends with an abstract and slightly sloppy version of "Playing in the Band." Overall the jam is impressive, but when examined closely, one sees that Garcia is operating at a deeper level than the rest of the band. Jerry seems to be constantly sending the jam toward a deeper level while Lesh and Weir struggle to maintain a structure. The result is some oddly formed themes with Garcia sounding a beat or two off. The effect is pleasant to the ear if you like lengthy atonal jams.

The second set begins with the Dead showing off a bit with a scorching "Promised" > "Bertha" > "Greatest." Later in the second set the band launches into an eerie version of "The Other One" after a rare "Cryptical" introduction. This version, like that of September 17, 1972, in Baltimore leaves "The Other One" and transforms into an improvisational beast. Initially the band fools around with a straightforward jam, but with the help of Weir plucking harmonics and Billy slowing the pace, the band hits rock bottom. Garcia picks them up and with Lesh's help wanders through several "Other One" funk jams. The final jam before the lyrics is towering intimidation. Garcia changes the band's pace back into the "Other One" chords and they rise higher than ever. At its peak Garcia erupts with a nasty "Other One" siren. Truly one of their best moments ever, featuring a stormmmmin' Jerry Garcia. After the first verse the theme changes to a frightening, dark tone. The band melts into a fanatical sprint toward the bowels of the Theatre. In some jams, like September 17, 1972, in Baltimore, the band sounds as though they are challenging, but during this jam it sounds as though they are being attacked and fleeing for their lives. Garcia seems to be the unfortunate soul taking the brunt of the attack. The feedback that he emits sounds as though he is in pain. Weir does an excellent job of masking Garcia by letting off strange sounds along with Lesh. The jam enters several off-beat atonal blasts that make no sense and should logically enter other jams. One is left wondering why and what is going on. Ultimately they wind this bliss back into "The Other One" and, instead of finishing off the "Cryptical" with the "He Had to Die" reprise (damn!), the band enters one of its finest "Wharf Rat"s. Weir provides a stellar performance at rhythm, letting off some awesome power chords. Garcia, though, turns this into one of his saddest performances. When he sings, "I wandered downtown, no place to go but just to hang around," it sounds as though he is crying. An excellent conclusion to another stellar September 1972 round-trip into the Dead's improvisational mind.

ROBERT A. GOETZ

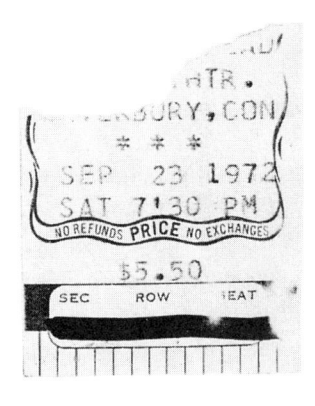

*Ticket stub for 9/23/72 at the Palace Theatre, Waterbury*

## 9/24/72
### The Palace Theatre, Waterbury, Connecticut

**Set 1:** Playing in// the Band
**Set 2:** Tomorrow Is Forever, Dark Star > China Cat Sunflower > I Know You Rider//, Sugar Magnolia

**Source:** SBD, **Quality:** A–, **Length:** 1:30, **Genealogy:** MR > RR > DAT

**Highlights:** Playing in the Band, Dark Star > China Cat Sunflower > I Know You Rider

This show is immortalized for another spectacular "Dark Star" masterpiece. The first set closes with a wide-ranging "Playing in the Band" that features some well-hit peaks by Lesh and Garcia. The second-set "Dark Star" steals the show. The pre-verse jam sounds like the band is a well-trained butterfly coasting through space at speeds faster than light. Lesh and Garcia bounce several themes off one another resulting in perhaps the best improvisational jams from this phenomenal month. They obviously reach an incredible plateau in what the band later called approaching "it." The final five minutes are genuinely awe-inspiring. While the rest of the band is soaring at a constant level, Lesh grumbles them to a low area that leads beautifully into what appears to be the verse. Garcia is teasing though, and through his guitar does a slow-motion back flip sending the band downward. Just as they catch up, Garcia has already landed back in the "Dark Star" theme. Lesh then takes another turn and opens another atonal theme that ultimately blends into the lyrics. This "Star" rivals those of July 18 in Jersey City, July 27, August 27 in Eugene, September 17 in Baltimore, and September 21, 1972, in Philadelphia, in the intense improvisational display by the omnipotent quintet. After the lyrics Lesh annihilates the Palace with a slow and massive bass solo. The band lets him reach a conclusion, then Garcia initiates a hypnotic "Tiger." This version develops slowly as if the band is savoring every second. Weir creates a tribal rhythm with Garcia plucking sinister licks and Godchaux providing the typical bizarre tonal horizon. They seem to me to have landed on a planet with a green sky and a purple sun—truly weird. Ultimately Garcia climaxes with an orgasmic and deranged screeching "Tiger." The band recovers for a moment in its aftermath, but Lesh refuses to let it die. He begins a sick and mutilated solo; As if this weren't enough, the band switches gears and enters a slightly psychotic jam that burns out into a wicked Kreutzmann solo. The band picks up at its conclusion and enters a funky strut jam. Near its conclusion Weir emits a single chord of "Sugar Magnolia," but the band doesn't follow. Shortly thereafter Weir calls out, " 'China Cat'?" and sure enough Garcia melts the band into it. This version is stellar. The jams are near perfect and Weir shines with an extended solo. The band reaches some excellent peaks in the transition into the "Rider," rivaling 8/27/72. The "Rider," although cut near the end, is flawlessly performed and concludes one of the Dead's finest and widest-ranging fifty minutes of improvisation.

ROBERT A. GOETZ

## 9/26/72
### Stanley Theatre, Jersey City, New Jersey

**Set 1:** Bird Song//
**Set 2:** Mississippi Half-Step, Greatest Story Ever Told, Tomorrow Is Forever, Truckin' > The Other// One > It's All Over Now, Baby Blue, Sugar Magnolia

**Source:** AUD, **Quality:** B–, **Length:** 1:30, **Taper:** Louis Falanga

**Highlights:** Greatest Story, The Other One, Sugar Magnolia

Entering the Stanley Theatre for the first of these three legendary shows, the band displayed a loose and almost laid-back attitude. Garcia takes the lead through most of this show, displaying at times lazy improvisation and at others serious jamming. The second-set "Half-Step" is played quite slowly, and the Garcia jams crackle with bop. The "Greatest Story" is really slow in comparison to other September 1972 versions. The final jam takes awhile to build up and gives Garcia ample opportunity to explore various dimensions and quacking sounds before ending it on a crazy note. The fireworks fly with the "Truckin'" > "Other One." Weir concludes the "Truckin'" song with some hair-raising screams before Garcia begins a patriotic marching strut through several jams. He slowly transfers the jam into "The Other One," and for a few minutes it is neither "Truckin'" nor "The Other One" but rather the in between. The transfer to "The Other One" enters through a back door into a deep jam. Jerry improvises at will for quite a while with the band right behind him. The aura is really laid-back and almost ambivalent. The jams are totally improvisational but not at all seriously powerful like the 9/28/72 Jersey City version. The result is a really impressive and quite rare version. Ultimately Garcia increases the pace, which leads to the first verse, but still it feels as if they didn't even want to enter it. After the verse, the band drifts for a little while before dropping into a Lesh solo. This solo is not the traditional "Other One" power solo but is rather atonal and resonant. Lesh drops a few bombs but mostly finds several tones and holds them. It is deep and contemplative. He concludes it with a thunder roll, and the band returns. Garcia takes the reins again and immediately enters a psychotic jam. It is short-lived, however, as he quickly brings it to a climax with an impressive "Tiger." During the aftermath the band drifts aimlessly as Garcia moans and Lesh hits some low notes. They decide to skip the final verse of "The Other One" and enter "Baby Blue." As with the 9/23/72 Waterbury version, Garcia forgets several of the lyrics but makes up for it with a great jam. The band finishes the set with an outstanding "Sugar Magnolia." Consistent with the show's pace, this one is slow and tasty. Garcia brings the "Sunshine Daydream" jam from the depths to monstrous heights. Weir and Donna close it with some great screams while Garcia creates an intense "wah-wah" rhythm.

ROBERT A. GOETZ

---

## 9/27/72

**Stanley Theatre, Jersey City, New Jersey**

**Set 1:** Morning Dew, Beat It on Down The Line, Friend of the Devil, Black-Throated Wind, Tennessee Jed, Mexicali Blues, Bird Song, Big River, Brokedown Palace, China Cat Sunflower > I Know You Rider, Playing in the Band

**Set 2:** He's Gone, Me and My Uncle, Deal, Greatest Story Ever Told, Ramble On Rose, Dark Star > Cumberland Blues, Attics of My Life, Promised Land, Uncle John's Band, Casey Jones

**Encore:** Around and Around

**1. Source:** SBD, **Quality:** A–, **Length:** 3:00, **Genealogy:** MR > C > DAT

**2. Source:** AUD, **Quality:** B–, **Length:** 3:00, **Taper:** Louis Falanga

**Highlights:** Morning Dew, Black-Throated Wind, Tennessee Jed, Bird Song, Playing in the Band, Greatest Story Ever Told, Dark Star > Cumberland Blues, Attics of My Life, Promised Land, Uncle John's Band, Casey Jones, Around and Around

This performance is easily one of the band's best ever. The first set opens with a strong "Morning Dew." Lesh stands out, dropping bombs galore throughout, but Garcia maintains a friendly and almost tame pace. The "Black-Throated Wind" has the typical melancholy Garcia-Weir conclusion, and the finale jam on the "Tennessee" is long and well done. The "Bird Song" jams are unusually long and well crafted; the band changes the evening's pace here from tight to *improvisationally* tight. This is certainly one of the better versions ever played! The band knows it too; before the last note of "Bird Song" fades away, one can clearly hear Lesh exclaim, "Dynamite!" The "Big River" is noteworthy because of the hot country Garcia jams and because it was the first performance that included a structured Godchaux solo during the second jam. The "China" > "Rider" features a hot Weir solo, an uneventful transition jam, and then an excellent "I Know You Rider." The set-closing "Playing in the Band" is scorching! The jam basically consists of four themes. The band is once again performing as one instrument, and the jams reach some great heights. During the third jam Garcia concludes with a variation on the "Tiger" chop, and Weir opens the fourth with a long solo.

The entire second set is noteworthy. A sweet "He's Gone" opens it and is followed with a "Deal" that features Garcia warming up for the remainder of the set with hot leads and unusual screams during the finale. Next the band pulls out a scalding "Greatest Story." The song itself is sung perfectly and the final jam sounds like a viciously dancing tornado that is swallowed by a whirlpool. Incidentally, 1972 "Greatest Story"s should be near the top of everyone's list for the best anthem of the Dead. After a boppy "Ramble On Rose" the band reaches some amazing levels with a legendary "Dark Star." The "Star" opens with about eight minutes of short jams featuring enthusiastic Lesh and Weir, but a careful and wise Garcia. Eventually Garcia creates enough inner tension, and the jam wanders into a vast open space. Keith Godchaux capitalizes on the opportunity and starts a lead that the band immediately follows. Garcia leads the band down a scorching path while effortlessly improvising to the max. This lasts for about ten minutes and is similar to other September 1972 "Dark Star"s before Lesh changes the pace with low bombs. Garcia matches him with moaning feedback, and Godchaux creates an intense effect with his outer space keyboard sounds. The ground beneath the band that has been created up to this point instantly vanishes, and they seem to be drifting in a thick and viscous tonal jelly. One would be hard pressed to find a "Dark Star" that reaches such an area. Lesh grumbles slowly and drops some deep bombs while Garcia lightly moans through feedback. Billy and Keith are absent: Bobby is lightly and barely strumming. Garcia begins to add a slight and innocent rhythm while Lesh opens up with more bombs. Lasting for about four minutes, this is probably one of the purest moments in Dead history. Labeling it is difficult, but perhaps it could be said that the band reached the nucleus of "Dark Star." It has an inspiring aura while hinting at demise. It is soft and tender and at the same time sad and gloomy. Not a sound is heard from the audience. Incredibly, just as the journey reaches an emotional zenith and silence ensues, Garcia *returns* to the formal structure of "Dark Star" and immediately sings the lone verse. Indeed, one of their most special moments has transpired. After the lyrics, the band opens an upbeat theme. An interesting contrast is immediately formed, however, as Garcia plucks a fast lead and the band pulls toward lower depths. Weir begins playing long power chords while Lesh is dropping long and resonant bombs. Eventually Weir joins Garcia's pace, and Lesh unexpectedly jumps into the opening of "Cumberland Blues." It takes the band a moment to catch up and the transition sounds like a cascading waterfall. One is left wondering why they never did this transition before or after this date. The "Cumberland" is intense. Garcia makes up for the missing "Tiger" through his jams; indeed the final jam is so hot that Garcia hints at a "Tiger" through it. This version should be known as the "Dark Starred" "Cumberland Blues."

Maintaining the special nature of this performance, the band next enters a bittersweet "Attics of My Life" that yearns for yesteryear. The band finishes the show up with amazing versions of "Promised Land," "Uncle John's Band," and "Casey Jones." Keeping up with the unusual set list, the band encores with "Around and Around," featuring some lightning Garcia leads and scary Weir screams. This is a must-have performance.

ROBERT A. GOETZ

---

## 9/28/72
**Stanley Theatre, Jersey City, New Jersey**

**Set 1:** Loser, Beat It on Down the Line, Brown-Eyed Women, Mexicali Blues, Mississippi// Half-Step, Black-Throated Wind, Don't Ease Me In, Big River, Tennessee Jed, Promised Land, China Cat Sunflower > I Know You Rider//, Playing in the Band
**Set 2:** //Bertha > Greatest Story Ever Told, Brokedown Palace, Me and My Uncle, Ramble On Rose, El Paso, He's Gone > The Other// One > Me and Bobby McGee > The Other One Reprise > Wharf Rat

---

**1. Source:** SBD, **Quality:** B+, **Length:** 3:20, **Genealogy:** MR > RR > RR > PCM > PCM > DAT
**2. Source:** AUD, **Quality:** B−, **Length:** 3:00, **Taper:** Louis Falanga
**Highlights:** Beat It on Down the Line, Brown-Eyed Women, Mexicali Blues, Mississippi Half-Step, Black-Throated Wind, Don't Ease Me In, Tennessee Jed, Playing in the Band, Greatest Story, Brokedown Palace, Me and My Uncle, Ramble On Rose, El Paso, He's Gone > The Other One > Me and Bobby McGee > The Other One Reprise > Wharf Rat

The previous evening's performance was surreal and perhaps one of their best of all time. The band faced a formidable task in attempting to create the same magic on September 28, 1972, but indeed rose to the occasion. As with most 1972 performances, these two alternated "Dark Star" and "The Other One" the 28th should be considered the fraternal twin of the 27th, featuring an "Other One" as ceremonious as the previous evening's "Dark Star."

In particular Lesh stands out among the quintet, providing a powerful presence through each song and jam. The first set is nearly flawless; it begins with a "Truckin'" that unfortunately is nowhere to be found on tape. Considering the remainder of the set one has to assume it was hot. "Beat It on Down the Line," "Brown-Eyed Women," "Mexicali," "Half-Step," "Black-Throated Wind," and "Big River" are all textbook stellar versions. The "Don't Ease Me In" has a monstrous Garcia solo, and the "Tennessee Jed" finale jam is delirious. The set-closing "Playing" is, like almost every other September 1972 version, mind-boggling. The jams are wise, jazzy, and explorative. Garcia improvises in a narrative tone while Lesh and Weir provide the animation. The band immediately reaches the necessary improvisational plateau and exploits it to a maximum. During the final jam Lesh is grumbling really low tones while Garcia howls a "Tiger" that reaches an exasperated emotional climax before drifting back to the reprise.

The second set begins with a rock 'n' roll version of "Bertha" that transfers into perhaps the most famous "Greatest Story" of all time. This "Greatest Story" contains a fully articulated "Saint Stephen" jam led by Garcia, but the jam that follows is ferocious and definitely rivals the intensity of August 27, 1972, in Eugene. After a soothing version of "Brokedown Palace," the band lets loose a maniacal "Me and My Uncle." Weir stands out on the following "Ramble On Rose" with a chopping rhythm. After the "Ramble On," Lesh starts playing "The Other One": here one can Garcia say, "Yah, yah, yah." The "He's Gone" is slow and hypnotic. The jams are jubilant, and just near its conclusion Lesh gets his wish as the band fades away for an "Other One" bass solo with Kreutzmann. This bass solo is powerfully funky. Lesh could have been a leading force in the Cold War considering the size of the bombs he was dropping. He concludes it with a massive thunder roll, providing the cue for the band to return. After some solid "Other One" jams, the band begins to drift to a deeper and slower state under Garcia's direction. An interesting contrast is developed here because Lesh just doesn't quit the muscular tone created in his bass solo. The result is a deep and notable "Other One" jam. Garcia and Lesh seem to be teasing each other and yet each having his own way. Jerry changes the pace again to a nonthreatening outer space tone. The jam gets way out there, reaching a point where just Garcia is plucking harmonics and Lesh is dropping bombs. This ultimately builds from the depths to a massive power jam into the first verse. After the verse Garcia and Lesh do become threatening; in fact they get downright evil. The jam molds into a sick and demented atonal jam. Garcia creates such terrifying and weird sounds with Lesh that it sounds as though they have reached the seventy-second dimension. This builds into a massive and devastating "Tiger." In its aftermath it sounds as though the Stanley Theatre was collapsing from the rafters. The band wallows in it for a moment before Weir brightens the mood by entering "Me and Bobby McGee." This version is incredible. The vocals are supreme and Garcia's solo sounds like a calming breeze deep in the Louisiana bayou. Lesh concludes the tune with a massive bomb, and the band immediately returns to another powerful "Other One" jam. This goes into a slow and transcendental "Wharf Rat." Garcia screams during the "everyone saaayyys I come to no good," and the final jam features an appropriately rowdy Weir on rhythm. This version is so calm and tender that it could be heard not as a story about a drunken bum but as the philosophical history of the human race. The concerts of September 27 and 28, 1972, reached some legendary moments. The versions of "Dark Star" and "Other One" performed are some of their very best ever.

ROBERT A. GOETZ

---

## 🌀 10/2/72 🌀
### Civic Center Arena, Springfield, Massachusetts

**Set 1:** Bird Song, Black-Throated Wind, El Paso, Greatest Story Ever Told, Jack Straw, Don't Ease Me In, Playing in the Band, Casey Jones
**Set 2:** Promised Land, China Cat Sunflower > I Know You Rider

**Source:** AUD, **Quality:** D+, **Length:** 1:20

**Highlights:** Black-Throated Wind, Playing in the Band

**Comments:** The sound here is hissy and very distant. The drums, for example, sound like they've got an expensive shag rug glued over the skins. The instruments can be made out if one refuses to give up.

This is probably a mix of first- and early second-set tunes. The playing is sharp, as was the norm for the fall of '72 tour, arguably the band's career peak. Wiping the mud from my ears reveals a decent, well-explored "Bird Song." "Black-Throated Wind," underrated and in need of attention from this era, typically sparkles with a long, hot closing jam led by Weir's emphatic singing.

Once again, "Playing in the Band" is a cave of wonders. This one has the band tossing up a variety of off-speed pitches behind Garcia, who chops and dices his leads in an urgent, frenzied fashion. While he wails, Lesh finds a form in playing slow but insistent "Ga-roo, Ga-roo"s. When Keith picks it up, Weir slows down to nail those strange chords only those huge hands of his can reach. When Garcia lets up to refocus, Billy goes wild. So it goes with this version.

MICHAEL M. GETZ

## 10/18/72
### Fox Theatre, St. Louis, Missouri
**Set List:** Dark Star

**Source:** FM-SBD, **Quality:** A, **Length:** 0:30, **Genealogy:** MC > DAT
**Highlights:** Dark Star

Along with 10/28/72, this was masterfully chosen and introduced by the Grateful Dead's archivist, Dick Latvala, when he hosted the *Grateful Dead Hour* for David Gans. The Dead sound like a polished quintet here: light, humble, and prone to sudden mood swings. Quickly dispensing with the song's intro, the band heads straight into the unknown. For five minutes or so, they play little games of tag, drawing each other in, making sure everyone's all ears. Garcia then hangs a quick left as a test: nobody's fooled. Good. A short, very controlled melt ensues before they rise up into the first and only verse. This is sung with an unusually serious cosmic conviction by Garcia, betraying the intensity of the mood onstage. More exploring follows. Patiently and thoughtfully the band moves as one organism. Garcia begins the pre-"Tiger" hiccup chops. Will Phil solo yet? Nope. Instead, the band drops off the map into ground zero. Finally, as sleigh bell sounds from Billy ring out Lesh rips into a highly melodic chordal solo. Latvala and Gans have nicknamed this solo the "Philo Stomp." Billy picks up the pace. Jerry comes in with some sweet licks. The whole band comes in to play off of Lesh's towering riffs. Lesh, of course, counters it by blasting the whole thing to smithereens and then marching them all into a gorgeous "Feelin' Groovy Jam." A few minutes later the faint notes of "Morning Dew" can be heard, but Dick quickly fades it out. Damn.

MICHAEL M. GETZ

## 10/19/72
### Fox Theatre, St. Louis, Missouri

**Set 1:** Promised Land, Mexicali Blues, Bertha, El Paso, China Cat Sunflower > I Know You Rider, Beat It on Down the Line, Dire Wolf, Around and Around, Casey Jones
**Set 2:** Big River, Bird Song, Truckin' > The Other One > He's Gone > The Other One Reprise, Greatest Story Ever Told, Not Fade Away > Goin' Down the Road Feelin' Bad > Not Fade Away Reprise

**Source:** AUD, **Quality:** B, **Length:** 1:35
**Highlights:** Around and Around, Casey Jones, Big River, Bird Song, Truckin' > The Other One > He's Gone > The Other One Reprise, Greatest Story, Not Fade Away > Goin' Down the Road Feelin' Bad > Not Fade Away Reprise

The band put forth a solid show on this evening, featuring their typical 1972 solid first set and explorative second set. Lesh, in particular, stands out during each song and arguably directs the entire "Other One." Noteworthy from set 1 are arousing versions of "Around and Around" and a stormin' "Casey Jones" closer. As with basically the entire tour, the set itself is nearly flawless. The second set opens with a really juicy "Big River." Garcia is on fire, and the only rest he takes from improvising is during the Keith Godchaux solo. The following "Bird Song" is, like almost every other 1972 version, outstanding. Lesh really wreaks havoc on this usually innocent and sweet song by forcing Garcia into raging themes that are indeed quite rare for it. Returning for the final verse, the calming effect of Garcia's voice seems almost out of place. The band enters solar exploration through a "Truckin'" vehicle. This solid version launches Garcia into a quality "Truckin'" strut jam that drives the band up and down at a ferocious pace for several minutes before they slow down for a *barking* transitional jam. Lesh begins teasing "The Other One" and, sure enough, begins it before the band drops all playing for a short drum solo. Lesh, the first to return, does a short but hypnotic bass solo before fully commencing "The Other One" with a massive thunder roll. The band follows a regular "Other One" jam for a little while before Garcia and Lesh begin meandering to a deeper level. Lesh is really in control here, dropping numerous bombs left and right. Garcia makes several different attempts to drive the jam to a really deep level, but Lesh refuses and consistently returns back to a powerful "Other One" theme jam. Indeed, it appears that Garcia and Lesh are challenging each other for the steering wheel. Ultimately, Garcia gets his way and the result is a strange melting sound before they surface for the first verse. After the verse the band enters a calm and nonthreatening drift. Each band member seems to be cautiously dipping a big toe into an unknown pool of fluid, testing for its temperature. Garcia is the first to take the plunge; he dives into an "Other One"–type strut jam with Lesh chasing behind with the rest of the band. This jam wanders for a while before Garcia burns it out with a "Tiger" jam foreshadow. The band takes a small break, leaving only Keith and Billy to fill the gap. Keith, not surprisingly, rises to the occasion and begins the "Tiger" space with a really bizarre solo. Weir is the first to return, beginning a fast and galloping rhythm. Lesh and Garcia join in and enter another lightning fast jam where once again it is difficult to tell who is leading. Ultimately the jam dies out, leaving Garcia with the task of building a monster from an almost silent base. He accomplishes this, carrying the band beneath him into a surging wave of energy or an approaching tidal wave. Just as it is reaching its massive peak, Garcia soars above it like a comet and does an impressive "Tiger" before annihilating the Fox Theatre. Lesh and Garcia really go all-out, and the result is a short medley of strange sounds. After its conclusion the two masters of this creation are trading epilogue thoughts through "Feedback" when Weir, whose most notable contribution to the jam up to that point was singing the first verse, decides to cut their conversation by returning the rhythm to a basic "Other One" theme. Lesh and Jerry are slow to follow this lead and, in fact, sound a little perturbed. Jerry wanders a bit and really makes the final decision as he enters, of all things, "He's Gone." This version is actually quite tender and well played. Typical at first, the final jam is slowly and carefully molded back into "The Other One" by Garcia. This transition is impressive, and it leads directly into the final verse. This particular "Other One" features the amazing duo of Lesh and Garcia and the incredible improvisational magic created through their taunting, challenging, tasting, and mind reading of each other. The "Greatest Story" that follows features the typical scorch jam finale, but what is noteworthy is that for the final few seconds it could be argued that Garcia does a "Saint Stephen" jam that is nowhere near as structured or defined as that of September 28, 1972, in Jersey City. The set-closing "Not Fade Away" > "Goin' Down the Road" > "Not Fade Away" is an all-encompassing masterpiece that is the twin of those played on August 22, 1972, in Berkeley and September 21, 1972, in Philadelphia. The transition to "Goin' Down the Road" is chunky and well improvised. The "Goin' Down the Road" finale jam features intense improvisational glee from Garcia, and during the final chorus Weir lets loose several screams. Of course the "Not Fade Away" reprise is exceptional. Garcia provides an impeccable rhythm, and Weir lets out about six deranged but in-tune yelps.

ROBERT A. GOETZ

---

### 10/23/72

**Performing Arts Center, Milwaukee, Wisconsin**

**Set 1:** Promised Land, Sugaree, Big River, Loser, Jack Straw, Deal, El Paso, Tennessee Jed, Black-Throated Wind, China Cat Sunflower > I Know You Rider, Mexicali Blues, Stella Blue, //Beat It on Down the Line, //Rockin' Pneumonia, Playing in the Band//
**Set 2:** //Bertha, Me and My Uncle, Brown-Eyed Women, Greatest Story Ever Told, Brokedown Palace, Dark// Star > Mississippi Half-Step > Me and Bobby McGee, Tomorrow Is Forever, Sugar Magnolia, Uncle John's Band
**Encore:** One More Saturday Night//

**Source:** AUD, **Quality:** A, **Length:** 3:00

**Highlights:** China Cat Sunflower > I Know You Rider, Stella Blue, Beat It on Down the Line, Rockin' Pnuemonia, Playing in the Band, Dark Star, Sugar Magnolia, Uncle John's Band, Saturday Night

This all-around solid show displays one of Garcia's finest improvisational efforts of the tour during "Dark Star." The first set begins with solid renditions through the first half, but they end the set rising well above normal expectations. The "China Cat" features a long Weir solo before Garcia takes over and does a fantastic transition jam into the "Rider," similar to that of August 27, 1972, in Eugene. The "Stella Blue," although adolescent in form, is performed with moving sadness. The finale jam soars through tears and remorse. Weir issues a wake-up call with a very well-sung "Beat It on Down the Line," and the "Rockin' Pneumonia" that follows steals the set. Garcia and Godchaux trade about four solos during the jam; they must have made everyone get up and groove. The "Playing in the Band" is unfortunately cut after about nine minutes, but we do get the beginning of the jam, which features several short but tasty themes.

The second set begins with a rousing version of "Bertha" and stays through "Brokedown," but the show explodes with the following "Dark Star." Usually during the pre-verse jam several different themes arise, but on this evening Garcia improvises incessantly up to the verse. Succinctly put, Jerry was totally on fire. The band provides a kaleidoscope-like aural landscape while Jerry simply soars up and down through melts, dives, leaps, and escapes. On several different occasions the band slows way down while Jerry employs a sparking meltdown. At times it sounds like a storm of colorful dust particles. After the verse Garcia picks up right where he left off with a deep "Dark Star" theme. This molds into a strange beast before Jerry pauses for a Godchaux lead. As Keith has done many times before, he titillates Garcia into a "Tiger" space. Jerry returns and follows the hint into a savage nonsensical jam that bursts into a screeching "Tiger." The epilogue features Garcia and Weir moaning through feedback while Lesh is emitting strange growls, as if to represent the beast that is slowly and painfully dying. Ultimately the misery is concluded, and Garcia aptly enters an uplifting and boppy "Half-Step." The band finishes this incredible show with stomping versions of "Sugar Magnolia," "Uncle John's Band," and "One More Saturday Night," which is unfortunately cut halfway through.

ROBERT A. GOETZ

---

### 10/26/72
**Music Hall, Cincinnati, Ohio**

**Set 2:** Playing in the Band, Deal, Me and My Uncle, Brokedown Palace//, Truckin' > Nobody's Fault but Mine Jam > Dark Star > Sugar Magnolia, Sing Me Back Home, One More Saturday Night

**Source:** SBD, **Quality:** B/B+, **Length:** 1:40
**Highlights:** Playing in the Band
**Comments:** There is a light buzz and a rather flat but clear presentation of the instruments. Billy, though, is playing with a very loose snare drum, giving him more percussive sounds and fewer of those jazzy rolls a tight snare gives; also, his bass drum is high in the mix while Lesh, unfortunately, is low.

The highlight of this set comes right away: a twenty-five-minute "Playing in the Band." The first part gallops briskly away, driven by Garcia and Billy. As the band prepares to descend into the reprise, part 2 begins when they blow it off and gobble some more space. Garcia continues to play aggressively, balancing on a wire with some searing, high-pitched notes. Then everyone bails out, leaving Billy to back up a strange Lesh solo. It sounds like the theme song for some TV action program. Weird. After a few minutes Garcia slips in behind Lesh and rides him for a while, escalating the music with more singeing notes. At this point the music explodes, reaching the desired peak. Garcia also comes up with some odd, alluring melodies along the way to the well-earned reprise.

"Truckin'" goes into an amalgram of "Nobody's Fault" and a blues jam, neither really dominant. Things slow down as Garcia's blues scale wails and fades. Sounds of a "Truckin' reprise" are teased until Billy plays that ceremonial tom-tom roll that usually means . . . "Dark Star." Lesh kicks it into gear and off they go . . . *nowhere*. For twenty-plus minutes they aimlessly noodle around with lethargic minds and arthritic fingers. Bottle this up and you've got a cure for insomnia. How *very* unusual for this period in their career!

The segue into "Sugar Magnolia" is slick, and the band jumps all over it, pouring out their frustration. "Sing Me Back Home" is well sung, with Donna doing a very nice job.

MICHAEL M. GETZ

## 10/27/72
**Veterans Memorial Auditorium, Columbus, Ohio**

**Set 1:** Bertha, Mexicali Blues, Loser, Jack Straw, Big Railroad Blues, El Paso, Sugaree, Beat It on Down the Line, Brown-Eyed Women, Box of Rain, Black-Throated Wind, Tennessee Jed, Me and Bobby McGee
**Set 2:** Tomorrow Is Forever, Promised Land

**Source:** SBD, **Quality:** B–, **Length:** 1:30
**Highlights:** Big Railroad Blues, Box of Rain, Black-Throated Wind

This standard but flawlessly played first set features Billy at his best. Highlights include above-average performances of "Big Railroad Blues," "Black-Throated Wind," and "Box of Rain." This tape is most likely missing a first-set-closing "Playing." The little bit of the second set we have contains a horrendously out-of-tune Donna and Jerry on "Tomorrow Is Forever."

ROBERT A. GOETZ

## 10/28/72
**Public Hall, Cleveland, Ohio**

**Set 2:** Dark Star//

**Source:** SBD, **Quality:** B+, **Length:** 0:22, **Genealogy:** MC > DAT
**Highlights:** Dark Star

From the relatively untapped October 1972 shows surfaces this incredible "Dark Star." Garcia immediately sets the pace at a calm level developing a surreal aura. The pre-verse jams are profoundly meditative and require constant attention to follow the intricacies. The band follows Garcia as he flows theme to theme, bringing them up and down. Several exceptional jams occur as a result of Garcia's effortless deep improvisational skill, then beautifully blend into the lyrics. Before the lyrics a placid pace has been set, but afterward, as if a huge thunderstorm cloud has surfaced, the theme turns grim. The band gets into a deep drift with Lesh dropping bombs. A calm sets in before the storm, then Lesh spontaneously begins a stomping bass solo with a definite strut theme. It is a groovy "something great just went my way" jam. Only Billy plays with him. Unfortunately, Lesh did this "Philo Stomp" jam only a couple of times in the band's history. Garcia picks up the theme and twists it back into the forecasted storm. A sinister, explosive jam results with Garcia melting into an electrocuted state. This jam is one for the record books. The band cools down and sets in for the remainder of the storm. The band moans a bit with Kreutzmann setting a chaotic pace. Ultimately Garcia falls into a exceptional and perhaps the longest "Tiger" ever. Afterward the tape drifts out and leaves the listener shivering. As with several of the omnipotent 1972 "Dark Stars," the Dead bring you through a palace of gardens only to turn the tables and drive you to unfathomable and mind-blistering heights.

ROBERT A. GOETZ

## 10/30/72
**Ford Hall, Detroit, Michigan**

**Set 1:** Bertha, Me and My Uncle, Deal, Black-Throated Wind, Sugaree, El Paso, Bird// Song, Big River, China Cat Sunflower > I Know You Rider, Jack Straw, Don't Ease Me In, Mexicali Blues, Box of Rain, //Playing in the Band
**Set 2:** Truckin', Ramble On Rose, Promised Land, Tomorrow Is// Forever, //Around and Around, Candyman, Greatest Story Ever Told, Mississippi Half-Step, Sugar Magnolia > Goin' Down the Road Feelin' Bad > Not Fade// Away Reprise
**Encore:** Uncle John's Band

**Source:** AUD, **Quality:** B+, **Length:** 3:20, **Genealogy:** MC > C > C > DAT
**Highlights:** Deal, Black-Throated Wind, Bird Song, Playing in the Band, Truckin', Ramble On Rose, Greatest Story, Sugar Magnolia > Goin' Down the Road > Not Fade Away, Uncle John's Band

On this final show in October 1972 the band delivered a solid performance in mostly rock 'n' roll format. The first set takes off during Garcia's final lead on "Deal." The "Black-Throated Wind" that follows is heart-wrenching. The contrast between Weir's wails and Garcia's guitar moans during the finale will deeply sadden the listener. The "Bird Song" midway through the set really soars during the jam. Garcia flies through the perfect rhythm provided. The "Playing in the Band" is definitely the highlight of the first set. Unfortunately it is cut, but despite the loss, we are left with about twenty minutes of solid improvisational jamming. At different times the band aimlessly falls into the bowels of the auditorium, reaching screeching lows before Garcia lifts them to the rafters. The theme is slightly haunted, which makes sense considering the next night is Halloween.

The second set begins with an outstanding performance of "Truckin'." The jam lasts about fifteen minutes and emits nothing but high-energy "Truckin'" particles. Garcia rips through several blistering themes with the band providing impeccable rhythm. The "Ramble On Rose" and "Greatest Story" are also exceptional. The remainder of the show is strictly tonal in nature. The final trio of "Sugar Magnolia," "Goin' Down the Road," and "Not Fade Away" are particularly impressive. Weir ends the show screaming his lungs out on the "Not Fade Away" while Garcia matches Weir's rhythm so precisely that one is left wondering if only one person is playing. The "Uncle John's Band" encore is sweet and appropriate, containing an extended Garcia jam to wrap it up.

ROBERT A. GOETZ

---

## 11/13/72

### Stars and Stripes Auditorium, Kansas City, Missouri

**Set 1:** Cold Rain and Snow, Beat It on Down the Line, Loser, Jack Straw, China Cat Sunflower > I Know You Rider, Box of Rain, Black-Throated Wind, Candyman, El Paso, Tomorrow Is Forever, Around and Around, Brown-Eyed Women, //Playing in the Band
**Set 2:** Promised Land, Ramble On Rose, Me and Bobby McGee, Dark// Star > Morning Dew, Sugar Magnolia, Casey Jones
**Encore:** Johnny B. Goode

---

**Source:** AUD, **Quality:** B–, **Length:** 3:00
**Highlights:** Dark Star > Morning Dew, Sugar Magnolia, Casey Jones, Johnny B. Goode

November 13 opened audaciously with "Cold Rain and Snow." The band's vocals created a sweet harmony even during the extended wails, but the musical rhythm created a frantic contrast that evidently foreshadowed the remainder of the evening. One wonders why the band didn't open with this more often in 1972. The first set is well done. Standing out is another classic version of "Black-Throated Wind" complete with livid jealousy screams, an eardrum-piercing harmonics solo during the "Loser," a "Tomorrow Is Forever" that is mostly in tune, and a scorching "Round and Round." Although mostly a solid first set, the jams during the songs seem to be yearning for a deeper challenge. Instead of finishing the set with "Round and Round," as they logically may well have done, they instead indulge themselves with "Playing in the Band" and provide the more-than-fortunate audience member with the first of two incredible mind odysseys. This "Playing" begins carefully as if the band is on guard or overly cognizant of their surroundings. Weir breaks this trend by leading them into a faster pace, which Garcia bites at. Soon the band falls into this groove and they are on their way to another one of their finest readings of this song. It really sounds as if the band was transformed into a strange human antibody and is scanning through the system in search of pathogens. Soon the band locates a virus and commences attack. The jams get hotter and faster, with Lesh grumbling, Weir plastering chord strums, and Garcia providing the laser therapy through his wah-wah sprints. What really makes this one of their finer "Playings," however, is that instead of having a finely crafted jam-to-jam structure, with each successively getting faster and faster, this version creates a certain tension that the band indeed may not survive this encounter—that they perhaps shouldn't have gone on this particular antibody trip. At times Garcia moans his feedback, Weir emits extended sounds slowing the pace, and Lesh hits higher pitched bombs suggesting a sense of lostness in their attack. Just when it seems that this pathogen may indeed take over, however, Jerry resorts to the last military power known to any of your common 1972 antibodies: Nuclear Tiger Power. Jerry switches on the "Tiger" and progressively scorches the jam systematically annihilating all sides of musical spectrum. The aftermath leaves the band feedbacking their way into the reprise and the listeners are left shaking their heads in remembrance of the days when the jams ruled, the singing apparently took second stage, and Garcia was literally a king.

After a solid second-set song introduction, the Dead explore the outer regions of their psyche again with a wide-ranging "Dark Star." The pre-verse themes are carefully constructed by Garcia. Several jams occur that reach some impressive heights, but what is noteworthy here is that they are all gloomy or melancholy in nature. This "Star" could be considered as an expression of grief or bereavement. Jerry carries the band up and down, ultimately culminating in saddening emotional zeniths. Garcia at times sounds as if he is crying through his improvisation. After the verse the band drifts for a little while before opening up an immense psychotic jam that rivals that of September 17, 1972, in its massive whirlpool form. Lesh and Garcia reach a torrential "Tiger" that sounds to me like a conscience burning in desire. Afterward they calm for a few seconds before Garcia opens yet another screaming and exasperated "Tiger." I would bet something must have been plaguing Garcia's mind on this evening, considering the emotional intensities he reached. This final "Tiger" is concluded by Lesh launching into a "Philo Jam." Unlike October 18 and 28, and November 19, 1972, this one is perfectly placed. The other versions, though impressive, seem to have been intentionally inserted into the jam. This Kansas City version fits in like a hot sun on a cloudless day. Lesh immediately hits all the stomping notes, and the band quickly follows suit, building into a funky jam. This rises into another massive nonpsychotic jam led by Garcia and Lesh. As it winds down, Weir initiates "Feelin' Groovy" notes and the band follows. This was the medication that Garcia needed, and he soars with it into a happy "now I feel better" jam. Appropriately this winds down and, as with a recurrent depression, Garcia enters a mourning "Morning Dew." Garcia seemingly cries through the lyrics and the jams resemble a monstrous firestorm. Indeed "Dark Star" may be one of the best unused psychiatric diagnostic tools. Through their improvisation, the band members are unable to hide their feelings, and the result is a quintet of sentiment culminating into one singular emotional expression. The band finishes the show with hot versions of "Sugar Magnolia," "Casey Jones," and "Johnny B. Goode."

ROBERT A. GOETZ

---

## 11/14/72
### Oklahoma City Music Hall, Oklahoma City, Oklahoma

**Set 1:** Promised Land, Sugaree, El Paso, Loser, Black-Throated Wind, Bertha, Mexicali Blues, Tennessee Jed, Big River, China Cat Sunflower > I Know You Rider, Box of Rain, Beat It on Down the Line, Friend of the Devil, Around and Around
**Two 2:** Greatest Story Ever Told, Brown-Eyed Women, Me and My Uncle, Deal, Me and Bobby McGee, He's Gone > Truckin' > The Other One > Sing Me Back Home, Sugar Magnolia//
**Encore:** Casey Jones

**Source:** SBD, **Quality:** B+, **Length:** 3:10, **Genealogy:** MC > C > C > C > DAT, **Taper:** Bear
**Highlights:** Me and Bobby McGee, Sing Me Back Home

Here's a story about different styles of tape trading and about perseverance. In 1992, I began lending a fellow some tapes to help start his collection. After close to a year, he'd borrowed and dubbed hundreds of my very best tapes. During this time he began telling me how he might be getting some uncirculated, rare tapes one day from an excellent source. Well, I *hoped*. But I knew better than to expect anything. Yet one day the bugger calls me and says that he did indeed receive these rare tapes.

"Just let me check them out first," he told me.

A few weeks later I finally called him, palms sweaty. "So, uh, how'd you like to bring over some of those new tapes for me to dub?"

"Oh," he replied. "I don't lend my tapes out."

Six months later—after returning most because they were both overrecorded and had unnecessary, harsh cuts—he dubbed me the last of the twenty-two tapes. Was it worth it? Here's the list: 12/26/69, 12/29/69, 12/30/69 (2), 7/21/72 (2), 8/20/72, 8/24/72 (2), 9/21/72 (2), 10/30/72 (2), 11/14/72 (2), 11/15/72, 11/18/72, 12/10/72 (2), 12/15/72 (2), 2/19/73, 3/19/73, and 6/29/73. Some of these have since been upgraded, of course. And as this fellow wasn't a trader, I did enjoy turning these tapes loose on the community. And when I listen to a show like the one below, then, yeah, it was worth it. Just different styles of tape trading.

I strongly recommend this entire show. The Dead are tuned into each nuance of every song, playing even the mundane pans with a creative zest. It feels as if the Dead's Marin living rooms have been transported to the stage in Oklahoma. This is not some blow-out, a Polanski nose slice, or the soundtrack to *Godzilla*. But it is one of the most sensitive, thoughtful musical conversations I've ever heard the Dead participate in.

Keith's keyboard sounds like it's underwater, strongly adding to the psychedelic flavor. Garcia, in particular, is barely able to contain all the ideas spilling from his guitar and nearly overplays at moments. The Dead play it perfectly and peak during the "He's Gone" through "Sing Me Back Home" sequence. Go out of your way to obtain a good copy of this and see how good the Dead were in the fall of '72.

MICHAEL M. GETZ

## 11/15/72
### Oklahoma City Music Hall, Oklahoma City, Oklahoma

**Set 1:** Promised Land, Ramble On Rose, Mexicali Blues, Brokedown Palace, Playing in the Band//

**Source:** SBD, **Quality:** A–, **Length:** 0:45, **Genealogy:** MC > C > C > C > DAT
**Highlights:** Playing in the Band

This high-quality forty-five minute soundboard is unfortunately all that exists of this apparently hot night. The previous evening included "The Other One," so one would logically predict that "Dark Star" was performed here, but alas, it's not on this tape. What we have is the probable tail end of the first set. The band sounds like a tight machine. The four songs before "Playing in the Band" are flawless. The "Playing" is quite impressive despite being cut. The first twenty-three minutes of jam exist on this tape before it fades out before the reprise. The jams are quite different from the improvisational jams of the previous evening, when Garcia's pace eliminated any deep jams. Weir, Lesh, Godchaux, Kreutzmann, and Garcia are all contributing, and the pace is anything but stable. While Lesh maintains a constant inquisitive tone, Garcia and Weir seem to be chasing each other through their jams and rarely catching one another. At one point, the jam turns slightly demented as Garcia is making strange quacking sounds, Weir and Lesh are pounding power chords, and Kreutzmann is frantically increasing the pace. The jam reaches a peak near its conclusion when the entire band is jamming at top speed and Garcia puts the icing on the cake with a variation on the "Tiger" jam. The band was reaching a peak with this improvisational masterpiece during its November through December run. Indeed, the November 15, 1972, "Playing in the Band" is impressive enough to leave the listener pondering what the probable "Dark Star" that evening was like.

ROBERT A. GOETZ

## 11/17/72
### Century II Convention Hall, Wichita, Kansas

**Set 1:** Promised Land, Sugaree, Me and My Uncle, Tennessee Jed, Black-Throated Wind, Bird Song, Jack Straw, Box of Rain, Don't Ease Me In, Beat It on Down the Line, Brown-Eyed Women, China Cat Sunflower > I Know You Rider, Around and Around, Casey Jones
**Set 2:** Cumberland Blues, El Paso, He's Gone > Truckin' > The Other// One > Brokedown Palace

**1. Source:** SBD, **Quality:** A, **Length:** 3:20
**2. Source:** AUD, **Quality:** C, **Length:** 1:40 ("Don't Ease Me In," "Beat It on Down the Line," "Brown-Eyed Women," "Big River," "China Cat Sunflower" > "I Know You Rider," "Around and Around," "Casey Jones," "El Paso," "He's Gone" > "Truckin'" > "The Other One," "Brokedown Palace"//)
**Highlights:** China Cat > Rider, Around and Around, Cumberland, He's Gone > Truckin' > The Other One

This high-quality soundboard tape features a raw and exceptional Grateful Dead performance. The first set is solid and, for the most part, structured. Although lacking expanding solos, each song is nearly flawless. The "Me and My Uncle," "Tennessee Jed," "China" > "Rider," and "Around and Around" stand out because of the band's uncharacteristically massive jams. After an excellent "Cumberland," this jamming frenzy is carried over into "Truckin'" and "The Other One." Through the song Garcia provides a fiendish rhythm while Weir screams. After a loose strut jam, Garcia brings the band into a pleasant "Truckin'" space that obviously yearns for something deeper. Following a brief and surreptitious transition to "The Other One," Garcia dives into a deep yet fast-paced jam with the band soaring behind him. This "Other One" is atypical for its lack of structured theme. Instead, Garcia and Lesh are improvising at will in and out of deep jams. After the first verse, the band enters a deep and viscous drift.

Garcia erupts from this into a ferocious jam where he emits several roars. At its conclusion, Keith picks up with a haunted piano solo, providing an appropriate plateau for Garcia to launch into a "Tiger" space. This resulting jam is long and twisted. Garcia attacks from several fronts and ultimately reaches two massive and tearing "Tiger" roars. The aftermath features a brief transition back into the final verse. This "Other One" differs from the other November versions, such as November 14 and 22 in Austin, which are quite structured. This version is a pure and demented improvisational drift, very similar to October 19, 1972, in St. Louis.

ROBERT A. GOETZ

far from your mind. The Dead chew up what is an odd second-set list for 1972. There is a great deal of tension onstage, and this is reflected in the music. Lesh, in particular, plays so much lead and has so much to get out of his system that Garcia is forced to fight back like a demon. Each tune here is chunky and dense, full of musical rage—yet that good ol' Grateful Dead swing is still present. In place of the usual "Dark Star" or "Other One" centerpiece is an extraordinary "Playing in the Band." Here the slugfest is taken to a peak. There's a priceless moment during the jam when the band slows down to a near halt from its furious pace. Billy waits a second or two before—bam!—he pops a few nasty karate chops on his snare. The rest of the band responds instantly, as if on cue, and off they trudge again into battle, shredding everything in their path. For this is not some peace 'n' love, hippy-dippy version to get mellow with, man. Rather, it feels like having a fellow in a ski mask holding a fully fueled chainsaw two inches from my genitals for twenty-four minutes. The Dead's music was unique in that it transformed all feelings—anger and rage or love and joy—safely through their music, without looking back. I love this tape because the relief following the tension . . . feels great!

MICHAEL M. GETZ

## 11/18/72

**Hofheinz Pavilion, Houston, Texas**

**Set 1:** Casey Jones//
**Set 2:** Bertha > Greatest Story Ever Told, He's Gone, Jack Straw, Deal, Playing in the Band, Mississippi Half-Step, Sugar Magnolia//, Sunshine Daydream, One More Saturday Night
**Encore:** Uncle John's Band

**1. Source:** SBD, **Quality:** A–, **Length:** 1:30 (missing "Casey" and "Deal"), **Genealogy:** MC > C
**2. Source:** SBD, **Quality:** B/B+, **Length:** 1:30 (missing "Uncle John's"), **Genealogy:** MC > C > C > C
**Highlights:** Playing in the Band, He's Gone, Greatest Story Ever Told

The mix on this tape wobbles just a tad with Lesh coming out on top (no complaints). But the quality of playing—muscular and brutish—leaves any shortcomings

## 11/19/72

**Hofheinz Pavilion, Houston, Texas**

**Set 1:** Bertha, Me and My Uncle, Sugaree, Beat It on Down the Line, Bird Song, Black-Throated Wind, Don't Ease Me In, //Shave and a Haircut Two Bits, Mexicali Blues, Box of Rain, Stars and Stripes Forever, Tomorrow Is Forever, Big River, China Cat Sunflower > I Know You Rider, Nickelodeon, Playing in// the Band, Casey Jones
**Set 2:** Promised Land, Ramble On Rose, El Paso, //Stella Blue, Jack Straw, Dark Star > Weather Report Suite Prelude > Dark// Star > Mississippi Half-Step, Around and Around, Big Railroad Blues, Sugar Magnolia > Goin' Down the Road Feelin' Bad

**Source:** SBD, **Quality:** B+, **Length:** 3:20, **Genealogy:** MR > RR > RR > DAT

**Highlights:** Bird Song, Black-Throated Wind, Box of Rain, Tomorrow Is Forever, Big River, China Cat Sunflower > I Know You Rider, Playing in the Band, Dark Star > Weather Report Suite Prelude > Dark Star > Mississippi Half-Step, Around and Around, Big Railroad Blues, Sugar Magnolia > Goin' Down the Road Feelin' Bad

Several attempts have been made to label the music created by the Dead with a simple catch phrase. One label that frequently surfaces is "cowboy rock 'n' roll." With the Weir-Barlow influence one would have to agree, but with the hodgepodge of other influences a lone cowboy rock label doesn't suffice. But, as we all know, this band loved the exception, and on November 19, 1972, the band was almost completely in a Southern-style country image. This monumental and legendary show rates as one of the longest and widest-ranging of all time; nearly every taste is satisfied here. The first set is nearly flawless and demonstrates how much the band had matured since the loss of Pigpen. This historic show was to have started with a set by the Allman Brothers Band, but due to the tragic death of Berry Oakley, the Dead had to perform alone. It is for this reason that Bobby steps to the microphone early in the first set and dedicates their show "to a brother." After a standard set of opening tunes, the flavor changes from flawless to spectacular with "Bird Song." A deep and spacey sound is created through Jerry's improvisational harmonics, inquisitive bass bombs from Lesh, and just plain weird organ notes from Godchaux. The jams are slow and thoughtful, yet at the same time energetic. The following "Black-Throated Wind" would have made any parent proud. Following its progression from July through November, one would have to conclude that this version certainly one of the finest ever. Weir's singing is neither too screamy nor too blunt, and Garcia's improvisations are superb. The finale jam combination of Weir's bellows and Garcia's guitar would bring anyone to tears.

Switching into a more upbeat tempo, Garcia makes "Don't Ease Me In" an exceptionally bouncy version by adding new lyrics, referring to the "Texas Blues." A very funny, half-assed attempt at "Shave and a Haircut Two Bits" follows immediately—just one of several ditties interjected between songs on this evening that prove the band was having at least as much fun as the audience. "Box of Rain," one of the better versions, is brilliant; the band seems to *march* through it triumphantly. Garcia and Donna do one of the few performances of "Tomorrow Is Forever" that doesn't make the listener wince. Sad, sweet, and tasteful. Keeping the country pace right in stride, the band next delivers a fantastic performance of "Big River." The Garcia jams are really tight and succinct, but it is the Keith Godchaux solo that steals this version. It is so indirect but carefully placed that it sounds as though he is four beats ahead of the rest of the band. Indeed, this is another example of how in only thirteen months Godchaux had risen from new band member to necessary ingredient. "China" > "Rider" is next, and as could have been guessed, this version is amazing. The Weir solo is quite long and simply deranged, but during the transition to the "Rider" Jerry really puts forth a square-dance-style jam that is so perfectly placed that it makes the listener laugh while stomping a left foot and screaming, "Yee-haaah!" The first set, along with the universe for that matter, comes to a standstill, during "Playing in the Band." This rendition rates among the finest examples of pure Jerry improvisation. The entire jam is completely controlled both in tempo and lead by Garcia. Jerry races through several smacking feedback moans, harmonic space-outs, and meltdowns. The result is one of their deepest and finely crafted jam sessions. At one point near its conclusion Jerry is emitting low-sounding roars like a lion warning an approaching predator. The previous evening Lesh was in control with Jerry following his lead, but on this evening the roles are reversed. Lesh, in contrast to his madman performance the previous night, plays carefully and consciously and seems to be teasing Jerry. These two "Playing in the Band"s demonstrate how "Playing" had evolved so dramatically in 1972 from a tame spacey tune to a way out, brain jam.

After a well-earned set break the band returns, retaining the same momentum and rendering exceptional performances of all the songs leading up to the "Dark Star." As with most of the concerts where it's played, however, the set is overpowered by the "Star." Jerry opens the jam by slowly and carefully crafting a sun-drenched mural. Eventually the band gets into his sync, and Jerry and Phil take over. Once again we have another mind-numbing example of one of the best musical duets in history: Phil and Jerry. Phil sets a constant and driving pace that Jerry improvises off of. The final twelve minutes before the lone verse features a constant jam that reaches and caresses the G-spot of "Dark Star." The jams are slow and windingly contemplative. In many respects this version is similar to that of November 11, 1973, in its incessant and unique jamming. After the verse we get a massive lecture on the true meaning of the Phil Zone. The band drifts for about a minute before transforming into complete silence with the exception of Lesh's quiet feedback. They hold this silence for about ten seconds, and indeed it is frightening. Lesh breaks it with a monstrous series of bombs that must have deafened the people in the front row. Jerry matches Phil for about a minute with some scary feedback screams but bows aside as Phil begins one of his all-time best solos. The length too is noteworthy: it lasts about ten solid minutes. During the middle, he includes a "Philo Jam" that is less structured than October 18 or 28 and not as integrated into the jam as on November 13. This "Philo" is also a lot meaner than the others.

Ultimately this comes to an end as Jerry and Bob return the feeling from grim and brutal to one that is happy and pleasant. They build a "Feelin' Groovy"–type jam that gives birth to a "Weather Report Suite Prelude" as Bobby delivers the infant. Actually, with Jerry's rhythm, it is surprisingly well done. As it concludes, the band wanders into a "Tiger" jam that is unfortunately cut. Once again we have here another omnipotent "Dark Star" that ranges in theme from a confusing contemplation of an evil dictator's cerebellum to "Feelin' Groovy." The aftermath drifts for a little while before wandering into a mellow and crowd pleasing Half-Step. The band ends the show on a exceptionally scalding note. The "Around and Around" and "Big Railroad Blues" feature Jerry sacrificing his fingers to the jam god. The "Sugar Magnolia" and "Goin' Down the Road" are also scorching in pace but epitomize the evening by closing on the cowboy rock 'n' roll notes that they began with. Indeed, this show is by far, from first set to finish, one of the Grateful Dead's grandest performances.

ROBERT A. GOETZ

---

## 11/22/72
**Municipal Auditorium, Austin, Texas**

**Set 1:** Sugaree, Mexicali Blues, Loser, Black-Throated Wind, China Cat Sunflower > I Know You Rider, Beat It on Down the Line, Candyman, El Paso, Bird Song, Playing in the// Band, Casey Jones
**Set 2:** He's Gone > Truckin' > The Other One > Stella Blue, //Big River, Ramble On Rose, Sugar Magnolia, Brokedown Palace, Around and Around, One More Saturday Night
**Encore:** Uncle John's Band//

**Source:** SBD, **Quality:** A–, **Length:** 3:00
**Highlights:** Sugaree, Mexicali Blues, Loser, Black-Throated Wind, Candyman, Bird Song, Playing in the Band, He's Gone > Truckin' > The Other One > Stella Blue

The exceptional momentum created in Houston was carried to Austin for this concert. The band displayed a powerful, flex-your-muscle performance. From the start the band is in a such a unique sync that standard songs like "Sugaree," "Mexicali," and "Loser" are played like masterpieces. As compared to the beautifully mournful November 19, 1972, version, this "Black-Throated Wind," is rageful. Weir screams the lyrics out while Lesh and Garcia provide an angry and fierce rhythm. Later in the set the band does a stellar "Candyman." The Garcia lead is deep and spaced-out and sounds as if he is attempting to communicate with dolphins. The "Bird Song," too, is exceptional not only because Garcia's soaring leads but because of Lesh's improvisation and appropriately placed bombs. The band must have felt slightly intimidated about performing "Playing in the Band," considering the legendary two previous versions, but they rise to the occasion. Instead of a Lesh- or Garcia-driven jam, this one is controlled by the whole band, similar to the 9/21/72 Philadelphia version. Before Garcia begins any sort of lead, the rhythm created by Lesh, Godchaux, and Billy is like an expanding amoeba. Garcia splits it open, however, and rages through several jams and themes. Godchaux, in particular, rises to the moment, providing exceptional rhythm and leads at times. There's a cut in the jam three-quarters of the way through, but we still have another fantastic version of "Playing in the Band," once again featuring peaking performances from Lesh and Garcia. This, the third of five monumental Texas 1972 "Playing"s, provides direct evidence that this jam reached a zenith in the fall of 1972. The band could do no wrong. The "He's Gone" from the second set is flawless, containing a massive finale jam led by Lesh and Garcia. The "Truckin'" > "Other One" that follows is slick and quite jazzy. The "Truckin'" jam begins with a light-speed strut that forms into a mad Garcia jam with a slight "Truckin'" flavor. After a great Billy solo, Lesh launches the band into "The Other One" with a massive thunder roll and resulting pace. Jerry races through jams, attempting to keep up with Lesh, winding in and out of some of their fastest and tightest "Other One" jamming ever. After the first verse, instead of entering the usual "Tiger" space, the band takes turns taking solos in between more impressive "Other One" jamming. No attempt is really made at the "Tiger," but the tradeoff is overwhelming. The band races through several short and tight jams that would be definitive for any acid jazz reference book. Lesh's solo, oddly placed in the middle of a pre-second-verse jam, is astounding. It is fast and chunky, with such well-placed bombs that one can only conclude that indeed the "Other One" genetic code is indigenous to his DNA. This version seems to be the culmination of the tight and rapid versions of that tour, such as those of September 15 in Boston and November 17 in Wichita. It is the most mature and flawless. The "Stella Blue" that flows from "The Other One" is raw and innocent and fortunately lacks the out-of-tune bellows from that of November 19 in Houston. The band ends the show with a series of standard tunes played once again to perfection.

ROBERT A. GOETZ

---

## 11/24/72
### Memorial Auditorium, Dallas, Texas

**Set 1:** Don't Ease Me In, Me and My Uncle, Brown-Eyed Women, Black-Throated Wind, Bertha, El Paso, Deal, Beat It on Down the Line, Tennessee Jed, Playing in the Band
**Set 2:** China Cat Sunflower > I Know You Rider, Truckin', Casey Jones, Sugar Magnolia, Not Fade Away > Goin' Down the Road Feelin' Bad > Not Fade Away Reprise

---

**Source:** SBD, **Quality:** B+, **Length:** 2:15, **Genealogy:** MR > RR > RR > DAT
**Highlights:** Playing in the Band, Truckin', Sugar Magnolia, Not Fade Away > Goin' Down the Road Feelin' Bad > Not Fade Away

This fourth out of five performances in Texas is noteworthy for three main reasons. First, the band took the evening off from "Dark Star" and "The Other One." Second, the second set is probably one of their best rock 'n' roll displays ever. Third is the first-set "Playing in the Band." A solid and standard first set indeed culminates in another fantastic Texas-flavored "Playing in the Band" jam. This one is led mostly by Garcia, but honorable mention again goes to Lesh. The themes are similar to 11/18/72 Houston but instead Garcia is at the helm. (11/19/72 Houston is led by Garcia, but the tempo is much different. Lesh's manic style on 11/18/72 is mirrored by Garcia on this version.) Jerry flows through several jams, effortlessly lifting the band from the depths of oblivion to the rafters of doom. This "Playing in the Band" is downright scary. The scorching meltdowns and intriguing improvisation from Lesh and Garcia are unnerving. The second set is similar to 10/30/72 Detroit, in that there is no deep improvisational exploration. Instead the band goes way out into the rock 'n' roll mode. The "Truckin'" is superb. The jam is the twin brother that of August 12, 1972, in Sacramento. Garcia puts forth a liquid portrayal of ecstasy. This jam reaches the peaks of "Truckin'" space in a jammed and nonexplorative fashion. Although not hypnotic, it grabs the listener and makes him stand, shake, and quiver. The "Sugar Magnolia" > "Sunshine Daydream" jams also reach superb heights. However, the highlight of the second set is "Not Fade Away." The jam leading into "Goin' Down the Road" features Garcia in a sick frenzy testing the limits of the band's ability to keep up with him. Unfortunately, as the jam reaches the final peak, Jerry does a screeching scald-out and breaks a string. Weir picks up the slack and does a great solo to fill in the gap preceding "Goin' Down the Road." The transition back to "Not Fade Away" features a rare jam in a blues format before the lyrics. The jam gets real quiet and almost furtive near the end until Jerry and Bob suddenly scream "I wanna tell you . . ." Jerry takes Bob to his vocal limits in the finale. As Bob is intensely trashing his lungs and vocal chords, Jerry just keeps on jamming away at a hyperpace. Ah, what a jam.

ROBERT A. GOETZ

## 11/26/72
### Civic Auditorium, San Antonio, Texas

**Set 1:** Promised Land, Deal, Mexicali Blues, Sugaree, Black-Throated Wind, Bird Song, China Cat Sunflower > I Know You Rider, Beat It on Down the Line, Box of Rain, El Paso, Big Railroad Blues, Around and Around, Casey Jones
**Set 2:** Playing in the Band, Brown-Eyed Women, Jack Straw, Don't Ease Me In, Big River, Dark Star > Me and Bobby McGee, Brokedown Palace, Sugar Magnolia > Goin' Down the Road Feelin' Bad > One More Saturday Night

**Source:** SBD, **Quality:** C/B, **Length:** 3:00
**Highlights:** Big Railroad Blues, Around and Around, Playing in the Band, Dark Star > Me and Bobby McGee, Sugar Magnolia > Goin' Down the Road Feelin' Bad > One More Saturday Night

This being the final show of the fall tour, the band members were most likely exhausted. If so, it certainly was not evident in their performance. The first set, unlike some other ones from the same period, is slick and tight. Throughout it Billy maintains a slappy presence, providing a faster-paced and highly structured platform. The result is a rowdy, well-performed set that doesn't reach the outer limits—they saved that for the second set. After solid versions of "Deal" (with great Jerry screams), "Sugaree," and "Black-Throated Wind," we get a unique "Bird Song." Instead of the typical jam featuring creepy exploration, this version features the rigorous Billy beat, causing Garcia to conform to a more controlled, funky theme. After the drum intermission, Jerry does soar a bit, but only shortly, with some sky high harmonics that effortlessly drift back to the first verse reprise. The finale jam is interesting because Jerry creates a slightly bluesy theme with perhaps a very distant hint of "Nobody's Fault but Mine." Jerry and Phil stand out during the "China Cat" that follows, but after a short Weir lead, Garcia opted not to enter a long transition into the "Rider." After a stellar Godchaux "Beat It on Down the Line" piano solo and a sweet "Box of Rain," the audience was treated to some incredible rock 'n' roll. "Big Railroad Blues" features the band maintaining a delirious pace (it is definitely faster than most "Big Railroad"s) that Jerry perfectly emits sparks off of. This pace just dives right into the "Around and Around," which is appalling in its own right with the contrast created by Weir's screams and Jerry's guitar screech. Finally the band blows the horn and drives into "Casey Jones" before a well-deserved break. Although not extraterrestrial in nature, this set was indeed extremely well played and deserves recognition.

The second set begins with the final "Playing in the Band" from the 1972 Texas run. Once again this version is a masterpiece. Jerry and Lesh take over and between the two of them race through numerous jams at frantic paces. As with the other versions, the jams reach monstrous heights including scorching meltdowns, hypnotic moaning, and top-notch improvising. This version is different from the previous four for two reasons. The speed is definitely not as fast and there is a lot more drift. It may just be that the magical injection they all got upon reaching the border of Texas on November 18th, 1972, in Houston was beginning to wear off. Nonetheless, this version is quite impressive. The band does a fantastic version of "Don't Ease Me In" with a scalding Garcia solo before the last non-Californian "Dark Star" of 1972. Garcia starts off the jam with a looping series of complex improvisational rifts. The band at first seems to be trying to figure him out. As they approach his groove, Garcia wanders severely into a chopping jam with only Billy following him. As this calms, the band and Jerry wander through some top-notch "Dark Star"–themed jams. Garcia puts forth another stellar performance. This pre-verse jam sounds as if the band is in slow motion while Jerry soars above and below them communicating with the outside universe. Lesh plays a calm and almost cautious rhythm throughout. All totaled, it is actually a beautiful nonstop improvisational theme from Jerry as he steps in and out of slow- and fast-paced themes. After the verse, Garcia performs "Feedback" with Lesh dropping sedating bombs. Lesh soon enters a solo that is yearning in nature at first but, with help from Billy, builds into a stomping, funky strut. Weir joins in at this point, followed by waddling sounds from Garcia. Garcia immediately soars upward, followed by Lesh into an explosive jam that blends into a "Feelin' Groovy Jam." Jerry really stands out during this jam with blistering leads. He concludes it with an volcanic meltdown into a psychotic space. Jerry begins digging deep into the space and erupts again into a "Tiger" roar. It sounds like Garcia's head is exploding. The aftermath is long and features Lesh dropping huge bombs while Garcia refuses to exit the jam. Ultimately, Garcia emits one last surge into oblivion and, like a spaceship returning to a familiar atmosphere, the band wanders under Weir's guidance into "Me and Bobby McGee." Here concludes another quality 1972 "Dark Star" roller coaster from the depths of fear through mystical ponds to towers of joy. The band ends the show on another scorching note. The "Sunshine Daydream" jam has Garcia once again taking this familiar theme and rewriting the book on which version may be the best. "This Goin' Down the Road" is unique. The second jam has Garcia once again putting forth an amazing jam but when the band sings the final chorus, instead of performing the familiar conclusion, Jerry melts the jam into a complete halt that immediately turns into a stomping "One More Saturday Night." Thus concluded the final Texas show of five. The band was cooking on this run as on few others. Almost every song was textbook hot, and the "Playing in the Band"s, "Other One"s, and "Dark Star"s are among the best of all time. These five shows are highly recommended.

ROBERT A. GOETZ

## 12/10/72
### Winterland Arena, San Francisco, California

**Set 1:** Bertha, Playing in the Band, Casey Jones
**Set 2:** Promised Land, Stella Blue//, Jack Straw, China Cat Sunflower > I Know You Rider, Truckin' > The Other// One > Deal, Sugar Magnolia, Ramble On Rose, Johnny B. Goode
**Encore:** Uncle John's Band

**Source:** SBD, **Quality:** A–, **Length:** 2:15, **Genealogy:** MC > C > C > C > DAT

**Highlights:** Bertha, Playing in the Band, Casey Jones, China Cat > Rider, Truckin' > The Other One, Sugar Magnolia, Ramble On Rose, Johnny B. Goode, Uncle John's Band

After a two-week vacation from touring, the band returned filled with the same vigor that made November 1972 legendary. In this reviewer's opinion December 10, 1972, may be the finest all-around Garcia performance between 1971 and 1974. Jerry dominates this concert in nearly all respects while the band also does an exceptional job. Most of the first set does not exist as a circulating tape, but what we have of it is amazing. Garcia's guitar solo on "Bertha" sounds like an improvisational beast trapped in a structured song. The following "Playing in the Band" allows Jerry the boundless playground he desires. This "Playing" goes a step deeper than the November 1972 versions and for all practical purposes is more difficult to listen to. Instead of a constant noodling jam created by Garcia or Lesh, this version is mostly atonal with some fantastic improvisation in between nonsensical explosions. Ultimately this "Playing" represents Garcia taking the Grateful Dead to the next higher level. For those of you with strong ears, this version is basically the thinking man's "Playing" according to Jerry Garcia. Impressive improvisational leads are overshadowed by cataclysmic guitar explosions unlike any created by Jerry before or after. By turns, the sound is angry, sad, curious, furious, paranormal, or savage. The band honorably attempts to follow Garcia in this quest but in many respects can't match his intensity. Attempting to summarize the overall creative nature is difficult. This version is peculiar because of Garcia's unique representation. Of all the 1971–74 versions, this "Playing" stands out alone for Garcia's explosive and atonal style. The audience that witnessed this must have melted into one large boiling primal soup.

Upon the conclusion of "Playing," however, the band quickly enters a "Casey Jones" that returns it and the audience back to our universe. Before the set ends, this "Casey Jones" cooks like a well-greased engine approaching light speed.

The second set begins with solid performances of "Promised Land," "Stella Blue," and "Jack Straw." The fireworks begin to fly with the "China Cat" transition into "Rider." After a trademark 1972 "China Cat" Weir solo, Garcia picks up the lead and, with Weir providing a fierce rhythm, creates one of the fastest, well-jammed transitions into "Rider." The following "Truckin'" displays the band once again launching into the rafters of oblivion. Jerry's long and fast-picked "Truckin'" strut slowly melds in and out of the interzone between "Truckin'" and "The Other One." Weir incessantly hints at the "Other One" theme, but Jerry and Lesh present a slight "Truckin'" flavor for a good five minutes, tempting and teasing the listener. Finally, after the foreplay is completed, the band drops suddenly, leaving only Billy to fill the space and provide a diving board for Lesh to launch from. Lesh takes his cue and takes the band back into deep jam. Garcia quickly takes the reins and sets forth on a course delineated by the typical fall 1972 "Other One" boundaries. After a five-minute series of structured but ferocious leads, the band takes a pit stop by moving into the first verse. Afterward they enter uncharted "Other One" territory. Weir and Lesh initially lead the band into a soft and tame theme marked by grumbling Lesh and snapping Weir sounds. Garcia jumps in, and the band changes into a cyclical series of funky jams that resemble "The Other One." The cyclical notion takes the listener from a happy groove to an unsettling nervous-breakdown-type feeling. This five-minute jam may be one of the finest Grateful Dead improvisation jams of all time. Unfortunately just at its conclusion the tape is cut, leaving the listener in the realm of a soft but notably pre-"Tiger" space. This builds into one of the more disturbing versions from 1972 with Garcia projecting a particularly deranged identity. The preorgasmic minute before the "Tiger" is simply grizzly! The transition back to reality begins when Garcia starts strumming an "Other One" theme that the band just melts around. At first the pace is slow, but it is molded into a monstrous platform that Jerry ultimately dives from. The resulting jam, like the evening's other improvisation jams, is ferocious. Jerry conveys the notion of all-out mental and physical attack as he changes from several haunting "Other One" sirens to blistering leads. This version indicates what "The Other One" had been changing into throughout 1972. The band's tight structure, intense communication, and inquisitive improvisation is clearly evident. The only fall 1972 versions that rival this one are September 17 in Baltimore and 28 in Jersey City and October 19 in St. Louis. The band ends this legendary performance with some of the finest readings of "Sugar Magnolia," "Ramble On Rose," and "Uncle John's Band" ever. On the "Sugar Mags" > "Sunshine Daydream" jam Garcia reaches a foot-stomping pace, while in the "Sunshine Daydream" verse, he takes Weir and Donna to their vocal limits with a pressing and intrusive rhythm. Finally, the closing Garcia lead in "Uncle John's Band" presents a soothing and heartwarming conclusion to an evening where the Dead have explored nearly every avenue of their psyches. Upon listening to the entire performance from start to finish, the listener develops a deep and intense respect for Jerry Garcia. Garcia attacked this concert like a voyage into the depths of his brain. On almost every single evening in 1972 Garcia was "on," but on a couple of evenings, he was so "on" that it makes you shake your head in utter amazement. Hats off, Jerry . . . Take a bow.

ROBERT A. GOETZ

---

### 12/11/72
**Winterland Arena, San Francisco, California**

**Set 1:** Sugaree, Mexicali Blues, Loser, Me and Bobby McGee, Brown-Eyed Women, Beat It on Down the Line, China Cat Sunflower// > I Know You Rider, Box of Rain, He's Gone, Around and Around, Friend of the Devil, Playing in the Band
**Set 2:** Mississippi Half-Step, Me and My Uncle, Dark// Star > Stella Blue, Big River, Deal//, Tomorrow Is Forever//

**Source:** SBD, **Quality:** A–, **Length:** 3:00, **Genealogy:** MC > C > C > C > DAT

**Highlights:** Sugaree, Mexicali Blues, Loser, Me and Bobby McGee, Brown-Eyed Women, Beat It on Down the Line, China Cat > I Know You Rider, Box of Rain, He's Gone, Around and Around, Friend of the Devil, Playing in the Band, Half-Step, Me and My Uncle, Dark Star > Stella Blue

Consistency is probably the best word to describe this evening at Winterland. The first set is phenomenal—easily one of their best ever. Each song is simply textbook hot. In particular "China Cat" > "Rider," "Box of Rain," "He's Gone," and "Playing in the Band" stand out. The "China Cat" begins definitively before Weir starts his solo, which unfortunately cuts into the final prelude to "Rider." One can only guess at how hot the transition jam was. The band really picks up the energy level for "Rider," which is easily a top version. The jams crackle and the chorus is perfect. The following "Box of Rain" also stands out as flawless and inspiring. "He's Gone" is unusually long, filled with sweet vocals and a series of pleasant jams, very similar to that of December 15, 1972, in Long Beach. Up to this point the set has been hot and really tight, but, as is so often the case, all bets go out the window with the subsequent "Playing in the Band." Compared to the previous evening's version, this is darker. "Playing" has evolved into a surreal catapult. Here they enter a morose and churlish area. It isn't psychotic like many others, just gloomy. The jams are tight and hot, but there is a lot of feedback, echoed piano, "Tiger" roars, and slow moments that give them a really high or dreamy sound. Lesh provides a lot of support in this theme, including several low notes that drive the band deeper into the bitter moon. This is a rare face of "Playing in the Band."

The second set begins with a fantastic version of "Half-Step" and features one of the finest versions of "Dark Star." This "Star" meanders at first, but soon the sound gets really deep. Garcia, Weir, and Lesh enter improvisational bliss. This "Star" isn't pleasant in the least; in fact, it's one of the most sinister performances around. The pre-verse jams reach several different themes with each band member apparently taking turns in the creation. After the lyrics, the theme turns into a vast wasteland. Godchaux provides a haunting keyboard effect throughout while Garcia and Kreutzmann noodle around awaiting the ever-approaching "Tiger." The effect is quite spaced-out, complete with hair-raising feedback and Lesh bombs galore. Ultimately the band returns from its nebulous state, and the final San Francisco "Dark Star" of 1972 comes to a conclusion. The "Stella" that follows is simply beautiful.

ROBERT A. GOETZ

## 12/15/72

### Long Beach Arena, Long Beach, California

**Set 1:** Black-Throated Wind, El Paso, Tennessee Jed, //Box of Rain, Mexicali Blues, Brown-Eyed Women, Beat It on Down the Line, Loser, Playing in the Band, Casey// Jones
**Set 2:** //Greatest Story Ever Told, //Deal, Me and My Uncle, He's Gone, Truckin' > Dark// Star > Morning Dew, Sugar Magnolia
**Encore:** Johnny B. Goode

**Source:** SBD, **Quality:** A–, **Length:** 3:00, **Genealogy:** MC > C > C > C > DAT

**Highlights:** Playing in the Band, He's Gone, Truckin' > Dark Star > Morning Dew

This final lone Grateful Dead road performance of 1972 features, once again, Jerry Garcia reaching mind-boggling improvisational heights. A fragmented first set is highlighted by a Lesh-and-Garcia-controlled "Playing in the Band." Lesh maintains a consistent open-ended structure that appears to be facilitating a rambunctious Garcia. After flowing through a few fast-paced leads marked by roars and feedback blasts, Lesh drops the band into a bottomless sound of delirium. Garcia also falls into this seeming spiderweb and intentionally drifts downward, carrying the rest of the band with him. Ultimately, as with many other type jams, Jerry turns the tables and suddenly starts an ascension with little help from a content-sounding band. An unreasonable Garcia settles for no compromise as he surges the band into a series of twisted jams complete with some bizarre and eerie feedback that sounds like rank flatulence. For the most part, as with December 10, 1972, at Winterland, this "Playing in the Band" is mostly the band taking a backseat to an astonishing series of bold improvisational statements by Jerry. The second set includes an extended "He's Gone" nearly identical in structure and intensity to the December 11, 1972, Winterland version. The fireworks of this show, however, erupt out of "Truckin'." Garcia casts the band into a patriotic "Truckin'" march that quickly is swallowed by a black hole created by massive Lesh bombs, a stumbling Kreutzmann beat, and tormenting feedback from Garcia. After a round of sinister mania from Garcia, Lesh, and Weir, Garcia wanders into a pleasant outer space theme. Impressively and beautifully, Lesh begins a rhythm that deeply hints at and yearns for "Dark Star." Jerry takes the cue and leaps forward into a series of "Dark Star" jams that rate among the band's finest. Unfortunately, just as Jerry calms down and Lesh begins a slight bass solo, the tape is cut and the listener is zapped into a deep "Dark Star" jam. Anywhere between seven minutes and one hour of music may be missing here. The tape picks up with Garcia improvising at such a lightning pace that only Billy and Keith are backing him up. Jerry's leads sound like a complex language that only he can understand. It is as if he has psychically reached nirvana onstage and followed it directly into the verse of "Dark Star." The five minutes of jam before the verse are truly amazing and should be listened to by all—it would bring world peace. After the verse the band wanders furtively into an impressive "Tiger" roar, which is overshadowed by the previous thirty minutes of Jerry jamming. This marks the conclusion of the last 1972 "Dark Star" as the band appropriately entered a inspiring "Morning Dew" with Jerry making sense of all in the finale. At this point in the band's career, they could do no wrong when entering any type of improvisational jam.

ROBERT A. GOETZ

Reviews: December 1972

> ❋ **12/31/72** ❋
>
> **Winterland Arena,
> San Francisco, California**
>
> **Set 1:** Around and Around, Deal, Mexicali Blues, Brown-Eyed Women, Box of Rain, Jack Straw, Don't Ease Me In, Beat It on Down the Line, Candyman, El Paso, Tennessee Jed, Playing in the Band, Casey Jones **Set 2:** //Promised Land, Mississippi Half-Step, //Big River, Sugaree, Truckin' > The Other One* > Jam* > Morning Dew*
>
> * with David Crosby on guitar

**1. Source:** FM-SBD (GDH 042, 222, 223, and 224), **Quality:** A–, **Length:** 3:00, **Genealogy:** MR > DR

**2. Source:** SBD, **Quality:** A–, **Length:** 3:00, **Genealogy:** MR > RR > RR > DAT

**Highlights:** Playing in the Band, Half-Step, Truckin' > The Other One > Morning Dew

This final show from 1972 actually begins with the first second of 1973. After a momentous countdown the band begins perhaps its poorest first set of the season. The set ends on a high note, however, with a fine version of "Playing in the Band." Garcia is barely present during the first-set songs, but during the improvisational "Playing" he is omnipresent. The jam consists of four themes. The first has Garcia playing in a relaxed and cautious state while the band taunts and jeers at him. Ultimately, after much meandering and exploring, Garcia penetrates the jam into a "Playing" frenzy. Garcia and Lesh work this together for a few minutes before Garcia emits a few strange but appropriate sounds. The descent to the reprise is long and well done. Just as the band concedes on the timing, it sounds as though one is looking at a small pond deep inside the north woods as the morning sun breaks.

The second set begins with solid but deep versions of "Promised Land," "Half-Step," "Big River," and "Sugaree." The jams, though structured, yearn for an inner level. "Truckin'" provides just the vehicle they desired. The jam out of the song sends the band way into outer space. A structured "Truckin'" strut quickly evaporates into a delirious "Truckin'" light-speed drift with the whole band displaying stellar form. Lesh seems to be controlling the flow as he fights to maintain "Truckin'" and not enter "The Other One." The result is easily the longest "Truckin'" > "Other One" interzone jams of the band's career. A stubborn Garcia attacks Lesh with an array of new and deeper themes, crying out for a "Cryptical" rhythm, but to no avail. Ultimately, the jam and Garcia begins to slow down for what would logically be a drums solo, but Lesh surprises the band with a sudden but calm bass roll into "The Other One." Garcia and the band race after Lesh, but the resulting "Other One" jams are dreamy and relaxed. This transition is quite impressive, allowing the listener to sneak into one of the Dead's more intimate moments. Entering the jam at this point is David Crosby, who for the most part plays a cautious and nonhindering rhythm. Crosby entered the jam at one of its drippiest moments: a daring feat. After a series of twisted and sedating "Other One" jams, the pace slowly comes to a close and Billy takes over. After an impressive drums solo, Lesh is the first to return and enter another classic 1972 bass solo. Instead of a fast pace, he creates a funky upbeat groove that for the most part exits "The Other One." Garcia and the band, still including Crosby, return on top of this Kreutzmann-Lesh creation and enter one of their finest improvisational jams. Garcia really holds the reins here, controlling not only the pace but the direction too. Jerry enters into an overdrive jam, digging deep into the annals of the Dead. The resulting jam features Garcia improvising at a mind-boggling pace and creating some beautiful sounds in between. The band retains a tight rhythm, but as with some other of that era jams, sometimes they do nothing but listen to Garcia in awe. Garcia appropriately dive-bombs the finale, spiraling down into a "Tiger" space. The drop is slow, however, and it feels like a strongman slowly dropping through the air. Lesh in particular provides some haunting bass bombs and along with Garcia creates yet another demented "Tiger" roar. During its aftermath Jerry enters another fast-paced jam, but the band doesn't catch the bait, and it quickly diminishes into a sensuous Weir solo that leads the band to an uncomfortable silence screaming for Lesh to take over. Lesh does seize the moment, returning the band to the monster that created its current space. An enormous bass roll launches Garcia and the band into a series of nasty "Other One" jams before entering the first "Other One" verse. After the lyrics Jerry wanders away from "The Other One" into a beautiful jam. Indeed this jam, which lasts about five minutes, is probably the most serene of that era. It is almost as if Garcia suddenly realized that the jams set up through their 1972 repertoire could no longer exist in the following years. This jam then, which I'll dub "Enlightenment Jam," is the final serenade for what may have been Garcia's finest year. All of the band's various 1972 explorations seemingly led them to this final dance with improvisation. Listened to closely, this theme will give the hearer a lump in the throat and a tear in the eye. Appropriately, this melts into "Morning Dew" and gives Jerry one last chance to moan through lyrics and his guitar. Garcia really puts forth an emotional display. The finale is monstrous: the band has finished its last 1972 quest. Although the following years would allow the band ample exploration, the fall of 1972 featured night in and night out explorative improvisational bliss. This truly was one of the band's peaks, and probably was Garcia's peak as an improvisational guitar player. New Year 1973 is completed with structured rock 'n' roll and in that respect foreshadows the upcoming years.

ROBERT A. GOETZ

## Flashback:
### December 31, 1972, Winterland

You may not believe this but by the time December 31, 1972, rolled around I was getting pretty down on the boys. As far as I was concerned, it had been downhill since Mickey left, and the first time I'd heard the band with Godchaux I about puked (at the Chicago Auditorium Theatre, October 21, 1971). They did "Dark Star" and "Saint Stephen" in that show—which ought to have been a thrill, right?, since I hadn't seen them do either before, but their performance was so lethargically abysmal, I thought they might as well just hang it up. It just didn't seem to me that the Dead were into making music anymore. My Deadfreak friends and I were pretty much agreed that the *Skull and Roses* album, which came out about the same time, was a downer: good songs, but bad renditions and odd selections (couldn't they tell good nights from bad ones anymore?). In short, it was becoming depressingly clear that '69–'70 would never happen again. Anyway, the good news was that I had caught them in Berkeley on August 22, 1972, and enjoyed myself. It seemed like they were getting a new style together, working Keith in a bit and even jamming respectably despite having only one drummer. And so when I found myself on the West Coast again at holiday time, I got tickets for the New Year's show at Winterland. However I was still thinking that I wasn't going to be interested in following the Dead much longer—it just wasn't fun anymore...

Winterland is packed: we are about in the middle of the floor... As things get close to starting time, these two guys—both wearing corduroy jackets, and one of them with a ponytail that comes down to his ass—are working their way through the crowd. They crouch down right in front of us and open a velour-lined briefcase—more like a large jewelry box—full of little white pills (mind you, it's hard to distinguish colors in that Day-Glo environment). One of them says, "Acid, courtesy of the Grateful Dead." It was eight months since my last trip, and it's tempting, but, no, not tonight, I say to myself.... Someone next to us takes one, and my companion, Kirk, saying, "Why turn down a free hit?," puts one in his pocket. Eventually, Bill Graham comes out and leads everyone in the countdown to midnight: 3, 2, 1, and the band breaks into "Around and Around." I was turned off from the start, as this song epitomized for me the metamorphosis of Bob Weir into a (pseudo-)rock star egotist ("Johnny B. Goode" usually made me cringe as well). "Deal" gets me dancing—one of my favorite Jerry tunes, and he's starting to rock 'n' roll on that one.... When Phil gets up and sings "Box of Rain," the crowd loses it—he really sings it pretty nice—and Donna chimes in with some fine harmonies to boot. "Jack Straw" really rocks—I'm getting off on this one. Then they blow me away, bringing out "Don't Ease Me In." I knew this from the '70 acoustic sets—but this is rock 'n' roll! At the end of the solo—which really rocked; Jerry's leads were tight, and right on the money—Jer dances from way back by the speakers all the way to the mike just in time to sing "The girl I love! She's sweet and true." I just crack up laughing: If Jerry's having a good time, then who am I to sulk over times gone by and paradise lost? "Playing in the Band" starts out as, well, just another song (I've never heard the expanded version before)—but the jam develops into a really cerebral thing ("So this is what happened to the 'Dark Star' energy," I'm thinking to myself) and then, at an uptempo place, they drop this mirrored ball around while they shine the spotlight on it: a new twist back then on the light show idea; people go wild. To me, it seems a little cheap, but I am digging the music and so I just close my eyes and go ride the music.... This is what I came for.

The second set builds up with some nice renditions of "Mississippi Half-Step," "Big River," and "Sugaree." I'm still pining for "the old days" of psychedelic, cosmos-pointing "Dark Star" highs and "Lovelight" rhythms. (Pigpen didn't make this show, and this too indicates to me that things won't ever be the same again—no Pig means no "Alligator," no "Lovelight," no "Hard to Handle," no "Good Lovin'"—no blues, no rappin'.) They come out with "Truckin'," and people are dancing again.... They move on into a jam, get lost in space, and suddenly the boys are all around Bill-the-Drummer and they're gettin' down!! Lesh is on the bottom, Jerry's sailing high above, Bobby's filling in the space betwixt and between, and Keith is just everywhere—first they paint wild, abstract textures and then, the unexpected, unanticipated, I-thought-it-couldn't-happen-again hard-driving jamming; following Kreutzmann's beat, they re-create something out of nothing—Void becomes Chaos, becomes Order. My friend Kirk—reacting at the same time as me, as the whole Winterland crowd—utters, "Oh, shiiiiit." It's pure, visceral, timeless awe, and wonder. Like Bill Graham says, "The Grateful Dead are not the best at what they do—they are the only ones who do what they do." In two or three minutes of that "Truckin'" jam, all my assumptions are proven false: they can still maintain intensity through a jam; Keith can support the momentum without dragging it down into the space-quagmire, and, yes, the boys can get it on with just one drummer. I'd gotten more than my money's worth ($4.50, as I remember).

P.S. "Morning Dew" was icing on that cake. After that I was ready to go home—I could do without the "Johnny B. Goode" encore, and "Uncle John's Band" (one of my favorite songs) seemed trite, forced, and formulaic. So be it—that image of Jer, Bobby, and Phil gathered tight in a semicircle around Billy K. and just smokin' from "Truckin'" all the way into "That's It for the Other One" will forever be etched in my mind as my final image of my last Grateful Dead concert, in the wee hours of 1973. (Note: This remained my last show until December 8 and 9, 1994, when I had the privilege of seeing the Dead at Oakland Coliseum.)

ROBERT A. GOETZ

---

## ??/??/72
### Unknown Location

**Studio Sessions:** //Track 1, Track 2, Track 3, Track 4, Track 5//

**Source:** SBD, **Quality:** B, **Length:** 0:45
**Highlights:** The first four tracks
**Personnel:** Tom Constanten, Jerry Garcia, Richard Green, Mickey Hart, Phil Lesh

**Comments:** Although the tape is labeled 1972, speculation has it that the date and location are April 1971, Electric Ladyland Studios, New York. The date speculation is derived from deduction based on Constanten's guest appearance at the Grateful Dead's Fillmore East performance on April 28, 1971.

An extremely unusual session, these outtakes from Tom Constanten's unreleased *Tarot Touch* LP feature an extraordinary blend of classical approaches, as well as a vast magnitude of cumbersome gibberish that propels directionlessly. Unfortunately, the former is kept disappointingly brief while the latter endures for what seems like forever. The first track begins with a divinely beautiful flute-guitar-piano trio, which gently sweeps the listener into an alluring aura of fantastic images and courtly romantic settings. Lasting only a few minutes, it leads into a rolling piano segment that quickly brings the energy to a climax with the aid of splashing cymbals from Hart and stoic spearing from Lesh. Garcia's lines are reminiscent of "Morning Dew" both in construction and execution, oozing raw emotion from each note.

Track 2 begins with a medieval classical guitar passage that serves as the prelude for the following jam. Slowly, the motif transforms from serenity to rage, as Garcia's spirals become more and more frenzied and Lesh's drive intensifies further. Constanten's organ contribution is subtly supportive, ranging from delicate to diabolical. Though the eruption is perhaps premature, it clearly establishes a continuity that flows gracefully into the next segment.

Track 3 continues with a similar medieval motif, except it's executed on organ rather than guitar. Of particular note is a distantly similar chord progression of what would years later be composed as "Unbroken Chain." Garcia's leads here are divinely simple as he hammers and pulls around a few basic riffs. And though his ability to coax milestones from only a few notes has been well documented, it is incomparably well illustrated by this passage.

The following track, which borders on operatic, begins with a divinely delicate string passage. Although at the onset the phrases are short and poignant, it takes only a few moments before they turn long and conversational. And, much like the instrumentalists, the dialogue is sophisticated, almost arrogant. Thematically, the passage is rather grand, and although the timing is a hair rushed in spots, the instrumentalists tackle the magnitude of the motif in undaunted heroic fashion. The final track, which ironically is both the most obscure and the most predictable selection of the album, is presumably indicative of the influence of Hart and Lesh. Beginning with a series of jagged screeches followed by synthetic applause, the material is premonitory of the material that would later evolve as "The Silent Flute" and "Seastones." However, unlike the aforementioned passages, this exhibition is both unrefined and immature. Poorly mixed, the segment contains a unique string melody in the left channel, which is not at all balanced by Hart's percussive racket in the right channel. Thus, although undoubtedly some elements of the maniacal prowess that Hart and Lesh would later define are present, disappointingly absent is their powerful grace.

BRIAN DYKE

---

### ??/72
**Unknown Location**
**Interview:** Bob Weir

---

**Source:** AUD, **Quality:** B, **Length:** 0:05
**Highlights:** "For about two months, Bill Graham used to call Billy up for advice, business advice, about, about putting on rock 'n' roll shows. None of us have ever been able to figure that one out."

Weir discusses the Grateful Dead's earliest gigs as well as their relationship with Bill Graham before the tape breaks off.

BRIAN DYKE

## 1973

At the beginning of 1973, new songs were introduced right away that continued to develop the Dead's unique sound. Songs like "Row Jimmy," "Eyes of the World," and "Here Comes Sunshine" included melodies and chord changes rarely, if ever, seen in the world of popular rock music. They were more a synthesis of jazz, rock, and folk into a new, distinct musical genre. As in 1972, shows were extremely long, with many sets approaching two hours each, even in the same show. The "Tiger" jam continued, by now well established as a feature of every show. However, instead of falling into a set-ending ballad, the band had the option of continuing the momentum with the jazzy, quintessential Dead tune, "Eyes of the World." The cycle had returned to a second set filled by one long continuous jam, many of the songs segueing into one another. From the time the Dead started to consistently perform two sets, and throughout the first half of 1973, the first set was sometimes used by the band simply as a warm-up. Consequently, many of the songs seemed as if the band was just running through their paces. Knowing they had plenty of time to pull it together, they seemed not always to see the need to pay each song its due. At some of the bigger outdoor shows of the early summer, where there were three full sets, this problem became even more apparent because they often did not hit full stride until the final set. However, by midyear, the band began to address the problem and to pay more careful attention to each song they played, shortening up their shows. The result was a tighter, more completely satisfying concert. On occasion, they would go back to playing monumentally long shows, but they seemed more selective about when that occurred.

In October the Dead released Wake of the Flood, the first album put out by their own record company. It was their first studio album in nearly three years and featured lots of guest appearances, including horns and fiddle on several songs. Just as they had brought the acoustic sound of Workingman's Dead to the concert hall in 1970, on the 1973 East Coast fall tour they tried it again, bringing along Martin Fierro and Joe Ellis to add the horn sound. For some of their fans, it gave a unique and fitting quality to the songs. "Sugar Magnolia" and "One More Saturday Night" were given entirely new meaning, and "Eyes of the World" seemed made for the jazz saxophone. Other fans, however, only heard ear-splitting "squonking" that ruined each song on which it appeared. Whatever one's tastes, there are several excellent quality soundboard tapes available to judge for oneself. One thing for certain is that there are no other shows that sound like the ones on this tour.

Throughout the year, some very good audience tapes were made by a small number of tapers across the country. Most of them come from the spring and fall East Coast tours and from the few West Coast shows played that year. By 1973, tapers were setting up at every show on either coast and in many places in between. It was not yet a practice accepted by the band and crew, so every effort had to be made to keep the microphones and equipment from being spotted by crew members. This, combined with the scarcity of high-quality portable recording equipment, meant that only by exceptional skill and a little luck could an outstanding audience tape be made. This was the beginning, however, of what would become a burgeoning tape-trading scene on both coasts.

Two significant developments occurred in the fall and winter of 1973 that make tapes from this era popular. First, "Playing in the Band" was transformed from a solitary song usually played in the first set to a showcase song from which other songs might be launched. Originally, on October 21 and 27, 1973, the band played "Mississippi Half-Step" and "Big River" sandwiched between "Playing," but afterward, they took the concept a step further by playing a fully recursive jam of "Playing in the Band" > "Uncle John's Band" > "Morning Dew" and then back through "Uncle John's" into "Playing in the Band" again. Through the remaining two decades of the Dead's career, "Playing in the Band" would serve as a frame within which a musical picture could be created.

Secondly, a new theme was introduced around the deep space jams. A lilting, breezy instrumental melody, known as the "Mind Left Body Jam" (due to its similarity to a song of the same name on the album *Baron Von Tollbooth and the Chrome Nun* by Paul Kantner, Grace Slick, and David Frieberg), it became a transition point for the band to dive from the main theme of a song like "Dark Star" or "Playing in the Band" to very deep space or to return therefrom. Having this transitional melody seemed to enable the band to travel further to the outer reaches of the musical galaxy. By December, these deep space explorations—where the band would lose all sense of the song's main theme and spiral into the "Tiger," punctuating the jam with relentless blasts of feedback and Lesh's massive bass notes—went on far longer than they had even a few months previous. The final month of 1973 contains some of the most awesome, mind-blowing jams ever recorded on tape, every one worth seeking out.

Tapes to get: 3/24, 3/28, 5/26, 6/10, 7/1, 7/27, 9/21, 9/26, 10/25, 11/10, 11/11, 12/2, 12/18.

---

### 2/9/73
**Maples Pavillion, Stanford University, Palo Alto, California**

**Set 1:** Promised Land, Row Jimmy, Black-Throated Wind, Deal, Me and My Uncle, Sugaree, Looks like Rain, Loose Lucy, Mexicali Blues, Brown-Eyed Women, El Paso, Here Comes Sunshine, Playing in the Band
**Set 2:** China Cat Sunflower > I Know You Rider, Jack Straw, They Love Each Other, Truckin' > Eyes of the World > China Doll, Big River, Ramble On Rose, Box of Rain, Wave That Flag, Sugar Magnolia, Uncle John's Band, Around and Around
**Encore:** Casey Jones

**1. Source:** SBD, **Quality:** A+, **Length:** 3:30, **Genealogy:** MR > RR > DAT
**2. Source:** FM-SBD (DHH 30 and 31, GDH 103), **Quality:** A+, **Length:** 2:00 ("Black-Throated Wind," "Loose Lucy" through "Here Comes Sunshine," "China Cat" > "I Know You Rider," "Big River," "Box of Rain," "Wave That Flag")
**Highlights:** Row Jimmy, Here Comes Sunshine, Playing in the Band, China Cat Sunflower > I Know You Rider, Jack Straw, They Love Each Other, Eyes of the World > China Doll

According to Dan Healy, this was the first Wall of Sound show. He says that on the first note of the first set, every tweeter blew. Notwithstanding, the tape sounds great. A definite departure from 1972's sound, this first show of '73 firmly establishes the band's sound through September '73: long first and second sets with most of the exploratory stuff happening toward the end of the show. This show is further significant in that it introduces several songs that would become staples for the rest of the Dead's career, especially "Eyes of the World," "China Doll," and "Row Jimmy." Set 1 includes "Loose Lucy" in its rowdy, burlesque pre-'74 incarnation, an excellent "Here Comes Sunshine," and a beautiful, spacey "Playing in the Band." However, this show doesn't really hit its stride until set 2.

After a memorable rap by emcee Wavy Gravy in which he invites the audience to help aid Vietnam War victims, he introduces the Grateful Dead as the "sunshine makers." They launch immediately into one of the tightest, spunkiest renditions of "China Cat" > "I Know You Rider" ever! The first "They Love Each Other" is also superlative—maybe the best ever with a funky, syncopated tempo that seriously bops. "Eyes of the World" > "China Doll" in its first appearance sounds like they've been playing it for years. "Eyes of the World" includes a slightly underdeveloped version of the minor arpeggio jam that signifies pre-'75 versions. Every song in this set is played with extreme competence, yet few of them truly stand out.

HARRY HAHN

---

### ❊ 2/15/73 ❊
#### Dane County Coliseum, Madison, Wisconsin

**Set 1:** Loose Lucy, Beat It on Down the Line, Mexicali Blues, Tennessee Jed, Looks like Rain//, Box of Rain, Row Jimmy, Jack Straw, China Cat Sunflower > I Know You Rider, Me and My Uncle, Bertha, Playing in the Band, Casey Jones
**Set 2:** Here Comes Sunshine, El Paso, You Ain't Woman Enough, They Love Each Other, Big River, Dark Star > Eyes of the World > China Doll, Promised Land, Sugaree, Sugar Magnolia
**Encore:** Uncle John's Band, One More Saturday Night

---

**Source:** SBD, **Quality:** A+, **Length:** 3:35, **Genealogy:** MR > RR > DAT

**Highlights:** Loose Lucy, Beat It on Down the Line, Playing in the Band, Here Comes Sunshine, Dark Star > Eyes of the World > China Doll, Sugaree, Sugar Magnolia

This show opens with a tasty, hip-grinding "Loose Lucy." It's the Grateful Dead just the way we like them: Jerry in command while Bobby, Phil, and Keith hold their own. Phil steps up boldly to lead them into a perfect, burbling "Beat It on Down the Line." The cut in "Looks like Rain" is quite bad. The rest of the songs in this set, not standouts in any way, are great archetypal renditions of Grateful Dead standard bearers. The set ends with a long, juicy "Playing in the Band" with the Dead at their best during the extended journey back from the deepest Milky Way to the final vocal break.

"Here Comes Sunshine" displays a lot of progress since February 9, 1973, the last time it was played. This version is more confident and more jammed out. The unfortunate "You Ain't Woman Enough" has failed to grow on anyone after all these years. The entire set is very good, but the real magic happens during "Dark Star." It's actually a relatively short and nondaring version until Phil takes a unique solo. It seems as though his notes are divided into two different registers. The Wall of Sound system eliminated the difference between PA and stage monitor; the two registers of Phil's sound seem to be delivered through two different sets of speakers within what was essentially a giant stage monitor. This creates something of a call-and-response quality that isn't replicated at any other show that I've heard (although tapes of early Michael Hedges concerts occasionally display the same effect). As his solo progresses, Phil begins to strongly suggest "Eyes." There is a stunning moment in which Jerry comes back in to build one of the sweetest jams the Dead ever played. The rest of the band falls into formation, and we find ourselves beautifully transported into the summer day that is "Eyes of the World." "China Doll" follows with equal beauty and the dead serious silences of a funeral. "Sugaree" and "Sugar Magnolia" are highlights of the rest of a nice set.

HARRY HAHN

---

### ❊ 2/17/73 ❊
#### St. Paul Auditorium, St. Paul, Minnesota

**Set 1:** Promised Land, He's Gone, Looks like Rain, Box of Rain, Wave That Flag, Mexicali Blues, El Paso, They Love Each Other, Playing in the Band
**Set 2:** Truckin', Row Jimmy, Big River, You Ain't Woman Enough, Here Comes Sunshine > China Cat Sunflower > I Know You Rider, Around and Around, Not Fade Away > Goin' Down the// Road Feelin' Bad > Not Fade Away, One More Saturday Night
**Encore:** Casey Jones

**Source:** SBD, **Quality:** A+, **Length:** 2:35, **Genealogy:** MR > RR > DAT

**Highlights:** Playing in the Band, Here Comes Sunshine > China Cat Sunflower > I Know You Rider

The first set may contain several more songs, but they haven't materialized on tapes in circulation. What is here is relatively uninspired. A false start renders "Promised Land" very disjointed. Problems persist during "He's Gone" with the mix giving us only Phil. More mix problems are apparent during a tepid version of "Looks like Rain." Mexicali Blues is badly cut, and at this point this tape becomes utterly frustrating. Fortunately, "Playing in the Band" puts us back on solid ground; it's definitely the high point here.

This is a much better effort in set 2 as things seem to go much more smoothly. The highlight is easily "Here Comes Sunshine" > "China Cat Sunflower" > "I Know You Rider." "Here Comes Sunshine" is hot but shortened by a seamless and astoundingly smooth transition into "China Cat." From there we hear a long, perfect "China Cat Sunflower" > "I Know You Rider." The run of three songs are absolutely album quality. The glitch in "Goin' Down the Road" is annoying but not horrible. As this song progresses, we hear some fun strumming with phased effects from Garcia. Bobby ruins his voice as usual at the end of "Not Fade" (how can he still be singing?).

HARRY HAHN

---

### ❄ 2/19/73 ❄

#### International Ampitheatre, Chicago, Illinois

**Set 2:** He's Gone > Truckin' > Other One// > Eyes of the World > China Doll, Sugar Magnolia, Casey Jones

**1. Source:** SBD, **Quality:** B+, **Length:** 1:30, **Taper:** Bear
**2. Source:** FM-SBD (GDH 408), **Quality:** A, **Length:** 0:26 ("Eyes of the World" > "China Doll"), **Genealogy:** MR > DR

**Highlights:** The entire tape

Fans of 1973-style Grateful Dead will eat this tape up like sherbet on a hot summer day. Why? Because this is a tape for Phil phreaks. "He's Gone" is sweet, and "Truckin'" rises steadily to a thrilling climax, but the highly memorable action starts shortly thereafter as Phil brings the band into "The Other One." As the post-"Truckin'" jam evolves from the familiar to the unknown, Phil starts to play his bass in a highly animated "plucky" style; the rest of the band responds and the energy rises. But then Jerry, Bob, and Keith step back to let Phil and Billy take a fast-paced duet. Phil then triumphantly states the official opening to "The Other One" (for the second time!), and they're all of in unison again. Somehow, this digresses into yet another spacey jam from out of which Phil and Billy let rip yet *another* duet! Eventually the song comes back around and Bobby sings the first verse. Off they fly into the unknown again—and, before the second verse, appear the tape cuts.

The music comes back in again with the opening chords of "Eyes of the World." Now Jerry seems to be the leader again. This version of "Eyes" is long and drawn out. The band knows it's in the groove, and they have no desire to leave such a delicious space quickly. This is the jazzy Grateful Dead at its finest. After a very long jam Jerry eventually brings the energy down to a slow throb with a heartfelt and emotional reading of "China Doll." But wait, the fun isn't over. "Sugar Magnolia" is nothing less than incredible—one of the better versions I've heard. "Casey Jones" isn't a slouch either. This tape leaves the listener wondering whether the rest of this show was as inspired.

JOHN R. DWORK

---

### ❄ 2/22/73 ❄

#### Assembly Hall, University of Illinois, Champaign-Urbana, Illinois

**Set 1:** Promised Land, They Love Each Other, El Paso, Bird Song, Mexicali Blues, Deal, Beer Barrel Polka, Looks like Rain//, //Looks like Rain, Tennessee Jed, Box of Rain, Playing in the Band
**Set 2:** U.S. Blues, Me and My Uncle, Dark Star > Eyes of the World > China Doll, Around and Around, Goin' Down the Road Feelin' Bad > One More Saturday Night
**Encore:** Casey Jones

**1. Source:** SBD, **Quality:** B/B+, **Length:** 1:30 ("Promised Land" through "Me and My Uncle")

**2. Source:** AUD, **Quality:** C/B–, **Length:** 1:00 ("Me and My Uncle" through "Casey Jones")

**Highlights:** Deal, Tennessee Jed, Playing in the Band, Dark Star > Eyes of the World > China Doll

It's not unusual that the opener sets the tone for the entire night, and this show is one example. A rockin' version of "Promised Land" gets things off to a great start, and the nice quality of this tape (at least the first set) really adds to the enjoyment. Amazingly, for the first song of a show, there are no obvious technical hang-ups with the sound quality, either in the hall or on the recording. This is a flawless rendition of a Berry classic. "They Love Each Other" is given a traditional '73 treatment: bright and uptempo with Jerry ringing out loud and clear. You can hear "El Paso" coming from a mile away during the tuning interlude; Phil really has fun with this one, his running bass lines providing a getaway route out Rose's back door. Then Jerry offers a peaceful "Bird Song" and takes off with a real spacey solo. The band has an opportunity to stretch out here, the first time this evening, and it sounds so sweet. Although really nice throughout the tape, the stereo separation adds to this segment in particular. Next is "Mexicali Blues," typically tight with Jerry ripping off two scalding hot solos that then put him in the mood for "Deal." This is a great version with the solo here going for two verses, the second one absolutely screaming. It comes complete with string-stretchin' overtones and a few chords crunched in for good measure. An unexpected and full "Beer Barrel Polka" tuning turns up next, leading directly into "Looks like Rain." A very pretty rendering, which unfortunately gets clipped at the end of side A of many cassette tapes, the last bit of the refrain starting out side B. "Tennessee Jed" starts right after, and Jerry, quite animated on vocals with lots of comical expression in his delivery, is holding back on guitar. He teases during the first and second solos, doing a little midrange chicken scratchin'. Then the third break comes 'round. It starts out like the first two, in a midrange octave, then builds slowly, moving to lower registers with a little "Shortnin' Bread" flavoring, then to ever higher registers and the denouement, with Keith and Bob providing wonderful support. Phil has seemed to be having a lot of fun singing backup all evening, and now he gets a chance to step to the fore with "Box of Rain." The moment is almost spoiled by Donna who is singing harmony on every other line. Somehow she restrains herself just enough so that Phil's lead vocal is mostly audible and the whole thing works pretty well. Phil ends with a hearty "Thank you!" as that last A-suspended-fourth fades out. It's the end of the set, so that must mean it's time for "Playin' in the Band"; this one is another jazzy interstellar meltdown starring the entire crew of psychonauts: mind-bending ensemble jamming at its cosmic best and it's still the first set!

The first two songs of set 2 are often found on the end of side B of the first-set cassette tape. Something happened to the mix during the set break because most of the band's vocals are largely inaudible throughout the first few verses of the "Wave That Flag" opener. The vocals kick in after the first break, and the band starts really cookin'. The second break has Jerry wailing away ferociously and nailing every note. Up to this point the tape is still a very nice soundboard recording, and would appear to be from the same source as the first set. Bob announces an "equipment malfunction" just seconds before they launch into a hot "Me and My Uncle," which then gets clipped right after Bob's "uncle started winnin' . . ."

Tape 2 of this show is from an unknown audience source and begins with "Me and My Uncle," from the top, including the malfunction announcement. The next segment is one of those magical moments that defines the attraction of this period of the band for me. "Dark Star," beginning mystically and heard via the medium of this murky audience recording, takes off for destination unknown and is immediately riveting, mesmerizing. The liquid introduction and opening statement of the main theme fuel the blast-off, which gives off sweet smokelike sound clouds wafting up to form a beautiful first verse. An incredible moment ensues where Jerry's guitar is transformed into a fire-breathing dragon. The reality check comes on rather quickly with a segue into "Eyes of the World" and unfortunately this coincides with a downturn in the sound quality. The jamming gets intense here as Jerry steers the ship back into uncharted space. What a way to travel! As the band continues its fascinating journey it discovers a "Stronger Than Dirt" jam beneath some cosmic debris. The end appears to be in sight however with the graceful and delicate development of "China Doll," closing out side A in gorgeous style.

All of side B serves as the finale, which basically rocks out. "Around and Around" starts it off in smokin' fashion. After this, a splice is heard just clipping the first note or two of "Goin' Down the Road Feelin' Bad." It's a heavy version that eventually winds down before

# Reviews: February 1973

yielding to "One More Saturday Night," during which the band completes a scorching reentry into the real world, splashing down in an ocean of adoration. The "Casey Jones" encore highlights the bouncy, clapping audience. You can feel the entire room smiling and bobbing along with the happy gratefulnauts as they wait for the next bus to come by, fish 'em outta the Champaign sea, and carry 'em to the next launch site.

TOM FERRARO

---

### 2/24/73
**Field House, University of Iowa, Iowa City, Iowa**

**Set 1:** El Paso
**Set 2:** Wave That Flag, You Ain't Woman Enough, Truckin', Nobody's Fault But Mine Jam > Eyes of the World// > Sugar Magnolia//

---

**1. Source:** AUD, **Quality:** C–, **Length:** 1:00
**2. Source:** FM (GDH364), **Quality:** A, **Length:** 0:15 (the jam out of "Eyes of the World")
**Highlights:** Truckin' > Nobody's Fault But Mine Jam > Eyes of the World > Sugar Magnolia

The tape begins with a rockin' rendition of "Wave That Flag," followed by a brief excerpt of "You Ain't Woman Enough" before moving into the heart of the set. Though solidly performed, "Truckin'" is pretty standard until the outro jam, where Garcia launches ferociously with an unusually energized interpretation of his standby licks. The timing on a few of the climaxes is missed, seemingly due to the band becoming aloof in the midst of the music. Slowly, Garcia and Lesh unwind the jam, falling into the "Nobody's Fault But Mine Jam," which contains a fantastic Garcia/Lesh standoff, each playing chops against the other's in contrasting fashion. As Garcia blazes, Lesh descends, each fighting for control of the tempo. After allowing Weir to throw in a brief allusion to "Wang Dang Doodle," Garcia embarks on a series of direct and methodical string bends that slice through the frenzied drive of Lesh's bass. After a brief eruption, Garcia quickly spirals the band into the meltdown, where Lesh begins to lay the bombs that segue into "Eyes of the World." The interplay among the three stringmen displayed here, both during and between the verses, is remarkably dynamic. While Lesh playfully counters the guitarists with curvy ascensions and regressions, Garcia and Weir trade some comfortable in-sync/out-of-sync rhythm chops that blend beautifully against Kreutzmann's percussive splashes. The outro jam, though brief, is comfortably chaotic. Attempting to segue into "The Other One," Garcia and Lesh strike up a complementary dialogue; Lesh emerges the victor, then steps forth for what is assuredly one of his finest solos ever. Combining authoritative doublestops with immaculately precise speed riffing, this is PURE LESH. Passionate and focused, he lets out a series of wandering phrases, pausing repetitively with authoritative grounding bombs. As he is rejoined by the ensemble, the jam segues effortlessly into the "Feelin' Groovy" theme, which features a sparkling Garcia solo full of innocent meandering and naive exploration that brings the jam to a graceful fade and light eruption. Hesitating briefly, the band launches into the set-closing "Sugar Magnolia." Sounding a tad exhausted, this rendition is delivered in standard fashion all around.

BRIAN DYKE

---

### 2/26/73
**Pershing Municipal Auditorium, Lincoln, Nebraska**

**Set 1:** Promised Land, Deal, Mexicali Blues, Loser, Jack Straw, Don't Ease Me In, Box of Rain, China Cat Sunflower > I Know You Rider, Looks like Rain, Loose Lucy, Beat It on Down the Line, Row Jimmy, El Paso, Big Railroad Blues, Playing in the Band
**Set 2:** They Love Each Other, Dark Star > Eyes of the World, Mississippi Half-Step, Me and My Uncle, Not Fade Away > Goin' Down the Road Feeling Bad > Not Fade Away
**Encore:** Truckin'//

---

**1. Source:** SBD, **Quality:** A–, **Length:** 1:30 ("Dark Star" through "Truckin'")
**2. Source:** AUD, **Quality:** D, **Length:** 1:30 ("Promised Land" through "They Love Each Other")
**Highlights:** Dark Star > Eyes of the World, Truckin'

If you want to hear some superb 1973-style jamming at its best, don't let this pass you by! While the whole show's performance is top-notch, the very lo-fi audience tape of the first set is only for the true completists—you have to strain so hard to make out the music, it's practically work. But the great, clear soundboard recording of the heart of the second set is outrageous. It kicks off with a "Dark Star" that is engaging from the get-go, with Garcia and Lesh making numerous strong statements one after the other. After some fifteen minutes the verses arrive, followed by some nice bass and drum solos and scary feedback-insect-chaos music for the next seven minutes—and then relief comes in the form of a wonderful "Eyes of the World." Great "Truckin'" encore, too.

TODD ELLENBERG

## 2/28/73
### Salt Palace, Salt Lake City, Utah

**Set 1:** Cold Rain and Snow, Beat It on Down the Line, They Love Each Other, Mexicali Blues, Sugaree, Box of Rain, El Paso, He's Gone, Jack Straw
**Set 2:** China Cat Sunflower > I Know You Rider, Big River, Row Jimmy, Promised Land, //The Other One > Eyes of the World

**Source:** SBD, **Quality:** B+, **Length:** 2:00
**Highlights:** The Other One > Eyes of the World

As has been previously stated, early 1973 was a transitional period for the Grateful Dead. In yet another attempt to remain stylistically fresh, the band gravitated from a young and chaotic psychedelic sound to a more sophisticated and smoother jazz-based sound, the result of the loss of Pigpen and the integration of the Godchauxs. The extended jams of manic disarray that often veered off in several directions at once were less emphasized, replaced by focused and concise jams that revolved around specific themes in ensemble format. Taking their time in warming up, the band performs the first set solidly but without any mind-blowing numbers. It is obvious that the frontmen are still adjusting to an additional singer in the band, and consequently the vocals are executed with a trace of uncertainty. Wisely, the band breaks after about fifty minutes, being cautious not to blow out early. From the first note of the second set "China" > "Rider" opener, it becomes evident that the band is ready to get serious. Garcia leads the way through "China Cat" authoritatively before tagging Weir, who handles the transition into "Rider." Throughout the transition the momentum builds steadily, like water against a dam and, after the band hits the first instrumental climax, is unleashed in a spiraling catharsis. Kreutzmann in particular does the work of two drummers, successfully confusing the rest of the band as the lead in to "Rider" occurs. The band uses the well-executed "Rider" to taper down from the jam as Garcia restlessly coaxes focused sixteenth-note runs from his axe. "Big River" is executed with the same amount of energy, and the band has trouble bringing the pace down through "Row Jimmy." Even so, this reading is extremely sweet, filled with passion, and even contains semiaccurate vocal blends. The following "Promised Land" is highlighted by a fantastically charged solo from Keith. Unfortunately, the heart of the second set is missing, and the second tape breaks in on the segue into "The Other One." Though not on the level of the jam in Iowa City four nights earlier, what follows is four minutes of pure Lesh at his finest. Aided by Kreutzmann's calculated drumming, Mr. Lesh takes the driver's seat and subtly stomps through the intro several times, breaking off with short phrases each time. Slowly, he begins to branch off from the theme with angular commands before dropping off into a circular jam that spirals rapidly around the theme. Suddenly launching back into "The Other One," he yields to Garcia, who continues the jam with some furious ascending and descending licks of his own. Godchaux softly tries to interject as the band begins to melt, but is overpowered by Garcia, who scrambles frantically as he leads the band back into the verse. Weir assumes the vocal chores flawlessly, inserting a "coming a circle" ad lib into the refrain. Switching to wah-wah mode, Garcia takes over on the jam out of verse one. Beginning with hesitation, he slowly unravels, loosening bit by bit, as the rest of the band fades into feedback. Finally he lands into a full chaos/paranoia jam that screams with intensity, and the band slowly begins to rejoin the jam, with Lesh inserting strong, descending, single-note lines against Garcia's blazing sixteenth-note runs. As the energy rises, Godchaux responds with soft jazzy chords that set the tone for the transition into "Eyes of the World," a perfect segue that shifts the mood like a morning sunrise. Although this is probably a result of immaturity more than anything, this version is noteworthy for the chord jamming from both guitarists, a nice alternative to the traditional "Garcia: lead," "Weir: rhythm" roles. Of course, Garcia begins to get friskier on the outro jam, hinting at "Stronger Than Dirt," before returning to "Eyes," where, unfortunately, the tape breaks off.

BRIAN DYKE

---

### ?/?/73
#### Unknown Location

**Apartment Demo:** I Believe, She's Mine, No Time

---

**Source:** AUD, **Quality:** C, **Length:** 0:15
**Highlights:** She's Mine
**Personnel:** Ron "Pigpen" McKernan
**Comments:** The "No Time" that appears on this tape is actually a fragmentary and inferior duplicate of the song labeled "So Long (No Tomorrow)" that appears on the tape circulating as "??/??/70 Pigpen in the Studio." This entire set appears on the tape circulating as "Bring Me My Shotgun" and "Pigpen Studio Demos 1964–73." The set also circulates separately labeled "2/73 Pigpen's Last Recordings." Tape is annotated "Pigpen's Final—Recorded 3/9/73." Ron "Pigpen" McKernan died on March 8, 1973, thus rendering that date obviously incorrect.

While this session sounds at first like little more than Pigpen clowning around with a guitar and a tape recorder, it takes only a few moments for the momentum to rise.

"I Believe," a somewhat morbid blues tune, is pretty sloppy, with rhythmic miscues galore and downright grumbling vocals. The following "She's Mine," however, is first class from start to finish, with its bouncy shuffle feel and nonchalant vocals. Interestingly, Pigpen downplays his traditional Texas influences, instead opting for a touch of Chicago in the rhythm delivery. The solo break begins with a series of cute pull-off phrases, simple yet effective, and unexpectedly graceful. After throwing in a few Muddy Waters licks followed by a brief Lightnin' Hopkins fingerpick, he returns to the main riff and final verses. Surprisingly, rather than utilizing a typical turnaround finish, the song fades on the outro.

BRIAN DYKE

---

### ?/?/73
#### Unknown Location

**Studio Sessions:** Playhouse, Walkin' Blues, Driving Wheel, Kansas City//, Kansas City > St. Louis Women//, Bluebird, My Property, So Long (No Tomorrow)

---

**Source:** AUD, **Quality:** B, **Length:** 1:00
**Highlights:** All
**Comments:** This tape is often mislabeled 3/10/73. Ron "Pigpen" McKernan died on March 8, 1973, thus rendering this date incorrect.

This tape contains a mixture of traditional blues and extraordinary ballads, all executed solo by Pigpen at the piano. From the opening notes of "Playhouse," the listener is grabbed by the authenticity of the delivery. Passionate, soulful, and remarkably melodic are Pigpen's vocals, giving the track a distinctive pre–World War II feel. "Walkin' Blues," which actually only contains one verse from Robert Johnson's definitive version, begins as a boogie-woogie stomp, but restarts as a common-time shuffle. Finding a comfortable niche, Pigpen showcases his improvisational skills by taking several liberties with the lyrics and masterfully ad-libbing several verses of his own. The instrumentation contains more than several shaky spots, but they are greatly overshadowed by the vocal delivery. The following "Driving Wheel" is unnecessarily brief, lasting only two verses, thus remaining disappointingly unremarkable. In contrast, Pigpen's interpretation of the classic "Kansas City" is a barrelhouse stomp from start to finish. Instrumentally, Pigpen chops at this with the rhythm of a choo-choo, and the tune is further complemented by vocals that are as sweet as a honeybee's nectar. On the second take, Pigpen uses the instrumental break to nonchalantly shift to "St. Louis Women," which is considerably saltier in execution, and certainly more characteristic of the Pigpen we're accustomed to. Unfortunately, the tape then breaks off midverse.

Side B begins with "Bluebird," a soulful, albeit extremely erratic, selection. Pigpen's attack on the verse is done with the passion of James Brown, filled to the brim with soul and emotion. However, the refrain is unusually lethargic, slower in tempo and noticeably less enthusiastic in delivery. The pattern repeats itself again on the second verse and refrain, although considerably less severe, before dissolving abruptly.

"My Property" is musically identical to the following "So Long (No Tomorrow)," similar in somberness but lyrically far less dreary. Like the preceding "Bluebird," this selection dissolves prematurely.

The tape concludes with "No Tomorrow," a deeply sad and introspective ballad. This could arguably be considered Pigpen's swan song, with its haunting melody and frighteningly forboding lyrics. The instrumentalism is classic melancholy, and eloquent throughout. Even so, it is far overshadowed by the moving emotion displayed in Pigpen's vocal. Crying out, "Don't make me live in this pain no longer / You know I'm getting weaker not stronger," it is as though the performer awakens through the music to the realization of the final curtain that lurks momentarily, leaving the listener with a touch of sadness deep and removed.

BRIAN DYKE

## 3/15/73
### Nassau Veterans Memorial Coliseum, Uniondale, New York

Mexicali Blues, They Love Each Other, Here Comes Sunshine//, Playing in the Band, Row Jimmy, Beat It on Down the Line, Truckin' > The Other One > Eyes of the World//

**Source:** SBD, **Quality:** F, **Length:** 1:30
**Highlights:** Playing in the Band (if you can stand the horrible quality!)
**Comments:** This tape is easily one of the worst live concert recordings in existence. This very butchered mix tape has songs arranged in no apparent order and wouldn't even add up to an amateurish cheesy greatest hits tape for a friend. The hiss, sounding like the old radiator in your grandmother's living room, is quite a bit louder than the music. As soon as the listener cranks up the volume on the stereo to hear the barely audible music, he or she just as quickly cranks it back down due to the painfully poor sound quality. Some of the songs are completely obscured through the undulating levels of distortion, resulting in only a few clear songs.

Musically there is nothing exceptional worth noting in depth. There is, however, some historical significance to this show, as this was the first show after Pigpen's death. On a happier note, it was a birthday show: Phil turned thirty-three. The version of "They Love Each Other" has a very interesting bridge between the verses that follow Jerry's solo. For some reason it was dropped from the later versions. The exceptionally well-performed "Playing in the Band" sounds as if it were leaking through the doors from a smoky, basement-type jazz club. If you're a person who just has to have every show on tape, then this will be quite a rarity for you! If that's not your goal, then don't waste your time—you can find so much more elsewhere.

COREY SANDERSON

*Ticket stub for 3/15/73 at Nassau Coliseum, Uniondale*

## 3/16/73
### Nassau Veterans Memorial Coliseum, Uniondale, New York

**Set 1:** China Cat Sunflower > I Know You Rider, Jack Straw, Wave That Flag, Looks like Rain, Ramble On Rose, Box of Rain, Beat It on Down the Line, They Love Each Other, El Paso, Row Jimmy, Mexicali Blues, Bird Song, Playing in the Band
**Set 2:** Promised Land > Bertha > Greatest Story Ever Told, Loser, Big River, Don't Ease Me In, Me and My Uncle, Dark Star > Truckin' > Morning Dew

**1. Source:** SBD, **Quality:** A (tapes were waterlogged), **Length:** 2:00 ("China Cat Sunflower" through "Playing in the Band," plus most of "Morning Dew")

**2. Source:** FM-SBD (DHH07), **Quality:** A, **Length:** "Wave That Flag"

**3. Source:** AUD, **Quality:** C, **Length:** 3:00, **Genealogy:** MC > C > DAT, **Taper:** Jerry Moore
**Highlights:** The entire show

The tape begins with a Garcia-led "China Cat Sunflower" > "I Know You Rider," showing the band to be on from the get-go. The transition from "China" into "Rider" is brief, but the jamming between Garcia and Weir is right on, complemented by Lesh's angular bass lines. The following jam smokes all the way through; again each band member is right on. "Rider" is strongly sung, with Weir and Garcia taking turns trading licks behind the other's verse. The Dead keep the mood constant with "Jack Straw." The vocals on this one really blend nicely, and again, the trading licks behind the other's verse is especially sweet here. Then turning to shuffle mode, the boys get the mood bouncy with "Wave That Flag."

After a few minutes of clowning around, the Dead shift gears with "Looks like Rain" followed by "Ramble On Rose." "Box of Rain" is wonderfully sweet, although Phil flubs the line before the solo, which is split between Garcia, Weir, and Godchaux. Nice touch. The set continues on a high energy level, and each tune has that little something extra; "They Love Each Other" bounces, "El Paso" swings, "Row Jimmy" flows, and "Mexicali" gallops.

The "Bird Song" jam is short and very focused, with Garcia handling the dreamy wandering while the band stays close to its home base. Just before returning for the final verse, a succinct back-and-forth jam erupts, echoing "Dark Star." Obviously in the mood for jamming, the Dead close this excellent set with a fantastically strong "Playing in the Band." Rather than fading, the jam remains steady out of the verse, with Garcia eliciting furious space tones behind Weir and Lesh's driving jazz-based rhythms. Lesh subtly ascends the jam bit by bit in teasing fashion, trading rapid steps into space with thundering staccato single notes. At the four-minute mark, the band becomes fully lost in deep space, each player screaming in a disoriented frenzy. At eight minutes they begin to work their way back to familiar territory, leading into a jam of indecision, further out or further back. Alas, at eleven minutes, it's back to the reprise, wrapping up an outstanding first set.

The Dead return to the bandstand confidently with a ferocious "Promised Land" > "Bertha" > "Greatest Story Ever Told." Make no mistake, this band means business! The jam on "Greatest Story" is maniacal, with Garcia hinting at the "Saint Stephen Jam" in between his picture-perfect one-and-a-half-note bends. The following "Loser," "Big River," "Don't Ease Me In," and "Me and My Uncle" are stokes to the fire, keeping the flame going without oversizzling. (Wouldn't it be sad if they ran out of gas on "Don't Ease?")

This "Dark Star" unravels slowly and methodically. The band takes its time wading through the main theme, cautiously measuring each note. Once it has firmly established its territory, the band begins the journey outward at about the four-minute mark, in spaghetti fashion, step by step, each triplet representing a further step outside the song's perimeter, with periodic stops along the way. The jam ascends at seven minutes, the pace rapidly increasing, with Weir and Lesh providing an expedited rhythm against Garcia's cautious leads. Minutes later, the jam peaks as each band member finds a spot in the groove, erupting in a brief, restrained frenzy, before fading back into the main theme and verse at thirteen minutes. Alas, the tape cuts forty-five seconds out of the first verse, picking up on side B with a great feedback before Billy takes the spotlight. The "Drums" segment is methodically dark, eliciting fear and chaos from the listener. Garcia joins in with a few minutes of disturbed noodling before returning to his previous decelerated pace. At twenty-three minutes, an enraged outburst of severe chaos erupts, combining feedback with screaming pick harmonics, which continues for a few minutes before ending abruptly. Instantaneously, the band switches themes, with a momentary jam that is way beyond the parameters of deep space, falling gracefully into a "Shufflin' Blues Jam." Of course, this sets the course for "Truckin'" which emerges at twenty-eight minutes, emitting an outburst of built-up energy. Triumphantly marching on, the band executes a powerful reading, and the following "Morning Dew" is a sweet lullaby to rest your head to, a cathartic release of joy.

BRIAN DYKE

## 3/18/73
### Felt Forum, Madison Square Garden, New York, New York

Cold Jordan, I Hear a Voice Callin', Swing Low, Sweet Chariot, //Portland Woman, I Don't Need No Doctor, Last Lonely Eagle, Louisiana Lady, Honky-Tonk Woman, The Race Is On, Willie and the Hand Jive, Truck-Driving Man, Bounty Hunter, Long Black Veil, Hello Mary Lou, Henry, Sutter's Mill, Connection, Whiskey

**Source:** SBD, **Quality:** B, **Length:** 1:30

**Highlights:** All except Portland Woman and I Don't Need No Doctor. Hand Jive is especially tasty!

**Personnel:** New Riders of the Purple Sage with Ramblin' Jack Elliot, Jerry Garcia, Donna Godchaux, Keith Godchaux, and Bob Weir

**Comments:** Taking stage banter into consideration, it may be presumed that all of the listed instrumentalists are not present on every selection. Actual personnel on a song-by-song basis is unknown.

A splendid reunion of old friends, this performance, like the October 1972 Scottie's Music Store jam, falls amid some of the Grateful Dead's finest performances, and illustrates quite a contrast in musical approaches. The performance begins with a perfect trifecta of familiar folk classics, "Cold Jordan," "I Hear a Voice Callin'," and "Swing Low, Sweet Chariot." Slightly rough around the edges, these tunes ooze with authenticity, and are complemented by the delicious banjo pickin' by Garcia. After a brief and unremarkable switch to electric instruments, the performers continue with a wondrous rendition of "Last Lonely Eagle." Though ordinarily John Dawson's vocals are nondescript, the reading he gives here is strong and heartfelt. Hardly missing a step, the following "Louisiana Lady" serves as an appropriate transition to a barroom country setting, resulting in the ol' standbys of "Honky-Tonk Woman," "The Race Is On," and the classic "Willie and the Hand Jive," the latter featuring a stunning pedal steel solo from Garcia. Continuing the country motif, the following versions of "Truck-Driving Man," "Bounty Hunter," and "Long Black Veil" are absolutely delightful, highlighted by Garcia's spectacular pedal steel solos and Keith Godchaux's pristine piano accompaniments. By the time the band rolls into a knee-slappin' "Hello Mary Lou," you'd think you'd died and gone to hillbilly heaven! Obviously enthused, the following "Henry" contains some absolutely ferocious fiddlin' from "Ramblin' Jack Elliot." Breathtakingly graceful and meticulously precise, this is truly the stuff that legends are made of. After catching their breath during "Sutter's Mill," the set concludes anticlimactically with "Connection" and "Whiskey."

BRIAN DYKE

## 3/19/73
### Nassau Veterans Memorial Coliseum, Uniondale, New York

**Set 1:** Promised Land, He's Gone, Mexicali Blues, They Love Each Other, Looks like Rain, Wave That Flag, Box of Rain, The Race Is On, Row Jimmy, El Paso, China Cat Sunflower > I Know You Rider, Around and Around

**Set 2:** Loose Lucy, Me and My Uncle, Brown-Eyed Women, Big River, Mississippi Half-Step > Stella Blue > Jack Straw, Truckin' > Nobody's Fault but Mine Jam > Drums > The// Other One > Eyes of the World > China Doll, Johnny B. Goode

**Encore:** Casey Jones//

**1. Source:** SBD, **Quality:** A–, **Length:** 3:20, **Genealogy:** MC > C > DAT

**2. Source:** AUD, **Quality:** B+, **Length:** 3:20

**Highlights:** He's Gone, Looks like Rain, China Cat Sunflower > I Know You Rider, Truckin' > Nobody's Fault but Mine Jam > The Other One > Eyes of the World

**Comments:** "Casey Jones" only lasts for about a minute.

Only a few days after Pigpen's death, and with the New Riders supporting them for almost the last time, this period marked the end of an era for the Dead. Fortunately it was also the beginning of a striking new one. A full band introduction from Bill Graham sets the scene in classic style and provides a link with the past before the band impatiently launches into "Promised Land." A long and well-jammed "He's Gone" is interesting so early in the set, and it seems for a while that it is unprecedentedly about to head into another tune. A hot "Mexicali" and a languid "Looks like Rain" that packs a heavy emotional punch follow. We then have an early example of the band bantering amusingly and somewhat sharply with their audience in an attempt to get them to take a step back. "The Race Is On" is reintroduced, with great success into Weir's repertoire for the first time since early 1970. It is unfortunate that it only lasted as a regular feature there for another year and a half. What we have of the set finishes with a "China" > "Rider" that features a long and intense jam in the transition. Another hot jam in "I Know You Rider" makes for a superlative version that must also rate as one of the longest ever. Naturally the crowd is wild in its appreciation. After this performance, it is a real shame we are missing the "Playing" that closed the set.

Set 2 starts off fairly slowly before hitting a unique sequence of jammed-together songs. An upbeat and energetic "Mississippi Half-Step" flows cleanly into a typically beautiful "Stella Blue" and then into "Jack Straw." The real jamming of the evening is yet to come, though, as a glorious fifty-minute sequence starts with a fiery "Truckin'." A pickin' solo from Garcia has Kreutzmann hammering home his support as the band slides swiftly into a clear "Nobody's Fault" jam. Phil's dramatic announcement of "The Other One" soon brings Garcia alongside and together they head into a fluid and rhythmic version that is mellower and shorter than those of 1972 but certainly not lacking in energy. It drops away into a standout "Eyes," whose slow-starting jam soon picks up with the rapid hallucinatory flight of Garcia's guitar tumbling and swirling effortlessly over strong backing from Phil and Keith, leading the band into a multitude of musical spaces before "China Doll" brings us all back to earth. After that a couple of rabble-rousing tunes are all that's needed to send the crowd home very happy.

JAMES SWIFT

### 3/21/73
**Memorial Auditorium, Utica, New York**

**Set 1:** //Bertha, Me and My Uncle, Wave That Flag, Looks like Rain, Tennessee Jed, Box of Rain, You Ain't Woman Enough, Jack Straw, Row Jimmy, Beat It on Down the Line, Here Comes Sunshine, The Race Is On, Loser, El Paso, China Cat// Sunflower > I Know You Rider, Playing in the Band
**Set 2:** Greatest Story Ever Told, They Love Each Other, Mexicali Blues, Brown-Eyed Women, Big River, Brokedown Palace, Me and Bobby McGee, Weather Report Suite Prelude > Dark Star > Eyes of// the World > Wharf// Rat > Sugar Magnolia, Casey Jones

**1. Source:** SBD, **Quality:** A, **Length:** 3:30, **Genealogy:** Betty Board, 10-inch reel, ½ track, 7½ ips, MR > PCM > DAT
**2. Source:** FM-SBD (GDH 008), **Quality:** A–, **Length:** Wave That Flag, Looks like Rain, Playing in the Band, They Love Each Other, Brown-Eyed Women, Big River
**Highlights:** Wave That Flag, You Ain't Woman Enough, Dark Star > Eyes of the World
**Comments:** Overall the sound quality is good, if a little light on bass. This gives a great sense of "being there"—it's not one of those soundboard recordings where the audience is a distant murmur. The band mix is generally good, with a tremendous clarity given to Billy's drums and Keith's piano—instrumentation that can sound distressingly flat in many recordings of this vintage. In fact, because of his clarity in the mix, Kreutzmann fans are going to have a real ball here; this is certainly one show to search out if you want to hear some prime-time Billy. The only drawbacks are no real Phil power for part of the time and thin, tinny vocals that unfortunately distort on a couple of the later tunes due to the Betty tapes suffering from water damage. ("Eyes of the World" is the main victim.)

One of the truly epic shows from '73, this date covers an awful lot of ground and despite several irritating

*Ticket stub for 3/19/73 at Nassau Coliseum, Uniondale*

cuts still provides a tremendous three and a half hours worth of High Dead Magick.

For those looking for unusual song selections, this show gives us fine readings of the proto–"U.S. Blues"/"Wave That Flag," as well as a confident "You Ain't Woman Enough," belted out by Donna in fine voice. In the same general category comes "The Race Is On" (why this never caught on as a regular in electric sets I really can't imagine), and I suppose you could also list "They Love Each Other" because it includes the extra bridge—a section they later dropped. The songs destined for *Wake of the Flood* are all performed in an assured manner and certainly don't sound like works in progress, even though they almost all received their debut on stage the previous month.

The jamming on all the numbers that stretch out is inspired, especially on "Dark Star," the beginning of which is imbued with a restless sense of inquiry, prodded and poked into a series of oblique twists by Billy's superb jazzy drumming. Check the section after the first verse, which is led by Kreutzmann playing cascading, free-flowing rolls with splashes of cymbals to accompany the unearthly scraped-string noises of the guitarists; the core of this "Star is pure free improv heaven. Instead of a sonic overload the band chooses a rapid transition into a speedy "Eyes of the World" that, on my copy at least, is spoiled by distorted vocals and a horrendous cut in the middle of Garcia's first utterly blazing solo. Relax, he gets in another one later on (and on and on . . .).

PAUL BODENHAM

## 3/22/73
### Memorial Auditorium, Utica, New York

**Set 1:** Promised Land, Sugaree, Mexicali Blues, They Love Each Other, Looks like Rain, Deal, Beat It on Down the Line, Bird Song, Jack Straw, Box of Rain, You Ain't Woman Enough, The Race Is On, Row Jimmy, El Paso, China Cat Sunflower > I Know You Rider, Playing in the Band
**Set 2:** Big River, Wave That Flag, Me and My Uncle, Here Comes Sunshine, Truckin' > The Other One > //Eyes of the World > China Doll, Sugar Magnolia
**Encore:** One More Saturday Night, Casey Jones

**1. Source:** AUD, **Quality:** B+, **Length:** 3:50, **Genealogy:** MR > DAT
**2. Source:** SBD, **Quality:** A+, **Length:** 2:20 ("Promised Land" through "El Paso" and "Eyes" through "Casey Jones"), **Genealogy:** Betty Board, MR 10-inch reel, ½ track, 7½ ips, MR > PCM > DAT
**Highlights:** Looks like Rain, Box of Rain, Truckin', The Other One
**Comments:** The soundboard of this show is a Betty Board. Reel 2 (of three) is missing. "China Cat" through "The Other One" is missing from the soundboard. My audience tape contains "Playing" through "The Other One," but not the "China Cat" > "Rider." An audience tape contains the entire show but is not widely available. This tape was one of the Betty Boards that suffered water damage (possibly during the floods of winter '81 in Marin County) and were covered with mold. Many of these tapes were left behind or thrown in a Dumpster. The second reel may have been one that was thrown away. However, these reels were in the best shape of all the salvaged ones and had relatively few problems during transfer. The sound is very crisp and is not distorted as the others from this group were. It is possible that the missing reel is among one of the other batches of Betty Boards that have yet to be released.

The show itself is very good. The band, warmed up from the previous night, comes out blazing. The first set, while not a stellar song selection, is all well played and is nearly two hours long. The band was engaged in an ongoing feud with the fire marshal who constantly threatened to close down the show. Phil was forced to give an extended explanation on the concept of fire lanes to the ever-surging crowd. There were several long elaborate "Take a step back" raps both here and the previous night. This is one of the best-sounding audience tapes from 1973; the tapes from the previous night as well as the 1981 show at this venue are also quite good. This crowd situation did not seem to affect the band's ability to deliver, however. In the second set, the "Truckin'" > "Other One" jam holds together very well and contains an early instrumental version of "Nobody's Fault but Mine" as well as a beautiful slowed-down version of the "Tiger Jam." The "Eyes" > "China Doll" is typical of the early versions, jazzy and surprisingly well developed.

DOUGAL DONALDSON

## 3/24/73

**The Spectrum, Philadelphia, Pennsylvania**

**Set 1:** Me and Bobby McGee, Loser, Playing in the Band, Promised Land
**Set 2:** China Cat Sunflower > I Know You Rider, Big River, Stella Blue, Me and My Uncle, He's Gone > Truckin' > Spanish Jam > Space > Dark Star > Sing Me Back Home, Sugar Magnolia
**Encore:** Johnny B. Goode

1. **Source:** AUD, **Quality:** B–, **Length:** 4:10, **Taper:** Jerry Moore
2. **Source:** SBD, **Quality:** A, **Length:** 2:40, **Genealogy:** Betty Board, MR > RR > DAT
3. **Source:** SBD, **Quality:** B–, **Length:** 2:40

**Highlights:** Playing in the Band, I Know You Rider, He's Gone > Truckin' > Spanish Jam > Space > Dark Star, Sugar Magnolia, Johnny B. Goode

**Comments:** Billy is very prominent in the mix. On many copies in circulation there is a swooshing sound somewhere in the high end, which sounds as though somewhere along the line this tape suffered from improper DBX noise reduction conditioning.

The jam in "Playing in the Band" starts with Phil and Billy clearly leading the way. After several minutes Jerry takes over the lead and brings the band through a typical early '73—spacey, but not mind-blowing—jazz-rock voyage. "Promised Land" starts with Bobby's vocals too high in the mix—this is even more of a shame, given that he flubs the words.

The jam between "China Cat" and "I Know You Rider" doesn't quite come together at first. It's not bad; it's just not as focused as many others of the time. "I Know You Rider," however, is *amazing*, with every musician playing with great emotion. Jerry screams, Billy goes nuts, and Phil drops the bombs.

In "He's Gone," Jerry's voice is ragged, but the band performs with believable passion. The highlight of this tape, however, is clearly the journey between "Truckin'" and "Sing Me Back Home." After "Truckin'" they descend into a melodic "Space" jam. Bobby hints at "Dark Star," but neither Jerry nor Phil actually makes the opening statement. Yet, just after Bobby teases the "Star," it's completely obvious that they're all playing it. They segue into a fairly hyperactive "Spanish Jam" due to Billy's upbeat tempo. Eventually we get a nice drum-bass duet with Phil playing fast and jazzy. When they finally play "Dark Star" and sing the words, it's almost an afterthought!

Hardly a few moments pass before Jerry delivers a reading of "Sing Me Back Home" so mellow one could mistake it for "China Doll." It's not distasteful, just so remarkably minimalist it's hard to believe that fewer than eight months had elapsed since the rip-roarin' version in Veneta, Oregon, during which Donna Jean and Garcia sang this song as though the world were ending.

This sleepy business complete, the band wakes up for a high-octane version of "Sugar Magnolia" > "Sunshine Daydream." As Bobby and Donna Jean scream louder and longer, the rest of the band follows suit. Barely five minutes have passed and the difference in energy onstage is like night and day. It is as though two different bands were playing! Obviously reenergized by the finale, the band continues on a theme and rips through one of the better "Johnny B. Goode"s I've ever heard. Jerry noodles away on a perfectly repetitive riff while Billy keeps the tempo in fifth gear throughout.

JOHN R. DWORK

## 3/26/73

**Baltimore Civic Center, Baltimore, Maryland**

**Set 1:** Promised Land, Mississippi Half-Step, The Race Is On, Wave That Flag, Jack Straw, Sugaree, Mexicali Blues, Box of Rain, Row// Jimmy, Beat It on Down the Line, Brown-Eyed Women, El Paso, China Cat Sunflower > I Know You Rider, //Looks like Rain, Don't Ease Me In, Playin' in the Band
**Set 2:** Ramble On Rose, Big River, Here Comes Sunshine, Greatest Story Ever Told//, Candyman, Mc and My Uncle, He's// Gone > Truckin' > Jam > Weather Report Suite Prelude > Wharf Rat, Bobby //McGee > Eyes of the World > Morning Dew, One More Saturday Night

**Source:** AUD, **Quality:** D+, **Length:** 4:30, **Taper:** Les Kippel

**Highlights:** Brown-Eyed Women, Playing in the Band, Truckin' > Jam > Weather Report Suite Prelude > Wharf Rat

**Comments:** This show, due to the immense amount of music, just fits on three ninety-minute cassettes. The quality is only fair, leaving the tapes at the barely listenable end of the spectrum.

This show has something to please just about everyone. It was a great year for the Dead, and this particular show is quite solid. Here are some of the highlights. The first set starts out on the right foot with an upbeat "Promised Land" and sweetly sung "Mississippi Half-Step." This version of "Sugaree," with its exceptionally smooth grooving manner, features Jerry's playing at his most melodic and passionate. It's a version that you can really get lost in. The tranquilizing "Row Jimmy" has such a warm sound that it fills up the room like the aroma of fresh-baked apple pie. Thirteen and a half beats (a slight goof-up that was nicely recovered) kick off this version of "Beat It on Down the Line," which is dominated by heavy piano and guitar work. "Brown-Eyed Women," loaded with rhythmically funky guitar strumming, features Jerry playing an extremely hot and fluid double-time lead through the solo section. This version is as good as it gets! "Playing in the Band," filled with passion and potency, starts out very solid with a straightforward direction. The band then abandons the safe structure in favor of a spacey, jazzy, adventuresome route. These jazzy versions of "Playing in the Band" from this year are phenomenally deep. The musical range and improvisational explorations in this song during 1973 are among the finest. This truly fantastic musical journey ranks right up there with any other top-notch version and is by far the highlight of the show.

Set 2 (introduced by someone who sounds just like Wolfman Jack!) starts with a slow, churning version of "Ramble On Rose" that is pure enjoyment. "Here Comes Sunshine," bubbling over with energy, is well played throughout, making it another highlight of the evening. The blistering version of "Greatest Story Ever Told" is a huge crowd-pleaser as it is belted out with power and energy. "He's Gone," which displays its usual comforting quality as it slowly sways along, gets interesting near the end. There's a great mini–vocal jam and another hot Garcia solo as things ease into yet another jam. The transition into "Truckin'" is right on the money, with the crowd immediately joining in with their rambunctious clapping and hollering. "Truckin'" gets my nod for most enjoyable song of the evening due to the gobs of energy exerted and the direction the jam takes as it veers from the safety of the structure. The momentum then slows down and a gorgeous "Weather Report Suite Prelude" is born. This version contains hints of the "Wharf Rat" that follows. The opening chords of "Wharf Rat" become the resolution for the incredibly satisfying "Weather Report Suite Prelude" jam that has built up a subtle tension. "Wharf Rat" digs way down deep with a heavy-laden feel, touching the sad and frustrated core of human experience. Jerry belts out the lyrics without the slightest hint of hesitation. A quick "Bobby McGee" precedes a hot and jazzy "Eyes of the World" that takes straight off into never-never land. Billy's playing becomes incredibly melodic, which causes the beat to become implicit and not actually played. The main chunk of the jam swims around the beat, sometimes touching it but never clinging or grasping to it. A long "Morning Dew" is born, slow and serious, filled with a controlled sense of power. "One More Saturday Night" closes the show, leaving in its wake a night of some truly great music. All told, this was an extremely solid show with some fine musical moments.

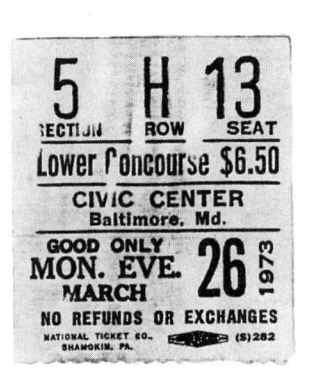

*Ticket stub for 3/26/73 at Baltimore Civic Center*

COREY SANDERSON

## 3/28/73
### Civic Center Arena, Springfield, Massachusetts

**Set 1:** //Cumberland Blues//, Here Comes Sunshine, Mexicali Blues, Wave That Flag, Beat It on Down the Line, Loser, Jack Straw, Box of Rain, They Love Each Other, El Paso, Row Jimmy, Around and Around, Brown-Eyed Women, You Ain't Woman Enough, Looks like Rain, China Cat Sunflower > I Know You Rider

**Set 2:** Promised Land, Loose Lucy, Me and My Uncle, Don't Ease Me In, The Race Is On, Stella Blue, Big River, Mississippi Half-Step, Weather Report Suite Prelude > Dark Star > Eyes of the World > Playing in the Band, Johnny B. Goode

1. **Source:** AUD, **Quality:** B+, **Length:** 3:30
2. **Source:** SBD, **Quality:** A, **Length:** 0:45 ("Weather Report Suite Prelude" through end), **Genealogy:** Betty Board 10-inch reel, ½ track, 7½ ips

**Highlights:** Cumberland Blues, Here Comes Sunshine, Mexicali Blues, Loser, They Love Each Other, China Cat Sunflower > I Know You Rider, Dark Star, Playing in the Band

"Cumberland" is a raging show-opener, and it's a shame it held this position only four other times. Here it has a particularly fierce tempo and an almost rockabilly feel to it. The harmonies in "Here Comes Sunshine" are more or less in tune but, as so often in 1973, sound rather strained. However, the band unwinds from the singing to a first jam that, while keeping a strict rhythm, builds up a real drive and flow. After the second verse the takeoff is rapid and ventures much further into space. The audience cheers loudly as the band launches triumphantly into the closing words; it's an excellent offering, especially so early in the show. "Mexicali" has a real party atmosphere and is also superb. The excitement and energy levels are kept up consistently until Garcia decides to slow things down somewhat with a "Loser" that is greeted rapturously by a crowd probably only too ready for its mellow reflectiveness. It is a great version that brings out the greatness of this song perfectly. "Box of Rain" has Phil in good enough vocal form, with Garcia fierce in his supporting twangy guitar runs. "They Love Each Other" is gloriously upbeat, with an extremely hot jam. The musicians sound almost cocksure at this stage; they can't seem to do any wrong and are filled with energy and commitment. "El Paso" is much less involving than what has gone before, but the crowd roars its appreciation louder than ever—but probably, on reflection, because they *are* less involved! "Row Jimmy" brings things back to form with an extremely graceful jam. However, the next highlight is not until the set-closing "China" > "Rider," which has a "Feelin' Groovy Jam" in the transition and another fine jam in "I Know You Rider." The crowd goes nuts during "I Know You Rider," feeding the band with energy, as they clap along with all-out abandon till the very end.

The second set opens with a long string of good-time songs, among which "Loose Lucy" drags as usual in its poor pre-1990 original arrangement and a well-sung "Stella Blue" provides a calming respite. The near-hour-long sequence that closes this show opens with a "Weather Report Suite Prelude" before "Dark Star" is introduced with an uptempo psychedelic jam. After the first verse there is a deep and carefully considered "Space" before the tempo heats up once more and then falls rather suddenly into "Eyes." The singing rather bogs them down here, but once they are free of it they launch into another jaunty, fast jam that again seems to fall into the next number rather sloppily and prematurely. "Playing" has a fine spacey jam, but overall these closing numbers promise more than they deliver, at least compared to other shows from the period, and you end up with the feeling that on this night the band may have used up too much vitality too early on.

JAMES SWIFT

## 3/30/73

**Community War Memorial, Rochester, New York**

**Set 1:** Promised Land, Deal, Looks like Rain, They Love Each Other, Mexicali Blues, Box of Rain, //Cumberland Blues, Candyman, Beat It on Down the Line, Don't Ease Me In, El Paso, Row Jimmy, Bird Song, Playing in the Band, The Race Is On

**Set 2:** China Cat Sunflower > I Know You Rider, Jack Straw, Wave That Flag, Greatest Story Ever Told, Truckin' > Eyes of the World > Not Fade Away > Goin' Down the Road Feelin' Bad > One More Saturday Night//

**Source:** AUD, **Quality:** C/B–, **Length:** 2:45
**Highlights:** Candyman, Don't Ease Me In, Playing in the Band, China Cat Sunflower > I Know You Rider, Greatest Story Ever Told, Truckin' > Eyes of the World

Here we go with another skeevy audience recording from 1973. Is there anything better? Completely mono, the initial thinness on this relatively hard-to-find tape actually begins to fatten up a little as the band roars through the opener. The first effort here is pretty tight as the usually obligatory sound problems are averted. Fingers loose, Jerry kicks off "Deal," stretching his vocal cords and a bunch of notes during the hot solo. The band really appears to be in sync, and they all have a lot of fun with the refrain on this one. But alas, they eventually let the deal go down. Then Bobby conjures up a romantic moment with a misty "Looks like Rain," and Jerry answers with a patented '73 "They Love Each Other," complete with bridge and upbeat. The break in this one is awesome as Jerry takes a couple of extra verses to finish his musical thought. Bob gets the message and keeps things rolling with a brisk "Mexicali Blues" wherein Jerry rips off a wild solo. Phil then takes a turn fronting the band with "Box of Rain," and it's during this song that Donna Jean makes her presence known. Jerry plays slide during the solo here to nice effect. Otherwise it's an unremarkable version. The recording fades out between each song on this tape. Next, Jerry is heard picking out a hot intro to "Cumberland Blues." A great high-energy version, but as has been true all night, the guys seem to be having more than a little trouble with their vocal harmonies. During "Row Jimmy" the tape is marred in several spots by noticeable speed fluctuations. Apparently the next song should be "The Race Is On," which is actually found on the set 2 tape. Never mind the reason, "Bird Song" comes next on my copy. This one is very spacey; it's clear the band is in a surreal mood so far this evening. "Bird Song" is followed by "Playing in the Band," which is very extended in its role as first-set closer. Not surprisingly, the band gets into typically amazing jamming, and though it's rather brief, it is is phenomenal.

My second cassette starts out with the first set's "The Race Is On," which features some nice work by Keith. Opening the second set is "China Cat Sunflower," and right off there seems to be a problem with Jerry's mike, causing some distraction. The band refocuses during the first instrumental break, where Jerry discovers a few really enchanting riffs and, after another verse, the whole band is off jamming hard. The instrumental segue leading up to "I Know You Rider" reaches a climax with a familiar little theme that often appears in this space, rolling briskly into the first verse and beyond. Jerry's northbound train gets a huge push from the audience as they're heard stomping and clapping along—and therein lies the beauty of the crappy audience recording: what a feel! The "Greatest Story Ever Told" flows in the same vein, rockin' out. Jerry offers up some really wild wah-wah stuff and then loses the pedal to take the whole jam to another level. Quite awesome. OK, time for "Truckin'." The crowd definitely approves, initially getting much more into it than the band does. And maybe it has something to do with the huge cheer that accompanies the "living on reds, vitamin C, and cocaine" line? "The party of the first part accuses the party of the second part," or something like that. Anyway, the post-"Truckin'" jam hints at "Nobody's Fault but Mine" before cranking back up briefly to ferocious intensity and then way, way down into the bowels of the beast, where Jerry finds his slide and embarks upon an ethereal journey accompanied only by Bob and Phil. Great great sounds ensue.

The first side of the tape ends at this point and a flip appears to pick up the jam in stride. Joined now by Keith, the space is incredibly deep and mind-bending, drifting effortlessly into "Eyes of the World." "Eyes" features a monster jam that includes a "Stronger Than Dirt" segment. The jam ultimately winds down until only a drumbeat is heard. It announces "Not Fade

Away," a standard version—which is to say it's great, rockin' hard but then easing softly into "Goin' Down the Road Feelin' Bad." The sound gets glitchy here with some major speed fluctuation and minor dropouts. The band keeps with the soft touch throughout "Goin' Down the Road," and as the wind-down jam is almost fully wound down, Bob suddenly breaks into "One More Saturday Night," which immediately fades to black on my tape, giving way to filler.

Overall, it's a superb show with highlights in both sets. The sound quality probably puts it in the category of "for hard-core collectors mostly," but really, once you tune in, it doesn't take long to get it. Check it out if you can.

TOM FERRARO

---

### 3/31/73

**War Memorial Auditorium, Buffalo, New York**

**Set 2:** He's Gone > Truckin' > Nobody's Fault but Mine Jam > Drums > The Other One > Spanish Jam > The Other One > Feelin' Groovy Jam > I Know You Rider

**Source:** FM-SBD (GDH), **Quality:** A+, **Length:** 0:50, **Genealogy:** MC > DAT
**Highlights:** All

---

Here we have a wide variety of musical styles that segue in and out of each other effortlessly. This is one of those shows where it seems that the band *must* have practiced this sequence for weeks; it just sounds that slick. But we all know better . . .

It starts out with a long, relaxed "He's Gone," featuring some playful, nearly goofy vocal harmonies by Lesh at the end. After sliding into the shuffle mode with a solid take on "Truckin'," the Dead unwind into the blues feel of a short "Nobody's Fault" instrumental. Billy solos for a few minutes before they all charge into the "Other One" chords. But before any singing occurs, Keith comes up with an irresistible groove to change the tempo; Garcia takes note of it, and so off they go into a fired-up, jazzy jam. This soon melts into a very slow jam with just Garcia, Lesh, and Billy. Garcia, as if recalling two sudden appointments he has to be at, suddenly starts playing both the "Other One" and the "Spanish Jam" themes simultaneously. The band soon opts for the latter, playing it short but brisk and rather unusual-sounding. This, of course, flows right back into "The Other One," where they sing verse one. In keeping with the program, they all bail out of this and dissolve into a drumless space that includes: Garcia doing his hiccup chops (not a "Tiger," though); Lesh dropping potentially fatal, precisely timed bombs; Weir's scraping, scab-pickin' feedback; and Keith playing what sounds like a harpsichord—though he may be strumming the inside of the piano strings à la Henry Cowell. Garcia switches to his wah-wah pedal and begins to play a vaguely familiar melody . . . until Lesh interrupts it all with a note of finality. Billy returns and immediately lays down some fresh jazz rolls as the band cruises joyfully into a "Feelin' Groovy Jam." As was the norm for this period, the Dead take this jam right into an inspired "Rider" to end a fascinating fifty-minute performance.

MICHAEL M. GETZ

---

### 4/2/73

**Boston Garden, Boston, Massachusetts**

**Set 1:** Promised Land, Deal, Mexicali Blues, Brown-Eyed Women, Beat It on Down the Line, Row Jimmy, Looks like Rain, Wave That Flag, Box of Rain, Big River, China Cat Sunflower > I Know You Rider, You Ain't Woman Enough, Jack Straw, Don't Ease Me In, Playing in the Band
**Set 2:** Ramble On Rose, Me and My Uncle, Mississippi Half-Step, Greatest Story// Ever Told, Loose Lucy, El Paso, Stella Blue, Around and Around, Here Comes Sunshine// > Space > Me and Bobby McGee > Weather Report Suite Prelude > Eyes of the World > China Doll, Sugar Magnolia, Casey Jones, Johnny B. Goode > We Bid You Goodnight

**Source:** SBD, **Quality:** A/A+, **Length:** 3:30, **Genealogy:** MR > DAT
**Highlights:** Greatest Story Ever Told, Stella Blue, Here Comes Sunshine, Me and Bobby McGee, Eyes of the World, China Doll

The first half of this show, plus the last few tracks, come as a crisp, clean, and clear soundboard recording that only just misses being perfect by the unfortunate lack of prominence given to Phil in the mix. He's still there, but I'm sure that most of us would prefer a more upfront bass sound. Just for us, most of the second set is of a higher generation and has an ever so slightly muddy bass sound, but for those seeking more than subliminal Phil, it is probably more satisfying. Unfortunately, although this mix has audible Lesh, it loses Weir . . . oh well. The playing is as sparkly as you would expect on a '73 date, but this is basically an extended showcase for a long, long list of great songs, with most of the jams kept relatively short.

The first set includes several interesting items such as an energetic "Wave That Flag," the prototype for "U.S. Blues"; Donna defiantly singing "You Ain't Woman Enough"; and a good-time romp through "Don't Ease Me In." There isn't a great deal in this set for those who like a bit of stretching out; "China" > "Rider" is kept on a short leash, and it's not until "Playing in the Band," clocking in at around a passably meaty sixteen minutes at the end of the set, that we get any improvisation that extends the song form. As "Playing"s go, this offers up few surprises, but it floats free over Kreutzmann's edgy, jazz-inflected drums and explores a few interesting polyrhythmic areas before returning to the theme.

Highlights of the second set begin with the hot "Greatest Story Ever Told" as Garcia pours out some wah-wah juju and Donna lets rip with some full-throated wails. "Stella Blue" is as dreamlike and ethereal as you could wish, and "Loose Lucy" is closer to the bluesy swagger of the late-eighties arrangement than the *Mars Hotel* version.

"Here Comes Sunshine" leads us into the serious fun with a performance that opens up majestically into a classic "Space" jam where edgy, unnerving scraped strings and Garcia's spooky shrieks (straight out of some B horror movie) unsettle and disorient the listener to the point that when Bobby suggests "Me and Bobby McGee" it comes as a blessed relief that the zombies aren't really coming for you! This is quite an accomplished take on "Bobby McGee," featuring excellent singing, an extraordinarily tight performance, and a flawless Garcia solo topped off with some wonderful harmonics. The "Weather Report Suite Prelude" is very brief, serving as little more than a breathing space before the launch into a totally kickin' "Eyes of the World" that's an irresistible lava flow of ideas. Wah! Now *this* is why you get out of bed in the mornings. Completing this jam sequence with a delicate "China Doll" is a master stroke; the fragility of this song complements the vitality of "Eyes" so well.

This is a Grade A Serious Business show, and though it doesn't become embroiled in gargantuan space jams like some '73 shows, it gives a pleasantly well-balanced view of Deadworld and includes some classic and concise performances.

PAUL BODENHAM

---

### 5/13/73
**Iowa State Fairgrounds, Des Moines, Iowa**

**Set 1:** //Promised Land, Deal, Mexicali Blues, They Love Each Other, Box of Rain, Loser, Beat It on Down the Line, China Cat Sunflower > I Know You Rider, El Paso, Row Jimmy, Me and My Uncle, Don't Ease Me In > Around and Around
**Set 2:** Tennessee Jed, Big River, Bertha, Jack Straw, Sugaree, Looks like Rain, Here Comes Sunshine, Brown-Eyed Women//, Playing in the Band
**Set 3:** Mississippi Half-Step, Greatest Story Ever Told, He's Gone > Truckin' > Drums > The Other One > Eyes of the World > China Doll, Sugar Magnolia
**Encore:** Casey Jones

---

**Source:** SBD, **Quality:** B/B+, **Length:** 4:30
**Highlights:** He's Gone > Truckin' > Drums > The Other One > Eyes of the World > China Doll

This is another one of those epic, far-out, stretched-out '73 shows. Unfortunately, it is not available in the stellar quality of the better-known marathon show tapes like the 2/9/73, 5/26/73, and 6/10/73 boards. But it is in the same league, and definitely merits at least a listen. The sound is mostly mid-range, and Phil's bass sounds rather remote. But Garcia's Stratocaster sounds crisp, and Keith comes through clearly as well; the peculiar sound quality of this tape serves to draw the listener's attention to the fascinating interplay between the guitars and the piano.

After the usual mix adjustments during the "Promised Land" opener, the first set starts to draw you in. An uptempo, bouncing, lilting "They Love Each Other" features a nice Weir countermelody riff that doesn't come through on other tapes. "Box of Rain" is spirited, polished, and flowing (it had made its debut only seven months before), and the "Big River" ranks up there with 11/19/72. Set 2 starts to get serious with a bubbly and nicely jammed "Here Comes Sunshine," and a typically great '73 "Playing in the Band."

The highlight of the show, however, is the set 3 "He's Gone" > "Truckin'" > "Drums" > "The Other One" > "Eyes of the World" > "China Doll" sequence. The fire is kindled during the undeniably classic "He's Gone" outro. After that, there's nothing left to do but smile, smile, smile as "Truckin'" dissolves into some good ol' Phil-Billy music that deconstructs into a loose, eerie jam into "The Other One" and then descends deeper into the maw of chaos, with scary primal sounds echoing deep into the core of your brain, only to coalesce into the newly composed "Eyes of the World," a tight, dancin' version that segues into a nice early-style "China Doll." After that, it's almost hard to listen to the closer and encore. Both sound a little lackluster, and Donna is way off-key. But I'm sure that all of the fans left the Iowa State Fairgrounds grinning!

PAUL J. PEARAH

## 5/20/73

**Campus Stadium, University of California at Santa Barbara, Goleta, California**

**Set 1:** Bertha, Me and My Uncle, Box of Rain, Deal, Looks like Rain, Tennessee Jed, The Race Is On, China Cat Sunflower > I Know You Rider, Beat It on Down the Line, They Love Each Other, Playing in the Band
**Set 2:** Promised Land, Brown-Eyed Women, Mexicali Blues, Row Jimmy, Jack Straw, Big Railroad Blues, Greatest Story Ever Told, Here Comes Sunshine, Big River, Loser, El Paso, Casey Jones
**Set 3:** Truckin' > The Other One > Eyes of the World > Stella Blue, Sugar Magnolia
**Encore:** Johnny B. Goode

**Source:** AUD, **Quality:** B–/C, **Length:** 3:45
**Highlights:** Playing in the Band, Here Comes Sunshine, Truckin' > The Other One > Eyes of the World > Stella Blue, Sugar Magnolia, Johnny B. Goode

Yes, Virginia, there was a time when it seemed as if the boys played all day! This is the second of four three-setters the Dead gave us in 1973. Due to the lack of a quality soundboard and the relative obscurity of this audience tape, this show is worth seeking out only if you can find a low-gen copy. (Mine is an eighth-generation with quite a bit of hiss, but it's very listenable.) This was the first of three afternoon shows the Dead played at UCSB, and it was the first show in that facility since the 1969 Crosby, Stills, Nash, and Young concert was marred by massive gate-crashing. Check it out: two twelve-song outdoor sets (with an eighteen-minute-long first set-closing "Playing in the Band"!), followed by a third set with "Truckin'" > "The Other One" > "Eyes of the World" > "Stella Blue," and "Sugar Magnolia." Tasty! The "Truckin'" is of special interest for the brief but very present "Nobody's Fault" jam as the band makes its way toward "The Other One." Phil is very present even in this audience tape. The most memorable moment of this show for me remains the sound of the metal stands vibrating at the break in "Sugar Magnolia" as the crowd stomped out its approval of an outstanding Garcia lead during the musical journey to "Sunshine Daydream." Walking out into the sunset after a rousing "Johnny B. Goode" was the perfect ending to an idyllic day in the sun.

DENNIS DONLEY

*At the University of California at Santa Barbara, 5/20/73* (photo credit: Michael Parrish)

*At the University of California at Santa Barbara, 5/20/73*

## 5/26/73

**Kezar Stadium, San Francisco, California**

**Set 1:** Promised Land, Deal, Jack Straw, Tennessee Jed, Race Is On, Sugaree, Mexicali Blues, Row Ji//mmy, Looks Like Rain, They Love Each Other, Playing in the Band
**Set 2:** Here Comes Sunshine, El Paso, Loser, Beat It on Down the Line, You Ain't Woman Enough, Box of Rain, China Cat Sun//flower > I Know You Rider, Big River, Bertha, Around and Around
**Set 3:** Mississippi Half-Step, Me and My Uncle, He's Gone > Truckin' > The Other // One > Eyes of the World > China Doll, Sugar Magnolia
**Encore:** Casey Jones

**Source:** SBD, **Quality:** A, **Length:** 1:20
**Highlights:** Playing in the Band, China Cat > Rider, He's Gone > end. The whole show, really.
**Comments:** The tape I have is a high-quality soundboard. Every instrument is clearly discernible, and there is a remarkable balance in the mix. Keith's piano and Bill's drums, especially the toms, are forward in the mix which, in my opinion, helps a great deal to balance this show. I am sure that excellent quality copies of this show are widely available, as it is a heavily traded show.

The Grateful Dead were playing an afternoon outdoor concert in their neighborhood's own stadium. The sun was out and people were dancing. Music had been going on all morning courtesy of the New Riders and Waylon Jennings, both of whom by all accounts put on exceptional shows. Around 2:00 in the afternoon Bill Graham kicked off the Dead's first set with a traditional "Please welcome the Grateful Dead" backed up by Bob's eager strumming of the opening chords to "Promised Land."

As is true of much of this show, the first group of songs are classic, easy-listening Grateful Dead. The music is solid and tight with only the occasional jam developing beyond the expected. Notable nonetheless are a sweet and simple "Sugaree," a strong "Jack Straw" and a very nice "Row Jimmy." "Row Jimmy" was a relatively new song at the time but had quickly matured, revealing the smooth, familiar groove that would guide it for years to come. The measured patience of Jerry's guitar, combined with some clever background work by Bobby and Keith and a gentle bass presence from Phil, set this song apart from the first portion of the show. The first set closes with a very nice series of songs including a great "Looks Like Rain" and a "They Love Each Other" that is even bouncier than usual. Thanks to Billy and his marvelous drumming, the "Playing" that closes has a fantastic pace and an unquestionably jazzy flavor for the entire jam. By the end of the first set, the solidity of the early songs had been channeled into jams with the high-speed, high-content, aggressive playing that allows songs like "Playing in the Band" to really sparkle. With such a closer, I'm sure I'm not the only one glad to hear Bobby say, "We'll be back in just a few minutes and play a lot more."

Right from the get-go, the second set maintains the remarkable pace and intensity of the previous set's end. A great jam during "Here Comes Sunshine" and the Jerry and Bob guitar back-and-forth during "Loser" are both worth mention. The jewel of the set (and perhaps the show) is a furious "China Cat Sunflower" > "I Know You Rider." A fun, fast, and elegant version, the band's playing is sharp and clear. The pace races and the jam never falters for more than ten minutes. Unfortunately, equipment problems force the set to end early, but not before it's properly wrapped up with a few quick tunes, including an unusually placed "Bertha."

The band returns to the stage and, after catching its stride on a "Half-Step" > "El Paso" combo, launch into one of the great hours in the history of the Grateful Dead. The interaction between band members is remarkable. Involvement is total, to the point that the band seems to be, and surely is, playing as one. The result is magical.

A long, rolling "He's Gone" leads the way with style. The group is clearly in top form as vocal harmonies are tight and the jam into "Truckin'" is longer but more up-tempo than usual. Out of "Truckin'," Phil takes a brief, surprisingly melodic solo before dropping the bomb into "The Other One." "The Other One" gradually builds to a tremendous climax that explodes into several minutes of spacey (but familiar) noodling. The pieces condense into an "Eyes of the World" that quickly returns the show to the feel of the "He's Gone" > "Truckin'" jams that came before. After three "Seven" breaks and thirteen glorious minutes, the "Eyes" slows into a "China Doll." A rowdy "Sugar Magnolia" closer and a "Casey Jones" encore wind up the show.

DAVID R. CECCHI

*The Dead's Sound System, 5/26/73* (courtesy of *The Grateful Dead Newsletter*)

Keith

PA tweeters   Bobby   Jerry

PA high mids

PA low mids

PA low Phil (Lesh on tour)

Keith
monitors
Keith
Bobby (extension)

## 6/3/73
### Gramercy Park Hotel, New York, New York
**Interview:** Jerry Garcia

**Source:** AUD, **Quality:** Varies from B to D, **Length:** 1:10
**Highlights:** All
**Comments:** Interview conducted by Alan Oronwitz and Dennis McNally.

In this interview, Garcia briefly discusses his formative influences before segueing gracefully into an extensive discussion of his experiences with Neal Cassady. Using personal experience, romanticized storytelling, and insightful characterization, Garcia gives a remarkably candid glimpse of the mythical hero who, after so many years and so many words, remains enigmatic.

BRIAN DYKE

## 6/9/73
### Robert F. Kennedy Stadium, Washington, D.C.

**Set 1:** Promised Land, Deal, Looks like Rain, They Love Each Other, Jack Straw, Loose Lucy, Mexicali Blues, Row Jimmy, El Paso, Box of Rain, Sugaree, Beat It on Down the Line, Tennessee Jed, Greatest Story Ever Told, China Cat Sunflower > I Know You Rider
**Set 2:** He's Gone > Truckin' > Space > Playing in the Band, Big River, Eyes of the World > China Doll
**Encore:** Sugar Magnolia > Sunshine Daydream//

1. **Source:** SBD, **Quality:** A/A−, **Length:** 2:50, **Genealogy:** MR > RR > PCM
2. **Source:** SBD, **Quality:** C+ (contains fade-in and -out cuts on nearly every song in the first set), **Length:** 2:40
**Highlights:** Loose Lucy, Space, Playing in the Band, China Doll

The first set here has a few moments to recommend it. "Loose Lucy," for one, is a keeper due to some bug-eyed ensemble vocals and a flubbed last verse that spontaneously leads into a spiffy, Garcia-led ("hey—you broke it, you fix it") blues jam containing echoes of "Let It Rock." "China Cat," too, finds a groove and serves as a launching pad for a sublime segue into a "Feelin' Groovy Jam." Pure velvet.

On a rather strange note, when "Rider" reaches the "wish I was a headlight" lyric, the band—as usual and with great anticipation from both themselves and the crowd—prepares to spit fire, knowing that Garcia will scream out the line. Instead, Garcia purrs it like a kitty on Valium, to the astonishment of everyone. The result is complete polarization, which nicely sums up this first set.

Set 2 opens with a long, slow "He's Gone." The audience—which can be heard unusually well for a soundboard tape—voice their disapproval with catcalls and groans. The Dead ride it out and deliver a focused, soulful rendition that eventually converts the crowd—especially with the fired-up four-part vocal harmonies at the song's closing. The beat picks up steadily and intentionally—until "Truckin'" busts out. This version is carefree to the point of sloppiness; the crowd loves it. After an emotional but poorly executed finale, a strange "Space" emerges. This seems to be what the band needs as they settle into it comfortably. Keith switches to an electric keyboard, and the effect blends in perfectly.

After six or seven minutes, the band begins to carefully weave around each other, a little more intensely each turn, until they pull the opening chords of "Playing in the Band" out of thin air! Simply stunning. *Nobody* could do this like the Grateful Dead.

Keith is all over this version. A swift, thoughtful jam runs freely until Garcia pops the wah-wah pedal,

*Ticket stub for 6/9/73 at Robert F. Kennedy Stadium, Washington, D.C.*

**Electric Factory Concerts Presents**

# Grateful Dead

# Allman Brothers Band

**R.F.K. Memorial Stadium
Washington, D.C.
Saturday June 9 & Sunday June 10**

*Program for RFK Stadium, Washington, D.C., 6/9/73 and 6/10/73*

usually signaling that it's time to try to bring this baby full circle. But they don't. A near "Tiger" roar occurs—but more space engulfs the band. After a while, the rest of the band create a net and wait for Garcia to join them. Instead, though, Garcia teases them, moaning and bending, suggestive and alluring. Phil gets itchy and barks out a few impatient bombs, implying, "Yo—let's either *do* it, or head back into space, man." Garcia complies, secretly pleased to have gotten Phil's goat. Then Donna wails! The crowd roars! The circle closes.

Both "Eyes" and "China Doll" are given a soft, tender touch by Garcia; the latter is especially emotive and well worth sitting down to. Though this isn't indicated on my tape, "Sugar Mag" is probably the encore. There are a long few minutes before they begin, as well as Weir telling the crowd to enjoy their suntans. Regardless, it cuts at "Sunshine Daydream."

MICHAEL M. GETZ

---

## 6/10/73

### Robert F. Kennedy Stadium, Washington, D.C.

**Set 1:** Morning Dew, Beat It on Down the Line, Ramble On Rose, Jack Straw, Wave that Flag, Looks like Rain, Box of Rain, They Love Each Other, The Race Is On, Row Jimmy, El Paso, Bird Song, Playing in the Band
**Set 2:** Eyes of//the World > Stella Blue, Big River, Here Comes Sunshine, Around and Around, Dark Star > He's Gone > Wharf Rat > Truckin' > Sugar Magnolia
**Set 3:** It Takes a Lot to Laugh*, That's Alright Mama*, Promised Land*, Not Fade Away* > Goin' Down the Road Feelin' Bad* > Not Fade Away Reprise*, Johnny B. Goode*

* with Merl Saunders and members of the Allman Brothers Band

**1. Source:** SBD, **Quality:** A–, **Length:** 4:25, **Genealogy:** MR > RR > RR > DAT

**2. Source:** FM-SBD (GDH 185), **Quality:** A, **Length:** 0:45 ("It Takes a Lot to Laugh," "Promised Land," "Not Fade Away" through "Johnny B. Goode")
**3. Source:** AUD, **Quality:** B–, **Length:** 4:25, **Taper:** Jerry Moore

**Highlights:** Morning Dew, The Race Is On, Row Jimmy, Bird Song, Playing in the Band, and the entire second and third sets

This was the last of the four three-set shows that the Dead played to kick off the summer of 1973; they were among the longest they ever played. The second of two nights co-headlining with the Allman Brothers Band at RFK Stadium, this show apparently kicked off at around 7 P.M. and lasted until about 2 A.M. During the evening the band managed about four and a half hours of music that covered the full range of styles and influences that they could call on at that time, generally played to the highest standard. You can hear the excitement of the crowd as they open the show with a majestic and measured "Morning Dew." As far as we know this has only been done three times since the nineteen sixties. Garcia is in fine voice, which always makes a lot of difference to this tune. Then Bob and Donna turn up the energy for "Beat It on Down the Line," which exhibits the ragged harmonies that are a feature of so many 1973 shows. With both Phil and Donna singing their hearts out, there's unfortunately plenty of room for backing vocals to go seriously off-key. This show is no exception, but hey, the enthusiasm's there. A brisk and rocking solo from Garcia tightens up the final version of "Wave That Flag" before its transmutation into "U.S. Blues" the following year. Bob wryly introduces an excellent "The Race Is On" as "a song for our times," before the band really settles into its stride for the closing numbers of the set. "Row Jimmy" is beautifully structured, with fine vocals from Garcia again and perfect accompaniment from Keith. The vocals of "Bird Song" subside into a wonderfully atonal jazzy jam with Garcia and Keith trading off each other. Whenever it seems about to slip back into vocals, either Kreutzmann or Lesh gently shoves it in another direction until Garcia finally slides in with the last verse. After this level of jamming, the long, spacey, bassy "Playing in the Band" that follows lets us forget we were listening to a mere first set.

The second set kicks off with an unusual and excellent "Eyes of the World." Garcia plunges into his first and second solos with real passion, and the jam that follows is intense as he keeps verging toward dissonance and the band continually pulls him back into the rhythmic swing that has by now taken hold. The result is a panoply of spacey jams and jam-filled spaces that run on the back of the established beat. A bluesy interlude brings us to an impeccably executed "Stella Blue," with Phil taking charge and establishing a rhythm that allows the lyrics to be showcased, as they should be. Garcia closes with a tender solo. "Here Comes Sunshine" wanders into a long, crystalline, hauntingly beautiful jam; it's certainly one of the finest ever versions, with Weir's playing particularly admirable. "Around and Around" has Weir in fine voice, and Garcia and Keith right alongside: another standout. "Dark Star" kicks off with a long and unusual, teasing but tight introductory jam that never loses its way. Gentle use of feedback and a bass solo bring the rest of the band back in for a curious jam that gives way to the first and only verse. More gentle feedback and space lead to an extraordinary period that starts with Garcia making incredible psychedelic runs up and down the neck of his guitar, then going into a "jungle space" that sounds like the chattering of monkeys. More space leads into "He's Gone," which is stately and once again features very prominent harmonies. A nice jam then precedes "Wharf Rat." "Truckin' " has a fiery solo, and the "Sugar Magnolia" that follows is particularly tight and exciting, with a surprising solo from Garcia that overlays the lead-out from the song into "Sunshine Daydream."

The fact that this is no mortal concert is underscored not only by the fact that the band then steps out for a third set, but also that some of the Allman Brothers Band as well as Merl Saunders join them for it. They start with the Bob Dylan tune "It Takes a Lot to Laugh, It Takes a Train to Cry," which was the only time they did this tune until the six versions of the early 1990s. It is, however, without any real fire—which is certainly *not* the case for the even more rare (only one other version) "That's Alright Mama" that follows it. It is a hot blend of Allmans and Dead that spins out the jams. "Promised Land" is tight, but necessarily a bit of a comedown. "Not Fade Away" soon makes up for it, though, with a long and gentle roller-coaster ride of intense jamming where the laid-back Allman feel really takes hold but is taken to another space entirely by the musicality and interaction of the Dead. Garcia toys with "Mountain Jam" for a while before "Goin' Down the Road," where Dickey Betts kicks the band into high gear. Garcia responds immediately and the two play furiously off of each other. After Phil plunges in to slow things down, "Drums" appears seamlessly and in turn leads to a Weir-screaming high-energy "Not Fade Away" reprise. "Johnny B. Goode" sends the crowd home.

Overall, although not quite every tune is a standout, if you had to take one show to a desert island . . .

JAMES SWIFT

---

### 6/22/73
**P.N.E. Coliseum, Vancouver, British Columbia, Canada**

**Set 1:** Bertha, Beat It on Down the Line, Deal, Mexicali Blues, Box of Rain, Bird Song, Sugaree, Looks like Rain, Row Jimmy, Jack Straw, China Cat Sunflower > I Know You Rider, Big River, Tennessee Jed, Playing in the Band

**Set 2:** Here Comes Sunshine, Promised Land, Brown-Eyed Women, El Paso, Black Peter, Greatest Story Ever Told, Big Railroad Blues, He's Gone > Truckin' > Nobody's Fault but Mine Jam > Phil Solo > Jam One > The Other One > Jam Two > Wharf Rat, Sugar Magnolia, Casey Jones

---

**1. Source:** SBD, **Quality:** A+, **Length:** 2:45 ("Bertha" through "The Other One"), **Genealogy:** Betty Board, 10-inch reel, ½ track, 7½ ips, MR > PCM > DAT

**2. Source:** AUD, **Quality:** B+, **Length:** 0:45 ("Jam Two" through "Casey Jones")

**Highlights:** Greatest Story Ever Told, rhythm guitar on Deal, Weir's playing throughout, improvisations

This is really a song-oriented show, but the two jams, one at the end of the first set and one at the end of the second set, are long and excellent. "Playing" gives us jam #1. These thirteen minutes are fast, dark, and mostly quiet. After eleven minutes on shifting minor-key tonal centers, an onstage voice (Jerry?) shouts, "Slow down," and the band negotiates a delicately crafted approach to the "Playing" reprise. The second jam, which begins with the end of "He's Gone," fills most of the third cassette. During the bluesy vocals at the end of the song, the gospel quartet delivers a sermon that winds down to a hot intro for a killer "Truckin'." The tail end of "Truckin'" fades into a long, high jam that features Lesh-Kreutzmann-Garcia > Lesh-Kreutzmann > a long Lesh solo, then back through Kreutzmann, adding Garcia and the rest for more long, rocking improvisation. "The Other One" pops up for a while, then dissolves quickly into the weirdest tweaky Mandelbrot chaos insect music. Only to return red hot from silence with a naked Phil "Other One" intro lick. Followed by a sweet floaty transition to "Wharf Rat."

WILLIAM POLITZ

---

## 6/24/73
### Memorial Coliseum, Portland, Oregon

Mississippi// Half-Step, You Ain't Woman Enough, El Paso, Stella Blue, Greatest Story Ever Told > Bertha//, //Row Jimmy, Beat It on Down the Line, China Cat// Sunflower > //I Know You Rider, Around and Around

---

**Source:** SBD, **Quality:** C, **Length:** 1:00

**Highlights:** The entire show except for Half-Step and Row Jimmy

**Comments:** The "Not Fade Away" > "Goin' Down the Road Feelin' Bad" > "Not Fade Away" reprise and "Johnny B. Goode" encore that often appear on this tape are actually from 6/10/73. There are cuts in the middle of "China Cat Sunflower," "I Know You Rider," and "Mississippi Half-Step." The beginning of "Row Jimmy" is missing, and the end of "Bertha" breaks off as well. "Mexicali Blues" > "Big Railroad Blues," as well as all of set 2, are missing entirely.

This fragmentary tape contains what appears to be a fantastic 1973 summer performance. Badly hampered by song cuts, we may never know just how hot it was.

The first set is a smoker all the way through. Following a hilariously chaotic "You Ain't Woman Enough" and deliciously sweet "Stella Blue," the Dead launch into a "Greatest Story Ever Told" > "Bertha" that bursts with energy. The jam between Garcia and Godchaux during "Greatest Story Ever Told" is heavenly. And how could you not love Donna's passionate cries from stage left? "Bertha" is driven relentlessly by the rhythm section as Garcia solos frantically while at the same time trying to keep up.

A spectacularly played "Beat It on Down the Line" precedes the set's highlight, "China Cat Sunflower" > "I Know You Rider." Starting normally, this version starts to take off on the bridge before the final verse. Garcia explodes on the outro jam, leading into a fast and furious "Rider" jam that smokes from start to finish. Aided by Weir's driving rhythm guitar, the band reaches the instrumental climax early, and this one is even more intense than usual, with Garcia and Weir struggling to outdo each other. Competition continues throughout the jam, as each member struggles to enter the frenzy in a race to see who can unveil the fastest lick. Eventually this turns into a battle to see which musician can confuse the others the most, with Godchaux the clear victor here, as his out-of-time chords force Garcia to surrender as he leads into the verse, which is comically out of tune. The set closing "Around and Around" features more of Godchaux's out-of-this-world jamming, perhaps as a cover for Garcia's ridiculously repetitive guitar licks.

BRIAN DYKE

---

## 6/26/73
### Seattle Center Arena, Seattle, Washington

**Set 1:** Casey Jones > Greatest Story Ever Told, Brown-Eyed Women, Jack Straw, Box Of Rain, Deal, Mexicali Blues, You Ain't Woman Enough, The Race Is On, Row Jimmy, China Cat Sunflower > I Know You Rider, Beat It on Down the Line, Loser, Playing in the Band

**Set 2:** They Love Each Other, El Paso, Black Peter, Here Comes Sunshine, Me and My Uncle, He's//Gone > Truckin' > The Other One > Me and Bobby McGee > The Other One > Space > Sugar Magnolia//

---

**1. Source:** AUD, **Quality:** B+/A−, **Length:** 3:00

**Highlights:** Greatest Story, Mexicali Blues, Row Jimmy, China Cat Sunflower > I Know You Rider, Playing in the Band, They Love Each Other, He's Gone > Truckin' > The Other One > Space

This is one of the best-sounding audience tapes from a year that featured some outstanding ones (9/11/73, 7/1/73, 7/27/73, etc.). It's also a very relaxed mellow Dead show; there's an unselfish, patient, and communal attitude both on the stage and in the crowd. Both sides are in sync; in fact, audience applause seems perfunctory, as if an afterthought ("oh yeah, we're supposed to clap now"). There aren't any sound problems, nervous stage banter, nor crowd heckling. Consequently, the Dead roll gracefully through this show.

"Casey Jones" gets things started here: it's slow but has a punchy kick to get the crowd wiggling. Right away it's evident that Weir is in a special place; he could earn a stack of patents for the multitude of inventive strokes he plays at this show. The same clever lead rhythm he came up with for the intro to "China Cat Sunflower" permeates nearly every song here. Lesh senses it as well and sticks close to Weir, playing off his sounds. The first set peaks with "Greatest Story," "Mexicali," "Row Jimmy," "China Cat" > "I Know You Rider" and, of course, "Playing in the Band."

"Playing" starts out quietly as the band slowly draws the audience in. The pressure is carefully increased—a girl in the audience screams at one point—and then stabilized to feel things out. Lesh teases the launching of a solo several times; Garcia mimics a saxophone beautifully, one with a nice, nasty squeeze in it. Then, Lesh mimics Garcia and they joyfully collide. What's left after this? Finish it off, take a break and get ready to really stretch it out in the second set. All of which they do.

"They Love Each Other" and "Big River" get the crowd galvanized; "Black Peter," though, collapses during a severely blown chord right at the "See here how everything..." peak of the song. But "Here Comes Sunshine" takes the biggest stride thus far: the first jam stretches and grasps for space at breakneck speed; the second features a brief "Dark Star" tease by Garcia, while the band jams furiously.

"He's Gone" sounds Eno-esque with its mellow, ambient flavor. The strong gospel closing sounds like some hip funeral chant. Garcia grabs the band with some kickin' string-bending and takes them right into the eye of a blazing "Truckin'." The closing jams rips the joint. The ensuing jam floats between a blues direction and the other soup of the day, "The Other One." Billy solos for ten seconds until Lesh picks the latter with one note. "The Other One" springs effortlessly for a while, despite Lesh's strange, savage, and seemingly spontaneous thumps on the E and D chords. Garcia just keeps peeling the onion, though, clearly on to something. Deeper and deeper he goes. Finally, he plays an E to D himself, corrals everyone's ears, holds up "The Other One" for all to see—and then slips beautifully right into "Bobby McGee" instead. Gotcha, Weir. Weir jumps to the mike, scowling at Garcia and already plotting his revenge. This version is given a typically spacey second-set rendering. When Lesh slams the band back into "The Other One" from the ashes of "Bobby McGee," another girl can be heard screaming.

At this point, Keith switches to the electric piano and a jazzy jam picks up. A theme develops: Keith, Lesh, and Weir hold it down while Garcia gets nasty. Then a familiar theme slips out: Lesh leads the charge into "The Other One" and finally they sing verse one. Garcia pumps the wah-wah pedal and within two minutes the Dead, minus Billy, melt down. Billy shivers and returns with some rhythm. As if on cue, Garcia goes nuts, revving up into a brief "Tiger Roar." Feedback erupts. Garcia then plays an astonishing array of sounds that could easily have been lifted from a '66 Coltrane performance: harsh, dissonant shrieks of life-affirming primal energy. The whole band is sucked into Garcia's spiraling vortex, at first stumbling and then willfully wrapping themselves around it, until they all squeeze at once. Oh my! And then it ends.

The tension is released, the relief evident in the tentative applause from the audience. A crunching "Sugar Magnolia" chord bursts forth suddenly and everyone lets out a big sigh. Too bad it cuts shortly.

MICHAEL M. GETZ

---

### 6/29/73

**Universal Amphitheater, Universal City, California**

**Set 1:** Jack Straw, Deal, Playing in//the Band
**Set 2:** Mississippi Half-Step, El Paso, Brown-Eyed Women, Promised Land, //He's Gone > Truckin' > The Other One > Space > Morning Dew

**Source:** SBD, **Quality:** B, **Length:** 1:50, **Genealogy:** MC > C > C > C
**Highlights:** Space, Morning Dew

The mostly static performance on this tape does have a few emphatic moments. The "Playing"—despite a minor cut—is clean and jazzy though it never gets stretched down very deep. "The Other One" starts out lackluster but builds to an indignant climax thanks to some scathing rhythm guitars. The "Space" segment features what one imagines could be the sound of a whale receiving a mighty enema. Forgoing the second verse of "The Other One" the band drops down into a dense, dirgelike "Morning Dew" that is short on the jam but contains some cavernous, heartfelt singing by Jonah—er, Jerry.

MICHAEL M. GETZ

## 6/30/73
### Universal Amphitheater, Universal City, California

**Set 1:** Promised Land, They Love Each Other, Mexicali Blues, Tennessee Jed, Looks Like Rain, Bird Song, Cumberland Blues, Row Jimmy, Jack Straw, Deal, Beat It on Down the Line, Black Peter, Playing in the Band
**Set 2:** Greatest Story Ever Told, Ramble On Rose, El Paso, Dark Star > Eyes of the World > Stella Blue, Sugar Magnolia
**Encore:** One More Saturday Night

**Source:** AUD, **Quality:** B–, **Length:** 1:20
**Highlights:** Dark Star > Eyes of the World

This three-night stand occurred before the venue was covered and the seating greatly expanded. My program from this show brags that the seat farthest from the stage is only one hundred fifty feet distant. A nice cozy venue indeed! This is another fairly obscure tape and well worth seeking out for the second set. Out of a relatively brief and chaotically ending Dark Star emerges one of the more interesting "Eyes of the World," exceeding twenty minutes in length and featuring many twists and turns not normally incorporated into that tune. "Eyes" is absolutely extraordinary in the way it swings, propelled by Billy's drumming (one forgets how different the rhythm section sounded with a single percussionist) and Jerry leading the band from one direction into another just as you think they're going bring it all to a close.

DENNIS DONLEY

## 7/1/73
### Universal Amphitheater, Los Angeles, California

**Set 1:** Mississippi Half-Step, Me and My Uncle, Sugaree, The Race Is On, Brown-Eyed Women, Looks like Rain, Don't Ease Me In, Big River, China Cat Sunflower > I Know You Rider, Around and Around
**Set 2:** Playing in the Band, Row//Jimmy, El Paso, Loose Lucy, Truckin' > Drums > The Other One > Wharf Rat > Me and Bobby McGee, Casey Jones

**Source:** AUD, **Quality:** B+, **Length:** 2:45, **Genealogy:** MC > RR > PCM > DAT
**Highlights:** China Cat > I Know You Rider, Playing in the Band
**Comments:** This is one of the best audience tapes of the early seventies. There is very little crowd noise except for the guy at the beginning of "China Cat" who wants to talk into the microphones. For the most part, the dynamics of the music are great. Jerry is more prominent in the mix than he should be, but he sounds crisper than on any other early seventies audience tape I've ever heard. Jerry is high in the mix, Bob and Keith are hard to hear, and Phil comes through mostly in the subsonics.

The band plays very well, though they are not on fire. This was the end of a three-show run in L.A., and in typical Southern California fashion, they took their time and crafted each song with care. "China Cat" is about as slow as it has ever been played. Instead of the building to a climax as was usually done, Jerry gives the transition jam long, deep strokes before finally releasing his hold on it, passing it off to Phil, who gives the song a quick scratch behind the ears as the band drops into "I Know You Rider." It's one of my favorite versions on tape. "Playing in the Band" is musically solid throughout, but "Loose Lucy" comes off as downright plodding. "Truckin'" is relatively uneventful but features some great slide leads. During a rare "Feedback" segment in "The Other One," the audience is caught in rapture. This "Feedback" dissolves into a short "Tiger" jam, at the end of which you can hear the audience release its collective breath. Finally, there is a long, powerful "Wharf Rat" that melts nicely into "Me and Bobby McGee." The band was obviously tired from the long weekend and quickly ended one of the shortest shows of the year with a perfunctory "Casey Jones."

DOUGAL DONALDSON

---

## 7/27/73

**Free "Soundcheck" concert, Grand Prix Racecourse, Watkins Glen, New York**

**First Set:** Promised Land, Sugaree, Mexicali Blues, Bird Song, Big River, Tennessee Jed
**Second Set:** Mississippi Half-Step, Jam > Wharf Rat, Around and Around

---

1. **Source:** SBD, **Quality:** A–, **Length:** 1:30
2. **Source:** FM-SBD (GDH 256), **Quality:** A, **Length:** 0:50 ("Half-Step" through "Around and Around")
3. **Source:** AUD, **Quality:** A, **Length:** 1:30

**Highlights:** Bird Song, Tennessee Jed, Jam > Wharf Rat

If the biggest Dead show ever played—with the Allman Brothers and the Band also on the bill—sounds like heaven on earth, you weren't there.

True: All three bands played with spunk and glory on both days of the "Summer Jam," a festival hosted by Bill Graham that attracted more than 600,000 people to the Watkins Glen racecourse. The sheer size of the crowd, however—one of the largest gatherings in history, magnetized by the vision of another Woodstock rising out of the psychic muck of the Watergate hearings—overwhelmed even Graham's ability to provide enough resources to keep everyone comfortable. Freakish weather also conspired against the assembled multitudes, alternately freezing and roasting the occupants of the field around the stage—in mid-July!—as thunderheads aimed daggers of lightning at the sound towers during the Band's heroic rendition of "Stage Fright," turning the ground underneath sleeping bags and blankets into slick ooze. By nightfall on Saturday, some poor souls had torched the Port-O-Sans for heat.

With 50,000 people between wherever you happened to be and the few toilets and showers available, and the only drinkable water around falling out of the sky, music and the kindness of strangers had to carry the day. The good news is that they did—though we may never hear some of the best of the music, which was played in a trailer backstage by a changing roster of members of all three bands on acoustic instruments.

The tape of the soundcheck (really an extra show, played for the thousands who braved clogged roads and arrived early) is much more widely appreciated than the tape of Saturday's show. The soundcheck jam is so spectacular, few have sought out the next day's performance. This is partly due to sound quality: a partial soundboard of the soundcheck has been in circulation for years, while Saturday's tape is an inferior audience source tape. There was a broadcast of Saturday's show on a local radio station—including the climactic jam by members of all three bands, which lasted until dawn—but regrettably, no tape of that broadcast has ever surfaced. Saturday's show deserves more attention, however, because it captures the Dead in a fertile period of transition, with foreshadows of their lean, fusion-inflected '75-era incarnation flashing in the jams.

The soundcheck begins with a spritely "Promised Land," which gets suddenly more interesting with Phil's aggressive entrance. Phil is obviously eager to play, tying the opening bars of "Sugaree" to the beat when they seem on the verge of floating away completely. "Mexicali Blues" finds Keith in a playful mood, with Garcia picking up the pace during his first lead, adding "Cumberland"-like accents during the verses.

The band's collective imagination begins to open up during "Bird Song." First, Weir plays an unexpected rephrasing of his familiar line; then the whole band gracefully drifts out during the jamming section, trading ideas that are never developed very far, but keeping their ears open to one another. Listen to Billy's attentive playing when the guitars ebb in a quiet few moments, offering hints of possible direction to the soloists, while making the whole thing cohere. There's a second, brief excursion into jamming after the vocals return, with some lovely, liquid playing, slightly behind the beat, by Keith.

"Big River," which sizzles like bacon in a pan over

moderate heat, reasserts the band's rockabilly roots. After a standard "Tennessee Jed," Phil blurts, "This is still a test, which means you'll forgive us anything tonight, won't you, folks?" "Half-Step" is taut and neat—a springboard for the leap to come.

The jam commences in a cloud of bass and cymbals, Garcia and Weir probing like lasers through the charged atmosphere. Garcia's first tentative idea fakes out Weir for a moment, who plays a chord of "Eyes" before he realizes that the destination is unmapped territory. Bill sounds amazingly confident as a groove comes into focus, greeted by some lovely harmonics by Weir. Within a couple of minutes, the band is completely on its own turf, in that place where there was all the time and space in the world for each player to add accents and emphasis.

The fabric of the groove unravels into a place that's chaotic but still gentle, like leaves drifting down in the light of stained-glass windows. Then things start to get edgier, when suddenly Bill and Keith—on electric—pull an idea out of that place where good ideas come from, and immediately the rest of the band is on the tip. It's a cooking groove, "Eyes"-like in its buoyancy, as joyous as the "Feelin' Groovy Jams" of '70—imagine coming onto the sight of a spring river rushing down a mountain—and eventually Garcia lays over the top a sweet riff that's one of his loveliest spontaneous inventions.

After Phil and Garcia reach one of those surprise meeting places in the middle of making-it-up-as-we-go—like a mutual "Why not?"—the jam loses its inner momentum. Phil, however, won't let the mood die and leads the band through a short, delightful "Feelin' Groovy Jam." Phil then throws down a couple of promising chords, but there's nothing underneath him anymore, and for a second Garcia almost seems ready to go into "Morning Dew." Instead, the floating suggestions coalesce into a soulful "Wharf Rat," with a tinge of melancholy that seems right after the sunburst of the jam, ending in fragile harmonics that harken back to the sounds in which the jam was born.

Bang—"Around and Around"—and that's all she wrote.

DARREN MASON

## 7/28/73
### Grand Prix Racecourse, Watkins Glen, New York

**Set 1:** Bertha, Beat It on Down the Line, Brown-Eyed Women, Mexicali Blues, Box of Rain, Here Comes Sunshine, Looks like Rain, Row Jimmy
**Set 2:** Around and Around, Loose Lucy, Big River, He's Gone > Truckin' > Nobody's Fault but Mine Jam > El Paso, China Cat Sunflower > I Know You Rider, Stella Blue, Eyes of the World, Sugar Magnolia//
**Encore:** Not Fade Away > //Mountain Jam

**Source:** AUD, **Quality:** C–, **Length:** 3:30, **Taper:** Barry Glassberg, Louis Faranga, and Jerry Moore. Jerry Moore taped this show with an Advent home deck altered to run off a car battery.

**Highlights:** Bertha, Beat It on Down the Line, Box of Rain, Here Comes Sunshine, Playing in the Band, Around and Around, Eyes of the World, Not Fade Away > Mountain Jam

One of the men that made it all possible—Mr. Bill Graham. Just a few words, Bill. "From Marin County, California, to Watkins Glen, New York, here we go, the Grateful Dead."

Thus begins the Dead's best-attended show. The roads leading into the Glen may have been at a standstill; the elbow-to-elbow dance floor may have been drenched and churned back to primordial ooze (the *New York Post* the next morning read, 600,000 HIPPIES IN SEA OF MUD); but there were surely more first-timers getting their initial flash of the Dead's magic that day at Watkins Glen than at any other venue in the band's history.

"Bertha" charges out of the gate with very aggressive playing by Phil, strong and solid. A spunky "Beat It on Down the Line" follows, with an ivory-throttling honky-tonk lead by Keith. "Brown-Eyed Women" is workman-like, but "Mexicali" is played so fast it verges on chaos, as vocals and instruments spin off into different time zones.

The band recovers its composure for "Box of Rain," a near-great performance with bright pedal-steel-like lines from Jerry, nice harmonies, and a surprising little build-up and crescendo after the line, "like a moth before a flame." "Here Comes Sunshine" boasts a lovely cascading jam punctuated by Jerry's stinging lines. It's not nearly as exploratory as the expansive performance on *Dick's Picks 1*, but it's still a substantial short-form version.

"Looks like Rain" meanders, but things start to pick up again with an earnest, low-key "Jack Straw." The band throws itself into "Deal" with abandon, a successful attempt to pick things up.

The set-closing "Playing in the Band" is the highlight of the show, and a major discovery, considering how little attention the show has gotten over the years from Deadheads. There are as many surprises and delights in it as in the jam of the previous day, if in a more familiar container.

After a tight reading of the vocals and the opening fanfares, the band launches into the jam with subdued dynamics but at full throttle, led by Weir, with Garcia employing his "underwater" tone. About four minutes in, there's a brief flurry of dueling lead lines by Jerry and Phil, followed by electric piano punctuations by Keith. The band is already in the Zone, and time starts to float, with martial drum and cymbal accents by Bill, who sounds like two drummers. Weir is frenetic but articulate, feeding syncopations to Bill while ideas stream through Phil and Jerry.

Bill shadows Jerry's staccato explorations, while Phil jumps in and out of the foreground with sudden thunderbursts. There's an ebb and flow of jazzy lines from Keith, as Jerry fires off strings of eighth and sixteenth notes that dart like hornets in a smoldering forest fire. In a wonderful shift in dynamics, instead of trailing Phil's harmonics back into the melody, the jam expands, then mellows, riding Jerry's unexpectedly elegaic lines down to a meditative shimmer. The next few minutes belong to Jerry, weaving one poignant idea after another out of the tune's uncanny riff. This is music for the ages—Miles Davis could have strolled out and blown a soul-searing cry from "*In a Silent Way*," and it wouldn't have sounded out of place.

There's a nod toward chaos in some playfulness between Jerry and Keith, and then Jerry fakes everyone out, dipping back to the restatement of the melody a fraction of a second early. It takes only that long for everyone to catch up. And the set is over.

The second set begins with an "Around and Around" that's better than the perfunctory set-closer of the previous day, an energetic version with great Hammond and rather brittle-sounding piano. "Loose Lucy" is slow but extremely funky, with some vocal flubs, sounding more than a little like the Talking Heads a few years ahead of schedule. (In perverse moods, I used to think the nineties-era Dead should have covered "Swamp," with Bob in the Big Suit growling, "Ahhh, we've come to take you home—*woo hoo!*")

"Thanks a lot, we're havin' a real good ol' time," Bob says, before racing off into a breakneck "Big River," with "Cumberland"-esque accents from Jerry, rising to a maniacal intensity that gets a rise out of Bob on his vocal re-entrance.

Keith rescues "He's Gone" from its unfocused beginning, with rolling New Orleans funk played under the gospel choruses of "Nothing's gonna bring him back" that are so charged up, it's sounds as if he wants to go into another song. Jerry responds with some unusual crying lines, and then a small tape glitch takes us right into "Truckin'."

After a punkishly fast and offhand beginning, Jerry solos only briefly before going quite straightforwardly

*Ticket stub for 7/28/73 at Grand Prix Racecourse, Watkins Glen*

into the "Nobody's Fault" riff. Then things get darker and spacier, with Phil and Jerry trading slow, fat, noirish phrases, until Bob cuts off further exploration by strumming "El Paso"—it's like stumbling into a brightly lit Western movie set on Mars.

"China Cat" begins airily, with three bombs from Phil at one of the turnarounds, before Bob takes some bust-out leads, which are hard to hear on the poor-quality tape. Jerry warps the little bridge over and over, the band getting pretty quiet before dropping into the '74-style transitional jam. An almost hushed, earnest "Rider" follows.

"Stella Blue" is given an unadorned, nicely emoted reading by Jerry, as the crowd talks loudly on the tape. The final descending lines hint at some nice Phil-Jerry possibilities, but then the song ends.

"Eyes of the World" is like a sudden shaft of sunlight—what an inspired call!—as if they had a whole show ahead of them. Immediately after the first chorus, the guitarists kick the tempo up with some inspired, choppy licks. Phil is offered a lead spot, but then Jerry steps in with a take-charge solo. By midjam, they're at their peak, mining the deep vein of golden possibility, but they're no longer trying to get somewhere: they've arrived. Jerry attempts to lead the band in various directions, skirting some interesting places, but never quite arriving.

They fall sloppily into the "Stronger Than Dirt" riff (for lack of a more precise name for it), but it's developed into some bluesy, spooky lines—the darker edge of the "Nobody's Fault" space they were in earlier—then Garcia whacks out some chords amazingly like "Help on the Way" two years before it was played, before "Eyes" disperses in a mist so luminous that Weir has to bring things down to earth with "Sugar Magnolia." Just as Bob's muse dances a Cajun rhythm, the tape cuts.

Members of the Band and the Allman Brothers join the Dead for the encores. "Not Fade Away" gets some slide embellishments, then someone—probably Band bassist Rick Danko—shouts a slightly addled rap about "all around the world, rock 'n' roll is all they play," as the guitarists dance around one another, looking for holes to fill with something worthwhile. Phil seems to be having a great time. Then a tape glitch slams us right into the first notes of "Mountain Jam."

Even the raggedness of this version is lovely and warm, sounding more like the Allmans by now, though Jerry's deftness flashes unmistakably. Working parallel tracks off Donovan's simple fable of a melody, on the brink of "Goin' Down the Road," the assembly of geniuses relaxes into the easy groove, with Jerry managing an astounding burst of notes a minute or so before the tape cuts.

It's during "Mountain Jam" that I have my clearest memory of that July morning, the last notes still rising out of the glen as I walked toward the highway to stick my thumb out, my clothes stiff with mud, under the reddening clouds of dawn. I was fifteen, and I had just seen—well, I didn't know what I had seen.

But I spent the next twenty-two years in the presence of that music, trying to figure it out.

STEVE SILBERMAN

---

## 7/31/73

### Roosevelt Stadium, Jersey City, New Jersey

**Set 1:** Ramble On Rose, Me and My Uncle, Don't Ease Me In, Beat It on Down the Line, Brown-Eyed Women, Mexicali Blues//, Loser, Jack Straw, They Love Each Other, Looks like Rain, Tennessee Jed, El Paso//, Row Jimmy, Playing in the Band
**Set 2:** China Cat Sunflower > I Know You Rider//, Promised Land > Bertha > Greatest Story Ever Told, Black Peter, Big River, Loose Lucy, Me and Bobby McGee//, Truckin' > Bass/Drums > Jam > Goin' Down the Road Feelin' Bad > Johnny B. Goode

**Source:** AUD, **Quality:** B–, **Length:** 3:20, **Tapers:** Barry Glassberg and Jerry Moore
**Highlights:** Ramble On Rose, Don't Ease Me In, Playing in the Band, China Cat Sunflower > I Know You Rider//, Promised Land > Bertha > Greatest Story Ever Told, Me and Bobby McGee, Truckin' > Bass/Drums > Jam > Goin' Down the Road > Johnny B. Goode

I went to Roosevelt Stadium that late July day still exhilarated from the two shows I had seen a few days earlier at Watkins Glen. I had just about caught up on my sleep when it was time to go to Jersey City. The traveling part didn't thrill me, for having seen a number of shows at Roosevelt Stadium, I knew what a pit it was. Until I got the tapes of the two shows ages ago, the memory of those July shows was a bit blurred, but it had always been my opinion that the Jerry birthday show made this show seem paltry.

But 7/31/73 is one of those shows that seems better on tape than it did live, and this show certainly has unfair competition from the next night's "Dark Star." This show is indeed a peppy one that bounces right along. The first set is a straight-ahead 1973 first set with the long set list and the usual inclusions. Of course, back then, folks weren't so picky about "song repeats," but rather just enjoyed whatever the Dead decided to serve up. However, this first set is unusual for the "Ramble On Rose" opener (it certainly confused me at the time). Also, the "Don't Ease Me In" two songs later was great. The rest of the set was uneventful, but there was a fine "Playing in the Band" to end the first set.

The second set continues in an upbeat mood. The song list and performance is standard for a first set of the time with less improvisation but a lot of energy. The "China Cat" > "Rider" and "Me and Bobby McGee" are superb. The "Truckin'" > "Bass/Drums" > "Goin' Down the Road" was certainly a great jam, but it was not the "deep space"–type jam that makes 1973 my favorite period. 7/31 is simply a rockin' good-timey show.

*DeadBase* has some song list errors: (a) there is a "Row Jimmy" before "Playing in the Band," and (b) "China Cat" > "I Know You Rider" opens the second set. The "Other One" mentioned in the set list is barely more than a forty-five-second tease that sets the pace for the bass and drums section.

But now for the tape itself. After a few upgrades, I now have an "A–" grade audience tape. After adjusting the pitch of the tape (a skill we should all learn, folks) and running it through my thirty-one-band equalizer, I made it into what I consider a "A" grade tape, but the problem here is the venue itself. After diddling with the tape for hours, what did it sound like? Roosevelt Stadium! Oy vey! The place is a WPA-era minor league baseball stadium with an overhang to shade the fans. And this overhang caught all the sound and sent it back, unimpeded, onto the Deadfreaks on the field. Due to the echo, you literally could not hear from the back of the field or the lower seats. Really bad. I can just close my eyes and remember the fun we had in the New Jersey smog swamps listening to the music cut through the thick fetid air.

JAY KERLEY

## 8/1/73
### Roosevelt Stadium, Jersey City, New Jersey

**Set 1:** Promised Land, Sugaree, The Race Is On, You Ain't Woman Enough, Bird Song, Mexicali Blues, They Love Each Other, Jack Straw, Stella Blue, Big River, Casey Jones
**Set 2:** Around and Around, Mississippi Half-Step, Me and My Uncle, Row Jimmy, Dark Star > El Paso > Eyes of the World > Morning Dew, Sugar Magnolia
**Encore:** Goin' Down the Road Feelin' Bad > One More Saturday Night

**1. Source:** AUD, **Quality:** C+/B–, **Length:** 3:00 (entire show)
**2. Source:** SBD, **Quality:** B/B+, **Length:** 2:35 ("Bird Song" through Encore), **Genealogy:** MR > RR > RR > RR > PCM > DAT
**Highlights:** Bird Song, Casey Jones, Dark Star

Here is one of the strongest shows from 1973. It's also Garcia's thirty-first birthday. Donna actually gets things going with a spunky, crowd-pleasing take on "You Ain't Woman Enough." The gorgeous, ten-minute-long "Bird Song" that follows features two fine jams. The band is relaxed and focused all the way through the set. They climax with a "Casey Jones" that has those extra singing efforts at the end to make it a special version.

The beginning of set 2 is highlighted by a smoking "Around and Around" and a sad, touching rendition of "Row Jimmy." Then we get "Dark Star." The band is poised. A spacey, summery grace is instantly felt. With this strong sensitivity so quickly established, they simply take off for the unknown right away. Why wait? A cunning, even-keeled jam rips off down the golden road. They milk it easily as it builds in momentum, never too high or low in the peaks, just a patient wait with a bucket beneath the cow. Yet it has a serious, meaningful side to it all. This eventually detours into a funk jam heavily laced with bass, very typical of 1973. Verse one appears out of this with a melancholy air to Garcia's voice: "*Can* we go . . . ," he sings, as if harboring some doubts. His voice trails off and a drumless meltdown takes form. It begins with some deep, rumbling bass blended into some guitar feedback. There's a strong sense of urgency here to get it just right; nobody hurries. The sounds become jaded and strange, as if originating from a dark crevice on the moon. Lesh runs out of patience first: he delivers a savage series of bone-chilling notes. Garcia reaches down and answers with notes like the cries of an amped seagull. Then it gets quiet again. Billy wants in so he taps his high hat innocently. But Garcia keeps it still with some painfully introspective playing. Suddenly his notes begin making circles around each other, faster and faster, until he erupts with a ferocious "Tiger" burst. After several shattering minutes, they take a collective sigh and then quickly slide into . . . "El Paso." This one has that extra juice in it not normally found when it's played in its usual first-set slot.

Up next is a short but dense "Eyes." Lesh mugs the song with some muscular, up-against-the-wall combos. A "Stronger Than Dirt" jam follows but quickly dissolves into a subtle variation, loaded with more space and fewer rules. Soon "Dirt" disappears completely as Garcia and Lesh take turns driving the Land Rover over new and bumpy terrain. After a nice cruise, Lesh slams head-on into "Dirt" again. This time the band fully immerses itself in it before spacing out yet again for a minute and then descending into "Morning Dew."

Unfortunately, Garcia tries too hard with the vocals—sounds like he's out in front of a change-up—while the band comes unglued behind him. The closing jam, though, comes together as it soars to splendid heights, despite missing the runway on the way down.

The gang clicks again with a thundering "Sugar Mag" as Weir and Donna give it their vocal all—especially in the cathartic ending. And as it's Jerry's birthday, he gets to play "Goin' Down the Road" as an encore. This one is very slow and mellow with the band showing signs of fatigue. They spill out their last drops of energy into a rockin' "Saturday Night" to finish off a fine hot summer day's worth of music.

MICHAEL M. GETZ

---

### 9/7/73
**Nassau Veterans Memorial Coliseum, Uniondale, New York**

**Set 2:** Beer Barrel Polka, Here Comes Sunshine, Me and My Uncle, Loser, Let It Grow > Stella Blue//, Truck//in' > Drums > The Other One Jam > Eyes of the World > Sugar Magnolia > Sunshine Daydream//

**Source:** AUD, **Quality:** B/B+, **Length:** 1:30, **Taper:** Jerry Moore

**Highlights:** Let It Grow > Stella Blue//, Truck//in' > Drums > The Other One Jam > Eyes of the World > Stronger Than Dirt Jam > Sugar Magnolia > Sunshine Daydream//

**Phil:** Doesn't everybody wanna feel more comfortable? After all, this place ain't sold out or nothin'. No reason y'all have to cram into six inches of space.
**Jerry:** All you people down back there by the soundboard move back and give these people some room so they can keep movin' back.
**Someone:** Get on it!

A few moments pass . . .

**Jerry:** It hasn't gotten any better down in front here.
**Phil:** They're just swayin' from side to side, fellas . . . No use . . .

So, figuring they've gotten about as much cooperation as they're going to get from this overeager audience, the band briefly reviews the "Beer Barrel Polka" and then marches straight into the second set with "Here Comes Sunshine," a really nice version if you can overlook some dubious vocal harmonies, the Donna Jean factor notwithstanding. The band has a chance to stretch out early on here, and Jerry, for one, takes nice advantage of it, developing a wonderful musical storyline with his first guitar solo. Very nice electric piano here as well.

It sounds as if Keith has been trying out some new gear during the previous month's hiatus. I don't know if Keith had played electric piano onstage before. Anyway, "Me and My Uncle" is up next and—wait! an organ?!—

and at the instrumental break, a switch to back to electric piano—weird—but a very hot rendition of this tune nonetheless. Keith surely is up to something new in this show. Next, a very convincing "Loser" sees Jerry in his element, soulful vocals and guitar with great accompaniment from everyone, including Keith on organ. The guitar solo is magnificent, all laden with ringing harmonic overtones.

At this juncture, Bob announces, "We just spent a month in the studio and we're gonna try something for you that we haven't done before," then leads the troops into the first-ever "Let It Grow" (no prelude here). Phil lends a monster bass line to this debut effort, and it seems like Jerry has been playing the tune his whole life. The flamenco feel is there and it sounds great. A spacey jam is built in, and Keith shifts from piano to organ just as the last bridge comes up. Jerry releases dazzling bursts of notes, and there's grand jamming that slows to a trickle and then flows and ebbs again, settling ultimately into "Stella Blue." This is a gorgeous rendering of "Stella," but unfortunately its ending is clipped. "Truckin'," kicked off from a standing start, gets a raucous treatment and includes a lot of great audience participation. There are some really nice piano fills during the verses and especially in the bridge.

The tape cuts off moments after the last verse when the band really starts to "get back truckin' on." A flip picks up the jam seemingly without missing a beat, and an awesome jam it is, Jerry trading licks with Keith on organ and stretching the soundscape ever further. "The Other One" theme is broached momentarily by Jerry and Bob, but the delicate concordance dissolves into a Kreutzmann drum solo. Using skins and cymbals, Bill works out a few neat rhythms before dropping into a long, low drum roll that Phil caps with his patented "Other One" run-and-bomb intro. This time, however, rather than augment Phil's explosion with the usual straight ahead E-major chord blast, one of the guitarists hits a weird E-derivative that sounds like it came from the theme of a sixties TV detective series. It might've even been an accident, but nonetheless it sounds way cool and somehow fits perfectly. This leaves the band rolling furiously into "The Other One" with Phil now leading the way. A red hot jam follows with Jerry, Bob, Phil, and Keith on electric piano taking serious care of business.

The band then makes a soft turn onto Jazz Alley with Bill swinging out on cymbals. An even gentler theme develops, and Bob is heard fingering a few chords reminiscent of the "Weather Report Suite Prelude." It becomes apparent that "The Other One" will go unsung as Phil steps forward to cauterize the segue with some really cruel chords, and Jerry follows with the opening to "Eyes of the World." A few sloppy moments in this latter tune can't detract from some great instrumental parts that feature lots of bass and electric piano. Of course Jerry is in command overall, navigating through all kinds of changing themes and rhythms including a hot "Stronger Than Dirt" jam. Just after this segment, the band again careens off into a wild and electric jamming sequence wherein Jerry gets into a piercing, bending, Neil Young–like one-note solo that he sustains for ten measures at least.

Eventually, the improvisational flame flickers out, and Bob suggests "Sugar Magnolia," a song that everyone, including the audience, readily agrees upon. This is a nice version of a standard closer with another incredible jam carved in just before the "Sunshine Daydream" epilogue. As Bob and Donna begin their vocal collaboration on "Sunshine Daydream," and with the band building toward a smashing finale, the tape regrettably runs out. Damn, this is one hot set though, with unique stuff from start to end and more than a few transcendental moments. It's certainly worth a listen if happenstance provides the opportunity.

TOM FERRARO

## 9/8/73

**Nassau Veterans Memorial Coliseum, Uniondale, New York**

**Set 1:** Ber//tha, Me and My Uncle, Sugaree, Beat It on Down the Line, Tennessee Jed, Looks like Rain, Brown-Eyed Women, Jack Straw, Row// Jimmy, Weather Report Suite Prelude > Weather Report Suite Part One// > Let It// Grow, Eyes of the //World > China Doll, Greatest Story Ever Told, Ramble On Rose, Big River
**Set 2:** Let Me Sing Your Blues Away, China Cat Sunflower > I Know You Rider, El Paso, He's Gone > Truckin'// > Not Fade Away > Goin' Down the Road Feelin' Bad > Not Fade Away Reprise//
**Encore:** Stella Blue > One More Saturday Night

**1. Source:** AUD, **Quality:** D+, **Length:** 3:30
**2. Source:** SBD, **Quality:** B, **Length:** 0:30 ("He's Gone" > "Truckin'," "Not Fade Away")

**Highlights:** Keith is very strong during most of this show as an individual and through some cooperative work with Jerry during "I Know You Rider" and the "He's Gone" jam. Also worth mention are "Eyes of the World," "China Cat" > "I Know You Rider," and the "He's Gone" > straight through the end of the show.

**Comments:** Most of this tape is a classic, rough-listening audience tape. Boomy fuzzy bass, distant vocals, and abundant hiss all work against an enjoyable listening experience. Some clever work with an equalizer to bring the midrange up and the bass and hiss down upgrade the sound quality only slightly to a D+. In addition, the "He's Gone" > "Truckin'" portion of the show circulates from the soundboard source, which has been patched in on my copy.

The first set opens with a rousing series of songs, including great versions of "Bertha" and "Me and My Uncle." Both are tight, well-played versions with heavy crowd and band enthusiasm. One very noticeable participant is Keith, who plays extremely well during most of the first set, including "Bertha," "Sugaree," and "Tennessee Jed." The rest of the band is tight and under control, playing it safe but not boring the audience. Jerry explores some extended jamming on "Me and My Uncle" and "Tennessee Jed," and Bobby takes over for a nice "Looks like Rain" and really shines during a smokin' "Jack Straw."

The "Weather Report Suite" that comes midway through the first set features the first "Part One" ever performed. The pace is fast, and Phil can't seem to catch the right groove to carry the band. Early on, the "Let It Grow" that follows suffers a similar fate, fortunately much less severely, and actually focuses into a nice jam near the end of the song. The band, now catching its stride, launches into a dazzling "Eyes of the World." Jerry, Bob, and Phil all have their moments during an intense jam that settles down into a nice, sweet "China Doll." The crowd sounds really into the show after the "Eyes" > "Doll" combo, and the band seems to reflect its attitude. A "Greatest Story Ever Told" keeps the pace going with a dose of vitamin Bobby, and a "Ramble On Rose" featuring large, extended notes by Phil, and Jerry "The King of Smooth" Garcia, settles the pace down to the logical conclusion of the set. But no, a one hundred-minute first set isn't enough, so they throw in a fun "Big River" just to ensure everyone goes into the break hungry for more.

The second set stumbles in with the first "Let Me Sing Your Blues Away," showing a need for much improvement. As with the "Weather Report" in the first set (and I suppose with new songs in general), the band doesn't sound comfortable with the new material. However, as in the first set, perhaps the highlight of the show comes out of a disaster. "China Cat" > "I Know You Rider" starts playfully with not much interest in going anywhere special. After the second verse, though, Bobby and Jerry have had enough playing-around time and really settle down into some serious jamming. Jerry takes the leads most of the time, but Bob is responsible for the general direction. His moves (guitar and otherwise, I suspect) turn the intensity up for the drums, Phil, and the crowd. The "Rider" that explodes out of the jam is great, with Jerry working well with Keith during the jam, trading lines in a way so rare with Keith but so common with Bruce Hornsby in the later years.

In what is truly a gift, the flip side of the second set features a soundboard portion that includes a "He's Gone" > "Truckin'" pair. The "He's Gone" is superb with big smooth Phil washing over the listener as Jerry croons away. In no hurry whatsoever, Jerry solos the band into a long lazy windup that is cut short on my tape by a splice. The splice picks up with the "Nothin's gonna bring him back" chant featuring more Jerry and Keith cooperation in what winds up as a slow but beautifully powerful jam. The "Truckin'" that follows takes a while to get going and, at first, lumbers slightly, but proves well worth the wait. The jam is smokin'. Jerry's solo is fast and furious, hanging on to certain phrases for much longer than we deserve. Bobby lays down excellent support and vocals, and the rhythm section pushes the jam at times to a fevered pace but never steers out of control.

The show winds up with a strong "Not Fade Away" > "Goin' Down the Road" > "Not Fade Away" that continues the energy of the previous "Truckin'" jam. The familiar series is played with energy and intensity rarely matched and closes the show in spectacular fashion. An outstanding second set. The Dead greet the roaring audience with an encore of . . . "Stella Blue"? Uh-huh. What balls! The crowd gradually eases up on the whistling to relax into a gorgeous and heartfelt rendition. The Dead pause a long moment at the end as if to tease the crowd, "That's it, folks," but then they pop into a crunching "Saturday Night," bringing a huge cry of relief and appreciation from the audience. Much of this show deserves to be listed with the best that '73 had to offer.

DAVID R. CECCHI

## 9/11/73

**College of William and Mary**
**Williamsburg, Virginia**

**Set 1:** Promised Land, Sugaree, The Race Is On, Loser, Looks like Rain, Tennessee Jed, Jack Straw, China Cat Sunflower > I Know You Rider, El Paso, Mississippi Half-Step, Playing in the Band
**Set 2:** Let Me Sing Your Blues Away*, Weather Report Suite Prelude*, Weather Report Suite Part One* > Let It Grow*, Row Jimmy, Big River, Deal, Beat It On down the Line, Dark Star > Morning Dew, Sugar Magnolia

* with Martin Fierro and Joe Ellis on horns

**Source:** AUD, **Quality:** B, **Length:** 3:00, **Genealogy:** MC > RR > DAT

**Highlights:** China Cat Sunflower > I Know You Rider, Mississippi Half-Step, Playing in the Band, Dark Star > Morning Dew

**Comments:** This is a very well recorded audience tape. The crowd makes its presence known but does not overwhelm the sound. It has a slight muffle, but all the instruments come through.

This is one of those shows that falls through the cracks in terms of style for the period. There is a tough, waterfront attitude here—especially from Lesh—that contradicts the tamer, cleaner, and jazzier playing that characterized much of 1973. The peaks and valley here are extreme, yet fully explored with great vigour. Garcia's solos bite to the bone; Lesh has his "hide 'n' seek" basslines working to perfection. Keith is wideawake, too, and plays that saloon style reminiscent of his first tour in the fall of '71.

The Dead finish their warm-up songs when they rip the tail off "China Cat." The ensuing jam finds Lesh darn near pushing Garcia off the stage. This struggle peaks in the final lap of the obligatory "Feelin' Groovy Jam" when the music explodes. "I Know You Rider" wails, too. The gang is playing like it's the end of the show. Even "El Paso" is a tour de force as Garcia solos from beginning to end with tremendous exhuberance. The first jam in "Half-Step" contains more energy than most entire versions.

"Playing" jumps out of the block, leading the band, squirming in delight at being called upon. As Weir finishes singing, immediately a rapid-fire, thick space takes over. Garcia steers the band at a furious pace, relentlessly, as if the hounds of hell were snapping at his heels (or, rather, for another finger). The music, thanks to Billy's expertise at handling the curves, cuts sharply left and right, repeatedly, with remarkable grace and stamina, as if they've traversed this road every day in practice. Right. But Garcia doesn't just play fast like speed-king Al Dimeola; he puts in beautiful pauses, sudden spins, and deep string bends to drive home his feelings.

Lesh counters Garcia's moves in the same strange vein but with even more unpredictable and abrupt patterns that somehow blend in just right. All this adds up to one of the most exciting versions of "Playing in the Band."

Set two has a "Weather Report Suite" that features some juicy horn-blowing by Martin Fiero and Joe Ellis. They know the song's structure well despite the fact that this is only the first gig of their nine-show run with the Dead. The intensity of "Playing" easily continues with "Let It Grow." Lesh seems to be in five places at once. The closing jam segues back into the "Weather Report Suite Prelude" chords to end the song with a twinkle.

The rest of the set continues to sparkle in this high-octane fashion leading up to . . . "Dark Star." Just how eager are they to get down? After only fifteen seconds they skip out of the song's introductory chords and vanish into instantly intense, we-mean-business space.

Soon the beat accelerates and speedballs into an ornery, steadily rising improvisation similar to a post-"Truckin'" jam; but instead of climaxing, they pull out and veer off into more new turf. Each twist and turn is intuited by the whole band. Lesh takes great pleasure in undercutting everyone else's ideas, including his own, like an ordained nihilist minister. Finally, something resembling 1973 emerges: a jazzy jam led by Keith on electric piano. Garcia blends into it with strums while Lesh steps to the forefront; Garcia comes back with a lead and Lesh disappears—only to resurface moments later with a blowtorch aimed at the tag on Jerry's Levi's. Soon an even-tempered jam takes form, shaped by everyone but Lesh, who takes pride in disfiguring it.

Finally, Garcia guides the band into verse one. After the final word fades away, Lesh impishly torpedoes the house with chords of raunchy, bruising notes. This turns into a cavity-popping solo. Garcia tries to get a piece but is drowned out. This could be the loudest, nastiest solo

Lesh ever played. Pure exposure. After only a few minutes, though, Lesh starts "Morning Dew." Lesh continues, however, to play bizarre, barely fitting notes as he's clearly not ready to return from his pilgrimage to Pluto. He's not playing notes so much as shoveling chunks of sound loose from his bass. Consequently, this is one strange-sounding "Dew." Garcia sings it sweetly as if nothing were going on. The closing jam creates page-turning suspense as Garcia joins Lesh for some moon-shooting riffs himself.

All in all, an exceptional show in every sense and surely a strong candidate for an official Vault release.

MICHAEL M. GETZ

Musically, the previous night was superior, although this night offered up a nice "Eyes of the World" with a fine jam afterward that moves in a few directions, returning to "Eyes" at each change, before slowing into "Stella Blue." Keith plays well in this show; his piano comes out strong on such songs as "Let Me Sing Your Blues Away," "Around and Around," and "Big River." Phil can also be heard playing quite well. Most of the show plays out as a fun dance concert, with a few slow pieces to let us enjoy the musical talent of the band. "Row Jimmy" is quite relaxed, almost reggae-ish at the start.

DAN DASARO

---

### 9/12/73
**College of William and Mary, Williamsburg, Virginia**

**Set 1:** Bertha, Mexicali Blues, Brown-Eyed Women, El Paso, //Don't Ease Me In, Looks like Rain, Beer Barrel Polka equipment break, Ramble On Rose, Me and My Uncle, Bird Song, Jack Straw, Big River
**Set 2:** Loose Lucy, Row//Jimmy, Let Me Sing Your Blues Away*, Around and Around//, Eyes of the World* > Stella Blue, Beat It on Down the Line, Casey Jones
**Encore:** One More Saturday Night//

* with Martin Fierro and Joe Ellis on horns

**Source:** AUD, **Quality:** B–, **Length:** 2:05
**Highlights:** Thirteen-and-a-half-minute "Bird Song," "Let Me Sing Your Blues Away," "Looks like Rain," "Eyes of the World"
**Comments:** Audience and tape noise is a distraction; missing "Here Comes Sunshine," "Loser," two lines from "Jimmy," and just a few seconds from "Saturday Night." The poor quality of the tape makes the show hard to enjoy. At times, the vocals sound as if they're far away and the horns are hard to distinguish, except in "Let Me Sing Your Blues Away." The gaps between songs are cut, which can be a distraction, and we lose a small amount of some starts and finishes. The tape quality is a little better for set 2.

---

### 9/15/73
**Providence Civic Center, Providence, Rhode Island**

**Set 1:** Beat It on Down the Line, Sugaree, Greatest Story Ever Told, Brown-Eyed Women, Me and My Uncle, Ramble On Rose, Looks like Rain, Deal, Jack Straw, Tennessee Jed, El Paso, Bird Song, Playing in the Band
**Set 2:** Mississippi Half-Step, Big River, Row Jimmy, Truckin' > Drums > Eyes of the World*, Let Me Sing Your Blues Away*, Weather Report Suite Prelude* > Weather Report Suite Part One* > Let It Grow* > Stella Blue, Sugar Magnolia
**Encore:** One More Saturday Night*

* with Martin Fierro and Joe Ellis on horns

**1. Source:** SBD, **Quality:** A–, **Length:** 3:15, **Genealogy:** MR > RR > RR > PCM > DAT (set 1); MR > DAT (set 2)
**2. Source:** AUD, **Quality:** B, **Length:** 3:15, **Taper:** Jerry Moore
**3. Source:** FM-SBD (GDH 063), **Quality:** A–, **Length:** "Let Me Sing Your Blues Away" through Encore, **Genealogy:** MR > DR
**Highlights:** Tennessee Jed, Bird Song, Playing in the Band, Row Jimmy, Truckin' > Drums > Eyes of the World, Weather Report Suite, Stella Blue, Sugar Magnolia, Saturday Night

The first-set song list is not unusual for the period, but all of the songs are played with vigor. An insistent throbbing Lesh bass line charges into a breathless "Greatest Story." A sing-song "Sugaree," a sentimental but upbeat "Brown-Eyed Women," a striding "Ramble On Rose," and an easygoing "Deal" counter the Bobby cowboy tunes "Me and My Uncle" and "El Paso." A slow and serious "Looks like Rain" lends some calm to the middle of the set. A classic "Tennessee Jed," with some wonderful Weir guitar fills, works up to a divine frenzy, before a textbook "El Paso" and a perfect "Bird Song." This is the last "Bird Song" the Dead played until they brought it back as an acoustic song on September 25, 1980. I consider it tragic that they abandoned "Bird Song" at this point, because, for me, this version exhibits the most poise, grace, and melodic line of any. The Providence version anchors the lovely and ethereal end of the "Bird Song" continuum, while the 8/27/72 Veneta, Oregon, version anchors the gutsy and dynamic end.

After "Bird Song," the fifteen-plus-minute "Playing in the Band" cruises through an energetic space (in a jam more reminiscent of a second-set "Dark Star") to glide serenely and deliberately into an energetic "Playing" reprise to end the set. The band emerges from the break with an upbeat but not exceptional "Mississippi Half-Step" and "Big River," followed by a hypnotic "Row Jimmy." I remember taking a walk around the Civic Center during that song and noticing that even the normally surly Providence security guards seemed to be lulled into a groove. During the next song, "Truckin'," Martin Fierro (sax mostly, flute on "Weather Report Suite") and Joe Ellis (trumpet) came onstage to join the band for most of the rest of the second set. Martin was placed too close to Weir onstage, and when he got to wailing on the sax and thrashing about, he kept bumping into Bobby, who glared at him in annoyance.

At the end of "Truckin'" is a splendid, balanced crescendo to climax breathlessly, ballistically in "the drop" onto the triumphant E chord. This is followed by a galloping jam with Fierro holding his own, but when he gets to wailing too enthusiastically he is abruptly quashed in the mix, several times. The jam fades into "Drums." It was an average Kreutzmann performance (but Mickey certainly would have added to it, had he been playing with the Dead during this period). The drums pause, and Jerry leads into an "Eyes of the World" that sparkles with life but with an exuberance born of inner calm. The brass adds thoughtful texture with long-held soulful droning notes. Emerging from the song proper, the band flirts easily with the minor, building energetically to resolve on schedule with exuberant confidence on those broad, satisfying E-major chords en route to the '73–'74 "Eyes" syncopated jam sequence. Fierro is caught unaware by the first warp-out and goes blustering on well into it. He goes silent at the beginning of the second jam and comes in late. By the third one he's ready and synchronized with the syncopation. The band canters happily away from "Eyes" with a spunky, jazzy jam with some playful back and forth between the sax and the guitars. The mood turns briefly serious and slows to a halt.

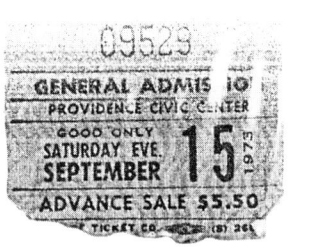

Next a clean but unencumbered "Let Me Sing Your Blues Away" arises, dogged by giddy, sarcastic saxophone energy. Fierro's flute adds serenity to the pristine "Weather Report Prelude" as the Dead go on to execute a virtually flawless performance of the suite, joined for much of it by Ellis. In "Let It Grow" Fierro switches back to saxophone, adding an eclectic jazzy feel. Coming out of "Weather Report Suite" he switches back to flute to complement the frenetic jam for about ten minutes until the mood slides through brief galactic space noodling into a slow, soulful "Stella Blue." Fierro and Ellis are not evident on the tape, and I suspect they left the stage during "Stella Blue." (I can't remember. . . .) The show finishes with a throbbing, pulsing "Sugar Magnolia" that starts out with a staggered entrance by the band members into the song: Weir, then Kreutzmann, Jerry, Keith, Phil, and finally Fierro (on sax) and Ellis, in a caricaturish, almost Motown brass chorus. Donna enters with the vocals. The band thunders through "Sugar Magnolia," caught between restraint and reckless abandon. The latter seems to dominate once they get to "Sunshine Daydream."

A proud, enthusiastic "Saturday Night" encore finishes the evening. The brass adds some extra spice to the mix. It's a resounding climax to an excellent show.

CHRIS ALLEN

*Ticket stub for 9/15/73 at the Providence Civic Center*

## 9/17/73
### Onondaga County War Memorial, Syracuse, New York

Me and My Uncle, They Love Each Other, Beat It on Down the Line, Sugaree, Mexicali Blues, Loser, Looks like Rain, Jack Straw//, //Let Me Sing Your Blues Away//*, Eyes of the World* > Weather Report Suite Prelude* > Weather Report Suite Part One* > Let It Grow* > Stella//Blue

* with Martin Fierro and Joe Ellis on horns

**Source:** SBD, **Quality:** B–, **Length:** 1:30
**Highlights:** Eyes of the World, Weather Report Suite > Stella Blue

This is a decent-sounding, though slightly hissy and occasionally warbly, soundboard cassette, of generally unremarkable musical quality. Respectable but not mind-blowing, the jams are good, but I didn't write home about 'em. A pensive early "Looks like Rain" stands out from the first set. A rare "Sing Your Blues Away," while it's cut substantially on each end, is distinguished by the horn section that played most of this September 1973 tour. The horn section still seems to be finding its bearings here, and sometimes it sounds better in theory than on tape. Intermittent but annoying tape flutter, sound fuzziness, and song cuts contribute to this tape's overall mediocrity. The horns of Martin Fierro and Joe Ellis are prominently featured in "Eyes of the World," ranging from horn-section-style accompaniment to free jazz wailing and screeching over the jam, which drops sweetly into the "Weather Report Suite Prelude." A well-played "Stella Blue" rounds out the tape, though haunted by a cut near the beginning.

ADAM HUNTER BAUER

## 9/17/73
### Unknown Location

**Interview:** Donna Godchaux, Keith Godchaux, Jon McIntyre, Bob Weir

**Source:** FM, **Quality:** B, **Length:** 0:45
**Highlights:** All; "A lot of times our onstage, uh, our onstage performances come off being something less than, uh, or bearing a little, bearing not too close scrutiny. I mean, you don't want to listen to it fifty or sixty times." (Weir)

This interview is noteworthy because it is conducted by Deadheads, and thus the questions are both remarkably insightful and considerably more fan-oriented. The discussion is a general "State of the Dead," covering a wide array of topics, including the upcoming *Wake of the Flood* release, current performance and gear status, touring logistics, tapers, songwriting, composition, and personnel interaction.

Of particular note is the interviewers' referring to "Eyes of the World" as "Wake Up and Find Out" and "Stronger Than Dirt" as "The Seven Four Jam." Also, Weir sheds light on the correct song titles for tracks on *Anthem of the Sun*, as well as the inside rib title "Alice D. Millionaire."

BRIAN DYKE

## 9/20/73
### The Spectrum, Philadelphia, Pennsylvania

**Set 1:** Promised Land, Tennessee Jed, Mexicali Blues, They Love Each Other, Looks like Rain, Loser, Beat It on Down the Line, China Cat Sunflower > I Know You Rider, El Paso, Row Jimmy, Greatest Story Ever Told, Deal, Around and Around//
**Set 2:** Truckin' > Nobody's Fault Jam > Eyes of the World > Stronger Than Dirt > Stella Blue, Sugar Magnolia

**Source:** AUD, **Quality:** B/B+, **Length:** 3:00
**Highlights:** China Cat Sunflower > I Know You Rider, Deal, Around and Around, Nobody's Fault Jam > Eyes of the World > Stella Blue, Sugar Magnolia

I'd seen the Dead for the first time exactly one year before (September 21, 1972), so this was my fifth GD show and my third at the Spectrum. Only halfway through high school, I was a pimply teenager but already on the bus... thanks to some positive older influences and some previous heavy doses of the band. One of my most vivid memories of September 20, 1973, is being able to stroll right up to center stage (or at least to the barricaded moat fronting it) at any time during the show. This is a phenomenon I experienced neither before nor after, and it was the other extreme from the mud-pit moshing I encountered on the infield of RFK Stadium a few months earlier. I think some of this peaceful easy feeling actually is borne out on the tape, too.

The tape of 9/20/73 is not widely circulated. I searched long and hard before finally copping it. Was it actually worth the trouble of tracking down? Let me say at the top: indubitably! As with nearly every tape I've heard from '73, this one has its magic moments that make it a valuable and joyous listening experience.

The "Promised Land" opener gets things going nicely, rockin' out through several distracting sound system and/or taper glitches (aren't these mandatory in "Promised Land" openers?), not the least of which is the taper's mike meddlings. The mike adjustment seems to have a beneficial effect, however, and "Tennessee Jed" gets a warm treatment, thick with Weir's half-rhythm, half-lead guitar style. Both the first, shorter instrumental break as well as the second, longer break are highlighted by typically great interplay between Bob and Jerry. Actually, all the players are heard very nicely in the mix here, with Keith blending in seamless accents and Phil covering the usual sonic expanse. The launching of "Mexicali Blues" is marked again by Bob and Jerry's excellent work and with Keith once more adding wonderfully colorful lines. Jerry then steps to the mike to give us a patented '73 uptempo rendition of "They Love Each Other," and if it wasn't clear before now, Jerry is simply nailing everything in sight, providing a great solo just before the bridge. "Looks like Rain" is given a soft and tender treatment and reminds us of the sincerity with which Bob used to sing love songs. Unfortunately, some warble in the recording leaks through to detract from this one. Jerry maintains a mellow feel by offering a "Loser" that features nifty crosspicking by Bob and an understated break by Jerry that's full of harmonic overtones. I love it when he does that! Next, a mood swing, as nineteen downbeats open "Beat It on Down the Line," and we

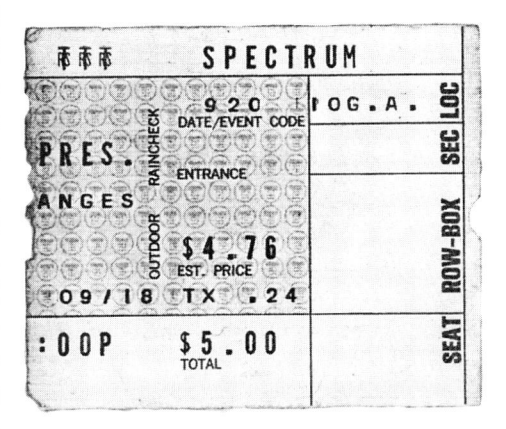

*Ticket stub for 9/20/73 at the Spectrum, Philadelphia*

hear Donna for the first time as she "harmonizes" with Bob on this little ditty that really never gets too far off the ground.

The next segment, which starts side B of my tape, is the real highlight of the set. A mini–false start quickly turns into "China Cat Sunflower": a lilting version, like a stream quickly running. The dynamic is in full gear as Bobby takes the lead and widens the segue with a wonderful chord and melody improvisation. There's a very subtle but real tape splice (which fortunately seems to cut only a few precious moments) just before he's joined by Jerry in the "Feelin' Groovy Jam," a very familiar and gorgeous sequence that introduces—what else?—"I Know You Rider." A soulful version, fat but fragile, the band does it with intensity, yet there is still a hint of restraint as melody lines and harmonies are drawn delicately rather than nailed confidently. This is what's it's all about, folks. Time to settle down easy with "El Paso." But no—they're rolling now, and after only two Robbins-esque verses, the energy level is building, Keith hitting his stride full on. "Row Jimmy" follows, and with this they are successful in allowing the faithful to catch their collective breath. Donna's back, but Jer takes the spotlight away with two shining solos. The "Greatest Story Ever Told," although suffering from a few gaffes and a wild, albeit brief, "vocal excursion" by Donna, contains incredible Jerry wah-wah stuff and a real powerful ending. Kicking back again, they swing into "Deal," a strong version with a great (but too short!) break where everyone has their moment, especially Phil, who goes into strumming mode. The set closes with "Around and Around," which also begins in a lope. Great rockin' ensues shortly, though—especially when they hit that key change. Jerry gets into a very unusual banging thing, which sets Keith to doing the same until it's practically grungy. Very wild. Unfortunately, the recording cuts out a few seconds before the last decibels of the final chord dissolve into space. Oh well, I guess that's part of the beauty of it all.

The second-set tape is actually a notch worse than the first in recording quality. The "Truckin'" opener deflects attention from this fact, though, first by revealing that there's a horn section on board for this part of the ride, and then by using the horns to light the way through a few shaky verses until they enter the Zone: that wonderfully delicious post-"Truckin'," epilogue-like Zone. Some warbly tape glitches crop up just about the time the band cuts a path to the "Nobody's Fault but Mine" jam, in which Jerry and Bob collaborate to particularly fine effect. The jam fizzles out abruptly, however, as the band launches right into "Eyes of the World." Again it's the horn section that immediately commands attention as trumpeter Joe Ellis blows a little sour. But by the first instrumental break, the crescendos and decrescendos of the horn section are working nicely and blending well with Jerry's intricate phrasings. More warbly tape detracts from the next jam, though, as Martin Fierro sneaks in a Coltrane squawk or two. A somewhat hypnotic ensemble swirling leads into the "Stronger Than Dirt" jam wherein Jerry and Martin weave a wonderful aural web over Phil's rumblings. Bob's playing gets really "thick" in this segment too, like pulling taffy but twice as sweet. Ultimately, Martin's sax highlights a climax that tumbles into a soft "Stella Blue." The extremely slow tempo here magnifies the dreamy essence of this tune. Jerry's vocal gets real emotional in spots, and each syllable seems more deliberate than the next. I remember being right up front for this part of the show. The lights were way low. It was difficult to see the band members even from right there at the rail, and that seemed to focus the power of the music all the more. This is a really fine version of "Stella" and a memorable moment, too. Then, a long delay and lots of suggestions from the audience precede the band's selection of the final song of the evening, "Sugar Magnolia," with Ellis and Fierro way out front. They chill on the chart stuff, fortunately, and the band proceeds to deliver a kick-ass closer with Bob blazing and Martin just wailing! A really high-powered rendering that's seems simply relentless until finally they give in to the inevitable and finish it off with Bob announcing, "Thank you, folks, that's all the time there is. We'll see you tomorrow night."

I remember not being able to concentrate well in school the following day. It was a Friday and I was going to another Dead show that night, just a pimply teenager but already on the bus. For good.

TOM FERRARO

---

### 9/21/73
**The Spectrum, Philadelphia, Pennsylvania**

**Set 1:** Big Railroad Blues, Me and My Uncle, Brown-Eyed Women, Beat It on Down the Line, Sugaree//, //Big River, Here Comes Sunshine, El Paso, Loose Lucy, Jack Straw, Black Peter, Playing in //the Band
**Set 2:** Let Me Sing Your Blues Away*, Weather Report Suite Prelude* > Weather Report Suite Part One* > Let It Grow*, He's Gone > Truckin' > The// Other One > Wharf Rat > Row Jimmy, Casey Jones*
**Encore:** One More Saturday Night*

* with Martin Fierro and Joe Ellis on horns

**Source:** SBD, **Quality:** A, **Length:** 3:00, **Genealogy:** MR > RR > RR > PCM > DAT
**Highlights:** The entire second set

Fall 1973 was an interesting period for the Grateful Dead. Incorporating Fierro and Ellis on brass, the jazz idioms hinted at throughout the year peaked on the September and October tours. This show provides a solid case for that. The first set begins bouncily with "Big Railroad Blues," which sets the pace for a very solid and well-played set. Moving steadily through their standard first-set material, the band shows its first signs of brilliance during "Sugaree" and "Big River," but as luck would have it, both contain severe cuts. Ah, well. Luckily, we are treated to a flawlessly executed reading of "Here Comes Sunshine" that shows the band beginning to jell. Long and thoughtful, the band, especially Garcia, slowly meanders away from the song's frame during the jam with well-placed slithering licks that are as sweet as nectar. The vocal harmonies are strongly executed and the emotional factor is overwhelming. Continuing the set at the same level of meticulous perfection, it becomes evident that Garcia and Keith Godchaux are performing at a level a notch above their colleagues. The consummate musicians, notes drip from the duo's instruments through otherwise average readings of "El Paso" and "Jack Straw." By "Black Peter," the rest of the band has risen to Garcia's level, resulting in a delightfully melancholy interpretation. This also sets the platform for the set-closing "Playing in the Band." As the jam unfolds, the guitarists take over, with Weir immediately finding a comfortable rhythm to groove on, as Garcia weaves his way around the theme. After finding the right space to wander in, Lesh and Godchaux rejoin the jam, acting as grounding devices in case one of the guitarists begins to stray. Inevitably, Weir disappears from the jam entirely, and Garcia heads straight for outer space, leaving Lesh and Godchaux to maintain the theme. As Garcia becomes firmly lost in a paranoia jam, Weir returns to the same place as before, transforming the moment into the Grateful Dead plus the Lost Garcia. Returning, Garcia begins to bring the band up to meltdown level when, unfortunately, the tape cuts.

The second set begins with "Let Me Sing Your Blues Away." Largely unpopular with Deadheads, this song might actually have matured gracefully had it been given more performance time, perhaps as a segue into "Tennessee Jed." This version, the band's last, hints at the song's potential, while illustrating why it was abandoned. Although slightly fast, the following "Weather Report" is sweet and gentle. Bobby's vocals are right on here, and Garcia carefully measures each lick without overplaying. As well, the horn accompaniment from Fierro and Ellis adds texture to the background. On the "Let It Grow" jam, Garcia lies back and lets Bobby take the lead with thick rhythms that sound great against the crescendos of Fierro and Ellis. Garcia snags the outro jam with racing sixteenth notes and precision bends. Slowing down, he is joined by the horn section, who add frenzied vibrato. The two guitarists then trade bars with the two brasses, with Bobby sticking out, coaxing deliciously lush sounds out of his ES-335. The band builds energy on the "He's Gone" outro, continuing throughout "Truckin'" and climaxing on the "Truckin'" jam, which unfortunately is ended by a premature transition into "The Other One." Lesh steps out for a few minutes of meandering, directionless leadership that only succeeds in adding tension to the jam. Frustrated, he launches back into "The Other One," instantaneously exploding the emotional rage characteristic of a bad solo. The psychotic jam that follows is led by Garcia, who returns the momentum with incessant sixteenth-note spirals. Weir's accompanies this with bright and jazzy rhythm guitar, rather than the distorted E riffs that we're accustomed to. As the band falls back into silence, Kreutzmann begins a funky groove that eventually brings the band into a phenomenal, well-formed yet untitled space jazz jam. This eventually dissolves into a meltdown that leads into a R&B jam that combines subtle elements of the "Feelin' Groovy" and "Mind Left Body" jams with enough twists to remain unique. This gracefully leads into the second "Other One" verse, which is notably softer in execution, an obvious preparation for the segue into "Wharf Rat," which delicately decreases the intensity to a somber state. Beautifully executed throughout, the interplay between Garcia and Godchaux on the transition will leave you breathless. "Row Jimmy," a questionable choice, is actually perfect in effectively retaining the somber mood that has been set, so much so that the set-closing "Casey Jones" and "Saturday Night" encore seem anticlimactic.

BRIAN DYKE

*Ticket stub for 9/21/73 at the Spectrum, Philadelphia*

## 9/24/73

**Civic Arena, Pittsburgh, Pennsylvania**

**Set 1:** Mexicali Blues, Loose Lucy, Looks like Rain, Row Jimmy, Big River, Greatest Story Ever Told, Beat It on Down the Line
**Set 2:** China Doll, Truckin' > Nobody's Fault but Mine > Eyes of the World*

* with Martin Fierro and Joe Ellis on horns

**1. Source:** SBD, **Quality:** C+, **Length:** 0:45 (first set material)
**2. Source:** FM-SBD (GDH), **Quality:** A, **Length:** 0:45 (second set material)
**Highlights:** Looks Like Rain, Row Jimmy, Greatest Story Ever Told, Truckin' > Nobody's Fault > Eyes of the World.
**Comments:** This tape contains segments of the first and second sets, resulting in a tape that luckily has pre-

served some quality music from this night. Unfortunately, there's quite a bit of hiss. The mix leans heavily toward the upper ranges, sadly leaving Phil's sound less present. The piano maintains a fantastic presence that fills out the mix, making this tape sound a lot better than it is.

The tape starts out with an incredibly spicy version of "Mexicali Blues." Keith's commanding piano work, combined with Phil's solid bass lines, leads this song to the fun side of the spectrum. "Loose Lucy" is slow-grooving, funky-sounding and played with plenty of feeling. This combination results in a sound completely different from the more familiar versions. It's easy to hear Jerry having fun singing this one. Donna and Bobby faithfully support him with their background vocals. A thoughtful and extremely pretty "Looks like Rain" follows, featuring Bobby singing with emotion and tenderness. Jerry's sustaining guitar chords echo Keith's subtle piano embellishments, making this a truly beautiful version. "Row Jimmy," with all of its hypnotic swaying, keeps the rhythmic pace floating upon the musical waves. It's a calming and soothing effort that easily rocks your soul into the great ocean of life. On the upswing, "Big River" is fun and energetic, and then the enthusiastically sung "Greatest Story Ever Told" is a real barn burner to boot. "Beat It on Down the Line," which had to be restarted due to Billy's miscounting of the opening beats, also turns out to be a fine version.

The second side of the tape, starting with "China Doll," has a blessedly incredible increase in sound quality. In all of its frailty and beauty, Keith converts this song into a beautifully perfect lullaby with his music-box-sounding piano lines. A solid and well-played "Truckin'" drives along, slowly transforming into the bluesy revival of "Nobody's Fault but Mine," which hadn't been played much recently. This is a superslick transition as they integrate "Nobody's Fault but Mine" slowly into "Truckin'." The magical, special moment happens when we find the band playing both songs simultaneously, then slowly fading out "Truckin'," leaving us with "Nobody's Fault but Mine." After they jam for a while, they ease into "Eyes of the World." Here we find the very nice horn accompaniments of Martin Fierro and Joe Ellis, laying out their soothing lines. The horns weren't very audible during "Nobody's Fault but Mine." Phil gets a chance to stretch out on this one, making his bass really sing. This version of "Eyes of the World," with horns, seems to foreshadow the times when Branford Marsalis would join them onstage. The jam briefly leads toward the spacey and weird side before it returns to the theme. With their aggressive horn parts, Martin and Joe really help to make this a great version. This tape is very solid musically and would be a fine place to start for those interested in hearing one of the last horn accompaniments from 1973.

COREY SANDERSON

### 9/26/73
### War Memorial Auditorium, Buffalo, New York

**Set 1:** Here Comes Sunshine, Beat It on Down the Line, Deal, Looks like Rain, Tennessee Jed, Mexicali Blues, Loser, Big River, Brown-Eyed Women, The Race Is On, Row Jimmy, El Paso, China Cat Sunflower > I Know You Rider, Around and Around
**Set 2:** Playing in// the Band†//, Sing Me Back Home, Me and My Uncle, He's Gone > Truckin' > Space > Eyes of the// World*† > Weather// Report Suite Prelude* > Weather Report Suite Part One* > Let It Grow* > Sugar Magnolia*
**Encore:** *One More Saturday Night

* with Martin Fierro on tenor sax and Joe Ellis on trumpet
† with AUD splices

**1. Source:** SBD, **Quality:** A, **Length:** 3:20, **Genealogy:** MR > DAT > C > C > DAT
**2. Source:** AUD, **Quality:** B, **Length:** Splices, **Genealogy:** MR > Reel > DAT, **Taper:** Barry Glassberg and Louis Falanga
**Highlights:** Here Comes Sunshine, Truckin' > Space > Eyes of the World > Weather Report Suite

Hearing the Dead play with a horn section or other special guests has been the dream of many Deadheads. Until the late eighties, this tour was the only example of how such additions changed the sound of the band. Despite the many cuts, not to mention the audience recordings spliced into the middle of "Eyes of the World" and "Playing in the Band" (done quite well), this soundboard tape is well worth tracking down as it's got a bright, clean sound—although maybe a little Lesh-lite in comparison to others of the period.

The first set is stuffed full of classy performances. The opener of "Here Comes Sunshine" is a total joy, and it sets the benchmark for the songs that follow. This show is brimming over with a sense of fun and an urge to *paaaarty*. It's not an overwhelmingly intense experience like some shows and at times the band seems to almost revel in a certain laid-back charm, but that isn't to say there aren't moments of exhilarating invention or consummate musicianship.

Horns add such a range of extra tonal colors to the Dead's palette that it's a mystery why the band didn't used them more: with the right musicians, the mix is dynamite. Here, both players get to solo, although Fierro is the more adventurous of the two. In fact, at times he's the most adventurous guy onstage, twisting strong melodic lines into a squall of grumbles and squeals. Their ensemble playing blends well with the band, especially on "Eyes of the World" and the uplifting "Weather Report Suite," but the repetitive simplicity of their contribution to "Sugar Magnolia" overstays its welcome by halfway through the song.

The appearance of the horns is reason enough to go out and hear this tape, but other moments of magic can be discovered on the spritely "Brown-Eyed Women" and the equally energetic "The Race Is On," and Bobby roars out the lyrics to "Around and Around." The performance of "Sing Me Back Home" was the band's last. It does sound rather tired here, though once the band steers its way out of "Truckin'" (with its several good-natured asides from Phil) into a tasty jazz space, you're unlikely to remember or care much about after the fact.

PAUL BODENHAM

---

### 10/19/73
**Fairgrounds Arena, Oklahoma City, Oklahoma**

**Set 1:** //Mexicali Blues, Tennessee Jed, Looks like Rain, Don't Ease Me In, Jack Straw, They Love Each Other, El Paso, Jimmy Row, Playing in the Band
**Set 2:** China Cat Sunflower > I Know You Rider, Dark Star > Mind Left Body Jam > Morning Dew > Sugar Magnolia, Eyes of the World > Stronger Than Dirt Jam > Stella Blue, Johnny B. Goode

**1. Source:** SBD, **Quality:** A–, **Length:** 1:30 ("Dark Star" through "Johnny B. Goode")
**2. Source:** AUD, **Quality:** B–/B, **Length:** 1:30 ("Mexicali Blues" through "I Know You Rider")
**3. Source:** FM-SBD (GDH 245), **Quality:** A, **Length:** 1:30 ("Dark Star" through "Sugar Magnolia"), **Genealogy:** MR > DR

**Highlights:** Tennessee Jed, Don't Ease Me In, Playing in the Band, and the entire second set

Every collector of live Grateful Dead music develops strong ties to certain tapes, and, as with other aspects of the band, this usually happens for reasons that can't easily be put into words. For me, 10/19/73 really embodies the musical essence of the Dead and is among my favorite shows. The second set, especially, is a monster, and it almost seems to consist of one long piece of music that touches all the bases, several times over. The majority of the second set is readily available as a nice quality soundboard recording, but the first set exists only as a rather poor quality audience tape that isn't widely circulated. Nonetheless, the music on the tape makes it well worth the hassle of tracking it down if you can.

The clipped intro to "Mexicali Blues" and subsequent clunk-clunk-clunk of tapers' microphones suggests that the fellows who are responsible for my first-set tape were a little late getting set up on this evening. The sound quality here definitely qualifies the tape as an archetypal '73 "skeevy aud" recording, but that doesn't take a thing away from the fact that the band is really cookin'. Jerry is first to test the water, casually ripping off a hot solo and then maintaining a poignant improvised guitar line to accompany Bob's vocal. It's quite a nice opener and one that suggests the band is really present tonight. A momentary tape cut loses the first note or two from the introduction to "Tennessee Jed," but once rolling, Jerry is heard delivering a typically corny but convincing rendering of the hayseed storyline. Bob meanwhile has some fun playing those rubbery fills. Phil's booming backdrop comes through nicely as they head into the instrumental verse, an incredible blend of improvised melodies from everyone. Jerry serves up a little "Shortnin' Bread" as he and Bob get into a bit of dual lead guitar that's oh so sweet, climaxing with the crowd loudly indicating its approval. An infectious song anytime, this version of "Tennessee Jed" gets a real high rating in my book.

"Looks Like Rain" begins with some more distracting mike "adjustments" by the tapers but gets off to an otherwise positive start with some heartfelt playing. Something goes awry when Jerry takes to the slide for his solo, though, and the song loses momentum. Deep-sixing the slide permits a nice recovery during the last few verses, and the ending is marked by Bob belting out the familiar refrain, once again accompanied by Jerry's soaring guitar. Bob's stupid Martian GooGoo joke gives way (after many tape cuts) to a blazing "Don't Ease Me In." The band really digs in on this one, with Keith playing a particularly emotional barrelhouse style throughout. Jerry cranks it up a notch, too, and is joined by Bob in another "two-guitar solo" during the second break. Way cool! Finally, Bob goes really boinky on his guitar while Jerry finishes off the last verse and chorus. "Jack Straw" requires some downshifting by both the band and the audience as a more mellow feel seeps in. However, during the instrumental break and beyond, that paradoxical and insidious tension generated by the seemingly effortless blending of four lead musical voices provides a glorious depth to this tune. Even though it may not make many "best of" lists, this version is still captivating, owing largely to its concise yet spacey nature. At first, the next song, "They Love Each Other," also seems more relaxed than usual. But again the energy level builds, and after a great solo by Jerry, Bob and Phil combine to create a wonderful musical framework upon which Jerry hangs the final verses. The heightened feeling is carried through to "El Paso," which closes side A in spicy Tex-Mex fashion. "Row Jimmy" is but a tranquil bridge between the former uptempo first-set standards and the magnificent music that follows. Especially notable, however, is the considerable color that Keith supplies to this tune. Closing the first set is "Playing in the Band." This is a version that

deserves special mention. Clocking in at just under nineteen minutes, it contains arguably some of the finest and most extended jamming this side of 1969. Not surprisingly, it's Jerry who leads the charge, and his playing is all Ornette and Coltrane—going places no man has gone before, and taking a stadium full of unsuspecting folks along for the ride. Playing the Arkestra to Jerry's Sun Ra, the band members are everywhere at once, going this way and that, up this scale and down the next, following the leader through every minor fault in the clouds of delusion. Finally, the "Playing" reprise comes around, and Jerry caps the package with several galloping glissandos turned on the "Playing" theme. Magnificent! This version certainly is a must-hear for any fan of this song.

Tacked on to the end of the first-set audience tape is the perennial second-set opening pair, "China Cat Sunflower" > "I Know You Rider," and it is immediately clear that the band is still feeling the energy flow initiated in the first set. The texture is dreamy, though, with floating melodies like strains from distant minstrels carrying the mind's ear past "China Cat's" lace bandannas and golden-stringed fiddles into that fine little jamming sequence that connects it to "Rider." The jam retains the familiar melody that became second nature to us from repeated listenings to the *Europe '72* album and other versions from that year. But there is that added melody here as well, a reexamination of the "Feelin' Groovy" Jam, this time at a faster tempo. It fits perfectly into the space between these two songs, closing one door while opening another. "I Know You Rider" is the beneficiary of this swinging jam, as sparks ignite the tinderbox of rhythms, harmonies, and leads, all coming together to convince us well beyond a reasonable doubt that we surely WILL miss them when they are gone. A fantastic piece of music that sends one scurrying for tape 2.

The second tape, vastly different from the first in sound quality, continues the second set. It begins straight away with a colossal "Dark Star": a sublime introduction, pensive, introspective with a long spacey jam trickling into the first verse, which Jerry carries out with an odd vocal modulation. Phil takes the wheel momentarily for a brief but out-front bass-fed jam, while the rest of the band constructs a backdrop of intricate melodies and rhythms. It's heady, mellow music, and Jerry moves from wah-wah to slide guitar as the band floats an ethereal "Mind Left Body" jam. This theme is given a strenuous but graceful workout before it dissolves into a wicked and angular musical interaction that evolves wondrously into "Morning Dew."

Bob's contribution to this jam is particularly noteworthy and includes some really interesting feedback sequences. The "Morning Dew" that follows is also inspired. Jerry's singing is full of heart and soul, and his deliberate vocal approach is incredibly evocative. His playing is also way out there, as evidenced by a truly cosmic jam in the middle of the song followed by a second instrumental segment near the end where he goes so far as to quote Bach's "Jesu, Joy of Man's Desiring"! On my tape, "Sugar Magnolia" is spliced right up close to the last strains of "Morning Dew"—so close that the first note or two of "Sugar Magnolia" get clipped off as we hear the band members fall quickly into place one by one. What starts out as a pretty standard and slightly haphazard rendering picks up a little by the first break and gains a real head of steam by the closing jam. Jerry starts it off a little tentatively but then gets into a wonderful swirling sonic synchrosystem sounding like he's gasping for the clusters of notes popping from his guitar. He finally gives it up and strums the last few measures that lead into "Sunshine Daydream." Bob and Donna are heard having a real good time belting out the vocals on this one, but alas, the big ending is lost to a tape cut shortly before it's due.

The flip side of my tape picks up with a lot of tuning. Then, from the dust and ashes rise the sweet chords of "Eyes of the World." Though the quality of the recording seems to have deteriorated considerably (and I don't think this is just my tape: cranking the volume here helps), it's obvious that Jerry is still in the Zone singing and playing with incredible feeling. The entire band has seemed really at ease during the whole show, and in this segment in particular, they're just lying back and lettin' it flow. It's some of the most natural, connected stuff I've heard, beautifully stretched out and inevitably running headlong into a "Stronger Than Dirt" jam that blows through the roof before braking suddenly to turn into "Stella Blue." Like sherbet on a seared palate, "Stella" is a little cognitive Kool-Aid for those jammed-out and burnt-out brain cells: a beautiful version, emotionally charged even in its tranquillity. "Johnny B. Goode" is the finale, and although they might be considered hackneyed by some, I think the Chuck Berry covers represent an important part of the Dead's musical menu. In this version, Jerry nails the first solo, and after Bob growls out the last verse, Keith has a shot at the second solo but kinda blows it. This one may not be the best version recorded but it's still rockin', and for me that's an important aspect of the Dead, too. In a peculiar way, "Johnny B. Goode" is a perfect complement to the other, more surreal music on this tape, and in the end it all combines to sound absolutely perfect to my ear. "Johnny B. Goode" and the show conclude with a psychedelic burst from Jerry's guitar and a "Thank y'all and good night!" from Bob. Thank you! Jesu!

TOM FERRARO

## 10/21/73
### Civic Auditorium, Omaha, Nebraska

**Set 1:** //Here Comes Sunshine, Beat It on Down the Line, Loser, Black-Throated Wind, They Love Each Other, Cumberland Blues, El Paso, You Ain't Woman Enough, Weather Report Suite Prelude > Weather Report Suit Part One > Let It Grow

**Set 2:** Playing in the Band > Mississippi Half-Step > Big River > Playing //in the Band, He's Gone > Truckin' > Wharf //Rat > Sugar Magnolia, Goin' Down the Road Feelin' Bad > One More Saturday Night

**Source:** SBD, **Quality:** A–, **Length:** 3:00, **Genealogy:** MR > RR > PCM > DAT

**Highlights:** Loser, You Ain't Woman Enough, Weather Report Suite, Playing in the Band, He's Gone

**Comments:** This tape sounds very much like a low-generation soundboard based on the dynamics of the music. However, there is an inordinate amount of hiss and splices. I have heard DAT tapes that originated from two different sources, and they both have these same defects.

Both band and crew are very untogether at the start of this show. The mix for "Here Comes Sunshine" has too much high cymbal, and the beginning is missing altogether. You can hear the crew talking into the mike. The start of "Beat It on Down the Line" is blown and must be restarted. Finally, "Loser" completely falls apart, leaving the band wandering until Jerry is able to pull it together to start the first chorus. From there, the band begins to pick up the pieces. The "You Ain't Woman Enough" is the finest version I have heard, but, unfortunately, it's also the last one the band ever did. "They Love Each Other" and "Cumberland" are also high energy. However, it's when they get to the "Weather

Report Suite" that the band finally gets into gear. This is an excellent version, both appropriate and heartfelt, with a huge Phil bomb to mark the transition into "Let it Grow." It's the first appearance of the song in the Midwest, and coming right in the middle of harvest season, it must have been well received by the crowd. The band decides to cut its losses here and end the set.

The second set opens with "Playing in the Band" where the space, for only the second time ever, segues into a different song, "Mississippi Half-Step." This is the kind of unexpectedness that characterized shows in the Midwest. Having listened to this tape (as well as the Indianapolis tape from the following week) before ever going to a Midwest show, I always looked forward to hearing unusual song selections whenever I traveled to a show in the heartland. From "He's Gone" through the end of the show (save for "Wharf Rat") is completely rocked out, with very little of the typical early seventies spaciness present. However, I believe that if a flawless version of this tape were to appear in circulation, the second set would most certainly be ranked as one of the best rocking shows of the year.

DOUGAL DONALDSON

---

### 10/25/73

**Dane County Coliseum,
Madison, Wisconsin**

**Set 1:** Here Comes Sunshine, Sugaree, Mexicali Blues, Tennessee Jed, Looks like Rain, Deal, El Paso, Playing in the Band
**Set 2:** China Cat Sunflower > I Know You Rider, Me and My Uncle, Dark Star > Mind Left Body Jam > Dark Star > Eyes of the World > Stella Blue, Weather Report Suite Prelude > Weather Report Suite Part One > Let It Grow > Goin' Down the Road Feelin' Bad, One More Saturday Night, Uncle John's Band

**Source:** SBD, **Quality:** A–/A+ ("Dark Star" > "Weather Report Suite" is A+), **Length:** 3:20, **Genealogy:** MR > DAT > C > VHS > DAT, MR > PCM > DAT ("Dark Star" > "Weather Report Suite")

---

**Highlights:** China Cat Sunflower > I Know You Rider, Dark Star, Eyes of the World, Weather Report Suite

At times during this show you will ask yourself, "Does life as we know it get any better than this?" The answer will invariably be, "Not very often." Most of the second set is the absolute epitome of the Grateful Dead's creativity as an improvising band without equal, and all this comes in a soundboard mix of tonal richness and gorgeous clarity. You need a copy of this show like you need a heartbeat.

This show also features one of the best Phil mixes around, not just because he's so prominent but because the recording captures something of the complexity of the tones that issue forth from Mr. Lesh and his bass: from the sound of fingers on strings to that unearthly rumble of low-end frequencies that all of a sudden seem to flood into your room from God knows where (though not obviously from the speakers).

The second set in particular is nothing short of a masterpiece of collective improvisation around several contrasting songs and moods. The "China Cat Sunflower" > "I Know You Rider" is easily one of the best renditions of 1973. Although it's played in a spritely fashion, nothing is rushed, and the long, long jam that snakes out of "China Cat" only resolves itself in the introduction to "Rider" when it's good and ready. The following "Me and My Uncle" is more than adequate, but its brevity makes it seem slightly out of place here—though it does set up a contrast to the following relaxed introduction into "Dark Star." Its slowly evolving soundworld drawing you in with a delicious "Mind Left Body Jam" between the main theme and the first verse (a very respectable thirteen minutes or so), this "Star" majestically unfolds, becoming more complex as it develops. The free-form section becomes all the more enjoyable because of the excellent sound quality, which helps you sort out just who is producing what unearthly noise in the midst of what is quite a restrained, considered space. Once again Phil manages to be in two distinctly different sonic places at the same time: providing both a keening whine of feedback and a earthshaking rumble of unknown origin. "Eyes of the World" is a total classic from the moment Phil's dissonance is layered over Garcia's introductory chords. This rendition is absolutely note-perfect, and like all the best performances of this song, it flows with a breathtaking logic as its different elements intertwine and suggest further improvisations. Garcia and Lesh are quite inspired here, each at a creative peak where it seems that every nuance in their playing is infused with beauty and their ability to turn a phrase in an unpredictable way. Utter delight. "Stella Blue" is performed with great delicacy, its dramatic effect enhanced by the preceding improvisations. In any other show, this version of "Weather Report Suite" would be the high point of the performance, but here it can't quite match the levels of creativity to be found in "Dark Star" > "Eyes of the World." It, like the rest of this show, is merely exceptionally wonderful. This show is essential, for life without it is just too gray and meaningless to contemplate.

PAUL BODENHAM

## 10/27/73
### Coliseum, Indianapolis, Indiana

**Set 1:** Promised Land, Sugaree, Mexicali Blues, Loser, Black-Throated Wind, They Love Each Other, Jack Straw, Ramble On Rose, El Paso, Brown-Eyed Women, Greatest Story Ever Told, Loose Lucy, Beat It on Down the Line, China Cat Sunflower > I Know You Rider
**Set 2:** Playing in the Band > Mississippi Half-Step > Big River > Playing in the Band Reprise, He's Gone > Truckin' > Nobody's Fault but Mine Jam > Wharf Rat//

**Source:** SBD, **Quality:** B+, **Length:** 3:00
**Highlights:** Loose Lucy, Playing in the Band > Mississippi Half-Step > Big River > Playing in the Band

A relatively muddy soundboard of this show surfaced in the mid-1990s. The first set is rather mundane until things kick into gear with a rockin' "Greatest Story," followed by an extremely funky, if ponderous, "Loose Lucy" on which Keith pumps out slow motion Jerry Lee Lewis riffs on his piano. A breakneck "Beat It on Down the Line" opens with twenty-nine beats. The second-set jam starts with the unusual placement of "Half-Step" and "Big River" inside "Playing in the Band." This is, of course, exactly the sort of novel set list we live for. "He's Gone" is sweet and solemn, with an extended, joyous vocal rave-up at the end before everyone swings into "Truckin'"—which eventually changes into a dark, ominous "Nobody's Fault" jam. The beginning and end of set 2 are missing on the soundboard tape.

PAUL BODENHAM

## 10/29/73
### Kiel Auditorium, St. Louis, Missouri

**Set 1:** Cold Rain and Snow, Beat It on Down the Line, Brown-Eyed Women, Mexicali Blues, Don't Ease Me In, Black-Throated Wind, Tennessee Jed, The Race Is On, Row Jimmy, El Paso, Eyes of the World > China Doll, Around and Around
**Set 2:** Promised Land > Bertha > Greatest Story Ever Told, Loser, Big River, Brokedown Palace, Truckin' > Other One > Wharf Rat//, Sugar Magnolia
**Encore:** Casey Jones

**Source:** AUD, **Quality:** B–, **Length:** 3:30
**Highlights:** Jerry on Tennessee Jed, Eyes of the World, Promised > Bertha > Greatest Story, Wharf Rat

October 1973 was a good time for the Grateful Dead. The St. Louis shows of the 29th and, especially, the 30th showcase some excellent songs and some masterful guitar work by Jerry that forecasts the gradual change of the band's sound to the smooth jazz feel so prominent in 1974. The 10/29/73 is an audience tape of regrettably low quality. Tape hiss is present but tolerable, and overall the sound is muffled with little to no high end. Fortunately, guitar and vocals are clear and the bass is not overpowering as is common on many early-seventies audience tapes. The show starts out by painfully dragging through "Cold Rain and Snow" and "Beat It on Down the Line," both of which are forgettable. Early on, it becomes evident that the energy level of the crowd is much higher than the band's and as one of the unwritten laws of Dead concerts states, "If you're not happy with the way things are going, yell about it." The crowd obediently follows the rules and dusts off old standbys including "Come ON!," "Let's go, Jerrrrrrrrrry!," "The 'Cum-Ber-Land Blues,' Jerry!," and of course my favorite, "Turn it UP!!" The group responds with a series of nice songs including a "Brown-Eyed Women" that really foreshadows the subtle shift to a more jazzy sound. Bobby and Jerry in particular both seem to have found the same groove. Although remaining slow and too short, what results is a song that feels very solid, one that I'm more than happy to remember. The same feeling is present in the "Black-Throated Wind" that comes later and even to some extent in a "Tennessee Jed" that finally showcases some great solo work by Jerry. Also worthy of mention is the "Eyes of the World" near the end of the set. Seemingly out of nowhere, everyone comes to play. The jamming is fast and furious, with Jerry playing exceptionally well. Lasting around ten minutes, this song is big and reassures both the audience and the listener that when necessary the band can really play.

One of the biggest issues in the first set is the pace. After a few listenings, I decided that what I took for laziness had been in some cases deliberate and careful instrumentation. It is true that some of the songs ("Cold Rain and Snow," "Beat It on Down the Line") lack energy and enthusiasm, but others ("Tennessee Jed," "Brown-Eyed Women") do not suffer the same fate. The second set, however, opens with "Promised Land" > "Bertha" > "Greatest Story" that sounds as though a new band has taken the stage. The pace is quick, the jamming is sharp, and the energy level is way up. Keith notably digs in early on and drives through both "Bertha" and "Greatest Story" with some great piano. After these three songs, the band somewhat regrettably falls back into the slower pace of the first set via "Loser," "Big River," and a poorly timed (but somehow always nice) "Brokedown Palace." The big sequence of the second set starts with a "Truckin'" that takes about six minutes to get on the road. The song does have its moments, with some nice Jerry-led jamming in predictable spots, winding up in a spacey Phil jam into "The Other One." Actually, the song becomes one big jam, more than thirty-five minutes long, and takes some long detours on the way to the end. For spaceheads, this is a must-hear, but a thirty-plus-minute "Other One" should have more intensity in my opinion. The show winds up with a powerful "Wharf Rat" that fits in well with the relaxed pace of the show. Superb guitar from Bobby and piano from Keith help build this song to a great crescendo that is worthy of note. The "Sugar Magnolia" closer and "Casey Jones" encore, however, continue the less energized pace of earlier songs.

DAVID R. CECCHI

---

## 10/30/73
### Kiel Auditorium, St. Louis, Missouri

**Set 1:** Here Comes Sunshine, Me and My Uncle, Ramble On Rose, Looks like Rain, Deal, Mexicali Blues, They Love Each Other, El Paso//, Row Jimmy, China Cat Sunflower > I Know You Rider, Playing in the Band
**Set 2:** Mississippi Half-Step, Big River, Dark Star > Mind Left Body Jam > Stella Blue > Eyes of the World//, Stronger Than Dirt Jam > Weather Report Suite Prelude > Weather Report Suite Part One > Let It Grow > Goin' Down the Road Feelin' Bad > Johnny B. Goode
**Encore:** One More Saturday Night

**1. Source:** AUD, **Quality:** C+, **Length:** 3:00
**2. Source:** FM-SBD (GDH 069), **Quality:** B+/A–, **Length:** 0:50 ("Dark Star" > "Stella Blue"), **Genealogy:** MR > RR > DR
**Highlights:** China Cat Sunflower > I Know You Rider, Dark Star > Stella Blue

My 10/30/73 tape is a moderately low grade audience tape with several generations on it. Even lacking nearly all the high end, the tape remains dynamic from the midrange through midbass and is easily listenable.

The show opens with a smattering of familiar songs, all of which are decent versions. "Hear Comes Sunshine," which as an opener I nearly always find to be a downer, is nevertheless played well. Among the remaining early songs, "Looks like Rain" in particular is notably mature, and "Ramble on Rose" features some particularly nice guitar work by Jerry.

After a somewhat quiet beginning, this show eventually begins to open up. A sweet "China Cat" loaded with both poignant Jerry and Bob jams segues into a brief but not forgettable "Rider." This two-song adventure would easily be the highlight of the first set if it weren't for the treat that follows. An immense "Playing in the Band" starts aggressively, the crowd clapping along in a feverish manner as the band winds up for the first reprise. Just as quickly, though, it settles into a slower groove featuring some long beautiful guitar work by Jerry, some rowdy piano by Keith, and some excellent drumming. Throughout the song, Phil, seemingly in his own world, moves from manic to mellow, and helps keep the edge going for well over twenty minutes.

As clichéd as it sounds, however, I'm going to say that the "Dark Star" that comes early in the second set takes the show. Available as a *Grateful Dead Hour* broadcast, the "Star" > "Stella" pairing is the perfect combination for this laid-back, jazzy show. Although I enjoy a screaming '69 "Dark Star" as much as anybody, versions like this, in their subtle, sweet way, are just about perfect. The song rises gracefully out of silence and evolves for twenty-seven minutes, much of which is highlighted by a strong performance by Phil. The last ten minutes become extremely spacey, losing the edge only slightly, before settling into the perfect choice, "Stella Blue." The *Grateful Dead Hour* segment cuts as the "Eyes" comes in, but the audience tape continues on and catches nearly all the "Let It Grow." This post–*Dead Hour* audience segment is definitely worth tracking down.

DAVID R. CECCHI

### 11/1/73
**McGraw Memorial Hall, Northwestern University, Evanston, Illinois**

**Set 2:** Morning Dew > Playing in the Band > Uncle John's Band > Playing in the Band Reprise

**Source:** FM-SBD, **Quality:** A+, **Length:** 0:45, **Genealogy:** MC > DAT

"Morning Dew" starts out with an awkward feel to it; Billy can't seem to make up his mind to play a straight ballad beat or spruce it up with some jazz chops. The result is distracting and takes away from the song's fine vocal power. The instrumental at the end, though, allows the band to regroup—and they do. A long, slowly building jam develops. As it begins to peak, Garcia steers the band elegantly into "Playing in the Band." Now, the final crescendo of "Morning Dew" is one of my favorite Dead pleasures. But this transition is so gorgeous I felt like I didn't miss a thing.

"Playing" is sung by Weir like he's got a mouth full of chewing tobacco. The jam is clean, friendly, jazzy: no "Tiger" roars, no meltdown, no scathing, perverse feedback, just well-executed ensemble work. Lesh is unusually unrepetitive, barely grazing the root notes. Garcia keeps the stream flowing with swift, sweet, hornlike notes that skip freely like flat stones.

"Uncle John's" sneaks in slickly. It, too, is very jazzy, though basically weightless. The reprising jam drops like a feather back into the vocals. Lesh doo-dee-doos the ensuing space with a frolicking wiggle to his runs. The "Playing" reprise comes quickly but earnestly and with excited anticipation. Garcia closes it all with some pretty strumming to finish off a very professionally played forty-five minutes of music.

MICHAEL M. GETZ

### 11/9/73
**Winterland Arena, San Francisco, California**

**Set 1:** Don't Ease Me In, Black-Throated Wind, Ramble On Rose, Mexicali Blues, Brown-Eyed Women, Beat It on Down the Line
**Set 2:** To Lay Me Down, The Race Is On, They Love Each Other, Me and Bobby McGee, Tennessee Jed, Big River, Row Jimmy, Mississippi Half-Step//, //Greatest Story Ever Told > Bertha, Weather Report Suite Prelude > Weather Report Suite Part One > Let It Grow > Eyes of the World > China Doll, Around and Around > Goin' Down the Road Feelin' Bad > Johnny B. Goode

**1. Source:** SBD, **Quality:** A–, **Length:** 1:30 ("Don't Ease Me In" through "Row Jimmy")
**2. Source:** AUD, **Quality:** B–, **Length:** 1:30 ("Half-Step" through "Johnny B. Goode"), **Taper:** Jerry Moore
**Highlights:** Don't Ease Me In, Around and Around > Goin' Down the Road > Johnny B. Goode

The first show of the three-night fall '73 run at Winterland is relatively sedate, but features some unique performances, including the first live "To Lay Me Down" since 1970. Starting with an energized "Don't Ease Me In," the first set mostly plows familiar territory, with high points including a speedy "Black-Throated Wind" and a midset grand slam of "Beat It on Down the Line";

"To Lay Me Down," which benefits greatly from Keith's grand piano; a loping "Race Is On;" and the original incarnation of "They Love Each Other," which I always felt was superior to its postretirement makeover. The soundboard covers the first part of the first set, terminating after a sedate "Row Jimmy."

The second set begins with an airy "Mississippi Half-Step." The first jam starts with an explosive "Greatest Story," which plows into "Bertha" and on into a beautiful "Weather Report Suite." A short, pretty instrumental segue bridges "Let it Grow" and "Eyes of the World," which is followed by a hushed "China Doll" that sounds as if it were being played in a cathedral rather than a hockey rink. Possibly as an antidote to overplayment of the "Not Fade Away" > "Goin' Down the Road" medley, the show finishes with a different all-American sequence consisting of "Around and Around," "Goin' Down the Road Feelin' Bad," and "Johnny B. Goode."

MICHAEL PARRISH

## 11/10/73

### Winterland Arena, San Francisco, California

**Set 1:** Bertha, Jack Straw, Loser, Looks like Rain, Deal, Mexicali Blues, Tennessee// Jed, El Paso, Brokedown Palace, Beat It on Down the Line, Row Jimmy, Weather Report Suite Prelude > Weather Report Suite Part One > Let It Grow//

**Set 2:** Playing in the Band > Uncle John's Band > Morning Dew > Uncle John's Band Reprise > Playing in the Band Reprise, Big River, Stella Blue, Truckin' > Wharf Rat > Sugar Magnolia//

**1. Source:** SBD, **Quality:** A–, **Length:** 3:00, **Genealogy:** (Set 1) Unknown; (Set 2) MR > RR > DAT

**2. Source:** FM-SBD (DHH 50), **Quality:** A, **Length:** "Weather Report Suite," "Playing in the Band" through "Playing in the Band" Reprise

**3. Source:** AUD, **Quality:** C+, **Length:** 3:00, **Taper:** Louis Falanga

**Highlights:** The entire second set, especially: Playing in the Band > Uncle John's Band > Morning Dew > Uncle John's Band Reprise > Playing in the Band Reprise, Big River, Stella Blue.

Greatly overshadowed by the following evening's performance, this late '73 piece is still one of the band's finest from that era. First sets in 1973, or any time for that matter, served mainly to warm up the band for the more adventurous second set, and this performance is no exception. While clearly a synchronicity exists among each other, from the opening notes of "Bertha," the band takes few risks and keeps improvisation to a minimum throughout, opting instead for tight renditions of each selection. Perhaps they were only pacing themselves. We've all seen or heard those unfortunate evenings when the band struggles through "Dark Star" or "The Other One" or "Playing in the Band," the result of having shot their wad during a first-set "Beat It on Down the Line" or what have you. The set-closing "Weather Report Suite" is the evening's first true sign of musical brilliance. Gently romantic, its soft tempo is sweet like a moonlight walk along an Acapulco beach. Combining beautiful vocal harmonies, with well-crafted musicianship, one cannot help but sigh at the serene feeling that is elicited. Carefully measured, "Let It Grow" soars in its magnificence, as Garcia solos in musical self-inquiry against Weir's confident vocal readings. The outro jam provides a brief glimpse of Garcia's frantic struggle to race ahead of the band, a characteristic that will be reiterated throughout the remainder of the performance. Unfortunately, as the jam builds to a climactic halt, the soundboard tape breaks off, forcing the listener to cry out in agony. After a few minutes of clowning around on the "Tico Tico" theme, the Dead open the second set with one of four, and arguably the most interesting, "Playing in the Band" > "Uncle John's Band" > "Morning Dew" > "Uncle John's Band" > "Playing in the Band" palindromes. Immediately out of the verse, the band fades into deep space, wandering calmly on the main theme. The three frontmen mesh perfectly here as they individually find the proper space to inhabit. Once established, the jam begins to accelerate, with Garcia being the first to launch. Abandoning all concepts of time, he methodically begins to ease his way ahead of the band, creating a confusing and disoriented conflict among the rest. Intuitively, Garcia veers off in a sudden spiral, leaving his bandmates hanging out to dry. At seven minutes, Weir and Garcia begin to butt heads, and the frenzy that emerges is like a cat-and-mouse chase through long, dark corridors without an exit. You can almost hear Garcia egging his bandmate on, saying, "Catch me if you can," with each ascending run. Weir's response, that of a true prankster, is a completely obtuse—if brilliant—segue into "Uncle John's Band." Approaching each verse tentatively, the band locks the groove flawlessly out of the first refrain. The band continues to play in angular, out of time off-beats against each other through the coda jam when again Garcia abandons the band, racing off in a desperate struggle of twirling sixteenth notes. His colleagues attempt to catch up, an out-of-control madness that only the Grateful Dead are capable of creating, erupts, progressing from playful to furious over the course of only a few minutes. Tapering down, perhaps from exhaustion as much as anything else, the Dead gracefully arrive at the resolution, a beautifully tranquil "Morning Dew." This version is filled with an emotional energy that words cannot describe. Although far from perfect, the combination of precision bends sweetly brushing against thick piano fills, backed by gentle rhythm sweeps, is truly stirring. As he begins building to the end crescendo, Garcia once again begins to race ahead of the others, his leads becoming swifter yet maintaining directness. On the verge of climax, Weir leads the band back into the "Uncle John's Band" coda. Successfully catching the band off-guard, the mischievous Mr. Weir leads the way through the final refrain and back into the "Playing" reprise theme, shuffling the jam around like a rag doll. This time, the Dead divide instantaneously, each band member veering off in a different direction. With Kreutzmann alone to hold the groove solid, chaos emerges. As the wandering becomes more frantic with each bar, the frontmen begin to compete with each other to see who can stretch out the most. When one comes closer to home, the other drifts further off into the next measure. Now the tempo is really cookin', with Kreutzmann keeping perfect time on the skins, masterfully increasing the tempo while at the same time subtly becoming softer in volume. As the jam dissolves into silence, Garcia, in perfect timing, leads the way back to the reprise. The final, joyous jam, after the words to the "Playing" reprise are sung, is played with the same confidence a Derby champion displays as it struts its way to the winner's circle to claim its prize. Signifying the end of the voyage, the following "Big River" cooks from start to finish. Widely considered to be among the band's finest, this rendition is again greatly overshadowed by that of the following night. Nonetheless, it is nearly flawless, albeit brief. "Stella Blue" is nothing short of heavenly, complemented by keyboard brushes from Godchaux that are powerful enough to bring one to tears. "Truckin'" > "Wharf Rat" > "Sugar Magnolia" concludes this performance in bold fashion. While this fails to match the level of intensity as the first half of the set, the boys sure give it a hell of a try. The jam out of "Truckin'" hints at "Nobody's Fault but Mine," but the band sticks to a straight blues guitarists' jam before segueing into "Wharf Rat." The Dead begin to show signs of fatigue at this point with slight missteps of clumsiness throughout. Looks like it's time to wrap this one up. Although the set-closing "Sugar Magnolia" sounds very promising at the onset, the tape breaks off during the first verse.

BRIAN DYKE

---

**11/11/73**

**Winterland Arena, San Francisco, California**

**Set 1:** Loose Lucy, Weather Report Suite Prelude > Weather Report Suite Part One > Let It Grow
**Set 2:** Mississippi Half-Step, Big River, Dark Star > Mind Left Body Jam > Eyes of the World > China Doll

---

**1. Source:** SBD, **Quality:** A– (middle of "Loose Lucy" to beginning of "Sugar Magnolia"), **Length:** 1:30, **Genealogy:** MR > RR > RR > DAT
**2. Source:** AUD, **Quality:** B–, **Length:** 3:20, **Taper:** Jerry Moore
**Highlights:** Every note
**Comments:** This tape contains a very scrambled song sequence to facilitate an uncut "Dark Star." The tape flip occurs during the "Eyes of the World" outro jam.

"Dark Star." Many words have been used to describe this storied selection, although words seldom can convey the effect that it produces. Joy, sorrow, anger, confusion, fear: we refer to the emotional thesaurus for an appropriate description of what happens when the Grateful Dead perform this composition. As various band members have stated over the years, the Grateful Dead is a nightly process of discovery and rediscovery. "Dark Star" is the most primitive example of this, a passage that can lead anywhere, an invitation into the unknown abyss of musical and spiritual exploration.

From the structured yet spatial versions of 1968 to the free-flowing, tone-inebriating readings of 1990, it is the belief of this reviewer that on November 11, 1973, the Grateful Dead played one of the the "darkest" musical passages of their illustrious career.

Reviewed chronologically, the first-set conclusion of "Loose Lucy" and "Weather Report Suite" seem irrelevant when compared to the vast magnitude of the second set. However, a close listen reveals these to be close-to-definitive renditions, confident yet slightly hesitant, a premonition of things to come. Set 2 begins with the band's strongest versions of "Mississippi Half-Step" and "Big River." While the former is executed with absolute precision, the latter is balls-out rockin' Grateful Dead at its finest. From the opening notes, the band is scalding hot, the energy unmatchable, the intensity oozing out of each lick. The centerpiece of the performance, "Dark Star," unravels slowly and methodically. Each band member cautiously wades through the introductory theme, measuring each note with a trace of hesitance. About a minute or so in, the interplay between Garcia, Lesh, and Weir begins to develop, with Garcia noodling while Lesh and Weir maintain the jam's footing. Lesh is the next to launch, reaching immediately to the outer parameters in a frisky yearning for further spatial exploration, leaving Weir with the difficult role of holding ground as Garcia swims around the fretboard in a naive and innocent exploration of triplet spaghetti licks. As Lesh rejoins Weir in maintaining structure, Garcia rapidly increases the pace of unraveling the "Star," with the rest of the band following his lead.

Having reached the first destination at the six-minute mark, the band melts momentarily before erupting simultaneously for the second journey. Starting frantically, Garcia and Weir masterfully ease their way down to a motionless state of grace as their bandmates continue the frenzy. Taking gravityless steps one by one, they span the circumference at nine minutes, and the guitarists rejoin the frenzy set by their colleagues. As fear becomes prominent, the speed is reduced and the Dead slowly retreat from their point of confusion back to the verse. After playing through the theme both at the normal register and one octave higher, Garcia gives the lyrical reading in hesitant fashion. A slight trace of nervousness is evident, each syllable dripping anxiety.

On the meltdown out of the verse, Lesh assumes the lead, dropping calculated bombs from his Alembic against the subtle feedback cries from the guitarists. Here the transformation begins, from black and white to color, from deaf, dumb, and blind to Awakened Buddha. Reaching into the octava register, Lesh's solitary statements turn quickly into unfinished thoughts and unanswered questions, almost assuredly the result of being trapped within a musical passage of such confusion. With perfect timing, Kreutzmann rejoins the jam with a mild chaos attack that serves as an invitation to the rest of the band. At this point the roles have polarized, with Garcia maintaining the jam as Lesh wanders innocently across the fretboard. As the tempo shifts to common time, Garcia begins a beautifully crafted feedback passage that is nothing short of brilliant. Perhaps inspired, Godchaux begins to assert himself at this point, playing curt paranoia licks that gracefully brush against Garcia's long and reverb-rich feedback howls. Taking the cue, Weir abruptly intervenes with a paranoia chord progression of his own that encourages the following jam of complete disorientation. The chemistry at this point dissolves in a chaotic frenzy, spawning in six directions, each band member taking a turn with short phrases, communicating their destination with each note. Seemingly inadvertent, the "Mind Left Body Jam" that results is boiling with kinetic energy, the excitement of the band clearly evident, expressing the delight of improvisational orgasm. Catharsis has now been reached, and the end is now appropriate. Winding down, the band hints momentarily at "Stella Blue," but Garcia shifts to "Eyes of the World" instead. Obviously anticlimactic, the band barely misses a beat as they march through one of the finest ever renditions of this classic piece. Garcia's presence is 100 percent, his chops every bit as animated as previously displayed, his vocals as sweet as honey. The band solidly behind him, Garcia marches the band militantly into the "Stronger Than Dirt" jam with coarse authority, shifting the mood from joyous to stern, a perfect prelude to the following "China Doll." Ahh . . . what a perfect landing for the night. Rich in melancholy, this morbid lullaby says goodnight in ways that words fail to justly describe.

BRIAN DYKE

## 11/14/73

### San Diego Sports Arena, San Diego, California

**Set 1:** Big Railroad Blues, Jack Straw, Sugaree, Mexicali Blues, Here Comes Sunshine, Black-Throated Wind, Cumberland Blues, Row Jimmy, The Race Is On, Brown-Eyed Women, Beat It on Down the Line, Tennessee Jed, El Paso, China Cat Sunflower > I Know You Rider, Around and Around
**Set 2:** //Truckin' > Jam// > The Other One > Big River > The Other One Jam > Eyes of the World > The Other One Reprise > Wharf// Rat, Me and My Uncle, Goin' Down the Road Feelin' Bad > One More Saturday Night

**Source:** SBD, **Quality:** A, **Length:** 3:00
**Highlights:** Overall quality of the music and the recording; Sugaree, Eyes of the World
**Comments:** Top quality sound, no noise, good mix. One line cut from "Wharf Rat," one verse from "Truckin'," negligible cut between "Truckin'" and "The Other One."

My first thoughts after listening to this show were "Wow, what a show." Not because of a superb solo, or a perfect rendition of one song, or powerful vocals that pegged a certain phrase. Those would simply have been moments. This is a quality show, start to finish. Finding the best description hasn't been easy, but I'll seek a metaphor in the world of baseball. Some shows achieve success through a mix of a few home runs with singles, doubles, triples, and the inevitable strikeouts. This is a night made up of a series of solid doubles. If you're looking for a quality show with a steady pace, check this one out.

A mellow tempo comes in with the second song and holds throughout the night, with a few uptempo songs to break the pace, but no screamers to change the relaxed mood. Jerry was there to play that night; he takes the time to throw in at least a short solo at every opportunity. There appears to be no hurry to get to the next song, yet we get some two dozen pieces this evening. A small break between the first-set songs gives you the opportunity to smile, sit back for a moment, and think, "That was nice." Inevitably, the next song picks up where the last stopped; none of the transitions seem jarring. Nice first-set versions of "Sugaree," "Black-Throated Wind," "Row Jimmy," even a piano solo on "The Race Is On."

The second set continues the trend, but the songs are woven together with one theme acting as the thread to the next. A meandering transition takes us from "Truckin'" to "The Other One," complete with thundering bass bomb, for the first verse. The music then slows way down and turns into some space noodling. Perhaps the band is taking a deep breath. Space dissolves into an uneventful "Big River," out of which Bobby heads back to "The Other One" for a jam that lasts a few minutes but then quiets down, and a nice version of "Eyes of the World" emerges. It continues the flow of the set, with a reasonable amount of playing, good singing, and a nice extended postlude jam, initially led by Phil. We then head back into "The Other One," and Phil drops another bomb as we get into it for the second verse. The song winds down and essentially comes to an end, but "Wharf Rat" comes up as "The Other One" disappears. Again, a nice rendition, played slowly, but ending with a slow fade to an unexpected halt in the music (but not before Phil throws in some bass feedback). Perhaps they didn't know where to go next, but they tune up and give us an oddly placed "Me and My Uncle," followed by a break, and then a nice, sweet, slow-paced "Goin' Down the Road," followed by a rockin' "One More Saturday Night" to close this Wednesday show.

DANIEL DASARO

## 11/17/73

**Pauley Pavilion, University of California at Los Angeles, Los Angeles, California**

**Set 1:** Me and My Uncle, Here Comes Sunshine, Looks like Rain, Deal, Mexicali Blues, Tennessee Jed, The Race Is On, China Cat Sunflower > I Know You Rider, Big River, Brown-Eyed Women, Around and Around
**Set 2:** Playing in the Band > Uncle John's Band > Morning Dew > Uncle John's Band Reprise > Playing in the Band Reprise, Stella Blue, El Paso, Eyes of the World, Sugar Magnolia
**Encore:** Casey Jones

   1. **Source:** SBD, **Quality:** A–, **Length:** 1:30 (second set), **Genealogy:** MR > DAT
   2. **Source:** AUD, **Quality:** B–, **Length:** 1:30 (first set)
   **Highlights:** Playing in the Band > Uncle John's Band > Morning Dew > Uncle John's Band Reprise > Playing in the Band Reprise

Although poor in sonic quality, set 1 of this epic show is high in musical quantity and quality. Jerry's playing throughout the evening is stellar; the extended segue from "China Cat Sunflower" into "I Know You Rider" is especially indicative of an "on" night, with many embellishments by Garcia propelling it along. "Here Comes Sunshine" is very similar to the big beefy version in Tampa a month later, now enshrined by Latvala on *Dick's Picks I*. Although a twelve-song first set seems generous by latter day standards, it was not unusual for this period; it is well paced and played with enthusiasm. First sets of this period also offer the listener some unusual song placements: a midset "Deal," for instance. However, it is what follows after the break that is truly stunning; set 2 features improvisational ensemble playing at its finest and really defines why I was on the bus for almost thirty years. This is a must-have second set!! The "Playing in the Band" > "Uncle John's Band" > "Morning Dew" > "Uncle John's Band reprise" > "Playing in the Band" reprise sequence is one of only three played (11/10/73 and 3/23/74 are the other two) and is absolutely flawless in its execution, with the songs flowing one into another almost effortlessly. This "Playing" palindrome, in comparison to those at Winterland and the Cow Palace, runs ten minutes longer than the former and almost seven minutes longer than the latter; the segues from song to song seem to be smoothest in this version. The harmonies at UCLA also seem to be much sharper than the others, although that could be as much a comment on the crispness of the tape as on the actual performances—this low-gen soundboard especially accentuates Keith's very nice punctuation throughout the set. In addition, the drop from "Uncle John's Band" into "Morning Dew" leaves one breathless. Even with the verse flubs in "Dew," Jerry never skips a beat, slowly building to an expected climax that instead drops right back into "Uncle John's Band." This sequence seems to have had its origin in the Northwestern show a few weeks prior; however, in that show "Morning Dew" opens the second set, then proceeds to "Playing in the Band" > "Uncle John's Band" > "Playing" reprise, an arrangement that, although interesting, pales in comparison to this.

And, as if that wasn't enough, after tasty excursions through "Stella Blue" and "El Paso," we get the set-closing "Eyes" > "Sugar Magnolia"! Though I was in my infancy as far as shows go, I realized at the time I had witnessed something special.

—DENNIS DONLEY

## 11/20/73

**Denver Coliseum, Denver, Colorado**

**Set 1:** Ramble On Rose, Black-Throated Wind, To Lay Me Down, //The Race Is On, They Love Each Other, Me and Bobby McGee, Tennessee Jed, Big River, Row Jimmy, Weather Report Suite Prelude > Weather Report Suite Part One > Let It Grow, Casey Jones
**Set 2:** Mississippi Half-Step > Dire Wolf, Promised Land > Bertha > Greatest Story Ever Told, Looks like Rain, China Cat Sunflower > I Know You Rider, Truckin' > The Other One > Mind Left Body Jam > Stella Blue

**1. Source:** SBD, **Quality:** A−, **Length:** 3:00

**2. Source:** FM-SBD (KPFA marathon), **Quality:** A, **Length:** ("Weather Report Suite," "Big River," "Truckin' " > "Stella Blue")

**3. Source:** FM-SBD (GDH 233), **Quality:** A, **Length:** 0:45 ("Truckin' " through "Mind Left Body Jam"), **Genealogy:** MR > DR > precirculation

**4. Source:** AUD, **Quality:** B+, **Length:** Ramble On Rose, Black-Throated Wind, To Lay Me Down

**Highlights:** China Cat Sunflower > I Know You Rider, Truckin > The Other One > Stella Blue

Late 1973 was a pinnacle period for the Grateful Dead that contained some of the finest shows ever. Indeed, nearly every show between September 7 and December 19 is well worth seeking out. This Denver performance is certainly no exception. The first set opens with a standard run of tunes that serve as the evening's warm-up. Although these are played quite competently, the band doesn't begin to unwind until the midset "They Love Each Other." Here the transition from sluggish to graceful occurs, with Garcia in particular showing signs of friskiness. Weir and Godchaux follow in shaking off the cobwebs during "Bobby McGee," with Godchaux switching from thickening Weir's lush rhythms to improvising underneath Garcia's sweet leads. Godchaux was a master at mediating between Garcia and Weir's often sparse and unquestionably spatial interplay. This is illustrated throughout the remainder of the set, which peaks near the conclusion with a luscious "Weather Report Suite." The opening prelude and following verse are warm and bright, like a breezy Saturday afternoon in April, with Weir's vocals a whisper away from perfection. "Let It Grow" is a soft darkening, like a thunderstorm that arrives unexpectedly, shifting from gentle on the bridge to furious on the outro. Hampered by a conclusion that falls a hair short, the band quickly shifts to "Casey Jones" for the set closing. Sigh.

Returning for the second set, the Dead begins with "Half-Step," starting sluggishly but gaining momentum throughout. By the end jam, the band is again in full swing. However, as things begin to look promising, the band falls into "Dire Wolf," which DRAGS. Not having played the tune for over a year, the band can be easily forgiven, but it drastically brings the mood down nonetheless. Their attempt to change the pace, the triad of "Promised" > "Bertha" > "Greatest Story," falls flat on its face. Perhaps this would have been better suited for the first set, which noticeably lacked any uptempo selections. Succumbing to the ambience, the following "Looks like Rain" is beautifully minimalistic. Weir's vocals are strong and clear, and Garcia's solo is delightful.

At this point the performance changes course drastically. Having barely achieved average status thus far, the band concludes this performance with sixty minutes of out-of-this-world musicianship, starting with "China Cat Sunflower" > "I Know You Rider." Beginning very cautiously, it takes only a few measures to get comfortable enough for takeoff. You can hear the change between Garcia's first and second solos, as he shifts from hesitant to authoritative. Weir joins his colleague in rising to the occasion by taking the lead on the transition into "I Know You Rider." This jam gets bluesier than usual, with Weir and Garcia trading a series of short phrases before resuming the standard themes. After hitting the instrumental climax, the band falls into a jazzy groove typical of the late '73 versions. Taking their time, they explore various motifs that subtly hint at the "Feelin' Groovy Jam," dancing in circles around the "I Know You Rider" theme before falling into the verse. Pacing themselves, they execute the verse in calm fashion, the music breezing by like a cool gust of wind. The following "Truckin'" continues the groove that's been set, beginning calmly and slowly reaching a boil by the second refrain. Here the transformation begins, with "Truckin'" the catalyst, into a dueling guitarists' jam that brings the energy to a peak. Garcia is the first to blast off, cranking the volume on his axe to ten. Feeling obnoxious, Captain Trips pulls out a hilariously appropriate Bob Weir imitation, before switching back to his traditional role with a solo that subtly hints at "Nobody's Fault but Mine." After a few minutes of teasing, the guitarists tag off to Mr. Lesh. Grabbing the spotlight with both hands, Lesh begins playfully but quickly becomes stern, making brisk, powerful statements that sound like the barking of an angry drill instructor. Perfectly, the mood is set for "The Other One." Immediately noticeable is Garcia's change of tone, resulting in sweet and hollow rather than acidic imagery. As he methodically sweeps up and down the fretboard, the transformation deepens, and Garcia and Company are reduced to components, the music having taken over, leading into a funky shuffle in common time that brings images of astronauts floating in the midst of space. One can't help but shake to the groove of this brief but delightful passage. As they attempt to reclaim their territory, the transition back into "The Other One" is rough, as if the boys have been displaced far enough outside the perimeter to not know how to return. Godchaux throws a few light bombs to establish the landing point, and Phil takes the cue leading to the verse. Following a militant vocal reading, Weir playfully weaves around the theme, methodically straying from its base. Signaling a change of course, Garcia cranks up the reverb and begins the meltdown. The band slowly fades into deep space, with Weir supplying frenzied rhythms, Garcia plucking paranoid chicken scratches, and Lesh innocently tiptoeing across the upper register. Fear and confusion begin to arise as the music becomes so intense that the listener begins to pluck hairs from the skull in bewilderment. Swoosh. Out of the ashes emerges a funk jam from Weir and Kreutzmann that gracefully transcends into the "Mind Left Body Jam." Role reversal occurs once again, with Garcia steadily supplying rhythm beneath Weir's antagonistic Garcia impersonations. After stating the theme, the guitarists return to their normal roles, and the interplay that follows is purely blissful. Fading, Weir takes the lead and spirals his way out of space into a picture-perfect "Stella Blue." Inevitably, tears begin to well up in the eyes of the listener; the emotion displayed is beauty in motion, the musical perfection a harmonious release.

BRIAN DYKE

---

### 11/21/73
**The Coliseum, Denver, Colorado**

**Set 1:** Me and My Uncle, Sugaree, Jack Straw, //Big Railroad Blues, Mexicali Blues, They Love Each Other, Looks like Rain, Here Comes// Sunshine, Big River, Brokedown Palace
**Set 2:** Mississippi Half-Step > Playing in the Band//, //Wharf Rat > Playing in the Band > Morning Dew, Truckin' > Nobody's Fault but Mine > Goin' Down the Road Feelin' Bad > One More Saturday Night
**Encore:** Uncle John's Band

---

**1. Source:** AUD, **Quality:** C, **Length:** 3:00
**2. Source:** SBD, **Quality:** A–, **Length:** 3:00
**Highlights:** Looks like Rain, Playing in the Band, Truckin', Goin' Down the Road

Here is another widely untraded audience tape from a wonderful tour. Though not as powerful as the show nine days later in Boston, this night at Denver has many shining moments, the best of which is tragically marred by a brutal cut and some apparently missing music.

The show starts out with some standard songs of the era, picking up by the time "Big Railroad Blues" appears. My tape cuts out the beginning of this song and picks up in midjam, with the first vocals being the "went down to the depot..." segment. This is a rousing version, with Jerry really punching the vocals as the song draws to a close. After a few more servings of some standard fare, the first true highlight of the show arrives with a killer version of "Looks like Rain." Dripping with emotional guitar work by Jerry, this passionate version is one of the finest I have ever heard. Melodic scales fill the air with a tapestry of sound as it builds and builds to a climatic conclusion; Bobby is in true form here. The "Here Comes Sunshine" that follows is also well played, characteristic of the era. The midsong jam is nicely structured, occasionally descending in some melodic scales. The only major flaw is a roughly ten-second dropout on the tape, as though the input knob had been spun to zero for a time and then returned to its original position. Worse still, just as the first set of vocals are sung, my tape cuts as the end of the side is reached. The other side picks up about where the previous side left off, leading me to guess that little music was lost. The first set draws to a close with a rousing version of "Weather Report Suite." I am a true fan of this song, and this one is very pleasing indeed. It's a great ending that serves as a preview to the improvisational music to follow.

The second set opens with a surprising combination of "Mississippi Half-Step" > "Playing in the Band." "Mississippi Half-Step" is aptly played, but pales in comparison to the huge "Playing in the Band" suite that follows. When I first traded for this tape, the second-set suite that begins with "Playing in the Band" was the enticing factor; it does not disappoint. This version gets off to a roaring start, fat with energy. The spacey jam that follows, so characteristic of the monumental versions of 1972–74, is very dynamic, with Jerry's nimble fingers and Billy's exceptional work on the drums leading the way. Unfortunately, just as things are getting good, my tape is cut—severely, picking up with "Wharf Rat" on the second tape of the two-tape set. From a personal e-mail from David Gans I have gathered that much is apparently missing from circulating tapes, namely the sequence of "Playing in the Band" > "El

Paso" > "Playing in the Band" that appears on the Vault's reels and should be sandwiched in where this harsh cut occurs. This omission is only one of the numerous reasons that soundboards of this show should someday find the light of day. In any event, at least the "Wharf Rat" is complete, somber, and well played. But I find myself wondering what turns the band took along the way to get to this mellow ballad. Once the lyrics of "Wharf Rat" are completed, the post-verse jam is completely snuffed out and replaced with a smooth transition to the frenetic jamming that, one imagines, preceded it. A quiet space develops from the jam, first becoming chaotic, then frenzied and full of distortion and mirth. Finally, the telltale chords of the "Playing in the Band" reprise are heard, marked by Donna Jean's signature wail (which I have actually grown quite fond of). As the final chords of the song are sounded, another "turn on a dime" transition descends into a well-received "Morning Dew."

To close the evening, the band pulls out one final explosive suite. First teased by Keith, the Dead launches into a quite appropriate "Truckin'," which is approved by the audible "Yeah!!" from the taper next to the mikes. As usual, the highlight is the postvocals jam. As one would expect, the jam is very lively with Jerry driving it hard—very hard. After a lengthy sequence filled with scales, notes of "Nobody's Fault but Mine" are heard, first played by Jerry. This version is fairly short, with no real development afterward, and Jerry soon leads the band off in a happier direction with "Going Down the Road Feelin' Bad." Here we find that awesome energy that dominated the earlier version of "Truckin';" the jam out of the chorus is hot! Lots of energy, with Keith going nuts on the keys and Jerry and Bobby following suit. The "One More Saturday Night" that follows fits nicely, closing out an exceptional set. "Uncle John's Band" is a fitting conclusion, quietly and sweetly ending the night.

DARREN E. MASON

## 11/25/73

### Feyline Field, Tempe, Arizona

**Set 1:** Sugaree, Beat It on Down the Line, Don't Ease Me In, Black-Throated Wind, Tennessee Jed, China Cat Sunflower > I Know You Rider, Big River, Row Jimmy, Me and My Uncle, Brown-Eyed Women, Playing in the Band
**Set 2:** Eyes of the World > Weather Report Suite Prelude > Weather Report Suite Part One > Let It Grow, Casey Jones, Sugar Magnolia > Goin' Down the Road Feelin' Bad > One More Saturday Night
**Encore:** We Bid You Goodnight

**Source:** SBD, **Quality:** B, **Length:** 3:00
**Highlights:** China Cat Sunflower > I Know You Rider, Me and My Uncle, Playing in the Band, Weather Report Suite Prelude > Weather Report Suite Part One > Let It Grow

Note for note, this performance is almost flawless. The play ranges from average to brilliant, and quickly at that, while the vocals are strong all around. What this show lacks is the emotional charge that is characteristic of so many late 1973 shows. The band seems hesitant, as if afraid to take the launch beyond the parameters of each selection. The first set breaks in at the beginning of "Sugaree," followed by an uninspired pairing of "Beat It on Down" and "Don't Ease." Although both versions are executed competently, is there a pairing of songs that you'd rather not hear played back to back? On the rebound, the band effortlessly brushes through "Black-Throated Wind," "Tennessee Jed," and "Mexicali Blues," all played confidently, if not spectacularly.

All right, it's the middle of the set, time to roll up the sleeves and play some hot music. "China Cat Sunflower" > "I Know You Rider" is brilliant, featuring an amazing conversation between Keith and Jerry. During the bridge, the band begins to unwind before coming back for the final verse. Rather than race into "I Know You Rider," the band takes its time, wandering, as if lost, through a bluesy jam led by Keith and Jerry. Each time it appears that the band is arriving, Garcia grabs the lead and heads a little further out. Rather than the typical "landing," the band eventually "finds" its way into "I Know You Rider." This version is well paced, allowing the musicians to catch their breath before jumping into "Big River." Bobby takes the lead in keeping the momentum here, throwing in chunky rhythm textures between each verse.

Okay, time to cool down a bit. "Row Jimmy" gets a little confusing. Some of the band is still cookin', particularly Billy, who's in an awful hurry to get to "Me and My Uncle," which smokes! Garcia solos nonstop behind each verse. If ever there were a time to imagine Jerry in a ten-gallon hat and a pair of steel-toed boots, this is it! Appearing tired, the band barely makes it through "Brown-Eyed Women." Oh well, it's about time to end the set anyway.

WRONG! "Playing in the Band" highlights this set. The jam begins, led by Phil, who passes it to Jerry. Time to meander for a while. Sometimes it just takes a little time and a little help to find what you're looking for. "Hmm, let's see what Bob thinks." Bobby's response is to gush out thick jazzy rhythm textures as if to say, "Well, here's one path we can try." Of course, rebel that he is, Jerry rebounds with "Okay, we seem to be getting close, better head off in the opposite direction." At this point Phil breaks in. "Uhh, I think we better stay closer to home." "Okay, but let's stretch it out a bit," says Jerry, who proceeds hungrily through a few minutes of paranoid exploration before suddenly shouting, "Hey, it's time to land," leading the band full circle back into the reprise.

Wow. Let's take a break.

Set 2 shows the band eager to jump back in where they left off. Now, many of us prefer a few numbers to warm up and shake off the cobwebs before diving into a lengthy jam, and this "Eyes" shows clearly that the band could have benefitted from just that. Cautiously sticking close to home base, this version of "Eyes" displays minimalism at its finest. No earth-shattering brilliance here; no embarassing flubs either. The end jam stays very basic before quickly falling into the outro "Stronger Than Dirt" jam, which again remains fairly basic. Just as things teeter on the verge of getting stale—and we all know how bad an "Eyes" that's not happening can be—the band gracefully glides into "Weather Report," the highlight of the show. Time to unwind. Bobby's vocals are right on here, even the tri-harmonies between Bobby, Jerry, and Donna are semiaccurate. At times, you can imagine how beautiful it must've been in Tempe that day. "Let It Grow" is very smooth, highlighted by Keith's piano fills that sound like bells skipping across water. Jerry's first solo doesn't quite "get It," but he authoritatively shows his resilience by hitting a scorcher on the pre-coda jam, each lick a succulent delight of simplicity. Unfortunately, the band is unable to maintain its momentum and the outro simply falls flat. Of course, good sports that they are, they immediately launch into "Casey Jones," as if to say, "All right, back to earth now."

The show closing trifecta of "Sugar Magnolia" > "Goin' Down the Road Feelin' Bad" > "One More Saturday Night" allows the band to pump the energy to the red line while at the same time resting their obviously tired faculties. No out of this world musicianship here, just good old house-rockin' Grateful Dead. Even "Sunshine Daydream" fails to solicit Bobby's trademark yawp. Hey, just because it's simple doesn't mean it's bad, as long as the band gives 100 percent, which they clearly do here. This passage is the kind that warms your heart rather than invades your soul. Feel-good music at its best, and even though this version is horrendously flat and out of tune, the rare "We Bid You Goodnight" encore sends this show off on a warm note.

BRIAN DYKE

---

**11/28/73**

**Palace of Fine Arts,
San Francisco, California**

Seastones

**Source:** SBD, **Quality:** A, **Length:** 2:15, **Genealogy:** MC > C > DAT

**Highlights:** All

**Personnel:** Jerry Garcia, Mickey Hart, Ned Lagin, and Phil Lesh

**Comments:** This tape is said to have been mixed by Phil Lesh.

This eclectic ensemble auspiciously combines the elements of electronic genius, intuitive improvisation, and incomprehensible incompetence. Based heavily around the experimental wizardry of Ned Lagin, the passages are slow and methodical. While it is traditional in the music of the Grateful Dead for the momentum to conflict and resolve on several occasions, this performance is one long passage where each measure only becomes more and more exploratory, failing to climax yet sustaining anticipation until the last minutes, when the resolution occurs. At times, it seems like the middle of a bad science fiction movie; at others one can envision moonwalking on a rainbow.

The first section of the performance, lasting around forty minutes, is simple and delicate. Garcia's fingerpicking is graceful and Lagin's electronic passages gentle. After several long passages of jagged commentary, Lesh leads the transition with a series of delay bombs that seem to confuse the rest of the performers, who fall into silence as if to say, "Well, what do we do next?" Turning the intensity up just a hair, the dragon is slowly awakened, and the subtle and often soothing passages turn suddenly poignant. After several minutes of methodically increasing momentum, the mood shifts to ridiculous with a brief passage of child's play, complete with recess bells ringing repetitiously. This dose of comic relief leads into the Hart-Lagin "Scottish Bagpipe" jam, which ranges from amusing to annoying within its brief time allotment. Following the waterfalls and bird whistles that appear on its heels is an eastern theme jam, with sitar sounds straight out of the bag of George Harrison and Ravi Shankar. Perhaps indicative of having completed the revolution, the mood returns to its original gentle tranquillity at about eighty minutes. The listener is then lured into a false sense of security, but from around the corner come the sirens, and now the arrest, or conclusion, may begin. Lesh's commanding yet indecipherable vocal quips seem to put one on trial for incomprehension, with Garcia, Hart, and Lagin as judge and jury. Tortuous but enlightened. Maniacal but melancholy. Sad yet serene. Accompanied by Hart, the listener/victim is marched to the dungeon for the thrashing, which ultimately results in the final taming of the jam.

BRIAN DYKE

---

## 11/30/73
### Boston Music Hall, Boston, Massachusetts

**Set 1:** Morning Dew, Mexicali Blues, Dire Wolf, Beat It on Down the Line, Brown-Eyed Women, Black-Throated Wind, Don't Ease Me In, El Paso, They Love Each Other, Big River, Loser, //Playing in the Band
**Set 2:** Row Jimmy, Jack Straw, Here Comes Sunshine, Weather Report Suite Prelude > Weather Report Suite Part One > Let It Grow > Dark Star Jam > Eyes of the World > Sugar Magnolia

**Source:** AUD, **Quality:** B/B+, **Length:** 3:00, **Genealogy:** MC > RR > DAT
**Highlights:** The entire show!

This show is transcendental. If asked why I am a Deadhead, I would probably reach for this tape, because it shows what the Dead could do when they were truly inspired. Throughout this masterful performance, they are both mellow and powerful. The show opens with an intro by Phil, who is ecstatic to be in a real concert hall. He begins, "We've been playin' ice rinks, basketball courts, multipurpose rooms, and shitholes all over America. . . ."

As for the tape itself, even though it's clearly not a high-fidelity recording, the midrange is quite crisp, and the magical, warm ambience of Boston Music Hall pervades the recording to its very marrow. I suspect that the soundboard would pale in comparison (but I would still love to hear it). Garcia's singing is jubilant. The guitar playing has even more energy (check out "Here Comes Sunshine!"), but isn't out of control.

After Phil's introduction comes a quintessential fifteen-minute-plus "Morning Dew" opener. The hall's acoustics enhance the determined, energetic, majestic vibe of the music, and make for blissful listening. The grand piano sounds elegant and beautiful. "Dire Wolf" exhibits a rare restraint and really hits a groove. "Playing in the Band" features persistently percussive piano and a very interesting segue into the final reprise. It's hard to believe that things are gonna get stranger, but they do!

A lyrical, flowing, and mellow ten-minute "Row Jimmy" opens the second set, but the smokin' "Here

Comes Sunshine" really sets the pace for the rest of the show. This just has to be heard! Garcia is all over it, without dominating, but everyone is in top form. The "Weather Report Suite," particularly "Let It Grow," is surging with creative energy. It's not the kind of thing that one describes with words; it evokes closed-eyed smiles and dancin' and swayin', and music playin'. . . .

The ensuing tasty "Dark Star" jam includes a Bach tease ("Jesu, Joy of Man's Desiring"), then segues into an epic, ethereal twenty-minute "Eyes of the World" that epitomizes the Dead. This tape is one of the best ever—get it!!!

PAUL J. PEARAH

## 12/1/73
### Boston Music Hall, Boston, Massachusetts

**Set 1:** Promised Land, Sugaree, Mexicali Blues, Tennessee Jed, Looks like Rain, China Cat Sunflower > I Know You Rider, Big River, Brokedown Palace, Weather Report Suite Prelude > Weather Report Suite Part One > Let It Grow, Casey Jones
**Set 2:** They Love Each Other, Me and My Uncle, Don't Ease Me In, Me and Bobby McGee, Mississippi Half-Step, Playing in the Band > Uncle John's Band > Playing in the Band Reprise, Not Fade Away > Goin' Down the Road Feelin' Bad > One More Saturday Night

**1. Source:** AUD, **Quality:** B+, **Length:** 2:40 (whole show)
**2. Source:** FM-SBD (GDH 217), **Quality:** A, **Length:** 0:45 ("They Love Each Other," "Me and My Uncle," "Mississippi Half-Step" through "Playing in the Band" Reprise), **Genealogy:** MR > RR > DR
**3. Source:** SBD, **Quality:** A, **Length:** 0:35 ("Playing" through "Playing" Reprise), **Genealogy:** MR > RR > PCM > DAT
**Highlights:** Playing in the Band > Uncle John's Band > Playing in the Band Reprise

This is the least circulated tape of this three-show run at the Music Hall in Boston. It is also the least impressive of the three performances. The audience recording is a very good recording tape from a venue with excellent sound. Consequently, this tape is relatively easy to listen to. Unfortunately, it is hampered by an unruly audience that detracts both from the otherwise good sound of the tape and from the band's performance. For much of the first half of the second set, the band attempts to get the crowd to cooperate with the local fire marshal and return to their seats. They begin with gentle cajoling, which escalates into a full-scale harangue by Phil. He correctly warns the audience that by continuing to fill the aisles, they risk losing the Music Hall as a venue and the band will have to play at the big ice arena. Of course, his warnings fall on deaf ears, as they would for the next twenty years until the only place left for the band to play would be the huge concrete stadiums. The Dead's next visit to Boston was at the huge, echoey Boston Garden. The distraction proves too much for the band as they muddle through a lackluster show. The only part worth listening to, other than the lengthy harangue, is the thirty-minute "Playing" > "Uncle John's" jam. Although missing "Morning Dew," which was included in every other occurrence of that jam in 1973, the "Playing" is sufficiently spacey and interesting. The transition to "Uncle John's Band" is pulled from the ether of the mid-"Playing" jam and settles effortlessly into a relaxed and pleasant version. No mind-blowing fireworks here, but it's certainly worth putting as filler on any tape. Fortunately, that jam is in circulation as a soundboard, and, really, that is all you need.

DOUGAL DONALDSON

## 12/2/73
### Boston Music Hall, Boston, Massachusetts

**Set 1:** Cold Rain and Snow, Beat It on Down the Line, Dire Wolf, The Race Is On, Brown-Eyed Women, Jack Straw, Ramble On Rose, El Paso, Row Jimmy, Big River, Deal, Weather Report// Suite Prelude > Weather Report Suite Part One > Let It Grow
**Set 2:** Wharf Rat > Mississippi Half-Step > Playing in the Band > He's Gone > Truckin' > Stella Blue > Sugar Magnolia > Sunshine Daydream//
**Encore:** Morning Dew

**1. Source:** AUD, **Quality:** B+, **Length:** 1:55 (first set plus encore)
**2. Source:** SBD, **Quality:** A, **Length:** 1:30 (second set), **Genealogy:** MR > DAT
**3. Source:** FM-SBD (GDH 071), **Quality:** A, **Length:** "Wharf Rat" through "He's Gone," **Genealogy:** MR > RR > DR
**Highlights:** Big River, Playing in the Band, Stella Blue

A very excited, friendly crowd greets the band as they take the stage. All during the first set Lesh chats amiably between nearly every number. Unfortunately, the person who did the recording kept pushing the pause button so most of what he has to say is unintelligible. He's clearly having fun, though. Too bad most of the first set is lackluster. "Big River" finally galvanizes the band. "Let It Grow" features some blistering leads by Garcia at the end, but he cuts these short to end the tune, bringing out woeful cries of "noooooooo!" from the audience.

"Wharf Rat" was a smart choice to open the second set: it's slow and simple, giving the band a change to get focused. But despite Garcia's impassioned singing and Weir's absolutely stellar picking, it limps along often in an amateurish way. Yet in the very long, mellow closing jam, the band finally comes comes together. "Half-Step" keeps it going and slips nicely into "Playing in the Band." During the singing parts, Keith plays a beautiful riff worth checking out.

Now comes one of the most inventive jams of the band's career. Immediately as "Playing in the Band" fades, a huge gust of inspiration descends upon the stage, sighing as if it has been waiting all night to appear. Some very, very careful playing by all members reveals their awareness of the gift that just dropped in their laps. They shrug and hop on board.

The jam creeps along slowly at first, nearly dirgelike. After a brief pitstop, they pick up the pace, pushing it, still carefully but with a few firm slaps on the proverbial elephant by all hands. The confidence level rises. Garcia plays a few hiccup chops rather lazily; Lesh strums a chord and then a brief bomb. The band starts spinning faster and faster as the drain opens and a whirlpool ensues. And then—all hell breaks loose.

Weir scrapes his strings with his pick while doing some feedback. Garcia screams a dozen notes per second, Neal Cassady–style. Lesh bellows like King Kong. But this passes suddenly as a series of slashing, John Cage–like random notes sets in. *Very* random, very odd, and seemingly unrelated. Acid, anyone? Lesh sounds like he's rehearsing for "Seastones" as his bass blares wildly. Keith stands out because he has to play it straight, gimmickless. Too bad he didn't get up, open the lid of his piano, and start tossing stuff in. Now Garcia joins Keith in some straight playing without effects processing. But this only makes Weir and Lesh's antics sound even weirder. Lesh goes over the top with some shredding, very dissonant shrieks. Perhaps if a Tyrannosaurus Rex got speared in the groin, such a sound would have emerged from his great throat.

But suddenly, as the noise recedes, a small flower pokes its head up defiantly amidst the carnage: Garcia and Weir stand alone, gracefully picking the beautiful introductory chords to the "Mind Left Body" instrumental. This moment of contrast between raging chaos and pure, childlike joy is truly breathtaking. Soon the whole band joins in for one of the most tender, spirited versions ever.

*Ticket stub for 12/2/73 at Boston Music Hall*

The rest of the set is very solid; "Stella Blue" stands out due to Garcia's poignant, soulful singing. The encore of "Morning Dew" is icing on the cake. This one doesn't explode but is played with great pride and a deliberate, well-balanced intensity.

MICHAEL M. GETZ

## 12/6/73
### Convention Center, Cleveland, Ohio

**Set 1:** Bertha, El Paso, Deal, They Love Each Other, Greatest Story, Ramble On Rose, Weather Report Suite Prelude > Weather Report Suite Part One > Let It Grow, China Cat Sunflower > I Know You Rider
**Set 2:** Dark Star > Eyes of the World > Stella Blue

**1. Source:** FM-SBD (GDH 270, 279, and 280), **Quality:** B+, **Length:** 1:40 ("They Love Each Other," "Greatest Story Ever Told," "China Cat Sunflower" > "I Know You Rider," "Dark Star" through "Stella Blue." "Greatest Story" and "China Cat" > "I Know You Rider" appear after "Stella Blue" on side 2 of cassettes of this show), **Genealogy:** MR > DR

**2. Source:** AUD, **Quality:** C, **Length:** 1:20 (first set only)

**Highlights:** What a Dark Star!!, Stella Blue

An inferior quality audience recording of the first set of this show has been around for a long time, but you really must acquire the decent soundboard excerpts that first appeared on the scene around 1994. The crème de la crème is, as you would expect, the "Dark Star"—which at forty-two minutes is one of the Dead's all-time longest. Metaphorically, "Dark Star" was a creative ship built by the band in order to sail the infinitely vast uncharted realms of the collective unconscious. Most of the time it was Garcia who stood at the bow of the ship, launching breathtaking volleys of aural pyrotechnics forward into the great unknown to illuminate the way. This version, however, is one of those rare ones from which both Phil and Keith launched the brightest volleys. Put headphones on and listen carefully as Phil alternates between plucking subtle, high, percussive notes as a deliberate counterbeat to Billy's drumming, and laying down deeply entrancing harmonic drones that seem to go on and on forever. This is Phil at his very, very best. Keith, for a change, is very loud in the mix. This allows the listener to clearly hear him inventing weblike melodic patterns against which Jerry's picking stands out strongly. At several points Keith is leading the band, something you just don't hear that often. This incredibly well-developed jam goes on for quite some time before Garcia steps forward with strong vocals. Back into space they fly. This evolves into one of the most beautiful explorations of feedback I've ever heard this band play. Neither minimalist like the "Dark Star" feedbacks of 1970, nor scary like many versions found in 1972, nor electronic-sounding like many played in '74, this feedback sounds mostly like something you'd expect as background music in a Stanley Kubrick film. After several delicious minutes of group feedback, Keith lays down a more structured riff and boom, the whole band rises up into structured melodic harmony again. Both Phil and Keith eventually find their way into "Wharf Rat," but Jerry wants no part of it—he cuts them off, launching into a long, spacey "Eyes." "Stella Blue" is particularly soulful, and at its conclusion Phil lays down one last long signature feedback note as if to signify he's well aware how special the past sixty minutes have been. The "Greatest Story" and "China Cat Sunflower" > "I Know You Rider," which appear on the end of my tape, are good, but not nearly as inspired.

JOHN R. DWORK

## 12/8/73
### Cameron Stadium, Duke University, Durham, North Carolina

**Set 1:** Me and My Uncle, Sugaree, Mexicali Blues, Dire Wolf, Black-Throated Wind, They Love Each Other, Me and Bobby McGee, Don't Ease Me In, The Race Is On, Brown-Eyed Women, Big River, Candyman, Weather Report Suite Prelude > Weather Report Suite Part One > Let It Grow, China Cat Sunflower > I Know You Rider

**Set 2:** Around and Around, Ramble On Rose, El Paso, Row Jimmy, Greatest Story Ever Told, Bertha, He's Gone > Truckin' > Nobody's Fault but Mine > //Jam > //The Other One// > Feedback > Wharf Rat > Stella Blue > Johnny B. Goode > Uncle John's Band

**Encore:** One More Saturday Night

**Source:** AUD, **Quality:** B–/B, **Length:** 3:10

**Highlights:** Candyman, Weather Report Suite Prelude > Weather Report Suite Part One > Let It Grow, China Cat Sunflower > I Know You Rider, Nobody's Fault but Mine > Jam > The Other One > Wharf Rat > Stella Blue > Johnny B. Goode > Uncle John's Band

**Comments:** The quality of the first-set recording could be a bit better. It seems as though the recordist simply could've had better seating. By the second set, the ambience of the tape has improved a solid notch and listening becomes more enjoyable.

A nice long, classic, late '73 show. The band drives hard and steady through the entire first set. It's obvious they've got lots of energy to burn. Bobby's tunes are particularly energized. "Candyman," though, is perhaps the sweetest reading in the set. "Weather Report" takes a while to get going, but once it does Jerry noodles furiously. The band caps this winner off with a strong "China Cat" > "Rider" featuring a requisite "Feelin' Groovy Jam."

The second set shines even brighter. The "Nobody's Fault but Mine" is one of the finer versions you'll hear.

*Ad for show at Duke University, 12/8/73*

This digresses into a jam that lacks melodic focus but nevertheless succeeds in captivating and holding one's attention due to Jerry's aggressive noodling. After a brief cut (the first of three before the next song appears), the jam continues with numerous hintings at "The Other One." Finally, they play the song, but only the first verse. The verse disposed of, the band melts reality with a classic brain-fry feedback jam. Then, from out of this tonal holograph, the band ascends *perfectly* into "Wharf Rat." The rest of the set is picture-perfect.

JOHN R. DWORK

## 12/12/73
### The Omni, Atlanta, Georgia

**Soundcheck:** Sleighride, Stay, Rip It Up, Blue Suede Shoes, Peggy-O, Cumberland Blues, 30 Days
**Set 1:** Promised Land, Sugaree, Mexicali Blues, Tennessee Jed, Don't Ease Me In, Looks like Rain, They Love Each Other, El Paso, Peggy-O, Beat It on Down the Line, Brown-Eyed Women, Big River, Deal, Playing in the Band
**Set 2:** Mississippi Half-Step, Me and Bobby McGee, China Cat Sunflower > I Know You Rider, Greatest Story Ever Told, Row Jimmy, Weather Report Suite Prelude > Weather Report Suite Part One// > Let It Grow, Wharf Rat > Me and My Uncle, Eyes of the World > Morning Dew, //Sugar Magnolia//, Casey Jones

**Source:** SBD, **Quality:** A–, **Length:** 3:55, **Genealogy:** Soundcheck: MR > RR > DAT
**Highlights:** China Cat Sunflower > I Know You Rider, Weather Report //Suite, Eyes of the World, Morning Dew

On the whole, soundchecks are thin on the ground, and although few people would consider them particularly enlightening, they can bring up interesting items, albeit in a fragmentary fashion. This date includes some oddities, and even though we only get to hear truncated versions of "Rip It Up," et al., it's all quite amusing in a very laid-back way. None of the songs performed in full have anything like a sense of urgency or intensity you'd expect in a proper concert performance, but they're nevertheless an enjoyable listen. Coming as an afterthought to "Cumberland Blues," "30 Days" does suggest an interesting pairing that was never followed up, more's the pity. Most of us will search this tape out for the last two tracks as any performances at all are so rare that a chance to check them out is hardly going to be passed up. Both are most definitely works in progress. Incidentally, "Peggy-O" is also an early run-through, complete with Garcia's comments on chord structure. No one would make great claims for the musical worth of this piece, but eavesdropping it is still good fun.

As for the show itself, there are some staggeringly fine performances to be heard, including a stunning "China Cat Sunflower" > "I Know You Rider" that is wrapped around a wonderful, undulating jam section, a magnificent "Weather Report Suite," the development of which is perfectly paced, leading up to a breathtaking jam (great drums, Billy). No music is lost with the break in this track as it's been faded out on side A and back in on side B to fit neatly onto a ninety-minute cassette, and you get a slight reprise. For my money the hottest segment of the show is the utterly sublime "Eyes of the World," a truly magnificent freewheeling exploration that brims over with sunburst guitars, liquid piano, and cascading drums. The bridge into "Morning Dew" is quite sudden, and this version contains some remarkably 3-D Phil: bass that lurches out of your speakers (whatever their size) to give your molecules a damn good shaking.

PAUL BODENHAM

## 12/18/73
### Curtis Hixon Hall, Tampa, Florida

**Set 1:** Tennessee Jed, Me and My Uncle, Don't Ease Me In, Looks like Rain, They Love Each Other, Me and Bobby McGee, Brown-Eyed Women, Beat It on Down the Line > Peggy-O, El Paso, Deal, Jack Straw, China Cat Sunflower > I Know You// Rider
**Set 2:** Promised Land > Bertha > Greatest Story Ever Told, Row Jimmy, Weather Report Suite Prelude > Weather Report Suite Part One > Let It Grow > Dark Star > Drums > Eyes of the World > Wharf// Rat > Sugar Magnolia, Uncle John's Band, Casey Jones//

**1. Source:** SBD, **Quality:** A, **Length:** 3:00, **Genealogy:** MR > DAT > C > C > DAT
**2. Source:** AUD, **Quality:** B–, **Length:** 3:00, **Genealogy:** MC > DAT

**Highlights:** The second-set jam, particularly Eyes of the World

For years I've been nuts about this concert, though until recently I've also been woeful that it was only available as an audience tape. In early 1996 the soundboard appeared, and I had a chance to experience this show in a whole new light.

The first-set performance is on the hot side of lazy: every song starts slow, builds steadily, and peaks impressively, though never reaching that mind-blowing level present so often just the year before. This whole concert sounds a bit more like a show from 1974 than one from 1973. Halfway through the short first set (are we missing songs?), Bobby tells a completely spaced-out, rambling, utterly senseless story while the roadies fix the piano.

The real magic starts in the second set. "Weather Report" is picture-perfect—not as energized as, let's say, the version from Fresno on 7/19/74, but beautiful nonetheless. Toward the end of the jam the whole band collectively rises to weave the first of several liltingly gorgeous melodic webs present throughout the rest of the concert. This is a Grateful Dead sound more on the side of electrified jazz than rock 'n' roll. Miles Davis' album *Bitches Brew* is what's going on here—not the Rolling Stones' *Sticky Fingers*.

Again, like the rest of this show, the pre-lyrics segment of "Dark Star" is rather mellow, with true inspiration to be found in the subtle intricacies and sensitive interplay. It's amazing how much more mellow this Grateful Dead is than the same band just one year before! After Jerry sings the words, however, the band transforms "Dark Star" into something much, much more strange. One by one they all start to play *extreme* "Feedback"—very much like the "Feedback" played in "Playing in the Band" at Oakland on 6/8/74. At first it's all rather minimalist. But then all of a sudden, from out of nowhere, the entire band ascends into one of the darkest, ugliest, scariest "Space Feedback" jams of their entire career. Phew! Heavy indeed! Bobby in particular plays some of the scariest sounds I've ever heard.

Like so many other songs in this show, "Eyes" starts slow. Steadily, it soars higher and higher until, during the post-lyrics jam, Phil starts to drop the serious bombs. The rest of the band soars even higher above this bellowing foundation. This may be one of the best "Eyes" jams ever. The finale is certainly as powerful as any I've heard.

"Wharf Rat" is strong, though marred by an obvious cut where the master reels were changed. "Sugar Mags" also starts slow, but again the jam is inspired. "Casey Jones" cuts early on.

This is one of those shows that perhaps is best listened to late at night while driving in a car. The gems to be mined here show up best when observed carefully with a mindset geared for introspection. Sacred, mellow, electrified jazz-rock indeed.

JOHN R. DWORK

## 12/19/73
### Curtis Hixon Hall, Tampa, Florida

**Set 1:** Promised Land, Sugaree, Mexicali Blues, Dire Wolf, Black-Throated Wind, Candyman, Jack Straw, Big Railroad Blues, Big River, Here Comes Sunshine, El Paso, Ramble On Rose, Playing in the Band
**Set 2:** Mississippi Half-Step, Me and Bobby McGee, Row Jimmy, Weather Report Suite Prelude > Weather Report Suite Part One > Let It Grow, He's Gone > Truckin' > Nobody's Fault but Mine > The Other One > Jam > Stella Blue > Around and Around
**Encore:** Casey Jones

**1. Source:** SBD, **Quality:** A+, **Length:** 2:10 ("Here Comes Sunshine," "Big River," "Mississippi Half-Step," "Weather Report Suite Prelude" > "Weather Report Suite Part One" > "Let It Grow," "Big Railroad Blues," "Playing in the Band," "He's Gone" > "Truckin'" > "Nobody's Fault but Mine" > "The Other One" > "Feedback" > "Stella Blue," "Around and Around"), **Genealogy:** MR > DAT

**2. Source:** AUD, **Quality:** B, **Length:** 2:55 ("Here Comes Sunshine" contains a cut) **Genealogy:** MC > DAT

**Highlights:** Here Comes Sunshine, Big River, Playing in the Band, Feedback > Stella Blue

There are two very good reasons why Dick Latvala put excerpts from this show out as *Dick's Picks I*. First, because "Here Comes Sunshine" is INCREDIBLE! It's the most emphatically embellished version this reviewer has ever heard. Second, because this finally got the *Dick's Picks* project off and running. Amen! As for the rest of the show—well, it's good, but not great. Still, it's all worth the investment as both a CD and an audience recording. Despite its overall low-key energy I applaud Dick for getting this show out. The "Here Comes Sunshine" alone is worth its weight in gold.

Dick did not put these songs onto the CD in the order they were performed. Nor did he include all the songs performed at this show. Personally, this doesn't bother me in the least, many Deadheads made a big stink about it. I must go on record supporting the producer's decision to edit out music that cannot be salvaged due to technical shortcomings in the original recordings and to arrange the music in an order that he thinks fits well on the disc. I think, however, it would serve history better if these "edited" releases contained liner notes that gave the original order. That way, while we may not get to enjoy all of the show, future listeners will at least know how it really went down.

I've also heard that Phil Lesh made the decision to edit out his bass solo from "The Other One" (which is captured on the audience recording). I'm not too wild about that. But I do want Phil to be happy with these releases, and if that's what he had to do in order to finally get this project going, then so be it. I hope, however, that in the future he sees the fault in this logic.

As for the music, well, this "Here Comes Sunshine" is nothing less than phenomenal! It's not the tightest version ever, but the jam keeps building and building and building for what seems like an eternity. I've played this cut for entire concert halls full of Deadheads and it never fails to make them scream in orgasmic delight. "Big River," with Keith Godchaux's tasty piano work and Jerry's jumpy lead, is superb, though average for the time.

"Mississippi Half-Step" is beautifully mellow, perhaps too much so. Dick fades it out during the final sleepy notes anyway. "Weather Report Suite," which actually builds some heat, features delicious slide work by Jerry during "Part One." "Big River" sleeps by comparison with so many other renditions from the previous two years. "Playing in the Band," however, is an intriguing, jazz-inflected, psychedelic romp through the wilds of the Dead's group mind. This version is dominated by Jerry's extremely noodly guitar work, which holds at a steadily hyperactive level throughout the jam. As a final adieu to space, Phil drops a single extended harmonic bomb over which Bobby brings in the familiar melody of the reprise. Yum!

Looking back at the set list, I would've been scratching my head if I was at this show. "Half-Step," "Me and Boby McGee," "Row Jimmy," "Weather Report Suite," and "He's Gone" to open the second set?! Regardless of how beautifully it's performed this is a textbook example of laid-back.

"He's Gone" > "Truckin'" > "Nobody's Fault" > "Other One" is all uneventful, though it's always a treat to hear Jerry fully articulate the lyrics on the fairly rare "Nobody's Fault but Mine." The "Feedback" segment is another matter altogether, with Phil laying down gigantic moaning monster tones. Very nice! A delicate "Stella Blue" emerges from out of this "Feedback" like a cold winter sunrise—lonely, sad, beautiful. "Around and Around," again, though played well enough, is unremarkable.

JOHN R. DWORK

---

### ❆ 12/31/73 ❆
**Cow Palace, San Francisco, California**

**Set 2:** Hideaway > You've Upset Me Baby > Hideaway > You've Upset Me Baby, Hey// Bo Diddley, Save My Life, Jam//
**Set 3:** You Don't Love Me > Will the Circle Be Unbroken > Mountain Jam

---

**Source:** SBD, **Quality:** A, **Length:** 1:45
**Highlights:** Hideaway, You Don't Love Me > Will The Circle Be Unbroken > Mountain Jam
**Personnel:** The Allman Brothers Band with Jerry Garcia, Bill Kreutzmann, and Boz Scaggs

The set begins with "Hideaway," a perfect standby to warm up on. The boys stick remarkably close to Freddie King's original through the first few bars, immediately shifting to an uptown B.B.-style jam following the break, which segues perfectly into "You've Upset Me Baby." Unfortunately, Garcia completely blows his solo, and the following vocal reading is less than confident. Managing to rebound for the second solo, Garcia nails some fine licks, though they're somewhat hampered by being buried in the mix. After briefly leading the boys back into "Hideaway," Dickey Betts then comes to the rescue with a sparkling solo, then returning to "You've Upset Me Baby" for a repeat of the verse and the trademark Allman Brothers triplet turnaround.

The tide then turns when, blown up, the boys stumble through a painfully disjointed rendition of "Hey Bo Diddley." Hampered by sloppy shuffles from the rhythm section and downright horrible vocals, this deceptively simple two-chord shuffle amounts to little more than a falling off the barstool stupor. Though the guitarists manage to coax a few appropriately pointed licks that contrast nicely with the rhythm, they are overshadowed by the foppish falsetto shrieking of an obviously inebriated Gregg Allman. As the boys segue into the "Mountain Jam," the conversation slowly evolves to a near acceptable level, sounding unsurprisingly similar to the "Not Fade Away" jams of 1970, even going so far as to tease a bar or two of "Goin' Down the Road Feelin' Bad." Unfortunately, what would be the highlight of the jam, a Q and A duet between Betts and Garcia, is plagued by Garcia's poor showing in the mix.

Somewhat resilient, the boys rebound with a solid rendition of "Save My Life" before rolling up their sleeves with a ritzy swing jam. Although this passage is loaded with stunning licks, Garcia's contribution is marginal at best, plagued both by more sound problems in the mix and by a fairly sleepy showing in composition. And to add insult to injury, the tape breaks off in the midst of a hot Dickey Betts solo.

Following the intermission and what appears to be an impromptu wedding ceremony, complete with kudos from Mr. Graham himself, the boys embark on an ever appropriate, though conspicuously instrumental "You Don't Love Me." Here Garcia showcases his finest licks of the evening, and both Kreutzmann and Scaggs make enthusiastic contributions as well. The finale is picture-perfect, featuring some ferociously precise "Heartbreaker" licks from Dickey Betts, segueing gracefully into "Will the Circle Be Unbroken." This ballad, a perfect selection for a New Year's Eve performance, is gently joyous, containing stunning lead guitar lines and even a few remote piano quotations from "Let It Be." For only a split second on the transition into the concluding "Mountain Jam," Garcia licks a few microscopic but noticeable phrases from "Big Railroad Blues," "Black-Throated Wind," and "Goin' Down the Road Feelin' Bad," all within a few bars! Momentarily confused, the band then launches into the finale jam, settling the momentum in an appropriate conclusion to the evening's festivities.

BRIAN DYKE

---

### ❆ 12/31/73 ❆
**Cow Palace, San Francisco, California**
**Interview:** Jerry Garcia

---

**Source:** FM, **Quality:** B, **Length:** 0:05
**Comments:** Interview was conducted by Tom Donahue.

Garcia discusses Grateful Dead Records and gives a quick promo for the "Eyes of the World" single.

BRYAN DYKE

# 1974

Arguably one of the Grateful Dead's greatest years, 1974, began with three marathon shows at Winterland in February, followed a month later by another one at the Cow Palace in San Francisco. The four shows contained well over three hours of music each and featured six brand new, original songs. The tapes of these shows have all been available for years as very good sounding audience tapes, with the final two shows at Winterland and parts of the Cow Palace Show are now available as excellent soundboards. They show the band having reached a place of musical craftsmanship far exceeding, in sound and tightness, the place from which they had started nine years earlier. Each musician maintained a distinct niche within the ensemble; they were well accomplished at their tasks. Even though the shows harkened back, in length, to those of the previous two years, they were much more consistent throughout. The band was able to overcome its problem with throwaway first sets as each song was given focus and played with care. By the second set of each of these four shows, they were able to produce monumental versions of "The Other One," "Dark Star," and the "Playing" > "Uncle John's" > "Morning Dew" sandwich.

As the year progressed, the band was able to continue this trend. It also tried to shake up the set structure from the past two years. Now, with over seventy songs in their regular rotation, they were being more creative in how the jams progressed. "Eyes of the World" could have appeared anywhere in either set, even as the centerpiece to the main second-set jam. "Truckin'" replaced "Dark Star" as the gateway to deep space. Indeed, "Dark Star" and "The Other One" became somewhat rare, and when they were played, it was not guaranteed that the verses would be sung. August 5 in Philadelphia and June 26 in Providence, Rhode Island, both contain strong "Other One" themes, but neither ever got close to a point where vocals would be sung. June 23 in Miami, Florida, and June 28 in Boston, Massachusetts, both have complete "Dark Star" jams without a single sung word. However, many times "Truckin'" would go places no "Dark Star" ever had. Listen to May 25 in Santa Barbara, July 31 in Hartford, August 5 in Philadelphia, and September 20 in Paris to hear how adept the band had become at completely deconstructing this rock 'n' roll song and transforming it into musical pudding. "Playing in the Band" remained, as it had since late 1973, a common second-set centerpiece, most significantly on May 21 in Seattle, June 8 in Oakland, July 21 in Los Angeles, and October 20, the last show at Winterland.

Part of the reason for such strong playing was the excellent sound being provided by the legendary "Wall of Sound" PA system. Unveiled in its full capacity for the first time at the Cow Palace on March 23, this sound system produced beautiful, clear music played quietly, but broadcast at very loud volume. It enabled the Dead to play their songs as if they were in a more intimate setting where they could interact more gracefully, knowing that they could hear every note and so could every member of the audience. The music could be put out so that even in the upper reaches of an arena or stadium every strum of the guitar, every plunk of the piano, and every crash of cymbal would appear to be right before one's face. Lesh's bass, too, became wonderfully overpowering as he produced subsonic notes that felt as if they were coming right out of the floorboards.

As with any system, however, there were drawbacks. The vocals, although clear, came out thin and reedy and lost some of the richness they possessed a few years before. In addition, such clear separation of each instrument sometimes prevented their blending in the overall soundscape, which gave the music an overly sparse quality. As a whole, however, the good qualities more than compensated for these drawbacks.

The Dead took this incredible PA system on the road with them the entire year. Coinciding with this dramatic increase in sound quality, tapers were appearing at shows with improved microphones and recorders. This became the first year in the band's history that is almost completely documented on tape. With the exception of September 14 in Munich, July 25 in Chicago, and August 4 in Philadelphia, there are tapes ranging in quality from listenable to outstanding of at least one set from every 1974 show. Many of the audience tapes are quite good, including March 23 from the Cow Palace, May 21 in Seattle, June 23 in Miami, June 30 in Springfield, Massachusetts, and July 21 in Los Angeles. They all demonstrate the unique loud clarity of the PA. During quiet parts, one may hear a nearby member of the audience while notes from a guitar are heard over the talking and appear to be just as close to the microphones. On the whole, these audience tapes provide one of the best means of experiencing what it was like to be at a pre-"retirement" concert. Even when soundboards exist, audience tapes should be sought out for this reason.

*Because this year was so well documented, there is an excellent opportunity for Deadheads to hear how the music evolved over the course of the year. Since the music could be heard so clearly, it seemed that each night's jam became a natural evolution of the previous night's. This phenomenon appeared to accelerate toward the end of the year. Also, by midyear, the "Spanish Jam," one of their earliest instrumental themes, had crept back into the space jams. It seemed that all the energy and creativity of the band's ten years was being put into each show. By the time of the Europe tour in September, they were reaching incredible peaks at every concert. Unfortunately, the price of lugging this mammoth sound system across the country and the ocean was costly. Because the band needed two separate crews to erect the scaffolding and the sound system, and due to the huge increases in the price of gasoline that summer, they made very little profit in 1974. In addition, they were limited to playing only the largest of stadiums and arenas. This brought with it the pressure of huge crowds, heightened security backstage, and frisk lines everywhere. The scene had grown to a size that nobody in the band cared to be part of. It was time for a break. Listening to the music, one can feel influencing the music the tension and energy that prompted the band to take time off from touring. Then, having made the decision to take time off, the final five shows at Winterland became a joyous celebration. The band was more relaxed and, consequently, performed some of the best music they had ever played. Each of the first four shows were very different from each other and played off a different aspect of the band's style from the previous three years. It was a fitting culmination to what would be only the first phase of the Dead's career.*

*Tapes to get: 2/24, 3/23, 6/16, 6/18, 6/23, 6/26, 6/28, 7/19, 9/10, 9/11, 9/20, 10/16, 10/18, 10/19.*

---

## 2/22/74
### Winterland Arena, San Francisco, California

**Soundcheck:** Let It Grow, They Love Each Other, U.S. Blues (2×), Attics of My Life, It Must Have Been the Roses (2×), Jam
**Set 1:** U.S. Blues, Beat It on Down the Line, Brown-Eyed Women, Mexicali Blues, It Must Have Been the Roses, Black-Throated Wind, They Love Each Other, Big River, Loose Lucy, El Paso, Row Jimmy, Playing in the Band
**Set 2:** Tennessee Jed, Me and My Uncle, Ship of Fools, The Race Is On, China Cat Sunflower > I Know You Rider, Truck//in' > Nobody's Fault but Mine > Goin' Down the Road Feelin' Bad
**Set 3:** Mississippi Half-Step, Promised Land, Brokedown Palace, Jack Straw//, Eyes of the World > China Doll > Wharf Rat > Sugar Magnolia
**Encore:** Uncle John's Band

**1. Source:** SBD, **Quality:** A, **Length:** 3:30, **Genealogy:** MR > DAT
**2. Source:** AUD, **Quality:** B–, **Length:** 3:30, **Taper:** Louis Falanga with a Sony TC-110 deck and an ECM-23 mike
**3. Source:** FM-SBD (GDH 068 and 203), **Quality:** A, **Length:** "They Love Each Other," "Mexicali Blues," "It Must Have Been the Roses," "Big River," **Genealogy:** MR > DR

**Highlights:** China Cat Sunflower > I Know You Rider, Mississippi Half-Step, Eyes > China Doll > Wharf Rat > Sugar Magnolia

Returning from what by all accounts, a fabulous year, the Dead kick off 1974 with a trio of performances at the Winterland Arena that show they haven't missed a beat. From the first note it is evident that the band has been itching to play; they roar confidently through the standard repertoire before prematurely shifting into overdrive with a highly energized if slightly rusty "Playing in the Band." Unwinding gently out of the verse, Garcia chooses a beautiful pseudo-trumpet sound from his pre-amp while floundering throughout the song's frame. He trades chops evenly with Weir, the theme is stated, and the band synchronizes perfectly. As Weir switches from beefy rhythms to single-note trills, Garcia grasps the opportunity to slyly begin hinting at "Slipknot," the jam that was later to reside between "Help on the Way" and "Franklin's Tower." However, as the band drifts further into space, Weir's swooshing rhythms begin to splash against Garcia's meticulous lines, creating a temporary chaos, before lying out and letting the rest of the band take over. Garcia's presence becomes prominent, quickly switching his trumpetlike pre-amp to his traditional, mildly distorted guitar sound. Noodling in and out but remaining fairly static, the jam begins to discombobulate momentarily before Phil furiously marches the jam back to order. Again Garcia attempts to integrate a "Slipknot" jam, but as the rest of the band tries to follow along, inevitably the synchronicity crumbles, and in frustration the band returns to the much safer main theme. Garcia immediately heads off into deep space as his colleagues lock into the groove of the main theme. Unfortunately, this only becomes more disoriented, and soon Kreutzmann is the sole remaining member playing in correct time, with Godchaux so far off on another wavelength that it becomes embarrassing. At this point the jam has completely strayed, with Weir and Lesh splashing random harmonics against Garcia's painfully out of tune bends. Finally realizing that enough's enough, the band slowly marches back into the reprise, wisely opting for a well-timed intermission.

Refreshed from the break, the band kick off set 2 with a smokin' "Tennessee Jed" and a "Me and My Uncle" that absolutely roars! The following "Ship of Fools" is sweet and steady, and of course, "The Race Is On" is always a nice treat. It should be mentioned that while the entire band is on, Godchaux is playing well above the earth. Ready to boogie the Dead break into "China Cat Sunflower" > "I Know You Rider." Here the guitarists take over, and Weir's steady rhythm meshes perfectly with Garcia's ingenious waltzes of simplicity. You can actually hear the trademark Garcia grin on this one. The segue into "I Know You Rider" isn't as exploratory as usual; rather the band locks into the groove instantly, taking their time riding it out. Ah, what precision! The simplicity displayed here is breathtaking, the interplay gorgeous. Peaking on "Rider," the jam shifts to furious for the finale, as the band comes full circle before launching into the set-closing "Truckin'" > "Nobody's Fault" > "Goin' Down the Road." While certainly competent, the play here is clearly a notch below that of the preceding material. Nonetheless, this is a fine way to close off the set, and the rare "Nobody's Fault but Mine" is always a treat.

On the third and final set of the evening, the Dead maintain the confidence displayed earlier. The opening "Half-Step" is stunningly gorgeous, especially sweetened by Weir's bright harmonics on the outro. The simplicity displayed, reminiscent of the second-set "China" > "Rider," is a perfect warm-up for a rip-roaring "Promised Land," highlighted again by Godchaux, who displays chops that would make Johnnie Johnson blush. Not to be outdone, Garcia responds with calculated soloing underneath each verse, while Weir handles the vocals perfectly. The flawless execution continues through "Brokedown Palace" and "Jack Straw" before the wrap up of "Eyes" > "China Doll" > "Wharf Rat" > "Sugar Magnolia." Starting slowly, the band takes its time through a picture-perfect reading of "Eyes," waiting until the outro to begin unwinding. The band then launches, trading thick chord jamming with spiraling leads that eventually lead into the "Stronger Than Dirt" jam. Here the band begins to stumble a bit, and they wisely shift to "China Doll," which is beautifully melancholy. Garcia's singing is superb, and the vocal harmonies are partially in tune. Keeping the mood morose, Garcia chooses "Wharf Rat" to follow. Again, the band gives a meticulous reading, highlighted by Godchaux, who uses rich piano textures to add warmth and color. Obviously impressed, Garcia allows Godchaux to showcase his chops here, rather than taking his usual solos between each verse. Then tagging to the guitarists, a light jam in the third register develops before Weir kick starts into "Sugar Magnolia." Oh, what a perfect way to wrap up such a performance. The "Uncle John's Band" encore is icing on the cake, as the Dead start off 1974 with a blast.

BRIAN DYKE

# Reviews: February 1974

## 🌀 2/23/74 🌀
### Winterland Arena, San Francisco, California

**Set 1:** Around and Around, Dire Wolf, Me and Bobby McGee, Sugaree, Mexicali Blues, Here Comes// Sunshine, Beat It on Down the Line, Ship of Fools, Jack Straw, Deal, Promised Land > Bertha > Greatest Story Ever Told
**Set 2:** Row Jimmy, Weather Report Suite Prelude > Weather Report Suite Part One > Let It Grow > Stella Blue, Big River, Ramble// On Rose, Me and My Uncle, He's Gone > Nobody's Fault Jam > Truckin' > Drums > Slipknot > The Other One > Eyes of the World, One More Saturday Night
**Encore 1:** Casey Jones
**Encore 2:** Johnny B. Goode > We Bid You Goodnight

**1. Source:** SBD, **Quality:** A+, **Length:** 3:20, **Genealogy:** MR > DAT
**2. Source:** AUD, **Quality:** B–, **Length:** 3:30, **Taper:** Louis Falanga with a Sony TC-110 deck and an ECM-23 mike
**3. Source:** FM-SBD (GDH 044, 045, 085, and 170), **Quality:** A, **Length:** "Around and Around," "Here Comes Sunshine," "Ship of Fools" through "Greatest Story," "Big River," "He's Gone through Eyes of the World," "Johnny B. Goode" > "We Bid You Goodnight," **Genealogy:** MR > DR
**Highlights:** Weather Report Suite, Eyes of the World, several Gizarno first set mixes

With the introduction of "the great, great Grateful Dead" from Bill Graham, the show kicks off with a no-nonsense "Around and Around" where Weir just about shouts himself hoarse inside the first five minutes. OK, it's gonna be one of *those* shows. . . . Keith is in fine form.

The second set features enough hardcore jamming to satisfy just about everyone: "Weather Report Suite" unfolds in its own exquisite fashion, leading to a climax that has all the instrumentalists streaming through liquid improvisations that seem to flow without effort, easing out of this epic into a pleasantly understated "Stella Blue." "Big River" and "Me and My Uncle" are both taken at a furious pace, skidding to a halt following concise bursts of invention. "Concise" is hardly the the word for the rest of the show, which develops in its own time, every number examined in minute detail before a transition leads into the next platform for improvisation. Onward and upward, peaking in the incandescent rush of "Eyes of the World." Sure, the recording of this show has more than a few glitches (odd mixes in the first set, cuts and a SBD/AUD change in the second), but rest assured that this is a fine performance.

PAUL BODENHAM

## 🌀 2/24/74 🌀
### Winterland Arena, San Francisco, California

**Set 1:** U.S. Blues, Mexicali Blues, Brown-Eyed Women, Beat It on Down the Line, Candyman, Jack Straw, China Cat Sunflower > I Know You Rider, El Paso, Loser, Playing in the Band
**Set 2:** Cumberland Blues, It Must Have Been the Roses, Big River, Bertha, Weather Report Suite Prelude > Weather Report Suite Part One > Let It Grow > Row Jimmy > Ship of Fools, Promised Land, Dark Star > Morning Dew, Sugar Magnolia > Not Fade Away > Goin' Down the Road Feelin' Bad > Not Fade Away
**Encore:** It's All Over Now, Baby Blue

**1. Source:** SBD, **Quality:** A, **Length:** 3:20, **Genealogy:** MR > DAT
**2. Source:** AUD, **Quality:** B+/B, **Length:** 3:20, **Taper:** Louis Falanga with a Sony TC-110 deck and an ECM-23 mike
**3. Source:** FM-SBD (GDH 286 and 287), **Quality:** A, **Length:** 1:00 ("U.S. Blues", "Brown-Eyed Women", "Beat It on Down the Line", "Jack Straw" through "Playing in the Band"), **Genealogy:** MR > DAT
**Highlights:** China Cat Sunflower > I Know You Rider, Playing in the Band, Dark Star (a mellow, introspective version), Not Fade Away > Goin' Down the Road Feelin' Bad > Not Fade Away Reprise

The last of a three-show run at Winterland that unleashed the transcendent phenomenon that was the

Dead in 1974, this was a good taste of what lay ahead. The arrangements are more tightly structured than ever before, yet this is combined with a sense of space that allow all band members to have their say without smothering the essence of the song they're playing. The most immediate practical consequence of this is that there is no dross among the song selections because they can throw you into the essence of a "Big River" as fully as they can a "Dark Star," and once you're there you just relax and enjoy it. There's no need to fast-forward to the jams or get past this or that tired old song—this was the year they were all brought back to life!

The show kicks off with the second ever "U.S. Blues," which makes for a great opener; triumphant but irreverent, upbeat but offbeat, it puts you in mind of nothing so much as the ol' Grateful Dead themselves. Not for nothing does it also open *The Grateful Dead Movie*. It's a shame it only ever held this position five other times before being relegated to being what was a sometimes rather tired encore. "Mexicali Blues" appears in a version second to none. The only "Candyman" of the year has a lovely solo, and there is a palpable sense of excitement about the band as they head into "China Cat" > "I Know You Rider." Garcia molds a wonderfully inventive rolling jam in the transition, spiraling up and down with truly vertiginous brilliance. Only the second, of course, of the all-time finest versions that will happen this year. In "Playing in the Band" Garcia starts the jam as he means to continue, with psychedelic chords rippling over a solid bed of undulating rhythm provided by Phil and Keith. The effect is sustained perfectly by the entire band as a reminder that virtuosity is as much an attitude or state of mind as a matter of force or rapidity. Remarkable, and the end of an interesting set. Much more is to come, though.

Set 2 boasts another rip-roaring set opener in the shape of a "Cumberland Blues" whose wonderful extended jam must place it among the longest-ever versions. The second-ever "Roses" is noticeably faster tempo than it later settled down to be. "Bertha" has a particularly enthusiastic vocal and a striking solo that rolls along with the furious beat so ably provided by Kreutzmann. "Weather Report Suite" starts off with particularly dramatic instrumental flourishes that complement Weir's carefully pitched singing, ably helped by Donna and Keith's spot-on accompaniment. The slow but inexorable buildup of this suite of songs, its greatest strength, is managed with consummate skill on this night, right up to the first solo of "Let It Grow." This produces a reeling cascade of notes from Garcia, which is then gently laid back to rest before the last verse. The jam that comes out of this does not, however, provide quite the cathartic climax expected after this display. Garcia takes a backseat as the band cooks up a bubbling cauldron of swirling themes that no one really takes the initiative on. The jam ends prematurely and falls into a "Row Jimmy" that one cannot help but be disappointed by at first. However, this is an elegant version, with a syncopated beat that takes hold partway and rocks you happily through to the end. It too, however, is without a real jam. The third-ever "Ship of Fools" follows with a very different intro and Weir-Kreutzmann backing that provide extra interest. It is the subsequent "Dark Star" > "Morning Dew" jam that puts the band in the space it has been aiming toward all evening. In "Dark Star" the alterations of pace and direction, seemingly at a moment's notice, are second to none, and yet such athletic prowess would mean little if it remained uncomplemented or unenlivened by a matching temperamental force and fire and a passionate, elemental, almost demonic quality. These are then themselves set off by the power, desolation, and majesty of a quintessential rendition of "Morning Dew," on whose final solo Garcia appears to reach new heights of expression. "Not Fade Away" provides a vehicle for free and rhapsodic exposition by the band, particularly Garcia, and the crescendo that leads up to "Goin' Down the Road" unleashes a positive firestorm of virtuosity from him. "Goin' Down" is as mean a piece of rock 'n' roll as the Dead ever produced, with Kreutzmann playing like a man possessed and Bobby screaming his way through the closing "Not Fade Away" reprise. The roaring crowd is sent home on a sweet and mellow vibe with an expressively constructed "Baby Blue," one of only three played between 1970 and 1981. This is the glorious last night of a stand of shows that provide a great musical welcome to the wonderful year ahead.

JAMES SWIFT

## Reviews: March 1974

### 🌀 3/23/74 🌀

**Official sound test for the Wall of Sound
Cow Palace, San Francisco, California**

**Set 1:** U.S. Blues, Promised Land, Brown-Eyed Women, Mexicali Blues, Tennessee Jed, Black-Throated Wind, Scarlet Begonias, It Must Have Been the Roses, El Paso, Deal, Cassidy, China Cat Sunflower > I Know You Rider, Weather Report Suite Prelude > Weather Report Suite Part One > Let It Grow
**Set 2:** Playing in the Band > Uncle John's Band > Morning Dew > Uncle John's Band Reprise > Playing Reprise, Ship of Fools, Big River, Ramble On Rose, Me and My Uncle, Bertha, Around and Around, Wharf Rat > Sugar Magnolia, Casey Jones
**Encore:** One More Saturday Night

**1. Source:** SBD, **Quality:** B+, **Length:** 4:00, **Genealogy:** MR > DAT
**2. Source:** AUD, **Quality:** B+, **Length:** 3:40, **Taper:** Louis Falanga with a Sony TC-110 deck and an ECM-23 mike
**3. Source:** FM-SBD (GDH), **Quality:** A, **Length:** 0:45 ("Playing" through "Playing" Reprise), **Genealogy:** MR > DAT
**4. Source:** FM-SBD (GDH 085), **Quality:** A, **Length:** 0:45 ("El Paso" through "Let It Grow"), **Genealogy:** MR > DAT
**Highlights:** The first-ever Cassidy, the first-ever Scarlet Begonias, China Cat > Rider, Weather Report Suite, Playing in the Band > Uncle John's Band > Morning Dew > Uncle John's Band Reprise > Playing in the Band Reprise, and, on the audience tape, the audience!

There are those Deadheads who swear by soundboards because they capture the musical artifact itself. Others swear by audience tapes, favoring the essence of the event and the overall flavor of being there. The latter explains why, despite their obvious sonic limitations, these tapes work. Their homey, intimate charm provokes nostalgia among the "real" old-time Deadheads while those who boarded The Bus from the Brent Mydland era on—myself included—are limited to imagination and fascination. Yes, Phil's bass booms with distortion on occasion, and you have to pay attention to catch Billy's cymbals and Keith's auspicious piano in a raw, rough mix; yet the rewards make the extra effort satisfying, deriving from the aura of an engaging, supportive audience.

Musically, these fine readings of "China Cat" > "I Know You Rider" and "Weather Report Suite" are not to be missed. But the meat of this exquisite show is the third and final "Playing" > "Uncle's John's Band" > "Morning Dew" > "Uncle John's" > "Playing" palindrome, complete with an amusing false start. Of course, moments after they restart with the vocals finally coming out of the PA, you have already forgotten about that technical snafu and been transported onto The Bus. Although my personal preference of these three palindromes is 11/17/73 UCLA, the transitions between "Playing" and "Uncle John" (and vice versa) are traversed here with an enthused confidence. The jamming is completely entrancing throughout, making this a must-have segment.

This evening also marked the debut of two concert staples that would remain intact and develop in the Dead's repertoire. "Scarlet Begonias" is confidently introduced here with a much greater sense of possibility for extensive embellishment than, for example, "Playing in the Band" displayed during its first flights in early 1971. "Cassidy" also took its first tentative flight on this evening in an abbreviated form—clearly revealing that the band hadn't discovered the song's strengths yet. It is interesting to note that this is the one and only live version during which Donna and Bobby sing the same "do, do, do, do, do" vocal riff found on the album version.

Yet what the audience tapes capture that many soundboards cannot—besides the debut of the Wall of Sound—is the subtle give-and-take between band and audience: the crowd cheering on a rollicking, tasty "China" > "Rider"; the warm-hearted bits of laughter at the false start on "Playing." The best way to listen to this tape is to close your eyes, concentrate on the details of the band's interplay, and then transport yourself via Mr. Peabody's Wayback Machine back to 1974 and become part of the crowd.

After all, being there was what "It" was all about!

JOHN WOOD

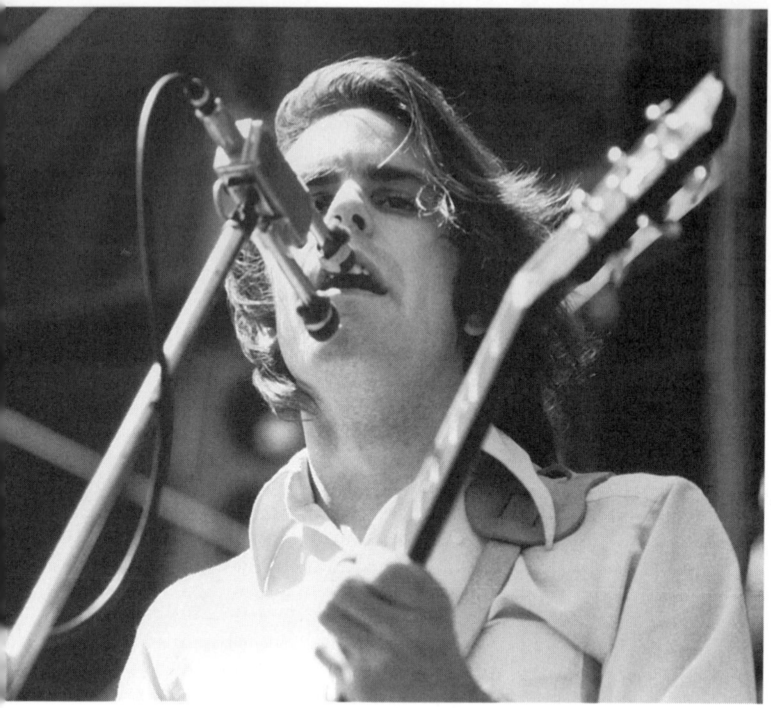

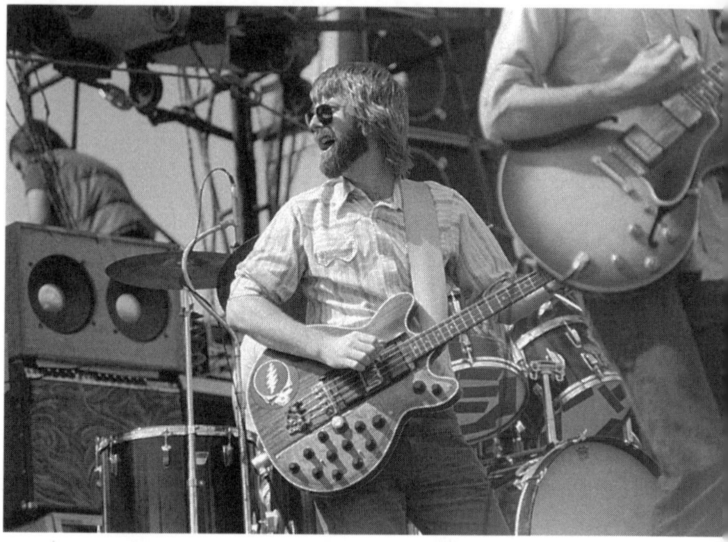

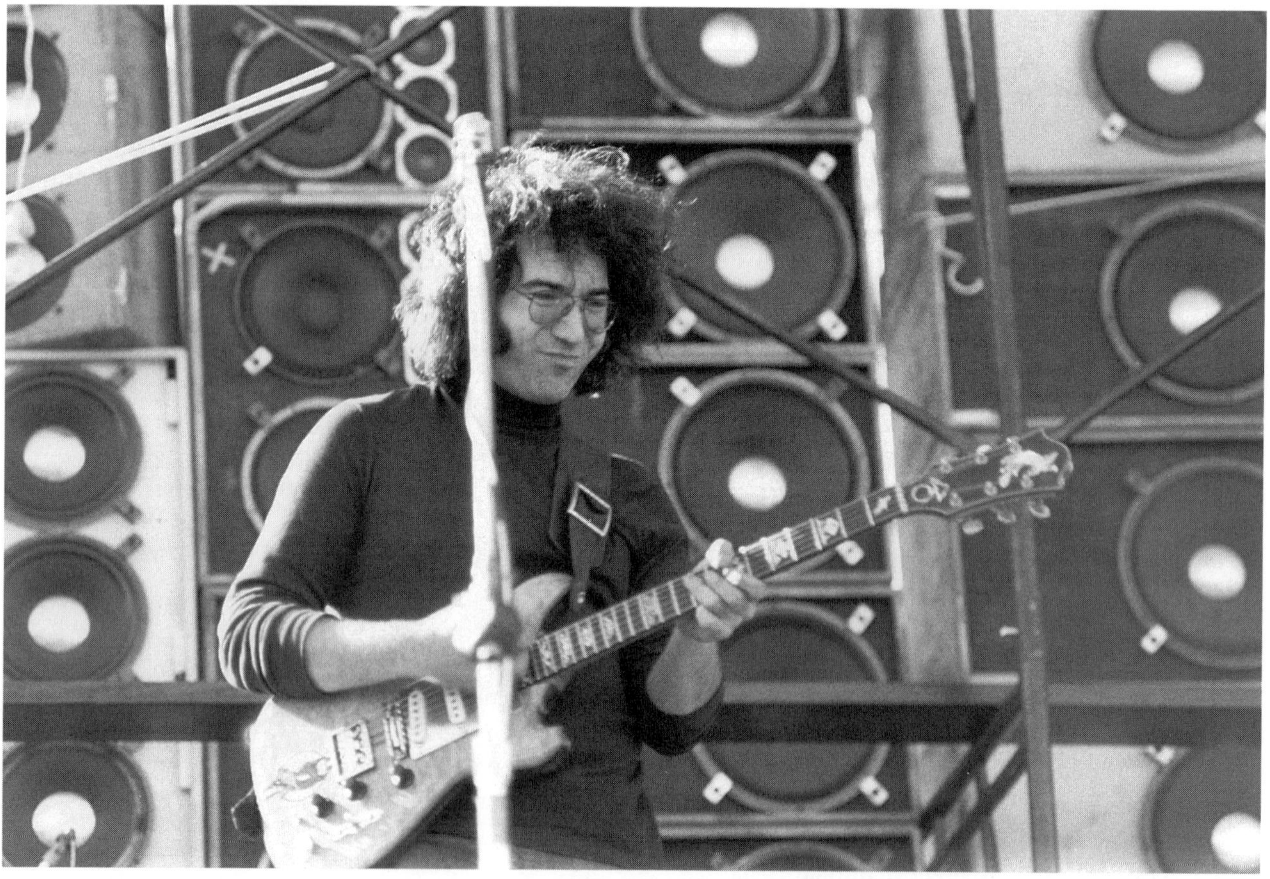

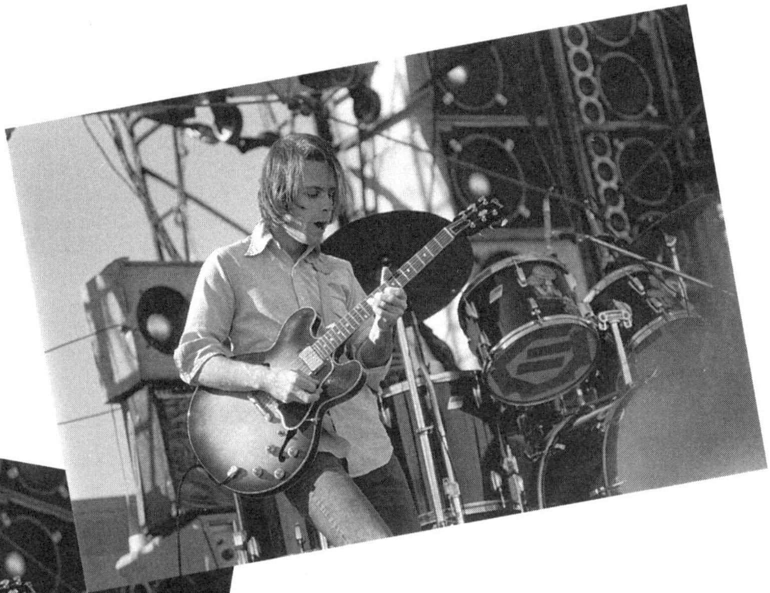

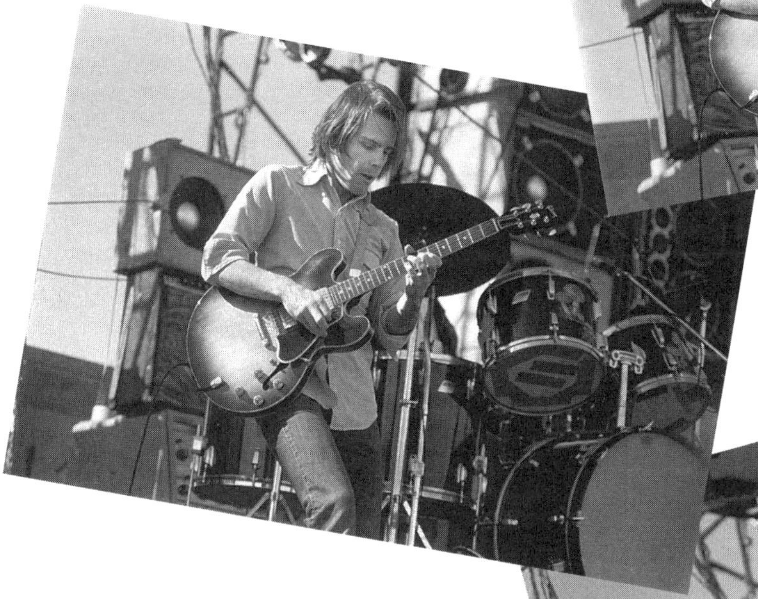

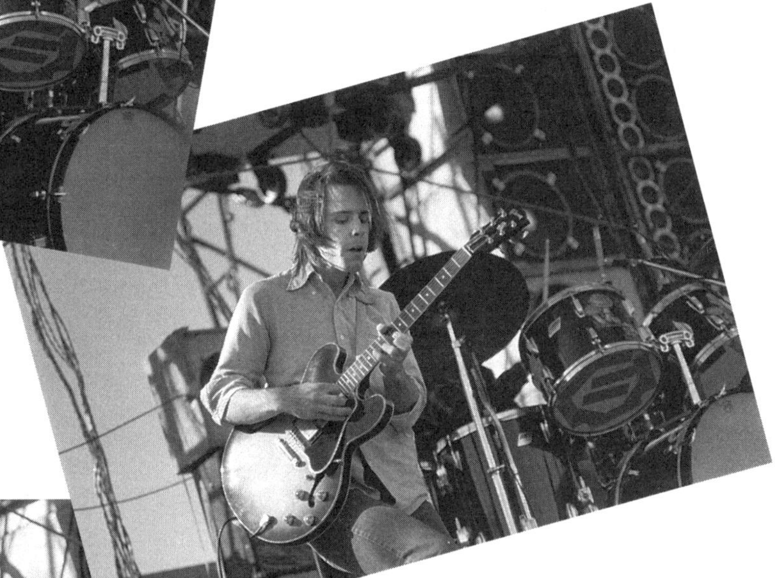

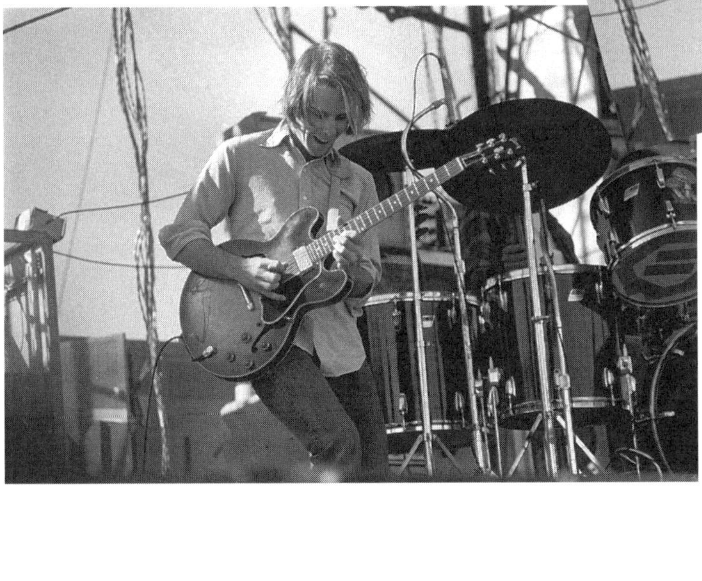

## 5/12/74
### University of Nevada, Reno, Nevada

**List:** Mississippi Half-Step, Truckin' > Lesh Solo > Jam > The Other One > Space > Row Jimmy, Big River, Ship of Fools, Sugar Magnolia

**Source:** AUD, **Quality:** B–, **Length:** 1:20
**Highlights:** Truckin' through Mind Left Body Jam
**Comments:** This tape features a boisterous crowd but also a full-bodied sound. The high end is a tad squashed, but it's easy to listen to.

A titanic, boisterous post-"Truckin'" jam collides head-on with the crowd; the result is a massive discharge of energy that fuels the next unique hour of music. Here comes true primal Dead at its best.

A blues theme develops with faint hints of "Nobody's Fault." Lesh is in fine spirits, to say the least, as he aggressively wiggles back and forth, seemingly gone one second and then glued to your face the next. Garcia picks up on this and pulls out, leaving only Billy to back a brief but emphatic Lesh solo. The band rejoins Lesh while he just continues to rattle away. A powerful jam takes form: no teases or current tour plottings here. This is a thundering, chunky rapids of energy. Finally, we get the "Other One" chords, teased and lightly grazed.

After moving downward into a quieter place, Lesh steps up and—out of nowhere—*hammers* the crowd with repeated "Other One" intros, one after the other. They sing verse one. Afterward, the band quickly dissipates into an atonal shriekfest. There is a serious feel here. They are astonishing us. Easier said than done. Lesh crushes without mercy any resistance he picks up on. Garcia delivers a short but revved-up "Tiger" roar. Then things mellow again.

Soon yet another pathway opens up. This one is also firm, unyielding, and determined to break new ground despite several "Uncle John's" teases. Billy shines, as he has all day, using his kit with an emphasis on percussive pops. Not sweet—but powerful, shamanistic callings. Amid the savage beauty an innocent melody arises: the "Mind Left Body" theme. Ah, but Lesh slashes his parts, denying the softness. Garcia gives up on it after only a few rounds but extracts his revenge by going into "Row Jimmy," of all songs. It's played delicately and is well-received by the crowd.

The last three songs, especially the raucous "Sugar Mags," cap off an amazing set of music. If you don't have this one—get it.

MICHAEL M. GETZ

## 5/14/74
### Adams Field House, University of Montana, Missoula, Montana

**Set 1:** Bertha, Me and My Uncle, Loser, Black-Throated Wind, Scarlet Begonias > It Must Have Been the Roses, Jack Straw, Tennessee Jed, Mexicali Blues, Deal, Big River, Brown-Eyed Women, Playing in the Band//
**Set 2:** U.S. Blues, El Paso, Row Jimmy, Weather Report Suite Prelude > Weather Report Suite Part One > Let It Grow > Dark Star > China Doll, Promised Land, Not Fade Away > Goin' Down the Road Feelin' Bad > One More Saturday Night

**1. Source:** AUD, **Quality:** C+, **Length:** 3:20
**2. Source:** FM-SBD (KPFA, GDH 290), **Quality:** A, **Length:** 0:50 ("Weather Report" through "China Doll"), **Genealogy:** MR > DAT
**Highlights:** Scarlet Begonias > It Must Have Been the Roses, Mexicali Blues, Deal, Tennessee Jed, Weather Report Suite > Dark Star > China// Doll, Not Fade Away > Goin' Down the Road > Saturday Night

For much of this show the band's energy level swings back and forth between sleepiness and heartfelt excitement. Things are very laid-back until "Scarlet Begonias," which is impressively tight though not stretched out. The segue into "Roses" is unexpected but very much appreciated by the audience, who drown out the beginning of the song with their applause. Things don't really get smokin' until "Tennessee Jed." By "Deal" Jerry is really belting out the words. Keith is playing hard behind him. "Mexicali Blues" is equally impressive with jumpy piano fills throughout. By this point you're sort of glad you've been patient with the lack of superior sound quality.

This dreamy combination of songs continues to be pretty sleepy until well into the "Dark Star," when Garcia finally gets around to doing his wah-wah pedal pushing, fingerpicking psychedelic meltdown "Tiger" shtick. At that point things finally get satisfactorily transportational. "China Doll" is exquisite. As a whole, this excerpt is worth having but not worth getting excited about.

Jerry finally comes alive during the "Not Fade Away" > "Goin' Down the Road" > "Not Fade Away" sequence—and how! Like I said: this show is hot and cold throughout.

JOHN R. DWORK

---

### 5/17/74

**P.N.E. Coliseum,
Vancouver, British Columbia**

**Set 1:** Promised Land, Deal, The Race Is On, Ramble On Rose, Jack Straw, Dire Wolf, Beat It on Down the Line, Loose Lucy, Big River, It Must Have Been the Roses//, Mexicali Blues, Row Jimmy, Playing in the Band
**Set 2:** U.S. Blues//, Big River, Ship of Fools, Money Money, China Cat Sunflower > I Know You Rider, Greatest Story Ever Told, Sugaree//, Truckin' > Nobody's Fault but Mine > Eyes of //the World > China Doll, Sugar Magnolia

---

**1. Source:** AUD, **Quality:** C+, **Length:** 3:00
**2. Source:** FM-SBD (GDH 049), **Quality:** A, **Length:** 0:20 ("Money Money," "China Cat" > "I Know You Rider"), **Genealogy:** MR > DAT

**Highlights:** Big River, Playing in the Band, China Cat Sunflower > I Know You Rider, Nobody's Fault but Mine

**Comments:** Sonically, my tape of this show is a newly circulating soundboard that has replaced the previously circulating audience tape. A major improvement on the audience tape, this tape has widespread dynamics, full bass, and the mix of Jerry, Bobby, and Keith is quite balanced. Perhaps my only complaint is that it takes until "Jack Straw" in set 1 before the mix balances out and the very high end cymbals kick in. No matter, this new soundboard is a pleasure for the ears of this old fan of 1974.

Three days into the summer tour of 1974, the Grateful Dead served up a balanced, and at times wonderful, musical performance. Indeed, as can be said of most dates from this banner year, it was not a question of whether the band would be good that night—just how good. On this evening the playing is even, occasionally phenomenal, and pleasing overall. Although significantly better nights can be found from this incredible year, this tape is well worth obtaining, if only to hear the "Playing in the Band."

The first set of this show begins with a solid version of one of my favorite show openers, "Promised Land." Always a crowd pleaser, the necessary fifties-like rhythm is welcome and serves to motivate both audience and band members to get in the mood. This particular offering is quite respectable and features a short but energetic solo at the end. Following this, with the exception of a ripping version of "Big River," the remainder of the first set consists of a wide variety of standard fare that, though aptly played, appears unnoteworthy. However, the time the band spends honing their chops on these various songs is well spent as it serves as a warmup exercise for the main event of the first set: "Playing in the Band."

For "Playing in the Band" 1974 was a banner year. Indeed, the song served as a newly maturing vehicle in which the band could explore true space while immersed in a jazz groove that was firmly anchored to Mr. Kreutzmann's four-sided schizophrenia. Brought to life that year by the growing musical versatility of the band and the sonic quality of the Wall of Sound, this song was characterized by richly textured and complex interactions among the band members. No one person truly dominated the improvisation; rather, as is intimated by the song title, a true collective conversation took place. What was truly unique here, when compared to many other songs of the era, was that all of the participants in this discourse, though speaking simultaneously, were completely and joyously understood by everyone involved. The listener and musician simply needed to become pleasurably drenched in the tapestry of swirling notes.

This night's version is truly wonderful. Like so many others of this year, it provides a focal point for the night's energy. At 22:50, the song is nearly the perfect length: long enough to provide breathing room to the musicians so that they may explore, journey, and take risks, yet short enough to prevent the proliferation of incoherent chaos that can divert this song into darkness. Indeed, following a well-orchestrated beginning that features some strong vocal work by Bobby and Donna, the mid-verse improvisation is rhythmic, structured, and a hell of a lot of fun. Nimble finger work by Jerry, combined with some eclectic keyboard jams by Keith, form a mosaic of which Billy, the master drummer, is the foundation. On this day, Billy is the backbone of the journey, providing subtle structure where otherwise there would be none, creating the road on which others can travel. By following his underlying current, the band improvises with incredible consonance, explores numerous landscapes, and delivers a wondrous performance. This song is quite easily the high point of the evening and provides a fitting end to the first set.

The second set, following the masterful work on "Playing in the Band," begins in a mellow mood. The first side of my tape begins sweetly, with a well-played "Ship of Fools," and ends just as sweetly, with "Sugaree." In between, the listener is treated to another signature suite from 1974: "China Cat Sunflower" > "I Know You Rider." This version is well played and a nice preview to such upcoming stellar versions as those from 6/26/74, and 8/5/74. (Technical note: This song is marred by sonic rolling problems from the soundboard that last throughout most of the song.)

The last major segment of the night begins with a nice, albeit short, version of "Truckin'." Here, Bobby appears to forget what he is singing and delegates the entire first verse of the song as a throwaway, prompting the crowd to react with cheers and laughter. After the final verse, rather than launch off into the more commonplace chordal jams that usually stretch the song's length and energy, this rendition suffers an immediate mood change that is characterized by a slowly worked blues/jazz jam, tailor-made for the upcoming "Nobody's Fault but Mine." Hauntingly, Jerry treats the audience to some delicate finger work and provides subtle direction to the others; so that by the time the first notes of "Nobody's Fault but Mine" are played, they are all in sync. Like the "Truckin'" that began this sequence, the subsequent "Eyes of the World" is also made unusually short (11:35) by a fairly harsh mid-song tape splice. Nevertheless, all the important aspects of the song are explored, with intricate and melodic scales forming a competent backbone to this compact rendition, before they decay into a sweetly sung "China Doll." Finally "Sugar Magnolia," though nearly ten minutes in length and slow in tempo, provides a well-received cap to an even, and occasionally spectacular, evening.

DARREN E. MASON

---

## 5/19/74

**Memorial Coliseum, Portland, Oregon**

**Set 1:** //Mississippi Half-Step, Mexicali Blues, Big Railroad Blues, Black-Throated Wind, Scarlet Begonias, Beat It on Down the Line, Tennessee Jed, Loose Lucy, Money Money, China Cat Sunflower > I Know You Rider

**Set 2:** Promised Land > Bertha > Greatest Story Ever Told, Weather Report Suite Prelude > Weather Report Suite Part One > Let It Grow > Wharf Rat, Big River, Peggy-O, Tico Tico, Truckin' > Jam > Not Fade Away > Goin' Down the Road Feelin' Bad, One More Saturday Night

**Encore:** U.S. Blues

**1. Source:** SBD, **Quality:** A, **Length:** 2:45, **Genealogy:** MR > PCM > DAT

**2. Source:** FM-SBD (GDH 001, 080, and 244), **Quality:** A, **Length:** "Black-Throated Wind," "Scarlet Begonias," "Loose Lucy," "Tico Tico" through "One More Saturday Night"

**Highlights:** Mexicali Blues, Big Railroad Blues, Beat It on Down the Line, China Cat Sunflower > I Know You Rider, the entire second set

Here, in one of the earlier Wall of Sound shows, we have all of the lightness of touch, fluidity, and control that characterized the Dead during this time. However, it was combined on this night with a furious energy that seemed to drain them somewhat as the effort of taking the world's most powerful sound system around the United States through that long hot summer took its toll. Kreutzmann's sinuous yet rock steady, almost military, drumming sweeps the band along. A proper appreciation of the music in this show must start with a consideration of his contribution. By 1974 the Dead had substantially adjusted their playing style to accommodate having only one drummer, and this gave them freedom to move in ways they never had before. In extended jams they could turn on a pin with speed and grace while in the middle of the deepest and most extraordinary "Space," a capacity that disappeared almost completely during the comparatively leaden shows of 1976, when Mickey Hart returned and the difficult readjustment to having two drummers took place.

In first sets in 1974 Kreutzmann's contribution meant that arrangements could be relatively sparse and uncluttered. This left plenty of space for lightning fills and delicate touches from the rest of the band, particularly Garcia, which, however, did not detract from the energy of the sound. It is the cowboy and country-tinged songs, which later would often become little more than time fillers, that benefit disproportionately, and this set is no exception. "Mexicali" rips along with a hot solo; "Big Railroad Blues" is wonderfully fluid; "Black-Throated Wind" has Garcia bubbling away behind what may be Barlow's best-ever lyric to great effect; and "Beat It on Down the Line" crackles with an incredible controlled energy. Things slow down for "Tennessee Jed," which nevertheless has a lovely solo, then they almost grind to a halt with "Loose Lucy," suffering in its poor pre-1990s arrangement, and the simply dreadful "Money Money," which should still be mentioned because it is a genuine rarity. Then, to close the set, we slide into one of the spectacular 1974 "China Cat" > "I Know You Riders." The incredibly muscular jam out of "China Cat" has Kreutzmann's rattling drumrolls holding together an awe-inspiring performance from the rest of the band. A classic moment.

Set 2 starts with a driving "Promised Land." Garcia's closing solo is pure raunch and slides into a perfect "Bertha," with Kreutzmann once again hopping on the beat. We then have one of the greatest-ever versions of "Greatest Story," with the guitarists shooting out streams of piercing notes underlaid with true funk underpinnings from the Leshmeister. The "Weather Report Suite"'s low-key intro is perfectly played, building up the tension. "Let It Grow" stays stately; you get the impression of a reined-in beast. Then, during his first solo, Garcia flicks a finger and we go off to a whimsical Spanish interlude with Keith right alongside. The final jam continues, still teasingly whimsical and downbeat though incredibly articulate, and ends mean and growling before Garcia slips into telling the story that is "Wharf Rat" with long pure guitar tones. "Big River" is furious in its energy, the band ripping out of the end of the song to a crazy new height of intensity. "Peggy-O" is merely extremely pretty by comparison. The colossal final jam, nearly forty minutes long, starts with a long and interesting Spanish-style tuning before Truckin', not mentioned in *DeadBase*, but probably needed because of the "technical difficulties" wryly announced by Weir. A count-in from him and they're into a standout but somehow still restrained version, which goes into a rolling, mellow, and mature "Jam." Everything changes very swiftly, though, as the "Mind Left Body Jam" takes hold, living fully up to its name with intensely vibrant space jamming, dizzy with possibilities as it nevertheless manages to stay on the hip-swaying rock 'n' roll path that has been created. Phil thoroughly in the driving seat by now, cuts off an attempt to go into "Goin' Down the Road," thrusting the band back into space and then soloing the full "Not Fade Away" theme. The band just falls in with him through an alarming crescendo of Garcia guitar that single-handedly hints at a "Spanish Jam" and then back at deep space before the band appears to literally drop as one into "Not Fade Away." "Not Fade" and the "Goin' Down the Road" that follows are once again standouts and even the "Saturday Night" and "U.S. Blues," crowd-pleasing farewell tunes, have remarkably different sounding solos from Garcia. These final few tunes also bring to mind the other area of consistent excellence throughout the evening, which is the singing. Both Weir and Garcia are in great voice, no certainty even in those days, and, perhaps most unusually, Donna is having a very good night, on key and rocking more or less throughout. A great show.

JAMES SWIFT

---

### 5/21/74
**Edmunson Pavillion, University of Washington, Seattle, Washington**

**Set 1:** Me and My Uncle, Brown-Eyed Women, Beat It on Down the Line, Deal, Mexicali Blues, It Must Have Been the Roses, The Race Is On, Scarlet Begonias, El Paso, Row Jimmy, Money Money, Ship of Fools, Weather Report Suite Prelude > Weather Report Suite Part One > Let It Grow > China Doll
**Set 2:** Playing in the Band, U.S. Blues, Big River, Stella Blue, Around and Around, Eyes of the World > Wharf Rat > Sugar Magnolia
**Encore:** Johnny B. Goode

---

1. **Source:** AUD, **Quality:** A–, **Length:** 3:00
2. **Source:** FM-SBD (GDH 299), **Quality:** A, **Length:** 1:00 ("Money Money," "Playing in the Band"), **Genealogy:** MR > DAT

**Highlights:** Scarlet Begonias, Row Jimmy, Playing in the Band, Big River, Sugar Magnolia

This show has been legendary for more than two decades for one reason; it contains the longest known version of "Playing in the Band." Now, as many of you self-educated Dead scholars will rush to announce when this fact is brought up in conversation, it's not the best version the Dead ever played. Nevertheless, this long jaunt through the wilds of jazz/rock space is most worthy of careful contemplation. But there's more worth checking out here than just "Playing in the Band"; most of the show is a gem, particularly the first set, which is nearly perfect in every way. This was a night for fans of Bob Weir songs. Every one of his songs shines, with Donna singing nicely and Keith playing many deliciously haunting lines. And Jerry didn't slack off either. "Scarlet Begonias" is especially uptempo, and "Row Jimmy" aches with sincerity.

A low-generation copy of the audience recording of this show is a surprisingly good listen. The highs are crystal clear, although there isn't much low end. Garcia's guitar and Keith's piano come through loud and clear. The only imperfection in the audience recording doesn't come at the hands of the recordist but from the audience itself: during the prelude to "Weather Report Suite" more than one bozo screams out "Dark Star."

The much ballyhooed "Playing in the Band" starts the second set with a triumphant wailing crescendo by Miss Donna Jean before setting off on what quickly becomes a wild ride through a dark and stormy sea of swirling musical chaos. As captain, Garcia quite intentionally steers the ship of the Dead through one wild tsunami after another. This is not pretty music. It is dark, ugly, even scary at times. But that's the beauty of the Dead. Sometimes they invite us to grok and groove on the underbelly, the shadow world, the dark side. As Garcia steers through each storm of notes and the frenetic pace subsides, Billy replies to the threat of impending calm with a rat-tat-tat and Bobby suggests another rhythmic direction, and once again Garcia takes his cue and sets course toward another storm front. This is most amazing! Eventually, after a beautiful climax lead by Phil, the band takes one more long, wild ride through chaos and then sails headlong toward the familiar land of the closing verses. Upon reaching port, Miss Donna Jean lets rip another truly triumphant wail and the band lowers the sails. Wow! Not the best or the most visionary version ever, but stunning in its dark power.

Several songs later, Jerry sounds either tired or too high in "Wharf Rat," during which he flubs the words. "Sugar Magnolia," which starts slow, builds to an enormous, drawn-out climax. All in all, a tremendous show.

JOHN R. DWORK

---

## 5/25/74

### Stadium, University of California, Santa Barbara, California

**Set 1:** U.S. Blues, Mexicali Blues, Deal, Jack Straw, Scarlet Begonias, Beat It on Down the Line, Brown-Eyed Women, Me and My Uncle, Sugaree, El Paso, China Cat Sunflower > I Know You Rider, Around and Around
**Set 2:** Promised Land, Ship of Fools, Big River, Tennessee Jed, Truckin' > Jam > Let It Grow > Wharf Rat, Beer Barrel Polka, Sugar Magnolia > Goin' Down the Road Feelin' Bad > One More Saturday Night
**Encore:** Casey Jones

**1. Source:** SBD, **Quality:** A, **Length:** 2:40, **Genealogy:** MR > DAT
**2. Source:** AUD, **Taper:** Louis Falanga with a Sony TC-110 deck and an ECM-23 mike
**Highlights:** Deal, Jack Straw, Scarlet Begonias, Brown-Eyed Women, Me and My Uncle, El Paso, China Cat > Rider, Truckin' > Jam > Let It Grow > Wharf Rat, Sugar Magnolia, One More Saturday Night

"One more round of applause for the light show" (Bob Weir before the encore.)

Yes, it was quite a light show, and it was quite a day: clear sunny skies, temperature in the seventies, and a light breeze coming off the ocean. I may be only slightly (!) prejudiced about this show because this is the show where I GOT it. This was my second show (first was May 20, 1973, at the same location). It was four days before I lost teenage status, and there wasn't a better way to start an early celebration of my birthday.

Other than in "U.S. Blues" (where it's hard to tell what's going on due to the mix), the Dead are tight, focused, and *very* energized from the start. The first set may lack a lot of jamming tunes, but the band is rockin' out. "Deal," "Jack Straw," "Scarlet Begonias," "Brown-Eyed Women," "Me and My Uncle," "El Paso," and "China Cat Sunflower" > "I Know You Rider" are guaranteed to get you dancing around your living room.

The second set continues where the first left off, and then we get to the meat of the show. "Truckin'" is a great example of what made this song arguably the quintessential leaping off point for the band's interstellar journeys in 1974. You just gotta love it when Phil vibrates every nerve ending in your body during the jam between "Truckin'" and "Let It Grow." Jerry solos exquisitely during "Let It Grow." The band performs a beautiful segue into a great "Wharf Rat." They then give us a near-perfect version of one of the greatest pure rock 'n' roll songs ever written: "Sugar Magnolia." Jerry's background filigrees during Bobby's vocals are simply amazing. "Goin' Down the Road" is a bit messy, but at this point, they have given everything they've got. A little forgiveness is in order. Off they go into a slam-bang "One More Saturday Night" and "Casey Jones," and one more time, the Grateful Dead have turned an audience into an oozing mass of delirium.

LARRY STEIN

---

## 6/8/74

**Day on the Green #1
Oakland Coliseum Stadium,
Oakland, California**

**Set 1:** Promised Land, Brown-Eyed Women, Me and Bobby McGee, Scarlet Begonias, Mexicali Blues, It Must Have Been the Roses, Me and My Uncle, Tennessee Jed, Greatest Story Ever Told, China Cat Sunflower > I Know You Rider, Around and Around
**Set 2:** U.S. Blues, Big River, Ship of Fools, Playing in the Band > Wharf Rat > Playing in the Band, Eyes of the World, Sugar Magnolia
**Encore:** Casey Jones > One More Saturday Night

---

**1. Source:** AUD, **Quality:** A–, **Length:** 2:30
**2. Source:** FM-SBD, **Quality:** A+, **Length:** 0:30 ("Playing" through "Playing"), **Genealogy:** MR > DAT
**3. Source:** AUD, **Quality:** B–, **Length:** 0:10 ("Casey Jones" > "Saturday Night")

**Highlights:** Greatest Story Ever Told, Playing in the Band > Wharf Rat > Playing in the Band

**Comments:** This whole show, except for the encore, is widely available as an excellent audience recording, biased toward the piano. The encore is available as a less excellent, but still decent audience recording. The *Grateful Dead Hour* has blessed us with the "Playing in the Band" sandwich.

This first Day on the Green was a "spontaneous concert" (to quote Mr. Lesh) and a "great afternoon for a ballgame" (to quote Mr. Weir). This is the Dead's first visit to this venue, the home of the Oakland A's, and they have themselves quite the fine time. This is definitely a Keith Godchaux showcase, although his being very heavily favored in the mix may influence this opinion. He drives many of the songs and quite a bit of the jamming, most unusual for 1974. The first set is not heavily jammed out, but Keith's excellent playing makes it memorable. He lights up "Promised Land," "Brown-Eyed Women," and "Greatest Story Ever Told" (check out his duet with Jerry in the jam).

The second set's "Playing in the Band" sandwich is the major event of the show. The jam starts with a strong Phil lead rather than the spaced meandering more common in 1974. Jerry introduces some spacey wah-wah, but Bobby quickly accelerates the jam. After a quiet Keith interlude, Phil and Jerry bring a hard, herky-jerky rhythm to the jam with their twin leads. Then Jerry takes three approaches to the "Tiger" before the band brings it to full roar. Out of the "Tiger," the band passes through some feedback into a series of fast jams driven by Billy and Keith and featuring drone themes from Jerry and Phil. Jerry starts to reintroduce the "Playing" theme. But the band slips smoothly into a passionate "Wharf Rat," riddled with Phil bombs. Jerry and Phil set up a blues jam out of "Wharf Rat" to lead back to the "Playing in the Band" jam and reprise. A rather short and undeveloped (for 1974) "Eyes of the World" follows, but Phil's leads are always a treat. The show closes strongly with a potent "Sugar Magnolia," and an interesting transition from "Casey Jones" to "Saturday Night" in the encore.

HUGH BARROLL

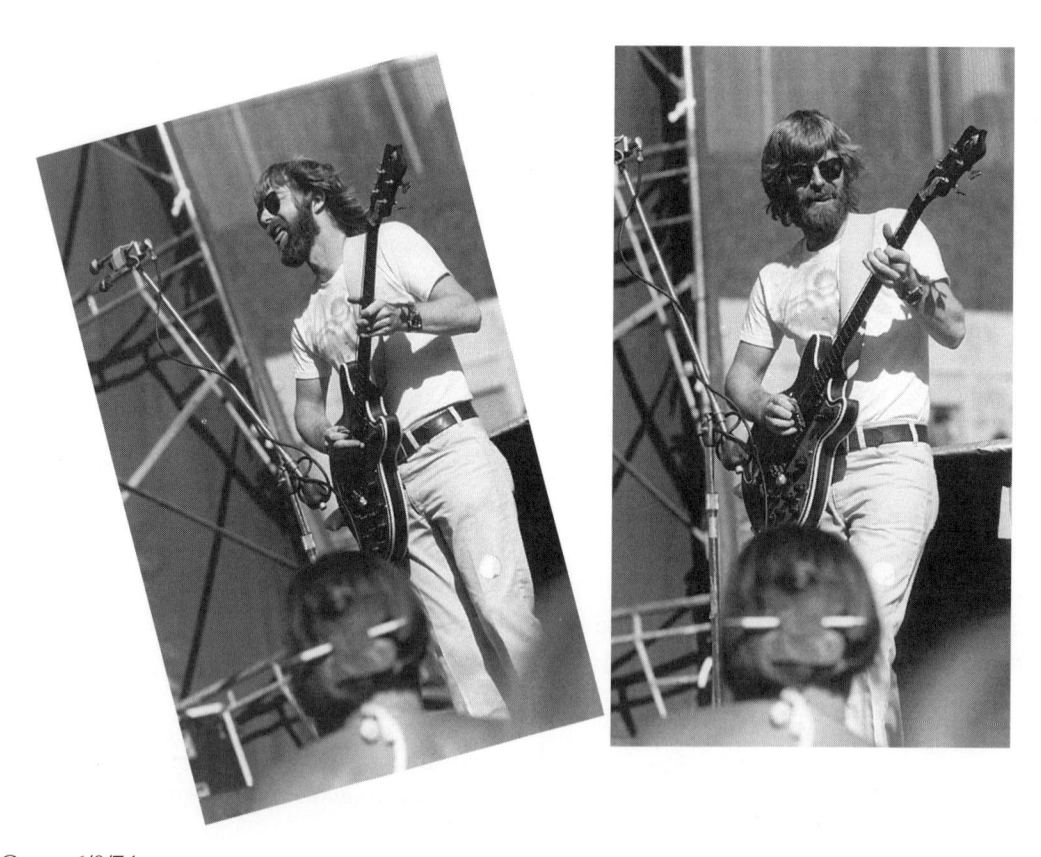

*Day on the Green, 6/8/74*

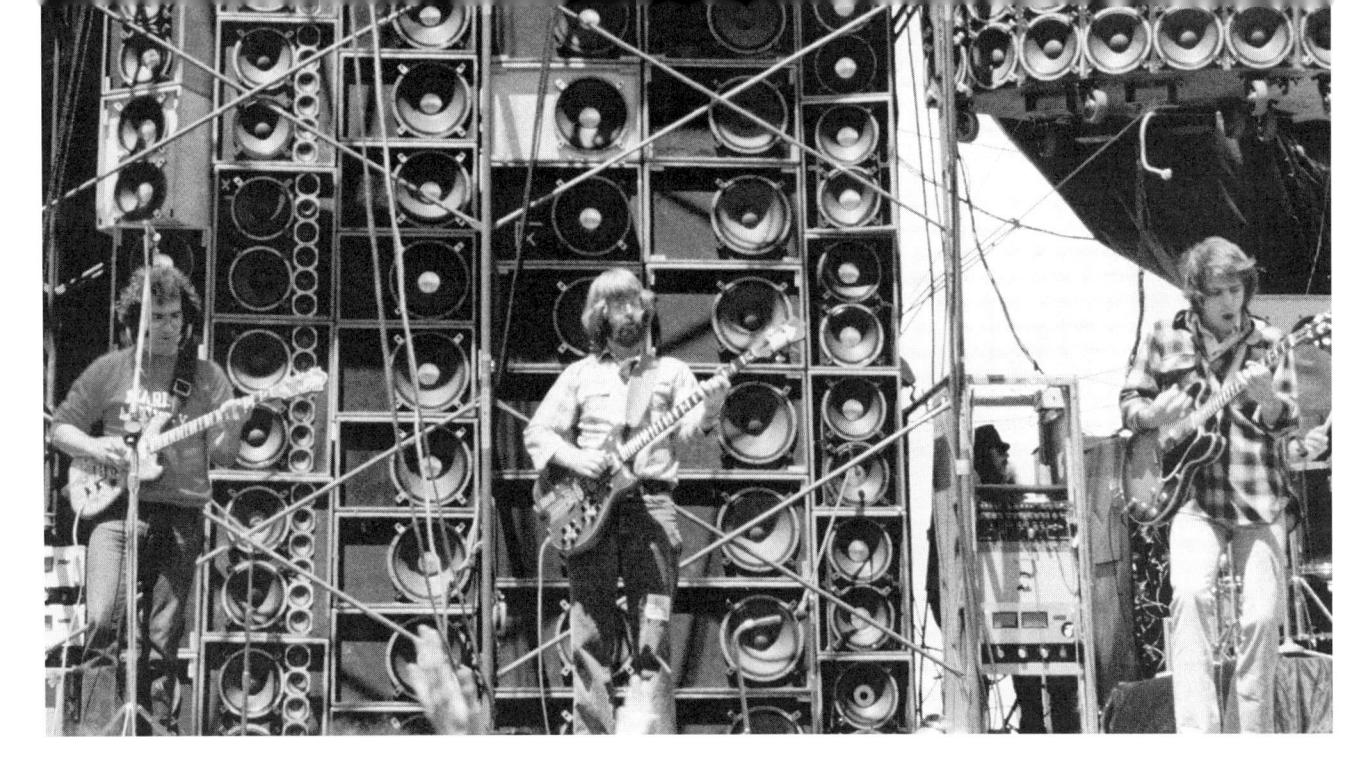

*Iowa State Fairgrounds, 6/16/74* (photo credit: Ray Ellingsen)

## ❦ 6/16/74 ❦

### State Fairgrounds, Des Moines, Iowa

**Set 1:** Bertha, Mexicali Blues, Row Jimmy, Beat It on Down the Line, Scarlet Begonias, Black-Throated Wind, Sugaree, El Paso, It Must Have Been the Roses, Jack Straw, China Cat Sunflower > I Know You Rider, Around and Around
**Set 2:** U.S. Blues, The Race Is On, Eyes of the World > Big River, Ship of Fools, Playing in the Band
**Set 3:** Truckin' > Wharf Rat > Nobody's Fault Jam > Goin' Down the Road Feelin' Bad//
**Encore:** Casey Jones

1. **Source:** SBD, **Quality:** B+/C, **Length:** 3:30
2. **Source:** AUD, **Quality:** B, **Length:** "Jack Straw"
3. **Source:** FM-SBD (DHH 29 and 52), **Quality:** A–, **Length:** "Scarlet Begonias," "Eyes of the World" > "Big River//"

**Highlights:** Eyes of the World, Playing in the Band, Truckin' Jam

**Comments:** This whole show is in wide circulation. "Jack Straw" is a B quality audience recording. The rest of the show is a B+ soundboard, except the start of the first set, which gets a C due to severe mix problems. The radio broadcast excerpts are a notch better sounding. Also, most tapes in circulation are close to random in their song sequencing. There are some painful chops in jams and wildly eccentric mix problems in the first set.

The June tour kicks off with a three-set monster led at many times by Mr. Lesh. The often misordered tapes do not do the show justice. Through it all though, the music glows. Phil is upfront and inventive through much of the first set, adding depth to "Beat It on Down the Line," "Black-Throated Wind," "El Paso," and "It Must Have Been the Roses." "Scarlet Begonias" is nicely jammed, led by Jerry.

The second set revolves around a nineteen-minute "Eyes of the World" and a twenty-eight-minute "Playing in the Band." Phil pushes "Eyes" into several beautiful jams, as he counterpoints Jerry's efforts to introduce the "Stronger Than Dirt" theme. The transition jam into "Big River" is, to my ears, unique. "Playing in the Band" is a classic example of why almost every 1974 version of this song is essential. It features a massive "Tiger" jam that devolves into deep space. The keyboards in this section remind me of "Seastones." Could Ned Lagin be sitting in for the space section? Jerry and Phil lead an intricate dance of themes on the way back to the "Playing" reprise, with Jerry offering a variety of "Playing"-based themes while Phil pushes back to space before finally relenting.

The third set puts away those left standing. "Truckin'" passes through a "Nobody's Fault" jam on the way to the edge of a "Caution" jam. Phil then redirects and slows the jam into material that later appeared in *Blues for Allah*. "Wharf Rat" and "Goin' Down the Road" close the show strongly. Unfortunately, there's a cut in "Goin' Down the Road."

HUGH BARROLL

---

### 6/18/74
#### Freedom Hall, Louisville, Kentucky

**Set 1:** Promised Land//, It Must Have Been the Roses, Black-Throated Wind, Ramble On Rose, Beat It on Down the Line, Loser, Eyes of the World > China Doll, Around and Around
**Set 2:** Loose Lucy, El Paso, Row// Jimmy, Weather Report Suite Prelude > Weather Report Suite Part One > Let It Grow > The Other One > It's a Sin Jam > Stella Blue > Big River, Tennessee Jed, Sugar Magnolia
**Encore:** Morning Dew

---

1. **Source:** SBD, **Quality:** B+/A–, **Length:** 3:00
2. **Source:** AUD, **Quality:** C+, **Length:** 3:00, **Taper:** Marty Steckler

**Highlights:** Beat it on Down the Line, Eyes of the World > China Doll, Weather Report Suite > It's a Sin Jam, Morning Dew

**Comments:** A very good soundboard to the entire show is in broad circulation. The start of the first set is downgraded for mix problems.

This show has long been a favorite from this era, and justly so. The band is in an adventurous mood, breaking out of conventional jamming structures. Phil and Jerry are in top form, inspiring and challenging each other throughout. The entertainment begins playfully, despite mix problems similar to those at Des Moines. We learn from Bobby about the Venusian spy in attendance. Jerry's solo livens up "Beat It on Down the Line" with a quote from "My Old Kentucky Home."

With "Eyes of the World," the action gets serious. Phil kicks off the jam with a buoyant lead, articulate and beautiful, followed by Jerry setting up the counter-theme. In the succeeding sections of the jam, Jerry and Phil each integrate elements from the other's leads into their leads. For 1974, this is a relatively short "Eyes," but it covers a lot of ground and ends up being one of the jazziest, most eloquent versions ever played. "China Doll" is also one of the great versions of that time.

Set 2 covers even more ground. A strong, Phil-led "Weather Report Suite" launches us on an amazing journey. "Let it Grow" leads into a brilliant jam that accelerates, breaks down into space, then accelerates again. Some choppy rhythms lead into a short "Other One." After the first verse, a hot jam develops that dives into deep space. This is a spare and dissonant space, not for the faint of heart. At times the band sounds as if it is trying to simultaneously play in as many different tempos as possible. Intensity builds through Phil's then Jerry's climbing patterns. The band then moves into a very unusual space blues jam, using a blues framework for space themes. This evolves into an instrumental version of "It's a Sin" before returning to more conventional terrain. Finally, the "Morning Dew" encore brings home what a special show this is. Jerry and Phil are in perfect communication, defining the structure for the song, developing its moods both instrumentally and vocally and pushing both jams to the heights. "Morning Dew" is an exceptional encore for a truly exceptional trip.

HUGH BARROLL

---

### 6/20/74
#### Municipal Auditorium, Atlanta, Georgia

**Set 1:** U.S. Blues, Beat It on Down the Line, Brown-Eyed Women, Mexicali Blues, It Must Have Been the Roses, Jack Straw, Scarlet Begonias, Me and My Uncle, To Lay Me Down, El Paso, China Cat Sunflower > I Know You Rider, Around and Around
**Set 2:** Big River, Ship of Fools, Truckin' > Eyes of the World > Slipknot Jam > China Doll, One More Saturday Night

---

1. **Source:** SBD, **Quality:** B+, **Length:** 1:30 (first set)

**2. Source:** AUD, **Quality:** C–, **Length:** 1:15 (second set), **Genealogy:** MC > DAT

**Highlights:** China Cat Sunflower > I Know You Rider, Truckin' Jam, Slipknot Jam

**Comments:** A decent soundboard of the first set of this show and an audience of the second set with washed-out vocals have just entered circulation.

As first sets go, this one is OK but nothing special. Phil is definitely the star. He offers some lively banter from the stage, enthusiastic vocals in "I Know You Rider," and some very fine playing. He lights up "It Must Have Been the Roses" and a sweet "To Lay Me Down." "Scarlet Begonias" is short, with a chop in the jam. "China Cat Sunflower" > "I Know You Rider" is the serious music of the set, and again Phil's in charge. His bombs launch Jerry's first "China Cat" lead. He and Bobby dominate the first section of the jam, then his lead intertwines with Jerry as the jam flows gracefully through to "I Know You Rider."

The second set features some fascinating jamming. A spirited "Truckin'" opens into a Jerry-led fast jam with "Nobody's Fault" hints. The band builds to the classic "Truckin'" crescendo, then moves in the direction of the "Nobody's Fault" jam. Billy and Bobby derail "Nobody's Fault" with a different blues pattern, while Jerry continues to skirt its edges. Bobby, Keith, and Billy then break the rhythm down and head toward space. Jerry launches a spacey solo with echoes of his "Love Theme from *Zabriskie Point*." Billy joins, then Bobby and Keith add gentle accents as Jerry leads a quiet space jam. Keith gives us some "Stella Blue" hints. Jerry moves to wah-wah and Phil enters to give us a lead that is alternately pounding and searching. Bobby and Jerry start to form a "Tiger" around Phil, but it never jells and quickly breaks down into a fast jam kicked off by Keith. Jerry escalates the jam. Phil joins in, then reasserts space themes. The fast jam dissolves as multiple tempos develop, leading into "Eyes of the World." "Eyes of the World" is its typically wonderful self. Phil's first lead is particularly sweet and extended. The high point of this jam, and of the show, comes after the final "Stronger Than Dirt" restatement. Here Keith and Jerry turn the band away from "Eyes," and the rhythm breaks down and reforms into a mid-tempo jam led by Keith, Billy, and Jerry. Jerry then establishes a very trippy "Slipknot" jam. The theme is clearly stated, but the tempo and melody get stretched in variety of strange directions. Finally, the "Slipknot" theme slows for the move into a Phil-led "China Doll."

HUGH BARROLL

---

## 🌀 6/22/74 🌀
### Jai Alai Fonton, Miami, Florida

**Set 1:** Promised Land > Bertha > Greatest Story Ever Told, Deal, Me and Bobby McGee, Scarlet Begonias, Jack Straw, Loose Lucy, Mexicali Blues, Sugaree, The Race Is On, It Must Have Been the Roses, Playing in the Band

**Set 2:** China Cat Sunflower > I Know You Rider, Me and My Uncle, Ship of Fools, El Paso, Eyes of the World > Wharf Rat > Sugar Magnolia

**Encore:** Johnny B. Goode

**1. Source:** SBD, **Quality:** A–, **Length:** 2:40 (complete show except for "Promised Land," //"Bertha," "Sugaree"//, "Ship of Fools"//)

**2. Source:** AUD, **Quality:** B+, **Length:** 0:20 ("Promised Land" > "Bertha," "Sugaree," "Ship of Fools"), **Taper:** Jerry Moore and Les Kippel with a Sony 152 deck and AKG D-200 mikes

**Highlights:** Scarlet Begonias, Eyes of the World

This a consistently good show that never quite soars to the heights of other shows from this era. The playing and song selection is strong throughout. The sense of adventure is missing. "Scarlet Begonias" features a high-energy solo and jam. "Playing in the Band" takes a while to develop, but its closing jam features some strong statements from Phil. Phil also makes "China Cat" > "Rider" a treat, and his lead in "Eyes of the World" is the highlight of the show. The "Eyes" jam ends with a delicate and beautiful space leading into "Wharf Rat."

HUGH BARROLL

# Reviews: June 1974

## 6/23/74
### Jai Alai Fonton, Miami, Florida

**Set 1:** Ramble On Rose, Black-Throated Wind, Mississippi Half-Step, Beat it on Down the Line, Row Jimmy, Jack Straw, Let It Rock, Cumberland Blues, El Paso, To Lay Me Down, Weather // Report Suite Prelude > Weather Report Suite Part One > Let It Grow
**Phil and Ned:** Seastones//
**Set 2:** Jam > Ship of Fools, Big River, Black Peter, Around and Around, Dark Star Jam > Spanish Jam > U.S. Blues, Uncle John's Band > One More Saturday Night
**Encore:** Casey Jones

1. **Source:** AUD, **Quality:** A–, **Length:** 3:10, **Taper:** Jerry Moore and Les Kippel with a Sony 152 deck and AKG D-200 mikes
2. **Source:** SBD, **Quality:** A–, **Length:** 1:00 ("Dark Star" through "Uncle John's")
3. **Source:** FM-SBD (GDH 016, 041, and 112), **Quality:** A–, **Length:** "Let It Rock," "Black Peter" through "U.S. Blues"
**Highlights:** Let It Rock, Jam > Ship of Fools, Dark Star Jam > U.S. Blues

For those who had seen a relatively conventional show the previous night, this show must have been a trip through the looking glass. It is a night of unusual song choices, weirdly placed jams, and the first assault of "Seastones." I doubt anyone was bored. The first set is well played throughout and features unusual song choices from Jerry. "Cumberland Blues" and "To Lay Me Down" are wonderful. "Let It Rock," a one-time occurrence, is spectacular! A well-jammed "Weather Report Suite" sets the stage for the weirdness to come. The debut of "Seastones" must have stunned the audience. It certainly stunned me three days later in Providence. With its harsh tones and unrelenting drones, this version makes a conventional Grateful Dead feedback jam seem very accessible. I love the ways this music bends my mind. I doubt many of those hearing it were prepared for the ride.

The second set brings still more surprises. An elegant, melodic jam leads into "Ship of Fools," with Phil in front and Jerry and Keith providing ornaments. The heart of the set is the hypnotic twenty-five-minute "Dark Star" jam > "Spanish Jam." The "Dark Star" jam features an extensive space centered on a revolving figure set up by Jerry and echoed by Keith. At one point, Jerry suggests a return to "Dark Star," but Billy emphatically moves into the "Spanish Jam." This features concurrent leads from Jerry and Phil that are radically different in tone and structure but still perfectly complementary. Out of the "Spanish Jam," the band kicks off an extended jam to open one of the all-time best versions of "U.S. Blues." "Uncle John's Band" leads a spirited close to the show.

HUGH BARROLL

## 6/26/74
### Providence Civic Center, Providence, Rhode Island

**Set 1:** Big River, Brown-Eyed Women, Beat It on Down the Line, Scarlet Begonias, Black-Throated Wind, Row Jimmy, Mexicali Blues, Deal, The Race Is On, Mississippi Half-Step, El Paso, Weather Report Suite Prelude > Weather Report Suite Part One > Let It Grow > It Must Have Been the Roses
**Phil and Ned:** Seastones
**Set 2:** U.S. Blues, Me and My Uncle, Jam > China Cat Sunflower > I Know You Rider, Beer Barrel Polka Tuning > Truckin' > The Other One Jam > Spanish Jam > Wharf Rat > Sugar Magnolia
**Encore:** Eyes of the World

1. **Source:** AUD, **Quality:** B+, **Length:** 3:00 (entire show), **Taper:** Jerry Moore
2. **Source:** SBD, **Quality:** A, **Length:** 1:30 (second set), **Genealogy:** MR > DAT > C > DAT
3. **Source:** FM-SBD (GDH 203), **Quality:** A+, **Length:** 0:30 ("Jam" > "China Cat Sunflower" > "I Know You Rider"), **Genealogy:** MR > DAT
**Highlights:** Jam > China Cat Sunflower > I Know You Rider, Truckin' > Spanish Jam, Eyes of the World

This night rages throughout. The energy starts high and never lets up. In addition, we are offered some unique and awe-inspiring jams. This was my first concert, and I'm biased—I love it! As the tapes show, so did the audience. The first set is very uptempo with good jams in "Scarlet Begonias" and "Weather Report Suite." Bobby also regales us with the story of the Tomb of the Unknown Speaker. The Wall of Sound suffered many casualties. "Seastones" wails with air raid and drone themes.

The second set takes us to new land. The jams opening "China Cat" are unique and magical. For two minutes, Phil, Jerry, and Keith take us on a gentle exploration of space. The "China Cat" theme ignites the crowd and leads to three more minutes of jamming reminiscent of some "Dark Star" jams. "China Cat" is delivered confidently with great bass lines, followed by a powerful performance of the classic '74 transition jam featuring the "Uncle John's Band" theme. "I Know You Rider" builds to a powerful climax. The band shows a great sense of dynamics in the "Wish I was a headlight" verse, and the audience responds ecstatically. Accordingly, this is one of the versions best loved by Deadheads near and far. "Beer Barrel Polka" was next. Given my last name, I've lived with that song my whole life. At my first concert, the Dead played it for me. This led straight to a kick-ass "Truckin'" followed by a jam that is yet another treasure of this show. Phil launches an amazing one-minute solo assault leading into his patented "Other One" intro. The "Other One" jam cooks, but we never hear the song, as Bobby and Billy lead us into the "Spanish Jam." "The Other One" resurfaces in the jam, but we still do not hear from the Spanish Lady as the jam develops a wide array of themes. I hear hints of a return to the "Spanish Jam," the "Tiger," and "Playing in the Band" before the band spaces into "Wharf Rat." Finally, the "Eyes of the World" encore, featuring strong bass leads, gives us our last treasure. Many tapes lack the complete encore. Track it down. Stand-alone "Eyes of the World"s are rare, and this one is hot.

HUGH BARROLL

## 6/28/74
### Boston Garden, Boston, Massachusetts

**Set 1:** Mississippi Half-Step, It Must Have Been the Roses > Jack Straw, Beat It on Down the Line, Deal, Mexicali Blues, Tennessee Jed, Me and Bobby McGee, Loose Lucy, El Paso, Sugaree, Around and Around
**Phil and Ned:** Seastones//
**Set 2:** Sugar Magnolia > Scarlet Begonias, Big River, To Lay Me Down, Me and My Uncle, Row Jimmy, Weather Report Suite Prelude > Weather Report Suite Part One > Let It Grow > Mind Left Body Jam > Dark Star Jam > U.S. Blues, Promised Land > Goin' Down the Road Feelin' Bad > Sunshine Daydream
**Encore:** Ship of Fools

1. **Source:** AUD, **Quality:** B, **Length:** 3:00, **Genealogy:** MC > RR > DAT, **Taper:** Jerry Moore with a Sony 152 deck and AKG D-200 mikes
2. **Source:** SBD, **Quality:** B+, **Length:** 1:30 (Set 2 and encore)
3. **Source:** FM-SBD (*GDH* 139 and 140), **Quality:** A, **Length:** 1:20, "Sugar Magnolia" > "Scarlet Begonias," "Weather Report Suite" > "Sunshine Daydream," **Genealogy:** MR > DAT
4. **Source:** AUD, **Quality:** D+, **Length:** 0:10 (Seastones)

**Highlights:** Weather Report Suite > Tiger Jam

**Comments:** A decent audience tape of the first set is in limited circulation. A terrible audience recording of "Seastones" recently circulated. My version is twenty minutes but consists of the same ten-minute section repeated twice. The *Grateful Dead Hour* has given us the critical second-set material in crisp soundboard quality. The rest of the second set and the encore circulate in hissy soundboard.

This show features a forty-three-minute brain-melting experience at the core of a stellar second set. The rest of the show pales by contrast. The first set never takes off, but "Seastones" soars with wild pitch variations, laser weapons, fire, and sirens. Regrettably, the audience tape source quality is pathetic. The second set is a giant, tasty "Sugar Magnolia" sandwich. The first ingredient is a glowing "Scarlet Begonias." This may be the finest "Scarlet" of the tour, and it was its first-ever second-set placement. Phil underpins the song and the jam with subtle and unending melodic soloing. Jerry leads the jam through alternating driving and spacy sections. Donna's scat is quite brief. "To Lay Me Down" is dominated by strong Phil lines. Jerry and Donna sound very sweet. The meat of this sandwich is a tremendous "Weather Report Suite" (the best of the June tour). Phil joins Bobby to lead us through an elegant "Prelude." Jerry's slide guitar work complements Bobby's fine delivery of "Part One." "Let It Grow" powerfully launches the jam. The first two instrumental breaks build beautifully. The third break adds space to the mix and kicks off half an hour of amazing jamming. The jam starts fast, building on "Let It Grow" themes. Jerry, Bobby, and Phil slow things down with abstract revolving patterns. Jerry starts a ghostly wah-wah as Phil drops out. Jerry and Bobby lead the band into a spacey then high energy "Mind Left Body Jam" with Billy pushing the pace. Phil's leads push the jam in the direction of "I Know You Rider." Jerry then brings the band into a brief statement of the "Dark Star" theme, followed by a couple of minutes of jamming on "Dark Star." After a breakdown into space, a jazzy ¾ tempo develops and takes us to an extended section of feedback and Billy leads. Full-throated feedback growls show the first hint of what becomes a brief but fiercely spacey "Tiger." The "Tiger" fades into a fast, light jam powered by Billy, which turns toward the blues on its way into a jammed-out opening to "U.S. Blues." Here we re-enter the solar system. The show rocks out nicely with its "Promised Land" > "Goin' Down the Road" > "Sunshine Daydream" close. The "Goin' Down the Road" jam strolls through its "We Bid You Goodnight" theme, stops, and then flawlessly steps up into "Sunshine Daydream" to finish our sandwich as we return to earth. Yummy!

HUGH BARROLL

*Ticket stub for 6/28/74 at the Boston Garden*

### 6/30/74
### Civic Center Arena, Springfield, Massachusetts

**Set 1:** Don't Ease Me In, Black-Throated Wind, Peggy-O, Jack Straw, Loser, Greatest Story Ever Told, Cumberland Blues, Dire Wolf//, Playing in the Band > Uncle John's Band > Playing in the Band
**Phil and Ned:** Seastones
**Set 2:** China Cat Sunflower > I Know You Rider, Big River, Scarlet Begonias, U.S. Blues > Truckin' > Nobody's Fault Jam > Eyes of the World > Stella Blue, Not Fade Away > Goin' Down the Road Feelin' Bad > One More Saturday Night

**Source:** AUD, **Quality:** B+, **Length:** 3:45, **Genealogy:** MC > RR > DAT, **Taper:** Jerry Moore with a Sony 152 deck and AKG D-200 mikes
**Highlights:** Cumberland Blues, Playing in the Band > Uncle John's Band > Playing in the Band, Eyes of the World

This was my second show. It's not as consistently great as Providence, but it's a very good show with some great highs. The first set is excellent. "Jack Straw," "Loser," "Greatest Story Ever Told," and "Cumberland Blues" are sung with passion and played with authority. Jerry's guitar is on fire throughout, and he goes nuts on "Cumberland." After a fumbled but endearing "Dire Wolf," "Playing" > "Uncle John's" > "Playing" sends the set into orbit. The first round of "Playing" goes way out to a point where Jerry and Phil are playing twin leads strongly reminiscent of Miami's "Spanish Jam." "Uncle John's Band" continues the twisted jamming, finding a beautiful space for the "Playing" reprise. "Seastones" is completely different from the earlier versions. Instead of an aural assault, Phil and Ned present us with a variety of tones and textures. This music is more engaging yet still filled with weird surprises. I think Jerry joins toward the end, adding melodic elements just before the tape cuts.

The second set takes a while to develop. "Eyes of the World" is the first effort that takes off. It's more of a full band effort than others from the tour, particularly with more Keith. After the standard closing jam, a wonderfully strange jam develops featuring a highly spacey Jerry lead. "Not Fade Away" > "Goin' Down the Road" rocks out strongly with a driving jam anchored by Keith. The end of this show remains a mystery to me. After the band left the stage, the crowd clapped diligently for several minutes. Then some idiot set off a cherry bomb (this also happened in the first set at Boston). After more clapping, someone (not a band member) came out and said something to the effect of "the Dead were going to come back and play for another forty-five minutes, but you folks blew it." Did we miss a third set? Was this guy just messing with our minds? I still wonder.

HUGH BARROLL

*Ticket stub for 6/30/74 at Civic Center Arena, Springfield*

---

### 6/??/74

### Mickey's Barn, Novato, California

Ghost Riders in the Sky*, Rock and Roll Nurse*, Unvicious Circle*, When You Do What You Do*, Fire on the Mountain†

* John Cippolina, Terry Dolan, Greg Douglas, Nicky Hopkins, Mickey Hart
† Mickey Hart, Phil Lesh, Steve Miller, and unidentified personnel

---

**Source:** SBD, **Quality:** Varies from B to D, **Length:** 0:30

**Highlights:** Unvicious Circle

**Comments:** This tape begins with a rendition of "Ghost Riders in the Sky" that is much muddier and poorly mixed than the definitive version appearing on *Area Code 415*.

These unique tracks from a mid-'74 jam session are an extremely uneven exhibition, hitting all points on the spectrum: breathtakingly luscious, pathetically lethargic, and unremarkably mediocre.

The pair of novelties, "Rock and Roll Nurse" and "When You Do What You Do," are uncharacteristically ordinary. The combination of unoriginal rhythm, rational yet restrained fills, and accurate vocals give these selections a solid yet unremarkable feel. While the execution is good across the board, there simply isn't anything about these tracks that would distinguish them from any other ordinary pop tune from the time. And rarely in Grateful Dead material will you find something that so stubbornly sticks within the parameters of appropriateness.

Conversely, "Unvicious Circle," an instrumental guitar passage, is simply monumental! Cippolina's leads here are considerably more subdued than is characteristic, gentle yet direct. The balance of country-flavored turnarounds with western-influenced slide solos is perfect, complemented further by Hopkins' supportive piano responses. Antithetical to the preceding selections, this track is a prime example of the fulfillment that can be attained when one blends the fundamentals of rock 'n' roll with the expression of pure emotion and intuition.

This rendition of "Fire on the Mountain," with alternate lyrics, is lethargic and ineffective. Though certainly distinct, the lead vocals by Steve Miller are lackluster, as are the unidentified female backup vocals. Musically speaking, Miller's solo is a fine effort, but is far overshadowed by his inability to ascertain an appropriate tone.

BRIAN DYKE

## 7/19/74
### Selland Arena, Fresno, California

**Set 1:** Bertha, Mexicali Blues, Deal, Beat It on Down the Line, Row Jimmy, Me and Bobby McGee, Scarlet Begonias, Tennessee Jed, Playing in the Band
**Phil and Ned:** Seastones
**Set 2:** Brown-Eyed Women, Me and My Uncle, It Must Have Been the Roses, Jack Straw, He's Gone > U.S. Blues, Weather Report Suite Prelude > Weather Report Suite Part One > Let It Grow > Spanish Jam > Eyes of the World > China Doll, Saturday Night

1. **Source:** AUD, **Quality:** B−, **Length:** 3:00
2. **Source:** SBD, **Quality:** A, **Length:** "He's Gone" through "China Doll"
3. **Source:** FM-SBD (GDH 049, 124, and 181), **Quality:** A, **Length:** 0:50 ("Jam" > "U.S. Blues," "Weather Report Suite" through "China Doll"), **Genealogy:** MR > DAT

**Highlights:** Scarlet Begonias, Playing in the Band, He's Gone > U.S. Blues, Weather Report Suite Prelude > Weather Report Suite Part One > Let It Grow > Spanish Jam > Eyes of the World > China Doll

The July leg of the 1974 summer tour starts with another classic show. The soundboard section is essential for any tape library. The audience tape suffers for sound quality and some painful chops, but it also includes amazing music. The first set features a very hot "Bertha," and a high-energy "Scarlet Begonias." "Scarlet" is played quite differently from on the June tour, though it definitely remains a Jerry-ied jam. The set closes with yet another incredible "Playing in the Band." This may be my favorite of the year, despite stiff competition. Phil kicks off the jam and is a very strong force throughout. A painful chop cuts off one early embellishment. Later, Phil leads the band into deep space. The space jam crests as Phil extends one high note while Jerry's lead pushes the band. This breaks down to a quiet space that passes through a blues jam reminiscent of "Smokestack Lightning" before the return to "Playing." "Seastones" returns to the drone/assault pattern of the early versions. Phil is dominant.

The second set kicks into gear where the soundboard starts, with a glorious "He's Gone." It is beautifully sung and jammed. Jerry's solo is stellar. Like the June Boston show, "Weather Report Suite" and its jams are the centerpiece of the show, even though the jams are totally different. The song is performed superbly; Phil gives us perfectly placed fills. Phil and Jerry launch a fast jam that develops into an eerie, angry space dominated by Phil and Keith. Phil then opens the "Spanish Jam" and presents one of his finest leads on tape. Unlike the Miami "Spanish Jam," Phil and Jerry trade leads until Jerry drops the chords from "Eyes of the World" into a Phil lead. Stunning!! "Eyes of the World" is well played and includes more excellent work from Phil, though it can't match the power of the "Spanish Jam." "China Doll" is an appropriately spiritual end to a very intense trip.

HUGH BARROLL

## 7/21/74
### Hollywood Bowl, Los Angeles, California

**Set 1:** Promised Land, Tennessee Jed, Me and My Uncle, Sugaree, Jack Straw, Mississippi Half-Step > It Must Have Been the Roses//, El Paso, Scarlet Begonias//, Around and Around//
**Phil and Ned:** Seastones
**Set 2:** China Cat Sunflower > I Know You Rider, Big River, Row Jimmy, Sugar Magnolia, U.S. Blues//, Playing in the Band > Wharf Rat > Truckin' > Nobody's Fault Jam > Playing in the Band, Ship of Fools

1. **Source:** AUD, **Quality:** A−, **Length:** 1:50 (second set), **Genealogy:** MC > PCM > DAT, **Taper:** Harvey Lubar
2. **Source:** AUD, **Quality:** B, **Length:** 1:10 (first set), **Genealogy:** MC > RR > DAT, **Taper:** Harvey Lubar

**Highlights:** Seastones and second set through Playing in the Band reprise

A terrific "Seastones" and second set make 110 minutes of this show essential. Little in the first set impresses, and the "Scarlet Begonias" jam is cut. It's for completists (like me) only. The first section of "Seastones" has Phil in assault mode, while Ned sets up a dizzying array of accents and counterthemes. One section reminds me of koto music. Toward the end, Phil and Ned unite in the rocket launch/air raid siren mode, capped by a wah-wah blast from Ned. Jerry comes into play in the second set. He fires up "China Cat" with pinpoint lead lines. Bobby joins in to drive the jam, but Jerry is in charge for a high-energy "I Know You Rider." Jerry is all over "Big River" as well. "Row Jimmy" calms things down as Phil finds room to explore in and around Jerry's slide lines. Next comes a "Playing in the Band" sandwich for the ages. Phil and Jerry shine throughout the verses, then blast through the jam. This is a driving and challenging "Playing in the Band" jam. The band throws each other enough curves to twist any mind. Phil and Jerry are out front from the start with varied high-energy themes. The band almost develops the "Tiger" jam twice in and around some dissonant and searching space. Toward the end, a fast jam develops with "Other One" hints. Weir tries to introduce the "Spanish Jam," but the jam breaks down into a monumental "Wharf Rat." After this, "Truckin'" is almost a relief from the intensity, featuring a fine "Nobody's Fault" jam. Phil, Keith, and Jerry are having big fun. Billy then picks up the tempo, and Jerry magically transports us to the depths of the "Playing in the Band" jam. After this journey, the "Playing in the Band" reprise is like coming home.

HUGH BARROLL

### 7/27/74
#### Civic Center, Roanoke, Virginia

**Set 1:** Bertha, Mexicali Blues, Row Jimmy, Jack Straw, Mississippi Half-Step > It Must Have Been the Roses, Me and Bobby McGee, //Tennessee Jed, Playing in the Band//
**Set 2:** China Cat Sunflower > I Know You Rider, Me and My Uncle, Ramble On Rose, Big River, Brokedown Palace, U.S. Blues > Promised// Land, Not Fade Away > Goin' Down the Road Feelin' Bad > Johnny B. Goode

**Source:** AUD, **Quality:** C–, **Length:** 2:30
**Highlights:** China Cat Sunflower > I Know You Rider, Brokedown Palace, jam between U.S. Blues and Promised Land

This is a largely uncirculated show with an uninspiring set list. The show does, however, have its intriguing features. First question: Where's Donna? After "Row Jimmy," I don't hear her at all. This leaves "Playing in the Band" without its customary wails and thins out the backing vocal on "Mississippi Half-Step" and "It Must Have Been the Roses." Second question: Where's Phil? He's subdued to the point of lethargy for the whole first set. This seriously weakens "Playing in the Band," which never develops any strong themes. He resurfaces in the second set and makes "China Cat Sunflower" > "Rider" a treat. He sets up parallel lead lines with Jerry in "China Cat Sunflower," and the transition jam shows their telepathic communication in fine form. "Brokedown Palace" is a gem. It's a rarity in 1974, and Jerry sings his heart out. Keith's Fender provides wonderfully spooky colors. Third question: Where did that jam between "U.S. Blues" and "Promised Land" come from? It's a high-energy blues jam, vaguely reminiscent of a "Truckin'" jam, but really quite unlike other 1974 jams. The "Not Fade Away" jam is more conventional, but still great fun. Last question: Where are "Seastones" and the encore? We need them.

HUGH BARROLL

### 7/29/74
#### Capital Center, Landover, Maryland

**Set 1:** Promised Land, Sugaree, Black-Throated Wind, It Must Have Been the Roses, Cumberland Blues, Scarlet Begonias, Jack Straw, Deal, El Paso, To Lay Me Down, Weather Report Suite Prelude > Weather Report Suite Part One > Let It Grow
**Set 2:** He's Gone > Truckin' > Nobody's Fault but Mine > The Other One > Spanish Jam > Wharf Rat, Around and Around, Peggy-O, U.S. Blues, Sugar Magnolia
**Encore:** Casey Jones

**Source:** AUD, **Quality:** A–, **Length:** 3:00, **Genealogy:** MC > RR > PCM > DAT, **Taper:** Jerry Moore with a Sony 152 deck and AKG D-200 mikes.
**Highlights:** Weather Report Suite through Wharf Rat

Landover is yet another fine summer show. Phil is strong throughout the first set. His soloing around the vocals in "Black-Throated Wind" is particularly delightful. "Cumberland" is another high point of the set. "Weather Report Suite" is a long (almost twenty minutes) and wild journey. The Prelude and Part One are both quite beautiful. "Let It Grow" builds subtly into a powerhouse. The first instrumental break is quite spacey, almost relaxed. The second break opens gently, but rises with a steady swell as Keith and Jerry push the tempo. The final jam starts with a very tight, full band fast jam driven by Jerry and Bobby. This unwinds into a Jerry-led jam to close out the suite. "He's Gone" gives the second set a strong kickoff. It features a closing vocal free-for-all anchored by Phil. After a brief bluesy jam, Bobby, Keith, and Billy launch "Truckin'." The jams into and out of "Nobody's Fault but Mine" show the band intricately interlinking its songs. Jerry's first solo out of "Truckin'" states the "Nobody's Fault" theme, moves back into a more standard "Truckin'" lead, then is followed by more "Nobody's Fault" hints. A descending figure then leads to the vocals. After the song, Jerry's lead rips apart the song, then rebuilds it. Bobby then moves the jam toward "The Other One," and the band follows. Jerry's lead then mixes "Nobody's Fault" and "Other One" themes, shifting back and forth almost bar by bar. Once "The Other One" is launched, it moves quickly into the first verse, much like 6/18/74. Jerry's "Other One" lead after the vocal breaks down into "Space," followed by an extended Jerry and Billy duet, with Jerry developing dissonant wah-wah patterns and Billy working variations on "Other One" patterns. Bobby and Keith rejoin amid "Tiger" hints. Phil is nearly absent. Jerry pushes the "Tiger," then Bobby joins, followed by Billy, as the ascending pattern builds. Jerry moves out of the "Tiger" into a fast wah-wah jam. The band restates the "Other One" theme, then moves directly into the "Spanish Jam." Phil finally steps up in the mix as a powerful jam develops capped by Jerry's piercing slide. The "Spanish Jam" dissolves into hints of "The Other One" and "Mind Left Body Jam" before "Wharf Rat" appears. "Wharf Rat," with some beautiful Phil parts, is the high point of the set-closing songs.

HUGH BARROLL

*Ticket stub for 7/29/74 at the Capital Centre, Washington, D.C.*

## 7/31/74

### Dillon Stadium, Hartford, Connecticut

**Set 1:** Scarlet Begonias, Me and My Uncle, Brown-Eyed Women, Beat It on Down the Line, Mississippi Half-Step > It Must Have Been the Roses, Mexicali Blues, Row// Jimmy, Jack Straw, China Cat Sunflower > I Know You Rider, Around and Around
**Set 2:** Bertha, Eyes of the World > China Doll, //Promised Land, Weather Report Suite Prelude > Weather Report Suite Part One > Let It Grow
**Phil and Ned:** Seastones
**Set 3:** El Paso, Ramble On Rose, Greatest Story Ever Told, To Lay Me Down, Truckin' > Mind Left Body Jam > Spanish Jam > Wharf Rat, U.S. Blues, //One More Saturday Night
**Encore:** Uncle John's Band

1. **Source:** SBD, **Quality:** A–, **Length:** 1:60 ("Scarlet" through "Big River" and "Truckin'" through "One More Saturday Night")

2. **Source:** AUD, **Quality:** B, **Length:** 3:30, **Genealogy:** MR > RR > RR > PCM > DAT

**Highlights:** Scarlet Begonias, Eyes of the World, Weather Report Suite, To Lay Me Down, Truckin' > Wharf Rat

**Comments:** The AUD source tape features noticeable wind noise.

This was my third show. It did not impress me the way June's Providence and Springfield shows did. Nevertheless, the tape does reveal a spectacular show. The first set is of soundboard origin. "Scarlet Begonias," in a rare opening position, becomes a showcase for Phil, who is out front throughout the verses and then kicks off and directs the jam. Phil continues to shine throughout the set, particularly in "Row Jimmy" and "Jack Straw." Closing the set, "China Cat" starts off delicately, with Jerry carefully stretching out the lines in his first lead. Bobby and Phil then drive the fast jam. When Jerry moves out, he suggests "I Know You Rider," but pulls the jam back to the "Feelin' Groovy" theme. A strong Phil lead brings the band back to a well-sung "I Know You Rider."

A low-key "Bertha" kicks off the second set. On the soundboard tape currently in circulation, this is followed by the end of the "Eyes of the World" jam—a wonderful fragment. The audience section includes the entire amazing "Eyes." Phil is dominant and inventive from the start, underpinning the verses and intertwining with Jerry's leads. In the jam, Phil takes the first lead with extensive variations on the "Eyes" theme, stretching melodic ideas in all directions. After anchoring this section, Jerry kicks off a brief duet with Phil to introduce the "Stronger Than Dirt" theme. Phil moves back out front, integrating the new theme as he trades off leads with Jerry. Jerry then moves the "Stronger Than Dirt" theme into "Space" before pulling back. To close the jam, Jerry introduces a descending figure punctuated by Phil bombs to introduce "China Doll." The set is capped by one of my very favorite "Weather Report Suites": not the major jamming vehicle of Boston or Fresno but a confident and strong delivery nonetheless. The song's power builds beautifully through the verses. Tight Jerry runs and Phil bombs build the tension as "Let it Grow" develops. Jerry echoes the slow building power of the verses with a relaxed opening to the first jam that gradually intensifies through waves of Jerry's lead lines. A fast jam develops, framed by Bobby, featuring intertwining Jerry and Phil leads. After the last verse, the fast jam returns then promptly slows. Jerry spaces out, while Phil inserts quick lead lines. The jam accelerates in the direction of "Caution" and builds to a nice climax.

"Seastones" is marred by exceptionally rude audience noises. It is an interesting one, with enormous thematic variations, and lots of Phil leads. I wish it sounded better.

The band then pulls out an excellent third set. Jerry's enthusiastic, wailing guitar lines highlight "Ramble On Rose." His croon and his singing guitar bring us a beautiful "To Lay Me Down." From here the band lauches into a spirited "Truckin'" > "Jam" with tasty hints at "Nobody's Fault but Mine." A hint of "The Other One" leads almost to "Wharf Rat," but Jerry redirects to a nervous pulse jam. This moves into a melodic jam, where my tape rejoins the soundboard. The jam then moves into extended versions of the "Mind Left Body Jam" and the "Spanish Jam." After this, the "Mind Left Body Jam" almost resurfaces, but the band slows for a powerful "Wharf Rat." After all this, it is not surprising that the "Uncle John's Band" encore sounds tired. By then the audience was pretty tired as well.

HUGH BARROLL

---

### 8/4/74
### Civic Convention Hall Auditorium, Philadelphia, Pennsylvania

**Set 1:** Bertha, Mexicali Blues, Scarlet Begonias, Black-Throated Wind, Beat it on Down the Line, Peggy-O, Jack Straw, Loser, El Paso, Row Jimmy, Playing in the Band//
**Set 2:** Ship of Fools, Big River, Loose Lucy, Me and My Uncle, It Must Have Been the Roses, Weather Report Suite Prelude > Weather Report Suite Part One > Let It Grow > Wharf Rat > U.S. Blues
**Encore:** Casey Jones

---

**Source:** AUD, **Quality:** B+, **Length:** 3:00, **Taper:** Jerry Moore with a Sony 152 deck and AKG D-200 mikes

**Highlights:** Playing in the Band, Weather Report Suite > Wharf Rat

The first set starts strong with a "Scarlet" jam that, while brief, is well developed. Jerry pushes hard on "Black-Throated Wind" and "Jack Straw" with intricate leads throughout. "Loser" is delivered strongly. And "Playing in the Band" gives us yet another monster jam. It starts slow and relaxed but doesn't stay that way. Billy pushes a fast framework that Jerry uses for an amazing variety of themes. The return of the "Playing in the Band" theme provides another jam structure as Jerry pushes the theme then backs away. Phil and Bobby also

*Program for show at Philadelphia Civic Convention Hall Auditorium, 8/4/74 and 8/5/74*

sparkle, but this is Jerry's showpiece. The tape cuts just before the reprise, but at least we get the jam. We have no tape of "Seastones," so the next exploration of the cosmos comes from "Weather Report Suite." As at Boston and Fresno this year, when "Weather Report Suite" is the core of the second set, a memorable jam results. This jam gives us Jerry and Phil in perfect communication, developing leads and melodic structures until Bobby introduces a descending figure that leads into the "Tiger." This roars massively until Phil leads the band in the direction of the "Spanish Jam." Jerry smashes the "Spanish" hints and forces the band into "Wharf Rat." He compensates for the lost jam with a beautiful closing jam featuring "Other One" hints.

HUGH BARROLL

---

### 8/5/74
#### Civic Convention Hall Auditorium, Philadelphia, Pennsylvania

**Set 1:** Promised Land, Brown-Eyed Women, Beat It on Down the Line, Dire Wolf, Me and Bobby McGee, Tennessee Jed, Jack Straw, Deal, El Paso, China Cat Sunflower > I Know You Rider, Around and Around
**Phil and Ned:** Seastones//
**Set 2:** Mississippi Half-Step > It Must Have Been the Roses, Big River, Ramble On Rose, Me and My Uncle, Scarlet Begonias, He's Gone > Truckin' > The Other One Jam > Stella Blue, One More Saturday Night
**Encore:** U.S. Blues

---

**1. Source:** SBD, **Quality:** A–, **Length:** 3:00
**2. Source:** AUD, **Quality:** B–, **Length:** 0:20 ("Stella Blue" through "U.S. Blues"), **Taper:** Jerry Moore with a Sony 152 deck and AKG D-200 mikes
**Highlights:** Brown-Eyed Women, Jack Straw, Truckin' Jam
**Comments:** The core of the jam after "Truckin'" circulates as 6/22/74 and as part of 6/23/74. This, however, is its real home.

August 5 is an unusual show for 1974 because the focus is much more on songs than on jamming (at least until the close). Don't fret, it's still well worth getting. The tape quality is good, and many of the songs are hot. The first set features standout versions of "Brown-Eyed Women," "Me and Bobby McGee," "Tennessee Jed," and "Jack Straw." The playing on "Big River" and the singing on "He's Gone" light up the second set. For hardcore Phil fans it's also nice to have another good soundboard of "Seastones" (at least eleven minutes of it), this one being of particular note due to a second section quite different from the standard drones. The jam out of "Truckin'" reminds us that this is 1974: it takes time to grow. For a while the band sounds stuck in a lumpy rhythm that doesn't develop. This eventually dissolves, and the fun starts as Phil leads the band into "The Other One" jam. This devolves into a yearning space, punctuated by Phil's harmonics. Then comes an angry full band jam and a brief "Tiger." From the "Tiger," a powerful and strange jam develops and passes through some wild mutations until it abruptly shifts into "Stella Blue."

HUGH BARROLL

## 8/6/74
### Roosevelt Stadium, Jersey City, New Jersey

**Set 1:** Bertha, Mexicali Blues, Don't Ease Me In, Beat It on Down the Line, Sugaree, Jack Straw, Eyes of the World, Promised Land, Deal, Playing in the Band > Scarlet// Begonias > Playing in the Band
**Phil and Ned:** Seastones
**Set 2:** Uncle John's Band, El Paso, Black Peter, Loose Lucy, Big River, Ship of Fools, Me and My Uncle, Row Jimmy, Sugar Magnolia > He's Gone > Truc//kin' > Spanish Jam > The Other One > Goin' Down the Road Feelin' Bad > Sunshine Daydream
**Encore:** U.S. Blues

**1. Source:** SBD, **Quality:** A–, **Length:** 2:40 ("Bertha" through "Truckin'"), **Genealogy:** MR > RR > RR > PCM > DAT
**2. Source:** AUD, **Quality:** A–, **Length:** 0:45 ("Truckin'" through "U.S. Blues"), **Taper:** Barry Glassberg
**3. Source:** FM-SBD (GDH 319), **Quality:** A, **Length:** Eyes of the World
**Highlights:** Eyes of the World, Playing in the Band > Scarlet Begonias > Playing in the Band, Uncle John's Band, Sugar Magnolia through Sunshine Daydream

This night would be a great choice for Dick's Picks. Once the band gets into sync halfway through the first set, the rest of the show features several stunning jams. The Dead finished up their last tour with the Wall of Sound in style. After the "Bertha" start, Bobby assures the audience it won't rain (as it did on the original concert date, August 2). He then remarks, "That wasn't the only news to come out today." This is almost certainly an allusion to the release of the Watergate "smoking gun" tape, which dominated the day's news. Tapers are everywhere—heh, heh. As to the music, a strong Phil-led "Sugaree" is an early highlight. A stand-alone "Eyes of the World" then launches the set into high orbit. Phil kicks off the main "Eyes" jam with a high-energy throbbing lead. He takes the band through subtle and powerful variations on the "Eyes" theme. After Jerry and Phil do their "Eyes"–"Stronger Than Dirt" tradeoffs, an unusual high-energy jam takes us to an even higher level. Jerry extends the jam into a variety of twisted dimensions. Amazingly, the jam stops almost abruptly as the Dead react to numerous audience members climbing onto the stage! Not satisfied with one major first-set jam, the band, having gained their composure, gives an incredible "Playing" > "Scarlet" > "Playing," featuring a "Playing" jam for the ages. Phil dominates the song, then kicks off the jam. Throughout the jam he develops with Jerry a series of wonderful musical conversations, with imaginative support from the rest of the band. Toward the jam's end, a "Tiger" almost develops, but Billy and Keith develop a jazzy theme that Jerry pushes toward the blues. Jerry then turns on a dime into a "Scarlet" blues jam, then launches into "Scarlet." (The soundboard recording, unfortunately, has a major splice smack in the middle of the lyrics.) The "Scarlet" jam builds in intensity until it transmutes back into a spacey "Playing" jam. This brings us to the "Playing" reprise, and the end of a monumental first set. If this concert ever does get released, I hope they include the "Seastones." This is one of the few we have in high-quality soundboard, and it is a good one. It is nicely varied, like the Hartford "Seastones." In addition, Phil takes a stunning solo roughly eight minutes in. Ned closes the jam with a spiraling electric pattern, his version of a "Tiger Jam."

In wonderful contrast, we get an stellar "Uncle John's Band" to open the second set. The harmonies are a bit ragged, but the playing is angelic. Next comes an unusual sequence where three of Bobby's cowboy songs are interspersed among three Jerry ballads and a bouncy "Loose Lucy." I might cut this section from my hypothetical Dick's Picks. The rest of the show is a keeper. It's a "Sugar Magnolia" sandwich every bit as tasty as Boston's. Bobby gives us a high-energy "Sugar Mags" followed with a pretty "He's Gone" that ends with an extended four-part vocal jam. A brief instrumental jam brings us to a sloppy but spirited "Truckin'." This is, regrettably, the end of the soundboard. A short "Truckin'" jam leads to "Other One" hints, but breaks down into space set up by Jerry, Billy, and Bobby. Jerry and Bobby go into a duet, joined by subtle Phil harmonics. Phil then takes charge with some of his finest playing on tape. He kicks off his lead with piercing throbs and bombs then builds an extended free-form solo. Billy and Bobby kick off the "Spanish Jam," but this version belongs to Phil. His lead voice dominates the jam beautifully. Jerry eventually breaks the "Spanish Jam" up and reintroduces "Other One" themes. After a Jerry-led fast jam, one verse of "The Other One" appears, then breaks down into space and a wailing "Tiger." This brings us to a mellow "Goin' Down the Road Feelin' Bad" and a happy "Sunshine Daydream" to rock us out.

HUGH BARROLL

## 9/9/74
### Alexandra Palace, London, England

Bertha, Promised Land, It Must Have Been the Roses, Jack Straw, Scarlet Begonias, Mexicali Blues, Row Jimmy, Playing in the Band, Deal, El Paso, Ship of Fools, Tennessee Jed, Truckin' > Wharf Rat > Uncle John's Band
**Encore:** U.S. Blues, One More Saturday Night

**1. Source:** SBD, **Quality:** A, **Length:** 2:30
**2. Source:** CD (*Dick's Picks VII*), **Quality:** A+, **Genealogy:** MR > DR > CD
**Highlights:** Playing in the Band, Truckin' > Wharf Rat > Uncle John's Band, U.S. Blues, One More Saturday night

Before the legendary October stand at Winterland Arena that signaled the band's hiatus as active performers, the Grateful Dead concluded 1974 with a brief tour of England, West Germany, and France. This show, the first of seven, served as the warmup gig for some of the band's finest performances of the year. Obviously pacing themselves, the Dead start off with a loose version of "Bertha," not too fast, but enough to get the mood a little bouncy. The band continues solidly through "Jack Straw" before beginning to unwind with "Scarlet Begonias." Still unmatured, this version stretches out into a short jam that aimlessly wanders around the song's frame, but ultimately fails to gets off the ground before being called to a halt by Garcia. The following "Mexicali Blues" is average, and "Row Jimmy" falls flat. The show's first highlight comes during the midset "Playing in the Band." From the opening notes, it is apparent that Lesh has taken the lead, dancing in circles around the rest of the band throughout the verse. As the final verse unravels, the Dead fall into an instant meltdown à la 12/2/73. After a few moments of methodical exploratory jamming from Garcia and Lesh, the launch begins. At the onset the band is fresh and bold, but as Garcia begins to stray, the jam begins to fall apart. Instantly, however, Godchaux comes to the rescue, bringing the jam back together by coaxing deep bassy tones out of his Rocket 88. However, when Garcia again attempts to take over, the result is several minutes of very uneven play that fluctuate between frantic and chaotic. Bowing for the second time, Godchaux again assumes the spotlight, this time in a higher register, and the synergy between Garcia and Godchaux begins to intertwine. This, of course, leads gracefully into deep space mode, with Garcia playing a beautiful melody of short jazzy lines, aided by haunting Fender Rhodes tones from Keith. Although Kreutzmann and Lesh make a valiant attempt to expedite the pace, they are overpowered by the undistractable duet of Garcia and Godchaux, who have by this time veered far enough into space that the rest of the band is left fading into silence. Slowly, the duo begins to ascend, leading the band back into a subdued execution of the song's reprise. Still riding the momentum of the preceding selection, Garcia and Godchaux lead the band through an otherwise nondescript rendition of "Deal," highlighted by Godchaux's energized piano riffing. Though the following "El Paso" is barely average, "Ship of Fools" is picture-perfect. Minutely hampered by sound problems, Garcia's solo is blissfully sweet, his perfectly intonated bends brushing gently against Godchaux's rich piano fills. Unfortunately, the band is unable to maintain the momentum, as "Tennessee Jed" falls embarrassingly flat on its face, musically lacking and vocally sloppy. Ever resilient, the Dead quickly shift into overdrive with a fine version of "Truckin'" > "Wharf Rat" > "Uncle John's Band." Although the verse section is executed rather lazily, the band bursts energetically on the outro. Backed by solid piano rhythms from Godchaux, Garcia showcases his hottest licks of the evening before being joined by Lesh, who asserts his position confidently as he and Garcia lead the band through a jam that hints at both

"Nobody's Fault but Mine" and "The Other One." Rapidly veering off into the direction of "The Other One," a pseudo-funk jam between Garcia, Lesh, and Kreutzmann emerges that brings the evening's energy to a frenzied peak. After a few hilariously unrealistic attempts at segueing directly into "Wharf Rat," Garcia enlists the assistance of Godchaux in easing the tension of the jam to ground level. Almost immediately, the jam is tranquilized, and an abrupt transition into "Wharf Rat" follows. The band sails effortlessly through this version, highlighted once again by the synchronicity between Garcia and Godchaux. Stumbling a tad on the song's conclusion, Lesh gives a quick "Thanks, folks" to the audience before proceeding directly into "Uncle John's Band," most notable for a partially solo verse sung by Lesh. Concluding with a fatigued "Johnny B. Goode," the band reasserts themselves by dealing out a pair of rockin' encores, "U.S. Blues" and "One More Saturday Night," sending this European performance off with a bang.

BRIAN DYKE

## 9/10/74

### Alexandra Palace, London, England

**Set 1:** //Peggy-O, Black-Throated Wind, China Cat Sunflower > I Know You Rider, Weather Report Suite Prelude > Weather Report Suite Part One > Let It Grow > Stella Blue
**Set 2:** Me and My Uncle, Dire Wolf, Not Fade Away, Big River, Dark Star > Morning Dew, Sugar Magnolia
**Encore:** U.S. Blues

1. **Source:** AUD, **Quality:** C, **Length:** 2:15
2. **Source:** CD-SBD (*Dick's Picks VII*), **Quality:** A+, **Genealogy:** MR > DR > CD

**Highlights:** Black-Throated Wind, China Cat > I Know You Rider, Weather Report Suite, Not Fade Away, Dark Star > Morning Dew

Although effortless is perhaps the most accurate description of the rare occasions when the band reaches ultimate Grateful Deadness, the words that follow often seem unnecessary. With just one warm-up gig under their belt, the Dead's second Europe '74 performance reached epic proportions that make it easily one of the year's finest. The tape breaks in on a beautifully gentle "Fennario." Quickly it becomes evident that the band is in sync, and the first emotional highlight follows with one of the finest renditions of "Black-Throated Wind" to date, so compelling that to remain seated throughout seems impossible. The momentum continues with "China Cat Sunflower" > "I Know You Rider," at which time the intuitive potential of the evening is achieved. Following a picture-perfect reading of verses one and two, Garcia assumes control with a short but exploratory solo that narrows the focus for the jam that follows. Taking the characterization to heart, Garcia truly begins to function as the headlight on a northbound train, authoritatively charging while the band steadily supplies the groove behind him. Although the first instrumental climax is reached abruptly, the band chooses to slowly ride the wave of the groove in a calculated and methodical transition, rather than the traditional immediate segue into "I Know You Rider." Again the momentum begins to rise, somehow falling into a perfectly timed "Feelin' Groovy Jam." With each note, the Dead become more locked into each other, finally bursting and leading into "I Know You Rider." Having peaked, a subdued reading follows, the band cautious not to overexert themselves so early in the performance. Not missing a beat, the Dead execute a breathtakingly luscious set-closing combination of "Weather Report Suite" > "Stella Blue." From June 1974 to its retirement on October 17, 1974, "Weather Report" was perfected, often reaching tear-eliciting proportions. This reading is no exception, combining all of the necessary elements; illustrious fingerpicking from Garcia, (at least) semiaccurate vocal harmonies from Weir and Donna Jean, and pulsating rhythms from Kreutzmann and Lesh. In the midst of confusion, Garcia gets a bit scrambled on the first solo, choosing a more direct and focused approach on the pre-coda jam. At times his blazing leads sound like the "Tiger," at half speed and a few octaves lower. The final outro, however, takes a deep swerve as the three frontmen immediately veer off in different directions, taking only a few moments to turn the music into complete and utter chaos. Of course this sets the path for a brief jazz jam that unbelievably hints at "King Bee" (yes, that's right folks), if only for a split second, before rapidly fading into a gorgeous "Stella Blue." Not remotely showing signs of fatigue, this version erupts on the bridge in another of the evening's many emotional climaxes.

Still brimming with confidence from the first set, the Dead return to the stage with a hilariously enthused "Me and My Uncle," featuring some of the finest Weir voice cracks on record. Obviously pacing themselves, they playfully segue through a standard song selection, most notable of which is a solo "Not Fade Away." Rather than be predestined by a segue, the band wisely chooses to remain stationary, laying down a simple but effective groove beneath a unique head-cuttin' duel between Garcia and Weir. Although played enthusiastically and at times spectacularly, the second-set prelude seems minute in comparison to the monstrous "Dark Star" > "Morning Dew" that highlights the performance, illustrating one of the most important characteristics of Grateful Dead composition: intuition. Unwinding very gently à la 11/11/73, the band circles around the song's main frame for a few minutes before each member begins to fade into space. Instinctually, it takes but four minutes before the band hits its first climax, a minute but distinct amount of franticism displayed by each member. Bewildered and unfocused, the EKGs on the jam begin to deviate, as the band swiftly begins a series of wide open throttle/slam on the brakes phrases. The gracefulness between each brief transition is breathtaking as it becomes evident that the sensory intuition level of the band is approaching its maximum facility level. Indeed, as each instrumentalist begins to stray into space, he is met at the destination by his colleagues. At nine minutes, Lesh assumes the wheel, and the jam quickly accelerates to jazz mode, complemented by Godchaux's finest Herbie Hancock "In a Silent Way" licks to date. As the synergy rises, the band falls into what is arguably the finest Grateful Dead sans Garcia jam of all time, eventually melting into a delightfully beautiful silence that meanders naively before fading into a brief pseudo-blues jam. Once again segueing gracefully, the band returns to the theme and verse at twenty minutes. After a second meltdown, the "Star" quickly ascends from the ashes into a paranoia jam, a trifle funkier than usual, and certainly bordering on orgasmic. After several attempts to overthrow the playful interplay of feedback screams from Garcia and psycho surf screeching from Weir, Godchaux and Lesh authoritatively bring the jam to an instantaneous halt. As Godchaux spirals in calculated precision beneath Lesh's pointed bomb dropping, the jam slowly melts, setting the path for the transition into "Morning Dew." Still riding the momentum of the "Star," the band struggles to taper the energy down, as the emotion continues to ooze from each note. After several consecutive, and quite probably inadvertent, ascensions into the realm of musical bliss, the Dead ascertain the spiritual conclusion of the voyage, timed perfectly for those needing to wipe the tears from their eyes. Exhausted and certainly anti-climactic, the conclusion of "Sugar Magnolia" and encore of "U.S. Blues" serve as little more than extra landing gear from the journey, always welcomed by those of us who need it.

BRIAN DYKE

---

## 9/11/74
### Alexandra Palace, London, England

**Set 1:** Scarlet Begonias, Mexicali Blues, Brown-Eyed Women, Beat It on Down the Line, Sugaree, Jack Straw, Row Jimmy, Me and Bobby McGee, Tennessee Jed, Big River, It Must Have Been the Roses, Playing in the Band
**Set 2:** Seastones* > Sp//ace* > Jam* > Space* > Eyes of the World* > Stronger Than Dirt* > Space* > Wharf Rat*
**Set 3:** Around and Around, Ship of Fools, Goin' Down the Road Feelin' Bad > Sugar Magnolia
**Encore:** U.S. Blues

* with Ned Lagin on keyboards.

**1. Source:** AUD, **Quality:** B, **Length:** 3:50
**2. Source:** SBD, **Quality:** A–, **Length:** 1:15 ("Playing," "Eyes" > "Space"//, "Jam" > "Wharf Rat," "Around and Around"), **Genealogy:** MR > DAT
**3. Source:** CD-SBD (*Dick's Picks VII*), **Quality:** A
**Highlights:** Row Jimmy, Playing, Set 2, Sugar Magnolia

Here is a very well recorded audience tape that puts you right in the middle of the Alexandra Palace to experience one of the most powerful, highly transformative shows the Grateful Dead ever played. Despite the available soundboard portions, I highly recommend listening to the audience tapes. This show has more pure improvisational material than any other Dead show. They were certainly feeling "It" across the board. Set 1 opens with a long, well-jammed "Scarlet" to set the pace. The opening lyric, "As I was walking 'round Grosvenor Square," though, elicited zero reaction from the crowd. The rest of the set is relaxed and articulate, with "Row Jimmy" standing out for its superb ensemble work.

The last song, "Playing in the Band," is easily one of their finest versions. Lesh foreshadows what's to come with some sonic booms to open the song. Soon a panoramic landscape unfolds, engineered to precision. Deep blues and velvet purples come to mind. The communion with the crowd—sadly missing from the soundboard portions—is a force of its own, acutely felt. The music is graceful, yet gritty, as it spins round and round, like a vortex sucking everyone into the source. The pressure is methodically increased and then leveled out.

Some staccato interplay comes in between Lesh and Billy—but still the circle holds. Garcia follows this with some streaking, intergalactic leads like comets shooting across the sky. Then he squeezes these into a strong "Tiger," but it's toothless in that it doesn't go over the top and break the spell—it merely intensifies it. More cyclical weaving patterns continue. At twenty-three minutes, Garcia swiftly and deftly stages the reprise, which goes down without a hitch. The nearly two-hour first set comes to a close, and the show's only half over.

Phil and Ned open set 2 with fifteen minutes' worth of their "Seastones," i.e., strange sounds. It doesn't get too out there. What's fun is eavesdropping on the crowd, which seems to take it all in stride. British accents pop up here and there with comments like "Eh, what's this then?"

Then the rest of the band comes out and starts spacing right off the bat. What's unique here is that Phil and Ned continue their squiggles to give us a "Seastones"/Dead jam. Amid Weir's feedback and Garcia's introspective, melancholic leads, Billy provides a downriver beat that's sparse and tribalistic. The film *Apocalypse Now* comes to mind—"Where's Kurtz?" the music is asking.

Soon Garcia picks up the pace: more circles within circles. Lagin counterpoints with his computerized keyboard of the future. After a drumless space, the pace picks up again. Lesh returns with his regular bass and greets the music with zigzagging mournful runs. When another drumless space follows, the crowd grows a bit restless and starts whistling and clapping. Sprouts, sprouts—who's got the meat?

Perhaps picking up on this, "Eyes" almost comes together several times—but different members bail out, shutting the door. Garcia gives up and leads the band into a careening, free-fall jam that gets to a dizzying height—peaks—and then drops back down into the valley once again. This space is more accentuated, sorrowful, and a little sinister. From this point, Garcia lifts the band quietly—with all hands on board—into "Eyes." The crowd reacts instantly with joy. A *very* long intro threatens to space out again (are these guys loose or what?) as Garcia wails and wails, further and further away with each cry. But he reels the song back in and finally—ten minutes after beginning—sings the first verse.

The crowd goes nuts. This version is, of course, spacey and mellow yet very strong-willed. Lesh snags the helm at the end and plays a bellowing lead. The crowd roars when he's done—in a jazzlike fashion—and "Dirt" appears. This one is long and sweaty, led fiercely by Lesh again. Just as the jam is taken to its highest peak, Lagin comes in with some "Seastones" notes that—don't work. The band staggers momentarily, almost comically, before dropping down into (can you guess?) another space.

This one has an otherworldly feel to it as it expands steadily outward like a rocket in slow motion. The segue into "Wharf Rat" is quite inventive; Garcia builds a firm ladder and clop-clop-clops down each rung like he's wearing clogs. He sings the song with tremendous warmth and confidence. After the line "But I'll get back on my feet some day," a mate in the audience comments loudly and sincerely, "Hope so, man." The closing jam soars and almost turns into another jam, but Garcia brings it down gently and carefully to close the set.

As the crowd goes into encore fever, Lesh comes out to say, "We'll be back for a few more numbers," delighting the fans. The final songs are solid, but signs of fatigue start to finally show. Amusingly, the crowd claps the "Not Fade Away" beat after "Around and Around"—just like they did at the Dead's last show from their Europe tour on May 26, 1972. Alas, this time the band ignores them. And amazingly, "Sugar Mag" nearly goes into the unknown as it has that same drive found in between "China" and "Rider," but Weir cuts it short. Before making a list of your favorite shows, make sure to get hold of this one. Mine is fifth-gen and sounds great. Good luck.

MICHAEL M. GETZ

## 9/14/74
### Olympiahalle, Munich, West Germany

**Set 1:** Bertha, Me and My Uncle, Deal, Jack Straw, Scarlet Begonias, Promised Land, Loser, El Paso, Row Jimmy, Weather Report Suite Prelude > Weather Report Suite Part One > Let It Grow, Tennessee Jed, Around and Around
**Phil and Ned:** Seastones
**Set 2:** Big River, Sugaree, Mexicali Blues, Mississippi Half-Step, It Must Have Been the Roses, Truckin' > Wharf Rat > Sugar Magnolia
**Encore:** Eyes of the World > One More Saturday Night, U.S. Blues

**Source:** AUD, **Quality:** B to B–, **Length:** 4:00, **Genealogy:** MR > RR > C > DAT > DAT
**Highlights:** Scarlet Begonias, Sugar Magnolia, Eyes of the World

The Wall of Sound was an awesome thing to behold, with its fifty-foot-high stacks of speakers from one end of the stage to the other. I mean, the thing just *looked* loud. It made you want to run and hide. But even more awesome was the sound that came out of it: loud, hell yes, but amazingly clean. No distortion. Wafer-crisp bass notes and bell-clear highs. The Wall of Sound provided the opportunity for some of the most amazingly precise audience recordings before the digital era. Unfortunately, this show's tape is not one of them. Even so, there are places in this concert where the squeaky-cleanness of the Wall leaves its mark on even a dull tape.

So let's skip through the first twenty minutes or so of this concert (competent but uncompelling versions of "Bertha," "Me and My Uncle," "Deal," and "Jack Straw") and focus on Garcia's first solo in "Scarlet Begonias." The notes that Garcia chooses to play are in and of themselves nothing special; he's basically playing a steady stream of sixteenth notes. But it's what he does with them, and how he works the Wall to his advantage. Garcia takes what in the hands of lesser guitarists would be an uninteresting stream of evenly spaced notes and creates rhythm and texture by accenting odd beats. No great trick there, but then he takes things to a more sophisticated level and changes the dynamics of *each* note. No two successive notes in the solo are attacked with the same degree of loudness. In doing so, Garcia creates a hypnotic swirl of loud-and-soft tonal runs. Pretty heady stuff, but Garcia goes the extra mile—and here's where the Wall's clarity of sound comes into effect—by finding the natural resonance of the concert hall and, through the dynamics of his solo, mimics the echoes of the music bouncing around the rafters! All this happens within the framework of a thirty-second solo over some very simple chord changes, but it's the clarity of the Wall that allows it to be captured on tape. You would *never* hear this on a soundboard recording, and most concert PA systems are too muddy to allow audience recording to reproduce these subtle shifts in dynamics.

That's a lot of words to expend on a thirty-second solo, isn't it? Well... unfortunately we need to, because Garcia is lost in action for a great part of the rest of the show. And yes, the Dead is more than Garcia, but Garcia is all we can really hear on this muddy audience recording; the rest of the band is indistinct and gets lost in the mix. Every now and then Keith or Bob rises above the morass, but for the most part it's difficult to focus on anything but Garcia's directionless playing. The low point of the first set comes at the end of "Let It Grow," where Garcia noodles aimlessly and is apparently unaware that the rest of the band is winding the song down.

Fortunately, we have Phil and Ned's "Seastones"—and this show contains my favorite version of this avant-garde exploration. Phil and Ned segments are very difficult to listen to on tape, they were meant to be experienced live. The feeling of an entire stadium vibrating—LOUDLY—until you thought your fillings were going to fall out just cannot be reproduced by a home stereo. And frankly, there is little to distinguish one Phil and Ned segment from another. So how can this one be my favorite? It's the audience's reaction that makes this one so endearing. Most audiences were split down the middle, with half of those in attendance sitting in awed silence and the other half totally oblivious to the music, merrily chatting away with their neighbors. But the Munich crowd, God love 'em, are *really* into the weirdness, hooting and cheering each odd zzzzzaaaaapppp and bbbuuuuzzzzzzz. It's hard to remain unaffected by the audience's affectionate reaction to this oddball music.

But once again we're focusing on a narrow part of the show in order to avoid the unpleasant fact that Garcia remains uninspired for most of the second set. There are a few rays of sunshine: Garcia and Godchaux trade some nice riffs at the end of "Mississippi Half-Step," and that song also includes a tasty, virtually a cappella "Across the Rio Gran-dee-oh" part. But so much potential here goes mostly untapped. The jam connecting "Truckin'" to "Wharf Rat" ("Truckin'" to "Wharf Rat"? Where's "The Other One"? Hey, I want my money back!) is short, and the band runs through its bag of melodic tricks—including a weird, begin-fast-and-end-slow "Mind Left Body Jam"—trying to find *something* upon which to hang their musical hats. But it isn't until "Sugar Magnolia" that Garcia snaps out of his trance, immediately bringing the excitement level up with him. (Again, one hates to give Garcia's playing more weight than the rest of the band, but again, this muddy tape doesn't allow us any other way to look at the musical big picture.) "Sugar Magnolia," fortunately, smokes! But unfortunately it's the final song of the second set.

The Dead must have felt a little guilty about the way the evening took shape, for they came out for a very good and unusually long three-song encore. "Eyes of the World" is tight as a drum (no pun intended) and sparkly, and segues niftily into a high-spirited "One More Saturday Night," and the show finally closes with a redeeming "U.S. Blues." If the rest of the show matched the excitement of the final twenty minutes, we'd be looking at one of the all-time bests. Sadly, this is a show with a lot of empty spaces.

JEFF TIEDRICH

---

### 9/18/74
#### Parc des Expositions, Dijon, France

**Set 1:** Uncle John's Band, Jack Straw, Black-Throated Wind, Scarlet Begonias, Mexicali Blues, Row Jimmy//, Beat it on Down the Line, Deal, The Race Is On, To Lay Me Down, Playing in the Band
**Set 2:** Loose Lucy, Big River, Peggy-O, Me and My Uncle, Eyes of the World > China Doll, He's Gone > Truckin' > Drums > Caution Jam > Ship of Fools, Johnny B. Goode
**Encore:** U.S. Blues

**1. Source:** SBD, **Quality:** A, **Length:** 2:45, **Genealogy:** MR > DAT

**2. Source:** FM-SBD (GDH 273 and 274), **Quality:** A+, **Length:** "Jack Straw" through "Scarlet Begonias," "The Race Is On," "To Lay Me Down," "He's Gone" through "Johnny B. Goode"
**3. Source:** AUD, **Quality:** C– (high-generation), **Length:** 0:10 (only "Johnny B. Goode" and "U.S. Blues")
**Highlights:** One of the better first sets

This one is a real gem. The accessibility of the music on this tape makes it an excellent choice for less experienced Deadheads. I often make this tape as one of several introductory tapes for newbies to sink their teeth into. In fact, all of the tapes from France in 1974 have a unique, airy quality. Every instrument seems perfectly imaged in the mix. No instrument steps on any other. One can easily focus on each instrument and follow it through an entire song. During this first set, the Dead seem to be in one of their calmest, most melodic moods. They start with what becomes one of the nicest-ever readings of "Uncle John's Band." Others nuggets include a perfect "Scarlet Begonias" and a "Race Is On" to which Keith and Jerry add ending flourishes that would do Nashville's finest proud. A beautiful "To Lay Me Down" is perfectly indicative of the gentle aesthetic of this set, with both Godchauxs giving career-high performances. Finally, a well-oiled "Playing in the Band" smoothly explores form and formlessness. Jerry eventually leads the band from spaceyness through a funk jam, and then leaves Keith and Phil to fool around in that idiom while he gets us back to the final verse.

Unfortunately, the very things that make set 1 so great are the downfall of set 2. In a second set we usually look for the Dead to uncork things a bit and do some deep exploration. Apparently on this night everybody was just too mellow to really get heavy. "Loose Lucy" appears in its less desirable fast variation. Both "Lucy" and "Big River" suffer from nearly inaudible vocals. "Peggy-O" is unremarkable but, as usual, beautiful. "Eyes" features some great Keith Godchaux work, but otherwise remains too straight and calm. The jam during "Eyes" is a bit confused and lacks the intensity that earlier '74 versions have. "China Doll" again finds Keith doing his best while the rest of the band can't seem to sync up. "Truckin'"—sans the usual climax—leads quickly into "Drums." Jerry and Phil eventually join Billy and begin an apocalyptic jam that comes into its own as Bobby chimes in. This leads very smoothly to a loose but superfunky instrumental rendition of "Caution." My better quality tape is cut before "Caution" finds its way to "Ship of Fools." "Johnny B. Goode" and the encore "U.S. Blues" are found on another tape. These two final songs were standards even at that time and are performed competently but not memorably.

HARRY HAHN

## 9/20/74
### Palais des Sports, Paris, France

**Set 1:** Cumberland Blues, Jack Straw, It Must Have Been the Roses, Beat It on Down the Line, Scarlet Begonias, Black-Throated Wind, Friend of the Devil, El Paso, Weather Report Suite Prelude > Weather Report Suite Part One > Let It Grow > Stella Blue, Around and Around
**Set 2:** China Cat Sunflower > I Know You Rider, Big River, Greatest Story Ever Told, Brokedown Palace, Truckin' > Eyes of the World > Not Fade Away > Goin' Down the Road Feelin' Bad/, One More Saturday Night
**Encore:** U.S. Blues

1. **Source:** SBD, **Quality:** A+, **Length:** 2:50 (my tape contains no "Brown-Eyed Women" and ends during "Goin' Down the Road")
2. **Source:** AUD, **Quality:** C– (high-generation), **Length:** 0:10 (only "One More Saturday Night" and "U.S. Blues")
**Highlights:** Black-Throated Wind, Friend of the Devil, Stella Blue, Brokedown Palace

Very similar in sound and feel to the first set from 9/18/74, this first set is an excellent adjunct to the mighty fine Dijon tape. Again, the performance is melodic, friendly, and executed perfectly. This time we get a smooth and sensational "Cumberland" to start and a more energetic version of "Scarlet" than on 9/18. Phil shines while Keith makes some abortive attempts at the synthesizer. "Black-Throated Wind" is defined by its silences on one hand and Bobby's exceptional vocals on the other. The ending crescendo is epic. We get to enjoy one of the final renditions of "Friend of the Devil" in its fast arrangement. The band does sweet justice to Bobby's masterpiece, "Weather Report Suite," offering up a tasty, mysterious rendition with feature work by Keith. Jerry answers back with a sweet, sad "Stella Blue." This "Stella" has those golden, morose silences that define the best versions of this song. Keith is again completely masterful, and we are reminded of how great Billy was as a solo drummer. Bobby, in an effort to keep everyone awake, finishes with a rousing and surprisingly unannoying "Around and Around."

A nice, bread and butter '74 "China Cat" > "Rider" is followed by an even more uptempo and well-played "Big River." Keith, Jerry, and Billy vie for Most Valuable Player on a beautiful "Brokedown Palace" (love those "da-da-da" vocals at the end). "Truckin'" includes the usual buildup and then becomes a very intricate jam that highlights Billy and Phil. The jam evolves into a more Jerry and Billy oriented exploration before Phil reawakens and starts sounding very ominous, recalling the apocalyptic feeling of the last few minutes of many 1972 "Dark Stars." From there the band quiets down, gently slides into "Eyes," and the planet feels safe again. While better than 9/18's, this short version of "Eyes" displays a strange, loose approach that is ultimately unsatisfying. The slack feeling persists throughout "Not Fade Away" and eventually gives way to a very funky "Goin' Down the Road" jam that features Jerry's repeating crescendos and prolific jamming by Keith and Phil. Finally they go into "Goin' Down the Road," which on my tape is cut after about four minutes. My very high-generation audience recording of "One More Saturday Night" and "U.S. Blues" offers tight versions of these standards and a remarkably enthusiastic audience response.

HARRY HAHN

## 9/21/74
### Palais des Sports, Paris, France

**Set 2:** Seastones > Playing in the Band > Drums > Playing in the Band, Row Jimmy, Big River, Ship of Fools, Uncle John's Band, Morning Dew, Sugar Magnolia
**Encore:** Casey Jones

**Source:** SBD, **Quality:** A+, **Length:** 1:30
**Highlights:** Playing in the Band, Row Jimmy, Uncle John's Band, Morning Dew

As usual, for many, "Seastones" here is a bit difficult to enjoy. However, it evolves very gradually into a notable

"Playing in the Band" that has a different jam than others during the same period and contains a drum solo, which is somewhat unusual. "Row Jimmy" and "Uncle John's Band," which features great work by Keith and a strong vocal presence by Phil, are both superb. Keith must've liked France; some of his best work appears during this run of shows. "Morning Dew" is as haunting and triumphant as ever.

HARRY HAHN

---

### 10/16/74
#### Winterland Arena, San Francisco, California

**Set 1:** //Deal, Mexicali Blues, It Must Have Been the Roses, Beat It on Down the Line, Scarlet Begonias, Me and Bobby McGee, Tennessee Jed, Cumberland Blues, Row Jimmy, Playing in the Band
**Set 2:** Seastones > Space > Wharf Rat > Space > Eyes of// the World, Big River, Ship of Fools, Truc//kin' > Goin' Down the Road Feelin' Bad > Uncle John's Band, Johnny B. Goode
**Encore:** Happy Birthday (for Bobby), U.S. Blues

---

**1. Source:** SBD, **Quality:** A, **Length:** 4:05
**2. Source:** AUD, **Quality:** B+, **Length:** 4:05, **Taper:** Louis Falanga with a Sony TC-110 deck and an ECM-23 mike
**3. Source:** FM-SBD (GDH 052 and 212), **Quality:** A, **Length:** "Scarlet Begonias," "Me and Bobby McGee," "It Must Have Been the Roses," "Big River," "Playing in the Band," "Happy Birthday," "U.S. Blues"
**Highlights:** The entire show
**Personnel:** with Ned Lagin as guest artist
**Comments:** It's hard to tell how significant the cut in "Eyes" is. "Happy Birthday" is sung for Bobby before "U.S. Blues."

The first of the five "retirement" shows at Winterland before the Dead's near-complete sabbatical from playing in the next year and a half, these shows should hold a special place in every Deadhead's heart because they are depicted in *The Grateful Dead Movie* and feature the return of Mickey Hart after an absence of nearly four years. Each show has something very special to recommend it, and together they form an unparalleled run of music. This particular night is in many ways the strangest and was also Bob Weir's twenty-seventh birthday—a nice age to retire at, wouldn't you say!

A controlled but flowing "Deal" kicks off the show, and immediately all the hallmarks of 1974 Dead at their finest are there. There is a wonderful sense of space in the arrangements and a lightness of touch that rides on the back of Kreutzmann's fluid and fluent drumming. The really unique thing about this particular night is the prominence of Phil's playing. He is in spectacular form throughout, almost completely in control in the first set in particular. "Mexicali Blues," like all the fast countryish tunes they played at this time, responds particularly well to that '74 sound. During "It Must Have Been the Roses," Phil plays a lovely and subtle underpinning, and although this song was probably even better served by the acoustic arrangements of 1980, it also works very well here. On "Scarlet Begonias" Phil's contribution is even more startling and can only be described as "lead bass." He and Garcia lock instruments over a glorious loping beat from Kreutzmann, and the resulting long fine jam is more of a duet between them. Unfortunately, it can't be said that Donna is in good voice on it. "Tennessee Jed" is rather poor by comparison with what has gone before, but a racy "Cumberland Blues" soon makes up for that. "Row Jimmy" is methodically explored with beautiful and expressive singing. "We all have new strings on our instruments, they need stretching," says Bob before they go on to do just that in one of the all-time great versions of "Playing in the Band," marred only slightly by Donna's trademark screeches, which on this occasion really do sound more like she is gargling antiseptic than anything else. The bass guitar introduces the jam before Garcia comes in and drops immediately into eloquent and rhythmic space, which is where he stays for the next twenty or so minutes. Over this Phil continually builds inventive lead lines, leaving Garcia to weave mellow magic underneath, ably supported by Keith, who stays right alongside him throughout.

The second set begins with the trademark spooky strangeness of Phil and Ned's "Seastones" adventure. The band ambles on and slowly turns it into a "Space" whose fifteen minutes of ambient jazzy ebbs and flows are best appreciated on headphones and which are complemented by an upfront Phil solo. By this time, however, the crowd is obviously getting a little restless at the fact that they've heard nothing but weirdness for the last fifty minutes; some start up a slow handclap to which the band soon responds with a gentle segue into "Wharf Rat." The reappearance of music that could almost be described as being of this earth, coupled with vocals, is quite startling, and the band is obviously shocked enough by it that afterwards they fall back into another "Space." This time, however, it is the two guitarists who are center stage—indeed, virtually alone for most of it—in a glorious sparkling duet with runs and explorations somehow reminiscent of both jazz and acoustic folk music. A bizarre "Eyes," lacking its usual rhythmic bounce but filled with inventive jamming, follows as the band once more seems to struggle to come to terms with actually having to play a song. Maybe feeling the lack of rhythm, Phil takes hold partway through, solos long and hard, and then never lets go until, apparently losing interest, the band slows down relatively abruptly and then drops away to nothing but Garcia noodling plaintively. No one seems to want to follow him, and he brings things to a quiet close in a really strange ending—one of the most unusual Dead song sequences ever, which, together with the "Seastones," clocks in at over seventy-five minutes.

After a long tuning they make another attempt to return to Planet Earth with a fine "Big River" that features hot playing from Garcia and Keith and is followed by an excellent "Ship of Fools." "Truckin'" kicks off their next bid for an extended jam and features exciting, indeed rather frenetic, playing by all of the band, as does the pumping "Goin' Down the Road" that follows. Nevertheless, they still sound wayward and rather disorganized, and as they slip into "Uncle John's Band," things rather fall apart, possibly under the strain of what is a tightly structured song. They close with "Johnny B. Goode," still sounding off-kilter. Bob's birthday is hilariously celebrated before the encore of "U.S. Blues" with someone, possibly Phil, singing "Happy Birthday" in a gloriously tuneless and lugubrious voice. A wonderfully eccentric ending to an eccentric but wonderful show.

JAMES SWIFT

---

### 10/17/74
**Winterland Arena, San Francisco, California**

**Set 1:** Promised Land, Mississippi Half-Step, Black-Throated Wind, Friend of the Devil, Jack Straw, Loser, El Paso, China Cat Sunflower > I Know You Rider, Me and My Uncle, It Must Have Been the Roses, Weather Report Suite Prelude > Weather Report Suite Part One > Let It Grow//
**Set 2:** //Scarlet //Begonias, Big// River, Ramble On Rose, Mexicali Blues, He's Gone > The Other One Jam > Space > The Other One > Spanish Jam > Mind Left Body Jam > The Other One > Stella Blue > Sugar Magnolia
**Encore:** Casey Jones, //U.S. Blues

**1. Source:** SBD, **Quality:** A–/B+, **Length:** 2:37, **Genealogy:** MR > RR > RR > PCM > DAT
**2. Source:** AUD, **Quality:** B/B+, **Length:** 1:29 (set 2, missing "U.S. Blues"), **Taper:** Louis Falanga with a Sony TC-110 deck and an ECM-23 mike
**Highlights:** Second set from He's Gone to the end, Weather Report Suite
**Comments:** The first source is the more commonly circulated tape; the song cuts mentioned in the set lists above refer to this tape. "Sugar Magnolia" and "Casey Jones" are missing. Generally good mix (everybody is there), but the bass is too strong in set 1, distorting at times.

This was the second of the five farewell shows filmed for *The Grateful Dead Movie*. The band sounds relaxed as they perform a few final shows before parking The Bus and taking a break. Bill Graham starts the night by pointing out the cameras in the auditorium. He asks the audience to be themselves and remarks that hopefully this will all end up in an X-rated movie. The first song is interrupted by a brief, loud burst of static, which throws Bobby off for just a moment. He recovers quickly and adds a "God willing" after "won't let the poor boy down." There are several references throughout the show to the technical glitches that plagued the mammoth Wall of Sound. The band steps from song to song for the rest of the set, which is competently played but not exceptional. The only musical extensions in this set are "China Cat Sunflower" > "I Know You Rider" and "Weather Report Suite." The latter can be considered a highlight due to the range of the song, from its subtle introduction to the power of "Let It Grow," here truncated a minute or two before the finish and thus not affording us closure to the song.

The second set would fit on a one-hundred-minute tape today, but both the board tape and the audience tape have omissions. The board tape is missing "Sugar Magnolia" and "Casey Jones," and "Scarlet Begonias" begins at "I knew right away she was not like other girls." There are barely noticeable breaks during "Scarlet Begonias" and "Big River." The audience tape does not have these gaps, but we miss the segue from "Stella Blue" to "Sugar Magnolia," which fades in right at its beginning, so it does not appear that much is missing. Also, "U.S. Blues" is missing. (Note that it was played as an encore four of the five nights of this run.)

Although the band stretches out a little on "Scarlet Begonias," set 2 doesn't really set itself apart from set 1 until "He's Gone," which starts a continuous flow of music that plays through to the end of the show. The set list doesn't do justice to what transpires here. After adding some deep down vocals to the end of "He's Gone," Phil takes the helm and thumps the band into what is definitely recognizable as "The Other One," but they just touch on it before taking off into a jam that quickly dissolves into a trip to the cosmos, an improvisation similar to the excursions often tied to "Playing in the Band." Phil then brings us back into "The Other One," and the Spanish lady makes her appearance. But then we're off again, into what becomes a "Spanish Jam" and then a "Mind Left Body Jam," which moves around a bit, as if we were lost in a valley, then climbs to a point where Garcia, by dropping in one perfectly inflected note, brings us over the hill and back home again. Phil soon guides us back into "The Other One" for its final verse, and shortly thereafter we find ourselves in the welcome quietness of "Stella Blue," some thirty-two minutes after the denouement of "He's Gone." And of course "Sugar Magnolia" perks us up as a finale.

DAN DESARO

---

### 10/18/74
**Winterland Arena, San Francisco, California**

**Set 1:** Around and Around, Sugaree, Mexicali Blues, Peggy-O, Beat It on Down the Line, Brown-Eyed Women, Cumberland Blues, El Paso, Tennessee Jed, Jack Straw, Row Jimmy, Weather Report Suite
**Set 2:** Seastones > Jam > Dark Star > Morning Dew
**Set 3:** Promised Land > Bertha > Greatest Story Ever Told, Ship of Fools, Not Fade Away > Goin' Down the Road Feelin' Bad > One More Saturday Night
**Encore:** U.S. Blues

**1. Source:** SBD, **Quality:** A, **Length:** 3:30, **Genealogy:** MR > RR > DAT
**2. Source:** AUD, **Quality:** B+, **Length:** 3:30, **Taper:** Louis Falanga with a Sony TC-110 deck and an ECM-23 mike
**3. Source:** FM-SBD (*GDH*), **Quality:** A+, **Length:** 0:58 ("Jam" through "Morning Dew" only), **Genealogy:** MR > DAT
**Highlights:** The whole second set

The Dead's Friday night performance during their "Farewell" series was a centerpiece in more than just a chronological sense. It was the first of the five-night stand that I was able to attend, and I was struck by the amount of extra gear stuck onto the already typically crowded stage by the film crews, including a rotating camera dolly adjacent to Keith's piano. The long, relatively low-key first set opens with a slow, stately couplet of "Around and Around" and "Sugaree." A good-natured "Roll Out the Barrel" leads into a barrelhouse piano-driven "Mexicali Blues." Next up is the slow, sweetly sung Bay Area debut of "Peggy-O," followed by a relatively turgid version of "Beat It on Down the Line." "Brown-Eyed Women" and "Cumberland Blues" are smooth and solid. The mournful "Row Jimmy" features some bittersweet slide guitar. The final version of the complete "Weather Report Suite" opens with a multilayered introduction featuring Weir, Lesh, and Keith, continues with some more fine Garcia slide during part 1, and ends with a relatively low-key "Let It Grow" that brings the first set to a close.

The show's masterpiece begins innocuously enough, with Ned Lagin's insectlike keyboard noises, joined in short order by Phil's musique concrète bass booms. After nearly a half hour of duo improvisation, the remaining band members troop on silently and join what becomes a strange, slow, and elegant jam that leads into what proves to be the last "Dark Star" for over four years and one of the most emotional versions ever. Garcia dances around the song's theme instrumentally for over ten minutes before slowly and surely moving into the single vocal verse that is performed. Whether it was Lagin's attempts at musical biofeedback or simply the state of group consciousness, the Dead's part of this set evoked one of the most intense audience responses I ever saw at a show; many of those around me were literally in tears by the time the band drove into the extended, and equally wrenching, version of "Morning Dew" that concluded the nearly seventy-five-minute improvisation that was that night's second set.

Probably by necessity, the third set is a more extroverted, rock 'n' roll outing including the then popular juxtaposition of "Promised Land" > "Bertha" > "Greatest Story Ever Told" and a shimmering "Ship of Fools." The high-energy concluding medley of "Not Fade Away" > "Goin' Down the Road" > "One More Saturday Night" is stretched way out, and notable for Keith's incredible Jerry Lee Lewis–style piano riffing. Having apparently shot their psychic wad, the band makes its escape after a quick but rollicking "U.S. Blues" encore.

MICHAEL PARRISH

---

## 10/19/74
### Winterland Arena, San Francisco, California

**Set 1:** Mississippi Half-Step, Me and My Uncle, Friend of the Devil, Beat It on Down the Line, It Must Have Been the Roses, El Paso, Loose Lucy, Black-Throated Wind, Scarlet //Begonias, To Lay Me Down, Mama Tried, Eyes of the World > China Doll, Big River
**Phil and Ned:** Seastones
**Set 2:** Uncle John's Band, Big Railroad Blues, The Race Is On, Tomorrow Is Forever, Mexicali Blues, //Dire Wolf, Sugar Magnolia > He's Gone > Truckin' Jam > Caution Jam > Drums > Space > Truckin' > Black Peter, Sunshine Daydream
**Encore:** One More Saturday Night, U.S. Blues

**1. Source:** SBD, **Quality:** A–, **Length:** 3:40, **Genealogy:** MR > RR > RR > PCM > DAT
**2. Source:** AUD, **Quality:** B+, **Length:** 3:40, **Taper:** Louis Falanga with a Sony TC-110 deck and an ECM-23 mike
**3. Source:** FM-SBD (DHH 39, GDH 197 and 198), **Quality:** A, **Length:** "Big River," the entire second set
**Highlights:** Eyes of the World, Uncle John's Band, Truckin' Jam > Black Peter
**Comments:** This tape is a nice stereo soundboard, most likely a rough mix-down tape mixed from the multitrack master tapes during the making of *The Grateful Dead Movie* in 1977. Although the tapes are very enjoyable, some distractions are apparent in the mix: besides obvious hiss and slightly muddy sound in places, there is a clear vocal echo throughout. Also, crowd noise is often present and occasionally bothersome, particularly when out-of-sync clapping is audible. DAT tapes from the master mix-down tapes circulate, as well as low-generation analogue copies. Portions of the show (from the same mix-down tapes) have been broadcast on David Gans' *Grateful Dead Hour* radio show over the years.

The show as a whole is very well played, and is my favorite of this week of Winterland shows. The first set has many fine renditions of songs. "Mississippi Half-Step," "El Paso," and "Black-Throated Wind" stand out, with "El Paso" being a really amazing version of an often disappointing song. This extremely fast version features demon cymbal work from Bill, stunningly quick leads from Garcia, and excellent dynamics that accentuate the tension of the cowboy song. Bob doesn't sound rushed even as he sings at a frenetic pace.

Of note for those who like to inject some humor into their Grateful Dead Experience is this version of "Mama Tried," the first in over three years. Bob flubs the words to both verses and ends up mumbling through the entire song; it is kind of fun to listen to him squirm as he fails essentially to recall any of the words. Earlier in the set, Garcia also engages in his own spontaneous arranging during "Friend of the Devil," but he seems to stumble through with a bit more grace than Bob manages.

The focus of the first set, and probably of the show, is the incredible version of "Eyes of the World"; this is the Grateful Dead at its best. The version here is punchy, ecstatic, and every musician is wonderfully light on his or her feet. At the same time that "Eyes" stretches out to a fully realized nineteen minutes long, there are no wasted notes or flabby jamming. Garcia's guitar sparkles, and he engages Keith's piano in a dazzling conversation that stretches out in a long and satisfying manner, ending just in time for Phil to lead the way into the dark "Slipknot"-type jams near the end. This version was born from some wise and joyous dream, and you should honor the space these musicians found themselves in by putting down this book and listening to it.

Phil and Ned's "Seastones" trip is pretty relaxing if you like that sort of thing, and there is some surprisingly enthusiastic audience response. The second set, on the other hand, is extremely energetic and exciting. It begins with a great version of "Uncle John's Band," ragged but full of piss and vinegar, wherein we find two really fine long jams. This is followed by a spot-on "Big Railroad Blues," with Lesh and Garcia chugging forward in inimitable fashion. "Tomorrow Is Forever" is also well sung and played, and seems to strike a heartfelt note with the musicians.

The major interest in the second set, however, lies in the big final jam. "Sugar Magnolia" and "He's Gone" start the jam, but the band really begins to move as it makes a leap into about a two-minute "Truckin'" jam that segues without audible effort into an intense, high-energy "Caution" jam. Phil belts it out for about five minutes until the band steps back and lets Bill play his drums for a bit. When the band rejoins our favorite skin-pounder, Garcia's watery guitar sound and Lesh's feedback create a sort of electronic "Prelude to the Afternoon of a Faun," very placid and very hypnotic. They eventually build a more conventional jam out of this space, and finally smoothly change time signatures to begin a second run at "Truckin'." After the vocal section and a bit of jamming, "Truckin'" breaks down into a wonderfully soulful and powerful "Black Peter." Overall, this sequence of jams has a concise, focused feel that never seems boring or directionless. I highly recommend this show.

BART WISE

---

## 10/20/74

**"Farewell" Show
Winterland Arena,
San Francisco, California**

**Set 1:** Cold Rain and Snow, Mama Tried, Deal, Beat It on Down the Line, Loser, Jack Straw, Tennessee Jed, El Paso, Brokedown Palace, China Cat Sunflower > I Know You Rider, Around and Around
**Phil and Ned:** Seastones
**Set 2:** Playing in the Band* > Drums* > Not Fade Away* > Drums* > The Other One* > Wharf Rat* > Playing in the Band*
**Set 3:** Good Lovin'*, It Must Have Been the Roses, Promised Land*, Eyes of the World > Slipknot > Stella Blue, Sugar Magnolia*
**Encore 1:** Johnny B. Goode*
**Encore 2:** Mississippi Half-Step* > We Bid You Goodnight

* with Mickey Hart

---

**1. Source:** SBD, **Quality:** A–, **Length:** 4:00, **Genealogy:** MR > RR > RR > PCM > DAT
**2. Source:** AUD, **Quality:** B+, **Length:** 4:00, **Taper:** Louis Falanga with a Sony TC-110 deck and an ECM-23 mike

Although in hindsight it seems like a humorous footnote, those of us in attendance at this Sunday show had every reason to believe that it might well be the Dead's last performance, so every note took on much greater significance than normal. A wakelike atmosphere prevailed as the crowd bade farewell to one familiar tune after another, with a few exciting surprises thrown into the mix as well. The first set opens with a slow, sure "Cold Rain and Snow" followed by a rocked-up "Mama Tried," brought out of retirement for one "last" time. Midset highlights include a feedback-drenched "Loser" and a reverent "Brokedown Palace." One of the liveliest "China Cat" > "Rider" pairings from that era precedes the perfunctory "Around and Around" that closes out the set.

The evening's Lesh-Lagin set was one of the shortest and noisiest of the five nights, and ended without any participation by the other group members.

As a second drum kit was set up on stage, the audience's excitement visibly mounted as it became clear that Mickey Hart was to be reunited with his bandmates onstage for the first time in nearly four years. The remarkable jam that was set 2, sandwiched between the two halves of "Playing in the Band," was a veritable drumfest. A first drum duel comes out of the lengthy jam, dominated by keyboard and lead guitar, following the intro to "Playing," which leads into a speedy "Not Fade Away," with Phil leading the charge and Bob shredding his vocal cords at the end, rolling into a brief statement of the "Other One" melody, after which the drummers take off again, with Lagin throwing in some synthesized sparks. Out of the "Drums" comes a relatively short, spacey version of "The Other One" that leads into a melodramatic "Wharf Rat" before everyone roars back into the "Playing" reprise to close out the continuous set.

After a third break, the band returns with another landmark, the first post-Pigpen version of "Good Lovin'." Much of the last set seems a bit anticlimactic by comparison with the second, but no one was in any hurry for the proceedings to end. A languid "Eyes of the World" features Phil's dancing bass and Keith on some dreamy electric piano noodling, and leads into an equally slow, poignant "Stella." Mickey's manic percussive fills give extra drive to the set-closing "Sugar Magnolia." The first encore, a roaring version of "Johnny B. Goode," clearly was not going to satisfy the crowd, so the group returns, after a very long pause, with what seemed a strange, but oddly fitting, final encore, an almost funereal version of "Half-Step" that leads into a very moving, if obvious, closer, "We Bid You Goodnight." As the crowd slowly and reluctantly funneled out into the early San Francisco morning, Bill Graham's staff took the unusual step of returning the crowd's tickets, with "The Last One" stamped on them. Fortunately, that proclamation turned out to be premature by a good twenty-one years.

MICHAEL PARRISH

---

## ??/??/74
### Unknown Venue

**Studio Sessions:** Unbroken Chain, Unbroken Chain, Scarlet Begonias, Pride of Cucamonga, Ship of Fools, Money Money, Loose Lucy, U.S. Blues, Crazy Fingers

---

**Source:** SBD, **Quality:** A–, **Length:** 0:45
**Highlights:** Unbroken Chain (both takes)
**Comments:** The "Crazy Fingers" that appears here is most probably from a different batch of outtakes than the rest of the tape.

This tape begins with two takes of "Unbroken Chain." The first is performed by Lesh, solo on acoustic guitar. Obviously a preliminary draft, Lesh actually names the chord progressions between verses. Though a tad hoarse, Lesh's vocals are warm and heartfelt. The instrumental jam is executed with delicate timing; sternly instructed Lesh, "The short length of the pause between the punch of this rhythm is correct." The second take is instrumental but with the complete ensemble, and it's stunningly perfect from start to finish. The instrumental jam is considerably more assertive than on the more commonly circulated version with vocals. Garcia's lead is without hesitation, and Kreutzmann's rhythm is simply furious. The segue back into the verse section contains some whispering bell-like licks from Godchaux that are heavenly. Most of the remaining tracks, all of which are instrumental, are perhaps best described as ordinary. Though none of the selections contain audible mistakes, they do little more than illustrate the basic framework of the material in a tight but somewhat sterile depiction. However, the tape's conclusion of "Crazy Fingers," which contains some very prominent Godchaux-Lesh interplay, has a distinctive calypso feel to it that is significantly more enthused than the soothing version that appeared are on the *Blues for Allah* LP.

BRIAN DYKE

# Reviews: 1974

> ✺ **??/??/74** ✺
>
> **Unknown Location.**
>
> **Studio Sessions:** Pride of Cucamonga, Pride of Cucamonga, Pride of Cucamonga, Money Money, Unbroken Chain, Unbroken Chain

**Source:** SBD, **Quality:** B+, **Length:** 0:25
**Highlights:** All
**Comments:** The final take of Unbroken Chain also circulates labeled "12-12-73 Soundcheck."

From its playful demeanor, we can perhaps assume that this material is from a rehearsal and not an actual session. Much looser than its their instrumental companion, the two vocal selections here could be considered among the Dead's most unjustifiably underperformed. "Pride of Cucamonga," vocal flubs aside, is well performed in every respect. Ever the perfectionist, however, Lesh halts and restarts on two occasions, once from the top and once following the second refrain. Although definitely among the Dead's least desirable selections, the following version of "Money Money" far surpasses both the version that appeared on the *Mars Hotel* LP and the few live performances it was given before its retirement. Weir's vocal reading is repetitive yet confident, with some comical falsetto attempts mixed in as well. And abandoning their backup responsibilities, Garcia and Godchaux choose to solo nearly all the way through, and become so seemingly aloof and lost in their own dialogue that they are reminded by Weir, "Bar eight," before the conclusion. This rendition of "Unbroken Chain"—which also receives a false start during which Garcia quips, "Fumble-fingers Godchaux!"—is perhaps the definitive version, and simply beautiful in execution. Again, Garcia and Godchaux strike a nice contrast with thick piano fills that mesh perfectly with prickly Garcia fingerpicking. The bridge jam is tight and flawless, with Garcia cautiously stretching a few curt phrases before returning to the verse and conclusion.

BRIAN DYKE

> ✺ **??/??/74** ✺
>
> **Unknown Location**
>
> **Studio Sessions:** 3 tracks, titles unknown

**Source:** SBD, **Quality:** A, **Length:** 0:40, **Genealogy:** Mickey Hart's unreleased *Silent Flute* LP
**Highlight:** Track 1

Unlike the very enigmatic efforts of *Area Code 415* and *Fire on the Mountain*, this unreleased Mickey Hart LP is precisely predictable in material. Cryptic, tranquil, naive, and exploratory, this solo effort consists of only three tracks, which represent a bipolar display of delicate genius and arrogant mercurialism. The standard chops are thought out and poignant, the avant-garde material focused and melodic. And, of course, the percussion contribution is incomparably dynamic, ranging from serenely silent to the threshold of pain. Track 1 begins with a distant space segment followed by a brief series of indecipherable quips à la "Seastones." In the background you can hear commanding bellows erupting rather quickly before they fade into silence. Arising abruptly, the tempo of the jam becomes erratic, the pattern like that of a bell curve. Though the ascensions are painstaking, the declines are demonic. Upon the arising, one can feel the motion of the jam flowing through the body. While descending, one can feel oneself being drained drip by drip. After failing to resolve, the jam is grounded with an eruptive bomb that is as chillingly haunting as the call of the reaper. Without warning, the jam abruptly shifts from possessed to enlightened, leading into a sparingly minimal jam with deep Asian overtones. Precise and refined, the jam meanders to a graceful fade, until all that is left are the empty and uncluttered whispers of the flute, and the silence in between. This is what it must sound like in the presence of the Buddha! Teasing the ascension, Garcia takes the lead with a heavenly solo of innocent inquiry. Rich in delay, each bend in the string seemingly expands the awakening further. The responding jam, which contains a brief lick resembling the "Star Wars" theme, sets the path for the final ascension. Slowly and gently the jam builds, savoring momentarily upon the arrival before once again fading to silence.

Track 2 is backward, and though at a glance it sounds like gibberish (remember "Revolution #9"?), it actually contains a quaint and soothing melody. Unfortunately, the track concludes before its motif can be assumed.

The concluding selection is a Hart-Lagin jam set with a primitive percussion rhythm accompanied by hollow electrosynthesizer-like bombs. Though appealing, this jam remains set in a specific pattern, and like track 2, it concludes prematurely, thus hampering it's effectiveness.

BRIAN DYKE

---

### ??/??/74
**Unknown Location**
**Interview:** Jerry Garcia

**Source:** FM, **Quality:** B, **Length:** 0:11
**Highlights:** "Every straight person that you see wandering around is, you know, taking three Valiums a day, or something."

This interview is fairly ridiculous in content, containing scattered discussion of Pigpen, Richard Nixon, musical philosophies and approaches, and drugs.

BRIAN DYKE

---

### ??/??/??
**Unknown Location**
**Interview:** Jerry Garcia

**Source:** FM, **Quality:** A, **Length:** 0:02
**Comments:** This tape was derived from *The Rock Years* radio program.

Garcia gives a brief, heartfelt description of his first encounters with Janis Joplin.

BRIAN DYKE

---

### ??/??/??
**Unknown Location**
**Interview:** Phil Lesh

**Source:** AUD, **Quality:** B, **Length:** 0:05
**Highlights:** "This was when we had all the time in the universe."

This fragmentary piece contains discussion of Lesh's first encounters with Garcia, both musically and personally.

BRIAN DYKE

# PART THREE

# Resources

# 8

# Recommended Listening

Deadheads are forever in search of the ultimate musical *peak* experience. Many of our conversations include discussion or debate about which versions of Dead songs are our favorites. After all, we're every bit as analytical and critical as the next bunch of fanatics. It's natural that we seek to quantify the Dead experience by coming up with a hierarchical list and a collection of the hottest versions of our favorite tunes.

There are, of course, no right or wrong choices. It is our hope, however, that this list will serve as a basic guide for those looking to fill their collections with music which we all can agree is inspirational and/or noteworthy.

How did these versions qualify to be recommended here? Most of them demonstrate the greatest technical virtuosity and/or elicit the greatest emotional response from the listener.

There are a few songs listed here that the Dead only played once. While some like "Let It Rock," "New Orleans," "Mystery Train," and "My Babe" are amazing, a few—"Peggy Sue," "Louie, Louie," and "That'll Be the Day" in particular—aren't performed well. However, we've listed them anyway for those who will not rest until they own at least one version of every song played by the Dead.

This list was compiled by polling the contributors to this book and the staff of *Dupree's Diamond News*. We welcome your continued suggestions for adding to this list.

*"Ain't It Crazy"* (otherwise known as "The Rub"): 4/28/71, Fillmore East, N.Y. (featuring some *crazy* harmonica playing by Pigpen); 5/30/71, Winterland, San Francisco.

*"Alice D. Millionaire":* 12/1/66, the Scorpio Sessions.

*"Alligator":* 2/28/69, Fillmore West (phenomenal jamming), 8/23/68 Shrine Auditorium (extremely psychedelic); 2/14/68, Carousel Ballroom, Calif.; 6/14/68, Fillmore East (not the best quality, but played with enormous gusto); 12/30/69, Boston Tea Party; 11/6/70, late show, Capitol Theater, Port Chester, N.Y. (Garcia's notes in his post-drum solo jam fly like liquid fire); 9/2/68, Sultan, Wash.; 8/22/68, Fillmore West.

*"Around and Around":* 11/19/72, Houston (Jerry's licks are classic rock 'n' roll at its best); 11/20/70, Rochester, N.Y. (with Jorma, although the only tapes of this show in circulation are of godawful quality); 6/18/74, Louisville, Ky.; 11/8/70, Capitol Theater, Port Chester, N.Y. (the first-ever version, played much like the way the Stones used to perform it).

*"Attics of My Life":* 6/24/70 late show, Capitol Theater, Port Chester (sandwiched inside "Dark Star"); 9/20/70, Fillmore East (very smooth); 5/15/70, Fillmore East; 11/9/70, Action House, N.Y.

*"Baby Blue":* 6/4/70, Fillmore West; 2/24/74, Winterland, San Francisco; 4/26/69, Electric Theater, Chicago.

*"Beat It on Down the Line":* 4/26/71, Fillmore East (with Duane Allman on slide guitar); 2/15/73, Madison, Wisc.; 6/18/74, Louisville, Ky. (contains a "My Old Kentucky Home" guitar solo).

*"Beer Barrel Polka":* 6/26/74, Providence, R.I. (> "Truckin' ").

*"Bertha":* 4/28/71, Fillmore East; 12/5/71, Felt Forum, N.Y.; 8/27/72, Oregon Country Fairgrounds, Veneta, Oreg. (Garcia's guitar is brought slightly out of

tune by direct exposure to the intense sun that afternoon, yet his playing is so intensely fast it will have you shaking your head in disbelief); the one on *Skull and Roses,* April 1971.

"*Big Boy Pete*": 9/6/69, Family Dog, San Francisco; 3/1/70, Family Dog; 9/20/70, Fillmore East.

"*Big Railroad Blues*": 11/19/72, Houston, Tex.; 12/10/71, St. Louis; 8/12/72, Sacramento; 9/20/70, Fillmore East (acoustic), 4/17/72, Copenhagen, Denmark.

"*Big River*": 11/10 and 11/11/73, Winterland; 5/25/74, Santa Barbara; 11/14/73, San Diego (sandwiched inside "The Other One"); 6/16/74, Des Moines, Iowa; 12/31/71, Winterland, SF (first version that Garcia sings).

"*Bird Song*": 8/27/72, Oregon Country Fairgrounds, Veneta, Oreg. (breathtaking, exquisite, this rendition soars as high as the band on that very cosmic afternoon); 9/19/72, Roosevelt Stadium, Jersey City, N.J. (a hard-to-find, decent audience tape proves this version to be only one degree less inspired than the version from 8/27/72); 7/31/71, New Haven, Conn. (this one *explodes* out of "Dark Star"); 9/27/72, Jersey City (Phil exclaims, "Dynamite!" during the final note); 6/22/73, Vancouver, British Columbia, 9/12/73, Williamsburg, Va.; 3/30/73, Rochester, N.Y.; 9/15/72, Boston.

"*Black Queen*": 12/10/69, Thelma Theater, La. (only version; performed with Stephen Stills).

"*Black-Throated Wind*": 11/19/72, Houston; 10/21/73, Omaha, Nebr.; 9/18/74, Dijon, France.

"*Blue Moon*": 9/7/69, Family Dog, San Francisco (the only one; not very memorable though).

"*Born Cross-Eyed*": 2/14/68, Carousel Ballroom.

"*Box of Rain*": 11/19/72, Houston (Phil's voice is so perfect, they could have put this one on an album. At one point it sounds like the band is *marching* triumphantly through this song).

"*Brokedown Palace*": 8/30/70, *Calibration* TV show (features truly spectacular three-part harmonies, perhaps the Dead's best ever in front of an audience; get the videotape of this performance as well); 9/28/72, Stanley Theater, N.J.; 12/15/71, Ann Arbor, Mich.; 9/18/70, Fillmore East (followed "Cryptical Envelopment," which means the words went "And you know he had to die" > "fare you well my honey").

"*Brown-Eyed Women*": 7/18/72, Roosevelt Stadium, N.J.; 12/5/71, Felt Forum, N.Y.; 3/26/73, Baltimore.

"*Candyman*": 8/30/70, *Calibration* TV show; 10/23/70, Georgetown University, Washington, D.C.

"*Casey Jones*": 11/7/71, Harding Theater, San Francisco; 4/11/72, Newcastle, England; 8/27/72, Oregon Country Fairgrounds, Veneta, Oreg.; 1/16/70, Springer's Ballroom, Portland, Oreg.; 9/6/69, Family Dog, San Francisco; 7/11/69, Flushing Meadows Park, Queens, N.Y.; 8/1/73, Jersey City, N.J.

"*Caution*": 2/14/70, Fillmore East (The Dead take no prisoners as this version explodes out of a perfect "Mason's Children" and melts down into one of the most hauntingly beautiful "Feedback" explorations of their career); 2/14/68, Carousel Ballroom, San Francisco; 5/11/72, Rotterdam, Holland; 4/14/72, Tivoli Gardens (sandwiched inside a very psychedelic "Good Lovin'"), 11/8/68, Fillmore (amazing "Feedback"), 4/8/72, Wembley, England (Garcia plays slide guitar); 11/8/69, Fillmore West.

"*China Cat Sunflower*" (without "I Know You Rider"): 2/3/68, Portland, Oreg.; 6/5/69, Fillmore West.

"*China Cat Sunflower*" > "*I Know You Rider*": 8/27/72, Oregon Country Fairgrounds (It is during this song that the boys find themselves beginning to "peak" on that special sunny summer day); 11/19/72, Houston; the *Europe '72* version; 7/31/73, Roosevelt Stadium, N.J.; 2/28/73, Salt Lake City, Utah (features a rip-roarin' "Feelin' Groovy Jam"), 6/26/74, Providence, R.I.; 5/17/74, Vancouver, B.C.

"*China Doll*": 6/18/74, Louisville, Ky.

"*Chinatown Shuffle*": 5/16/72, Radio Luxembourg; 12/31/71, Winterland, San Francisco.

"*Clementine*": 1/26/69, Avalon Ballroom, San Francisco; 2/2/68, Portland, Oreg.

"*Cold Jordan*": 5/15/70, Fillmore East; 5/2/70, Binghamton, N.Y.

"*Cold Rain and Snow*": 6/7/69, Fillmore West; 3/25/66, Trouper's Hall, La. (old, fast, weird); 3/18/67, Winterland; 11/7/70, Capitol Theater, Port Chester, N.Y.

"*Comes a Time*": 10/19/71, Minneapolis (with extra verses); 12/5/71, Felt Forum, N.Y.; 7/26/72, Portland, Oreg.

"*Cosmic Charlie*": 3/1/69, Fillmore West (screaming guitars and an almost manic tone in their falsetto voices make this version the one to beat); 5/2/70, Harpur College, Binghamton, N.Y. (the singers have a triumphant tone in their voices); 5/15/70, Fillmore East.

"*Cream Puff War*": 10/7/66, Winterland, San Francisco (goes on for what seems like forever); 11/19/66, Fillmore, 3/18/67, Winterland.

"*Cryptical Envelopment*": 2/13/70, Fillmore East (absolute perfection! The reprise is apocalyptic); 5/2/70, Harpur College, Binghamton, N.Y.; 3/1/69, Fillmore West.

*"Cumberland Blues":* 11/19/72, Houston; 9/27/72, Stanley Theater (out of "Dark Star"—this version is *extremely* fast); the *Europe '72* version; 4/8/71, Boston; 6/30/74, Springfield, Mass.; 5/2/70, Harpur College (acoustic); 2/24/74, Winterland.

*"Dancin' in the Streets":* 5/2/70, Harpur College, Binghamton, N.Y. (an all-time classic, the favorite of many); 4/12/70, Fillmore West (listen carefully: the jam, which includes a full "Feelin' Groovy Jam," is just as inspired as the one from Harpur!); 2/14/70, Fillmore East (beautiful set opener, nice vocals); 5/6/70, MIT, Cambridge, Mass.; 9/18/70, Fillmore East (long and hot, even with a big tape glitch).

*"Dark Star":* 8/27/72, Old Renaissance Fairgrounds, Veneta, Oreg. (may very well be the most *serious*—or at least the most *out there*—psychedelic space exploration by any band ever. It's downright apocalyptic and it features a hair-raising Phil bass solo. Do not pass go without a copy of this tape); 2/13/70, Fillmore East (this is most folks' favorite, and the "Feelin' Groovy Jam" contained within is one of the most *heavenly* melodies ever played by the Dead); 2/27/69, Fillmore West (the *Live Dead* version); 9/27/72, Stanley Theater (it goes into "Cumberland Blues"!); 4/8/72, Empire Pool, England (next to 2/13/70 this version has some of the prettiest instrumental melodies ever played during "Dark Star"); 12/6/73, Cleveland (breathtaking harmonics and "Feedback" by Phil); 4/14/72, Tivoli Garden (completely *manic*—features an aggressive "Feelin' Groovy Jam"); 7/18/72, Roosevelt Stadium (Jerry plays as though he's possessed); 5/23/72, Lyceum, London, England; 5/15/70, Fillmore East (another very pretty "Feelin' Groovy Jam"); 9/10/74, London (a funky "Dark Star" > "Morning Dew"); 9/24/72, Waterbury, Conn.; 4/22/69, the Ark, Boston, 9/17/70, Fillmore East.

*"Darkness Jam":* 9/19/70, Fillmore East; 5/7/70, MIT.

*"Deal":* 7/2/71, Fillmore West; 8/6/71, Hollywood Palladium; 6/16/74, Des Moines, Iowa (many feel this song did not mature until many years later).

*"Death Don't Have No Mercy":* 5/24/69, West Hollywood, Fla.; 2/22/69, Dream Bowl, Vallejo, Calif.

*"Deep Elem Blues":* 10/10/70, Queens College, N.Y. (they actually jam on it).

*"Dire Wolf":* 11/8/69, Fillmore Auditorium; 6/27/69, Santa Rosa, Calif. (Bobby sings while Jerry plays the pedal steel).

*"Doin' That Rag":* 6/7/69, Fillmore West; ?/?/69, Action House, N.Y. (Many have this listed as 9/28/69, Café a Go-Go. This version goes into "The Seven"); 2/28/69, Fillmore West; 4/21/69, Boston Tea Party; 4/26/69, Electric Theater, Chicago.

*"Don't Ease Me In":* 11/19/72, Houston (a truly Texan rendition with different lyrics); 5/2/70, Binghamton, N.Y.

*"Dupree's Diamond Blues":* 6/7/69, Fillmore West; 7/11/69, Flushing Meadows Park, Queens, N.Y.

*"Early Morning Rain":* 1/7/66, Matrix Coffeehouse, San Francisco.

*"Easy Wind":* 9/20/70, Fillmore East (The hands-down winner, this incendiary version features some of Bobby's all-time best lead guitar work); 12/26/70, El Monte Legion Stadium, Calif.; 2/27/70, Family Dog; 10/24/69, Winterland.

*"El Paso":* 8/27/72, Old Renaissance Fairgrounds (out of an apocalyptic "Dark Star" meltdown jam—a perfect segue); 8/1/73, Roosevelt Stadium, N.J. (another out-of-"Dark Star" beauty); 12/15/71, Ann Arbor, Mich., 6/18/74, Louisville, Ky.

*"The Eleven":* 2/27/69, Fillmore West (the version from *Live Dead*); 2/28/69, Fillmore West; 6/14/69, Monterey, Calif.

*"Empty Pages":* 8/26/71, Gaelic Park, the Bronx, N.Y.

*"Eyes of the World":* 6/18/74, Louisville (the Dead at their jazziest); 6/16/74, Des Moines, Iowa; 12/18/73, Tampa, Fla.; 6/9 and 6/10/73, RFK Stadium, Washington, D.C.; 4/2/73, Boston Garden; 3/28/73, Springfield, Mass.; 6/22/74, Miami; 7/19/74, Fresno, Calif. (out of a killer "Spanish Jam"); 9/11/74, London (perhaps the spaciest), 8/6/74, Jersey City, N.J.; 6/26/74, Providence, R.I.; 10/25/73, Madison, Wisc., 10/19/74, Winterland.

*"Feelin' Groovy Jam":* 2/13/70, Fillmore East; 5/15/70, Fillmore East; 4/12/70, Fillmore West (inside "Dancin' in the Streets"); 4/29/72, Hamburg, Germany; 4/14/72, Copenhagen, Denmark (the fastest).

*"Friend of the Devil":* 9/23/72, Waterbury, Conn. (electric); 5/2/70, Harpur College, Binghamton, N.Y. (acoustic).

*"The Golden Road (to Unlimited Devotion)":* 5/5/67, Fillmore Auditorium.

*"Good Mornin', Li'l Schoolgirl":* 7/10/70, Fillmore East (good show opener; it's long, and most excellent-quality audience tapes of this feature a sexy, catlike female meowing in the background!); 4/9/70, Fillmore West.

*"Good Lovin'":* 4/26/71, Fillmore East (In Phil we trust! A "Saint Stephen" jam, hyper drum solo, and pounding bass beat make this a favorite of many); 4/17/71, Princeton, N.J. (certainly one of the longest,

funniest, most inspired Pigpen raps ever!); 4/11/72, Newcastle, England (enormous jam and rap); 5/2/70, Harpur College, Binghamton, N.Y.; 11/6/70, Capitol Theater, Port Chester, N.Y.; 4/14/72, Tivoli Garden, Copenhagen; 10/24/70, St. Louis (each band member takes a solo).

*"Greatest Story Ever Told"*: 9/28/72, Stanley Theater, Jersey City, N.J. (hot "Saint Stephen" jam, wailing Donna, and crisp Garcia licks); 8/27/72, Old Renaissance Fairgrounds (this hot set-closer is a close second); 5/20/73, Santa Barbara, Calif. (another "Saint Stephen" jam! Decent audience tapes of this show are out there, but you may have to look hard); 6/16/74, Des Moines, Iowa.

*"Green, Green Grass of Home"*: 6/21/69, Fillmore East (opens the show); 6/27/69, Santa Rosa, Calif. (slipped into an aborted "The Eleven").

*"Hard to Handle"*: 4/29/71, Fillmore East (features one of the Dead's all-time tightest rock 'n' roll climaxes); 8/6/71, Hollywood Bowl (Jerry supposedly fell down on his knees at the peak of this version), 4/24/71, Duke University; 4/28/71, Fillmore East; 12/28/69, Miami.

*"He Was a Friend of Mine"*: 5/24/69, Miami (out of "Doin' That Rag" and into "China Cat").

*"Help Me Rhonda"*: 4/27/71, Fillmore East (with the Beach Boys—the only one).

*"Here Comes Sunshine"*: 12/19/73, Tampa, Fla.; 2/15/73, Madison, Wisc.; 6/22/73, Vancouver, B.C.; 2/17/73, St. Paul, Minn. (into "China Cat" > "Rider"); 4/2/73, Boston (into "Space" > "Bobby McGee"); 6/10/73, Washington, D.C.

*"He's Gone"*: 6/22/73, Vancouver, B.C.; 5/13/73, Des Moines, Iowa; 12/2/73, Boston.

*"Hey Bo Diddley"*: 5/23/72, Lyceum Theater, London; 7/16/72, Dillon Stadium, Hartford, Conn. (with the Allman Brothers); 3/25/72, Academy of Music, N.Y. (with Bo Diddley himself).

*"Hey Jude"*: 2/11/69, Fillmore East (off-key, but one of only two versions in circulation).

*"Hey Little One"*: 3/25/66, Trouper's Hall, Los Angeles (better than Glen Campbell ever sang it).

*"Hideaway"*: 11/7/71, Harding Theater, San Francisco (the one and only—but picture-perfect).

*"High Heeled Sneakers"*: 11/19/66, Fillmore Auditorium.

*"High Time"*: 2/14/70, Fillmore East (straight out of "I Know You Rider").

*"I Hear a Voice a Callin'"*: 5/15/70, Fillmore East.

*"I Know You Rider"* (separate from "China Cat"): 5/15/70, Fillmore East; 3/31/73, Buffalo, N.Y.; 5/2/70, Binghamton, N.Y. (acoustic); 7/3/66, Fillmore.

*"I'm a Hog for You Baby"*: 3/25/66, Trouper's Hall, Los Angeles.

*"In the Pines"*: 7/15/66, Fillmore.

*"It Hurts Me Too"*: 5/18/72, Munich, West Germany; 4/26/71, Fillmore East (with Duane Allman).

*"It Takes a Lot to Laugh, It Takes a Train to Cry"*: 6/10/73, RFK Stadium (with the Allman Brothers).

*"It's All Over Now, Baby Blue"*: see "Baby Blue."

*"It's a Man's World"*: 5/2/70, Harpur College, Binghamton, N.Y. (gnarly background vocals and a bluesy bass line make this one the classic); 4/9/70, Fillmore West (first one and hot).

*"Jack Straw"*: The *Europe '72* album version; 11/19/72, Houston.

*Jam*: By "jam" we mean those melodic and often unnameable musical explorations that do not fall within the band's regularly identifiable repertoire:

7/27/73, Watkins Glen, N.Y.: Watkins Glen "soundcheck jam." The band pulls off a phenomenal twenty-minute-long jam that starts up out of silence and, after a tremendous series of melodic explorations, including a "Feelin' Groovy Jam," segues into "Wharf Rat."
4/29/71, Fillmore East: between "Alligator" and "Goin' Down the Road" the boys play a tasty nugget that more than just hints at "Saint Stephen."
?/?/69, Action House, Brooklyn, N.Y.: "The Seven" jam. Many have this labeled as 9/29/69—Cafe à Go-Go. This shockingly fast jam is sandwiched between "Doin' That Rag" and "Good Lovin'." "The Seven" is a jam that is also found on several Mickey Hart and the Hartbeats tapes.
10 and 11/68, Matrix, San Francisco: Hartbeats jams. All of these shows featuring Garcia, Hart, Lesh, Jack Casady, and friends feature fascinating, extended jams. We particularly recommend those shows with Jack Casady on bass.
4/2/73, Boston: out of "Here Comes Sunshine."
10/16/74, Winterland, San Francisco: out of "Seastones."

*"Johnny B. Goode"*: 11/7/71, Harding Theater, San Francisco; 3/24/73, Philadelphia; 11/17/72, Wichita, Kans.; 7/2/71, Fillmore West; 9/7/69 (unusual because Jerry sings).

*"King Bee"*: 2/21/71, Capitol Theater, Port Chester, N.Y.; 11/19/66, Fillmore Auditorium, San Francisco, (comes out of "Smokestack Lightning"); 11/23/70, Anderson Theater, N.Y.

# Recommended Listening

*"Let It Rock"*: 6/23/74, Miami (the one and only time Jerry did this with the Dead—but it's textbook perfect).

*"Let Me Sing Your Blues Away"*: 9/11/73, College of William and Mary, Williamsburg, Va.; 9/15/73, Providence, R.I.

*"Lindy"*: 9/16/66, Avalon Ballroom, San Francisco.

*"Long Black Limousine"*: 12/26/69, Dallas, Tex. (acoustic).

*"Loose Lucy"*: 2/15/73, Madison, Wis.; 4/2/73, Boston; 6/9/73, RFK Stadium, Washington, D.C. (features a long blues jam tacked on due to blown verses).

*"Louie, Louie"*: 9/7/69, Family Dog, San Francisco (the only pre-'75 version—not well-played though).

*"Main Ten Jam"*: 11/8/70, Capitol Theater, Port Chester, N.Y. (sandwiched in between "Dark Star" and "Dancin' in the Streets").

*"Mason's Children"*: 2/14/70, Fillmore East (out of "Not Fade Away" and into "Caution"); 12/28/69, Miami (raw energy jamming goes on and on); 2/2/70, St. Louis; 12/29/69, Boston (à la "Viola Lee Blues").

*"Master's Bouquet"*: 12/26/69, Dallas, Tex.

*"Me and Bobby McGee"*: 9/28/72, Stanley Theater, N.J. (out of and then back into "The Other One"); 5/26/72, Lyceum, England (out of and then back into "The Other One"); 4/2/73, Boston (out of "Here Comes Sunshine" > "Space"); 11/14/72, Oklahoma City, Okla.

*"Me and My Uncle"*: 11/7/71, Harding Theater (sandwiched inside of "The Other One"); 12/31/71, Winterland, San Francisco (also sandwiched inside of "The Other One"); 6/14/69, Monterey, Calif.; 12/1/71, Boston (also sandwiched inside of "The Other One"); 10/24/70, St. Louis.

*"Mexicali Blues"*: 12/31/72, Winterland; 8/27/72, Old Renaissance Fairgrounds (as with the version of "Bertha" played at this show, the direct glare of the sun mistuned Garcia's guitar, yet the man is so brimming with energy that this frighteningly fast version is transcendent); 12/4/71, Felt Forum, N.Y. (sandwiched inside "The Other One").

*"Midnight Hour"*: 9/3/67, Dance Hall, Rio Nido, Calif.—thirty minutes long! (Many have this incorrectly listed as Russian River Festival '68); 4/29/71, Fillmore East (a classic, despite one single off-note by Garcia; everyone loves this one); 2/14/68, Carousel Ballroom, San Francisco; 6/17/67, Winterland (*very* jumpy!).

*"Mindbender"* (*"Confusion's Prince"*): 11/3/65, Warlocks demo recording, Golden State Studios, San Francisco; 11/29/66, Matrix, San Francisco.

*"Mind Left Body Jam"*: 6/28/74, Boston; 5/12/74, Reno, Nev.

*"Money Money"*: 5/19/74, Portland, Oreg. (one of only three versions).

*"Monkey and the Engineer"*: 2/13/70, Fillmore East (acoustic); 12/31/70, Winterland, San Francisco (electric).

*"Morning Dew"*: 4/28/71, Fillmore East (crisp and tight enough to be put on CD); 5/23/72 and 5/26/72, Lyceum, London, England; 10/13/68, Avalon Ballroom, San Francisco (KSAN broadcast); 11/10/73, Winterland, San Francisco; 9/21/72, Philadelphia; 9/10/74, London, England; 11/7/69, the New Old Fillmore, San Francisco, Calif.; 6/18/74, Louisville, Ky.; 1/14/67, Human Be-In, San Francisco; 5/6/70, MIT, Cambridge, Mass.

*"Mountains of the Moon"*: 7/10/69, *Playboy After Dark* TV show; 6/7/69, Monterey, Calif.; 2/22/69, Dream Bowl, Vallejo, Calif.

*"Mr. Charlie"*: 5/4/72, Paris, France; 8/6/71, Hollywood Palladium, Los Angeles.

*"My Babe"*: 11/8/70, Capitol Theater, Port Chester, N.Y. (the only version).

*"Mystery Train"*: 11/8/70, Capitol Theater, Port Chester, N.Y. (the only version).

*"Next Time You See Me"*: 5/6/70, MIT, free outdoor concert; 12/5/71, Felt Forum, N.Y.

*"New Minglewood Blues"*: 5/15/70, Fillmore East (This early show encore features Bobby *screaming* his lungs out); 11/9/70, Action House, N.Y.

*"New Potato Caboose"*: 8/24/68, Shrine Auditorium, Los Angeles (simply incredible—a must-have piece of Dead music); 10/3/68, Avalon Ballroom, San Francisco; 3/1/69, Fillmore West; 2/14/68, Carousel Ballroom, San Francisco.

*"New Orleans"*: 11/8/70, Capitol Theater, Port Chester, N.Y. (the only version and it's great).

*"New Speedway Boogie"*: 9/20/70, Fillmore East (acoustic); 6/12/70, Honolulu; 7/16/70—San Rafael, Calif.

*"Nobody's Fault but Mine"*: 9/24/73, Pittsburgh.

*"Not Fade Away"* (without "Goin' Down the Road Feelin' Bad"): 2/14/70, Fillmore East (out of "Me and My Uncle" and into "Mason's Children." So fast and so electric, it may leave you breathless); 2/11/70—Fillmore East.

*"Not Fade Away" > "Goin' Down the Road" > "Not Fade Away"*: 11/7/71, Harding Theater, San Francisco (another absolutely must-have piece for every collection. Rock music simply doesn't get any hotter than this); 5/3/72, Olympia Theater, Paris; 10/31/71, Ohio Theatre (At one point Jerry plays faster on this version than on

any other, although the band, as a whole, shines brighter on 11/7/71 and 5/3/72); 6/10/73, RFK Stadium, Washington, D.C. (with Dicky Betts and at least one drummer from the Allmans—this version is simultaneously summertime hot *and* mellow); 9/28/72, Stanley Theatre, Jersey City, N.J.

*"Okie from Muskogee":* 4/27/71, Fillmore East (with the Beach Boys—the only one).

*"One Kind Favor":* 12/1/66, Matrix, San Francisco.

*"One More Saturday Night":* 11/7/71, Harding Theater, San Francisco (Phil is a monster! Another all-time classic rock 'n' roll masterpiece); 5/3/72, Olympia Theater, Paris; 4/26/72, Frankfurt; 9/26/73, Buffalo, N.Y. (with horns!); 5/7/72, Bickershaw, England; and just about any version from the fall '71 tour!

*"Operator":* 9/18/70, Fillmore East (electric!).

*"The Other One"* (in its various forms): 2/13/70, Fillmore East; 2/28/69, Fillmore West; 5/2/70, Binghamton, N.Y.; 5/26/72, Lyceum; 12/31/72, Winterland; 9/28/72, Stanley Theater, N.J.; 4/11/72, Newcastle, England (features a "Feelin' Groovy Jam"); 2/28/73, Salt Lake City (Phil goes nuts); 1/20/72, Winterland; 9/17/72, Baltimore; 11/17/72, Wichita, Kans. (as heavy as the "Playing in the Band," from the next evening, though it suffers from a brutal cut); 5/7/72, Wigan, England; 10/22/67, Winterland (different lyrics); 11/14/71, Fort Worth, Tex. (sounds like the fall of '79).

*"Peggy Sue":* 9/7/69, Family Dog, San Francisco (the only one, not very memorable though).

*"Playing in the Band":* 8/27/72, Old Renaissance Fairgrounds (This version is simply astounding—one of the most visionary jams ever played by the Dead! Jerry is operating at his all-time peak optimal mechanical facilities level); 11/18/72, Houston, Tex.; 9/10/72, Hollywood, Calif.; 11/19/72, Houston; 12/10/72, Winterland; 9/24/72, Waterbury, Conn.; 9/23/72, Waterbury; 11/18/72, Houston; 7/18/72, Roosevelt Stadium, N.J.; 5/21/74, Seattle (46 minutes long); 6/22/73, Vancouver; 2/15/73, Madison, Wis.; 11/17/72, UCLA; 6/8/74, Oakland Coliseum; 12/2/73, Boston Music Hall (screaming whales—honest); 10/26/72, Cincinnati; 6/16/74, Des Moines, Iowa; 9/11/74, Alexandra Palace, London.

*"Promised Land":* 8/27/72, Old Renaissance Fairgrounds; 9/28/72, Stanley Theater, N.J.; 2/15/73, Madison, Wis.

*"Ramble On Rose":* 4/11/72, Newcastle, England; 7/31/74, Hartford; 9/28/72, Stanley Theater, N.J.; 12/10/72, Winterland, San Francisco.

*"Riot in Cellblock #9":* 4/27/71, Fillmore East (with the Beach Boys—the only one).

*"Ripple":* 9/20/70, Fillmore East (acoustic); 2/21/71, Capitol Theater, Port Chester, N.Y.; 2/?/70, Pacific Heights Recording Studio, San Francisco.

*"Run, Rudolph, Run":* 12/15/71, Ann Arbor, Mich.; 12/10/71, St. Louis.

*"Rockin' Pneumonia":* 5/23/72, Lyceum, England.

*"Row Jimmy":* 9/18/74, Dijon, France; 9/11/74, Alexandra Palace, London.

*"Saint Stephen":* 2/28/69, Fillmore West; the *Live Dead* version; 6/24/70, Capitol Theater, Port Chester, N.Y.; 10/24/70, Kiel Auditorium, St. Louis; 4/28/71, Fillmore East (even the vocal mistake is great); 4/5/69, Avalon Ballroom, San Francisco.

*"Scarlet Begonias":* 6/16/74, Des Moines, Iowa; 9/18/74, Dijon, France; 7/31/74, Hartford, Conn.; 6/28/74, Boston; 8/6/74, Jersey City, N.J. (tucked inside "Playing in the Band").

*"Searchin'":* 11/8/70, Capitol Theater, Port Chester, N.Y.

*"Seasons":* 12/31/69, Boston Tea Party.

*"Seastones":* 8/6/74, Jersey City, N.J.; 10/16/74, Winterland.

*"Second That Emotion":* 4/29/71, Fillmore East (this version could be put on an album as is); 4/18/71, Cortland, N.Y.

*"See That My Grave Is Kept Clean":* see "One Kind Favor."

*"Ship of Fools":* 6/16/74, Des Moines, Iowa (Keith Godchaux launches this version onto the high seas of mythos with mystical Fender Rhodes perfection).

*"Sing Me Back Home":* 8/27/72, Old Renaissance Fairgrounds (could this be the most spiritual, bittersweet, emotional moment in their entire career? An absolutely must-have item); 7/2/71, Fillmore West.

*"Sittin' on Top of the World":* 6/7/69, Fillmore West; 12/10/71, St. Louis; 5/23/72, Lyceum, London; 12/5/71, Felt Forum, N.Y. (out of and then back into "Dark Star").

*"Slewfoot":* 6/28/69, Santa Rosa (Jerry on pedal steel); 6/21/69, Fillmore East; 7/12/69, Flushing, Queens, N.Y.

*"Smokestack Lightning":* 2/13/70, Fillmore East (this is the version featured on *Bear's Choice*); 2/8/70, Fillmore West; 3/3/68, Haight Street free jam; 11/8/67, Shrine Auditorium, Los Angeles.

*"Spanish Jam":* 2/11/70, Fillmore East (which features Duane and Greg Allman and Peter Green—this jam will make the blind see and the lame walk!); 6/23/74, Jai Alai Fronton, Miami; 7/19/74, Fresno, Calif. (out of "Let It Grow" and into "Eyes"); 2/14/68,

Carousel Ballroom, San Francisco; 8/6/74, Jersey City, N.J. (Phil takes charge).

*"Stealin' "*: 3/25/66, Trouper's Hall, Los Angeles.

*"Stella Blue"*: 11/19/72, Houston; 12/6/73, Cleveland.

*"Sugar Magnolia"*: 8/27/72, Old Renaissance Fairgrounds; 12/10/72, Winterland; 11/17/72, Wichita, Kans.; 8/19/70, Fillmore West; 9/26/73, Buffalo, N.Y. (not tight, but unique because of the horn section sitting in).

*"Swing Low, Sweet Chariot"*: 8/5/70, San Diego, Calif.; 7/30/70, Matrix, San Francisco.

*"Tennessee Jed"*: 7/18/72, Roosevelt Stadium, Jersey City, N.J. (perhaps the twangiest version of all time).

*"That'll Be the Day"*: 9/7/69, Family Dog, San Francisco (the only one—not memorable though).

*"That's Alright Mama"*: 6/10/73, RFK Stadium (with the Allman Brothers and Merl Saunders).

*"The Race Is On"*: 6/16/74, Des Moines, Iowa; 9/18/74, Dijon, France; 5/26/73, Kezar, San Francisco.

*"The Same Thing"*: 3/18/67, Winterland, San Francisco; 12/31/71, Winterland.

*"They Love Each Other"*: 2/9/73, Stanford U., Palo Alto, Calif.; 2/24/74, Winterland; 10/21/73, Omaha, Nebr.; 6/26/73, Seattle.

*"Till the Morning Comes"*: 10/4/70, Winterland.

*"To Lay Me Down"*: 7/31/74, Hartford.

*"Tomorrow Is Forever"*: 11/19/72, Houston (a beautifully bittersweet duet by Jerry and Donna); 10/19/74, Winterland.

*"Truckin' "*: 4/11/72, Newcastle, England; 12/31/72, Winterland; 7/18/72, Roosevelt Stadium, N.J.; 5/26/72 London, England; 12/10/71, St. Louis; 6/16/74, Des Moines, Iowa (funky, with a kazoo even!); 10/26/71, Rochester, N.Y.

*"Turn On Your Lovelight"*: This is another tough one, there are so many. 1/26/69, Avalon Ballroom (the *Live Dead* album version); 6/7/69, Fillmore West, with Janis Joplin; 6/14/69, Monterey (opens and closes the show!); 10/31/69, San Jose, Calif.; 2/11/70, Fillmore East (featuring Duane and Greg Allman and Peter Green); 2/1/70, New Orleans; 2/13/70, Fillmore East (this unusually slow version is smooth and sweet, like love in the afternoon); 5/7/72, Bickershaw, England (Jerry plays a bluesy slide guitar).

*"Two Souls in Communion"*: 5/23/72, Lyceum, London; 5/26/72, Lyceum, London; 2/28/72, Academy of Music, N.Y.

*"Unbroken Chain"*: ?/?/74, acoustic studio work tape (Phil teaches it to the band while playing it on an acoustic guitar).

*"Uncle John's Band"*: 11/20/70, Anderson Theater, N.Y. (beautiful harmonica intro); 9/18/74, Dijon, France; 11/18/72, Houston; 11/17/72, UCLA; 12/10/72, Winterland; 9/21/72, Philadelphia.

*"U.S. Blues"*: 6/28/74, Boston; 6/16/74, Des Moines, Iowa; 6/23/74, Jai Alai Fronton, Miami (out of a fantastic "Spanish Jam").

*"Viola Lee Blues"*: 5/2/70, Harpur College, Binghamton, N.Y. (BLISTERING!! Garcia has his amp turned all the way up); 3/3/68, Haight Street free jam; 7/9/70, Fillmore East; 12/28/70, El Monte, Calif.; 4/26/69—Electric Theater, Chicago.

*"Wake Up, Little Susie"*: 2/13/70, Fillmore East.

*"We Bid You Goodnight"*: 2/13/70, Fillmore East (Jerry sings all the verses to cap off this legendary show); 5/2/70, Binghamton, N.Y.

*"Weather Report Suite"*: 7/19/74, Fresno, Calif. (into an unbelievable "Spanish Jam"); 6/18/74, Louisville, Ky. (an album-perfect version; Bobby and Donna's voices are beautiful throughout); 3/28/73, Springfield, Mass.; 12/18/73, Tampa, Fla.; 6/28/74, Boston; 7/31/74, Hartford, Conn.

*"Wharf Rat"*: 9/28/72, Stanley Theater, N.J.; 9/9/74, London; 9/23/72, Waterbury, Conn.; 12/2/73, Boston, Mass.; 11/17/71, Albuquerque, New Mex.; 6/16/74, Des Moines, Iowa; 6/8/74, Oakland, Calif. (tucked inside "Playing in the Band"); 9/11/74, Alexandra Palace, London (great Phil Lesh lines).

*"What's Become of the Baby"*: 4/26/69, Chicago (the only one and what a beauty. Actually, Bear played a studio version of this song while the Dead layered live "Feedback" over it).

*"Who Do You Love"*: 4/14/72, Tivoli Gardens, Copenhagen ("Good Lovin'" > "Caution" > "Who Do You Love" > "Caution" > "Good Lovin'"—need we say more?); 5/11/72, Rotterdam, The Netherlands.

*"You Ain't Woman Enough"*: 2/15/73, Madison, Wisc., 10/21/73, Omaha, Nebr.

*"You Don't Have to Ask"*: 3/25/66, Trouper's Hall, Los Angeles.

*"You See a Broken Heart"*: 3/12/66, Danish Center, Los Angeles.

*"You Win Again"*: 12/31/71, Winterland; 12/15/71, Ann Arbor, Mich.

# 9

# Video and Film Guide, 1959–1974

Unlike the vast selection of Grateful Dead audiotape from before 1975, very little film and video imagery of the band is in circulation from that period. As you'll read in this chapter's accompanying interview with film/video researcher Jonathan Platt, there is still some very desirable footage stashed away in film/video vaults around the globe, but from pre-1975 even that adds up to slim pickin's. Still, a good deal of what does circulate is thoroughly fascinating and well worth tracking down. Unfortunately, VHS video (the format used by most collectors until a few years ago when Hi-8mm and Beta tape came out) doesn't copy well, and much of the older video that's been passed down over the years through multiple generations is usually pretty horrible looking. However, most serious collectors have been rerecording the more classic footage mentioned here on the improved tape formats as it is rebroadcast or recirculated from lower-generation sources. If you don't like what you find, keep searching for better quality. Almost everything we've listed here has eventually come around in better condition.

The earliest known footage, which comes from **Ken Kesey's Acid Test at Muir Beach** on **12/18/65**, offers an amazing glimpse of the early Grateful Dead. The soundtrack (also from that period) is overdubbed and doesn't correspond with what one sees, but the visuals offer a fantastic view of the band in its infancy. There's even a snippet of Garcia sweeping up the floor after the gig.

**Be-In,** a twenty-minute-long 16mm film shot and edited by light show veteran Jerry Abrams of the Heavy Water Light Show, briefly offers a powerful but fleeting glimpse of the Dead playing at the Human Be-In on **1/14/67** at the Polo Grounds in San Francisco. Don't get your hopes up, for while *Be-In* is a well-done experimental film, the Dead fly by at light speed in staccato pixilation with no matching soundtrack. Still, it's a priceless, mythic image frozen in time.

Another real tease is an even smaller snippet of the Dead playing on **6/18/67** at the **Monterey International Pop Festival,** complete with a light show pulsating behind them. This three-second clip was included in a retrospective of the festival that was shown years later on TV (the source is unknown). This footage is followed by several seconds of an interview with a much older Garcia beginning to explain what it was like to play at the festival. On the copies that circulate widely, Garcia is cut off in midsentence.

There are brief clips of the Dead performing in Lindley Meadow in **Golden Gate Park** on **8/28/67**. This raw footage, which comes from KRON's news cameraman on the scene at Hell's Angel Chocolate George's funeral/wake, shows just a portion of the Dead performing "Viola Lee Blues."

Another nugget from KRON's vault shows the Dead performing at the **Pan Handle** just East of **Golden Gate Park** (at Ashbury and Fulton) sometime in **1967**. This footage is also very brief, unedited news film bytes, but it gives an incredible view of the Dead playing the Pan Handle on a Sunday afternoon as hippies dance in utter delight while straight people walk by as though nothing is going on. The Dead perform "Yonders Wall," "King Bee," and several other tunes unidentifiable due to the briefness of the clips.

Some of the best-known early footage of the Dead is from the **1967** film *Hippie Temptation*. This "acid scare" documentary shows the Dead in their house at 710 Ashbury, including a priceless moment of Jerry practicing guitar in his room. Bob, Phil, Jerry, Bobby, and their managers, Danny Rifkin and Rock Skully, are interviewed about their feelings about LSD. A clip of the Dead playing "Dancin' in the Streets" in Golden Gate Park is also shown. In 1997 this film was re-aired on VH1.

*Journey in Time* is another anti-drug film that features a thirty-second clip of Jerry, Phil, and Danny Rifkin smoking pot at 710 Ashbury in **1967**.

Yet another drug-related snippet is the footage from the Dead's **marijuana arrest press conference** on 10/3/67. This ten-minute series of unedited bites comes from the KRON vault. All of the Grateful Dead are present, along with their managers Rifkin and Scully and their lawyer, answering questions with great humor.

The Robert Nelson film, *The Grateful Dead,* a seven-minute-long experimental film done in **1967**, gives a somewhat humorous look at the Dead as polarized, chopped up, looped, strobed images of each band member are edited together to create a quasi-psychedelic dream. At one point, there is a amusing clip of the Dead in a canoe à la "Alligator."

A four-minute-long silent color clip, circa **1967**, shows members of the Grateful Dead, the Jefferson Airplane, Quicksilver Messenger Service, and other Bay Area musicians walking from 710 Ashbury to Golden Gate Park for a **group photo session** (the photo appeared in *Rolling Stone* magazine).

*Petulia,* a strange feature film released in **1968** starring George C. Scott and Julie Christie, shows the Dead playing a minute of "Viola Lee Blues" in a trippy, staged concert setting complete with liquid light show. Bobby and Jerry each have insignificant one-line speaking roles in the film.

A segment from the CBS show *West 57th Street* profiling Bill Graham features a ten-second clip of the Dead walking down to the stage to perform at the Fillmore East on 2/11 or 12/69.

The Dead are featured in a black-and-white clip from the film *Columbia Revolt* filmed on 5/3/68. They perform "Cold Rain and Snow" and "Sittin' on Top of the World" at the Loew Library plaza at Columbia University.

One of the great classics is the episode of *Playboy After Dark* broadcast on 7/10/69. Hugh Hefner interviews Garcia, who is dressed in a delightfully gaudy Mexican poncho. Garcia then plays "Mountains of the Moon" on acoustic guitar with T.C. on organ and Bobby on acoustic. Jerry, who looks high as a kite, is absolutely *beaming*. Jerry and Bobby quickly switch to electric guitar for a raw, high-powered reading of "Saint Stephen" (which cuts, rumor has it, just as a Playboy bunny—who drank some of the punch that the Dead supposedly spiked—takes her top off).

Twenty-two minutes of full color outtakes from the film *Woodstock* exist of the Dead performing on 8/16/69 including complete versions of "Mama Tried" and "High Time," a short clip of "Saint Stephen" and the last eight minutes of "Lovelight." Additionally, a few minutes of very cut-up black-and-white footage (from a camera in the audience) with time code burned into it shows the Dead playing onstage. Fifteen seconds of footage of Jerry jamming on acoustic guitar in the backstage area also circulates. There are also two different clips of miscellaneous festival activities, including footage of the Prankster bus and Jerry and Mickey arriving and hanging out, set to the Dead playing "Lovelight" at Woodstock.

Another much more obscure film of the Dead playing at Woodstock on 8/16/69 is Jud Yalkut's *China Cat Sunflower.* Yalkut, a seminal figure in the expanded cinema movement of the 1960s, filmed the Dead while *shaking* the camera. The result of this technique is that all one sees is beautiful, abstract patterns of red and yellow light dancing across the screen. You'd never know it was the Dead from just looking at it.

In the Rolling Stones classic rock documentary *Gimme Shelter,* shot on 12/6/69 at the Altamont Racetrack, Jerry and Phil are shown reacting to the news that the concert has gotten out of hand. They wisely decide not to perform.

A PBS broadcast of *A Night at the Family Dog,* filmed on 2/4/70, shows the Dead jamming strong on "Hard to Handle" and "China" > "Rider." Jerry also participates in an eight-minute segment of the show's closing jam along with Jorma Kaukonen, Jack Casady, Paul Kantner, Carlos Santana, and the drummers from Santana's band.

A four-minute-long silent clip of the Dead performing on 5/16/70 at Temple Stadium in **Philadelphia** circulates.

Over ninety hours of footage of the Dead from the **June-July 1970 Trans-Continental Pop Festival** tour across Canada was shot. We are told that some of this footage may be released soon as an edited film (see the accompanying interview with Jonathan Platt). A stunning segment of the Dead (with Bobby in a cowboy hat) performing "Don't Ease Me In" in a train yard has appeared as part of a program entitled "**Cinerock: Loud Film, Rare Music**" at New York's Lincoln Center in 1996. Expect to see more of this footage in the future.

The **8/30/70** episode of the *Calibration* music TV show, broadcast by KQED in the Bay Area, features the Dead playing tight readings of vintage *Workingman's Dead* material as they are bathed in the drippy effects of the Heavy Water Light Show. This is very tasty footage, both visually and musically. Highlights include a memorable image of Pigpen singing "Easy Wind" as his head appears in a sea of swirling light show imagery. Also notable is the "Brokedown Palace," which offers some of the best vocal harmonies the Dead ever sang.

The **1970** PBS show *Go Ride the Music* contains several short cuts of Garcia commenting on the San Francisco music scene.

On the 4/19/97 episode of VH1's show *Album Classics* Phil Lesh, Bob Weir, Mickey Hart, sound engineer Steven Barncard, and Grateful Dead historian Dennis McNally reflect on the making of *Anthem of the Sun, American Beauty,* and *Workingman's Dead.* This is one of the better documentaries ever done on the Dead. There's plenty of old footage of Jerry, Pigpen, and Robert Hunter way back in the early 1960s as well as never-before-seen footage of the Dead in the studio making these albums. This hour-long show was produced by the BBC (though the version of this show that played in England is fifteen minutes longer). This documentary contains a priceless scene in which Phil Lesh is talking about playing "Box of Rain" for his dying father in the hospital in 1970 while Steven Barncard plays the master tape of this song from *American Beauty.* As Phil reflects, Barncard "solos" Phil's voice. Stunning. A must-get tape.

*The Last Days of the Fillmore,* a film about the closing of Bill Graham's legendary venue, features complete versions of the Dead performing "Casey Jones" and "Johnny B. Goode" on **7/2/71**. There is an amusing segment filmed backstage in which Jerry and Bobby kid around with Bill Graham. Jerry is also shown sound-checking on pedal steel guitar and rehearsing with the New Riders.

Danish TV's *TV from the Tivoli* captures the Dead on **4/17/72** at Tivoli Gardens in Copenhagen, Denmark, playing "Hurt Me Too," "Ramble On Rose," "El Paso," "Big Railroad Blues" (complete with the Dead donning Bozo and Bollo clown masks), "Truckin'," "Me and Bobby McGee," "Chinatown Shuffle," "China Cat" > "Rider," "Jack Straw," "He's Gone," "Lied and Cheated," "Saturday Night," and a portion of "Black-Throated Wind." This is a remarkable eighty-minute color broadcast of the band steamrolling through their classic 1972 repertoire. The clown mask scene is priceless. More of this concert exists in the Danish television station's vaults.

Only one song, "One More Saturday Night," has circulated from the Dead's performance on **4/21/72** on *The Beat Club* TV show in Bremen, West Germany. This one cut has been broadcast many different times, including as part of a Casey Kasem compilation tape and on MTV.

Almost sixty minutes of Super-8 black-and-white **home movies,** purportedly from the **1972** tour of Europe, circulate. This footage is very haphazard in its compilation. You really have to want to watch this to stick with it all the way through to the end. When some of this footage appeared in dramatically better quality on the 1997 VH1 documentary on the making of *American Beauty,* it was questioned whether this was really from Europe as the buildings appear to be somewhere in America. It does seem, however, from the clothing and hairstyles of the band, to be definitely from 1972.

One of the most important and certainly most captivating films ever to feature the Grateful Dead is the yet-to-be-released **Sunshine Daydream.** This landmark film was shot at the Old Renaissance Fairgrounds in Veneta, Oregon, on **8/27/72** during the Dead's legendary "Field Trip" concert produced by Ken Kesey and the Merry Prankster family. It is a thoroughly entrancing time capsule that will transport the viewer back to a very, very special time and place: hippie heaven on earth. "Sunshine Daydream" starts off with great Acid Test and "Furthur" Bus Trip footage, jumps to footage of the event setup, and then finally brings us to the stage as the band tears through blistering versions of "Promised Land," "China Cat Sunflower" > "I Know You Rider," "Jack Straw," and "Dark Star" > "El Paso." The "China Cat Sunflower" is both fascinating and awkward in that it features numerous close-ups of the many naked women dancing on that field on that day—obviously an unusual sight in Western culture, even two decades later (though it comes off now as being a bit sexist). The "Jack Straw" and "Dark Star" provide one of the most hypnotic images of the Dead you'll ever see; a tight closeup of Jerry singing is framed by a naked, long-haired hippie, balanced on a pole, undulating in obvious bliss. Very heavy! And even more significant is the "Dark Star," which is not only shown in its entirety but is also the only pre-1978 version known to exist on film (the 4/17/72 "Dark Star," which does not circulate yet, was shot on videotape). Though it is handicapped by some very simple, dated animation (not nearly psychedelic enough for the music being played), the image of Jerry tripping at sunset, seemingly in trance state as he channels deep space music, is so totally mesmerizing, so ethereal, it may leave you stunned. And the editor comes back from the animation sequence just in time to offer a nice closeup of Jerry's fingers as he plays the "Tiger" meltdown jam (a must-see moment for guitar players). Although the Dead refused to allow its release two decades ago (ironically, they only remember how hard it was to keep their instruments in tune under the hot sun that day), there is rumor of it being partially reedited and then finally released. One of the film's main protagionists, Phil De Guerre, recalls that the "Bird Song" from that day (certainly one of the better versions ever performed) was edited but never made it in to the final film due to time considerations.

On **3/16/73** Deadhead Chris Allen filmed Super-8 clips of his trip to **Nassau Coliseum** to see the Dead. These are silent images. There is a short snippet of the band wearing Nudie Suits during the first set, some very vacant second-set hall scenes (no hall dancers, no ponytails, only one Dead shirt), and then a few more moments of the Dead, this time wearing normal clothes again, onstage playing during the second set.

*Hell's Angels Forever,* a movie produced by Jerry Garcia, documents the **9/5/73** Hell's Angels cruise on the S.S. *Bay Belle* as it sails around New York harbor while a wedding and concert take place onboard. The Jerry Garcia Band plays "That's Alright Mama," and Garcia is interviewed about the Hell's Angels. An unreleased studio version of "It Takes a Lot to Laugh, It Takes a Train to Cry" plays over the credits at the end of the film.

Thirty seconds of very poor quality color cartoon animation of an unreleased commercial for the 1974 *Mars Hotel* album circulate. The famous Grateful Dead crow flies around and that's about it.

*The Grateful Dead Movie* is perhaps the most well-known moving imagery of the Dead from before 1975. The *waay* trippy animation by Gary Gutierrez is top notch—no doubt the best part of the film. It's a shame there isn't a lot more of this animation as it captures the psychedelic crazy wisdom of the pre-1975 Grateful Dead perfectly. This movie documents the Dead's final shows of 1974 at Winterland. Featured are live performances of "Goin' Down the Road," "Eyes of the World," "Stella Blue," "He's Gone," "Morning Dew," "Saturday Night," "Truckin'," "Sugar Magnolia," "Playing in the Band," "Casey Jones," and "Johnny B. Goode." There's also plenty of footage of Deadheads, band interviews, stage setup, and some juicy soundcheck action.

## Interview with John Platt

John Platt is a researching archive consultant for documentaries. He has written a biography of Hendrix with Mitch Mitchell, a biography of the Yardbirds, a book called *London's Rock Roots,* and a portfolio of psychedelic art called *Psychedelia.* John has also been collecting concert posters since 1967.

*John R. Dwork: Would you fancy yourself a video archivist?*

**John Platt:** It's certainly one of the things I do. I've been working in television and related fields coming up on eighteen years now. I do the research for various documentaries and films.

*Would you find a specific piece of footage or do you search for footage by general category?*

It just depends. Sometimes, because of previous knowledge, I know the extent of footage there is on a particular band. Sometimes my clients say, "I want them doing that particular number." And you go off in search of them doing that. But there are a number of obvious sources that you would try. Obviously TV is a good start. I've got lists of most of the old European TV shows' holdings, and although that's obviously not complete I have a good working knowledge of what *might* exist in the vaults. Sometimes you think, well, maybe they did do that on one of the Dutch TV stations, so you would fax that particular Dutch TV station and ask them if they have it.

On other things, like when I was researching Hendrix for a documentary about six years ago, I knew there was some stuff in the French TV archives, an archive that had never really been exploited. So I went over to Paris and spent a bizarre yet fulfilling week with the French going through their archives. And they're the most difficult people to deal with, but I discovered in that week a whole series that nobody had ever mentioned before from '67 in which I found live footage of Cream and Fairport Convention and a whole bunch of other people. There was even a Jefferson Airplane promo that I had never seen before as well. So you'd find things like that.

With other things it's really just a question almost of accident. Particularly live things that were filmed. Quite often I would have read that such and such a festival was filmed or whatever, and if you're lucky you can find the people that have got the footage. The problem with that is—unlike the TV thing where if it still exists it's probably usable in the sense that it was done for TV and it's edited and finished and that's it—a lot of festivals' films were shot without permission from the bands or at least without a final signature so they never had any rights to the film. If it was a multicamera shoot, which it probably was, it was never edited. There are cans of film, cans of sound, and so once you've established that somebody's got the film it doesn't necessarily mean that it's in a usable state. It depends. So getting back to your question, it depends what's required on any given occasion.

**In what condition do you usually find this old footage from the sixties and early seventies?**

It varies mostly on how it's been stored, what it's been stored on. If it's been under someone's bed for thirty years, then it's probably in a rusty can and the oxide is falling off the video for that matter. The film may be disintegrating, but it can be restored usually if it's not too far gone. It's an expensive process, and it depends on what it's for. If someone is looking for a whole film and actually wants that film, then presumably if they've got the money, they will spend it.

**Would it be preferable to you to transfer 16-millimeter footage to video in order to do the editing?**

It's almost inevitable these days. In fact, this is something that came up a lot in the summer when I was doing the Cinerock season at Lincoln Center. We were getting various complaints from people when we were showing video presentations if something was originally shot on 16- or 35-millimeter film. I understand completely what they're saying; for example, we did show the recently restored version of the Beatles' *Hard Day's Night*, which looks absolutely incredible. I've never seen a print of that film look that good. Even when I saw it in the theater in 1964, it was hardly a virgin print. So that was incredible. But then the Beatles have got the money to do that, and it really does cost thousands and thousands of dollars to restore a complete film. What's much easier and cheaper, to take another example of something we'd shown, was a film called *Tonite Let's All Make Love in London*, which was made in 1966. The last time I'd shown that was at the National Film Theater in London. And we showed the director, Peter Whitehead's own 16-millimeter print, the only one that he'd got, and it was shot to pieces. It was scratched and the sound kept jumping. When I asked him for a copy to show in New York, he said the only copy now is on video. And he'd had it digitally transferred to one-inch video. And in the process he was able to clean up 95 percent of the problems. Although it was not cheap to digitally transfer to video and clean it up, it's much cheaper than doing a film transfer and cleaning that up.

**Film emulsion looks better than video.**

That's right, but you just have to accept, unless you're the Beatles, it's just not possible anymore.

**Now tell me about, for example, the Calibration TV show. That's a great example of the Grateful Dead doing amazing readings of their Workingman's Dead tunes. Apparently, someone went back into the television station's vault and surreptitiously liberated the Grateful Dead segment. Obviously they had to play it back on the same type of ancient open reel video machines it was recorded on. And this duping process didn't go very smoothly because there are giant glitches on it that seem to be the result of the tape not tracking properly.**

I should say that that sounds very likely. I've encountered this problem before. It was probably on two-inch, also known as quad video. And that's the worst stuff for the oxide falling off it. It's possible today to do something about that. You bake it and that seals the oxide back onto the base stock as it were.

**Yeah, Dick Latvala has been doing that with a lot of the Grateful Dead's audiotapes.**

Absolutely. Then you've got a few months to transfer it to Beta SP or one-inch, whatever it is you want to do with them. So it sounds like that's what happened. There was a similar case with *The Allman Brothers at the Fillmore East*, which was also a PBS film from about the same era. No one knows exactly where the master of that is, but someone made a copy back in the early days onto three-quarter-inch tape, and that's OK. There are a couple of bad glitches in that and at the end the picture quality goes very fuzzy. In the absence of a master, that is very acceptable. I've been meaning to pursue that *Calibration* show for ages—whilst I do a certain amount for love, it's not only financially expedient to do it when someone is paying me to do it. It also means I have more legitimate reasons to do it. But my suspicion is that if it exists anywhere, it's in the PBS archive that is somewhere near Washington, 'cause that's where we got not the Allman Brothers, but the *Welcome to the Fillmore East* documentary.

**So how do you get permission to go in there and research this stuff, and is there a cost associated with it?**

Well, I wanted to show *Welcome to the Filmore East* [at the Cinerock film festival] for fairly obvious reasons: in part because it's fairly rare and partly because of its association with New York. So I didn't think that Bill Graham Presents (BGP) had a copy although they should've. I contacted Jerry Pompili and he said, "No, we haven't got a copy but if you find one we'd like to hear about it." So I contacted Channel 13 here, the local PBS affiliate, and they said, "Yes we should have a copy," and indeed they did. Now this is an interesting story; they said I had to get permission from the copyright owners. And all the contracts had changed. It turned out that BGP did indeed own it, which BGP was very delighted to hear, so the deal was struck. On this occasion that Lincoln Center paid for a new Beta SP copy to be made. We would then show it and then we would give the copy to BGP, who have done very nicely out of this because they got a free tape of something they didn't have before that they actually owned. So everyone was happy. It turned out, however, that when Channel 13, WNET, was making the transfer, the tape snapped, really badly, and it wasn't like old film stock where you could splice it, you can't with this stuff, three or four minutes was just gone forever. Well, then they said that there was probably a copy in the PBS archives near Washington. We said, OK, fine, if you can find it we'll carry on and do the same again. I think they were so embarrassed that there were no extra charges involved; they just had it done for us.

*So usually what happens is someone would employ your services as a researcher to find something. You would then go to a television station archive or find the archivist and put in a request saying that you represented one or more of the parties that owned the copyright and you'd like to purchase the rights to use the piece.*

Yes, although it depends on what the source of the material is. Some people won't even give you a time-coded one-inch VHS copy without written authority from the artist or their representative or something. Other people will say that you can have a screening copy, but if you want to license it, you'll have to clear it before we give you the master. Others will say that clearing it with the artist is your responsibility.

*So in virtually every circumstance you would need to obtain a signed release from the band, or the estate of the artists?*

That's right. Most TV stations today—and this goes for virtually every place in the world—will cover their butts. And who can blame them? And if you're talking about anybody particularly famous—the Beatles, the Stones, the Dead, the Who—no TV station is likely to say, "OK you can have it," because they know that they'll get sued. Copyright is a very gray area in certain respects. They're not stupid. There are all kinds of fundamental questions involved in this that are enormously complicated, like do the TV stations really own any copyright in these things? The fact is they actually have it so you could argue that possession is nine-tenths of the law. They are the people with the master copy. They are demanding X amount of money and you need to make certain clearances. Therefore, if you want it, you comply with those regulations. It's as simple as that.

*Let's say you get the permission; what generally is the fee associated with doing a transfer?*

Before you even think about doing that, the cost involved is staggering. In Europe the theoretical copyright owner of the physical footage tends to be the actual TV station like the BBC, Granada, Belgian National Television. Here of course it's slightly different. NBC doesn't tend to own most of those things; mostly it's reverted to whoever the production company was. So Dick Clark Media Archives owns the *American Bandstand* footage. It amounts to the same thing in the end because they're the ones that initially say, OK, you can license this material from us for X amount. X amount can be anything up to about $10,000 a minute. This is what most people don't understand: why you don't get more complete clips in a program.

*If a television station had in its possession a rare television performance by the Beatles, that TV station would try to get $10,000 per minute. Where as, if it were the 13th Floor Elevators, it might try to move a copy of the footage out the door without a big pricetag attached.*

Actually no. There is a certain correlation between the two but not much. Dick Clark Media Archives—who actually does own a 13th Floor Elevators clip by the way—they have a basic rate. It's a standard contract and it goes up every year and it's around $10,000 per minute. It depends what you're using it for. If it's a one-time showing on BBC will be different from showing it on various stations around the world.

*A film that generates continuous money.*

That's right. Like a home video. Most people today, if they have any sense, when they clear something with the copyright holder they clear it for all media, regardless of whether you intend to use it for one station TV. Such as with any major production like the recent PBS *History of Rock and Roll* series. It would cost you more to go back in three years' time to say, "Well, we want it for the rest of the world and home video." So, most people now say that they want it for everything, and that's going to cost you considerably more. You've got the physical footage copyright holder charges, which are the people that own it; you then have to clear it with the artist, and they can charge you anything. That again is dependent on any number of factors. You have to negotiate that. They can also withhold permission if they don't like what you're doing or if they don't like the clip. They have the perfect right to say no, you can't use it.

*So, because of this expense, you must also have to be in on the budget meeting. You have to be brought in and say, you want five minutes of Country Joe and the Fish, it's going to cost you this much money and has to be put into the budget.*

Absolutely. But there are yet more clearances to be dealt with and paid, including the music publishers. The whole thing with publishing rights and mechanical copyrights is a very complicated specialist field. So I often have to say, "Look, I can advise you on this, but you need to bring in a specialist in music publishing copyright clearance." And I try not to have anything to do with it beyond telling them what it will cost them. But yes, you're right, I tell people that I should be around and tell people what their budget is going to be. The only problem with that is that it changes so quickly that I can offer them a ballpark figure, but it is quite often the case where I tell them, "Look, the only way I can tell you exactly is if you give me a list of what you want and we'll get you some kind of figure and you'll have to figure out what to do."

*So often, I would imagine, a documentary on the music of the sixties would be in part shaped by budgetary restrictions as opposed to the script. There'll be something out there that's amazing and at a certain point they realize that they can only afford so much of it.*

It happens all the time. Or something where they say, we're going to use complete songs, and halfway through the production they're already into debt. It suddenly gets to the point where they only use thirty seconds, if that.

*So you might get half an hour of performances from Dick Clark, but you're charged only what goes into the film.*

Absolutely.

*You're charged for duplication and all that sort of stuff.*

And you're charged for any viewing copies. It varies a little bit; some people will say that the technical costs will be deducted from the final licensing fee. Or costs of the viewing cassettes will be deducted from the licensing fee. Not many people would just give you video cassettes. Even if once it's allowed, they'll probably charge you $100 to $150 a time. And if you're lucky, it may be deducted if you actually license something from them, but sometimes not. It really does vary.

*Let's talk about video and film of the Grateful Dead. I'd love to go over some things. Obviously everybody's seen the clips of the Grateful Dead from the famous 1967 CBS show* Hippie Temptation *with the Grateful Dead playing in the Pan Handle doing "Dancin' in the Streets." Do you know if there's more of that?*

As far as I know, no. It's highly unlikely. Funnily enough, I've got a friend in the CBS archive so I could always check those things. Highly unlikely: most TV stations don't keep that kind of stuff. You're lucky if they've still got the show as broadcast. I'll tell you a horror story about that kind of thing. There was a famous English documentary called *All My Loving* directed by Tony Palmer. It's partly unwatchable these days—it's all very fast cut and of the era and abstract. But it's got some good performances. And what is known is that Tony Palmer was in America at about March of 1968. He's best known here for directing the *Farewell Cream* show at the Albert Hall. This documentary features, among other things, footage of the Who, Cream, and Hendrix filmed around February or March of 1968 from various locations in America. I asked Tony Palmer if he shot whole concerts by these people, because there's only one number by each of the artists in the film. He said, "Yeah," but what happened was that he was contracted by the BBC. He was actually BBC staff at that point. And when he got back from America and did the program, he had to give the finished program to the BBC and all of his rushes and outtakes because that was part of the deal. They kept the film but junked or lost everything else. Part of the reason for that is, for most TV stations the central filing thing is the program as broadcast and each program is allocated a number. That's how they think. They can't deal with things that weren't finished. If it isn't bad enough that Cream, Who and Hendrix footage is missing, there's also quite a bit of Dead footage missing as well. I didn't realize this because I had first seen the film in 1968 on TV. I didn't see it again, because it was never really repeated, but I managed to get a copy out of the BBC when I was working there in the early eighties. I was sitting watching it at home, and there's suddenly a pan down this street with thousands of people on it. And I recognized that this was Haight Street. Then suddenly there is a very fast pan across a flatbed truck with the Grateful Dead on it! And this lasts about 1.5 seconds. I stopped it, rewound the film, and looked at it again. It's March of '68. There's no sound for the Grateful Dead; it's some other song completely. At some point Tony Palmer's crew filmed that gig. So there you are.

*Well, that's a juicy piece of disappointing news.*

Kesey released footage of the Dead at one of the Acid Tests, but it's got no soundtrack.

*Then of course there's the actual* Acid Test *video that Key-Z Productions has put out that's phenomenal. There's amazing footage with all the lights on with everybody doing the early Grateful Dead swirling, twirling, wiggling dancing with this giant Acid Test banner hanging in the background. The bus drives up, and it's really remarkably good quality by comparison to a lot of the stuff that was shot back then.*

Another early TV show was *The Maze*. Now I'm not sure that that can be the show with the still of Phil playing the broom handle. I say that because the audiotape that I've had for years, of *Maze*, is live. All the bands on the show do a version of "Walkin' Blues." Which implies that Phil with the broom is from a different show unless it was a publicity shot from the show and they just hammed it up for the publicity shot . . . *The Maze* featured chat by Ralph Gleason, who presented the show. So what I'm saying is that if it was a joke publicity shot from that show, then it must be a different TV thing.

*Well, the story goes that Phil was pissed because they had to lip-sync so he played the broom instead of the guitar. That's the story that's been around.*

The other thing is the Bob Nelson film of the Dead, the wacky film, has stuff shot off of TV of the Dead in it.

*Do you know if there are outtakes or more footage from the film* Petulia *with the Grateful Dead playing?*

There used to be. I worked with Dick Lester for a while and I remember one afternoon sitting in his office at Twickenham Film studios talking about *Petulia* and he said, "You're interested in that?" I said that I was. I asked, "Is there more footage that you shot of the Dead and Big Brother?" He said yes but that it all ended up on the cutting room floor. It just got junked immediately, and it never survived. He said, "You should have been at the closing night party." And I said, "Why?"

"Because," he said, "we had Country Joe and the Fish and Quicksilver playing."

*Do you know where the footage of the Grateful Dead playing "Viola Lee Blues" was from? It was a very small room.*

I asked Dick and he said that he didn't remember. Big Brother is at the Fairmont Hotel. I have a still of them playing there and you can see the flight of stairs behind them. I think it's the Matrix, though. You know the Alan Wicker thing from the BBC from '67. I think that is the Avalon. Again, there's not extra footage of that one either.

*In 1969, the Grateful Dead played* Playboy After Dark. . . .

Which was, funnily enough, on one of the local community access channels. I wish I had my machine switched on because, although it wasn't brilliant, it was better than my copy. There is a certain amount of *Playboy After Dark* stuff in circulation.

*As the rumor goes, the punch was spiked and the TV show cut to a commercial as one of the bunnies, who was starting to get high, took off her shirt.*

I talked to Tom Constanten about this last year, but he was a little vague—he just chuckled a lot. But he remembered the occasion very well. I think that's probably true; the Dead were spiking everyone in those days. Not something that I desperately approve of.

*Then there's the Dead at Monterey in '67.*

Now, the only bit of footage that I've [seen] is a quasi-edited version of a complete "Viola Lee Blues." I say quasi-edited because it was a multicamera shoot, and the edit, I think, is only one camera, but it is with the sound. And they've never actually done a complete edit on it.

*D. A. Pennebaker?*

Yes, Pennebaker supplied me with a list of all the Monterey outtakes. My understanding is that this list contained everything that they had film of with a note as to what state of editing it was in. Some of them said completely unedited, others said rough edited, like the Grateful Dead, and others said complete set edited. Two things surprised me. One is that I fondly imagined that they filmed virtually everybody and just didn't use them in the film. This turned out not to be true. I also assumed that they did film entire sets. That's not true either, seemingly. I think that "Viola Lee Blues" is the only thing on the list, maybe "Cold Rain and Snow" as well. Seemingly from the conversation that you and I had previously, Pennebaker had once indicated to you that he had the complete set as well as the free set at the football field.

***The Anarchy Stage or the Protest Stage, yes. What other footage do you know of pre-1970 that's out there of the Grateful Dead?***

Well, there are bits of things from various sources at the San Francisco News Archive. Not a lot but there's three or four bits of them where they've got a news of the day thing, something happening in the park. Invariably they did "Viola Lee Blues." There's a bit of Chocolate George's funeral and there's another thing from the Summer of Love, the event with the big banner across the stage that says Summer of Love.

***There is a great experimental film by Jerry Abrams about that called*** Be-In.

Oh, everybody and his mother had a camera at the Be-In including Jerry, who used to do the Avalon light show. But they didn't use ambient sound, they used overdub sound.

***Exactly. In the Abrams film there is great pixilated footage of the Grateful Dead playing, and of course it was a brilliantly sunny day and all the colors are just perfect.***

Yeah, that stuff is great. There were also two British TV films about San Francisco as it were. The Wicker's World one, the BBC one, that's the one we mentioned with the color footage of the Dead at the Avalon. And there's another film from ITN's Independent Television News' Roving Reporter Series, which I think has got some Dead in it. Again I think they're doing "Viola Lee Blues" in the park as well as the usual interviews with stoned hippies.

***And then there are all those little bits and pieces from the Grateful Dead's less than shining performance at Woodstock.***

Oh yes, although I was recently given a copy of that with a much better sound mix. A friend of mine worked on the staff when they did the Woodstock lost performances. He went through all the footage and got most of it for himself, and he's given me some bits and pieces. It sounds better to me than any of the other mixes that I've ever heard. It sounds quite tolerable.

***Well, there were several things. One there was the film crew, but there was also an independent guy in the audience rolling at least what ended up being black and white tape.***

Yes. I think I've seen that.

***And there's time code on that, and it cuts all over the place and is basically individual thirty-second sound bites.***

Is that not the security camera that they had mounted at the edge of the stage? Maybe it's not.

***I'm not sure.***

A friend of mine made a documentary about Woodstock and he got hold of all that footage, although I don't think he used the Dead in his film because he couldn't get permission. So I have seen other chunks of that film, because it is black and white.

***Now there's February 4th at the Family Dog with the Dead, Santana, and Jefferson Airplane.***

You mean the *Night at the Family Dog*?

***Yes. And, after the Dead played "China Cat" > "Rider" and "Hard to Handle" there's a clip at the end where all the bands are jamming together onstage. The question is, where's that entire jam?***

Well, I talked to Bob Zagone, the man who made that, and he told me that it was not a great night and everybody was really late. They didn't actually start until about two A.M. or something and I think it was supposed to be a fund-raiser for the Family Dog because they were going through one of their many financial crises. Chet may remember more. I think there was a problem with the filming. You really have to talk to Bob about this, but I don't know how long the whole jam was. He may still have his outtakes, it's possible. Bob still has a lot of stuff down in his basement. He's kind of iffy about all the stuff he shot of that period. What happened was, when I was doing "Cinerock," I thought we'd have a San Francisco evening, the core of which would be the Zagone footage because he made several films for KQED starting back in about '66. The most famous one he did early on was in early '67 for a KQED series called *Come Up Through the Years*. One of the episodes was Big Brother and the Holding Company live in the TV studio. That was actually released on home video as *Ball and Chain*. But he also shot other stuff. He did various promos; there's one for Quicksilver, two for Steve Miller, and a bunch of other stuff. He did B.B. King in the studio for KQED, although that's really not San Francisco material. And later there's *Night at the Family Dog* and *Go Ride the Music*. There's also the *Day in the Life of Country Joe and the Fish*, which is a quasi–Dick Lester look at Country Joe and the Fish. It's a very funny film actually. It has them getting up in the morning all in sleeping bags in the same room. It's all done very fast so it looks like an old silent film. Then they drive to Sausalito Airport for their rehearsal. It's literally a day in the life of Country Joe and the Fish. So I figured we'd use a whole batch of the stuff, but we could never come to an agreement with Zagone because he doesn't like a lot of the stuff. He finds it embarrassing.

*Sort of like Jordan Belson, the famous filmmaker who, after making some of the most visionary films ever, withdrew virtually every copy in circulation?*

Yeah. So in the end he wanted to show a fifty-minute compilation reel of his stuff, which has a few good things in it, but nothing from *A Night at the Family Dog*. There were a couple of clips from *Go Ride the Music*. One of the Steve Miller promos. So about half of it was what I wanted to show, and then the other half included about four minutes of a girl having her hair cut in San Francisco in 1967. Interesting sociological piece but not what I want to show. So in the end we couldn't decide on a compromise. Then he said he'd let us show *Night at the Family Dog* if we would pay him to reedit it and we said no. That's Zagone. He did tell me that he probably had some other stuff that we might be interested in. He said he'd have a look through his vault and see if there's anything relevant, but I don't think he really did.

*There's another film that is done of the Grateful Dead called* China Cat Sunflower. *It's a film of the Grateful Dead done onstage at Woodstock. The interesting thing about it is that it is basically done with the person shaking the camera from halfway up the hill. What you basically get is this beautiful set of squiggles of the stage lights as if you were taking a time exposure with moving a light around. It doesn't look like the Grateful Dead at all.*

There's also a film of the Grateful Dead in the park with no sound. This guy that eventually became a real documentary filmmaker shot it when he was sixteen or something. It's delightful but there's no sound. And there's the Columbia University student strike footage from 1968 as well which may or may not have sound.

*Now of course there are two things that people have yet to see from 1970—at least, that we know of. One is rumored to be film footage of the Grateful Dead on 5/24/70 at the Hollywood Festival in Newcastle-upon-Tyne, England.*

I could tell you a lot about that.

*Please do.*

Sadly, and it's my eternal regret, I was not at the show. I remember distinctly I was going to be going because I'd been a Dead fan for three years at that point and I got sick. It was just one of those things. But anyway about six years later I ended up working on a show of Rick Griffin art at the Roundhouse in London for which I wrote the catalogue notes and stuff like that. But the two main organizers, this was a sideline for them, they actually worked in TV. One was a freelance cameraman, the other a freelance soundman. And the one who was the cameraman, Dick Pope—when he was just starting out six years earlier, he'd been part of an independent production company hired by the BBC to film the Dead at the Hollywood Festival. The story he tells me I think makes a certain amount of sense. They were all set to film it for the BBC's then hit rock show *Disco Too* which evolved into something called *The Old Grey Whistle Test,* which people may have heard of. But what happened was that shortly before the Dead came on, someone from the Dead—he said Garcia, but it might have been one of the roadies—handed out acid to anyone that wanted it. Including the film crew. And the result was a disaster. The film consisted mainly of trees and god knows what else. It was unusable. Dick managed to get it together enough to remind the head sound guy that he should turn on his tape machine, but it was halfway through the set before they got into position to do it later. So Dick ended up with the sound tape of half of the set, minus some because the tape ran out about two minutes before "Lovelight" did. He gave me a dub from the sound tape, but unfortunately this was early on in my tape days and I just thought cassette tape is cassette tape and put it on Agfa tape which is like really awful cassette tape. It's OK, but if I'd known what I know now, I'd have it on Maxell tape. So it's slightly degenerated over the years, but it's still a remarkable artifact.

*Thankfully, a good soundboard from that show is in circulation.*

It never occurred to me in England that people had all this stuff, and then suddenly I've got this one tape that no one else has got. I advertised in *Relix* saying that I had this tape to trade and was anybody interested. I got all these people sending me lists of things I couldn't believe existed. That's how I started, by trading that. Which is quite funny in retrospect. The other thing which I've never been able to confirm, because I could never find the guy who was actually the head cameraman, was whether or not, as Dick Pope always maintained, the day before or maybe two days before the May 24 show the Dead used the Roundhouse to rehearse in acoustically. At least Lesh, Weir, and Garcia were sitting around playing acoustically and running through stuff. They filmed that and *that* would have been part of the final film. Who knows? I never found that footage.

*And then of course there's footage that you recently helped bring to light, which is the great trans-Canadian tour with the Band and Janis Joplin. Can you tell us about that?*

Absolutely. I'd known about this for many years, if nothing else I'd read about it in *Rolling Stone*—there was an article called "Million Dollar Bash." I knew it had happened. Then in the *Janis* documentary from '73 or '74 there was at least one number credited to the Festival Express. So when I started working in film and TV and people wanted San Francisco material, I started looking for it. Over the years I would make periodic stabs at phoning people and no one knew where it was until about a year ago when I contacted a guy I know from the company ARIQ. They're an archive place in East Hampton, New York, on Long Island. They're one of these places that—apart from the obvious places like TV stations and Dick Clark Media Archives, there are a few places that represent other archives, as it were. Certain TV shows, they either buy them outright or represent whoever the copyright holder is, they will theoretically legitimately represent them so that you can go to ARIQ or Research Video in Los Angeles, and they've got loads and loads of stuff. ARIQ is one such institution and the guy that runs it, Joe Lauro, said to me one day, "We just got this footage of the Dead and Janis and the Band from the Festival Express." And I was just like, "My God, you've got it! What is it? How did you come by it?" He said, "Don't get too excited because at the moment there's only about fifteen minutes' worth, but we are representing the company that is making the documentary." I asked him who it was and he told me about this production company in Canada. I phoned them up and the guy there, Garth Douglas, told me what had happened, which was that he and his partner had done research themselves. They knew this stuff existed and that it was probably still in Canada somewhere. He did actually tell me the whole story, but it's long and convoluted. But what it boiled down to was that they found the original producer, and he told them that it had been in storage in a warehouse in Toronto for twenty-five years or something. It was there and they found virtually all of it.

*How many hours?*

About ninety hours approximately. This included everything: various concerts along the way, stuff on the train, people jamming, people getting drunk and throwing up, the whole bit. I said this is great, but you haven't got the whole film. He said that they were making it, but there were some rights problems and things. I said that I would like to show the fifteen minutes that exist. What they had done was take one number from the Dead, one number from Janis, and one number from the Band, edited them properly, and got Eddie Kramer to redo the sound, kind of as a taster for what was to come. He said that I could show it but that I would have to clear it with the relevant parties. There were no theatrical rights signed over to anybody, so they still had to get permission from the bands. I phoned up Dennis McNally, whom I'd known for many, many years and said, "Look I want to show this." He said, "We're aware of this, we'll get back to you." Turned out that what happened was the production company came to an agreement with the Grateful Dead whereby the Dead are allowing these people to use X amount of Dead footage in their finished documentary. The quid pro quo is that all the remaining Grateful Dead footage will be returned to the Grateful Dead.

*I heard that what you showed was this classic scene of the Dead playing in a train yard playing an acoustic version of "Don't Ease Me In."*

That's right. There's a whole set of that apart from anything else. I wished I'd written it down because he told me where it was. Vancouver maybe. It was a free afternoon show, and they're playing in front of a set of carriages, presumably the Festival Express carriages, and they're in this train yard. It's absolutely stunning. They're in tune, Bobby's wearing a cowboy hat, and it sounds tremendous. They've got a bunch of other concerts by the Dead. I asked him one very important question: Was there a version of "Dark Star"? And he said that there wasn't, at least not in any of the footage that they've got. The upshot of it is that they've been given permission to go ahead, but they are still negotiating rights with other people for the publishing. Assuming they do get the final go-ahead, it should be finished by Christmas of next year, which is unfortunately too late for me to show it at this year's Cinerock festival. But that's the latest situation.

*Then of course there was* Calibrations *in August of '70. Moving on to '71 there's the clips of the Grateful Dead in* The Last Day of the Fillmore *movie.*

I'll tell you a horror story about that too. I had lunch with the associate director of that a couple of months ago. He told me the story—it's a very funny story, actually—about the Dead coming in to watch the rushes and everything. You'll love *and* hate this story. He told me that for ten years he was carrying around, whenever he moved, thousands of feet of film, outtakes. Other material by the people that were in the film and also footage of people that they didn't include in the film at all. He tried at various times to get people interested, by putting up money, to do a new version or a sequel. Finally he said that it was costing him too much money in the storage and transport, and by the early eighties, he didn't want to do this, but he junked the lot of it. So that's gone now.

*Wow! I would imagine that BGP would've wanted that footage. There was a great "Other One" played that night.*

That was on the first illegal bootleg I ever heard, I think.

*I don't know of any other footage from '71. Do you know if BGP recorded any more tapes at the Fillmore?*

BGP only really started to get their archives together in the past five years, with a view to licensing clips of things. They employed a company—the company is actually based in New York—who act as their agents for licensing clips. The first list of stuff I saw I was shown very briefly. It had all kinds of stuff that was later removed from the list, and included was everything of the Grateful Dead, subsequently they told me, "No, we can't represent Grateful Dead material," and gave it all back to the Dead. I do remember there was an early New Year's Eve show, '70, '71, that was on television.

*It was 12/31/70, broadcast by KQED.*

It may have been that. On the other hand, my feeling is that it wasn't, but anyway almost nothing before that. In fact most of their archive starts around '71, when they started filming in-house. A lot of the early stuff is in black and white, security camera stuff really. There's almost nothing before that.

*There's a television station in Copenhagen that has a whole concert from Tivoli Gardens in April of 1972.*

Yes, they do. It's Danish National TV.

*I heard that the Grateful Dead now have all of it but that they are having problems getting to use it from Danish TV who own the rights.*

They do. They filmed it, they own it. They'll just have to work out some kind of compromise. There is at least one home video with a clip from that on it that came out of England. I'm sure the rights were never cleared: it was a legal English release but from a company that was notorious for not clearing the rights with the artist. I think it was called *California Screaming,* but I wouldn't swear to that title. It's one of a series of sixties compilations, except the Dead of course is '72. They've got the whole show. There's the Beat club from that tour too.

"Truckin'" *and "Saturday Night," the latter of which was then reedited for showing on Casey Kasem and then later for MTV where they put in more psychedelic postproduction effects which actually make it look much better even though it's not very inventive.*

Someone once told me that there was a film of the Bickershaw Festival, which was the English festival they did on that tour. Now whether the whole festival was filmed, the guy was actually a Flamin' Groovies fan and that's what he was after, but he was told that they'd filmed all that stuff.

*Yeah. Supposedly it rained for days prior.*

I'm glad I wasn't at that one.

*The field was mud, and the rain finally cleared for the Grateful Dead. By that point everybody was soaked to the bone.*

Absolutely.

*Great show though. That just recently came out as pristine audio tapes.*

I think I only heard really dreadful tapes of it years ago.

*Then of course we go to 8/27/72, the infamous* Sunshine Daydream *film. That Deadheads know pretty much about because Phil De Guerre, one of the gents who made it and a longtime Deadhead, I know he has been very frustrated that the Dead have not allowed him to finally release that film. Amazingly, he told me at one point that the "Bird Song" from this show was edited (and is in storage) and that when they were finishing the editing he and Sam Field decided that the film was too long so they didn't include it. Of course, the Dead vetoed that release anyway. So there's yet another priceless moment that's in a Vault with all the sound all synched up to it that no one's ever seen. All the more frustrating for people like myself who hold that "Bird Song" to be the best version they ever did. I've also seen numerous outtakes from the other cameras.*

*Interestingly that was another show where the water was dosed, and after a while the camera people had to work extra hard to keep things in focus. But there's more footage of cameras just walking through the crowd and all sorts of footage that nobody's seen. Then there's—who knows how much more Prankster footage wasn't used for this project? Then of course there are all sorts of home movies shot of the Grateful Dead throughout their career. Particularly in 1972 there's all sorts of footage shot by Billy. And there's some classic footage of pixilation that Parish, the roadie, tying up* one of the members of the Dead with rope and then boom, they lift the bag up and the musician is gone.

I just remembered another thing, speaking of extraneous Dead footage. I think Justin Kreutzmann used some of it in *Backstage Pass*, footage of all the bands going up to the Panhandle to be photographed by Jim Marshall with Bill Graham. There's all the bands, the Charlatans, Big Brother, Quicksilver, and some of the footage in *Backstage Pass* has them walking up Haight Street that day. It was filmed by this guy named Lavell Benford. I talked to him about a year ago and he thought that he might have more, but none of it's got sound, of course. It's nice footage. Another film that you might be interested in but it isn't really the Dead. I'll tell you what it is. As I mentioned, my wife worked at the Fillmore East, and the reason I know her is because I was working with a woman called Amalie Rothschild who also worked there. Did you know that Amalie shot a film that was specifically made for the Grateful Dead?

**No.**

It's the "Casey Jones" film. Amalie heard that there was going to be a last run of this steam locomotive somewhere in upstate New York. She and a friend followed this train in a car, it was like an old-fashioned steam locomotive, doing hair-raising things to get ahead of it and film it. She did it, edited it, and without telling the Dead. So when they started playing "Casey Jones" she showed this film and it completely blew the Dead's minds. All of the Dead turned around with their mouths open, watching the film while they're playing. There's no Grateful Dead in the film, but the Dead loved the film. And they showed it whenever the Dead played "Casey Jones."

*Well, what's your feeling about unexplored territory and the race against time? Do you still think that there's stuff out there to be found?*

The recent VH1 show about the Dead (*Album Classics*) had some footage of them recording *American Beauty* in the studio with synched sound. Just a little snatch. How much of that footage there actually is I don't know. There's that stuff and then in the PBS *History of Rock and Roll* was this show that's not identified, but I believe it was Gaelic Park in the Bronx.

*1971!*

Because Pigpen is in the band and there's a subway train running along behind it.

*Yeah, that would be Gaelic Park in 1971.*

But how much there is of that I have no idea. There's always the possibility, and with a band like the Dead there's more likely to be.

*Because there's actually a filmmaker going through their archives who's likely to say, "Hmmm, Grateful Dead? I bet I could sell that."*

With a band like the Grateful Dead, most of it is going to be odd privately shot stuff from the studio or a festival or something like that because they did so little TV. They weren't much of a commercial proposition. Whereas with other bands, you think, well, there might be some footage—Cream comes to mind because I'm doing a Cream book. Someone just showed me some footage from an American TV show of Cream that I never knew existed. I thought that with a band as famous as Cream, all the footage would be out there. It wasn't particularly wonderful, it was a lip-sync thing, but it can turn up. With the Dead I think that all the old TV stuff is known about except some very early stuff that we were talking about. But there is always the possibility that people have got stuff under their beds that they shot. Although the likelihood of that being professionally shot with sync sound is small.

*There's also got to be a large number of outtakes from the October '74 run which was shot for the Grateful Dead movie.*

I think so because they filmed every night completely. I read that all that stuff existed.

*They could put out a whole second movie!*

I know of other things too. Like the last days of Winterland: I guess all that stuff existed at one point as well. Although that perhaps is less likely because that was a TV thing. Although it's possible the good news is that if it was filmed it's usable because it's all done at once as opposed to film, where you have to do all this stuff with editing later. It can still happen to a certain extent with TV. So they may have filmed stuff that they didn't use even though it was for TV. Generally speaking, though, what they've got is what they've got.

# 10

# The Compleat Guide to Collecting and Trading Tapes

*by Jeff Tiedrich*

### Tapes Are Where You Find Them

Ever since the first Cro-Magnon man lumbered out of his cave and crudely affixed iron oxide particles to a thin acetate backing . . .

Well, OK, tape collecting doesn't date back that far, but for as long as recording devices have existed, people have been collecting and trading tapes of live music. Why do they do it? Some folks, myself included, feel that live music is more compelling to listen to than the sterile, overproduced sound of studio recordings. Some folks, myself included, do it for sentimental reasons; they like to be able to listen to shows they've attended. Other folks, myself included, just enjoy the ego boost of staring at large stacks of tapes.

This guide is written with the beginner in mind. As with any subculture, the tape-trading world has over the years evolved accepted standards of behavior that govern how its citizens behave. Unfortunately, there are very few resources to help a newcomer learn the ropes. Most of us learned "on the job," making well-meaning mistakes and stepping on a more than a few toes along the way. Wouldn't it be nice to know in advance where the potential pitfalls lie? Read on . . .

### Shhhh! The Big Secret to Successful Tape Trading

That's right. I'm going to give it all away, right at the top. Here's the secret: be a good neighbor. Be the kind of person whom other people enjoy dealing with. Approach all trade situations cheerfully. Don't be rude, don't be paranoid, don't be secretive. That's it! Make trading tapes with you a pleasant experience and people will come back for more.

(Did it sound like I just belabored the obvious? Believe me, I wouldn't mention this if it wasn't necessary.)

Now, on to the details . . .

First off, a few words about tape formats. After all, before you make this considerable investment in time and money, you're going to want to figure out what you'll be spending your money on. Here is a *very* brief overview of the the major tape formats.

### Cassettes

Cassette tape is far and above the most widely used format in all of tapedom. You probably already own a cassette deck—most folks do. People who now use other media almost always started with cassettes. The main advantage of cassettes are that decks and tapes are omnipresent and relatively inexpensive. Everyone has them and everyone knows what to do with them. Most people trade cassettes, and you'll never have a hard time finding trading partners.

Cassettes do have their drawbacks. Most obvious is the certain amount of hiss that is added every time a tape is copied. This can build up to a distracting amount of noise over only a few generations.

### DAT (Digital Audio Tape)

The primary advantage of digital tape is that it is . . . well, *digital*. Copies of digital tapes ("clone" is the hip term) are, like floppy disks and other computer media, identical to the original. (Well, except for the introduction of errors—but more about that later.) Since there is no hiss to begin with and none added from generation to generation, a twentieth-generation will theoretically sound identical to the original. You just can't achieve that kind of fidelity from cassette tapes. Another plus is that DAT tapes are painfully easy to clone: there are no levels to set, and since DAT tapes are one-sided, there is no interruption to flip tapes. Once you start recording a DAT tape, you can pretty much walk away and not come back for a couple of hours.

However, there are many disadvantages to using DAT media. Decks and blank tapes are generally more expensive than their cassette counterparts. They are also harder to find. Unless you live in a major metropolitan area, you're not going to be able to wander into your local electronics store and walk out with a DAT deck. Most people rely on mail order. The DAT tape transport mechanism is very fragile and breaks easily. Tapes degrade very easily, and it is recommended that tapes be recopied every five years to ensure that they remain playable. Copy protection circuitry is built into the most inexpensive decks.

This all sounds very daunting, but the sound quality of digital tape is so stunning that many people feel that that alone outweighs all the negatives.

### Reel-to-Reel Tape
Open reel tape offers great dynamic range and less tape hiss, but reel tape is expensive and bulky to store. In the pre-DAT days, reel-to-reel was best format for ensuring a mimimum of generational degradation of sound quality, but nowadays very few people trade reel tapes.

### Mini-disc
Mini-discs, while sharing DAT's lack of tape hiss, are hobbled by a loss-compression scheme that throws away pieces of the music in order to squeeze it all onto the small-format disks. The loss from compression is inaudible in the originals but builds up quickly from generation to generation. Serious tape collectors shun this format.

### OK, now it's time to get some tapes. But where . . . ?
You're salivating. You *know* that there are all these great tapes out there and you just have to get your hands on them. How do you get tapes? Simple: you trade for them. But, hey, wait a minute, you say. If I don't have any tapes to trade in the first place, how am I going to trade for tapes? Seems like a bit of a catch-22, doesn't it?

Rest easy. Remember, all of us started with no tapes at all. Someone somewhere took pity on us and simply *gave* us a small pile of tapes to get started with. And most of us, to pay back the karma, consider it our ethical duty to find "newbies" (that's what we call you) and shower them with kindness. Your mission is to *find those people and make yourself known*.

Here's how to do it:

(But first a word from the Department of No Free Lunches: I exaggerated a bit back there. Almost no one will just *give* you tapes. The accepted practice is that you buy blank tapes in advance and give them to your benefactor, who in turn records onto them and returns them to you. When sending tapes through the mail, it is expected that you will also provide return postage for the package coming back to you. This is the mysterious "blanks and postage" reference which you will be seeing.)

### Look in Your Own Backyard.
No doubt you already have friends who trade tapes. Don't be shy; speak up and ask them to help you out.

### It Pays to Advertise.
There are many fan-oriented music magazines (for Deadheads, *Dupree's Diamond News* comes immediately to mind) that have page after page of classified ads placed by people looking for trading partners. You, the newbie, can also take advantage of this avenue. A concise ad works. Your ad doesn't need to be flowery or drawn out. A nice "Newbie, just getting started, will provide blanks and postage for a kind soul who will make me a few tapes." A little goes a long way.

### Get on the Net.
These days, most serious tape trading is done over the Internet. There are dozens of on-line discussion groups dedicated to discussing music and trading tapes. This is where's it's all happening now, and this is by far the easiest avenue for a newbie to quickly build up a tape collection. Here are the best places to look:

*On-line Services That Have Forums for Trading Tapes:*
The Well
America On Line
Compuserve

Do not overlook the Usenet newsgroup rec.music.gdead. Heavily trafficked, generating hundreds of posts a day, this is an excellent place to look for tapes. (See the resource guide of this book for information on how to access these services and forums.)

## Participate in Tape Trees.

If you spend any time at all on the Net, something you'll see constant reference to are *tape trees*. This is a popular method of distributing tapes on a mass basis. The person at the base of the tree makes a certain number of copies of a tape and sends the tapes up to the first level of branches. Each branch makes a number of copies, and the process continues to repeat itself. As you can see, quite a large number of tapes can quickly be passed out to a large group of people. Participate in as many trees as you responsibly can. If you have nothing to trade, etiquette dictates that your "parent" on a tree accept the familiar "blanks and postage."

## And Now, an Unabashed Plug for . . . Me.

I maintain a Web page where newbies and people who want to make tapes for newbies can find each other. It's part of my larger "Resources for Tape Traders" site and is regularly visited by people who are willing to make tapes. Browse the URL

http://www.tiedrich.com/tapelist/

and click on the link for "Adopt-A-Newbie."

*Hey, why can't I just buy some tapes (or bootleg CDs, for that matter)?*

Because it's unethical. For now, let's not wade into any polemics about bootlegging and whether we fans have an inalienable right to the music. Let's just point out while many bands (more and more all the time) allow people to tape and trade their shows, NO band wants you to sell tapes or CDs of their performances. As good neighbors, we ought to respect their wishes. Right?

*OK, I've got a connection for some tapes. How do I know what to ask for?*

Simple: you don't. Trust me. Most people's first inclination is to get tapes of shows they've attended, and there's nothing wrong with that. It's a natural urge and we all do this.

But what most newcomers lose sight of is a simple fact: people will be most interested in trading with you if you have interesting and off-beat tapes of your own to offer. In other words, you need to have what's known as trade-bait. You want to be able to say, "Hey, look at me—I have such-and-such tape *and you don't*. Want a copy?" (Including "nyeah-nyeah-nyeah" is optional.) What I recommend to people when starting out, is to ask the person making your tape what he or she thinks are their most desirable tapes. One thing about tape traders: they *love* it when someone asks them to choose their best tapes. What better excuse for them to listen to a good show all over again?

## Traders, Traders Everywhere . . .

*I've got some tapes!*

Congratulations rookie! See, now that wasn't so hard, was it? And now you've managed to nab a small pile of tapes. Pat yourself on the back!

*So now I can jump right in and trade tapes, right?*

Well . . . not exactly. But you're *almost* ready to trade.

*What do you mean, "almost?"*

Well, you need to do two things. First, you're going to need to listen to the tapes. "Well, DUH," you say. Obviously. I mention this only to introduce the next topic: evaluating and grading tapes.

The vast majority of your trading partners are going to want to know how your tapes sound. You mission, Jim, is to get it right—to more-or-less accurately describe the sound quality of your tapes. But people aren't going to want to wade through descriptions such as "well, it's a pretty good tape but it's a little bit hissy and you can't hear all the intruments all the time," or "WOW, this tape sounds GREAT!" And so the common practice of using letter (or number) grades has been developed over the years. It's not perfect but it works. And it's an undeniable A-plus when everyone is working from the same reference point.

*An Oversimplified Guide to Tape Ratings:*

A = strong recording levels, low tape hiss, a clean and clear mix of music

B = fair recording levels, a bit of tape hiss, perhaps slightly muddy-sounding music

C = low recording levels, distracting hiss levels, indistinct music

D = a sonic nightmare, virtually unlistenable.

*Ewww, why would anyone want to collect D-grade tapes?*

Some very rare tapes just don't circulate in any other condition. Many very old audience tapes were made under less-than-optimal conditions on less-than-optimal equipment. Those of us who just have to have *everything* have learned to accept the fact that sometimes we have to settle for less-than-optimal sound quality.

*Guess what: no two people rate tapes the same way.*

This unfortunate fact of tape trading gives more collectors indigestion than anything else. To a small extent, you've got to take other people's grading system with a grain of salt. Most people are as honest as they can be when grading tapes, but remember that we're dealing with people's opinions. It's just not a precise science.

Enter into tape trades with the idea that the other person's tape ratings are not exact, but rather *in the ballpark*. And when you grade your own tapes, err on the side of caution. If you think it's an A, list it as A–. Your trading partners would rather be surprised by a tape sounding better than its rating than the opposite.

Now for the second of the two things you need to do before you're ready to trade tapes. Once you've evaluated your tapes, you've got to make yourself a tape list.

*Awww, do I have to?*

Yes. Very few tape traders will take you seriously if you don't maintain an up-to-date tape list. It's a chore, but the sooner you get started, the less work it will be to keep it current.

*And with what shall I make this list?*

The vast majority of tape lists are composed on a computer, either with a word processing program or a specialized tape-list program. (See the resources section of this book for more information on such programs.) It's possible to keep a list by using a typewriter, but updating such a list is pretty much a logistical nightmare. I've even seen handwritten tape lists, but *please* don't do this.

*What information goes on a tape list?*

Your tapes, obviously. But more about that later.

A well-organized tape list will also include a bit of additional information at the top:

- Your name. It seems obvious to mention this, but I've seen tape lists that have no name attached to them.
- Your mailing address. People are going to need this eventually, so why not give it to them right away.
- Your e-mail address, if you're on the Internet.
- A brief explanation of how you grade your tapes.
- The date that your list was last updated. This is a nice courtesy.

Other stuff that people like to see on a list:

- The brand and model of your tape decks.
- The kind of tapes you like to collect. Are you only interested in shows that were held on Saturdays in Chicago? Put that on your list, let people know.
- A "wish list" of specific shows or bands that you're looking for.

*Yeah yeah yeah, but what about the tapes?*

OK, let's talk about listing your tapes (finally)! You mission is to pack as much information as you can about your tapes into a well-organized and easy-to-understand format. Folks aren't going to spend much time pondering over a cryptical list; they'll put yours aside and go on to the next one.

Let's look at an excerpt from a minimal tape list:

### GRATEFUL DEAD

| | | | | | |
|---|---|---|---|---|---|
| 5/2/70 | Harpur College | all | SBD | A–/B+ | 225 |
| 5/6/70 | Kresge Plaza | all | SBD | A– | 90 |
| 5/7/70 | DuPont Gym | all | AUD/6 | B+ | 270 |
| | includes NRPS set | | | | |
| 11/23/70 | Anderson Theatre | part | AUD | B | 180 |
| | missing Casey J, FOTD, Lovelight | | | | |

This is a good example of the all the basic information, concisely laid out. What's nice about this list is that it's pretty self-explanatory.

First we have the name of the band in question.

Next comes the date of the show, followed by the name of the venue. Some people include the location as well.

The next column represents how much of the show is in this person's possession.

Following that comes the type of recording. SBD refers to "soundboard," meaning the master tape was recorded from a deck patched into the band's PA. An AUD tape is one that was recorded through microphones into a portable deck by an audience member. Also common in tape lists is FM, a tape recorded from a radio broadcast.

Note the AUD/6 designation under the 5/6/70 entry. The 6 is the *generation* of the tape; in this case the tape in question is 6 copies down the line from the original, or *master*, tape. Tape generations are very important to serious collectors; the lower the generation number, the more crisp the music and the lower the buildup of tape hiss from copy to copy. Low-generation (1–3) tapes are prized by collectors—always list the generation, if known, of your tapes.

The final two columns are, respectively, the grade of the tape and the total running time of the music. Most people round this up to the length of the tapes on which the music is recorded.

Also helpful on this list is the notation that 5/7/70 includes the New Riders' set, and that songs are missing from 11/23/70. The information about missing songs is particularly helpful: it prevents people who looking for an upgrade from an equally incomplete tapes from trading for the exact same tape.

*Hey, wait—how do I know if any songs are missing from my tapes?*

Well. If they're Grateful Dead tapes, you're in luck. You can compare them to the set lists in this book, n'est-ce pas?

Now let's check out a list that's a little more complete:

JERRY GARCIA AND BOB WEIR:
11/21/70   Jerry Garcia, Bob Weir and Duane Allman—WBCN Studios, Boston, MA—complete—35min, FM > ? > ?C 3.5 [ea]
12/27/70   Jerry Garcia, Bob Weir, David Nelson, John Dawson—KPPC Studios, Pasadena, CA—interview and live acoustic performance (4 songs)—90min, MSR > 2C 4.0 [bs]
10/??/72   Jerry Garcia, Bob Weir, John Dawson, possibly other New Riders Scotty's Music Store, St. Louis, MO—Instrumental, Country Roads, Instrumental, Is Anybody Going to San Antone, Instrumental, Seasons of My Heart—30min, MST > ? > ?C 3.7 [dw] {on Raitt 10/17/72}

OK. I confess: This is from my own tape list. It's much more extensive than most people's, and frankly there's more information here than most people will ever need in order to conduct successful tape trades. But if you are so inclined, there's no such thing as having too much information.

To explain the more esoteric notations: First off, my collection includes enough tapes of Garcia and Weir playing together to break them out of the general Grateful Dead listings and give them their own subcategory. This is helpful to people looking for only such recordings.

In 11/21/70, "FM > ? > ?C" means that the original FM broadcast was taped onto an unknown medium, and was copied onto cassette an unknown amount of times. 3.5 is the rating—some people use numbers instead of letters—3.5 being equivalent to "B" in my scheme.

The letters in brackets are the initials of the person with whom I traded for this tape. (This helps to prevent me from asking the same person for the same tape twice.)

12/27/70 includes an explanation that not all of the material on the tape is music. It also notes that the tape in my possession is the second cassette copy off the master soundboard reel (MSR).

10/??/72 notes that the exact personnel of the show is unknown. And since it is unknown exactly how many songs were played here, it is impossible to simply say "complete" or "missing x songs," so all the songs that appear on the tape are listed.

Check out the information in the braces: {on Raitt 10/17/72}. This tells me that I can find this thirty-minute snip of music at the end of my Bonnie Raitt 10/17/72 tape. It is a very good habit to make such notes. You will find that eventually your tape collection will grow to a point where you can no longer keep track in your head of where every tiny fragment of tape is located. I wasted many hours digging through boxes of tapes—"uh . . . is it on this one? This one? Hmmm . . . this one?"—before I realized this was the only way to fly.

*Now I've finished my tape list. Who am I going to trade with?*

Remember everything you learned when you were a newbie depending on the kindness of strangers? Guess what: you're going to find tape traders in the exact same places: friend, magazines, the Internet. Use the same skills you learned in groveling for tapes to approach potential traders.

But first and foremost: Get in touch with the people who gave you your freebie tapes. Send them your fledgling list and offer to repay their kindness through a few good trades.

## The Anatomy of a Tape Trade

Now, on to the meat and potatoes (tempeh in a soy vinaigrette for you vegetarians out there). You've contacted a few traders, made some deals, and now it's time to actually copy a few tapes. So, without further ado . . .

### How to Make a Good (Cassette[1]) Tape

1. **Start with high-quality tape.** Use chromium dioxide or metal tapes—they're formulated for high-fidelity music. Using cheaper tape will result in muddy music. You and your trading partner should agree beforehand on what brand and type of tape to use.

---
1. DAT tapers are lucky—tapes are copied digitally and there are no levels to set and no added hiss to worry about.

2. **Use new tapes.** This is a common courtesy. Don't record for trades over old tapes.
3. **Keep the recording levels high—but not too high.** The idea here is to keep the music as loud as possible without "saturating" the tape. High levels are important because as the music becomes louder, tape hiss is less obvious. Music that is too quiet will get lost in the hiss, particularly since every time a tape is copied, the level of hiss grows. On the other hand, music that is too loud will become muddy and broken up. This is known as "oversaturation." For chromium tape, the loudest parts of the tape you make should register at +3db on your deck's meters. Metal tape can peak at +5.
4. **Should I use Dolby noise reduction?** The short answer is no. Without getting technical, Dolby is a way of minimizing audible tape hiss. Although this is a good thing, in practice it works best when tapes are played back on the same equipment they were recorded on. However, when trading tapes, obviously that's not what's going to happen.
5. **If you screw up, start over.** If you notice halfway into a tape that all of a sudden the levels are too loud and the tape is saturating, bite the bullet and go back to the beginning. Don't just hope that your trading partner won't notice—they will.
6. **Keep your decks in good working order.** Every twenty hours or so, clean the heads of your decks. Use a liquid cleaner—the abrasive cleaning tapes can wear down your heads. Once a year (or every six months if you're paranoid), bring your decks to a repair shop for routine maintenance—have your decks cleaned and checked out to make sure they're running at the correct speed.

## How to Mail Tapes

**Use insulated mailers.** Tapes need protection from rough handling, obviously, or else they'll arrive at their destination horribly smashed. The preferred method is to use bubble-padded mailers, available at almost any stationery or office supply store. The bubble variety offers the most protection. Fiber-filled mailers are frowned upon, for if they're accidentally ripped open (which does happen often), tiny fiber particles can get all over the tapes—and they're impossible to clean up after!

**Use new or almost-new mailers.** There is a tradition in the taping world of recycling: using mailer bags repeatedly in order to help protect the environment. This is a Good Thing Indeed. But don't go overboard. If a bag starts to become threadbare, throw it away and start with a fresh mailer. The idea is to ensure that your tapes arrive intact.

**Don't pack tapes loosely.** If you're mailing more than one tape (and you probably will be), don't just toss them into a mailer without securing them. Otherwise, they'll knock against each other in transit and arrive with the cases cracked and shattered. Rubber-banding tapes together is one method of making sure they arrive in one piece. Another popular method is to wrap the tapes in newspaper "gift wrap" style, to hold them immobile within the mailer bag.

**Use first class mail.** This is another courtesy. You'll want to make sure that the tapes you mail arrive at their destination promptly. Priority mail is another good option.

## Other Trading-Related Issues

**Be prompt.** Try to mail out finished tapes within a week of agreeing to trade.

**Don't bite off more than you can chew.** Try not to agree to more trades than you can comfortably finish in a reasonable amount of time. And "work off" trades in the same order that you arrange them.

The other side of the coin is to be patient with your trading partner. Every now and then, the "real world" intrudes and trades have to be shuffled into the background (this is a hobby, remember?).

**No surprises.** Discuss tape type, Dolby, etc., beforehand. If you're copying a tape and you discover flaws that you never noticed before, be up front about it and give your trading partner the opportunity to pick a different tape.

**Keep first-time trades modest.** When trading with someone who's a stranger to you, don't swap more than four tapes at one time. In the rare case of personality conflicts or outright thievery (see below), at the worst you'll only be out a few dollars.

**Someone mailed me tapes and they never arrived—who's responsible?** Until the moment they arrive at their destination, tapes are the responsibility of the person who mailed them. Fortunately, presuming that you didn't use a mailer that was falling apart, tapes are rarely lost.

**Someone sent me tapes and they were horrible!** Unfortunately, this happens from time to time. Usually this is an honest disagreement over how two people grade tapes. If you get a batch of dodgy tapes, first and foremost shine it on as One of Those Things. C'est la vie. Life is too short to get worked up over it. The best thing to do is to (politely!) try to educate your trading partner. Be specific: "Gee, the tapes you sent had a lot of hiss and no high end—do you really think they deserved to be rated A–?"

**I think I got ripped off!** It's extremely rare, but every now and then you will encounter the dreaded "bad trader"—someone who arranges a trade but has no intention of ever mailing anything out to you, in essence stealing your tapes.

But while genuine thieves exist, 99 percent of "bad trader" situations turn out to be nothing more than innocent miscommunication—someone's decks broke, they lost their Internet access, something happened to keep them from finishing their end of the trade and/or telling you about it. Your goal is to have infinite patience.

And in the rare cases where you actually lose tapes—did you remember what I said a few paragraphs back about keeping first-time trades down to a small number of tapes?

## A Final Word

You know the story: the snake has *got* to eat his tail. Yin's gotta yang. What goes around comes around. So now that you're a seasoned veteran, don't forget where it all began. It's your karmic responsibility, so to speak, to be on the lookout for newbies and help them get started.

# Resource Guide

### The Official Grateful Dead Home Page (www.dead.net/)

If you decide you wanna go Net-surfing for waves of GD info, this is the obvious diving board from which to spring. Elegantly designed with detailed graphics and vibrant colors, the space-themed site is maintained by the Dead organization itself. This is the place to go for the latest on releases from the Vault, this summer's Furthur tour, GD news, Hunter's recent travels and thoughts (his ongoing on-line journal is a fascinating and almost candid glimpse into the man better known for formal lyrics than one-on-one conversations), as well as other entertaining tidbits including recipes, Deadhead humor, envelope art, Phil's version of Classical Music 101, Deadhead history and relics (newsletters sent from the office back in the early seventies), and the contents of band members' personal music collections. You can also find the on-line version of the *GD Almanac*, Mickey's definition of rhythm, past and present photos of Billy, Hunter's poignant and stirring elegy for Garcia, links to the Rex Foundation and Hulogosi Books (a publishing company founded by GD alumni), a Grateful Dead merchandising on-line store, handwritten lyrics, photos from Furthur and Robert Hunter's latest nationwide tour, and the DeadNet Central discussion group, among other things. There's plenty to poke around for, and plenty of heart to match.

### rec.music.gdead

The official Grateful Dead newgroup, rec.music.gdead, is a hugely popular Usenet site where connected Deadheads often post requests for tape trades, share news and opinions on the latest and greatest GD rumors, discuss the virtues and downfalls of shows, debate the hottest versions of tunes, share insights, and in general, keep the Deadhead community alive in such a way that only HOL (Heads On-Line) can do.

### ftp://gdead.berkeley.edu

This FTP (file transfer protocol) is the file collector's dream come true. Stuffed with downloadable files including set lists, interviews, graphics, sounds, tape labels, trees and lists, current tour dates, and statistics, this Berkeley archive also includes (as does Tiedrich's site—see Jeff Tiedrich's resource for tape traders) Ihor Slabicky's discography, the most comprehensive and accurate discography of both Grateful Dead music and the individual members' solo projects, to date.

### The Annotated Grateful Dead Lyrics Web Site (www.ucsc.edu/gdead/agdl)

Has it occurred to you to wonder about the significance of the rose as a recurring Grateful Dead motif? Or what choice exactly a buck dancer makes? Have you ever pondered the verses of "China Cat Sunflower" and what they mean? Having trouble figuring out the exact words to "Sugar Magnolia"? If there's anyone who might have the answer, it would probably be David Dodd, an assistant professor who, while at the Kraemer Family Library at the University of Colorado at Colorado Springs, put together an extensive collection of Grateful Dead lyrics. Aside from this (quite a feat in itself given the number of songs the Grateful Dead have written and performed), he attempts to provide footnotes for the literary, mythical, biblical, and historical references within the songs themselves. Even more impressively, Dodd has written and collected quite a few thematic essays not only providing answers to the questions asked above, but also discussing such things as the origin of Franklin's Tower, the idea of the life cycle contained in *Aoxomoxoa*, and the nonsense verse and even nursery rhymes contained in Grateful Dead lyrics. Dodd also includes a search index (by phrase, theme, or motif), bibliographies, discographies, and a film- and videography. Reader comments and anecdotes are regularly integrated into his substantial body of work, and each month, when the site is updated, changes are noted and sent via e-mail to Dodd's mailing list (to be added to the mailing list, e-mail Dodd at ddodd@well.com).

### Roots of the Grateful Dead
### (www.taco.com/roots/)

While David Dodd's annotated lyrics site may put your mind at ease over some of the questions Hunter, Barlow, and the boys might have raised in listening to GD originals, a good portion of the Dead's repertoire, the covers, isn't even considered. Here, Randy Jackson's (ajax@well.com) Roots of the Dead site gives the origin and evolution of all non–Dead originals. The site contains topics including original authors, anecdotes explaining myths and characters, original recording artists, and the impact on the Dead's style made by both folk and country music genres. The site also catalogs the origins of non-Dead Jerry covers, such as "Don't Let Go," "Tangled Up in Blue," and "Dear Prudence"; the names of Garcia-Grisman tunes and their original sources; and reviews, lineups, and song origins of pre–Grateful Dead bands. Another remarkable feature of this site is the song archives (a list of virtually all covers and their original recording artists) as well as profiles, short bios, and photos of many of these original artists.

### The DeadLists Project
### (www.deadlists.com)

This site is an attempt by an ever-growing number of on-line Heads to create on the World Wide Web the most accurate collection of set list information for Dead performances. Set lists not only include names of songs, but also timings, song maps, recording information, etc. You can download the project's files, set lists for each year of the Grateful Dead's existence, and search engines as well, allowing you to search for certain songs, certain venues, etc., on your own computer. The project is a work-in-progress, and as it stands, the immediate results of the fruits of many persons' labors, but because it is composed of entirely original research, there is ample opportunity for you to get involved. For more information, and to become a part of the DeadLists project, join the Project Mailing List by sending mail to majordomo@gdead.berkeley.edu with the text "Subscribe DeadLists" in the body of the message.

### The Jerry Site
### (www.deadlists.com/jerry/index.html)

What makes JGB different from the Acoustic Jerry Band? When did the Legion of Mary play most of its shows? What's the best way to find solo-Jerry set lists from the mid-seventies? Interested in Jerry Garcia's music outside of the Grateful Dead? Curious about a tape's set list accuracy? Think it'll take nothing short of a miracle to satisfy your Jerry Garcia curiosity?

An excellent companion to the DeadLists project, the Jerry site can answer all of these questions and more. Ryan Shriver's (ryan@digicol.com) Web site tracks set lists and recordings for Jerry Garcia's non–Grateful Dead work from 1971 to 1995. These include the various conglomerations of musicians that made up the Legion of Mary, Garcia-Saunders, Old and In the Way, the Great American String Band, the Jerry Garcia Band, Reconstruction, Garcia-Kahn, the Jerry Garcia Acoustic Band, and Garcia-Grisman. This site includes lineups and dates for each of the bands as well as a Garcia resource guide. It provides useful information, especially for identifying mislabeled tapes and seeing which shows are the most popular, or rare, in general circulation.

### Tapes in Circulation Site
### (www.winternet.com/~edoherty/)

Aside from interesting personal anecdotes and photographs from site author Eric Doherty, you'll find a detailed collection of show and tape history. The most current and accurate tape genealogy and circulation information resides here, providing an informative picture of current tapes floating around the Deadhead circuit. The pre–Grateful Dead era is also covered, as are Garcia's shows with the Legion of Mary, and the site rounds itself off with the section "Commonly Mislabeled Tapes," a must-read for any serious taper.

### Jim Denaro's Grateful Dead Tapelist Site
### (www.demonsys.com/jim/tapelists.html)

One-stop shopping for tapers, whether they consider themselves to be beginners, intermediate, or advanced, Denaro's seed of an idea to build a comprehensive network of earnest, dead-icated tapers, collections large or small, has grown into one sweet-smelling flower. Hundreds, if not thousands, of lists, both DAT and analog, reside here, organized by the number of hours in each collection and further denoted by each taper's name and how often they update their lists. There is also a taper's chat room, a how-to guide for getting your foot in the door in the ever-complex neighborhood of taping, taper's wish lists, discussion groups on such topics as the future accuracy of DAT trading, and a trader's resource guide.

You can add your list to the many and, with the click of a button, update it as often as you like.

### Jeff Tiedrich's Resource for Tape Traders
### (www.tiedrich.com/tapelist/)

It's obvious that hours and hours and hours of painstaking research have gone into Tiedrich's Web site. The pinnacle of the site's success is the categorized list of Grateful Dead tapes in circulation, including ideas on the quality you can expect to find upon acquiring one of these tapes. This site also includes a tape exchange where you can post requests to find that ever-elusive show you've been looking for since that night, as well as technical info on cassette decks and DAT tape machines and tapes. There's a list of bands that allow in-concert taping as well as a conclusive GD discography (compiled by Ihor Slabicky), a section on tape-trading etiquette and another devoted exclusively to commonly mislabeled tapes. Tiedrich, a perfectionist and an impressive researcher, has created an honest, down-to-earth, direct-to-the-point site that in a couple of tens of thousands of bytes manages to answer virtually every question you might have about taping and trading.

### The Dead Sled
### (www.voicenet.com/~yakko/gdead.html)

Your metaphorical sticker-covered VW hippie-van to cruise the Internet Superhighway, without fear of being pulled over just for having Dead stickers on your car. In reality, this site, maintained by Aaron Richardson (arichard@acs.bu.edu), serves as your basic HOL (Heads On-Line) starter kit. It offers, in vibrant, psychedelic colors and using Stealies, Dancing Bears, and Skulls and Roses, links to Deadhead homepages across the Net, access to screen savers, J-cards, GD icons and sounds for your computer, chat rooms, lifestyle surveys, humor, connections to well-known Head shops, boutiques and environmental activist causes, even an informative text on "How to Tie-Dye." Some of the site's more notable links are those to the Tie-Died homepage, DeadBase, Liquid Blue, Sunflower Studios (a site that's managed to create a name for itself by offering some of the most astoundingly beautiful J-cards to be downloaded, free of charge) as well as the Web site of Steve Silberman, coauthor of *Skeleton Key: A Dictionary for Deadheads*. One last notable feature allows you to listen to pleasantly muzaked versions of "Scarlet Begonias," "The Golden Road," "Ramble On Rose," "Dear Prudence," "Johnny B. Goode," "Uncle John's Band," and several other tunes. The essence of the site is to remind Deadheads that the community spirit will live on forever—if the Dead Sled is any proof, right on!

### www.rukind.com

This site has a little bit of something for everyone. Geared for musicians, there are links to on-line music magazines like *Rolling Stone, Billboard,* the *Bluegrass Connection, Cybergrass,* and *MandoZine* (a magazine for mandolin players) as well as a music chat room. However, if your mind starts to wander, there's also a connection to ESPN's Sport Zone, a hippie site (for hippies by hippies), and a separate psychedelic art show, even a link to *High Times* on-line. However, this site's most notable feature is its tiny bit of guitar player's heaven on earth: tons and tons of guitar tablature, including, but not limited to, the Grateful Dead, the Beatles, Neil Young, Frank Zappa, Pink Floyd, Bob Dylan, and Chuck Berry. All you need to do is pick a song, any song, and up pops the tab. It's that simple. It was previously known and renowned as Ed Bick's Grateful Guitar Page, put together by Bick and other music-minded Heads. Presumably it's still the same site, and then some. Regardless, play like Jerry!

## DeadBase
## (www.deadbase.com)

Though not as comprehensive as the actual hard- and softcover versions, DeadBase on-line is what you'd expect, and a little bit more. The site offers complete and thorough set lists from the 1990s, the results of the first and second electronic surveys, a bulletin board service (called DeadBase Forum), and Web space (at a reasonable price) for traders to post their lists and for related businesses and services to advertise.

## Magazines and Books

*Dupree's Diamond News.* Published quarterly, *DDN* has been documenting the Deadhead Experience since 1987. Available in 2,000 stores nationwide, and by mail through reader subscriptions, *Dupree's* provides high-quality, in-depth articles on Grateful Dead tape trading, the latest GD news and tour reviews, interviews with band members and organization family, as well as coverage on related bands (Dylan, Hot Tuna, Allmans, Phish, moe, Medeski Martin & Wood, Blues Traveller, Strangefolk, etc.) and the Deadhead community. With its yearly "Tape Trading in Review" articles and the largest tape-trading classified ads section in print, *DDN* is a great way to keep up-to-date on what's happening in the taping and trading worlds and the general Deadhead scene as well. Four-issue subscriptions (with free twenty-five-word tape trade or personal ad): $16 ($21 Canadian, $29 Europe, $33 Asia); sample issue, $5 ($7 Canadian, $8 Europe, $8 Asia). Mail check or money order to DDN, PO Box 936, Northampton, MA 01060.

*Taper's Quarterly: The Magazine of Live Music and Concert Taping*

Though not specifically geared toward Deadheads, *Taper's Quarterly* is an excellent twenty-five-page 'zine dedicated to live concert taping. With articles on the hows and whys of taping; trading; trees and vines; taping history, anecdotes, and memorabilia from readers regarding recent shows; even lists and highlights of bands (large and small, nationwide) that allow in-concert taping, *TQ* is a interesting and informative way to learn about and keep up with the live-show taping scene. *Taper's Quarterly* relies heavily on reader submissions (including articles, reviews of memorable recent or shows from the past, album or equipment reviews, and memorabilia—fliers, ticket stubs, setlists, photos, etc.) on live music and encourages folks to get involved. For more information or to make a submission, write: *LAVA/Taper's Quarterly,* PO Box 641191, San Francisco CA 94164-1191 or e-mail lava@well.com. Four issues: $10 (US, Canada and Mexico), $19 (elsewhere, includes one twenty-five-word classified ad for one issue).

*The Complete Guide to High-End Audio,* by Robert Harley, Acapella Publishing, 1995, 450 pp. $29.95 plus $4.95 shipping and handling.

Sooner or later, if you get into music seriously, it's necessary to learn about serious audio equipment and basic sound theory. This can be quite a daunting process, as high-end audio seems to have nearly become rocket science. Robert Harley, a technical editor for *Stereophile Magazine,* has authored the easy-to-understand *Complete Guide to High-End Audio*. It's all here: from the basics of sound and hearing to learning how to become a better listener. You'll learn how to choose the stereo components that are right for you, and how to make your stereo sound up to 50 percent better in ten minutes. In short, it's the bible for those who want to become serious music listeners. To order, call 800-848-5099.

*DeadBase* (hardcover, softcover, and junior editions).

Published ten times to date, *DeadBase,* in its various incarnations, has for years been the definitive answer to set list and show statistics questions. Not only does it include every set list for every show (accurate to the day of the week the show occurred) but it set the stage for Deadhead lifestyle surveys and boggled the minds of Heads across the country with its lists upon lists upon lists: songs played, number of times played (including jams), venues played (even including seating charts for many of the major ones!), exhaustive discographies, etc. The appearance of the hardcover and softcover versions remind you of the college textbook you wish you could have studied in school! Available through the DeadBase company: DeadBase, P.O. Box 499, Hanover, NH 03755, 603-542-2945, or at Head shops and retail stores across the country.

*The Grateful Dead and the Deadheads: An Annotated Bibliography,* by David Dodd and Rob Weiner. Greenwood Press, 1997. $75.

Though $75 is rather pricey for the average Deadhead to shell out of his/her pocket, this 430-page annotated bibliography is well worth every penny. An exhaustive tome, the bibliography includes notations on and text from all books written about the band and its followers, as well as articles from every major magazine and journal, newspaper articles from the *San Francisco Chronicle* and the *San Francisco Examiner,* and all entries and chapters from books mentioning the Dead or Deadheads from the band's creation in 1965 to September 1996. Another remarkable innovation is the chronicle of material from Grateful Dead fanzines such as *Dupree's Diamond News, Relix, Unbroken Chain,* and *The Golden Road,* among others.

*Skeleton Key: A Dictionary for Deadheads,* by David Shenk and Steve Silberman, Doubleday Books, 1994, 388 pp. $14.95.

More than just a dictionary of lingo, *Skeleton Key* is the first in-depth map of the Deadhead subculture. In pithy entries from "Acid Tests" to "the Zone," the authors interweave historical narrative, tour stories, and interviews to produce a many-textured quilt of observations on touring, psychedelics and spirituality, Deadhead books and magazines, Heads on-line, jargon and humor, taping and trading, and many other aspects of Deadhead tribal life. *Skeleton Key* includes reviews of the band's albums by Robert Hunter, Blair Jackson, Bob Bralove, and David Gans, as well as reminiscences by Bruce Hornsby, Elvis Costello, John Dwork, and others. Many colorful Deadhead characters—from Bear to Cassady to the Pineapple Guys—are portrayed in the context of the unfolding history of the scene, traced from the Beat coffeehouse days on the Peninsula to arena shows of the nineties. By combining personal perspectives with historical overview, *Skeleton Key* preserves a wealth of Deadhead lore and offers readers—from newbies to longtime tourheads—a lively and affectionate meditation on Deadhead spirit.

### Others

*Terrapin Tapes*
336 Federal Road
Brookfield, CT 06804
WWW.TTapes.Com
(800) 677-8650

Terrapin Tapes is a mail-order *blank* tape and DAT equipment company that works with live-music tape traders. Terrapin offers great pricing if you order tapes in bulk quantities. The company also understands and supports the Deadhead community by sponsoring concerts and music festivals. Most importantly, Terrapin's run by a bunch of Heads and is a great way of keeping your money in the community instead of doing business with someone who says, "Jerry who?"

# The Contributors

CHRIS ALLEN, 43. Favorite "Dark Star": 4/28/71 (It's short, but reveals the ultimate synchronistic intuition). First Show: 10/23/70 Georgetown University, Washington, D.C. Favorite GD Period: '69–'73. Interests: Psychology/Nonsense audio/Geology/Meteorology/Environmental consulting/GIS-programming. Still, got into 119 GD shows. Why wasn't *Anthem* remix used for CD instead of original? Contact: callen2@clarku.edu

HUGH BARROLL, 40. Favorite "Dark Star": 4/29/72. Lawyer for the Environmental Protection Agency, specializing in wetlands protection. Married, father of Daniel and Mark. Personal hero: Bullwinkle.

ADAM BAUER, 32. Favorite "Dark Star": Silly question; why attempt to quantify the ineffable? What is the sound of one guitar silenced? Bauer, whatever his genuine peculiarities might be, at least looks out for opportunities to shine a light in the world. And he grows a sweet bed o' basil. Could be worse. Contact: ahunterb@crocker.com

PAUL BODENHAM. Favorite "Dark Star": 5/11/72. Lives in Bristol, UK, and works in a hospital as a medical artist. Loves of my life: Linda, travel, and music. Favorite/most inspiring destinations: West Africa, Indonesia, India (go!). "If the Dead Experience teaches us anything it's to be forever open to the New, to actively search it out and to be aware of it enough to know when it bites yer bum." Oh yeah, and don't forget, folks, "The pig's head does not get lost in the soup."—Akan proverb. Contact: paul.bodenham@ukonline.co.uk

ELIZA BUNDLEDEE, 35. Favorite "Dark Star": 9/19/70. Eliza is a musician known for her innovative vocalizations and unusual, eclectic songwriting style. She performs in the Bay Area as a soloist and with her band. In 1986, she initiated her "Musical Medicine" program that brings music to hospice, bedbound, and acute rehab patients. It's now established in several local hospitals and care facilities. Contact: mgoetz@well.com

DAVID CECCHI, 23. Favorite "Dark Star": 4/29/72. "We're sittin' here stranded, though we're all doin' our best to deny it."—B. Dylan. Geologist, computer scientist, hiker, biker, golfer, skier, 318. Contact: cecc0003@gold.tc.umn.edu

CHRISTIAN CRUMLISH (GATEFOLD SLEEVE), 32. Favorite "Dark Star": 6/24/70b. First show: 6/24/84 SPAC. Last show: 6/4/95 Shoreline. Writer, artist, raconteur. Publisher of *Enterzone* at http://ezone.org/ez and Kind Veggie T-Shirt in Usenet posts, e-mail, and netsam everywhere. See you at JazzFest. Contact: xian@ezone.org *or* General Delivery, Saturn

DANIEL J. DASARO, 32. Favorite "Dark Star": 10/31/91. First show: 6/23/84. Favorite event: 4/26/88. Computer systems engineer (financial industry), former Virtual Realist, sports car enthusiast. East Coaster who spent five music-filled years in the Bay Area. Thanks. Contact: daniel_dasaro@techsol.com

ERIC DOHERTY, 24. Favorite "Dark Star": 09/17/70. "Get up off your ass and dance!" ;) Contact:

edoherty@winternet.com *or* 2110 S. Rosewood Ln., Roseville, MN 55113

DOUGAL DONALDSON, 38. Favorite "Dark Star": *Live Dead*, silly. First discovered there was something special about the Dead: 3/29/75. First show: 9/25/76. Last (387th) show: 6/4/95. I'm a software developer living in Berkeley with my wife, Poppy, and Mad Dog, my annoying cat. Anyone know where there are any live Camper Van Beethoven tapes?! Contact: dougal@well.com.

DENNIS DONLEY, 46. Favorite "Dark Star": 2/27/69. First show: 4/29/67. Last show: 6/4/95. Best show: 10/18/74. Librarian and educator, husband of Ruth, father of Eric and Evan. Collector of books, music, and posters; contributor to various publications. ". . . and leave it on!" Contact: Dennis Donley, Hoover High School, 4474 El Cajon Blvd., San Diego, CA 92115

BRIAN DYKE, 24. Favorite "Dark Star": 11/11/73. First show: 14/17/89. First tapes: 11/19/71 and 6/28/86. Deeply indebted: To Che for showing, to Rob for giving, to Michael for accepting, and to Patricia, with whom I share the gift of music. Contact: BDyke@cris.com

ROB EATON, 36. Favorite "Dark Star": 4/8/72. First show: 8/2/76. Recording producer/engineer/musician, Vermont transplant in Jersey, collecting DATs, Border Legion, hanging with wife Tina and dogs Redzers and Chief. Contact: kingbeemusic@earthlink.net

TODD ELLENBERG, 41. Favorite "Dark Star": 4/8/72. Life on the rails: "If we continue in the same direction down this track, we'll probably wind up where we're headed. . . . We need to lay some new track." Communicator/writer/public relations counselor. Forever grateful to Chris, Kerry, and Spencer, my partners in the ever-continuing "long strange trip."

TOM FERRARO, 41. Favorite "Dark Star": 2/27/69. First Show: 9/21/72. Ph.D. Pharmacology, 1985; associate professor, University of Pennsylvania, 1997: neurogenetics, neuropharmacology. My Main Ten: family, friends, heart, inquiry, discovery, head, work, play, soul, life!

JAKE FROST. Favorite "Dark Star": *Live Dead* version. Discovered *Live Dead* in 1970, became enamored, first show 1972, became hooked. Most fun at shows: summer and fall tours 1989. Late seventies in the UK saw a tail-off: the lean years here. The Dead came back in 1981 and so did my interest—and a lot of other people's. Found out about tape trading in a big way and never looked back. Became involved in the UK fanzine *Spiral Light* in 1983; continued until 1996 when we folded it. Since Jerry's death have found solace in the early years 1968–74.

EVELYNN GETZ, 15. I love music, especially Portishead! I love mysteries, like the Loch Ness monster, vampires, weird spirits, death, and UFOs. I go to San Francisco Waldorf School.

BARRY GLASSBERG, 46. Favorite "Morning Dew": 9/18/87. First show: 10/31/70 late Stony Brook. Shows attended: 352. Grateful Dead shows personally taped: 300+. I am still actively taping, i.e., Allman Brothers Band. Contact: PO Box 538, Larchmont, NY 10538-0538

ROBERT A. GOETZ. I mostly appreciate the 1972 "Dark Star"s, and have been into the Dead since 1987. Here is a music that created challenging and sinister sounds yet also soothes through a nurturing side. Contact: goetz017@goetz017.email.umn.edu

JOLIE GOODMAN, 36. Favorite "Dark Star": 7/13/84. First show: 4/27/77. "The enemy is listening."—sticker on Jerry's Travis Bean guitar, circa 1977. Special education teacher, wife, mother, amateur musician. Contact: Jerrapin@aol.com

HARRY HAHN, 31. Favorite "Dark Star": 8/27/72. First show: 3/9/81. Favorite shows: 10/11/83, 4/14/84, 3/27/85, 6/14/85, 11/1/85. Favorite tapes: 8/27/72, 6/16/74, 9/18/74, 9/25/76. What I miss most is the feeling in the room just after the lights went down and before the band came on.

SCOTT HAYMAKER, 32. Favorite "Dark Star": 7/13/84. First show: Cap Center, 1982. "One of the unusual suspects."—Scott Haymaker. Systems engineer, poet, and patriot. Contact: the_Saint@trellis.net

DWIGHT HOLMES, 45. Favorite "Dark Star" (besides the *Live Dead* version, of course): 6/24/70b. First show: 3/14/71. Profession: Teacher, educationist. Goal: To resist and undermine the system's penchant for giving the least in school to those who already get the least in life. Avocation: Escaping the samsaric realm of birth and rebirth. Contact: dholmes@mailer.fsu.edu (STARBASE: http://garnet.acns.fsu.edu/~dholmes/starbase.html)

# The Contributors

BLAIR JACKSON has been writing about the Dead for more than 25 years. He is the author of two books about the band, *The Music Never Stopped* (Delilah Books, 1982, out of print) and *Goin' Down the Road: A Grateful Dead Traveling Companion* (Harmony Books, 1992), and for nine years he was editor/publisher/writer of the Dead fanzine *The Golden Road*. God willing, his biography of Jerry Garcia will be published by Viking Books in the fall of 1998.

JAY KERLEY, 43. Favorite "Dark Star": 10/18/74. I've been Dead for 28 years. I first heard the Dead on NYC FM radio in '69 and began collecting tapes in the summer of '71. I finally escaped and saw them live on 7/18/72. Nowadays I spend my time teaching, traveling and/or taping. Jerry lives!

CHERIE CLARK-KING, 35. Favorite "Dark Star": 4/28/71 Fillmore East, New York City. Editor/author/tarot reader living in New York City; I have done work for *Dupree's Diamond News*, *Garcia: A Grateful Celebration*, *Dead-Base*, *Terrapin Tapes*, and other publications. I was blessed with eighteen touring years on the bus. Now all that is left is the music. Contact: cherie@well.com

BILL KRISTI, 38. Favorite "Dark Star": 8/24/72. (I love how wild that "Star" is!) First show: 12/30/79. Favorite show (of 110): 12/30/82. Favorite tape: 11/8/69. Backpacker, database manager at UC Berkeley. Happy trails! Contact: bck@dev.urel.berkeley.edu

HARVEY LUBAR, born 11/11/53. Forget "Dark Star," gimme "Viola Lee Blues" 5/2/70 Harpur. First show: 12/6/71 Felt Forum. Biggest shock of my life: I expected "Lovelight," "Viola Lee Blues," and "Cream Puff War" at my first show and got "Bertha," "Mr. Charlie," and "Jack Straw."

JEFF MATTSON, 38. Favorite "Dark Star": 12/6/73. First show: 9/8/73. "Peculiar travel suggestions are dancing lessons from God."—Kurt Vonnegut. Guitarist with the Zen Tricksters. Contact: zen.tricksters@juno.com, Web site: http://ada.hofsta.edu/~bseis24/zen.html

DARREN E. MASON, 28. Favorite "Dark Star": 5/25/72 & 10/28/72 (tie). First show: 6/26/86 Hubert H. Humphrey Metrodome, Minneapolis, Minnesota. Visiting mathematics professor, CMU. Maxim: Never panic. Especially when real life is concerned. Contact: dmason+@andrew.cmu.edu

NICHOLAS G. MERIWETHER, 32. Favorite "Dark Star": 2/27/69 Fillmore West. A student of American bohemianism, he lives in San Francisco. He has written about the American South, the San Francisco Bay Area, and American music and culture from the sixties to the present.

ALEXIS MUELLNER, 35. Favorite "Dark Star": 8/27/72. First show: 5/8/80, Glens Falls, NY. Print journalist, writer, radio producer, satirist, ham, listener, master of the pick 'n' roll, actor, french pastry chef. Creed: Loyalty, truth, tact, caring, creativity, spontaneous expression, art, word jazz, and an occasional pad Thai with chicken. "Play hard, play fair, nobody gets hurt." Contact: alexis@icanect.net

JOHN OLEYNICK, 32. Favorite "Dark Star": 4/22/69. John grew up in Bucks County, Pennsylvania, but now lives in the San Francisco Bay Area with his wife, Julie. He enjoys listening to music (Dead, Ramones, Clegg, N'Dour, Miles, Mulligan) and hiking through the redwoods and along the ocean. Contact: http://www.geocities.com/SunsetStrip/Palms/5270/

MICHAEL PARRISH, 43. Favorite "Dark Star": 2/27/69. First show: 3/1/69. Last show: 7/9/95. "Fear is excitement minus the breath."—F. Perls. Paleontologist/biologist/freelance music writer. Contact: mparrish@niu.edu

PAUL J. PEARAH, 36. Favorite "Dark Star": 9/21/72. First show: 11/17/78 Uptown. The music of the Dead has enriched my life with great gifts of insight, joy, and friendship. As another tape collector remarked, they have been playing the soundtracks of our lives for decades. I bid you peace, and enjoy the music! SCUBA diver, tape trader, engineer.

BARRY EDGAR PILCHER, 54. Favorite "Dark Star": 9/24/72. Born southeast London; poet, musician, mail artist. Current creative base: magical Inishfree in Ireland. For news of future albums, poetry, books, and projects, write to: Raven's Cottage, Inishfree Upper, Burton Port, Nr. Letterkenny, County Donegal, Ireland

WILLIAM E. POLITS, 37. Favorite "Dark Star": 12/21/2012. Occupation: musician, educator. Favorite quote: Anything can happen . . . and it always does. Fan mail: 2903 San Mateo St., Richmond, CA 94804

COREY SANDERSON, 26. Favorite "Dark Star": 8/27/72 Veneta, Oregon. First show: 7/2/89 Foxboro, MA. Professional student. "If you have to ask what jazz is, you'll never know."—Louis Armstrong. Tape trading, transcending yourself in a DEEP space jam, and the adventure of it all! Groove Rock bands, reading, muscle car restorations, playing drums. Contact: 210 Herrick Rd-Box 73, Newton Centre, MA 02159

STEVE SILBERMAN, 39. Favorite "Dark Star": Every "Dark Star" ever played, heard as a single evolving piece of music. First show: Watkins Glen soundcheck, 7/27/73. Coauthor with David Shenk of *Skeleton Key: A Dictionary for Deadheads*. Also wrote the liner notes for *How Sweet It Is*, "The Only Song of God," "Who Was Cowboy Neal?" and other Dead-ly texts. Happy contributor to *Dupree's Diamond News*. Observer of online culture for *Wired News* (www.wired.com) and *Packet* (www.packet.com/silberman). "Stoke the fires of paradise with coals from Hell to start."—R. Hunter. Contact: digaman@hotwired.com *or* home page at www.levity.com

IHOR SLABICKY. Favorite "Dark Star": 2/27/69. Sure, all "Dark Star"s are good, and some are even better than others! But the spaces this one takes you, the emotions you experience, the aural vistas—they make this the definitive version, against which all others are compared! Contact: Ihor Slabicky, 35 Hathaway Drive, Portsmouth, RI 02871

LARRY STEIN, 42. Favorite "Dark Star": Pick only one?!?! You gotta be kidding! First show: 5/20/73. Computer professional, ex-wine retail geek, married to Deadhead, one beautiful baby daughter who I predict in about three or four years will ask, "Daddy, what's that noise you're playing?"

JAY STRAUSS, 39. Favorite "Dark Star": 4/8/72. Dead-Headhunter, living on a rock in the Puget Sound with my sweetie, Sharon the indulgent, kids, Josh and Taylor, and Jerry the smiling dog. Mine ears have heard the glory of the jamming of the Dead. Contact: piggar@ix.netcom.com

JAMES SWIFT, 29. Favorite "Dark Star": 9/19/70. I live in London (England!) and love music from folk to ambient dub and many writers, especially William Burroughs. "To achieve complete freedom from past conditioning is to be in space. Techniques exist for achieving such freedom. These techniques are being concealed and withheld."—W.B. Contact: James@Gaisford.demon.co.uk

ERIC TAYLOR, 48. First show: 9/67, Denver City Park. Sunny afternoon. Fire-eaters. Conga lines. Strange goodness. Some band members even took off their shirts. Now: Live near NYC and work as free-lance film/TV director. Miss the Love/Music of the shows. "Nothing left to do but smile, smile smile." Contact: et@bestweb.net

JEFF TIEDRICH, 40. Favorite "Dark Star" (this week): 9/24/72. Tape collecting is a wonderful hobby for obsessive-compulsive list-makers. I'm glad you all agree. Now if you'll excuse me, I have to go buy some more shelves. Contact: jeff@tiedrich.com

ERIC M. VANDERCAR, 36. Favorite "Dark Star": 4/8/72. First show: 11/5/79. Last show: 7/9/95. "In the end there's still that song..."—Garcia-Hunter 8/9/95 RIP. Strategist, skier, kayaker, whitewater guide, rock climber, taper, artist, poet/lyricist, procrastinator, dog lover, NoHo, MP/NTAP.

MICHAEL WANGER, 50. Favorite "Dark Star": 9/10/74. Film and video producer. Music programs on PBS. Emmy nominations. Former member of "The Uncalled Four." "If you get confused, listen to the music play." Contact: vidkid@well.com, www.vidkid.com

MICHAEL P. WEITZMAN, 27. Favorite Dark Star: 7/26/72. "I think that my schooling interrupted my education."—Winston Churchill. This is probably more than you need to know about me. Contact: Mpw@access.digex.net

BART WISE, 30. Favorite Dark Star: 2/13/70. Seen many a high point in my time, hope to rejoice in a number more before I'm done. Been an archaeologist, union drive instigator, writer, server administrator, traveler; now hoping to heal a few people's bodies. Awake in joy!

JOHN J. WOOD, 32. Favorite "Dark Star": The last one I heard. "All good things in all good time."—Robert Hunter. "And in the end, the love you take is equal to the love you make."—John Lennon, Paul McCartney. Computer geek. Longtime music junkie. Always living for the moment by being ready for IT! Contact: johnw@newscorp.com

STEPHEN WADE, 44. Favorite "Dark Star": 4/26/70 Poynette, Wisconsin. First show: 11/17/68. Performer, writer, and musician. Jerry Garcia represents to me the heart of musicianship, a pursuit he filled with grace, mystery, and delight. Contact: dholmes@mailer.fsu.edu

# Acknowledgments

First and foremost we would like to thank the Grateful Dead for providing thirty years worth of music from the heart. Dead concerts were islands of freedom, places to let go, rituals of introspection, and gatherings to communally share peak experiences. Dead music erased the moat between band and audience. We participated and influenced the music.

And this book would not exist without the band's generosity in sharing tapes of its performances as well as allowing us to record the shows ourselves. Rest assured, fellas: the music is being put to good use through continued celebration, wonderment, and lots of fun.

## Research

Next, we must vociferously thank Nicholas G. Meriwether, Dougal Donaldson, Brian Dyke, Jeff Tiedrich, and Eric Doherty. The gargantuan efforts of these Grateful Dead scholars in helping to research, write, and fact-check this book cannot be overstated. If a Deadhead's Hall of Fame is ever launched you gentlemen surely deserve to be among the first inductees.

Nick Meriwether, who wrote so eloquently of the Dead's early years, left no stone unturned (or turn unstoned). His scholarship of the pre-1966 material for this book is of the highest order. All the librarians in the Bay Area and Palo Alto know him well. His ongoing feedback for many areas of the *Compendium* was not only astute and kindly presented—it was inspirational and positively infectious. Thanks, Nick.

Dougal Donaldson was an essential *Compendium* team member from day one, offering excellent suggestions, making solid referrals, and bringing accuracy to the book. He was a complete support during the ups and downs and gave consistently to the project on a variety of levels—in addition to his meticulous reviews and insightful pioneering of the year by year summaries for this book. He's also a class-act tape trader. Thanks so much, Dougal.

Brian Dyke went above and beyond the call of duty as we zapped him with an endless stream of outtake tapes; unreleased, semi-Dead jams; and regular show reviews. With tremendous patience he took it all in stride and churned out stellar work. Brian: you can wail, man. Thank you.

And then there's Jeff Tiedrich. He not only provided too many tapes to count, but was present—acerbic wit in tow—for helping to hunt down tapes, facts, and data of all kinds. Jeff also designed the *Compendium's* Web site and wrote the witty "Compleat Guide to Collecting and Trading Tapes." His sense of humor was always present in his correspondence, regardless of how busy he was, and was something we came to count on and look forward to. He didn't disappoint. Jeff is as much a part of this book as anyone and without him we'd still be working on it. Many thanks, sir.

In the beginning may have been the Word, but for us it was Eric Doherty. After seeing his excellent Tapes in Circulation list, we contacted him and instantly connected. Eric was a resource guide for Web info and put us in touch with many big Web traders. Soon the domino effect took over and the Web ship was sailing. Eric also provided constructive criticism. useful ideas, tapes, friendship, and even ice-fishing trips. Eric: thank you so much.

The many dead-icated Web folk and Michael's Bay Area cronies were crucial in helping us build the tape list database. Dozens and dozens of people contributed tapes and referrals. But special honor goes to Dr. Michael Parrish (from Chicago) and Hugh Barroll. Besides writing wonderful reviews these two fellers either lent or dubbed an amazing number of tapes with no strings attached—only goodwill and that wonderful feeling that comes from participating in a community project. To Michael and Hugh: we tip our hats to you both. This book would have taken much, much longer without your help. Thank you.

Once the database was flowing, questions arose as to the accuracy of certain shows in regard to the right venue, proper date, correct set list, etc. Darren Mason has tediously worked on this front with his excellent "Mislabeled Tapes" Web site (see "Resources"). Great work and thanks, Darren.

Many thanks to Dwight Holmes, too, for his fine detective work and overall support and enthusiasm for the project on many fronts. And thanks also for introducing us to Fred Ordower.

And thanks to all the people who have done research over the years and shared this with all the community: good ol' Harvey Lubar, Christian Crumlish, Rob Bertrando, Barry Glassberg, Dwight Holmes, Pete Gelpke, David Gans, Rob Eaton, Blair Jackson, Dario Wolfish, Hugh Barroll, and the DeadBase crew. There are many names missing here, we know. For those we've neglected, please forgive us and let us know: we'll mention you in the revised edition because you deserve it.

An extra special thank-you goes to kindhearted Rob Eaton for contributing in this area as well.

Another special thanks to Dead archivist and fellow Deadhead Dick Latvala. Dick was invaluable to us as he donated hours and hours of his time checking facts and giving lengthy interviews for this project. Dick is the ultimate dead-icated Deadhead.

When we were writing the history chapter, in the bottom of the ninth, Alexis Muellner went to bat with bases loaded and hit the ball out of the park.

A hearty round of applause goes to all those who came forward to tell their tales for the history chapter: Bear, for having the patience to put up with three interviews; and, of course, Dick Latvala, as well as Barry Glassberg, Les Kippel, Eddie Claridge, Jerry Moore, R.T. Carlyle, Bob Cohen, Bob Matthews, Rob Eaton, Louis Falanga, Peter Abram, Kenn Babbs, David Cooks, Harry Ely, Alan Mande, Gene Estribou, Kidd Candelario, Ed Perlstein, John Platt (out of the blue!), Steve Brown, Michael Wanger, Cary Wolfson, Steve Rolphe, Bill Belmont, Alain Hartmann, Richard Raffel, Zane Kesey, Chet Helms, and last but not least: Dan Healy for those wonderful lectures in 1985.

David Gans was a tremendous help as he promptly answered our steady stream of questions. He generously shared info on all *Grateful Dead Hour* programs, tapes, tapers, and various resources, and gave up a long afternoon to give us an honest, thoughtful interview. Thanks, David.

We are grateful to Les Kippel, founder of *Relix* magazine, not only for the great interview, but for the hours he clearly put in preparing for it and for helping later with proper names, dates, and other important editing. His referrals, copies of Free Underground Tape Exchange literature, and thoughtful suggestions for this project were also extremely helpful. Thanks, Les.

Many librarians and student newspaper staffers at colleges up and down the Eastern U.S. took the time to help with research. Thanks to Darcy Duke, Lori Mary, and Milan Merhar from MIT; Dianne Perron at Wesleyan University; Beth Kilmarx at SUNY Binghamton; Lynn Konnay at Georgetown University; Lora Brueck at Worcester Polytechnic Institute; Tracy at William Paterson College; and Kevin Grace at University of Cincinnati. Ari Ellberg spent many hours on the phone pursuing many leads.

Greg Shaw, thanks for the essential tidbits of particularly obscure arcana, especially the proof that the Dead did indeed play early shows on February 11, 13, 14, 1970. Thanks also to David Dodd for the tiny essential facts.

Our photographers came forward with a wealth of never-before-seen jewels: Amalie Rothschild, Michael Parrish, Fred Ordower, Don Snyder, David Spitzer, Harvey Lubar, David Lemieux, Susanna Millman, and Ed Perlstein—hip, hip hooray. And thanks to Jeff Harrison for the yearbook.

Special thanks to Fred Ordower for opening his home to us and taking the time to dig through those dusty boxes of killer photos.

Douglas Tinney at Ampex Corporation. Wow! Nice photo stash. Thank you.

Ticket stubs, programs, and posters were generously provided by Chris Allen, Ed Perlstein, Marc Blaker, Eddie Claridge, and Sue Kesey.

# Acknowledgments

## Writing Team

Once the ongoing database had established deep roots, we set out searching for writers. A special thanks here goes to Dario Wolfish for putting together a list of prospective writers based on his exchanges with them. Many of these people came on board. Dario also provided positive feedback and good vibes for the book since day one. You've got a big heart, Dario.

Our dead-icated writing team: Nick Meriwether, Dougal Donaldson, Brian Dyke, Robert A. Goetz, Michael Parrish, Jeff Tiedrich, Eric Doherty, Paul Bodenham, Hugh Barroll, Chris Allen, Adam Bauer, Marc Blaker, Eliza Bundledee, David Cecchi, Cherie Clark-King, Christian Crumlish, Daniel Dasaro, Dennis Donley, Rob Eaton, Todd Ellenberg, Tom Ferraro, Evelynn Getz, Bill Giles (for the poem!), Jolie Goodman, Harry Hahn, Scott Haymaker, Dwight Holmes, Blair Jackson, Jay Kerley, Bill Kristi, Andrew Lemieux, Harvey Lubar, Darren Mason, Jeff Mattson, Don Oldenberg, John Oleynick, Paul Pearah, William Polits, Corey Sanderson, Steve Silberman, Ihor Slabicky, Larry Stein, Jay Strauss, James Swift, Eric Taylor, Eric Vandercar, Stephen Wade, Michael Wanger, Bart Wise, Dario Wolfish, and John Wood.

## Production

Any project this size cannot see the light of day without the concerted efforts of a plethora of production experts. This project is no exception.

A giant high five goes to our way cool editor, Tracy Brown, a fan of the band since 1969. We couldn't have been luckier. This project shines because of your sage wisdom, steady demeanor, and upbeat attitude. You taught us a great deal, Tracy. Thanks are also in order for Tracy's faithful assistant, Alessandra Bocco.

The wonderful layout and design were crafted by Lucy Albanese and Paula Szafranski. How you put so much text in so little room and keep it not only readable, but beautiful, too, is a wonderful mystery.

Our production and copy editors did a phenomenal job making sure every *t* was crossed and *i* was dotted. Kathleen Fridella and Susanna Sturgis, you are goddesses!

Jean Sienkewicz and Adam MacConnell get medals of honor for their many hours of formatting, fact checking, transcribing, spell-checking, and all around word massaging. Tom Perry and Eric Doherty also helped with transcriptions.

And thanks to the talented Kevin Peake, artist extraordinaire, who birthed our wonderful cover art.

## Business

And to our agent Eileen Cope, as well as Barbara and Tom of Lowenstein-Morel Associates, a bow of gratitude. And a nod and a wink goes to Danny Goleman for the recommendation.

Thanks to our legal staff: Adrienne Crew—"literal girl" and guardian angel—and Richard Wiel, both of the California Lawyers for the Arts; the bright, lovely Gabrielle Sellei and the quick-witted Jeff Hofferman (of Mesirov, Gelman, Jaffe, Cramer & Jamieson); the savvy Dick Evans of Northampton, Massachusetts; the fog-cutting abilities of Tim Bak from Tommy Conner and Associates in San Francisco; Joe De Fazio of Northampton, Massachusetts; Tom Canova from New York; and Boston's suave David Marglin (of Skadden/Arps).

## Personal Acknowledgments

### MICHAEL M. GETZ:

My work might well have been tardy without the support, understanding, and scheduling acrobatics of my day-job boss (and fellow writer) Vito Chiala, of the Westin St. Francis. Thanks so very much, Vito. Thanks are in order to Orlando Bell, too. And thanks go to Myrna Padilla, Donald Anderson, Evis Rosales, and Carol Junsay for working these shifts for me. And I'd like to tip my hat in return to the servers who appreciate the skill, precision, and dark humor required to be a good host: Manny Panis, Joseph Wing, Connie Hibbard, Michelle Duvall, Ogee Baltazar, Sam Wong, Chris Schmidt, Ernie Castaneda, Elizabeth Farmer, and Mary Lee Chambers. Your generosity goes deeper than you know.

Super thanks to Josie Hipolita, Ofelia Palma, and Richard "Mean Guy" Kuscinski for all the belly laughs that *almost* made it too hard to eat. Finally, many thanks to Rex, Adib, Francisco, and Omar for their kindness in the kitchen.

In the beginning these people opened their hearts: Chris Stanton, Herbert and Janice Egli, and Gregory and Constance "The Nibbler" Alexander. Your kindness and generosity were truly inspiring. Thank you.

Special thanks to Nick Meriwether. A fellow companion in the battle against Sauron, Nick provided me with an elven cloak. My deepest gratitude.

EARWORK: The following people were there listening, always believing, some in special moments, some all along the way, when I dearly needed it: Eliza Bundledee; Evelynn Getz; Bill Clark; Elsa and Alexander Murray-Clark; Crayton Bedford; William Polits; Nick Meriwether; Karla, Jamil, and Kalin Downing; Dave Rannefeld and Patricia Buckenmeyer; Tim Bak; Laurel Norsetter; Sally Ansorge Mulvey; Tracy Brown; Scott and Kelly Boggs; Eric Doherty; Jeff Tiedrich; Dwight Holmes; Penina Taesali; Darren Mason; Christian Crumlish; Michael Parrish; Paul Bodenham; Dario Wolfish; Hugh Barroll; Dougal Donaldson; Herbert and Janice Egli; and Gregory and Constance Alexander. You folks are the binding for this book and kept my heart warm. Many, many thanks.

Thanks must go to Peets Coffee, Green Apple Books, Cinema Video and Le Video. And, of course, Corinne Fendell and everybody at the San Francisco Waldorf School for providing real education, real caring, and real magic for my daughter.

And finally, to my wife and daughter, Eliza and Evelynn: your love and support make everything possible. Every man should be so lucky. From my heart to yours, thank you for the zillions of things you did to help with this book—and especially for the ones I didn't notice.

In memory of my mother, Evelyn M. Goetz (1937–1977).

**JOHN R. DWORK:**
I am continually amazed that the universe has allowed me to make a profession out of listening to and writing about the music I love. I am GRATEFULLY DEDICATED.

I must give humble thanks to the divine inspiration provided by the miraculous music played by the Dead in Veneta, Oregon, on August 27, 1972. This music (with the help of some little men—especially Mr. Natural—and a small push from Big George) was the catalyst which inspired me to devote a big chunk of my time on this planet to sharing my enthusiasm about the Dead's music with all of you. Woosh! Vroom! *Comprenez-vous*? (Cotter does!).

I owe a lot to my guardian angels: Jean Sienkewicz, Adam "Compendium Boy" MacConnell, Leda Barasch O'Callahan, Christine Austin, Ari Ellberg, Graham Ridley, Trish Stankowicz, Alexis Muellner, F. Lee Badillion, Molly Yeaton, and Rasa Fuda Nabi Badillion. Special credit goes to Adrienne Crew and Dougal (both of you were patient and exceedingly generous with your time), Michael Sammet, and Alex Thomson. There are no words to convey how much I am in debt to all of you. And a hearty Hoi M'Noi! to the rest of the Badillions who also provided essential emotional support.

*Domo arigato* Linda West and Peter Schlossberg for the digs. You warmly opened your homes to me on numerous research field trips. I love you both very much.

The biggest thanks of all goes to Bonnie and Kerry Dwork who taught me by example the value of working hard. And to Trudy Englander, who taught me how to live life as art. I love you more than words can tell.

DON'T EVER FORGET:
MUSIC IS LOVE